A Cuisine of Spices

For a listing of these spices, please see chart on page 42.

Vibrant Curries

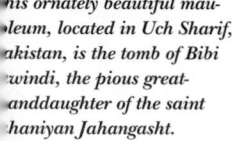

Griddle-cooked stuffed potato cakes are topped with contrasting sauces of tamarind, red chiles, yogurt, and fresh mint (page 45).

A bashful Muslim newlywed on her honeymoon.

PUNJABI, KASHMIRI, AND PAKISTANI CURRIES: Abundant

kohlrabi, beets, garbanzo beans, lotus root, and turnips mottle many of this area's succulent and hearty curries. As fields of mustard greens dot the landscape here, it is no wonder this plant, in all its

mustard

glory, punctuates their saucy offerings. Pureed greens with garlic and butter get swooped into pieces of griddle-cooked corn bread in India's bread basket of Punjab. In Kashmir, spiced lamb chops pan-sear in mustard oil and nestle in cream-kissed fenugreek leaves along with this area's other prized offering—perfectly steamed white basmati rice. The Sindhis, who straddle the Indian-Pakistani border stuff potato shells with sprouted beans and smother them with contrasting sauces to create sublime mouthfuls of obsession.

A teenaged Kashmiri beckons passersby with his sensuous display of ground Kashmiri chiles and turmeric.

This ornately beautiful mausoleum, located in Uch Sharif, Pakistan, is the tomb of Bibi Jiwindi, the pious great-granddaughter of the saint Jahaniyan Jahangasht.

A party pleaser, these rib lamb chops will excite your taste buds with garlic, mustard oil, and the allure of perfumed fenugreek leaves (page 92).

The juicy tenderness of ivy gourd squash blends with the sweetness of fresh coconut and the citrus aroma of curry leaves (page 610).

tAMILIAN, SRI LANKAN, AND KERALITE CURRIES: Coconut, chiles, legumes, and curry leaves are hallmarks of the curries here with roasted mustard seeds as a key spice infusing nutty flavor. Fish and seafood are staples along the

Luxurious lobster tails are poached in creamy coconut milk redolent of cinnamon, ginger, and black peppercorns (page 284).

seafood

Freshly netted fish along Kerala's coastline wait for the highest bidder at a Cochin beach.

coastal areas of the southwest, and rice is a constant accompaniment in this land where it is cultivated two or three times a year. Fresh vegetables, legumes, and thin-bodied curries permeate Tamilian home kitchens; shrimp with unripe mango, chiles, and coconut milk peppers the Keralite's palate; while crab, tart leaves, and local cinnamon perfume the Sri Lankan home kitchen.

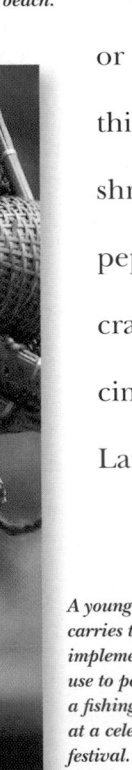

A young woman carries the fishing implements she'll use to perform a fishing dance at a celebratory festival.

A look of heartfelt disgrace is painted on the face of a Kathakali dancer.

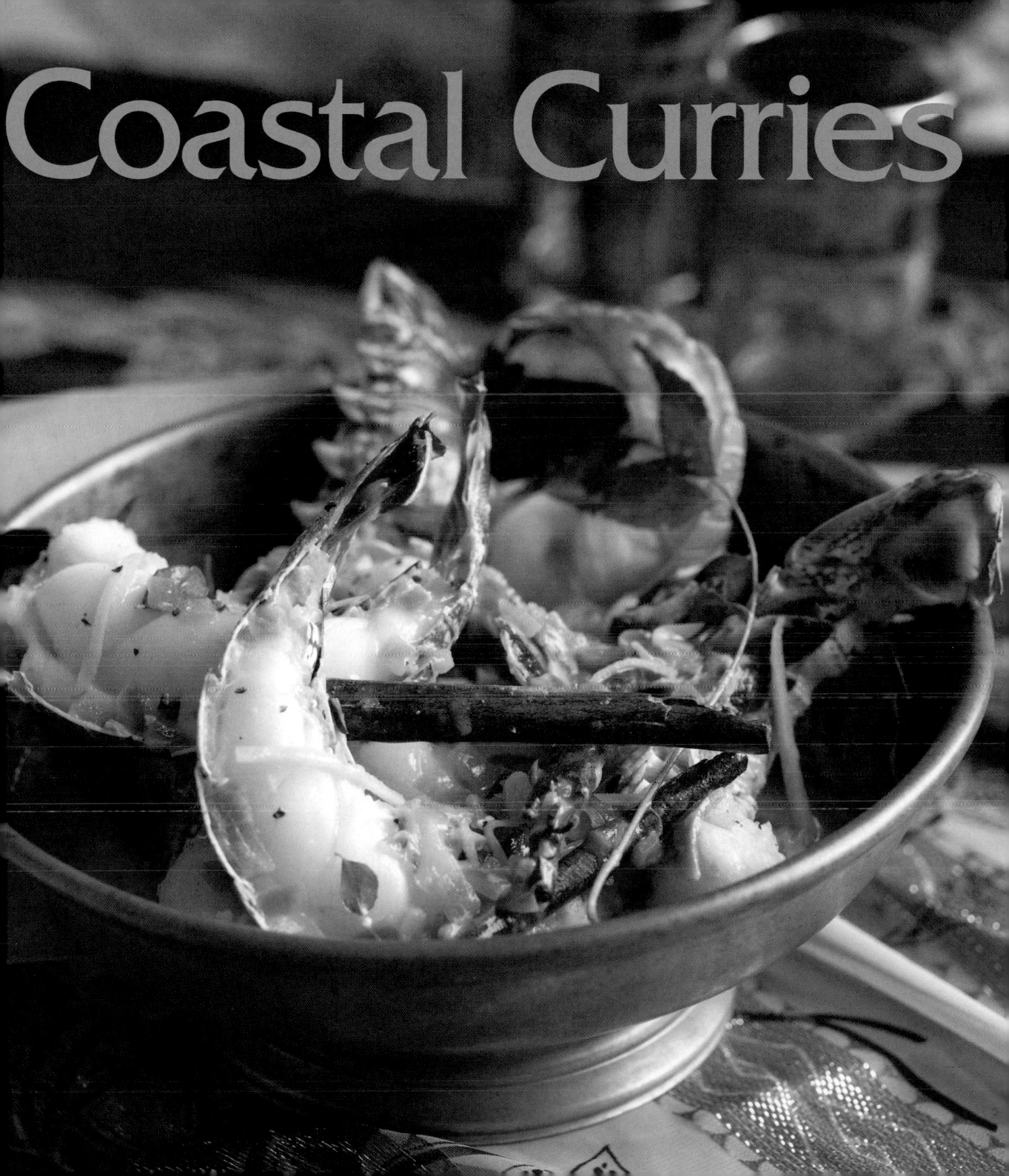

Coastal Curries

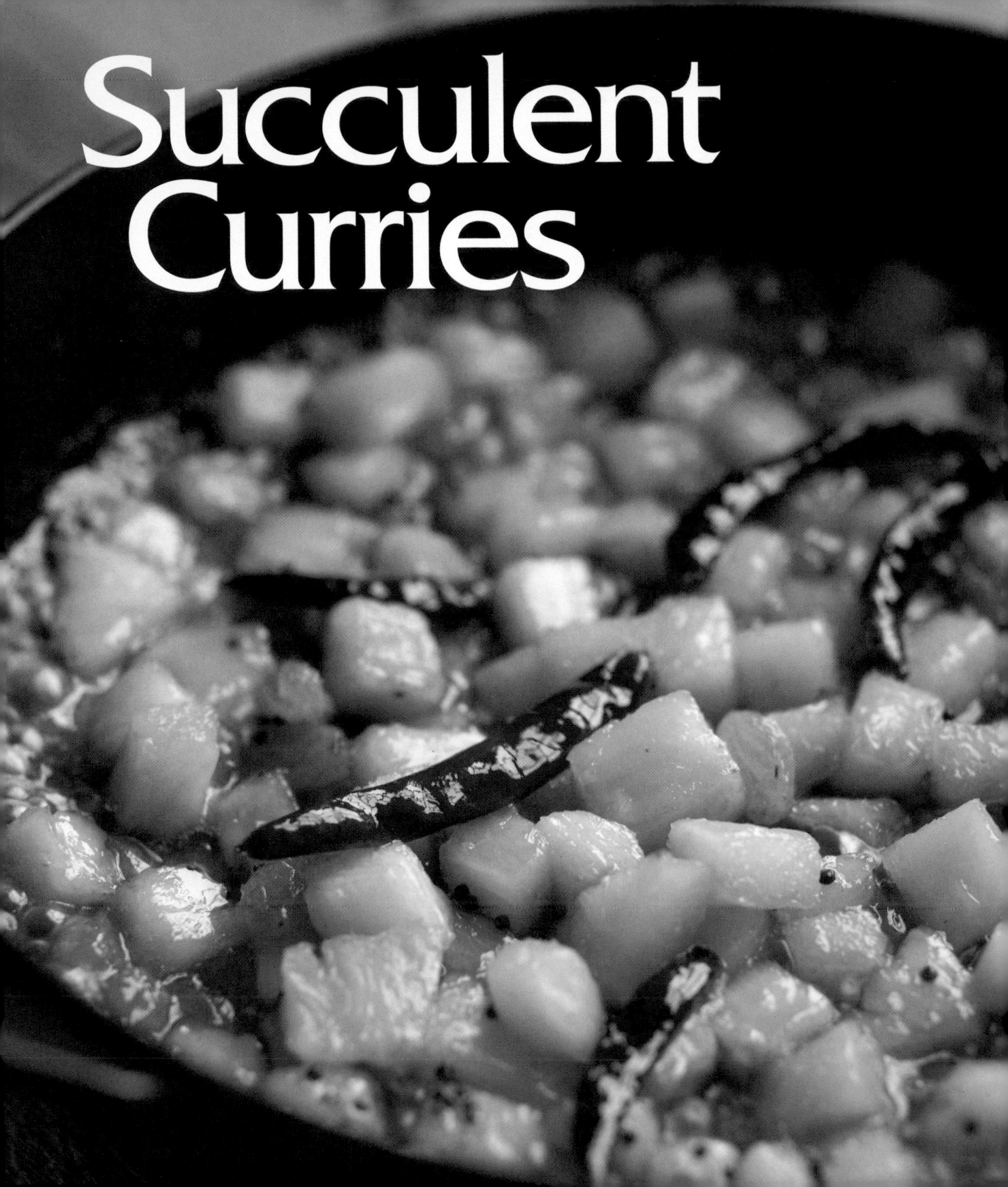

Succulent Curries

Two siblings from the same capsicum family, one sweet, the other pungent, balance out jumbo prawns dusted with turmeric (page 258).

Sweet-tart pineapple stewed with golden raisins and red chiles may well top your next bowl of premium vanilla ice cream (page 744).

LUCKNOWI, BENGALI, NEPALESE, AND ASSAMESE CURRIES:

The Muslim Nawabs of Lucknow wrote the book on living it up as choice cuts of meat, rich-tasting nuts, and cream swathe many of their succulent kebabs. Bengalis, who can and do consume fish and seafood at all their meals, cherish

opulence

bitter-tasting ingredients like mustard oil to complement them, but the end result is magically sweet with spices like fennel and cardamom. The Nepalese love to stuff Chinese flour dumpling wrappers with cabbage, turmeric, and assertive spices. The Assamese stew red lentils with scallions and tomatoes and their love for fish is unmistakable as they poach carp steaks in fenugreek and lime juice.

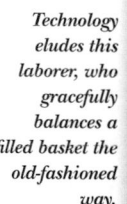

Technology eludes this laborer, who gracefully balances a filled basket the old-fashioned way.

The frying sizzle of artfully-piped funnel cake-like jalebis in a street confectioner's wok invites you to freely salivate.

The hardships of a pilgrimage illuminate the lives of these elderly **sadhus** (mendicants).

MAHARASHTRIAN, GUJARATI, AND GOAN CURRIES:

While Gujaratis are masters at magical flavors with legumes and vegetables, Maharashtrians and Goans treat the fruits of the sea with utmost reverence. Fresh coconut and chiles blanket jumbo prawns in the home state of Mumbai (formerly Bombay) and just south of the metropolis, homemade sausage links stew

chiles

in black-eyed peas, hinting at Goa's Portuguese influence. You would think chickpea flour is blah, but sift it into a Gujarati's bowl, and revel in its inclusion in steamed roulade of taro leaves topped with roasted mustard seeds and juicy tomatoes.

Layers of taro leaves harboring ginger and chile-spiked chickpea flour have been steamed, pan-fried, and smothered with fresh coconut and tomatoes (page 107).

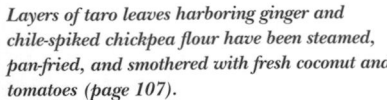

Plum sea scallop nestle i peanut-flecke spinach spice with a poter chile-coconut blen (page 280

A sunny open- market is wh this vendor har tomatoes gar

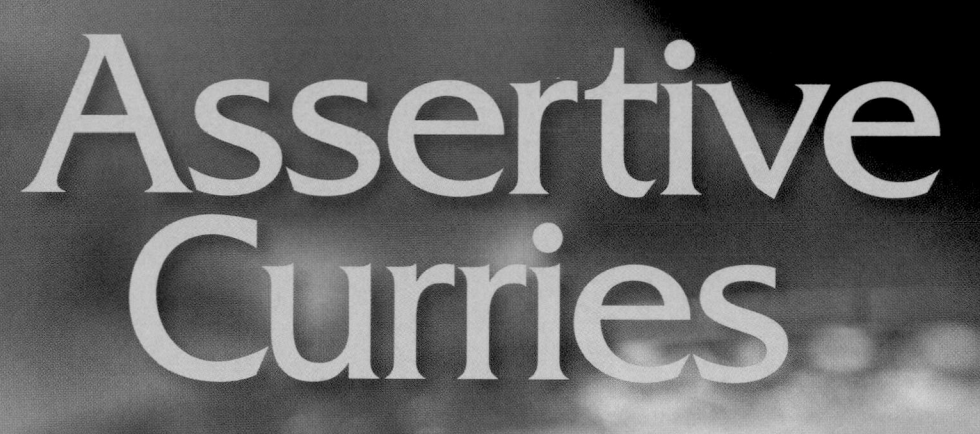

Assertive Curries

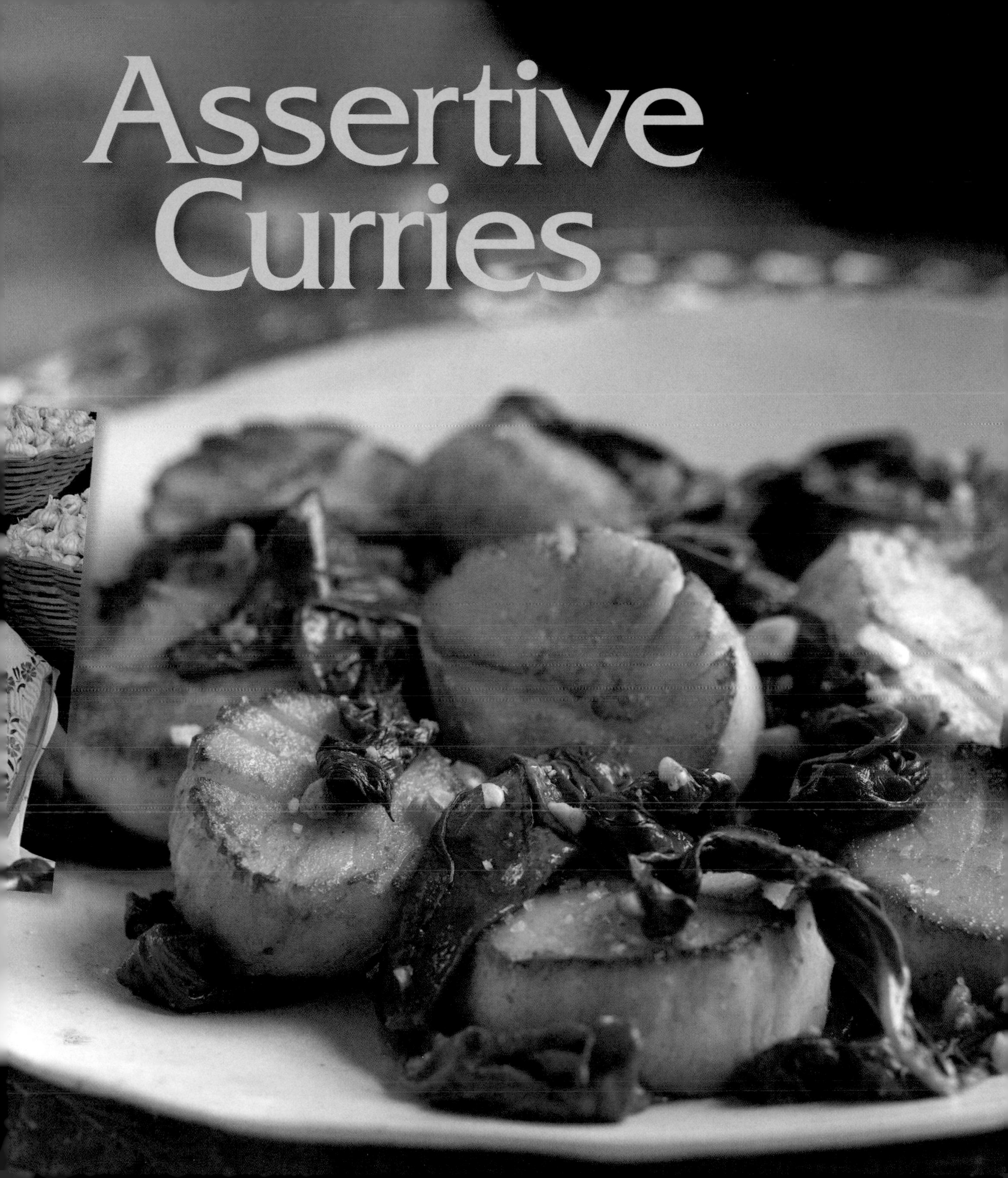

Wholesome
Curries

RAJASTHANI AND PARSI

CURRIES: Even though the desert climate of Rajasthan in western India gives it a short rainy window for growing legumes and vegetables, Rajasthanis extend that season by drying them to eat in the months when rain is sacred. They stew them with nutritious chickpea flour dumplings and this area's year-around

Hearty and nutty chickpea flour nuggets provide nurturing comfort (page 349).

A grassy-fresh sprinkling of mint, coconut, and cilantro envelop fillets of sole steamed in packets of banana leaves (page 249).

chickpeas

opulence: milk, yogurt, and ghee (clarified butter). The Parsis in Mumbai and Gujarat cherish their Persian roots as they whip up steamed fillet of sole wrapped in banana leaves at every auspicious gathering while pumpkins stew in multi-legume curries redolent with cinnamon, cloves, and red chiles.

A turbaned Rajasthani mahout and his decked elephant greet tourists in Jaipur at Amber Fort.

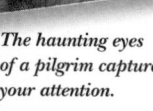

The haunting eyes of a pilgrim capture your attention.

An adorable Rajasthani boy's charm is enough to make any father proud.

The stir-frying techniques of China and hearty spices of India come alive in these egg noodles of the Hakka coated with a soy-chile sauce (page 675).

BLENDING CULTURES:

I am the perfect hybrid as I have split my life almost equally between India and the United States. How could I not combine my childhood's flavors with those of my adult years as I prepare with ease a

fusion

Grilled salmon never loses its subtle flavors amid sweet honey, tart tamarind sauce, and holy basil (page 668). You may well utter "Om!"

tandoori filet mignon with a mushroom-cream sauce and scalloped potatoes baked in coconut milk and chiles? My love for Mexican cuisine seeps into my obsession for potato-stuffed peppers in a guajillo chile sauce. One of the oldest fusion cuisines in India has been Indo-Chinese and the noodles of the Hakka twirl around crisp-tender vegetables that are sauced with malt vinegar, Kashmiri chiles, and cilantro.

The block printed fabric of a tribal woman as an equal mate for her hand painted up and sensuous jewelry.

Contemporary Curries

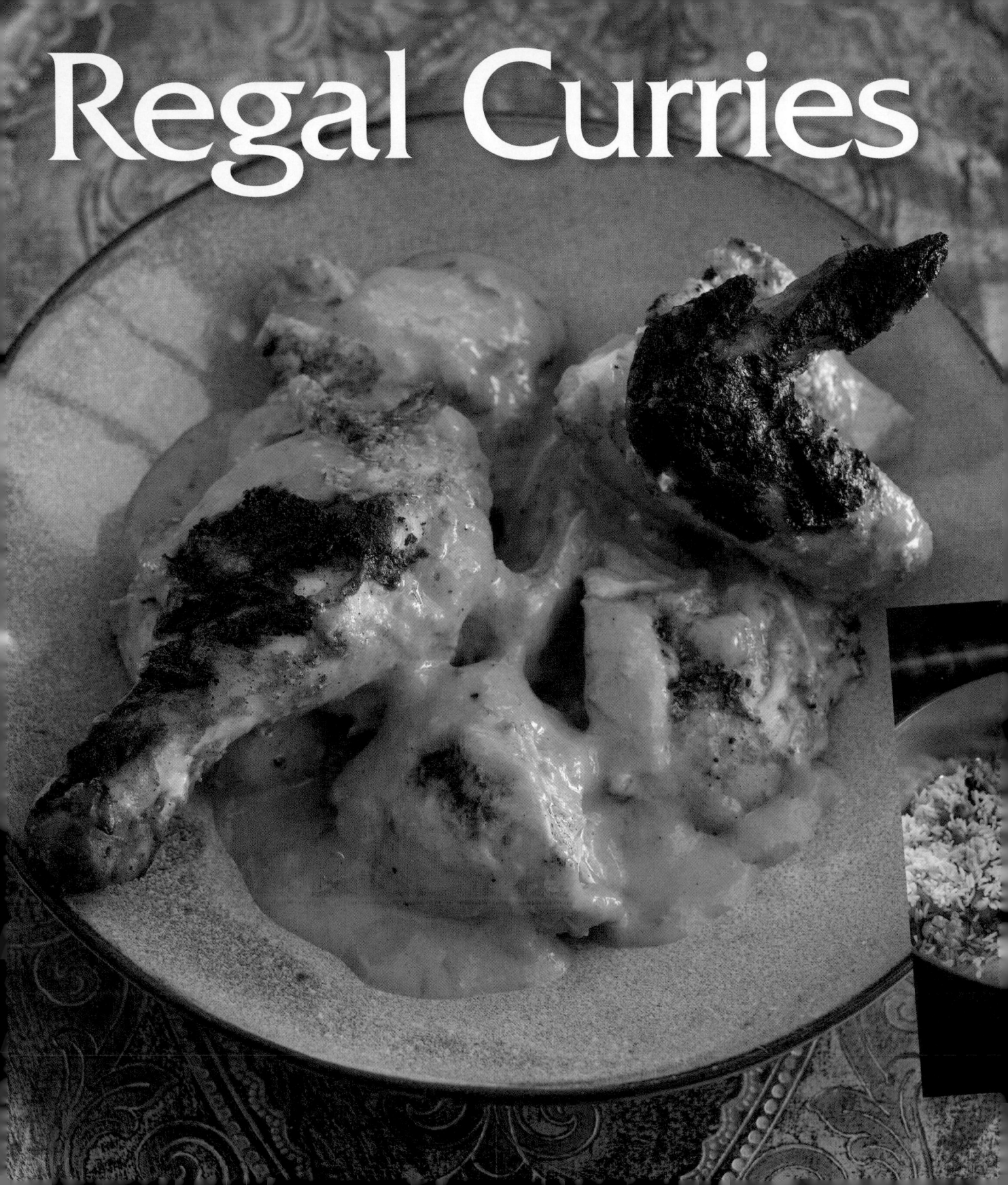

Regal Curries

Chickens in India are close in flavor to Cornish hens and these birds glow under the blanket of a tomato-fenugreek sauce (page 163).

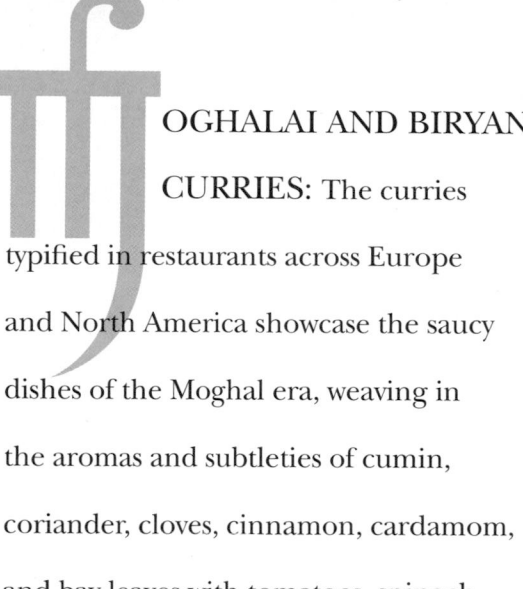

MOGHALAI AND BIRYANI

CURRIES: The curries typified in restaurants across Europe and North America showcase the saucy dishes of the Moghal era, weaving in the aromas and subtleties of cumin, coriander, cloves, cinnamon, cardamom, and bay leaves with tomatoes, spinach,

A beautiful woman wishes (perhaps) for the same depth of love that went into building the magnificent Taj Mahal.

harmony

A one-pan meal that will appease your inner royalty, this layered saffron-kissed rice with garlicky vegetables makes for an elegant meal (page 698).

cream, and nut purees. Ginger, garlic, and onion are the pungent base for curries like Aloo mutter, Chana masala, and Badam murghi. Biryanis combine rice, legumes, meats, and vegetables in one-pot meals, and flatbreads scoop the curries as edible flat-ware—all coming together to create harmonious balance.

A detail from the ceiling of the Taj Mahal.

Herbs and Vegetables

TARO LEAVES

IVY GOURD SQUASH

BITTER MELON

BOTTLE GOURD SQUASH

GREEN PAPAYA

CURRY LEAVES

YAMS

UNRIPE MANGO

LUFFA SQUASH

TARO LEAVES

FENUGREEK

GINGER

660
curries

by Raghavan Iyer

Food Photography by Ben Fink

WORKMAN PUBLISHING · NEW YORK

Library of Congress Cataloging-in-Publication Data is available.
ISBN: 978-0-7611-3787-0 (pb); ISBN: 978-0-7611-4855-5 (hc)

Cover and book design by Lisa Hollander with Carolyn Casey
Cover food photography by Ben Fink
Author photograph by Manoj Vasuevan

Photo Credits:

Color Insert: Jon Arnold 2/3 (center), Pakistan Images 3
(middle); **Ben Fink:** 1, 2, 3 (bottom), 4 (top), 5, 6, 7 (top), 8
(bottom), 9, 10, 11 (top), 12 (bottom), 13, 14, 14/15 (center);
Corbis: Peter Adams/zefa 4 (middle), epa 4 (lower left), Frans
Lemmens/zefa 11 (bottom), Hugh Sitton/zefa 12 (top), Paule
Seux/Hemis 12/13 (center); **Getty Images:** Jason Edwards/Na-
tional Geographic 15 (bottom), Paul Harris/Stone 15 (top);
Raghavan Iyer: 3 (top), 4 (bottom right), 7 (middle and bottom), 8 (top), 8/9 (center), 10/11 (center).

Chapter Openers: **age fotostock:** Dinodia 169, Sean Sprague 311,
Dennis Cox 647, Tolo Balaguer 750; **Alamy Images:** Hugh Wil-
liamson 285, Chris Fredriksson 459; **Getty Images:** Rouf Bhat/
AFP 235; **Lonely Planet Images:** Greg Elms 119; **Raghavan Iyer:**
1, 11, 43, 687.

Workman books are available at special discounts when
purchased in bulk for premiums and sales promotions as well
as for fund-raising or educational use. Special editions or book
excerpts can be created to specification. For details, contact
the Special Sales Director at the address below.

Workman Publishing Company, Inc.
225 Varick Street
New York, NY 10014-4381

Manufactured in the United States of America

First printing March 2008
10 9 8 7 6 5 4 3 2 1

dedication

. . . .

My mother's death,
before she could see the finished book,
deeply saddens me.
I take solace in her memory,
kept alive through some of her
saucy offerings which you'll find
in these pages.

. . . .

What fulfills me is my
almost-nine-year-old son, Robert,
who is unconditionally the best thing that
has happened to me in my
46 years of living. He tasted *all*
of the recipes in this book
(extraordinarily commendable when I tell
you all the testing happened during the
fourth, fifth, and sixth years of his life).

. . . .

So I dedicate this book to a generation
that slipped away, and one
that continues to spice up my life every
step of the way. And to my partner of
twenty-five years, Terry Erickson, who has
supported me through all my
ups and downs.

acknowledgments

Many have compared bringing a book from inception to publication to the birthing process, and I for one cannot agree more. True, I may not know much about "birthin' babies," but I sure do know a thing or two about the conceiving, nurturing, evolution, and the ultimate publication of a cookbook—but nobody warned me this one would be a horse. And yes, after all the huffing and puffing, when it was finished, I fell in love with this gargantuan "baby," full of well-balanced and saucy glow.

My partner, Terry Erickson, sowed the idea for a curry book, "a big one," he said, "nothing like any before." Easy for him to say! So off I went and called my friend and literary agent extraordinaire, tenacious Jane Dystel, who said, "Raghavan, I think you are ready for a big book." I blurted out "How about *1,001 Curries?*" without even thinking, and she said, "I love it." The next few months, and with Jane's help, I slaved over a proposal (this is where I bid adieu to my ego). Once satisfied, off she went, saying, "Workman Publishing is the ideal match for you." She garnered the interest of a wise editor at Workman, Suzanne Rafer, who—along with Peter Workman's support—immediately said, "Yes" (or at least I'd like to think so). Jane called and said, "You better get to work, kid, 'cause they want, well, maybe not 1,001 curries, but between 600 and 800." Shaking with excitement, complete with morning nausea, I felt the curry seed planted in me, germinating and hungering for saucy recipes from the Indian subcontinent.

I called my family in India and my mother was thrilled, along with my two sisters, Dr. Lalitha Iyer and Mathangi Gopalkrishnan, and all four brothers, my siblings' respective spouses, and their children. Ideas flowed, connections were made, and the recipes started to filter in from many friends and acquaintances. It does take a village to gather over 650 curry recipes, and the crew that nourished my baby was impressive: Gangabai Iyer, Alamelu Iyer, Dr. Lalitha Iyer, Mathangi Gopalkrishnan, Geeta Iyer, Lalitha Nateshan-Iyer, Meena Iyer, Anuradha Iyer, Perinne Medora, Sakina Munaim, Zohair Motiwalla, Kumud Desai, Mithu Mukherjee, Leela Rao, Sharon Naik, Monica and Devjyoti Kataky, Pratima Revenkar, Geeta Dash-Larson, Usha Raikar, Chef Kartikai, Piyumi and Priyantha Samaratunga, Bina Toniyat, Radhika Sharma, Preeti Mathur, Balki Radhakrishnan, Swetal Sindhvad, Bharati Sindhvad, Sanjita Carriappa, Chef Mahipal Singh Rathore, Abdul and Geetanjali Contractor, Mrs. Chandwani, Varsha Chandwani, Mrs. Joshi, Shirley Matthew, Mrs. Vakharia, Vidya Subramani, Sangha Mitra Roy, Dr. Jeffrey Mandel, R. J. Singh, Jiten Gori, Ambuja Balaji Rao, Rajni Kedia, Dr. Kiran and Dr. Kumar Belani, Dr. Jyotsana Rayadurgh, Dr. Ashlesha Tamboli-Madhok, Dr. Manu Madhok, Nimmy Paul, Norton Cunningham, Jairam Das, Bhavesh Kumar Thapa, Shankar and Rekha Singh, Ranee Ramaswamy, Razia Syed, Farida Kathawalla, and Padma Chintapalli.

The lonesome work of creating, testing, and writing consumed my years, as my son Robert tried every dish I made, with the occasional "not curry again, Papa." Terry gave his opinion on each (sometimes cautioning me that it was PDE—pretty darn ethnic) as I took copious notes. I enlisted the volunteer services of friends, Kathryn Tempas, Dr. Joel Wagener, Mary Evans, Sharon Sanders, the boys' night group— R. J. (Molu) Singh, Jiten Gori, Dr. Jeffrey Mandel, Ben Martin, and Raymond Vaughn, to test many of these creations, tweaking each dish as warranted.

As it grew alarmingly huge, I had to share my fears, successes, weight gain, advice, and gossip with my friends and colleagues of the food world: David Joachim, Sharon Sanders, Mary Evans, Paulette Mitchell, Crescent Dragonwagon, Lynne Rossetto Kasper, Lee Dean, Judy Bart Kancigor, Beth Dooley, Lucia Watson, Cathy Cochran-Lewis, Sara Monick, Barbara Jo Davis, Lois Tlusty, Kim Walter, Jeanne Kozar, Karen Coune, Andi Bidwell, Maya Kaimal, Nathan Fong, Lance Sanders, Nick Malgieri, Shirley Corriher, Madhur Jaffrey, Florence Lin and many others, not to mention the cooking schools' staff and tens of thousands of students that I had the fortune of teaching over the years.

Once the recipes were tested and written, then came the introduction, and I couldn't find a more resourceful, competent, and giving person to help me than my friend and colleague Phyllis Louise Harris, the founder of the Asian Culinary Arts Institutes, Ltd., and an incomparable researcher who traced the role of spices back to 20 million B.C.

The manuscript (a whopper at 2,000 pages) went to Workman, my new *mishpuchah* (that's family in Yiddish, in case you didn't know), and the massaging began, similar to Kobe beef, in the supple, strong, capable, and overworked mind of Suzanne Rafer, the leader of my personal Dream Team. She brought in Kathie Ness, an unbelievably detailed copy editor, who questioned every possible element that could go wrong when it does get delivered for the world to peruse. Assistant editor Helen Rosner was diligent as well. Production editor Carol White made sure things moved along for a timely delivery, while indexer Cathy Dorsey made sure anyone looking for a specific recipe would find it. Barbara Peragine got the whole thing typeset and ready for the printer. Copywriter David Schiller breathed excitement into the back cover. None of this would have been possible without art director Lisa Hollander, who designed an entirely gorgeous and elegant book (My own font? Well, you shouldn't have). She had the incredible talents and assistance of Carolyn Casey, photo department director Anne Kerman, photographer Ben Fink, prop stylist Roy Finamore, and food stylist Jamie Kimm. Manoj Vasuevan was kind enough to shoot the author photo and some of the location shots, as were Marcia Rogers, Pamela Workman, and Peggy and David Lucas. Of course, I needed someone to announce the birth, and who better than savvy and hardworking Ron Longe and Jen Pare Neugeboren, along with the myriad of sales and marketing staff, to beat the drums and make some noise?

My dear friend and colleague, the compassionate and kind Jim Dodge of Bon Appetit Management Company held my hand and, along with Marc Zammit and Christine Seitz, promised partnership through his company. In return I pledged to train all their 200 corporate chefs in the not-so-mysterious ways of the curry world. The folks at CanolaInfo were very sweet as well, promising to soothe my baby with oiled hands when the time came—Leah Mann, Dorothy Long, Robert Hunter, and Ellen Pruden.

And yes, it finally arrived—vivacious, boisterous, saucy, and sensational—a chip off the old block, you say? Please, you are making me blush. Savor it just as I do, you'll love it! And do visit me on my website: www.raghavaniyer.com.

contents

Spice blends and pastes are the backbone of India's curries. Easy and quick to make—and easy to store—these combinations will open the world of curry to you.

The curry version of small plates will spice up everyday snacks, cocktail party nibbles, or a weekend tailgating party. Onion-Studded Lentil and Split Pea Fritters, Grilled Chicken with Cashew-Tomato Sauce, and Wok-Cooked Beef Cubes with a Chile-Yogurt Sauce are just a few to enjoy.

In India, chicken is turned into a multitude of delectable curries—juicy, succulent, and vibrant with ginger, garlic, chiles, coconut, and an array of spices and fresh herbs. But it doesn't stop there: Curries are also made with Cornish game hen, duck, and even eggs.

Despite its reputation as a vegetarian paradise, many Indians eat meat and here is a delicious catalog of curries to prove it: Fall-Apart Beef Cubes with Spinach and Coconut, Spicy Ground Beef with Peas and Chiles, Saffron-Scented Lamb with an Almond Sauce, Pork with Potatoes, Peppers, and Apples, and many, many more.

With some 4,700 miles of coastline, India has a long tradition of seafood curries. Shrimp, crabs, mussels, scallops, and saltwater fishes combine with coconut, tamarind, chile, ginger, onion, yogurt, fenugreek, and lime to become succulent dishes for all fish and shellfish lovers.

A staple of northern India, *paneer*—India's only kind of cheese—can be fried and spiced, covered with delicious sauces, crumbled and cooked with an assortment of vegetables, marinated with herbs, or made into dumplings.

the curry quest

As a naïve twenty-one-year-old, I found myself enrolled in a college program in hotel, restaurant, and institutional management in my newly adopted country, the United States. I had arrived with a degree in chemistry, but was pretty clueless about cooking. At my neighborhood supermarket, which catered to a town of 10,000 locals and 2,000 students, I piled familiar potatoes,

onions, and tomatoes into my cart and meandered over to the spice aisle. Ground cumin and turmeric were the only spices I instantly recognized from my mother's Tamilian kitchen. A rectangular container, lurking alongside the cumin, caught my attention: *Durkee Curry Powder.* I had no idea what that meant.

I reached for the tin and read the description. This particular blend of spices promised to create authentic

Indian flavors by currying your favorite meats, poultry, and vegetables. Granted, I did not know much about cooking, but I did know what curries were. To us Indians, a curry is a sauce-based dish—which frankly had nothing much to do with this generic blend of spices. Nevertheless, curiosity got the better of me and I walked out of the grocery store with lofty hopes of being transported back to my mother's kitchen.

As the onions sizzled in the skillet, I added the potatoes and tomatoes along with the manna from the Durkee container. Alas, the aromas and tastes kept me imprisoned in the tundra of Minnesota. I wept for the curry powder's yellow betrayal and yearned for the true curries devoured in the kitchens of my friends and family.

To find a true curry, especially one from my southern Indian roots, I didn't have to look beyond my mother's and grandmother's kitchen. But to research India's multiregional offerings, I had to expand my horizons a bit— an expansion that took years to achieve and that was punctuated with a degree in hotel and restaurant management and a stint as a chef at an Indian restaurant in the United States. My growing curiosity about regional Indian cuisine led to a career as a cooking teacher and as a food writer, which provided a strong reason to delve into that multiregion research. I traveled extensively in India, knocking on doors of friends, extended family, acquaintances, and even total strangers. I interviewed numerous folks (was even bitten by a stray dog) and invited myself, without an iota of shame, to their homes for meals. I pored through books, studied hundreds of sources, and put on eight pounds (which may not seem a lot to you, but on my wispy-thin body, it's serious)—all in the name of research. It's a tasty job, so I was glad to be your sacrificial lamb. I sliced, stir-fried, stewed, steamed, and spiced hundreds of meals for over a year to arrive at this juncture in my curried expedition.

That can of curry powder sent me back twenty million years, to a time when coconuts bobbed their way across the southern seas to implant themselves along what are now India's coastal shores. In order for you to comprehend what a curry is (and more importantly, what it isn't), we must track the evolution and journey of its key ingredients: the spices. So sit back and be my travel companion.

what is a curry?

before I try to define that word, let me create an image for you from my college days in India, when I was pursuing a degree in chemistry. As I busied myself in the laboratory, I happened to knock a mercury thermometer onto the tile floor. Tiny pieces of glass and droplets of liquid mercury dispersed, and I tried to pick up the pieces. The glass was easy, but not the mercury. The shining, silvery liquid was elusive (not to mention dangerous) and defied containment and form (we had no mercury spill kits back then). It moved freely with even the slightest nudge and affected everything it touched. Which brings me back to the task at hand: Defining curry is like trying to grasp liquid mercury and gather it into a neat pile.

The word "curry" itself is unknown in the Indian vocabulary. It doesn't appear in any of India's twenty-three officially recognized languages and sixteen hundred dialects. Words like *kari* and *kadhi* refer to sauce-based or gravy-laden dishes that existed in India well before the Aryans got there—and with a civilization that spans six thousand years, you can well imagine their longevity. James Trager, in his book *The Enriched, Fortified, Concentrated, Country-Fresh, Lip-Smacking, Finger-Licking, International, Unexpurgated Foodbook* (and I thought I was the hyphen king), mentions the seasoning habits of the Mohenjo-Daro people who lived in the Indus Valley c. 4000 B.C. They used mortars and pestles to pound the sun-dried "seeds of mustard, fennel, and most especially cumin and the rinds of tamarind pods" to create the "earliest curry powder" (the use of the term "curry powder" here applies modern terminology to an ancient, but very real, spice blend). *Kari,* a Tamil (southern Indian) word that was widely in use by 1500 B.C., according to the renowned Indian food historian K. T. Achaya, meant animal meat stewed with "wet dressings" and spiced with black pepper. From where I sit, I see the transformation of *kari* to *curry* as the possible result of mispronounced happenstance.

Perhaps, as some believe, it was King Richard II's palace cooks who invented the word "curry" in Britain around A.D. 1390, as they built layers of flavors and textures with sophisticated spicing techniques that involved cloves, cinnamon, ginger, coriander, cumin, and cardamom, among others. Some of these recipes are well documented in the book *The Forme of Cury* (published in the late fourteenth century). Since there is no evidence that they knew either the word *kari* or *kadhi* in the 1300s, how then did the English know to bastardize those terms to "cury"? Well, the British were involved in the spice trade before they set up shop in India in the early 1600s. I can only speculate that they picked up one of the Indian words and adapted it to "cury." After all, it was the British who tried to capture the flavors of a *kari* years later with a generic blend of ground spices called "curry powder."

In spite of this theory—and a raft of others—concerning the origination of the word "curry," there is an agreement that the concept of this sauce-based, spice-laden dish has been India's legacy for thousands of years. Spices, you see, are the backbone of these dishes, and with India's six-thousand-year tradition of using them in cooking, I consider the Indian sub-

continent to be their master. Indians toasted, roasted, pounded, and mixed their spices to provide complex flavors to the sauces that bathed, swathed, steeped, stewed, and simmered meats, vegetables, and legumes well before the Europeans did.

So, what is a curry? In England and the rest of the world, "curry" describes anything Indian that is mottled with hot spices, with or without a sauce, and "curry powder" is the blend that delivers it. In keeping with my culture, I define a curry as any dish that consists of meat, fish, poultry, legumes, vegetables, or fruits, simmered in or covered with a sauce, gravy, or other liquid that is redolent of spices and/or herbs. In my India, curry is never added—it just *is*! In order to share this with you, I have focused on recipes that are accessible to the home cook. To help navigate, you'll find comprehensive ingredient glossaries, cooking tips, clearly explained cooking terms, and appealing yet simple spicing techniques. Welcome to a saucy repertoire and a world beyond curry powders.

the elements of a curry

"flavor" is a complex word—although maybe not quite as multifaceted as "curry." It seems so very simple to us when we use it to describe what we eat and drink, interchangeably with "taste."

Wikipedia describes "flavor" as "the sensory impression of a food or other substance, determined by the three chemical senses of taste, olfaction (smell), and the so-called trigeminal senses (a merging of the ophthalmic, maxillary, and mandibular nerves), which detect chemical irritants in the mouth and throat." You weed

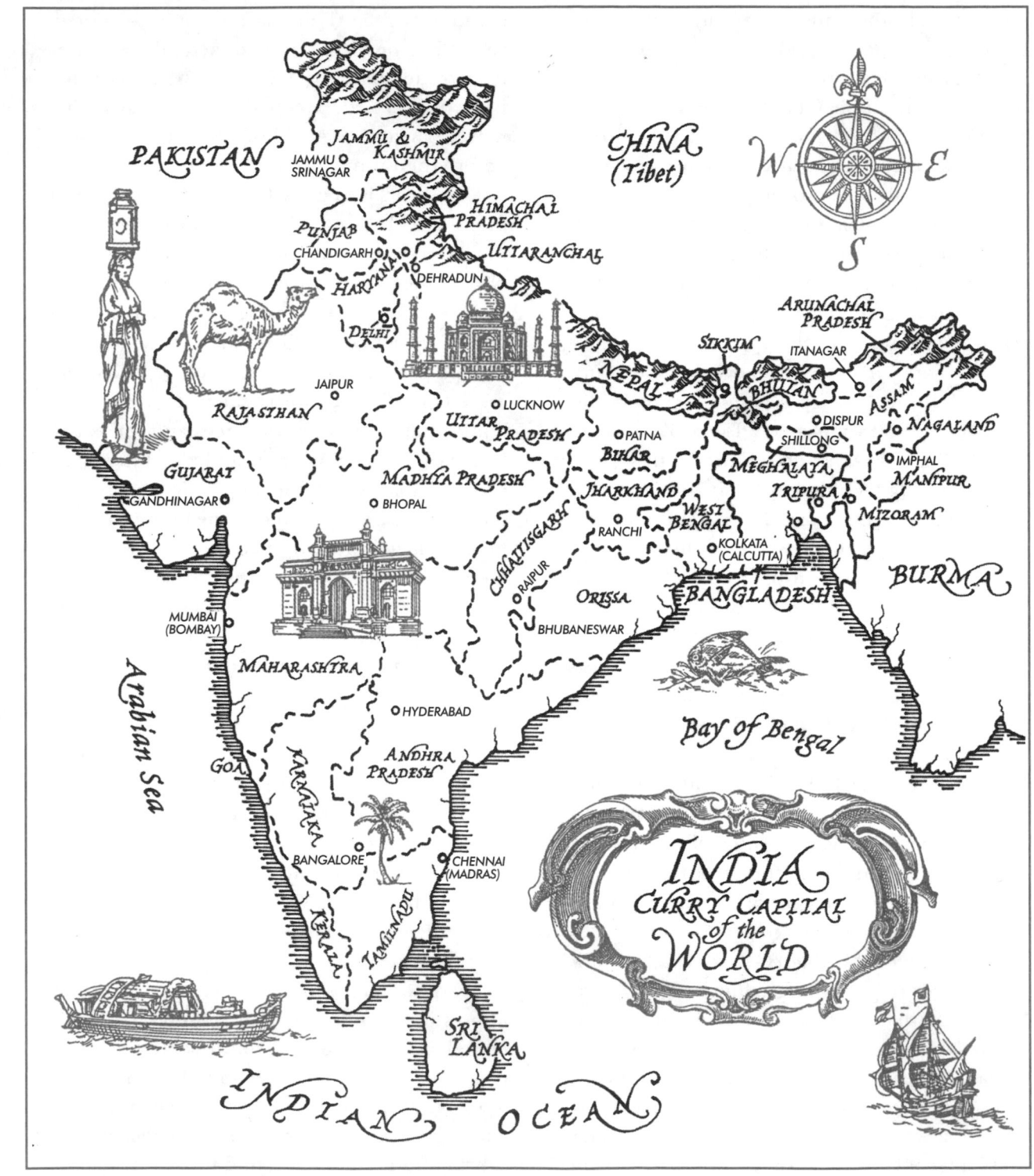

PAKISTAN

CHINA
(Tibet)

JAMMU &
KASHMIR
JAMMU
SRINAGAR

HIMACHAL
PRADESH

PUNJAB
CHANDIGARH

UTTARANCHAL

HARYANA
DEHRADUN

DELHI

JAIPUR

RAJASTHAN

ARUNACHAL
PRADESH
ITANAGAR

SIKKIM

NEPAL

BHUTAN

ASSAM

NAGALAND

LUCKNOW

UTTAR
PRADESH

PATNA

BIHAR

DISPUR

SHILLONG

MEGHALAYA

TRIPURA

IMPHAL
MANIPUR

GUJARAT
GANDHINAGAR

MADHYA PRADESH

BHOPAL

JHARKHAND

RANCHI

WEST
BENGAL

MIZORAM

CHHATTISGARH

RAIPUR

KOLKATA
(CALCUTTA)

BANGLADESH

BURMA

ORISSA

BHUBANESWAR

MUMBAI
(BOMBAY)

MAHARASHTRA

HYDERABAD

Bay of Bengal

GOA

ANDHRA
PRADESH

Arabian Sea

KARNATAKA

BANGALORE

KERALA

TAMILNADU

CHENNAI
(MADRAS)

INDIA
CURRY CAPITAL
of the
WORLD

SRI
LANKA

INDIAN OCEAN

through all that scientific talk and end up at the old adage "You eat with all your senses."

When I create curries in my kitchen I look for that perfect balance of sizzle, taste, smell, texture, and visual appeal. My workspace becomes an aromatic laboratory as measuring cups judiciously dole out onions, garlic, and ginger, spoons sprinkle salt, turmeric, and spices, cooking gadgets mince and puree, and pots and pans hold frying or stewing vegetables, legumes, and meats.

In the *Oxford Companion to Food*, Alan Davidson defines "flavor" as the combined effects of taste and aroma. Using that as my guide, I decided to analyze the composition of an Indian curry by examining its taste and aromatic components. I also broke down the elements that give it form, texture, and body. My reason for doing this is a simple one: I wish to share with you all my available tools in order to empower you to create and shape your own curries. So come along; we have much to do.

When you spoon a curry into your mouth, your taste buds identify its ingredients as being *bitter, sour, salty,* and *sweet* (the four primary taste elements). More recently, scientists consider *umami* (a Japanese term) to be the fifth primary element. Speak to Asians and you will find that they consider the additional elements of *pungent* (hot) and *astringent* to be equally significant.

There are ten thousand taste buds in your tongue that recognize the primary taste elements. It is true that there are specific parts of the mouth that taste one element more so than any other, but it's not all that cut-and-dried, as those taste centers (and their sensitivities) change with age. Children are very responsive to pungent chiles and bitter greens, but those same areas have diminished capacity when those babies and toddlers enter their second childhood phase, more commonly known as the senior years. Taste does not work in isolation, as temperature and aroma play pivotal roles in how you experience flavor.

Bitter In general, and I know that generalizing is risky, Americans and Western Europeans find the bitter taste to be very unpleasant. But the same taste is manna to the palates of Southeast Asians and folks from the Indian subcontinent. The Bengali-speaking community, in addition to others from eastern India, usually starts a meal with bitter-tasting curries or perhaps slices of bitter melon, salted and pan-fried. Other regions mask the bitterness so it plays a supporting role in balance with the other taste elements. Spices, herbs, and other ingredients that infuse bitterness in our curries include fenugreek, mustard, amaranth, turnip, and bitter melon, among many others.

Sour Many of us love sour tastes, even though their lips-puckering quality provides slight discomfort. My eight-year-old son, Robert, constantly begs for a piece of lime to suck on, as he draws pleasure not only from its tartness but also from my reaction. The acidic component in Indian curries is a strong one, and each region has its favorite. Tamarind sours its way into the coastal areas along the south, west, and east, while kokum and kudampuli provide smoked acidity in a few communities along the Konkan coast on the west. The Sri Lankans, just south of India, steep kudampuli (they call it goraka), while the Goan Christians use palm, cashew, malt, and distilled vinegars in their Portuguese-influenced fare. Tomato, a late arrival on the scene (late eighteenth century A.D.), spread instant acidic joy, saucing its way into every region. Yogurt and buttermilk blanket all of India, while limes, unripe mangoes, and pineapple give sour comfort to some northern, northwestern, and southern communities. Gongura leaves are a favorite in south central India, not because of their close relationship to the marijuana plant, but because the tart-tasting leaves impart valuable nutrients to curries and provide acidic balance to hot chiles.

Salty In many ways, I consider this the most significant taste element. Salt is the catalyst that lets you taste everything else (when recipes say "Salt to taste," this is what they mean). Of course you can oversalt something, and that can be a downer (but definitely an upper when it comes to your blood pressure)—which makes me want to get back on that soapbox of mine, preaching the virtues of balance in the world of Indian curries. Two main ingredients in Indian curries bring forth the salty taste: salt and black salt.

Sweet In the world of Indian curries, ingredients that infuse sweetness in a sauce tone down its bitter and hot tastes. This is especially true in curries from the eastern regions, where folks love bitter things. Each region has its sweetener of choice, some more complex-tasting than others.

A multitude of ingredients sweeten our curries. Jaggery, white granulated sugar, and both dried and fresh fruits sweeten the pot, while spices like fennel, nutmeg, and mace start by sweetly tempering the oil.

White granulated sugar imparts a one-dimensional sweetness to curries, and that's fine when you want a nonassertive sweetness to sit on the sidelines while bolder flavors bask in the limelight. Jaggery, which also comes from sugarcane but more closely resembles brown sugar, imparts a more complex flavor (see page 765).

Umami To define umami, a Japanese term, I resort to describing its coating effect, its succulence that drapes the tongue. Glutamate (also known as free glutamate), an essential amino acid, is the reason for umami. Its best-known form is deeply entrenched in the foods of China, in the additive known as MSG (monosodium glutamate). In Indo-Chinese fare, MSG (known as ajinomoto in India) is sprinkled on every curry. Knowing that many are allergic to this flavor enhancer, I have chosen to exclude it in my Indo-Chinese curries. If you like, you can throw it in (instead of the salt) in those recipes. Free glutamate is found in aged cheeses, meats, fish and shellfish, mushrooms, dairy products, nuts, legumes, and tomatoes. With the exception of aged cheeses, all these foods play a gargantuan role in Indian curries, asserting their protein-rich presence and contributing umami.

Beef, lamb, pork, fish, shellfish, chicken, duck, and quail are some of the proteinaceous products in curries. The succulence that they supply is a big factor in the curry's flavor. Each protein source tastes different, and you can take the same sauce and simmer a different meat (or even a different cut of the same meat) in it to experience a completely new taste sensation.

Mushrooms are a meat analogue, in terms of texture and chewiness. No wonder many vegetarian curries use them for that satiating trait. The recipe for Cheese-Stuffed Mushroom Caps with a Creamy Onion Sauce (page 108) shows a contemporary way of using traditional ingredients, while Mushrooms and Peas in a Fenugreek-Cream Sauce (page 519), a northern Indian classic, demonstrates mushroom's role as the meat stand-in.

The free glutamate in whole milk, yogurt, cream, and clarified butter fulfills the umami experience. Dough-soft milk solids (*Khoya,* page

nonassertive canola

❖ ❖ ❖

I use canola oil (extracted from canola flowers, a relative of mustard, cabbage, and broccoli) for my everyday Indian cooking for a multiplicity of reasons:

❖ Canola has a high smoke point that makes it ideal since most of Indian cooking starts on medium-high heat when we heat oil to roast spices or to stir-fry onions, ginger, or garlic.

❖ Canola has no flavor and does not assert itself or compete in the presence of the ingredients used to showcase a dish.

❖ Most Indian home cooking is healthy and low in fat. Canola has the lowest amount of saturated fats among all the oils, making it my choice for a healthier lifestyle.

❖ Many of our rice pulaos (pilafs) and legume curries rely on flavoring the oil with whole spices like cardamom pods, cinnamon sticks, bay leaves, and cumin seeds—which need to roast at high temperatures to release their essential oils, a technique known as tadka. As a cooking medium, canola works perfectly for this.

24) are silky, rich, and smooth. This protein-rich medium is lower in fat than cream, and when pureed with yogurt and simmered as a sauce, it acts as a stabilizer, preventing the yogurt from curdling, as it is apt to do. At times cream and half-and-half act as heat diffusers in a curry, wrapping around the sauce to tone it down. When you employ ghee (a special form of clarified butter) as a cooking medium to sear and stir-fry ingredients, it yields a mild taste. But fold the ghee in just before you serve the curry, and it drapes a buttery, fatty coating on your tongue. You don't need a lot—even a table-spoon or two is enough to provide succulence.

We tend to overlook the importance of nuts as proteinaceous, umami-satisfying ingredients in the world of curries. Cashews, pistachios, almonds, pine nuts, walnuts, and peanuts (which are actually a member of the legume family but are placed in this category for their nutty trait—crazy, isn't it?) are tapped for their hearty taste, nutty aroma, and sauce-thickening qualities.

Pistachios and almonds are imported from the Mediterranean countries, and they are used sparingly in curries in India because of their cost.

Poppy seeds and sesame seeds both have a nutlike quality that contributes to umami.

In a country that boasts of over sixty kinds of lentils, beans, and peas, legumes provide valuable protein, infusing curries with the creamy, satiating quality so essential for that umami experience. When certain legumes are toasted and roasted, then blended with spices to create signature blends like *Sambhar masala* (page 33), you realize how that is possible.

Pungent (hot) This very Asian taste element is a key one in my world of curries, and it is one that instills fear (and dislike), especially among those who wince at the mention of curry. Don't worry, the pungency is balanced out by the presence of other ingredients that diminish its presence. Black peppercorns, chiles, ginger, and cloves all breathe fire, but they all have different hot points in your mouth. Peppercorns are throat-hot, chiles cover the lips and sides of the tongue, ginger has that nose-tingling thing going, while cloves exude numbing heat.

Astringent

This particular group of ingredients is in your face, hard-hitting, and pushy. They are not a primary taste element, but their presence in a curry is definitely noticeable. They are always used in minute amounts, since a little goes a long way. When you look at words like "harsh," "severe," "caustic," and "acerbic," used to describe the taste of astringency, ingredients like asafetida, turmeric, teflam seeds, and baking powder come to mind. Don't shy away from sprinkling these ingredients into sauces and spice blends, as they are essential flavor-building elements.

Aromatic

The sense of smell is a powerful force, and aromas leave imprints in your memory bank that last for a lifetime (the smell of honey elicits a bitter taste memory for me because I was given crushed pills swirled in honey during a childhood illness). Smell helps us analyze taste. If we have a cold and can't smell, it affects our taste, since we can truly "taste," in the technical sense, only a few things. Smell helps the taste buds "taste" hundreds of ingredients, and this group of aromatic spices and herbs breathe life into our curries. When you enter a kitchen where the aroma of spices hangs in the air, it sets off a tasty anticipation of what's to come.

Among India's favorite aromatic herbs are bay leaves, cilantro, curry leaves, dill, fenugreek, and mint. In the world of spices, these rule the roost: cardamom, cumin, coriander seed, and cinnamon. I call them the high C's, as their presence is felt all over India in thousands of dishes. Another spice, *ajowan,* or bishop's weed, drapes curries with an aromatic heat, and

I include it with this group. And let's not forget the sensuous "s" (or maybe it should be $) spice that colors a perfumed trail—saffron.

Oils, liquids, thickeners, and stabilizers

When I think about curry as a structure, I look at these ingredients as its essential building blocks (its infrastructure) while the spices, herbs, and other flavorings are what make the house a home. You can't have one without the other.

The dribbling of oil into a pan usually is the start of a curry buildup. Sometimes the oil is insignificant from a flavor standpoint, its role being that of a provider of fat to sear ingredients. Flavorless oils with a high smoke point (the temperature at which oil starts to smoke) are essential for sizzling whole spices and searing meat, fish, and poultry before we stew them in sauce. Vegetable-based oils, including canola (which is not rapeseed oil, although it is often described that way), work perfectly for this. Low in saturated fats, they also have a re-use quality that I like, especially when I deep-fry nonmeat ingredients (meats leach a lot of liquid into the oil, lowering its smoke point). Peanut and corn oil also work well for this purpose, but if you are allergic to peanuts, it's best to avoid the oil too. I recently sampled rice oil and found it to be part of this "flavorless" category, and since it is rich in antioxidants, contains no trans fat, and has a smoke point of 490°F, it too suits my cooking style, although I don't find it readily available.

Every region of India has its favorite oils, many of which not only provide fat for searing and sizzling but also infuse flavor. When you look toward the southwest and Sri Lanka, you find that cooks use coconut oil in their curries. The dried meat from the coconut yields an amber-colored oil, rich with buttery taste and saturated fats. There are many schools of thought as to whether this is good for you or not. One school points out that coconut oil is made up of medium-chain triglycerides (fatty acids), which are not stored in the body as fat as readily as the long-chain triglycerides found in other oils. The lauric acid in coconut oil also makes it appealing for some because of its ability to fight infections; this is the same acid found in mothers' breast milk. When you taste the rich covering of coconut oil drizzled atop Mixed Vegetables with a Potent Coconut Chile Sauce (page 630), you will see why we adore it.

The southeast prefers unrefined sesame oil, called gingelly oil, for its delicate nutty taste that is crucial to many of their curries. Mustard oil, much valued in India's northeast, north, and northwest, is essential for a vital, bitter taste in their curries. Ghee (page 21) is also crucial to many of our curries. It is great for deep-frying because of its high smoke point. Just before you serve a curry, drizzle a tablespoon or two of ghee over it to experience that "tongue-coating," satiating quality we look for in our meats.

Once you perfume an oil with spices, it's hard not to notice the role of garlic and onion in providing fodder for the subsequent layer of sauce. Garlic and onion, indigenous to the regions in and around Afghanistan and Egypt, were considered by the Aryans in India to get in the way of seeking spiritual joy. Garlic, even now, is markedly absent in certain communities (the Jains in the northwest and the Brahmins in the south). In fact, garlic had no place in my mother's Tamil kitchen. However, it is used in many other regions. When ground into a potent paste (page 15), it marinates strong-tasting meats, and when stewed with lentils, it delicately flavors them and imparts valuable nutrients.

how to approach the recipes (besides with great joy)

❖ ❖ ❖

❖ Read the recipe from start to finish—including the headnote, which gives you a little background about the curry and a clue to its taste. This read-through will help you picture what's happening in the recipe from start to finish. The Tips at the end of the recipe provide some extra help; they shed light on techniques and ingredients, offer suggestions for alternative ingredients, and note serving suggestions.

❖ The French have a wonderful phrase, mise-en-place, which means put in place. It is especially appropriate for cooking the Indian way: Measure all the ingredients and get them prepped before you start to cook. If the recipe contains a spice blend or a paste that you don't have on hand, put it together (most take less than 5 minutes) and line it up with the other ingredients. Some spices, especially when they're sizzled in oil, take less than a minute to cook. You don't want the spices to burn while you are scurrying around for the next ingredient.

Onions have a similar role, and although there are many varieties, the red onion is the most common in India. I use only red onions and shallots in my curries, but feel free to employ any kind that appeals to you. When consumed raw or pureed, onions taste pungent, but when stir-fried long enough so that the starches change to sugars, their sweet personality takes over, giving a curry incredible sweetness. And when chunky onions brown and stew in an onion sauce, I find them meaty and very tasty.

Next in the lineup is the array of liquids that bulk up the curry's base (I always tell my students that if it weren't for liquids, there would be no Indian curries). The obvious and most pervasive of all the liquids is water. Many of our legume curries use water to cook the grains, with a simple seasoning of spices to give flavor to the water. Acidic liquids like tomato sauces, pastes, and purees dot the curry landscape, providing not only valuable moisture but also tartness and color. Dairy products like yogurt, buttermilk, cream, half-and-half, and reduced milk solids not only provide a sauce base but also lower the hot tastes in curries.

When nut purees get involved, they provide not only the textural element but also the sauce for the meats to stew in. Vegetable and fruit purees breathe abundant flavor in curries. Legume purees supply the proteins for potatoes and, in conjunction with vegetable purees, they shine in the Parsi community's signature Chicken Simmered in a Pumpkin-Lentil Sauce with Fenugreek (page 140). Smooth coconut milk is the medium for simmering vegetables like potatoes and carrots, while vinegars poach shrimp.

Once you understand the liquids that create waves in the curry's sauce, you can start thinking about its body, thickness, and viscosity. Some curries are meant to be thin-bodied, and some are naturally thick because of the inclusion of a nut, vegetable, fruit, or legume puree. Then there are a few that need to bulk up, and for that we look to flours made from chickpeas, rice, and wheat. Starches help too: Some curries employ cornstarch, and other harbor potatoes as a natural built-in thickener, especially when you mash a few of the cooked tubers.

So now you know all the elements that shape a curry. Each ingredient is described further in the Glossary of Ingredients (page 758) and I encourage you to have a read-through. I have also included a Shopping Cheat Sheet (pages 762 and 763) that tells you an ingredient's name in English and Hindi. As the saying goes, if you build it, they will come. Do experiment on your own if you are so inclined. Meanwhile, there are hundreds of curries right here for you to savor.

spice blends and pastes

to say that spices and herbs are the backbone of India's curries is an understatement. This chapter will give you some practical guidance on how to buy, store, and use them. You will find yourself coming back to the recipes time and again, because many of these pastes, blends, and sauces shape the curries and their accompaniments. Almost all of them take five minutes or less to put together. The beauty of the

blends and pastes is in their ability to be stored for lengthy periods—some even for two months. A majority do not even require refrigeration.

how to buy & store spices

these tasks seem simple—for the most part. But, like draping and unraveling a saree, there's much more to them than meets the eye. Many of the spices are easy to find in your everyday grocery store. Some, however, will necessitate a trip to an Indian or Pakistani store, which you will be able to find in any midsize city. If you are someone who enjoys shopping via the Internet, or if you don't live near a city, there are hundreds of websites that will be happy to send you (even the next day) spices, legumes, and herbs. On page 758 you will find a glossary of ingredients, including their more common Indian names, that will help you along as you walk down the aisles, or browse through the catalogs, of these stores.

When you buy spices, I strongly recommend that you buy them, as much as possible, in their whole form—for example, cumin seeds (as opposed to ground), black peppercorns (as opposed to ground), and so on. Now, some spices—like turmeric, asafetida, and mango powder—you will find only in their ground form, and I identify them as such in the recipes where they appear. Less is always more—in other words, to ensure freshness and optimum quality, buy small quantities of spices and replenish your stock as needed. If a spice package contains more than you will ever use, gather some friends and split the package among yourselves—it will save money and guarantee that you all have the freshest spices. Some natural food stores and cooperatives make it easy to purchase spices in bulk. I have found spices in these stores to be far less expensive than the bottled ones in the supermarket.

The reason I am so emphatic about procuring spices whole is a simple one, although the reasoning itself appears complex. When we Indians (by which I mean all of us in the subcontinent, including Pakistanis, Nepalese, and Sri Lankans) use spices, we can extract at least eight different flavors from any single spice, depending on the technique we use. Here's an example:

❖ Coriander seed, a member of the parsley family, is a commonly available spice. When you use it as is, you get a specific flavor.

❖ Take the whole seed and toast it (dry-toast, with no oil), and you experience a nutty-citrus aroma.

❖ Take that toasted seed and grind it, and it smells nothing like any of its previous incarnations.

❖ Grind it after you roast it, and it seems to lose its citrus bouquet.

❖ Heat a little oil and roast the seed, and discover yet another flavor—almost pungent-smelling and smoky.

❖ When you grind the seed and sprinkle it in a curry, its flavor is more pronounced and quite different.

❖ Soak the whole seed in a liquid, use it in a curry, and its presence will be surprisingly subtle.

❖ And when you grind it after you soak it, it not only takes on the liquid's taste but also imparts the spice's eighth flavor: The strong citrus-like aroma reappears, enhanced by the flavor of the liquid.

Folks, this is one spice! With the plethora of spices and herbs we have in our repertoire, from which we can extract similar numbers of flavors, you begin to realize the impact they have on the world of Indian curries. Simply put, our curries taste so complex because one ingredient (or a mere handful of ingredients) is treated in different ways to extract layers of flavors. This is the secret to the magic of Indian, Pakistani, Nepalese, and Sri Lankan curries.

Now that I have convinced you to buy whole spices, I'll give you my suggestions about storing them: Store your spices, whole or ground, in airtight jars in a cool, dry spot in your kitchen or pantry. That convenient shelf next to the hot stove is not such a good idea, even if it is handy. Refrigeration is neither necessary nor recommended since the moisture it creates affects the spice's flavor and aroma. Whole spices have a very long shelf life if properly stored; they can last up to a year (during my college days I kept whole spices for even three or four years and ground them later to unleash their robust flavors). Buying ground spices, on the other hand, is like driving a new car out of

Incidentally, I teaspoon freshly ground cumin seeds (or any other spice) is not the same as I teaspoon ground cumin from a jar. If a recipe calls for I teaspoon of a ground whole spice and you are using the bottled ground version of that spice, use about 3/4 teaspoon. In general, there's about 15 percent more volume in the freshly ground whole spice.

the dealer's lot—the moment you get behind that wheel and drive away, its value depreciates. The oils in the spice are optimum when freshly ground or heat-treated, and their flavor tends to dissipate within two months. In my recipes, I have you grind whole spices fresh for that maximum effect.

grinding spices

Ideally, a well-equipped kitchen will have a variety of grinders to serve various needs: grinding small or large amounts of spices; combining dry spices with fresh herbs; obtaining fine or coarse grinds; making a dry spice blend; and making a blend that will be turned into a paste or puree. To meet all these needs, I strongly recommend that you invest in an electric spice grinder (or a coffee grinder), a mortar and pestle, a blender, and a food processor or mini chopper.

Electric spice grinder: The ability of electric coffee grinders to grind hard coffee beans also makes them ideally suited for grinding a wide range of spices, such as dried bay leaves, cumin seeds, cloves, and broken-up cinnamon sticks. They can grind from as little as a teaspoon of spice to as much as half a cup, and they can produce both fine and coarse grinds. It is not necessary to clean the grinder after each spice. And if a recipe calls for multiple spices to go into a curry

at the same time, you can certainly plunk them all in and grind them together. (However, I often encourage my students to grind spices individually so they can see for themselves how different each spice smells before and after grinding. Over time, you should be able to identify a spice by smell alone.) If you do want to clean the grinder, wipe the inside with a slightly damp paper towel, taking extra care to clean underneath the metal blades. The blades are sharp, so be careful not to cut yourself (and unplug the grinder before you start to clean it!). Another way to eliminate any spice residue is to grind dried bread cubes in the grinder. This not only cleans out the grinder but also provides flavored breadcrumbs that you can use to coat fish, meat, and poultry.

Blends of whole spices, whether they are raw, toasted, or even stir-fried in a little oil, can be ground in a spice grinder. However, fresh herbs like chiles, cilantro, and mint cannot be minced or ground in a coffee grinder because of their high moisture content.

One word of caution: Do not use the same grinder for spices and coffee beans. The oils in the coffee beans leave a residue that is difficult to clean out, and your spices will taste and smell different.

Mortar and pestle: The familiar concave dish called a mortar, and its "pounder," the pestle, have been around for centuries. Many cultures, including mine, still rely on the mortar and pestle for their daily pounding and grinding needs. Mortars and pestles come in various shapes, sizes, and materials, including ceramic (both porous and nonporous surfaces), marble, stoneware, cast iron, stainless steel, and even brass. Some are as big as large mixing bowls, while a few are only large enough to hold a scant half teaspoon of whole spices (now that's

Here are six blends and pastes that are great to have on hand. They will curry many a dish in this book and are a cinch to put together.

- ◆ Ginger Paste (Adrak ka lep) (page 15)
- ◆ Garlic Paste (Lasoon ka lep) (page 15)
- ◆ Punjabi-Style Warming Spice Blend (Punjabi garam masala) (page 25)
- ◆ Toasted Cumin-Coriander Blend (Dhania-jeera masala) (page 33)
- ◆ Roasted Chile, Spice, and Legume Blend (Sambhar masala) (page 33)
- ◆ Ghee (Clarified butter) (page 21)

kick-sand-in-your-face wimpy). Some "floor models" in India can weigh as much as 250 pounds. Most mortars and pestles are midsize: They're wide enough and deep enough to hold a cup of spices and herbs. My favorite, hands-on, is the porous Mexican *molcajete* (it's made of lava stone) that's sold in kitchenware shops. It is very similar to the ones we use in India.

Because the ingredients that you put into mortars are pounded and ground with the force of your hand and arm, the consistency of the final product can vary dramatically. While using a mortar and pestle can be time-consuming, it does have a distinct advantage over other grinders: both dried and fresh spices and herbs can be combined in this tool and pounded to form wonderful pastes with complex textures. The mortar and pestle is also ideal when combining dry and fresh herbs that should be crushed just enough to release their essential oils. And if you are grinding small amounts of spices, such as cloves, cardamom, peppercorns, cumin seeds, or

dried chiles, the mortar and pestle is ideal because you can control the coarseness.

Blender: There is nothing more effective than a blender when combining liquids with dry spices, fresh herbs, onions, garlic, or ginger for sauces, pastes, or purees. Glass blender jars, unlike plastic, will not absorb the aromas and flavors of spices and herbs. Large volumes of whole spices can be ground in a blender with surprisingly great results. However, blenders fail to do the job when all you need is a small quantity of a freshly ground spice. No two blenders are the same. Blenders with a narrow base effectively puree sauces and pastes. The broader-base models are better suited for blended drinks (which is why I have one of each: I can puree that Ginger Chile Paste in one while I sip a glass of blended margarita made in the other). I also adore the handheld stick blenders known as immersion blenders, especially if I need to puree legumes and vegetables after they cook (it saves cooling time and avoids messing up a blender jar).

Food processor and mini chopper: When it comes to mincing garlic, ginger, onions, and fresh herbs, food processors and mini choppers are a time-saving boon for busy cooks. There are many well-known brands of electric food processors. Handheld non-electric mini choppers rely on the user's strength to pulverize and mince herbs and spices. When making purees and coarsely chopped pastes, both appliances work well, especially when combining dry spices, fresh herbs, and liquids. Large and small food processors, and handheld mini choppers, don't do a good job with small amounts of fresh chiles; this is one instance where you're

What is jaggery? Where to find mango powder? Check the Glossary of Ingredients on page 758 for a complete description of Indian ingredients.

better off with a sharp chef's knife. These appliances do work well for mincing large volumes of chiles, ginger, garlic, onion, and fresh herbs. Use the pulsing action to mince herbs, onions, and so on, especially if you do not want too much of the ingredients' moisture in the mix.

Food processors and mini choppers do not work well for grinding dried whole spices by themselves.

So, if I were to equip your kitchen (with your hard-earned money, of course), I would arm it with an electric spice grinder, a mortar and pestle, a blender, and a food processor. You do want your kitchen to look like mine, don't you?

Ginger Paste

Adrak Ka Lep

those gnarly knobs of ginger contain a phenomenally pungent flavor and aroma. (The term "ginger root" is a misnomer because it is technically a rhizome, the bulbous stem end of the plant from which the roots emerge.) You can find fresh ginger in the produce department of most supermarkets. Look for bulbs with smooth brown skin and a hard surface; the bulb should feel heavy. Avoid ginger that is light, soft, and wrinkled. And do not be afraid of snapping off what you need at the store (no ginger police will be lurking in the aisles) if the root is too big. Fresh ginger has a relatively long shelf life, especially when kept loosely wrapped in a plastic bag in your refrigerator's humidity-controlled vegetable bin. Do not freeze pieces of fresh ginger; it becomes unmanageable, unpalatable, and rubbery when

thawed. (You can, however, freeze minced ginger.) Wash the ginger before use. If the skin is clean, smooth, and doesn't appear dry, you don't have to bother peeling it. Simply slice off any dry *ends* before using it. If the skin is tough and appears slightly woody, it's best to peel it, using a swivel peeler or a paring knife. **MAKES ABOUT 1¼ CUPS**

8 ounces coarsely chopped fresh ginger

Pour ½ cup water into a blender jar, and then add the ginger. (Adding the water first will ensure a smoother grind.) Puree, scraping the inside of the jar as needed, until it forms a smooth, light brown paste. Store the paste in a tightly sealed container in the refrigerator for up to 1 week. (I often divide the paste into smaller containers and freeze them for up to 1 month. Another option is to freeze 1-tablespoon portions in ice cube trays; once they are frozen, pop them out and transfer them to freezer-safe self-seal bags.)

Garlic Paste

Lasoon Ka Lep

twenty-two years ago, when I first landed on the shores of the United States, I had two large suitcases filled with memories from my home, including a strong abhorrence for garlic. Years later, I admit, I have seen the light. Now I keep a jar of garlic paste in my refrigerator to bestow its pungent presence on many a curry (especially those from the north of India) at a moment's notice. **MAKES ABOUT 1¼ CUPS**

50 medium-size to large cloves garlic, peeled

Pour ½ cup water into a blender jar, and then add the garlic. (Adding the water first will ensure a smoother grind.) Puree, scraping the inside of the jar as needed, until if forms a smooth paste. Store the paste in a tightly sealed container in the refrigerator for up to 1 week. (I often divide the paste into smaller containers and freeze them for up to 1 month. Another option is to place 1-tablespoon portions in ice cube trays and freeze them; once they are frozen, pop them out and transfer them to freezer-safe self-seal bags.)

Tip: Yes, you can spend the time and peel your own garlic cloves, but given the fact that your favorite grocery store carries whole peeled garlic cloves in plastic jars, right there in the refrigerated section next to the produce, wouldn't you want to save some time? (And do I like the pre-minced garlic in jars that are so readily available? No. It usually sits in oil or vinegar, affecting the flavor.)

Fried Onion Paste

Pyaaz ka Lep

fried Onion Paste is a key ingredient in many curries from the northern regions of India and Pakistan. It provides a smooth, sweet, dark brown base that mellows out the harsh flavors of ginger and garlic, two other common items in those curries. You can use yellow or white onions, but the red ones are *it* in classic Indian cooking.

MAKES 3 CUPS

¼ cup canola oil
2 pounds red onions, cut in half lengthwise
and thinly sliced

1. Preheat a wok or a large, deep frying pan over medium heat. Pour in the oil and swish it around gently to coat the bottom of the pan. The oil will immediately get hot and appear to shimmer. Add the onions and cook them, stirring occasionally, until they are caramel-brown with a deep purple hue, 25 to 30 minutes. Initially they will stew in the oil, but once they start to cook down in volume, you will need to stir them more often as they start to stick to the bottom. Transfer the onions to a plate to cool.

2. Pour 1 cup water into a blender jar. Add the caramelized onions and puree, scraping the inside of the jar as needed, to make a smooth, reddish-brown paste. (If you won't be using all of the onion paste, divide it into smaller batches and freeze them for up to 2 months. Leftover onion paste, stored in a tightly sealed container, will keep in the refrigerator for up to 1 week.)

Tip: The key to this recipe is the slow cooking of the onions, which releases their sugars. The more caramel-colored the onions, the richer the paste. Some households (and a larger number of restaurants) deep-fry the onions to get that particular shade of brown. You can do this if you're in a rush, but you must be careful not to overly crisp them, as the resultant paste can be bitter. You can also buy vacuum-sealed packages of fried onions in Pakistani and Indian grocery stores. I often keep a bag of these in the refrigerator (as they may turn rancid at room temperature if kept a long time) for those moments when I am fresh out of onions. Puree 1 cup of these fried onions with 1 cup water to yield 1 cup of onion paste.

Red Chile and Vinegar Paste

balchao masala

A pickle-like blend of ingredients called *balchao,* is crucial to many of Portuguese Goa's meat dishes, and usually incorporates Goa's other passion, *feni,* a potent alcoholic brew made from either cashew nuts or palm fruit. Also omnipresent in Goan dishes is the highly acidic *feni* vinegar, which reduces the potency of dried red chiles—as does tart tamarind, another key element in this layered, complex, and fiery-hot paste that peppers its way into many of Goa's curries. Unfortunately, neither the alcohol nor the vinegar is available outside of India (maybe even outside of Goa), and so my offering is devoid of both. Nonetheless, it is very flavorful, with cider or malt vinegar standing in as a perfectly acceptable substitute. **MAKES ½ CUP**

½ cup cider vinegar or malt vinegar

1 teaspoon tamarind paste or concentrate

1 cup dried red Thai or cayenne chiles,
   stems removed

1 tablespoon cumin seeds

1 teaspoon black peppercorns

½ teaspoon whole cloves

½ teaspoon ground turmeric

12 medium-size cloves garlic

2 lengthwise slices fresh ginger (each 2½ inches long,
   1 inch wide, and ⅛ inch thick)

2 cinnamon sticks (each 3 inches long), broken into
   smaller pieces

1. Pour the vinegar into a blender jar, and then add all the remaining ingredients. Puree, scraping the inside of the jar as needed, until it forms a highly pungent, reddish-brown paste.

2. Store the mixture in a tightly sealed nonreactive container in the refrigerator for up to 2 weeks, or in the freezer for up to 2 months.

Tip: Pouring the liquid into the blender jar first ensures a smooth puree, so do make sure you follow the recommended order for adding ingredients to the jar. If you are making only a half batch, you might need to add an extra tablespoon of vinegar (5 tablespoons total rather than ¼ cup) to get the blades to do a decent job of pureeing, just because of the sheer volume of chunky ingredients.

Ginger Chile Paste

Adrak Hara Mirch ka Lep

Sampled on its own, this paste will feel like a slap in the face, but when it's combined with the right components in a curry, it hurts so good. Even though both these ingredients generate heat, they feel different on your palate. Chiles have an immediate burn, especially around the sides of the tongue, while ginger has a throatier glow. Whether you stir-fry, steam, stew, or incorporate the Ginger Chile Paste in a marinade, each technique will extract a different level of gusto from the light green paste. **MAKES 1 CUP**

8 ounces coarsely chopped fresh ginger
12 fresh green Thai, cayenne, or serrano chiles,
    stems removed

Pour ½ cup water into a blender jar, and then add the ginger and chiles. (Adding the water first will ensure a smoother grind.) Puree, scraping the inside of the jar as needed, until it forms a smooth, light green paste. Store the paste in a tightly sealed container in the refrigerator for up to 1 week. (I often divide the paste into smaller containers and freeze them for up to 1 month. Another option is to freeze 1-tablespoon portions in ice cube trays; when they are frozen, pop them out and transfer them to freezer-safe self-seal bags.)

Simmered Tomato Sauce
WITH CHILES AND CARDAMOM

tamatar ka lep

Even though many recipes in the book use tomato sauce, I'm not going to insist that you make your own. I certainly want you to make these curries, but I am all for cutting corners to save time if it doesn't mean a compromise in the flavor. However, store-bought canned tomato sauce won't contain the spices this one does, so if you happen to have a few spare minutes on an uneventful Saturday afternoon, double or even triple the batch and freeze it in half-cup sizes for future use. The ingredients are easy to come by, and you won't have to labor over the stove for hours on end. **MAKES 2 CUPS**

2 tablespoons Ghee (page 21) or canola oil
6 green or white cardamom pods
2 fresh or dried bay leaves
2 cinnamon sticks (each 3 inches long)
1 can (15 ounces) tomato sauce
2 teaspoons ground Kashmiri chiles; or
    ½ teaspoon cayenne (ground red pepper)
    mixed with 1½ teaspoons sweet paprika

1. Heat the ghee in a small saucepan over medium heat. Sprinkle in the cardamom pods, bay leaves, and cinnamon sticks, and let them sizzle, crackle, and expand a bit, 1 to 2 minutes.

2. Carefully pour in the tomato sauce (stand back, as it will splatter). Sprinkle in the chiles and stir to blend. Lower the heat to medium-low, cover the pan, and simmer, stirring occasionally, until an oily layer forms on the surface and around the edges, 25 to 30 minutes. The sauce will be deep red, thanks to the Kashmiri chiles.

3. Discard the cardamom, bay leaves, and cinnamon sticks, and let the sauce cool completely. Store the sauce in a tightly sealed container in the refrigerator, where it will keep for up to 2 weeks, or in the freezer for up to 2 months.

Mint-Yogurt Sauce
WITH CHILES

pudhina dahi chutney

One of the essential sauces in the world of *chaat* (pages 44–50), this condiment is also great as a minty green, yogurt-tart, chiles-hot bed for silky smooth Chickpea Flour "Cigars" (page 114). **MAKES ½ CUP**

½ cup firmly packed fresh cilantro leaves and
    tender stems
½ cup firmly packed fresh mint leaves
1 tablespoon plain yogurt
½ teaspoon coarse kosher or sea salt
6 fresh green Thai, cayenne, or serrano chiles,
    stems removed
1 lengthwise slice fresh ginger (2½ inches long,
    1 inch wide, and ⅛ inch thick)

1. Pour ¼ cup water into a blender jar, and then pile in the remaining ingredients. Puree, scraping the inside of the jar as needed, until it forms a smooth, bright green sauce.

2. Store this minty-hot sauce in a tightly sealed container in the refrigerator for up to 5 days, or in the freezer for up to 1 month.

Cilantro-Mint Blend
WITH GARLIC

hara masala

this gritty, bright green *(hara)* herb blend *(masala)* is best when processed just before using. If you need only half of it for a recipe, make half a batch. I often make a whole batch and use some for stir-frying my morning fix of pan-fried potatoes, especially on weekends. The garlic will linger on your breath, but as long as everyone else at the table is in cahoots with you, there's no cause for embarrassment. **MAKES 1 CUP**

1 cup firmly packed fresh cilantro leaves and
    tender stems
1 cup firmly packed fresh mint leaves
    (see Tips)
8 medium-size cloves garlic
4 lengthwise slices fresh ginger
    (each 2½ inches long, 1 inch wide,
    and ⅛ inch thick)

1. Stuff all the ingredients into a food processor and chop, using the pulsing action, until they appear well minced. (This fresh-cut-grass-like herb blend should not be watery. If you allow the machine to run continuously, rather than pulse, that is exactly what will happen.)

2. Use the mixture immediately, or store it in a tightly sealed container in the refrigerator for up to 2 days. You can freeze it for up to 1 month, but the flavors and aromas will dissipate and the thawed herb blend will be discolored and watery.

Tips:

❖ Either spearmint or peppermint will be fine for this blend. *Fresh* is the key. Grow a pot of mint in the summertime; considered a weed by some gardeners, it is manna for connoisseurs of fine cooking.

❖ Since this herb blend has no acid or oil to preserve it, it will have a short shelf life in the refrigerator. Adding a few tablespoons of distilled white vinegar or lime juice to any leftovers will preserve it for a longer period, but the flavors will change sharply.

Red Chile, Garlic, and Shallot Sauce

Lal Mirch Lasoon Chutney

Its saucy, fiery, orange-red color is a clue to its dragon-breath-like quality, puffing wisps of burning heat in every single drop. My version tries to calm the flames by incorporating shallots and a tiny bit of sugar, but you will be the judge of their effectiveness. This is often the second sauce layer in some of the *chaats* (pages 44–50), India's popular street foods.

MAKES ⅓ CUP

> 1 cup boiling water
> 20 dried red Thai or cayenne chiles, stems removed
> ¼ cup thinly sliced shallots or red onion
> 1 teaspoon white granulated sugar
> ½ teaspoon coarse kosher or sea salt
> 6 medium-size cloves garlic

1. Pour the boiling water over the chiles in a small bowl, and set aside until the chiles have softened and the water has turned light reddish-orange, 1 to 2 hours. (I have certainly forgotten it and left it overnight, and everything has worked just fine.)

2. Drain the chiles, reserving ¼ cup of the liquid.

3. Pour the reserved liquid into a blender jar, and then add the chiles and all the remaining ingredients. Puree, scraping the inside of the jar as needed, until it forms a smooth, orange-red, pulpy paste.

4. Transfer this knock-your-socks-off-hot sauce to a tightly sealed container and refrigerate it for up to 5 days, or freeze it for up to 1 month.

Sweet-Tart Tamarind-Date Sauce

Sonth

Addictively sweet-tart, this sauce is the crucial one to blanket India's *chaats* (pages 44–50), making sure the hot flavors get tilted toward sweet and tart, proving that dichotomous tastes can and do exist harmoniously in the same dish. **MAKES 1 CUP**

> 1 teaspoon tamarind paste or concentrate
> ¼ cup crumbled or chopped jaggery or
>   firmly packed dark brown sugar
> 10 pitted dates (each about 2 inches long),
>   coarsely chopped

1. Pour 1½ cups water into a small saucepan, add the tamarind, and whisk until it has dissolved and formed a tart, muddy brown liquid. Add the jaggery and dates, and bring to a boil over medium heat. Boil, uncovered, stirring occasionally, until the liquid has evaporated by almost half, about 10 minutes. Remove the pan from the heat and allow the sauce to cool for about 5 minutes.

2. Transfer the dark brown, thin sauce and cooked-but-chunky dates to a blender jar and puree, scraping

the inside of the jar as needed, until it forms a pancake-batter-thick, milk-chocolate-colored, tart-sweet sauce.

3. Transfer the sauce to a tightly sealed container (preferably glass, stainless steel, ceramic, or plastic because of the highly acidic tamarind) and store it in the refrigerator for up to 5 days or in the freezer for up to 2 months.

Yogurt Sauce
WITH BLACK SALT

Kala Namak Dahi

t his yogurt-based sauce blankets all *chaat* recipes (pages 44–50), mellowing out the harsh chiles in some of the other sauces. Black salt is available in any Indian grocery store and has a unique flavor—don't try to substitute kosher or sea salt. **MAKES ½ CUP**

½ cup plain yogurt
2 teaspoons white granulated sugar
½ teaspoon black salt

Whisk the yogurt, sugar, and black salt together in a small bowl. Transfer the sweet-tasting sauce (with an aroma similar to that of hard-boiled eggs, thanks to the black salt) to a tightly sealed container and store in the refrigerator for up to 10 days. (I do not recommend freezing it because once thawed, yogurt has a slight, unappealing grittiness—and the sauce will be too watery.)

ghee

Clarified Butter

W e Indians do not always use ghee in our cooking, because we, too, are concerned about our diet. But its nutty flavor, the result of gentle browning, is the key taste in many curries, and often even a mere tablespoon is enough to provide succulence. Since the Vedic times (over 6,000 years ago) of the Indo-Aryan culture, ghee has played a role in many facets of Hinduism, including fueling the eternal flame associated with birth, marriage, and death. Ghee evolved thousands of years ago, when there was no refrigeration (actually, many Indians still don't have refrigerators today). Milk solids and water promote rancidity in butter, and when they are removed, gone is the need for a refrigerator. Middle Eastern and Arabic *samneh* is made the same way, as is *smen* from North Africa (as much as the word processing software wants to add an e between "s" and "m," don't let it!). **MAKES ABOUT 12 OUNCES (1½ CUPS)**

1 pound unsalted butter

1. Line a fine-mesh tea strainer with a piece of cheese-cloth, set it over a clean, dry glass measuring cup or pint-size canning jar, and set it aside.

2. Melt the butter in a small, heavy-bottomed saucepan over low heat, stirring it occasionally to ensure an even melt (otherwise, the bottom part of the block melts and starts to bubble while the top half remains firm). Once it melts, you will notice that a lot of foam is gathering on the surface. Scoop the foam out with

a spoon or just let it be; the melted butter will eventually stop foaming and start to subside. Now you can start to carefully skim off the foam. Some of the milk solids will settle at the bottom and start to brown lightly. This light browning is what gives Indian ghee its characteristic nutty flavor. This process will take 15 to 20 minutes.

3. Once the liquid appears quite clear (like oil) with a light amber hue, pour it through the cheesecloth-lined strainer, leaving the browned milk solids behind, and set it aside to cool.

4. When the ghee is cool, pour it into a storage jar (if it isn't already in one) and shut it. Keep it at room temperature, right next to your other bottled oils; it will solidify, even at room temperature. (I don't find it necessary to refrigerate ghee, but if you wish, by all means do so. I have kept mine at room temperature for many months, without any concern for rancidity or spoilage. Because ghee has no milk solids in it, and that's what can turn butter rancid, I do as millions in India do, and leave it out.)

Tips:

❖ A few do's and don'ts. First, *don't* use margarine or any butter substitutes that want you to think they're just like the real deal. *Do* use a heavy-bottomed pan to prevent the butter from scorching. Cast iron, stainless steel, carbon steel, and ceramic-coated cast iron are all fair game. In fact, I use a cast-iron or carbon steel wok if I happen to be making a large batch, as the fat seasons the pan. *Don't* turn up the heat beyond the low setting, as much as you may be tempted to do so; if you do, the milk solids will start to burn. *Do* make sure the glass jar is clean and dry before pouring in the ghee. Moisture will promote the growth of mold, which is the same reason why you should let the ghee cool completely before screwing on that jar's lid.

❖ Here's a Cliff Claven–style tidbit for all of you *Cheers* fans who adored the mailman's life, filled with inane banalities: You cannot deep-fry in butter because it has a low smoke point (that's the temperature at which oil starts to smoke). However, remove the milk solids and moisture, and you have elevated butter's smoke point, making it safe for deep-frying (of course, we are not talking about measuring fat calories when you do decide to splurge on fried foods this way).

❖ Ghee is widely available in stores. It is not easy on the pocketbook, so be prepared to plunk down your hard-earned money for the convenience, should you not have 15 to 20 minutes of free time to spend in the kitchen. I often splurge and buy ghee that is imported from India, only because the cows (or water buffalo, depending on where the milk came from) graze on a different diet and the ghee has a unique flavor not found in America's dairy land.

Thick Yogurt

gaada dahi

Silky-thick yogurt is made by separating as much of the whey from the curds as possible to create a thickened product that has the consistency of smooth whipped butter. Thick yogurt provides great texture to some curries, especially when meats marinate in it before stewing. Some Greek and Middle Eastern grocery stores stock thick yogurt (also called "yogurt cheese"), because it is widely used in many of their sauces and dips. **MAKES 3 CUPS**

4 cups plain yogurt

1. Line a colander with a generous piece of cheese-cloth (a single layer is fine), its edges hanging over by at least 3 to 4 inches. (Once you plop the yogurt in, it weighs down the cloth, reducing a good portion of the overhang. It's a rather messy operation to retrieve the edge of the cheesecloth if you haven't left enough extra.)

2. Place the colander in the sink or a bowl, and pour the yogurt into it. Cover the colander loosely with plastic wrap, and allow the whey to drip out for 3 to 5 hours at room temperature, or overnight in the refrigerator (I like to save the whey and use it in place of water in curries).

3. Transfer the thick yogurt to a container and refrigerate it, covered. It will easily keep for up to 2 weeks. Freezing is not an option.

Tip: Milk from cows and water buffalo are both common in India, with the buffalo milk yielding richer-tasting, creamier milk. Buffalo milk is naturally more homogenous (the fat globules are more evenly distributed) than cow's and has a higher amount of cream, lactose, and protein, with lower cholesterol. It has a lesser amount of carotene, and as a result, the milk is snow-white in appearance. Cup for cup, buffalo milk yields more curds and less whey in the yogurt than cow's milk.

making your own yogurt

❖ ❖ ❖

There are some good brands of yogurt, and I have no reason to push you into making your own. (If I insisted on it, you might put this book down and walk away. Now, why would I want that?) Having said that, I wouldn't be a good teacher if I didn't show you a foolproof way to make yogurt at home, should you wish to do it. I recommend starting with 2 cups of milk for a small family, 4 cups if there are a lot of yogurt enthusiasts. I make mine with standard homogenized, pasteurized whole milk because it gives the best mouth feel. You can make yours with lower-fat milk or even skim milk, but I find the results to be slightly chalky-tasting. To make the first batch of yogurt, you will also need some store-bought yogurt; read the label to make sure it contains live cultures like Streptococcus thermophilus and/or Lactobacillus bulgaricus. Place the milk in a small saucepan over medium or medium-high heat and bring it to a boil, uncovered, stirring frequently so that it does not stick to the bottom of the pan. As soon as it comes to a boil, pour the hot milk into a medium-size glass bowl (stainless steel, ceramic, or pottery will also do), and let it cool down to around 110°F. Then stir 1 to 2 tablespoons of the store-bought yogurt into the warm milk. Cover the bowl with plastic wrap and set it in an oven with the heat off. The goal is to create and maintain a warm, slightly humid, draft-free environment for the bacteria to do its magic. I usually leave the oven light on, which is enough to create that atmosphere. In about 6 hours you will be rewarded with a cream-on-top yogurt that is naturally sweet and not too tart. (In fact, once the yogurt sets, the longer it sits out, the tarter it turns, resulting in the production of more watery whey.)

Before your family devours all your delicious yogurt, reserve a couple of tablespoons to use for creating your next batch—you'll never have to buy store-bought again!

So, if you can boil milk, you can make yogurt! It's that simple.

Whole Milk Solids

khoya

Luxurious *khoya* provides a complex-tasting, rich, nutty flavor, with an underlying sweet-salty quality, creamy as heavy cream with far less fat. **MAKES ¼ CUP**

2 cups whole milk

1. Bring the milk to a boil in a medium-size saucepan over medium-high heat, stirring frequently to prevent it from scorching. Once it comes to a boil, lower the heat to medium. Continue boiling the milk down, scraping the sides of the pan occasionally to release the milk solids and stirring them back into the liquid, until 99 percent of the liquid has evaporated and only creamy light yellow solids remain, about 30 minutes.

2. Now keep stirring constantly until the remaining moisture dissipates and the solids have come together into a loose ball. Remove the pan from the burner and transfer the ball of milk solids to a plate to cool. The "dough" should feel very satin-soft and not very sticky. The more it cools, the more dough-like it will feel.

3. The milk solids will keep, covered, in the refrigerator for up to 1 week. Any longer than that, and a light green mosslike fungus may form on its surface—at which point it's best to discard it. You can freeze the milk solids, wrapped in plastic wrap and stored in a freezer-safe self-seal bag, for up to 2 months. To thaw it, leave it overnight in the refrigerator.

ENGLISH-STYLE Madras Curry Powder

Angrezi Curry Masala

there is no Indian name (the above is my loose translation) for this blend because it doesn't exist in any home kitchen in India, let alone in the southeastern city after which it is named. So what makes it a Madras curry powder? Probably the inclusion of dried red chiles, bitter fenugreek seeds, and nutty-strong mustard seeds—all signatures of Madrasi cuisine. Madras curry powder is the almost iconic representation of Indian cuisine in Western eyes. Some commercial mixes may contain as many as twenty spices, but the one I have devised brings home the essence of that blend with just eight.

The English prepared and sold commercial curry powders back in the 18th century, during the era of the East India Company. But in 1889, according to *Larousse Gastronomique,* the Universal Paris Exhibition determined a formula for curry powder that was to include set portions of tamarind, onion, coriander, chile pepper, turmeric, cumin, fenugreek, black pepper, and mustard. In honor of the awareness of "Indian curry" created by the East India Company, I have included a few recipes in this book that call for this mixture.

You can easily substitute a store-bought brand of Madras curry powder if you don't want to bother grinding your own (although there is really no comparison in terms of flavor). **MAKES ⅓ CUP**

1 tablespoon coriander seeds

2 teaspoons cumin seeds

1 teaspoon black or yellow mustard seeds

½ teaspoon whole cloves

½ teaspoon fenugreek seeds

½ teaspoon black peppercorns

5 to 7 dried red Thai or cayenne chiles, to taste,
  stems removed

1 teaspoon ground turmeric

1. Place all the ingredients except the turmeric in a spice grinder or coffee grinder, and grind until the texture resembles that of finely ground black pepper. Stir in the turmeric (which will give the mixture its characteristic yellow hue).

2. Store the blend in a tightly sealed container, away from excess light, heat, and humidity, for up to 2 months. (In my opinion, refrigerating the blend adversely affects its flavors.)

PUNJABI-STYLE
Warming Spice Blend

Punjabi Garam Masala

Indian cooking in the eyes of the Western world has become synonymous with *garam* (meaning "warm," as in the internal warmth generated by the body when it imbibes certain spices) *masala* ("blend"). In India *garam masala* is known as a blend of warming spices that is prepared in homes all around the northern, eastern,

and western regions of the country. Each cook weaves in his or her personal cooking style and regional ingredients, resulting in thousands of signature blends. Punjabis from northern India have made great strides in the culinary world, placing Indian restaurant cooking on the Western map, and have made their garam masala a household name. This version toasts whole spices, and when they are ground, the blend is amazingly complex.

MAKES ABOUT ¼ CUP

1 tablespoon coriander seeds

1 teaspoon cumin seeds

1 teaspoon whole cloves

½ teaspoon black peppercorns

½ teaspoon cardamom seeds from black pods

3 cinnamon sticks (each 3 inches long), broken into
  smaller pieces

3 fresh or dried bay leaves

1. Preheat a small skillet over medium-high heat. Add all the spices and the bay leaves, and toast, shaking the skillet every few seconds, until the coriander and cumin turn reddish brown, the cloves, peppercorns, and cardamom turn ash-black, the cinnamon and bay leaves appear brittle and crinkly, and the mixture is highly fragrant, 1 to 2 minutes.

2. Immediately transfer the nutty-smelling spices to a plate to cool. (The longer they sit in the hot skillet, the more likely it is that they will burn, making them bitter and unpalatable.) Once they are cool to the touch, place them in a spice grinder or coffee grinder, and grind until the texture resembles that of finely ground black pepper. (If you don't allow the spices to cool, the ground blend will acquire unwanted moisture from the heat, making the final blend slightly "cakey.") The ground blend will be reddish brown and the aroma will be sweet and complex, very different from that of the pre-toasted and post-toasted whole spices.

3. Store in a tightly sealed container, away from excess light, heat, and humidity, for up to 2 months. (In my opinion, refrigerating the blend adversely affects its flavor.)

EASTERN INDIAN
Sweet Scented Blend

bangala garam masala

Simple combinations can yield astonishingly complex flavors, as is evident in this easy-to-prepare spice blend. This sweet-smelling mixture enlivens many curries from the not-so-simple congested city of Calcutta, which hugs the Bay of Bengal on the eastern coast of India. Because of the small amount of spices and the fact that they are not toasted (which would make them brittle and easy to grind), you will not get a fine grind the first time you put them through the grinder. A few repeats should do it.

MAKES ABOUT 3 TABLESPOONS

- 1 teaspoon whole cloves
- 1 teaspoon cardamom seeds from green or white pods
- 4 cinnamon sticks (each 3 inches long), broken into smaller pieces

1. Place all the ingredients in a spice grinder or coffee grinder, and grind until the texture resembles that of coarsely ground black pepper. Sift this mixture through a fine-mesh strainer (like a tea strainer) into a small bowl. Regrind the coarse mixture left behind in the strainer. Repeat the straining and grinding two or three times more, until you have at least 3 tablespoons finely ground blend. Discard any coarse residual blend that cannot be ground any more. (Or, if you are as frugal as I am, dump the uncooperative pieces into a mortar and pound them into submission.)

2. Store the blend in a tightly sealed container, away from excess light, heat, and humidity, for up to 2 months. (In my opinion, refrigerating the blend adversely affects its flavor.)

Aromatic Minty Blend
WITH MACE AND NUTMEG

Rajasthani garam masala

Rekha was between twenty and twenty-five years of age (she didn't remember the exact age, she said, as it was not important, alluding to life before marriage) when she was given away in marriage to Shanker Singh. Both came from a small rural village near the bustling but relaxed city of Jaipur in the northwestern state of Rajasthan. Now they have an eighteen-year-old son, Pawan, and the family works on a farm owned by a travel agency, tending to peas, carrots, spinach, eggplant, beans, limes, and mustard. Shanker and Rekha cook special meals for those fortunate enough to receive an invitation to the farm, using produce from the backyard. Pawan acts as waiter. While the farm's owners entertained the guests in my group, I hung around in the sparsely equipped, open-air kitchen, talking with Shanker and Rekha about food, cooking, and spices. This blend is a finishing spice (which means that, to preserve the aromatic flavors, it is usually not cooked into a dish) that they use as they cook and weave passion into all that they touch. **MAKES 3 TABLESPOONS**

- ½ teaspoon black peppercorns
- ½ teaspoon black cumin seeds (see Tip)
- ¼ teaspoon whole cloves
- ¼ teaspoon cardamom seeds from green or white pods
- 1 or 2 dried bay leaves
- 2 tablespoons dried mint leaves, crushed or crumbled
- 1 teaspoon ground Kashmiri chiles; or ¼ teaspoon cayenne (ground red pepper) mixed with ¾ teaspoon sweet paprika
- ½ teaspoon ground ginger
- ½ teaspoon ground nutmeg
- ½ teaspoon ground mace
- ¼ teaspoon ground cinnamon

1. Place the peppercorns, cumin, cloves, cardamom, and bay leaves in a spice grinder or coffee grinder, and grind until the texture resembles that of finely ground black pepper. Dump the mixture into a small bowl and stir in the remaining ingredients.

2. Store the minty-smelling mixture in a tightly sealed container, away from excess light, heat, and humidity, for up to 2 months. (In my opinion, refrigerating the blend adversely affects its flavor.)

Tip: Black cumin imparts a smoky flavor to this mix, but if it's not at hand in your pantry, use the more commonly available cumin instead. I would recommend toasting the standard cumin seeds briefly, until they are reddish brown, before adding them to the other whole spices in the spice grinder.

Roasted Spices
WITH CHILES AND STAR ANISE

Usha Raikar's Garam Masala

You immediately adore some people, the moment you meet them. Usha Raikar is one of those people. Her toss-your-head-back-and-laugh vivaciousness and her attention to detail, especially when it comes to food, won and kept my attention for the evening. While entertaining friends in her spacious apartment in one of suburban Mumbai's high-rises, she shared many of her family's favorites with me, including this spice blend. Usha's beautiful daughter, Urmi (literally meaning "you are mine"), hovered in the kitchen, a combination of her mother's intelligence and beauty and her father's quiet charm. This garam masala reflects the warmth of that family, full of spicy life. **MAKES A SCANT 1 CUP**

- ½ cup dried red Thai or cayenne chiles, stems removed
- 4 dried bay leaves
- 2 tablespoons coriander seeds
- 1 tablespoon white poppy seeds
- 1 tablespoon black peppercorns
- 1 teaspoon cumin seeds
- 1 teaspoon black cumin seeds (see Tips)
- 1 teaspoon black or yellow mustard seeds
- 6 green or white cardamom pods
- 2 whole star anise
- 2 black cardamom pods
- 2 cinnamon sticks (each 3 inches long), broken into smaller pieces
- 5 blades mace
- 1 teaspoon canola oil
- ½ teaspoon ground asafetida (see Tips)

1. Combine the chiles, bay leaves, and all the whole spices, including the mace, in a medium-size bowl. Drizzle the oil over the ingredients and toss them well to coat them evenly with the oil. (This is much easier to do in a bowl than in a skillet.)

2. Preheat a medium-size skillet over medium-high heat. Add the mixture and roast, stirring constantly, until the chiles blacken slightly, the spices darken a bit, and the mixture is highly aromatic, 3 to 4 minutes.

3. Immediately transfer the pungent, nutty-smelling mixture to a plate to cool. (The longer they sit in the hot skillet, the more likely it is that the spices will burn, making them bitter and unpalatable.) Once they are cool to the touch, place half the ingredients in a spice grinder or coffee grinder, and grind until the texture resembles that of finely ground black pepper. (If you don't allow the spices to cool, the ground blend will acquire unwanted moisture from the heat, making the final blend slightly "cakey.") Transfer the ground mixture to a small bowl and repeat with the remaining batch. Thoroughly combine the two ground batches. The blend will be dark brown and the aroma will be sweet and complex, very different from that of the pre-toasted and post-toasted whole spices. Stir in the asafetida.

4. Store the blend in a tightly sealed container, away from excess light, heat, and humidity, for up to 2 months. (In my opinion, refrigerating the blend adversely affects its flavor.)

Tips:

❖ Black cumin seeds provide a smoky flavor to this blend. All Indian and Pakistani grocery stores stock these black tea-leaf-like flat seeds right next to the more widely known plump, grayish cumin seeds.

❖ Asafetida, often found in the ground form in the United States, is added after all the whole spices have been roasted and ground. If the asafetida were roasted with the rest of them, the intense and prolonged heat would instantly burn the strong-smelling spice. Indian stores also sell a block form of asafetida. If you have some, chisel off a small piece, the size of a green pea, and roast it along with the whole spices in the recipe.

❖ Some of Usha's family favorites, like Minty Chicken Strips with Coconut (page 155), call for this masala. I have also used it in some other curries, including Boneless Pork Cooked with Toasted Coconut in Coconut Milk (page 230) and Whole Fish Poached in a Stewed Onion Sauce (page 236). You could also perk up your morning scrambled eggs with this masala, or stir it into crème fraîche and serve it alongside a piece of grilled salmon.

Sesame-Flavored Blend
WITH PEANUTS AND COCONUT

Maharashtrian Garam Masala

this version of garam masala, markedly different from the Punjabi garam masala (page 25), weaves in coconut, peanuts, and sesame seeds, flavorings charactcristic in Marathi-speaking homes, especially in the home state of Maharashtra, in western India. There are similar blends from this region called *kala* (black) or *goda* (sweet) *masala*. These masalas contain dark-toasted coconut (hence the "black"), which has an inherent sweetness (*goda*).

I love the presence of this blend's peanuts and sesame seeds in two appetizer curries:

Yellow Split Pea and Peanut Cakes with a Tamarind Chile Sauce (page 117) and Crispy Vegetable Rolls with a Cucumber Yogurt Sauce (page 100). The blend also works as a great alternative to any of the curries that call for Usha Raikar's garam masala (page 27).

MAKES ABOUT 1 CUP

- ¼ cup raw peanuts (without the skin)
- 2 tablespoons white sesame seeds
- 1 tablespoon coriander seeds
- 1 teaspoon cumin seeds
- 8 to 10 dried red Thai or cayenne chiles, to taste, stems removed
- ¼ teaspoon nutmeg shavings (see Tips)
- 2 to 3 blades mace
- ¼ cup shredded dried unsweetened coconut

1. Preheat a small skillet over medium-high heat. Add all the ingredients except the coconut, and toast, shaking the skillet every few seconds, until the peanuts (in spots) and sesame seeds turn honey-brown, the coriander and cumin seeds turn reddish brown, and the chiles blacken slightly and smell pungent, 3 to 4 minutes; the chiles' aroma will be masked by the sweet-smelling nutmeg and mace.

2. Immediately transfer the nutty-smelling spices to a plate to cool. (The longer they sit in the hot skillet, the more likely it is that they will burn, making them bitter and unpalatable.) Return the skillet to the heat and toast the coconut for about 15 seconds; it will immediately start to turn almond-brown. Add the coconut to the pile of toasted peanuts and spices.

3. Once it is cool to the touch, place half the mixture in a spice grinder or coffee grinder, and grind until the texture resembles that of finely ground black pepper. (If you don't allow the spices to cool, the ground blend will acquire unwanted moisture from the heat, making

the final blend slightly "cakey.") Transfer this to a small bowl. Repeat with the remaining batch. Thoroughly combine the two ground batches. The aroma of the light reddish-brown ground blend will be sweet and complex, very different from that of the pre-toasted and post-toasted whole spices.

4. Store in a tightly sealed container, away from excess light, heat, and humidity, for up to 2 months. (In my opinion, refrigerating the blend adversely affects its flavors.)

Tips:

❖ To shave a nutmeg, hold it down firmly with the fingers of one hand, and with a sharp knife in the other, carefully slice off thin shavings. There are two key things you always want to remember to ensure an accident-free task: a sharp knife and a well-anchored cutting board, held in place with a wet cloth or a rubber mat.

❖ If whole nutmeg or weblike blades of mace are not at hand, substitute ⅛ teaspoon of the ground spice. Just remember not to toast them with the whole spices (they will burn); simply stir them into the cooled, ground toasted blend.

Untoasted and Toasted Spice Blend

kashmiri garam masala

In this unusual masala, some of the spices are toasted and some not, which is typical of everyday Kashmiri cooking. Most of the spices in this mélange are aromatics (see page 8), and it is sprinkled in meat, poultry, vegetable, and legume curries as a finishing blend, usually toward the end of the cooking. **MAKES ¼ CUP**

1 teaspoon cumin seeds

2 cinnamon sticks (each 3 inches long),
*   broken into smaller pieces*

1 teaspoon fennel seeds

1 teaspoon black peppercorns

1 teaspoon ground ginger

½ teaspoon black cumin seeds

½ teaspoon whole cloves

½ teaspoon ground nutmeg

4 blades mace, or ¼ teaspoon
*   ground mace*

Seeds from 4 black cardamom pods

1. Preheat a small skillet over medium-high heat. Add the cumin and cinnamon, and toast, shaking the skillet every few seconds, until the cumin seeds turn reddish brown, the cinnamon sticks appear brittle, and the mixture is highly fragrant, 1 to 2 minutes.

2. Immediately transfer the nutty-smelling spices to a plate to cool. (The longer they sit in the hot skillet, the more likely it is that they will burn, making them bitter and unpalatable.) Once they are cool to the touch, place them in a spice grinder or coffee grinder, add all the remaining spices, and grind until the texture resembles that of finely ground black pepper.

3. Store the dark brown spice blend in a tightly sealed container, away from excess light, heat, and humidity, for up to 2 months. (In my opinion, refrigerating the blend adversely affects its flavors.)

Coriander-Scented Untoasted Blend

Bin Bhuna Hua Garam Masala

The heady aromas emanating from the released oils of just-pulverized spices give you a hint of fresh and complex flavors that are sorely missing from store-purchased pre-ground spices. This version of garam masala does not involve toasting the whole spices. It is added to a dish early on in the cooking, allowing time for the spices to add their subtle flavors.

This blend is the primary source of flavors in Spiced Ground Beef Sandwiches (page 91) and Roasted Leg of Lamb with Raisin-Mint Sauce (page 184). In Spinach and Mustard Greens with Cheese (page 295), it is combined with the toasted Punjabi garam masala to create a complexity that bowls you over.

I find this blend to be a perfectly acceptable alternative in any recipe that calls for a commercial curry powder. **MAKES ⅓ CUP**

2 tablespoons coriander seeds

1 teaspoon cumin seeds

1 teaspoon black peppercorns

½ teaspoon whole cloves

½ teaspoon cardamom seeds from green
*   or white pods*

2 dried bay leaves

3 or 4 dried red Thai or cayenne chiles,
*   to taste, stems removed; or 1 teaspoon*
*   cayenne (ground red pepper)*

1. Place all the ingredients in a spice grinder or coffee grinder, and grind until the texture resembles that of finely ground black pepper.

2. Store the mixture in a tightly sealed container, away from excess light, heat, and humidity, for up to 2 months. (In my opinion, refrigerating the blend adversely affects its flavors.)

Tip: I usually stock both whole cardamom pods and cardamom seeds (sometimes called decorticated cardamom seeds) in my pantry. You do pay much more for the seeds, but it's worth every penny since it saves having to pry each pod open for those menthol flavor–like tiny black seeds.

Fennel-Flavored Toasted Spice Blend

balti masala

Hindi/Urdu word for "bucket" is *balli* and here it's not a vessel for cooking. This is coined terminology that originated with an enterprising Pakistani restaurant owner in Birmingham, England, and ended up back in restaurants in India. The food is actually cooked and served in a *karhai*, not a bucket: a *karhai* is the Indian version of a wok. Wherever it came from, some of the spices used in this blend are typical in Pakistani cooking. On occasion, when I have run out of Kashmiri garam masala (page 29), I have substituted Balti masala with equally satisfying results. **MAKES ⅓ CUP**

2 teaspoons fennel seeds

2 teaspoons coriander seeds

I teaspoon cumin seeds

I teaspoon black or yellow mustard seeds

½ teaspoon whole cloves

½ teaspoon cardamom seeds from black pods

½ teaspoon nigella seeds

3 fresh or dried bay leaves

2 cinnamon sticks (each 3 inches long),
   broken into smaller pieces

2 teaspoons cayenne (ground red pepper)

½ teaspoon ground nutmeg

1. Preheat a small skillet over medium-high heat. Add all the whole spices (reserving the cayenne and nutmeg), and toast, shaking the skillet every few seconds, until the fennel, coriander, and cumin turn reddish brown, the mustard, cloves, and cardamom turn ash-black, the cinnamon and bay leaves appear brittle and crinkly, and the mixture is highly fragrant, 1 to 2 minutes. (The nigella will not change color.)

2. Immediately transfer the nutty-smelling spices to a plate to cool. (The longer they sit in the hot skillet, the more likely it is that they will burn, making them bitter and unpalatable.) Once they are cool to the touch, place them in a spice grinder or coffee grinder, and grind until the texture resembles that of finely ground black pepper. (If you don't allow the spices to cool, the ground blend will acquire unwanted moisture from the heat, making the final blend slightly "cakey.") The ground blend will be a deep reddish brown and the aroma will be sweet and complex, very different from those of the pre-toasted and post-toasted whole spices. Stir in the cayenne and nutmeg.

3. Store the mix in a tightly sealed container, away from excess light, heat, and humidity, for up to 2 months. (In my opinion, refrigerating the blend adversely affects its flavors.)

Red-Hot Chile and Coconut Blend

kolhapuri masala

kolhapur, a vibrant community of artists and sportsmen (especially wrestlers) in the western state of Maharashtra, is best known for its hand-sewn, open-toed, flat-bottomed leather sandals known as *chappals*. Culinarily, the city is overshadowed by its neighbor Ratnagiri, where the world's best mango, the Alphonso, is grown. Don't expect that to last much longer, however, because Kolhapur's bold masala finds its way into many fish, chicken, vegetable, and legume curries. **MAKES 1¼ CUPS**

1 cup dried red Thai or cayenne chiles, stems removed

½ cup shredded dried unsweetened coconut

2 tablespoons white sesame seeds

1 tablespoon coriander seeds

1 tablespoon cumin seeds

1 tablespoon black peppercorns

1 teaspoon black or yellow mustard seeds

1 teaspoon fenugreek seeds

4 blades mace (see Tip)

2 fresh or dried bay leaves

1 teaspoon canola oil

2 tablespoons ground Kashmiri chiles; or ½ tablespoon cayenne (ground red pepper) mixed with 1½ tablespoons sweet paprika

1. Combine all the ingredients except the ground Kashmiri chiles in a medium-size bowl, and stir to coat with the oil. (Coating the whole spices evenly with the oil ensures an even roast, and is much easier to do in a bowl rather than in a skillet.)

2. Preheat a medium-size skillet over medium heat. Pour the oiled spices into the skillet and roast the blend, stirring constantly, until the whole chiles blacken slightly, the coconut turns dark brown, the sesame, coriander, cumin, and fenugreek turn reddish brown, the mustard seeds pop, swell up, and look ash-black, and the bay leaves appear dry (especially if using fresh ones), 3 to 4 minutes.

3. Immediately transfer the pungent nutty-smelling spices to a plate to cool. (The longer they sit in the hot skillet, the more likely it is that they will burn, making them bitter and unpalatable.) Once they are cool to the touch, place half of the spices in a spice grinder or coffee grinder, and grind until the texture resembles that of finely ground black pepper. (If you don't allow the spices to cool, the ground blend will acquire unwanted moisture from the heat, making the final blend slightly "cakey.") Pour the ground mixture into the same medium-size bowl and grind the remaining half. Add the remaining ground mixture to the bowl. (Alternatively, since you have a large quantity of whole spices, put them all in a blender jar and grind them in one batch.) Stir in the ground Kashmiri chiles. The ground blend will be a deep saffron red and the aromas will be sweet and complex, very different from those of the pre-toasted and post-toasted whole spices.

4. Store in a tightly sealed jar, away from excess light, heat, and humidity, for up to 2 months. (In my opinion, refrigerating the blend adversely affects its flavors.)

Tip: In the absence of mace blades, use ¼ teaspoon ground mace. Add it along with the ground Kashmiri chiles after roasting and grinding the whole spices. A hot pan will burn ground spices on contact, yielding unpalatable flavors.

Toasted Cumin-Coriander Blend

dhania-jeera Masala

Many of the curries in this book call for this two-spice blend, and you wouldn't think you'd need a recipe for something this simple. However, my students often reveal a slight fear when it comes to toasting spices, so this is a perfect opportunity to reiterate that easy technique. This blend is available in Indian and Pakistani grocery stores, where the spices are often not toasted (because they deal with large volumes of spices, toasting them en masse might not yield best results). In Indian home kitchens, on the other hand, where the blend is made in smaller quantities, the spices are toasted, yielding a nutty quality that is quite crucial to many of our regional curries. **MAKES ¼ CUP**

2 tablespoons coriander seeds

1 tablespoon cumin seeds

1. Preheat a small skillet over medium-high heat. Add the whole spices and toast them, shaking the skillet every few seconds, until they start to crackle and turn reddish brown and the aroma is highly nutty-fragrant with citrus undertones, 1 to 3 minutes.

2. Immediately transfer the spices to a plate to cool. (The longer they sit in the hot skillet, the more likely it is that they will burn, making them bitter and unpalatable.) Once they are cool to the touch, place them in a spice grinder or coffee grinder, and grind until the texture resembles that of finely ground black pepper. (If you don't allow the spices to cool, the ground blend will acquire unwanted moisture from the heat, making the final blend slightly "cakey.") The ground blend will be a deep reddish brown and the aromas will be sweet and complex, very different from those of the pre-toasted and post-toasted whole spices.

3. Store the masala in a tightly sealed container, away from excess light, heat, and humidity, for up to 2 months. (In my opinion, refrigerating the blend adversely affects its flavors.)

Roasted Chile, Spice, and Legume Blend

sambhar Masala

There are as many *sambhar* masalas as there are kitchens in south India. This combination of roasted spices and legumes (yellow split peas in this instance) is used to flavor a thin stewlike dish called *sambhar* (page 77), often considered southern India's signature dish. Normally when you cook legumes, you boil them in water until they are tender. But here they are roasted and then ground with traditional spices to create a blend of complex aromas and flavors. The southerners are probably the only people in the world to do this. The lentils provide not only flavor but also texture when added to a sauce. **MAKES 1½ CUPS**

*½ cup firmly packed medium-size to large
fresh curry leaves*

*½ cup dried red Thai or cayenne chiles,
stems removed*

*¼ cup yellow split peas (chana dal), picked
over for stones*

¼ cup coriander seeds

2 tablespoons cumin seeds

I tablespoon fenugreek seeds

I tablespoon black or yellow mustard seeds

I tablespoon white poppy seeds

*2 cinnamon sticks (each 3 inches long), broken into
smaller pieces*

I tablespoon unrefined sesame oil or canola oil

1. Combine all the spices in a medium-size bowl. Drizzle the oil over them and toss well, coating the spices evenly with the oil.

2. Preheat a medium-size skillet over medium-high heat. Add the mixture and roast, stirring constantly, until the curry leaves curl up and appear dry and brittle, the chiles blacken slightly, the split peas turn dark brown, the coriander, cumin, and fenugreek turn reddish brown, the mustard seeds pop, swell up, and look ash-black, and the poppy seeds are tan, 3 to 4 minutes.

3. Immediately transfer the pungent, nutty-smelling spices to a plate to cool. (The longer they sit in the hot skillet, the more likely it is that they will burn, making them bitter and unpalatable.) Once they are cool to the touch, pour half of the mixture into a spice grinder or coffee grinder, and grind until the texture resembles that of finely ground black pepper. (If you don't allow the spices to cool, the ground blend will acquire unwanted moisture from the heat, making the final blend slightly "cakey.") Transfer the ground blend to a small bowl. Repeat with the remaining spices, and thoroughly combine the two ground batches. The aromas of the light reddish-brown ground blend will be sweet and complex, very different from those of the pre-toasted and post-toasted whole spices.

4. Store in a tightly sealed container, away from excess light, heat, and humidity, for up to 2 months. (In my opinion, refrigerating the blend adversely affects its flavors.)

Tips:

❖ Sprinkle this masala on everyday stir-fries and stews to yield highly flavorful results.

❖ Because of the large quantity of chiles, make sure you use proper ventilation when roasting this blend. I am always amazed how sweet the ground blend smells after I've been thrown into a coughing fit while roasting them.

Roasted Spice Blend
WITH BLACK PEPPER

Rasam Powder

this combination of spices is used in thin, peppery-flavored, tart broths from southern India called *rasam*. I have included a few versions of this popular second-course offering in this book, even though a multiple-course meal is not a common way of dining in Indian homes. A dinner including *rasam* would go something like this: The first course would be a thicker *sambhar* (a type of stew) fortified with pigeon peas and studded with fresh vegetables; the second, the thin, tamarind-based *rasam;* and the third course, a yogurt-based curry speckled with roasted mustard seeds and fresh curry leaves. All three courses would be served over rice. **MAKES 1 CUP**

¼ cup coriander seeds

¼ cup black peppercorns

2 tablespoons cumin seeds

2 tablespoons fenugreek seeds

1 teaspoon whole cloves

2 tablespoons yellow split peas
    (chana dal), picked over for stones

1 teaspoon unrefined sesame oil
    or canola oil

1. Combine all the spices and the split peas in a medium-size bowl. Drizzle the oil over them and toss well, coating them evenly with the oil.

2. Preheat a medium-size skillet over medium-high heat. Add the mixture and roast, stirring constantly, until the split peas turn light brown, the coriander, cumin, and fenugreek turn reddish brown, and the peppercorns look slightly ash-black, 3 to 4 minutes.

3. Immediately transfer the pungent, nutty-smelling spices to a plate to cool. (The longer they sit in the hot skillet, the more likely it is that they will burn, making them bitter and unpalatable.) Once they are cool to the touch, place half the mixture in a spice grinder or coffee grinder, and grind until the texture resembles that of finely ground black pepper. (If you don't allow the spices to cool, the ground blend will acquire unwanted moisture from the heat, making the final blend slightly "cakey.") Pour the ground blend into a small bowl. Repeat with the remaining batch, and thoroughly combine the two ground batches. The aromas of the light reddish-brown blend will be sweet and complex, very different from those of the pre-toasted and post-toasted whole spices.

4. Store in a tightly sealed container, away from excess light, heat, and humidity, for up to 2 months. (In my opinion, refrigerating the blend adversely affects its flavors.)

Roasted Curry Leaf Spice Blend

karuvapillai podi

fresh curry leaves provide a mildly citruslike flavor and give off an intense aroma, especially when you rub a leaf between your fingertips and smell your fingers. Fresh leaves are found in the refrigerated section of Indian grocery stores and are quite inexpensive. The leaves come off the sprig very easily when you slide your fingers down the stem, moving in the opposite direction of the upward-growing leaves. **MAKES ABOUT ½ CUP**

2 tablespoons oily or unoily skinned split
    yellow pigeon peas (toovar dal), picked
    over for stones

1 teaspoon canola oil

½ cup firmly packed medium-size to large
    fresh curry leaves

2 tablespoons skinned split black lentils
    (cream-colored in this form, urad dal),
    picked over for stones

6 to 8 dried red Thai or cayenne chiles,
    to taste, stems removed

¼ teaspoon ground turmeric

¼ teaspoon ground asafetida

1. If you are using oiled pigeon peas, thoroughly rinse off the oil and pat them dry.

2. Toss all the ingredients except the turmeric and asafetida in a small bowl, making sure they all get a thin coating of the oil (which ensures an even roasting).

3. Preheat a small skillet over medium-high heat. Add the mixture and stir-fry until the leaves feel dry and crinkly (they appear wet but feel dry when touched), the pigeon peas and lentils turn golden brown, the chiles blacken slightly and smell pungent, and the blend is nutty-fragrant, about 2 minutes.

4. Immediately transfer the spices to a plate to cool. (The longer they sit in the hot skillet, the more likely it is that they will burn, making them bitter and unpalatable.) Once they are cool to the touch, place them in a spice grinder or coffee grinder, and grind until the texture resembles that of finely ground black pepper. (If you don't allow the spices to cool, the ground blend will acquire unwanted moisture from the heat, making the final blend slightly "cakey.") Mix in the turmeric and asafetida. The ground blend will be yellow-brown with specks of green, and the aromas will be sweet and complex, very different from those of the pre-toasted and post-toasted whole spices.

5. Store in a tightly sealed container, away from excess light, heat, and humidity, for up to 2 months. (In my opinion, refrigerating the blend adversely affects its flavors.)

Bengali Five-Spice Blend

Panch Phoron

Every Bengali-speaking kitchen in the world has this five-spice blend on a shelf, although its constitution differs slightly in each kitchen. Oftentimes in eastern India, in the state of Bengal, a spice known as *radhuni* is part of the blend, but it's not as well known or easily found outside of Bengal. *Radhuni* looks sort of like celery seeds, tastes a bit like thyme-flavored bishop's weed, and has a bitterness reminiscent of fenugreek seeds (which is often the ingredient in many commercial *panch phoron* mixtures). This whole-spice mix is often sizzled in mustard oil for many Bengali fish curries, providing a slightly sweet backdrop to the nose-tingling, bitter mustard oil.

MAKES ABOUT ¼ CUP

2 teaspoons fennel seeds

I teaspoon cumin seeds

I teaspoon fenugreek seeds

I teaspoon nigella seeds

I teaspoon black or yellow mustard seeds

Thoroughly combine all the ingredients in a small bowl and transfer them to a tightly sealed container. Store them in your pantry, away from excess light, heat, and humidity for up to a year (which I hope will not be the case).

Toasted Twenty-Spice Blend

East Indian Bottle Masala

The East Indians are a small group from one of the seven islands that make up Mumbai, and they consider themselves to be among the first Indians to convert to Christianity, well before the Goans and Mangoloreans from India's southern coast. This community of Roman Catholic Christians, who speak Marathi, are now bunched in just a few sectors of Mumbai. In order to make sure the ruling English never confused them with the other immigrant-community converts farther south (such as the Portuguese traders in Goa), they adopted the name East Indians, possibly in reference to the British East India Company.

East Indian foods are very much meat-, fish-, and seafood-based, with a spice blend known as *bottle masala* being their signature mix. Recipes for this blend pass from mother to daughter in great secrecy, and each family pounds its own version in deep wooden mortars, the number of ingredients often ranging from twenty to an astounding seventy-five. Because the spices are sun-dried before being toasted, *bottle masalas* are always made during the summer months just before the monsoons arrive. Then they are stored in airtight bottles, perfuming curries throughout the year. My version incorporates twenty ingredients, most of them found in any grocery store.

MAKES 2 CUPS

1 cup dried red Thai or cayenne chiles, stems removed

2 tablespoons yellow split peas (chana dal), picked over for stones

2 tablespoons kanak or wheat berries (see Tip)

1 tablespoon uncooked long-grain white rice

½ cup coriander seeds

1 tablespoon black or yellow mustard seeds

1 tablespoon white sesame seeds

1 tablespoon white poppy seeds

1 tablespoon black peppercorns

1 teaspoon cumin seeds

1 teaspoon fennel seeds

1 teaspoon fenugreek seeds

1 teaspoon whole cloves

½ teaspoon cardamom seeds from green or white pods

½ teaspoon nutmeg shavings (see Tips, page 29)

3 whole star anise

3 cinnamon sticks (each 3 inches long), broken into smaller pieces

3 blades mace, or ¼ teaspoon ground mace

2 fresh or dried bay leaves

2 tablespoons ground Kashmiri chiles; or 1½ teaspoons cayenne (ground red pepper) mixed with 1½ tablespoons sweet paprika

1 tablespoon ground turmeric

1. Combine all the ingredients except the ground mace, if using, the ground Kashmiri chiles, and turmeric, in a medium-size bowl.

2. Preheat a wok or a large skillet over medium-high heat. Add the mixture and toast, shaking the pan every few seconds, until the chiles blacken slightly, the coriander and cumin turn reddish brown, the rice and yellow split peas turn light brown in patches, the cloves, peppercorns, and cardamom turn ash-black, the cinnamon and bay leaves appear brittle and crinkly, and it is highly fragrant, 4 to 6 minutes.

3. Immediately transfer the nutty-smelling spices to a plate to cool. (The longer they sit in the hot skillet, the more likely it is that they will burn, making them bitter and unpalatable.) Once they are cool to the touch, place them, in batches, in a spice grinder or coffee grinder and grind until the texture resembles that of finely ground black pepper. (If you don't allow the spices to cool, the ground blend will acquire unwanted moisture from the heat, making the final blend slightly "cakey.") As each batch is ground, pour it into the same medium-size bowl. (Alternatively, because you have a large quantity of ingredients, pour them all into a blender jar and grind them in one batch.) When all the spices are ground, stir in the ground mace, the ground Kashmiri chiles, if that's what you used, and the turmeric. The ground blend will be a deep reddish brown and the aromas will be sweet and complex, very different from those of the pre-toasted and post-toasted (pre-ground) whole spices.

4. Store in an airtight container, away from excess light, heat, and humidity, for up to 2 months. (In my opinion, refrigerating the blend adversely affects its flavors.)

Tips:

❖ Golden Indian wheat berries, called *kanak,* have a lesser amount of protein and elasticity than the ones grown in the United States. This is the grain that is turned into flour for making India's tortilla-like rotis and *chappatis.* (Until recently, many Indians made a trip out to family-run flour mills to have their wheat freshly ground in large stone grinders called *chakkis.*) Indian grocery stores in the United States stock this grain, but the wheat berries found in the bulk foods aisle of a natural food store will suffice for this spice blend. You can omit the wheat altogether if necessary.

❖ Since you do end up with a large quantity of the blend, share it with your loved ones. You are not limited to using it on just the recipes from the East Indian community. Sprinkle it in everyday stir-fries, soups, salad dressings, and even pasta sauces for that extra flavor punch that will have your family and friends wondering why a mundane offering has taken on a new and exciting persona.

Vegetable Pâté Spice Blend

Paav Bhajee Masala

Let me preface this recipe by saying that *paav bhajee masala* is commonly available in any store that sells Indian groceries, and it is perfectly okay to use it. In fact, I have done so on numerous occasions. However, my chemistry background got the better of me as I looked at the list of ingredients on the box. All of these spices were in my pantry, and so I experimented with the proportions a few times. This version surpasses the flavor of the store-bought blend, I think. **MAKES ALMOST ½ CUP**

1 tablespoon coriander seeds
1 teaspoon cumin seeds
½ teaspoon black peppercorns
½ teaspoon fenugreek seeds
½ teaspoon anise seeds
¼ teaspoon cardamom seeds from green or white pods
6 whole cloves
2 tablespoons cayenne (ground red pepper)
1 tablespoon mango powder
2 teaspoons coarse kosher or sea salt
1 teaspoon black salt
¼ teaspoon ground nutmeg

1. Place the coriander, cumin, peppercorns, fenugreek, anise, cardamom, and cloves in a spice grinder or coffee grinder, and grind until the texture resembles that of finely ground black pepper.

2. Transfer the aromatic blend to a small bowl and mix in the remaining ingredients.

3. Store in a tightly sealed container, away from excess light, heat, and humidity, for up to 2 months. (In my opinion, refrigerating the blend adversely affects its flavors.)

Clove-Scented Spice Blend

dabeli Masala

E ven though this blend is designed to flavor a specific curry—Spiced Potatoes and Pomegranate Sandwiches (page 105)—the spices in it are an elaborate version of the Coriander-Scented Untoasted Blend (*Bin bhuna hua garam masala*, page 30). Use *Dabeli masala* as an alternative should you happen to have a little left over after you binge on the sandwiches. You can also rub the masala on meat or fish before grilling it.

MAKES A GENEROUS 2 TABLESPOONS

1 teaspoon whole cloves
½ teaspoon fennel seeds
½ teaspoon black peppercorns
½ teaspoon coriander seeds
4 dried red Thai or cayenne chiles, stems removed
4 blades mace, or ¼ teaspoon ground mace

2 or 3 whole star anise
1 or 2 dried bay leaves
Seeds from 1 or 2 black cardamom pods
½ teaspoon ground ginger
⅛ teaspoon ground turmeric

1. Place the cloves, fennel, peppercorns, coriander, chiles, mace, anise, bay leaf, and cardamom in a spice grinder or coffee grinder, and grind until the texture resembles that of finely ground black pepper.

2. Transfer the aromatic blend to a small bowl and stir in the ground ginger and turmeric (and ground mace, if using).

3. Store in a tightly sealed container, away from excess light, heat, and humidity, for up to 2 months. (Refrigerating the blend adversely affects its flavors.)

Cooling Spice Blend

WITH BLACK SALT

Chaat Masala

I n Hindi, *chaat* means "lick" and this finger-licking blend has a salty, addictive edge to it. The sulfurlike aroma and the flavor reminiscent of hard-cooked eggs are thanks to the black salt (not a true salt but a mineral in crystal form, found in mines). Mango powder and dried pomegranate seeds contribute tartness, while the heat from black peppercorns balances out the blend. Nutty cumin, in addition to its obvious flavor when toasted, helps the digestion, as does black salt. Put them all together, and you have a mélange that sprinkles its way into many of Mumbai's and Delhi's street foods, all now popularized under the catchy name *chaat*.

MAKES ¼ CUP

2 teaspoons cumin seeds

1 teaspoon dried pomegranate seeds (see Tips)

½ teaspoon black peppercorns

1 tablespoon mango powder

2 teaspoons black salt

1 teaspoon coarse kosher or sea salt

1. Preheat a small skillet over medium-high heat. Sprinkle the cumin seeds into the hot pan and toast, shaking the skillet every few seconds, until they start to crackle, turn reddish brown, and are highly fragrant, about 1 minute. Transfer the toasted cumin to a spice grinder or coffee grinder, and allow it to cool completely.

2. Add the pomegranate seeds and peppercorns to the cumin, and grind until the texture resembles that of finely ground black pepper.

3. Transfer the ground spices to a small bowl and stir in the remaining ingredients; the blend will be light brown in color. Store in a tightly sealed container, away from excess light, heat, and humidity, for up to 2 months. (In my opinion, refrigerating the blend adversely affects its flavors.)

Tips:

❖ Dried pomegranate seeds can be a hard nut to crack (sorry, grind), and your spice grinder may not be able to pulverize them to the right consistency. Often, once I run the seeds through the grinder, I transfer them to a mortar and then pound and grind them to a finer texture.

❖ Boxes of *chaat masala*, already blended for your convenience, are found in the spice aisle of every Indian grocery store. Purchase it in a heartbeat, but if you wish to make your own, try my version. Its flavor is exactly the same—no, it's better!

Untoasted Sri Lankan Curry Powder

Sinhalese Kari Masala

I find this version of a Sri Lankan blend, which consists of predominantly dark-colored spices, to be highly aromatic. Since the spices in this blend are neither toasted nor roasted, it's best to combine it with onion or garlic before cooking it. If you throw the blend directly into hot oil, it will burn and yield a bitter-tasting mix that can ruin a curry. **MAKES ¼ CUP**

1 tablespoon coriander seeds

1 teaspoon cumin seeds

1 teaspoon fennel seeds

1 teaspoon fenugreek seeds

½ teaspoon cardamom seeds from green or white pods

½ teaspoon nutmeg shavings (see Tip, page 29)

2 cinnamon sticks (each 3 inches long), broken into smaller pieces

1. Place all the ingredients in a spice grinder or coffee grinder, and grind until the texture resembles that of finely ground black pepper.

2. Store in a tightly sealed container, away from excess light, heat, and humidity, for up to 2 months. (In my opinion, refrigerating the blend adversely affects its flavor.)

2. Once the flour is reddish brown and smells nutty, immediately transfer it to a plate to cool.

3. Store in a tightly sealed jar or self-seal plastic bag in the refrigerator, and use as needed. It will keep for up to 6 months.

Toasted Chickpea Flour

bhuna hua besan

toasting chickpea flour is neither an art nor a science, but maintaining control over the pan's heat is crucial in producing the nutty-tasting result you want. What you will need is patience and muscle. Relentlessly stirring the flour for at least a quarter of an hour to prevent it from burning (okay, that sounds like a lot, but it's only 15 minutes—it's more dramatic in hour segments) will bring you priceless joy, for this is used in many curries. If your arm gets tired, pass the task on to someone else who wouldn't mind the exercise. **MAKES 1 CUP**

1 cup chickpea flour

1. Preheat a wok or large skillet over medium heat. Add the flour and toast it by stirring it constantly (I use a spatula), scraping the flour from the bottom to make sure none collects there, for 15 to 20 minutes. This may seem tedious, but do not hurry the process by cranking up the heat. Slow toasting is what brings out the nutty flavor, so crucial to some of the curries in this book.

Matchstick-Thin Fried Potatoes

saliya

india's Parsi community loves to top its curries with these addictive shreds (what's not to love about salted fried potatoes?). They are a cinch to make and will keep for a week or two. Try to restrain yourself from eating the potatoes before you top your favorite Parsi curry with them—but then, I can't claim such restraint! **MAKES 2 CUPS**

2 medium-size potatoes, such as russet or
*   Yukon Gold*
Canola oil for deep-frying
1 to 2 teaspoons coarse kosher or sea salt

1. Peel the potatoes and shred them into matchstick-thin pieces (see Tips). Place the shredded potatoes in a large bowl of cold water to keep them from turning brown while you heat the oil.

2. Pour oil to a depth of 2 to 3 inches in a wok, Dutch oven, or medium-size saucepan. Heat the oil over

medium to medium-high heat until a candy or deep-fry thermometer registers 350°F (don't let the thermometer touch the bottom of the pan). If you don't have a thermometer, you can tell if the oil is at the right temperature for deep-frying by gently flicking a drop of water over the oil's surface; if the drop skitters across the surface, the oil is ready.

3. Once the oil is ready, drain the potatoes and pat them very dry with paper towels.

4. Line a plate or a cookie sheet with three or four sheets of paper towels. Sprinkle a handful of potato shreds into the oil and fry, turning them occasionally to ensure even browning and to prevent them from sticking to one another, until they are caramel brown and crisp, about 5 minutes. Remove them with a slotted spoon or a Chinese-style skimmer (gadget-shopping time again) and allow them to drain on the paper towels. Repeat until all the shreds are fried. You may need to adjust the heat to maintain the oil's temperature at 350°F.

5. Transfer the potatoes to a bowl and salt them while they are still warm. When they have cooled, store them in self-seal plastic bags in a cool, dry spot for up to 2 weeks. Use on your favorite Parsi curry.

Tips:

❖ These days you have a few gadget options for shredding the potatoes. The larger holes on a box grater yield the perfect thickness. I usually shred the potato lengthwise, to create long, elegant strips. If you are using a chef's knife, cut the potatoes lengthwise into cardboard-thin slices, stack a few of the slices at a time, and cut them into long, thin shreds. Specialty kitchen stores now carry a julienne peeler that shreds potatoes; use it as you would a swivel peeler. A mandoline will also do the trick.

❖ Cooking just a handful of potato shreds at a time produces the best crispy, nongreasy results. Overcrowding the pan not only will lower the oil's temperature, but also will yield greasy shreds that are, frankly, yucky (nice technical term).

1. Indian dried hot red chile
2. Jaggery
3. Black salt
4. Star anise
5. Saffron (kashmiri)
6. Mace
7. Birdseye chile
8. Cayenne
9. Cardamon pods
10. Cardamon seeds
11. Fenugreek seeds
12. Dried fenugreek leaves
13. Fennel seeds
14. Dried pomegranate seeds
15. Coriander seeds
16. Turmeric
17. Deggi chile
18. Bishop's weed (ajowan)
19. Brick tamarind
20. Kudampuli
21. Kokum

appetizer curries

We Americans are a "noshing" bunch, picking up foods on the run. The plethora of fast-food eateries, plus all those establishments that dole out small plates of delicacies, like the Spanish tapas joints, Chinese dim-sum cafes, and even upscale fine-dining restaurants with tasting menus (small portions of full-

blown menu items) are all evidence of that trend.

Now, curries may not immediately jump out at you as satisfying munchies, but soon I'm going to have you thinking differently. So, when that chips-and-dip bell goes off in your head, it will be for something a little more exotic— like garlicky potato finger sandwiches in a bun with sweet-hot sauces, or skewers of chicken, beef, or lamb with flavorful sauces. Or spiced lamb chops, grilled and topped with a dollop of fenugreek-scented cream sauce—elegant enough to

serve at fancy cocktail parties to guests draped in pearls and flowing evening gowns. If I have my way, you'll be passing around tapioca fritters with coconut-sesame seed sauce at your next outdoor summer party. How convenient to set a pan of hot oil on the grill and fry them while chatting with friends between sips of Vouvray, Sancerre, or Côtes-du-Rhône! For an unusual tail-gating party serve grilled chicken with cashew-tomato sauce—it goes great with beer. Include these appetizer curries in your own noshing lifestyle.

Trispy Vegetables
WITH HOT, SWEET, AND COOLING SAUCES

Subzi Pakora Chaat

fried, batter-dipped vegetable nuggets—called *pakoras*—are dunked in savory, tart, and sweet chutneys and traditionally munched as a late-afternoon snack. Delhi-ites have taken this a step further and turned the experience into a layered nirvana, in which the vegetables form the bed for the hot, tart, pungent, and soothing sauces that blanket them. No wonder *chaat* has captured the palates of Western audiences, fueled by features in national newspapers.

If you want to simplify this appetizer, make just two of the sauces—the Mint-Yogurt and the Tamarind-Date—for that dichotomous, yet harmonious, flavor. **SERVES 6**

For the sauces:

¼ cup Mint-Yogurt Sauce with Chiles (page 18)

¼ cup Red Chile, Garlic, and Shallot Sauce (page 20)

¾ cup Sweet-Tart Tamarind-Date Sauce (page 20)

¾ cup Yogurt Sauce with Black Salt (page 21)

For the batter:

1 cup chickpea flour, sifted

¼ cup rice flour

2 tablespoons cornstarch

¼ teaspoon baking soda

1 teaspoon coarse kosher or sea salt

1 teaspoon cayenne (ground red pepper)

½ teaspoon ground turmeric

For the vegetables:

8 ounces cauliflower, cut into 1-inch florets

1 medium-size russet or Yukon Gold potato, peeled, cut crosswise into ¼-inch-thick slices, and submerged in a bowl of cold water to prevent browning

1 medium-size green bell pepper, stemmed, seeded, and cut into 1-inch-wide strips

Canola oil for deep-frying

¼ cup finely chopped fresh cilantro leaves and tender stems for garnishing

Chaat masala (page 39) for dusting

1. Prepare the sauces before you begin making the patties (see Tip, page 46).

2. To make the batter, mix the two flours, cornstarch, baking soda, salt, cayenne, and turmeric in a medium-size bowl. Pour in about ⅓ cup warm water, whisking the ingredients together to form a thick batter. Add more warm water, a few tablespoons at a time, whisking after each addition, to make a smooth, thick batter that coats a spoon. You will need about ¾ cup water altogether.

3. Pour oil to a depth of 2 to 3 inches into a wok, Dutch oven, or medium-size saucepan. Heat the oil over medium heat until a candy or deep-frying thermometer inserted into the oil (without touching the pan's bottom) registers 350°F. (An alternative way to see if the oil is at the right temperature for deep-frying is to gently flick a drop of water over it. If the pearl-like drop skitters across the surface, the oil is ready.)

4. Line a large plate or a cookie sheet with several layers of paper towels. Once the oil is ready, drop a few of the vegetables into the batter, completely coating each piece. Carefully slide each piece into the hot oil as you finish coating it. Fry the vegetables, turning them occasionally, until they are golden brown and crisp all over, 5 to 10 minutes. Remove them with a slotted spoon and allow them to drain on the towel-lined plate. Repeat

with the remaining vegetables. You may need to adjust the heat to maintain the oil's temperature at 350°F.

5. To serve the *chaat*, place 3 or 4 pieces of *pakoras* on each individual serving plate. Atop each *pakora*, spoon ½ teaspoon Mint-Yogurt Sauce, followed by ½ teaspoon Red Chile Sauce, then 1 teaspoon Tamarind-Date Sauce, and finally 1 teaspoon Yogurt Sauce. A little cilantro and a light dusting of the *chaat masala* complete the layered creation. Instruct your guests to fork right through (or better yet, to use their fingers to eat), getting the complete package in each addictive mouthful. It's okay to lick your fingers because that's what *chaat* means—"to lick.""

so appealed to Mrs. Chandwani. These are very substantial and can easily be the centerpiece for an evening dinner. The night I made them it was only my six-year-old son Robert and I at the table, and he queried, "That's all you are giving me, Papa?" Once I assured him that he could have as many as he wanted, he gobbled down four more, full-bodied sauces and all.

If you wish to simplify this appetizer, make just two of the sauces: the Mint-Yogurt and the Tamarind-Date. **SERVES 6**

SINDHI-STYLE Stuffed Potato Shells

Aloo tikki Chaat

My childhood neighbor in Mumbai (Bombay), Mrs. Chandwani, whose ancestral roots were embedded in Sindh (now Pakistan), purchased her *aloo tikkis* from the same woman, also a Sindhi, every week for fifteen years. It was her way of showing support for the hardworking widowed mother of two. It was also her opportunity to complain, in Sindhi, about the growing cost of vegetables, and about not being able to see her children and grandchildren often enough.

Years later those patties made it into my American kitchen, with the traditional filling that

For the sauces:

¼ cup Mint-Yogurt Sauce with Chiles (page 18)

¼ cup Red Chile, Garlic, and Shallot Sauce (page 20)

¾ cup Sweet-Tart Tamarind-Date Sauce (page 20)

¾ cup Yogurt Sauce with Black Salt (page 21)

For the shells:

1 pound russet or Yukon Gold potatoes, peeled, boiled until tender, and mashed

1 teaspoon coarse kosher or sea salt

4 to 6 slices firm white bread

1 tablespoon canola oil

For the filling:

2 tablespoons canola oil

½ cup finely chopped red onion

1 cup red cowpeas or whole green lentils (sabud moong), partially sprouted (see Tip, next page), or store-bought bean sprouts

2 tablespoons finely chopped fresh cilantro leaves and tender stems

½ teaspoon Toasted Cumin-Coriander Blend (page 33)

½ teaspoon cayenne (ground red pepper)

½ teaspoon coarse kosher or sea salt

About 6 tablespoons canola oil for frying

Chaat masala (page 39) for dusting

1. Prepare the sauces before you begin making the patties (see Tip).

2. To make the shells, place the mashed potatoes and salt in a large bowl. Hold the bread slices under running water to drench them, and then squeeze out as much water as possible. You should end up with a rolled-up wad of moist but firm bread. Work the bread into the potatoes by squeezing handfuls of potato and bread together to blend them and then kneading the mixture, creating a slightly sticky dough; the softer the bread, the more slices you will need to get the right consistency. (This technique of creating instant dough with moist bread slices works well as a binder to hold the patties together while pan-frying.) Rub the oil over the dough and allow it to rest, covered with plastic wrap or with a clean, moistened paper towel, for 15 to 20 minutes.

3. Meanwhile, make the filling: Heat the oil in a medium-size skillet over medium-high heat. Add the onion and stir-fry until it is light brown around the edges, 3 to 4 minutes.

4. Add the sprouted peas, cilantro, spice blend, cayenne, and salt. Cook, stirring frequently, to warm up the sprouts and cook the spices, about 2 minutes. Set the filling aside.

5. To assemble the shells, use your hands to shape the dough into a 12-inch-long log. Cut it, crosswise, into twelve 1-inch-thick pieces, and shape each piece into a ball. Working with one piece at a time, flatten it between the palms of your hands and shape it with your fingers into a dumpling-like wrapper roughly 3 inches in diameter and ¼ inch thick. Spoon about 2 teaspoons of the filling in the center of the wrapper. Gather the edges and bring them together to the center, pinching the seam to seal it tightly, forming a mound that looks like a Hershey's Kiss. Gently flatten the top, making sure the filling stays completely covered. Press and shape it into a patty roughly 3 inches in diameter and ½ inch thick. Set it aside on a plate, and repeat with the remaining rounds.

6. Line a large plate or a cookie sheet with several layers of paper towels.

7. Heat about 3 tablespoons canola oil in a large nonstick skillet or a well-seasoned cast-iron skillet over medium heat. Arrange 6 patties in a single layer in the skillet (do not crowd them), and cook until they are golden brown and crisp on the underside, about 5 minutes. Flip them over to cook the other side until golden brown and crisp, about 5 minutes. Transfer the cooked patties to the paper-towel-lined plate, and repeat with the remaining patties, adding more oil as needed.

8. Place 2 patties on each individual serving plate. Atop each patty, spoon 1 teaspoon of the Mint-Yogurt Sauce, followed by 1 teaspoon Red Chile Sauce, 1 tablespoon Tamarind-Date Sauce, and finally 1 tablespoon Yogurt Sauce. A little cilantro and a light dusting of the *chaat masala* complete the layered creation. Instruct everyone to fork right through to get the complete package in each addictive mouthful.

Tips:

❖ The secret to making this a quick deal is to have all the sauces prepared a few days ahead of time. Each sauce takes no more than 5 minutes to assemble, and some barely 2 minutes.

❖ It takes 3 to 4 days to sprout the cowpeas or lentils, so you'll want to start them ahead of time—or simply substitute store-bought bean sprouts. (See box, page 328.) If the sprouts are long, I would recommend coarsely chopping them so they don't poke out of the patties when they are stuffed with the filling.

Crispy Shells

FILLED WITH POTATO AND CHICKPEAS

dahi Chaat

ere's the deal with this layered *chaat:* As soon as they are ready, grab one and pop it in your mouth in one fell swoop. Don't look at it, don't admire its beauty, don't take a bite from it, don't ponder what's in it, don't be afraid that it won't fit in your dainty mouth (open wide and in it will go). Why? Because the moment the sauces start pooling at the bottom of the *poori* (which is within seconds), they will soften it and its inner wall will cave in, making for a messy experience. Having someone to help you fill the shells will expedite the process and keep the shells crispy, making for a crunchier experience. The *poori* should fall apart in your mouth and not in your hands because you want to experience the cracking of the shell followed by a gush of soft potatoes, nutty chickpeas, fiery sauces cooled off by tamarind and yogurt, and a final burst of cayenne heat with the lip-puckering black salt in the *Chaat masala.* And you know, you just can't eat only one. **SERVES 6**

For the sauces:

¼ cup Mint-Yogurt Sauce with Chiles (page 18)
¼ cup Red Chile, Garlic, and Shallot Sauce (page 20)
½ cup Sweet-Tart Tamarind-Date Sauce (page 20)
½ cup Yogurt Sauce with Black Salt (page 21)

For the filling:

1 medium-size russet or Yukon Gold potato, peeled, boiled until tender, and coarsely mashed
1 cup cooked chickpeas
1 teaspoon coarse kosher or sea salt

For the crispy shells and topping:

30 round poori shells (see Tip)
Cayenne (ground red pepper) for sprinkling
Chaat masala (page 39) for sprinkling (optional)
Finely chopped fresh cilantro leaves and tender stems for sprinkling

1. Prepare the sauces before you begin assembling the *pooris.*

2. Combine the potato, chickpeas, and salt in a medium-size bowl, and blend well, mashing the chickpeas.

3. Working with one *poori* at a time, cup a shell in the palm of one hand, and with the forefinger of the other hand, gently tap the thin surface to form a finger-width hole, letting the crumbs and small pieces fall in. Repeat with the remaining shells, and place them in a single layer on a serving platter.

4. Carefully spoon a scant teaspoon of the potato-chickpea filling into a shell. Then drop in ¼ teaspoon of the Mint-Yogurt Sauce, followed by ¼ teaspoon of the Red Chile Sauce, ½ teaspoon of the Tamarind-Date Sauce, and finally ½ teaspoon of the Yogurt Sauce. Lightly dust the filled shell with cayenne and *chaat masala,* sprinkle with cilantro, and serve immediately. Repeat with the remaining shells. (Or, if you're prepared to move speedily, set this up assembly-line style so you can fill and serve a number of the shells at once.)

Tip: These hollow *pooris,* 1- to 2-inch rounds, are made of all-purpose flour and Cream of Wheat. Every Indian grocery store carries them in the snack aisle, labeled *paani pooris* or *gol gappa pooris* (the names of another street food that fills the shells with cool spiced water).

They sometimes come as part of a *paani poori* kit; I just discard the accoutrements and keep the *pooris*. For an even crisper shell, preheat the oven to 300°F, place the *pooris* on an ungreased cookie sheet, and warm them for 5 minutes. Once they are cool to the touch, proceed with filling them.

Poori Shells

FILLED WITH CHILE-SPIKED WATER AND COOLING SPICES

Gol Gappe Chaat

I love to see the widened eyes of guests and students who trust me well enough to open their mouths wide, as I offer up, communion-style, a round *poori* filled with chickpeas and hot-sweet-tart-cool water. I serve it this way because I don't want them to ponder the marvelous liquid in the delicate shell for even a second, as the shell will cave in with the watery weight, creating a mess in their (or my!) hands.

In India this street food is also a one-bite deal, as the vendor pokes a hole in the *poori* with his finger, dunks it into the pot to fill it with the spiked water, and transfers inviting mouthful to plate in one sweeping motion. No, he does not feed you, as you are supposed to know how to eat it—although it may require some bravery to trust the dubious water source in that earthen pot of his.

Now, my water source is safe, so you can trust my priestly way of feeding you. Go ahead, indulge my pious fantasy, and serve your guests as I do. Remember to tell them to open wide! **SERVES 6**

2 cups well-chilled water
½ cup Sweet-Tart Tamarind-Date Sauce (page 20)
¼ cup Mint-Yogurt Sauce with Chiles (page 18)
¼ cup Red Chile, Garlic, and Shallot Sauce (page 20)
2 teaspoons chaat masala (page 39)
30 round poori shells (see Tips)
1 cup cooked chickpeas (see Tips)

1. Pour the cold water into a pitcher or into a large measuring cup, and add the three sauces and the *chaat masala.* Whisk well to mix the potent concoction. You will need to stir it again before you fill each *poori,* as the flavorings settle at the bottom of the pitcher rather quickly.

2. Working with one *poori* at a time, cup a shell in the palm of one hand, and with the forefinger of the other hand, gently tap the thin surface to form a finger-width hole, letting the crumbs and small pieces fall in. Repeat with the remaining shells, and place them in a single layer on a serving platter.

3. Just before you serve them, stuff each *poori* with 2 or 3 chickpeas (or you can instruct your guests to fill their own). Then instruct everyone how to continue: Stir the spiked water, fill a *poori* to the brim, and immediately pop the entire thing into the mouth to experience a gush of flavored water.

Tips:

❖ If you are using canned chickpeas, drain them and rinse off the brine before using them. Then pat them dry before placing them in the shells.

❖ For a more profound impact, preheat the oven to 350°F (no, that's not the shocking part). After you poke a hole in each one, place the *pooris* on a cookie sheet and bake until they are warm to the touch and crisper, about 5 minutes. (Be careful not to leave them in too long, as they can turn black and unpalatable in minutes.) This crispier shell has a crunchier collapse, a warm contrast to the ice-cold spicy water within.

❖ If the water is too chile-heavy for you, add more of the Tamarind-Date sauce to create your own balance.

Puffed Rice
WITH POTATO, UNRIPE MANGO & SWEET-HOT SAUCES

bhel poori chaat

A Mumbai street food original, *bhel* reflects the nature of that city's residents: opposites attract, anything and everything goes, all with great harmony. This sauce-topped snack is a great first course. If you don't prepared the sauces in advance, start on them as soon as you start to cook the potato. You will get them done just around the time the potato is ready (they are a cinch to make). For an unusual presentation, pile it atop crisp baby greens as a salad offering.

SERVES 10

> 1 medium-size russet or Yukon Gold potato, peeled, cut into ¼-inch cubes, and submerged in a bowl of cold water to prevent browning
>
> 1 large rock-firm unripe mango, peeled, seeded, and cut into ¼-inch cubes
>
> ½ cup finely chopped red onion
>
> 1 package (14 ounces) bhel mix (see Tips)
>
> 1 teaspoon chaat masala (page 39)
>
> 2 tablespoons Mint-Yogurt Sauce with Chiles (page 18)
>
> 2 tablespoons Red Chile, Garlic, and Shallot Sauce (page 20)
>
> ½ cup Sweet-Tart Tamarind-Date Sauce (page 20)
>
> ¼ cup finely chopped fresh cilantro leaves and tender stems

1. Drain the potato cubes, place them in a small saucepan, and add fresh water to cover. Bring the water to a boil over medium-high heat. Then reduce the heat to medium-low and simmer until the pieces are tender but still firm-looking, 5 to 10 minutes.

2. Drain the potato cubes in a colander and rinse them under cold water to cool them off and stop the cooking.

3. Combine the potato, mango, and onion in a large serving bowl. Just before you are ready to eat, empty the *bhel* mix into the bowl, pour in the sauces, and add the *chaat masala*. Toss the mélange well and serve sprinkled with the cilantro.

Tips:

❖ *Bhel* mix, a hodgepodge of turmeric-stained puffed rice *(murmura/moori)*, vermicelli-thin fried chickpea-flour noodles *(sev)*, and pieces of flat crisp bread *(poori),* is easy to find among all the other snacks in Indian and Pakistani grocery stores. It has a relatively long shelf life (like potato chips) and is great to snack on au naturel (I meant the *bhel* mix, not your state of dress or undress). I usually stash mine in the refrigerator if I don't plan to use it for a while, because the oil used to fry the snack can go rancid rather quickly. This is especially true if you've opened the bag and used some of it.

❖ You want to highlight the effect of the airy, crispy *bhel* mix against the moist drench of sauces and juicy vegetables, so mix the dry and wet just before you plan to eat it. If you don't plan to eat it all, use only half the vegetables, sauces, and *bhel* mix, saving the rest for a later time.

Pan-Fried Potatoes
WITH
SCALLIONS AND HOT-SWEET SAUCES

Aloo Chaat

Even though this is a great teatime snack, I often serve it as a late breakfast on Sunday morning after having a leisurely read through the newspaper (whatever that means when you're the parent of a young boy). This may remind you of an upscale version of the fried potatoes found on some American breakfast menus, but my take is anything but (upscale or American). This is peasant food found on the streets of Mumbai and Delhi: layers of hot, sweet, tart, and creamy sauces over thin-cut, crispy-fried potatoes. **SERVES 6**

For the sauces (see Tips):

2 tablespoons Mint-Yogurt Sauce with Chiles (page 18)

2 tablespoons Red Chile, Garlic, and Shallot Sauce (page 20)

¼ cup Sweet-Tart Tamarind-Date Sauce (page 20)

¼ cup Yogurt Sauce with Black Salt (page 21)

For the potatoes:

1 pound russet or Yukon Gold potatoes, peeled, cut into quarters, thinly sliced crosswise, and submerged in a bowl of cold water to prevent browning

2 tablespoons canola oil

½ cup finely chopped scallions (green tops and white bulbs)

Chaat masala (page 39) for sprinkling (optional)

2 tablespoons finely chopped fresh cilantro leaves and tender stems for garnishing

1. Drain the potatoes and pat them dry. Heat the oil in a large nonstick skillet over medium heat. Add the potatoes and fry, turning them occasionally, until they are crisp and brown, 5 to 10 minutes. Set the potatoes aside.

2. To assemble the *chaat*, spread one fourth of the potatoes on a small serving platter. Dot or drizzle the Mint-Yogurt Sauce evenly over them. Spread another fourth of the potatoes over the sauce, and drizzle or dot the Red Chile Sauce over the second layer. Spread another fourth of the potatoes over that hot sauce, topping this layer with the Tamarind-Date Sauce. Layer the last of the potatoes over the tamarind sauce, and top off with the Yogurt Sauce. Scatter the scallions over the top, dust with *chaat masala,* and serve sprinkled with the cilantro.

3. When you serve the *aloo chaat,* make sure folks scoop out all four layers to experience the complete package.

Tips:

❖ Prepare the sauces before you begin pan-frying the potatoes.

❖ For an unusual and more colorful presentation, pan-fry 8 ounces of sliced sweet potatoes along with 8 ounces white potatoes. The sweet potatoes impart more sweetness to the dish, so you may wish to use less of the tamarind sauce. However, that's entirely up to your taste buds.

Potato-Filled Pastry Shells

OVER SWEET-TART STEWED YELLOW PEAS

Ragada Samosas

There is no dish more synonymous with Indian food than samosas—those flaky, crispy shells housing spicy mashed potatoes and peas. My version includes carrots and mint, adding color, flavor, and texture. On the streets of large cities like Mumbai and Delhi, samosas are broken open and soused with a hearty stew, then topped with sweet-hot chutneys. When you snack on these in the evening before dinner, it's no wonder you don't have much of an appetite for anything else! Now, I am the first to admit that making samosas and their accoutrements is a labor of love. So gather a few friends and family who enjoy cooking and divvy up the tasks. You not only will have a great time (yes, wine and cocktails are fair game), but you'll also get done that much faster. Because this is rather substantial, serve it as the signature dish with maybe a salad alongside, should you wish for some greens. **MAKES 24 SAMOSAS (SERVES 12)**

For the samosa shells:

3 cups unbleached all-purpose flour
1 teaspoon coarse kosher or sea salt
8 tablespoons (1 stick) butter, chilled,
cut into thin slices
About ½ cup ice water

For the filling:

8 ounces russet or Yukon Gold potatoes,
peeled, diced, and submerged in a bowl
of cold water to prevent browning
2 large carrots, peeled and diced
1 cup frozen green peas, thawed and drained
¼ cup finely chopped fresh mint leaves
¼ cup finely chopped fresh cilantro leaves and
tender stems
1 teaspoon coarse kosher or sea salt
2 fresh green Thai, cayenne, or serrano chiles,
stems removed, finely chopped
(do not remove seeds)
2 tablespoons canola oil
1 teaspoon cumin seeds
1 cup finely chopped red onion
1 tablespoon finely chopped fresh ginger

For the stew and sauce:

2 tablespoons canola oil
½ cup finely chopped red onion
1 tablespoon white granulated sugar
2 teaspoons coriander seeds, ground
1½ teaspoons coarse kosher or sea salt
1 teaspoon cumin seeds, ground
½ teaspoon cayenne (ground red pepper)
½ teaspoon ground turmeric
3 cups cooked dried whole yellow peas
(safed vatana; see box, page 53) or
cooked chickpeas
1 tablespoon tamarind paste or concentrate
¾ cup crumbled or chopped jaggery or
firmly packed dark brown sugar
2 fresh green Thai, cayenne, or serrano chiles,
stems removed
2 lengthwise slices fresh ginger
(each 2½ inches long, 1 inch wide,
and ⅛ inch thick), coarsely chopped

Canola oil for deep-frying

1. To make the samosa shells, combine the flour and salt in a food processor, and pulse to blend. Add the butter and cut it into the flour by pulsing until the butter forms pea-size rounds. (It's these clumps of butter that will provide fat for a flaky shell.)

2. Drizzle in the cold water, a few tablespoons at a time, continuing to pulse the crumbly flour-butter mixture until it just starts to come together to form a soft ball. Stop the processor and transfer the dough to a cutting board or other dry surface. Knead it gently to form a smooth ball, and then roll it to form a 12-inch-long log. Cut the log crosswise into 12 pieces, and shape each piece into a ball. Press each ball flat to form a patty. Cover them in plastic wrap and refrigerate until ready to use.

3. To make the filling, bring a medium-size saucepan of water to a boil over medium-high heat. Drain the potatoes. Add the potatoes and carrots to the pan, and bring to a boil again. Lower the heat to medium and cook, partially covered, until the vegetables are very tender, 5 to 8 minutes; drain. Coarsely mash the vegetables in a medium-size bowl, and then stir in the peas, mint, cilantro, salt, and chiles.

4. Heat the oil in a medium-size skillet over medium-high heat. Add the cumin seeds and let them sizzle until they turn reddish brown and are aromatic, 5 to 10 seconds. Add the onion and ginger, and cook until the vegetables are light brown around the edges, 3 to 5 minutes. Add this to the potato filling, thoroughly stirring it in. You will have an orange-hued, bumpy mixture with specks of green. Set the filling aside.

5. To make the stew and sauce, heat the oil in a medium-size saucepan over medium-high heat. Add the onion and cook until it is light brown, about 2 minutes. Sprinkle in the sugar, coriander, salt, cumin, cayenne, and turmeric, and stir for 5 to 10 seconds. The ground spices will instantly sizzle and cook, turning the onion aromatic.

6. Immediately add the peas and 1 cup water. Heat the curry to a boil. Lower the heat to medium and simmer the peas, covered, stirring occasionally, to allow them to absorb the spicy flavors and to thicken the sauce, 25 to 30 minutes.

7. While the peas are stewing, make the sauce: Whisk the tamarind paste and 1 cup water together in a small saucepan. Stir in the jaggery, chiles, and ginger. Bring to a boil over medium heat. Continue boiling, uncovered, stirring occasionally, until the sauce is slightly thickened, 10 to 12 minutes. Remove the pan from the heat and allow the sauce to cool for just a few minutes. Then transfer it to a blender and puree, scraping the inside of the jar as needed, to form a smooth, dark chocolate brown sauce. Transfer the sauce to a nonreactive bowl (like glass or stainless steel) and refrigerate to chill and thicken it, about 30 minutes (or to speed it up, 15 minutes in the freezer).

8. Remove the stewed peas from the heat and cover the pan to keep the curry warm while you are assembling and frying the samosas.

9. Place a small bowl of water right next to the bowl of filling. Remove a firm, chilled patty from the refrigerator and place it on a lightly floured board. Roll it out to form a round roughly 4 to 5 inches in diameter, dusting it with flour as needed. Slice the round in half. Lay one half across the fingers of one hand (the best position is when your four fingers are together and your thumb is pointing skyward) with its straight edge in line with your forefinger. Dab a little water over the dough, leaving a ¼-inch border. Lift the edge closest to your thumb and twist it, laying the flipped side against the wet side, fashioning a cone. Spoon a heaping tablespoon or two of filling into the cone, pushing

it down. Wet the top round edge of the cone, and press it together to seal it tightly shut. Place the triangular-shaped samosa on a floured plate. Repeat with the remaining patties and filling.

10. Pour oil to a depth of 2 to 3 inches into a wok, Dutch oven, or medium-size saucepan. Heat the oil over medium heat until a candy or deep-frying thermometer inserted into the oil (without touching the pan's bottom) registers 350°F. (An alternative way to see if the oil is at the right temperature for deep-frying is to gently flick a drop of water over it. If the pearl-like drop skitters across the surface, the oil is ready.)

11. Line a large plate or a cookie sheet with several sheets of paper towels. Once the oil is ready, gently slide in 6 samosas (do not crowd the pan). Fry, turning them occasionally, until they are caramel-brown and crisp all over, about 5 minutes. Remove them with a slotted spoon and place them on the paper-towel-lined plate to drain. Repeat until all the samosas are fried. You may need to adjust the heat to maintain the oil's temperature at 350°F.

12. Ladle a scoop of the stewed peas onto an individual serving plate to form a small lumpy bed, and drizzle a teaspoon of the chilled sauce over it. Place 2 samosas over the *ragada,* and serve. If you wish, break open the samosas and ladle the saucy pea stew over them to allow the flavors to permeate the filling.

Tips:

❖ One way to skirt around the work of making your own dough is to purchase thin egg or spring roll wrappers to hold the filling. I have done that on occasion, and I have been immensely satisfied with the results. In fact, they resemble the thin samosa shells that are favored in Mumbai.

how to cook yellow peas
❖ ❖ ❖

Place 1 cup dried peas in a medium-size bowl. Fill the bowl halfway with water and rinse the peas by rubbing them between your fingers. The water will become slightly cloudy. Drain this water. Repeat three or four times, until the water remains relatively clear; drain. Now fill the bowl halfway with hot water, and allow the peas to soften by letting them sit at room temperature, covered, overnight (at least 8 hours); drain. (An alternative for a quicker soak is to bring the pea and hot water mixture to a boil in a pressure cooker, without the lid in place. Then turn off the heat, cover the cooker, and allow the peas to swell and become tender in that steam-room-like environment, 3 to 8 hours).

Drain the peas and place them in a pressure cooker. Add 4 cups water and bring to a boil, uncovered, over high heat. Skim off and discard any foam that forms on the top. Seal the cooker and allow the pressure to build up. Once the weight begins to jiggle or whistle, lower the heat to medium-low and cook for about 30 minutes. Turn off the heat and allow the pressure to subside naturally before opening the lid, about 15 minutes. You will see that many of the peas have shed their skin, which will float to the top. Do not discard the skins. Drain the peas into a colander. If you wish, save the cooking liquid and use it instead of the water called for in stewing the curry.

❖ If you use canned chickpeas, make sure you drain them and rinse off the brine before use.

❖ Want to cut down on the work? You can prepare the samosa patties, through Step 2, up to 4 days ahead. And you can prepare the sauce (Step 7) and chill it up to 2 days ahead.

Breaded Potato Shells
WITH CHICKPEA STEW

Ragada Patties

Daunting-looking recipe: yes. Difficult: no. This classic Mumbai street food is layered, complex, very simple to execute, and definitely easy on the pocketbook. In fact this delicacy is a complete meal that will appease any die-hard nutritionist. If you get most of it put together two or three days before you plan to serve it, the work doesn't seem burdensome. **MAKES 12 PATTIES (SERVES 6)**

cooking times
❖ ❖ ❖

Cooktops vary: electric, gas, flat-top—they all put out different levels of heat. Pots and pans vary, too, in the way they conduct heat. When you are following a recipe, pay more attention to the cooking technique, and to the results you want to achieve, than to the exact amount of time specified.

For the patties:
I pound russet or Yukon Gold potatoes, peeled, boiled until tender, and mashed
I teaspoon coarse kosher or sea salt
4 to 6 slices white bread (choose a bread that is not too soft or "wondrous")
About 5 tablespoons canola oil

For the chickpea stew:
2 cups cooked chickpeas
2 tablespoons Fried Onion Paste (page 16)
I tablespoon Garlic Paste (page 15)
I teaspoon coarse kosher or sea salt

For the sauce:
I tablespoon tamarind paste or concentrate
20 pitted dates (each about 2 inches long), coarsely chopped
½ cup firmly packed fresh cilantro leaves and tender stems
8 lengthwise slices fresh ginger (each 2½ inches long, I inch wide, and ⅛ inch thick)
3 to 5 fresh green Thai, cayenne, or serrano chiles, to taste, stems removed

For garnishing:
I small red onion, finely chopped
¼ cup finely chopped fresh cilantro leaves and tender stems

1. To make the patties, place the mashed potatoes and salt in a large bowl. Hold the bread slices under running water to drench them, and then squeeze out as much water from the slices as possible. You should end up with a wad of moist but firm bread. Squeeze handfuls of the potato and bread together to combine them, and then knead the mixture, creating a slightly sticky dough; the softer the bread, the more slices you will need to get the right consistency. (This technique of creating instant dough with moist bread slices helps

to hold the patties together while pan-frying.) Rub 1 tablespoon canola oil over the dough and allow it to rest, covered with plastic wrap or with a clean, moistened paper towel, for 15 to 20 minutes.

2. Using your hands, shape the dough into a 12-inch-long log. Cut the log crosswise into 12 pieces, and shape each piece into a ball. Press each ball between the palms of your hands to form a patty roughly 3 inches in diameter and ¼ inch thick. Lay the patties on a plate or tray.

3. Line a large plate or a cookie sheet with several layers of paper towels. Heat 2 tablespoons canola oil in a large nonstick skillet, or a well-seasoned cast-iron skillet, over medium heat. Arrange 6 patties, without crowding, in a single layer in the skillet and cook until they are golden brown and crisp on the underside, about 5 minutes. Flip them over and cook the other side until golden brown and crisp, about 5 minutes. Transfer the patties to the paper-towel-lined plate to drain. Repeat with the remaining patties, adding more oil as needed. Keep the patties warm, uncovered, in a low oven.

4. To make the stew, combine the chickpeas, Fried Onion Paste, Garlic Paste, salt, and 2 cups water in a medium-size saucepan. Bring to a boil over medium heat. Reduce the heat to a vigorous simmer and cook the thin curry, uncovered, stirring occasionally, until the liquid has reduced by half, 8 to 10 minutes.

5. While the chickpeas are stewing, prepare the sauce: Whisk the tamarind paste and 2 cups water together in a small saucepan. Stir in the dates and bring to a boil over medium heat. Boil, uncovered, stirring occasionally, until the liquid has reduced by half, 8 to 10 minutes. Set aside.

6. When the stew is ready, remove the pan from the heat and coarsely mash some of the chickpeas, leaving

the rest of them whole. (This thickens the curry, making it almost chowderlike.)

7. Transfer the sauce, including the chunky dates, to a blender. Add the cilantro, ginger, and chiles, and puree, scraping the inside of the jar as needed, until the mixture forms a thick, smooth, green-speckled, fudge-brown sauce. Transfer it to a serving bowl.

8. Arrange the crisp patties in a single layer on a serving platter. Cover each patty with a mound of the chickpea stew, topped with a tablespoon of the tamarind sauce. Sprinkle with the onion and cilantro, and serve.

Onion-Studded Lentil and Split Pea Fritters
WITH A CHUNKY TOMATO-NIGELLA SAUCE

Mung Aur Chana Dal ke Pakoday

these fritters are not only addictive, they are also pretty to look at. A crispy crust encases a soft interior with slightly crunchy red onion and hot chiles; all of it is blanketed with sweet-hot tomatoes, making for one finger-licking appetizer. Don't be put off by the fact that these are deep-fried, because they are not at all greasy—especially if your oil has not been recycled one too many times and its temperature is just right. **SERVES 6**

For the fritters:

- ¾ cup skinned split green lentils (yellow in this form, moong dal), picked over for stones
- ¼ cup yellow split peas (chana dal), picked over for stones
- 6 fresh green Thai, cayenne, or serrano chiles, stems removed
- 4 large cloves garlic
- 2 lengthwise slices fresh ginger (each 2½ inches long, 1 inch wide, and ⅛ inch thick)
- ½ cup finely chopped red onion (see Tip)
- 2 tablespoons finely chopped fresh cilantro leaves and tender stems
- 1 teaspoon coarse kosher or sea salt
- 1 teaspoon bishop's weed; or ½ teaspoon dried thyme mixed with ¼ teaspoon freshly ground black pepper
- Canola oil for deep-frying

For the sauce:

- 1 tablespoon mustard oil or canola oil
- 1 teaspoon nigella seeds
- 2 dried red Thai or cayenne chiles, stems removed, gently pounded to release some of the seeds
- 1 large tomato, cored and finely chopped
- 1 tablespoon crumbled or chopped jaggery or firmly packed dark brown sugar
- ½ teaspoon coarse kosher or sea salt

bishop's weed? Nigella seeds? Jaggery? See the Glossary of Ingredients, page 758.

1. Place the lentils and split peas in a medium-size bowl. Fill the bowl halfway with water, and rinse the legumes by rubbing them between your fingers. The water will become cloudy. Drain this water. Repeat three or four times, until the water remains relatively clear; drain. Now fill the bowl halfway with warm water and allow the lentils and split peas to soften by letting them sit at room temperature, covered, for at least 1 hour or up to 4 hours.

2. Drain the lentils and split peas. Pour ½ cup water

into a blender jar, and add the lentils and split peas, chiles, garlic, and ginger. Puree, scraping the inside of the jar occasionally to ensure even pureeing, until the mixture is smooth and pastelike. Transfer the thick, chile-speckled, yellow batter to the same bowl you used for the legumes, and fold in the onion, cilantro, salt, and bishop's weed.

3. Pour oil to a depth of 2 to 3 inches into a wok, Dutch oven, or medium-size saucepan. Heat the oil over medium heat until a candy or deep-fry thermometer inserted into the oil (without touching the pan's bottom) registers 350°F. (An alternative way to see if the oil is at the right temperature for deep-frying is to gently flick a drop of water over it. If the pearl-like drop skitters across the surface, the oil is ready.)

4. Line a large plate or a cookie sheet with several layers of paper towels. Once the oil is ready, gently slide in teaspoonfuls of the batter without overcrowding (about 10 at a time). Fry, turning the fritters occasionally, until they are golden brown and crisp all over, 3 to 5 minutes. Remove them with a slotted spoon and place them on the paper-towel-lined plate to drain. Repeat with the remaining batter. You may need to adjust the heat to maintain the oil's temperature at 350°F.

5. While the fritters are frying, make the sauce: Heat the oil in a small saucepan over medium-high heat. Sprinkle in the nigella seeds and chiles (seeds and all), and let them sizzle and waft their pungent aromas until the chiles blacken, 10 to 15 seconds. Add the tomato, jaggery, and salt. Cook, uncovered, stirring occasionally, until the tomato pieces soften but still retain their shape, 5 to 7 minutes.

6. Place 3 *pakoras* on each individual serving plate, and spoon about ½ teaspoon of the sweet-spicy, chunky tomato sauce over each one. Chances are people will ask for a second round.

Tip: Onion is not your only option for the batter. Chopped spinach, carrots, green peas (if using frozen, thaw them and drain any excess water), chopped unripe papaya, chopped unripe mango, and chopped potato are all fair game.

Spinach Fritters
IN A YOGURT-CHILE SAUCE

Palak Pakodi Kadhi

These fritters are highly addictive even without the vibrant yogurt-based sauce, but do enjoy them together: You will see why millions of people in homes all across northern India savor this combination on special occasions like weddings and family gatherings. I often serve them as a first course with dark beer or even a glass of a buttery white wine.

MAKES ABOUT 35 FRITTERS (SERVES 10)

For the fritters:

Canola oil for deep-frying
2 cups chickpea flour, sifted (see Tips)
8 ounces fresh spinach leaves, well rinsed and finely chopped
2 teaspoons bishop's weed; or 1 teaspoon dried thyme leaves mixed with ½ teaspoon freshly ground black pepper
2 teaspoons coarse kosher or sea salt
½ teaspoon cayenne (ground red pepper)
¼ teaspoon ground turmeric

For the sauce:

1 cup plain yogurt
1 tablespoon chickpea flour
1 teaspoon Garlic Paste (page 15)
½ teaspoon coarse kosher or sea salt
¼ teaspoon ground turmeric
2 tablespoons finely chopped fresh cilantro leaves and tender stems
3 or 4 fresh green Thai, cayenne, or serrano chiles, to taste, stems removed, finely chopped (do not remove the seeds)
1 tablespoon Ghee (page 21) or unsalted butter
1 teaspoon cumin seeds

1. Pour oil to a depth of 2 to 3 inches into a wok, Dutch oven, or medium-size saucepan. Heat the oil over medium heat until a candy or deep-fry thermometer inserted into the oil (without touching the pan's bottom) registers 350°F. (An alternative way to see if the oil is at the right temperature for deep-frying is to gently flick a drop of water over it. If the pearl-like drop skitters across the surface, the oil is ready.)

2. While the oil is heating, mix together the flour, spinach, bishop's weed, salt, cayenne, and turmeric in a medium-size bowl. Pour in ½ cup water and quickly stir the ingredients together with a spoon to thoroughly combine them and make a moist, slightly thick batter.

3. Line a large plate or a cookie sheet with several layers of paper towels. Once the oil is ready, gently slide in teaspoonfuls of the batter without overcrowding (about 10 at a time). Fry, turning the fritters occasionally, until they are golden brown and crisp all over, about 7 minutes. Remove them with a slotted spoon and place them on the paper-towel-lined plate to drain. (It's okay to snitch a fritter and taste it to make sure it is tasty.) Repeat with the remaining batter. You may need to adjust the heat to maintain the oil's temperature at 350°F.

4. While the fritters are frying, make the sauce: Whisk the yogurt with 1 cup water in a medium-size bowl. Beat the chickpea flour into the yogurt mixture, making sure there are no lumps (the flour is essential because it will prevent the yogurt from curdling upon heating). Fold in the Garlic Paste, salt, turmeric, cilantro, and chiles.

5. Heat the ghee in a small saucepan over medium-high heat until it appears to shimmer. Scatter in the cumin seeds and let them sizzle until they are nutty-fragrant and look reddish brown, 5 to 10 seconds. Lower the heat to medium and pour in the spiced yogurt. Simmer, uncovered, stirring occasionally, until the sauce thickens slightly, about 15 minutes.

6. Place 3 to 4 fritters on each individual serving plate. Pour about 1 tablespoon of the sauce over each fritter, and serve immediately (although they are equally tasty when served with the sauce at room temperature). Make sure you do not pour the entire sauce over the complete batch of fritters. If you do, eat them all quickly!

Tips:

❖ Sifting provides lump-free and airily light flour, which is crucial to the texture of these fritters. There are many varieties of sifters available in any store that sells kitchen gadgets. Rotary-cranked and battery-operated sifters are popular. However, I don't have a sifter in my kitchen—I simply use a fine-mesh strainer to sift flour.

❖ Bishop's weed imparts an essential pungent, thyme-like flavor to these fritters. It helps in the digestion of the chickpea flour, and its peppery undertone bestows a unique zest. If you don't have any, use the thyme-pepper mixture.

❖ Triple-washed spinach leaves are available in the produce section of any supermarket. If you like, use thawed frozen chopped spinach,

but make sure you squeeze out all the water before adding it. But please, no matter what, do not use canned spinach. Its insipid flavor and metallic taste do nothing to enhance the dish.

❖ Ideally, these fritters are best when fried just before they're served. But if you don't want the hassle of deep-frying at the last minute, make them ahead of time and hold them (or reheat them) in a preheated oven at 250°F. The sauce will thicken as it sits. Beat in a tablespoon or two of water to bring it back to a syruplike consistency.

Mung Bean Fritters
WITH A TAMARIND-JAGGERY SAUCE

Mung dal bhujiyas

Bite-size morsels of batter-fried vegetable or lentil dumplings are called *bhujiyas*. These addictive fritters are a cinch to make, and are especially useful to serve as a snack when unexpected visitors drop by. Even though the fritters contain an alarming number of chiles, you will be amazed at their mellowness.

MAKES ABOUT 30 FRITTERS (SERVES 8 TO 10)

For the fritters:

1 cup skin-on split green lentils (moong dal), picked over for stones and rinsed (see Tip)
10 fresh green Thai, cayenne, or serrano chiles, stems removed

Tamarind paste? See the Glossary of Ingredients, page 758.

2 lengthwise slices fresh ginger (each 2½ inches long,
   1 inch wide, and ⅛ inch thick)
1½ teaspoons coarse kosher or sea salt
1 teaspoon cumin seeds
¼ teaspoon ground turmeric
Canola oil for deep-frying

For the sauce:

1 teaspoon tamarind paste or concentrate
¼ cup chopped or crumbled jaggery or
   firmly packed dark brown sugar
2 tablespoons Toasted Chickpea Flour (page 41)
1 teaspoon cumin seeds
½ teaspoon coarse kosher or sea salt
2 fresh green Thai, cayenne, or serrano chiles,
   stems removed

1. Place the lentils in a medium-size bowl, and fill the bowl halfway with water. Rinse the lentils by rubbing them between your fingertips. The water will become cloudy and some of the skin will separate and float to the top. Drain this water. Repeat three or four times, until the water remains relatively clear; drain. Now fill the bowl halfway with hot water and allow the lentils to soften by letting them sit at room temperature, covered, for at least 15 minutes.

2. Drain the lentils. Pour ½ cup water into a blender jar and add the lentils, chiles, and ginger. Puree, scraping the inside of the jar occasionally to ensure the even pureeing, until the mixture is smooth and pastelike. Transfer the thick, olive-green batter to the bowl you used for soaking the lentils. Fold in the salt, cumin, and turmeric.

3. Pour oil to a depth of 2 to 3 inches into a wok, Dutch oven, or medium-size saucepan. Heat the oil over medium heat until a candy or deep-fry thermometer inserted into the oil (without touching the pan's bottom) registers 350°F. (An alternative way to see if the oil is at the right temperature for deep-frying is to gently flick a drop of water over it. If the pearl-like drop skitters across the surface, the oil is ready.)

4. Line a large plate or a cookie sheet with several layers of paper towels. Once the oil is ready, gently slide in teaspoonfuls of the batter without overcrowding (about 10 at a time). Fry, turning the fritters occasionally, until they are golden brown and crisp all over, 3 to 5 minutes. Remove them with a slotted spoon and place them on the paper-towel-lined plate to drain. Repeat with the remaining batter. You may need to adjust the heat to maintain the oil's temperature at 350°F.

5. To make the sauce, dissolve the tamarind paste in 1 cup water in a small saucepan. Stir in the jaggery and sprinkle in the Toasted Chickpea Flour, whisking to make sure there are no lumps.

6. Place the cumin, salt, and chiles in a mortar and pound until the chiles are crushed and the cumin is partially ground but still gritty. Scrape this mixture into the sauce. Bring the sauce to a boil over medium-high heat, uncovered, stirring occasionally until the jaggery dissolves and the mixture thickens slightly, about 5 minutes.

7. Place 3 fritters on each individual serving plate, and blanket them with the syrup-thick, sweet-spicy sauce.

Tip: I have noticed a higher amount of stones with skin-on lentils, so please take extra care to pick them over. I also rinse the skin-on lentils once or twice before I soak them, to wash off any dust or grit that might adhere to the skins. If I forget, I am duly punished with a gritty, grainy texture, reminiscent of unwashed spinach leaves, when I bite into a fritter.

Tapioca Fritters
WITH A COCONUT–SESAME SEED SAUCE

Sabudana Vada

tapioca (*sago*), a starch, is processed from the stem of the cassava plant. Pushing tapioca through special molds yields its pearl-like shape. The snowy-white Indian tapioca pearl is often larger in size than its Southeast Asian counterpart, which also comes in assorted pastel colors. In the U.S., tapioca pearls are widely available in natural food stores, supermarkets, and Asian grocery stores. Tapioca is more familiar in this country as a sweet, thickened pudding, but the same pearls offer a savory backdrop to the vibrant, nutty, spicy flavors in this classic dish from Maharashtra.

MAKES 20 FRITTERS (SERVES 10)

For the fritters:

- 1 cup uncooked medium-size white tapioca pearls
- 1 cup unsalted dry-roasted peanuts
- ½ cup firmly packed fresh cilantro leaves and tender stems
- 10 fresh green Thai, cayenne, or serrano chiles, stems removed
- 6 medium-size to large cloves garlic
- 2 lengthwise slices fresh ginger (each 2½ inches long, 1 inch wide, and ⅛ inch thick)
- 1 pound russet or Yukon Gold potatoes, peeled, boiled until tender, and mashed
- 2 teaspoons coarse kosher or sea salt
- Canola oil for deep-frying

For the sauce:

- 1 tablespoon canola oil
- ¼ cup shredded dried unsweetened coconut
- 1 tablespoon white sesame seeds
- ½ cup unsalted dry-roasted peanuts
- 2 tablespoons fresh cilantro leaves and tender stems
- 1 teaspoon coarse kosher or sea salt
- 1 medium-size tomato, cored and coarsely chopped
- 2 to 4 fresh green Thai, cayenne, or serrano chiles, to taste, stems removed

1. Place the tapioca pearls in a medium-size bowl. Fill the bowl halfway with water and rinse the hard, pebble-like, starchy grains by rubbing them between your fingertips. The water will become cloudy. Drain this water. Repeat three or four times, until the water remains relatively clear; drain. Fill the bowl halfway with hot water and let the pearls soak for 30 minutes. They will swell and soften. (Press a pearl between your fingers: it should squish easily. If the grain is old and hasn't softened enough, you might have to soak it a little longer.) Drain the softened pearls thoroughly in a colander.

2. While the tapioca is soaking, grind the peanuts in a food processor, using the pulsing action to break them up into a coarse breadcrumb-like texture. Transfer them to a large bowl.

3. Combine the cilantro, chiles, garlic, and ginger in the same food processor bowl, and process until minced. Add the herb mixture to the peanuts.

4. Once the tapioca has completely drained, add it to the peanut-herb mixture, along with the mashed potatoes and salt. Bring the ingredients together into a ball and knead it, just as you would while making bread dough. It will resemble a soft and maybe slightly sticky dough (albeit bumpy because of the tapioca pearls). Grease your palms, if need be, with

a little cooking oil or spray. Take 2 tablespoons of the dough and shape it into a tight round ball. Press the ball between the palms of your hands to form a patty roughly 2½ inches in diameter and ½ inch thick. Lay it on a plate or tray. Repeat with the remaining dough. You should end up with about 20 light green, bumpy-looking patties.

5. Pour oil to a depth of 2 to 3 inches into a wok, Dutch oven, or medium-size saucepan. Heat the oil over medium heat until a candy or deep-fry thermometer inserted into the oil (without touching the pan's bottom) registers 350°F. (An alternative way to see if the oil is at the right temperature for deep-frying is to gently flick a drop of water over it. If the pearl-like drop skitters across the surface, the oil is ready.)

6. Line a large plate or a cookie sheet with several layers of paper towels. Once the oil is ready, gently slide 6 patties into the pan (do not crowd the pan). Fry, turning them occasionally, until they are caramel brown and crisp on both sides, about 5 minutes. Remove them with a slotted spoon and place them on the paper-towel-lined plate to drain. Repeat until all the patties are fried. You may need to adjust the heat to maintain the oil's temperature at 350°F.

7. To make the sauce, heat the oil in a small saucepan over medium-high heat. Add the coconut and sesame seeds and roast, stirring constantly, until the combination is caramel brown and smells incredibly nutty, about 1 minute.

8. Immediately transfer the coconut mixture to a blender, and add 1 cup water plus all the remaining sauce ingredients. Puree, scraping the inside of the jar as needed, until the mixture forms a relatively smooth reddish-green sauce. Pour this into a small saucepan, making sure you scrape every drop from the blender jar. Feel free to add a few tablespoons of water to the jar and swish it around to wash it out, adding this to the sauce. Bring the sauce to a boil over medium-high heat. Remove from the heat.

9. Place 2 fritters on each individual serving plate, and cover them with the spicy sauce. You will marvel at the fritter's crispy exterior and the soft, zesty, gooey interior.

Tip: If you don't wish to fry them all, store the remaining uncooked patties, tightly wrapped in plastic wrap, in the refrigerator for up to 2 days; or store them in resealable freezer bags in the freezer for up to 1 month. You can fry them while they are still frozen, but keep them in the hot oil for a few extra minutes to make sure the center gets cooked.

Pigeon Pea Fritters
WITH A YOGURT-TOMATO SAUCE

toram Paruppu Vadai

This combination of fritter and sauce, referred to as *vadai-pachadi* in Tamil-speaking kitchens, is an absolute must for weddings and auspicious religious functions. The yellow split peas, left whole but soaked until tender, provide a delicious crunch to these spicy fritters.

MAKES ABOUT 25 FRITTERS (SERVES 10 TO 12)

For the fritters:

I cup oily or unoily skinned split yellow pigeon
    peas (toovar dal), picked over for stones
3 or 4 dried red Thai or cayenne chiles, to taste,
    stems removed
¼ cup yellow split peas (chana dal), picked
    over for stones, soaked in hot water for
    30 minutes and drained
¼ cup finely chopped red onion
¼ cup finely chopped fresh cilantro leaves and
    tender stems
1½ teaspoons coarse kosher or sea salt
½ teaspoon ground asafetida
Canola oil for deep-frying

For the sauce:

I cup plain nonfat yogurt
½ teaspoon coarse kosher or sea salt
I tablespoon canola oil
I teaspoon black or yellow mustard seeds
I medium-size tomato, cored and finely
    chopped
I or 2 fresh green Thai, cayenne, or serrano chiles,
    to taste, stems removed, finely chopped
    (do not remove the seeds)
I tablespoon finely chopped fresh cilantro leaves
    and tender stems

1. Place the pigeon peas in a medium-size bowl. Fill the bowl halfway with water and rinse the peas by rubbing them between your fingertips. The water will become cloudy. Drain this water. Repeat three or four times, until the water remains relatively clear; drain. Now fill the bowl halfway with warm water and add the chiles to the peas. Allow the peas and chiles to soften by letting them sit at room temperature, covered, for at least 30 minutes or up to 4 hours.

2. Drain the pigeon peas and chiles, transfer them to a food processor, and process to form a red-speckled,

Asafetida? Black mustard seeds? See the Glossary of Ingredients, page 758.

slightly gritty paste. Scrape this paste into a medium-size bowl. Fold in the yellow split peas, onion, cilantro, salt, and asafetida, forming a paste that looks like wet sand.

3. Grease your palms with a little cooking oil or spray. Take a heaping tablespoon of the paste and shape it into a tight round ball. Press the ball between the palms of your hands to form a patty roughly 1½ inches in diameter and ½ inch thick. Lay it on a plate or tray. Repeat with the remaining paste. You should end up with about 25 patties.

4. Pour oil to a depth of 2 to 3 inches into a wok, Dutch oven, or medium-size saucepan. Heat the oil over medium heat until a candy or deep-fry thermometer inserted into the oil (without touching the pan's bottom) registers 350°F. (An alternative way to see if the oil is at the right temperature for deep-frying is to gently flick a drop of water over it. If the pearl-like drop skitters across the surface, the oil is ready.)

5. Line a large plate or a cookie sheet with several layers of paper towels. Once the oil is ready, gently slide 8 patties into the pan (do not crowd the pan). Fry, turning them occasionally, until they are caramel-brown and crisp on both sides, about 5 minutes. Remove them with a slotted spoon and place them on the paper-towel-lined plate to drain. Repeat until all the patties are fried. You may need to adjust the heat to maintain the oil's temperature at 350°F.

6. To make the sauce, whisk the yogurt, salt, and ¼ cup water together in a medium-size bowl.

7. Heat the oil in a small skillet over medium-high heat. Add the mustard seeds, cover the skillet, and

wait until the seeds have stopped popping (not unlike popcorn), about 30 seconds. Immediately add the tomato, chiles, and cilantro. Cook, uncovered, until the tomato has broken down and formed a chunky sauce, 2 to 4 minutes. Stir this spicy sauce into the watered-down yogurt.

8. Place 2 fritters on each individual serving plate, and cover each one with a heaping teaspoon of the tart-hot, mustard-spiked yogurt sauce.

Tip: If you don't wish to fry them all, keep the remaining uncooked patties, tightly wrapped in plastic wrap, in the refrigerator for up to 2 days; or store them in resealable freezer bags in the freezer for up to 1 month. Partially thaw them before frying, and keep them in the hot oil for a few extra minutes to make sure the center cooks.

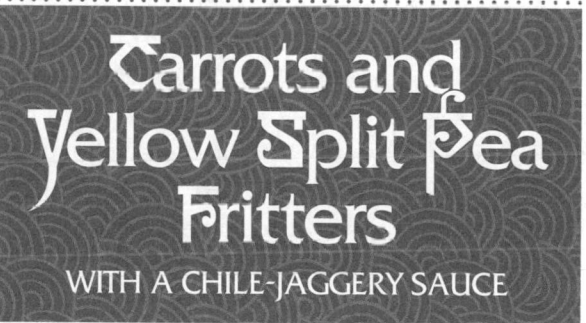

Carrots and Yellow Split Pea Fritters
WITH A CHILE-JAGGERY SAUCE

Aamai Masala Vadai

A version of the pigeon pea fritters on page 61, these incorporate slightly chunky vegetables to create delectably crunchy, moist fritters. Don't stop if you feel compelled to keep on noshing—give in to temptation and just let it go. You will love every overindulged bite.

MAKES ABOUT 18 FRITTERS (SERVES 6)

For the fritters:

1 cup yellow split peas (chana dal), picked over for stones
6 dried red Thai or cayenne chiles, stems removed
1 cup frozen green peas, thawed
½ cup finely chopped carrots
2 teaspoons coarse kosher or sea salt
½ teaspoon ground asafetida
Canola oil for deep-frying

For the sauce:

1 tablespoon tamarind paste or concentrate
5 tablespoons crumbled or chopped jaggery or firmly packed dark brown sugar
2 dried red Thai or cayenne chiles, stems removed
1 tablespoon rice flour

1. Place the split peas in a medium-size bowl. Fill the bowl halfway with water and rinse the split peas by rubbing them between your fingertips. The water will become cloudy. Drain this water. Repeat three or four times, until the water remains relatively clear; drain. Now fill the bowl halfway with warm water and add the chiles to the split peas. Allow the chiles and split peas to soften by letting them sit at room temperature, covered, for 1 to 4 hours.

2. Drain the split peas and chiles, place them in a food processor, and process to form a red-speckled, slightly gritty paste. Transfer this paste to the same medium-size bowl (why dirty another one?), and fold in the peas, carrots, salt, and asafetida.

3. Grease your palms with a little cooking oil or spray. Take 1 heaping tablespoon of the paste and shape it into a tight round ball. Press the ball between the palms of your hands to form a patty roughly 1½ inches in diameter and ½ inch thick. Lay it on a plate or tray. Repeat with the remaining paste. You should end up with about 18 patties.

4. Pour oil to a depth of 2 to 3 inches into a wok, Dutch oven, or medium-size saucepan. Heat the oil over medium heat until a candy or deep-fry thermometer inserted into the oil (without touching the pan's bottom) registers 350°F. (An alternative way to see if the oil is at the right temperature for deep-frying is to gently flick a drop of water over it. If the pearl-like drop skitters across the surface, the oil is ready.)

5. Line a large plate or a cookie sheet with several layers of paper towels. Once the oil is ready, gently slide 6 patties into the pan (do not crowd the pan). Fry, turning them occasionally, until the fritters are caramel-brown and crisp on both sides, about 5 minutes. Remove them with a slotted spoon and place them on the paper-towel-lined plate to drain. Repeat until all the patties are fried. You may need to adjust the heat to maintain the oil's temperature at 350°F.

6. To make the sauce, dissolve the tamarind paste in 2 cups water in a small saucepan. Stir in the jaggery and chiles. Bring the sauce to a boil over medium-high heat. Allow the sauce to boil vigorously, uncovered, stirring occasionally, until the liquid has reduced by half, 8 to 10 minutes.

7. Transfer the hot liquid to a blender jar. Puree, holding the blender lid down with a towel (to prevent it from bursting open because of the pressure built up from the hot liquid), to form a smooth liquid. Pour this back into the pan and sprinkle in the rice flour, quickly whisking it in to prevent any lumps from forming. Rewarm the sauce over medium-low heat, uncovered, whisking occasionally, until thickened, 3 to 5 minutes.

8. Place 3 fritters on each individual serving plate, and cover them with the syrup-thick, sweet-spicy sauce.

Tip: If you don't wish to fry them all, keep the uncooked patties, tightly wrapped in plastic wrap, in the refrigerator for up to 2 days; or wrap them in freezer paper or self-seal plastic freezer bags, and freeze for up to 1 month. Partially thaw the patties before frying them, and keep them in the hot oil for a few minutes extra to make sure the centers are cooked.

Lentil Fritters
WITH RAISINS IN A YOGURT SAUCE

dahi Vada

These creamy, sweet, hot, fluffy lentil fritters will have your guests speculating about the ingredients. I can safely bet that raisins and cashews will never appear on their radar screen! The only slightly time-consuming task in this recipe is frying the *vadas*. The sauce takes all of thirty seconds to put together. What is also great about these fritters is that you can make them up to two days ahead. **MAKES 30 FRITTERS**

Asafetida? Tamarind paste? Jaggery? See the Glossary of Ingredients, page 758.

For the fritters:

1 cup skinned split black lentils (cream-colored in this form, urad dal), picked over for stones
½ cup golden raisins
½ cup raw cashew nuts
10 to 12 fresh green Thai, cayenne, or serrano chiles, to taste, stems removed
1½ teaspoons coarse kosher or sea salt
½ teaspoon ground asafetida
Canola oil for deep-frying

For the sauce:
   1 cup Yogurt Sauce with Black Salt (page 21)
   Cayenne (ground red pepper) for sprinkling
   Chaat masala (page 39) for sprinkling (optional)
   2 tablespoons finely chopped fresh cilantro leaves
      and tender stems for garnishing

1. Place the lentils in a medium-size bowl. Fill the bowl halfway with water and rinse the lentils by rubbing them between your fingertips. The water will become cloudy. Drain this water. Repeat three or four times, until the water remains relatively clear; drain. Now fill the bowl halfway with warm water and allow the lentils to soften by letting them sit at room temperature, covered, for at least 30 minutes or up to 4 hours.

2. Drain the lentils. Pour ¾ cup water into a blender, and add the lentils, raisins, nuts, and chiles. Puree, scraping the inside of the jar occasionally, until the mixture is smooth and pastelike. Transfer the thick batter to the same bowl. Add ¼ cup water to the blender jar and run the blender to wash out any remnants of batter; add this to the batter in the bowl, and stir in the salt and asafetida. (If you use the entire 1 cup water to grind the soaked lentils, the resulting batter might be gritty and slightly watery.) Using a spatula, vigorously beat the batter in a circular motion for 2 to 3 minutes (this incorporates air, ensuring a fluffy but crispy fritter).

3. Pour oil to a depth of 2 to 3 inches into a wok, Dutch oven, or medium-size saucepan. Heat the oil over medium heat until a candy or deep-fry thermometer inserted into the oil (without touching the pan's bottom) registers 350°F. (An alternative way to see if the oil is at the right temperature for deep-frying is to gently flick a drop of water over it. If the pearl-like drop skitters across the surface, the oil is ready.)

4. Fill a medium-size bowl with hot water and place it near the stove. Once the oil is ready, gently slide in teaspoonfuls of the batter without crowding (about 10 at a time). (I usually fill one spoon with the batter and use another spoon to slide the batter into the oil.) Fry, turning them occasionally, until the fritters are golden brown and crisp all over, about 5 minutes. Remove them with a slotted spoon and drop them into the hot water. Repeat until all the fritters are cooked and transferred to the hot water. You may need to adjust the heat to maintain the oil's temperature at 350°F. (Do not leave any fritters in the water for longer than 5 minutes.)

5. Place the yogurt sauce in a medium-size bowl.

6. Working with one *vada* at a time, press them between the palms of your hands to squeeze out every bit of water. Drop them into the yogurt sauce, dunking and coating them evenly, and then place them on a serving platter. If there's any sauce remaining in the bowl, pour it over the *vadas*.

7. Sprinkle some cayenne and *chaat masala* over the blanketed *vadas*, top them off with the cilantro, and serve. They will keep, covered, in the refrigerator for up to 2 days.

Tips:

❖ If nut allergies are a cause for concern, eliminate the cashews.

❖ The more you incorporate air into the lentil batter by beating it, the fluffier your fritters will be. The fluffy fritter will absorb more grease, but the water-soaking will remove all the excess fat, making for a guilt-free fritter.

❖ One reason why many legume-based recipes include the strong-smelling (but not strong-tasting) spice asafetida is its ability to help break down the complex indigestible sugars that cause gas, making this an Indian's "Beano."

Coconut-Flavored Fritters
WITH A
BUTTERMILK–PIGEON PEA BROTH

More Rasam Mysore Bonda

Similar in ingredients to the Lentil Dumplings in a Spicy Tamarind-Lentil Broth (page 75) but surprisingly different because of a change in some key elements, these fritters deliver a bowlful of addiction. The coconut in the fritters is a trademark of these nibblers from Mysore, a city in south central India not too far from India's Silicon Valley—Bangalore. The buttermilk gives the curry a pleasant tartness and mellows out the peppercorns. "Buttermilk" is *more* in Tamil, with the "e" pronounced "uh," and yes, you will ask for more of it. If you wish to turn this into a soup course, plan on this feeding six.

MAKES ABOUT 30 DUMPLINGS (SERVES 10)

For the fritters:

- 1 cup skinned split black lentils (cream-colored in this form, urad dal), picked over for stones
- 1 teaspoon black peppercorns
- 1 cup shredded fresh coconut; or
  - ½ cup shredded dried unsweetened coconut, reconstituted (see Note and Tips)
- ¼ cup coarsely chopped medium-size to large fresh curry leaves (see Tips)
- 1 teaspoon coarse kosher or sea salt
- ½ teaspoon ground asafetida
- Canola oil for deep-frying

For the broth:

- ¼ cup oily or unoily skinned split yellow pigeon peas (toovar dal), picked over for stones
- 1 large tomato, cored and cut into 1-inch chunks
- 2 teaspoons sambhar masala (page 33)
- 1 teaspoon coarse kosher or sea salt
- ¼ teaspoon ground asafetida
- ¼ teaspoon ground turmeric
- 15 medium-size to large fresh curry leaves (see Tips)
- 1 tablespoon unrefined sesame oil or canola oil
- 1 teaspoon black or yellow mustard seeds
- 2 dried red Thai or cayenne chiles, stems removed
- 1 cup nonfat buttermilk

1. Place the lentils in a medium-size bowl. Fill the bowl halfway with water and rinse the lentils by rubbing them between your fingertips. The water will become cloudy. Drain this water. Repeat three or four times, until the water remains relatively clear; drain. Now fill the bowl halfway with warm water and allow the lentils to soften by letting them sit at room temperature, covered, for at least 30 minutes or up to 4 hours.

2. Drain the lentils. Pour ½ cup water into a blender jar, and add the lentils and peppercorns. Puree, scraping the inside of the jar occasionally, until the mixture is smooth and pastelike. Transfer the thick batter to the same medium-size bowl. Pour ¼ cup water into the blender jar and run the blender to wash out any remnants of batter; add this to the batter in the bowl. (If you use the entire ¾ cup water to puree the soaked lentils, the resulting batter may be slightly watery and gritty.) Stir in the coconut, curry leaves, salt, and asafetida. Using a spatula, vigorously beat the batter in a circular motion for 2 to 3 minutes (this incorporates air, ensuring a fluffy but crispy fritter).

3. Pour oil to a depth of 2 to 3 inches into a wok, Dutch oven, or medium-size saucepan. Heat the oil over medium heat until a candy or deep-fry thermometer inserted into the oil (without touching the pan's bottom) registers 350°F. (An alternative way to see if the oil is at the right temperature for deep-frying is to gently flick a drop of water over it. If the pearl-like drop skitters across the surface, the oil is ready.)

4. Line a large plate or a cookie sheet with several layers of paper towels. Once the oil is ready, gently slide in teaspoonfuls of the batter without crowding (about 10 at a time). Fry, turning them occasionally, until the fritters are golden brown and crisp all over, about 5 minutes. Remove them with a slotted spoon and place them on the paper-towel-lined plate to drain. Repeat until the fritters are cooked. You may need to adjust the heat to maintain the oil's temperature at 350°F.

5. To make the broth, place the pigeon peas in a medium-size saucepan. Fill the pan halfway with water and rinse the peas by rubbing them between your fingertips. The water will become cloudy. Drain this water. Repeat three or four times, until the water remains relatively clear; drain. Now add 2 cups water and bring it to a boil, uncovered, over medium-high heat. Skim off and discard any foam that forms on the surface. Reduce the heat to medium-low and simmer, covered, stirring occasionally, until the peas are tender, about 20 minutes.

6. While the peas are cooking, combine 1 cup water with the tomato, *sambhar masala,* salt, asafetida, turmeric, and curry leaves in another small saucepan.

Bring to a boil over medium heat and continue cooking, uncovered, stirring occasionally, until the tomato chunks are tender but still hold their shape, 5 to 8 minutes.

7. Transfer the cooked pigeon peas and the residual cooking water to a blender and puree, scraping the inside of the jar as needed, until smooth. Set aside.

8. Heat a small skillet over medium-high heat, and pour in the oil. Add the mustard seeds, cover, and wait until all the seeds have stopped popping (not unlike popcorn), about 30 seconds. Remove the skillet from heat, add the chiles, and toss until the chiles blacken, 10 seconds. Scrape the nutty-pungent mixture into the simmering tomato broth, along with the pureed pigeon peas.

9. Remove the pan from heat and allow it to cool for about 5 minutes. Stir in the buttermilk, which may curdle slightly.

10. Place 3 to 5 fritters in each individual serving bowl, and ladle the hot buttermilk curry over them. Serve immediately.

Note: To reconstitute coconut, cover with ½ cup boiling water, set aside for about 15 minutes, and then drain.

Tips:

❖ If you use reconstituted dried coconut instead of fresh, the slightly larger amount of water in the batter will make the fritters greasy. To prevent this, press the fritters between paper towels before sousing them with the buttermilk curry.

❖ I have substituted finely chopped fresh cilantro leaves and tender stems for the curry leaves at times when I did not have curry leaves on hand.

Batter-Fried Chile-Smothered Vegetables
WITH A COCONUT SAUCE

thenga bonda

Some version of these addictive fritters is a must at breakfast on the day of a Tamil wedding. Occupying the center position on the platter that is lined with a cut-out piece of banana leaf, these golden brown *bondas* are served with a mound of coconut sauce alongside. When the server with the plateful of these *bondas* walks by, it's no wonder you can never refuse "just one more," alternating mouthfuls of chile-hot *bondas* with sips of strong coffee.

MAKES 20 FRITTERS (SERVES 10)

For the vegetable mixture:

1 pound russet or Yukon Gold potatoes,
    peeled, boiled until tender, and
    mashed
½ cup finely chopped red onion
½ cup frozen green peas (no need to thaw)
¼ cup finely chopped fresh curry leaves
2 tablespoons finely chopped fresh ginger
1½ teaspoons rock salt, pounded;
    or 2 teaspoons coarse kosher or sea salt
½ teaspoon ground turmeric
6 to 8 fresh green Thai, cayenne, or serrano chiles,
    to taste, stems removed, finely chopped
    (do not remove the seeds)

For the coconut sauce:

1 cup shredded fresh coconut; or ½ cup shredded
    dried unsweetened coconut, reconstituted
    (see Note)
2 tablespoons dry-roasted yellow split peas
    (see Tip)
1 teaspoon coarse kosher or sea salt
¼ teaspoon tamarind paste or concentrate
1 or 2 fresh green Thai, cayenne, or serrano chiles,
    to taste, stems removed
1 tablespoon canola oil
1 teaspoon black or yellow mustard seeds

For the batter:

1 cup chickpea flour, sifted
½ cup rice flour
1 teaspoon coarse kosher or sea salt
1 teaspoon cayenne (ground red pepper)
¼ teaspoon ground asafetida
¼ teaspoon ground turmeric

Canola oil for deep-frying

1. Combine all the ingredients for the vegetable mixture in a medium-size bowl, and mix them together thoroughly. Divide the mixture into 20 portions, and shape each portion into a tight golf-ball-size ball; they will be bright yellow with specks of green and purple. Set these balls aside until you finish making the sauce and the batter. (In fact, you can assemble these a day or two ahead and refrigerate them, covered, until ready to cook.)

2. To make the coconut sauce, pour 1 cup water into a blender jar, followed by the coconut, split peas, salt, tamarind paste, and chiles. Puree, scraping the inside of the jar as needed, until the mixture forms a slightly gritty, spicy-tart sauce.

3. Heat the oil in a small saucepan over medium-high

heat. Add the mustard seeds, cover, and wait until all the seeds have stopped popping (not unlike popcorn), about 30 seconds. Carefully pour the coconut sauce into the saucepan, and allow it to come to a boil. Once it does, remove it from the heat.

4. To make the batter, mix the two flours, salt, cayenne, asafetida, and turmeric in a medium-size bowl. Pour in about ⅓ cup warm water, whisking the ingredients together to form a thick batter. Continue adding warm water, a few tablespoons at a time, whisking them in after each addition, to make a smooth batter that coats a spoon. You will need about ¾ cup warm water altogether.

5. Pour oil to a depth of 2 to 3 inches into a wok, Dutch oven, or medium-size saucepan. Heat the oil over medium heat until a candy or deep-fry thermometer inserted into the oil (without touching the pan's bottom) registers 350°F. (An alternative way to see if the oil is at the right temperature for deep-frying is to gently flick a drop of water over it. If the pearl-like drop skitters across the surface, the oil is ready.)

6. Line a large plate or a cookie sheet with several layers of paper towels. Once the oil is ready, dip a vegetable ball into the batter, coating it all over, and then carefully slide it into the hot oil. Repeat with about 6 more vegetable balls; do not crowd the pan. Fry, turning them occasionally, until they are golden brown and crisp all over, about 5 minutes. Remove them with a slotted spoon and place them on the paper-towel-lined plate to drain. Repeat with the remaining rounds. You may need to adjust the heat to maintain the oil's temperature at 350°F.

7. Place 2 fritters on each individual serving plate, spoon the coconut sauce over them, and serve immediately.

Note: To reconstitute coconut, cover with ½ cup boiling water, set aside for about 15 minutes, and then drain.

Tip: Dry-roasted yellow split peas *(dahlia)* are available in Indian grocery stores. When yellow split peas (which are actually split and hulled black chickpeas) are dry-roasted or fried, they are sold under the label *pottu kadala* (Tamil) or *dalia* (Hindi). These are perfectly edible as is, and when pureed with other ingredients they provide body to the sauce, along with valuable proteins. If they are unavailable, use unsalted dry-roasted peanuts as an alternative.

Green Pea Croquettes
WITH A PEANUT-CHILE SAUCE

Mutter Patties

When you cast your eyes at the presentation, you may very well say, "Ooooh, looks like crab cakes under that sauce." However, biting into a morsel will make you eat those words, much to the pleasure of the vegetarians at the table. But you will not care one bit about your mistake—and a serving of seconds may very well have your name on it. These croquettes are truly flavorful and full of texture, with the nutty-tart peanut sauce, crisp patty, and soft sweet peas mottled with chiles going "wild-n-crazy" in your mouth. **MAKES 12 CROQUETTES (SERVES 6)**

For the croquettes:

2 cups frozen green peas, thawed and drained

1 small red onion, coarsely chopped

3 to 5 fresh green Thai, cayenne, or serrano chiles,
to taste, stems removed

2 lengthwise slices fresh ginger (each 2½ inches long,
1 inch wide, and ⅛ inch thick)

¼ cup rice flour

2 teaspoons Toasted Cumin-Coriander Blend (page 33)

1 teaspoon coarse kosher or sea salt

¼ cup finely chopped fresh cilantro leaves
and tender stems

Canola oil for pan-frying

½ cup uncooked Cream of Wheat (do not use instant)
or unseasoned fine dry breadcrumbs

For the sauce:

1 cup firmly packed fresh cilantro leaves
and tender stems

½ cup unsalted dry-roasted peanuts

2 or 3 fresh green Thai, cayenne, or serrano chiles,
to taste, stems removed

1 teaspoon white granulated sugar

1 teaspoon coarse kosher or sea salt

Juice of 1 medium-size lime

1. Combine the peas, onion, chiles, and ginger in a food processor and pulse to mince—do not overprocess or the mixture will become watery. Transfer the mixture to a medium-size bowl and stir in the flour, Cumin-Coriander Blend, salt, and cilantro.

2. Line a large plate or a cookie sheet with several layers of paper towels. Heat about 2 tablespoons canola oil in a nonstick skillet, or in a well-seasoned cast-iron skillet, over medium heat.

3. While the oil is heating, scoop out about ¼ cup of the pea mixture, place it in the palm of your hand, and shape it into a ball. Press it down to make a bumpy, slightly unmanageable patty, about ½ inch thick. Shower some of the Cream of Wheat liberally over the patty, to form a gritty covering. Flip the patty over and sprinkle Cream of Wheat on the other side. Place the coated patty in the skillet, and quickly shape and coat another three or so, adding them to the skillet as you prepare them. Cook the croquettes until the underside is light brown and crisp, 5 to 8 minutes. Then turn them over and cook the other side, another 5 to 8 minutes. Transfer the cooked croquettes to the paper-towel-lined plate to drain. Shape, coat, and cook the remaining croquettes, and set them aside to drain.

4. To make the sauce, pile the cilantro, peanuts, chiles, sugar, and salt into the same food processor bowl, and process to form a chunky sauce. With the processor running, slowly drizzle 1 cup water through the feed tube, letting the water thin out the sauce. Continue processing to form a slightly smoother (albeit still gritty) texture (a technique very similar to making basil pesto).

5. Scrape the sauce into a small saucepan and heat it gently over medium-low heat, uncovered, until it is warm and slightly thick, 5 to 7 minutes. Remove the pan from heat and stir in the lime juice.

6. Place 2 croquettes on each individual serving plate and cover them with the spicy-tart peanut sauce. Enjoy the crispy crunch of the exterior as it gives way to the soft, surprisingly sweet interior.

Tip: Sprinkling the Cream of Wheat over the patty while it is in the palm of your hand (as opposed to rolling the patty in a plate of Cream of Wheat) has to do with the patty's delicate texture. Overhandling them causes the croquettes to fall apart. So, once you place a patty in your hand to shape it, it makes perfect sense to keep it there until it slides into the hot skillet. When the coating browns, it forms a protective shell, making it easier to flip them.

Potato-Pea Croquettes
WITH A TOMATO-JAGGERY SAUCE

Aloo Mutter ki tikki

bite-size savory morsels are called *tikkis*. These easy-to-make croquettes are a favorite in northwestern India. The layers of sweet, hot, tart, and nutty, created with simple ingredients, exemplify what a curry is all about. A few pointers on what kinds of bread *not* to use in this recipe: none with flavors, whole-wheat grain, or bran, and definitely no overly soft white bread. Pepperidge Farm and Arnold loaves are perfect. It's all right to use the heels of the bread.

MAKES ABOUT 24 CROQUETTES (SERVES 12)

For the croquettes:

- 1 pound russet or Yukon Gold potatoes, peeled, boiled until tender, and mashed
- ½ cup finely chopped fresh cilantro leaves and tender stems
- 1 small red onion, coarsely chopped
- 4 to 6 fresh green Thai, cayenne, or serrano chiles, to taste, stems removed
- 4 lengthwise slices fresh ginger (each 2½ inches long, 1 inch wide, and ⅛ inch thick)
- 2 teaspoons coarse kosher or sea salt
- ½ cup frozen green peas (no need to thaw)
- 4 to 6 slices firm white bread
- Canola oil for pan-frying

For the sauce:

- 1 tablespoon canola oil
- 1 teaspoon cumin seeds
- 1 can (14.5 ounces) diced tomatoes (do not drain)
- 2 tablespoons crumbled or chopped jaggery or firmly packed dark brown sugar
- 1 teaspoon cayenne (ground red pepper)
- 1 teaspoon coarse kosher or sea salt

1. Place the mashed potatoes in a large bowl.

2. Combine the cilantro, onion, chiles, and ginger in a food processor, and process until the ingredients are minced. Add the herb mixture to the potatoes, along with the salt and green peas.

3. Hold the bread slices under running water to drench them, and then squeeze out as much water from the slices as possible. You should have a rolled-up wad of moist but firm bread. Work the bread into the potato mixture by squeezing handfuls of potato and bread together to combine them, and then knead the mixture to create a slightly sticky dough; the softer the bread, the more slices you will need to get the right consistency. (This technique of creating an instant dough with moist bread slices helps to hold the croquettes together while pan-frying.)

4. Grease your palms with a little cooking spray or oil. Take a heaping tablespoon of the dough and shape it into a tight round ball. Press the ball between the palms of your hands to form a patty roughly 2 inches in diameter and ¼ inch thick. Lay it on a plate or tray. Repeat with the remaining dough. You should end up with about 24 of these light-green, pea-studded croquettes.

5. Line a large plate or a cookie sheet with several layers of paper towels. Heat 2 tablespoons canola oil in

a large nonstick skillet over medium heat. Arrange 8 croquettes, without crowding, in a single layer in the skillet and cook until the underside is golden brown and crisp, about 5 minutes. Turn them over and cook the other side until it is golden brown and crisp, about 5 minutes. Slide the croquettes onto the paper-towel-lined plate to drain. Repeat until all the croquettes are fried.

6. To make the sauce, heat the oil in a small sauce-pan over medium-high heat. Add the cumin seeds and let them sizzle until they turn reddish brown and fragrant, about 10 seconds. Stir in the remaining sauce ingredients and bring to a boil. Lower the heat to medium and simmer, uncovered, stirring occasionally, until the jaggery dissolves and the tomatoes soften, about 5 minutes. Let the sauce cool for about 5 minutes, and then transfer it to a blender and puree, scraping the inside of the jar as necessary, to make a smooth sauce.

7. Place 2 croquettes on each individual serving plate, and cover them with the deep red, sweet-spicy sauce.

Tip: If you don't wish to fry them all, you can keep the remaining uncooked croquettes, tightly wrapped in plastic wrap, in the refrigerator for up to 2 days. Any extra sauce will keep, too.

If you want to freeze them, pan-fry them first and then freeze them, securely wrapped in freezer paper or in resealable freezer-safe bags, for up to 1 month. To rewarm them, place the frozen croquettes on an ungreased cookie sheet in a preheated 300°F oven and bake until they are warm in the center, about 15 minutes.

Potato and Yellow Split Pea Croquettes
WITH AN ONION-MACE SAUCE

Aloo Shaami Kebab

My vegetarian friends felt cheated when I served the traditional Kashmiri *shaami kebab* (page 94) with ground lamb. So the next time they invited themselves over (when it comes to food, they don't feel shy), I made this vegetarian kebab with potatoes and yellow split peas. Though not the same as a *shaami kebab* (since this recipe includes neither raisins nor tomato), I love the fact that it includes the split peas, making it a nutritionally sane alternative to appease the vegetarians. I must say the nonvegetarians at the table were equally bowled over by these.

MAKES 20 CROQUETTES (SERVES 10)

For the croquettes:

1 cup yellow split peas (chana dal), picked over for stones
1 pound russet or Yukon Gold potatoes, peeled, cut into 1-inch cubes, and submerged in a bowl of cold water to prevent browning
1½ teaspoons coarse kosher or sea salt
½ cup firmly packed fresh cilantro leaves and tender stems
6 large cloves garlic
6 fresh green Thai, cayenne, or serrano chiles, stems removed
½ cup rice flour
Canola oil for pan-frying

For the sauce:

- 2 tablespoons canola oil
- 1 cup finely chopped red onion
- 1 teaspoon white granulated sugar
- ½ teaspoon coarse kosher or sea salt
- ½ teaspoon ground mace
- ½ teaspoon ground nutmeg
- ½ teaspoon cayenne (ground red pepper)
- 2 tablespoons finely chopped fresh cilantro leaves and tender stems

1. To make the croquettes, place the split peas in a medium-size bowl. Fill the bowl halfway with water and rinse the split peas by rubbing them between your fingertips. The water will become cloudy. Drain this water. Repeat three or four times, until the water remains relatively clear; drain. Now fill the bowl halfway with warm water and allow the split peas to soften by letting them sit at room temperature, covered, for at least 1 hour.

2. Drain the split peas and the potatoes, and place them in a medium-size saucepan. Add water to cover and bring to a boil over medium-high heat. Skim off and discard any foam that forms on the surface. Stir in 1 teaspoon of the salt. Reduce the heat to medium-low and simmer, covered, stirring occasionally, until the potatoes and split peas are tender, 15 to 20 minutes. Reserving 1 cup of the cooking water, drain them in a colander.

3. Place the cilantro, garlic, and chiles in a food processor, and pulse until the mixture is minced. Add the potatoes and split peas, and process until pureed. The mixture will appear sticky, thanks to the potatoes. Transfer it to a bowl, and fold in the rice flour along with the remaining ½ teaspoon salt.

4. Refrigerate the dough-like mixture, covered, to allow the starch to cool and to make the dough manageable enough to handle (although it will be slightly sticky), about 1 hour.

5. With greased hands, shape the dough into a 10-inch-long log. Cut it in half lengthwise, and then slice each half crosswise into 10 pieces, so you end up with twenty 1-inch-thick pieces. Shape one piece into a ball. Press the ball between the palms of your hands to form a patty roughly 2 to 3 inches in diameter and ½ inch thick. Lay it on a plate or tray. Repeat with the remaining pieces, greasing your hands as often as needed.

6. Line a large plate or a cookie sheet with several layers of paper towels. Heat 2 tablespoons canola oil in a large nonstick skillet, or in a well-seasoned cast-iron skillet, over medium heat. Arrange 6 patties, without crowding, in a single layer in the skillet and cook until the underside is golden brown and crisp, about 5 minutes. Turn them over and cook on the other side until golden brown and crisp, about 5 minutes. Slide them onto the paper-towel-lined plate to drain. Repeat with the remaining patties, adding more oil as needed.

7. To make the sauce, heat the oil in a small saucepan over medium heat. Add the onion and stir-fry until it is soft and a light caramel-brown with a light purple hue, 8 to 10 minutes.

8. Sprinkle the sugar, salt, mace, nutmeg, and cayenne over the onion, and stir once or twice. Pour in the reserved cup of potato cooking water, and scrape the bottom of the pan to release any browned bits of onion.

9. Pour this mixture into a blender jar and puree, scraping the inside of the jar as needed, to form a thick, muddy brown, red-tinted sauce. Pour the sauce into a small bowl and stir in the cilantro.

10. Place 2 croquettes on each plate, cover them with the slightly bitter, sweet-spicy sauce, and serve.

Thickpea Flour Troquettes
WITH A
BLACKENED CHILE-TOMATO SAUCE

Besan Thawal Vadi

These spicy croquettes are a perfect choice for friends who are wheat-intolerant. The flours used in this recipe are not only healthful and gluten-free, they are also easily available. The croquettes are a cinch to make, but if you want to take an even easier route, any store-bought dipping sauce—even a robust salsa—will make a great condiment.

These croquettes do taste best when they are freshly fried. If you don't plan to eat them all at once, store the uncooked patties in the refrigerator, covered, for about 4 days, or in the freezer for up to a month. **MAKES 20 CROQUETTES**

For the croquettes:

- 1 cup chickpea flour
- ½ cup rice flour
- 1 cup finely chopped red onion
- ¼ cup finely chopped fresh cilantro leaves and tender stems
- 1½ teaspoons coarse kosher or sea salt
- ½ teaspoon bishop's weed; or 1 teaspoon dried thyme leaves mixed with ½ teaspoon freshly ground black pepper
- ¼ teaspoon ground asafetida
- 8 fresh green Thai, cayenne, or serrano chiles, stems removed, finely chopped (do not remove the seeds)
- Canola oil for deep-frying

For the sauce:

- 1 tablespoon canola oil
- 1 teaspoon black or yellow mustard seeds
- 1 tablespoon skinned split black lentils (cream-colored in this form, urad dal), picked over for stones
- 4 or 5 dried red Thai or cayenne chiles, to taste, stems removed
- 8 ounces tomatoes, cored and finely chopped
- 2 tablespoons finely chopped fresh cilantro leaves and tender stems
- 1 teaspoon coarse kosher or sea salt

1. Combine the two flours, onion, cilantro, salt, bishop's weed, asafetida, and chiles in a medium-size bowl. Pour in 2 tablespoons warm water, mixing the colorful blend of flours, onion, spices, and herbs until it comes together in a ball. Add more warm water as needed, a tablespoon at a time, to turn the ball into a soft, slightly bumpy dough. If the dough feels too sticky, dust it with a little extra rice flour.

2. Roll and stretch the dough to form a log roughly 20 inches long. Cut the log crosswise into 20 pieces, and shape each piece into a tight ball. Press a ball between the palms of your hands to form a patty roughly 1½ inches in diameter and ½ inch thick. Lay it on a plate or tray. Repeat with the remaining balls.

3. Pour oil to a depth of 2 to 3 inches into a wok, Dutch oven, or medium-size saucepan. Heat the oil over medium heat until a candy or deep-fry thermometer inserted into the oil (without touching the pan's bottom) registers 350°F. (An alternative way to see if the oil is at the right temperature for deep-frying is to gently flick a drop of water over it. If the pearl-like drop skitters across the surface, the oil is ready.)

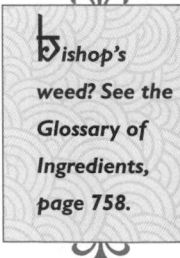

Bishop's weed? See the Glossary of Ingredients, page 758.

4. Line a large plate or a cookie sheet with several layers of paper towels. Once the oil is ready, gently slide 6 patties into the pan (do not crowd the pan). Fry, turning them occasionally, until they are caramel-brown and crisp all over, about 5 minutes. Remove the croquettes with a slotted spoon and place them on the paper-towel-lined plate to drain. Repeat until all the patties are fried. You may need to adjust the heat to maintain the oil's temperature at 350°F.

5. To make the sauce, heat the oil in a small saucepan over medium-high heat. Add the mustard seeds, cover the pan, and wait until all the seeds have stopped popping (not unlike popcorn), about 30 seconds. Then add the lentils and stir-fry until they turn golden brown, 15 to 20 seconds. Stir in the chiles and stir-fry until they blacken and smell pungent, 15 to 20 seconds.

6. Add the tomatoes, cilantro, and salt. Reduce the heat to medium-low and simmer, covered, stirring occasionally, until the tomatoes turn soft but are still chunky-looking, about 5 minutes.

7. Place 2 croquettes on each individual serving plate and top each one with a tablespoon of the sauce.

Fresh curry leaves? Asafetida? See the Glossary of Ingredients, page 758.

Lentil Dumplings
IN A SPICY TAMARIND-LENTIL BROTH

Rasa Vadai

If you were to ask me to identify the one recipe that is closest to my heart, I would pick this one. Yes, it looks complicated, but I assure you, all you have to do is follow my instructions, and the result will bring you much comfort, as it does me, time and again. **MAKES ABOUT 30 DUMPLINGS (SERVES 10)**

For the dumplings:

1 cup skinned split black lentils (cream-colored in this form, urad dal), picked over for stones
1½ teaspoons coarse kosher or sea salt
Canola oil for deep-frying

For the broth:

¼ cup oily or unoily skinned split yellow pigeon peas (toovar dal), picked over for stones
½ teaspoon plus 1 tablespoon canola oil
1 tablespoon uncooked long-grain white rice
2 tablespoons yellow split peas (chana dal), picked over for stones
1 teaspoon coriander seeds
½ teaspoon cumin seeds
½ teaspoon fenugreek seeds
½ teaspoon black peppercorns
2 or 3 dried red Thai or cayenne chiles, to taste, stems removed
1 teaspoon tamarind paste or concentrate
2 teaspoons coarse kosher or sea salt
½ teaspoon ground turmeric
½ teaspoon ground asafetida
1 medium-size tomato, cored, cut into 1-inch cubes
15 to 20 medium-size to large fresh curry leaves
1 teaspoon black or yellow mustard seeds
2 tablespoons finely chopped fresh cilantro leaves and tender stems

1. Place the lentils in a medium-size bowl. Fill the bowl halfway with water and rinse them by rubbing them between your fingertips. The water will become cloudy. Drain this water. Repeat three or four times, until the water remains relatively clear;

drain. Now fill the bowl halfway with warm water and allow the lentils to soften by letting them sit at room temperature, covered, for at least 30 minutes or up to 4 hours.

2. Drain the lentils. Pour ½ cup water into a blender, add the lentils, and puree, scraping the inside of the jar occasionally, until the mixture is smooth and pastelike. Transfer the thick batter to the same medium-size bowl. Pour ¼ cup water into the blender jar and run the blender to wash out any remnants of batter; add this to the batter in the bowl. Stir in the salt. (If you use the entire ¾ cup water to puree the soaked lentils, the resulting batter may be slightly watery and gritty.) Using a spatula, vigorously beat the batter in a circular motion for 2 to 3 minutes (this incorporates air, ensuring a fluffy dumpling).

3. Pour oil to a depth of 2 to 3 inches into a wok, Dutch oven, or medium-size saucepan. Heat the oil over medium heat until a candy or deep-fry thermometer inserted into the oil (without touching the pan's bottom) registers 350°F. (An alternative way to see if the oil is at the right temperature for deep-frying is to gently flick a drop of water over it. If the pearl-like drop skitters across the surface, the oil is ready.)

4. Line a large plate or a cookie sheet with several layers of paper towels. Once the oil is ready, gently slide in teaspoonfuls of the batter without crowding them (about 10 at a time). Fry, turning the dumplings occasionally, until they are golden brown and crisp all over, about 5 minutes. Remove the dumplings with a slotted spoon and place them on the paper-towel-lined plate to drain. Repeat until all the dumplings are cooked. You may need to adjust the heat to maintain the oil's temperature at 350°F.

5. To make the broth, place the pigeon peas in a small saucepan. Fill the pan halfway with water and rinse the peas by rubbing them between your fingertips. The water will become cloudy. Drain this water. Repeat three or four times, until the water remains relatively clear; drain. Now add 2 cups water to the pan and bring it to a boil, uncovered, over medium-high heat. Skim off and discard any foam that forms on the surface. Reduce the heat to medium-low and simmer, covered, stirring occasionally, until the pigeon peas are tender, about 20 minutes.

6. While the pigeon peas are cooking, heat a small skillet over medium-high heat. Add the ½ teaspoon oil, and then add the rice, yellow split peas, coriander seeds, cumin seeds, fenugreek seeds, peppercorns, and chiles. Stir-fry until the rice appears shriveled and light brown around the edges, the split peas turn light brown, the spices are fragrant, and chiles blacken slightly, 2 to 3 minutes. Transfer the roasted blend to a plate to cool. Once it is cool to the touch, grind the mixture in a spice grinder until the texture resembles that of finely ground black pepper.

7. Combine the tamarind paste with 4 cups water in a medium-size saucepan, whisking until the tamarind dissolves, turning the tart liquid a dark chocolate color. Stir in the spice blend, salt, turmeric, asafetida, tomato, and curry leaves, and bring to a boil over medium-high heat. Lower the heat to medium and continue simmering, uncovered, to cook the tomatoes, about 15 minutes.

8. Transfer the cooked pigeon peas and the residual cooking water to a blender and puree, scraping the inside of the jar as needed, until smooth. Pour this thin, creamy-yellow broth into a bowl. (If you have an immersion blender, you can puree the peas and water right in the saucepan.)

9. Heat the same small skillet over medium-high heat, and add the remaining 1 tablespoon oil. Add the mustard seeds, cover the skillet, and wait until all the seeds have stopped popping (not unlike popcorn), about 30 seconds. Scrape the nutty-smelling mixture into the simmering tamarind broth, and add the pureed pigeon peas. Stir in the cilantro.

10. Place 3 dumplings in each individual serving bowl and ladle the hot tamarind broth over them, filling the bowls to the brim. Serve immediately.

Tips:

❖ You can easily substitute the more commonly available yellow split peas for the pigeon peas. The cooking time will be the same.

❖ If you have broth left over, warm it in a microwave and ladle it over bowls of steamed white rice.

❖ Cooks in southern India normally shape these dumplings in the form of a doughnut before frying them. It sure looks pretty, but I don't bother with the hassle and the time it takes to shape each savory fritter. Trust me, they will taste the same no matter what their form. Purists will tsk-tsk, however, and if you are one of them, or have invited one of them to dinner, here's how you can create those doughnut-shaped *vadais:* Lightly spray a piece of wax paper with vegetable cooking spray. Plop a tablespoon of the batter onto the wax paper. Grease your hand with cooking spray, and spread the batter out to form a ½-inch-thick patty. Poke a finger through its center, creating the familiar doughnut shape. Gently slide the patty off the paper directly into the hot oil, and fry until it is golden brown and crispy.

Lentil Dumplings
IN A VEGETABLE STEW

Vadaa Sambhar

ade popular in restaurants in southern India, the combination of bold flavors, fried dumplings, and nutritious legumes in this appetizer curry is a must every time I visit. Even though the dumplings are the same as those in Lentil Dumplings in a Spicy Tamarind-Lentil Broth (page 75), the flavors in the curry are far apart, reminding you of the marvels of extracting disparate tastes from the same items.

MAKES ABOUT 30 DUMPLINGS (SERVES 10)

For the dumplings:

1 recipe Lentil Dumplings (see Step 1)

For the stew:

¼ cup oily or unoily skinned split yellow pigeon peas (toovar dal), picked over for stones

1 tablespoon tamarind paste or concentrate

1 tablespoon sambhar masala (page 33)

1½ teaspoons coarse kosher or sea salt

½ teaspoon ground asafetida

1 medium-size red or green bell pepper, stemmed, seeded, and cut into 1-inch pieces

1 small red onion, cut into 1-inch chunks

15 to 20 medium-size to large fresh curry leaves

1 tablespoon unrefined sesame oil or canola oil

1 teaspoon black or yellow mustard seeds

2 tablespoons finely chopped fresh cilantro leaves and tender stems

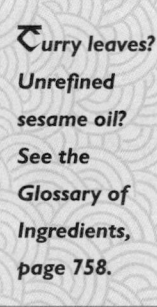

Curry leaves? Unrefined sesame oil? See the Glossary of Ingredients, page 758.

1. Prepare and cook the dumplings as described on page 75, through Step 4.

2. Place the pigeon peas in a small saucepan. Fill the pan halfway with water and rinse the peas by rubbing them between your fingertips. The water will become cloudy. Drain this water. Repeat three or four times, until the water remains relatively clear; drain. Now add 2 cups water to the peas and bring it to a boil, uncovered, over medium-high heat. Skim off and discard any foam that forms on the surface. Reduce the heat to medium-low and simmer, covered, stirring occasionally, until the peas are tender, about 20 minutes.

3. While the peas are cooking, whisk the tamarind paste with 2 cups water in a medium-size saucepan. Sprinkle in the *sambhar masala*, salt, and asafetida, and add the bell pepper, onion, and curry leaves. Stir the murky brown curry and bring it to a boil over medium heat. Continue boiling, uncovered, stirring occasionally, until the bell pepper and onion are fork-tender, about 15 minutes.

4. Transfer the cooked pigeon peas and the residual cooking water to a blender, and puree, scraping the inside of the jar as needed, until smooth. Pour this thin, creamy-yellow broth into a bowl. (If you have an immersion blender, you can puree the peas and water right in the saucepan.)

5. Heat a small skillet over medium-high heat, and add the oil. Add the mustard seeds, cover the skillet, and wait until all the seeds have stopped popping (not unlike popcorn), about 30 seconds. Scrape the nutty-smelling mixture into the simmering stew, along with the pureed pigeon peas. Stir in the cilantro.

6. Place 3 to 5 dumplings in each individual serving bowl and ladle the hot-tart stew over them, filling the bowls to the brim. Serve immediately.

Tip: With the exception of leafy greens, any vegetable is fair game for this stew—try sweet potatoes, eggplant, carrots, or squash. Each vegetable imparts its own flavor and texture, and you will need to adjust the cooking time accordingly. Just make sure to cut them into bite-size pieces.

Lentil Dumplings
IN A BUTTERMILK-COCONUT SAUCE

Vadai Morekozhambu

South Indians reserve this delicacy for special occasions, and I confess that when I make it, it becomes my sole mission to eat every one of the dumplings. But sharing is a good thing, as we all learn in kindergarten. Some of the other appetizer curries start with these same dumplings, but because they absorb the sauce they're in, they taste different in each case. Here it's a creamy buttermilk sauce that's loaded with flavor: coconut, chiles, curry leaves, coriander, fenugreek . . . Who could resist them?

MAKES ABOUT 30 DUMPLINGS (SERVES 10)

For the dumplings:
1 recipe Lentil Dumplings (see Step 1)

For the sauce:
2 cups buttermilk
½ cup heavy (whipping) cream
½ teaspoon plus 1 tablespoon canola oil
1 tablespoon coriander seeds
1 teaspoon fenugreek seeds

½ cup shredded fresh coconut; or ¼ cup shredded dried
   unsweetened coconut, reconstituted (see Note)
3 or 4 fresh green Thai, cayenne, or serrano chiles,
   to taste, stems removed
1 tablespoon rice flour
1 teaspoon coarse kosher or sea salt
1 teaspoon black or yellow mustard seeds
2 dried red Thai or cayenne chiles, stems removed
12 to 15 medium-size to large fresh curry leaves
2 tablespoons finely chopped fresh cilantro leaves
   and tender stems

1. Prepare and cook the dumplings as described on page 75, through Step 4.

2. To make the sauce, whisk the buttermilk and cream together in a medium-size bowl.

3. Heat the ½ teaspoon oil in a small skillet over medium-high heat. Sprinkle in the coriander and fenugreek seeds, and stir-fry to roast the spices until they crackle, turn reddish brown, and have a nutty-citrus aroma, about 1 minute.

4. Scrape the roasted seeds into a blender jar and add the coconut, ¼ cup water, the green chiles, rice flour, and salt. Puree, scraping the inside of the jar as needed, until the mixture forms a green-speckled, slightly gritty paste. Transfer this paste to the creamy buttermilk, stirring to combine the ingredients.

5. Heat the remaining 1 tablespoon oil in a medium-size saucepan over medium-high heat. Add the mustard seeds, cover, and wait until all the seeds have stopped popping (not unlike popcorn), about 30 seconds. Immediately pour the spiked buttermilk into the saucepan, and add the red chiles, curry leaves, and cilantro. Heat to a boil. Once it boils, the sauce will thicken slightly—but it will never curdle, thanks to the heavy cream and flour. Remove the pan from the heat.

6. Flatten each cooled fried dumpling by pressing it between the palms of your hands, or between paper towels, to form a disk that is about ½ inch thick. Lay them in a single layer on a serving platter (preferably one with a lip to contain the sauce). Spoon about 2 tablespoons of the sauce over each *vadai,* and serve.

Note: To reconstitute coconut, cover with ¼ cup boiling water, set aside for about 15 minutes, and then drain.

Tip: The sauce will continue to thicken as it stands, especially when kept refrigerated; you can prepare it up to 2 days ahead. Thin it with water to bring it back to a hollandaise like consistency. I usually sauce the *vadais* just before serving them because saucing them all ahead of time allows the dumplings to absorb the sauce, making for a drier curry. Warm the sauce-topped *vadais* in a microwave oven for barely a minute to help thin the sauce to the right succulent consistency.

Boiled Cabbage-Filled Dumplings
IN A LIGHT VEGETABLE BROTH

Momos

Nepalese and Tibetans savor *momos* with the same fervor that the northern Chinese do with their dumplings. Most *momos* swell with spiced ground meat and float in meaty broths. I love this vegetarian version, and I serve it more as a substantial soup course. I do admit that the night I made this, it was my only offering for dinner and no one complained. I pan-fried the leftover dumplings (see Tips) the next day for a midmorning snack.

MAKES 24 DUMPLINGS (SERVES 8)

For the dumpling wrappers:

2 cups unbleached all-purpose flour

1 teaspoon coarse kosher or sea salt

About ¾ cup boiling water

For the filling:

3 cups shredded green cabbage

2 teaspoons coarse kosher or sea salt

½ cup finely chopped fresh cilantro leaves and tender stems

2 teaspoons shredded fresh ginger

½ teaspoon ground turmeric

4 fresh green Thai, cayenne, or serrano chiles, stems removed, finely chopped (do not remove the seeds)

4 scallions (green tops and white bulbs), thinly sliced

For the broth:

2 tablespoons canola oil

1 small red onion, finely chopped

1 large tomato, cored and cut into ½-inch cubes

1 teaspoon English-Style Madras Curry Powder (page 24)

4 fresh green Thai, cayenne, or serrano chiles, stems removed, thinly sliced crosswise (do not remove the seeds)

4 cups vegetable stock or water

¼ cup finely chopped fresh cilantro leaves and tender stems

1. To make the wrapper dough, combine the flour and salt in a medium-size bowl. Add the boiling water, drizzling in a few tablespoons at a time and stirring with a spoon (because the water is hot, it will be difficult to use your fingers to mix the dough). Add just enough water to bring the flour together to form a ball. It should feel neither sticky nor dry. Remove any dough clinging to the spoon and add it to the dough ball. Knead the dough right in the bowl for 2 to 3 minutes, to form a smooth ball. Shape it into a log roughly 12 inches long. Cut the log into ½-inch-wide pieces, cover them with plastic wrap, and set aside.

2. To make the filling, stir the cabbage and salt together in a medium-size bowl. Set the bowl aside so the salt can leach the liquid from the cabbage, at least 1 hour but no longer than 2 hours.

3. Squeeze handfuls of the cabbage to get rid of the excess water, and place the drained cabbage in a medium-size bowl. Add the cilantro, ginger, turmeric, chiles, and scallions, and mix thoroughly.

4. To make the dumplings (see box, facing page), shape each piece of dough into a 1-inch ball. Flatten it out to form a patty, and then roll it out to form a round that is 2 to 3 inches in diameter. Dust the patty with flour as needed while rolling it out. Repeat with the remaining pieces, stacking the wrappers after liberally dusting each one with flour to prevent them from sticking together.

5. Place a teaspoonful of the filling in the center of each wrapper, and then fold the edge over to make a half-moon shape. Press the edges tightly together with your thumb and forefinger, sealing the dumpling completely. As they are filled and sealed, lay the dumplings on a floured plate. When they are all formed, cover them with plastic wrap.

6. As soon as the dumplings are formed, make the broth: Heat the oil in a medium-size saucepan over

medium-high heat. Add the onion and stir-fry briefly to reduce the raw taste, 1 to 2 minutes. Then add the tomato cubes, curry powder, and chiles, and cook, uncovered, stirring occasionally, until the tomatoes soften slightly, 2 to 4 minutes.

7. Pour in the stock and bring it to a boil. Reduce the heat to low and keep the broth warm, covered, while you boil the dumplings.

8. Fill another medium-size saucepan halfway with water and bring it to a vigorous boil over medium-high heat. Gently slide 6 to 8 dumplings into the water, stirring gently once or twice to prevent them from sticking to each other. They will sink to the bottom. Once the water comes to a boil again, the dough will start to absorb some of the water and appear puffed up, and the dumplings will float to the surface. All this takes 5 to 7 minutes. As they rise to the surface, scoop the dumplings out with a strainer and transfer them to a plate.

9. Place 3 or 4 dumplings in each soup bowl, ladle a scoop or two of the broth over them, sprinkle with some cilantro, and serve.

Tips:

❖ I tried steaming the dumplings in a steamer basket, but found that the wrapper's texture became a bit tough.

❖ For a meat-filled option, use ground pork, beef, lamb, chicken, or turkey instead of the cabbage. There is no need to cook the meat before filling the wrappers, as boiling them will cook it just right. You can also vary the stock by using chicken or beef broth.

❖ All Asian grocery stores and supermarkets have packages of potsticker wrappers either in the refrigerator section or in the freezer. Use them as a perfectly acceptable alternative.

making perfect dumplings

I was fortunate enough to have the opportunity to spend some time with Florence Lin, the grande dame of Chinese cooking, who taught the classic foods of her homeland and authored numerous authoritative cookbooks on the subject. At a series of events for the Asian Culinary Arts Institutes, Florence, along with two master chefs from northern China, shared some great techniques while working with flour to shape, fill, steam, boil, and pan-fry numerous varieties of dumplings. The skills I learned there helped me years later when I created this recipe.

To shape the dumpling wrappers into a perfect round, thin around the edges and thicker in the center to comfortably house the filling, use the type of thin rolling pin that looks like a dowel. First, roll the patty out to form a 2-inch round. Then, to create the perfect wrapper, as she says in her **Complete Book of Chinese Noodles, Dumplings, and Breads,** "roll the pin with the palm of one hand while you feed and turn the wrapper with the other hand's fingers. Roll from the edges to the center so that the edges are thinner than the center." It will take a few tries, and slow you down, to master this technique, but with practice your speed will soon pick up and your wrappers will be perfect.

❖ If you plan to freeze your dumplings for later use, fill and seal them. Then arrange them in a single layer on a sheet of lightly floured wax paper on a tray. Freeze the tray for 2 to 3 hours. Once they are solidly frozen, lift the dumplings one by one and place them in a freezer-safe self-seal bag; they will keep in the freezer for up to 2 months. Boil them without thawing (otherwise the filling, once thawed, will moisten the wrapper, creating unwanted rips).

❖ For a snack, pan-fry the dumplings: Lightly oil a nonstick skillet, or a well-seasoned cast-iron skillet, and heat it over medium heat. Add the dumplings in a single layer, and cook until they are browned on the underside, 3 to 5 minutes. Flip them over and repeat on the other side. (For a moister result, once both sides are browned, pour 2 to 3 tablespoons water into the skillet and braise the dumplings, covered, until all the water has been absorbed, 2 to 3 minutes—this is the technique used in making potstickers.)

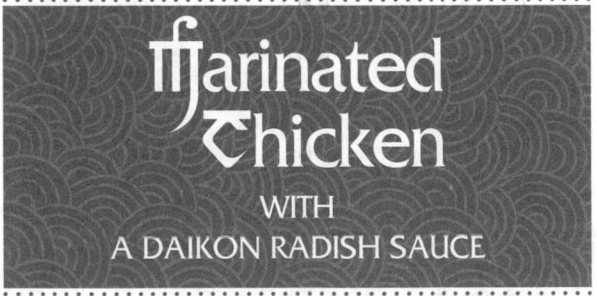

Marinated Chicken
WITH A DAIKON RADISH SAUCE

haree murghi kebab

Creamy, complex, and outright delicious, these bite-size morsels *(kebabs)* of chicken showcase the cuisine of Hyderabad, in south-central India. Double the recipe and make it your dinner, served with Grilled Flatbread Studded with Chile-Spiked Onions (page 736) and lightly salted slivers of raw red onion, smothered in chiles. **SERVES 8**

For the kebabs:

Bamboo or metal skewers
¼ cup tightly packed fresh mint leaves
¼ cup tightly packed fresh cilantro leaves and tender stems
1 tablespoon fresh lime or lemon juice
3 or 4 fresh green Thai, cayenne, or serrano chiles, to taste, stems removed
2 tablespoons heavy (whipping) cream
1 teaspoon coarse kosher or sea salt
1 pound boneless, skinless chicken breasts, cut lengthwise into 1-inch-wide strips

For the sauce:

1 medium-size tomato, cored and coarsely chopped
1 cup thinly sliced peeled daikon radish
2 tablespoons packed fresh cilantro leaves and tender stems
2 large cloves garlic
2 fresh green Thai, cayenne, or serrano chiles, stems removed
1 tablespoon Ghee (page 21) or unsalted butter
1 teaspoon cumin seeds
¼ cup heavy (whipping) cream
½ teaspoon coarse kosher or sea salt

Vegetable cooking spray

1. If you are using bamboo skewers, place them in a flat dish filled with water and let them soak for an hour (see Tip, page 84).

2. While the skewers are soaking, prepare the mari-

nade: Combine the mint, cilantro, lime juice, and chiles in a food processor, and pulse until minced. Transfer this herb mix to a medium-size bowl, and stir in the cream and salt.

3. Add the chicken strips to the bowl and stir to coat them completely with the tart, light green marinade. Refrigerate, covered, for at least 30 minutes or up to 6 hours.

4. When you are ready to cook the kebabs, make the sauce: Put the tomato, radish, cilantro, garlic, and chiles into a blender jar and puree, scraping the inside of the jar as needed, to make a smooth (albeit slightly gritty) mixture.

5. Heat the ghee in a small saucepan over medium-high heat. Add the cumin seeds and let them sizzle until they turn reddish brown and smell nutty, 5 to 10 seconds. Carefully pour the pureed sauce into the pan (it will splash in the hot oil). Once the sauce starts to boil, stir in the cream and salt and warm it for a minute. Then remove the pan from the heat.

6. Preheat a gas (or charcoal) grill, or the broiler, to high.

7. While the grill is heating, thread the chicken strips (covered with the thick marinade), accordion-style, onto the skewers.

8. *If you are grilling*, lightly spray the grill rack with vegetable cooking spray. Grill the chicken, covered, turning the skewers occasionally, until the pieces are light brown, 6 to 8 minutes. (To test for doneness, slice into a piece with a paring knife; the meat should no longer be pink and the juices should run clear.) *If you are broiling*, position a rack so the top of the chicken will be 2 to 3 inches from the heat. Lightly spray the rack of a broiler pan with cooking spray, place the skewers on the rack, and broil, turning them occasionally, until the chicken pieces are light brown, the meat is no longer pink inside, and the juices run clear, 6 to 8 minutes.

9. Slide the chicken off the skewers onto a serving plate. Spoon the sauce over the chicken and serve immediately. (If the sauce has cooled while the chicken was grilling, rewarm it over low heat before using it.)

Tip: This recipe makes more sauce than you will need for the kebabs. Leftover sauce can be refrigerated for up to a week or frozen for up to a month. Pour the rewarmed sauce over cooked red rice (page 706) or serve it as a dip for bread.

Grilled Chicken
WITH
MUSTARD GREENS SAUCE

Sarson Murghi Kebab

this appetizer curry features Punjab's two passions: those bite-size morsels of chicken called *kebabs*, and pungent, tasty, nutritionally blessed mustard greens (they are a rich source of iron). To make it your dinner, double the amount of chicken; there will be plenty of sauce.

SERVES 8

Bamboo or metal skewers

8 ounces fresh mustard greens, coarsely chopped
   (see Tip, page 606)

3 tablespoons canola oil

2 tablespoons Ginger Paste (page 15)

I tablespoon Garlic Paste (page 15)

I teaspoon dill seeds, ground

I teaspoon coarse kosher or sea salt

I teaspoon Punjabi garam masala (page 25)

½ teaspoon cayenne (ground red pepper)

I pound boneless, skinless chicken breasts, cut
   lengthwise into 1-inch-wide strips

½ cup finely chopped red onion

I medium-size tomato, cored and coarsely chopped

Vegetable cooking spray

1. If you are using bamboo skewers, place them in a flat dish filled with water and let them soak for an hour (see Tips).

2. While the skewers are soaking, prepare the marinade: Place the mustard greens, in batches so as not to overcrowd them, in a food processor and process until minced. Transfer the pungent minced greens to a medium-size bowl, and stir in 1 tablespoon of the oil. Add the Ginger Paste, Garlic Paste, ground dill seeds, salt, garam masala, and cayenne. Stir well.

3. Add the chicken strips and stir to coat them completely with the dark green marinade. Refrigerate, covered, for at least 30 minutes or up to 6 hours.

4. Preheat a gas (or charcoal) grill, or the broiler, to high.

5. While the grill is heating, thread the chicken strips, accordion-style, onto the skewers, saving the residual marinade.

6. Make the sauce by heating the remaining 2 table-spoons oil in a small saucepan over medium-high heat. Add the onion and stir-fry until it is lightly browned, 2 to 3 minutes. Add the reserved marinade and simmer over medium-low heat, uncovered, stirring occasionally, for 8 to 10 minutes (this cooks the raw chicken juices in the marinade). Add ½ cup water and the tomato, and bring the mixture to a boil. Remove the pan from the heat and pour the contents into a blender jar. Puree, scraping the inside of the jar as needed, until the mixture forms a smooth, reddish-green sauce.

7. *If you are grilling*, lightly spray the grill rack with vegetable cooking spray. Grill the chicken, covered, turning the skewers occasionally, until the pieces are light brown, 6 to 8 minutes. (To test for doneness, slice into a piece with a paring knife; the meat should no longer be pink and the juices should run clear.) *If you are broiling*, position a rack so the top of the chicken will be 2 to 3 inches from the heat. Lightly spray the rack of a broiler pan with cooking spray, place the skewers on the rack, and broil, turning them occasionally, until the chicken pieces are light brown, the meat is no longer pink inside, and the juices run clear, 6 to 8 minutes.

8. Slide the chicken off the skewers onto a serving plate. Spoon the sauce over the kebabs before serving. If you have some sauce left over, save it for future use (see Tips).

Tips:

❖ Soaking bamboo skewers in water will prevent them from catching on fire over the grill or under the broiler.

❖ Chances are you will have some extra sauce left over. Leftover sauce can be refrigerated for up to a week or frozen for up to a month. Savor it with flaky griddle-cooked *paranthas* (page 731) or spoon it over a bowl of steamed white rice.

Skewered Chicken
WITH A CREAMY FENUGREEK SAUCE

Malai Methi Kebab

A curry this easy is a good choice for an outdoor gathering. It appeals to the stand-around-the-grill-and-munch crowd, and as the creamy sauce that clings to each morsel drips to the ground, the host won't think twice about the mess because Fido will be busy mopping it up with his eager tongue. Serve it over boiled red rice (page 706) for an unusual combination. Turkey breasts make an excellent alternative, should you wish to cluck a different tune. **SERVES 8**

Bamboo or metal skewers
¼ cup Thick Yogurt (page 22)
2 tablespoons finely chopped fresh cilantro
    leaves and tender stems
1 tablespoon coriander seeds, ground
1 tablespoon Ginger Paste (page 15)
1 teaspoon Garlic Paste (page 15)
1 teaspoon cumin seeds, ground
½ teaspoon punjabi garam masala (page 25)
1 teaspoon coarse kosher or sea salt
1 pound boneless, skinless chicken breasts,
    cut lengthwise into 1-inch-wide strips
1 tablespoon Ghee (page 21) or melted butter
½ cup tomato sauce, homemade (page 18) or
    canned
2 tablespoons dried fenugreek leaves,
    soaked in a bowl of water and skimmed
    off before use (see box, page 473)

½ teaspoon cayenne (ground red pepper)
¼ cup heavy (whipping) cream or half-and-half
Vegetable cooking spray

1. If you are using bamboo skewers, place them in a flat dish filled with water and let them soak for an hour. (See Tips on facing page.)

2. While the skewers are soaking, whisk the yogurt, cilantro, coriander, Ginger Paste, Garlic Paste, cumin, garam masala, and salt together in a medium-size bowl. Add the chicken strips, stirring to coat them well with the creamy marinade. Refrigerate, covered, for at least 30 minutes or up to 6 hours.

3. Preheat a gas (or charcoal) grill, or the broiler, to high.

4. While the grill is heating, thread the chicken strips, accordion-style, onto the skewers, making sure you do not scrape any marinade off the meat. There should be no leftover marinade.

5. Make the sauce by heating the ghee in a small saucepan over medium heat. Pour in the tomato sauce, fenugreek leaves, and cayenne. Simmer the sauce, covered, stirring occasionally, to allow the leaves to perfume the sauce, 5 to 8 minutes. Some of the ghee will start to separate from the sauce.

6. Gently stir in the cream.

7. *If you are grilling,* lightly spray the grill rack with vegetable cooking spray. Grill the chicken, covered, turning the skewers occasionally, until the pieces are light brown, 6 to 8 minutes. (To test for doneness, slice into a piece with a paring knife; the meat should no longer be pink and the juices should run clear.) *If you are broiling,* position a rack so the top of the chicken

dried fenugreek leaves? See the Glossary of Ingredients, page 758.

will be 2 to 3 inches from the heat. Lightly spray the rack of a broiler pan with cooking spray, place the skewers on the rack, and broil, turning them occasionally, until the chicken pieces are light brown, the meat is no longer pink inside, and the juices run clear, 6 to 8 minutes.

8. Slide the chicken off the skewers onto a serving plate. Spoon the sauce over the kebabs, and serve.

Grilled Chicken
WITH A
CASHEW-TOMATO SAUCE

kaaju murghi kebab

ven though I highly recommend this as a starter to a curry dinner, don't feel boxed in with the suggestion. By all means make this a main-course offering—with the realization that the recipe will then serve 4 and not 8.

Whenever I use bamboo skewers, I get the ones that are 6 inches long, which hold a single strip of chicken. For an appetizer curry, I normally portion 2 skewers per person. **SERVES 8**

Bamboo or metal skewers
½ cup Thick Yogurt (page 22)
2 tablespoons finely chopped fresh cilantro leaves
*   and tender stems*
2 teaspoons Ginger Paste (page 15)
1 teaspoon Garlic Paste (page 15)
1 teaspoon balti masala (page 31)
1½ teaspoons coarse kosher or sea salt
1 pound boneless, skinless chicken breasts,
*   cut lengthwise into 1-inch-wide strips*
1 tablespoon Ghee (page 21) or canola oil

¼ cup raw cashew nuts, ground
½ cup canned tomato sauce
½ teaspoon cayenne (ground red pepper)
Vegetable cooking spray
¼ cup heavy (whipping) cream or half-and-half

1. If you are using bamboo skewers, place them in a flat dish filled with water and let them soak for an hour. (See Tips on page 84.)

2. While the skewers are soaking, combine the yogurt, 1 tablespoon of the cilantro, the Ginger Paste, Garlic Paste, *balti masala,* and 1 teaspoon of the salt in a medium-size bowl, and stir together. Add the chicken strips, and stir to coat them well. Refrigerate, covered, for at least 30 minutes or up to 6 hours.

3. Preheat a gas (or charcoal) grill, or the broiler, to high.

4. While the grill is heating, thread the chicken strips, accordion-style, onto the skewers, making sure you do not scrape any marinade off the meat. There should be no leftover marinade.

5. Make the sauce by heating the ghee in a small saucepan over medium heat. Sprinkle in the ground cashews and cook, stirring constantly to make sure the nuts brown but do not burn, for about 1 minute. Pour in the tomato sauce, and sprinkle in the cayenne and the remaining ½ teaspoon salt. Reduce the heat to medium-low and simmer the sauce, covered, stirring occasionally, until some of the ghee starts to separate around the edges, 6 to 8 minutes.

6. While the sauce is simmering, cook the chicken: *If you are grilling,* lightly spray the grill rack with vegetable cooking spray. Grill the chicken, covered, turning the skewers occasionally, until the pieces are light brown, 6 to 8 minutes. (To test for doneness, slice into a piece with a paring knife; the meat should no longer be pink and the juices should run clear.) *If you are broiling,* position a rack so the top of the chicken will be 2 to 3 inches from the heat. Lightly spray the rack of a broiler pan with cooking spray, place the skewers on the rack, and broil, turning them occasionally, until the chicken pieces are light brown, the meat is no longer pink inside, and the juices run clear, 6 to 8 minutes.

7. Stir the cream into the sauce and continue simmering, covered, stirring occasionally, to warm it, about 2 minutes. Stir in the remaining 1 tablespoon cilantro.

8. Slide the chicken off the skewers onto a serving plate. Spoon the sauce over the kebabs, and serve.

Tips:

❖ Although I have used *balti masala* in this recipe, any garam masala (including store-purchased) will work.

❖ For a more complete package, serve the curry with a piece of Naan (page 729) and my favorite Cabbage and Cucumber "Slaw" with Roasted Peanuts (page 741). This makes for a perfect summer main course.

Breaded Ginger Beef
WITH A CUCUMBER–PIGEON PEA SAUCE

Malai tikka Sarki

When Sakina Munaim and Sakina Motiwalla met during a six-month secretarial course, the only things they had in common (in addition to their first names) were their Bohri Muslim heritage and a passion for food. Nevertheless, perennially eating lunch from your mother's home kitchen can get boring, so they swapped their daily lunches, each savoring the other's meals. Their friendship grew, and as each got married and became a mother, they became more of a close-knit family. Their dream of further cementing their families via matrimony came into fruition when Ranee Munaim married Zohair Motiwalla. Now that penchant for cooking and for family favorites, like this one, is re-created in the wedded couple's home in Minneapolis, while the Sakinas wait patiently for the grandchildren to arrive.

Note that the meat is marinated in the ginger paste a day ahead. **SERVES 6**

¼ cup Ginger Chile Paste (page 17)
2 teaspoons coarse kosher or sea salt
1 pound boneless beef, from the sirloin or a similar
　choice cut, cut into 1-inch cubes
¼ cup oily or unoily skinned split yellow pigeon peas
　(toovar dal), picked over for stones
1 large English cucumber, peeled, cut in half
　lengthwise, seeded, and shredded
2 to 4 fresh green Thai, cayenne, or serrano chiles,
　to taste, stems removed, finely chopped
　(do not remove the seeds)
2 scallions (green tops and white bulbs),
　finely chopped
1 tablespoon Ghee (page 21) or unsalted butter
1 teaspoon cumin seeds
Canola oil for deep-frying
2 large eggs, lightly beaten
1 cup fine dry breadcrumbs
Juice of 1 small lime
2 tablespoons finely chopped fresh cilantro
　leaves and tender stems

1. Combine the Ginger Chile Paste and 1 teaspoon of the salt in a medium-size bowl. Add the beef and stir to coat it with the mixture. Refrigerate, covered, for 24 hours (this allows the flavors to permeate the meat and, more important, to tenderize it).

2. Next, prepare the sauce: you can do this 24 hours ahead, at the same time that you start the meat marinating, or you can do it the next morning. Place the pigeon peas in a small saucepan. Fill the pan halfway with water and rinse the peas by rubbing them between your fingertips. The water will become cloudy. Drain this water. Repeat three or four times, until the water remains relatively clear; drain. Now add 1 cup water and bring it to a boil, uncovered, over medium-high heat. Skim off and discard any foam that forms on the surface. Reduce the heat to medium-low and simmer, covered, stirring occasionally, until the peas are tender, about 20 minutes.

3. Transfer the pigeon peas and the residual cooking water to a blender and puree, scraping the inside of the jar as needed, until smooth. Pour this thin, creamy-yellow broth into a bowl. (If you have an immersion blender, you can puree the peas and water right in the saucepan.)

4. Stir in the cucumber, chiles, scallions, and remaining 1 teaspoon salt.

5. Heat the ghee in a small skillet over medium-high heat. Sprinkle in the cumin seeds and let them sizzle until they turn reddish brown and smell nutty, 5 to 10 seconds. Immediately pour the skillet's contents into the pigeon pea mixture, and stir once or twice. Cover and refrigerate the sauce.

6. When you are ready to cook the meat, pour oil to a depth of 2 to 3 inches into a wok, Dutch oven, or medium-size saucepan. Heat the oil over medium heat until a candy or deep-fry thermometer inserted into the oil (without touching the pan's bottom) registers 350°F. (An alternative way to see if the oil is at the right temperature for deep-frying is to gently flick a drop of water over it. If the pearl-like drop skitters across the surface, the oil is ready.)

7. Line a large plate or a cookie sheet with several layers of paper towels. Put the eggs and the breadcumbs in separate shallow bowls. When the oil is ready, dip half of the marinated beef cubes into the beaten egg and then roll them in the breadcrumbs to coat them completely. Carefully lower them into the hot oil and fry, turning them occasionally, until they are reddish brown and crisp, about 5 minutes. Remove them with a slotted spoon and place them on the paper-towel-lined plate to drain. Repeat with the remaining beef. You may need to adjust the heat to maintain the oil's temperature at 350°F.

8. Just before serving it, stir the lime juice and cilantro into the chilled sauce.

9. Serve these addictive *tikkis* with the cold sauce, highlighting the temperature contrast between the two. Be sure to souse each cube with ample sauce.

Yellow pigeon peas? See the Types of Legumes, page 313.

Tips:

❖ There is no *malai* (cream) in this appetizer. The use of the word in the recipe title refers to the creamy tenderness of the meat, the result of the long marinating time. (Often, if the cut of meat is an inferior one, the Bohris in India add ¼ cup pureed unripe papaya to the marinade; or they rub the meat with it and after a few hours or overnight, wash it off and then do the marinade. Unripe papaya contains an enzyme called papain, an excellent meat tenderizer.)

❖ Substitute chunks of extra-firm tofu or *paneer* (homemade cheese, page 287) for the beef for a meatless option. Fry the *paneer* first in the oil, before the beef, so as not to contaminate the oil for the vegetarian at the table.

Beef Cubes
WITH A TAMARIND-MINT SAUCE

Gosht Kebab Aur
Pudhinay Ki Chutney

this wickedly hot appetizer can throw its eaters for a loop if they are not adequately warned. The effect of the chiles will linger on the palate for minutes, but it's nothing a cold beer won't take care of. **SERVES 4**

For the kebabs:

½ cup plain yogurt

6 to 8 green Thai, cayenne, or serrano chiles,
   to taste, stems removed

6 medium-size cloves garlic

2 lengthwise slices fresh ginger (each 2 inches long,
   1 inch wide, and ⅛ inch thick)

1 pound boneless beef (chuck, or "stew meat"),
   cut into 2-inch cubes

1 teaspoon ground Deggi chiles (see box, page 290);
   or ½ teaspoon cayenne (ground red pepper)
   mixed with ½ teaspoon sweet paprika

1 teaspoon coarse kosher or sea salt

½ teaspoon ground turmeric

½ teaspoon whole cloves, ground

For the sauce:

¼ cup firmly packed fresh mint leaves

¼ cup firmly packed fresh cilantro leaves and
   tender stems

1 teaspoon white granulated sugar

½ teaspoon coarse kosher or sea salt

½ teaspoon tamarind paste or concentrate

1 or 2 fresh green Thai, cayenne, or serrano chiles,
   to taste, stems removed

Bamboo or metal skewers
Vegetable cooking spray

1. To make the marinade, pour the yogurt into a blender jar. Add the chiles, garlic, and ginger, and puree, scraping the inside of the jar as needed, to make a smooth paste. Place the beef in a bowl and pour the marinade over it. Stir in the ground chiles, salt, turmeric, and cloves. Refrigerate, covered, for at least 1 hour or overnight, to allow the meat to absorb the flavors.

2. If you are using bamboo skewers, place them in a flat dish filled with water and let them soak for an hour. (See Tips on page 84.)

3. To make the sauce, pour ¼ cup water into a blender jar, and then add all the sauce ingredients. Puree, scraping the inside of the jar as needed, until smooth.

4. Pour the sauce into a small saucepan and allow it to warm over low heat. Keep it warm while you cook the kebabs.

5. Preheat a gas (or charcoal) grill, or the broiler, to high.

6. While the grill is heating, thread the beef cubes, covered with the thick marinade, onto the skewers (there should be no leftover marinade).

7. *If you are grilling,* lightly spray the grill rack with vegetable cooking spray. Grill the beef, covered, turning the skewers occasionally, until the pieces are light brown and the interior is still pink and tender-looking, 6 to 8 minutes. *If you are broiling,* position a rack so the top of the beef will be 2 to 3 inches from the heat. Lightly spray the rack of a broiler pan with cooking spray, and place the skewers on the rack. Broil, turning them occasionally, until the pieces of beef are light brown and the interior is still pink and tender-looking, 6 to 8 minutes.

8. Slide the beef off the skewers onto a serving plate. Spoon the sauce over the beef, and serve immediately. (If the sauce has thickened too much, thin it to the right consistency with a tablespoon or more of hot water.)

Tip: Cubes of lamb and pork make perfectly acceptable alternatives. For the vegetarian, serve browned chunks of tofu, *paneer,* tempeh, or steamed potatoes.

Wok-Cooked Beef Cubes
WITH A CHILE-YOGURT SAUCE

kadhai gosht kebab

These quick-cooking kebabs are neither skewered nor grilled. The bite-size chunks of beef are wok-seared, providing a great alternative for those who do not wish to mess with a grill. What I love about this dish is that the marinade not only tenderizes and flavors the meat, but also forms the basis for the creamy yogurt sauce.

Note that you start the marinating a day ahead. **SERVES 4**

For the marinade and the meat:
½ cup plain yogurt
1 tablespoon Ginger Paste (page 15)
1 tablespoon Garlic Paste (page 15)
2 teaspoons ground Deggi chiles (see box, page 290); or 1 teaspoon cayenne (ground red pepper) mixed with 1 teaspoon sweet paprika
1 teaspoon ground Kashmiri chiles; or ¼ teaspoon cayenne (ground red pepper) mixed with ¾ teaspoon sweet paprika
1 teaspoon coarse kosher or sea salt
½ teaspoon ground turmeric
1 pound boneless beef, from the sirloin or a similar choice cut, cut into 2-inch cubes (see Tip)
2 tablespoons canola oil

For the sauce:
¼ cup plain yogurt
¼ cup heavy (whipping) cream
½ cup finely chopped fresh mint leaves

1. To make the marinade, whisk the yogurt, Ginger Paste, Garlic Paste, both kinds of chiles, salt, and turmeric together in a medium-size bowl. Add the beef cubes and toss to thoroughly coat them with the spicy-hot marinade. Refrigerate, covered, overnight to allow the flavors to mingle and, more important, to allow the meat to further tenderize. I left my batch to marinate for 24 hours.

2. Preheat a wok or a well-seasoned cast-iron skillet over medium-high heat. Dribble the oil down the sides of the wok as it heats. When the oil has formed a shimmering pool in the bottom of the wok, add the beef, marinade and all, and cook, stirring frequently, until the beef is tender when cut with a fork, 15 to 20 minutes. As it cooks, the reddish-orange marinade will be absorbed into the meat, creating a pungent-smelling oily sheen on the surface. (Use adequate ventilation.) Transfer the cooked kebabs to a plate.

3. Pour 1 cup water into the wok, boiling it vigorously and scraping the browned bits of meat and spice from the bottom. Continue boiling the liquid down, uncovered, stirring occasionally, until it starts to thicken, 5 to 8 minutes.

4. Quickly whisk the yogurt and cream together, and add this to the liquid in the wok. Keep stirring until the sauce has reduced and thickened, 5 to 8 minutes. Stir in the mint.

5. Add the beef to the sauce, coating it well. Transfer it to a serving platter, and serve with toothpicks.

Tip: I cannot emphasize enough the importance of a good cut of meat for these kebabs. Because they are quick-cooking and not done over very high heat (when compared to a grill), you want to start with a tender piece of beef. Lamb is also a great alternative, as are chicken breasts and pork tenderloin.

Spiced Ground Beef Sandwiches

kheema paav

Sloppy Joes—those sandwiches of tomato-infused ground beef in hamburger buns—may well be as American as apple pie, but *kheema paav*, often made with ground mutton or lamb, is the equivalent in Mumbai and Delhi, a street food invented by vendors of the Muslim faith and devoured by all who eat meat. Both sandwiches are designed to be eaten on the run, at a picnic, or even at a simple family dinner, with the Indian version—no surprise—packing more oomph. **SERVES 4**

2 tablespoons canola oil

1 teaspoon cumin seeds

1 cup finely chopped red onion

2 large cloves garlic, finely chopped

2 lengthwise slices fresh ginger
  (each 2 inches long, 1 inch wide,
  and ⅛ inch thick), finely chopped

2 fresh green Thai, cayenne, or serrano chiles,
  stems removed, finely chopped
  (do not remove the seeds)

2 tablespoons tomato paste

1 teaspoon Bin bhuna hua garam masala
  (page 30)

1 teaspoon coarse kosher or sea salt

8 ounces lean ground beef

2 tablespoons finely chopped fresh cilantro
  leaves and tender stems

Butter for spreading on the buns

8 small white finger-sandwich-style buns,
  about 3 inches in diameter

½ cup finely chopped scallions
  (green tops and white bulbs) for sprinkling

1. Heat the oil in a medium-size skillet over medium heat. Add the cumin seeds and let them sizzle until they turn reddish brown and smell nutty, 10 to 15 seconds. Immediately add the onion, garlic, ginger, and chiles. Stir-fry until the onion is light brown around the edges, 3 to 5 minutes.

2. Stir in the tomato paste, garam masala, and salt. Reduce the heat to medium-low and simmer, partially covered, stirring occasionally, until there is an oily sheen

on the surface and around the edges of the sauce, 3 to 5 minutes.

3. Break up the ground beef, if necessary, and add it to the skillet along with the cilantro. Cook, uncovered, stirring occasionally, until the meat is partially cooked, 5 to 10 minutes.

4. Stir in ½ cup water and continue simmering the curry, covered, stirring occasionally, to let the flavors mingle, 5 to 8 minutes. Remove the curry from the heat and keep it covered so it stays warm.

5. Preheat a griddle or skillet over medium heat. Butter the cut side of each slice of bun and place them, butter side down, on the griddle. Cook until the underside is browned, 2 to 3 minutes. Remove the buns from the griddle.

6. To serve, place the bottom half of 2 buns on each plate. Spoon a liberal serving of *kheema* onto each bun, top it with a sprinkling of scallions, and set the other half of the bun on top.

Spiced Lamb Chops
WITH A FENUGREEK SAUCE

Mulayam Methi Gosht

this elegant, blow-your-socks-off-delicious first-course curry is sure to set a high standard for the meal's remaining courses. Fortunately nowadays one can purchase racks of lamb at most supermarkets. If you do not want the hassle of cutting your own chops from the rib rack, have the butcher do it for you. This is a great curry to serve because it requires no silverware—your guests can hold the convenient rib bone and munch away on the tender, succulent, full-flavored meat. Licking your fingers is perfectly acceptable—in fact, it's the best way to relish every bit of lingering flavor.

SERVES 4

2 tablespoons Ginger Paste (page 15)
1 tablespoon Garlic Paste (page 15)
2 teaspoons coriander seeds, ground
1 teaspoon cumin seeds, ground
1 teaspoon black cumin seeds, ground
Seeds from 2 black cardamom pods, ground
1 teaspoon cayenne (ground red pepper)
1 teaspoon coarse kosher or sea salt
1 pound rack of lamb (from ribs), cut into chops
2 tablespoons mustard oil or canola oil
1 cup half-and-half
½ cup chopped fresh or (thawed) frozen fenugreek leaves; or ¼ cup dried fenugreek leaves, soaked in a bowl of water and skimmed off before use (see box, page 473)
½ teaspoon Kashmiri garam masala (page 29)

1. Thoroughly combine the Ginger Paste, Garlic Paste, coriander, both kinds of cumin, cardamom, cayenne, and ½ teaspoon of the salt in a small bowl, stirring to make a moist (and potent) rub. Coat the lamb chops with this rub and refrigerate, covered, for at least 30 minutes or as long as overnight.

2. Heat the oil in a large skillet over medium-high heat. Add the lamb chops, rub and all, to the hot oil and sear each side until browned, about 2 minutes per side. Transfer the chops to a serving platter.

3. Pour the half-and-half into the skillet and bring to a simmer, scraping the bottom of the pan to release any browned bits of rub. Add the fenugreek leaves, garam masala, and the remaining ½ teaspoon salt. Simmer, uncovered, stirring occasionally, until the sauce thickens, 2 to 4 minutes.

4. Pour the sauce over the chops, and serve.

Almond-Rubbed Lamb Chops

WITH A SAFFRON CREAM SAUCE

Zaffran Chaamp

◆

I have often wondered whether the word *chaamp* is the Hindi language's nasal adaptation of "chop"—it's too close to think otherwise. In any case, call it what you want, because after one mouthful of these rich, slightly gamey, sweet flavors, you will be asking for *chaamp* time and again.

SERVES 4

¼ cup plain yogurt

½ cup slivered blanched almonds: ¼ cup left as is, the other ¼ cup ground

1½ teaspoons coarse kosher or sea salt

1 teaspoon cumin seeds

1 teaspoon fennel seeds

½ teaspoon whole cloves

½ teaspoon cayenne (ground red pepper)

1 pound rack of lamb (from ribs), cut into chops

1 tablespoon Ghee (page 21) or butter

4 large cloves garlic, finely chopped

½ cup half-and-half

½ teaspoon Punjabi garam masala (page 25)

¼ teaspoon saffron threads

Vegetable cooking spray

1. Pour the yogurt into a blender jar, followed by the slivered almonds, salt, cumin, fennel, cloves, and cayenne. Puree, scraping the inside of the jar as needed, to form a thick, gritty paste. Smear the paste over both sides of each chop and refrigerate them, covered, for at least 30 minutes or as long as overnight to allow the flavors to permeate the meat.

2. Preheat a gas (or charcoal) grill, or the broiler, to high.

3. Heat the ghee in a small skillet or saucepan over medium heat. Add the garlic and stir-fry until it is light brown, 2 to 4 minutes. Stir in the ground almonds and cook, stirring constantly, until the mixture is light brown and nutty-smelling, about 2 minutes.

4. Pour in the half-and-half, and then stir in the garam masala and saffron. Once the half-and-half starts to boil, the saffron will bloom into the sauce, perfuming it and turning it into a sunset-orange curry. The sauce will also thicken within a minute or two, thanks to the almonds. Remove the pan from the heat and set it aside.

5. *If you are grilling,* lightly spray the grill rack with vegetable cooking spray. Place the chops, marinade and all, on the rack and grill until the meat is seared on both sides and is still medium-rare in the center, 2 to 4 minutes per side. *If you are broiling,* position a rack so the tops of the chops will be 2 to 3 inches from the heat. Lightly spray the rack of a broiler pan with cooking spray, and place the chops, marinade and all, on the rack. Broil until the meat is seared on both sides and is still medium-rare in the center, 2 to 4 minutes per side.

6. Transfer the chops to a serving platter, pour the sauce over them, and serve. (If the sauce has cooled too much, rewarm it briefly in the saucepan until it is warm to the touch.)

Tips:

❖ This sauce has a tendency to thicken as it sits, because of the ground almonds. If need be, thin it with an additional tablespoon or two of half-and-half to bring it back to a pancake-syrup consistency.

❖ Saffron threads, albeit break-your-bank-expensive, will last a very long time when stored in a cool, dry place, and a little bit of saffron goes a long way. Refrain from purchasing ground saffron, or even threads from dubious vendors, for fear of acquiring an inferior-quality or even adulterated product.

Raisin-Stuffed Lamb Patties

WITH A TOMATO-RAISIN SAUCE

Kashmiri Shaami kebab

My Kashmiri version of a Lucknowi specialty hides sweet golden raisins within its classic meat-legume mixture, making for a pleasant surprise in each bite. To create a crispy shell, cooks often deep-fry these kebabs after dipping them in beaten eggs. I went with a pan-frying option, *sans* eggs, to keep the fat content down. However, you may wish to go skipping down the deep-fry trail.

MAKES 20 PATTIES (SERVES 10)

For the kebabs:

> ½ cup yellow split peas (chana dal), picked over for stones
> ½ teaspoon ground turmeric
> ½ cup golden raisins

> ¼ cup firmly packed fresh cilantro leaves and tender stems
> 2 or 3 fresh green Thai, cayenne, or serrano chiles, to taste, stems removed
> 1 pound ground lamb
> 1½ teaspoons coarse kosher or sea salt
> 1 teaspoon Kashmiri garam masala (page 29)

For the sauce:

> 2 tablespoons mustard oil or canola oil
> 4 medium-size cloves garlic, coarsely chopped
> ½ cup golden raisins
> 1 large tomato, cored and coarsely chopped
> 1 teaspoon fennel seeds, ground
> 1 teaspoon ground ginger
> 1 teaspoon ground Kashmiri chiles; or ¼ teaspoon cayenne (ground red pepper) mixed with ¾ teaspoon sweet paprika
> 1 teaspoon coarse kosher or sea salt

> *Canola oil for pan-frying*

1. Place the split peas in a medium-size saucepan. Fill the pan halfway with water and rinse the peas by rubbing them between your fingertips. The water will become cloudy. Drain this water. Repeat three or four times, until the water remains relatively clear; drain. Now add 3 cups water and bring to a boil, uncovered, over medium-high heat. Skim off and discard any foam that forms on the surface. Stir in the turmeric. Reduce the heat to medium-low and simmer, covered, stirring occasionally, until the split peas are tender, 30 to 35 minutes. Reserving 1 cup of the cooking water, drain the split peas in a colander.

2. Place the split peas in a food processor and pulse to mince. Transfer them to a medium-size bowl. In the same processor bowl (no need to rinse it out), combine the raisins, cilantro, and chiles; pulse to mince. Scrape this mixture into a small bowl and set it aside.

3. Add the lamb, salt, and garam masala to the split peas, and mix thoroughly. (If you are comfortable doing so, use your hands to mix it, since they're the best tool around.) Set the meat mixture aside while you make the sauce.

4. To make the sauce, heat the oil in a small saucepan over medium heat. Add the garlic and raisins, and stir-fry until the garlic turns light brown and the raisins swell, 2 to 4 minutes. Add the tomato, fennel, ginger, chiles, and salt. Cook, uncovered, stirring occasionally, until the tomato softens, about 5 minutes. Pour in the reserved split pea cooking water and bring to a boil. Continue simmering the sauce vigorously, uncovered, stirring occasionally, until it has thickened slightly, 3 to 5 minutes.

5. Transfer the sauce to a blender and puree, scraping the inside of the jar as needed, to form a smooth, reddish-brown sauce. (Alternatively, if you have an immersion blender, you can puree the sauce right in the saucepan.) Return the sauce to the saucepan and keep it warm.

6. Lightly grease your hands and scoop out about 2 tablespoons of the lamb mixture. Flatten it and shape it into a round, rather like a bumpy-looking wonton wrapper, about 2 inches in diameter. Place a scant teaspoon of the raisin filling in the center, and fold the edges of the meat wrapper over it to enclose it. Reshape it to form a ½-inch-thick patty. Repeat with the remaining lamb and filling.

7. Line a large plate or a cookie sheet with several layers of paper towels. Heat about 1 tablespoon oil in a large nonstick skillet, or in a well-seasoned cast-iron skillet, over medium heat. Arrange 6 patties, without crowding, in a single layer in the skillet and cook until the underside is reddish brown, about 5 minutes. Turn them over and cook on the other side until reddish

brown, about 5 minutes. Remove them with a slotted spatula and allow them to drain on the paper-towel-lined plate. Repeat with the remaining patties, adding more oil as needed.

8. Place 2 kebabs on each plate, blanket them with the sweet-hot sauce, and serve.

Ground Lamb
WITH SCALLIONS
IN A SAFFRON-ROSE SAUCE

Gulab Seekh Kebab

An appetizer curry like this one can easily turn out to be a main-course offering, especially if you serve it with Nimmy Paul's Tomato Rice (page 694). The mellow spices in the lamb, drenched with the aromas from the rich saffron-rose sauce, offer a great contrast to the gamey flavor of the meat. For those of you who prefer a different ground meat, beef or pork can be used as an alternative. **SERVES 8**

Bamboo or metal skewers
1 pound ground lamb
¼ cup firmly packed fresh mint leaves, finely chopped
½ teaspoon cayenne (ground red pepper)
6 medium-size cloves garlic, finely chopped
3 scallions (green tops and white bulbs), finely chopped
1 teaspoon Kashmiri garam masala (page 29)
1¼ teaspoons coarse kosher or sea salt
Vegetable cooking spray
1 cup half-and-half
¼ cup dried rose petals, crumbled (see Tip)
¼ teaspoon saffron threads

1. If you are using bamboo skewers, place them in a flat dish filled with water and let them soak for an hour. (See Tips on page 84.)

2. While the skewers are soaking, combine the lamb, mint, cayenne, garlic, scallions, ½ teaspoon of the garam masala, and 1 teaspoon of the salt in a medium-size bowl. Mix well, cover, and refrigerate until ready to use.

3. Divide the meat mixture into 8 portions, and shape each portion into a ball. Holding a ball in your hand, carefully poke a skewer through the center of the dense mass. Press the meat tightly against the skewer, spreading it and shaping it alongside the skewer, akin to a corn dog at the state fair. Repeat with the remaining balls of meat.

4. Preheat a gas (or charcoal) grill, or the broiler, to high.

5. *If you are grilling,* lightly spray the grill rack with vegetable cooking spray. Grill the lamb, covered, turning the skewers occasionally, until the sausage-like links are reddish brown and the interior is barely pink, 6 to 10 minutes (slice into a piece with a sharp paring knife). *If you are broiling,* position a rack so the top of the lamb will be 2 to 3 inches from the heat. Lightly spray the rack of a broiler pan with cooking spray, and place the skewers on the rack. Broil, turning the skewers occasionally, until the sausage-like links are reddish brown and the interior is barely pink, 6 to 10 minutes.

6. Transfer the grilled meat to a serving platter. (You can serve it on or off the skewers.)

7. Combine the half-and-half, rose petals, saffron, remaining ½ teaspoon garam masala, and remaining ¼ teaspoon salt in a small saucepan and bring to a boil over medium-high heat. Simmer, uncovered, stirring occasionally, to allow the aromas of saffron and rose to infuse the now slightly thickened sauce, 2 to 3 minutes.

8. Pour the deep yellow curry over the grilled meat, and serve.

Tip: Dried rose petals are usually found in the spice or tea aisle of natural food, Indian, Pakistani, and Middle Eastern grocery stores. If you can't locate any, make the sauce without them.

If you grow roses in your garden and don't spray them with either fertilizer or pesticide, pluck the petals when the flowers have bloomed but not yet faded. Rinse them under cold water, and then spin them in a salad spinner. Pat them dry between paper towels and let them dry in full sunlight. Store them in airtight jars in your pantry.

Natural food stores also stock dried rose hips. Crumble them for an acceptable alternative.

Herb-Stuffed Shrimp

Sharlele Kolumbi

This appetizer curry is an easy prelude to either a tasting menu or a full-blown, multiple-course meal—especially since you can assemble the shrimp and the sauce a day or two in advance. "Colossal" shrimp are essential only because they look impressive and because it is easier to stuff a few shrimp rather than more. If you can't find this size, select the largest shrimp available. Very small shrimp won't hold enough of the filling to be worthwhile.

Even though the sauce contains many of the same ingredients as the filling for the shrimp, the nutty-tasting peanuts and tart-sweet tomato provide great balance to the hot chiles. The texture of the sauce resembles basil pesto, and I often make an extra batch to toss with fresh-cooked penne pasta for a simple dinner. **SERVES 4**

For the stuffed shrimp:

8 colossal shrimp (11 to 15 per pound),
   peeled (tail shell left on), and deveined
½ cup shredded fresh coconut; or ¼ cup shredded
   dried unsweetened coconut, reconstituted
   (see Note)
¼ cup firmly packed fresh cilantro leaves and
   tender stems
½ teaspoon coarse kosher or sea salt
4 medium-size cloves garlic
2 or 3 fresh green Thai, cayenne, or serrano chiles,
   to taste, stems removed

For the sauce:

½ cup shredded fresh coconut; or ¼ cup shredded
   dried unsweetened coconut, reconstituted
   (see Note)
¼ cup unsalted dry-roasted peanuts
¼ cup firmly packed fresh cilantro leaves and
   tender stems
1 teaspoon white granulated sugar
½ teaspoon coarse kosher or sea salt
1 large tomato, cored and coarsely chopped
2 fresh green Thai, cayenne, or serrano chiles,
   stems removed
½ teaspoon rock salt, coarsely pounded

2 tablespoons canola oil

1. To prepare the shrimp, use a small sharp knife to make a deep gash down the back of each shrimp, keeping the tail shell intact and making sure not to cut through to the underside. Set the shrimp aside.

2. Combine the coconut, cilantro, salt, garlic, and chiles in a food processor. Pulse to form a slightly gritty paste, speckled green with the herbs. (My garlic cloves refused to mince thanks to the coconut, which interfered with the blades. I removed as much of the processed paste as possible, pulverized the garlic, and then mixed the garlic into the paste.)

3. Divide the paste into 8 portions, and press a portion into the gash on the back of each shrimp—the filling will be sticky and will stay put in its place. (This can be done even a day or two before you plan on serving them.) Refrigerate the stuffed shrimp, covered, until ready to cook.

4. To make the sauce: Combine all the sauce ingredients except the rock salt in a small saucepan. Add ½ cup water and bring it to a boil over medium-high heat. Once it starts to boil, lower the heat to medium and continue vigorously simmering the chunky curry, uncovered, stirring occasionally, until the tomato softens and the mixture thickens, about 5 minutes.

5. Transfer the mixture to a blender and puree it, scraping the inside of the jar as needed, to form a smooth sauce. Pour the sauce into a bowl, and fold in the rock salt. (The sauce can be made up to 2 days ahead and refrigerated, covered; reheat it before serving.)

6. Heat the oil in a medium-size skillet over medium-high heat. Arrange the shrimp in a single layer in the skillet, and cook until the underside is salmon-orange, about 2 minutes. Now turn the shrimp on their backs, stuffing side down with the tails sticking up in the air, and gently press each piece down (a pair of tongs works great for this) to sear the paste 2 minutes. Then lay the shrimp on the uncooked side, and cook until that side is salmon-orange, about 2 minutes. Transfer the shrimp to a serving platter.

7. Either spoon the curry onto individual plates and place the shrimp on top, or pass the shrimp and sauce around separately, instructing your friends to do it themselves. Either way, they will wolf them down.

Note: To reconstitute coconut, cover with ¼ cup boiling water, set aside for about 15 minutes, and then drain.

Grilled Cheese Fingers
WITH AN ALMOND CREAM SAUCE

Paneer Pasanda

A Lucknowi specialty, *pasandas* usually involve tender slices of premier cuts of meat in a nutty, creamy sauce. This version appeals to vegetarians, incorporating coconut milk with a little half-and-half for a rich-tasting sauce fortified with almonds (vegans can use water instead of the half-and-half). The spices are delicate and aromatic, with black pepper providing just the right bit of heat to create a comfortable balance. **SERVES 4**

I can (13.5 ounces) unsweetened coconut milk
¼ cup half-and-half
¼ cup slivered blanched almonds, ground

I teaspoon coarsely cracked black pepper
I teaspoon coarse kosher or sea salt
10 to 12 medium-size to large fresh curry leaves
6 whole cloves
4 green or white cardamom pods
I cinnamon stick (3 inches long)
8 ounces Doodh or Malai paneer (pages 286 or 287), cut into pieces about 3 inches long, 1 inch wide, and 1 inch thick
2 tablespoons canola oil
½ cup finely chopped red onion
Vegetable cooking spray

1. Pour the coconut milk into a small saucepan. Stir in the half-and-half, almonds, pepper, salt, curry leaves, cloves, cardamom pods, and cinnamon stick. Bring to a simmer over medium heat, stirring occasionally. Remove the pan from the heat and add the *paneer* fingers. Set the pan aside so the *paneer* can steep, absorb the flavors, and soften up, about 30 minutes (there is no need to refrigerate it).

2. Remove the *paneer* pieces from the pan and transfer them to a bowl, reserving the creamy soaking liquid.

3. Heat the oil in a medium-size sauté pan over medium-high heat. Add the onion and cook until it is light brown around the edges, 2 to 4 minutes. Pour in the reserved sauce, reduce the heat to medium, and simmer, uncovered, stirring occasionally, until the sauce thickens, 3 to 5 minutes.

4. Preheat a gas or charcoal grill, or the broiler, to high.

5. *If you are using a grill,* lightly spray the grill rack with cooking spray. Grill the *paneer* fingers, covered, turning them every 2 to 3 minutes, until the grill marks are reddish brown, 8 to 12 minutes. *If you are using the broiler,* set the rack so the *paneer* fingers will be 2 to 3 inches from

the heat, and lightly spray the rack in a broiler pan with cooking spray. Broil the *paneer* fingers, turning them every 2 to 3 minutes, until they are light reddish brown, 8 to 12 minutes. (When you remove the *paneer* fingers from the bowl, there will be a little pool of soaking liquid at the bottom of the bowl. Add this to the thickened sauce—there won't be enough to thin it down again.)

6. Transfer the *paneer* slices to a serving platter and pour the sauce over them. (If the sauce is not warm enough, rewarm it, covered, before pouring it.) Serve immediately.

Tips:

❖ Grilling or broiling is an option for the silky *paneer*, but pan-frying also works really well: Heat 1 tablespoon oil in a skillet, preferably nonstick, over medium heat. Pan-fry the *paneer* fingers, broad side down, until golden brown, 3 to 5 minutes. Then turn them over and fry the other side, another 3 to 5 minutes.

❖ If you like, remove the curry leaves, cloves, cardamom pods, and cinnamon stick before pouring the sauce over the *paneer* slices.

Battered Cheese
WITH A RAISIN–RED CHILE SAUCE

Paneer Kishmish

f or those who wish to get away from eating too much meat but crave its texture and succulence, this appetizer curry will fill the bill. The *paneer* has a chewy texture, especially when cut thick and then stacked with other ingredients. A layer of sweet-hot raisin-chile spread holds together two slices of cheese, and when dipped into a nutty-tasting batter, the combination is addictive. You can augment the appetizer with a green salad or even a Cabbage and Cucumber "Slaw" with Roasted Peanuts (page 741) for a simple meal. **SERVES 8**

½ cup golden raisins
3 or 4 dried red Thai or cayenne chiles, to taste,
*   stems removed*
1 cup boiling water
4 large cloves garlic
1 teaspoon coarse kosher or sea salt
1 pound Doodh paneer (page 286), cut into pieces
*   roughly 3 inches long, 1½ inches wide,*
*   and ¼ inch thick*
Canola oil for deep-frying
¼ cup chickpea flour
2 tablespoons rice flour
¼ teaspoon ground turmeric
¼ cup heavy (whipping) cream
2 tablespoons finely chopped fresh cilantro
*   leaves and tender stems*

1. Place the raisins and chiles in a small heatproof bowl, and pour the boiling water over them. Set the bowl aside until the raisins and chiles have swelled and softened, about 15 minutes. Drain, reserving the soaking water. You should have about ¾ cup slightly cloudy liquid; if not, add enough water to bring it to that level.

2. Pour ¼ cup of the reserved liquid into a blender jar, followed by the raisins, chiles, garlic, and ½ teaspoon of the salt. Puree, scraping the inside of the jar as needed, until the mixture forms a smooth, light brown, red-speckled paste. Transfer the paste to a bowl.

3. Spread this hot-sweet paste over half the *paneer*

slices, covering one side. There should be some paste left over in the bowl. Stack the remaining *paneer* slices on top of the paste-covered ones, making little finger sandwiches. Don't worry if some of the paste oozes out from the sides.

4. Pour oil to a depth of 2 to 3 inches into a wok, Dutch oven, or medium-size saucepan. Heat the oil over a medium heat until a candy or deep-fry thermometer inserted into the oil (without touching the pan's bottom) registers 350°F. (An alternative way to see if the oil is at the right temperature for deep-frying is to gently flick a drop of water over it. If the pearl-like drop skitters across the surface, the oil is ready.)

5. While the oil is heating, combine the two flours, the remaining ½ teaspoon salt, and the turmeric in a small bowl. Pour in ¼ cup of the reserved soaking water, whisking quickly to make a thick, sun-yellow batter.

6. Line a large plate or a cookie sheet with several layers of paper towels. Once the oil is ready, dip a *paneer* sandwich into the thick batter, coating it. Gently slide it into the hot oil. Repeat with about 3 more sandwiches; don't crowd the pan. Fry, turning them occasionally, until they are golden brown and crisp all over, 5 to 7 minutes. Remove them with a slotted spoon and place them on the paper-towel-lined plate to drain. Repeat with the remaining sandwiches.

7. Combine the leftover raisin paste, remaining ¼ cup soaking water, cream, and cilantro in a small saucepan, and bring to a boil over medium-high heat. Cook the sauce, uncovered, stirring occasionally, until it thickens slightly, 2 to 3 minutes.

8. Arrange the mouth-watering fried *paneer* sandwiches on a platter. Pour the sauce over them, and serve.

Trispy Vegetable Rolls
WITH A CUCUMBER-YOGURT SAUCE

Subzi Kebab

In India these kebabs are sometimes roasted in a tandoor (a clay oven), with incredibly juicy results. Given that tandoors are not everyday equipment in American households (not yet, at least), I have created a skillet-friendly version, yielding equally addictive results. The Cream of Wheat gives these cigar-shaped kebabs a delectable crunch, and the spicy-hot flavors find solace blanketed under the cooling yogurt sauce.

MAKES 16 KEBABS (SERVES 8)

For the kebabs:
- *1 pound russet or Yukon Gold potatoes, peeled*
- *1 small red onion, coarsely chopped*
- *4 fresh green Thai, cayenne, or serrano chiles, stems removed*
- *4 ounces Doodh paneer (page 286), shredded or crumbled*
- *½ cup finely chopped fresh cilantro leaves and tender stems*
- *1 tablespoon Maharashtrian garam masala (page 28)*
- *1½ teaspoons coarse kosher or sea salt*
- *1 cup Cream of Wheat (not instant)*
- *Canola oil for pan-frying*

For the sauce:
- *1 cup plain yogurt*
- *1 large cucumber, peeled, seeded, and shredded*

2 fresh green Thai, cayenne, or serrano chiles,
   stems removed, finely chopped

2 tablespoons finely chopped fresh cilantro leaves
   and tender stems

½ teaspoon Toasted Cumin-Coriander Blend
   (page 33)

½ teaspoon coarse kosher or sea salt

1. To make the kebabs, bring a medium-size saucepan of water to a rolling boil. Add the potatoes, return to a boil, and continue to boil, uncovered, until they are partially cooked, barely 5 minutes. Drain the potatoes and rinse them under cold water to stop the cooking. Once they are cool to the touch, shred the potatoes in either a food processor or a handheld box grater. Transfer the shredded potatoes to a medium-size bowl.

2. Combine the onion and chiles in the same food processor bowl and pulse until minced (if you run the machine continuously, you will end up with unwanted excess moisture from the onion). Add this to the potatoes, along with the *paneer,* cilantro, garam masala, and salt. Combine the ingredients to make a slightly sticky "dough." Divide the mixture into 16 portions.

3. Place the Cream of Wheat in a shallow dish. Working with one portion at a time, shape the potato mixture into a cigar-like shape, roughly 2 to 3 inches long, by pressing and rolling it against a hard surface. Then roll it around in the Cream of Wheat to encase it in the gritty grain. Set it aside on a plate, and repeat with the remaining portions.

4. Line a large plate or a cookie sheet with several layers of paper towels. Heat 2 tablespoons canola oil in a large nonstick skillet, or in a well-seasoned cast-iron skillet, over medium heat. Arrange 6 rolls, without crowding, in a single layer in the skillet and cook until golden brown and crisp on the underside, 3 to 5 minutes. Turn the rolls over and cook the remaining sides until they are

evenly golden brown and crisp, about 3 minutes each side. Remove them with a slotted spatula and allow them to drain on the paper-towel-lined plate. Repeat with the remaining rolls, adding more oil as needed.

5. To make the sauce, thoroughly combine all the sauce ingredients in a medium-size bowl.

6. Place 2 kebabs on each plate, and cover them with the cucumber-cool, chile-hot sauce.

Tips:

❖ The *paneer* helps to hold the kebabs together; shredded firm tofu or even mozzarella cheese will do the same thing.

❖ Adding shredded carrot (1 medium, peeled and shredded) makes the kebabs more festive-looking.

BUTTER-ROASTED
Mashed
Vegetables
WITH GRIDDLE-BROWNED BREAD

Paav Bhajee

the 1970s witnessed the popularity of disco music here in the United States, but in the streets of Mumbai (then called Bombay), a much spicier melody swept through the metropolis. Street vendors hawked an unusual combination of simple vegetables, slow-roasted with an abundance of butter and spices and served them with browned slices of soft white bread. Disco fever may have down-spiked after a few years, but not this addictive curry, which still soars in many a Mumbai-ite's heart. **SERVES 10**

I pound russet or Yukon Gold potatoes, peeled, diced, and submerged in a bowl of cold water to prevent browning

8 ounces cauliflower, cut into florets

I large green bell pepper, stemmed, seeded, and coarsely chopped

½ cup frozen green peas (no need to thaw)

I large red onion, coarsely chopped

4 fresh green Thai, cayenne, or serrano chiles, stems removed

8 tablespoons (I stick) salted butter, plus more for spreading on the bread

I can (15 ounces) tomato sauce

I tablespoon Ginger Paste (page 15)

I tablespoon Garlic Paste (page 15)

I tablespoon Paav bhajee masala (page 38)

I teaspoon coarse kosher or sea salt

¼ cup tomato paste

½ cup finely chopped fresh cilantro leaves and tender stems

10 white hamburger-style buns

Optional garnishes:

I cup finely chopped red onion

I teaspoon cayenne (ground red pepper)

I large lime, cut into wedges

1. Drain the potatoes. Combine the potatoes, cauliflower, bell pepper, peas, and 4 cups water in a medium-size saucepan, and bring to a boil over medium-high heat. Lower the heat to medium and stew the vegetables, covered, stirring occasionally, until tender, 18 to 20 minutes.

2. While the vegetables are cooking, combine the

onion and chiles in a food processor and pulse to form a nose-tingling, eye-watering, pungent blend.

3. Preheat a wok or a large skillet over medium-high heat. Add 2 tablespoons of the butter; it will instantly melt and start to bubble. Add the onion-chile blend and cook, stirring, until the mixture is honey-brown with a light purple hue, 5 to 8 minutes.

4. Add the tomato sauce, Ginger Paste, Garlic Paste, *Paav bhajee masala*, and salt to the onion mixture. Lower the heat to medium and allow the sauce to simmer, partially covered, stirring occasionally, until a thin film of oil forms on the surface, 8 to 10 minutes. (You will have to stir more frequently as the sauce thickens because it tends to stick.)

5. Meanwhile, reserving 1 cup of the cooking water, drain the potatoes and other vegetables in a colander. Transfer them to a medium-size bowl, add the tomato paste, and coarsely mash the vegetables.

6. Add the mashed vegetables, ¼ cup of the cilantro, and the reserved cup of vegetable cooking water to the sauce. As the curry warms, it will start to bubble, geyser-like, because of its thick consistency. Reduce the heat to medium-low and cook, covered, stirring frequently for about 15 minutes. Add 2 tablespoons of the butter and allow it to melt. Stir the butter into the paste and cook, uncovered, stirring frequently, for about 5 minutes. Repeat twice more, adding 2 tablespoons butter each time.

7. Sprinkle the remaining ¼ cup cilantro over the curry and keep it warm.

8. Preheat a griddle or skillet over medium heat. Butter the cut side of each slice of bun and place them, butter side down, on the griddle. Cook until the underside is browned, 2 to 3 minutes, and remove the buns.

9. If you are using the garnishes, toss the onion and cayenne together in a medium-size bowl. Instruct folks to sprinkle the spicy-hot onion garnish over their plate of curry, followed by a squirt of fresh lime juice and 2 pieces of toasted bun.

Fried Potato Sandwiches

Vadaa paav

Let me be the first to tell you that this is a production. On the day I make it, it's all I eat for breakfast, lunch, and dinner—oh, and let's not forget afternoon tea.

I find myself in seventh heaven when I am eating carbohydrates with more carbohydrates, especially when it is potato with bread. *Vadaa paav* flooded the streets of Mumbai during the 1970s, taking roadside dining to a new level. I call it Mumbai's veggie burger, complete with toppings and a soft square bun (*paav*).

SERVES 8

For the roasted garlic-spice blend:

- 1 tablespoon canola oil
- ½ cup raw peanuts (without the skin)
- 1 tablespoon coriander seeds
- 1 teaspoon cumin seeds
- 8 to 10 dried red Thai or cayenne chiles, to taste, stems removed
- 1 tablespoon white sesame seeds
- 6 medium-size cloves garlic, thinly sliced
- 1 teaspoon coarse kosher or sea salt

For the cilantro-peanut sauce:

- ½ cup firmly packed fresh cilantro leaves and tender stems
- 2 tablespoons shredded dried unsweetened coconut
- ½ teaspoon coarse kosher or sea salt
- 6 to 8 fresh green Thai, cayenne, or serrano chiles, to taste, stems removed

For the garlic potatoes:

- 1 pound russet or Yukon Gold potatoes, peeled, boiled until tender, and mashed
- ½ cup frozen green peas (no need to thaw them)
- 1 teaspoon coarse kosher or sea salt
- ½ teaspoon ground turmeric
- ½ cup firmly packed fresh cilantro leaves and tender stems
- ¼ cup firmly packed medium-size to large fresh curry leaves
- 5 fresh green Thai, cayenne, or serrano chiles, stems removed
- 4 medium-size cloves garlic
- 3 lengthwise slices fresh ginger (each 1½ inches long, 1 inch wide, and ⅛ inch thick)

For the batter:

- ½ cup chickpea flour, sifted
- ½ cup rice flour
- 2 tablespoons cornstarch
- 1 teaspoon coarse kosher or sea salt
- ½ teaspoon ground turmeric
- Canola oil for deep-frying

16 small, white, finger sandwich–style buns

1. To make the spice blend, heat the oil in a small skillet over medium-high heat. Add the peanuts and roast, stirring them constantly, until they start to smell nutty and turn reddish brown, 2 to 4 minutes. Transfer half the peanuts to a plate to cool. Put the other half in a blender jar and set it aside.

2. Add the coriander, cumin, chiles, and sesame seeds to the same skillet and roast, stirring constantly, until the chiles blacken slightly and the spices turn reddish brown, 1 to 3 minutes. Add this mixture to the peanuts on the plate.

3. Now add the garlic to the remaining oil in the skillet and cook, stirring the slices around occasionally, until they are a sunny brown color, 2 to 4 minutes. Spread the garlic slices over the spices on the plate, and leave them until they are cool and dry, 5 to 10 minutes. (If you don't allow the garlic and spices to cool, the ground blend will acquire unwanted moisture from the heat, making it slightly "cakey.")

4. Place half the garlic-spice mixture in a spice grinder and grind until the texture resembles that of finely ground black pepper. Scrape this into a small bowl. Repeat with the remaining batch. Thoroughly combine the two ground batches, and mix in the salt. This light reddish-brown dry chutney will keep, tightly covered, in the refrigerator or at room temperature for up to a week.

5. To make the cilantro-peanut sauce, pour ¼ cup water into the blender jar containing the roasted peanuts. Pile in the cilantro, coconut, salt, and chiles. Puree, scraping the inside of the jar as needed, to form a light green sauce, gritty with the freshly roasted peanuts. Transfer this to a small bowl. Add 2 tablespoons water to the blender jar and swish it around to loosen up every last bit of sauce; add the washings to the sauce. Stir well and refrigerate, covered, until ready to use. (I prefer to keep it at room temperature if I am planning on using it right away, or if I make it a day or two earlier, to bring it to room temperature before serving. Refrigerating it will thicken the sauce, but stirring a tablespoon or two of water into it will bring it back to its right, "souse-able" consistency.)

6. To prepare the potatoes, combine them with the peas, salt, and turmeric in a medium-size bowl.

7. Combine the cilantro, curry leaves, chiles, garlic, and ginger in a food processor and pulse to mince, creating a slightly wet, grassy-fresh blend. Add it to the potato mixture, combining them well to make a slightly sticky, bumpy, yellow-green dough.

8. Divide the dough into 16 portions. Shape each portion into a round, pressing it between the palms of your hands to flatten it into a ½-inch-thick patty. Set the patties aside.

9. To make the batter, mix the two flours, cornstarch, salt, and turmeric in a medium-size bowl. Pour in about ⅓ cup warm water, whisking the ingredients together to start forming a thick batter. Continue adding water, a few tablespoons at a time, whisking them in after each addition, to make a smooth, thick batter. You will need about ¾ cup warm water altogether.

10. Pour oil to a depth of 2 to 3 inches into a wok, Dutch oven, or medium-size saucepan. Heat the oil over medium heat until a candy or deep-fry thermometer inserted into the oil (without touching the pan's bottom) registers 350°F. (An alternative way to see if the oil is at the right temperature for deep-frying is to gently flick a drop of water over it. If the pearl-like drop skitters across the surface, the oil is ready.)

11. Line a large plate or a cookie sheet with several layers of paper towels. Once the oil is ready, dip a patty into the batter, coating it, and carefully slide it into the hot oil. Repeat with about 5 more patties (do not crowd the pan). Fry, turning them occasionally, until they are golden brown and crisp, about 5 minutes total. Remove them with a slotted spatula and allow them to drain on the paper-towel-lined plate. Repeat with the remaining *vadaas.* You may need to adjust the heat to maintain the oil's temperature at 350°F.

12. To serve the appetizer curry, slice open each bun and spread on a liberal amount of the cilantro-peanut sauce. Sprinkle it with the garlic-spice blend. Place a patty between the slices, close the bun, and serve.

Tips:

❖ The good news is that the spice blend and the cilantro-peanut sauce can be made ahead, even up to 2 days in advance. The patties are best when served hot off the stove, but they are also good when made ahead and served at room temperature.

❖ The cornstarch in the batter gives the coating a crisper edge. I have also poured a ladle of hot oil into the batter, stirring it in just before dipping the patties, for crispy results. A pinch of baking soda helps too.

Spiced Potato and Pomegranate Sandwiches

dabeli

aharashtrians are very creative when it comes to combining multiple sources of carbohydrates in the same dish. This curry-in-a-bun is love at first bite—topped with fresh, luscious-red, juicy-tart pomegranate seeds. It's really a cinch to make as a do-ahead dish. Just lay everything out in bowls assembly-line style, in the same order as they go into the bun, and folks can help themselves by making their own. Those ho-hum taco parties will make a run for the border.

SERVES 6

For the sauces:
½ cup Sweet-Tart Tamarind-Date Sauce (page 20)
½ cup firmly packed fresh cilantro leaves and tender stems
½ teaspoon coarse kosher or sea salt
4 medium-size cloves garlic
2 lengthwise slices fresh ginger (each 2 inches long, 1 inch wide, and ⅛ inch thick)
2 fresh green Thai, cayenne, or serrano chiles, stems removed
2 dried red Thai or cayenne chiles, stems removed

For the filling:
1 pound russet or Yukon Gold potatoes, peeled, boiled until tender, and mashed
1 tablespoon Dabeli masala (page 39; see Tips)
1½ teaspoons coarse kosher or sea salt
1 teaspoon white granulated sugar
2 tablespoons canola oil

For assembling the sandwiches:
Butter for spreading
6 white hamburger-style buns
Seeds from 1 small to medium-size ripe pomegranate (see box, page 106)
About 6 tablespoons spicy-hot roasted peanuts (store-bought is just fine)
About 6 tablespoons finely chopped red onion
About 6 tablespoons finely chopped fresh cilantro leaves and tender stems
Thin chickpea-flour noodles for sprinkling (optional; see Tips)

1. Pour the tamarind-date sauce it into a small bowl, and set it aside.

2. To make the hot cilantro sauce, pour ⅓ cup water into a blender jar, followed by the cilantro, salt, garlic, ginger, and the two kinds of chiles. Puree, scraping the inside of the jar as needed, to form a smooth, bright green, vibrant-hot sauce. Pour it into a small bowl, and set it aside.

3. To make the potato filling, combine the mashed potato, masala, salt, and sugar in a medium-size bowl. Mix well.

4. Heat the oil in a medium-size skillet over medium-high heat. Add the potato mixture and cook, stirring occasionally, until the potatoes have warmed and the spices are cooked, 5 to 8 minutes. Return the potato mixture to the medium-size bowl.

5. To assemble the sandwiches, first preheat a griddle or skillet over medium heat. Butter the cut side of each bun and place them, butter side down, on the griddle. Cook until the underside is browned, 2 to 3 minutes. Remove the buns from the griddle.

6. To make a sandwich, spread a scant teaspoon-ful (less or more, depending on your tolerance for chiles) of the cilantro-chile sauce on the bottom of a toasted bun. For the second layer, spread a generous teaspoonful of the tamarind-date sauce. On top of that pile in and spread out one sixth of the spiced potatoes.

the glorious pomegranate

❖ ❖ ❖

My weakness in life (next to potatoes and chocolate) is a bowlful of fresh pomegranate seeds, each encased in its ruby-red, gel-like, juicy liquid. Each squishy crunch squirts out a burst of sweet-tart flavor, and if you spoon in a mouthful at the same time, you just might experience nirvana. Of course, if you chase it down with a fistful of crispy, thin, kettle-cooked potato chips and then a bite of rich dark chocolate, that zen state is a guarantee.

A fresh pomegranate, with its apple shape and crownlike stem, will keep in the refrigerator for up to a week. Once you have removed the seeds, they will keep for only 2 to 3 days. Choose a fruit that is very firm to the touch, with a blood-red color and an orange glow. Ones that look shriveled and are dull in color have probably been sitting around for too long, their unhappy appearance a premonition of the dried and rotten seeds inside. (The sun-dried seeds of slightly unripe pomegranate, dark reddish brown in color, are the tart flavoring of choice in northern Indian kitchens; this spice known as anardana.)

To get the seeds out of a pomegranate, here's what I do: I cut the fruit in half lengthwise, and then each half again in half lengthwise. Working with one quarter at a time, I turn it inside out over a bowl, so the seeds and flesh are pushed out, like a puffed-up chest. Using my fingers, I cajole the juicy seeds in their red pulp out into the bowl, discarding the thin off-white membranes that house them. Soon I have a bowlful of near-nirvana.

The pomegranate was heralded as the fruit of choice of Venus, the goddess of love. The Egyptians turned it into a fermented beverage, consuming it like wine. Concentrated pomegranate extract is found in grenadine syrup, a crucial ingredient in the Tom Collins— at least in the version I drank way, way back during my early college years. You could rationalize that the cocktail is healthy, because pomegranates are rich in vitamin C and fiber (yes, it's a stretch, I admit).

Sprinkle a tablespoon of the juicy red pomegranate seeds over the potatoes, followed by the peanuts and onion. Cover this with the top of the bun, and sprinkle the cilantro and noodles on top of that. Repeat with the other sandwiches.

Tips:

❖ You can make your own *Dabeli masala*—a combination of several spices, all of which are readily available—using the recipe on page 39. It is also available, premixed, in any Indian grocery store's spice aisle. Or, if you happen to have made the *Paav bhajee masala* (page 38), use it as an alternative. Most of the garam masalas in this book also are acceptable options.

❖ Crunchy chickpea-flour noodles (*sev*) are widely available in the snack aisle of Indian grocery stores. They come in various degrees of thickness and spiciness. For this recipe, choose the ones that are wispy thin, pale yellow, and mildly spicy. (Some of the cayenne-spiked noodles, which are spaghetti-thick and crunchy, are great as a snack, perfect for teatime.)

Roulade of Taro Leaves
WITH A TOMATO-MUSTARD SAUCE

Patra Masala

I have made this dish with taro leaves (on the rare occasion when I see these Dumbo-ears-like leaves in the produce section of an Indian grocery store) and also with collard greens. The only teeny, tiny difference is in the very slightly chewy texture of the collard greens, because the leaves are a wee bit thicker than taro. But other than that, the rolls have the same incredibly complex flavors: a tart, spicy-sweet interior with the juicy succulence of tomatoes made nutty by mustard and cumin seeds. **SERVES 6**

> 8 medium-size to large taro leaves or collard leaves
> 1 cup chickpea flour
> 2 teaspoons Toasted Cumin-Coriander Blend (page 33)
> 1 teaspoon coarse kosher or sea salt
> 1 teaspoon white granulated sugar
> ½ teaspoon cayenne (ground red pepper)
> ½ teaspoon ground turmeric
> 1 tablespoon Ginger Chile Paste (page 17)
> ½ teaspoon tamarind paste or concentrate
> Vegetable cooking spray
> ¼ cup canola oil
> 1 teaspoon black or yellow mustard seeds
> 1 teaspoon cumin seeds
> ¼ teaspoon ground asafetida
> 1 medium-size tomato, cored and finely chopped
> 2 tablespoons finely chopped fresh cilantro leaves and tender stems
> 6 to 8 medium-size to large fresh curry leaves
> ½ cup shredded fresh coconut (optional)

1. Rinse the leaves (taro or collard) under cold water to wash off any dirt. Working with one leaf at a time, fold them in half lengthwise, alongside the stem. Slice off the tough stem end. When you unfold the leaf, you will have a V-shaped base.

2. Combine the chickpea flour, cumin-coriander blend, salt, sugar, cayenne, and turmeric in a medium-size bowl. Gradually add about ¼ cup warm water, a couple of tablespoons at a time, whisking until the mixture forms a thick paste with the consistency of smooth peanut butter. Whisk in the Ginger Chile Paste and tamarind paste.

3. Place a leaf on a work surface and place about a tablespoon of the mixture on it. Using a spatula, spread it out to cover as much of the leaf as possible. Use a little more of the paste if needed, but keep in mind that you need enough for the remaining leaves. Place a second leaf on top of the first, with its base at the opposite end of the bottom one, and spread the mixture over this leaf. Repeat the layering twice more. Rolling from one end, roll the 4 layered leaves into a tight log. Repeat with the remaining 4 leaves and paste.

4. Lightly spray a steamer basket with cooking spray, and place it in a pan filled halfway with water; or prepare a bamboo steamer for steaming by placing it into a wok filled halfway with water. If you are using a bamboo steamer, line the bottom with wax paper and lightly spray the paper with cooking spray.

5. Place the 2 rolled logs in the steamer basket and bring the water to a boil. Once the water comes to a gentle boil, cover the pan and steam until the leaves are olive green and the filling peeking around the edges is opaque and has lost its wet sheen, 20 to 25 minutes. Transfer the logs to a cutting board and allow them to cool for 5 to 10 minutes. Then cut them crosswise into ½-inch-thick slices.

6. Heat the oil in a large skillet over medium-high heat. Add the mustard seeds, cover, and cook until the seeds have stopped popping (not unlike popcorn), about 30 seconds. Sprinkle in the cumin and asafetida, which will instantly sizzle, turn reddish brown, and smell nutty-garlicky. Add the *patra* slices, arranging them in a single layer, and cook until the undersides are lightly browned, about 1 minute. Flip the slices over and brown the other side, about 1 minute.

7. Spread the chopped tomato over the slices, followed by the cilantro and curry leaves. Lower the heat to medium and cover the skillet. Cook for about 5 minutes, during which time the steam rising from within, thanks to the juicy tomatoes, will infuse the *patra* slices with flavor. Do not stir the slices while this is happening.

8. Use a spatula to gently transfer the slices to a platter, and spoon the chunky tomatoes and the pan drippings over them. Serve sprinkled with the fresh coconut, if desired.

Tips:

❖ These rolls are great to prepare ahead: they will keep, covered and refrigerated, for up to 3 days. If you wish to freeze them, steam them, slice them, and then freeze them in airtight freezer-safe self-seal bags for up to 2 months. Thaw them before proceeding with Step 6.

❖ Even though the coconut is optional, do use it—it nudges the curry to a greater, even tastier height.

Cheese-Stuffed Mushroom Caps
WITH A CREAMY ONION SAUCE

bharwaan dhingri

Mushroom caps are nature's perfect way of saying "Stuff me." This curry makes an excellent first course, appealing to the carnivore and herbivore alike, the mushrooms' meatlike firm flesh providing a chewy contrast to the creamy, minty filling. Go ahead and use your fingers to eat them, because there is no greater joy than licking off all that earthy sauce. You do realize that eating with silverware is like making love through an interpreter, don't you? **SERVES 6**

For the mushrooms:

12 large button mushrooms (either white or
   brown) with stems
8 ounces Doodh paneer (page 286), crumbled
¼ cup finely chopped fresh mint leaves
1 teaspoon Punjabi garam masala (page 25)
1 teaspoon coarse kosher or sea salt
2 tablespoons canola oil

For the sauce:

½ cup Whole Milk Solids (page 24); or ½ cup heavy
   (whipping) cream
½ teaspoon Punjabi garam masala
   (page 25)
½ teaspoon coarse kosher or sea salt
¼ cup finely chopped fresh cilantro leaves
   and tender stems
2 tablespoons canola oil
1 cup finely chopped red onion

1. Remove the mushroom stems by pulling them out, leaving a cavity. Scrub the stems with a vegetable brush to get rid of any debris, or rinse and dry them. Finely chop them and set them aside.

2. Combine the *paneer*, mint, garam masala, and salt in a medium-size bowl, and mix thoroughly. Stuff the mushroom caps with this full-flavored, cheesy mix. Try to use up all the stuffing. It's all right to sample some.

3. Heat the oil in a large skillet over medium-high heat. Arrange the mushroom caps, stuffed side up, in a single layer in the skillet and cook until they are browned on the underside, 2 to 3 minutes.

Reduce the heat to medium-low, cover the skillet, and cook until the mushrooms are slightly shriveled and spongy but are still springy when gently poked with a finger, 8 to 10 minutes. Transfer them to a plate.

4. To make the sauce, pour ½ cup water into a blender jar, followed by the milk solids, garam masala, and salt. Puree, scraping the inside of the jar as needed, to form a smooth, light brown sauce. Pour it into a bowl and stir in the cilantro. (I prefer not to puree the leaves.)

5. Heat the oil in the same (unwashed) skillet over medium-high heat. Add the onion and the chopped mushroom stems and stir-fry until the onion is light brown around the edges and the mushrooms are soft, 5 to 8 minutes.

6. Add the sauce to the skillet and stir once or twice. Place the mushroom caps, stuffed side up, in the skillet, and spoon the sauce over them. Reduce the heat to medium-low, cover the skillet, and braise the mushroom caps until the mushrooms are easily pierced with a fork, 5 to 7 minutes.

7. Transfer the mushrooms to a serving platter, spoon the sauce over them, and serve.

Tips:

❖ In a bind, I have substituted crumbled feta or extra-firm tofu when I didn't have any *paneer* on hand. With feta being so salty, eliminate the salt from the filling.

❖ If you don't have 1 minute to spare to make your own Punjabi garam masala, plunk down some dollars to purchase the premixed garam masala that some major spice companies now stock in the spice aisle in large supermarkets.

Griddle-Cooked Eggplant
WITH A GARLIC-YOGURT SAUCE

Baingan Bhurani

this room-temperature curry reflects the cooking of Persia and the Middle East, thanks to the influence of the ruling Moghuls in northern India, where the combination of yogurt and eggplant is as natural as strawberries dipped in chocolate (okay, that's not natural—but it should be, don't you think?). This version is more reflective of cooking the Hyderabadi way, using southern Indian curry leaves and northern Indian mint, made fiery hot with potent chiles. **SERVES 6**

I to 1½ pounds eggplant, stem removed,
   sliced lengthwise into ¼-inch-thick slices
1½ teaspoons coarse or kosher salt
2 tablespoons canola oil
I cup plain yogurt
2 tablespoons finely chopped fresh cilantro leaves
   and tender stems
2 tablespoons finely chopped fresh mint leaves
2 tablespoons finely chopped fresh curry leaves
2 large cloves garlic, finely chopped
2 fresh green Thai, cayenne, or serrano chiles,
   stems removed, finely chopped
   (do not remove the seeds)

1. Lay the eggplant slices in a shallow, medium-size pan (glass, stainless steel, or plastic). Sprinkle the salt over them and set them aside to allow the salt to leach out the bitter-tasting water, about 1 hour.

2. Squeeze the slices of the eggplant between the palms of your hands to get rid of any excess water, and set them aside.

3. Line a large plate or a cookie sheet with several layers of paper towels.

4. Drizzle 1 tablespoon of the oil into a large non-stick skillet and heat it over medium heat. Arrange half the eggplant slices in a single layer in the skillet, without crowding them. Cook until the slices have softened and turn medium brown on the underside, 5 to 8 minutes. Flip them over and repeat on the other side, another 5 to 8 minutes. Slide them onto the paper-towel-lined plate to drain. Heat the remaining 1 tablespoon oil in the skillet, and repeat with the remaining eggplant.

5. To make the sauce, whisk the yogurt, cilantro, mint, curry leaves, garlic, and chiles together in a medium-size bowl.

6. Arrange the eggplant slices in a single layer on a large serving platter. Drape the herb-scented yogurt sauce over them, and serve.

Tips:

❖ Even though this is a great starter course, I often serve it as a chilled accompaniment during summer months. I like it with grill-friendly Ground Lamb with Scallions in a Saffron-Rose Sauce (page 95) and Cabbage and Cucumber "Slaw" with Roasted Peanuts (page 741).

❖ You can make a curry like this up to 2 days ahead. Keep the eggplant and sauce separate (just like the bride and groom before their nuptials), bringing them together just before serving. You don't want the eggplant to be all sloshed up before the party, do you?

Steamed Chickpea Flour Cake
WITH MINT SAUCE

dhokla Sudhina Chutney

Known as *khaman dhokla* in Gujarati-speaking kitchens, these fluffy yellow cakes are served at any and every occasion. Some recipes call for yellow split peas, which are soaked overnight, ground into a batter, allowed to ferment, and then steamed. My version gratifies us without the wait. **SERVES 8**

For the cake:

I cup chickpea flour

I tablespoon uncooked Cream of Wheat (not instant)

2 teaspoons white granulated sugar

I teaspoon coarse kosher or sea salt

I cup plain yogurt, whisked (see Tips)

2 tablespoons Ginger Chile Paste (page 17)

Juice of I medium-size lime

Vegetable cooking spray

1½ teaspoons Eno salt (see Tips)

2 tablespoons canola oil

I teaspoon black or yellow mustard seeds

¼ cup shredded fresh coconut; or 2 tablespoons shredded dried unsweetened coconut, reconstituted (see Note)

2 tablespoons finely chopped fresh cilantro leaves and tender stems

For the sauce:

I cup firmly packed fresh cilantro leaves and tender stems

I cup firmly packed fresh mint leaves

2 tablespoons heavy (whipping) cream

I teaspoon coarse kosher or sea salt

6 fresh green Thai, cayenne, or serrano chiles, stems removed

2 lengthwise slices fresh ginger (each 2 inches long, I inch wide, and ⅛ inch thick)

1. To make the cake, combine the chickpea flour, Cream of Wheat, sugar, and salt in a medium-size bowl. Whisk in the yogurt and ¾ cup water to form a slightly thin, lumpfree, pancakelike batter. Stir in the Ginger Chile Paste and lime juice.

2. Spray the bottom and sides of a large, deep, round cake pan, such as a 6- to 8-inch-diameter soufflé dish, with cooking spray.

3. Pour 4 cups water into a stockpot that is wide enough to hold the cake pan. Fill a small heatproof bowl with water and set it inside the stockpot to form a base for the cake pan. The rim of the small bowl should extend above the level of the water in the stockpot. Bring the water in the stockpot to a gentle boil over medium-high heat.

4. Stir the Eno salt into the cake batter, which will immediately rise up, thanks to the chemical reaction between the lime juice and the sodium bicarbonate. Pour the batter into the prepared cake pan, and set it on the small bowl in the stockpot. Cover the pot tightly, and steam until a knife inserted in the center of the cake comes out clean, 45 minutes to 1 hour. Have a teakettle of boiling water on standby, to replenish the water in the stockpot so it stays at the same level. When it is done, the cake will be an opaque yellow, look spongy, and spring back when gently touched with a finger.

5. Lift the cake pan out of the pot and set it aside to cool for about 15 minutes. Then invert the pan over a serving platter, and lift it off the cake.

6. Heat the oil in a small skillet over medium-high heat. Add the mustard seeds, cover the skillet, and cook until the seeds have stopped popping (not unlike popcorn), about 30 seconds. Pour the seedy oil over the cake, and top it off with the coconut and cilantro. Cut the cake into serving pieces.

7. To prepare the sauce, pour ½ cup water into a blender jar, and then add all the sauce ingredients. Puree, scraping the inside of the jar as needed, to form a smooth, bright green sauce.

8. Transfer this minty-hot sauce to a small saucepan and warm it gently over medium heat. (Too hot, and the herbs in the sauce will be mellow.)

9. Spoon 1 to 2 tablespoons of the sauce on each plate, top with a piece of cake, and serve.

Note: To reconstitute the coconut, cover with 2 tablespoons boiling water, set aside for about 15 minutes, and then drain.

Tips:

❖ The sourer the yogurt the better, as it contributes to the yeasty, sourdoughlike flavor characteristic of this cake.

❖ Eno "salt" (not a mineral but a combination of chemicals—good ones), widely available in Indian grocery stores, is often consumed for relief from indigestion, flatulence, and nausea. Created by well-known pharmacist James Crossley Eno, these fruit salts also became the cure in Britain for seasickness and change of climate, and were thus much revered by sailors. Dissolve some of the crystalline salty-tasting powder in a glass of water, and as it fizzes, gulp it down for instant relief. Because it contains sodium bicarbonate and citric acid (an alkali and an acid), the chemicals react to produce carbon dioxide, which leavens the batter for the *dhokla*. The same quantity of Alka-Seltzer produces similar results.

Steamed Chickpea Flour Cake
WITH PEANUTS AND SPINACH

Sengdana Palak Dhokla

Even though the technique and some of the ingredients are the same, the texture and flavor of this cake are poles apart from those of the Chickpea Flour "Cigars" with Coconut-Mint Sauce (page 114). I love the nutty crunch that coarsely ground peanuts offer. This is a great do-ahead dish, quichelike (without a crust) in appearance with that same egglike firmness. Warm it in a microwave for a hassle-free appetizer course. **SERVES 8**

For the cake:

½ cup unsalted dry-roasted peanuts
1 cup chickpea flour
1 teaspoon coarse kosher or sea salt
½ teaspoon ground turmeric
½ cup plain yogurt, whisked
2 tablespoons Ginger Chile Paste
  (page 17)

4 ounces fresh spinach leaves, well rinsed, patted dry,
  and cut into thin strips (see Tip)
Vegetable cooking spray
1 teaspoon Eno salt (see Tip, page 112)

For the sauce:

2 tablespoons canola oil
1 teaspoon black or yellow mustard seeds
1 teaspoon cumin seeds
¼ teaspoon ground asafetida
½ cup finely chopped red onion
1 large tomato, cored and finely chopped
½ cup finely chopped fresh cilantro leaves and
  tender stems
1 teaspoon white granulated sugar
½ teaspoon coarse kosher or sea salt
½ teaspoon cayenne (ground red pepper)

Asafetida? See the Glossary of Ingredients, page 758.

1. To make the cake batter, place the peanuts in a food processor and pulse to grind them to the consistency of coarse breadcrumbs. Transfer the ground peanuts to a medium-size bowl, and stir in the chickpea flour, salt, and turmeric. Whisk in the yogurt and 1 cup water to make a slightly thin, lumpfree, pancakelike batter. Stir in the Ginger Chile Paste and spinach.

2. Spray the bottom and sides of a large, deep, round cake pan, such as a 6- to 8-inch-diameter soufflé dish, with cooking spray.

3. Pour 4 cups water into a stockpot that is wide enough to hold the cake pan. Fill a small heatproof bowl with water and set it inside the stockpot to form a base for the cake pan. The rim of the small bowl should extend above the level of the water in the stockpot. Bring the water in the stockpot to a gentle boil over medium-high heat.

4. Stir the Eno salt into the cake batter, which will immediately rise up, thanks to the chemical reaction between the lime juice and the sodium bicarbonate. Pour the batter into the prepared cake pan, and set it on the small bowl in the stockpot. Cover the pot tightly, and steam until a knife inserted in the center of the cake comes out clean, 1 to 1¼ hours. Have a teakettle of boiling water on standby, to replenish the water in the stockpot so it stays at the same level. When it is done, the cake will be opaque yellow with olive green ribbons, look spongy, and spring back when gently touched with a finger.

5. Lift the cake pan out of the pot and set it aside to cool for 15 to 30 minutes. The cake will firm up considerably as it cools, making it easier to slice it into wedges. Invert the pan over a serving platter and tap it gently to loosen the cake; lift the pan off the cake. Slice the cake into wedges.

6. Meanwhile, to make the sauce, heat the oil in a small saucepan over medium-high heat. Add the mustard seeds, cover, and cook until the seeds have stopped popping (not unlike popcorn), about 30 seconds. Sprinkle in the cumin and asafetida, which will instantly sizzle, turn reddish brown, and smell nutty-harsh.

7. Add the onion and cook, stirring, to reduce the raw taste, 2 to 3 minutes. Add the tomato, cilantro, sugar, salt, and cayenne. Cook over medium heat, uncovered, stirring occasionally, until the tomato is softened but still firm-looking, about 5 minutes.

8. Warm the steamed cake in a microwave for a few seconds, and serve it mounded with the sweet-hot sauce.

Tip: To cut fresh spinach into thin strips, stack a few leaves together, and roll them into a log. Cut them into thin slices, forming lush green ribbons—a simple technique with the froufrou name "chiffonade."

Thickpea Flour "Cigars"
WITH A COCONUT-MINT SAUCE

khaandvi

I watched carefully as Bharati Sindhvad, my friend Swetal's mother, made *khaandvi*. As the batter thickened in the pan and started to separate from the sides, she spread a little of it on the counter next to the stove, spreading it out with her finger to see if it was the right consistency. "Almost there," she said in Gujarati, and continued her clockwise stirring for an additional 1 to 2 minutes. Within minutes, the thin, flat lasagnalike sheets lay spread out on foil, cooling. After slicing them, she rolled them into loose cigar shapes and placed them on a serving platter ready to be seasoned, then served. **SERVES 8**

For the "cigars":
- *1 cup chickpea flour*
- *1 teaspoon white granulated sugar*
- *1 teaspoon coarse kosher or sea salt*
- *½ teaspoon ground turmeric*
- *1¼ cups buttermilk*
- *4 tablespoons canola oil*
- *1 tablespoon Ginger Chile Paste (page 17)*
- *Vegetable cooking spray*
- *1 teaspoon black or yellow mustard seeds*
- *¼ teaspoon ground asafetida*
- *2 tablespoons finely chopped fresh cilantro leaves and tender stems*
- *1 or 2 fresh green Thai, cayenne, or serrano chiles, to taste, stems removed, finely chopped (do not remove the seeds)*

For the sauce:
- *1 cup firmly packed fresh mint leaves*
- *½ cup firmly packed fresh cilantro leaves and tender stems*
- *¼ cup shredded fresh coconut; or 2 tablespoons shredded dried unsweetened coconut, reconstituted (see Note)*
- *1 teaspoon white granulated sugar*
- *1 teaspoon coarse kosher or sea salt*
- *Juice of 1 medium-size lime*

1. To make the *khaandvi,* combine the chickpea flour, sugar, salt, and turmeric in a medium-size bowl.

2. Pour in half of the buttermilk, quickly whisking it in to make a thick, lump-free batter. Then add the remaining buttermilk, whisking it in to form a thinner batter. Whisk in 2 tablespoons of the oil and the Ginger Chile Paste.

3. Tear off two large sheets of aluminum foil about the size of a cookie sheet, and lay them side by side on the counter next to the stove. Lightly spray them with cooking spray.

4. Pour the batter into a small saucepan and heat it gently, stirring constantly, over medium-low heat. Keep stirring until its color changes from shiny yellow to a dull, opaque yellow and it starts to thicken and pull away from the sides of the pan, 10 to 15 minutes.

5. Using a spatula, transfer a walnut-size wad of the soft dough-like batter to the prepared foil and quickly (and that's the key) spread it out to form a thin, flat sheet, about the same length, thickness, and width as a single lasagna noodle. Repeat (working quickly so the batter doesn't cool) until all the batter is spread out. Don't worry if the edges are ragged and not straight (I, for one, never could draw a straight line). Cut each sheet of dough in half crosswise. Allow the dough to cool until you can handle it, 5 to 10 minutes. Then roll each half-sheet into a loose cigar shape and place it on a serving platter.

6. Heat the remaining 2 tablespoons oil in a small skillet. Add the mustard seeds, cover, and cook until the seeds have stopped popping (not unlike popcorn), about 30 seconds. Sprinkle in the asafetida, which will instantly sizzle and smell strong, with garlicky undertones. Pour this seedy oil evenly over the rolled *khaandvi*. Top them with the cilantro and chiles.

7. To make the sauce, pour ½ cup water into a blender jar, and then add all the sauce ingredients. Puree, scraping the inside of the jar as needed, to form a light green sauce. Pour it into a serving bowl.

8. Pass individual plates and have folks dip the *khaandvi*, fondue-style, into the sauce before taking a bite.

Note: To reconstitute coconut, cover with 2 tablespoons boiling water, set aside for about 15 minutes, and then drain.

Steamed Rice-Lentil Cakes
WITH A COCONUT–PIGEON PEA SAUCE

Idli Sambhar

If you have ever visited a South Indian home, or a restaurant that features dishes from that area, chances are that you have sampled these fluffy, pillow-soft, steamed rice-lentil cakes, the color of pure snow. It's not difficult to make these airy delights. What you need is a pound of patience, an ounce of the right ingredients, and a dash of kitchen accoutrements. With my method, I seem to have found the right mix to create feathery-soft magic without the usual wait for the batter to ferment. And no, I haven't sold my soul to the dark side to achieve these results. A little alchemy goes a long way, that's all.

MAKES ABOUT 40 *IDLIS* (SERVES 10)

½ cup skinned split black lentils (cream-colored in this form, urad dal), picked over for stones
3 cups fine rava rice (see Tip)
½ cup plain yogurt, whisked
1 tablespoon coarse kosher or sea salt
2 teaspoons Eno salt (see Tip, page 112)
Vegetable cooking spray
Boiling water
1 recipe Coconut-Smothered Pigeon Peas with Pumpkin (page 429)

1. Place the lentils in a medium-size bowl. Fill the bowl halfway with water and rinse the lentils by rubbing them between your fingertips. The water will become cloudy. Drain this water. Repeat three or four times, until the water remains relatively clear; drain. Now fill the bowl halfway with warm water and let it sit at room temperature, covered, until the lentils have softened, at least 30 minutes (you can let them soak longer, but no longer than 4 hours).

2. Drain the lentils. Pour ½ cup water into a blender jar, add the lentils, and puree, scraping the inside of the jar as needed, until the mixture is smooth and paste-like. Transfer the thick batter to the same medium-size bowl. Pour about 1 cup water into the blender jar and run the blender to wash out any remnants of batter; add this to the batter in the bowl.

Stir another 1 cup water into the batter, and add the rice, yogurt, and salt. Whisk thoroughly to create a homogenous, if gritty, blend. Stir in the Eno, which will instantly aerate the batter, making it bubble and appear fermented.

3. *If you don't have an idli pan,* you will need to create one: Set a standard muffin tin (with cups 2 to 3 inches wide and 1 to 1½ inches deep) in a larger flameproof baking pan. Lightly spray the muffin cups with cooking spray. Fill the cups three-quarters full with the *idli* batter. Pour boiling water into the baking pan so it reaches halfway up the sides of the muffin tin. Cover the entire baking pan tightly with aluminum foil, and set it on a burner over medium heat. Steam for 20 to 25 minutes, or until a toothpick or knife stuck in an *idli* comes clean. Remove the muffin tin from the hot water bath and allow it to cool for at least 5 minutes. Then slide the *idlis* out, giving them a nudge with a butter knife. Repeat with the remaining batter.

If you do own an idli pan, spray the individual concave disks with cooking spray and fill them three-quarters full with batter. Stack them (there are usually 4 plates with 4 concave-shaped discs on each plate) around the *idli* stand, placing the small metal rods between the plates to separate them; set the device in a large stockpot filled with hot water to a depth of about ½ inch. Cover, and steam over medium-high heat until a toothpick or knife stuck in an *idli* comes out clean, 20 to 25 minutes. Remove the *idli* stand from the stockpot and allow it to cool for at least 5 minutes. Then slide the *idlis* out, giving them a nudge with a butter knife. Repeat with the remaining batter.

4. Serve the *idlis* in individual serving bowls, with the pigeon pea stew ladled on top.

> **Black lentils?**
> See the Types
> of Legumes,
> page 313.

Tips:

❖ *Rava* rice—sometimes labeled *idli rava*—is available in any store that sells Indian groceries. It is a combination of parboiled and uncooked long-grain rice that is ground either coarse or fine—hence the name *rava* (Cream of Wheat) rice. (The coarser grind works just as well; the *idlis* will just differ in texture.) This convenience product lets you shortcut the soaking and grinding required in the traditional recipe (as mentioned in the Tip below).

❖ The Eno "salt" is the cheater's way to create carbon dioxide without having to let the *idli* batter ferment. In India the batter is often a combination of soaked skinned split black lentils and parboiled (converted rice). We soak and grind the rice separately from the lentils because rice takes a lot longer than lentils to grind to a paste. In this country, I have had better results using equal proportions of parboiled and uncooked long-grain rice (1 cup each) and ½ cup lentils, with enough water to make a pancake-type batter. To ferment the batter naturally, place it in a large bowl, cover, and leave it in a warm place until it has risen, smells yeasty, and has bubbles forming on the surface. I usually cover the bowl and stick it in a turned-off oven with the pilot light lit (if it's a gas oven) or the oven light on. With the door shut, the conditions in there are warm and humid, perfect for the fermentation to occur. Depending on the conditions, the process can take anywhere from 8 to 24 hours.

❖ If you don't have any Eno in your pantry, you can ferment the batter as described in the above Tip.

❖ The Pigeon Peas with Pumpkin and Coconut is a cinch to make and can even be made a day or two in advance. It can also be frozen for up to a month.

❖ *Idlis,* in either batter form or steam-cooked, have a

relatively long shelf life in the refrigerator (up to 10 days). They can also be frozen for up to 2 months. To thaw frozen steamed *idlis*, I usually re-steam them in a steamer basket (5 to 10 minutes until piping hot and soft) or cover them with a wet paper towel and microwave them on high power for 3 to 5 minutes.

Yellow Split Pea and Peanut Cakes
WITH A TAMARIND-CHILE SAUCE

dal Sengdana Vadi

Wonderfully textural and full of flavor, these nutty, slightly flaky, addictive cakes are my vegetarian answer to crab cakes—which means they're also a perfect choice for those who keep kosher or are allergic to shellfish. And the fact that they are pan-fried, rather than deep-fried, makes them healthy too (they fall apart in the oil if deep-fried). The peanuts help hold the patties together without the need for eggs or flour as a binder.

MAKES 20 CAKES (SERVES 10)

For the cakes:

I cup yellow split peas (chana dal),
    picked over for stones
¼ cup raw peanuts (without the skin)
I cup shredded fresh coconut; or ½ cup
    shredded dried unsweetened coconut,

Holy basil?
See the
Glossary of
Ingredients,
page 758.

    reconstituted (see Note)
4 to 6 fresh green Thai, cayenne, or serrano chiles,
    to taste, stems removed
4 lengthwise slices fresh ginger (each 2½ inches long,
    I inch wide, and ⅛ inch thick)
½ cup finely chopped fresh cilantro leaves
    and tender stems
I½ teaspoons coarse kosher or sea salt
½ teaspoon ground turmeric
¼ teaspoon ground asafetida
Canola oil for pan-frying

For the sauce:

½ teaspoon tamarind paste or concentrate
I cup coconut milk
2 teaspoons Maharashtrian garam masala
    (page 28)
½ teaspoon coarse kosher or sea salt
I or 2 dried red Thai or cayenne chiles,
    to taste, stems removed, pounded in
    a mortar to release some of the seeds
    (do not remove the seeds)
2 tablespoons finely chopped fresh holy basil or
    sweet basil leaves, or finely chopped
    fresh cilantro leaves and tender stems

1. Place the split peas and peanuts in a medium-size bowl. Fill the bowl halfway with water and rinse the legumes (yes, botanically speaking, the peanut is a legume and not a nut) by rubbing them between your fingertips. The water will become cloudy. Drain this water. Repeat three or four times, until the water remains relatively clear; drain. Now fill the bowl halfway with warm water and allow the legumes to soften by letting them sit at room temperature, covered, for at least 1 hour.

2. Drain the split peas and peanuts, and transfer them to a food processor. Add the coconut, chiles, and ginger, and process the

gritty paste. Scrape this into the same medium-size bowl (why dirty another one?). Fold in the cilantro, salt, turmeric, and asafetida.

3. Scoop out a tablespoon of the wet sand-like paste and form it into a ball. Press the ball between the palms of your hands to form a patty roughly ½ inch thick. Place the patty on a plate. Repeat with the remaining paste. You should have about 20 patties.

4. Line a large plate or a cookie sheet with several layers of paper towels. Heat 2 tablespoons canola oil in a large nonstick skillet or a well-seasoned cast-iron skillet over medium heat. Arrange 6 patties, without crowding, in a single layer in the skillet and cook until the undersides are golden brown and crisp, about 5 minutes. Flip them over and cook the other side until golden brown and crisp, about 5 minutes. Using a slot-ted spatula, transfer the patties to the paper-towel-lined plate to drain. Repeat with the remaining patties, adding more oil as needed.

5. To make the sauce, whisk the tamarind paste and coconut milk together in a small saucepan. Stir in the garam masala, salt, chiles, and basil. Bring the sauce to a boil over medium-high heat, stirring occasionally, and cook until it is thick and viscous, akin to cold pancake syrup.

6. Place 2 cakes on each individual serving plate and cover them with the creamy, tart, slightly hot sauce.

Note: To reconstitute coconut, cover with ½ cup boiling water, set aside for about 15 minutes, and then drain.

poultry, game & egg curries

In the pre-Aryan days (before 1500 B.C.), everyone in India ate meats freely, from over 250 kinds of animals. It's only with the arrival of the Aryans, and their beliefs as described in the holy scriptures of the Hindus known as the *Vedas,* that certain meats become forbidden. Vegetarianism played a big role, especially among the Hindu Brahmins, but other castes and religions continued to eat meats. Specific meats were taboo

in some religions, but the one that defied all prohibitions was the chicken, in all its forms and glory (except the cluck perhaps). Its wide availability and easy to raise qualities make chicken, even in modern times, the most sought-after meat.

It is very common in India, at many of the open-air markets, to see cages of live poultry stacked on top of each other. The chicken are huddled en masse, awaiting quick death at the hands of their butcher, to be stuffed into

cloth sacks and taken—still feathered and undressed—on a one-way journey to the kitchen fires. It is here that they are transformed into delectable curries—juicy, succulent, and vibrant with ginger, garlic, chiles, coconut, and a myriad of fresh herbs and spices. Many chickens are stewed as bone-in pieces (always skinned, because the skin is considered unhealthy).

The chickens in India are much smaller than those in the U.S.—similar to Cornish game hens (1½ to 2 pounds)—and, yes, they taste like chicken: assertive, slightly gamey, and chock-full of flavor. In this country, I tend to shy away from those birds that are pumped with antibiotics and look as though they're on steroids, and stick to the ones that are labeled "grain-fed," "organic," or "free-range" (although with this third classification, I wonder about the size of the actual "range").

When I am looking for a quick fix to feed my hungry carnivorous child after a long day at school, I whip up Cubed Chicken with Wok-Seared Vegetables (page 145) or Stir-Fried Chicken with Green Beans (page 148), targeting meat and vegetables in one easy swoop. For a relaxing Sunday evening, I will spend the extra time to prepare Chicken Simmered in a Pumpkin-Lentil Sauce with Fenugreek (page 140) while sipping a glass of pinot noir. If you are entertaining guests or family for a laid-back Sunday brunch, try Halved Eggs with Garlic, Curry Leaves, and Tamarind (page 167) or Sri Lankan–Style Hard-Cooked Eggs with Coconut Milk (page 166) instead of the usual scrambled eggs. And if you want to bowl someone over with a remarkable duck curry, serve Duck Stew with Black Cardamom and Cherries (page 165) and watch them relish every succulent morsel. Whatever the occasion, make one of these flavorful poultry curries, even if you think you are "chickened out." You will never look at chicken in the same light—and yes, you may cluck with joy.

Coconut Chicken
WITH POTATOES

batata murghi

Marathi-speaking households from the state of Maharashtra (home to the bustling metropolis Mumbai) savor this curry at family gatherings or special weekend meals. Chickens in India are close in flavor and size to the Cornish game hen, so feel free to use the smaller hens as an alternative. **SERVES 6**

1 can (13.5 ounces) unsweetened coconut milk (see Tips)

2 tablespoons coarsely chopped fresh ginger

2 tablespoons unsalted dry-roasted peanuts

1½ teaspoons coarse kosher or sea salt

¼ teaspoon ground turmeric

5 large cloves garlic

4 to 6 fresh green Thai, cayenne, or serrano chiles, stems removed

1 tablespoon coriander seeds

½ teaspoon cardamom seeds from green or white pods

1 or 2 cinnamon sticks (each 3 inches long), broken into smaller pieces

1 chicken (3½ pounds), skin removed, cut into 8 pieces (see box, next page)

2 medium-size potatoes, such as russet or Yukon Gold, peeled, cut into 1-inch cubes, and submerged in a bowl of cold water to prevent browning

2 tablespoons peanut or canola oil

1 medium-size red onion, cut in half lengthwise and thinly sliced

2 tablespoons finely chopped fresh cilantro leaves
and tender stems

12 to 15 medium-size to large fresh curry leaves
(see Tips)

1. Pour ½ cup of the coconut milk into a blender jar. Add the ginger, peanuts, salt, turmeric, garlic, and chiles. Puree, scraping the inside of the jar as necessary, to make a slightly smooth but still gritty paste. Transfer the paste to a medium-size bowl.

2. Preheat a small skillet over medium-high heat. Add the coriander, cardamom, and cinnamon, and cook, shaking the pan occasionally, until the coriander turns reddish brown, the cardamom looks ash-gray, and the blend smells fragrant, about 30 seconds. Transfer the spice mixture to a plate and let it cool for about 5 minutes. Then grind the mixture in a spice grinder until it has the texture of finely ground black pepper. Fold the ground spices into the coconut-milk mixture.

3. Place the chicken pieces in a baking dish and thoroughly coat them with this marinade. Cover and refrigerate for at least 30 minutes or as long as overnight.

4. Drain the potatoes and pat them dry.

5. Heat the oil in a nonreactive wok (if it isn't nonreactive, the coconut milk, which you will add later, will discolor), large skillet, or Dutch oven over medium heat. Add the potatoes and cook, stirring, until they turn golden brown, 8 to 10 minutes. Using a slotted spoon, transfer them to a plate.

6. In the same pan, cook the onion until it is light brown around the edges, 5 to 8 minutes; add the onion to the potatoes.

7. Arrange the chicken pieces in a single layer in the same pan (make sure you reserve the marinade), and cook until the underside is golden brown, 3 to

how to skin and cut up a chicken

❖ ❖ ❖

Skinning and cutting up a whole chicken is simple, albeit a bit messy. From its cavity remove all the gizzards and innards (these are usually contained in a small paper sack). You can save them for another use. Using one hand, hold the chicken in a squatting position (the chicken, not you) on a firm surface or on a clean, damp dishtowel. With the other hand, firmly peel the skin away from the bird, starting at its neck and moving toward its legs. It's not possible to remove the skin completely from the wings; just remove what you can. Trim off and discard the excess fat. (Some cooks save the trimmed fat and render it for other uses.)

To cut the chicken into 8 pieces, I usually start at the legs. Hold the legs clasped together with one hand, and slip the other hand into the neck cavity for leverage. Now wring the chicken, as you would a wet towel, twisting and separating the two halves. Separate the 2 legs and cut each leg in half at the joint, creating thigh and drumstick pieces. Stick your thumb in the neck cavity and pull off the neck bone and cartilage. Slice each breast alongside the breastbone. Cut each breast in half crossways so that one half of the piece has the wing attached to it. You can cut the wing off at the joint if you wish.

5 minutes; turn the pieces over and sear that side to a golden brown color, 3 to 5 minutes.

8. Stir the potatoes, onion, remaining coconut milk, reserved marinade, cilantro, and curry leaves into the pan. Reduce the heat to medium-low, cover, and simmer, turning the chicken occasionally and basting it with the sauce, until the meat in the thickest parts is no longer pink inside and the juices run clear, 15 to 20 minutes.

9. Remove the chicken pieces and arrange them on a serving platter. Skim off any excess oil that may be floating on the surface of the curry, and then ladle the sauce, along with the vegetables, over the chicken pieces.

Tips:

❖ Make sure to shake the can of coconut milk before you open it to ensure an evenly thick liquid. The fat often separates from the wheylike liquid and collects at the top half of the can.

❖ Curry (*karhi*) leaves are very easy to find in the refrigerated section of a store that carries Indian groceries. If they are unavailable, leave them out of the recipe. No other herb resembles curry leaves' unmistakable subtle aroma and flavor, thus defying substitution.

❖ I always serve a big bowl of steamed rice with this dish to mop up all that rich-tasting curry. This is a great "do-ahead" recipe, as the flavors mature over time. Leftover cooked chicken can be refrigerated for up to 2 days or frozen for up to a month.

Yogurt-Marinated Chicken
IN A BLACK PEPPERCORN SAUCE

Chettinad Kozhi

Chettinad, a region in Tamil Nadu, in the southeast of India, is known not only for its fiery foods showered with black peppercorns, red chiles, tamarind, and coconut, but also for its inhabitants, the Tamil-speaking, industrious Chettiars: bankers and businessmen, many of whom traveled to what were then called Ceylon and Burma during the 19th and 20th centuries to conduct commerce. This is a classic curry of the Chettiar community. Savor it over a mound of steamed white rice to absorb some of the curry's heat. **SERVES 6**

2 tablespoons yellow split peas (chana dal),
    picked over for stones
½ cup plain yogurt
2 teaspoons black peppercorns
1½ teaspoons coarse kosher or sea salt
¼ teaspoon ground turmeric
6 medium-size cloves garlic
6 green or white cardamom pods
3 to 5 dried red Thai or cayenne chiles,
    to taste, stems removed
1 cinnamon stick (3 inches long), broken into
    smaller pieces
1 chicken (3½ pounds), skin removed,
    cut into 8 pieces (see box, page 121)
2 tablespoons canola oil
1 teaspoon black or yellow mustard seeds

1 small red onion, cut in half lengthwise and
　　thinly sliced
12 to 15 medium-size to large fresh curry leaves
2 fresh green Thai, cayenne, or serrano chiles,
　　stems removed, cut in half lengthwise
　　(do not remove the seeds)
1 teaspoon tamarind paste or concentrate
½ cup shredded fresh coconut; or ¼ cup shredded
　　dried unsweetened coconut, reconstituted
　　(see Note)

1. Preheat a small skillet over medium-high heat. Add the split peas and cook, stirring them constantly or shaking the skillet every few seconds, until they are reddish brown in patches and smell nutty, 2 to 3 minutes. (They will not be evenly brown because there is no oil to coat them and provide a uniform heating surface.)

2. Transfer the toasted split peas to a blender jar, and add the yogurt, peppercorns, salt, turmeric, garlic, cardamom pods, dried chiles, and cinnamon stick. Puree, scraping the inside of the jar as needed, to make a sun-yellow marinade, mottled with black and red speckles.

3. Arrange the chicken pieces in a single layer in a baking dish, and spread the marinade over them, making sure you coat the meat completely. Refrigerate, covered, for at least 1 hour or as long as overnight, to allow the spices to permeate the meat.

4. Heat the oil in a large skillet over medium-high heat. Add the mustard seeds, cover the skillet, and cook until the seeds have stopped popping (not unlike popcorn), about 30 seconds. Then uncover the skillet, lower the heat to medium, and add the onion, curry leaves, and fresh chiles. Cook, stirring, until the onion is light purple-brown around the edges, 6 to 10 minutes.

5. Add the chicken pieces, marinade and all, meat side down. Sear until the pieces are light brown on both sides, about 5 minutes per side.

6. While the meat is searing, combine the tamarind paste with 1 cup water in a small bowl, and stir to dissolve the paste. Pour this murky brown water over the chicken and allow it to pool around the meat. Turn the chicken so it is meat side down, cover the skillet, and simmer, basting occasionally with the thin curry, until the meat in the thickest parts of the chicken is no longer pink and the juices run clear, 15 to 20 minutes. Remove the chicken and arrange it on a serving platter.

7. Raise the heat to medium-high and simmer the sauce, uncovered, stirring it occasionally, until it has thickened, 3 to 5 minutes. Then stir in the coconut, pour the sauce over the chicken, and serve.

Note: To reconstitute coconut, cover with ¼ cup boiling water, set aside for about 15 minutes, and then drain.

Almond Chicken
WITH A YOGURT-MINT SAUCE

dahi pudhina murghi

for a simple dinner, serve this curry with either white rice or nutty red rice (page 708). I love the burst of fresh mint with the initial mouthful, and equally relish the gentle cayenne burn as it slides down smooth and easy, thanks to the tart yogurt. **SERVES 4**

½ cup plain yogurt

¼ cup slivered blanched almonds

8 large cloves garlic

3 lengthwise slices fresh ginger (each 2 inches long,
   1 inch wide, and ⅛ inch thick)

1 tablespoon coriander seeds

2 teaspoons black or yellow mustard seeds

1 teaspoon fennel seeds

2 teaspoons coarse kosher or sea salt

1 teaspoon cayenne (ground red pepper)

¼ cup finely chopped fresh cilantro leaves
   and tender stems

1 chicken (3½ pounds), skin removed, cut into 8 pieces
   (see box, page 121)

2 tablespoons canola oil

1 medium-size red onion, cut in half lengthwise
   and thinly sliced

2 fresh or dried bay leaves

½ cup firmly packed fresh mint leaves, finely chopped

1. Pour the yogurt into a blender jar, and then add the almonds, garlic, and ginger. Puree, scraping the inside of the jar as needed, to make a slightly gritty, tart-tasting marinade. Pour this into a medium-size bowl.

2. Combine the coriander, mustard, and fennel seeds in a spice grinder, and pulverize until the blend has the texture of finely ground black pepper. Stir this into the yogurt mixture, along with the salt, cayenne, and cilantro. Add the chicken pieces to the marinade and turn them to make sure they are well coated. Refrigerate, covered, for at least 2 hours or as long as overnight, to allow the flavors to permeate the meat.

3. Heat the oil in a large skillet over medium-high heat. Lift the chicken pieces out of the marinade, reserving whatever liquid is left, and place them, meat side down, in the skillet. Cook until the pieces are light brown, 3 to 5 minutes. Turn the chicken over and brown the other side, 3 to 5 minutes. Transfer the chicken to a plate.

4. Add the onion and the bay leaves to the skillet and cook, stirring and scraping the bottom to deglaze it, releasing any brown bits of chicken. Pour ½ cup water into the skillet, along with the reserved marinade. Bring to a boil, and scrape up any remaining browned bits of meat. Return the chicken to the skillet, meat side down, and pile the onion slices over the pieces to blanket them.

5. Once the curry comes to a boil, reduce the heat to medium-low, cover, and simmer, basting the chicken frequently, until the meat in the thickest parts is no longer pink inside and the juices run clear, 15 to 20 minutes.

6. Transfer the chicken to a serving platter. Stir the mint into the sauce. If the sauce is not thick enough, crank up the heat to medium-high and simmer it, uncovered, stirring occasionally, until the curry is thick, 3 to 5 minutes.

7. Pour the sauce over the chicken, and serve.

Roasted Cashew Chicken
WITH A FENUGREEK SAUCE

kaaju methi murghi

This velvety-smooth sauce is a winning combination of the sweetness of roasted cashews and the perfumed bitterness of fenugreek leaves. Serve the chicken with a bowl of steamed basmati rice for a comforting meal. **SERVES 6**

4 tablespoons canola oil

I medium-size red onion, cut in half lengthwise and
thinly sliced

¼ cup raw cashew nuts

I teaspoon cumin seeds

½ teaspoon whole cloves

¼ teaspoon cardamom seeds from green or white pods

2 fresh green Thai, cayenne, or serrano chiles,
stems removed, coarsely chopped
(do not remove the seeds)

I cinnamon stick (3 inches long), broken into smaller
pieces

I chicken (3½ pounds), skin removed, cut into 8 pieces
(see box, page 121; see also Tips)

1½ teaspoons coarse kosher or sea salt

¼ teaspoon ground turmeric

½ cup chopped fresh or frozen fenugreek leaves
(thawed if frozen); or 2 tablespoons dried fenugreek
leaves, soaked in a bowl of water and skimmed off
before use (see box, page 473)

1. Heat 2 tablespoons of the oil in a Dutch oven over
medium-high heat. Add the onion, cashews, cumin
seeds, cloves, cardamom seeds, chiles, and cinnamon
stick, and stir-fry until the onion slices are brown, the
cashews turn dark brown, and the spices smell fragrant,
4 to 6 minutes. Remove the pan from the heat.

2. Pour ½ cup water into a blender jar, and then add
the caramelized onion mixture. Puree, scraping the
inside of the jar as needed, to make a smooth, light
purple sauce.

3. Heat the remaining 2 tablespoons oil in the same
pan over medium heat. Add the chicken pieces in a single layer (it will be a tight squeeze). Cook, turning the
pieces every 2 minutes, until they are evenly browned,
5 to 7 minutes.

4. Add the onion sauce to the chicken. Wash out

the blender jar with ¼ cup water, and add this to the
pan. Stir in the salt, turmeric, and fenugreek. Stir the
chicken pieces, coating them evenly with the green-
speckled sauce and scraping up any browned bits on
the bottom of the pan. Reduce the heat to medium-low,
cover, and simmer, turning the chicken occasionally,
until the meat in the thickest parts is no longer pink
inside and the juices run clear, 15 to 20 minutes.

5. Transfer the chicken to a serving platter. Pour the
sauce over the chicken and serve.

Tips:

❖ You can use boneless, skinless chicken breasts as
an alternative, but watch the cooking time closely
because they will cook much faster (usually in less
than 10 minutes, including the browning stage).

❖ Even though bunches of fresh fenugreek leaves may
not be a common sight, even in the produce section
of Indian grocery stores, the chopped frozen ones
are readily available. Manufacturers freeze them in
square blocks (akin to large ice cubes). Two of these
blocks, when thawed, will yield ½ cup fragrant leaves.

Creamy Chicken
WITH KASHMIRI CHILES AND FENNEL

kashmiri Mirchi Waale Murghi

Everyday Kashmiri cooking is neither
complex nor time-consuming. Mustard
oil, black cardamom, black cumin, and
the omnipresent vermilion-red Kashmiri chiles
(colorful but not hot) make their presence
in just about every dish to weave in pungent,

smoky, and sweet flavors. This dish is quite mild, made creamier by the milk solids, an ingredient that is very easy to make but does require a little time. I often make a large batch of milk solids and freeze them; then I can thaw them out at a moment's notice to add depth to many of this region's curries.

I like to complement this curry's mellow presence with the slap-in-your-face, potent Skinned Split Black Lentils with Chiles and Black Pepper (page 369). White basmati rice will soak up those antithetical sauces. **SERVES 4**

2 tablespoons Ginger Paste (page 15)

2 tablespoons Garlic Paste (page 15)

2 teaspoons ground Kashmiri chiles; or
    ½ teaspoon cayenne (ground red pepper)
    mixed with 1½ teaspoons sweet paprika

1 chicken (3½ pounds), skin removed,
    cut into 8 pieces (see box, page 121)

4 tablespoons mustard oil or canola oil

1 teaspoon black cumin seeds (see Tips)

1 teaspoon fennel seeds

2 black cardamom pods (see Tips)

1 large red onion, cut in half lengthwise and
    thinly sliced

1½ teaspoons coarse kosher or sea salt

¼ cup Whole Milk Solids (page 24) or
    heavy (whipping) cream

1. Combine the Ginger Paste, Garlic Paste, and Kashmiri chiles in a medium-size bowl, and mix well. Add the chicken pieces and turn them to make sure they get well coated with the mixture. Refrigerate, covered, for at least 30 minutes or as long as overnight, to allow the flavors to permeate the meat.

2. Heat 2 tablespoons of the oil in a large saucepan or Dutch oven over medium-high heat. Sprinkle in the cumin seeds, fennel seeds, and cardamom pods, and allow the spices to sizzle and slightly sweeten the pungent mustard oil, 10 to 15 seconds.

3. Add the onion and stir-fry until it is honey-brown, about 5 minutes. Remove the onion slices, including any spices that cling to them, and pile them on a plate.

4. Heat the remaining 2 tablespoons oil in the same pan over medium heat. Add the chicken pieces in a single layer. Cook until they are browned all over, 2 to 3 minutes on each side. Transfer the chicken to a plate.

5. Pour 1 cup water into the pan, and scrape the bottom to deglaze it, releasing the collected bits of spice and meat; the liquid will turn into a reddish-orange broth. Stir in the salt.

black cumin seeds? See the Glossary of Ingredients, page 758.

6. Return the chicken and the spiced onion to the pan. Cook, covered, basting the chicken occasionally with the broth, until the meat in the thickest parts of the chicken pieces is no longer pink inside and the juices run clear, 18 to 20 minutes. Remove the chicken and arrange it on a serving platter.

7. Raise the heat to medium-high and simmer the sauce vigorously, uncovered, stirring occasionally, until the curry is gravy-thick, 3 to 5 minutes. Then stir in the milk solids and allow them to warm, about 2 minutes. The sauce will be creamy but curdled-looking.

8. Pour the sauce over the chicken pieces, and serve.

Tips:

❖ Black cumin yields a musky, smoky flavor to the curry. If it's unavailable, use the more common grayish variety.

❖ I often remove the cardamom pods before I serve them to my non-Indian guests. Biting into one of the pods can overpower the taste buds and make for an unpleasant experience. We Indians of course know not to eat them, and set them aside should they land on our plate.

Mangalorean Chicken Curry
WITH TAMARIND AND COCONUT MILK

kori gassi

thick, coconut milk–based curries from Mangalore, in southwestern India are called *gassis*. They are made tart with tamarind and are spiced with roasted assertive spices like chiles, fenugreek, and peppercorns. This classic curry incorporates poultry, but fish and other meats are also fair game. Two forms of coconut, one as shreds, the other its milk, surprisingly do not overpower the curry, so any of you coconut-phobes out there, go ahead and indulge in this. Mound it over red or white rice. **SERVES 6**

¼ cup shredded dried unsweetened coconut

1 tablespoon coriander seeds

1 tablespoon white poppy seeds

1 teaspoon black or yellow mustard seeds

1 teaspoon fenugreek seeds

1 teaspoon black peppercorns

4 to 6 dried red Thai or cayenne chiles,
    to taste, stems removed

1 teaspoon plus 2 tablespoons canola oil

1 large red onion, cut in half lengthwise and
    thinly sliced

6 large cloves garlic, finely chopped

1 chicken (3½ pounds), skin removed,
    cut into 8 pieces (see box, page 121)

1 cup unsweetened coconut milk

1 teaspoon tamarind paste or concentrate

1½ teaspoons coarse kosher or sea salt

12 to 15 medium-size to large fresh curry leaves

1. Combine the coconut, coriander seeds, poppy seeds, mustard seeds, fenugreek seeds, peppercorns, and chiles in a small bowl and drizzle the 1 teaspoon oil over them. Stir well to make sure the spices get well coated (to try to do this in a skillet may not be the best way).

2. Preheat a large skillet over medium-high heat. Add the oil-coated spices and cook, stirring them constantly to prevent them from burning, until the coconut turns reddish brown, the chiles blacken slightly, and most of the remaining spices turn reddish brown, 1 to 2 minutes. Scrape this mixture into a blender jar.

3. While the skillet is still hot, drizzle in the remaining 2 tablespoons oil, which will instantly heat up and appear to shimmer. Add the onion and garlic, and stir to coat them with the oil. Lower the heat to medium, cover the skillet, and cook, stirring occasionally, as the vegetables initially sweat and release their moisture, and once that evaporates, start to brown and soften, 15 to 20 minutes.

4. While the onion and garlic are cooking, add ¼ cup water to the roasted spices that are waiting patiently in the blender jar. Puree, scraping the inside of the jar as needed, to make a thick, slightly gritty paste. With the blender running, drizzle in another ¼ cup water and grind the paste to a smoother consistency. (If you pour the entire ½ cup water

White poppy seeds? Fresh curry leaves? See the Glossary of Ingredients, page 758.

in at once, the spices will be swimming in too much liquid and the blender won't be able to grind the ingredients.)

5. Once the onion and garlic have browned, push them to the sides of the skillet to make room for the chicken pieces. Add the chicken, meat side down. Pile the onion mixture on top of the chicken to blanket the pieces, cover the skillet, and cook until the chicken is browned, 5 to 7 minutes on each side.

6. Push the chicken and onion to the sidelines (or transfer them to a plate for the moment if the skillet is too crowded), and add the spice paste to the skillet. Pour the coconut milk into the blender jar, swish it around to wash the inside, and add the washings to the skillet. Stir in the tamarind paste, salt, and curry leaves. Scrape the bottom of the skillet to deglaze it, releasing any browned bits of chicken and onion.

7. Bring the chicken and onion back into the lime-light, in the center of the skillet. Tilt the skillet to scoop the sauce into a spoon, and baste the chicken. Cover the skillet and simmer, basting the chicken occasionally, until the meat in the thickest parts is no longer pink inside and the juices run clear, 15 to 20 minutes. Remove the chicken pieces from the skillet and arrange them on a serving platter.

8. Continue to simmer the sauce vigorously, uncovered, stirring occasionally, until the curry is gravy-thick, 5 to 8 minutes.

9. Pour the sauce over the chicken, and serve.

> Jaggery? See the Glossary of Ingredients, page 758.

Apricot Chicken
WITH POTATO STRAWS

Murghi Jardaloo

A tradition in the Parsi community of Mumbai, this recipe uses apricots, an ingredient that reveals the Parsis' Persian roots, combined with cloyingly sweet jaggery and pungent chiles, ingredients that reflect the cooking of the community they now live in. Top it off with crunchy shoestring-thin potatoes, and you have a texturally pleasing and highly complex-tasting curry. **SERVES 6**

8 to 10 dried apricots

½ cup boiling water

2 tablespoons Ghee (page 21) or canola oil

1 medium-size red onion, cut in half lengthwise
    and thinly sliced

4 lengthwise slices fresh ginger (each 1½ inches
    long, 1 inch wide, and ⅛ inch thick), cut into
    matchstick-thin strips (julienne)

4 medium-size cloves garlic, thinly sliced

4 fresh green Thai, cayenne, or serrano chiles,
    stems removed, cut crosswise into ¼-inch-
    thick slices (do not remove the seeds)

1 chicken (3½ pounds), skin removed,
    cut into 8 pieces (see box, page 121)

1 tablespoon Bin bhuna hua garam masala
    (page 30)

2 teaspoons coarse kosher or sea salt

¼ cup distilled white vinegar

2 tablespoons crumbled or chopped jaggery or
    firmly packed dark brown sugar

2 cups Matchstick-Thin Fried Potatoes
   (page 41; see Tip)
2 tablespoons finely chopped fresh cilantro leaves
   and tender stems for garnishing

1. Place the apricots in a small heatproof bowl, add the boiling water, and set it aside to allow the apricots to soften.

2. Meanwhile, heat the ghee in a large saucepan over medium-high heat. Add the onion, ginger, garlic, and chiles and cook, stirring, until they turn light brown around the edges, 5 to 8 minutes.

3. Add the chicken, garam masala, and salt. Allow the meat to brown lightly and the spices to cook gently without burning, turning the chicken frequently to ensure even browning, 5 to 8 minutes.

4. Add the softened apricots along with their soaking water. Stir in the vinegar and jaggery. Scrape the bottom of the skillet to deglaze it, releasing any browned bits of onion, spice, and chicken, and stir to incorporate those intense flavors into the curry. Once it comes to a boil, reduce the heat to medium-low, cover the skillet, and simmer, turning the chicken occasionally and basting it with the sauce, until the meat in the thickest parts is no longer pink inside and the juices run clear, 20 to 25 minutes.

5. Transfer the chicken pieces to a serving platter, and pour the sweet-hot sauce over them. Top with the fried potatoes and cilantro, and serve.

Tip: I know it's not the real deal, but if you don't wish to make your own matchstick-thin fried potatoes, sneak in a can of shoestring potatoes from the snack aisle of your neighborhood supermarket to top off the curry. I won't tell if you won't.

Stewed Chicken
WITH BROWNED ONION AND FRESH POMEGRANATE

Murghi Anardana

I often talk about ingredients like tamarind, mango powder, or lime juice that infuse tartness into a curry to provide a crucial balance and cut down the heat from chiles. That's exactly what the fresh, juicy, tart-sweet pomegranate does to this sauce, and in addition, it studs it with its ruby-red luminescence to make for a stunning presentation. During the months when pomegranates are not in season, I have made this with fresh tart cherries, pitted and cut in half. **SERVES 6**

1 tablespoon Ginger Paste (page 15)
1 tablespoon Garlic Paste (page 15)
1 chicken (3½ pounds), skin removed,
   cut into 8 pieces (see box, page 121)
2 tablespoons canola oil
6 whole cloves
2 cinnamon sticks (each 3 inches long)
2 black, green, or white cardamom pods
2 fresh or dried bay leaves
1 medium-size red onion, cut in half
   lengthwise and thinly sliced
1 cup half-and-half
2 teaspoons Rajasthani garam masala
   (page 26)
1 teaspoon coarse kosher or sea salt
2 tablespoons finely chopped fresh cilantro
   leaves and tender stems
1 medium-size fresh pomegranate, seeds separated
   from the flesh (see box, page 106)

1. Combine the ginger and garlic pastes in a small bowl. Smear a little of this mixture evenly over both sides of each piece of chicken. Refrigerate, covered, for 30 minutes or as long as overnight, to allow the flavors to permeate the chicken.

2. Heat the oil in a large skillet over medium heat. Once the oil appears to shimmer, sprinkle in the cloves, cinnamon sticks, cardamom pods, and bay leaves. Cook until they sizzle and perfume the oil, about 1 minute. Then add the onion and cook, uncovered, stirring frequently, until it softens and then turns brown with a light purple hue, 10 to 15 minutes.

3. Once the onion has browned, push it to the side in the skillet and add the chicken pieces, meat side down. Pile the onion over the chicken to blanket the pieces, cover the skillet, and cook until the chicken has browned on the underside, 5 to 7 minutes. Turn the chicken pieces over and cook for another 5 to 7 minutes. Transfer the chicken to a plate.

4. Pour a little of the half-and-half into the skillet and deglaze it, scraping up any browned bits of meat and onion. Then add the rest of the half-and-half. Stir in the garam masala and salt. The sauce will turn a light reddish brown with specks of green, thanks to the dried mint in the masala.

5. Return the chicken, meat side down, to the skillet, and add any juices that pooled in the plate. Spoon the creamy sauce over the chicken pieces. Reduce the heat to medium-low, cover the skillet, and simmer, turning the pieces over once and basting them occasionally, until the meat in the thickest parts is no longer pink inside and the juices run clear, 15 to 20 minutes. Remove the chicken and arrange it on a serving platter.

6. Stir the cilantro and pomegranate seeds into the sauce. Raise the heat to medium and simmer the sauce vigorously, uncovered, stirring occasionally, until the curry is gravy-thick, 3 to 5 minutes.

7. Remove and discard the cardamom pods, bay leaves, cinnamon sticks, and if you can find them, the cloves. Pour the ruby-studded, creamy sauce over the chicken pieces, and serve.

Razia Syed's Chicken
WITH AN ALMOND YOGURT SAUCE

Murghi Korma

Razia sat next to her highly successful executive husband, Badruddin Syed, on the couch in their modern, well-furnished home in Bangalore, India's Silicon Valley. She was demure, not sure what to think of this man with a thick American accent who was probing her with questions about her culinary upbringing in a traditional Lucknowi home. She kept looking at her husband with questioning eyes, but once she was comfortable that I could speak her "lingo," she opened up to share some incredible curries with me. Razia's memories and recipes filled my diary's pages with nut-based kormas, thinly sliced tender cuts of meats called *pasandas*, and richly layered rice *biryanis* perfumed with screw-pine extract—all hallmarks of the meat-heavy Lucknowi cuisine from north central India. Here is her chicken korma: tender cooked pieces of bone-in chicken covered with a red-hued, light brown nutty sauce that brims with aromatic spices. **SERVES 4**

¼ cup plain yogurt

2 tablespoons Ginger Paste (page 15)

I tablespoon Garlic Paste (page 15)

I chicken (3½ pounds), skin removed, cut into
    8 pieces (see box, page 121)

2 tablespoons canola oil

½ teaspoon whole cloves

½ teaspoon black peppercorns

6 green or white cardamom pods

3 black cardamom pods

3 cinnamon sticks (each 3 inches long)

2 fresh or dried bay leaves

I medium-size red onion, cut in half lengthwise
    and thinly sliced

½ cup slivered blanched almonds

1½ teaspoons coarse kosher or sea salt

½ teaspoon cayenne (ground red pepper)

2 tablespoons finely chopped fresh cilantro leaves
    and tender stems for garnishing

1. Combine the yogurt, Ginger Paste, and Garlic Paste in a small bowl, and blend well. Place the chicken pieces in a baking dish and smear the mixture over them, covering all sides. Refrigerate, covered, for at least 1 hour or as long as overnight, to allow the chicken to tenderize and acquire the flavors.

2. Heat the oil in a large skillet over medium-high heat. Sprinkle in the cloves, peppercorns, green and black cardamom pods, cinnamon sticks, and bay leaves. Cook until they sizzle and smell aromatic, 1 to 2 minutes.

3. Add the onion and cook until it is light brown around the edges, 5 to 7 minutes. Transfer the onion and all the spices to a blender jar and pour in 1 cup water. Add the almonds, salt, and cayenne. Puree, scraping the inside of the jar as needed, to make a light purple, gritty paste, speckled brown with spices.

4. Place the chicken, including any marinade, in the skillet and cook over medium-high heat until the meat is lightly browned, 4 to 6 minutes on each side.

5. Add the onion paste to the skillet. Pour ½ cup water into the blender jar and wash out the remaining paste; add this to the skillet. Make sure the chicken is blanketed under the rich-tasting sauce. Once it starts to bubble, mud-bath-like, reduce the heat to medium-low and cover the skillet. Cook, turning the chicken pieces to keep them evenly basted with the sauce, until the meat in the thickest parts of the chicken pieces is no longer pink inside and the juices run clear, 15 to 20 minutes.

6. If you wish, remove the cinnamon sticks, bay leaves, cardamom pods, and cloves. Sprinkle the cilantro over the curry, and serve.

Ginger Chicken
WITH PEANUTS AND COCONUT

Murghi Ni Curry

this is a version of a recipe from a dear family friend, Perin Irani, who is a colleague of my sister Lalitha. Perin has a strong presence that fills any room she is in with enthusiasm, and she is as passionate about food as she was about her work as an ob/gyn specialist in the Parsi community of Mumbai (she is now retired). The Parsis trace their roots back to a group of Persians who fled Iran when the Islamic powers took over, because they wanted to protect their religion, which is based on the teachings of Zoroaster, worshiper of the sacred fire. Zoroastrians, later known as Parsis, eventually settled in Mumbai and Navsari (Gujarat). Their food habits and religious backgrounds are an interesting blend of their roots (Iran) and influences from their migration (Gujarat and Mumbai). **SERVES 4**

2 tablespoons Ginger Paste (page 15)

1 tablespoon Garlic Paste (page 15)

1 chicken (3½ pounds), skin removed, cut into 8 pieces (see box, page 121)

2 tablespoons canola oil

¼ cup raw peanuts (without the skin)

1 tablespoon coriander seeds

3 to 5 dried red Thai or cayenne chiles, to taste, stems removed

½ cup shredded fresh coconut; or ¼ cup shredded dried unsweetened coconut reconstituted (see Note)

1 can (14.5 ounces) diced tomatoes

2 teaspoons coarse kosher or sea salt

2 tablespoons finely chopped fresh cilantro leaves and tender stems

1. Combine the ginger and garlic pastes in a small bowl, and blend well. Smear the paste over the chicken pieces, covering all sides.

2. Heat the oil in a large skillet over medium heat. Add the chicken, including any residual paste, and immediately cover the skillet to contain the splattering. Cook, covered, turning the chicken pieces occasionally, until they are evenly browned, 5 to 7 minutes.

3. While the chicken is searing, preheat a small skillet over medium-high heat. Toss in the peanuts, coriander seeds, and chiles. Toast, stirring constantly, until the peanuts turn patchy brown and slightly glistening (from the oil they release), the coriander turns reddish brown, and the chiles blacken, 2 to 3 minutes. Immediately transfer the nutty-smelling mixture to a blender jar. (The longer the ingredients sit in the hot skillet, the more they will burn, making them unpalatable.) Pour in ¼ cup water, and add the coconut. Puree, scraping the inside of the jar as needed, to make a paste.

4. Spread this paste over the chicken, making sure you use every last bit of it. Add the tomatoes, with their liquid, and the salt. Lift the chicken pieces and allow the chunky sauce to run under them and deglaze the skillet. Reduce the heat to medium-low, cover, and simmer, basting the chicken every few minutes, until the meat in the thickest parts of the chicken pieces is no longer pink inside and the juices run clear, 18 to 20 minutes. Remove the chicken from the skillet and arrange it on a serving platter.

5. Stir the cilantro into the sauce and raise the heat to medium. Simmer the sauce vigorously, uncovered, stirring occasionally, until it is gravy-thick, 5 to 8 minutes.

6. Pour the sauce over the chicken, and serve.

Note: To reconsitute coconut, cover with ¼ cup boiling water, set aside for about 15 minutes, and then drain.

Fennel-Kissed Chicken
SIMMERED IN A GINGER–POPPY SEED SAUCE

Murghi Poshto

I like to serve this Bengali curry with Bengal's well-kept secret, a short-grain rice known as *Govindo bhog*, which has a sweetish flavor and slightly starchy appearance (see page 708). Indian stores carry this variety of rice, as do some specialty gourmet stores and mail-order sources. The creamy-tasting rice offsets the assertive curry's gusto to create a balanced meal. **SERVES 6**

- ¼ cup plus 1 tablespoon mustard oil or canola oil (see Tips)
- ¼ cup coarsely chopped fresh ginger
- 2 teaspoons fennel seeds
- 1½ teaspoons coarse kosher or sea salt
- 10 medium-size cloves garlic
- 3 to 5 dried red Thai or cayenne chiles, to taste, stems removed
- 1 chicken (3½ pounds), chicken skin removed, cut into 8 pieces (see box, page 121)
- ¼ cup heavy (whipping) cream
- 2 tablespoons white poppy seeds, toasted (see Tips)

1. Pour the ¼ cup oil into a blender jar, followed by ¼ cup water and the ginger, fennel seeds, salt, garlic, and chiles. Puree, scraping the inside of the jar as needed, to make a potent-smelling, pungent-tasting, yellowish cream-colored marinade speckled with flecks of red chiles and light green bits of fennel.

2. Place the chicken pieces in a medium-size bowl, pour the marinade over them, and turn the chicken to coat it well. Refrigerate, covered, for at least 30 minutes or as long as overnight, to allow the flavors to permeate the meat.

3. Heat the remaining 1 tablespoon oil in a large skillet over medium-high heat. Arrange the chicken pieces, marinade and all, in a single layer in the skillet. Cook until the underside is light brown, 5 to 7 minutes. Turn the chicken over and brown the other side, 5 to 7 minutes. There will be bits of the meat sticking to the skillet. Transfer the chicken pieces to a plate.

4. Pour about ¼ cup water into the skillet and scrape the bottom to deglaze it, loosening the browned bits of meat and spices. Once you have deglazed the pan, stir in ¾ cup water (if you were to have poured all the water in at once, deglazing the pan would be messy), the cream, and the poppy seeds. Return the chicken to the skillet, and arrange it meat side down. Spoon some of the thin sauce over the chicken. Reduce the heat to medium-low, cover, and simmer, basting the chicken every few minutes, until the meat in the thickest is no longer pink inside and the juices run clear, 20 to 25 minutes. Lift the chicken pieces out of the skillet and arrange them, meat side up, on a serving platter.

5. Raise the heat to medium-high and boil the sauce vigorously, uncovered, stirring occasionally, until it thickens to a gravy consistency, 3 to 5 minutes.

6. Pour the sauce over the chicken, and serve.

Tips:

❖ If you make that trip to the Indian grocery store, make sure you stock up on mustard oil, since it contributes an earthy bitterness along with an underlying sweetness. Its amber color also provides the marinade's yellowish tone. If you decide to use canola oil, add 1 tablespoon prepared mustard (such as Dijon) to the blender when you prepare the marinade, to approximate the flavor and color of mustard oil.

❖ To toast poppy seeds, preheat a small skillet over medium-high heat. Sprinkle in the seeds and toast them, shaking the skillet very often to keep them moving as they crackle and brown evenly; this takes about 1 minute. Immediately transfer them to a plate to cool (they will continue to burn if they remain in the hot skillet).

Chicken
SIMMERED IN A COCONUT MILK– VINEGAR SAUCE

Murghi Vindaloo

If you have 1 million Portuguese Goans cooking vindaloos, chances are you will be able to sample 1 million versions of this famous curry, should you be fortunate enough to live that long. I love the inclusion of Kashmiri chiles; their vibrant red color and mellow flavor make for a mighty tasty, good-looking sauce. The Goan Christians don't use coconut milk in their cooking, but the Hindu Konkan locals do, and I do love its effect on the vinegar. **SERVES 4**

2 tablespoons canola oil

I medium-size red onion, cut in half lengthwise and thinly sliced

I chicken (3½ pounds), skin removed, cut into 8 pieces (see box, page 121)

¼ cup distilled white vinegar

I tablespoon Garlic Paste (page 15)

I tablespoon coriander seeds, ground

2 teaspoons cumin seeds, ground

I teaspoon cayenne (ground red pepper)

I teaspoon ground Kashmiri chiles; or ¼ teaspoon cayenne (ground red pepper) mixed with ¾ teaspoon sweet paprika

I teaspoon coarse kosher or sea salt

¼ teaspoon ground turmeric

I cup unsweetened coconut milk

1. Heat the oil in a large skillet over medium-high heat. Add the onion and cook, stirring, until it is light brown around the edges, about 5 minutes.

2. Lower the heat to medium and add the chicken pieces, meat side down. Cook until they have browned, 2 to 3 minutes per side. Transfer the chicken and onion to a plate.

3. Pour the vinegar into the skillet, and add the Garlic Paste, coriander, cumin, cayenne, Kashmiri chiles, salt, and turmeric. Scrape the bottom of the skillet to deglaze it, releasing any browned bits of onion and meat; this will incorporate a rich flavor and color into the sauce. Reduce the heat to medium-low, cover, and simmer the sauce, stirring occasionally, until some of the oil, now a deep vermilion-red color, starts to separate around the edges of the skillet and on the surface, 5 to 6 minutes.

4. Stir in the coconut milk, and return the chicken to the skillet. Cook, covered, stirring and basting occasionally, until the meat in the thickest parts of the chicken is no longer pink inside and the juices run clear, 18 to 20 minutes. Transfer the chicken to a serving platter.

5. Raise the heat to medium and simmer the sauce vigorously, uncovered, stirring occasionally, until the creamy, reddish-brown curry is gravy-thick, 5 to 8 minutes.

6. Pour the sauce over the chicken, and serve.

Tips:

❖ Bone-in pieces of chicken are commonly used in Indian curries. The marrow in the bone adds to the meat's juicy succulence. If you wish, you can use boneless pieces, but do make sure to decrease the cooking time by at least 50 percent. Dark meat is always gamier-tasting than white; either one will work for this curry.

❖ For a sweeter-tasting sauce, use malt or cider vinegar instead of the distilled white variety.

❖ There is no need to grind the coriander and cumin seeds separately. Place them together in a spice grinder for a strongly aromatic blend. (I do, however, always recommend that my students grind them separately at first, so they can learn to recognize the difference between the two. One should be able to identify ground spices by smell alone—it's a great way to get acquainted with them and to appreciate their subtleties.)

Fresh curry leaves? See the Glossary of Ingredients, page 758.

Tart Chicken
WITH ROASTED CHILES, TAMARIND, AND COCONUT MILK

Puli Kozhi

The Moppalahs, inhabitants of the southwestern state of Kerala who follow the doctrines of the Islamic faith, consume chicken, mutton, fish, and other seafood as part of their special-occasion meals. This curry combines roasted and ground spices—a typically southern Indian technique—with coconut milk, the other Keralite staple, to provide the base for plump chicken. Serve it with the nutty and aromatic basmati rice *Kaaju badam chawal* (page 712) for a satisfying meal. **SERVES 6**

4 tablespoons canola oil
1 tablespoon yellow split peas (chana dal), picked over for stones
1 tablespoon coriander seeds
2 dried red Thai or cayenne chiles, stems removed
1 cup unsweetened coconut milk
2 teaspoons coarse kosher or sea salt
3 lengthwise slices fresh ginger (each 2½ inches long, 1 inch wide, and ⅛ inch thick)
4 large cloves garlic
1 chicken (3½ pounds), skin removed, cut into 8 pieces (see box, page 121)
1 medium-size red onion, cut in half lengthwise and thinly sliced
1 teaspoon tamarind paste or concentrate
12 to 15 medium-size to large fresh curry leaves
2 tablespoons finely chopped fresh cilantro leaves and tender stems

1. Heat 2 tablespoons of the oil in a large skillet over medium-high heat. Add the split peas, coriander seeds, and chiles, and roast the blend, stirring constantly, until the slit peas and coriander are reddish brown and the chiles have blackened slightly, 1 to 2 minutes. Remove the pan from the heat, and use a slotted spoon to skim off the spice blend and transfer it to a blender jar. Set the pan aside.

2. Add ½ cup of the coconut milk to the blender jar, along with the salt, ginger, and garlic. Puree, scraping the inside of the jar as needed, to form a smooth, creamy yellow, red-speckled paste.

3. Transfer the nutty-smelling marinade to a medium-size bowl. Add the chicken pieces and thoroughly coat them with the marinade. Refrigerate, covered, for at least 30 minutes or as long as overnight, to allow the flavors to liven up the chicken.

4. Add the remaining 2 tablespoons oil to the skillet containing the residual spiced oil, and heat it over medium-high heat. Add the onion and stir-fry until its edges are light brown, 3 to 5 minutes. Add the chicken pieces in a single layer, saving the residual marinade. Lower the heat to medium, and cook until the chicken is browned on the underside, 3 to 4 minutes. Turn

the pieces over and brown on the other side, 3 to 4 minutes.

5. Pour the reserved marinade into the skillet and add the remaining ½ cup coconut milk and the tamarind paste. Stir, making sure the tamarind is thoroughly mixed in with the liquid. Lift the chicken pieces to ensure that the sauce runs underneath. Scrape the bottom to deglaze the pan, releasing all the cooked-on chicken bits, spices, and onion. Reduce the heat to medium-low, cover the skillet, and braise the chicken, basting it occasionally and turning the pieces every few minutes, until the meat in the thickest parts is no longer pink inside and the juices run clear, 15 to 20 minutes. Remove the chicken and arrange it on a serving platter.

6. Stir the curry leaves and cilantro into the sauce and raise the heat to medium. Simmer vigorously, uncovered, stirring occasionally, until the curry is gravy-thick, 5 to 8 minutes.

7. Pour the sauce over the chicken, and serve.

Rock salt? See the *Glossary of Ingredients,* page 758.

Stewed Chicken
IN A MUSTARD GREENS–SPINACH SAUCE

Saag Murghi

Cooks in north Indian restaurants in the United States (and in many parts of the Western world) stew boneless pieces of chicken with pureed spinach, cream, and spices. I like to include mustard greens for a more complex-tasting sauce with a slightly bitter edge to it.

I leave the cream out to make sure the dish is not only healthier, but also an unusual one that you can enjoy frequently without guilt. Some naan (see page 729) would be just great with the meal. **SERVES 4**

½ cup plain yogurt
2 tablespoons finely chopped fresh cilantro
    leaves and tender stems
1 tablespoon coriander seeds, ground
1 teaspoon cumin seeds, ground
1 teaspoon cayenne (ground red pepper)
1 teaspoon coarse kosher or sea salt
¼ teaspoon ground turmeric
1 chicken (3½ pounds), skin removed,
    cut into 8 pieces (see box, page 121)
4 tablespoons canola oil
1 medium-size red onion, finely chopped
5 large cloves garlic, finely chopped
8 ounces fresh mustard greens, well rinsed
    and coarsely chopped (see Tip, page 606)
8 ounces fresh spinach leaves, well rinsed
    and coarsely chopped
1 teaspoon rock salt, pounded

1. Whisk the yogurt, cilantro, coriander, cumin, cayenne, kosher salt, and turmeric together in a small bowl. Place the chicken in a baking dish and coat the pieces well with the creamy marinade. Refrigerate, covered, for at least 1 hour or as long as overnight, for the flavors to permeate the meat.

2. Heat 2 tablespoons of the oil in a large skillet over medium-high heat. Add the chicken pieces, reserving any remaining marinade in the dish. Cook the chicken until light brown on both sides, about 5 minutes per side. Transfer the chicken pieces to a plate.

3. Pour the remaining 2 tablespoons oil into the skillet and heat it over medium-high heat. Add the onion and garlic. Stir, scraping the bottom of the skillet to deglaze it, releasing any browned bits of chicken and marinade. Reduce the heat to medium-low, cover the skillet, and cook, stirring occasionally, until the onion and garlic turn caramel brown and the onion acquires a deep purple hue, 15 to 20 minutes.

4. Add the mustard greens and spinach, a handful at a time, to the skillet, cover, and allow the steam to wilt them. Repeat until all the greens have been wilted. The water leached from the greens will deglaze the skillet to create a rich-tasting base for the chicken. Stir in the reserved marinade and ½ cup water. Cook, uncovered, stirring occasionally, to allow the greens to soften and the marinade to cook, 3 to 7 minutes.

5. Return the chicken to the skillet, meat side down, along with any liquid that pooled on the plate. Spoon greens and sauce over the chicken pieces to blanket them. Cover the skillet and simmer, basting the chicken occasionally, until the meat in the thickest parts is no longer pink inside and the juices run clear, 15 to 20 minutes. Remove the chicken and arrange it on a serving platter.

6. Carefully transfer the greens and any liquid in the skillet to a food processor, and process to create a slightly smoother-textured sauce. Spoon this sauce over the chicken, sprinkle with the rock salt, and serve.

Tip: Salt, when used the right way, can push a curry from being just okay to being sublime. When you add it at different cooking steps, it creates a layered effect. I love the initial burst of pounded rock salt that comes with each spoonful, followed by the subtle hint of the salt that the chicken absorbed from the marinade.

Vibrant Chicken
WITH A SPICY TOMATO SAUCE

tari Waali Murghi

Sometimes a new student will ask me to share a "basic chicken curry." They may as well ask me to come up with a peace plan for the Middle East! Curries are so dynamic that pinning down a fundamental sauce for the ubiquitous bird is truly not possible. Westerners often think of tomato-based dishes as essential curries, and maybe this recipe appeals to that perception. Whatever the reason, this deep red, full-bodied curry, delicious with bowls of steamed basmati rice, represents to many Westerners the quintessential northern Indian chicken curry. **SERVES 4**

¼ cup Ginger Paste (page 15)
2 tablespoons Garlic Paste (page 15)
1 chicken (3½ pounds), skin removed,
    cut into 8 pieces (see box, page 121)
2 tablespoons canola oil
1 can (14.5 ounces) tomato sauce
½ cup Fried Onion Paste (page 16)
1 tablespoon coriander seeds, ground
2 teaspoons sweet paprika
1½ teaspoons coarse kosher or sea salt
1 teaspoon cumin seeds, ground
½ teaspoon ground turmeric
½ teaspoon cayenne (ground red pepper)
2 tablespoons finely chopped fresh cilantro
    leaves and tender stems for garnishing

1. Combine the ginger and garlic pastes in a medium-size bowl, and mix well. Add the chicken pieces and smear them all over with the paste.

2. Heat the oil in a large skillet over medium-high heat. Add the chicken pieces, meat side down in a single layer, and cook until they are lightly browned, about 3 minutes. Turn the pieces over and cook on the other side until lightly browned, about 3 minutes. Transfer the chicken to a plate.

3. Add the tomato sauce, onion paste, coriander, paprika, salt, cumin, turmeric, and cayenne to the skillet. The sauce will immediately start to bubble and boil. Reduce the heat to medium-low, cover the skillet, and simmer, stirring occasionally, until a thin layer of oil separates from the sauce, forming a spice-colored film on the surface, 20 to 25 minutes.

4. Return the chicken pieces to the skillet and coat them with the sauce. Cook, covered, turning the chicken occasionally, until the meat in the thickest parts is no longer pink inside and the juices run clear, 20 to 25 minutes.

5. Serve the chicken with its vermilion-red sauce, sprinkled with the cilantro.

Coconut Chicken
WITH MUSTARD SEED

thenga kozhi

When you are faced with an abundance of coconut, a predicament (albeit a tasty one) common to many homes along India's coastlines, you find every possible excuse to incorporate them in spice blends, pastes, sauces, rice, desserts, seafood, and meats.

This mellow curry showcases the richness of fresh coconut with a hint of chiles rounded out by the other coastline favorite—tart, cooling tamarind.

SERVES 4

> 1 cup shredded fresh coconut; or ½ cup shredded dried unsweetened coconut, reconstituted (see Note)
> ¼ cup firmly packed fresh cilantro leaves and tender stems
> 1½ teaspoons coarse kosher or sea salt
> 1 teaspoon tamarind paste or concentrate
> 4 fresh green Thai, cayenne, or serrano chiles, stems removed
> 3 tablespoons canola oil
> 1 teaspoon black or yellow mustard seeds
> 1 chicken (3½ pounds), skin removed, cut into 8 pieces (see box, page 121)

1. Pour 1 cup water into a blender jar. Add the coconut, cilantro, salt, tamarind paste, and chiles, and puree, scraping the inside of the jar as necessary, to make a smooth but slightly gritty paste.

2. Heat the oil in a large skillet over medium-high heat. Add the mustard seeds, cover, and cook until the seeds have stopped popping (not unlike popcorn), about 30 seconds. Immediately add the chicken pieces, meat side down in a single layer, cover, and cook the chicken until the underside is golden brown, 3 to 5 minutes. Turn the pieces over, cover, and cook until the other side is golden brown, 3 to 5 minutes.

3. Pour the coconut sauce over the chicken pieces, making sure the sauce covers each piece in addition to forming a small pool under them. Lower the heat to medium and simmer, uncovered, turning the chicken occasionally and basting it every 3 to 4 minutes, for about 15 minutes. Then reduce the heat to medium-low, cover the skillet, and simmer until the meat in the thickest parts of the chicken is no longer pink inside and the juices run clear, 10 to 12 minutes.

4. Transfer the chicken to a serving platter, pour the sauce over them, and serve.

Note: To reconstitute coconut, cover with ½ cup boiling water, set aside for about 15 minutes, and then drain.

Chicken
WITH RED CHILES AND COCONUT MILK

thenga paal kozhi

Even though the chiles are potent, the vinegar and coconut milk in this dish bring it down many notches to make a hot, sweet, creamy curry. Ladle it over mounds of cooked red rice (page 708) for a down-home comfort, southern Indian-style. **SERVES 6**

¼ cup distilled white vinegar
1 teaspoon coarse kosher or sea salt
¼ teaspoon ground turmeric
1 small red onion, coarsely chopped
6 medium-size cloves garlic
3 dried red Thai or cayenne chiles, stems removed
1 chicken (3½ pounds), skin removed, cut into 8 pieces
  (see box, page 121)
2 tablespoons canola oil
¾ cup unsweetened coconut milk
1 can (14.5 ounces) diced tomato
¼ cup finely chopped fresh cilantro leaves
  and tender stems

1. Pour the vinegar into a blender jar, followed by the salt, turmeric, onion, garlic, and chiles. Puree, scraping the inside of the jar as needed, to make a smooth, yellow-hued, light purple marinade.

2. Place the chicken in a baking dish and spoon the marinade over it, turning the chicken pieces to coat them thoroughly. Refrigerate, covered, for at least 30 minutes or up to 2 hours, to allow the flavors to penetrate the meat. (Because vinegar is sharply acidic, you do not want to marinate the chicken for any longer because it might break down the meat's texture, rendering it unappetizing.)

3. Heat the oil in a large skillet over medium-high heat. Add the chicken, including the marinade, meat side down, in a single layer. Cook, allowing the meat to sear after some of the nose-tingling marinade boils off, until browned, 5 to 7 minutes. Turn the chicken over and brown on the other side, about 5 minutes.

4. Pour in the coconut milk and lift the chicken pieces slightly to allow it to coat the bottom of the skillet and to loosen the browned bits, deglazing the skillet. Add the diced tomatoes, with their juice, stirring to incorporate them into the curry. Once it comes to a boil, reduce the heat to medium-low, cover, and simmer, turning the chicken pieces occasionally and basting them every 3 to 4 minutes, until the meat in the thickest parts is no longer pink inside and the juices run clear, 20 to 25 minutes. Transfer the chicken to a serving platter.

5. Stir the cilantro into the sauce, raise the heat to medium, and simmer vigorously, uncovered, stirring occasionally, until the chunky, reddish-brown curry is slightly thick, 5 to 8 minutes.

6. Pour the sauce over the chicken, and serve.

Chicken
SIMMERED IN A PUMPKIN-LENTIL SAUCE WITH FENUGREEK

Murghi dhansaak

What gumbo is to a New Orleanean (if that's not a word, it should be), *dhansaak,* which means "grains and vegetables," is to a Parsi. There are *dhansaaks* with chicken, with mutton, or sometimes with fish— just ask Mrs. Medora, the mother of my friend and webmaster, Zubin. And yes, there is a version for vegetarians too.

This hearty rendition seems a perfect fit for a chilly wintry day, combining juicy-sweet pumpkin, aromatic mint, and headstrong fenugreek with the ubiquitous bird that will leave you clucking for more. Even though I recommend using a pressure cooker for cooking the legumes (see box, page 314), you can use a stockpot if you don't have one. You will have to cook the legumes longer, and they will also require an additional 1 to 2 cups water, until they are tender. **SERVES 8**

1 cup oily or unoily skinned split yellow pigeon
   peas, picked over for stones
4 cups cubed fresh red pumpkin
   (1-inch cubes; see Tips) or sweet potatoes
2 large red onions: 1 coarsely chopped,
   1 cut in half lengthwise and thinly sliced
¼ cup firmly packed fresh cilantro leaves
   and tender stems
¼ cup firmly packed fresh mint leaves
1 teaspoon ground turmeric
½ teaspoon cayenne (ground red pepper)

2 to 2½ pounds cut-up bone-in chicken,
   skin removed
4 tablespoons Ghee (page 21) or canola oil
4 cups loosely packed finely chopped fresh or
   frozen fenugreek leaves (thawed and
   drained if frozen; see Tips)
2 tablespoons Ginger Paste (page 15)
1 tablespoon Garlic Paste (page 15)
2 teaspoons Sambhar masala (page 33)
2 teaspoons coriander seeds, ground
1 teaspoon ground Kashmiri chiles; or
   ¼ teaspoon cayenne (ground red pepper)
   mixed with ¾ teaspoon sweet paprika
1 teaspoon English-Style Madras Curry Powder
   (page 24)
½ teaspoon cardamom seeds from black pods
½ teaspoon cardamom seeds from green or
   white pods
1 large tomato, cored and finely chopped
2 teaspoons coarse kosher or sea salt

1. Place the pigeon peas in a pressure cooker. Fill the cooker halfway with tap water and rinse the peas by rubbing them between your fingertips. The water may appear slightly dirty. Drain this water. Repeat three or four times, until the water is relatively clear; then drain. Add 3 cups water and bring to a boil, uncovered, over high heat. Skim off and discard any foam that rises to the surface. Stir in the pumpkin, chopped onion, cilantro, mint, turmeric, and cayenne. Seal the cooker shut and allow the pressure to build up. Once steam starts to escape from the regulating valve and the bell-shaped weight begins to jiggle or whistle, reduce the heat to medium-low and cook for about 15 minutes. Remove the cooker from the heat and allow the pressure to subside naturally, about 15 minutes, before opening the lid.

2. While the vegetables are pressure-cooking, place the chicken in a saucepan that is large enough to

accommodate the pieces without overcrowding. Add water to cover, and bring it to a boil over medium heat. If any foam forms on the surface, skim it off. Simmer the chicken, uncovered, until the meat in the thickest parts is no longer pink inside and the juices run clear, 15 to 20 minutes. Transfer the chicken pieces to a platter, reserving 1 cup of the broth. (Save the remaining broth for another use.)

3. Once the pressure cooker's lid is opened, coarsely mash the (already pulpy) lentils and pumpkin with the back of a spoon, or with a potato masher, to break down some of the larger pumpkin pieces.

4. Heat 2 tablespoons of the ghee in a medium-size skillet over medium heat. Add the sliced onion and stir-fry until it is soft and brown with a deep purple hue, 8 to 10 minutes. Add the onion to the lentil mixture.

5. Heat the remaining 2 tablespoons ghee in the same skillet over medium heat. Add the fenugreek leaves, ginger and garlic pastes, *sambhar masala*, coriander, Kashmiri chiles, curry powder, and both kinds of cardamom seeds. Cook, uncovered, stirring occasionally, until the fenugreek leaves appear olive green, about 5 minutes. Add this to the dal (the lentil mixture), along with the tomato, salt, chicken, and reserved 1 cup of broth. Bring the *dhansaak* to a simmer over medium heat and cook, uncovered, stirring occasionally, to allow the chicken to reheat and the flavors to blend, 8 to 10 minutes. Then serve.

Tips:

❖ There are so many varieties of pumpkin in the world that I cannot even begin to expound on them. One that is widely used in India we call *kaddu*—the orange-red pumpkin. We see them squatting in open fields just before Halloween. The seeds (once you get them disentangled from the weblike strands) are edible when toasted. The pumpkin's skin is very hard, typical of winter squash, and is best removed with a chef's knife. Canned pumpkin is not a good substitute because it is way overcooked and mushy. Use sweet potatoes instead.

❖ In recipes that call for fresh or frozen fenugreek leaves, I always suggest dried fenugreek as an alternative—except for this one. The fenugreek is a key flavor in this curry and I strongly suggest you make a trip out to that *desi* (our slang for "Indian or Pakistani") store to procure either fresh (seasonal) or frozen chopped (all year long) leaves. One 12-ounce bag of frozen chopped leaves will yield 4 loosely packed cups.

Bone-In Chicken
WITH SQUASH AND PICKLING SPICES

Achari Murghi

Indian pickles (*achar*) are very potent, packing assertive flavors in small bites. We never eat them as is; rather, we use them to enhance mellow-tasting foods like breads and rice. I have used some of the ingredients that go into pickling—mustard oil, ground mustard, fenugreek, cayenne pepper, turmeric—to enliven ho-hum Chicken Little in this dish. The squash in the curry adds juicy tenderness, and together the dish will keep you happy, even if the sky does fall. **SERVES 6**

¼ cup mustard oil or canola oil

2 tablespoons Ginger Paste (page 15)

1 tablespoon Garlic Paste (page 15)

1 tablespoon black or yellow mustard seeds, ground

1½ teaspoons fenugreek seeds, ground

1½ teaspoons coarse kosher or sea salt

1 teaspoon cayenne (ground red pepper)

½ teaspoon ground turmeric

1 chicken (3½ pounds), skin removed,
    cut into 8 pieces (see box, page 121)

1½ pounds bottle gourd squash
    (see Tip and box, page 596)

¼ cup finely chopped fresh cilantro leaves and
    tender stems

1. Thoroughly combine the oil, Ginger Paste, Garlic Paste, mustard, fenugreek, salt, cayenne, and turmeric in a medium-size bowl. Put the chicken pieces into the bowl and smear them well with the thick paste. Refrigerate, covered, for at least 1 hour or even overnight, to allow the flavors to permeate the flesh.

2. Cut off and discard the stem and heel ends of the squash. Peel the squash with a vegetable peeler, and then cut it in half lengthwise. Scoop out the seeds and the surrounding spongy mass, using with a spoon or melon baller, to create two firm-fleshed, pale green, squash "boats." Cut the squash into 1-inch pieces, and set aside.

3. Preheat a large skillet over medium heat. Add the chicken pieces, marinade and all, meat side down, in a single layer. Sear until the pieces are light brown, about 5 minutes. Turn the pieces over and sear the other side, about 5 minutes. Transfer the chicken to a plate.

4. Pour about ¼ cup water into the skillet and scrape the bottom to deglaze it, releasing the browned bits of meat and spice. Then stir in ¾ cup water, and add the squash. Return the chicken to the skillet, placing the pieces meat side down. Pour in any juices that accumulated in the plate. Tilt the skillet and spoon some of the thin sauce over the chicken. Then reduce the heat to medium-low, cover, and simmer, turning the pieces over once and repeating the basting, until the meat in the thickest parts is no longer pink inside and the juices run clear, 25 to 30 minutes. The squash should be fork-tender. Remove the chicken pieces and arrange them on a serving platter.

5. Raise the heat to medium-high and boil the sauce, uncovered, to thicken it, 5 to 8 minutes. Stir in the cilantro.

6. Spoon the sauce and squash over the chicken, and serve.

Tip: Yellow summer squash is an acceptable alternative to bottle gourd squash. There is no need to peel them, or to scoop out the seeds.

Yogurt-Almond Chicken
WITH A SPINACH SAUCE

badam murghi

The almonds here help to thicken the sauce as well as providing flavor. The number of chiles in the marinade might alarm you, but never fear: the same almonds come to the rescue to lower the chiles' capsaicin effect. **SERVES 6**

For the marinade:

1 cup plain yogurt

¼ cup slivered blanched almonds

6 lengthwise slices fresh ginger (each 1½ inches long, 1 inch wide, and ⅛ inch thick)

6 large cloves garlic

5 to 7 fresh green Thai, cayenne, or serrano chiles, to taste, stems removed

¼ cup finely chopped fresh cilantro leaves and tender stems

1 tablespoon coriander seeds, ground

2 teaspoons cumin seeds, ground

2 teaspoons coarse kosher or sea salt

½ teaspoon cardamom seeds from green or white pods, ground

½ teaspoon whole cloves, ground

1 chicken (3½ pounds), skin removed, cut into 8 pieces (see box, page 121)

4 tablespoons canola oil

1 medium-size red onion, cut in half lengthwise and thinly sliced

4 fresh or dried bay leaves

1 bag (5 ounces) fresh prewashed baby spinach leaves

1. To make the marinade, combine the yogurt, almonds, ginger, garlic, and chiles in a blender jar. Puree, scraping the inside of the jar as needed, to make a smooth, albeit slightly gritty, sauce. Transfer the contents to a medium-size bowl. Fold in the cilantro, coriander, cumin, salt, cardamom, and cloves to make a marinade freckled with dark brown spices.

2. Add the chicken pieces to the bowl and coat them well with the marinade. Refrigerate, covered, for at least 1 hour or as long as overnight.

3. Heat 2 tablespoons of the oil in a large skillet over medium-high heat. Add the onion and bay leaves, and cook, stirring, until the onion slices are soft and light brown around the edges, 3 to 4 minutes. Transfer the onion and bay leaves to a plate.

4. Pour the remaining 2 tablespoons oil into the same skillet. The skillet will still be hot enough for the oil to instantly heat up. Remove the chicken from the marinade (it's okay if some is still clinging to the pieces) and add it to the skillet, meat side down, in a single layer. Reserve the remaining marinade. Sear the meat until it is lightly browned, about 3 minutes. Turn the pieces over and sear the other side until lightly browned, about 3 minutes.

5. Spread the reserved marinade over the chicken, and add the cooked onion and ½ cup water. Lift the chicken pieces and allow the liquid to flow underneath them; it should deglaze the skillet, releasing any bits of browned chicken and spices. Reduce the heat to medium-low, cover, and braise the chicken, basting it with the sauce occasionally, until the meat in the thickest parts is no longer pink inside and the juices run clear, 25 to 30 minutes. Transfer the chicken and onions to a serving platter.

6. Raise the heat to medium-high and boil the sauce, uncovered, stirring occasionally, until it is slightly thickened, 5 to 8 minutes. Then stir the spinach, a handful at a time, into the sauce. Cook just until the leaves have wilted, 1 to 2 minutes.

7. Spoon the spinach sauce over the chicken pieces, and serve.

Tips:

❖ For a creamier sauce, try sour cream instead of the yogurt as the marinade's base.

❖ You really don't have to grind the whole spices one at a time. Put them all in a spice grinder and pulverize them together for a full-bodied flavor.

Chicken
WITH YELLOW SPLIT PEAS

Murghi dalcha

Lentil-based curries called *dalchas* hail from the south-central city of Hyderabad. Combining meats with legumes may seem redundant to the protein-conscious among us, but the textural differences make perfect sense to the Hyderabadis, especially when the curry's base relies, as this one does, on yellow split peas for body, color, and flavor. **SERVES 6**

1 cup yellow split peas, picked over for stones

1 teaspoon tamarind paste or concentrate

1 small red onion, coarsely chopped

6 medium-size cloves garlic

4 lengthwise slices fresh ginger (each 2 inches long, 1 inch wide, and ⅛ inch thick)

4 fresh green Thai, cayenne, or serrano chiles, stems removed

4 tablespoons canola oil

1 teaspoon cumin seeds

3 fresh or dried bay leaves

2 cinnamon sticks (each 3 inches long)

2 pounds cut-up bone-in chicken, skin removed (see Tips)

2 teaspoons coarse kosher or sea salt

¼ teaspoon ground turmeric

2 tablespoons finely chopped fresh cilantro leaves and tender stems

1 teaspoon black or yellow mustard seeds

12 to 15 medium-size to large fresh curry leaves

1. Place the split peas in a medium-size saucepan. Fill the pan halfway with tap water and rinse the peas by rubbing them between your fingertips. The water will become cloudy. Drain this water. Repeat three or four times, until the water is relatively clear; drain. Now add 3 cups water and bring to a boil, uncovered, over medium-high heat. Skim off and discard any foam that forms on the surface. Lower the heat to medium and simmer, uncovered, stirring occasionally, until the split peas are partially tender, about 10 minutes. Stir in the tamarind paste, making sure it dissolves; it will turn the water chocolate-brown.

2. While the split peas are cooking, combine the onion, garlic, ginger, and chiles in a food processor and process until minced.

3. Heat 2 tablespoons of the oil in a large skillet over medium-high heat. Sprinkle in the cumin seeds, bay leaves, and cinnamon sticks, and cook until they sizzle and smell aromatic, 10 to 15 seconds. Add the onion-chile blend and stir-fry, with adequate ventilation, until the pungent onion mixture turns honey-brown, 3 to 5 minutes.

4. Arrange the chicken pieces, meat side down, in a single layer on top of the onion blend. Cook until the chicken turns light brown, 2 to 4 minutes. Sprinkle in the salt and turmeric. Pour in the split peas, with their cooking water, and stir once or twice. Heat to a boil. Then reduce the heat to medium-low, cover, and simmer, stirring occasionally, until the meat in the thickest parts of the chicken is no longer pink inside and the juices run clear, 40 to 45 minutes. Stir in the cilantro.

5. Heat the remaining 2 tablespoons oil in a small skillet over medium-high heat. Add the mustard seeds, cover the skillet, and cook until the seeds have stopped popping (not unlike popcorn), about 30 seconds. Remove the skillet from the heat and throw in the curry leaves—carefully, as they will spatter upon contact.

6. Pour this nutty citrus-smelling oil over the chicken curry, stir once or twice, and serve.

Tips:

❖ Cut-up bone-in chicken can be found in every grocery store's meat department. These skin-on pieces are easy to work with, compared to the messy process of skinning a whole chicken and cutting it into smaller pieces. Hold the chicken piece in one hand, and with a piece of paper towel in the other hand, pull off the skin, using the paper towel to help you grip the skin. Sometimes, partially freezing the chicken also helps to make the skinning easy. While buying pre-cut pieces makes for less work, it may not be the most frugal option when compared to buying a whole chicken. If you decide to buy a whole bird, see box on page 121 on how to skin it and cut it up.

❖ You can remove the cinnamon sticks and bay leaves before you serve the curry. Curry leaves are usually left in the mix, but if you wish, you can fish them out too. We Indians, on the other hand, relish sucking each leaf dry, getting every last bit of flavor we possibly can. There is a reason why we eat with our fingers!

Cubed Chicken
WITH WOK-SEARED VEGETABLES

balti dahi murghi

the beauty of a well-seasoned *kadhai* (Indian wok) is its ability to sear in the juices and flavors of meats and vegetables as they stir-fry in the pan's capacious, concave-shaped base. The cooking happens quickly over near-high heat, which is why it is a good idea to measure out and prepare all the ingredients in the recipe before you fire up the wok. Enjoy the smoky aromas that emanate from the pan and the combination of spices that titillate the taste buds. Don't worry about all the chiles, whole and ground, here—the cream-coated yogurt will bring the heat down a notch. **SERVES 8**

2 tablespoons canola oil

1 large green bell pepper, stemmed, seeded, and cut into 1-inch pieces

1 small red onion, cut into ½-inch cubes

4 large cloves garlic, thinly sliced

4 dried red Thai or cayenne chiles, stems removed

2 pounds boneless, skinless chicken breasts, cut into 1-inch pieces

¼ cup finely chopped fresh cilantro leaves and tender stems

2 teaspoons balti masala (page 31)

½ cup plain yogurt

2 tablespoons heavy (whipping) cream

1 large tomato, cored and finely chopped

1. Preheat a wok or a well-seasoned cast-iron skillet over medium-high heat. Drizzle the oil down its sides, so it heats quickly and then pools at the bottom. When the oil is shimmering, add the bell pepper, onion, garlic, and chiles. Stir-fry this colorful mélange until the peppers blister in spots, the onion cubes brown around the edges, the garlic turns honey-brown, and the chiles blacken, 5 to 8 minutes.

2. Add the chicken and continue to stir-fry until the meat is seared, 3 to 5 minutes.

3. Sprinkle in the cilantro and *Balti masala*. Stir-fry to cook the spice blend without burning it, about 1 minute (the cooking will also take the strong-tasting edge off the cilantro).

4. Reduce the heat to medium and continue to cook, uncovered, stirring occasionally, until the chicken is fork-tender and no longer pink inside, 10 to 15 minutes.

5. While the mixture is cooking, combine the yogurt and cream in a small bowl, stirring thoroughly (evenly distributing the cream in the yogurt stabilizes the yogurt and prevents curdling when it hits the heat).

6. Fold the yogurt mixture into the chicken and vegetables. Stir in the tomato, stir for just a minute to warm it, and serve immediately.

Breast of Chicken
WITH
TOMATO AND COCONUT MILK

Chicken Curry

This simple curry can be made with store-bought Madras curry powder—all the better to make it an authentic British East Indian adaptation of "curry." Serve it with an English bottled mango chutney (usually sweet) and steamed white rice for a true Anglo-Indian experience.

SERVES 6

2 tablespoons canola oil
1 small red onion, cut in half lengthwise and thinly sliced
4 medium-size cloves garlic, finely chopped
2 lengthwise slices fresh ginger (each 2½ inches long, 1 inch wide, and ⅛ inch thick), cut into matchstick strips (julienne)
1½ pounds boneless, skinless chicken breasts, cut into 1-inch pieces
2 teaspoons English-Style Madras Curry Powder (page 24)
1½ teaspoons coarse kosher or sea salt
¼ cup unsweetened coconut milk
1 large tomato, cored and finely chopped
2 tablespoons finely chopped fresh cilantro leaves and tender stems

1. Preheat a wok or a well-seasoned cast-iron saucepan over medium-high heat. Drizzle the oil down its sides. Add the onion, garlic, and ginger, and stir-fry until the vegetables are light brown, 3 to 5 minutes.

2. Add the chicken pieces and the curry powder, and cook until the meat is seared all over, about 5 minutes.

3. Sprinkle the salt over the chicken and pour in the coconut milk, which will immediately come to a boil. Cover, lower the heat to medium, and simmer, stirring occasionally, until the chicken is fork-tender and no longer pink inside, 5 to 7 minutes. Remove the chicken pieces from the thin yellow sauce and place them in a serving bowl.

4. Raise the heat to medium-high heat and boil the sauce, uncovered, stirring occasionally, until it thickens, 3 to 5 minutes. Stir in the tomato and cilantro. Pour the sauce over the chicken and toss to bathe it with the curry. Serve immediately.

Marinated Chicken
WITH AN ONION-PEPPER-ALMOND SAUCE

Chicken Tikka Masala

I contemplated giving this dish a Hindi title (especially the "chicken" part) but decided against it because Chicken Tikka Masala is, after all, the proclaimed national dish (drum roll, please) of Britain, a testimony to that country's love affair with curry. With over eight thousand curry houses in the United Kingdom, this particular fusion dish appears on diners' plates in many variations. I find this version particularly pleasing because the mellow heat from the Kashmiri chiles does not compete with the sauce's delicate, nutty, creamy flavors. **SERVES 4**

For the chicken tikkas:

Bamboo or metal skewers
½ cup plain yogurt
2 tablespoons Ginger Paste (page 15)
2 tablespoons Garlic Paste (page 15)
2 tablespoons finely chopped fresh
*   cilantro leaves and tender stems*
2 teaspoons coriander seeds, ground
1 teaspoon cumin seeds, ground
2 teaspoons ground Kashmiri chiles; or
*   ½ teaspoon cayenne (ground red pepper)*
*   mixed with 1½ teaspoons sweet paprika*
1½ teaspoons coarse kosher or sea salt
½ teaspoon Punjabi garam masala
*   (page 25)*
½ teaspoon ground turmeric

1½ pounds boneless, skinless chicken breasts,
*   cut lengthwise into 1-inch-wide strips*

For the sauce:

2 tablespoons Ghee (page 21) or canola oil
1 small red onion, coarsely chopped
1 small red bell pepper, stemmed, seeded, and
*   cut into ½-inch pieces*
¼ cup slivered blanched almonds
¼ cup golden raisins
1 cup diced tomatoes, fresh or canned
*   (no need to drain)*
¼ cup heavy (whipping) cream or half-and-half
½ teaspoon coarse kosher or sea salt
¼ teaspoon cayenne (ground red pepper)
¼ teaspoon Punjabi garam masala (page 25)
Vegetable cooking spray
2 tablespoons finely chopped fresh cilantro leaves
*   and tender stems for garnishing*

1. If you are using bamboo skewers, place them in a flat dish filled with water and let them soak for an hour (see Tip, page 84).

2. While the skewers are soaking, make the marinade: Combine the yogurt, Ginger Paste, Garlic Paste, cilantro, coriander, cumin, Kashmiri chiles, salt, garam masala, and turmeric in a small bowl. Whisk to blend.

3. Put the chicken strips in a large bowl and pour this full-flavored, red-hot-looking marinade over them. Toss to thoroughly coat the meat. Refrigerate, covered, for at least 30 minutes or up to 6 hours.

4. When you are ready to cook the chicken, make the sauce: Heat the ghee in a small saucepan over medium-high heat. Add the onion, bell pepper, almonds, and raisins, and cook, stirring frequently, until the vegetables soften and then acquire honey-brown patches, 10 to 12 minutes.

The nuts and raisins will turn reddish brown, and a thin film of brown will coat the bottom of the pan. (Forcing the vegetables into a small pan allows them to sweat a little, creating moisture that prevents burning.)

5. Stir the tomatoes into the pan and scrape the bottom to deglaze it. Pour this chunky sauce into a blender jar, and add the cream, salt, cayenne, and garam masala. Puree, scraping the inside of the jar as needed, to make a thick, nutty-gritty, reddish-brown sauce.

6. Pour the sauce into a medium-size saucepan and simmer it over low heat, stirring it occasionally, while you grill the chicken.

7. Preheat a gas or charcoal grill, or the broiler, to high.

8. While the grill is heating, thread the chicken strips, covered with the marinade, onto the skewers, accordion-style. *If you are grilling,* lightly spray the grill grate with cooking spray. Grill the chicken, covered, turning the skewers occasionally, until the pieces are light brown, the insides are no longer pink, and the juices run clear, 6 to 8 minutes. *If you are broiling,* position an oven rack so the top of the chicken will be 2 to 3 inches from the heat. Lightly spray the rack of a broiler pan with cooking spray, place the skewers on the rack, and broil, turning the skewers occasionally, until the chicken is light brown, the meat is no longer pink inside, and the juices run clear, 6 to 8 minutes.

9. Slide the chicken off the skewers into the sauce. Stir once or twice to make sure the sauce drenches the tender, juicy meat, and then serve, sprinkled with the cilantro.

Stir-Fried Chicken
WITH GREEN BEANS

farasvi Murghi

I adore green beans, especially the tender, thin ones that snap with a juicy crispness when broken in two. Pairing them with chicken in this full-bodied, complex-flavored (thanks to the bottle masala) stew makes perfect sense (not to mention color), a union that sings magic when you gobble down forkfuls of the curry served over steamed white rice. And speaking of gobble, breast of turkey is fair game for a switcheroo in the absence of chicken. **SERVES 6**

1 pound boneless, skinless chicken breasts, cut into 1-inch pieces

2 teaspoons East Indian bottle masala (page 37; see Tip)

1 medium-size potato, such as russet or Yukon Gold, peeled, cut into 1-inch cubes, and submerged in a bowl of cold water to prevent browning

2 tablespoons canola oil

4 medium-size cloves garlic, cut into thin slivers

3 lengthwise slices fresh ginger (each 1½ inches long, 1 inch wide, and ⅛ inch thick), cut into matchstick strips (julienne)

1½ teaspoons coarse kosher or sea salt

1 cup fresh or frozen French-cut green beans (if frozen, no need to thaw)

2 teaspoons cornstarch

2 tablespoons finely chopped fresh cilantro leaves and tender stems for garnishing

1. Toss the chicken pieces with the bottle masala in a medium-size bowl.

2. Drain the potato and pat it dry with paper towels.

3. Heat the oil in a large skillet over medium-high heat. Add the garlic, ginger, and potato, and stir-fry until the vegetables are light brown around the edges, 5 to 8 minutes.

4. Add the chicken and stir-fry to lightly brown and sear it, 3 to 5 minutes.

5. Pour in 1 cup water, sprinkle with the salt, and scrape the bottom of the skillet to deglaze it. Stir in the green beans and heat the curry to a boil. Then lower the heat to medium, cover, and simmer, stirring occasionally, until the chicken is no longer pink inside and the potato is fork-tender, 15 to 20 minutes.

6. Combine the cornstarch with 2 tablespoons water in a small bowl, and stir well. Stir this mixture into the curry. You will see the starchy magic at work as it thickens the sauce almost instantaneously.

7. Sprinkle the cilantro over the curry, and serve.

Tips:

❖ Bottle masala brings the flavors of the East Indian community of Mumbai into your Western kitchen, but if you are fresh out of this masala, use the equally tasty (but not as complex) English-style Madras curry powder instead.

❖ Instead of the potato, try cubed turnips or parsnips for a slightly bitter-sweet alternative.

❖ The second time I tested this recipe, I made it with fresh-picked yellow wax beans, which were overflowing from the vegetable baskets at my neighborhood farmers' market. I also picked up some young free-range chicken from a nearby vendor, which I cut into bone-in, serving-size pieces. I found the flavors to be exceptionally good. I added 5 to 8 minutes to the simmering time to ensure that the meat had safely cooked through to the bone.

Wok-Seared Chicken Breasts
WITH A FENNEL-TOMATO SAUCE

kadhai tamatar murghi

Wok-like vessels called *kadhais,* with curved bases and slightly higher sides than their Chinese counterparts, have helped many an Indian to stir-fry, deep-fry, and stew their foods, including curries, for centuries. Cast-iron *kadhais* are my pick for even heat transfer, but carbon steel and stainless steel ones are equally functional. Some *kadhais* have no handles, which makes them trickier to hold, but there are Indian tongs designed for just that. When you sear meat and spices together in a *kadhai* over high heat, and then simmer the mixture in a sauce, you get a smoky flavor without the use of charcoal. This curry is a perfect example of that smoky sear. Serve it with that other north Indian specialty, naan (page 729)—warm, buttery pieces of bread that you tear and wrap around the succulent meat in order to devour it. **SERVES 4**

2 tablespoons canola oil

1 teaspoon cumin seeds

1 teaspoon fennel seeds

1 small red onion, finely chopped

4 large cloves garlic, finely chopped

3 lengthwise slices fresh ginger
   (each 2½ inches long, 1 inch wide,
   and ⅛ inch thick), finely chopped

1 pound boneless, skinless chicken breasts,
   cut into 1-inch pieces

1 medium-size tomato, cored and
   finely chopped

2 tablespoons dried fenugreek leaves,
   soaked in a bowl of water and skimmed
   off before use (see box, page 473)

2 tablespoons finely chopped fresh cilantro leaves
   and tender stems

1½ teaspoons coarse kosher or sea salt

½ teaspoon cayenne (ground red pepper)

¼ teaspoon ground turmeric

½ teaspoon Punjabi garam masala
   (page 25)

1. Preheat a wok or a well-seasoned cast-iron skillet over medium-high heat. Drizzle the oil down its sides—it will heat on contact and also season the wok all around. Sprinkle in the cumin and fennel seeds, which will sizzle and turn reddish brown on contact, 5 to 10 seconds.

2. Add the onion, garlic, and ginger, and stir-fry until the vegetables turn light brown, about 2 minutes.

3. Add the chicken pieces and allow them to sear and turn light brown, about 5 minutes.

4. Add the tomato, fenugreek leaves, cilantro, salt, cayenne, and turmeric. Cook, uncovered, stirring occasionally, until the tomato has softened, about 2 minutes. Then pour in ¼ cup water and stir once or twice. Reduce the heat to medium-low, cover, and simmer, stirring occasionally, until the chicken is fork-tender and no longer pink inside, 5 to 7 minutes.

5. Stir in the garam masala, and serve.

Moghalai-Style Chicken
WITH
SPINACH, ALMONDS, AND RAISINS

Kishmish Waale Murgh

this sweet-hot sauce, with an underlying nuttiness thanks to the almonds, is a perfect accompaniment to mellow-tasting chicken. I served this the day I made Okra Curry with Toasted Chickpea Flour (page 527) and steamed Nimmy Paul's Tomato Rice (page 694), to appease many an appetite. **SERVES 6**

¼ cup canola oil

1 large red onion, finely chopped

½ cup golden raisins

½ cup slivered blanched almonds

2 pounds boneless, skinless chicken breasts,
   cut into 1-inch pieces

1 tablespoon Punjabi garam masala (page 25)

2 teaspoons coarse kosher or sea salt

½ teaspoon cayenne (ground red pepper)

½ teaspoon ground turmeric

8 ounces fresh spinach leaves, well washed and
   finely chopped; or 1 package (8 to 10 ounces)
   frozen chopped spinach, thawed (no need to drain)

1. Heat the oil in a large skillet over medium heat. Add the onion, raisins, and almonds, and cook until the onion softens and then turns dark brown with deep purple hues and the raisins turn honey-brown and look succulent, 15 to 20 minutes.

2. Stir in the chicken and cook until it sears and turns light brown, 8 to 10 minutes.

3. Stir in the garam masala, salt, cayenne, and turmeric, and cook for 20 to 30 seconds.

4. Stir in the spinach and ½ cup water. Bring to a boil. Then reduce the heat to medium-low, cover the skillet, and simmer, stirring occasionally, until the chicken is no longer pink inside, 5 to 10 minutes. Transfer to a large platter and serve.

Cubed Chicken
WITH TOMATOES AND FRESH COCONUT

Nariyal Chi Kombdi

I am the first to admit that the *kolhapuri* masala is a potent one—vibrantly red and full-bodied, akin to fine aged wine. Sprinkle it in anything, and watch the sparks fly! But have no fear, 'cause coconut is here. That's why I have you add it toward the end, after the chicken cooks: its creamy quality will tame the chiles to a pleasantly manageable piquancy. **SERVES 4**

2 tablespoons canola oil

I teaspoon black or yellow mustard seeds

4 medium-size cloves garlic, cut into thin slivers

1¼ pounds boneless, skinless chicken breasts, cut into 1-inch pieces

I large tomato, cored and finely chopped

2 tablespoons finely chopped fresh cilantro leaves and tender stems

2 teaspoons Kolhapuri masala (page 32)

1½ teaspoons coarse kosher or sea salt

½ teaspoon ground turmeric

I cup shredded fresh coconut; or ½ cup shredded dried unsweetened coconut, reconstituted (see Note)

1. Heat the oil in a large skillet over medium-high heat. Add the mustard seeds, cover the skillet, and cook until the seeds have stopped popping (not unlike popcorn), about 30 seconds. Then throw in the garlic slivers, which will turn light brown almost immediately because of the hot oil. Quickly add the chicken and stir-fry it to sear the meat evenly, 3 to 5 minutes.

2. Add the tomato, cilantro, masala, salt, and turmeric. Stir once or twice. Once the curry starts to boil, reduce the heat to medium-low, cover the skillet, and simmer, stirring occasionally, until the meat is no longer pink inside, 8 to 10 minutes.

3. Stir in the coconut, which will instantly thicken the sauce. Let it warm for a minute or two, and then serve.

Note: To reconsititute the coconut, cover with ½ cup boiling water, set aside for about 15 minutes, and then drain.

Chicken
WITH
ONION, BELL PEPPER, AND MACE

Murghi Jalfrezie

Versions of this curry dot many a north Indian restaurant menu, with bell pepper and onion acting as the key ingredients and the tomato-based sauce speckled with a variety of spice blends. My version enhances the simple vegetable flavors with only a few spices. The blackened chiles provide a sharpness that is offset by sweet mace, a surprise ingredient in this easy-to-make dish for a weekday evening.

SERVES 4

1 tablespoon Ginger Paste (page 15)
2 teaspoons Garlic Paste (page 15)
1 pound boneless, skinless chicken breasts,
    cut into ½-inch pieces (see Tip)
2 teaspoons coriander seeds
1 teaspoon cumin seeds
2 dried red Thai or cayenne chiles, stems removed
2 blades mace, or ¼ teaspoon ground mace
4 tablespoons canola oil
1 cup cubed red onion (½-inch cubes)
1 large green bell pepper, stemmed, seeded,
    and cut into ½-inch pieces
2 tablespoons tomato paste
1 teaspoon coarse kosher or sea salt
2 tablespoons finely chopped fresh cilantro
    leaves and tender stems for garnishing

1. Combine the ginger and garlic pastes in a medium-size bowl. Add the chicken pieces and toss to coat them with the paste. Refrigerate, covered, for at least 30 minutes or as long as overnight, to allow the flavors to permeate the meat.

2. Preheat a small skillet over medium-high heat. Add the coriander seeds, cumin seeds, chiles, and mace, and toast, shaking the skillet every few seconds, until the coriander and cumin turn reddish brown, and the chiles blacken slightly and smell pungent (their aroma masked by the sweet-smelling mace), 1 to 2 minutes.

3. Immediately transfer the spice mixture to a plate. Once it is cool to the touch, transfer the mixture to a spice grinder and grind until the texture resembles that of finely ground black pepper. (If you don't allow the spices to cool, the ground blend will acquire unwanted moisture from the heat, making the final blend slightly "cakey.")

4. Heat 2 tablespoons of the oil in a large skillet over medium-high heat. Add the chicken and stir-fry until the cubes turn light brown, about 2 minutes. Transfer the partially cooked chicken to a plate.

5. Heat the remaining 2 tablespoons oil in the same skillet over medium-high heat. Add the onion and bell pepper and cook, stirring, until the onion is lightly brown around the edges, about 2 minutes. Add them to the plate of chicken.

6. Add the tomato paste and 1 cup water to the hot skillet and whisk the two together to make a smooth sauce. Scrape the bottom of the skillet to deglaze it, releasing any collected bits of ginger, garlic, chicken, and vegetables. Stir in the ground spice blend and the salt.

7. Return the chicken and vegetables to the skillet, and stir to coat them evenly with the sauce. Continue to cook the curry, uncovered, stirring occasionally, until the sauce thickens and the chicken is no longer pink inside, 3 to 5 minutes.

8. Sprinkle with the cilantro, and serve.

Tip: Bone-in chicken pieces are an acceptable stand-in in this recipe, especially if you desire a more succulent curry. In Step 7, braise the pieces, covered, over medium-low heat until the meat in the thickest parts of the chicken pieces is no longer pink inside and the juices run clear, 25 to 30 minutes.

Breast of Chicken
IN AN ONION-TURMERIC SAUCE

Pyaaz Murghi

Simmered with quick-cooking boneless chicken breasts, this is one of those curries that will take care of your craving for spicy satisfaction at a moment's notice. If you prefer, however, or if you're not in a rush, you can certainly use bone-in skinless chicken pieces; just be sure to allow an extra 10 to 15 minutes of simmering time to make sure the meat cooks through.

SERVES 4

4 tablespoons canola oil

1 small red onion, coarsely chopped

1 teaspoon coarse kosher or sea salt

¼ teaspoon ground turmeric

1 pound boneless, skinless chicken breasts, cut into 1-inch pieces

2 tablespoons finely chopped fresh cilantro leaves and tender stems

1 teaspoon Punjabi garam masala (page 25)

3 lengthwise slices fresh ginger (each 2½ inches long, 1 inch wide, and ⅛ inch thick), cut into matchstick-thin strips (julienne)

1. Pour 2 tablespoons of the oil into a blender jar, followed by the onion, salt, and turmeric. Puree, scraping the inside of the jar as needed, to form a smooth, light purple-yellow paste. (When you pour the oil in first, it provides much-needed liquid for the blender blades to perform their task.)

2. Spoon the onion puree into a medium-size bowl, add the chicken pieces, and coat them well with the marinade. Refrigerate, covered, for 30 minutes to 1 hour, to allow the chicken to absorb some of the marinade's flavors.

3. Heat the remaining 2 tablespoons oil in a medium-size skillet over medium-high heat. Add the chicken, paste and all, and cook, stirring, until the chicken pieces turn honey-brown and some of the onion paste turns dark brown and sticks to the bottom of the skillet, 5 to 6 minutes. Lower the heat to medium if the pan gets too hot and the paste starts to burn.

4. Pour in ½ cup water and scrape the bottom to deglaze the skillet, releasing the collected bits of chicken and onion. The curry will come to a boil quickly. Lower the heat to medium, cover, and simmer, stirring occasionally, until the chicken pieces are no longer pink in the center, 5 to 7 minutes.

5. Stir in the cilantro, garam masala, and ginger. Raise the heat to medium-high and simmer, uncovered, stirring occasionally, until the sauce thickens slightly, 2 to 3 minutes. Serve immediately.

Red-Hot Chicken
WITH OKRA AND POTATOES

tambda bhindi kombdi

The word "red" in Marathi is *tambda,* and this chicken will have you experience it, both in its appearance and in its gusto. This curry is not for those wary of heat, and you can see why this is a delicacy in Kolhapur, the land of wrestlers who are energized by its warmth.

SERVES 6

I pound boneless, skinless chicken breasts,
   cut into I-inch pieces
I teaspoon ground Kashmiri chiles; or ¼ teaspoon
   cayenne (ground red pepper) mixed with
   ¾ teaspoon sweet paprika
2 medium-size potatoes, such as russet or Yukon Gold,
   peeled, cut into I-inch cubes, and submerged in a
   bowl of cold water to prevent browning
2 tablespoons canola oil
I teaspoon cumin seeds
8 ounces fresh okra, rinsed, completely dried, the caps
   pared off, cut crosswise into I-inch lengths
I tablespoon Kolhapuri masala (page 32)
I½ teaspoons coarse kosher or sea salt
I medium-size tomato, cored and cut into
   I-inch pieces
¼ cup finely chopped fresh cilantro leaves
   and tender stems

1. Place the chicken in a medium-size bowl, add the Kashmiri chiles, and toss to coat the chicken.

2. Drain the potatoes and pat them dry with paper towels.

3. Heat the oil in a large skillet over medium-high heat. Add the cumin seeds, and as soon as they sizzle, turn reddish brown, and smell nutty, throw in the okra and potatoes. Stir-fry until the vegetables have acquired light brown patches, 5 to 8 minutes.

4. Add the chicken and continue to stir-fry until the meat is seared, 2 to 4 minutes. The chiles coating the chicken will also cook, and the fumes will be quite strong, so make sure to have adequate ventilation.

5. Pour 1 cup water into the skillet, and sprinkle in the masala and salt. Scrape the bottom of the skillet to deglaze it, releasing any browned bits of vegetable and meat. Once the curry comes to a boil, lower the heat to medium, cover the skillet, and simmer, stirring occasionally, until the meat is no longer pink inside and the vegetables are fork-tender, 5 to 10 minutes.

6. Stir in the tomato and cilantro and continue to simmer, uncovered, stirring occasionally, until the tomato warms through, 3 to 5 minutes. Then serve.

Tips:

❖ Pan-frying okra will prevent it from getting slimy. If you don't like okra, use asparagus, even though it is not classically Indian.

❖ Dark meat yields a more succulent curry, and skinless, boneless chicken thighs work great in this recipe. If you want to use bone-in pieces, pan-fry them separately in a little oil until the meat is cooked halfway; then add the chicken to the curry and simmer until it cooks through.

Cashew Chicken
WITH A CILANTRO SAUCE

dhania murghi

I look at this curry and realize how well it fits in with our eight-ingredients-or-less way of cooking, not to mention how easily and quickly the tender strips of breast meat come to the table, cloaked in the nutty cashew-cilantro sauce. Even though the curry has an abundance of cilantro, the long simmering yields a mellow incarnation of this controversial herb. For an unusual combination, ladle it over fresh-cooked noodles tossed with olive oil. "Yummski, deelish," as a friend of mine would say. **SERVES 4**

2 small red onions; I coarsely chopped,
   I cut in half lengthwise and thinly sliced
¼ cup raw cashew nuts
¼ cup firmly packed fresh cilantro leaves and
   tender stems
2 tablespoons canola oil
1¼ pounds boneless, skinless chicken breasts,
   cut lengthwise into 1-inch-wide strips
I teaspoon coarse kosher or sea salt
½ teaspoon Punjabi garam masala (page 25)
½ teaspoon cayenne (ground red pepper)

1. Pour ½ cup water into a blender jar, and add the coarsely chopped onion, cashews, and cilantro. Puree, scraping the inside of the jar as needed, until smooth; it will resemble a watered-down pesto.

2. Heat the oil in a medium-size skillet over medium-high heat. Add the sliced onion and cook, stirring, until it is light honey-brown, 3 to 5 minutes. Pour in the cilantro-cashew puree and cook over medium heat, stirring occasionally, until most of the liquid has evaporated. The sauce should be a darker green, with some of the oil starting to separate around the edges and on the surface; and a thin coat of browned onion-cashew paste will have formed on the bottom of the skillet.

3. Add the chicken strips and stir-fry until the meat is seared and the brown layer on the bottom has darkened, 2 to 4 minutes.

4. Pour in ½ cup water and scrape the skillet to release the browned layer, creating an intensely robust sauce. Stir in the salt, garam masala, and cayenne. As soon as the sauce comes to a boil, reduce the heat to medium-low, cover, and simmer, stirring occasionally, until the chicken is no longer pink inside, 5 to 8 minutes.

5. Uncover the skillet, raise the heat to medium-high, and cook, stirring occasionally, until the sauce has thickened, about 5 minutes. Serve immediately.

Minty Chicken Strips
WITH COCONUT

Murghi hara Masala

Even though Usha Raikar, my sister's vibrantly colorful neighbor in Mumbai, uses bone-in pieces of chicken in her recipe, I have taken the liberty of substituting much quicker-cooking boneless breasts. (All Indians who eat chicken always skin it, because the skin is considered unhealthy.) For a weekday meal, this means I don't have to spend too much time in the kitchen. For a more relaxed weekend meal, I do highly recommend making this with succulent bone-in pieces—just allow more cooking time.

The green *(hara)* in the perfumed *Hara masala* comes from fresh mint and cilantro leaves. **SERVES 6**

½ cup Hara masala (page 19)

¼ cup plain yogurt, whisked

1½ teaspoons coarse kosher or sea salt

2 pounds boneless, skinless chicken breasts, cut lengthwise into 1-inch-wide strips

4 tablespoons canola oil

1 large red onion, finely chopped

1 large tomato, cored and finely chopped

2 teaspoons Usha Raikar's garam masala (page 27)

¼ teaspoon ground turmeric

½ cup shredded fresh coconut; or ¼ cup shredded dried unsweetened coconut, reconsituted (see Note)

1. Combine the masala, yogurt, and salt in a medium-size bowl. Add the chicken strips, and toss to coat them well. Refrigerate, covered, for at least 30 minutes or up to 2 hours, to allow the flavors to permeate the meat. (You can marinate the chicken overnight, but if you do, leave the salt out of the marinade. Stir it in after you have finished marinating the chicken. Salt will break down the already tender breast meat if left overnight in the marinade.)

2. Heat 2 tablespoons of the oil in a large skillet over medium-high heat. Add half the onion and stir-fry until it is light brown around the edges, 2 to

3 minutes. Add the tomato, garam masala, and turmeric. Stew, uncovered, stirring occasionally, until the tomato softens and the mixture appears sauce-like but still chunky, 3 to 5 minutes.

3. Add the chicken, marinade and all, and cook, uncovered, over medium heat, stirring occasionally, until the meat is no longer pink inside, 8 to 10 minutes.

4. While the chicken is simmering, heat the remaining 2 tablespoons oil in a medium-size skillet over medium-high heat. Add the remaining onion and stir-fry until it is light brown around the edges, 3 to 5 minutes. Stir in the coconut and cook, stirring occasionally, until it has lightly browned, about 2 minutes. Pour in ½ cup water and scrape the skillet to deglaze it, releasing the browned bits of onion and coconut. Transfer this mixture to a blender and puree, scraping the inside of the jar as needed, to form a slightly gritty paste.

5. Add the paste to the cooked chicken, stir once or twice, and serve.

Note: To reconstitute coconut, cover with ¼ cup boiling water, set aside for about 15 minutes, and then drain.

Tips:

❖ Turkey strips are a perfectly acceptable alternative, and so are drumsticks (either chicken or turkey).

❖ For the vegetarian, use cubes of *paneer* (page 287) or even chunks of extra-firm tofu. Marinate them just as you would the meat, although you will not need to cook them as long (5 minutes will be just fine).

Cardamom-Scented Chicken
WITH GINGER AND GARLIC

Murghi Elaichi

If you are a fan of cardamom, you will fall in love with this finger-licking curry. The menthol-like cardamom, with its sweet undertones, combines with slow-cooked onions to create a mellow sauce. The cayenne kicks in some heat to provide balance, a hallmark of truly delectable fare.

SERVES 4

2 tablespoons Ginger Paste (page 15)
1 tablespoon Garlic Paste (page 15)
2 teaspoons cardamom seeds
  from green or white pods, ground
1 teaspoon cayenne (ground red pepper)
1 teaspoon coarse kosher or sea salt
¼ teaspoon ground turmeric
8 chicken drumsticks, skin removed (see Tip)
2 tablespoons canola oil
1 medium-size red onion, cut in
  half lengthwise and thinly sliced
4 fresh or dried bay leaves
2 cinnamon sticks (each 3 inches long)
2 tablespoons finely chopped
  fresh cilantro leaves and tender stems

1. Combine the Ginger Paste, Garlic Paste, cardamom, cayenne, salt, and turmeric in a small bowl and mix well to form a wet paste. Smear each drumstick with the paste and refrigerate, covered, for at least 30 minutes or as long as overnight.

2. Heat the oil in a large saucepan over medium heat. Add the paste-smeared drumsticks and the onion, bay leaves, and cinnamon sticks. Allow the chicken to sear all over and the onion to soften and brown lightly, stirring occasionally, until the bottom of the pan acquires a thin brown layer of spice and onion and the mixture smells menthol-like, 18 to 20 minutes.

3. Pour 1 cup water into the pan and scrape the bottom to deglaze it, releasing the thin layer of browned spices, chicken, and onion. Reduce the heat to medium-low, cover the pan, and braise the chicken, spooning the juicy, saucy onion slices over the drumsticks frequently, until the meat is fall-apart tender, 25 to 30 minutes. Transfer the chicken to a serving platter.

4. Raise the heat to medium-high and cook the sauce, uncovered, stirring occasionally, until it has thickened, about 5 minutes.

5. Remove the bay leaves and cinnamon sticks if you wish. Stir in the cilantro, spoon the sauce over the drumsticks, and serve.

Tips:

❖ Yes, you can substitute other bone-in chicken pieces. However, drumsticks make it especially easy to bite into a yummy morsel of tender chicken while you lift it with eager fingers by its convenient bone handle—not to mention their economic advantage. To skin them before you marinate them, pull the skin off with a paper towel—it will give you a better grip.

❖ If you wish, stir in 8 ounces well-rinsed fresh baby spinach leaves in Step 4. Cook until the sauce has thickened without overcooking the spinach.

Yogurt-Marinated Chicken
WITH PEAS

Mutter Murghi

I have prepared this recipe when fresh peas are in season, which makes the combination extra-special. Often I will add cream to yogurt for a smoother consistency. The fat in the cream prevents the yogurt from curdling, making way for a creamier-looking and -tasting sauce. For a quick weekday meal, this curry is delicious with a bowl of steamed white rice, basmati or otherwise. **SERVES 6**

½ cup plain yogurt

2 tablespoons heavy (whipping) cream

2 tablespoons finely chopped fresh ginger

1 teaspoon coarse kosher or sea salt

¼ teaspoon ground turmeric

6 medium-size cloves garlic

2 fresh green Thai, cayenne, or serrano chiles,
    stems removed, finely chopped
    (do not remove the seeds)

1½ pounds bone-in chicken thighs,
    skin removed

2 tablespoons canola oil

1 medium-size red onion, cut in half
    lengthwise and thinly sliced

1 cup frozen green peas (no need to thaw)

2 tablespoons finely chopped fresh cilantro
    leaves and tender stems

1 tablespoon Maharashtrian garam masala
    (page 28)

1. Combine the yogurt, cream, ginger, salt, turmeric, garlic, and chiles in a medium-size bowl, and mix well. Add the chicken and turn the pieces to coat them completely. Refrigerate, covered, for at least 30 minutes or as long as overnight.

2. Heat the oil in a large skillet over medium-high heat. Add the onion and stir-fry until it is light brown around the edges, about 3 minutes.

3. Arrange the chicken pieces, including the marinade, in a single layer on top of the onions, and cook until the chicken is golden brown on the underside, 4 to 6 minutes. Turn the pieces over and cook until the other side is golden brown, 4 to 6 minutes.

4. Pour in ½ cup water and scrape the bottom of the skillet to deglaze it, releasing any browned bits of onion and chicken. Add the peas, cilantro, and garam masala, and stir once or twice to incorporate them into the curry. Reduce the heat to medium-low, cover the skillet, and simmer, turning and basting the chicken occasionally, until the meat in the thickest parts of the chicken is no longer pink inside and the juices run clear, 15 to 18 minutes. Remove the chicken from the skillet and arrange it on a serving platter.

5. Raise the heat to medium-high and boil the sauce until it has thickened, about 5 minutes.

6. Pour the sauce over the chicken, and serve.

Tip: Instead of using all thighs, you can use a whole chicken, cut into small pieces. My son loves it when I use drumsticks because he derives immense pleasure in picking one up with his young fingers and devouring it ("just like the Flintstones, Papa").

Chicken Thighs
WITH A PEANUT SAUCE

Sengdana Murghi

Peanut curries are often associated with foods from Thailand. In India, they are most common in the states of Gujarat and Maharashtra—where, in fact, this flavor combination originated. Fresh coconut, another local abundance, smoothes out the chiles in this curry, as do the yogurt and cream. Together they magically balance this addictive dish that is a cinch to make, especially if you already have the garam masala in your pantry. **SERVES 4**

2 tablespoons peanut oil or canola oil

¼ cup raw peanuts (without the skin)

¼ cup shredded dried unsweetened coconut

¼ cup firmly packed fresh cilantro leaves
    and tender stems

4 to 6 medium-size garlic cloves, to taste

2 or 3 fresh green Thai, cayenne, or serrano chiles,
    to taste, stems removed

I tablespoon white sesame seeds

I teaspoon cumin seeds

8 bone-in chicken thighs (2½ to 3 pounds),
    skin removed

I½ teaspoons coarse kosher or sea salt

½ cup plain yogurt

2 tablespoons heavy (whipping) cream

I teaspoon Maharashtrian garam masala (page 28)

1. Heat the oil in a medium-size skillet over medium heat. Add the peanuts and roast, stirring them constantly to prevent them from burning, until they turn nutty brown, 2 to 3 minutes. Scoop them out with a slotted spoon, leaving behind as much of the oil as possible, and place them in a food processor. Add the coconut, cilantro, garlic, and chiles to the processor. Pulse to mince, creating a nutty-smelling rub.

2. Reheat the oil in the skillet over medium heat. Sprinkle in the sesame and cumin seeds. As soon as they sizzle, turn reddish brown, and smell nutty-sweet, stir in the peanut blend. Stir-fry until the mixture smells nutty-pungent, 1 to 2 minutes.

3. Push the mixture to the edge and arrange the chicken pieces in a single layer in the skillet. Cover the chicken with the mixture and cook until the chicken is light brown on the underside, 2 to 4 minutes. Turn the chicken over, topping the pieces with the peanut mixture, and brown on the other side, 2 to 4 minutes. Keep the peanut mixture atop the chicken to prevent it from burning as the meat browns.

4. In a small bowl, stir the salt into ½ cup water. Pour this solution over the chicken, and heat it to a boil. Cover the skillet and simmer, periodically basting the chicken and turning the pieces, until the meat in the thickest parts is no longer pink inside and the juices run clear, 20 to 25 minutes. Transfer the chicken to a serving platter.

5. Stir the yogurt, cream, and garam masala into the sauce. Raise the heat to medium-high and simmer, uncovered, stirring occasionally, until the creamy green sauce thickens, 3 to 5 minutes.

6. Pour the sauce over the chicken, and serve.

Tips:

❖ Anyone who is allergic to peanuts should avoid peanut oil too. If peanuts are an issue, cashews work well in this recipe.

❖ Dark-meat chicken exudes more succulence than white meat, but if you prefer, you can use bone-in chicken breasts; just reduce the cooking time by about 7 or 8 minutes to prevent rubbery overcooked meat.

Chicken Curry
WITH WHOLE SPICES, CREAM, AND TOMATOES

Garam Masala Murghi

Working in an Indian restaurant kitchen can be brutal. I want to expunge the memory of those long hours on my feet. Let me also forget about repeatedly lowering my arm into a 700°F tandoor to slap a piece of dough for naan. I have almost managed to erase the rec-ollection of scrubbing pots when the dishwasher chose to quit on the busiest Saturday night, not to mention that hard-to-get-along-with boss who gave new meaning to the term "hell's kitchen." What I do enjoy reminiscing about are the aromas and flavors of many of my creations that brought satisfaction to our customers. There was a simple chicken curry on the menu that was the restau-rant's most popular dish, especially among those just starting to acquaint themselves with tastes that were foreign to their midwestern palate. Here is a slightly different version, decades later, as I relive those memories, both good and bad, that shaped my food career over the years. **SERVES 6**

2 tablespoons canola oil
½ teaspoon whole cloves
4 green or white cardamom pods

2 fresh or dried bay leaves
2 cinnamon sticks (each 3 inches long)
4 medium-size cloves garlic, finely chopped
2 lengthwise slices fresh ginger (each 2 inches long,
    1 inch wide, and ⅛ inch thick), finely chopped
1 large tomato, cored and finely chopped
2 teaspoons Punjabi garam masala (page 25)
1 teaspoon coarse kosher or sea salt
1½ pounds boneless, skinless chicken thighs,
    cut into 1-inch pieces
½ cup low-sodium canned chicken broth or water
¼ cup heavy (whipping) cream
2 tablespoons finely chopped fresh cilantro leaves
    and tender stems for garnishing

1. Heat the oil in a medium-size skillet over medium-high heat. Sprinkle in the cloves, cardamom pods, bay leaves, and cinnamon sticks, and cook until they sizzle, crackle, and smell aromatic, 10 to 15 seconds. Add the garlic and ginger, and stir-fry until they are light brown, 1 to 2 minutes.

2. Quickly add the tomato to the skillet (this stops the ginger and garlic from browning further), and then sprinkle in the garam masala and salt. Cook, uncov-ered, stirring occasionally, until the tomato softens a bit but is still firm-looking, 3 to 5 minutes.

3. Stir in the chicken and pour in the broth. Bring the curry to a boil. Then reduce the heat to medium-low, cover the skillet, and simmer, stirring occasionally, until the meat is no longer pink inside and the juices run clear, 10 to 15 minutes.

4. Fold in the cream and allow it to warm, uncovered, stirring occasionally, for 2 to 4 minutes.

5. Remove the cardamom pods, bay leaves, whole cloves, and cinnamon sticks. Sprinkle the cilantro over the curry, and serve.

Tips:

❖ Boneless chicken thighs are an underrated cut; the thigh has a slightly stronger flavor than the other parts of the chicken and asserts itself in the company of equally sturdy spices. Of course you can use breast meat or any other cut that suits your fancy; just be careful not to overcook breast meat, as it tends to get rubbery and quite unpalatable.

❖ If you don't have low-sodium broth on hand, lower the salt in the recipe by ½ teaspoon. Conversely, if you're using water, throw in an additional ½ teaspoon salt while the tomato is simmering.

Cornish Game Hens

WITH AN ALMOND-MACE SAUCE

Javintri Murghi

The assertive flavor of Cornish hens is a great match for this robustly spiced marinade. Even though there are quite a few chiles in the marinade, its pungency tends to dissipate, especially when the hens are soused with the creamy sauce. The initial burst of mint is a pleasant surprise, adding perfume to the mace-nutmeg combination. **SERVES 4**

For the hens and marinade:

2 Cornish game hens (about 1½ pounds each), skin removed, cut in half lengthwise (see Tip, page 163)
8 medium-size cloves garlic, sliced in half lengthwise
¾ cup plain yogurt
¼ cup slivered blanched almonds
2 teaspoons coarse kosher or sea salt
½ teaspoon ground turmeric
¼ teaspoon ground nutmeg
5 blades mace, or ½ teaspoon ground mace
6 dried red Thai or cayenne chiles, stems removed
¼ cup finely chopped fresh cilantro leaves and tender stems

Vegetable cooking spray

For the sauce:

2 tablespoons Ghee (page 21) or canola oil
½ cup finely chopped red onion
¼ cup slivered blanched almonds, ground
¼ teaspoon ground mace
½ cup half-and-half
½ teaspoon rock salt, pounded
2 tablespoons finely chopped fresh mint leaves for garnishing

1. Using a sharp knife, make four slits in each hen half: two into the breast meat, one in the outer thigh meat, and one in the inner thigh meat. Stuff a piece of garlic into each of the slits. Place the hens in a baking dish, meat side up.

2. To make the marinade, combine the yogurt, almonds, salt, turmeric, nutmeg, mace, and chiles in a blender jar. Puree, scraping the inside of the jar as needed, to create a slightly gritty, colorfully tart sauce. Pour it into a small bowl and fold in the cilantro.

3. Pour the marinade over the hens, lifting them up to make sure it coats their underside too. Refrigerate, covered, for at least 1 hour or as long as overnight, to allow the flavors to permeate the meat.

4. Preheat a gas or charcoal grill to high, or preheat the oven to 350°F.

5. *If you are grilling,* spray the grill grate with cooking spray. Place the hens, meat side down, on the grate. (There shouldn't be very much marinade left in the dish, but if there is—which is more likely if the yogurt you used is nonfat or low-fat—reserve it for basting the hens.) Cover, and grill the hens, basting them occasionally with the remaining marinade (if any) and turning them over halfway through, until the meat in the thickest parts is no longer pink inside and the juices run clear, about 30 minutes. Transfer them to a serving platter and cover them with aluminum foil to keep them warm while you quickly make the sauce.

If you are oven-roasting the hens, place a rack in a roasting pan and spray it with cooking spray. Place the hens, meat side down, on the rack. (There shouldn't be very much marinade left in the dish, but if there is—which is more likely if the yogurt you used is nonfat or low-fat—reserve it for basting the hens.) Roast, basting them occasionally with the remaining marinade (if any) and turning them over halfway through, until the meat in the thickest parts is no longer pink and the juices run clear, 45 minutes to 1 hour. Transfer them to a serving platter and cover them with aluminum foil to keep them warm while you quickly make the sauce.

6. To make the sauce, heat the ghee in a small saucepan over medium-high heat. Add the onion and stir-fry until it is light brown around the edges, 3 to 5 minutes. Then stir in the ground almonds and cook, stirring frequently, until they brown, about 2 minutes.

7. Sprinkle in the mace and pour in the half-and-half. Bring to a boil and cook until the sauce thickens, 2 to 3 minutes.

8. Stir in the rock salt, and pour the sauce over the hens. Sprinkle with the mint leaves, and serve.

Fiery Game Hens
WITH SCALLIONS

kadipatte Chi Murghi

The flavors in this curry bring to your home the subtleties of Kolhapur, a city in Maharashtra. Green chiles, garlic, and scallions enliven these Cornish hens, along with the southern Indian–influenced fresh curry leaves. The fiery Maharashtrian garam masala provides added dimension and sassiness to this tomato-based curry. One taste and you will utter, "Saucy!"

SERVES 4

½ cup plain yogurt
6 fresh green Thai, cayenne, or serrano chiles,
    stems removed
6 medium-size cloves garlic
1½ teaspoons coarse kosher or sea salt
2 Cornish game hens (about 1½ pounds each),
    skin removed, cut in half lengthwise
2 tablespoons canola oil
1 teaspoon black or yellow mustard seeds
1 can (14.5 ounces) diced tomatoes
¼ cup loosely packed medium-size to large
    fresh curry leaves
1 cup finely chopped scallions (green tops
    and white bulbs)
2 teaspoons Maharashtrian garam masala (page 28)

1. Combine the yogurt, chiles, garlic, and salt in a blender jar. Puree, scraping the inside of the jar as needed, to make a smooth, green-speckled, tart-hot marinade.

2. Place the hens in a baking dish and pour the marinade over them, turning the pieces in the marinade to thoroughly coat them. Refrigerate, covered, for at least 30 minutes or up to 6 hours, to allow the flavors to permeate the meat.

3. Heat the oil in a large skillet over medium-high heat. Add the mustard seeds, cover the skillet, and cook until the seeds have stopped popping (not unlike popcorn), about 30 seconds. Then add the hen halves, meat side down, marinade and all (although there won't be that much residual marinade), in a single layer. Lower the heat to medium, and cover the pan as the hens' juices will make the oil sputter. Cook until the hens have turned caramel-brown on the underside, about 5 minutes. Turn the pieces over and brown on the other side, about 5 minutes.

4. Add the tomatoes, with their juices, and spread the curry leaves over the hens. Reduce the heat to medium-low, cover the skillet, and stew the hens, basting them occasionally with the sauce and turning the pieces every few minutes to ensure even cooking, until the meat in the thickest parts is no longer pink inside and the juices run clear, 20 to 25 minutes. Remove the hen pieces and arrange them on a serving platter.

5. Stir the scallions and garam masala into the sauce, and raise the heat to medium. Simmer the sauce vigorously, uncovered, stirring occasionally, until the curry is gravy-thick, albeit chunky, 5 minutes.

6. Pour this festive-looking sauce over the hens, and serve.

Tips:

❖ Specially bred Rock Cornish hens, also known as game hens, are a cross between the Cornish and White Rock breeds of chicken. They are naturally small (weighing no more than 2 pounds) and have a slight "gamey" quality to the meat. They are more similar to the chickens in India than the larger, blander-tasting chickens used in the U.S. Rock Cornish hens are usually to be found in the freezer section of your grocery store. Thaw them in the refrigerator overnight or under cold tap water, still wrapped, for 2 to 3 hours. I find it's much simpler to peel off their skin when they are still slightly frozen. A couple of dry paper towels afford a better grip when you pull off the skin. If Rock Cornish hens are unavailable in your area, substitute 1 small chicken (about 3 pounds).

❖ You can leave the curry leaves in the sauce when you serve the birds. They are perfectly edible, but we usually eat around them. Bay leaves make for an interesting alternative, but use only 3 or 4, fresh or dried, as they do have a sharper flavor. Discard the bay leaves before serving the curry.

Grilled Cornish Game Hens
WITH A TOMATO-FENUGREEK SAUCE

tandoori murgh makhani

In many Western countries, the U.K. and U.S. included, tandoori chicken is considered *the* signature dish of Indian cooking. Maybe so in those parts of the world, but in India, it was confined to the cooking associated with the

Moghals, who dominated the northern regions just before the British took over their raj, and now it is associated with Punjab and Pakistan. Tandoori chicken showed up on restaurant menus in Old Delhi and soon spread to other parts of the world, roasting its way into people's hearts. The chickens in India are much smaller than those in the U.S. and have a stronger flavor, so Cornish game hens are the perfect substitute. **SERVES 4**

*2 Cornish game hens (about 1½ pounds each),
    skin removed, cut in half lengthwise
    (see Tip, page 163)*
⅓ cup plain yogurt
1 tablespoon Ginger Paste (page 15)
1 tablespoon Garlic Paste (page 15)
2 teaspoons Balti masala (page 31)
*2 teaspoons ground Kashmiri chiles; or ½ teaspoon
    cayenne (ground red pepper) mixed with
    1½ teaspoons sweet paprika*
1¼ teaspoons coarse kosher or sea salt
Vegetable cooking spray
2 tablespoons Ghee (page 21) or butter
½ cup tomato sauce
*½ cup chopped fresh or frozen fenugreek leaves
    (thawed if frozen); or 2 tablespoons dried
    fenugreek leaves, soaked in a bowl of water
    and skimmed off before use (see box, page 473)*
½ teaspoon cayenne (ground red pepper)
½ cup half-and-half

1. Using a sharp knife, make four slits in each hen half: two into the breast meat, one in the outer thigh meat, and one in the inner thigh meat. Place the hens in a baking dish, meat side up.

2. Combine the yogurt, Ginger Paste, Garlic Paste, *balti masala,* Kashmiri chiles, and 1 teaspoon of the salt in a small bowl, and whisk to blend. Smear the hen halves with this orange-red marinade, making sure to

stuff some of it into the slits. Refrigerate, covered, for at least 1 hour or as long as overnight, to allow the flavors to permeate the meat.

3. Preheat a gas or charcoal grill to high, or preheat the oven to 350°F.

4. *If you are grilling,* spray the grill grate with cooking spray. Place the hens, meat side down, on the grate. (Reserve any marinade for basting the hens.) Cover, and grill the hens, basting them occasionally with the remaining marinade and turning them over halfway through, until the meat in the thickest parts is no longer pink inside and the juices run clear, 30 to 40 minutes. Transfer the hens to a serving platter and cover them with aluminum foil to keep them warm while you quickly make the sauce.

If you are oven-roasting the hens, place a rack in a roasting pan and spray it with cooking spray. Place the hens, meat side down, on the rack. (Reserve any marinade for basting the hens.) Roast, basting them occasionally with the remaining marinade and turning them over halfway through, until the meat in the thickest parts is no longer pink inside and the juices run clear, about 45 minutes. Transfer the hens to a serving platter and cover them with aluminum foil to keep them warm while you quickly make the sauce.

5. To make the sauce, heat the ghee in a small saucepan over medium heat. Add the tomato sauce, fenugreek, cayenne, and the remaining ¼ teaspoon salt. Cover and simmer, stirring occasionally, to allow the flavors to meld, 5 to 10 minutes. Then stir in the half-and-half and continue to simmer, uncovered, stirring occasionally, to let it warm, 2 to 4 minutes.

6. To serve the curry, cut the hens into smaller pieces and toss them with the sauce.

Tip: It's easier to roast larger pieces of the bird and then cut them into smaller serving pieces, and it retains their juiciness. Once the halves are slightly cool to the touch, cut each one into four pieces.

Duck Stew
WITH
BLACK CARDAMOM AND CHERRIES

kashmiri batak

this complex-tasting curry combines all things good about Kashmir, the state that grows India's black walnuts and cherries. Strong-tasting duck meat absorbs the tart-sweet juices of the cherries along with the meaty walnuts while it stews in sweet fennel and pungent ginger to create what we chefs like to refer as a "flavor profile"—in this case, one that blows your mind (or your palate). Serve it with Kashmir's other prized delicacy, steamed white basmati rice, for a truly scrumptious meal. **SERVES 8**

I duck (5 pounds), skin removed, cut into 8 pieces
   (see box on cutting up a chicken, page 121)
2 tablespoons Ginger Paste (page 15)
2 tablespoons Garlic Paste (page 15)
2 teaspoons coarse kosher or sea salt
I teaspoon ground turmeric
2 tablespoons canola oil
I small red onion, cut in half lengthwise
   and thinly sliced
6 black cardamom pods
2 fresh or dried bay leaves
2 cinnamon sticks (each 3 inches long)
2 teaspoons fennel seeds, ground

I½ teaspoons ground Kashmiri chiles;
   or ½ teaspoon cayenne (ground red pepper)
   mixed with I teaspoon sweet paprika
I teaspoon ground ginger
I bag (12 ounces) frozen pitted cherries,
   partially thawed and sliced in half
½ cup chopped black walnuts
2 tablespoons finely chopped fresh cilantro leaves
   and tender stems for garnishing

1. Combine the duck pieces, ginger and garlic pastes, 1½ teaspoons of the salt, and the turmeric in a large bowl, making sure all the duck pieces get well coated with the mixture. Cover and refrigerate for at least 1 hour, or as long as overnight, to allow the meat to absorb the flavors.

2. Heat the oil in a large skillet over medium heat. Add the duck pieces, including any paste mixture that is clinging to them, meat side down, in a single layer. Cook until the pieces are seared and have turned light caramel-brown, about 10 minutes. Flip the pieces over (this side will be more bone than meat) and let whatever meat there is turn light brown, about 5 minutes. Transfer the duck pieces to a plate.

3. Add the onion, cardamom pods, bay leaves, cinnamon sticks, and ½ cup water to the skillet. Scrape the skillet to deglaze it, releasing any stuck-on pieces of meat and paste. Raise the heat to medium-high and cook, uncovered, stirring occasionally, until the liquid is reduced by half, about 5 minutes.

4. Stir in the ground fennel, chiles, ginger, and the remaining ½ teaspoon salt, and cook for about 30 seconds.

5. Pour in 1½ cups water, and stir in the cherries and walnuts. Heat the liquid to a boil. Then lower the heat to medium and add the duck pieces, meat

side down, including any liquid that has pooled on the plate. Baste the duck with the curry, cover the skillet, and simmer, basting very occasionally, until the meat is tender and no longer pink inside, 35 to 40 minutes.

6. Transfer the duck to a serving platter and cover it with plastic wrap or aluminum foil to keep warm. Raise the heat under the skillet to medium-high and cook, uncovered, stirring occasionally, until the sauce is thick, about 10 minutes.

7. Pour the sauce over the duck pieces, top with the cilantro, and serve immediately.

SRI LANKAN–STYLE
Hard-Cooked Eggs
WITH COCONUT MILK

bittarai kirihodi

this simple curry is made in many home kitchens in Sri Lanka—this version came to me from Piyumi Samaratunga (see page 282). Typical of Sri Lankan cooking, the coconut milk provides not only the base but also a creamy balance to the pungent chiles. The eggs are left whole, and they look deceptively like peeled new potatoes (which by the way is a great alternative if you don't eat eggs). Serve it over steamed white rice, or if you have

a chance to procure the Sri Lankan pearly-white rice called *Muttu sambha* (page 721), use that in a heartbeat. **SERVES 6**

2 tablespoons canola oil
½ teaspoon fenugreek seeds
1 or 2 cinnamon sticks (each 3 inches long)
1 cup finely chopped red onion
1 or 2 fresh green Thai, cayenne, or serrano chiles,
    to taste, stems removed, cut in half lengthwise
    (do not remove the seeds)
2 teaspoons Untoasted Sri Lankan Curry Powder
    (page 40)
1 can (13.5 ounces) unsweetened coconut milk
1 teaspoon coarse kosher or sea salt
½ teaspoon ground turmeric
6 extra-large or jumbo eggs, hard-cooked
    and peeled (see box, facing page)

1. Heat the oil in a medium-size saucepan over medium heat. Sprinkle in the fenugreek seeds and cinnamon sticks, and cook until the spices sizzle, the fenugreek turns reddish brown, and the cinnamon smells fragrant, 15 to 30 seconds. Add the onion and chiles, and stir-fry until the onion is light brown around the edges, 5 to 8 minutes.

2. Sprinkle in the curry powder, stirring to cook the spices without burning them (the onion provides a cushion that prevents that from happening), about 30 seconds. Then add the coconut milk, salt, and turmeric.

3. Gently add the eggs and simmer the yellow curry, uncovered, basting the eggs very often, until the sauce thickens slightly, 5 to 10 minutes.

4. Serve immediately, spooning the sauce over the eggs. (Remove the cinnamon sticks if you like.)

Halved Eggs
WITH GARLIC, CURRY LEAVES, AND TAMARIND

Muttai kari

Eggs were never part of my family's repertoire when I was growing up in a somewhat rigid Tamilian Brahmin home—at least not when my tenacious grandmother was still alive. With her passing, and with new generations of children pervading the kitchen in these global times, taboos like this have fallen by the wayside to make way for a completely new array of offerings. Savor this curry for breakfast with south India's rice-lentil pancakes called *Vengayam adai* (page 724). **SERVES 4**

2 tablespoons firmly packed fresh cilantro leaves and tender stems

8 to 10 medium-size to large fresh curry leaves

4 medium-size cloves garlic

1 or 2 fresh green Thai, cayenne, or serrano chiles, to taste, stems removed

2 tablespoons unrefined sesame oil or canola oil

1 teaspoon black or yellow mustard seeds

2 medium-size to large shallots, thinly sliced

½ teaspoon ground turmeric

1 teaspoon coarse kosher or sea salt

½ teaspoon tamarind paste or concentrate

4 extra-large or jumbo eggs, hard-cooked, peeled, and cut in half lengthwise (see box below)

2 teaspoons rice flour

1. Pile the cilantro, curry leaves, garlic, and chiles into a mortar. Pound the ingredients with a pestle, scraping the interior of the mortar to contain the herbs in the center for a more concentrated pounding, until the

the perfect hard-cooked egg
❖ ❖ ❖

If you can boil water, you can make perfect hard-cooked eggs. It starts with an egg that is not so fresh, maybe 7 days old. (Over time, the shell and the egg white separate slightly, making it easier to peel the egg.) Of course, you don't want an egg that is really old. If it floats in the water, it is one rotten egg. Choose eggs that have a smooth shell with no cracks. Let the eggs sit at room temperature for about 15 minutes before you cook them.

Fill a small saucepan three-quarters full with water and bring it to a rolling boil over medium-high heat. Gently place the eggs in the water and reduce the heat to medium. (To avoid cracking the shell, I usually place the egg in a spoon and lower the spoon into the water.)

Simmer the eggs, without letting the water come to a boil (which is why I prefer the term "hard-cooked" because they really are not "hard-boiled"), for 15 to 18 minutes, depending on how hard you actually want them to be. You don't want to overcook the eggs, or you will find an unpleasant green ring of hydrogen sulfide around the sun-yellow yolk.

Remove the eggs with that same spoon and plunge them into a bowl filled with cold water. If you want the eggs to be quite cold, continue to cool them by replacing the water with more cold tap water for about 5 minutes. Shocking the eggs (submerging the hot eggs in cold water) stops the cooking and also makes the shell easier to peel.

mixture forms a paste. (Alternatively, place the ingredients in a food processor and process until minced.)

2. Heat the oil in a medium-size skillet over medium-high heat. Add the mustard seeds, cover, and cook until the seeds have stopped popping (not unlike popcorn), about 30 seconds. Then add the paste and shallots and stir-fry until lightly browned, 1 to 2 minutes. Sprinkle in the turmeric, which will instantly color everything sun-yellow.

3. In a small bowl, quickly combine the salt, tamarind paste, and 1 cup water, whisking to dissolve the paste and create a muddy-brown liquid. Pour this into the skillet; it will instantly start to boil, thanks to the hot pan. Sink the eggs, cut side up, into the liquid and spoon the sauce over them. Bring the curry to a boil over medium-high heat. Cook, basting the eggs with the sauce (don't actually stir the eggs), for 3 to 5 minutes. Using a slotted spoon, transfer the eggs to a serving platter.

4. Sprinkle the rice flour into the thin sauce, stirring to prevent any lumps from forming. The sauce will immediately start to thicken; cook for about 1 minute. Pour the sauce over the eggs, and serve.

Easter Eggs
WITH AN ONION-GARLIC SAUCE

Pyaaz Waale Unday

Egg curries like this are a cinch to make. Around Easter, I find an abundant supply of hard-cooked eggs lying around our house. Gently simmering the cooked eggs in a robust onion-tomato sauce makes for a delicious quick lunch, especially when accompanied by slices of buttered toast. I particularly enjoy dunking the crusty pieces into the sauce before I devour them. **SERVES 4**

2 tablespoons canola oil

1 cup finely chopped red onion

6 medium-size cloves garlic, finely chopped

2 teaspoons bin bhuna hua garam masala (page 30)

2 tablespoons finely chopped fresh cilantro leaves and tender stems

1 teaspoon coarse kosher or sea salt

2 fresh green Thai, cayenne, or serrano chiles, stems removed, cut in half lengthwise (do not remove the seeds)

1 medium-size tomato, cored and finely chopped

4 extra-large or jumbo eggs, hard-cooked, peeled, and cut in half lengthwise (see box, page 167)

1. Heat the oil in a medium-size skillet over medium-high heat. Add the onion and garlic, and stir-fry until the onion is honey-brown around the edges with a deep purple hue, 8 to 10 minutes.

2. Stir in the garam masala and cook for 30 seconds to 1 minute. Transfer the mixture to a blender jar, and pour in 1 cup water. Puree, scraping the inside of the jar as needed, to make a smooth sauce.

3. Pour the sauce back into the skillet and stir in the cilantro, salt, chiles, and tomato. Lower the eggs into the sauce, cut side up. Spoon the sauce over the eggs and bring the curry to a boil over medium-high heat. Don't stir the sauce, but keep basting the eggs with it until it starts to thicken, 5 to 8 minutes.

4. Lift the eggs onto a serving platter, spoon the sauce over them, and serve.

beef, lamb & pork curries

Many people think that all Indians are vegetarians, but in fact a large number of India's 1.2 billion population do consume lamb, mutton, beef, and pork. Religious tenets are what usually dictate eating habits, especially when it comes to meats. For example, a majority of Hindus refrain from eating meat (or anything that has

eyes, for that matter). But within Hinduism (the most widespread religion in India) some groups abstain from beef but will eat lamb, mutton, and pork. (It's interesting to note that when Rama, one of the most widely worshiped Hindu gods, and his wife, Sita, were banished to the forest for fourteen years, Sita enjoyed eating deer meat stewed with vegetables and spices. Her father-in-law periodically sacrificed and consumed mutton and pork sim-

mered in fruit juices, or fried in clove-scented butter and then stewed with lentils.)

Muslims, who comprise the second largest religious group in India, relish beef. Bottle Gourd Squash Stuffed with Ground Beef and Golden Raisins (page 181), for example, is a specialty of the Bohri Muslims in northwestern India. Lamb and mutton are revered among the Islamic community, and every major religious event within that community witnesses their sacrifice with utmost sanctity. It comes as no surprise, then, that lamb is treated with the choicest of ingredients and elaborate preparations in curries like Saffron-Scented Lamb with an Almond Sauce (page 202) and Roasted Leg of Lamb with Raisin-Mint Sauce (page 184).

Like the Jews, Muslims avoid pork. But leave it to the Goan Christians to concoct Nutty-Tart Pork with Cider Vinegar, Cashews, and Onions (page 228) and the Portuguese-influenced Goan-Style Spicy Pork Sausage with Kidney Beans and Black-Eyed Peas (page 232). The warrior clan of Kodavas, in the southwestern state of Karnataka, enjoy stewed Cubed Pork with Potatoes, Yogurt, and Tamarind (page 222).

The Syrian Christians of southwestern India do eat beef curries (Beef with Bell Peppers, Onions, and Mushrooms, page 171), as do the Portuguese Christians in Goa, just north of Kerala (Curried Beef Stew with Potatoes, Shallots, and Malt Vinegar, page 172).

The Parsis, followers of Zoroastrianism who fled Iran and settled in Mumbai, devour lamb with equal gusto. You will savor their Coconut-Smothered Lamb with Shoestring Potatoes (page 195).

Whatever your leanings in the carnivorous world, you will never go wrong with any of these succulent, vibrant, saucy dishes.

{ beef }

Stewed Beef
WITH PICKLING SPICES

Achar Gosht

Pickles in India are made with large amounts of mustard (oil and ground), cayenne, and turmeric—it's these flavorings that make this curry so memorable. Strong, machismo beef stands up to those bold flavors to provide an unequivocal answer to the question "What's for dinner?" Serve it with either store-bought or homemade naan (page 729) for a complete experience. **SERVES 6**

2 tablespoons mustard oil

2 tablespoons Ginger Paste (page 15)

1 tablespoon Garlic Paste (page 15)

1 tablespoon black or yellow mustard seeds, ground

1 teaspoon cayenne (ground red pepper)

1 teaspoon coarse kosher or sea salt

1 teaspoon ground turmeric

1 pound boneless beef (chuck, or "stew meat"), cut into 1-inch cubes

1 large red onion, cut into 1-inch cubes

1 large green bell pepper (8 ounces), stemmed, seeded, and cut into 1-inch pieces

2 tablespoons tomato paste

2 tablespoons finely chopped fresh cilantro leaves
and tender stems for garnishing

1. Combine the mustard oil, Ginger Paste, Garlic Paste, ground mustard, cayenne, salt, and turmeric in a medium-size bowl. Add the beef and toss to coat it well. Refrigerate, covered, for at least 30 minutes or as long as overnight.

2. Preheat a large saucepan over medium-high heat. Add the beef, onion, and bell pepper to the pan and cook, stirring, until the beef is browned all over, 8 to 10 minutes. (The beef and vegetables will brown in the mustard oil that is released from the beef.)

3. Add the tomato paste and 1 cup water, and stir to make a smooth sauce. Cover the pan and braise the meat over medium-low heat, stirring occasionally, until the beef cubes are very tender when cut with a fork, 1¼ to 1½ hours.

4. Sprinkle with the cilantro, and serve.

Beef
WITH BELL PEPPERS, ONIONS, AND MUSHROOMS

dhingri gosht

the Jews of Cochin (now called Kochi) had a major impact on the economic scene in southwestern India, starting as early as the 4th century. Though only a mere handful remain in the city today, an entire section of the town, still known as "Jew Town," continues to harbor an array of vibrant stores as well as the oldest synagogue in India. Some of the Cochin Jews ate beef (although not so often, in deference to their Hindu neighbors), but they followed their religious prohibition regarding combining dairy with meat. Local spices and ingredients like mustard seeds and coconut milk made their way into their kitchens, as is evidenced in this easy-to-make curry.

SERVES 4

¼ cup unsweetened coconut milk

¼ teaspoon ground turmeric

8 ounces boneless beef (chuck, or "stew meat"),
cut into 1-inch cubes

2 tablespoons coconut oil or canola oil

1 teaspoon black or yellow mustard seeds

4 ounces button mushrooms or brown cremini
mushrooms, quartered

1 large red bell pepper (8 ounces), stemmed, seeded,
and cut into 1-inch pieces

1 small red onion, cut into 1-inch cubes

12 to 15 medium-size to large fresh curry leaves

1½ teaspoons coarse kosher or sea salt

½ teaspoon cayenne (ground red pepper)

1. Stir the coconut milk and turmeric together in a medium-size bowl. Add the beef and stir to coat it. Refrigerate, covered, for at least 30 minutes or as long as overnight, to allow the meat to absorb the flavors.

2. Heat the oil in a large skillet over medium-high heat. Add the mustard seeds, cover, and cook until the seeds have stopped popping (not unlike popcorn), about 30 seconds. Immediately add the mushrooms, bell pepper, onion, curry leaves, and beef (including any residual marinade). Cook, uncovered, stirring occasionally, until the meat releases its liquid and browns and the vegetables turn light brown, 12 to 15 minutes.

3. Pour in 1 cup water. Scrape the bottom of the skillet to deglaze it, releasing any browned bits of vegetables and meat, to create a deep-flavored base for the curry. Stir in the salt. Once the curry comes to a boil, reduce the heat to medium-low, cover the skillet, and simmer, stirring occasionally, until the meat is fork-tender, 18 to 20 minutes.

4. Stir in the cayenne, and serve.

Tip: Even though there is only a small amount of cayenne pepper in this recipe, it has a sharp presence because you sprinkle it in just before you serve the curry. The coconut milk normally would have masked its heat, but it has already been absorbed into the meat and vegetables, making for a not-so-creamy curry.

Curried Beef Stew

WITH POTATOES, SHALLOTS, AND MALT VINEGAR

Soan Gosht Curry

this is one curry that will appeal to even the most finicky eater, the one who does not like "spicy" food, the one who turns up his/her nose at Indian food, the one who fails to taste even a small forkful of anything "foreign." Why? Because the ingredient mix appeals to their meat-and-potato, Sunday-beef-stew senses. The spicing is delicate yet complex-tasting, the malt vinegar providing an unusual depth that's mellowed by the creamy coconut milk. Serve it with a hunk of freshly baked crusty bread (store-bought is just fine too) as a simple dinner, or over steamed white rice for something more satiating. The dinner guests at my house used words like "robust," "juicy," "succulent," and "downright yummy" to describe this curry. **SERVES 6**

1 pound boneless beef (chuck, or "stew meat"),
cut into 1-inch cubes
1 teaspoon cayenne (ground red pepper)
½ teaspoon ground turmeric
8 ounces russet or Yukon Gold potatoes,
peeled, cut into 1-inch cubes,
and submerged in a bowl of
cold water to prevent browning
2 tablespoons canola oil
4 green or white cardamom pods
2 fresh or dried bay leaves
2 cinnamon sticks (each 3 inches long)
4 ounces shallots, thinly sliced
2 teaspoons cumin seeds, ground
2 teaspoons coriander seeds, ground
1 can (13.5 ounces) unsweetened
coconut milk
1 can (14.5 ounces) diced tomatoes
¼ cup malt vinegar
2 teaspoons coarse kosher or sea salt
2 tablespoons finely chopped fresh cilantro
leaves and tender stems for garnishing

1. Toss the beef in a medium-size bowl with the cayenne and turmeric. Refrigerate, covered, for at least 30 minutes or as long as overnight, to allow the spices to flavor the meat. (The turmeric does tenderize the beef, so the longer you marinate it, the more tender the meat curry.)

2. Drain the potatoes and pat them dry with paper towels.

3. Heat the oil in a large saucepan or skillet over medium-high heat. Add the cardamom pods, bay leaves, and cinnamon sticks, and cook until they sizzle and are aromatic, 5 to 10 seconds. Toss in the beef, shallots, and potatoes. Stir-fry until the beef is seared and the shallots and potatoes are lightly browned, about 5 minutes.

4. Sprinkle in the cumin and coriander, and continue to stir-fry for about 2 minutes.

5. Pour in the coconut milk, tomatoes with their juices, vinegar, and salt. Stir once or twice to deglaze the skillet, releasing any collected bits of spice and shallots. Reduce the heat to medium-low, cover, and simmer, stirring occasionally and gently, until the beef cubes are very tender when cut with a fork, the potatoes are tender but still firm, and the sauce is thick, 1¼ to 1½ hours.

6. Sprinkle with the cilantro, and serve.

Tips:

❖ The first time I tested this recipe, I was certain that the potatoes would fall apart with overcooking. Beef for stew comes from the tougher cuts of the animal, which require longer cooking times to break down the connective tissue, so when I added the potatoes and the beef at the same time, I was confident that I would have to retest it by adding the potatoes at a later stage. Imagine my surprise when the potatoes held their form after almost an hour and a half! It dawned on me that the acidity of the tomatoes helped to keep the starchy cubes firm.

❖ If you like, discard the cardamom pods, bay leaves, and cinnamon sticks before you serve the curry.

Aromatic Beef Stew
WITH MUSTARD GREENS, FENUGREEK, AND MINT

Gosht Hariyali

I celebrate the abundance of greens widely cultivated all across India, in this beef curry that combines the bitterness of mustard with the perfume of fenugreek and the allure of mint. Serve it with Saffron-Laced Basmati Rice (page 716). **SERVES 4**

2 tablespoons Ginger Paste (page 15)
1 tablespoon Garlic Paste (page 15)
1 teaspoon coarse kosher or sea salt
1 pound boneless beef (chuck, or "stew meat"),
    cut into 1-inch cubes
2 tablespoons canola oil
2 fresh green Thai, cayenne, or serrano chiles,
    stems removed, cut in half lengthwise
    (do not remove the seeds)
8 ounces fresh mustard greens, finely chopped
    (see Tip, page 606)
½ cup chopped fresh or frozen fenugreek leaves
    (thawed if frozen)
½ cup finely chopped fresh mint leaves
¼ cup finely chopped fresh cilantro leaves
and tender stems

Fenugreek leaves? See the Glossary of Ingredients, page 758.

1. Stir the Ginger Paste, Garlic Paste, and salt together in a medium-size bowl. Add the beef and stir to coat it with the paste. Refrigerate, covered, for at least 30 minutes or as long as overnight, to allow the flavors to permeate the meat.

2. Preheat a wok or a well-seasoned cast-iron skillet over medium-high heat. Drizzle the oil down its sides. When the oil has formed a shimmering pool at the bottom, add the beef, paste and all, and the chiles. Cook, stirring, until the meat is seared all over and the chiles are lightly browned, 8 to 10 minutes.

3. Pile the mustard greens and the fenugreek leaves into the wok, and cook, stirring occasionally, until the mustard has wilted and its liquid has deglazed the wok, releasing the browned bits on the bottom, 8 to 10 minutes.

4. Pour in 1 cup water and heat to a boil. Reduce the heat to medium-low, cover the wok, and simmer, stirring occasionally, until the beef is fork-tender, about 15 minutes.

5. Stir in the mint and cilantro, and serve.

Tart-Hot Beef
WITH MALT VINEGAR AND CAYENNE

Gosht Vindaloo

Goan vindaloos rely on fermented palm vinegar or cashew vinegar to tone down (just a tad) the cayenne, found in two forms in this curry: whole and ground. In the absence of those two kinds of vinegar in this country, I am using sweet malt vinegar for an equally satisfying balance. I usually make sure there is a bowl of plain yogurt on the table for those who may not be bold enough to savor the heat of the vindaloo. **SERVES 4**

½ cup malt vinegar
2 teaspoons cayenne (ground red pepper)
½ teaspoon ground turmeric
1 pound boneless beef (chuck, or "stew meat"), cut into 1-inch cubes
2 tablespoons canola oil
4 ounces pearl onions, peeled and cut in half lengthwise
5 medium-size cloves garlic, finely chopped
6 dried red Thai or cayenne chiles, stems removed
1 teaspoon coriander seeds, ground
1 teaspoon cumin seeds, ground
1 teaspoon coarse kosher or sea salt
2 tablespoons finely chopped fresh cilantro leaves and tender stems for garnishing

1. Combine the vinegar, cayenne, and turmeric in a medium-size stainless steel or glass bowl. Add the beef and toss to coat it with the mixture. Refrigerate, covered, for at least 1 hour or preferably overnight, to allow the acidic vinegar to tenderize the beef.

2. Heat the oil in a medium-size saucepan over medium-high heat. Add the onions, garlic, and chiles, and cook, stirring, until the onion halves are light honey-brown, about 5 minutes.

3. Add the beef and marinade. Cook, stirring occasionally, until the beef has absorbed the spiced vinegar and seared, and the oil is starting to separate from the meat, 12 to 15 minutes. Sprinkle in the coriander, cumin, and salt, and cook, stirring, for 1 to 2 minutes.

4. Pour in 1 cup water and bring to a boil. Reduce the heat to medium-low, cover the pan, and cook, stirring occasionally, until the meat is fork-tender and the sauce is reddish brown and thick, 40 to 45 minutes.

5. Remove the chiles if you like. Sprinkle with the cilantro, and serve.

Minty Beef
WITH CRACKED WHEAT AND LENTILS

haleem

Y ou might wonder if the amount of beef called for here is correct—could 1 pound of meat be enough for eight folks? But fear not: the legumes and cracked wheat add bulk to the curry and provide more protein as well. This curry is a substantial meal all on its own. Serve it with a few slices of crusty French bread on a cold wintry night. **SERVES 8**

1 pound boneless beef (chuck or "stew meat"),
*   cut into 1-inch cubes*
2 tablespoons Ginger Paste (page 15)
1 tablespoon Garlic Paste (page 15)
½ cup cracked wheat
½ cup skinned split green lentils (yellow in this form,
*   moong dal), picked over for stones*
½ cup skinned split brown lentils (salmon-colored in
*   this form, masoor dal), picked over for stones*
½ teaspoon ground turmeric
¼ cup canola oil
6 whole cloves
2 cinnamon sticks (each 3 inches long)
2 fresh or dried bay leaves
2 black cardamom pods
8 to 10 fresh green Thai, cayenne, or serrano chiles,
*   to taste, stems removed, cut in half lengthwise*
*   (do not remove the seeds)*
1 large red onion, cut in half lengthwise and thinly sliced
1½ teaspoons Kashmiri garam masala (page 29)
½ cup finely chopped fresh mint leaves
½ cup finely chopped fresh cilantro leaves
*   and tender stems*

1. Combine the beef, Ginger Paste, and Garlic Paste in a medium-size bowl, and toss to mix. Refrigerate, covered, to allow the flavors to permeate the meat, 6 to 8 hours.

2. At the same time, place the cracked wheat in a medium-size bowl. Fill the bowl halfway with water, and rinse the coarse grains by rubbing them between your fingertips. The water will become slightly cloudy. Drain this water. Repeat three or four times, until the water remains relatively clear; drain. Now cover the wheat with water and let it sit at room temperature, covered, until it softens and swells, 6 to 8 hours.

3. When you are ready to make the curry, place the green and brown lentils in a medium-size bowl. Fill the bowl halfway with water and rinse the lentils by rubbing them between your fingertips. The water will become cloudy. Drain this water. Repeat three or four times, until the water remains relatively clear; drain.

4. Drain the cracked wheat, and transfer it to a large saucepan. Add the drained lentils, and pour in 4 cups water. Bring the water to a boil, uncovered, over medium heat. Skim off and discard any foam that rises to the surface. Stir in the turmeric. Then lower the heat to medium, cover the pan, and simmer, stirring occasionally, until the lentils and wheat are tender, 20 to 25 minutes. Remove from the heat and set aside.

5. While the grains are cooking, heat the oil in a large saucepan over medium-high heat. Sprinkle in the cloves, cinnamon sticks, bay leaves, and cardamom pods. Cook until they sizzle and crackle and the cinnamon sticks swell, about 30 seconds. Then add the chiles and onion. Lower the heat to medium, cover the pan, and cook until the onion is starting to brown (the onion will release its liquid first, and then start to brown once it evaporates), 15 to 20 minutes. Uncover the pan and brown the onion further by stir-frying until it is reddish brown with a deep purple hue, 5 to 10 minutes.

6. Add the beef cubes, including the clinging pastes, raise the heat to medium-high, and cook until the meat is starting to turn light brown, 12 to 15 minutes. (At first the meat will sear, then it will release its liquid, and then after that evaporates, it will start to brown.)

7. Pour in 1 cup water, stir in the garam masala, and bring to a boil. Then reduce the heat to medium-low, cover the pan, and simmer, stirring occasionally, until the meat is fork-tender, 15 to 20 minutes.

8. Add the wheat and lentils, along with their liquid. Let the curry simmer, uncovered, stirring occasionally, until the flavors mingle, 10 to 15 minutes.

9. Remove the cloves, cinnamon sticks, bay leaves, and cardamom pods if you wish. Stir in the mint and cilantro, and serve.

Tamarind Beef
WITH SHALLOTS AND MANGO

Ḿoppalah Ǵosht Ḱootan

Ḿoppalahs (also spelled Moplah, Mapilla, Mappila . . .) are the Muslim community in Kerala, whose male ancestors, descendants of Arab traders, married the local women and settled there in the 7th century, well before the advent of Islam. They were very recep-tive to conversion and incorporated not only the Islamic dietary laws that prohibited the inclusion of pork but also kept the local fondness for coconut, curry leaves, shallots, and mustard seeds. This beef curry combines all those ingredients with chunks of beef and two acidic ingredients, tamarind and seasonal unripe mango. Serve it over rice noodle nests (*Idiappam,* page 723) or the other northern Kerala favorite, flaky griddle-cooked bread (*Malabar parantha,* page 731).

SERVES 4

> 2 tablespoons Ginger Paste (page 15)
> 1 tablespoon Garlic Paste (page 15)
> ½ teaspoon ground turmeric
> 1 pound boneless beef (chuck, or "stew meat"),
>   cut into 1-inch cubes
> 2 tablespoons coconut oil or canola oil
> 1 teaspoon black or yellow mustard seeds
> 1 cup thinly sliced shallots
> 4 dried red Thai or cayenne chiles, stems removed
> 2 tablespoons coriander seeds, ground
> 1½ teaspoons coarse kosher or sea salt
> ½ cup unsweetened coconut milk
> 1 teaspoon tamarind paste or concentrate
> 1 large, rock-firm, unripe mango, peeled
>   and cut into ¼-inch cubes
> 12 to 15 medium-size to large fresh curry leaves
> 2 tablespoons finely chopped fresh cilantro
>   leaves and tender stems for garnishing

1. Combine the Ginger Paste, Garlic Paste, and turmeric in a medium-size bowl and mix well. Add the beef and toss to cover it with the paste. Refrigerate, covered, for at least 30 minutes or as long as overnight, to allow the flavors to permeate the meat.

2. Heat the oil in a large skillet over medium-high heat. Add the mustard seeds, cover, and cook until the seeds have stopped popping (not unlike popcorn),

about 30 seconds. Immediately add the shallots and chiles, and stir-fry until the shallots are light brown around the edges, 3 to 4 minutes.

3. Add the turmeric-stained beef, along with the coriander and salt. Cook, stirring, until the meat has released its liquid and started to sear and turn light brown, 10 to 12 minutes.

4. Whisk the coconut milk and tamarind paste together in a small bowl. As soon as the beef is seared, pour in the coconut milk mixture. Scrape the bottom of the skillet to deglaze it, releasing any browned bits of meat and shallots. Stir in the mango and curry leaves. Reduce the heat to medium-low, cover the skillet, and simmer, stirring occasionally, until the beef is fork-tender, 12 to 15 minutes.

5. Remove the chiles if you like. Sprinkle with the cilantro, and serve.

Fall-Apart Beef Cubes
WITH SPINACH AND COCONUT

Nariyal Palak Gosht

The secret of this simple but succulent curry is in the simmering of a slightly tough cut of meat over a long period of time, which yields a fall-apart texture. The spinach greens and the shower of coconut add freshness, and the last-minute jolt of tamarind balances it all out with its tart flavor. Serve it with steamed rice noodles

(*Idiappam*, page 723) or with griddle-cooked *roti* (page 727) for a winning combination. **SERVES 6**

- 2 tablespoons plain yogurt
- 1 tablespoon Ginger Paste (page 15)
- 1 tablespoon Garlic Paste (page 15)
- 1 teaspoon coarse kosher or sea salt
- ½ teaspoon ground turmeric
- ½ teaspoon cayenne (ground red pepper)
- 1 pound boneless beef (chuck, or "stew meat"), cut into 1-inch cubes
- 2 tablespoons canola oil
- 1 pound fresh spinach leaves, well rinsed
- 1 cup shredded fresh coconut; or ½ cup shredded dried unsweetened coconut, reconstituted (see Note)
- 1 teaspoon tamarind paste or concentrate

1. Whisk the yogurt, Ginger Paste, Garlic Paste, salt, turmeric, and cayenne together in a medium-size bowl. Add the beef cubes, tossing to coat them with the creamy, spicy marinade. Refrigerate, covered, for at least 1 hour or as long as overnight, to allow the flavors to come together and the meat to tenderize.

2. Heat the oil in a medium-size saucepan over medium-high heat. Add the beef, marinade and all. Cook, uncovered, stirring occasionally, until the liquid gets absorbed and the oil starts to separate from the beef, 10 to 15 minutes.

3. Pour 1 cup water into the pan and scrape the bottom to deglaze it, releasing any browned bits of meat. Continue to simmer, uncovered, until the water is absorbed and the oil once again separates from the meat, 10 to 15 minutes.

4. Now pour in 2 cups water, stirring once or twice. After it comes to a boil, lower the heat to medium, cover the pan, and simmer, stirring occasionally, until the beef absorbs the liquid and is very tender, 30 to 40 minutes.

5. Grab a handful of spinach and add it to the pan. Cover, and allow the steam to wilt the spinach. Mix it in before you add the next batch of spinach. Repeat until all the greens are wilted, about 5 minutes.

6. Stir in the coconut and tamarind paste. Simmer, uncovered, stirring occasionally, to warm the coconut, about 5 minutes, and serve.

Note: To reconstitute coconut, cover with ½ cup boiling water, set aside for about 15 minutes, and then drain.

Skewered Beef
WITH AN ONION–MALT VINEGAR SAUCE

"Stick" Curry

Norton Cunningham, an Anglo-Indian now settled in Bangalore, shared some of his family history with me (his family resided for a number of years in Ooty, a hill station in south central India—a beautiful landscape filled with tea plantations and botanical gardens that was popular with the British during the Raj). Then Norton shared a little of his culinary history and gave me this curry recipe. Asked about the name "stick," he explained that it referred to the top halves of broomsticks, which were used to skewer meats. It may be presumptuous of me to assume that you may have a number of broomsticks lying around, in lieu of a vacuum cleaner, so I suggest using skewers instead. **SERVES 6**

1 pound boneless beef (chuck, or "stew meat"), cut into 1-inch cubes
About 12 small cloves garlic
4 to 6 fresh green Thai, cayenne, or serrano chiles, to taste, stems removed, cut crosswise into ¼-inch-thick slices (do not remove the seeds)
About 12 thin slices fresh ginger (cut in rounds roughly the size of a nickel)
12 to 15 bamboo skewers (preferably 6 inches long)
2 tablespoons canola oil
1 teaspoon cumin seeds
1 large red onion, cut in half lengthwise and thinly sliced
2 large tomatoes, cored and finely chopped
1 tablespoon Toasted Cumin-Coriander Blend (page 33)
½ teaspoon ground turmeric
1½ teaspoons coarse kosher or sea salt
¼ cup malt vinegar
2 tablespoons finely chopped fresh cilantro leaves and tender stems for garnishing

1. Place the meat in a medium-size saucepan and add water to cover. Bring it to a boil over medium-high heat. Lower the heat to medium, cover the pan, and simmer, stirring occasionally, until the meat is fork-tender, 20 to 25 minutes. Drain the beef, reserving the broth for another use if you wish, and set the meat aside until it is cool enough to handle.

2. Line up the beef cubes, garlic cloves, chile slices, and ginger slices in a row, so you can skewer them in sequence, assembly-line-style. Thread a piece of meat on a skewer, followed by a garlic clove, a slice of chile, and a ginger round. Repeat the sequence on the same skewer. Fill the remaining skewers the same way. If you have some remnant garlic, chile, and ginger left, save them for another curry.

3. Heat the oil in a large skillet over medium heat. Add the cumin seeds and cook until they sizzle, turn reddish brown, and smell nutty, 10 to 15 seconds. Immediately add the onion. Cover the skillet and cook, stirring occasionally, until the onion starts to soften and turn caramel-brown with a deep purple hue, 15 to 20 minutes.

4. Add the tomatoes, cumin-coriander blend, turmeric, and salt. Cook, uncovered, stirring occasionally, until the tomatoes soften but still look chunky, 5 to 8 minutes.

5. Add the skewers to the skillet and blanket them with the sauce. Reduce the heat to medium-low, cover the skillet, and simmer, without stirring, until the flavors permeate the meat and the ginger, garlic, and chiles season the sauce, about 10 minutes. Transfer the skewers to a serving platter.

6. Pour the vinegar into the sauce, stirring it well. Spoon the sauce over the skewers, sprinkle with the cilantro, and serve.

Ground Beef
WITH SWEET POTATO AND WHOLE-WHEAT RIBBONS

Thicoli

there is a reason why Zohair Motiwalla loves this childhood favorite and insists that his mother make it each time he visits her in Australia. It takes time to put it together, but the result is a comforting one-dish meal that includes meat, vegetables, and bread. Zohair recommends savoring it over rice. **SERVES 8**

For the curry:

- 2 tablespoons canola oil
- 3 teaspoons cumin seeds; 2 left whole, 1 ground
- 1 small red onion, cut in half lengthwise and thinly sliced
- 2 tablespoons finely chopped fresh ginger
- 3 to 5 fresh green Thai, cayenne, or serrano chiles, to taste, stems removed, finely chopped (do not remove the seeds)
- 3 large cloves garlic, finely chopped
- 2 cinnamon sticks (each 3 inches long)
- 2 fresh or dried bay leaves
- 1 pound lean ground beef
- 2 teaspoons coriander seeds, ground
- 2 teaspoons coarse kosher or sea salt
- 1 teaspoon ground turmeric
- 1 medium-size russet or Yukon Gold potato, peeled, cut into 1-inch cubes, and submerged in a bowl of cold water to prevent browning
- 1 medium-size sweet potato, peeled, cut into 1-inch cubes, and submerged in a bowl of cold water to prevent browning
- 1 medium-size carrot, peeled and cut into 1-inch lengths
- 1 small Japanese eggplant (about 6 inches long and 1 inch in diameter), stem removed, cut in half lengthwise, and cut into 1-inch lengths
- 1 cup cut-up fresh green beans (1-inch lengths)
- ½ cup cubed fresh red pumpkin (1-inch pieces; see Tip, page 141)
- 1 recipe Whole-Wheat Ribbons (recipe follows)

To finish the curry:

- 1 tablespoon Ghee (page 21) or canola oil
- 1 teaspoon cumin seeds
- ½ teaspoon cayenne (ground red pepper)
- 2 tablespoons finely chopped fresh cilantro leaves and tender stems for garnishing

1. First, start the curry: Heat the oil in a large saucepan over medium-high heat. Add the 2 teaspoons whole cumin seeds, and cook until they sizzle, turn reddish brown, and smell nutty, 5 to 10 seconds. Then stir in the onion, ginger, chiles, garlic, cinnamon sticks, and bay leaves. Stir-fry until the onion is light brown around the edges and the spices perfume the mixture, about 5 minutes.

2. Break up the ground beef if it is not already loose, and mix it in. Cook, stirring occasionally, until the meat has browned, 8 to 10 minutes.

3. Drain the potatoes.

4. Sprinkle the ground coriander, the 1 teaspoon ground cumin, the salt, and turmeric over the meat mixture, and stir to coat the meat with the spices. Then stir in the potatoes, carrot, eggplant, beans, pumpkin, and 2 cups water. Bring the curry to a boil. Reduce the heat to medium-low, cover the pan, and simmer, stirring occasionally, until the vegetables are fork-tender and the meat has absorbed the complex flavors, 10 to 12 minutes.

5. Once the vegetables are fork-tender, add the Whole-Wheat Ribbons to the stew.

6. To give the curry its final seasoning, heat the Ghee in a small skillet over medium-high heat. Sprinkle in the cumin seeds and cook until they sizzle, turn reddish brown, and smell nutty, 5 to 10 seconds. Immediately remove the skillet from the heat and sprinkle in the cayenne. Pour this spiced ghee over the curry, and stir it in gently once or twice.

7. Remove the cinnamon sticks and bay leaves if you like. Sprinkle the cilantro over the curry, and serve.

Tip: This is a great do-ahead curry and can be the only offering at your Sunday dinner table, with either rice (in addition to the noodles) or a loaf of crusty bread.

Whole-Wheat Ribbons

Seon Kay Sev

Prepare the dough for the ribbons (Steps 1 and 2) 2 to 3 days in advance and refrigerate it, covered. Bring it to room temperature and proceed with Step 3. **SERVES 8**

½ cup roti flour (see Tip, page 728)
I teaspoon coarse kosher or sea salt
I teaspoon coriander seeds, ground
½ teaspoon cumin seeds, ground
½ teaspoon ground tumeric
I tablespoon canola oil
About ¼ cup plain yogurt, at room
    temperature, whisked

1. Combine the roti flour, salt, coriander, cumin, and turmeric in a medium-size bowl. Drizzle the oil over the flour mixture, and rub the flour through your hands to evenly distribute the oil.

2. Add the yogurt, a tablespoon or two at a time, stirring until the flour comes together to form a soft ball. Using your hand (as long as it's clean, I think it's the best tool), gather up the ball, pick up any dry flour in the bottom of the bowl, and knead the dough to form a smooth, slightly stiff ball. If it's a little too wet, dust it with a little flour and knead it in after every dusting until you get the right dry consistency. (If you have been using your hand to make the dough from the start, your hand will be caked with clumps of dough. Scrape that off your hand back into the bowl. Wash and dry your hands thoroughly and return to the dough to knead it. You will get a much better feel for the dough's consistency when your hand is dry.

3. Using your hands, roll the dough out to form a 12-inch-long log. Cut it crosswise into ½-inch-thick pieces, and shape each piece into a small ball. Then press each ball flat to form a patty. Cover the patties with a sheet of plastic wrap.

4. Fill a medium-size saucepan halfway with water, and bring it to a rolling boil over medium-high heat.

5. Lightly flour a small work area near the stove, and place a dough patty on it. (Keep the remaining patties covered with the plastic wrap.) Roll the patty out to form a round that is 2 to 3 inches in diameter, dusting it with flour as needed. Cut the round into ¼-inch-wide strips. Repeat with the remaining patties.

6. Scatter a handful of the dough strips into the boiling water and bring it to a boil again. Once the strips float to the top, 3 to 5 minutes, skim them off with a slotted spoon and add them to the curry. Repeat with the remaining strips until all have been added.

Tip: Making these pasta-like ribbons can be a bit time-consuming. You can use cooked whole-wheat pasta for a much easier alternative. The only difference is that the homemade ribbons have a spicy bite to them which the store-bought pasta does not. One cup broken-up dried pasta, cooked al dente and stirred into the curry, should be enough to feed your hungry family.

Stuffed Bottle Gourd Squash
WITH GROUND BEEF AND GOLDEN RAISINS

Kheema Lauki

The diet of Bohri Muslims, who occupied the northwestern borders of India for centuries, away from the fruits of the sea more abundant to their south, leans heavily toward meat—ground beef, mutton, or lamb being the most popular. The spices are always subtle, in sharp contrast to the seasonings in neighboring states. This thin-bodied curry uses no spices, in fact; herbs, bulbs, and nuts, along with sweet golden raisins, perfume the beef. Serve it as the main course along with a bowl of Yellow Split Peas with Tomato and Chiles (page 420), Chunky Potatoes with Buttermilk (page 547), and the usual accoutrements of rice and/or bread. (The pan juices are great spooned over cooked white rice.) **SERVES 6**

*1 medium-size to large (1½ to 2 pounds) bottle
  gourd squash or eggplant*
4 tablespoons canola oil
1 pound lean ground beef
¼ cup Ginger Chile Paste (page 17)
1½ teaspoons coarse kosher or sea salt
½ cup golden raisins
*¼ cup fried onion pieces, coarsely crushed
  (see Tip, page 201)*
¼ cup raw pine nuts, ground
*¼ cup finely chopped fresh cilantro leaves
  and tender stems*

1. Cut off and discard the stem and heel ends from the squash. Peel the squash with a vegetable peeler. Slice the squash crosswise into 3-inch-thick pieces. Working with 1 piece at a time, use a paring knife to make a circular cut around the inner spongy flesh and seeds, and push it out to create a cylindrical cavity. Repeat with the remaining pieces.

2. Heat 2 tablespoons of the oil in a large skillet over medium heat. Add the squash circles, broad side down, and cook, moving them around occasionally, until they are evenly light brown, 5 to 10 minutes. Transfer them to a plate.

3. Pour the remaining 2 tablespoons oil into the same skillet; it will instantly heat up in the hot skillet. Break up the ground beef (if it is not already loose) and add it to the skillet along with the Ginger Chile Paste. Cook, stirring occasionally, until the meat browns, 8 to 10 minutes. Then stir in the salt, raisins, fried onion, pine nuts, and cilantro. Transfer the meat mixture to a medium-size bowl.

4. Pour ½ cup water into the skillet and scrape the bottom to deglaze it, releasing any bits of browned meat. Place the hollowed-out squash pieces in the skillet, cut side down. Spoon the meat filling into each cavity.

Cover the skillet with a lid, if it will fit over the squash, or with aluminum foil. Cook over medium heat until the squash is tender, 20 to 25 minutes. (To test it, break off a corner with your asbestos-tough finger or cut off a small piece with a knife.)

5. I usually serve the stuffed squash straight from the skillet, offering a spatula for folks to reach in and lift one out.

Spicy Ground Beef
WITH PEAS AND CHILES

kheema mutter

More often than not, lamb, mutton, or goat meat is used to make *kheema* (minced or ground meat) curries. In many non-Hindu households, beef is also an option. In this country, I have found the quality of beef to be quite high (especially the beef from grass-fed cows). Lean ground meat makes for a lower-fat curry without compromising on its succulence. Serve it with a basket of store-bought or homemade rotis (page 727). **SERVES 6**

2 tablespoons canola oil
2 teaspoons cumin seeds
*1 small red onion, cut in half lengthwise
  and thinly sliced*
2 tablespoons finely chopped fresh ginger
*3 to 5 fresh green Thai, cayenne, or serrano chiles,
  to taste, stems removed, finely chopped
  (do not remove the seeds)*

3 large cloves garlic, finely chopped

2 cinnamon sticks (each 3 inches long)

2 fresh or dried bay leaves

1 pound lean ground beef

2 teaspoons coriander seeds, ground

1 teaspoon cumin seeds, ground

2 teaspoons coarse kosher or sea salt

1 teaspoon ground turmeric

1 cup frozen green peas (no need to thaw)

2 tablespoons finely chopped fresh cilantro
leaves and tender stems

1. Heat the oil in a medium-size saucepan over medium-high heat. Add the cumin seeds and cook until they sizzle, turn reddish brown, and are fragrant, 5 to 10 seconds. Immediately add the onion and stir-fry until the slices are limp and light brown, 5 to 10 minutes.

2. Add the ginger, chiles, garlic, cinnamon sticks, and bay leaves. Cook, stirring, until the mixture is caramel-brown, 5 minutes.

3. Break up the ground beef (if it is not already loose) and add it to the pan. Cook, stirring occasionally, until the meat browns, 8 to 10 minutes.

4. Sprinkle in the coriander, cumin, salt, and turmeric, stirring to coat the meat with the spices. Reduce the heat to medium-low, cover the pan, and simmer, stirring occasionally, for 10 to 12 minutes, to allow the meat to absorb the complex flavors.

5. Stir in 1 cup water, and add the peas and cilantro. Continue to simmer, covered, stirring occasionally, until the peas are cooked, 5 to 8 minutes. Then serve.

Tip: Feel free to remove the cinnamon sticks and bay leaves before you serve the curry. If you wish to leave them in (as is always the case in India), make sure you warn your guests (or family) of their presence. I like to leave them in because the whole spices continue to flavor the curry.

19TH-CENTURY English-Style Veal Curry

Angrezi bari Waale bachade ki Maas

William Makepeace Thackeray, an English journalist and novelist born in Calcutta, achieved fame and fortune with his novel *Vanity Fair,* a story of the women in two middle-class London families doing what it takes to make it in materialistic London. Written before *Vanity Fair,* Thackeray's "Poem to Curry" (see page 185) gives a hint of his passion for India, and especially for India's curries. Based on his musings, here is my rendition of his veal curry flavored with English-style "curry powder." **SERVES 6**

8 tablespoons (1 stick) butter

1 large red onion, cut in half lengthwise
and thinly sliced

1½ pounds boneless veal, cut into
1-inch cubes

1½ tablespoons English-Style Madras Curry Powder
(page 24)

1 cup heavy (whipping) cream

1½ teaspoons coarse kosher or sea salt

Juice of 1 medium-size lemon

1. Melt the butter in a large skillet over medium heat. Add the onion, cover, and cook, stirring occasionally, until it turns a caramel color with a deep purple hue, 20 to 25 minutes. (At first the onion sweats, releasing its moisture. Then as the liquid evaporates, it starts to brown.)

2. Add the veal and the curry powder, raise the heat to medium-high, and cook, uncovered, stirring occasionally, until the meat is seared a light brown (it's a hard color to see in all that yellow curry powder), 5 to 8 minutes.

3. Pour in the cream, reduce the heat to medium-low, and cover the skillet. Simmer, stirring occasionally, until the veal is fork-tender, 25 to 30 minutes.

4. Stir in the salt and lemon juice, and serve.

{ lamb }

Roasted Leg of Lamb
WITH RAISIN-MINT SAUCE

Raan

A specialty of Pakistan and Lucknow, *raan* is often roasted in tandoors or makeshift grills. In India, this special-occasion dish often requires a long marinating time because the meat used is mutton—a mature sheep—or goat. Cooks apply ground unripe papaya to the meat because the chemical papain, a natural tenderizer present in the fruit, breaks down the tough tissues to yield fall-off-the-bone meat when it is cooked.

However, lamb in Western countries is quite tender, making the papaya application unnecessary. The acidity from the yogurt is enough to tenderize it, especially when marinated overnight. This is a dry roast, often served in India with slivers of raw red onions, cilantro, and wedges of lime, with tandoor-cooked naan alongside. I have taken it a step further and serve it, curry-style, with a mint-enriched tomato sauce laced with cashews and golden raisins. This was my featured offering at a recent holiday meal, a different rendition of the traditional roast leg of lamb.

SERVES 8

For the roast:

1 boneless leg of lamb roast (3½ pounds)

1 cup plain yogurt

½ cup slivered blanched almonds

1 tablespoon Bin bhuna hua garam masala (page 30)

1½ teaspoons coarse kosher or sea salt

1 medium-size red onion, coarsely chopped

4 lengthwise slices fresh ginger (each 2 inches long,
 1 inch wide, and ⅛ inch thick)

4 large cloves garlic

4 fresh green Thai, cayenne, or serrano chiles,
 stems removed

2 tablespoons finely chopped fresh cilantro
 leaves and tender stems

Vegetable cooking spray

For the sauce:

2 tablespoons canola oil

1 teaspoon cumin seeds

1 small red onion, coarsely chopped

½ cup raw cashew nuts

¼ cup golden raisins

½ cup canned tomato sauce

¼ cup heavy (whipping) cream

¼ cup firmly packed fresh mint leaves,
 finely chopped

1. To prepare the lamb, first ensure that it is tied into a compact shape, either with cooking twine or in the oven-safe netted bag used by most supermarkets today. Make 4 to 6 gashes, about ¼ inch deep, in the meat (cut through the mesh if necessary). Place the roast in a shallow pan and set it aside while you prepare the marinade.

2. Pour the yogurt into a blender jar, and then add the almonds, garam masala, salt, onion, ginger, garlic, and chiles. Puree, scraping the inside of the jar as needed, to make a light purple, slightly gritty paste.

3. Pour the marinade over the lamb and sprinkle the cilantro over it. Using your hands, massage the marinade into the meat, making sure you get it into the gashes. Refrigerate, covered, overnight, to allow the yogurt to tenderize the lamb and the spices to permeate the meat.

poem to curry

❖ ❖ ❖

Three pounds of veal my darling girl prepares,
And chops it nicely into little squares;
Five onions next procures the little minx
(The biggest are the best, her Samiwel thinks),
And Epping butter nearly half a pound,
And stews them in a pan until they're brown'd.
What's next my dexterous little girl will do?
She pops the meat into the savoury stew,
With curry-powder table-spoonfuls three,
And milk a pint (the richest that may be),
And, when the dish has stewed for half an hour,
A lemon's ready juice she'll o'er it pour.
Then, bless her! Then she gives the luscious pot
A very gentle boil—and serves quite hot.
PS—Beef, mutton, rabbit, if you wish,
Lobsters, or prawns, or any kind fish,
Are fit to make a CURRY. 'Tis, when done,
A dish for Emperors to feed upon.

—William Makepeace Thackeray, 1846

4. When you are ready to roast the lamb, preheat the oven to 450°F. While the oven is preheating, bring the lamb to room temperature. I usually set the pan on the kitchen counter close to the oven to quicken the process.

5. Set a rack in a roasting pan, and spray the rack with cooking spray. Place the lamb, including the marinade that clings to its surface, on the rack. Reserve the remaining marinade, pooled on the bottom of the marinating pan, for basting. Roast the lamb until it is seared and lightly browned on the outside, 10 to 15 minutes.

6. Lower the heat to 325°F and continue to roast the meat. About 15 minutes into the roasting time, spoon the reserved marinade over the lamb. Intermittently check the roasting pan to see if the meat drippings are starting to burn off. I usually pour a little water into the pan so the moisture can maintain the meat's succulence and also prevent the drippings from burning. Roast until the meat's internal temperature, measured in the center of its thickest part, registers around 135°F for medium-rare, 1½ to 1¾ hours.

7. While the lamb is roasting, make the sauce: Heat the oil in a medium-size saucepan over medium-high heat. Add the cumin seeds and cook until they sizzle, turn reddish brown, and smell nutty, 5 to 10 seconds. Immediately add the onion, cashews, and raisins. Stir-fry until the cashews turn light brown, the raisins swell, and the onion browns around the edges, about 5 minutes.

8. Add the tomato sauce and ¼ cup water. Scrape the bottom of the skillet to deglaze it, releasing any browned bits. Once the curry comes to a boil, reduce the heat to medium-low, cover the skillet, and simmer, stirring occasionally, until some of the oil has separated and glistens on its surface and at the edges, 8 to 10 minutes.

9. Transfer the sauce to a blender jar, and pour in the cream. Puree, scraping the inside of the jar as needed, to make a nutty-sweet, creamy red sauce that will be slightly grainy to the touch. Pour it back into the saucepan.

10. Remove the roasting pan from the oven and let the meat rest for about 10 minutes. Its internal temperature will rise about 5 degrees. While the meat is resting, gently rewarm the sauce, covered, over low heat. Just before serving, stir the mint leaves into the sauce.

11. Cut off the cooking twine, or the webbing, with a pair of kitchen shears and transfer the lamb to a cutting board. Cut the meat into ½-inch-thick slices, and arrange them on a serving platter. Serve the sauce separately, so folks can spoon on as much as they wish.

Tip: Bone-in roasts work just as well here. In fact, the *raans* in India are usually bone-in, to provide the slightly more succulent, stronger flavor found in the meat that is closest to the bone. Save the bone and use it in soups for a rich flavor.

Braised Lamb Shanks
IN A FENNEL AND CUMIN BROTH

Nehari

This curry, a favorite in Pakistan and Kashmir, is an acquired taste. The hearty sauce and the strong, gamey flavor of the meat just might bring out your chest-thumping, machismo qualities. Because of the higher amount of connective tissue in the meat, the best method for cooking this cut is usually to braise or stew it for an extended time.

The spices in this curry hold their own against the dark meat, as would a glass of full-bodied cabernet sauvignon or Côtes du Rhône. If you are comfortable doing so, you can suck the rich marrow from the bone for an even more intense experience. **SERVES 6**

½ cup plain yogurt

2 tablespoons Ginger Paste (page 15)

2 tablespoons Garlic Paste (page 15)

1 teaspoon cayenne (ground red pepper)

1 teaspoon coarse kosher or sea salt

½ teaspoon ground turmeric

6 small lamb shanks (2½ to 3 pounds)

¼ cup mustard oil or canola oil

1 medium-size red onion, cut in half
    lengthwise and thinly sliced

2 teaspoons fennel seeds

2 teaspoons cumin seeds

1 teaspoon black cumin seeds

2 whole star anise

1 teaspoon ground ginger

2 tablespoons rice flour

2 tablespoons finely chopped fresh mint leaves
    for garnishing

2 tablespoons finely chopped fresh cilantro
    leaves and tender stems for garnishing

Star anise?
See the
Glossary of
Ingredients,
page 758.

1. Combine the yogurt, the ginger and garlic pastes, cayenne, salt, and turmeric in a large bowl. Add the lamb shanks and turn to coat them with the marinade. Refrigerate, covered, overnight, to allow the flavors to permeate the meat and tenderize it.

2. Heat the oil in a large saucepan over medium heat. Add the lamb shanks, marinade and all. Cook, turning them occasionally, until the marinade evaporates, the meat releases a little liquid, and the shanks start to brown, 8 to 10 minutes. Then reduce the heat to medium-low, cover the pan, and cook, occasionally stirring gently, until the oil starts to separate from the meat, about 15 minutes. Transfer the shanks to a plate.

3. Stir the onion into the same pan. Cook, stirring occasionally, letting the onion absorb the meaty flavors from the pan, until it softens, 8 to 10 minutes.

4. While the onion is cooking, combine the fennel seeds, both kinds of cumin seeds, and the star anise in a spice grinder, and grind until the texture resembles that of finely ground black pepper. (You may have a belligerent piece or two of anise that refuse to break down. Just remove them from the mix.) Stir in the ginger. The blend will have a licorice aroma with smoky undertones.

5. Once the onion has softened, stir in the ground spice blend and let it cook, without burning, for 1 to 2 minutes. Pour in 2 cups water and scrape the bottom of the pan to deglaze it, releasing the collected bits of meat, onion, and spices.

6. Lower the shanks into this broth and heat it to a boil. Spoon the onion slices over the meat and cover the pan. Braise, occasionally basting the shanks with the broth and turning them every so often (keep the onion blanketed over the meat each time you turn them), until the meat is almost falling off the bone, 2 to 3 hours.

7. Gently transfer the lamb to a serving platter.

8. Sprinkle 1 tablespoon of the rice flour into the broth, whisking it in quickly to dissolve it evenly. Repeat with the remaining 1 tablespoon flour. As soon as the sauce boils, it will instantly thicken. Pour this meaty sauce over the shanks, sprinkle the mint and cilantro on top, and serve.

Tips:

❖ Any cuts of lamb (preferably bone-in) will be a good alternative. You will need to vary the braising time to fit the cut you have chosen.

❖ This curry is ideal for a slow cooker: Prepare the shanks for simmering through Step 5. Then dump the pan's contents into the slow cooker and stew the shanks on low heat until the meat almost starts to fall off the bone, 6 to 8 hours. Transfer the shanks to a platter and thicken the sauce as described in Step 8.

Lamb Chops
WITH AN ALMOND–POPPY SEED SAUCE

Badam Khus Khus Champ

t he ingredients and flavors in this recipe will certainly appeal to lovers of Bengali cooking, satisfying their passion for mustard oil, fennel, and poppy seeds. You don't want to overcook the tender, expensive lamb as it will turn rubbery. Medium-rare is the way to go for this prime cut.

SERVES 4 (8 IF SERVED AS AN APPETIZER)

¼ cup Garlic Paste (page 15)

2 teaspoons fennel seeds, ground

1½ teaspoons coarse kosher or sea salt

½ teaspoon cardamom seeds from black pods, ground

1 pound rack of lamb (from ribs), cut into chops

½ cup slivered blanched almonds, ground (see Tip)

1 tablespoon white poppy seeds, ground

½ teaspoon cayenne (ground red pepper)

6 tablespoons mustard oil or canola oil

1 cup finely chopped red onion

2 tablespoons finely chopped fresh cilantro leaves and tender stems

½ teaspoon Punjabi garam masala (page 25)

1. Combine the Garlic Paste, fennel, 1 teaspoon of the salt, and the cardamom in a small bowl, stirring to form a thick, greenish-brown paste. Smear this over the meaty part of the chops, making sure each gets well coated with the smoky, licorice-smelling paste. Refrigerate, covered, for at least 30 minutes or as long as overnight, to allow the flavors to penetrate the tender meat.

2. While the meat is marinating, combine the almonds, poppy seeds, cayenne, and the remaining ½ teaspoon salt in a small bowl. Stir well and set aside.

3. When you are ready to cook the lamb, heat 2 table-spoons of the oil in a large skillet over medium-high heat. Add half the chops, including the caked-on marinade, arranging them in a single layer in the skillet without overcrowding. Sear until light brown on each side, 2 to 3 minutes per side. Transfer the chops to a serving platter and cover it with foil to keep them warm. If some of the leftover oil in the skillet appears burnt, wipe it out with a dry paper towel. Pour in 2 more tablespoons oil and sear the remaining chops. Add them to the platter.

4. Wipe out the skillet with a paper towel, and pour in the remaining 2 tablespoons oil. Heat it over medium-high heat, and add the onion. Stir-fry until the onion is light brown around the edges, 3 to 5 minutes. Then stir in the almond-spice blend and allow it to lightly brown, 1 to 2 minutes. Add the mixture to the chops on the platter.

5. Pour 1 cup water into the skillet, and add the cilantro and garam masala. Let the curry come to a boil and thicken, 1 to 2 minutes. Pour this over the chops, and serve.

Tip: I usually grind the almonds in a spice grinder, in two batches, until powder-like. Do not cram all those nuts into the jar at once—it will yield an uneven grind, not to mention the caked-on powder at the bottom that could turn wet from the compressed heat. A food processor will not work: it won't grind them to a powder, and as a result the sauce will be grainy.

Rib Lamb Chops
WITH A
CURRY LEAF–COCONUT SAUCE

East Indian–Style Lamb Chops

◆

In a culture that thrives on fish, seafood, and all kinds of meat, it is no wonder that this delicate cut of lamb is highly revered within the East Indian community in Mumbai. Once you have the *bottle masala* prepared (it's really not that daunting, the spices are easy to procure even in your everyday grocery store), these chops will make you smack your own. You can gnaw on the rib bones, too, to make sure you get it all. **SERVES 4**

2 tablespoons Ginger Paste (page 15)

2 tablespoons Garlic Paste (page 15)

½ teaspoon ground turmeric

½ teaspoon cayenne (ground red pepper)

1½ teaspoons coarse kosher or sea salt

1½ pounds rack of lamb (from the ribs),
　　cut into chops (about 12)

2 tablespoons canola oil

1 small red onion, coarsely chopped

10 to 12 medium-size to large fresh curry leaves

2 teaspoons East Indian bottle masala (page 37)

1 cup shredded fresh coconut; or ½ cup shredded dried
　　unsweetened coconut, reconstituted (see Note)

1 teaspoon tamarind paste or concentrate

Vegetable cooking spray

2 tablespoons finely chopped fresh mint leaves for
　　garnishing

1. Combine the Ginger Paste, Garlic Paste, turmeric, cayenne, and ½ teaspoon of the salt in a small bowl, stirring to make a thick, yellowish-red paste.

2. Smear both sides of each lamb chop with the paste (dole the paste out judiciously to make sure you have enough for all the chops). Refrigerate, covered, for at least 30 minutes or as long as overnight, to allow the spices to permeate the meat.

3. Just before you start up the grill to cook the chops, make the sauce: Heat the oil in a small saucepan over medium heat. Add the onion and curry leaves, and cook, stirring occasionally, until the onion softens and acquires a caramel color with a deep purple hue, 10 to 12 minutes. Stir in the *bottle masala*.

4. Pour ½ cup water into a blender jar, and then add the coconut, tamarind paste, and the onion mixture. Puree, scraping the inside of the jar as needed, to make a slightly gritty sauce. Pour this back into the same small saucepan and stir in the remaining 1 teaspoon salt. Keep the sauce on a low simmer while you grill the chops.

5. Preheat a gas (or charcoal) grill, or the broiler, to high.

6. *If you are grilling,* lightly spray the grill rack with cooking spray. Place the chops, marinade and all, on the rack and grill both sides until the meat is seared and is still medium-rare in the center, 2 to 4 minutes per side. *If you are broiling,* position an oven rack so that the top of the chops will be 2 to 3 inches from the heat source. Lightly spray the rack of a broiler pan with cooking spray. Place the chops, marinade and all, on the rack and broil on both sides until the meat has seared and is still medium-rare in the center, 2 to 4 minutes per side.

7. Transfer the chops to a serving platter, and ladle the sauce over them. Sprinkle with the mint, and serve.

Note: To reconstitute coconut, cover with ½ cup boiling water, set aside for about 15 minutes, and then drain.

Tip: When you purchase the rack of lamb, you can have the butcher separate it into individual chops or you can easily do that at home. Just make sure you cut off the excess fat from the back side. Too much fat can melt and drip into your grill, creating flames that will burn the chops before they cook.

Lamb Curry
IN A SWEET ONION-TOMATO SAUCE
Pyaaz tamatar Gosht

When students ask me to teach them a "basic lamb curry," I turn to this recipe, which I used in the restaurant kitchen where I slaved during the early years of my career. The flavors are typical of versions found in many a north Indian, particularly Punjabi, restaurant—the type that seems to dominate the American and European Indian restaurant scene. In the restaurants, this curry is usually served with baskets of hot buttered naan (page 729) and white basmati rice. The Indian customer would always request slices of raw onion, fresh green chiles, and wedges of lime to eat alongside the meal, and you may choose to do the same. **SERVES 4**

2 teaspoons coriander seeds, ground

1 teaspoon cumin seeds, ground

1 teaspoon sweet paprika

1 teaspoon coarse kosher or sea salt

½ teaspoon cayenne (ground red pepper)

½ teaspoon ground turmeric

4 lengthwise slices fresh ginger (each 2 inches long, 1 inch wide, and ⅛ inch thick), finely chopped

4 medium-size cloves garlic, finely chopped

1¼ pounds boneless leg of lamb, fat trimmed off and discarded, cut into 1-inch cubes

2 tablespoons canola oil

4 black cardamom pods (see Tips)

2 fresh or dried bay leaves

1 cup canned tomato sauce (see Tips)

¼ cup Fried Onion Paste (page 16)

2 tablespoons finely chopped fresh cilantro leaves and tender stems

1. Combine the coriander, cumin, paprika, salt, cayenne, turmeric, ginger, and garlic in a medium-size bowl. Add the lamb and toss to coat it with the spices. Refrigerate, covered, for about 30 minutes, to allow the flavors to mingle a bit.

2. Heat the oil in a medium-size saucepan over medium-high heat. Add the cardamom pods and bay leaves, and allow the leaves to sizzle and the pods to swell slightly, about 30 seconds. Add the lamb and stir-fry to sear it and cook the spices without burning them, 5 to 8 minutes. The juices from the meat will release the stuck-on spices that coat the bottom of the pan.

3. Stir in the tomato sauce, Fried Onion Paste, and cilantro. Once the curry comes to a boil, reduce the heat to medium-low, cover the pan, and simmer, stirring occasionally, until the meat is fork-tender, about 45 minutes. Then serve.

Tips:

❖ Black cardamom injects smoky undertones into the sauce, but green or white cardamom pods are perfectly all right as an alternative. Feel free to discard them, along with the bay leaves, before serving.

❖ Most canned tomato sauce is salted, so I have added

only a teaspoon of salt to the curry. If the kind you use is unsalted, add an extra ½ teaspoon salt to the recipe to bring alive the spices and their incredible flavors.

Garlicky Lamb
WITH POTATOES

Aloo Gosht

folks who shy away from "exotic" and unfamiliar foods will love this curry because it plays on the comfortable meat-and-potatoes theme. A great curry to serve with a bowl of basmati rice, this is equally comforting with a baguette and a glass of red burgundy. **SERVES 6**

For the marinade:

2 tablespoons Garlic Paste (page 15)

2 teaspoons cumin seeds, ground

2 teaspoons coriander seeds, ground

2 teaspoons coarse kosher or sea salt

1 teaspoon black cumin seeds, ground

1 teaspoon fennel seeds, ground

1 teaspoon cayenne (ground red pepper)

For the lamb:

1 pound boneless leg of lamb, fat trimmed
    off and discarded, cut into 1-inch cubes

8 ounces russet or Yukon Gold potatoes, peeled,
    cut into 1-inch cubes, and submerged in a
    bowl of cold water to prevent browning

4 tablespoons canola oil

¼ cup Fried Onion Paste (page 16)

2 tablespoons tomato paste

2 tablespoons finely chopped fresh cilantro leaves
    and tender stems for garnishing

> Black cumin seeds? See the Glossary of Ingredients, page 758.

1. Combine all the marinade ingredients in a medium-size bowl. Add the lamb and toss to coat it with the marinade. Refrigerate, covered, for at least 30 minutes or as long as overnight, to allow the flavors to permeate the meat.

2. Drain the potatoes and pat them dry with paper towels.

3. Heat 2 tablespoons of the oil in a large skillet over medium heat. Add the potatoes and immediately place a lid on the skillet to contain the spattering. Cook, covered, stirring occasionally, until they are light brown and slightly crispy (some scraps will be sticking to the skillet), 5 to 8 minutes. Use a slotted spoon to transfer the potatoes to a plate.

4. Add the remaining 2 tablespoons oil to the hot skillet. Add the lamb, marinade and all, and cook, uncovered, stirring, until the meat is seared and honey-brown all over, and there is a thin layer of browned garlic, spices, and potato remnants on the bottom of the skillet, about 5 minutes.

5. Stir in the Fried Onion Paste and tomato paste, and scrape the bottom of the skillet to deglaze it, releasing the browned bits. Pour in 1 cup water and stir once or twice. Bring the slightly thin curry to a boil. Reduce the heat to medium-low, cover, and simmer, stirring occasionally, until the lamb is tender when cut with a fork, 20 to 25 minutes.

6. Add the potatoes and cook, covered, stirring occasionally, until they are fork-tender, about 5 minutes.

7. Sprinkle with the cilantro, and serve.

Vinegar-Marinated Lamb
WITH
POTATOES AND MUSTARD SEEDS

Syrian Christian Lamb Curry

When the followers of the Apostle Thomas landed off the coast of Malabar (now known as Kerala) almost 2,000 years ago to spread the word of Christianity, they successfully converted a sect of Hindu Namboodri Brahmins. These Nazranis (followers of Christ from Nazareth who used the rituals and traditions of the Jewish faith) conducted their sermons in the Syrian and Aramaic languages; hence they came to be known as Syrian Christians. Now they are all members of the Roman Catholic Church. Another group of converts, particularly from the lower castes, embraced Latin Christianity around the 1500s, thanks to the influence of St. Francis Xavier. To this day intermarriages between the two communities are frowned upon, forming yet another religious divide within this third-widely-practiced faith in India. The eating habits of the Syrian Christians are different from those of the locals, and all meats are fair game, including beef and pork. A liberal use of locally grown spices and acidic vinegars (especially from the coconut palm) are the trademarks of their cooking style, and this curry provides a robust testimony to that tradition. **SERVES 6**

2 teaspoons coriander seeds

2 teaspoons fennel seeds

2 teaspoons black peppercorns

1 teaspoon cumin seeds

1 cinnamon stick (3 inches long), broken into smaller pieces

1 pound boneless leg of lamb, fat trimmed off and discarded, cut into 1-inch cubes

½ cup distilled white vinegar, cider vinegar, or malt vinegar

1½ teaspoons coarse kosher or sea salt

1 teaspoon cayenne (ground red pepper)

½ teaspoon ground turmeric

1 small red onion, coarsely chopped

4 lengthwise slices fresh ginger (each 2 inches long, 1 inch wide, and ⅛ inch thick)

4 large cloves garlic

1 pound russet or Yukon Gold potatoes, peeled, cut into 1-inch cubes, and submerged in a bowl of cold water to prevent browning

5 tablespoons canola oil

¼ cup finely chopped fresh cilantro leaves and tender stems

1 teaspoon black or yellow mustard seeds

15 to 20 medium-size to large fresh curry leaves

1. Combine the coriander seeds, fennel seeds, peppercorns, cumin seeds, and pieces of cinnamon stick in a spice grinder, and grind until the texture resembles that of finely ground black pepper.

2. Empty the aromatic blend into a medium-size bowl and add the lamb, vinegar, salt, cayenne, and turmeric. Stir to thoroughly combine. Refrigerate, covered, for at least 1 hour or as long as overnight, to allow the meat to tenderize (thanks to the vinegar) and absorb the pungent spices.

3. While the lamb is marinating, combine the onion, ginger, and garlic in a food processor, and pulse to mince the mixture.

4. Drain the potatoes and pat them dry with paper towels.

5. Heat 2 tablespoons of the oil in a large nonstick skillet over medium-high heat. Toss in the potatoes (careful, as they will splatter initially) and stir-fry until they are honey-brown and crisp on the outside but still slightly undercooked, 10 to 12 minutes. Set them aside, still in the pan.

6. Heat another 2 tablespoons of the oil in a large skillet over medium-high heat. Add the onion blend and stir-fry until it is light brown, 3 to 5 minutes. Then add the lamb, marinade and all, and cook, uncovered, stirring occasionally, until the meat is seared and the oil is starting to separate from the chunks, 12 to 15 minutes.

7. Pour in 1 cup water and bring to a boil. Cover and cook over medium-low heat, stirring occasionally, until the lamb is fork-tender, about 30 minutes.

8. Stir in the potatoes, including any residual cooking oil. Add the cilantro. Continue to simmer the curry, covered, stirring occasionally, until the potatoes are fork-tender, about 5 minutes.

9. While the curry is in its final cooking stages, heat the remaining 1 tablespoon oil in a small skillet. Add the mustard seeds, cover, and cook until the seeds have stopped popping (not unlike popcorn), about 30 seconds. Remove the skillet from the heat and add the curry leaves. They will spatter and crackle, so watch out for oil splatters. Add this nutty-smelling spiked oil to the lamb curry, stirring once or twice to blend in the flavors, and serve.

Jaggery? See the Glossary of Ingredients, page 758.

Sweet and Sour Lamb
WITH SHOESTRING POTATOES

Sali Boti

This is my version of Mrs. Medora's lamb curry, for which I took the liberty of adding and subtracting a couple of ingredients, all the while keeping the essence intact. The first time I made this, I served it for a quick lunch with Dirty Rice with Caramelized Onion and Pounded Spices (page 711), another contribution from Mrs. Medora (see more about her on page 249). Serve it with Sautéed Spinach and Yogurt (page 743) for a complete meal. **SERVES 6**

¼ cup firmly packed fresh mint leaves, coarsely chopped

2 tablespoons Ginger Paste (page 15)

2 tablespoons Garlic Paste (page 15)

1½ teaspoons coarse kosher or sea salt

½ teaspoon ground turmeric

½ teaspoon cayenne (ground red pepper)

1¼ pounds boneless leg of lamb, fat trimmed off and discarded, cut into 1-inch cubes

¼ cup canola oil

4 cups finely chopped red onion

1 tablespoon crumbled or chopped jaggery or firmly packed dark brown sugar

2 tablespoons malt or cider vinegar

¼ cup finely chopped fresh cilantro leaves and tender stems for garnishing

2 cups Matchstick-Thin Fried Potatoes (page 41)

1. Combine the mint, Ginger Paste, Garlic Paste, salt, turmeric, and cayenne in a medium-

size bowl, and mix well. Add the lamb and toss to coat it with the marinade. Refrigerate, covered, for at least 30 minutes or as long as overnight, to allow the meat to absorb the flavors.

2. Preheat a wok or a well-seasoned cast-iron skillet over medium-high heat. Drizzle the oil down its sides. As soon as it forms a shimmering pool at the bottom, add the onion and cook, stirring occasionally, while it stews in its own juices, about 5 minutes. Once the liquid evaporates, reduce the heat to medium and stir-fry until the onion turns honey-brown with a deep purple hue, 15 to 20 minutes.

3. Add the lamb and raise the heat to medium-high. Cook, stirring frequently, until the meat sears and starts to brown, 8 to 10 minutes. Some of the oil will separate from the onion and lamb, and glisten on top of the mixture.

4. Add 1 cup water and stir once or twice. Once it comes to a boil, which will be almost instantaneously, reduce the heat to medium-low, cover the wok, and simmer, stirring occasionally, until the lamb is fork-tender, about 30 minutes. Transfer the lamb and onion to a serving bowl.

5. Stir the jaggery into the wok. The heat from the curry will melt the raw cane sugar. Pour the sauce over the lamb, and stir in the vinegar. Sprinkle the cilantro over the curry, top with the fried potatoes, and serve.

Tips:

❖ The intense heat and ease of cooking in a wok have no parallel in other pots and pans—especially if you are using an old-fashioned carbon steel wok. *The Breath of a Wok*, my friends Grace Young and Alan Richardson's award-winning cookbook, takes an in-depth look at this ancient cooking vessel. If you do not have a wok, use a large, well-seasoned cast-iron skillet instead.

❖ When using a wok or a cast-iron skillet, it's important not to stir in the highly acidic vinegar until after you have transferred the curry to a serving bowl, because the vinegar can strip the wok's seasoning within seconds. Of course you can always re-season it if you forget, but my greater concern is the metallic taste that misstep could impart to the curry.

Lamb
WITH POTATOES AND ONION IN MUSTARD OIL

Mangsho Jhol

Meat-and-potatoes is a mix that appeals to many as a one-pot meal, prepared with minimal effort. This Bengali classic, simmered in pungent mustard oil, is no exception, although the flavors belie the ease of preparation: subtle cinnamon, cardamom, and cloves in the spice blend, combined with assertive ginger and garlic in the marinade, balance out the bitter-hot mustard. Serve it with Buttery Basmati Rice with Spinach and Onion (page 713) for a weekday family dinner. Beef or pork is a fine alternative to lamb for this recipe. **SERVES 6**

1 tablespoon Ginger Paste (page 15)
1 tablespoon Garlic Paste (page 15)
½ teaspoon ground turmeric
1 pound boneless leg of lamb, fat trimmed off and discarded, cut into 1-inch cubes
2 medium-size russet or Yukon Gold potatoes, peeled, cut into ½-inch cubes, and submerged in a bowl of cold water to prevent browning

¼ cup mustard oil or canola oil

2 teaspoons Panch phoron (page 36)

4 to 6 dried red Thai or cayenne chiles,
    to taste, stems removed

1 medium-size red onion, cut in half lengthwise
    and thinly sliced

1½ teaspoons coarse kosher or sea salt

½ teaspoon Bangala garam masala
    (page 26)

2 tablespoons finely chopped fresh cilantro
    leaves and tender stems

1. Combine the Ginger Paste, Garlic Paste, and turmeric in a medium-size bowl, and mix well. Add the lamb and toss to coat it with the paste. Refrigerate, covered, for at least 30 minutes or as long as overnight, to allow the flavors to permeate the meat.

2. Drain the potatoes and pat them dry with paper towels.

3. Heat the oil in a large skillet over medium-high heat. Sprinkle in the *Panch phoron* and chiles. Cook until the spices sizzle, crackle, and pop and the chiles blacken, 15 to 20 seconds. Immediately add the lamb, marinade and all, and the potatoes and onion. Cook, uncovered, stirring occasionally, until the meat is seared, the potatoes are lightly browned, and the onion has softened, 15 to 20 minutes.

4. Add 1 cup water and sprinkle in the salt. Scrape the bottom of the skillet to deglaze it, releasing the browned bits of meat, vegetables, and spice, to incorporate the flavors into the curry. Once it comes to a boil, reduce the heat to medium-low, cover the skillet, and simmer, stirring occasionally, until the meat and potatoes are fork-tender, 20 to 25 minutes.

5. Stir in the garam masala and cilantro, and serve.

Coconut-Smothered Lamb
WITH SHOESTRING POTATOES

Nariyal Saliya Gosht

Parsis have a passion for three things: lamb, coconut, and shoestring potatoes—combined here in one spicy curry. Serve it with Perfumed Basmati Rice with Black Cardamom Pods (page 709). **SERVES 6**

2 tablespoons Ghee (page 21) or canola oil

1½ pounds boneless leg of lamb, fat trimmed
    off and discarded, cut into 1-inch cubes

2 tablespoons Ginger Paste (page 15)

1 tablespoon Garlic Paste (page 15)

1½ teaspoons coarse kosher or sea salt

½ teaspoon ground turmeric

6 black, green, or white cardamom pods

2 cinnamon sticks (each 3 inches long)

2 fresh or dried bay leaves

1 cup shredded fresh coconut; or ½ cup
    shredded dried unsweetened coconut,
    reconstituted (see Note)

½ cup raw cashew nuts

3 to 5 fresh green Thai, cayenne, or serrano chiles,
    to taste, stems removed

2 cups Matchstick-Thin Fried Potatoes (page 41)

¼ cup finely chopped fresh cilantro leaves and
    tender stems for garnishing

1. Heat the ghee in a large skillet over medium-high heat. Add the lamb, ginger and garlic pastes, salt, turmeric, cardamom pods, cinnamon sticks, and bay leaves. Cook, stirring occasionally, until the lamb browns, 15 to

20 minutes. (Initially the lamb starts to sear, the spices flavor it, and the pastes begin to brown slightly. Then the meat releases its liquid, which deglazes the skillet. Once the liquid evaporates, the meat starts to brown.)

2. While the lamb is browning, pour 1 cup water into a blender jar, followed by the coconut, cashews, and chiles. Puree, scraping the inside of the jar as needed, to make a smooth (albeit slightly gritty), light green paste.

3. Once the lamb has browned, add the coconut paste. Pour ½ cup water into the blender jar, and swish it around to rinse out the remaining paste. Add this to the meat. Stir once or twice, and bring the curry to a boil. Then reduce the heat to medium-low, cover the skillet, and simmer, stirring occasionally, until the lamb is fork-tender, 25 to 30 minutes.

4. Remove the cardamom pods, cinnamon sticks, and bay leaves if you wish. Top the curry with the golden-crispy shoestring potatoes and cilantro, and serve.

Note: To reconstitute coconut, cover with ½ cup boiling water, set aside for about 15 minutes, and then drain.

Lamb Stew
WITH A SPINACH SAUCE

Palak Gosht

Yes, you have seen this dish in every north Indian restaurant all across the United States and the United Kingdom. Is it good in those eateries? That's for to you to decide. I don't puree the spinach, as is done in the restaurant versions, and I incorporate a tiny bit of yogurt instead of heavy cream, to make it appealing not only in appearance but also in healthfulness. A bite of the lamb will help you come to a decision about which refectory serves the tastiest version of this curry.

SERVES 6

- 1¼ pounds boneless leg of lamb, fat trimmed off and discarded, cut into 1-inch cubes
- 2 tablespoons plain yogurt
- 2 tablespoons canola oil
- 1 medium-size red onion, cut in half lengthwise and thinly sliced
- 6 medium-size cloves garlic, coarsely chopped
- 4 lengthwise slices fresh ginger (each 2 inches long, 1 inch wide, and ⅛ inch thick), coarsely chopped
- 2 teaspoons Bin bhuna hua garam masala (page 30)
- ½ teaspoon ground turmeric
- 2 tablespoons tomato paste
- 1 pound fresh spinach leaves, well rinsed and finely chopped
- 1½ teaspoons coarse kosher or sea salt

1. Place the lamb in a bowl, add the yogurt, and stir to coat the meat with the yogurt. Refrigerate, covered, for at least 30 minutes or as long as overnight. (This allows the yogurt to absorb some of the fat from the lamb and make for a curdle-free sauce.)

2. Heat the oil in a large skillet over medium heat. Add the onion, garlic, and ginger, and stir-fry until the onion is dark brown, 8 to 10 minutes. Remove the skillet from the heat and stir in the garam masala and turmeric. (The heat from the browned onion will be just right for cooking the spices without burning them.) Transfer this mixture to a blender jar, and add

the tomato paste and ¼ cup water. Puree, scraping the inside of the jar as needed, to make a smooth, reddish-brown paste. Set it aside.

3. Return the same skillet, as is, to the burner. Add the yogurt-coated lamb and raise the heat to medium-high. (The whey-like liquid from the yogurt and the liquid released from the lamb will help to deglaze the skillet and incorporate the flavors into the meat.) Simmer the meat, uncovered, as it initially stews in its own juices. Once the liquid boils off, the lamb will start to brown and a thin brown layer from the drippings will start to stick to the skillet. All this should take 10 to 12 minutes.

4. Now add the spinach, a handful at a time, and stir it in. (The heat will make the leaves release their liquid, which will deglaze the skillet once again.) Add the onion-spice paste. Pour ¾ cup water into the blender jar, swish it around to wash the jar, and add that to the skillet, stirring once or twice. Stir in the salt.

5. Reduce the heat to medium-low, cover the skillet, and simmer, stirring occasionally, until the lamb is fork-tender, 28 to 30 minutes. Then serve.

Tips:

❖ Chunks of beef, including chuck or "stew meat," make an excellent alternative to the lamb.

❖ For the vegetarian, pan-fried cubes of *Doodh paneer* (page 286) are great; in that case, eliminate the yogurt from the recipe. Add the *paneer* pieces after the spinach wilts, and allow them to warm through and absorb some of the saucy goodness.

❖ For the individual who may not like garlic, and there are a few (like my family in India), leave it out of the recipe.

Hearty Lamb
WITH
YELLOW SPLIT PEAS

Chana dal Gosht

Cold winter months in Kashmir call for stick-to-your-ribs, comforting meals. While the curry simmers in one pot, steaming basmati rice is usually being prepared in another, to be topped with the curry and consumed with enthusiasm. Before too long, the fingers of the right hand scoop and feed eager mouths and hungry stomachs. **SERVES 6**

1 teaspoon cayenne (ground red pepper)
½ teaspoon ground turmeric
1 pound boneless leg of lamb, fat trimmed off and discarded, cut into 1-inch cubes
¼ cup yellow split peas (chana dal), picked over for stones
1 medium-size red onion, coarsely chopped
6 lengthwise slices fresh ginger (each 2 inches long, 1 inch wide, and ⅛ inch thick)
6 large cloves garlic
3 to 5 fresh green Thai, cayenne, or serrano chiles, to taste, stems removed
2 tablespoons Ghee (page 21) or canola oil
2 teaspoons cumin seeds
1 teaspoon black cumin seeds
4 fresh or dried bay leaves
4 black cardamom pods
2 cinnamon sticks (each 3 inches long)
1½ teaspoons coarse kosher or sea salt
2 teaspoons coriander seeds
2 tablespoons finely chopped fresh cilantro leaves and tender stems

1. Combine the cayenne and turmeric in a medium-size bowl. Add the lamb and toss to coat it with the spices. Refrigerate, covered, for at least 30 minutes or as long as overnight (see Tip).

2. Place the yellow split peas in a medium-size bowl. Fill the bowl halfway with water, and rinse the peas by rubbing them between your fingertips. The water will become cloudy. Drain this water. Repeat three or four times, until the water is relatively clear; then drain. Now cover the split peas with hot tap water and allow them to soak for about 30 minutes.

3. While the split peas are soaking, place the onion, ginger, garlic, and chiles in a food processor and pulse to mince, creating a pungently aromatic blend that is not watery. (If you don't use the pulsing action and allow the blades to run constantly, you will create a soggy blend.)

4. Heat the ghee in a large saucepan over medium-high heat. Add 1 teaspoon of the cumin seeds along with the black cumin seeds, bay leaves, cardamom pods, and cinnamon sticks. Cook until the oil is flavored, 15 to 20 seconds. Immediately add the onion blend to the spiced oil and stir-fry until the pungent mix is lightly browned around the edges, 4 to 5 minutes.

5. Drain the split peas.

6. Add the lamb and the split peas to the skillet. Cook, stirring, until the lamb is seared and the split peas have absorbed the heady flavors and aromas, 5 to 7 minutes.

7. Pour in 2 cups water, scraping the skillet to deglaze it, releasing any collected bits of spice. Heat to a boil. Then reduce the heat to medium-low, cover the skillet, and simmer, stirring occasionally, until the lamb is fork-tender and the peas are softened but still firm-looking, 40 to 45 minutes.

8. While the lamb is simmering, heat a small skillet over medium-high heat. Add the remaining 1 teaspoon cumin seeds and the coriander seeds, and toast, shaking the pan frequently, until the spices turn reddish brown and are very fragrant, 30 seconds to 1 minute. Transfer the blend to a spice grinder or a mortar, and grind it to the texture of finely ground black pepper.

9. Once the lamb curry is cooked, stir in the ground toasted spices and the cilantro. Remove the cardamom pods, cinnamon sticks, and bay leaves, and serve.

Tip: If you have the time, allow the lamb to marinate overnight in the dry rub of turmeric and cayenne. The turmeric not only flavors the curry but also tenderizes the meat, helping it achieve that fall-apart texture we so desire in our stewy dishes.

Tender Braised Lamb
WITH TURNIPS AND MINT

Shalgam Gosht

turnips are a sweet, crunchy, juicy delicacy in Kashmir and root their way into many of this region's curries. They offer a pleasant backdrop to gamey-tasting lamb. Turnips also retain a lot of liquid, which provides valuable moisture for the meat to braise in. The smaller the turnip, the sweeter the vegetable. Overly large, dried-looking turnips are quite bitter, and people exposed to that undesirable quality once may refrain from using turnips ever again. The vegetable not only has a chameleon-like ability to absorb the flavors of whatever dish it is in, it also contributes a pleasant texture and juiciness.

Serve this curry with wedges of store-bought or homemade naan (page 729) for a simple, satisfying meal. **SERVES 6**

6 tablespoons mustard oil or canola oil

1 pound turnips, peeled and cut into 1-inch cubes

1 large red onion, cut in half lengthwise and thinly sliced

5 large cloves garlic, coarsely chopped

4 lengthwise slices fresh ginger (each 2 inches long, 1 inch wide, and ⅛ inch thick), coarsely chopped

1¼ pounds boneless leg of lamb, fat trimmed off and discarded, cut into 1-inch cubes

4 black cardamom pods

1 tablespoon Bin bhuna hua garam masala (page 30)

2 teaspoons coarse kosher or sea salt

1 cup firmly packed fresh mint leaves

3 dried red Thai or cayenne chiles, stems removed

1 large tomato, cored and coarsely chopped

½ cup finely chopped fresh cilantro leaves and tender stems

1. Heat 2 tablespoons of the oil in a large saucepan over medium heat. Add the turnips and stir-fry until they are light brown around the edges (they won't evenly color, and that's okay), 5 to 8 minutes. Use a slotted spoon to transfer them to a plate.

2. Add another 2 tablespoons of the oil to the same saucepan, and heat it over medium heat. Add the onion, garlic, and ginger, and stir-fry until the vegetables appear to soften and the onion turns honey-brown with a light purple hue, 8 to 10 minutes. Transfer this mixture to a blender jar.

3. Add 1 cup water to the ingredients in the blender and puree, scraping the inside of the jar as needed, to make a smooth paste.

4. Heat the remaining 2 tablespoons oil in the same pan over medium heat. Add the lamb and cardamom pods, and cook, stirring, until the meat is evenly browned, about 15 minutes. (At first the meat will sear; then it will release some of its liquid; the liquid will evaporate; and finally the meat will start to brown, all the while absorbing the black cardamom's smoky flavors.)

5. Transfer the onion paste to the pan. Add the garam masala and salt. Cover the pan and braise the meat, stirring occasionally, until it starts to become tender, about 15 minutes.

6. While the lamb is braising, pile the mint and chiles into a mortar. Pound the ingredients into a pasty blend, using a spatula to contain it in the center to ensure a more concentrated pounding. Add a few tomato pieces, and pound them into the paste. Remove and discard the tomato skin as it separates during the pounding. Repeat until all the tomato is incorporated into the soupy mixture.

7. Add the tomato mixture to the lamb, and stir in the turnips and the cilantro. Cook, covered, stirring occasionally, until the turnips and lamb are fork-tender, 15 to 20 minutes. Then serve.

Tip: Pounding the tomato into the herb-spice blend creates the base for this curry. If fishing for skins in a juicy pool is not your idea of fun, don't chop the tomato. Instead, first dunk the whole tomato into boiling water for a minute to blanch it; then core it and slip off its skin. Gently pound in the juicy pieces—carefully, to keep the squirting contained. (Don't blanch the tomato for too long or you might end up with an unmanageable mess.)

Cubed Lamb
WITH TURNIP GREENS

Gosht Aur Shalgam ka Saag

In the Midwest, turnip greens seem to be available only in the summer months, so I make it a point to buy copious amounts when I see them. I love their mellow bitterness, high nutritional value, and ease of cooking, and find them a perfect match for strong-tasting lamb. (I have also made this curry with beef, with equally satisfying results.) Even though turnip greens are not classic to the western region of India (they are much sought after in Kashmir, however), I think the Kolhapuri spice, with its coconut, assertive spices, and chiles, is a tasty choice. **SERVES 4**

2 tablespoons Ginger Paste (page 15)
2 tablespoons Garlic Paste (page 15)
1¼ pounds boneless leg of lamb, fat trimmed
*   off and discarded, cut into 1-inch cubes*
¼ cup canola oil
1 medium-size red onion, finely chopped
1 pound turnip greens, tough center ribs removed,
*   cut into thin shreds (see Tip)*
1 tablespoon Kolhapuri masala (page 32)
1½ teaspoons coarse kosher or sea salt
1 cup shredded fresh coconut; or ½ cup shredded
*   dried unsweetened coconut, reconstituted*
*   (see Note)*

1. Combine the ginger and garlic pastes in a medium-size bowl, and stir to blend. Add the lamb and toss it in the paste. Refrigerate, covered, for at least 30 minutes or as long as overnight, to allow the flavors to penetrate the meat.

2. Heat the oil in a large skillet over medium heat. Add the lamb, with the paste, and the onion. Cook, uncovered, stirring occasionally, until the lamb and onion brown, 15 to 20 minutes. (The lamb will sear a bit, then release its liquid, and once the liquid evaporates, start to brown.)

3. Pile in several handfuls of the greens, cover the skillet, and let them wilt, 2 to 4 minutes. Repeat, adding the remaining greens. Once they have wilted, stir in the masala and salt. Reduce the heat to medium-low, cover the skillet, and simmer, stirring occasionally, until the greens are dark olive-green and the meat is fork-tender, 20 to 25 minutes.

4. Stir in the coconut, and serve.

Note: To reconstitute coconut, cover with ½ cup boiling water, set aside for about 15 minutes, and then drain.

Tips:

❖ To prepare these large-leafed, thin-textured greens, cut out and discard the tough rib that runs down the center of each leaf (slice along the sides of the rib, making a V-shaped cut up to the point where it thins down). Stack a few leaves on top of one another, and roll them into a tight log. Cut the log into thin slices, and then separate them into ribbon-like shreds (chiffonade). Plunk them into a colander and rinse them well. There is no need to dry them before you add them to the lamb, since the extra moisture will provide more liquid for the curry's base.

❖ Collard, dandelion, mustard, kale, green chard, beet greens, and kohlrabi greens all provide that same hint of bitterness, so use any of them in this curry. (Spinach is more mellow-tasting, so it would not be as good a choice for this curry.)

Lamb Stew
WITH A TRIPLE-NUT PASTE

Awadhi Gosht

Nuts are a sign of opulence, a luxury not within everyday reach of the average home in India. The wealthy nawabs of Lucknow knew how to live in style, and every excuse to entertain warranted the inclusion of rich foods (in both flavor and cost), tender cuts of meat, and sweet fermented beverages extracted from golden raisins. Three varieties of nuts puree their way into this curry of slow-cooked lamb (where they also act as a thickener). With the first mouthful, you will experience the subtle flavors of almonds, pistachios, and cashews—the "three tenors" of poetic Lucknowi cuisine. **SERVES 4**

1 tablespoon Ginger Paste (page 15)
1 tablespoon Garlic Paste (page 15)
1¼ pounds boneless leg of lamb,
   fat trimmed off and discarded,
   cut into 1-inch cubes
2 tablespoons Ghee (page 21) or canola oil
1 medium-size red onion, cut in half
   lengthwise and thinly sliced
1 teaspoon Rajasthani garam masala
   (page 26)
1 teaspoon coarse kosher or sea salt
½ cup half-and-half
¼ cup raw cashew nuts
¼ cup shelled raw pistachio nuts
¼ cup slivered blanched almonds
2 tablespoons finely chopped fresh cilantro
   leaves and tender stems

Crisp-fried onions, homemade or store-bought, for sprinkling (optional; see Tip)

1. Combine the ginger and garlic pastes in a medium-size bowl, and mix well. Add the lamb and toss to coat it with the paste. Refrigerate, covered, for at least 30 minutes or as long as overnight, to allow the flavors to penetrate the meat.

2. Heat the ghee in a large skillet over medium heat. Add the lamb, including the paste, and the onion. Cook, uncovered, stirring occasionally, until the lamb and onion have browned, 15 to 20 minutes. (The lamb will sear a bit, then release its liquid—in the process deglazing the bits stuck on the bottom of the skillet—and once the liquid evaporates, start to brown.)

3. Pour in 1 cup water and scrape the skillet to deglaze it once again. Stir in the garam masala and salt. Once the thin broth comes to a boil, reduce the heat to medium-low, cover the skillet, and simmer, stirring occasionally, until the meat is fork-tender, 15 to 20 minutes.

4. While the lamb is stewing, pour the half-and-half into a blender jar, and then add the three kinds of nuts. Puree, scraping the inside of the jar as needed, to make a thick, slightly gritty, light green paste.

5. Once the lamb is tender, add the paste to the sauce, which will instantly thicken. Stir in the cilantro, top with the crispy onions, and serve.

Tip: You can buy packages of fried onions in Pakistani and Indian grocery stores. I often keep a bag in the refrigerator (as they may turn rancid if kept for a long time at room temperature) to sprinkle on curries like this one to add that extra *je ne sais quoi*.

To make your own, thinly slice a handful of onions and dust the slices with a coating of cornstarch (2 teaspoons cornstarch for about 1 cup sliced onions). Either deep-fry or shallow-fry the slices in canola oil until crisp. If you want to cheat (ssshhh), pick up a can of French-fried onions in the supermarket snack aisle, right next to the potato chips, and use it for the crunch.

Saffron-Scented Lamb
WITH AN ALMOND SAUCE

badam zarda gosht

I believe lamb, saffron, and almonds are a culinary ménage à trois that is meant to be together at all times. The earthy meat, creamy almonds, and perfumed saffron bring in elements characteristic of Moghal cooking—the cuisine of the Muslim emperors who had a profound cultural influence in northern India. Smoky black cardamom adds another twist, along with the other aromatic ingredients in the spice blend. Remove the whole spices from the curry before serving it, or instruct your guests to set them aside should they land on their plate. **SERVES 4**

2 tablespoons Ghee (page 21) or canola oil
1 teaspoon cumin seeds
3 cinnamon sticks (each 3 inches long)
3 fresh or dried bay leaves
3 black cardamom pods
1 medium-size red onion, cut in half lengthwise and thinly sliced
1½ pounds boneless leg of lamb, fat trimmed off and discarded, cut into 1-inch cubes
1 cup slivered blanched almonds
¼ teaspoon saffron threads
1½ teaspoons coarse kosher or sea salt
2 tablespoons finely chopped fresh cilantro leaves and tender stems

1. Heat the ghee in a large skillet over medium-high heat. Sprinkle in the cumin seeds, cinnamon sticks, bay leaves, and cardamom pods. Cook until they sizzle, crackle, and are aromatic, about 1 minute. Then immediately add the onion and lower the heat to medium. Stir-fry until the onion is soft and honey-brown, about 10 minutes.

2. Add the lamb and cook, stirring occasionally, until it starts to brown and some ghee separates from the mixture, 15 to 20 minutes. (The meat will sear a bit, then release its liquid, and once the liquid evaporates, start to brown.)

3. While the lamb does its thing, pour ½ cup water into a blender jar. Add the almonds and puree, scraping the inside of the jar as needed, to form a slightly gritty, milky white paste.

4. Once the lamb has browned, pour in the almond paste. Pour 1 cup water into the blender jar, and swish it around to wash it out. Add this to the skillet, along with the saffron and salt. Once the curry comes to a boil, reduce the heat to medium-low, cover the skillet, and simmer, stirring occasionally, until the lamb is fork-tender, 25 to 30 minutes.

5. Stir in the cilantro, and serve.

Perfumed Lamb
WITH
FENUGREEK AND FRIED ONION

Methi Gosht

Meats cut from the leg of lamb yield tender results when stewed for an extended cooking time. Lamb's gamey flavor holds its own against the perfumed bitterness of fenugreek in this curry. The surprise crunch of crisp-fried onion makes the combination all the more memorable, especially when it is served with Fragrant Basmati Rice with Curry Leaves (page 715). **SERVES 6**

1 tablespoon Ginger Paste (page 15)

2 teaspoons Garlic Paste (page 15)

1½ teaspoons coarse kosher or sea salt

1 teaspoon cayenne (ground red pepper)

½ teaspoon ground turmeric

2 pounds boneless leg of lamb, fat trimmed
   off and discarded, cut into 1-inch cubes

2 tablespoons canola oil, plus more for deep-frying

½ cup chopped fresh or frozen fenugreek
   leaves (thawed if frozen); or ¼ cup dried
   fenugreek leaves, soaked in a bowl of water
   and skimmed off before use (see box, page 473)

1 small red onion, cut in half lengthwise and thinly sliced

1 tablespoon cornstarch

1 tablespoon Toasted Cumin-Coriander Blend (page 33)

1. Combine the Ginger Paste, Garlic Paste, salt, cayenne, and turmeric in a medium-size bowl, and mix well. Add the lamb and toss to coat it with the paste. Refrigerate, covered, for at least 30 minutes or as long as overnight, to allow the flavors to penetrate the meat.

2. Heat the 2 tablespoons of oil in a large skillet over medium-high heat. Add the lamb and cook until it starts to brown, 15 to 20 minutes. (It will sear a bit, then release its liquid, and once the liquid evaporates, start to brown.)

3. Add 1 cup water and scrape the bottom of the skillet to deglaze it, releasing the browned bits of meat and spice. Stir in the fenugreek leaves. Once the liquid comes to a boil, lower the heat to medium, cover the skillet, and simmer, stirring occasionally, until the lamb is fork-tender, 25 to 30 minutes.

4. While the lamb is stewing, pour oil to a depth of 2 to 3 inches into a wok, Dutch oven, or medium-size saucepan. Heat the oil over medium heat until a candy or deep-fry thermometer inserted into the oil (without touching the pan's bottom) registers 350°F. (An alternative way to see if the oil is at the right temperature for deep-frying is to gently flick a drop of water over it. If the pearl-like drop skitters across the surface, the oil is ready.)

5. Line a plate or a cookie sheet with three or four sheets of paper towels.

6. When the oil is ready, toss the onion and cornstarch together in a small bowl, coating the slices evenly. Use your hands to separate the slices as you gently drop them into the hot oil. Cook, stirring occasionally, until the slices are honey-brown and crispy, about 5 minutes. Remove them with a slotted spoon and place them on the paper towels to drain.

7. If the curry is not thick enough, raise the heat to medium-high, uncover the skillet, and vigorously boil the sauce, stirring occasionally, until thickened, about 5 minutes.

8. Stir the cumin-coriander blend into the curry, top with the crisp fried onion, and serve.

Tip: It's very easy to fry your own onion slices, but if you wish, stop by your Indian or Pakistani grocery store and grab a bag of fried onions and use them. Half a cup of the onions should be adequate for this curry. Cans of French-fried onions, found in the snack aisle of your everyday supermarket, will work too, especially if you don't want to deep-fry or to make a trip to the specialty store.

Nutty-Tasting Lamb
WITH A ROASTED POPPY SEED SAUCE

Gosht Poshto

A specialty in many a Bengali-speaking home kitchen, this curry is flavored with one of Bengal's key spices: poppy seeds (*poshto*). When roasted and ground, poppy seeds are very nutty and sweet, with an ever-so-slight bitterness. I like to serve this with some Lime-Flavored Rice with Roasted Yellow Split Peas (page 717) and Nutty Cheese in a Spinach–Chickpea Flour Sauce (page 298). **SERVES 4**

2 tablespoons Ginger Paste (page 15)
2 tablespoons Garlic Paste (page 15)
1 cup finely chopped fresh cilantro leaves
*   and tender stems*
1 pound boneless leg of lamb, fat trimmed
*   off and discarded, cut into 1-inch cubes*

2 tablespoons mustard oil or canola oil
1 tablespoon Panch phoron (page 36)
2 to 4 dried red Thai or cayenne chiles, to taste,
*   stems removed*
1 small red onion, cut in half lengthwise
*   and thinly sliced*
4 fresh or dried bay leaves
1 teaspoon coarse kosher or sea salt
2 tablespoons white poppy seeds
½ teaspoon Bangala garam masala (page 26)

> *White poppy seeds? See the Glossary of Ingredients, page 758.*

1. Combine the Ginger Paste, Garlic Paste, and cilantro in a medium-size bowl. Add the lamb and toss to coat it with the mixture. Refrigerate, covered, for at least 1 hour or as long as overnight.

2. Heat the oil in a large skillet over medium-high heat. Sprinkle in the *Panch phoron* and chiles. Cook until the seeds crackle, sizzle, and pop, and the chiles blacken, 10 to 15 seconds.

3. Add the lamb, onion, and bay leaves, and cook, stirring, until the meat is browned around the edges and the onion is softened and lightly browned, 8 to 10 minutes. Stir in the salt.

4. Pour in 1 cup water and scrape the bottom of the skillet to deglaze it, releasing any browned bits of spice and meat. The water will come to a boil quite quickly. Reduce the heat to medium-low, cover the skillet, and cook, stirring occasionally, until the lamb is fall-apart tender, 30 to 35 minutes. By this point the meat will have absorbed almost all the water.

5. While the lamb is stewing, heat a small skillet over medium-high heat. Sprinkle in the poppy seeds and toast them, shaking the skillet every 5 seconds, until the seeds are nut-brown, 1 to 2 minutes. Immediately transfer the poppy seeds to a plate to cool. (The longer they stand in the hot skillet, the darker they turn, creating an unpalatable burnt flavor.) Once the poppy seeds are cool to the touch, place them in a spice grinder and grind until the texture resembles that of finely ground black pepper.

6. Once the lamb is tender, stir in the ground poppy seeds and the garam masala. Pour in ½ cup water, and stir once or twice to blanket the succulent lamb with the dark brown, thick sauce. Serve immediately.

Aromatic Lamb
WITH POUNDED SPICES

Lucknowi Gosht Korma

This lamb curry has an intense aroma and flavor that is as complex as its city of origin, Lucknow, in the northern state of Uttar Pradesh. Known for its opulence, not only in wealth but also in its foods, Lucknow is also the hotbed of Awadhi cuisine, named after the Muslim rulers who had a strong foothold there well after the Moghal empire had started to crumble in the surrounding cities and states. Aromatic spices like star anise, cloves, and black cardamom are the foundations upon which meats, poultry, and even vegetables are simmered, enhanced by strong aromatics like rosewater and *kewra* (screwpine). My friend and colleague Madhur Jaffrey reminisces about the foods of this community, almost her childhood's backyard, in her book *A Taste of India*. In it she vividly recounts, in mouthwatering detail, a lamb korma she sampled in Lucknow. Based on her memory, I have created a recipe that extols the city's rich tastes. Madhur

did a lot for me in the past, when I was a budding foodie. I hope I have done justice to her memory of that lamb korma with this rendition.

SERVES 6

- 2 tablespoons plain yogurt
- 2 tablespoons Ginger Paste (page 15)
- 1 tablespoon Garlic Paste (page 15)
- 1¼ pounds boneless leg of lamb, fat trimmed off and discarded, cut into 1-inch cubes
- 2 tablespoons Ghee (page 21) or canola oil
- 1 teaspoon black cumin seeds
- 2 black cardamom pods
- 2 fresh or dried bay leaves
- 2 cinnamon sticks (each 3 inches long)
- 1 medium-size red onion, cut in half lengthwise and thinly sliced
- 1 tablespoon coriander seeds, ground
- 4 dried red Thai or cayenne chiles, stems removed
- ½ cup crispy fried onions (see Tip, page 201)
- ½ teaspoon ground nutmeg
- ¼ teaspoon whole cloves
- ¼ teaspoon cardamom seeds from green or white pods
- 4 blades mace, or ¼ teaspoon ground mace
- 1 whole star anise
- 1 teaspoon kewra water (see Tip)

1. Combine the yogurt, Ginger Paste, and Garlic Paste in a medium-size bowl, and mix well. Add the lamb and stir to coat it with the marinade. Cover and refrigerate for at least 30 minutes or as long as overnight, to allow the flavors to permeate the meat.

2. Heat the ghee in a large skillet over medium-high heat. Sprinkle in the cumin seeds, cardamom pods, bay leaves, and cinnamon sticks. Cook until they sizzle, crackle, and are aromatic, about 1 minute. Immediately add the onion and stir-fry until it is honey-brown with a deep purple hue, 10 to 15 minutes.

3. Add the lamb, marinade and all, and cook, stirring occasionally, until the meat is lightly browned, 10 to 15 minutes. (It will sear a bit, then release its liquid, and once the liquid evaporates, start to brown.)

4. Stir in the coriander and chiles, and roast them for 30 seconds to 1 minute. Then add 1 cup water and scrape the bottom of the skillet to deglaze it, releasing the browned bits of onion, spices, and lamb. Heat the curry to a boil. Reduce the heat to medium-low, cover the skillet, and simmer, stirring occasionally, until the lamb is fork-tender, 25 to 30 minutes.

5. While the lamb is stewing, place the fried onions in a mortar and add the nutmeg, cloves, cardamom seeds, mace, and star anise. Sprinkle the *kewra* water over the spices and pound away, scraping the sides of the mortar to keep the mass in the center for a more contained, forceful pounding, until the blend has the texture of wet sawdust. In the event you do not have a mortar and pestle, pulse the mixture in a food processor (a mini processor is ideal, if you have one) to create that same wet, pulpy blend.

6. Once the lamb is tender, add the pounded spice blend and stir once or twice. If you wish, remove the cardamom pods, bay leaves, and cinnamon sticks before serving the curry.

Tip: *Kewra* water, a highly perfumed, clear liquid, is derived from the tropical screwpine tree. Its aroma (which is the main reason why it is used in sweet and savory dishes) has been described as a cross between rose and sandalwood. Even though the plant is pervasive in India, its usage is limited to the northern regions and Pakistan. It is widely available in the essences and extracts section of Indian and Pakistani grocery stores. Rosewater will work as an alternative.

Lamb
WITH
PICKLED MANGOES AND YOGURT

dahi Achar Gosht

Don't be alarmed by the amount of pickles I am asking you to use in this curry. Indian pickles are indeed potent, especially the savory ones, which are flavored with lots of ground red chiles and salt. But you'll find that the yogurt mellows out the curry to make for a tart, slightly hot lamb that's great with the clay-oven-baked bread called naan, either store-bought or homemade (page 729). **SERVES 4**

2 tablespoons canola oil

1 pound boneless leg of lamb, fat trimmed
 off and discarded, cut into 1-inch cubes

2 tablespoons Garlic Paste (page 15)

½ cup plain yogurt

¼ cup spicy mango pickles, either store-bought
 or homemade (page 746), finely chopped

2 tablespoons finely chopped fresh cilantro
 leaves and tender stems for garnishing

1. Heat the oil in a large skillet over medium-high heat. Add the lamb and Garlic Paste, and cook, stirring occasionally, until the meat is lightly browned, 5 to 8 minutes. (The lamb will sear a bit, then release its liquid, and once the liquid evaporates, start to brown.)

2. Stir in the yogurt and pickles, and deglaze the skillet, releasing the browned bits of meat and paste. Reduce the heat to medium-low, cover the skillet, and simmer, stirring occasionally, until the lamb is fork-tender and most of the sauce has evaporated, 25 to 30 minutes.

3. Sprinkle with the cilantro, and serve.

Tip: Store-bought Indian pickles are easy to find not only in any grocery store that sells Indian products, but also in larger supermarkets that stock some Indian goods. Mango, lemons, limes, eggplant, ginger, gooseberry, and garlic are a small handful of the pickle varieties that perk up millions of palates. Even though I have specified tart mango pickles, you can use any kind that tickles your fancy and of course excites your soul (does my coming of age during the disco era show?).

Spicy Lamb
WITH
YOGURT, CREAM, AND FENUGREEK

dahi malai methi gosht

this curry combines dairy in two forms: yogurt, playing the dual role of tenderizer and provider of tart flavor, and cream, mellowing the lamb's robust flavors. Serve it with a basketful of hot-buttered naan (page 729) for a simple dinner. **SERVES 4**

½ cup plain yogurt

1½ teaspoons coarse kosher or sea salt

¼ teaspoon ground turmeric

1 medium-size red onion, cut in half lengthwise; one
    half coarsely chopped, the other half thinly sliced

8 medium-size cloves garlic

6 fresh green Thai, cayenne, or serrano chiles,
    stems removed

3 lengthwise slices fresh ginger
    (each 1½ inches long, 1 inch wide,
    and ⅛ inch thick)

1 pound boneless leg of lamb, fat trimmed
    off and discarded, cut into 1-inch cubes

2 tablespoons Ghee (page 21) or canola oil

1 cup chopped fresh or frozen fenugreek leaves
    (thawed if frozen); or ½ cup dried fenugreek
    leaves, soaked in a bowl of water and skimmed
    off before use (see box, page 473)

¼ cup heavy (whipping) cream

1. Place the yogurt, salt, turmeric, coarsely chopped onion, garlic, chiles, and ginger in a blender jar. Puree, scraping the inside of the jar as needed, to make a smooth, light saffron-orange marinade with flecks of green. Transfer this to a medium-size bowl and toss the lamb in it. (You will have an abundance of marinade.) Refrigerate, covered, for at least 30 minutes or as long as overnight.

2. Heat the ghee in a large skillet over medium-high heat. Add the thinly sliced onion and stir-fry until the edges turn light brown, 3 to 5 minutes.

3. Add the lamb, with all the marinade, and cook, uncovered, stirring occasionally, until the liquid in the marinade evaporates and the oil starts to separate from the lamb, about 15 minutes.

4. Add the fenugreek leaves and 1 cup water, and stir once or twice. Allow the curry to come to a boil. Then reduce the heat to medium-low, cover the skillet, and simmer, stirring occasionally, until the lamb is fork-tender and the sauce has thickened and turned olive-green, 25 to 30 minutes.

5. Fold in the cream and allow it to warm, 1 to 2 minutes. Then serve.

Marinated Lamb Stew
IN A CLAY POT

hyderabadi Matki gosht

Archeological evidence of clay-pot cooking has been traced back 6,000 years; it is a functional, nature-friendly, and flavorful way to infuse meats, rice, legumes, and vegetables over a slow fire. I look at it as the exotic and earthy precursor to modern-day slow cookers. This curry combines the Hyderabadi flavors of coconut, chiles, and curry leaves with a northern blend of garam masala. It is a no-fuss curry that you can truly "fix and forget" (but it's certainly not forgettable). **SERVES 6**

½ cup plain yogurt

I small red onion, coarsely chopped

I cup shredded fresh coconut; or ½ cup shredded
    dried unsweetened coconut, reconstituted
    (see Note)

1½ teaspoons coarse kosher or sea salt

6 to 8 fresh green Thai, cayenne, or serrano chiles,
    to taste, stems removed

1½ pounds boneless leg of lamb, fat trimmed
    off and discarded, cut into 1-inch cubes

2 tablespoons Ghee (page 21) or canola oil

15 to 20 medium-size to large fresh curry leaves

I teaspoon Punjabi garam masala
    (page 25)

¼ cup firmly packed fresh mint leaves,
    finely chopped

¼ cup finely chopped fresh cilantro leaves
    and tender stems

1. Place the yogurt in a blender jar, and then add the onion, coconut, salt, and chiles. Puree, scraping the inside of the jar as needed, to yield a gritty, curdled-looking marinade, light purple in color, full of pungency and heat. (When you add the yogurt first and then the watery onion, you will have enough moisture to puree the rest of the ingredients without having to add water for the blades to do their magic.)

2. Place the lamb in a medium-size bowl and pour the marinade over it. Toss to coat the meat well. Refrigerate, covered, for at least 1 hour or as long as overnight, for the flavors to permeate the meat and the yogurt to tenderize it.

3. Position a rack in the center and preheat the oven to 300°F.

4. Drizzle the ghee into a clay pot. Add the meat, marinade and all, along with the curry leaves. Place the pot, uncovered, in the oven and let the lamb stew, stirring occasionally, until the juices are absorbed into the meat and it is starting to brown in the fat, 45 minutes to 1 hour.

5. Remove the pot from the oven (make sure you do not place it on a cold surface—a hot pad or cutting board will help to prevent it from cracking). Pour ½ cup hot tap water into the pot (if you pour in cold water, it will shock the clay pot and end up cracking it because of the temperature difference), and sprinkle in the garam masala. Stir once or twice. Cover the pot, return it to the oven, and bake, stirring occasionally, until the meat is very tender, 15 to 20 minutes.

6. Remove the pot from the oven (again making sure you do not place it on a cold surface), stir in the mint and cilantro, and serve.

Note: To reconstitute coconut, cover with ½ cup boiling water, set aside for about 15 minutes, and then drain.

Tip: Unglazed clay pots are widely available in gourmet kitchen shops and in the kitchenware section of department stores. With proper care and handling (follow the manufacturer's instructions for seasoning it before use), you will have a pot that will benefit you with years of pleasure. Certain imported glazed pots have leached toxic levels of lead into the foods of unsuspecting consumers, especially when the foods contained enough acid to strip the glaze and expose the powdery lead underneath the finish. If you prefer a glazed pot, make sure it comes from a reputable source.

Cashew Lamb
WITH A COCONUT MILK SAUCE

Kaaju Nariyal Gosht

There is a lot of sauce in this curry—all the more reason to serve it atop a mound of steamed white rice. The addition of ground red pepper at the end provides a sharp flavor, prized by many a Christian Goan, especially when it comes to vinegar-based dishes like this one.

SERVES 4

½ cup raw cashew nuts

1½ teaspoons coarse kosher or sea salt

1 pound boneless leg of lamb, fat trimmed off and
   discarded, cut into 1-inch cubes

2 tablespoons canola oil

1 large red onion, cut in half lengthwise and then into
   ¼-inch cubes

1 tablespoon coriander seeds

1 teaspoon cumin seeds

½ teaspoon fennel seeds

¼ teaspoon cardamom seeds from green
   or white pods

6 whole cloves

½ teaspoon ground turmeric

7 lengthwise slices fresh ginger (each 1½ inches long,
   1 inch wide, and ⅛ inch thick), finely chopped

6 large cloves garlic, finely chopped

½ cup unsweetened coconut milk

¼ cup distilled white vinegar

1 teaspoon cayenne (ground red pepper)

2 tablespoons finely chopped fresh cilantro
   leaves and tender stems for garnishing

1. Combine the cashews, ⅓ cup water, and the salt in a blender jar. Puree, scraping the inside of the jar as needed, to make a smooth marinade. Pour this into a medium-size bowl, add the lamb, and stir to coat the lamb with it. Refrigerate, covered, for 30 minutes or as long as overnight, to allow the mellow cashew flavor to penetrate the meat.

2. Heat the oil in a large skillet over medium-high heat. Add the onion and stir-fry until it is caramel-brown, 8 to 10 minutes.

3. While the onion is browning, combine the coriander, cumin, fennel, and cardamom seeds in a spice grinder. Add the cloves and grind until the texture resembles that of finely ground black pepper. Set it aside.

4. Add the lamb, including the marinade, to the skillet. Cook over medium heat, uncovered, stirring occasionally, until the sauce is completely absorbed into the meat, 8 to 10 minutes.

5. Sprinkle in the ground spices along with the

turmeric, ginger, and garlic. Cook, stirring, until the spices are aromatic, 1 to 2 minutes. Pour 1 in cup water and stir to deglaze the skillet, releasing any collected bits of spice and onion. Reduce the heat to medium-low, cover the skillet, and simmer, stirring occasionally, until the lamb is fork-tender, 18 to 20 minutes.

6. Stir in the coconut milk, vinegar, and cayenne, and continue to simmer, uncovered, to allow the added flavors to blend in, 2 to 4 minutes.

7. Sprinkle with the cilantro, and serve.

Tip: If you are allergic to cashew nuts, feel free to substitute any other nut that might be safe for you. If all nuts are taboo, puree ½ cup coarsely chopped onion instead of the cashew nuts. It is obviously not a substitution for the nuts, making for a more pungent flavor, but it is an acceptable alternative that provides yet another layer of flavor to the wide world of curries.

Creamy Lamb
WITH GREEN PEAS

khoya mutter gosht

In Hindi *khoya* means "lost," but in cooking it refers to whole milk cooked down until all its liquid evaporates and it turns into off-white, creamy, nutty, clumpy milk solids. This technique provides for a rich-tasting product that affords the same rich, silky succulence as heavy cream, without the equivalent fat. Every bite of this lamb curry will make you aware of the *khoya*'s opulence.

SERVES 6

2 tablespoons plain yogurt
2 tablespoons Ginger Paste (page 15)
1 tablespoon Garlic Paste (page 15)
2 teaspoons ground Kashmiri chiles; or
     ½ teaspoon cayenne (ground red pepper)
     mixed with 1½ teaspoons sweet paprika
½ teaspoon ground turmeric
1½ pounds boneless leg of lamb, fat trimmed
     off and discarded, cut into 1-inch cubes
2 tablespoons canola oil
1 teaspoon whole cloves
3 cinnamon sticks (each 3 inches long)
2 fresh or dried bay leaves
1 medium-size red onion, finely chopped
¼ cup Whole Milk Solids (page 24) or
     heavy (whipping) cream
1½ teaspoons coarse kosher or sea salt
2 cups frozen green peas (no need to thaw)

1. Combine the yogurt, Ginger Paste, Garlic Paste, Kashmiri chiles, and turmeric in a medium-size bowl, and mix well. Add the lamb and toss to coat it with the marinade. Refrigerate, covered, for at least 30 minutes or as long as overnight, to allow the flavors to permeate the meat. (The longer it marinates, the tenderer the meat, thanks to the yogurt.)

2. Heat the oil in a large saucepan over medium-high heat. Sprinkle in the cloves, cinnamon sticks, and bay leaves, and cook until they sizzle, crackle, and are aromatic, 15 to 30 seconds. Immediately add the lamb, including any residual marinade, and the onion. The meat will start to stew once its water is released and mixes in with the yogurt. Keep stirring the curry occasionally until the liquid evaporates and the red-tinted oil starts to separate from the meat, 10 to 12 minutes; the meat will be lightly browned. Don't worry about the yogurt curdling—the fat from the lamb protects it from breaking apart.

3. Stir in the Whole Milk Solids, which will have a crumbly appearance, and the salt. Pour in 1 cup water and bring to a boil. Then reduce the heat to medium-low, cover the pan, and simmer, stirring occasionally, until the lamb is tender, 20 to 25 minutes.

4. Stir in the peas, cover the pan, remove it from the burner, and let it sit for about 5 minutes. The heat in the pan will be just right to steam the peas but still keep them bright green.

Tip: When you bite into a mouth-tingling, slightly numbing whole clove, it is no fun. So when you serve this curry, do warn your friends and family to fork them aside. Of course you can also remove them—and the cinnamon sticks and bay leaves—from the curry before you serve it.

Onion-Marinated Lamb
WITH COCONUT

Kolhapuri Gosht

In addition to the citizens of Kolhapur's mastery at hammering out hand-stitched, open-toed leather slippers and sandals, they stew some incredible curries featuring local coconuts, mangoes (in season), and complexly layered spice blends made with exotic ingredients like *dagad phool,* or stone flower. (Even to Indians this spice is relatively unknown beyond its provincial boundaries. It is a blackish-purple, mosslike ingredient,

technically a lichen, that is found on stones. It is normally toasted and ground in spice blends to yield a woodsy flavor.) **SERVES 4**

2 small red onions: I coarsely chopped,
   I finely chopped
4 to 6 large cloves garlic
2 lengthwise slices fresh ginger (each 2 inches long,
   I inch wide, and ⅛ inch thick)
I tablespoon coriander seeds
1¼ pounds boneless leg of lamb, fat trimmed
   off and discarded, cut into I-inch cubes
2 tablespoons canola oil
2 fresh green Thai, cayenne, or serrano chiles,
   stems removed and cut in half lengthwise
   (do not remove the seeds)
I small to medium-size rock-firm unripe mango,
   peeled and cut into I-inch cubes
I tablespoon Kolhapuri masala (page 32)
1½ teaspoons coarse kosher or sea salt
I cup shredded fresh coconut; or ½ cup shredded dried
   unsweetened coconut, reconstituted (see Note)
¼ cup finely chopped fresh cilantro leaves
   and tender stems

1. Place the coarsely chopped onion and the garlic, ginger, and coriander seeds in a food processor. Process constantly (as opposed to pulsing) to create a pulpy, slightly watery marinade. Transfer this to a medium-size bowl and add the lamb to it. Stir to make sure the meat is covered with the marinade. Refrigerate, covered, for at least 1 hour or as long as overnight, to allow the flavors to permeate the meat.

2. Heat the oil in a large skillet over medium-low heat. Add the finely chopped onion and the chiles and cook, covered, stirring frequently, until the onion is a caramel color with a deep purple hue, 15 to 20 minutes.

3. Add the lamb, marinade and all, and stir once or

twice. Raise the heat to medium and cook, uncovered, stirring occasionally, until the marinade is absorbed and the meat is starting to brown, 15 to 20 minutes.

4. Stir in 1 cup water along with the mango, masala, and salt. Cover the skillet and simmer, stirring occasionally, until the mango pieces have softened but still appear firm-looking and the lamb is fork-tender, 20 to 25 minutes.

5. Stir in the coconut and cilantro, and serve.

Note: To reconstitute coconut, cover with ½ cup boiling water, set aside for about 15 minutes, and then drain.

Tip: If you are willing to try a stronger-tasting meat, use mutton (a mature sheep, usually more than 2 years old) instead of lamb. The meat department at your local grocery store might be willing to get it for you, should you not find any butchers in town that cater to Indian, Pakistani, African, or Middle Eastern immigrants.

Smoky Lamb
WITH VINEGAR AND COCONUT MILK

kudampuli maas

Notice how two strong souring agents can join forces to make a curry actually a tad sweet? When you use a sweeter vinegar like malt (or even cider) and smoky-tart kudampuli, the sweet and smoky counterparts play off each other to tone down the acidity. This lamb swims in a good amount of sauce, so do make sure you serve some white or red rice to mop it up. **SERVES 4**

- ¼ cup malt or cider vinegar
- 1 tablespoon coriander seeds, ground
- 1 teaspoon cumin seeds, ground
- 1 teaspoon cayenne (ground red pepper)
- 1 teaspoon coarse kosher or sea salt
- ½ teaspoon ground turmeric
- 1¼ pounds boneless leg of lamb, fat trimmed off and discarded, cut into 1-inch cubes
- 1 whole smoked kudampuli (see Tip, page 248)
- 2 tablespoons canola oil
- 4 medium-size cloves garlic, finely chopped
- 2 lengthwise slices fresh ginger (each 2 inches long, 1 inch wide, and ⅛ inch thick), finely chopped
- 1 can (13.5 ounces) unsweetened coconut milk
- 2 fresh green Thai, cayenne, or serrano chiles, stems removed, cut in half lengthwise (do not remove the seeds)
- 2 tablespoons finely chopped fresh cilantro leaves and tender stems for garnishing

1. Mix the vinegar, coriander, cumin, cayenne, salt, and turmeric together in a medium-size bowl. Add the lamb and stir to coat the pieces with the marinade. Refrigerate, covered, for at least 1 hour or as long as overnight, to allow the spices to penetrate the meat and the vinegar to tenderize it.

2. Bring ½ cup water to a vigorous boil in the microwave or in a small saucepan over medium-high heat. Put the kudampuli in it and set it aside until the black-brown pulp has seeped into the water and a haunting smokiness emanates from the liquid, about 15 minutes. Squeeze the fruit, which will still be firm to the touch, to extract some more of its juices. (I usually then wrap the fruit and refrigerate it to use for another extraction or two.) Set the kudampuli water aside.

3. Heat the oil in a large skillet over medium-high heat. Add the garlic and ginger, and stir-fry until light brown, about 1 minute. Add the lamb, marinade and all. Cook, uncovered, stirring occasionally, until the paste is absorbed and the meat has seared, 10 to 15 minutes.

4. Pour in the coconut milk and scrape the skillet to deglaze it, releasing any browned bits of meat and spice. Stir in the kudampuli water and the fresh chiles. Bring the curry to a boil. Then reduce the heat to medium-low, cover the skillet, and simmer, stirring occasionally, until the lamb is fork-tender, 20 to 25 minutes. (If you want a thicker sauce, remove the cover, raise the heat to medium, and simmer, stirring occasionally, for about 5 minutes.)

5. Sprinkle with the cilantro, and serve.

Tip: If kudampuli is unavailable, use ½ teaspoon easier-to-find tamarind paste or concentrate, dissolved in ½ cup water. For that distinct smoky flavor, stirring in a drop or two of bottled natural smoke flavor will do the trick.

Lamb
WITH
STAR ANISE AND COCONUT CHIPS

ᴹutton ◊lathel

A specialty of the Syrian Christian community in the southwestern state of Kerala, this curry (usually made with mutton) is not as cumbersome to make as the list of ingredients might lead you to believe. These are all commonly available items that prove yet again that unusual techniques applied to easy-to-find spices can result in outstanding flavors. I love the textural contrast that the coconut chips offer against the tender lamb. **SERVES 4**

¼ cup plain yogurt

2 small red onions: 1 coarsely chopped,
*   1 finely chopped*

3 or 4 dried red Thai or cayenne chiles, to taste,
*   stems removed*

1 pound boneless leg of lamb, fat trimmed off and
*   discarded, cut into 1-inch cubes*

1 cup finely chopped fresh coconut (see Tip)

2 tablespoons canola oil

¼ teaspoon whole cloves

4 black cardamom pods

2 whole star anise

2 cinnamon sticks (each 3 inches long)

4 large cloves garlic, finely chopped

1 tablespoon finely chopped fresh ginger

10 to 12 medium-size to large fresh curry leaves

2 fresh green Thai, cayenne, or serrano chiles, stems
*   removed, finely chopped (do not remove the seeds)*

½ teaspoon coarse kosher or sea salt

¼ teaspoon ground turmeric

2 teaspoons coriander seeds

1. Place the yogurt, the coarsely chopped onion, and the dried chiles in a blender jar. Puree, scraping the inside of the jar as needed, to make a light purple, red-speckled marinade. Spoon this into a medium-size bowl and add the lamb. Toss, making sure the meat is well coated with the spicy-hot marinade. Refrigerate, covered, for at least 1 hour or as long as overnight.

2. Heat a medium-size skillet over medium-high heat. Add the lamb, marinade and all, and the coconut to the hot skillet and cook, stirring occasionally, until the lamb browns, about 10 minutes. (The meat will release some liquid, which will evaporate, and then it will brown in its oil.)

3. Add 1 cup water and scrape the bottom of the skillet to deglaze it, releasing any browned bits of meat. Once the liquid comes to boil, reduce the heat to medium-low, cover the skillet, and simmer, stirring occasionally, until the lamb is tender, 45 to 50 minutes.

4. Heat the oil in a large skillet over medium-high heat. Sprinkle the cloves, cardamom pods, star anise, and cinnamon sticks into the hot oil and cook until they sizzle and are aromatic, 10 to 15 seconds. Immediately add the finely chopped onion and the garlic, ginger, curry leaves, and fresh chiles. Stir-fry until the onion is golden brown, 3 to 5 minutes. Add the lamb, salt, and turmeric, and cook, stirring, for 1 minute.

5. Pour in 1 cup water and heat the curry to a boil. Then reduce the heat to medium-low, cover the skillet, and simmer, stirring occasionally, until the sauce thickens slightly, 10 to 15 minutes.

6. While the curry is simmering, heat a small skillet over medium-high heat. Sprinkle in the coriander seeds and toast them, shaking the skillet often, until they turn reddish-brown and are aromatic. Transfer the seeds to a plate to cool. Once they are cool to the touch, grind them in a spice grinder, or with a mortar and pestle, until the texture resembles that of finely ground black pepper.

7. Stir the sweet-smelling coriander into the curry, and serve.

Tip: After you crack the coconut shell (see page 760) and catch the water in a bowl, score the coconut meat with a paring knife, cutting as deep as the shell will allow. Pop the scored pieces out by wedging a butter knife between the scored meat and the shell. Use the same paring knife or a swivel peeler to peel the thin, tough, brown skin from the coconut meat (the part that was against the coconut shell). Cut the white flesh into thin slices (about ⅛ inch thick), and then chop each slice into ¼-inch pieces. (You can do this up to 4 days ahead of time and store the coconut pieces in a zip-top plastic bag in the refrigerator. You can even freeze them for up to a month.)

Yogurt-Marinated Lamb
WITH GINGER AND GARLIC

Roghan Josh

The recent years have seen plenty of turmoil and mayhem in Kashmir, but let's not lose sight of this classic curry that showcases the state's pristine flavors. This red, robust-looking curry acquires its hearty *(josh)* looks from Kashmiri chiles, which are a cross between paprika and cayenne. Serve this over Kashmir's other prized offering—aromatic white basmati rice. **SERVES 6**

¼ cup Thick Yogurt (page 22)
1 tablespoon Ginger Paste (page 15)
2 teaspoons Garlic Paste (page 15)
2 teaspoons Bin bhuna hua garam masala (page 30)
2 teaspoons coarse kosher or sea salt
1½ pounds boneless leg of lamb, fat trimmed off and
    discarded, cut into 1-inch cubes

2 tablespoons Ghee (page 21) or canola oil

1 teaspoon black cumin seeds

1 teaspoon fennel seeds

12 whole cloves

4 black cardamom pods

2 fresh or dried bay leaves

2 cinnamon sticks (each 3 inches long)

1 cup finely chopped red onion

2 tablespoons tomato paste

1 tablespoon ground Kashmiri chiles; or ¼ tablespoon
   cayenne (ground red pepper) mixed with
   ¾ tablespoon sweet paprika

1. Whisk the yogurt, Ginger Paste, Garlic Paste, garam masala, and salt together in a medium-size bowl. Add the lamb and stir to coat it with the marinade. Refrigerate, covered, for at least 1 hour or as long as overnight.

2. Heat the ghee in a large saucepan or skillet over medium-high heat. Sprinkle in the cumin seeds, fennel seeds, cloves, cardamom pods, bay leaves, and cinnamon sticks, and stir-fry until the spices start to sizzle and are aromatic, 15 to 30 seconds. Immediately add the onion and cook, stirring frequently, until it is light brown, 4 to 6 minutes.

3. Add the lamb, marinade and all, and cook, stirring occasionally, until the yogurt is absorbed by the lamb and the ghee is starting to separate from the meat, about 15 minutes.

4. Stir in the tomato paste and Kashmiri chiles, and stir to make sure the lamb pieces get coated with the paste. Pour in 1 cup water and stir once or twice to deglaze the skillet, releasing any browned bits of lamb and spices. Bring it to a boil. Reduce the heat to medium-low, cover the pan, and simmer, stirring occasionally to prevent the curry from sticking to the bottom, until the lamb is tender, 15 to 20 minutes. Then serve.

Tips:

❖ This curry uses two kinds of garam masala—one left whole, the other ground—showing us, yet again, the multiple flavors that can come from any one spice.

❖ If you wish, remove the cinnamon, bay leaves, cardamom pods, and cloves before you serve the curry. Back home, we leave them intact and simply move them to the side of the plate.

❖ The fat from the lamb prevents the yogurt from curdling. If you have not had time to make thickened yogurt, use a good-quality full-fat plain yogurt (drain some of the excess whey) as an alternative.

❖ If you are like me, you will in all likelihood wrap the opened can of tomato paste, stick it in the refrigerator, and forget about it. Weeks later, you'll peek in to see black paste and fungus lining the walls of the can. In disgust, you'll throw it away and kick yourself for not being frugal. Today supermarkets sell tubes of tomato paste, letting you squeeze out just as much as you need and save the rest, without spoilage, for months in the refrigerator.

Creamy Lamb Meatballs

Goshtaba

Just as love and marriage are inseparable, so are *Rista* and *Goshtaba* at Kashmiri weddings—the same flavored meatballs with two different sauces. This one bathes the spicy lamb with a creamy sauce perfumed with saffron and a fennel-kissed spice blend. I often serve *Rista* and *Goshtaba* together, to allow my dining companions to marvel at their dissimilarities, even though the meatballs are flavored with the same intriguing spice combination. **SERVES 4**

8 ounces lean ground lamb

1 teaspoon coarse kosher or sea salt

½ teaspoon fennel seeds, ground

½ teaspoon black cumin seeds, ground

½ teaspoon ground ginger

½ small red onion, finely chopped

2 large cloves garlic, finely chopped

2 tablespoons mustard oil or canola oil

1 cup half-and-half

½ teaspoon Kashmiri garam masala
   (page 29)

¼ teaspoon saffron threads

Black cumin seeds? See the Glossary of Ingredients, page 758.

1. Mix the lamb, salt, fennel, cumin, ginger, onion, and garlic together in a medium-size bowl. (I have no qualms using my clean hands to do it—all the better to knead and massage the ingredients thoroughly into the meat.) Divide the spiced meat into 10 equal portions, and shape each portion into a tight round. (I usually compress it in one hand to shape and press it into a taut ball.)

2. Heat the oil in a medium-size saucepan over medium heat. Add the meatballs in a single layer and cook, gently moving them around every few seconds, until they are evenly browned, 5 to 7 minutes. Drain off the excess oil into a small bowl (you can reserve it for another recipe that calls for oil—just make sure it isn't a vegetarian dish).

3. Pour the half-and-half over the meatballs, and sprinkle in the garam masala and saffron. Raise the heat to medium-high and simmer the curry vigorously, uncovered, bathing the meatballs every minute or two,

until the lamb is barely pink inside and the sauce has thickened, 8 to 10 minutes.

4. Scoop out the meatballs and transfer them to a serving bowl. Pour the creamy-yellow, highly perfumed sauce over them, and serve.

Tip: In Kashmir, making these meatballs is a labor of love and patience. Cooks pound a handful of lamb or mutton cubes at a time in a mortar, creating a pasty-textured meat. This technique yields a silky-smooth meatball that literally melts in your mouth. You could do the same if you wish to do it the old-fashioned way and not use the convenient store-bought ground lamb.

Ground Lamb Meatballs
WITH A SAFFRON SAUCE

Rista

I was lucky enough to be able to witness the way cooks pounded small chunks of lamb on a cutting board in a restaurant kitchen in Old Delhi that served authentic Kashmiri foods. This pounding was the beginning of silky-smooth meatballs that later simmered in a thin broth steeped with vermilion-red cockscomb flowers (called *pran* in Kashmir). It's an ingredient rarely found outside Kashmir, so to re-create the color and flavor, I have combined ground Kashmiri chiles, a hint of saffron, and black cardamom pods—a near-perfect match. The flavors of this thin curry are potent, sinus-clearing, and intense. Make sure to serve it with basmati rice to bring down its intensity to a perfect balance. **SERVES 4**

- *8 ounces lean ground lamb*
- *1 teaspoon coarse kosher or sea salt*
- *½ teaspoon fennel seeds, ground*
- *½ teaspoon black cumin seeds, ground*
- *½ teaspoon ground ginger*
- *½ small red onion, finely chopped*
- *2 large cloves garlic, finely chopped*
- *1 teaspoon ground Kashmiri chiles; or ¼ teaspoon*
  cayenne (ground red pepper) mixed with
  ¾ teaspoon sweet paprika
- *¼ teaspoon saffron threads*
- *4 or 5 black cardamom pods*
- *6 whole cloves, crushed*
- *2 tablespoons mustard oil or canola oil*

1. Mix the lamb, salt, fennel, cumin, ginger, onion, and garlic together in a medium-size bowl. (I like to use my clean hands to do this, as I can knead and massage the ingredients thoroughly into the meat.) Divide the spiced meat into 10 equal portions, and shape each portion into a tight round. (I usually compress it in one hand, to shape and press it into a taut ball.) As you form them, place the meatballs on a plate.

2. Pour 2 cups water into a small saucepan, and add the Kashmiri chiles, saffron, cardamom pods, and cloves. Bring to a rolling boil over medium-high heat. Cook, uncovered, until the spices infuse the water and turn it into an aromatic, reddish-orange broth, about 5 minutes. Set it aside.

3. Heat the oil in a medium-size saucepan over medium heat. Add the meatballs, arranging them in a single layer, and cook, gently moving them around every few seconds to ensure even browning, until they are seared all over, 5 to 7 minutes. Drain off the excess fat into a small bowl (you can use it in another recipe, as long as it's not for vegetarians).

4. Pour the spiced broth over the meatballs. Raise the heat to medium-high and vigorously simmer the thin curry, uncovered, basting the meatballs every minute or two, until the lamb is barely pink inside, about 10 minutes. Use a slotted spoon to scoop the meatballs from the broth and transfer them to a serving bowl.

5. Continue to simmer the broth until it reduces to about ½ cup, 8 to 10 minutes. Pour this bright red, potent broth over the meatballs, and serve.

Lamb-Almond Dumplings
IN A TOMATO CREAM SAUCE

Shahi Kofta Curry

A dish fit for royalty *(shahi)* deserves a comparable companion, and I highly recommend that you serve this with Buttery Basmati Rice with Spinach and Onion (page 713). This will appeal even to the ones who are shy of anything out of the ordinary. Or serve it over fresh-cooked pasta strands for an Indian spaghetti-and-meatballs dinner. **SERVES 6**

1 pound lean ground lamb

½ cup finely chopped red onion

¼ cup slivered blanched almonds, ground

¼ cup firmly packed fresh mint leaves,
*   finely chopped*

2 tablespoons finely chopped fresh cilantro
*   leaves and tender stems*

6 medium-size cloves garlic, finely chopped

1 tablespoon Punjabi garam masala (page 25)

1½ teaspoons coarse kosher or sea salt

2 tablespoons Ghee (page 21) or canola oil

1 teaspoon cumin seeds

1 cup canned tomato sauce

½ teaspoon cardamom seeds from green
*   or white pods, ground*

½ teaspoon cayenne (ground red pepper)

½ cup heavy (whipping) cream

1. Thoroughly combine the lamb, onion, almonds, mint, cilantro, garlic, garam masala, and salt in a medium-size mixing bowl. Divide the spiced meat into 12 equal portions, and shape each portion into a compact meatball.

2. Heat the ghee in a large skillet over medium-high heat. Add the cumin seeds and cook until they sizzle, turn reddish brown, and smell nutty, 5 to 10 seconds. Immediately add the meatballs to the pan in a single layer. Cook, gently shaking the pan every 2 to 3 minutes, until the meatballs have browned evenly all over,

5 to 8 minutes. Using a slotted spoon, transfer the meatballs to a plate.

3. Pour the tomato sauce into the same skillet and scrape the bottom to deglaze it, releasing any browned bits of meat. Stir in the cardamom and cayenne. Reduce the heat to medium-low, cover, and simmer, stirring occasionally, until a thin film of oil starts to form on the surface and at the sides, 5 to 8 minutes. Stir in the cream.

4. Add the meatballs to the skillet and spoon the sauce over them. Cover the skillet and simmer, basting the meatballs occasionally, until they are light pink in the center, 10 to 15 minutes. Then serve.

Tips:

❖ The ground almonds in the meatballs act as the binder, so no eggs are required to hold them together. However, if your meatballs fall apart when you try to shape them, incorporate 1 large egg, lightly beaten, into the meat mixture.

❖ For the vegetarian at the table, make the mixture with shredded potatoes (from 2 large white baking potatoes) instead of the meat, and incorporate 2 tablespoons chickpea flour and 1 large egg (potatoes need an egg for binding), lightly beaten, to hold the meatballs together. For a more meatlike texture, use textured vegetable protein for that slightly grainy quality.

{ pork }

Pork Tenderloin Strips
WITH ONIONS AND BOTTLE MASALA

Pork do Pyaaz

This curry has no added liquid; instead, it relies on the onion's liquid to create its sweet magic. *Bottle masala* boosts this to a completely new level, but if you don't have any, use the less complex English-style Madras curry powder.

SERVES 4

2 tablespoons canola oil

2 medium-size red onions, cut in half lengthwise and thinly sliced

1 medium-size green bell pepper, stemmed, seeded, and cut into thin strips

1 pound pork tenderloin, sliced crosswise into ¼-inch-thick pieces, and the slices cut into ¼-inch-wide strips

2 teaspoons East Indian bottle masala (page 37)

1½ teaspoons coarse kosher or sea salt

¼ cup finely chopped fresh cilantro leaves and tender stems

1. Heat the oil in a large skillet over medium heat. Add the onions and bell pepper, stir once or twice, and cover the skillet. Cook, stirring, until the onions turn caramel brown with a deep purple hue and appear very soft, 25 to 30 minutes. (Stir occasionally at first, but once the onions cook down and the liquid evaporates, stir more frequently.)

2. Stir in the pork, *bottle masala,* and salt. Raise the heat to medium-high and cook, uncovered, stirring occasionally, until the pork browns, 8 to 10 minutes.

3. Stir in the cilantro, and serve.

Tip: Premium pork tenderloin not only contributes great flavor but also cuts your cooking time to mere minutes.

Pork
WITH POTATOES, PEPPERS, AND APPLES

Aloo Aur Simla Mirch Gosht

Bring this curry's hearty, rich, comforting flavors into your kitchen on a cold, wintry Saturday night. Stack a few logs in the fireplace and relish that glass of pinot noir by the fire as the pork stews slowly. Once it's ready, ladle yourself a bowl, cut yourself some warm, crusty bread, and pour yourself a second glass of wine. As your body warms, inside from the warming spices and outside from the blazing fire, think about how fortunate you are. (As Rosalind

Russell's character of Auntie Mame says in the old classic, "Life is a banquet and most poor suckers are starving to death.") **SERVES 6**

2 medium-size russet or Yukon Gold potatoes, peeled,
    cut into 1-inch cubes, and submerged in a bowl
    of cold water to prevent browning
1¼ pounds boneless pork loin chops, cut into 1-inch cubes
2 tablespoons plain yogurt
1½ teaspoons coarse kosher or sea salt
1 teaspoon fennel seeds, ground
1 teaspoon ground ginger
1 teaspoon black cumin seeds, ground
1 teaspoon dill seeds, ground
2 teaspoons ground Kashmiri chiles; or ½ teaspoon
    cayenne (ground red pepper) mixed with
    1½ teaspoons sweet paprika
6 large cloves garlic, finely chopped
Seeds from 2 black cardamom pods, ground
2 tablespoons mustard oil or canola oil
1 medium-size green bell pepper, stemmed, seeded,
    and cut into 1-inch pieces
2 tablespoons tomato paste
1 large, tart-sweet, crisp apple (such as Braeburn),
    cored and cut into 1-inch pieces
2 tablespoons finely chopped fresh cilantro
    leaves and tender stems

1. Drain the potatoes and pat them dry with paper towels.

2. Combine the pork, potatoes, yogurt, salt, fennel, ginger, cumin, dill, Kashmiri chiles, garlic, and cardamom in a medium-size bowl. Toss to mix well. Refrigerate, covered, for at least 30 minutes or as long as overnight, to allow the flavors to permeate the meat.

3. Heat the oil in a large saucepan over medium-high heat. Add the bell pepper and stir-fry until the intense heat causes the pieces to blister, 3 to 5 minutes.

4. Add the pork and potatoes, including any residual marinade. Cook, stirring occasionally, until the meat is seared and the potatoes are browned, 5 to 8 minutes.

5. Stir in the tomato paste and 1 cup water, and scrape the bottom of the pan to deglaze it, releasing any browned bits of meat, vegetables, and spice.

6. Fold in the apple pieces and heat to a boil. Then reduce the heat to medium-low, cover the pan, and simmer, stirring occasionally, until the meat is fork-tender, 20 to 25 minutes. (The vegetables will be tender too, but surprisingly maintain their shape.)

7. Stir in the cilantro, and serve.

Tip: Beef and lamb are both excellent alternatives to pork here, but do adjust for a longer stewing time to yield tender meat. If you want to try chicken, I recommend using bone-in pieces to maintain the meat's succulence.

Spicy Pork
WITH
CIDER VINEGAR AND FRIED POTATOES

Batata Dukkar Vindaloo

An easy meat-and-potato curry to please everyone, this offering packs quite a punch in every bite. Serve it with a slightly starchy, newer crop of long-grain white rice to soak up some of the potent capsaicin in the chiles. I often serve a bowl of plain, cooling yogurt for my eight-year-old, who appreciates its comfort-giving quality. Does that make him refrain from eating more of the curry? Not at all, as he surprises me with a request for seconds. **SERVES 6**

4 tablespoons canola oil

1½ pounds russet or Yukon Gold potatoes, peeled, cut in half lengthwise, thinly sliced, and submerged in a bowl of cold water to prevent browning

2 teaspoons coriander seeds

1 teaspoon cumin seeds

½ teaspoon black or yellow mustard seeds

½ teaspoon black peppercorns

6 whole cloves

3 to 5 dried red Thai or cayenne chiles, to taste, stems removed

1 cinnamon stick (3 inches long), broken into smaller pieces

½ cup cider vinegar or malt vinegar

8 medium-size cloves garlic

2 small red onions: 1 coarsely chopped, 1 cut in half lengthwise and thinly sliced

1 or 2 fresh green Thai, cayenne, or serrano chiles, to taste, stems removed, thinly sliced crosswise (do not remove the seeds)

1¼ pounds boneless pork loin chops, cut into 1-inch cubes

1½ teaspoons coarse kosher or sea salt

½ teaspoon ground turmeric

2 tablespoons finely chopped fresh cilantro leaves and tender stems for garnishing

1. Heat 2 tablespoons of the oil in a large nonstick skillet over medium heat.

2. Drain the potatoes and pat them dry with paper towels.

3. Spread the potato slices out in the skillet (there will be some overlapping). Cook until they are brown and crisp on the underside, and then flip them over to brown on the other side, about 15 minutes in all. Not all the slices will be perfectly crispy, but almost all will be fork-tender. Set the potatoes aside.

4. Heat a large skillet over medium-high heat. Sprinkle in the coriander seeds, cumin seeds, mustard seeds, peppercorns, cloves, dried chiles, and pieces of cinnamon stick. Toast the spices, shaking the skillet frequently, until they crackle and are aromatic, 1 to 2 minutes. Transfer them to a blender jar.

5. Pour the vinegar over the spices. Add the garlic and then the coarsely chopped onion. Puree, scraping the inside of the jar as needed, to make a beautiful light purple sauce, speckled with aromatic spices.

6. Heat the remaining 2 tablespoons oil in the same large skillet over medium-high heat. Add the thinly sliced onion and the fresh chiles, and stir-fry until the onion is light brown around the edges, 3 to 4 minutes.

7. Stir in the pork and stir-fry until it is light brown, about 5 minutes. Pour in the pureed sauce. Pour ½ cup water into the blender jar, swish it around to wash it out, and add this to the skillet. Stir the curry, scraping the bottom of the skillet to deglaze it, releasing the browned bits of meat and onion. Stir in the salt and turmeric.

8. Reduce the heat to medium-low, cover the skillet, and simmer, stirring occasionally, until the meat is fork-tender, 18 to 20 minutes.

9. Stir in the remaining ½ cup water and the fried potatoes. Cover the skillet and continue to simmer, stirring occasionally (carefully, so as not to break up the potatoes), until the potatoes are completely cooked, about 5 minutes.

10. Sprinkle with the cilantro, and serve.

Boneless Pork Loins

WITH ONIONS, POTATOES, AND CARROTS

Pork Batata Curry

A pleasantly spicy alternative to the pork roasts that brown in many an American oven, this curry is perfect for a Sunday dinner. Serve it alongside Sweet-Hot Basmati Rice with Jaggery and Chiles (page 715)—the sweet jaggery in the rice offers a nice balance to the chiles in the curry. **SERVES 6**

2 tablespoons canola oil

1¼ pounds boneless pork loin chops, cut into
      1-inch cubes

2 tablespoons Ginger Paste (page 15)

1 tablespoon Garlic Paste (page 15)

1 tablespoon Balchao masala (page 17)

1 teaspoon ground Deggi chiles (see box, page 290);
      or ½ teaspoon cayenne (ground red pepper)
      mixed with ½ teaspoon sweet paprika

1 large carrot, peeled and cut into ½-inch-thick rounds

1 large russet or Yukon Gold potato, peeled,
      cut into ½-inch cubes, and submerged
      in a bowl of cold water to prevent browning

1 small red onion, cut into ½-inch cubes

1½ teaspoons coarse kosher or sea salt

2 tablespoons finely chopped fresh cilantro
      leaves and tender stems for garnishing

1. Heat the oil in a large saucepan over medium-high heat. Add the pork, Ginger Paste, Garlic Paste, and masala. Cook, stirring, until the pork sears and turns light brown, 5 to 7 minutes. (Adequate ventilation will help ease the discomfort caused by cooking the pungent masala.)

2. Stir in the Deggi chiles and cook, without burning, for about 15 seconds.

3. Pile in the carrot, potato, onion, and salt. Stir once or twice. Cook, stirring occasionally, for 4 to 6 minutes.

4. Add ½ cup water. Once the curry comes to a boil, lower the heat, cover the pan, and simmer, stirring occasionally, until the meat and vegetables are fork-tender, 18 to 20 minutes.

5. Sprinkle with the cilantro, and serve.

Tips:

❖ If you prefer a thicker, stewlike consistency to the sauce, sprinkle 2 teaspoons rice flour into the pan about 5 minutes before the vegetables and meat are fork-tender. The rice flour also diminishes some of the spicy heat in the curry.

❖ During the winter months, when sweet potatoes are in abundance, use them in addition to, or instead of, the carrots.

Cubed Pork

WITH POTATOES, YOGURT, AND TAMARIND

Coorgh-Style Pork Curry

The Kodavas, a tiny, close-knit community in the southwest corner of the state of Karnataka, are thought to trace their ancestry back to around 300 B.C., when Alexander the Great invaded India. Their physical features belie that heritage. This proud cultural group, which has produced many warriors and generals, is Hindu but not highly religious, as meats and alcohol flow freely at many of their celebrations. This curry is an adaptation of their classic Pandhi curry (cubes of pork cooked in a spicy, red-hot sauce with vinegar), and its sour taste usually comes from kudampuli (the smoked fruit of *Garcinia camboge*), a member of the mangosteen family. The fruit is relatively hard to come by outside Karnataka, but the more widely available tamarind makes a perfectly acceptable alternative. To give the dish a sharper zing, use ½ cup malt or cider vinegar instead of the tamarind. **SERVES 8**

1½ teaspoons cayenne (ground red pepper)

½ teaspoon ground turmeric

2 pounds boneless pork loin chops,
    cut into 1-inch cubes

1 pound russet or Yukon Gold potatoes,
    peeled, cut in half lengthwise, thinly sliced,
    and submerged in a bowl of cold water
    to prevent browning

2 tablespoons canola oil

1 teaspoon cumin seeds

1 large red onion, cut in half lengthwise
    and thinly sliced

3 fresh or dried bay leaves

1 teaspoon tamarind paste or concentrate

2 teaspoons coarse kosher or sea salt

½ cup Thick Yogurt (page 22)

1 teaspoon Punjabi garam masala
    (page 25)

1. Combine the cayenne and turmeric in a medium-size bowl. Add the pork and toss to coat it with the spices. Cover and refrigerate for at least 30 minutes or as long as overnight, to allow the spices to flavor and tenderize the meat.

2. Drain the potatoes and pat them dry with paper towels.

3. Heat the oil in a large saucepan over medium heat. Add the potatoes carefully and cook, stirring occasionally, until they are light brown around the edges and some are sticking to the bottom, 5 to 8 minutes. Transfer the potatoes to a plate.

4. Add the cumin seeds, onion, bay leaves, and pork to the same pan, still over medium-high heat, and cook, stirring occasionally, until the pork releases its juices and the onion slices start to sweat, 5 to 10 minutes. The combined liquid will be just enough to deglaze the pan, releasing the stuck-on bits of potatoes and cumin. Once the liquid evaporates, lower the heat to medium and continue to cook, stirring more frequently, until the pork starts to brown, 5 to 10 minutes.

5. In a small bowl, stir the tamarind paste into ½ cup water. Stir this muddy-looking liquid into the pan. Add the salt and heat to a boil. Then reduce the heat to medium-low, cover the pan, and simmer, stirring occasionally, until the meat is slightly tender, 10 to 15 minutes.

6. Stir in the potatoes and continue to simmer, covered, stirring occasionally, until both meat and potatoes are fork-tender, 25 to 30 minutes.

7. Fold in the yogurt and masala, and serve.

Pork and Cashews

WITH A
BLACK PEPPERCORN SAUCE

kaaju kala miri pork

Pork and Goa go hand in hand. This Portuguese-influenced community has a love affair with pork and also with two of its bountiful harvests: cashew nuts and coconut. No wonder this nutty-tasting, slightly pungent curry appeals to a wide array of taste buds. Enjoy it with some steamed rice and Lime Wedges Pickled in Cayenne Pepper and Mustard Oil (page 745) for a simple meal. **SERVES 6**

2 tablespoons Ginger Paste (page 15)

1 tablespoon Garlic Paste (page 15)

¼ teaspoon ground turmeric

1¼ pounds boneless pork loin chops,
    cut into 1-inch cubes

2 tablespoons canola oil

½ cup raw cashew nuts

1 cup shredded fresh coconut; or ½ cup
    shredded dried unsweetened coconut,
    reconstituted (see Note)

¼ cup cider vinegar

2 teaspoons black peppercorns

1½ teaspoons coarse kosher or sea salt

1 teaspoon cumin seeds

1 small red onion, cut into ½-inch cubes

1 large tomato, cored and finely chopped

2 tablespoons finely chopped fresh cilantro
    leaves and tender stems for garnishing

1. Combine the Ginger Paste, Garlic Paste, and turmeric in a medium-size bowl. Add the pork cubes and toss to coat them with the paste. Refrigerate, covered, for at least 30 minutes or as long as overnight.

2. Heat the oil in a large skillet over medium-high heat. Add the cashews and stir-fry until they turn honey-brown, 1 to 2 minutes. Remove the skillet from the heat, and use a slotted spoon to transfer the nuts to a blender jar. Add the coconut, ½ cup water, the vinegar, peppercorns, and salt to the jar. Puree, scraping the inside of the jar as needed, to make a smooth but slightly gritty pepper-speckled sauce.

3. Reheat the nut-flavored oil in the skillet over medium-high heat. Sprinkle in the cumin seeds and let them sizzle for about 10 seconds. Then stir in the onion and the pork. Cook, stirring, until there is a thin layer of browned paste on the bottom of the skillet and the meat is light brown around the edges, 3 to 5 minutes.

4. Add the cashew sauce to the skillet. The sauce will immediately start to boil. Stir the curry, scraping the bottom of the skillet to deglaze it, releasing any collected browned bits of ginger and garlic. Reduce the heat to medium-low, cover the skillet, and braise the pork, stirring occasionally, until the meat is fork-tender, 12 to 15 minutes.

5. Stir in the tomato and allow it to warm, uncovered, for 2 to 3 minutes.

6. Sprinkle with the cilantro, and serve.

Note: To reconstitute coconut, cover with ½ cup boiling water, set aside for about 15 minutes, and then drain.

Mangalorean Pork Curry
WITH
ONION AND COCONUT MILK

Pork Gassi

If it's a crime to be both beautiful and intelligent, then Sharon Naik is guilty beyond any reasonable doubt. Originally from Mangalore, now settled in Minneapolis via Chicago and Cleveland, Sharon reminisced about her childhood as she ladled a hearty-looking *kori gassi* (chicken curry) over pieces of dried rice crackers called *rotti* (not to be confused with roti). It's not easy to find *rotti* in the United States, so serve rice or bread as a perfectly acceptable alternative. Even though Sharon cooked chicken that day, she said that any meat or vegetable works with this coconut-based curry. Here's my version with pork, another Mangalorean favorite. **SERVES 4**

4 tablespoons canola oil

I cup shredded fresh coconut; or ½ cup shredded dried
   unsweetened coconut, reconstituted (see Note)

10 to 12 dried red Thai or cayenne chiles, to taste,
   stems removed

5 or 6 black peppercorns

3 or 4 whole cloves

I cinnamon stick (3 inches long)

I can (13.5 ounces) unsweetened coconut milk

2 cups finely chopped red onion

2 tablespoons coriander seeds

I teaspoon cumin seeds

I teaspoon black or yellow mustard seeds

I teaspoon tamarind paste or concentrate

½ teaspoon fenugreek seeds

4 medium-size cloves garlic

2 lengthwise slices fresh ginger (each 2 inches long,
   I inch wide, and ⅛ inch thick)

1¼ pounds boneless pork loin chops,
   cut into 1-inch cubes

1½ teaspoons coarse kosher or sea salt

10 to 12 medium-size to large fresh curry leaves

1. Heat 2 tablespoons of the oil in a medium-size skillet over medium heat. Add the coconut, chiles, peppercorns, cloves, and cinnamon stick. Stir-fry until the coconut is reddish brown and the spices smell fragrant, about 5 minutes. Then transfer the mixture to a blender jar and pour in 1 cup of the coconut milk, 1 cup of the onion, the coriander seeds, cumin seeds, mustard seeds, tamarind, fenugreek seeds, garlic, and ginger. Puree, scraping the inside of the jar as needed, to form a thick, gritty paste.

2. Heat the remaining 2 tablespoons oil in a large skillet over medium-high heat. Add the remaining 1 cup onion and stir-fry until it is light brown around the edges, about 5 minutes.

3. Add the coconut paste, and then stir in the pork, salt, and curry leaves. Cook, uncovered, stirring occasionally, until the pork starts to sear, about 10 minutes. (At first it will stew in the juices it releases, along with the liquid from the coconut paste, and then as the liquid evaporates, it will start to brown.)

4. Pour the remaining coconut milk into the skillet and scrape the bottom to deglaze it, releasing any browned bits of onion, spice, and meat. Bring to a boil, and then reduce the heat to medium-low, cover the skillet, and simmer, stirring occasionally, until the meat is fork-tender, 45 to 50 minutes. Then serve.

Note: To reconstitute coconut, cover with ½ cup boiling water, set aside for about 15 minutes, and then drain.

Tip: The day I made this curry, I made it twice—one version with pork, the other with eggplant because I was entertaining nonvegetarians and vegetarians alike for a weekend meal. I cut the eggplant into 1-inch cubes (with the skin), and added it in Step 3 as described. It was tender within 10 to 15 minutes. Even though both dishes had the same sauce, the flavors could not have been more dissimilar. The large number of chiles did not faze anyone at the table because the coconut and coconut milk both help to tame the heat.

Sweet-Tart Pork
WITH CHILES

Pork Balchao

Surprisingly, this curry is sweet—with of course a strong hint of zing coming from the red chiles in the masala. If the kick isn't enough for your adventurous palate, use an additional tablespoon or more of the masala—that will surely make you break into a capsaicin-sweat. Serve the curry over a plate of starchy rice to soak up the sauce and spice. **SERVES 4**

2 tablespoons canola oil
1 medium-size red onion, finely chopped
1 tablespoon Balchao masala (page 17)
1 pound boneless pork loin chops, cut into 1-inch cubes
1 teaspoon tamarind paste or concentrate
2 teaspoons white granulated sugar
1 teaspoon coarse kosher or sea salt

1. Heat the oil in a large skillet over medium heat. Add the onion and stir-fry until it is dark brown and caramel-colored, about 10 minutes.

2. Stir in the masala and allow the spices in the paste to roast until the aroma is throat-clearing pungent (use ample ventilation) and some of the garlic and chiles (in the masala) are sticking to the bottom, about 1 minute.

3. Toss in the pork and stir-fry until it sears and turns light brown, about 5 minutes.

4. In a small bowl, whisk the tamarind paste with ½ cup water. Pour this murky brown water into the skillet and scrape the bottom to deglaze it, releasing the browned bits of spice and meat. Stir in the sugar and salt. The watery curry will instantly start to boil. Lower the heat to medium, cover, and cook until the pork is fork-tender, 18 to 20 minutes. Then serve.

Pork
WITH ONIONS, VINEGAR, AND COCONUT MILK

Pork Vindaloo (version 1)

Vinegar made from fermented cashew liquor *(feni)* infuses this particular curry in Christian Goa, providing acidity with an underlying sweetness, a technique that reflects the area's Portuguese culinary heritage. I would be hard-pressed to find that particular vinegar in this country, so the sweeter cider or malt vinegar will have to do. **SERVES 4**

¼ cup cider vinegar or malt vinegar

I tablespoon coarsely chopped fresh ginger

I teaspoon cumin seeds

6 large cloves garlic

2 small red onions; I coarsely chopped, I finely chopped

2 dried red Thai or cayenne chiles, stems removed

2 fresh green Thai, cayenne, or serrano chiles, stems removed

I teaspoon coarse kosher or sea salt

¼ teaspoon ground turmeric

2 tablespoons canola oil

I pound boneless pork loin chops, cut lengthwise into strips I inch wide and ¼ inch thick

⅔ cup unsweetened coconut milk

2 tablespoons finely chopped fresh cilantro leaves and tender stems for garnishing

1. Pour the vinegar into a blender jar, and then add the ginger, cumin seeds, garlic, the coarsely chopped red onion, and the dried and fresh chiles. Puree, scraping the inside of the jar as needed, to make a smooth, light purple paste. Transfer the paste to a small bowl, and fold in the salt and turmeric.

2. Heat the oil in a large skillet over medium-high heat. Add the finely chopped onion and stir-fry until it is light honey-brown, 5 to 10 minutes. Then stir in the pungent vinegar paste and cook, uncovered, stirring frequently, until the vinegar evaporates and the paste appears slightly dry, 3 to 5 minutes.

3. Add the pork strips and cook, stirring occasionally, until the meat is seared, about 2 minutes. Pour in the coconut milk and stir three or four times to deglaze the skillet, releasing any browned bits of spices and onion.

4. Reduce the heat to medium-low, cover, and simmer, stirring occasionally, until the sauce thickens slightly and the pork is fork-tender, 7 to 10 minutes. (If the sauce is not thick enough for you, remove the lid and cook over medium heat, stirring occasionally, for an additional 3 to 5 minutes.)

5. Sprinkle with the cilantro, and serve.

Tips:

❖ This curry finds the onions cooked in two different ways: one purees and cooks down with the vinegar, while the other stir-fries to provide a caramelized flavor.

❖ Dried and fresh chiles provide differing levels of heat, the dried being more pungent than the fresh.

❖ Coconut milk is not usually used in the Goan Christian community's vindaloos, but I have taken liberties with that unspoken rule because I find the creamy liquid to be a perfect partner in reducing the vinegar's sharp gusto. If you count calories as part of your diet, use a reduced-fat canned coconut milk for a very similar flavor. The coconut milk soothes the palate once the chiles take over. And of course, a plate of steamed white or red rice also helps to pacify the heat.

pork vindaloo
❖ ❖ ❖

I feel obliged to share multiple versions of this insanely popular curry from Goa, because there are so many of them. Every Indian restaurant menu includes a vindaloo of some sort, and many wrongly allow their customers to think this curry is spicy hot. In reality, vindaloos, adapted from the Portuguese vinh d'alho ("wine of garlic"), are not always chile-hot.

Nutty-Tart Pork

WITH CIDER VINEGAR, CASHEWS, AND ONIONS

Pork Vindaloo (version 2)

this version of the famed Goan vindaloo incorporates a locally grown commodity, originally brought in by the Portuguese traders and settlers and prized not only in India, but also all over the world: cashew nuts. In this curry, the cashews are stir-fried with the onion to provide a nutty-roasted component to the sauce's flavor.

One night when I served this curry, I also made the green beans curry *Vengayam avarai* (page 509) and served the combination with store-bought Indian flatbreads (rotis). (No, it is not a crime to do so occasionally if you are pressed for time. On the other hand, you can certainly make a stack of them at home—see page 727—and freeze them for use on days like this.)

SERVES 6

½ cup cider vinegar or malt vinegar

1 tablespoon Garlic Paste
    (page 15)

2 teaspoons coriander seeds, ground

2 teaspoons cumin seeds, ground

1½ teaspoons coarse kosher or sea salt

1 teaspoon cayenne (ground red pepper)

¼ teaspoon ground turmeric

2 tablespoons canola oil

1 medium-size red onion, cut into
    ½-inch cubes

¼ cup raw cashew nuts (see box), coarsely chopped

"raw" cashews

the cashew nut is encased in an inedible thick shell that contains the allergen urushiol—the same allergen that is present in poison oak, and which may cause dermatitis in hypersensitive people. The nuts are steamed at very high temperatures to get rid of the shell, and this process "cooks" them to yield sweet, white nuts. So, technically speaking, these nuts are not raw, but are steam-cooked. Every company that sells cashews in this form labels them "raw" to differentiate them from those that are roasted golden brown.

1½ pounds boneless pork loin chops,
    cut into 1-inch cubes

½ cup unsweetened coconut milk

2 tablespoons finely chopped fresh cilantro
    leaves and tender stems for garnishing

1. Pour the vinegar into a measuring cup. Stir in the Garlic Paste, coriander, cumin, salt, cayenne, and turmeric.

2. Heat the oil in a large skillet over medium-high heat. Add the onion and cashews, and cook, stirring, until the onion turns light brown and the nuts toasty brown, 5 to 8 minutes.

3. Stir the spiked vinegar, and then pour it into the skillet. Cook the pungent-smelling, chunky, onion-vinegar sauce over medium heat, stirring frequently, until the vinegar evaporates and the spices cling to the onion cubes, 3 to 5 minutes.

4. Add the pork and cook, stirring, until the cubes are seared, 1 to 2 minutes. Pour ½ cup water into the skillet and stir two or three times to deglaze it, releasing the browned bits of onion and spices. Heat to a boil. Then reduce the heat to medium-low, cover the skillet, and cook, stirring occasionally, until the meat is tender, about 30 minutes.

5. Stir in the coconut milk and raise the heat to medium. Cook, stirring occasionally, until the sauce thickens, 8 to 10 minutes.

6. Sprinkle with the cilantro, and serve.

Chile-Smothered Pork
WITH VINEGAR

Pork Vindaloo (version 3)

fiery-hot and most authentic of the vindaloos here, this version is my favorite. The Goan Christian community also makes this with beef, mutton, and seafood—all of which play a major role in their diet. For a more succulent experience, use bone-in pieces of chunky meat—in which case, extend the braising time and increase the amount of water to allow for a fall-off-the-bone conclusion. **SERVES 4**

½ cup cider vinegar or malt vinegar
1 tablespoon cumin seeds
8 lengthwise slices fresh ginger (each 2 inches long, 1 inch wide, and ⅛ inch thick)
8 medium-size cloves garlic
8 dried red Thai or cayenne chiles, stems removed
1 cinnamon stick (3 inches long)
1 pound boneless pork loin chops, cut into 1-inch cubes
1 teaspoon coarse kosher or sea salt
½ teaspoon ground turmeric
2 tablespoons canola oil
2 tablespoons finely chopped fresh cilantro leaves and tender stems for garnishing

1. Pour the vinegar into a blender jar, and then add the cumin seeds, ginger, garlic, chiles, and cinnamon stick. Puree, scraping the inside of the jar as needed, to form a pulpy, gritty paste that smells potent-hot.

2. Place the pork in a bowl and pour the paste over it. Sprinkle with the salt and turmeric, and stir it all together. Refrigerate, covered, for at least 30 minutes or as long as overnight, to allow the flavors to mingle.

3. Heat the oil in a medium-size skillet over medium-high heat. Add the pork, marinade and all, and cook, uncovered, stirring occasionally, until it is browned, 10 to 12 minutes. (The meat will stew initially; then once the liquid evaporates, it will sear and brown.)

4. Pour in ½ cup water and scrape the bottom of the skillet to deglaze it. Reduce the heat to medium-low, cover, and simmer, stirring occasionally, until the pork is tender, about 15 minutes.

5. Stir in the cilantro, and serve.

Boneless Pork
COOKED WITH TOASTED COCONUT IN COCONUT MILK

Pork Saguti

My version of this classic from the Konkan community of Goa is not as fiery as the ones I sampled during a recent visit. If you do prefer the authentic heat, up the ante by doubling the amount of chiles, both fresh and dried. Note how the coconut makes its presence known in two different ways, as it eloquently layers the flavors of nutty and creamy: First, the nuttiness comes from the dried form of fresh coconut shreds, toasted reddish brown and used more as a spice to provide flavor. Second, the coconut milk not only provides body to the curry but also absorbs some of the capsaicin-induced heat from the chiles. **SERVES 6**

Juice of 1 medium-size lime
½ cup firmly packed fresh cilantro leaves
and tender stems
4 medium-size cloves garlic
4 lengthwise slices fresh ginger
(each 2 inches long, 1 inch wide,
and ⅛ inch thick)
2 fresh green Thai, cayenne, or serrano
chiles, stems removed
1¼ pounds boneless pork loin chops,
cut into 1-inch cubes
4 tablespoons canola oil
1 small red onion, cut in half lengthwise
and thinly sliced
2 dried red Thai or cayenne chiles, stems removed
½ cup shredded dried unsweetened coconut

1½ teaspoons coarse kosher or sea salt
1 cup unsweetened coconut milk
1 teaspoon Usha Raikar's garam masala (page 27)

1. Pour the lime juice into a blender jar, and then add the cilantro, garlic, ginger, and fresh chiles. Puree, scraping the inside of the jar as needed, to make a bright green, tart-hot paste. (Depending on the lime's juiciness, you may need to add a tablespoon or so of water to get the blades to do a thorough job of pureeing.)

2. Transfer the paste to a medium-size bowl, add the pork cubes, and toss to thoroughly coat them. Refrigerate, covered, for 30 minutes to 2 hours, to allow the pork to marinate and absorb some of the paste's flavors.

3. While the meat is marinating, heat 2 tablespoons of the oil in a large skillet over medium-high heat. Add the onion and dried chiles, and stir-fry until the onion is light honey-brown, 5 to 8 minutes. Stir in the shredded coconut and continue to stir-fry until the coconut is toasty brown, about 1 minute. Transfer this mixture to a blender jar. Add the salt and ½ cup water. Puree, scraping the inside of the jar as needed, to make a smooth, light brown, red-speckled paste.

4. Heat the remaining 2 tablespoons oil in the same skillet over medium-high heat. Add the pork, marinade and all, and cook, stirring occasionally, until the meat is seared, about 10 minutes. (The meat will stew initially; then once the liquid evaporates, it will sear and brown.)

5. Add the onion-coconut paste to the skillet. Pour ½ cup water into the blender jar and swish it around to wash it out. Add this to the skillet and stir once or twice. Once the curry comes to a boil, reduce the heat to medium-low, cover the skillet, and cook, stirring occasionally, until the meat is fork-tender, 45 to 50 minutes.

6. Stir in the coconut milk and garam masala. Raise the heat to medium-high and simmer the curry, uncovered, stirring occasionally, until the sauce thickens, 5 to 7 minutes.

7. Serve immediately.

Tips: If pork is not your cup of tea, lamb, beef, chicken, or even turkey will fill the bill just fine. Just remember to check the meat for doneness during the final simmering stages since their timing will vary.

Pork
WITH
SPINACH AND CREAM

Saag Pork

I used to cook a version of this curry during my five-year stint at a north Indian restaurant in the United States, an arduous life I'd just as soon forget. Standing on my feet twelve hours a day behind a hot commercial stove got dreadfully old very quickly. When the days got long and tiresome and next day's lunch buffet had to be prepped, this pork dish met all my requirements (quick, hassle-free, and inexpensive) and my customers' needs (tasty, robust, familiar, and cheap) within minutes. **SERVES 4**

1¼ *pounds boneless pork loin chops, cut into*
 1-inch cubes
¼ *cup heavy (whipping) cream*
2 *tablespoons Garlic Paste (page 15)*
2 *teaspoons Bin bhuna hua garam masala (page 30)*

1½ *teaspoons coarse kosher or sea salt*
2 *tablespoons canola oil*
1 *teaspoon cumin seeds*
½ *cup tomato sauce, canned or homemade*
 (see page 18)
8 *ounces fresh spinach leaves, well rinsed*
 and finely chopped

1. Combine the pork, cream, Garlic Paste, garam masala, and salt in a medium-size bowl, and stir together well. Refrigerate, covered, for 30 minutes to 2 hours to allow the meat to tenderize and the flavors to mingle.

2. Heat the oil in a large saucepan over medium-high heat. Add the cumin seeds and cook until they sizzle and are fragrant, 5 to 10 seconds. Immediately add the pork, including its marinade. Cook, stirring occasionally, until the pork turns light brown and the spices are aromatic, about 5 minutes.

3. Stir in the tomato sauce, which will instantly appear creamy, thanks to the cream in the marinade. Lower the heat, cover the skillet, and simmer, stirring occasionally, until the sauce thickens and some oil starts to separate on the surface, 12 to 15 minutes.

4. Pile the spinach atop the curry and cover the skillet once again. Let it cook until the rising steam has wilted the greens, 3 to 5 minutes. Then stir the spinach into the curry and continue to simmer, covered, stirring occasionally, until the pork is fork-tender, 8 to 10 minutes. The spinach will release enough moisture to thin the fairly thick sauce, making its consistency just right—not too thick, not too thin.

5. Serve immediately.

Tip: For a somewhat different and slightly bitter flavor, use mustard greens instead of the spinach as an iron-rich alternative.

Goan-Style Spicy Pork Sausage
WITH KIDNEY BEANS AND BLACK-EYED PEAS

feijoada

This is the national dish of Brazil, so what is it doing here? Well, thanks to the colonization of Goa by the Portuguese—who introduced not only chiles and tomatoes to India, but also the Portuguese way of cooking with pork, vinegar, and spices—this classic dish of beans and pork is now omnipresent among the Christian Goan community. Serve it as they do, with their soft bread called *pao* (a soft yeast-leavened bread similar to White Castle's square hamburger buns)—yum!

SERVES 4

¼ cup malt vinegar or cider vinegar

4 medium-size cloves garlic

4 dried guajillo chiles, stems removed

2 to 4 dried red Thai or cayenne chiles, to taste, stems removed

2 lengthwise slices fresh ginger (each 2 inches long, 1 inch wide, and ⅛ inch thick)

2 tablespoons canola oil

1 teaspoon cumin seeds

1 large red onion, cut in half lengthwise and thinly sliced

1 large tomato, cored and finely chopped

½ teaspoon ground turmeric

1 cup cooked black-eyed peas (see Tips)

1 cup cooked red kidney beans (see Tips)

1½ teaspoons coarse kosher or sea salt

1 pound seasoned pork sausage (such as chorizo), cut into ½-inch-thick rounds

2 tablespoons finely chopped fresh cilantro leaves and tender stems for garnishing

1. Pour the vinegar into a blender jar, and add the garlic, both kinds of chiles, and the ginger. Puree, scraping the inside of the jar as needed, to make a thick, blood-red paste, fairly smooth in texture.

2. Heat the oil in a medium-size saucepan over medium heat. Sprinkle in the cumin seeds and cook until they start to sizzle, turn reddish brown, and smell nutty, 10 to 15 seconds. Immediately add the onion, cover the pan, and cook, stirring occasionally, until it softens and turns caramel-brown with a deep purple hue, 15 to 20 minutes.

3. Add the pureed sauce and continue to simmer, uncovered, stirring occasionally, until the liquid thickens, about 5 minutes.

4. Stir in the tomato and turmeric. Cook, uncovered, stirring occasionally, until the tomato softens but still appears firm-looking, 5 to 8 minutes.

5. Pour in ½ cup water and the black-eyed peas, kidney beans, salt, and sausage slices. Once the curry comes to a boil, reduce the heat to medium-low, cover the pan, and simmer, stirring occasionally, until the sauce thickens, the beans absorb the spicy flavors, and the sausage cooks through, 10 to 15 minutes.

6. Sprinkle with the cilantro, and serve.

Tips:

❖ Guajillo chiles (see Tips, page 686) are not classic to Indian cooking, but when pureed, they are very similar to Kashmiri chiles in color. The Kashmiri chiles tend to pack more heat than the guajillos, so to get a similar balance, I have used a combination of guajillo and Thai.

❖ If you use canned beans, make sure to drain and rinse them before you add them to the curry. A can normally contains 15 ounces of beans, so if you want to bulk up the curry and feed two more hungry folks, add the full can.

Goan-Style Spicy Pork Sausage
WITH VINEGAR

Pork Sausage Curry

A recent trip to Goa took me to the hot spot in town on a Friday morning—the Mapsa market, bustling with vendors hawking everything you need to run an efficient home: clothing, kitchen equipment, vegetables, spices, fruits, meat, fish, live poultry, straw broomsticks, and rugs. I felt the presence of all of Goa in this market square, the size of one city block. As I maneuvered through the sea of humanity, I stumbled across a string of women who were squatting on the blistering concrete under the blazing sun, their *saree pullow* draped over their heads as a futile shield against the hot rays. Perched atop makeshift racks, links of blood-red Goan pork sausages—ballooned with ground meat, cumin, and freshly ground spices—grabbed my attention. As the women fanned the sausages to keep the flies at bay, Portuguese-speaking shoppers stuffed their cloth bags with plastic-wrapped spicy links. One citizen, in impeccable Queen's English, told me how his wife cooked these delicacies. The instructions stuck in my mind, and months later, in my not-so-humid midwestern United States kitchen, my family savored every morsel, drenched with sweet-tart vinegar and potent spices. **SERVES 6**

2 tablespoons canola oil

1 small red onion, cut in half lengthwise and thinly sliced

4 medium-size cloves garlic, thinly sliced

1 large tomato, cored and finely chopped

2 teaspoons coriander seeds, ground

1 teaspoon cumin seeds, ground

1 teaspoon ground Kashmiri chiles; or ¼ teaspoon cayenne (ground red pepper) mixed with ¾ teaspoon sweet paprika

1 teaspoon coarse kosher or sea salt

½ teaspoon ground turmeric

1 pound seasoned pork sausage (such as chorizo), cut into ½-inch-thick rounds (see Tip)

¼ cup cider vinegar or malt vinegar

2 tablespoons finely chopped fresh cilantro leaves and tender stems

1 or 2 fresh green Thai, cayenne, or serrano chiles, to taste, stems removed, finely chopped (do not remove the seeds)

1. Heat the oil in a medium-size skillet over medium-high heat. Add the onion and garlic, and stir-fry until they are light brown around the edges, 5 to 8 minutes.

2. Stir in the tomato, coriander, cumin, Kashmiri chiles, salt, and turmeric. Reduce the heat to medium-low, cover the skillet, and simmer, stirring occasionally, until the tomato breaks down and the oil from the spices glistens on the surface, about 5 minutes.

3. Stir in the sausage and the vinegar. Raise the heat to medium and simmer the tart-sweet curry, covered, stirring occasionally, until the sausage is cooked through, 8 to 10 minutes.

4. Fold in the cilantro and fresh chiles. Continue to simmer, uncovered, stirring occasionally, until the sauce thickens, about 5 minutes. Then serve.

Tip: Goan sausages are not that easy to come by in this part of the world, but I have found chorizos (similar to the Portuguese *chouricos*) to be readily available and quite acceptable as an alternative. The spices used in chorizos are similar to the ones in Goa, providing balance to this robustly flavored tomato sauce.

fish & seafood curries

Look at a map of India and you will instantly realize why fish and seafood dishes are a staple in much of the country. Prawns, crabs, lobsters, mussels, and a myriad of saltwater fishes populate the warm tropical waters of the Arabian Sea to the west, the Indian Ocean to the south, and the Bay of Bengal to the east. All the coastal states show great creativity in incorporating these fruits from the seas into their curries.

In the west of India, the Maharashtrians make Pan-Grilled Mackerel with a Tamarind Sauce (page 245) and Mussels in a Coconut-Chile Sauce (page 282), while the Parsis whip up Steamed Fillet of Sole Wrapped in Leaves (page 249) at every auspicious gathering. Just to the south, in Goa, the Portuguese Christians relish Pan-Seared Shrimp with a Spicy-Hot Chile Vinegar Paste (page 270) and the Karwars savor

Toasted Tamarind-Rubbed Shrimp with a Coconut-Ginger Sauce (page 262). I adore the saucy flavors of Nimmy Paul's Fish Fillets Poached in a Tomato-Vinegar Sauce (page 254), which reflects the cuisine of the Syrian Christians in the state of Kerala. Travel to Sri Lanka, the tear-shaped island just south of India, and you won't be able to resist the Sri Lankan Crabs with Tart Leaves and Coconut Milk (page 282). Meander along to the east coast of India and notice how the Bengalis from Calcutta revere fish and seafood at any time of the day. Their simple fish curries, such as Tilapia with a Yogurt Sauce (page 250) and Carp Poached with Onion, Whole Spices, and Chiles (page 238), showcase their favorite spices—mustard, fenugreek, and turmeric—while their close neighbors to the north, the Assamese, create their own rendition of carp in their signature Carp Steaks with Fenugreek and Lime Juice (page 237).

The beauty of these fish and seafood curries is that they are not only simple to make, but also simply divine in the arenas of flavor and eye appeal. And let's not forget they are quick-cooking. What's not to love?

Poached Whole Fish

IN A STEWED ONION SAUCE

Paplet Gassi

Although I have written this Mangalorean recipe using pomfret, don't let that preclude you from making this curry if you cannot find it in your Indian or Pakistani grocer's freezer. Any saltwater fish like yellowfin tuna, mackerel, bluefish, or striped bass will work just fine; adjust the poaching time according to their thickness. Serve it over a bed of boiled red or black rice (page 708) for a simple dinner. **SERVES 4**

½ teaspoon ground turmeric

2 medium-size frozen whole pomfrets (about 1 pound each), thawed and cleaned (see Tips)

2 tablespoons peanut oil or canola oil

1 small red onion, cut in half lengthwise and thinly sliced

4 dried red Thai or cayenne chiles, stems removed, coarsely chopped (do not remove the seeds)

1 large tomato, cored and finely chopped

2 tablespoons finely chopped fresh cilantro leaves and tender stems

6 pieces (each roughly 2 inches long and 1 inch wide) dried black kokum (see Tips, page 251); or ½ teaspoon tamarind paste or concentrate

1 teaspoon coarse kosher or sea salt

1 teaspoon Usha Raikar's garam masala (page 27)

1. Sprinkle the turmeric over both sides of the fish and pat it into the skin. Refrigerate, covered, to allow the turmeric to flavor the fish at least 30 minutes or as long as overnight.

2. Heat the oil in a large skillet over medium-high heat. Add the fish and cook until they are seared on both sides, 3 to 5 minutes per side. Transfer to a plate.

3. Add the onion, chiles, and tomato to the skillet. Scrape the bottom to deglaze it, releasing any browned bits of fish. Lower the heat to medium and cook, stirring occasionally, until most of the liquid from the tomato has been absorbed and the sauce appears dry, 5 to 8 minutes.

4. Pour in 1 cup water and bring the curry to a boil. Cover the skillet, reduce the heat to medium, and cook until the onion is tender when cut with a fork but still looks firm, 10 to 12 minutes. Stir in the cilantro.

5. While the onion is stewing, bring ½ cup water to a boil in a microwave oven or in a small saucepan. Place the kokum in the hot water and set it aside to steep until the liquid is a murky brown color, about 5 minutes. Squeeze the kokum slices to extract as much of their earthy tartness as you can before you discard them. Set the kokum liquid aside. Alternately, dissolve the tamarind in the ½ cup water.

6. Stir the cilantro, salt, and garam masala into the onion mixture. Return the fish to the skillet, and spoon the onion and sauce over them to barely blanket them. Cover the skillet and poach the fish over medium heat, turning them over once and covering them again with sauce, until the skin is soft when pierced and the flesh inside is barely starting to flake, 5 to 10 minutes. Scrape the onion and sauce off the fish, and transfer the fish to a serving platter. Keep warm.

7. Pour the kokum liquid into the skillet and raise the heat to medium-high. Cook, uncovered, stirring occasionally, until the sauce thickens, 3 to 5 minutes.

8. Spoon the sauce over the fish, and serve.

Tips:

✤ Pomfret, also known as butterfish (a name that clearly tells you what the taste is), pompano, or dollarfish, is highly prized along India's coast. Here in the United States, you can find them swimming in Pacific Northwest waters. In her lavishly illustrated book *Cooking Ingredients*, Christine Ingram describes this silvery fish as looking "rather like coins as seen through the eyes of Salvador Dali." Don't be afraid to ask your fishmonger to clean them for you if you buy them whole. Get rid of the head, fins, and tail, as well as the scales, gills, and innards. (Some folks like to keep the head attached, since they consider the meat inside a delicacy.)

Carp Steaks
WITH FENUGREEK AND LIME JUICE

Maasor Tenga

Monica and Devjyoti Kataky were married almost two decades ago up in the Shillong hills in northeastern India—one of the places the British liked to visit during the Raj days, to escape the oppressive summer heat. Meghalaya, a picturesque state wedged between Bhutan, Bengal, and Bangladesh, boasts an unusual history (it was ruled by the Ahoms, of Thai ancestry, before the British) and an even richer culinary heritage, rarely experienced beyond its provincial borders. Monica shared her recipes with me in her suburban home in St. Paul—a far cry from the hills of Assam. **SERVES 4**

1½ teaspoons coarse kosher or sea salt

1 teaspoon ground turmeric

4 carp steaks, or 1 whole carp (1½ to 2 pounds), cleaned (see headnote, page 238, and Tips)

2 small red onions; 1 coarsely chopped, 1 cut in half lengthwise and thinly sliced

2 lengthwise slices fresh ginger (each 2 inches long, 1 inch wide, and ⅛ inch thick)

2 large cloves garlic

4 tablespoons mustard oil or canola oil

½ teaspoon fenugreek seeds

3 scallions (green tops and white bulbs), cut into ¼-inch-thick rounds

1 large tomato, cored and finely chopped

2 tablespoons finely chopped fresh cilantro leaves and tender stems

Juice of 1 medium-size lime

1. Combine 1 teaspoon of the salt and ½ teaspoon of the turmeric in a small bowl. Sprinkle the mixture over both sides of each fish steak, pressing it into the flesh to "seal" it in.

2. Place the coarsely chopped onion in a food processor, and add the ginger and garlic. Pulse until the mixture is minced.

3. Heat 2 tablespoons of the oil in a large skillet over medium heat. Add the carp steaks and sear until they are light brown with a deep yellow hue, 2 to 3 minutes per side. Transfer them to a plate.

4. Heat the remaining 2 tablespoons oil in the same skillet over medium heat. Add the fenugreek seeds and cook until they sizzle, turn reddish brown, and smell slightly bitter with nutty undertones, 30 to 45 seconds. Add the minced onion blend, thinly sliced onion, and scallions, and cook, uncovered, stirring occasionally, until the onions are light brown around the edges, 8 to 10 minutes.

5. Sprinkle in the remaining ½ teaspoon salt and ½ teaspoon turmeric. Add the tomato and 1 cup water. Cook, uncovered, stirring occasionally, until the tomato is softened but still slightly firm, 10 to 15 minutes.

6. Add the fish steaks and blanket them with the sauce. Poach the steaks, covered, keeping them submerged by basting them occasionally with the sauce, until they are barely starting to flake, 5 to 10 minutes.

7. Transfer the fish to a platter. Stir the cilantro and lime juice into the sauce, pour the sauce over the fish, and serve.

Tips:

❖ Because the sauce is tart, I recommend using fish fillets or steaks that have a firm, meaty texture. Monica used the classic *ruhu* (carp/buffalo fish), but I find that to be a not-so-common fish in your everyday grocery store. Meaty bass, pollock, red snapper, or even halibut works well as an alternative and cooks in about the same amount of time.

❖ The double tang *(tenga)* from tomatoes and lime juice works great with the assertive carp, and it does balance out with all the onions.

Poached Carp
WITH ONION, WHOLE SPICES, AND CHILES

Ruhu Maacher Jhol

A member of the carp family, which in turn is part of the minnow entourage, *ruhu, rui, roho, rohu,* and more specifically *labeo roho* or *rohita,* are all names for the same full-lipped fish (very Angelina Joli-esque). Its silvery black scales conceal a firm flesh that makes it ideal for poaching with robust spices. Carp are often sold whole in the marketplace, or you can buy them cut into steaks. (Don't feel shy about asking your fishmonger to cut it for you.) The cooking time varies according to whether it's a whole fish or fish steaks, as described below. Once the flesh is barely starting to flake, remove the fish from the heat and serve it with *Govindho bhog* (page 708), Bengal's short-grain rice. **SERVES 4**

½ teaspoon ground turmeric

4 carp steaks, or 1 whole carp (1½ to 2 pounds),
    cleaned

2 tablespoons mustard oil or canola oil

2 teaspoons Panch phoron (page 36)

4 to 6 dried red Thai or cayenne chiles, to taste,
    stems removed

1 small red onion, cut in half lengthwise and
    thinly sliced

2 teaspoons coriander seeds, ground

1 teaspoon cumin seeds, ground

1 teaspoon coarse kosher or sea salt

½ teaspoon cayenne (ground red pepper)

2 tablespoons finely chopped fresh cilantro
    leaves and tender stems for garnishing

1. Sprinkle the turmeric over both sides of each steak, or the whole fish, and press it into the fish. Refrigerate, covered, for at least 1 hour or as long as overnight, to allow the flavor to permeate the fish.

2. Heat the oil in a large skillet over medium-high heat. Sprinkle in the *Panch phoron* and cook until the spices sizzle, turn reddish brown, and are aromatic, 10 to 15 seconds. (If some of the mustard seeds start to pop, cover the skillet until the popping subsides.) Add the chiles and onion, and stir-fry until the onion is lightly browned at the edges, 3 to 5 minutes.

3. Stir in the coriander, cumin, salt, and cayenne, and cook the ground spices without burning them, thanks to the cushioning provided from the onion, for 30 seconds to 1 minute.

4. Add the carp to the skillet. *If you are using steaks,* sear them until they are light brown, 1 to 2 minutes per side. Pour in ½ cup water and scrape the bottom of the skillet to deglaze it. Spoon the sauce and onion over the fish and cover the skillet. Reduce the heat to medium and braise the fish, continuing to baste it with the pan

drippings, until the steaks are barely starting to flake, 5 to 10 minutes.

If you are using a whole fish, sear it until the skin looks slightly shriveled, 3 to 6 minutes per side. Pour in ½ cup water and scrape the bottom of the skillet to deglaze it. Spoon the sauce and onion over the fish and cover the skillet. Reduce the heat to medium and braise the fish, continuing to baste it with the pan drippings, until the flesh is barely starting to flake, 8 to 15 minutes.

5. Transfer the fish to a serving platter, and spoon the pan juices and onion over each piece. Sprinkle with the cilantro, and serve.

Tip: The second time I made this curry, I used thin fillets of tilapia. I seared them for barely 30 seconds per side, and then poached them, covered, for 3 to 4 minutes. They have a very short cooking time and make for an expedient evening at the stove. Tilapia has a subtle flavor when compared to the more assertive freshwater *ruhu.*

Poached Catfish
IN A CARAMELIZED ONION– TOMATO SAUCE

maacher jhol

Cooks from Bengali-speaking homes are masters at creating magic with fish. *Jhols* are saucy dishes, usually incorporating pungency, sweetness, and tartness in one harmonious curry. **SERVES 4**

½ teaspoon ground turmeric

Juice of 1 medium-size lime

1 pound skinless catfish fillets

2 tablespoons mustard oil or canola oil

1 tablespoon Panch phoron (page 36)

3 dried red Thai or cayenne chiles, stems removed

1 small red onion, cut in half lengthwise and
  thinly sliced

1 medium-size tomato, cored and finely chopped

2 tablespoons finely chopped fresh cilantro
  leaves and tender stems

1½ teaspoons coarse kosher or sea salt

½ cup shredded fresh coconut (see Tip)

1. Combine the turmeric and the lime juice in a small bowl, and stir to dissolve the turmeric. Place the catfish fillets in a baking dish, and pour this thin, tart, yellow juice over the fish. Lift the fillets to allow the liquid to pool underneath. Refrigerate, covered, for 30 minutes to 2 hours. (Do not leave it overnight—the acidic lime juice will break down the flesh, creating an unappealing texture.)

2. Heat the oil in a large skillet over medium-high heat. Sprinkle in the *Panch phoron* and the dried chiles, and cook until the spices sizzle and are aromatic, and the chiles blacken, 15 to 20 seconds. Immediately add the onion and stir-fry until it is dark brown, 4 to 5 minutes.

3. Mix in the tomato, cilantro, and salt. Push the chunky curry to the side to make room for the fish in the center. Lift the fillets from the lime marinade and arrange them in the center of the skillet, allowing them to sear briefly as they make contact with the pan. Pour the lime marinade over the tomato-onion sauce. Spoon the sauce over the fillets, covering them completely. Reduce the heat to medium-low and poach the fish, uncovered, until it is barely starting to flake, 6 to 8 minutes.

4. Transfer the fillets, sauce and all, to a platter. Top them with the coconut, and serve.

Tip: This is one recipe where I have not recommended using shredded dried coconut as an alternative. The sweet fresh coconut is a must to round out this curry's flavors.

PRATIMA REVENKAR'S
Poached Catfish
IN A
COCONUT-CORIANDER SAUCE

baridaar Copray Chi Muchee

One benefit of writing a cookbook is that it gives you permission to invite yourself into total strangers' houses for a meal. Mrs. Pratima Revenkar is my sister-in-law's neighbor in a high-rise in Borivili, a suburb of Mumbai. She and her husband had moved from Goa in search of a fruitful career, leaving behind the resort state's beaches, cashew plantations, and natural beauty but bringing along her love for fruits from the sea. Her aged but very nimble mother-in-law stood next to her, her white hair covered with her ample saree, and animatedly chimed in as Pratima shared this fish curry recipe with me, making sure I wrote down every bit of valuable information between mouthfuls of the addictive, sweet-spicy sauce. **SERVES 6**

1 teaspoon coarse kosher or sea salt

1½ pounds skinless catfish fillets, cut in half
   to form roughly 4-inch pieces

½ cup shredded fresh coconut; or ¼ cup
   shredded dried unsweetened coconut,
   reconstituted (see Note)

2 tablespoons long-grain or medium-grain
   white rice

1 tablespoon coriander seeds

½ teaspoon black peppercorns

½ teaspoon ground turmeric

2 to 4 dried red Thai or cayenne chiles, to taste,
   stems removed

5 pieces dried black kokum, each roughly
   2 inches long and 1 inch wide
   (see Tip, page 251)

¼ cup boiling water

2 tablespoons canola oil

1 cup finely chopped red onion

2 or 3 fresh green Thai, cayenne, or serrano chiles,
   to taste, stems removed, thinly sliced crosswise
   (do not remove the seeds)

1. Sprinkle the salt over both sides of the catfish fillets, and arrange them in a single layer in a baking dish. Refrigerate, covered, for 15 to 30 minutes.

2. Meanwhile, pour ½ cup water into a blender jar, and add the coconut, rice, coriander seeds, peppercorns, turmeric, and dried chiles. Puree, scraping the inside of the jar as needed, to make a thick, gritty paste mottled with chiles.

3. Combine the kokum and the boiling water in a small bowl, and set it aside to steep for 10 to 15 minutes. Squeeze the fruit to extract all its tart, slightly bitter juices, and discard the skin.

4. Heat the oil in a large skillet over medium-high heat. Add the onion and chiles, and stir-fry until the onion is light brown around the edges and the chiles smell pungent, 2 to 3 minutes.

5. Add the coconut paste to the skillet and stir-fry until the spices and coconut form a thin yellow film on the bottom, 1 to 2 minutes. Pour ½ cup water into the blender jar and swish it around to wash it out. Add this to the skillet and scrape the bottom to deglaze it, releasing the browned bits of spice and coconut.

6. Submerge the fish fillets, in a single layer, in the sun-yellow sauce, and cover the skillet. Poach, gently turning them over halfway into the poaching, until they are barely starting to flake, 12 to 15 minutes.

7. Gently lift the fillets out of the skillet and arrange them on a serving platter.

8. Pour the kokum water into the sauce, and stir once or twice. Pour the sauce over the fillets, and serve.

Note: To reconstitute coconut, cover with ¼ cup boiling water, set aside for about 15 minutes, and then drain.

Tips:

❖ The uncooked rice is an interesting ingredient in the sauce, acting as a thickener with its starchy presence. Because the rice is uncooked, the kernels are quite hard, and when pureed with the coconut, they retain a slight grittiness akin to coarsely cracked wheat.

❖ Even though I have used skinless fillets, feel free to use skin-on, bone-in, cleaned catfish (trout is an excellent alternative too). You may need an additional 5 minutes of poaching time to ensure that it is cooked through.

Simmered Catfish
IN AN UNRIPE MANGO–COCONUT MILK SAUCE

meen kootan

You won't find anything "mean" about this delicate coconut milk sauce with small bits of tart unripe mango, aromatic curry leaves, and three sources of heat—fresh green chiles, dried red ones, and black peppercorns—dotting its creamy landscape. Kerala, a state on the southwestern coast of India, has an unbridled love for coconut and fish, and this curry proves why. Enjoy it as the Keralites do, over slightly starchy long-grain white rice. **SERVES 4**

2 tablespoons coconut oil or canola oil

1 teaspoon black or yellow mustard seeds

1 can (13.5 ounces) unsweetened coconut milk

1 large, rock-hard unripe mango, peeled
    and cut into ¼-inch cubes (see Tips)

2 tablespoons finely chopped fresh cilantro
    leaves and tender stems

1 tablespoon finely chopped fresh ginger

1½ teaspoons coarse kosher or sea salt

½ teaspoon black peppercorns, coarsely crushed

10 to 12 medium-size to large fresh curry leaves

2 to 4 fresh green Thai, cayenne, or serrano chiles,
    to taste, stems removed, finely chopped
    (do not remove the seeds)

1¼ pounds skinless catfish fillets (see Tips)

1. Heat the oil in a large skillet over medium-high heat. Add the mustard seeds, cover, and cook until the seeds have stopped popping (not unlike popcorn), about 30 seconds.

canned coconut milk
❖ ❖ ❖

*N*ot all cans of unsweetened coconut milk are the same. Some float way above the rest with creamy, naturally sweet qualities. Canned coconut milk, when well stirred to reincorporate the milky white extract (the fat separates from the thin wheylike fluid), should be fairly thick, its viscosity similar to that of heavy cream. Coconut cream is usually the first extract from shredded coconut and is much richer in texture and flavor. If you have no unsweetened coconut milk but happen to have some coconut cream lying around, dilute the cream with a few tablespoons of water to get the desired consistency. Powdered unsweetened coconut milk is also available, and allows you to add a larger proportion of powder to water for a heavier coconut flavor (not my first choice, however).

2. Lift the lid and carefully pour in the coconut milk, which will instantly come to a boil because of the skillet's intense heat. Add all the remaining ingredients except the fish, and bring to a boil.

3. Arrange the fillets in the skillet in a single layer, and make sure the creamy-tart-spicy sauce completely covers the fish. Lower the heat to medium, cover the skillet, and simmer the fillets, basting them with the sauce every 2 minutes to make sure they stay submerged, until they are barely starting to flake, 8 to 10 minutes. Then serve.

Tips:

❖ Unripe mangoes, especially the kind used in Indian curries, are not that hard to come by. Check your local Asian grocery store for a variety commonly referred to as Haitian mangoes. They are stone-firm and oval-shaped with an olive green skin, easily peeled with a swivel peeler. The light green flesh is very tart. (When no one is watching, slice off a hunk, sprinkle it with coarse salt and cayenne pepper, and devour it. Makes my mouth pucker just writing about it.) Or you can always go to your neighborhood supermarket and choose the firmest mango you can find from one of the commonly available varieties called Kent, Haden, or Tommy Atkins.

❖ As is most often the case, any firm-fleshed fish will do as an alternative to the catfish. For any vegetarians who feel left out, simmer slices of lightly fried *paneer* (page 286) or even tofu for an equally satisfying experience.

Mustard Paste– Smothered Cod
AND
MUSHROOMS WRAPPED IN LEAVES

Satara Soda

An unusual curry, this is an adaptation of a vegetarian recipe that Geeta Dash-Larson shared with me at a recent potluck gathering. Her father came from a small village in the eastern state of Orissa, her mother from the western Konkan coast. They married, emigrated, and settled in Missouri to raise a beautiful and gifted daughter, Geeta, now an internist, who lives with her psychiatrist husband and two teenage children in Minneapolis. Geeta fondly remembers a visit to Orissa—her father's home and the source of this recipe. **SERVES 6**

> 2 tablespoons black or yellow mustard seeds, ground
> ¼ cup boiling water
> 1 pound skinless fillet of cod, cut into 2-inch pieces
>   (halibut, swordfish, bass, and pollock make great
>   alternatives)
> 2 tablespoons mustard oil or canola oil
> 1½ teaspoons coarse kosher or sea salt
> ½ teaspoon ground turmeric
> 8 ounces brown cremini mushrooms, thinly sliced
> 1 small red onion, cut in half lengthwise and thinly sliced
> 1 medium-size tomato, cored and cut into 2-inch cubes
> 4 medium-size cloves garlic, thinly sliced
> 2 or 3 fresh green Thai, cayenne, or serrano chiles,
>   to taste, stems removed, finely chopped
>   (do not remove the seeds)
> 1 piece of banana leaf large enough to cover
>   the grill grate, or a handful of collard greens
> 2 tablespoons finely chopped fresh cilantro
>   leaves and tender stems for garnishing

1. Combine the mustard and boiling water in a large heatproof bowl, and stir to make a thick, yellow paste (black mustard seeds are yellow inside, so the paste will be yellow whichever type you use). Add the pieces of cod and all the remaining ingredients except the banana leaf and the cilantro. Toss them together to ensure that everything is evenly coated.

2. Preheat a gas (or charcoal) grill to high.

3. Tear off a sheet of aluminum foil that is large enough to cover most of the grill grate. Place the foil on the grate and pierce it in numerous places with a knife. Spread the banana leaf or collard leaves over the foil, making sure you have spread the greens wide enough to accommodate the fish and vegetables.

4. Spread the fish and vegetables over the greens. Cover the grill and cook until the fish is barely starting to flake and the vegetables are fork-tender, 15 to 20 minutes.

5. Transfer the thick fish curry, still on the greens, to a serving bowl. Sprinkle with the cilantro, and serve.

Poached Cod
IN A
COCONUT-ONION SAUCE

Meen Pulusu

this curry from the southern state of Andhra Pradesh is tart, thanks to the tamarind, and chile-hot. I like to serve it with Squash with a Chickpea Flour-Lime Sauce (page 597) for a quick meal. **SERVES 4**

½ teaspoon ground turmeric

4 boneless, skinless pieces of cod fillet
   (about 6 ounces each)

½ cup shredded fresh coconut; or ¼ cup shredded
   dried unsweetened coconut, reconstituted
   (see Note)

2 small to medium-size shallots, coarsely chopped

I teaspoon black or yellow mustard seeds

¼ teaspoon whole cloves

2 dried red Thai or cayenne chiles, stems removed

2 medium-size cloves garlic

2 tablespoons canola oil

8 to 12 medium-size to large fresh curry leaves

½ teaspoon tamarind paste or concentrate

1. Sprinkle the turmeric on both sides of each fillet and press it into the flesh to ensure that it evenly flavors and colors the fish. Refrigerate, covered, for 30 minutes or as long as overnight.

2. Pour ¼ cup water into a blender jar, and then add the coconut, shallots, mustard seeds, cloves, chiles, and garlic. Puree, scraping the inside of the jar as needed, to make a slightly gritty paste, speckled with potent spices.

3. Heat the oil in a large skillet over medium heat. Add the yellow-stained cod fillets and sear until they are light brown on both sides, about 30 seconds per side. Transfer the fillets to a plate and keep warm.

4. Pour the coconut paste into the skillet, add the curry leaves, and simmer, uncovered, stirring occasionally, until the water evaporates and the coconut and spices start to roast, 5 to 8 minutes.

5. While the sauce is simmering, combine the tamarind paste with ¼ cup water in a small bowl, and whisk together. Once the coconut sauce is ready, pour this muddy-brown, tart liquid into the skillet, and add ½ cup water. Return the fillets to the skillet and spoon the sauce over to blanket them. Poach the fillets, uncovered, basting them with the sauce, until they are barely starting to flake, 3 to 5 minutes. Transfer them to a serving platter and keep warm.

6. Continue to simmer the sauce, uncovered, stirring occasionally, until it starts to thicken, 3 to 5 minutes.

7. Spoon the sauce over the fillets, and serve.

Note: To reconstitute coconut, cover with ¼ cup boiling water, set aside for about 15 minutes, and then drain.

Halibut Fillets
WITH A COCONUT MILK–MUSTARD SEED SAUCE

meen thenga paal kari

I can't think of a better match for this delicate but rich-tasting sauce than firm-fleshed halibut fillets. Serve the curry over a bed of slightly sticky long-grain white rice to mop up all the succulent flavors. **SERVES 4**

½ teaspoon ground turmeric

1 pound skinless pieces of halibut fillet
   (2 to 3 inches thick)

2 tablespoons canola oil

½ teaspoon black or yellow mustard seeds

1 tablespoon skinned split black lentils (cream-colored
   in this form, urad dal), picked over for stones

1 cup finely chopped red onion

1 cup unsweetened coconut milk

2 tablespoons finely chopped fresh cilantro
   leaves and tender stems

1 teaspoon sambhar masala (page 33)

1 teaspoon coarse kosher or sea salt

10 to 12 medium-size to large fresh curry leaves

1 large tomato, cored and finely chopped

1. Sprinkle the turmeric over both sides of the halibut fillets, gently pressing the yellow spice into the flesh. Refrigerate, covered, for about 30 minutes.

2. Heat 1 tablespoon of the oil in a small saucepan over medium-high heat. Add the mustard seeds, cover, and cook until the seeds have stopped popping (not unlike popcorn), about 30 seconds. Add the lentils and stir-fry until they turn golden brown, 15 to 20 seconds.

Skinned split black lentils? See the Types of Legumes, page 313.

Immediately add the onion and cook, stirring, until it is reddish brown, 5 to 7 minutes.

3. Add the coconut milk, cilantro, masala, salt, and curry leaves. The coconut milk will immediately start to boil. Lower the heat to medium and simmer, uncovered, until the sauce thickens slightly, 5 to 10 minutes. Some of the oil may start to separate from the sauce.

4. Stir in the tomato and cook just until it is warmed through but remains firm, about 2 minutes.

5. Heat the remaining 1 tablespoon oil in a medium-size skillet over medium heat. Add the halibut fillets and sear until light brown on each side, 2 to 3 minutes per side. Pour the sauce over them, making sure they are completely blanketed. Push the fillets aside and scrape the bottom of the skillet to release any bits of fish and incorporate them into the sauce.

6. Cover the pan and poach the fish, basting frequently with the sauce, until the fillets are barely starting to flake, 5 to 8 minutes. Then serve.

Pan-Grilled Mackerel
WITH A TAMARIND SAUCE

bangada chi hooman

Rich-tasting mackerel, *bangada,* blanketed under *hooman* (a Maharashtrian coconut-flavored sauce), is a version of Usha Raikar's family favorite. She normally uses fresh coconut in her sauce, but I went for a lighter approach, using a spice blend that incorporates toasted coconut for a sweeter flavor with a hint of smokiness. Serve it with Lime-Flavored Rice with Roasted Yellow Split Peas (page 717). **SERVES 4**

- *2 tablespoons Ginger Chile Paste (page 17)*
- *2 teaspoons coarse kosher or sea salt*
- *4 skinless fillets of mackerel, cod, or mahi-mahi (about 6 ounces each)*
- *4 tablespoons canola oil*
- *1 medium-size red onion, finely chopped*
- *1 large tomato, cored and finely chopped*
- *1 teaspoon tamarind paste or concentrate*
- *2 teaspoons Maharashtrian garam masala (page 28)*
- *¼ cup finely chopped fresh cilantro leaves and tender stems*
- *½ cup Cream of Wheat (not instant) or fine dried breadcrumbs*

1. Combine the Ginger Chile Paste and 1 teaspoon of the salt in a small bowl. Smear each side of the 4 fillets with the pungent mix. Refrigerate, covered, for 30 minutes to 1 hour, to allow the flavors to permeate the flesh.

2. Heat 2 tablespoons of the oil in a medium-size skillet over medium heat. Add the onion and stir-fry until it is soft and light brown around the edges with a light purple hue, about 10 minutes.

3. Stir in the tomato, tamarind paste, garam masala, and the remaining 1 teaspoon salt. Cook, uncovered, stirring occasionally, until the tomatoes soften but still appear firm-looking, 5 to 10 minutes. Stir in the cilantro. Remove the skillet from the heat and cover it.

4. Spread the Cream of Wheat out on a plate. One by one, press the marinade-coated fillets into the Cream of Wheat, covering both sides with a gritty armor.

5. Heat the remaining 2 tablespoons oil in a large nonstick skillet over medium heat. Add the coated fish fillets and fry until crispy brown on both sides, 4 to 8 minutes per side (depending on the fillets' thickness). The inside, under the coating, should be barely starting to flake.

6. To serve the curry, place the fillets on a platter and top them with the tart-spicy hot-sweet sauce. If, during serving, you feel the fish is not cooked through, top them with the sauce, wrap the platter in plastic wrap, and microwave on high power for no more than 1 minute to give you a piece of mind. You worrywart, you!

Tip: The mackerel family of fish is ubiquitous, found in oceans all over the world including the Pacific, Atlantic, and Mediterranean. They contain a large amount of oil, making them shelf-unstable, meant to be consumed within hours of being caught. Mackerel's firm flesh and fatty taste make it an ideal match for assertive spices—and thus it is enjoyed by many in India on a regular basis. Some alternatives such as mahi-mahi, cod (only because it is so easy to find), striped bass, and even tuna work well with the spicy *hooman*.

Salmon
WITH GARLIC AND TURMERIC

Lasoon Aur Haldi Waale Mucchi

Salmon is not native to India, even though the subcontinent is cupped by three large bodies of water that school many a variety of fish and shellfish, but it works well with the subtle flavorings in this curry (I hate to mask salmon with assertive spices). This creamy yellow curry with a delicate taste offers a stunning-looking backdrop for the saffron-hued fish. **SERVES 4**

1½ teaspoons coarse kosher or sea salt

1 teaspoon ground turmeric

6 medium-size cloves garlic, finely chopped

1 pound boneless, skinless salmon fillet

2 tablespoons canola oil

½ cup unsweetened coconut milk

½ teaspoon black peppercorns, coarsely crushed

2 fresh green Thai, cayenne, or serrano chiles,
   stems removed, cut in half lengthwise
   (do not remove the seeds)

1. Mix the salt, turmeric, and garlic together in a small bowl. Sprinkle this rub over the top of the salmon fillet, and rub it in. Refrigerate the fish, covered, for at least 30 minutes or as long as overnight, to allow the flavors to permeate the flesh.

2. Heat the oil in a large skillet over medium heat. Add the salmon, spice-covered side down, and sear it for about 2 minutes (this will brown the fish and the garlic in the rub, and also cook the turmeric). Turn the fillet over and sear the underside until browned, about 2 minutes.

3. Measure out the coconut milk in a measuring cup, and add the peppercorns and the chiles. Stir, and pour this over the fish. Lift the fillet with a spatula and tilt the skillet slightly to allow the spiced coconut milk to run under it and release the browned bits of garlic, spice, and fish. Reduce the heat to medium-low, cover the skillet, and braise the salmon, spooning the sauce over it occasionally, until the flesh is barely starting to flake, 3 to 5 minutes.

4. Transfer the fish to a platter, pour the curry over it, and serve.

Tips:

✤ Shrimp or scallops make an excellent alternative to the salmon, as does any firm-fleshed fish like cod, bass, or catfish. Farm-raised tilapia is also a palatable option.

✤ The two sources of heat in this curry, chiles and peppercorns, should not deter you from trying this recipe—they exude a hushed presence in the unsweetened coconut milk. The fresh chiles are slit open to reveal the vein that harbors the potent capsaicin, but since they are not chopped, they will generate less heat.

Red Snapper
IN A
SMOKY-TART COCONUT MILK SAUCE

Meen Kudampuli

Occasionally, a few sauces stand out in my mind, and this is definitely in the top five: tart, smoky, spicy-hot, and appealing to look at. Credit goes to the blackish-purple fruit of the kokum family, smoked and dried, which gives this curry its distinct flavor. During a recent stay at the Coconut Lagoon resort in Kumarakom, Kerala, I attended a cooking class on a hot, lazy afternoon. Strikingly handsome, tall, and thick-mustached, with his tall French chef's hat perched on his charcoal-black hair, Chef Kartikai chopped, pounded, stirred, and poached as he explained the marvels of a good fish curry—made the Keralite way. This version of his curry has graced our kitchen on a weekend night and has drawn many an ooh and aah from our dinner guests. **SERVES 4**

1 teaspoon Ginger Paste (page 15)

1 teaspoon Garlic Paste (page 15)

1 teaspoon coriander seeds, ground

½ teaspoon cayenne (ground red pepper)

½ teaspoon ground turmeric

1 whole smoked kudampuli (see Tips)

2 tablespoons coconut oil or canola oil

½ teaspoon fenugreek seeds

4 large cloves garlic, finely chopped

1½ teaspoons coarse kosher or sea salt

10 to 12 medium-size to large fresh curry leaves

6 medium-size shallots, thinly sliced

*2 lengthwise slices fresh ginger (each 2½ inches long,
    1 inch wide, and ⅛ inch thick), cut into matchstick-
    thin strips (julienne)*

*2 fresh green Thai, cayenne, or serrano chiles,
    stems removed, cut in half lengthwise
    (do not remove the seeds)*

*1½ pounds skinless fillets of red snapper
    (or similar fish)*

½ cup thick unsweetened coconut milk (see Tips)

1. Combine the ginger and garlic pastes, coriander, cayenne, turmeric, and 2 tablespoons water in a small bowl, and stir to form a thick slurry.

2. Bring ½ cup water to a vigorous boil in a microwave oven or in a small saucepan. Place the smoked kudampuli in the water and set it aside to steep until a haunting smokiness emanates from the mixture, about 15 minutes. Then squeeze the dried fruit, which will still be firm to the touch, to extract some more of its juices. Set the liquid aside. (I usually wrap the fruit and refrigerate it for another extraction or two.)

3. Heat the oil in a large skillet over medium-high heat. Sprinkle in the fenugreek seeds and cook until they sizzle and turn reddish brown, 5 to 10 seconds. Immediately add the garlic and stir-fry until it turns reddish brown, about 1 minute.

4. Add the spice slurry and cook, stirring occasionally to allow the liquid to evaporate, until a glistening sheen forms on the surface, 2 to 4 minutes.

5. Pour in the kudampuli liquid and ½ cup water. Add the salt, curry leaves, shallots, ginger, and chiles. Scrape the bottom of the pan to deglaze it, releasing the browned bits of spice and paste. Bring the thin curry to a boil. Place the fillets in the skillet, in a single layer, and spoon the sauce over them. Poach the fish, uncovered, basting the fillets every 30 seconds or so with the yellow-orange sauce, for about 5 minutes (do not stir the fish).

6. Pour the coconut milk over the fish; the sauce will turn creamy. Continue to baste the fish with the sauce until the fillets are barely starting to flake, 2 to 3 minutes. (If the sauce is not thick enough, gently lift the fillets with a spatula and place them on a serving platter. Cook the sauce down until it is creamy-thick, 2 to 4 minutes.)

7. Pour the sauce over the fillets, and serve.

Tips:

❖ Kudampuli (*Garcinia camboge* or *cambogia,* depending on your source), also known as Malabar tamarind, is a tree that is found in abundance in Kerala, off the coast of Malabar. It is difficult to find this smoked fruit in the United States, even in Indian stores. Some large Indian supermarkets stock it, as do some Thai and Vietnamese grocery stores. If you can't locate it, dissolve ½ teaspoon tamarind paste or concentrate in ½ cup water for this recipe, and for that distinct smoky flavor, stir in a drop or two of bottled natural smoke flavor.

❖ To get thick coconut milk from a can of unsweetened coconut milk, simply do not shake the can before you open it. Carefully open the can and scoop out the top thick portion of the coconut milk, leaving behind the thin, watery, wheylike liquid.

Steamed Fillet of Sole
WRAPPED IN LEAVES

Patra Ni Macchi

No Parsi wedding is complete without this fish, smothered in a coconut-chile sauce, wrapped in banana leaves, and served steaming hot. This version is a favorite of Mrs. Perinne Medora and her family. Of Persian ancestry, they emigrated to America after many years in Mumbai. They now lead successful lives in the fields of banking, technology (her son, Zubin, keeps my website functioning), and other professions. Perinne's instruction to use sole (a cabernet among fishes) gives a clue to her desire for excellence—not just in food, but in all walks of her life. **SERVES 4**

1 cup shredded fresh coconut; or ½ cup shredded
   dried unsweetened coconut, reconstituted
   (see Note)
1 cup firmly packed fresh cilantro leaves
   and tender stems
¼ cup firmly packed fresh mint leaves
1 tablespoon crumbled (or chopped) jaggery
   or firmly packed dark brown sugar
1 teaspoon cumin seeds
1 teaspoon tamarind paste or concentrate
1 teaspoon coarse kosher or sea salt
6 to 8 fresh green Thai, cayenne, or serrano
   chiles, to taste, stems removed
4 medium-size cloves garlic
1 banana leaf, cut into 4 pieces; or 4 turnip leaves
   or collard leaves, each one large enough
   to wrap around a fillet (see Tips)

1½ pounds skinless fillets of sole, flounder,
   haddock, cod, whiting, or similar fish
   (4 fillets, or cut into 4 pieces if large)

1. Pour 1 cup water into a blender jar, and then add all the ingredients except the leaves and the fish. Puree, scraping the inside of the jar as needed, to make a thick, gritty, dark green sauce. Transfer the sauce to a small bowl.

2. Fill a large saucepan halfway with water and bring it to a rolling boil. Fill a medium-size to large bowl with cold water, and set it near the stove. Trim off and discard the tough bottom inch of the leaves' ribs (especially if you use collard or turnip greens). Dunk the leaves in the boiling water to soften them, 1 to 2 minutes. Remove them from the hot water and immerse them in the cold water to cool them off quickly. Drain the leaves in a colander.

3. Place a fillet in the center of a leaf. Spoon one fourth of the sauce over the fillet and spread it over both sides of the fish. Wrap the leaf around the fish, making sure the fish is completely cocooned. Repeat with the remaining fish and leaves.

Jaggery?
See the
Glossary of
Ingredients,
page 758.

4. Fill a saucepan halfway with water, insert a steamer basket, and bring the water to a boil. (Or fill a wok halfway with water, set a bamboo steamer in the wok, and bring the water to a boil.) Place the leaf bundles in the basket, cover, and steam until the fillets are barely starting to flake, 10 to 15 minutes. (Unwrap a leaf to peek in.)

5. Transfer the wrapped fillets to a serving platter, and serve. Allow your guests to unwrap their own packets as the spicy steam, fragrant with herbs, wafts up in the air to titillate their taste buds.

Note: To reconstitute coconut, cover with ½ cup boiling water, set aside for about 15 minutes, and then drain.

Tips:

✥ Connoisseurs of fish consider sole, a saltwater fish, to be the top of the line among fishes—juicy-firm in texture and sweet in taste. An entire family of sole, under the name *Solea solea,* swims in the waters of the Mediterranean, the North Sea, the Atlantic, the English Channel, and the Norwegian Sea. Unlike most fish, which is best consumed hours after it is caught, sole is ideal 2 to 3 days after it is netted. Numerous varieties are available in markets all over the world, but Dover sole is the favorite of many.

✥ Banana leaves impart a subtle flavor to food when used for steaming, as do turmeric leaves, which are sometimes used in Parsi homes to swathe fish but are rarely found in the United States. Large-leafed turnip and collard greens make excellent alternatives. Parchment paper works too, and you can also use aluminum foil.

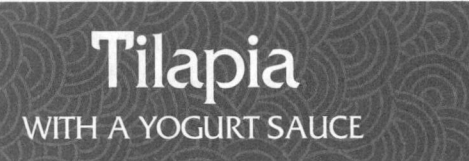

Tilapia
WITH A YOGURT SAUCE

doi maach

A common sight in Calcutta's streets are vendors hawking little clay pots of perfectly set plain yogurt, a layer of light yellow cream over the naturally sweet yogurt within. Spoon this rich yogurt into your mouth for a moment of joy, or, even better, use it to poach the Calcuttan's other passion: fish. **SERVES 4**

½ teaspoon ground turmeric
1 pound skinless tilapia fillets
1 cup plain yogurt
1 teaspoon white granulated sugar
1 teaspoon coarse kosher or sea salt
2 tablespoons mustard oil or canola oil
1 tablespoon Panch phoron (page 36)
2 dried red Thai or cayenne chiles, stems removed
1 cup finely chopped red onion
1 teaspoon finely chopped fresh ginger
2 tablespoons finely chopped fresh cilantro
    leaves and tender stems for garnishing

1. Sprinkle the turmeric over both sides of the fillets and rub it in. Refrigerate, covered, for at least 30 minutes, or as long as overnight, to allow the spice to flavor and color the fillets.

2. Whisk the yogurt, sugar, and salt together in a bowl.

3. Heat the oil in a large skillet over medium-high heat. Sprinkle in the *Panch phoron* and dried chiles. Cook until the spices sizzle and are aromatic, and the chiles blacken, 15 to 20 seconds. Immediately add the fillets and sear them on both sides on the bed of roasted spices, 30 seconds per side. Transfer the fish to a plate.

4. Add the onion and ginger to the skillet and stir-fry, scraping the skillet to release any browned bits of fish, until the onion is light brown around the edges, about 2 minutes.

5. Pour in the yogurt mixture and stir to incorporate the onion mixture into it. Bring the sauce to a boil, and add the fillets. Spoon the sauce over the fillets and poach them, uncovered, until the fish is barely starting to flake, 3 to 5 minutes.

6. Sprinkle with the cilantro, and serve.

Tip: I am the first to admit that the average American kitchen will rarely see plain yogurt being cultured on the counter with freshly heated milk. Hectic lives, convenience products, and a desire for immediate gratification preclude that from happening. The good news is that there is a plethora of plain yogurts lining the shelves in your favorite grocer's refrigerator section, and especially in natural food stores, that are just as good as homemade. Look especially for the cream-on-top kind.

Poached Tilapia
WITH
TART COCONUT MILK AND GARLIC

Kokum Muchee

I sampled this curry back in Mumbai at the home of Mrs. Desai, my Marathi teacher from my childhood's Jesuit-run private school. She poached skin-on, bone-in, whole pomfrets, but my version eliminates the frustration of having to pick out the bones from each mouthful. **SERVES 4**

½ teaspoon ground turmeric
1 pound skinless tilapia fillets (see Tips)
5 pieces dried black kokum, each roughly 2 inches long and 1 inch wide (see Tips)
¼ cup boiling water
2 tablespoons canola oil
4 medium-size cloves garlic, thinly sliced
2 fresh green Thai, cayenne, or serrano chiles, stems removed, cut in half lengthwise (do not remove the seeds)

1 cup unsweetened coconut milk
2 tablespoons finely chopped fresh cilantro leaves and tender stems for garnishing

1. Sprinkle the turmeric over both sides of the fillets, rubbing it in. Refrigerate, covered, for at least 30 minutes, to allow the spice to flavor and color the fillets.

2. Combine the kokum and the boiling water in a small heatproof bowl, and let it steep for 10 to 15 minutes to extract the kokum's slightly bitter juices. Then squeeze the kokum pieces to extract all their tart goodness. Discard the skin and reserve the liquid.

3. Heat the oil in a large skillet over medium-high heat. Add the fillets and sear them on both sides until barely browned, about 1 minute per side. Transfer the fish to a plate.

4. Add the garlic and chiles to the skillet and stir-fry, scraping the bottom to release any browned bits of fish, until the garlic is light brown around the edges, about 1 minute.

5. Pour in the coconut milk and deglaze the skillet, scraping the bottom to release browned bits of garlic. Stir in the purplish-brown kokum liquid.

6. Return the fish to the skillet. Continue to boil the curry, uncovered, spooning the sauce over the fillets, until they are barely starting to flake, 3 to 5 minutes.

7. Sprinkle with the cilantro, and serve.

Kokum? See the Glossary of Ingredients, page 758.

Tips:

❖ If you can't obtain kokum, you can dissolve ½ teaspoon tamarind paste or concentrate in the boiling water instead. Lime or lemon juice provides a clean, crystal-clear sharpness but lacks the earthy complexity of kokum or tamarind. However, you can use the juice from 1 medium-size lime for an "okay" as opposed to a "wowee" dish.

❖ Tilapia is a mild-tasting fish, and the thin fillets effectively absorb the tart, creamy sauce in barely 5 minutes. Any other white fish fillets will be fine, but their thickness will determine how much time it will take to poach them, adding anywhere from 5 to 10 minutes to the recipe.

Breaded Tilapia
WITH A MUSTARD SEED–COCONUT MILK SAUCE

Meen Curry

The lime juice in this curry provides a clean tartness when compared with the more complex, earthy tamarind—the latter often being the souring agent of choice in southern India. Farm-raised tilapia is a mellow-tasting fish and its fillets are very thin. It's easy to overcook them, so do take extra precaution while you fry or poach them. **SERVES 4**

Juice of 1 large lime
½ teaspoon ground turmeric
1 pound skinless tilapia fillets
2 teaspoons Roasted Curry Leaf Spice Blend (page 35)
1 cup plain dried breadcrumbs
4 tablespoons unrefined sesame oil or canola oil
1 teaspoon black or yellow mustard seeds
1 cup unsweetened coconut milk
1 teaspoon coarse kosher or sea salt
10 to 12 medium-size to large fresh curry leaves

1. Stir the lime juice and turmeric together in a small bowl. Lay the tilapia fillets in a single layer in a shallow platter. Pour the yellow-stained lime juice over them, and lift them to allow the juice to run under and coat the underside.

2. Sprinkle the spice blend over the top of each fillet. Refrigerate the fillets, covered, for 30 minutes to 2 hours to allow the flavors to marry.

3. Spread the breadcrumbs out on a plate. Lift the tilapia fillets from the marinade and coat them evenly on both sides with the breadcrumbs. Reserve any residual lime juice marinade.

4. Heat 2 tablespoons of the oil in a large skillet over medium-high heat. Add the fillets and fry on each side to seal in the flavors, about 1 minute per side. Transfer them to a serving plate and keep warm.

5. Heat the remaining 2 tablespoons oil in the same skillet. Add the mustard seeds, cover, and cook until the seeds have stopped popping (not unlike popcorn), about 30 seconds.

6. Lift the lid and carefully pour in the coconut milk, which will instantly come to a boil because of the skillet's intense heat. Add the salt, the curry leaves, and any residual lime juice marinade. Bring to a boil. Then lower the heat to medium and simmer, uncovered, stirring occasionally, until the sauce thickens.

7. Pour the sauce over the fillets, and serve.

Tip: If you would like to try for a crispier crust, use Cream of Wheat (the non-instant kind) instead of the breadcrumbs.

Fish Fillets
WITH A CILANTRO-CREAM SAUCE

dhaniawaale ffuchee

Cilantro-lovers will find they make this dish repeatedly, while the haters will balk at the quantity of the herb in the recipe. The cooking does help to lower the sharpness of cilantro, which a few find distressing. Therefore, haters go ahead and try it. I see no need to egg on the lovers, who are reaching over for seconds as we speak. **SERVES 4**

1 cup firmly packed fresh cilantro leaves
  and tender stems

¼ cup firmly packed medium-size to large fresh
  curry leaves

6 medium-size cloves garlic

4 fresh green Thai, cayenne, or serrano chiles,
  stems removed

1½ teaspoons coarse kosher or sea salt

1½ pounds skinless, firm-fleshed fish fillets,
  such as cod, halibut, swordfish, bass,
  or pollock

2 tablespoons canola oil

½ cup plain yogurt

½ cup half-and-half

Fish (especially fillets) changes from translucent to opaque when it is done. When you gently lift the cooked fish with a knife or fork, the flesh will break open and appear opaque throughout. When this happens, the fish is perfectly cooked. Don't let it cook to the point that it is falling apart—it will be overdone.

1. Pack the cilantro, curry leaves, garlic cloves, chiles, and salt into a food processor. Process until the ingredients are minced, forming a highly aromatic blend. Spread the blend over both sides of the fish fillets, patting it into the flesh. Refrigerate, covered, for 30 minutes to 1 hour, to allow the flavors to permeate the flesh.

2. Heat the oil in a large skillet over medium-high heat. Add the fish and sear the fillets, 1 to 2 minutes on each side. Transfer them to a plate.

3. Whisk the yogurt and half-and-half together in a small bowl. Pour this into the skillet, and scrape the bottom to deglaze it, releasing the browned bits of herbs and fish. Return the fillets to the skillet and spoon the sauce over them. Simmer, basting the fillets every few seconds (without stirring them), until they barely start to flake and the sauce is thick, 3 to 5 minutes (see Tips). Then serve.

Tips:

❖ The thickness of the fillets varies with the type of fish you use, so be prepared to adjust the simmering time in Step 3: lower for the thin-fleshed ones and slightly longer for the heftier ones. Tilapia fillets, for example, are only about ¼ to ½ inch thick. For such thin fillets, reduce the simmering time by half, and if the fish cooks before the sauce thickens, remove the fillets from the curry and then simmer the sauce down to the desired thickness. Pour it over the fillets, and serve.

❖ The half-and-half provides essential fat to the yogurt, helping it stabilize and not fall apart (curdle) when heated.

Poached Fish
IN A MUSTARD-CHILE SAUCE

Sorshe Maach

A simple spicing combination, this is meant to cater to every Bengali's penchant for the combination of fish and mustard. The more pungent the mustard and the firmer the fish, the better the dish will be. The thickness of the fillets will determine how much time they take to cook; allow at least 5 minutes of poaching for the flavors to permeate the flesh. Serve the thin curry with a slightly sticky boiled white rice. **SERVES 4**

½ teaspoon ground turmeric

1 pound skinless firm-fleshed fish fillets, such as cod, halibut, swordfish, sea bass, or pollock

1 tablespoon black or yellow mustard seeds

4 fresh green Thai, cayenne, or serrano chiles, stems removed

3 tablespoons mustard oil (see Tip)

1 teaspoon coarse kosher or sea salt

1 teaspoon white granulated sugar

2 tablespoons finely chopped fresh cilantro leaves and tender stems for garnishing

1. Sprinkle the turmeric over the fish, rubbing both sides of the fillets. Refrigerate, covered, for at least 30 minutes or as long as over night, to allow the spice to flavor the fillets.

2. Combine the mustard seeds and chiles in a mortar, and grind and pound them with the pestle to release the mustard's nose-tingling aroma and to create a yellowish-green, slightly gritty paste. (Alternatively, you can grind the mustard seeds in a spice grinder until the texture resembles that of finely cracked black peppercorns. Finely chop the chiles, seeds and all, and add them to the ground mustard seeds.)

3. Heat 2 tablespoons of the oil in a large skillet over medium-high heat. Add the pungent paste and stir-fry until it is sunny brown, about 1 minute. Quickly pour in ½ cup water, scraping the skillet to deglaze it, releasing the browned bits of spice. Stir in the salt and sugar.

4. Lay the fish fillets in a single layer in the skillet, and spoon the sauce over them. Lower the heat to medium, cover the skillet, and poach the fillets until they are barely starting to flake, 5 to 7 minutes.

5. Sprinkle with the cilantro, drizzle with the remaining 1 tablespoon oil, and serve.

Tip: I have not recommended an alternative to the mustard oil in this recipe. Unlike canola oil, its pungency will enliven this curry, so please make the effort to make a trip to your Indian grocery store.

NIMMY PAUL'S
Poached Fish Fillets
IN A TOMATO-VINEGAR SAUCE

Meen Pullikaach

Nimmy Paul runs a very successful cooking school out of her modest bungalow near Cochin in the southwestern state of Kerala, whose hills are studded with peppercorns, cloves, cardamom, nutmeg, and cinnamon. The foods of her Syrian Christian ancestry hold a special place in her heart as she effortlessly prepares lacy crepes, steamed noodles, and curries on a daily basis. Nimmy, the youngest of eight children, started teaching cooking to the newly married women in the neighborhood in 1991, and about eight years ago she reached out to the international community. Now she teaches the foods her mother taught her to groups from all over the world. Her husband, Paul (whose name she combined with hers for the cooking school), makes the daily trip to the markets and assists Nimmy with her flourishing business. **SERVES 4**

¼ cup coconut oil or canola oil

1 cup thinly sliced shallots

6 lengthwise slices fresh ginger
(each 1 inch long, 1 inch wide, and
⅛ inch thick), cut into matchstick-thin
strips (julienne)

4 large cloves garlic, cut into thin slivers

12 to 15 medium-size to large fresh curry leaves

3 to 5 fresh green Thai, cayenne, or serrano chiles,
to taste, stems removed, cut lengthwise into
thin strips (do not remove the seeds)

2 large tomatoes, cored and finely chopped

¼ cup distilled white vinegar

2 teaspoons ground Kashmiri chiles;
or ½ teaspoon cayenne (ground red pepper)
mixed with 1½ teaspoons sweet paprika

1½ teaspoons coarse kosher or sea salt

1½ pounds skinless fillets of halibut, sea bass,
or similar fish

1. Heat the oil in a large skillet over medium heat. Add the shallots, ginger, and garlic, and cook, stirring, until the vegetables are soft and light brown around the edges, 5 to 8 minutes.

2. Stir in the curry leaves and fresh chiles, and cook, stirring, for about 30 seconds. Then add the tomatoes, vinegar, ground chiles, and salt. Simmer, uncovered, stirring occasionally, until the tomatoes soften slightly but are still firm-looking, 2 to 4 minutes.

3. Add the fish fillets and spoon the sauce over to blanket them. Reduce the heat to medium-low, cover the skillet, and poach the fish, without stirring, until the fillets are barely starting to flake, 12 to 15 minutes. Then serve.

Tip: Nimmy suggests using whole fresh sardines as an alternative for this recipe. For the vegetarians at the table, she highly recommends eggplant slices (if you use the large American variety, salt them to leach their bitter juices before you poach them in the sauce).

POPPY AND MUSTARD SEED–RUBBED
Fish Fillets

Sorshe Poshto Maach

Bengalis adore their bitterness (in food, never in personalities), especially when the taste originates from various forms of mustard. In this curry, even though ground black mustard seeds and mustard oil provide an acrimonious and nose-tingling aroma to the catfish fillets, the resulting balance with nutty poppy seeds, pungent chiles, and slightly acidic tomato makes this recipe quite addictive. **SERVES 4**

1 tablespoon white poppy seeds, ground

2 teaspoons black or yellow mustard seeds,
   ground

1 teaspoon coarse kosher or sea salt

1 pound skinless fillets of catfish (see Tip)

2 tablespoons mustard oil or canola oil

1 tablespoon Panch phoron (page 36)

3 dried red Thai or cayenne chiles, stems
   removed

4 lengthwise slices fresh ginger (each 2 inches long,
   1 inch wide, and 1/8 inch thick), finely chopped

1 large tomato, cored and finely chopped

2 tablespoons finely chopped fresh cilantro
   leaves and tender stems for garnishing

White poppy seeds? See the Glossary of Ingredients, page 758.

1. Combine the poppy, mustard, and salt in a small bowl, and stir well. Rub this bitter spice blend over both sides of the catfish fillets. Refrigerate, covered, for at least 30 minutes or as long as overnight, to allow the flavors to permeate the fish.

2. Heat the oil in a large skillet over medium-high heat. Sprinkle in the *Panch phoron* and the chiles, and cook until the spices sizzle and are aromatic, and the chiles have blackened slightly, 15 to 20 seconds. Immediately add the ginger and stir-fry until it is golden brown, 30 seconds to 1 minute.

3. Add the catfish fillets and sear on each side to cook the spices, about 1 minute per side. Pour in 1/4 cup water and deglaze the skillet, releasing any browned bits of spice and fish. Spoon the tomato over the fillets, blanketing them. Reduce the heat to medium-low, cover the skillet, and braise the fillets, basting them with the sauce every 2 minutes, until the flesh is barely starting to flake, about 6 minutes.

4. Transfer the fillets to a serving platter and spoon the chunky sauce over them. Top with the cilantro, and serve.

Tip: Use any firm-fleshed fish fillet as an alternative to the catfish. Swordfish, halibut, shark, pollock, and even tuna will fill the bill. Refrain from using salmon—it's too delicate.

Shrimp
WITH BISHOP'S WEED

Ajwaini Jhinga

bishop's weed is the key flavor in this curry, and you will be reminded of it with each bite. Thyme makes an acceptable alternative, although it lacks the peppery, musky complexity of bishop's weed. Serve the curry atop fresh-cooked pasta for an unexpected out-of-this-world combination. **SERVES 4**

Bishop's weed? Black salt? See the Glossary of Ingredients, page 758.

1 pound large shrimp (16 to 20 per pound),
   peeled and deveined but tails left on

1 teaspoon white granulated sugar

1 teaspoon coarse kosher or sea salt

1 teaspoon bishop's weed or dried thyme

1 teaspoon ground Deggi chiles (see box,
   page 290); or 1/2 teaspoon cayenne
   (ground red pepper) mixed with
   1/2 teaspoon sweet paprika

1/2 teaspoon ground turmeric

2 tablespoons canola oil

1 cup finely chopped red onion

1 cup finely chopped tomato

1/2 cup half-and-half

2 tablespoons finely chopped fresh cilantro
   leaves and tender stems for garnishing

1. Combine the shrimp, sugar, salt, weed (it's, like, totally legal, dude), ground chiles, and turmeric in a medium-size bowl. Toss to coat the shrimp with the seasonings. Cover the shrimp and refrigerate it for at least 30 minutes. (If you wish, you can leave it as long as overnight. The flavors will permeate the shellfish, and since there is no acid in the spice rub to break down the structure, it's okay to marinate it for that length of time.)

2. Heat the oil in a large skillet over medium-high heat. Add the shrimp in a single layer, and sear them on each side, about 30 seconds per side. Transfer them to a plate.

3. Add the onion to the same skillet (there will be a little spiced oil left in the skillet, enough for the onion) and stir-fry until it is light brown around the edges, 5 to 8 minutes.

4. Add the tomato and cook, uncovered, stirring occasionally, until it softens and appears saucelike, 3 to 5 minutes.

5. Transfer the onion-tomato mixture to a blender jar. Puree, scraping the inside of the jar as needed, to make a smooth red sauce tinted with light purple. Add this sauce, the half-and-half, and the shrimp to the skillet. Bring the curry to a simmer over medium heat and cook, uncovered, stirring occasionally, until the shrimp curl and turn salmon-orange in color, 3 to 5 minutes.

6. Sprinkle with the cilantro, and serve.

Tip: For a totally "fusion" restaurant-style presentation, I cook the shrimp completely in the oil, adding an extra minute of cooking time per side. I simmer the sauce separately (without the shrimp in it) and set it aside after I puree it. Then I grab about 1 pound of fresh greens (spinach, kale, collard, mustard, or a combination) and either sauté them in vegetable oil or wilt them in a pot of hot water. Once drained, they become a bed for the seared shrimp and creamy sauce, to create a festive-looking curry.

Poached Shrimp
IN A SLOW-COOKED ONION SAUCE
bhuna hua jhinga

The technique of *bhuna*-ing (when you combine English and Hindi, it becomes the hybrid Hinglish) is easy to re-create: it means to stew a sauce slowly over medium-low heat in order to cook the spices long enough for their essential oils to be released, making for a very complex-tasting curry. Here a puree of fried onions, tomato paste, and a few spices simmers gently for almost half an hour to yield a sweet, slightly tart base for large shrimp. **SERVES 8**

2 tablespoons canola oil

4 lengthwise slices fresh ginger (each 2 inches long, 1 inch wide, and ⅛ inch thick), coarsely chopped

4 medium-size cloves garlic, coarsely chopped

I cup Fried Onion Paste (page 16)

2 tablespoons tomato paste

2 teaspoons mango powder (see page 763) or fresh lime juice

2 teaspoons coriander seeds, ground

I teaspoon cumin seeds, ground

I teaspoon fine black salt (see Tip)

½ teaspoon ground turmeric

½ teaspoon cayenne (ground red pepper)

I pound large shrimp (16 to 20 per pound), peeled and deveined but tails left on

2 tablespoons finely chopped fresh cilantro leaves and tender stems for garnishing

how to peel and devein shrimp

❖ ❖ ❖

Peeled and deveined shrimp (fresh or frozen) are easy to find at any large supermarket. If you need to do the peeling and deveining yourself, it is simple: Remove the thin shell with your fingers, leaving intact the tail shell and the last segment attached to the tail. (If you wish, you can get rid of the tail shell too—I leave it on for purely aesthetic reasons.) Using a paring knife, make a shallow incision down the center of the back of each shrimp. Wedge the tip of the knife under the black vein that runs down the back to lift it, and pull it out and discard it. Clean the deveined shrimp under cold running water before use.

1. Heat the oil in a medium-size saucepan over medium heat. Add the ginger and garlic, and stir-fry until golden brown, 1 to 2 minutes.

2. Using a slotted spoon, transfer the garlic and ginger to a blender jar. Pour in ¾ cup water, followed by the onion paste and tomato paste. Puree, scraping the inside of the jar as needed, to form a thick, reddish-brown paste. Transfer the paste to the same saucepan. Pour ¼ cup water into the blender jar and swish it around to wash it out. Add this to the pan.

3. Stir in the mango powder, coriander, cumin, black salt, turmeric, and cayenne. Cover the pan and simmer the sauce over medium heat, stirring occasionally, until the oil starts to form a few shiny drops around the edges, 5 to 8 minutes.

4. Stir in ½ cup water, cover the pan, and simmer, stirring occasionally, until there is a thin film of oil on the surface, 8 to 10 minutes.

5. Pour in ½ cup water and repeat one last time: cover the pan and simmer, stirring occasionally, until there is a thin film of oil on the surface, 8 to 10 minutes.

6. Add the shrimp and stir once or twice. Cover the pan and poach, stirring occasionally, until the shrimp are salmon-orange, curled, and tender, 8 to 10 minutes.

7. Sprinkle with the cilantro, and serve.

Tip: You can use coarse kosher or sea salt for this recipe if you don't have black salt, but you will lose out on the smoky, earthy flavor that sulfur-based black salt provides.

Chile-Hot Shrimp
WITH BELL PEPPERS

Thingri Maach Simla Mirchi

A slightly watery curry, this contains enough chiles to make you reach for a glass of milk, a bowl of yogurt, or a cool beer to douse the flame. By all means use fewer chiles if you prefer. For a creamier curry, I like to use unsweetened coconut milk instead of the usual water. Not only does it add body to the sauce, it diffuses some of the heat from the chiles. **SERVES 6**

1 pound large shrimp (16 to 20 per pound), peeled and deveined but tails left on

1 teaspoon ground turmeric

1 teaspoon coarse kosher or sea salt

2 tablespoons mustard oil or canola oil

2 teaspoons Panch phoron (page 36)

2 medium-size green bell peppers, stemmed,
seeded, and cut into 1-inch pieces

4 to 6 fresh green Thai, cayenne, or serrano
chiles, to taste, stems removed, cut
crosswise into ¼-inch-thick slices
(do not remove the seeds)

½ cup unsweetened coconut milk or water

2 tablespoons finely chopped fresh cilantro
leaves and tender stems for garnishing

1. Place the shrimp in a medium-size bowl, sprinkle with the turmeric and salt, and toss. Refrigerate, covered, for about 30 minutes.

2. Heat the oil in a wok or in a large skillet over medium-high heat. Sprinkle the *Panch phoron* into the skillet and cook until the spices sizzle and are aromatic, 10 to 15 seconds. Add the bell peppers and chiles, and stir-fry until they acquire brown patches and the chiles smell very pungent, 4 to 6 minutes.

3. Add the shrimp and continue to stir-fry for 1 to 2 minutes. Then add the coconut milk or water, and simmer until the shrimp are slightly curled and salmon-orange in color, 2 to 3 minutes.

4. Serve, sprinkled with the cilantro.

Tip: If you are using the coconut milk, I recommend cooking in a large skillet instead of a wok (especially if you have an old-fashioned iron wok). Oftentimes the iron in a not-so-well-seasoned wok reacts with coconut milk to produce an unappetizing-looking sauce with a slight metallic taste.

East Indian Shrimp
WITH RIPE MANGO

bottle masala jhinga

East Indians wait with bated breath, not for the monsoon floods, but for the onslaught of mangoes, so they can toss them with their new stash of summer-pounded *bottle masala* and plump, succulent tiger shrimp, freshly netted in the Arabian Sea. **SERVES 4**

2 tablespoons canola oil

1 small red onion, cut in half lengthwise and
thinly sliced

8 to 10 medium-size to large fresh curry leaves

6 medium-size cloves garlic, finely chopped

1 pound large shrimp (16 to 20 per pound),
peeled and deveined but tails left on

2 teaspoons East Indian bottle masala (page 37)

1 large, ripe but firm mango, peeled, seeded, and
cut into long matchstick-thin strips (julienne)

1½ teaspoons coarse kosher or sea salt

1. Heat the oil in a large skillet over medium heat. Add the onion, curry leaves, and garlic, and cook slowly, stirring occasionally, until the onion is soft and honey-brown with a deep purple hue, 10 to 15 minutes.

2. Raise the heat to medium-high, and add the shrimp and *bottle masala*. Cook, stirring, to coat the shellfish with the spice blend, 1 to 2 minutes.

3. Pour in ½ cup water and scrape the bottom of the skillet to deglaze it, releasing the browned bits of onion and spice. Continue the vigorous simmer, uncovered, stirring occasionally, until the shrimp curl and turn salmon-orange in color, 3 to 5 minutes.

4. Stir in the mango and salt and let the curry simmer, uncovered, stirring occasionally, to warm the mango strips, 1 to 2 minutes. Then serve,

Fragrant Ginger Shrimp
WITH
SHALLOTS AND CURRY LEAVES

Cochin Jhinga

Shrimp, called prawns in India, are abundant in the country's three oceans—the Arabian Sea, the Bay of Bengal, and the Indian Ocean. Cooks from the southwestern state of Kerala are masters at creating saucy magic with locally processed coconut oil, shallots, and of course prawns (which they cook with the head on). They cook many of their curries in *urulis:* wide-mouthed, slightly deep pots that have no handles but do have an impressive lip that makes them easy to lift. Brass, stainless steel, copper, iron, and even clay form the exterior of an *uruli*, with its interior made from acceptable cooking materials such as stainless steel, iron, or even aluminum. Hands-on, my favorite is the *uruli* made of clay. The earthy flavors and sensuously warm colors that emanate from these pots make for an impressive presentation. **SERVES 4**

2 tablespoons coconut oil or canola oil

½ cup finely chopped shallots

8 to 10 medium-size to large fresh curry leaves

2 fresh green Thai, cayenne, or serrano chiles, stems removed, cut in half lengthwise (do not remove the seeds)

1 large tomato, cored and finely chopped

2 tablespoons distilled white vinegar

1½ teaspoons coarse kosher or sea salt

1 teaspoon ground Kashmiri chiles; or ¼ teaspoon cayenne (ground red pepper) mixed with ¾ teaspoon sweet paprika

1 pound large shrimp (16 to 20 per pound), peeled and deveined but tails left on

3 lengthwise slices fresh ginger (each 2½ inches long, 1 inch wide, and ⅛ inch thick), cut into matchstick-thin strips (julienne) for garnishing

1. Heat the oil in a deep, medium-size skillet over medium-high heat. Add the shallots, curry leaves, and chiles, and stir-fry until the shallots are lightly browned, 1 to 2 minutes.

2. Stir in the tomato, vinegar, salt, and ground chiles, and heat to a boil. Stir in the shrimp, making sure they get well coated with the vermilion-red sauce.

3. Lower the heat to medium, cover the skillet, and poach, stirring occasionally, until the shrimp are slightly curled and salmon-orange in color, 3 to 5 minutes. (If the sauce is too thin for your liking, use a slotted spoon to transfer the cooked shrimp to a serving platter. Raise the heat to medium-high and cook the sauce, uncovered, stirring occasionally, until it has thickened, about 2 minutes.)

4. Pour the sauce over the shrimp, sprinkle with the ginger, and serve.

Prawns
WITH ONIONS IN A
PEANUT–COCONUT-SPICED CURRY

Copray Chi Kolumbi

If you make the spice blend ahead of time (which takes barely 5 minutes, by the way), this curry could not be any easier. Prep is next to nothing, especially if you purchase already peeled and deveined shrimp, and you know the cooking time is minimal because you don't want to overcook this delicate shellfish. Just a few minutes at the stove and you get to savor the curry's nutty, hot, and citrus undertones. **SERVES 4**

1 pound large shrimp (16 to 20 per pound),
   peeled and deveined but tails left on
1 teaspoon coarse kosher or sea salt
½ teaspoon ground turmeric
2 tablespoons peanut oil or canola oil
½ cup finely chopped red onion
2 teaspoons Maharashtrian garam masala (page 28)
¼ cup finely chopped fresh curry leaves

1. Place the shrimp in a medium-size bowl, and sprinkle them with the salt and turmeric. Toss to coat them with the spices. Refrigerate, covered, for 15 to 30 minutes to allow the shellfish to absorb the spices' flavor and color.

2. Heat the oil in a large skillet over medium-high heat. Add the onion and stir-fry until it is light brown around the edges, 3 to 5 minutes.

3. Add the shrimp, arranging them in a single layer in the skillet. Sear on each side to seal in the flavors, about 1 minute per side. Add ½ cup water and the garam masala, and stir once or twice to deglaze the skillet, releasing any browned bits of onion. Bring to a boil. Then continue to simmer vigorously, uncovered, stirring occasionally, until the sauce has thickened slightly and the shrimp are salmon-orange, curled, and tender, 3 to 5 minutes.

4. Stir in the curry leaves, and serve.

Tip: Once you get to know fresh curry leaves, you will realize there is no substitute for their delicate aroma and flavor. But not having them in your refrigerator should not preclude you from making this easy easy easy (did I say easy?) recipe. As a green alternative, use 2 tablespoons finely chopped fresh cilantro leaves and tender stems for a similar-looking sauce.

Spicy Shrimp
WITH BLACK PEPPER AND
BLACKENED CHILES

Jhinga Masala

While Americans call them shrimp and the rest of the world knows them as prawns (sometimes the size is the deciding point for the nomenclature), this well-loved shellfish, a member of the crustacean family (its skeleton is outside, masking succulent, sweet flesh underneath), is ubiquitous, with many popular varieties being farm-raised to meet burgeoning appetites. The prawns found in Indian waters, grayish green in color, are called tiger prawns—especially the larger ones that pile in at 16 to 20 pieces (without their heads) per pound.

This particular combination of ingredients breathes fire into every juicy piece, while the final squirt of fresh lime juice brings the heat down a level or two. **SERVES 4**

1 pound large shrimp (16 to 20 per pound),
  peeled and deveined but tails left on
4 medium-size cloves garlic, finely chopped
1 teaspoon Bin bhuna hua garam masala
  (page 30)
1 teaspoon coarse kosher or sea salt
1 teaspoon black peppercorns
2 or 3 dried red Thai or cayenne chiles, to taste,
  stems removed
2 tablespoons canola oil
6 to 8 medium-size to large fresh curry leaves
1 tablespoon rice flour
Juice of 1 medium-size lime

1. Combine the shrimp, garlic, garam masala, and salt in a medium-size bowl, and toss to mix. Refrigerate, covered, for at least 30 minutes or as long as overnight, to allow the spices to perk up the shellfish (since there is nothing acidic in the rub that might break down the fish's texture, it's okay to leave it overnight).

2. Heat a medium-size skillet over medium-high heat. Add the peppercorns and chiles and toast them, shaking the skillet very frequently, until the peppercorns appear slightly smoky gray and the chiles blacken (use adequate ventilation when you do this), 2 to 3 minutes. Transfer the peppercorns and chiles to a mortar, and pound them with a pestle to coarsely crack the peppercorns and break open the blackened skin of the chiles to unleash its heated capsaicin (far stronger than when it is not toasted). The blend does not have to be finely ground.

3. Drizzle the oil into the same skillet and heat it over medium-high heat. Add the shrimp, arranging them in a single layer, and sear the underside to seal in the flavors, about 1 minute. Flip them over and repeat. Pour in 1 cup water, and sprinkle in the curry leaves along with the pounded spices. Stir once or twice, and bring to a boil. Cook, uncovered, stirring occasionally, until the shrimp are salmon-orange, curled, and tender, 3 to 5 minutes.

4. Sprinkle the rice flour evenly across the surface so when you stir it in, it won't come together in clumps. As soon as you stir it in, the sauce will thicken, 10 to 15 seconds.

5. Stir in the lime juice, and serve.

Toasted Tamarind–Rubbed Shrimp

WITH A COCONUT-GINGER SAUCE

karwari jhinga

Karwar is a resort community along the Konkan coast, just south of Goa. Dotted with must-see beaches and vacation hot spots, Karwar is a tranquil community that forces you to slow down and savor the culinary fruits that swim ashore from the sea. Punchy crabs, clawing lobsters, scurrying prawns, and chubby fishes find themselves wrapped in sauces flavored with an abundance of local sweet coconuts and assertive chiles. Even though I use shrimp here, any of the aforementioned seafood would be a great stand-in for this curry. Serve it with *Malabar paranthas* (page 731), a flaky bread from the neighboring state of Kerala, for a winsome meal. **SERVES 4**

1 tablespoon coriander seeds

1 teaspoon rock salt

3 dried red Thai or cayenne chiles, stems removed

1 walnut-size ball of dried seedless tamarind, cut into smaller pieces

1 pound large shrimp (16 to 20 per pound), peeled and deveined but tails left on

4 medium-size cloves garlic, finely chopped

4 tablespoons canola oil

1 cup shredded fresh coconut; or ½ cup shredded dried unsweetened coconut, reconstituted (see Note)

2 lengthwise slices fresh ginger (each 2 inches long, 1 inch wide, and ⅛ inch thick)

¼ cup finely chopped fresh cilantro leaves and tender stems

½ teaspoon coarse kosher or sea salt

½ teaspoon black peppercorns, coarsely cracked

1. Heat a large skillet over medium-high heat. Sprinkle in the coriander seeds, rock salt, chiles, and tamarind. Toast, stirring constantly, until the coriander is reddish brown, the chiles have blackened slightly, and the tamarind appears a little dry, 3 to 5 minutes. Immediately transfer the spices to a plate and set them aside to cool for about 5 minutes.

Rock salt? See the Glossary of Ingredients, page 758.

2. Transfer the spices to a spice grinder, and grind until the texture resembles finely ground black pepper. Some of the tamarind may refuse to cooperate and not break down. Simply discard those pieces.

3. Place the shrimp in a bowl, and sprinkle the ground spice blend, along with the garlic, over them. Mix to make sure the shrimp is well coated. Then refrigerate, covered, until ready to use.

4. Heat 2 tablespoons of the oil in the same skillet over medium-high heat. Add the coconut and ginger, and roast, stirring constantly, until the coconut is toasty brown, 2 to 3 minutes. Stir in the cilantro and cook, stirring, to dry it out a bit, about 30 seconds. Then add ½ cup water and scrape the pan to deglaze it. Stir in the salt. Pour the green-speckled sauce into a blender jar and puree, scraping the inside of the jar as needed, to grind the coconut a little bit more and to puree the ginger. The sauce will feel gritty.

5. Heat the remaining 2 tablespoons oil in a clean skillet over medium-high heat. Add the shrimp, arranging them in a single layer, and allow the underside to sear for about 1 minute. Turn them over and sear the other side, about 1 minute. Add the sauce; it should almost instantly deglaze the pan and come to a boil. Continue to cook, uncovered, stirring occasionally, until the shrimp are salmon-orange, curled, and tender, 3 to 5 minutes.

6. Stir in the cracked peppercorns, and serve.

Note: To reconstitute coconut, cover with ½ cup boiling water, set aside for about 15 minutes, and then drain.

Fennel-Flecked Shrimp
WITH GROUND GINGER

kashmiri jhinga

Shrimp is not an ingredient in Kashmiri cooking, but I think the delicate spices used up north make a perfect combination for a shrimp curry. The smoky backdrop of black cardamom and black cumin enhances the mixture. The sauce will be on the thin side, so make sure you have plenty of basmati rice to go around to absorb it all. **SERVES 6**

2 teaspoons ground Kashmiri chiles; or ½ teaspoon
    cayenne (ground red pepper) mixed with
    1½ teaspoons sweet paprika
1½ teaspoons coarse kosher or sea salt
1 teaspoon fennel seeds, ground
½ teaspoon ground ginger
½ teaspoon ground turmeric
1½ pounds large shrimp (16 to 20 per pound),
    peeled and deveined but tails left on
¼ cup mustard oil or canola oil
2 teaspoons black cumin seeds
6 black cardamom pods
1 large red onion, cut in half lengthwise and
    thinly sliced
2 tablespoons finely chopped fresh cilantro
    leaves and tender stems for garnishing

1. Combine the ground chiles, salt, fennel, ground ginger, and turmeric in a medium-size bowl. Add the shrimp and toss to coat them with the seasonings.

Refrigerate, covered, for 30 minutes to 1 hour, to allow the flavors to permeate the shellfish.

2. Heat the oil in a large skillet over medium heat. Sprinkle in the cumin seeds and cardamom pods, and cook until they sizzle and smell smoky, 15 to 20 seconds. Add the onion and cook, stirring, until it is soft and honey-brown, about 15 minutes. Don't hurry this process—the slow cooking gently releases the onion's sugars to form an essential sweet base for this curry.

3. Raise the heat to medium-high and add the shrimp. Cook, stirring them once or twice, to seal in the juices and cook the spices, about 2 minutes.

4. Pour in 1 cup water and bring to a boil. Continue to boil, stirring occasionally, until the vermilion-red sauce thickens slightly and the shrimp are slightly curled and salmon-orange in color, 3 to 5 minutes.

5. Sprinkle with the cilantro, and serve.

Garlic Shrimp
WITH A COCONUT SAUCE

Lasoon jhinga

I introduced this curry to a group of friends during the Labor Day holiday. It required no real labor but still managed to elicit unconditional love from all, including the vegetarian, who fell off her wagon just this once. To further minimize my time in the kitchen, I brushed ghee over a batch of frozen whole-wheat griddle breads that I had purchased at my favorite Indian grocery store, and pan-fried them. If you want to make your own, prepare *Malabar paranthas* (page 731) on a day when you have some extra time, and freeze the unused breads for days like this. **SERVES 4**

I pound large shrimp (16 to 20 per pound), peeled and deveined but tails left on

¼ teaspoon ground turmeric

¼ cup distilled white vinegar, slightly warmed

2 teaspoons cumin seeds

½ teaspoon black peppercorns

4 large cloves garlic

3 dried red Thai or cayenne chiles, stems removed

½ cup shredded fresh coconut; or ¼ cup shredded dried unsweetened coconut, reconstituted (see Note)

2 tablespoons canola oil

I teaspoon coarse kosher or sea salt

¼ cup finely chopped fresh cilantro leaves and tender stems for garnishing

1. Place the shrimp in a medium-size bowl, sprinkle the turmeric over them, and toss. Refrigerate, covered, for 15 to 30 minutes, to allow the shellfish to absorb the spice's flavor and color.

2. While the shrimp is marinating, pour the warm vinegar into a small bowl and add the cumin seeds, peppercorns, garlic, and chiles. Soak until the chiles soften slightly, about 30 minutes. Then transfer the vinegar and the soaked ingredients to a blender jar, and add the coconut and ¼ cup water. Puree, scraping the inside of the jar as needed, to form a smooth, red-speckled paste.

3. Heat the oil in a large skillet over medium-high heat. Add the shrimp, arranging them in a single layer. Sear on each side to seal in the flavors, about 1 minute per side. Then add the coconut-garlic sauce and the salt. Stir once or twice, lower the heat to medium, and sim-

mer, uncovered, stirring occasionally, until the shrimp are salmon-orange, curled, and tender, 3 to 5 minutes.

4. Sprinkle with the cilantro, and serve.

Note: To reconstitute coconut, cover with ¼ cup boiling water, set aside for about 15 minutes, and then drain.

Priyanka's Shrimp
WITH A
SWEET ONION SAUCE

kolumbi Shanaupkari

I have always loved the name Priyanka, which means "pretty," and hoped to call a baby girl (if I ever had one, which I never did) by that name. So when I got a cat, I named him Priyanka (of course he never knew he strutted around all ten years of his life with a girl's name).

Years later, I met a stunningly beautiful woman, Leela Rao, at a mutual friend's house. She had started a chocolate business, Raga ("Tune") Chocolates, where she hand-made bite-size, truffle-shaped desserts of Indian origin with the help of her equally stunning young daughter, Priyanka. That mother-daughter bond was cruelly cut short by leukemia, which took eight-year-old Priyanka to a place where she no longer had to endure the pain and suffering caused by the disease. Leela said this curry brought her pretty Priyanka much pleasure, even during her down-and-out days. Savor it in her memory. **SERVES 4**

4 dried guajillo chiles, stems removed (see Tip, page 686)

¼ cup shredded fresh coconut; or 2 tablespoons shredded dried unsweetened coconut, reconstituted (see Note)

1 tablespoon coriander seeds

1 teaspoon tamarind paste or concentrate

4 medium-size cloves garlic

2 tablespoons canola oil

1 large red onion, cut in half lengthwise and thinly sliced

1 pound large shrimp (16 to 20 per pound), peeled and deveined but tails left on

1 teaspoon coarse kosher or sea salt

2 tablespoons finely chopped fresh cilantro leaves and tender stems

1. Heat a large skillet over medium-high heat. Add the chiles and toast them, shaking the pan frequently and turning them over occasionally so that all sides turn a darker shade of red, 3 to 5 minutes. Transfer the chiles to a blender jar and pour in ½ cup water. Add the coconut, coriander seeds, tamarind paste, and garlic. Puree, scraping the inside of the jar as needed, to make a thick, reddish-brown paste, packed with gusto.

2. Heat the oil in the same skillet over medium heat. Add the onion, cover the skillet, and cook, stirring occasionally, until the onion softens and turns caramel-brown with a deep purple hue, 15 to 20 minutes.

3. Add the paste to the skillet, and then add the shrimp and salt. Stir once or twice. Cover the skillet and cook, stirring occasionally, until the shrimp are salmon-orange, curled, and tender, 3 to 5 minutes.

4. Sprinkle with the cilantro, and serve.

Note: To reconstitute coconut, cover with 2 tablespoons boiling water, set aside for about 15 minutes, and then drain.

Bottle Gourd Squash
WITH SHRIMP AND CHILES

Lau Chingri Maach

bengali cooks are masters at vegetable-seafood combinations, and they are privy to an abundance of fish and shellfish off the coast of the Bay of Bengal. The original version of this curry has no dairy in it, but I love the tart hint of yogurt, added after the shrimp and squash are cooked, that rounds out the flavors. **SERVES 6**

1 pound large shrimp (16 to 20 per pound), peeled and deveined but tails left on

1½ teaspoons coarse kosher or sea salt

¼ teaspoon ground turmeric

1½ pounds bottle gourd squash or yellow squash

3 tablespoons mustard oil or canola oil

½ teaspoon cumin seeds

½ teaspoon fennel seeds

½ teaspoon fenugreek seeds

4 dried red Thai or cayenne chiles, stems removed

¼ cup plain yogurt, whisked (optional)

2 tablespoons finely chopped fresh cilantro leaves and tender stems for garnishing

1. Place the shrimp in a medium-size bowl. Sprinkle 1 teaspoon of the salt and the turmeric over them, and toss to mix. Refrigerate, covered, for about 30 minutes.

2. Cut off and discard the stem and heel ends from the squash. Peel the squash with a vegetable peeler, and then cut it in half lengthwise. Scoop out the seeds and the surrounding spongy mass with a spoon or a melon baller, creating a firm-fleshed, pale green, squash "boat." Cut the squash into ½-inch pieces. If using yellow squash, trim the ends and out it into ½-inch pieces (no need to peel or scoop out the seeds).

3. Heat 2 tablespoons of the oil in a large skillet over medium-high heat. Add the shrimp, arranging them in a single layer, and sear for 1 minute on each side. Transfer the shrimp to a plate.

4. Add the remaining 1 tablespoon oil to the same skillet, and heat it over medium-high heat. Sprinkle the cumin seeds, fennel seeds, fenugreek seeds, and chiles into the hot oil and cook until they sizzle and are aromatic, 5 to 10 seconds. Immediately add the squash and the remaining ½ teaspoon salt. Stir-fry until the squash is partially tender, 1 to 2 minutes.

5. Pour in ½ cup water, stir once or twice, and cover the skillet. Cook over medium-low heat, stirring occasionally, until the squash is fork-tender, 5 to 8 minutes.

6. Add the shrimp to the skillet (including any liquid that pooled in the plate) and cook, uncovered, stirring occasionally, until the shrimp are salmon-orange, curled, and tender, 3 to 5 minutes.

7. Fold in the yogurt (if you are using it) and let it warm, about 30 seconds. Sprinkle with the cilantro, and serve.

Fenugreek leaves? See the Glossary of Ingredients, page 758.

Shrimp
WITH BELL PEPPERS, FENUGREEK, AND SCALLIONS

Methiwaale Jhinga

Scallions make their presence known in many of Bengal's curries and provide pungent, crispy crunch in every mouthful. Their succulence matches the shrimp's, against the cinnamon backdrop of the garam masala. Serve this with the slightly starchy *Govindo bhog* rice (page 708), another of Bengal's prized commodities. **SERVES 6**

1 pound large shrimp (16 to 20 per pound), peeled and deveined but tails left on
½ teaspoon ground turmeric
4 tablespoons canola oil
2 medium-size green bell peppers (1 pound), stemmed, seeded, and cut into 1-inch pieces
1 cup shredded fresh coconut; or ½ cup shredded dried unsweetened coconut, reconstituted (see Note)
½ cup chopped fresh or frozen fenugreek leaves (thawed if frozen)
1 teaspoon coarse kosher or sea salt
½ teaspoon cayenne (ground red pepper)
½ teaspoon Bangala garam masala (page 26)
8 ounces scallions (green tops and white bulbs), finely chopped

1. Place the shrimp in a bowl, sprinkle the turmeric over them, and toss to coat them with the spice. Refrigerate, covered, for at least 30 minutes or as long as overnight (there is nothing acidic in the rub, so the shrimp won't break down if marinated overnight).

2. Heat 2 tablespoons of the oil in a large skillet over medium-high heat. Add the shrimp, arranging them in a single layer, and sear for about 30 seconds on each side. Slide them onto a plate.

3. Pour the remaining 2 tablespoons oil into the same skillet and heat it over medium-high heat. Add the bell peppers and stir-fry until they sear, blister, and acquire brown patches, 5 to 8 minutes.

4. Stir in the coconut, fenugreek leaves, salt, and cayenne. Allow the mixture to warm through. Then add 1 cup water, stir in the garam masala, and bring the curry to a boil. Simmer, uncovered, stirring occasionally, to allow the flavors to blend, 2 to 4 minutes.

5. Stir in the shrimp. Continue to simmer, uncovered, stirring occasionally, until the sauce thickens and the shrimp curl and turn salmon-orange in color, 5 to 8 minutes. Toss in the scallions, and serve.

Note: To reconstitute coconut, cover with ½ cup boiling water, set aside for about 15 minutes, and then drain.

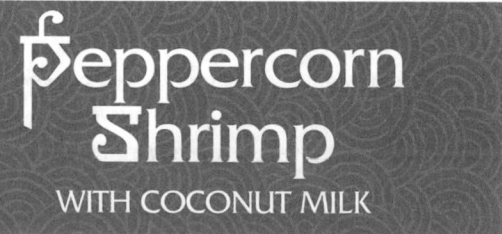

Peppercorn Shrimp
WITH COCONUT MILK

ffolaghu jhinga

1 remember getting a Tamil lesson from my sister, who insists that I speak my mother tongue with a heavy American accent (true). The object of her dissertation was to clarify the difference between *molagha* and *molaghu,* the former meaning chiles, the latter peppercorns. To this day I have to pause before I use the correct word, for fear of that lesson resurfacing. Whatever words I have misused in the past, I can vouch for the fact that the quantity of potent black peppercorns in this curry can seem mild when doused by rich, creamy, smooth coconut milk. **SERVES 4**

½ teaspoon ground turmeric
6 medium-size cloves garlic, finely chopped
1 pound large shrimp (16 to 20 per pound),
    peeled and deveined but tails left on
2 tablespoons coconut oil or canola oil
1 teaspoon black or yellow mustard seeds
1 can (13.5 ounces) unsweetened coconut milk
¼ cup coarsely chopped fresh curry leaves
2 teaspoons black peppercorns, coarsely cracked
1½ teaspoons coarse kosher or sea salt

1. Combine the turmeric and garlic in a bowl, add the shrimp, and toss to coat. Refrigerate, covered, for at least 30 minutes or as long as overnight (there is nothing acidic in the rub, so the shellfish will not break down if marinated overnight).

2. Heat the oil in a large skillet over medium-high heat. Add the mustard seeds, cover, and cook until the seeds have stopped popping (not unlike popcorn), about 30 seconds. Immediately add the shrimp, arranging them in a single layer, and sear them for about 30 seconds on each side.

3. Pour in the coconut milk, and add the curry leaves, peppercorns, and salt. Bring the curry to a boil and continue to cook, uncovered, stirring occasionally, until the shrimp curl and turn salmon-orange in color, 3 to 5 minutes. Using a slotted spoon, transfer the shrimp to a serving platter, and keep warm.

4. Continue to cook the sauce until it has thickened, 2 to 4 minutes. Spoon the sauce over the shrimp, and serve.

Coconut Shrimp
WITH MUSTARD GREENS

Narkol Chingri Maach

I have seen this curry prepared with baby shrimp at my friend Mithu's house. They were succulent, but I felt they got lost in the robust mustard greens. The larger prawns not only hold their own flavor, but they also look gorgeous against the backdrop of olive-green leaves and ruby red tomato. Each bite reminds me that bitter-tasting mustard greens cooked in harsh mustard oil can still taste sweet in the presence of a hint of sugar and some licorice-tasting fennel (in the *Panch phoron*). **SERVES 6**

2 tablespoons mustard oil or canola oil
1 tablespoon Panch phoron (page 36)
4 dried red Thai or cayenne chiles, stems removed
8 ounces fresh mustard greens, rinsed and finely chopped (do not pat dry; see Tip, page 606)
2 tablespoons Garlic Paste (page 15)
1 large tomato, cored and finely chopped
1½ teaspoons coarse kosher or sea salt
1 teaspoon white granulated sugar
½ teaspoon ground turmeric
½ teaspoon Bangala garam masala (page 26; see Tips)
1 pound large shrimp (16 to 20 per pound), peeled and deveined but tails left on
½ cup shredded fresh coconut; or ¼ cup shredded dried unsweetened coconut, reconstituted (see Note)

1. Heat the oil in a large skillet over medium-high heat. Sprinkle in the *Panch phoron* and cook until the spices sizzle and are aromatic, 10 to 15 seconds. Toss in the chiles and cook until they blacken and smell pungent, 5 to 10 seconds.

2. Pile the mustard greens into the skillet. Add the Garlic Paste. Stir-fry until any moisture clinging to the greens, as well as the water from the Garlic Paste, evaporates and some of the mixture starts to brown on the bottom of the skillet, 8 to 10 minutes.

3. Add the tomato, salt, sugar, turmeric, and garam masala. Cook, stirring occasionally, until the tomato has softened, 2 to 3 minutes.

4. Stir in the shrimp and ¼ cup water, and bring to a boil. Then lower the heat to medium and simmer, uncovered, stirring occasionally, until the shrimp are slightly curled and salmon-orange in color, about 5 minutes.

5. Stir in the coconut, and serve.

Note: To reconstitute coconut, cover with ¼ cup boiling water, set aside for about 15 minutes, and then drain.

Tips:

❖ Mustard greens are available year-round in supermarkets. If you can't find them, use either collard greens or kale for an equally iron-rich alternative with comparable bitterness.

❖ I have tried this curry both ways, with fresh coconut and the reconstituted dried kind. Even though they are both good, fresh coconut adds that extra juicy sweetness that's hard to replicate in its other forms. I could have insisted on the fresh, but I don't want to discourage you from making this curry if dried coconut is all that's on hand.

❖ If you do not have some *Bangala garam masala* on hand, use a store-bought garam masala (or any other kind left over from one of the recipes in this book) as an alternative.

Pan-Seared Shrimp
WITH A
SPICY-HOT CHILE VINEGAR PASTE

jhinga balchao

ishes with a vinegar-based acidic aggressiveness are called *balchaos* and have that slap-your-face feel. But it hurts so good, and it is no wonder you fall in love with its sadistic nature. Serve this curry not with rice, but with Portuguese Goa's other national gift: fluffy squares of warm, fresh-baked yeast buns called *pao*. (If you don't happen to have a Portuguese bakery nearby, try White Castle. Their hamburger buns are a close match!) **SERVES 4**

1 pound large shrimp (16 to 20 per pound),
    peeled and deveined but tails left on
2 tablespoons Balchao masala (page 17)
4 tablespoons canola oil
1 small red onion, cut in half lengthwise and
    thinly sliced
8 to 10 medium-size to large fresh curry leaves
2 tablespoons tomato paste
1 teaspoon coarse kosher or sea salt

1. Toss the shrimp with the *Balchao masala* in a medium-size bowl. Refrigerate, covered, for 30 minutes to 2 hours, to allow the acidic flavor and pungent heat to soak into the shellfish.

2. Heat 2 tablespoons of the oil in a medium-size skillet over medium-high heat. Add the shrimp (the paste is quite thick, so there will not be any marinade left in the bowl) in a single layer and sear the underside, about 1 minute. Turn the shrimp over quickly and sear the other side, 30 seconds to 1 minute. Slide them onto a plate.

3. Heat the remaining 2 tablespoons oil in the same skillet over medium heat. Add the onion and curry leaves, and cook slowly, stirring occasionally, until the onion softens and acquires a caramel color with a deep purple hue, 10 to 12 minutes.

4. Stir in the tomato paste and salt to make a thick, chunky sauce. Add the shrimp, stir once or twice, and cover the skillet. Cook, stirring occasionally, until the shrimp are salmon-orange, curled, and tender, 3 to 5 minutes. Then serve.

Seared Shrimp
WITH A PEARL ONION SAUCE

jhinga Chinnay Vengayam

Rice flour plays a crucial role here, thickening the tamarind-based sauce that forms a velvety-smooth sheen on each succulent shrimp. Serve the curry with Fragrant Basmati Rice with Curry Leaves (page 715) for a simply great meal. **SERVES 4**

I pound large shrimp (16 to 20 per pound),
   peeled and deveined but tails left on (see Tip)

I tablespoon rice flour

½ teaspoon ground turmeric

3 tablespoons coconut oil or canola oil

I teaspoon black or yellow mustard seeds

4 ounces pearl onions, peeled and cut into quarters

6 to 8 medium-size to large fresh curry leaves

2 dried red Thai or cayenne chiles, stems removed

½ teaspoon tamarind paste or concentrate

I teaspoon coarse kosher or sea salt

1. Place the shrimp in a bowl, sprinkle the rice flour and turmeric over them, and toss to coat the shrimp.

2. Heat 2 tablespoons of the oil in a large skillet over medium-high heat. Add the shrimp, arranging them in a single layer. Sear on each side to seal in the flavors and slightly cook the shellfish, about 30 seconds per side. Remove them from the skillet.

3. Drizzle in the remaining 1 tablespoon oil, and reheat the pan over medium-high heat. Add the mustard seeds, cover, and cook until the seeds have stopped popping (not unlike popcorn), about 30 seconds. Immediately add the onions, curry leaves, and chiles. Stir-fry until the onions turn light brown, 1 to 2 minutes.

4. While the onions are browning, quickly whisk the tamarind paste with 1 cup water in a small bowl.

5. Pour the chocolate-brown liquid into the skillet and scrape the bottom to deglaze it, releasing any browned bits of spice. The liquid will immediately come to a boil.

6. Add the shrimp and the salt, and continue to cook the curry, which will quickly start to thicken because of the rice flour that blankets the shrimp, uncovered, until the shrimp start to curl and turn salmon-orange in color, 2 to 3 minutes. Then serve.

Tip: Make sure you pat the shrimp completely dry between paper towels to absorb all the moisture that lingers after being thawed (if frozen) or cleaned. This provides for an even dusting when the shrimp are tossed with the rice flour. If not, clumps of the flour will stick unevenly to the shellfish, yielding a not-so-memorable sauce.

Sesame Shrimp
WITH BELL PEPPERS
IN A TAMARIND SAUCE

jhinga ka Salan

Cooks from Hyderabad, in south central India, balance the northern Indian Moghalai way of browning onions, garlic, and ginger with southern India's reliance on curry leaves, chiles, and tamarind. The result is nothing short of scrumptious and proves that north and south can coexist harmoniously—not only in food, but also in culture. **SERVES 6**

2 tablespoons white sesame seeds

2 teaspoons cumin seeds

25 medium-size to large fresh curry leaves

2 or 3 fresh green Thai, cayenne, or serrano chiles,
*   to taste, stems removed*

1 teaspoon tamarind paste or concentrate (see Tip)

1½ teaspoons coarse kosher or sea salt

2 tablespoons unrefined sesame oil or canola oil

1 medium-size green bell pepper, stemmed, seeded,
*   and cut into ½-inch pieces*

1 small red onion, cut in half lengthwise
*   and thinly sliced*

1¼ pounds large shrimp (16 to 20 per pound),
*   peeled and deveined but tails left on*

2 tablespoons finely chopped fresh cilantro
*   leaves and tender stems for garnishing*

1. Heat a medium-size skillet over medium-high heat. Add the sesame and cumin seeds and toast them, shaking the pan every few seconds, until they are reddish brown and nutty-smelling, about 1 minute. Slide the seeds into a small bowl.

2. Toast the curry leaves and chiles in the same skillet, shaking the skillet every few seconds, until the chiles blister and the curry leaves appear dry and crinkly, 2 to 3 minutes. Add them to the toasted seeds.

3. In a small bowl, dissolve the tamarind paste in ¼ cup water. Pour this into a blender jar, and add the toasted spice mixture. Puree, scraping the inside of the jar as needed, to make a thin, green-speckled blend containing bruised sesame seeds. (Because the amount of liquid and spice is low, the

blender will not puree it to a smooth consistency.) Pour the tamarind blend back into the same small bowl. Pour ¼ cup water into the blender jar and swish it around to wash it out. Add this to the blend. Stir in the salt.

4. Heat the oil in the same skillet over medium heat. Add the bell pepper and onion, and cook, uncovered, stirring frequently, until they are honey-brown and fork-tender, 8 to 10 minutes.

5. Raise the heat to medium-high and add the shrimp, arranging them in a single layer. Sear the shrimp evenly on both sides, about 30 seconds per side. Pour in the tamarind blend and heat the curry, uncovered, stirring occasionally, until the dark brown sauce thickens and the shrimp are salmon-orange, curled, and tender, 3 to 5 minutes.

6. Sprinkle with the cilantro, and serve.

Tip: Tamarind provides complex sourness to a curry. Sharp, acidic, and murky brown, this bean-pod-like tropical fruit is widely used in many regions of India. You can use not-so-multifaceted lime or lemon juice as an alternative, should you have the urge to whip up this simple curry at a moment's notice.

Garlic Shrimp
WITH UNRIPE MANGO

jhinga maangai kari

in this recipe the curry's base (the chile-spiked onion-garlic paste) is cooked initially to evaporate its liquid and then roasted in the oil to create a nutty-hot flavor. The tart mango cuts down the chiles' pungency and makes the curry downright tasty. Serve this with Fragrant Basmati Rice with Curry Leaves (page 715) for a winning combination. **SERVES 4**

> 1 small red onion, coarsely chopped
>
> 4 large cloves garlic
>
> 2 dried red Thai or cayenne chiles,
>   stems removed
>
> 1 teaspoon coarse kosher or sea salt
>
> ½ teaspoon fenugreek seeds, ground
>
> ½ teaspoon black or yellow mustard seeds,
>   ground
>
> ¼ teaspoon ground turmeric
>
> 2 tablespoons canola oil
>
> 1 large, rock-firm unripe mango, peeled, seeded,
>   and finely chopped
>
> 1 pound large shrimp (16 to 20 per pound),
>   peeled and deveined but tails left on
>
> 2 tablespoons finely chopped fresh cilantro leaves
>   and tender stems

1. Combine the onion, garlic, and chiles in a food processor, and process until minced. Pour in ½ cup water and pulse once or twice to turn the mixture into a chunky paste. Transfer the pungent paste to a small bowl and fold in the salt, fenugreek, mustard, and turmeric.

2. Heat the oil in a large skillet over medium-high heat. Add the onion paste and cook, stirring occasionally, until the liquid from the paste evaporates and a bit of spiced oil starts to form on the surface of the sauce and around the edges, 5 to 7 minutes.

3. Add the mango and stir to coat it with the paste. Pour in 1 cup water and scrape the bottom of the skillet to deglaze it, releasing any browned bits of paste.

4. Add the shrimp and stir once or twice. Cook, uncovered, stirring occasionally, until they curl and turn salmon-orange in color, 3 to 5 minutes. Using a slotted spoon, transfer the shrimp to a serving platter. Keep warm.

5. Continue to cook the sauce, uncovered, until it has thickened, 3 to 5 minutes. Stir in the cilantro, spoon the sauce over the shrimp, and serve.

Tip: Sea scallops make a great substitution for shrimp and take the same amount of time to cook. If you wish to impress someone or just to splurge, use a combination of the two for a special-occasion meal.

Easy Minty Shrimp
WITH PEAS AND COCONUT

jhinga mutter

A Maharashtrian-influenced curry, this is incredibly delicious if you use blue-gray tiger prawns, available in the seafood aisle of many large supermarkets. In my opinion, they are far more succulent than the more common farm-raised shrimp. Serve it with the mashed potato curry *Limboo podi maas* (page 561) and the black cardamom–scented basmati rice *Kala elaichi pulao* (page 709) for an amazingly easy-to-make meal that will charm one and all at the dinner table. **SERVES 6**

1 pound large shrimp (16 to 20 per pound),
     peeled and deveined but tails left on

¼ teaspoon ground turmeric

½ teaspoon tamarind paste or concentrate

2 tablespoons canola oil

1 tablespoon white sesame seeds

6 large cloves garlic, finely chopped

2 to 4 fresh green Thai, cayenne, or serrano chiles,
     to taste, stems removed, finely chopped
     (do not remove the seeds)

1 cup frozen green peas (no need to thaw)

2 teaspoons coarse kosher or sea salt

½ cup shredded fresh coconut; or ¼ cup
     shredded dried unsweetened coconut,
     reconstituted (see Note)

¼ cup tightly packed fresh mint leaves,
     finely chopped

¼ cup fresh cilantro leaves and tender stems,
     finely chopped

1. Toss the shrimp with the turmeric in a medium-size bowl. Refrigerate, covered, for 15 to 30 minutes, to allow the shellfish to absorb the spice's flavor and color.

2. While the shrimp is marinating, whisk the tamarind paste into ½ cup water in a small bowl.

3. Heat the oil in a large skillet over medium-high heat. Add the sesame seeds, garlic, and chiles, and stir-fry until the seeds and garlic are browned, about 1 minute. Immediately pour in the tamarind water, which will come to a rapid boil on contact with the hot pan. Stir in the peas and salt. Cook, uncovered, stirring occasionally, to warm the peas, 1 to 2 minutes.

4. Add the shrimp and continue to simmer, uncovered, turning the shellfish occasionally, until they are salmon-orange and slightly curled, 3 to 4 minutes.

5. Fold in the coconut, mint, and cilantro, and serve.

Note: To reconstitute coconut, cover with ¼ cup boiling water, set aside for about 15 minutes, and then drain.

Shrimp
WITH CASHEW NUTS AND VINEGAR

jhinga Vindaloo

uick-cooking and great, this curry is it when you are pressed for time. In the time the shrimp is marinating, you can cook some long-grain or basmati rice and the equally expedient Mustard Greens with Sweet Corn (page 520). **SERVES 4**

¼ cup distilled white vinegar

1 tablespoon coriander seeds, ground

1 teaspoon cumin seeds, ground

1 teaspoon cayenne (ground red pepper)

1 teaspoon coarse kosher or sea salt

¼ teaspoon ground turmeric

10 raw cashew nuts, ground (see Tip)

1 pound large shrimp (16 to 20 per pound),
     peeled and deveined but tails left on

2 tablespoons canola oil

2 tablespoons finely chopped fresh cilantro
     leaves and tender stems for garnishing

1. Combine the vinegar, coriander, cumin, cayenne, salt, turmeric, and cashews in a small bowl, and stir to make a smooth, slightly thin paste. Pour this over the shrimp in a medium-size bowl, making sure you scrape in every spicy, acidic drop. Toss well to coat the shellfish with the marinade. Refrigerate, covered, for about 15 minutes.

2. Heat the oil in a medium-size skillet over medium-high heat. Add the shrimp, arranging them in a single layer and reserving the residual marinade in the bowl. Sear the shrimp on each side to seal in the flavors, about 1 minute per side. Pour in the residual marinade and stir once or twice. Lower the heat to medium and simmer the curry, uncovered, stirring occasionally, until the shrimp are salmon-orange, curled, and tender and the sauce is almost entirely absorbed, 3 to 5 minutes.

3. Sprinkle with the cilantro, and serve.

Tip: I grind the cashew nuts in a spice grinder. Oftentimes, a few small pieces refuse to cooperate. When that happens, I remove some of the packed cashew powder, especially around the blades, to free up more space for the remaining pieces to end up powdered.

Tamarind Shrimp
WITH COCONUT MILK

Puli Jhinga

this simple-to-make curry is complex-tasting and maintains the subtle flavors of the shrimp in a tart, creamy sauce. Savor it over Lime-Flavored Rice with Roasted Yellow Split Peas (page 717) for a quick but elegant meal that will impress your guests. **SERVES 4**

2 teaspoons Sambhar masala (page 33)
1½ teaspoons coarse kosher or sea salt
1 teaspoon tamarind paste or concentrate

1 pound large shrimp (16 to 20 per pound), peeled and deveined but tails left on
2 tablespoons coconut oil or canola oil
½ cup unsweetened coconut milk
12 medium-size to large fresh curry leaves

1. Combine the masala, salt, and tamarind paste in a medium-size bowl. Add the shrimp and toss them with the mixture. Refrigerate, covered, for 30 minutes to 2 hours. (Be careful not to over-marinate the shrimp, as the highly acidic tamarind will start to break down the shellfish, resulting in an unappealing, almost rubberlike texture.)

2. Heat the oil in a medium-size skillet over medium-high heat. Add the shrimp, arranging them in a single layer. There shouldn't be any residual marinade, but if there is some (usually if you used previously frozen shellfish), reserve it. Sear the shrimp on each side to seal in the flavors, 30 seconds to 1 minute per side.

3. Pour the coconut milk and any residual marinade over the shrimp, add the curry leaves, and stir once or twice. Cook the milk-brown curry, uncovered, stirring occasionally, until the shrimp are salmon-orange, curled, and tender, and the sauce is slightly thick, about 3 minutes. Then serve.

Shrimp
WITH A PEANUT-GARLIC SAUCE

Sengdana Lasoon Jhinga

you may feel that there are one too many chiles in this curry, but that fear will be dispelled when you taste the sauce—the creamy-smooth coconut milk alleviates the heat. This Maharashtrian curry loses even more of the capsaicin-generated heat when it is piled onto steamed white rice. **SERVES 4**

1 pound large shrimp (16 to 20 per pound),
    peeled and deveined but tails left on

¼ teaspoon ground turmeric

¼ cup raw peanuts (without the skin)

4 large cloves garlic

3 fresh red Thai or cayenne chiles, stems removed

2 tablespoons canola oil

1 cup unsweetened coconut milk

1½ teaspoons coarse kosher or sea salt

2 tablespoons finely chopped fresh cilantro
    leaves and tender stems for garnishing

1. Toss the shrimp with the turmeric in a medium-size bowl. Refrigerate, covered, for about 30 minutes, to allow the shellfish to absorb the spice's color.

2. While the shrimp is marinating, combine the peanuts, garlic, and chiles in a mortar and pound them with the pestle, occasionally scraping and mixing the chunky blend with a spatula to ensure an even, pea-like texture. (Alternatively, pile them all into a food processor and pulse until you get that same pea-textured blend.)

3. Heat the oil in a medium-size skillet over medium heat. Add the spicy peanut mixture and cook until the garlic is browned, 2 to 3 minutes.

4. Pour in the coconut milk, stir in the salt, and bring the curry to a boil. Cook, uncovered, for 1 to 2 minutes. Then add the shrimp and bring the sauce once again to a boil. Continue to simmer, uncovered, stirring occasionally, until the shrimp are salmon-orange, curled, and tender, 3 to 5 minutes.

5. Sprinkle with the cilantro, and serve.

Mustard Shrimp
WITH CAULIFLOWER

Sorshe diyea Phulkopir Chingri Maach

Here's a one-dish curry for a quick evening meal and it's great too! I served it with nutty-tasting boiled red rice (page 708) for something different from humdrum white rice. Notice the use of cornstarch as a thickening tool—it is rarely used in classic Indian cooking. It reveals the strong influence of the Chinese immigrants during their two hundred years in Calcutta. **SERVES 6**

1 pound large shrimp (16 to 20 per pound),
    peeled and deveined but tails left on

½ teaspoon ground turmeric

1 pound cauliflower, cut into 1-inch florets

2 tablespoons black or yellow mustard seeds,
    ground

2 tablespoons mustard oil or canola oil

1 teaspoon Panch phoron (page 36)

2 to 4 dried red Thai or cayenne chiles, to taste,
    stems removed

1 teaspoon cornstarch

¼ cup firmly packed fresh mint leaves,
    finely chopped

¼ cup firmly packed fresh cilantro leaves
    and tender stems, finely chopped

1½ teaspoons coarse kosher or sea salt

1. Toss the shrimp with the turmeric in a medium-size bowl. Refrigerate, covered, for about 30 minutes to allow the shellfish to absorb the spice's color.

2. While the shrimp is absorbing the yellow spice, fill a medium-size saucepan three-quarters full with water, and bring it to a boil over medium-high heat. Add the cauliflower, lower the heat to medium, and cover the pan. Boil until the florets are fork-tender, 8 to 10 minutes. Set aside 1 cup plus 2 tablespoons of the hot cooking water, and drain the cauliflower in a colander. Run cold water over it to stop the florets from continuing to cook.

3. Mix the ground mustard with the 2 tablespoons cauliflower water in a small bowl to make a thick paste.

4. Heat the oil in a large skillet over medium-high heat. Sprinkle in the *Panch phoron* and the chiles. Cook until they sizzle, are aromatic, and are slightly smoky-hot, 10 to 15 seconds. Stir in the pungent mustard paste and cook, uncovered, stirring frequently, to take the raw edge off the mustard, 1 to 2 minutes.

5. Add the shrimp and cook for about 1 minute. Pour in the 1 cup reserved cauliflower water, and add the cauliflower florets. Heat the thin curry to a boil and continue to cook, uncovered, stirring occasionally, until the shrimp are slightly curled and salmon-orange in color, 3 to 4 minutes.

6. While the shrimp are cooking, stir the cornstarch and 1 tablespoon cold water together in a small bowl.

7. As soon as the shrimp are cooked, stir in the dissolved cornstarch. This will almost instantly thicken the sauce, providing the right body for the curry.

8. Stir in the mint, cilantro, and salt, and serve.

Beginner Almond Shrimp
WITH TOMATOES

tamatar jhinga

When my students, especially those who approach spices with trepidation, ask me to show them a "really simple" curry, I put this together while they watch in total amazement at the minimalism of it all. Even the garam masala, one of the recipe's components, consists of only three spices. Once they whet their appetite this way, the students are often ready to graduate to the next level, much to my satisfaction. **SERVES 4**

2 tablespoons canola oil
¼ cup slivered blanched almonds, ground
4 medium-size cloves garlic, finely chopped
I large tomato, cored and finely chopped
½ teaspoon cayenne (ground red pepper)
I½ teaspoons coarse kosher or sea salt
I teaspoon white granulated sugar
½ teaspoon Bangala garam masala
  (page 26)
I pound large shrimp (16 to 20 per pound),
  peeled and deveined but tails left on
½ cup heavy (whipping) cream
2 tablespoons finely chopped fresh cilantro
  leaves and tender stems for garnishing

1. Heat the oil in a medium-size skillet over medium-high heat. Sprinkle in the almonds and garlic, and cook, stirring constantly, until the nuts brown, 1 to 3 minutes.

2. Stir in the tomato, cayenne, salt, sugar, and garam masala, scraping the skillet to make sure nothing sticks to the bottom. Cook, uncovered, stirring occasionally, until the tomato softens but is still firm-looking, 2 to 4 minutes.

3. Add the shrimp and pour in the cream, stirring once or twice. Lower the heat to medium, cover the skillet, and simmer, stirring occasionally, until the shrimp are salmon-orange, curled, and tender and the creamy-rich sauce is thick, 5 to 8 minutes.

4. Sprinkle with the cilantro, and serve.

Savory Garlic Shrimp
WITH CHILES, TAMARIND, AND SESAME SEEDS

teekhat til jhinga

Shrimp has a delicate flavor that should not be masked. A quick glance at the ingredients here might make you wonder if the chiles and garlic are overpowering. However, a mouthful of this curry will squelch that initial doubt. The acidic tamarind lowers the chiles' sharpness while the coconut naturally sweetens the base, to let you savor each plump, juicy, subtle, rich-tasting shrimp.

SERVES 4

1 pound large shrimp (16 to 20 per pound), peeled and deveined but tails left on
¼ teaspoon ground turmeric
6 medium-size cloves garlic, coarsely chopped
4 fresh red Thai, cayenne, or serrano chiles, stems removed, coarsely chopped
1 tablespoon white sesame seeds
¼ cup shredded fresh coconut; or 2 tablespoons shredded dried unsweetened coconut, reconstituted (see Note)
½ teaspoon tamarind paste or concentrate
2 tablespoons canola oil
1½ teaspoons coarse kosher or sea salt
2 tablespoons finely chopped fresh cilantro leaves and tender stems for garnishing

1. Toss the shrimp with the turmeric in a medium-size bowl. Refrigerate, covered, for 15 to 30 minutes, to allow the shellfish to absorb the spice's flavor and color.

2. While the shrimp is marinating, combine the garlic, chiles, and sesame seeds in a mortar. Using the pestle, pound the contents into a pulpy but gritty mass, scraping the paste from the bottom and folding it in to ensure an even mix. Pound in the coconut, using the same folding technique, to make a coarse paste.

3. Dissolve the tamarind paste in ½ cup water in a small bowl.

4. Heat the oil in a medium-size skillet over medium heat. Add the spicy coconut paste and stir-fry until the coconut and garlic are browned and the chiles are pungent, 1 to 2 minutes. Pour in the tamarind water and the salt. Scrape the bottom of the skillet to deglaze it, releasing any browned bits of coconut and garlic.

5. Add the shrimp and cook, uncovered, stirring occasionally, until the sauce has thickened slightly and the shrimp are salmon-orange, curled, and tender, 3 to 5 minutes.

6. Sprinkle with the cilantro, and serve.

Note: To reconstitute coconut, cover with 2 tablespoons boiling water, set aside for about 15 minutes, and then drain.

Fenugreek-Scented Coconut Shrimp

thenga jhinga

the nibs of fenugreek will pucker your mouth, but the next wave of sweet coconut and spicy-hot chiles mellows out the obtrusive spice to make way for a well-balanced curry. **SERVES 4**

I teaspoon tamarind paste or concentrate

I teaspoon coarse kosher or sea salt

¼ teaspoon ground turmeric

I pound large shrimp (16 to 20 per pound), peeled and deveined but tails left on

I cup shredded fresh coconut; or ½ cup shredded dried unsweetened coconut, reconstituted (see Note)

I teaspoon fenugreek seeds

I teaspoon cumin seeds

4 fresh green Thai, cayenne, or serrano chiles, stems removed

2 tablespoons coconut oil or canola oil

I teaspoon black or yellow mustard seeds

10 to 12 medium-size to large fresh curry leaves

1. Combine the tamarind paste, salt, and turmeric in a medium-size bowl. Add the shrimp and toss to combine. Refrigerate, covered, for 30 minutes to 2 hours, to allow the flavors to meld. (Do not marinate too much longer, because the highly acidic tamarind and salt will break down the shellfish and turn its texture unappealing and rubbery.)

2. Put the coconut, ½ cup water, the fenugreek and cumin seeds, and the chiles in a blender jar. Puree, scraping the inside of the jar as needed, to make a gritty, chile-speckled paste (the seeds will be bruised, not totally ground).

3. Heat the oil in a large skillet over medium-high heat. Add the mustard seeds, cover, and cook until the seeds have stopped popping (not unlike popcorn), about 30 seconds. Immediately add the shrimp, arranging them in a single layer, and sear them on each side for about 30 seconds. Transfer the shrimp to a plate.

4. Add the coconut paste and the curry leaves to the skillet, and bring to a boil. Add the shrimp and cook, uncovered, stirring occasionally, until they curl and turn salmon-orange in color, 3 to 5 minutes. Then serve.

Note: To reconstitute coconut, cover with ½ cup boiling water, set aside for about 15 minutes, and then drain.

Tip: Coconut oil has a much lower smoke point (the temperature at which oil starts to smoke) than vegetable oil. It has a strong aroma when heated, which will linger like a heavy cloud if the ventilation is inadequate. So do yourself a favor and open a window or turn the hood fan on high—or both.

Pan-Grilled Sea Scallops

Scallops Palak Bhajee

Whenever I see peanuts and spinach in a menu item, I order it. I just love the combination—and I know I'm not alone since I find myself in good company with the millions of Maharashtrians. Shrimp or any other firm-fleshed fish works well as an alternative in this curry. **SERVES 6**

> 1 pound large sea scallops (about 12 to 15 per pound)
> ½ teaspoon ground turmeric
> ½ cup unsalted dry-roasted peanuts
> 2 tablespoons canola oil
> 6 medium-size cloves garlic, finely chopped
> 1 pound baby spinach leaves, well rinsed
> 1 tablespoon Kolhapuri masala (page 32)
> 1 teaspoon coarse kosher or sea salt

1. Combine the scallops with the turmeric in a medium-size bowl. Refrigerate, covered, for 30 minutes or as long as overnight, to allow the flavor to permeate the thick muscle (since there is nothing acidic to break down the mollusk's texture, it's fine to marinate them overnight).

2. Pour the peanuts into the bowl of a food processor and pulse until they have the consistency of coarse breadcrumbs.

3. Heat the oil in a large skillet over medium heat. Add the scallops, marinade and all (there won't be much at the bottom of the bowl), arranging them in a single layer. Sear the scallops' two broad sides until light brown, 3 to 5 minutes per side. Transfer them to a plate.

4. Add the garlic to the same skillet and stir-fry until it is light brown, about 1 minute. Pile in the spinach leaves, cover the skillet, and cook until the spinach is wilted, 5 to 8 minutes. (As the steam rises from within, the leaves will sweat and release their liquid, which will deglaze the pan and build yet another layer of flavor.) Stir in the masala and salt.

5. Add the scallops (including any liquid pooled in the plate), and cover them with a blanket of the wilted greens. Cover and cook, without stirring, until the scallops are firm to the touch but not rubbery, 3 to 5 minutes.

6. Transfer the scallops to a serving platter. Add the peanuts to the spinach in the skillet, and stir to combine. Simmer, uncovered, stirring occasionally, to allow the nuts to absorb the excess liquid and thicken the sauce, 2 to 4 minutes.

7. Spoon the spinach-peanut mixture over the scallops, and serve.

When you realize that spinach was cultivated around the 4th century A.D. in Persia and later greened its way toward China and then Europe around the 11th century, the popularity of its mellow flavor, deep green color, and ease of cooking is clear. In India, especially in Punjab, villagers press pureed spinach greens onto the inner walls of their tandoor ovens to season them so the naans bake quickly and perfectly.

Jubilee Scallops
WITH ONIONS, BELL PEPPERS, AND TOMATO

Scallops Jalfrezie

A medley of red (actually purple) onion, green bell pepper, red tomato, and light brown seared scallops, this curry makes for a sexy-looking dish. Serve it over rice noodles, either store-bought or homemade (page 709), for a great combination. **SERVES 6**

1 pound large sea scallops
   (about 12 to 15 per pound; see Tips)
1 tablespoon Ginger Paste (page 15)
1 tablespoon Garlic Paste (page 15)
2 teaspoons Balti masala (page 31)
1½ teaspoons coarse kosher or sea salt
2 tablespoons canola oil
1 large red onion, cut into ½-inch cubes
1 medium-size green bell pepper, stemmed,
   seeded, and cut into ½-inch pieces
½ cup tomato sauce
1 medium-size tomato, cored and cut into
   ½-inch cubes
¼ cup finely chopped fresh cilantro leaves
   and tender stems

1. Combine the scallops, Ginger Paste, Garlic Paste, 1 teaspoon of the masala, and 1 teaspoon of the salt in a medium-size bowl. Toss to coat. Refrigerate, covered, for about 30 minutes or as long as overnight, to allow the flavors to mingle.

2. Heat the oil in a large skillet over medium heat. Add the scallops, marinade and all (there won't be much), arranging them in a single layer, and sear them on their two broad sides until light brown, 3 to 5 minutes. Transfer them to a plate.

3. Add the onion and bell pepper to the same skillet, and cook until the vegetables start to turn light brown around the edges, 5 to 8 minutes.

4. Add the tomato sauce and the remaining ½ teaspoon salt. Simmer, uncovered, stirring occasionally, until there is a light sheen of oil on the surface of the sauce, 2 to 4 minutes.

5. Add the seared scallops (including any liquid pooled on the plate), the tomato, the cilantro, and the remaining 1 teaspoon *balti masala*. Cover the skillet and simmer, basting the scallops with the sauce but not stirring too often, until the scallops are firm to the touch but not rubbery, 3 to 5 minutes. Then serve.

Tip: Scallops are the abductor muscle of the mollusk (the flesh that the bivalve uses to open and shut its shell), and range in color from ivory to orange to light pink. They usually come shucked (and you thought corn had the monopoly on that word), and are sold either fresh or individually quick-frozen. They vary in size, with sea scallops being larger than bay scallops and not as sweet as the latter. "Bay," "sea," "calico," "king," and "queen" are some of the varieties sold in supermarkets. Bay scallops are delicious raw, as you can savor their natural sweetness.

The shells, in bright brown and pastel colors, resemble unfurled Japanese fans and are sold in some stores as decorative pieces. Shrimp are a great alternative to scallops, and so are chunks of lobster meat (especially the tail), monkfish, and cod.

mussels
IN A COCONUT-CHILE SAUCE

thisri hooman

this specialty from the Konkani-speaking community of Hindu Goa, along India's west coast, could not be any easier to prepare. The delicate flavor of the mussels is enhanced by sweet coconut, and the chiles add a mellow pungency. Pass around hot steamed white rice so your guests can pour the delicious broth over it to savor every last drop. **SERVES 4**

5 pounds mussels, in the shells
1 cup shredded fresh coconut; or ½ cup
  shredded dried unsweetened coconut,
  reconstituted (see Note)
½ cup firmly packed fresh cilantro leaves
  and tender stems
1 teaspoon coarse kosher or sea salt
2 large cloves garlic
2 fresh green Thai, cayenne, or serrano chiles,
  stems removed

1. Pile the mussels into a large bowl. Quickly go through them and discard any broken or cracked shells. Scrub each mussel (although the ones available at any supermarket are actually quite clean) and remove the beards (2 or 3 strands dangling from one end of the shell—rather like a straggly goatee on a pubescent boy's chin). Tap the shell if it's slightly ajar. If it closes shut, the mussel is alive and usable. If it does not shut, discard it, since this means it is dead. Plunk the prepared mussels into a colander and give them a good rinse.

2. Pour 1 cup water into a blender and add the coconut, cilantro, salt, garlic, and chiles. Blend, scraping the inside of the jar as needed, to form a puree.

3. Bring 1 cup water to a boil in a large stockpot over high heat. Add the mussels and cover the pot. Cook, shaking the pot occasionally so they cook evenly, until they all open up to reveal plump, off-white meat, about 5 minutes. Discard any mussels that remain shut.

4. Add the pureed mixture to the stockpot and stir it into the mussel-flavored broth, which will now turn green. Ladle some of the broth over the mussels to baste them a bit as you cook, uncovered, until the broth has warmed up, 1 to 2 minutes.

5. Pour the mussels and broth into a large serving bowl, and serve.

Note: To reconstitute coconut, cover with ½ cup boiling water, set aside for about 15 minutes, and then drain.

Sri Lankan Crabs
WITH SPINACH & COCONUT MILK

kekada Curry

lmost every daughter thinks that her mother is the best cook in the world, and Piyumi Samaratunga is no exception. She reminisced with me about her childhood days in Colombo, Sri Lanka, and particularly about her mother's culinary prowess. This family favorite drew my attention for the way it showcased the delicacy of crabmeat in creamy-rich coconut milk.

Ladle it over the Sri Lankan pearl rice called *muttu* (page 721) for a truly divine experience. **SERVES 6**

8 live blue crabs, each 6 to 8 ounces (see Tip)

5 large cloves garlic

2 lengthwise slices fresh ginger (each 2 inches long,
    1 inch wide, and ⅛ inch thick)

1 teaspoon black peppercorns

1 teaspoon black or yellow mustard seeds

2 tablespoons canola oil

1 small red onion, finely chopped

1 tablespoon Untoasted Sri Lankan Curry Powder
    (page 40)

1 teaspoon cayenne (ground red pepper)

1 large tomato, cored and finely chopped

1½ teaspoons coarse kosher or sea salt

2 fresh green Thai, cayenne, or serrano chiles,
    stems removed, cut in half lengthwise
    (do not remove the seeds)

2 cinnamon sticks (each 3 inches long)

3 cups unsweetened coconut milk

1 pound baby spinach leaves, well rinsed

Juice of 1 medium-size lime

1. Bring a large pot of water to a rolling boil over medium-high heat. Drop the live crabs into the pot (yes, you can feel sorry for them, and yes, this is humane—so say many a fishmonger, cook, and seafood expert). Cover the pan and return the water to a boil. Allow it to boil for 30 seconds to 1 minute. Immediately drain the crabs (yes, they are now at peace) into a colander and run cold water over them to stop the cooking.

2. Separate as much of the meat as possible from each crab: Place a crab on its back (that's shell side down) and yank off the front claws. Crack them open, remove the meat, and set it aside in a bowl. Make sure you get the meat nuggets toward the head. Pull and tear off the flap (called the apron) on the underbelly and discard it. Now place the crab on its belly and remove the flap off the entire back; it should come off in a single piece. Discard the feathery gills inside the crab's shell (these are called "dead man's fingers"). Using a sharp knife, cut the crab's body in half lengthwise. Lift the meat out, discarding any bits of shell and cartilage. Add this to the meat from the front claws. Crack the remaining claws with a rolling pin (or the flat side of a heavy knife or cleaver) and pull out the meat, adding it to the pile in the bowl. Cut some of the bigger chunks into bite-size morsels.

3. Put the garlic, ginger, peppercorns, and mustard seeds in a mortar, and pound with the pestle to form a pulpy, gritty-feeling paste.

4. Heat the oil in a large saucepan over medium-high heat. Add the onion and stir-fry until it is light brown around the edges, 3 to 5 minutes. Sprinkle in the curry powder and the cayenne, stir, and cook for about 1 minute.

5. Stir in the tomato, salt, chiles, cinnamon sticks, and coconut milk. Once the milk comes to a boil, stir in the crabmeat. Lower the heat to medium, cover the pan, and simmer, stirring occasionally, until the crabmeat is just cooked and tender, 6 to 8 minutes.

6. Stir in half of the spinach and simmer, uncovered, stirring occasionally, until it wilts, 2 to 4 minutes. Repeat with the remaining spinach.

7. Stir in the lime juice, and serve immediately.

Tip: Live blue crabs are available (usually from June through October) in any supermarket that has a decent seafood department and in Southeast Asian stores. Most of our supply comes from the multitude of fisheries along the western Atlantic. If you don't want the hassle of dealing with live crabs, you can very easily procure uncooked crabmeat (already cut up) and use it in the recipe. Each live 6-ounce crab yields approximately 2 ounces of usable meat, so for this recipe you'll need 1 pound crabmeat.

Lobster Tails
WITH CRACKED BLACK PEPPER AND CINNAMON

Lobster Kari

Dealing with live lobsters can be messy and tedious (and some of us may squirm at the prospect of killing them). Fresh or frozen lobster tails, which contain a large chunk of the meat, are perfectly acceptable. In fact, they are gorgeous when served against the backdrop of creamy coconut milk studded with ginger slivers, coarsely cracked black peppercorns, and sweet-smelling cinnamon. The beauty of this curry (sauce) is that it never overshadows the delicate flavor of the lobster meat. I like to serve this with the steamed rice nests called Coconut-Dusted Rice Noodles (page 723). Steamed red rice or even basmati rice is fine as an alternative. **SERVES 4**

2 small fresh or frozen lobster tails
   (about 1 pound total; thawed if frozen)
2 tablespoons canola oil
1 cup finely chopped red onion
2 green or white cardamom pods
2 cinnamon sticks (each 3 inches long)
1 can (13.5 ounces) unsweetened coconut milk
1 teaspoon black peppercorns, coarsely cracked
1 teaspoon coarse kosher or sea salt
12 to 15 medium-size to large fresh curry leaves
2 lengthwise slices fresh ginger (each 1 inch long,
   1 inch wide, and ⅛ inch thick), cut into
   matchstick-thin strips (julienne)

1. Cut the lobster tails in half lengthwise, through the shell, using either kitchen shears or a cleaver. (The meat will remain in the shells as you poach them, making for an attractive presentation.)

2. Heat the oil in a large saucepan over medium-high heat. Add the onion, cardamom pods, and cinnamon sticks, and stir-fry until the onion is partially browned and smells aromatic, about 3 minutes.

3. Pour in the coconut milk and add the pepper, salt, curry leaves, and ginger. Stir once or twice to incorporate the flavors. Place the four lobster halves, meat side up, in a single layer in the pan. Anoint the tails with the creamy sauce. Reduce the heat to medium-low, cover the pan, and poach, basting the tails occasionally, until the meat is white and firm and the tails curl up slightly (akin to shrimp), 7 to 9 minutes.

4. Lift the tails onto a serving platter, and cover with plastic wrap or aluminum foil to keep warm. Raise the heat under the pan to medium-high and cook, uncovered, stirring occasionally, until the sauce has thickened, 1 to 2 minutes.

5. Pour the sauce over the lobster tails, and serve immediately.

paneer curries

he rest of the world may find it surprising that a country the size of India has only one cheese in its culinary repertoire—and it is not even the melting kind! Fresh, firm, and chewy (especially when pan-fried or deep-fried), not unlike a block of extra-firm tofu (yes, in fact, you may very well substitute tofu for the moments when you don't have

any *paneer* on hand), *paneer* is northern India's signature meat-analogue for its vegetarians, providing valuable proteins through a myriad of curries.

In India *paneer* is always made with either cow or buffalo milk. I have also splurged a bit and made a version of it with half-and-half to create Creamy Homemade Cheese (page 287). Whether it is crumbled (Crumbled Creamy Cheese with Scallions and Tomatoes, page 302), panfried (Cashew Cheese with a Bell Pepper Sauce, page 289), or grilled (Grilled

Cheese with a Cashew-Tomato Sauce, page 303), I have grown to love this *fromage*—although I admit I disliked it in my youthful days because its fried texture reminded me of meat, something I couldn't relate to, having grown up in my mother's vegetarian kitchen. Now, of course, I've seen the light!

Even though the flavors in all these *paneer* curries are typical of north Indian kitchens (that includes northeast and northwest), you will be amazed at how markedly different each one is.

Whole-Milk Cheese

doodh paneer

Whole-milk *paneer* is a common ingredient in every north Indian kitchen. People are a bit daunted by the idea of making their own cheese, but let me assure you—there is nothing easier than this. If you can boil milk on the stove, you can make *paneer*.

MAKES 1¼ POUNDS

1 gallon whole milk
¼ cup distilled white vinegar

1. Pour the milk into a large saucepan and bring it to a boil over medium-high heat, stirring frequently to prevent the milk from scorching. When it comes to a boil, stir in the vinegar. Remove the pan from the heat and set it aside until the cheese separates and leaves behind a pale green, thin, watery whey, 15 to 30 seconds.

2. Line a colander with a double layer of cheese-cloth or a clean dishcloth, making sure there is about 2 to 3 inches hanging over the rim of the colander. Place the colander in the sink, then pour the cheese and whey into the colander, and let it drain. Once the

fried paneer

To fry paneer, you have two options: one is deep-frying; the other is pan-frying (my preferred method).

To deep-fry paneer, cut the fresh cheese into 1-inch cubes (or any other size). Pour canola oil to a depth of 2 to 3 inches into a wok, Dutch oven, or medium-size saucepan. Heat the oil over medium heat until a candy or oil thermometer inserted into the oil (without touching the pan's bottom) registers 350°F. (An alternative way to see if the oil is at the right temperature for deep-frying is to gently flick a drop of water over it. If the pearl-like drop skitters across the surface, the oil is ready.) Line a plate or cookie sheet with three or four sheets of paper towels. Once the oil is ready, gently slide in the paneer cubes. Fry, turning them occasionally, until they are golden brown and crispy, 3 to 5 minutes. The oil will spatter because of some moisture in the cheese, so please be careful. Remove the fried paneer cubes with a slotted spoon, and allow them to drain on the paper towels.

To pan-fry the cubes, heat 1/4 cup canola oil in a large nonstick skillet over medium heat. Add the cubes in a single layer and cook, turning them occasionally, until all sides are honey-brown and crispy, 7 to 10 minutes. Transfer them to a paper-towel-lined plate to drain.

One and a quarter pounds of fresh paneer will yield about 3 cups fried cheese (1-inch cubes). To store fried paneer, place the cubes in a bowl of water and refrigerate for up to a week, changing the water daily. You can also freeze the cubes (without immersing them in water) in a freezer-safe self-seal bag for up to 2 months.

cheese is slightly cool to the touch, gather the edges of the cloth and fold them over to cover it.

3. Fill a heavy pot with water, and set it directly on top of the cloth-wrapped cheese in the colander. Set this aside until the cheese is firm, 3 to 5 hours. (The weight will press on the cheese and force out almost all of its moisture.)

4. Remove the weight and unwrap the firm, milky-white cheese. Wrap it in plastic wrap and refrigerate it for up to 1 week. (You can also freeze the cheese, sealed in a freezer-safe self-seal bag, for up to 2 months. Thaw the *paneer* in the refrigerator before using it.)

Tip: Even though I've showed you how simple it is to make *paneer*, I have to point out that there is an alternative: Many Indian grocery stores and mail-order sources will be more than happy to take your money in return for frozen *paneer*, either in block form or as fried cubes. Thaw them before use.

Creamy Homemade Cheese

Malai Paneer

A vital source of protein for many vegetarians, whole-milk *paneer* is fine for most recipes. However, in the thousands of samples I have tasted, I could always detect an ever-so-slight chalky aftertaste. So I embarked on a cheesy journey, searching for that perfectly smooth mouth-feel. I found it in this version using half-and-half. I think you will agree too, once you sample a piece. **MAKES 1 POUND**

2 quarts half-and-half
¼ cup distilled white vinegar

1. Pour the half-and-half into a medium-size saucepan and bring it to a boil over medium-high heat, stirring frequently to prevent the cream from scorching. Once it comes to a boil, stir in the vinegar. Remove the pan from the heat and set it aside until the cheese separates and leaves behind a pale green, thin, watery whey, 15 to 30 seconds.

2. Line a colander with a double layer of cheesecloth or a clean dishcloth, making sure there is about 2 to 3 inches hanging over the rim of the colander. Place the colander in the sink, then pour the cheese and whey into the colander, and let it drain. Once the cheese is slightly cool to the touch, gather the edges of the cloth and fold them over to cover it.

3. Fill a heavy pot with water, and set it directly on top of the cloth-wrapped cheese in the colander. Set this aside until the cheese is firm, 3 to 5 hours. (The weight will press on the cheese and force out almost all of its moisture.)

4. Remove the weight and unwrap the firm, milky-white cheese. Wrap it in plastic wrap and refrigerate it for up to 1 week. (You can also freeze the cheese, sealed in a freezer-safe self-seal bag, for up to 2 months. Thaw the *paneer* in the refrigerator before using it.)

Spiced Pan-Fried Paneer
WITH MINT

Masala Pudhina Paneer

Even though I have spiced the cheese here for an extra burst of flavor with each bite, you can use plain *paneer* if you already have some in your refrigerator or freezer (just start the recipe at Step 6). The sharp mint flavor shines through the creamy sauce, making it the perfect "dunkable" curry for wedges of naan (page 729) or even slices of French baguette. It is a rich curry, so a little goes a long way. **SERVES 6**

> 1 gallon whole milk
> ¼ cup distilled white vinegar
> ½ cup finely chopped fresh cilantro leaves
>   and tender stems
> 2 teaspoons Balti masala (page 31)
> 2½ teaspoons coarse kosher or sea salt
> 6 tablespoons canola oil
> 1 cup finely chopped red onion
> ¼ cup tomato paste
> ¼ cup firmly packed fresh mint leaves, finely
>   chopped
> 2 fresh green Thai, cayenne, or serrano chiles,
>   stems removed, thinly sliced crosswise
>   (do not remove the seeds)
> 1 cup half-and-half

1. Pour the milk into a large saucepan and bring it to a boil over medium-high heat, stirring frequently to prevent the milk from scorching. Once the milk comes to a boil, stir in the vinegar. Remove the pan from the heat and set it aside until the cheese separates and leaves behind a pale green, thin, watery whey, 15 to 30 seconds.

2. Line a colander with a double layer of cheesecloth or a clean dishcloth, making sure there are about 2 to 3 inches hanging over the rim of the colander. Place the colander in the sink, then pour the cheese and whey into the colander, and let it drain for about 5 minutes.

3. Add ¼ cup of the cilantro, the masala, and 1½ teaspoons of the salt to the crumbly cheese, making sure that you do a decent job of incorporating them into the cheese. Once the cheese is slightly cool to the touch, gather the edges of the cloth and fold them over to cover it.

4. Fill a heavy pot with water and set it directly on top the cloth-wrapped cheese in the colander. Set this aside until the cheese is firm, 3 to 5 hours. (The weight will press on the cheese and force out almost all of its moisture.)

5. Remove the weight and unwrap the now firm, spice-speckled cheese. (You can make the cheese up to 1 week ahead, swath it in plastic wrap, and refrigerate it. You can also freeze the block, sealed in a freezer-safe self-seal bag, for up to 2 months. Thaw the *paneer* in the refrigerator before use.) Cut the *paneer* into 1-inch cubes.

6. Line a plate with several layers of paper towels.

7. Heat 4 tablespoons of the oil in a large nonstick skillet over medium heat. Add the *paneer* cubes in a single layer and cook, turning them occasionally, until all sides are honey-brown and crispy, 7 to 10 minutes. Transfer them to the paper-towel-lined plate to drain.

8. Heat the remaining 2 tablespoons oil in a medium-

size saucepan over medium-high heat. Add the onion and stir-fry until it is light brown around the edges, 5 to 8 minutes.

9. Stir in the tomato paste, remaining ¼ cup cilantro, remaining 1 teaspoon salt, the mint, and chiles. Lower the heat to medium and simmer the thick paste, uncovered, stirring occasionally, until there is an oily sheen on the surface, 2 to 4 minutes.

10. Pour in 1 cup water, stirring to make a luscious red sauce. Add the *paneer* and stir once or twice. Reduce the heat to medium-low, cover the pan, and simmer, stirring occasionally and gently, until the cheese cubes soak up some of the sauce and soften, 8 to 10 minutes.

11. Pour in the half-and-half and stir once or twice. Raise the heat to medium and simmer the curry, uncovered, stirring occasionally, until the creamy red sauce thickens, 8 to 10 minutes. Then serve.

Tip: Any garam masala will work as an alternative for the *balti masala.*

Cashew Cheese
WITH A BELL PEPPER SAUCE

Simla Mirch Paneer

this beautiful, lush red sauce, with its natural sweetness and pungent-spicy undertones, offers an addictive backdrop to pan-fried *paneer*. And did I mention how embar-

rassingly easy it is? The ingredients speak for themselves. Serve the curry with either homemade or store-bought rotis (page 727) or with slices of hot buttered toast—an easier alternative. **SERVES 8**

¼ cup raw cashew nuts
2 large red bell peppers (1 pound), stemmed, seeded, and cut into 1-inch pieces
6 green or white cardamom pods
2 to 4 fresh green Thai, cayenne, or serrano chiles, to taste, stems removed, coarsely chopped (do not remove the seeds)
1½ teaspoons coarse kosher or sea salt
1 teaspoon cayenne (ground red pepper)
8 ounces Doodh paneer (page 286), cut into 1-inch cubes and fried (see box, page 286)
2 tablespoons finely chopped fresh cilantro leaves and tender stems for garnishing

1. Pour 2 cups water into a medium-size saucepan, and add the cashews, bell peppers, cardamom pods, and chiles. Bring to a boil over medium-high heat. Reduce the heat to medium-low, cover the pan, and cook, stirring occasionally, until the bell peppers are fork-tender, 20 to 25 minutes. Transfer half of the ingredients, including half of the cooking water, to a blender and puree until smooth. Pour this creamy blend into a bowl. Repeat with the remaining ingredients and cooking water. Return the first and second batches of puree to the saucepan. (If you have an immersion blender, you can puree the mixture right in the saucepan.)

2. Stir in the salt, cayenne, and *paneer.* Cover the pan and simmer over medium-low heat, stirring occasionally, until the *paneer* is warmed through, about 5 minutes.

3. Sprinkle with the cilantro, and serve.

Cabbage
WITH PAN-FRIED CHEESE AND TOMATO

bund gobhi paneer

Joel Wegener, a physician and an intuitive cook, along with his then wife, Jordan, their two daughters, Selana and Frances, and my friend Marty, stopped by to help me cook one night—and to sample the results. I served this curry in addition to Pan-Grilled Sea Scallops (page 280). Of course the scallops were a big hit, but this dish caught everyone's attention too, because the cabbage offers an interesting textural backdrop to the meaty but tender homemade cheese. The milky, creamy cheese also offset the heat in the sauce, and everyone was sad to see that there wasn't much left over for a third helping. **SERVES 6**

2 tablespoons canola oil

I teaspoon cumin seeds

2 fresh green Thai, cayenne, or serrano chiles,
    stems removed, cut in half lengthwise
    (do not remove the seeds)

I pound cabbage, cut into thin shreds
    (see Tip, page 468)

2 teaspoons Toasted Cumin-Coriander Blend
    (page 33)

2 teaspoons white granulated sugar

I teaspoon coarse kosher or sea salt

I teaspoon ground Deggi chiles (see box, this page);
    or ½ teaspoon cayenne (ground red pepper)
    mixed with ½ teaspoon sweet paprika

½ teaspoon ground turmeric

I medium-size tomato, cored and
    finely chopped

8 ounces Malai paneer or Doodh paneer
    (pages 287, 286), cut into I-inch cubes
    and pan-fried (see box, page 286)

¼ cup finely chopped fresh cilantro leaves
    and tender stems

1. Heat the oil in a medium-size saucepan over medium-high heat. Add the cumin seeds and fresh chiles, and cook until the cumin seeds sizzle, turn reddish brown, and smell nutty, and the chiles blister slightly, 15 to 30 seconds. Immediately pile in the cabbage, cumin-coriander blend, sugar, salt, ground chiles, and turmeric. Cook, uncovered, stirring occasionally, to allow the ground spices to cook and the cabbage to wilt, 3 to 5 minutes.

2. Stir in ½ cup water and the tomato, *paneer,* and cilantro. Lower the heat to medium and simmer, uncovered, stirring occasionally, until the cabbage is tender, the cheese is spongy-soft, and the tomato is soft but still firm-looking, 10 to 15 minutes. (The sauce will never thicken, as there is nothing among the ingredients to make that happen.) Then serve.

deggi chiles
❖ ❖ ❖

Ground "Deggi chiles" is a mixture of dried mild red chile varieties, prized for its deep red-orange color and gentle heat. Most of the red color comes from dried red capsicum (bell pepper) and Kashmiri chiles. It is available in boxes (100 grams) under the brand name "MDH," found in any Indian grocery store. As an alternative, I suggest a combination of cayenne (ground red pepper) and sweet paprika for a near color and taste match.

Chile-Hot Cheese
WITH CAULIFLOWER AND CILANTRO

Phool Gobhi Paneer

I love cauliflower—along with the rest of the cruciferous vegetables like broccoli, cabbage, and collard greens—not only because it contains elements thought to fight cancer, but also because it is downright tasty. Throw in protein-rich *paneer*, and you have the makings of a complete, nutritious, vegetarian-friendly curry. (I have been known to spread leftover curry between slices of toast for a scrumptious sandwich. Most of the sauce is absorbed during cooking, so this isn't as sloppy as it sounds.) **SERVES 6**

2 tablespoons canola oil

1 cup finely chopped red onion

1 pound cauliflower, cut into ½-inch florets

¼ teaspoon ground turmeric

1 cup finely chopped fresh cilantro leaves
and tender stems (see Tips)

4 fresh green Thai, cayenne, or serrano chiles,
stems removed, thinly sliced crosswise
(do not remove the seeds)

8 ounces Doodh paneer (page 286), cut into
1-inch cubes and fried (see box, page 286)

1 medium-size tomato, cored and finely chopped

1½ teaspoons coarse kosher or sea salt

½ teaspoon Punjabi garam masala (page 25)

1. Heat the oil in a medium-size skillet over medium-high heat. Add the onion and stir-fry until it is light brown around the edges, 2 to 3 minutes.

2. Add the cauliflower and turmeric, and stir-fry to cook the spice, about 1 minute. Then add ½ cup water, the cilantro, and the chiles. Heat the thin curry to a boil. Reduce the heat to medium-low, cover the skillet, and braise, stirring occasionally, until the cauliflower is fork-tender, 10 to 12 minutes.

3. Stir in the *paneer*, tomato, salt, and garam masala. Simmer, covered, stirring occasionally, until the cheese and tomato are warmed through, about 5 minutes. Then serve.

Tips:

❖ Indians devour red onions because that is what is available in the markets across the vast subcontinent—not yellow, white, Walla Walla, or Vidalia. Not to say you can't use any of these types, but do keep in mind that each variety will provide its own distinct flavor to this addictive curry and to any other.

❖ For the cilantro naysayer: don't fret. True, there is a large amount of the controversial herb in this dish, but because it is cooked, the resulting flavor is mellow and provides a hushed presence, very different from its sharp character in its uncooked form.

Chickpeas
WITH PAN-FRIED CHEESE

Chana Paneer

A protein powerhouse of a curry, this is great with a simple starch accompaniment—such as rice or slices of toast (usually my vice of choice at lunch). I love to cut the toast into sticks and dip them in the curry to soak up the spicy flavors. A bite of that along with a mouthful of *paneer* and chickpeas does the trick. The motivation to work after a lunch like that is quite low, even though the ingredients should be having the opposite effect. **SERVES 6**

> 2 tablespoons canola oil
> I teaspoon cumin seeds
> I cup finely chopped red onion
> I or 2 fresh green Thai, cayenne, or serrano chiles,
>   to taste, stems removed
> I large tomato, cored and finely chopped
> I½ teaspoons coarse kosher or sea salt
> I teaspoon balti masala (page 31)
> ½ teaspoon ground turmeric
> I cup cooked chickpeas (see Tip)
> 8 ounces Doodh paneer (page 286), cut into I-inch
>   cubes and pan-fried (see box, page 286)
> ¼ cup heavy (whipping) cream
> 2 tablespoons finely chopped fresh cilantro
>   leaves and tender stems for garnishing

1. Heat the oil in a medium-size saucepan over medium-high heat. Add the cumin seeds and cook until they sizzle, turn reddish brown, and smell fragrant, 5 to 10 seconds. Add the onion and chiles, and stir-fry until the onion is light brown around the edges, 2 to 3 minutes.

2. Stir in the tomato, salt, masala, and turmeric. Lower the heat to medium and cook, uncovered, stirring occasionally, until the tomato softens, about 3 minutes.

3. Add the chickpeas and 1 cup water. Bring the curry to a boil. Then reduce the heat to medium-low, cover the pan, and simmer, stirring occasionally, until the sauce has thickened slightly, about 10 minutes.

4. Fold in the *paneer* and the cream, and simmer, uncovered, stirring occasionally, until the cheese and cream are warmed through, 2 to 3 minutes.

5. Sprinkle with the cilantro, and serve.

Tip: If you are using canned chickpeas, make sure you drain them and then rinse them in a colander to remove the brine. I often make extra when I am cooking chickpeas in a pressure cooker, and then freeze them in 1-cup amounts in freezer-safe self-seal bags for up to 2 months. Not only are they tastier, they are also easier on your pocketbook.

Fenugreek-Scented Cheese
WITH CREAM

Methi Malai Paneer

Once you have fried *paneer* cubes on hand in your refrigerator or freezer, this curry is a cinch to make. (Extra-firm tofu, fried golden brown, provides the same crispy exterior and soft, protein-rich interior.) The crunchy almonds offer textural contrast to the cheese, while the tomato paste leaves a tart aftertaste. **SERVES 4**

> 2 tablespoons canola oil
> I teaspoon cumin seeds
> I tablespoon slivered blanched almonds
> I cup chopped fresh or frozen fenugreek leaves
>   (thawed if frozen); or 2 tablespoons dried
>   fenugreek leaves, soaked in a bowl of water
>   and skimmed off before use (see Tip, page 473)
> ½ cup heavy (whipping) cream
> 2 tablespoons tomato paste

1 teaspoon coarse kosher or sea salt

½ teaspoon Punjabi garam masala (page 25)

8 ounces Doodh paneer (page 286), cut into
1-inch cubes and fried (see box, page 286)

1. Heat the oil in a medium-size saucepan over medium-high heat. Add the cumin seeds and cook until they sizzle, turn reddish brown, and are aromatic, 5 to 10 seconds. Stir in the almonds and stir-fry until they are golden brown, 1 to 2 minutes.

2. Add the fenugreek leaves and the cream. Stir the tomato paste into the creamy green curry, adding an intense red to the color scheme. Sprinkle in the salt and garam masala.

3. Fold in the *paneer* and heat to a boil. Then reduce the heat to medium-low, cover the pan, and simmer the curry, stirring occasionally, until the *paneer* feels soft and spongy, 5 to 8 minutes. Then serve.

Cheese
IN A BUTTER-CREAM SAUCE WITH FENUGREEK

Paneer Makhani

If you recently had a heart attack, this is not the curry for you—sorry. With ingredients like cheese, butter, and heavy cream, no wonder each mouthful can expedite that angioplasty. So why is this curry addictive? Do not analyze, but just enjoy—albeit in small portions, because it is very filling. My favorite accompaniment to this curry is the saffron-perfumed basmati rice *Zarda chaawal* (page 716). **SERVES 6**

3 tablespoons unsalted butter

1 cup tomato sauce (see Tips)

½ cup fresh or frozen fenugreek leaves
(thawed if frozen); or ¼ cup dried
fenugreek leaves, soaked in a bowl
of water and skimmed off before use
(see box, page 473)

1 teaspoon cayenne (ground red pepper)

1 teaspoon white granulated sugar

½ teaspoon coarse kosher or sea salt

8 ounces Doodh paneer (page 286), cut into
1-inch cubes and fried (see box, page 286)

½ cup heavy (whipping) cream

1 teaspoon cumin seeds, toasted and ground
(see Tips)

1. Melt 2 tablespoons of the butter in a small saucepan over medium heat. As soon as the butter melts (make sure it does not brown), pour in the tomato sauce. Then stir in the fenugreek leaves, cayenne, sugar, and salt. Reduce the heat to medium-low, partially cover the pan, and simmer, stirring occasionally, until the butter starts to separate from the sauce, 12 to 15 minutes.

2. Fold in the *paneer*, cream, and cumin. Cover the pan and simmer, stirring occasionally but gently to make sure you do not break up the cheese cubes, until the cheese absorbs some of the rich flavors from the sauce, 6 to 8 minutes.

3. Add the remaining 1 tablespoon butter. Once it melts, fold it into the thick, creamy *paneer*, accentuating the *makhan* (butter) in the *paneer makhani*.

Tips:

❖ Canned tomato sauce is usually salted. Some organic brands are either not salted or contain reduced amounts of salt. If you are using one of those, you may want to add an additional ½ teaspoon salt to the recipe.

❖ Students often ask me whether they can use something other than heavy cream. Half-and-half works okay, but whole or low-fat milk does not. Vegans and those who are lactose-intolerant can use extra-firm tofu instead of the *paneer*, oil for the butter (not quite the same), and instead of the cream, a smooth puree of ½ cup raw cashew nuts or slivered almonds and ¼ to ½ cup water. You can rename the curry too, while you're at it.

❖ To toast cumin seeds, heat a small skillet over medium-high heat. Sprinkle in the seeds and toast them, shaking the pan more frequently than not, until the aromas emanating from the skillet are nutty and the seeds are reddish brown, about 1 minute. Transfer them to a plate to cool. Grind the cooled seeds in a spice grinder or in a mortar (because of the small quantity of seeds, the blades of the grinder might not do the best job) until the texture is similar to that of ground black pepper.

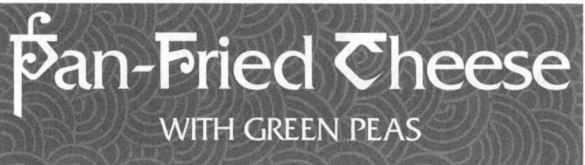

Pan-Fried Cheese
WITH GREEN PEAS

Mutter Paneer

S how me one north Indian restaurant menu, or any special-occasion meal from that region, that does not include *mutter paneer*, and I will personally come to your house and cook it for you. That's how confident I am that this pervasive curry will never stand me up. What's not to love about cream, cheese, onion, and garlic?

Throw in some perfumed spices, freshly ground, and you have yourself a winner, even if there are green peas in it. Trust me, your adventurous child will eat it and ask for seconds. I often serve this with store-bought (or restaurant take-out) naan and relive that restaurant experience at half the cost (plus, it's much tastier). **SERVES 6**

1 small red onion, coarsely chopped

3 lengthwise slices fresh ginger (each 1½ inches long, 1 inch wide, and ⅛ inch thick)

3 large cloves garlic

1 or 2 fresh green Thai, cayenne, or serrano chiles, to taste, stems removed

2 tablespoons canola oil

1 teaspoon cumin seeds

1 fresh or dried bay leaf

1 cup tomato sauce, canned or homemade (see page 18)

2 teaspoons Bin bhuna hua garam masala (page 30)

1 teaspoon coarse kosher or sea salt

1½ cups frozen peas (no need to thaw)

¼ cup heavy (whipping) cream

8 ounces Doodh paneer (page 286), cut into 1-inch cubes and pan-fried (see box, page 286)

2 tablespoons finely chopped fresh cilantro leaves and tender stems

1. Combine the onion, ginger, garlic, and chiles in a food processor, and pulse until they are minced.

2. Heat the oil in a medium-size saucepan over medium-high heat. Sprinkle in the cumin seeds and bay leaf, and cook until the cumin sizzles, turns reddish brown, and smells nutty, 5 to 10 seconds. Immediately add the minced onion blend and stir-fry until it is light reddish brown, 5 to 7 minutes.

3. Stir in the tomato sauce, garam masala, and salt.

The sauce will quickly start to bubble up and splatter, so lower the heat to medium. Simmer the sauce, partially covered, stirring occasionally, until some oil appears on the surface and around the edges, providing a glistening sheen, 5 to 10 minutes.

4. Pour in ¼ cup water and add the peas. Cover the pan and simmer, stirring occasionally, until the peas are tender and olive green in color, 8 to 10 minutes.

5. Fold in the cream, *paneer*, and cilantro. Cover the pan and simmer, occasionally stirring gently, until the cream and cheese have warmed through, about 5 minutes.

6. Remove the bay leaf, and serve.

Spinach and Mustard Greens
WITH CHEESE

Saag Paneer

I like to combine spinach and mustard greens in this classic Punjabi curry, the mellow and bitter-tasting greens providing a nice balance with the creamy, protein-rich cheese. (In many homes and almost all restaurants, this is made solely with spinach.) For the vegetarian at the table (who conforms to a lacto-friendly diet), this is a great main-course offering when coupled with one of the rice dishes in the Curry Cohorts chapter. **SERVES 6**

2 tablespoons canola oil

1 medium-size red onion, cut in half lengthwise and thinly sliced

6 medium-size cloves garlic, coarsely chopped

4 lengthwise slices fresh ginger (each 2 inches long, 1 inch wide, and ⅛ inch thick), coarsely chopped

2 teaspoons Bin bhuna hua garam masala (page 30)

½ teaspoon ground turmeric

2 tablespoons tomato paste

8 ounces fresh spinach leaves, well rinsed and coarsely chopped

8 ounces fresh mustard greens, well rinsed and finely chopped (see Tip, page 606)

1½ teaspoons coarse kosher or sea salt

1¼ pounds Doodh paneer (page 286), cut into 1-inch cubes and pan-fried (see box, page 286)

½ cup heavy (whipping) cream

½ teaspoon Punjabi garam masala (page 25)

1. Heat the oil in a large skillet over medium heat. Add the onion, garlic, and ginger, and stir-fry until the onion is light brown, 8 to 10 minutes. Remove the skillet from the heat, and stir in the *Bin bhuna hua garam masala* and the turmeric. (The heat from the browned onion will be just right to cook the spices without burning them.)

2. Transfer the mixture to a blender jar, and add the tomato paste and ¼ cup water. Puree, scraping the inside of the jar as needed, to form a smooth, reddish-brown paste. Return the paste to the skillet. Pour ¾ cup water into the blender jar, and whir the blades to wash it out. Add this to the skillet.

3. Place the skillet over medium heat. Pile handfuls of the greens into the skillet, cover it, and let the steam wilt them. Stir, and repeat with the remaining greens. Once they are all wilted, cover the skillet and cook, stirring occasionally, until the greens are broken down to a sauce-like consistency and are olive green in color, 10 to 15 minutes.

4. Stir in the salt, *paneer* cubes, cream, and *Punjabi garam masala*. Continue simmering the curry, covered, stirring occasionally, until the cheese and cream are warmed through, 5 to 8 minutes. Then serve.

Tip: You will notice that I use two garam masalas here in different ways. Initially, you add the untoasted blend early on, soon after the onion browns, to make sure the raw spices cook, providing the first spice layering. Then you swirl in the toasted garam masala toward the end, after the curry has cooked. This blend is a finishing spice (and does not need to cook since you toasted it before grinding it), yielding a second tier of flavors that are aromatic, smooth, and assertive. Both blends contain similar spices, but what you did with them at various stages creates a complex-tasting sauce.

Restaurant-Style Fried Cheese Cubes

WITH A SPINACH SAUCE

Palak Paneer

Restaurant-style *palak paneer* has a very smooth texture because the spinach leaves are pureed. I prefer to leave the spinach leaves whole, providing a better textural backdrop for the fried cubes of *paneer*. Serve this curry with either homemade rotis (page 727) or store-bought whole-wheat tortillas. **SERVES 6**

1 small red onion, coarsely chopped

4 lengthwise slices fresh ginger
(each 2 inches long, 1 inch wide,
and ⅛ inch thick)

2 tablespoons canola oil

1 teaspoon cumin seeds

½ teaspoon fennel seeds

2 dried red Thai or cayenne chiles, stems removed

1 tablespoon coriander seeds, ground

1½ teaspoons coarse kosher or sea salt

½ teaspoon cayenne (ground red pepper)

¼ teaspoon ground turmeric

1 large tomato, cored and finely chopped

1½ pounds fresh spinach leaves, well rinsed

1¼ pounds Doodh paneer (page 286), cut into
1-inch cubes and pan-fried (see box, page 286)

½ cup Thick Yogurt (page 22)

1. Combine the onion and ginger in a food processor, and pulse until minced.

2. Heat the oil in a large saucepan over medium-high heat. Sprinkle in the cumin seeds, fennel seeds, and chiles. Cook until they sizzle, turn reddish brown, and smell nutty-pungent, 10 to 15 seconds. Immediately add the minced blend and stir-fry until the onion is light brown around the edges, 5 to 7 minutes.

3. Stir in the coriander, salt, cayenne, and turmeric, and cook the spices without burning them (thanks to the cushioning from the onion medley), 10 to 15 seconds. Add the tomato and cook, uncovered, stirring occasionally, until it softens but is still chunky, about 3 minutes.

4. Add the spinach, in batches if it won't all fit, stirring until it is wilted, 4 to 6 minutes. Once all the spinach has wilted, the water it releases will deglaze the pan.

5. Stir in the *paneer,* cover the skillet, and simmer, stirring occasionally, until the cheese is warmed through, 2 to 3 minutes.

6. Remove the skillet from the heat and fold in the yogurt, which will look slightly curdled because the heat will break it down. Remove the chiles if you wish.

7. Serve immediately.

Tip: If you find a slightly curdled sauce unappealing, use ¼ cup heavy (whipping) cream instead of the yogurt. If you would rather maintain the yogurt's tartness, then stir 2 tablespoons heavy (whipping) cream into the yogurt. The fat stabilizes the yogurt, creating a smoother-looking sauce.

Cheese Tubes
WITH SPINACH AND MUSTARD SEEDS

Mathura Palak Paneer

What are the chances of two beautiful souls—one born in Chennai (formerly Madras), the other born in Queens, New York—meeting at an Indian professionals' conference in Chicago and uniting in wedded bliss within months of the encounter? No, it is not a hackneyed Bollywood movie plot, but a reality show starring my dear friend Balki Radhakrishnan and his bride, Swetal Sindhvad. When they met, one of the many things they found they had in common was a love of Indian food and cooking. The kitchen in their new home in a suburb of Minneapolis puffs out a distinctive mix of Tamilian spices (from Balki's southern childhood) mottled in cream (from Swetal's family roots in Gujarat, India's dairy capital). Balki named this succulent curry *Mathura palak paneer* because the dairy state is close to Krishna's birth land, Mathura. To round out your curry dinner, try the Mango Cardamom Cheesecake with a Pistachio Crust (page 751)—my gift to them and to you. **SERVES 4**

Mango powder? See the Glossary of Ingredients, page 758.

1 pound fresh spinach leaves, well rinsed
2 tablespoons canola oil
1 teaspoon black or yellow mustard seeds
1 small red onion, finely chopped
6 medium-size cloves garlic, finely chopped
½ teaspoon ground turmeric
½ teaspoon cayenne (ground red pepper)
1 teaspoon mango powder or fresh lime juice
1 teaspoon coarse kosher or sea salt
½ teaspoon Punjabi garam masala (page 25)
8 to 10 cherry or grape tomatoes, cut in half
8 ounces Doodh paneer (page 286), cut into
    1-inch cubes and pan-fried (see box, page 286)
½ cup half-and-half

1. Fill a medium-size saucepan halfway with water and bring it to a rolling boil over medium-high heat. A few handfuls at a time, stir the spinach leaves into the water and let them wilt. Repeat until all the leaves have wilted. Then drain them in a colander and run cold water through them to cool them (this will also shock the chlorophyll in the leaves, allowing them to retain their bright green color). Finely chop the spinach and put it in a bowl—and don't worry about the water that continues to pool at the bottom of the bowl.

2. Heat the oil in a small saucepan over medium heat. Add the mustard seeds, cover, and cook until the seeds have stopped popping (not unlike popcorn), about 30 seconds. Add the onion, garlic, turmeric, and cayenne. Cook, uncovered, stirring occasionally, until the onion

starts to soften and brown, 10 to 12 minutes. (The deep orange-yellow spices mask the color of the onion, but you will definitely sense its softness and smell the deep-roasted aroma emanating from the skillet.)

3. Stir in the spinach, including any of its green-tinted water, and the mango powder, salt, garam masala, and tomatoes. Simmer, uncovered, stirring occasionally, for about 5 minutes.

4. Fold in the *paneer* and simmer, uncovered, stirring occasionally, to let the cheese warm through, 1 to 2 minutes.

5. Stir in the half-and-half, cover the skillet, and simmer, stirring occasionally, until the cheese has softened and the sauce has thickened slightly, 8 to 10 minutes. Then serve.

Asafetida? See the Glossary of Ingredients, page 758.

Nutty Cheese
IN A
SPINACH–CHICKPEA FLOUR SAUCE

kutchi paneer

Mrs. Bikhalal Patel, whose family operates a successful grocery store and restaurant in Minneapolis, is a die-hard vegetarian and an extraordinary cook. Like so many women from Kutch, she breathes passion into many of the curries from her homeland, a tortoise-shaped district that spans much of the northwestern state of Gujarat. Their foods are simple, dairy-based, and rich with legumes and spices. An absence of onion, garlic, and even ginger in her dishes sheds light on Mrs. Patel's

Jain-based religious upbringing. A quick lunch of this curry, accompanied with handkerchief-thin *rotlis* (the thinner, fluffier Gujarati version of rotis), in her Minneapolis kitchen during a recent visit left a lasting impression. **SERVES 6**

2 tablespoons canola oil
1 teaspoon cumin seeds
2 teaspoons white granulated sugar
1½ teaspoons coarse kosher or sea salt
1 teaspoon cumin seeds, ground
1 teaspoon coriander seeds, ground
1 teaspoon cayenne (ground red pepper)
½ teaspoon ground turmeric
½ teaspoon ground asafetida
1 medium-size green bell pepper, stemmed, seeded, and cut into 1-inch pieces
1 large tomato, cored and finely chopped
8 ounces fresh spinach leaves, well rinsed and finely chopped
8 ounces Doodh paneer (page 286), cut into 1-inch cubes and pan-fried (see box, page 286)
2 tablespoons Toasted Chickpea Flour (page 41)

1. Heat the oil in a large saucepan over medium-high heat. Add the cumin seeds and cook until they turn reddish brown and are fragrant, 5 to 10 seconds. Remove the skillet from the heat and sprinkle in the sugar, salt, ground cumin, coriander, cayenne, turmeric, and asafetida. The spices will instantly sizzle and smell aromatic, the heat from the oil being just right to cook, but not burn, them.

2. Immediately add the bell pepper and tomato, and return the skillet to medium-high heat. Cook, uncovered, stirring, until the tomato softens slightly and the mixture looks sauce-like, about 2 minutes.

3. Pour 2 cups water into the skillet and bring to a boil. Pile in the spinach, stirring occasionally to wilt the

leaves. Reduce the heat to medium-low, cover the skillet, and cook, stirring occasionally, until the spinach is olive green and soft and the bell pepper is fork-tender, 12 to 15 minutes.

4. Stir in the fried *paneer* and cook, covered, stirring occasionally, until the cheese has softened, about 5 minutes.

5. Sprinkle in the flour, stirring it in quickly to prevent any lumps from forming in the sauce. Bring to a boil and cook, uncovered, stirring once or twice, until the sauce thickens slightly, 3 to 5 minutes. Then serve.

Tips:

✤ The fried *paneer* cubes provide essential proteins for the vegetarian diet, but if you don't have any, don't worry. Use extra-firm tofu, drained and pan-fried, as a perfectly acceptable alternative.

✤ You will be amazed at how much of a nutty taste you get by stirring in the toasted chickpea flour, which incidentally also provides smooth body to the spicy-sweet sauce.

Sweet-Tart Cheese
WITH POTATOES AND CAULIFLOWER IN A VINEGAR SAUCE

Sirka Paneer

You will find this to be an easy curry to make for a quick lunch, especially if you are entertaining a bunch of vegetarians. I have served it with slices of toasted French bread, perfect dunkers for the creamy, spicy-hot, sweet-tart sauce. The soft vegetables and chewy-but-tender *paneer* offered great contrasts to the soaked dunked toast, making for a successfully executed recipe and, more importantly, happy guests. **SERVES 8**

¼ *cup malt vinegar or cider vinegar*

¼ *cup tomato paste*

1 tablespoon coriander seeds

1 teaspoon cumin seeds

2 fresh green Thai, cayenne, or serrano chiles, stems removed

2 dried red Thai or cayenne chiles, stems removed

2 large cloves garlic

2 lengthwise slices fresh ginger (each 2 inches long, 1 inch wide, and ⅛ inch thick)

2 tablespoons canola oil

½ *cup finely chopped red onion*

2 cups cut-up cauliflower (1-inch florets)

2 medium-size russet or Yukon Gold potatoes, peeled, cut into 1-inch cubes, and submerged in a bowl of cold water to prevent browning

1 teaspoon coarse kosher or sea salt

1 cup unsweetened coconut milk

8 ounces Doodh paneer (page 286), cut into 1-inch cubes and fried (see box, page 286)

¼ *cup finely chopped fresh cilantro leaves and tender stems (see Tips)*

1. Pour ¼ cup water into a blender jar, and then add the vinegar, tomato paste, coriander seeds, cumin seeds, fresh and dried chiles, garlic, and ginger. Puree, scraping the inside of the jar as needed, to make a smooth, reddish-brown paste.

2. Heat the oil in a medium-size saucepan over medium-high heat. Add the onion and stir-fry until it is light brown around the edges, 3 to 5 minutes.

3. Add the paste to the pan and lower the heat to

medium. Cook the thick paste, uncovered, stirring frequently, until a thin oily sheen coats the surface and a thin film of paste forms on the bottom of the pan, 2 to 4 minutes.

4. While the paste is cooking, pour 1 cup water into the blender jar and whir the blades to wash it out.

5. When the paste has cooked, add the washings from the blender and scrape the bottom of the pan to release the collected film of paste.

6. Add the cauliflower, potatoes, and salt. Heat the curry to a boil. Then cover the pan and simmer, stirring occasionally, until the vegetables are almost tender, 15 to 20 minutes.

7. Pour in the coconut milk and stir in the *paneer*. Simmer, uncovered, stirring occasionally, until the sauce is thick and the vegetables are fork-tender, about 10 minutes.

8. Stir in the cilantro, and serve.

Tips:

❖ For a sweeter, more aromatic alternative, use ½ cup finely chopped fresh basil leaves instead of the cilantro.

❖ One day when I made this, I found myself scrambling for a can of coconut milk, which was nowhere to be found on my pantry shelf. Fortunately I happened to have bought powdered coconut milk, shelf-stable and convenient, a few months earlier for a moment like this one. Stirring ⅔ cup of the powder into 1 cup of boiling water gave me the required amount of coconut milk for the recipe, and I was quite pleasantly surprised at its quality. It certainly was not the best, when compared to certain brands of canned coconut milk, but it was good enough to cream my cause with dignified taste.

Asafetida? See the Glossary of Ingredients, page 758.

Pan-Fried Cheese
WITH POTATOES AND FENUGREEK

Aloo Methi Paneer

When protein (from *paneer*), starch (from potatoes), and iron (from fenugreek leaves) come together in one curry, it qualifies as a substantial main-course offering, satisfying for both the herbivore and the carnivore at your dinner table. A bowl of aromatic Dirty Rice with Caramelized Onion and Pounded Spices (page 711) and a side dish of plain yogurt make the whole experience special.

SERVES 6

1 pound russet or Yukon Gold potatoes, peeled, cut into ½-inch cubes, and submerged in a bowl of cold water to prevent browning
2 tablespoons canola oil
1 teaspoon black or yellow mustard seeds
1 teaspoon cumin seeds
2 teaspoons white granulated sugar
2 teaspoons coarse kosher or sea salt
2 teaspoons coriander seeds, ground
1 teaspoon cumin seeds, ground
1 teaspoon cayenne (ground red pepper)
½ teaspoon ground turmeric
¼ teaspoon ground asafetida
1 cup chopped fresh or frozen fenugreek leaves (thawed if frozen); or ½ cup dried fenugreek leaves, soaked in a bowl of water and skimmed off before use (see box, page 473)
8 ounces Doodh paneer (page 286), cut into 1-inch cubes and fried (see box, page 286)

1. Drain the potatoes.

2. Heat the oil in a medium-size saucepan over medium-high heat. Add the mustard seeds, cover, and cook until the seeds have stopped popping (not unlike popcorn), about 30 seconds. Sprinkle in the cumin seeds, which will instantly turn reddish brown and smell fragrant.

3. Remove the pan from the heat and sprinkle in the sugar, salt, coriander, ground cumin, cayenne, turmeric, and asafetida. Immediately add the potatoes, 2 cups water, and the fenugreek leaves. Return the pan to the heat and bring the watery curry to a boil. Reduce the heat to medium-low and simmer, uncovered, stirring occasionally, until the potatoes are almost tender and some of the liquid has evaporated, making the sauce slightly thick, 28 to 30 minutes.

4. Stir in the *paneer* cubes, cover the pan, and simmer, stirring occasionally, until the cheese is softened, the potatoes are cooked through, and the sauce has thickened, 8 to 10 minutes.

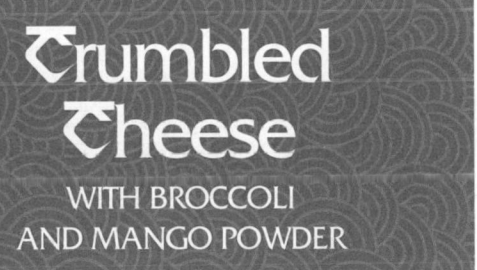

Crumbled Cheese
WITH BROCCOLI AND MANGO POWDER

ħaree ᵽhool ᵹobhi ᵽaneer

his curry has a thin, brothlike quality since there is nothing among its ingredients to thicken it. Broccoli, never part of traditional Indian cuisine (because it's not grown there), is now found in many of India's trendy, Western-style supermarkets. **SERVES 8**

2 tablespoons canola oil
1 teaspoon cumin seeds
1 pound broccoli, cut into 1-inch florets
1 tablespoon mango powder or lime juice
¼ teaspoon ground turmeric
4 ounces Doodh paneer or Malai paneer (pages 286–287), crumbled
1 teaspoon coarse kosher or sea salt
1 large tomato, cored and finely chopped
¼ cup finely chopped fresh cilantro leaves and tender stems
½ teaspoon Punjabi garam masala (page 25)

1. Heat the oil in a large skillet over medium-high heat. Add the cumin seeds and cook until they turn reddish brown and are aromatic, 5 to 10 seconds. Immediately add the broccoli, mango powder, and turmeric. Stir-fry the broccoli to cook the spices without burning them, about 1 minute.

2. Add 1 cup water along with the *paneer*, salt, and tomato. Bring to a boil. Then reduce the heat to medium-low, cover the skillet, and simmer, stirring occasionally, until the broccoli is fork-tender, 12 to 15 minutes.

3. Stir in the cilantro and garam masala, and serve.

Tips:

❖ Even though I have recommended using only broccoli florets, feel free to use their stems too. Since the stems are more fibrous, peel them with a vegetable peeler. Then trim off and discard the ends of the stems, and cut the stems crosswise into ¼-inch-thick rounds. Add them to the pan before the quicker-cooking florets, and allow them to sear and partially cook, about 5 minutes. Then add the florets and spices and continue with the recipe.

❖ If fresh turmeric root—usually available in any Asian grocery or natural food stores—is in season, cut a piece roughly ½ inch long into paper-thin slices and add them with the broccoli instead of the ground turmeric. The root's carrotlike quality provides both color and texture, giving you ample fodder to surprise your guests with an out-of-the-ordinary ingredient, seasoning the dinner conversation.

Crumbled Cheese
WITH MINT, CILANTRO, AND CHILES

Paneer Hariyali

Hindi for "green" is *hariyali,* and this curry will lead you down that lush, fresh-tasting path. Peas, cilantro, mint, and chiles offer a potent backdrop for the mellow cheese in this dish, a great main course for that lacto-vegetarian at your table. Serve store-bought or homemade rotis (page 727) alongside. **SERVES 6**

2 tablespoons Ghee (page 21) or canola oil

1 small red onion, finely chopped

2 teaspoons cumin seeds, coarsely cracked (see Tip)

2 cups frozen green peas (no need to thaw)

8 ounces Doodh paneer (page 286), crumbled

½ cup finely chopped fresh cilantro leaves and tender stems

¼ cup finely chopped fresh mint leaves

1 teaspoon coarse kosher or sea salt

½ teaspoon Punjabi garam masala (page 25)

4 to 6 fresh green Thai, cayenne, or serrano chiles, to taste, stems removed, finely chopped (do not remove the seeds)

1. Heat the ghee in a medium-size saucepan over medium-high heat. Add the onion and cumin seeds, and stir-fry until the onion is translucent and the cumin is aromatic, 2 to 3 minutes.

2. Stir in the peas, cover the pan, and cook, stirring occasionally, until they are tender, about 5 minutes.

3. Add all the remaining ingredients. Stir in 1 cup water, and bring to a boil. Then serve.

Tip: To coarsely crack cumin seeds, pile them onto a cutting board and using a sharp knife, chop them as you would a bunch of fresh herbs. Some of them will fly off the board, but doing it gently will contain most of them on the surface. You can also use a food processor, a mini chopper, or a spice grinder. Just make sure to use the pulsing action—not a steady grinding—to yield a coarse texture. The bruised spice does have a distinct nutty-peppery flavor, different from the whole seed.

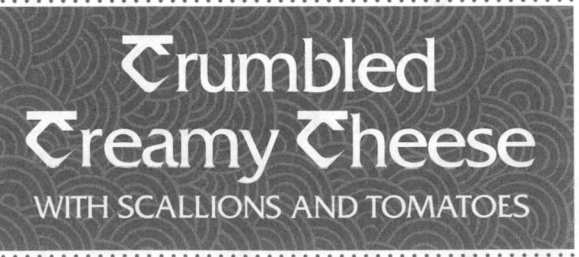

Crumbled Creamy Cheese
WITH SCALLIONS AND TOMATOES

Mulayam Paneer Bhurjee

Unbelievably quick, this creamy-tasting curry makes for a quick and delicious weekday meal. Serve fluffy homemade rotis (page

727) alongside, or even store-bought whole-wheat tortillas warmed in a skillet and lightly buttered. Add the crunchy Chopped Cucumber, Tomato, and Onion with Lime Juice (page 741), and you can go to bed with a satisfied palate and a full tummy. **SERVES 4**

2 tablespoons canola oil

1 teaspoon cumin seeds

8 ounces Malai paneer (page 287), crumbled
   (see Tip)

8 ounces scallions (green tops and white bulbs),
   finely chopped

8 ounces tomatoes, cored and finely chopped

2 tablespoons finely chopped fresh cilantro
   leaves and tender stems

1 teaspoon coarse kosher or sea salt

1 teaspoon Balti masala (page 31)

¼ teaspoon ground turmeric

2 to 4 fresh green Thai, cayenne, or serrano chiles,
   to taste, stems removed, thinly sliced crosswise
   (do not remove the seeds)

Heat the oil in a large skillet over medium-high heat. Sprinkle in the cumin seeds and cook until they sizzle, turn reddish brown, and smell fragrant, about 10 seconds. Add all the remaining ingredients and simmer, uncovered, stirring occasionally, until the flavors infuse the cheese, about 5 minutes. Then serve.

Tip: If you have not had a chance to make the *paneer*, use crumbled feta cheese for an excellent alternative. Because feta is salty, reduce the amount of salt in the recipe by half. And because it melts rather quickly, fold it in just before you plan to serve the curry.

Grilled Cheese
WITH A
CASHEW-TOMATO SAUCE

Paneer Tikka Masala

A staple at numerous north Indian restaurants that serve Moghalai foods—not only in India but also in the United States and the United Kingdom—this vegetarian-friendly curry packs intense flavors in small bites. Eating more than two slices at Sunday lunch can prove to be heavy, but what a fine excuse for an afternoon nap! **SERVES 6**

8 ounces Doodh paneer (page 286), cut into
   finger-like pieces about 3 inches long,
   1 inch wide, and 1 inch thick

2 tablespoons plain yogurt

2 tablespoons finely chopped fresh
   cilantro leaves tender stems

1 tablespoon Ginger Paste (page 15)

1 tablespoon Garlic Paste (page 15)

1 teaspoon Balti masala (page 31)

1 teaspoon ground Kashmiri chiles; or
   ¼ teaspoon cayenne (ground red pepper)
   mixed with ¾ teaspoon sweet paprika

1½ teaspoons coarse kosher or sea salt

2 tablespoons Ghee (page 21) or canola oil

½ cup finely chopped red onion

10 raw cashew nuts

2 tablespoons tomato paste

½ teaspoon ground turmeric

½ teaspoon cayenne (ground red pepper)

½ teaspoon Punjabi garam masala
   (page 25)

Vegetable cooking spray

1. Arrange the *paneer* fingers in a single layer in a baking dish.

2. Combine the yogurt, cilantro, ginger and garlic pastes, masala, ground chiles, and 1 teaspoon of the salt in a small bowl. Whisk together to form a smooth, orange-red marinade. Pour this over the cheese fingers, making sure each piece gets completely bathed in it. Refrigerate, covered, for at least 30 minutes or as long as overnight, to allow the flavors to permeate the dense cheese.

3. While the cheese is marinating, heat the ghee in a medium-size skillet over medium-high heat. Add the onion and cashews, and stir-fry until the onion is light honey-brown around the edges and the nuts are light brown too, 5 to 8 minutes.

4. Stir in the remaining ½ teaspoon salt, tomato paste, turmeric, and cayenne. Stir, and simmer to allow the spices to cook, about 30 seconds. Then pour in ½ cup water and scrape the skillet to deglaze it, releasing the browned bits of spice and onion.

5. Transfer the onion-cashew mixture to a blender jar and puree, scraping the inside of the jar as needed, to make a smooth, orange-red paste. Return the paste to the skillet. Pour ½ cup water into the blender, swish it around to wash it out, and add this to the skillet.

6. Add the garam masala to the skillet. Stir to mix well, and set aside.

7. Preheat a gas (or charcoal) grill, or the broiler, to high. *If you are grilling*, spray the grill grate lightly with cooking spray. Arrange the *paneer* fingers, marinade and all, on the grate. Cover, and grill, turning them every 2 to 3 minutes, until the grill marks are reddish brown, 8 to 12 minutes. *If you are broiling*, place an oven rack so the top of the cheese will be 2 to 3 inches from heat. Spray the rack of a broiler pan lightly with cooking spray. Arrange the *paneer* fingers, marinade and all, on the broiler pan and broil, turning them every 2 to 3 minutes, until they are light reddish brown, 8 to 12 minutes.

8. Transfer the cheese fingers to the skillet and spoon the sauce over them. Simmer the curry over medium-low heat, uncovered, without stirring, until the sauce thickens, 3 to 5 minutes. Then serve.

Turmeric-Soaked Grilled Cheese
WITH MILK AND CARDAMOM

Peela Thaaman

Manu Madhok, a successful pediatrician now living in a suburb of Minneapolis, has ancestral roots in Kashmir and was born and raised in Delhi. His love of cooking is reflected in the gleam in his eyes as he talks about the foods of his childhood. As it happens, he is able to enjoy those childhood foods in his adult life because his mother continues to make them for Manu and his family, ever since she and her husband immigrated to the United States. This three-generation family prospers as the grandmother cooks; the grandfather nurtures the garden, tending to the abundant basil plants, tomatoes, and chiles; the mother is busy pursuing a career as a dentist; and the two children flourish with parental and grandparental involvement.

At their house, I was treated to a lunch of simply prepared curry of fried cheese in milk, Stewed Radishes with Tamarind (page 587), Pan-Fried Bottle Gourd Slices with Yogurt and Aromatic Spices (page 604), and white basmati rice. Every curry was thin-sauced, devoid of onions and garlic, uncluttered with spices, the vegetable or cheese being the showcase. The culmination of the meal was the aromatic classic *Kehawa* (page 755)—Assamese green tea gently brewed with cardamom, saffron, and ground almonds. What's not to love about that? **SERVES 4**

> *8 ounces Doodh paneer (page 286), cut into slices*
>   *2 inches long, 1 inch wide, and ½ inch thick*
>   *and pan-fried (see box, page 286)*
> *1 teaspoon coarse kosher or sea salt*
> *½ teaspoon ground turmeric*
> *2 tablespoons canola oil*
> *3 or 4 black cardamom pods*
> *1 or 2 cinnamon sticks (each 3 inches long)*
> *½ teaspoon ground ginger*
> *½ teaspoon ground fennel*
> *½ cup whole milk or half-and-half*
> *4 to 6 green or white cardamom pods*

1. Place the pan-fried *paneer* pieces in a medium-size bowl, and pour 1 cup warm water over them. Sprinkle in the salt and turmeric, stirring to make sure the spices disperse evenly. Set the bowl aside to allow the slices to soak and soften, about 30 minutes.

2. Heat the oil in a medium-size saucepan over medium heat. Add the black cardamom pods and the cinnamon sticks, and cook until they sizzle and swell, 30 seconds to 1 minute. Then pour in the *paneer* and its soaking liquid. Add the ginger, fennel, and milk. Heat the thin curry to a boil. Reduce the heat and simmer,

uncovered, stirring occasionally, until the spices get a chance to flavor the cheese and the sauce, 5 to 10 minutes.

3. Stir in the green cardamom pods and simmer, still uncovered, stirring occasionally, until they perfume the sauce, about 5 minutes. Then serve.

Tip: If the whole cardamom pods are bothersome for you or your guests, remove them from the curry before you serve it. If you leave them in the curry, you may want to instruct your friends and family not to eat the pods. They are by no means poisonous, but are extremely strong-tasting and will hinder the taste buds from experiencing any other flavors. The black pods infuse a smoky flavor into the curry while the green ones are sweet-smelling. I love the contrast the two pods offer, making this curry complex-tasting without a plethora of spices.

Herb-Marinated Cheese
WITH A BLACKENED-CHILE SAUCE

haree bharee paneer

nce you secure the ingredients for the curry, creating this stunningly beautiful and full-flavored masterpiece is easy. Even though the proliferation of fresh and dried chiles may signal a pungent-hot dish, rest assured that that perception will dissipate, thanks to the dairy-rich, meaty but tender homemade cheese. **SERVES 6**

For marinating the paneer:

¼ cup firmly packed fresh cilantro leaves and tender stems

¼ cup firmly packed fresh mint leaves

¼ cup firmly packed fresh curry leaves

4 to 6 fresh green Thai, cayenne, or serrano chiles, to taste, stems removed

⅓ cup plain yogurt

I teaspoon coarse kosher or sea salt

8 ounces Doodh paneer (page 286), cut into finger-like pieces about 3 inches long, I inch wide, and I inch thick

For the sauce:

I teaspoon coriander seeds

I teaspoon cumin seeds

2 large cloves garlic, coarsely chopped

2 dried red Thai or cayenne chiles, blackened, stems removed (see Tip)

2 tablespoons canola oil

I teaspoon black or yellow mustard seeds

I large tomato, cored and finely chopped

I teaspoon white granulated sugar

½ teaspoon coarse kosher or sea salt

2 tablespoons finely chopped fresh cilantro leaves and tender stems

Vegetable cooking spray

1. To make the marinade, pile the cilantro, mint, curry leaves, and chiles into a food processor. Using the pulsing action, mince to form a green, intensely aromatic blend. Transfer the blend, each whiff bursting with minty chiles and citrus undertones, to a small bowl. Fold in the yogurt and salt to make a creamy-tart, pesto-like marinade.

2. Using a skewer, poke a few holes on the broad sides of each piece of cheese. Place the cheese in a baking dish and coat it on all sides with the marinade. Cover, and refrigerate for at least 1 hour or as long as overnight.

3. To make the sauce, combine the coriander seeds, cumin seeds, garlic, and blackened chiles in a mortar. Pound the spices to a pulpy, gritty mass. (Alternatively, use a food processor—just make sure to use the pulsing action to create a similar texture.)

4. Heat the oil in a small skillet over medium-high heat. Add the mustard seeds, cover, and cook until the seeds have stopped popping (not unlike popcorn), about 30 seconds. Immediately add the pounded spice blend and stir-fry to brown the garlic, about 1 minute.

5. Stir in the tomato, sugar, and salt. Lower the heat to medium and cook, uncovered, stirring occasionally, until the tomato is soft but still firm-looking, 3 to 5 minutes.

6. Fold in the cilantro, and keep the sauce warm while you grill the *paneer*.

7. To cook the *paneer*, preheat a gas (or charcoal) grill, or the broiler, to high. *If you are grilling*, lightly spray the grill grate with cooking spray. Place the *paneer* fingers, marinade and all, on the grate, cover the grill, and cook, turning them every 2 to 3 minutes, until the grill marks are reddish brown and the slices feel soft when gently prodded, 8 to 12 minutes. *If you are broiling*, set an oven rack so the top of the cheese will be 2 to 3 inches from the heat. Lightly spray the rack of a broiler pan with cooking spray. Arrange the *paneer* fingers, marinade and all, on the broiler pan and broil, turning them every 2 to 3 minutes, until they are light reddish brown, 8 to 12 minutes.

8. Transfer the grilled *paneer* fingers to a serving platter, top them with the sauce, and serve.

Tip: Blackening dried red chiles is a cinch. Nevertheless, I do want to warn you that the fumes will send you into a coughing fit if you do not have adequate ventilation. (Even though the number of chiles you are using here is minimal, the capsaicin in them is incredibly strong.) *If you have a gas burner,* use tongs to hold a chile pepper over the flame, turning the chile as necessary, until it is blackened all over, 5 to 10 seconds. *If you have an electric cooktop,* preheat a small skillet over medium-high heat. Add the chiles to the skillet and toast them, shaking the skillet very frequently, until they are evenly blackened, 1 to 2 minutes.

Creamy Cheese
WITH
RED ONION AND BELL PEPPERS

Paneer Jalfrezie

The word *jalfrezie,* a coined term that originated in Indian restaurants catering to the English, has come to mean many things. Some associate it with "chiles-hot," while to others it indicates the inclusion of bell peppers and onions as key ingredients that contribute to the curry's gusto. So I offer you an old English favorite, this version with homemade cheese.

SERVES 6

2 tablespoons canola oil

1 large red onion, cut into 1-inch cubes

1 medium-size green bell pepper, stemmed, seeded, and cut into 1-inch pieces

6 large cloves garlic, finely chopped

2 tablespoons finely chopped fresh ginger

½ cup tomato sauce, canned or homemade (see page 18)

1 tablespoon Balti masala (page 31)

1 teaspoon coarse kosher or sea salt

2 tablespoons finely chopped fresh cilantro leaves and tender stems

8 ounces Malai paneer, cut into 1-inch cubes (page 287)

1. Heat the oil in a wok or large skillet over medium-high heat. Add the onion, bell pepper, garlic, and ginger, and stir-fry until the onion is light brown around the edges, 3 to 5 minutes.

2. Stir in the tomato sauce, masala, and salt. Reduce the heat to medium and simmer, uncovered, stirring occasionally, until a bit of oil starts to form on the surface and around the edges, 5 to 8 minutes.

3. Stir in 1 cup water and the cilantro. (The water thins the curry to accommodate the cheese.)

4. Gently fold in the *paneer,* raise the heat to medium-high, and simmer, uncovered, stirring every so often, until the sauce starts to thicken, 10 to 12 minutes. Then serve.

Tip: You can make the same sauce and substitute any meat you like for the cheese. I would recommend using cuts that are easy to cook, and also lowering the amount of water to ½ cup, since meats contain their own water and tend to leach it while simmering, adding moisture to the curry.

Sanjita's Coorgh-Style Cheese
IN A SWEET-TART TOMATO SAUCE

tamatar paneer

Since I was her sous-chef that night, Sanjita Carriappa asked me to cut the *paneer* into 1-inch cubes. She kept apologizing for using store-bought cheese, and marveled at the way I could slice a red onion in seconds. Sanjita's chiseled features reveal her ancestral warrior heritage. She kept me regaled with stories of her Coorghi community as she instructed me on making the curry: Its key strength depended on the onion's slow cooking, preparing it redolent with sweetness. In her original recipe, she used both tomato sauce and paste. I eliminated the sauce and kept the paste, making the final curry not as tart. **SERVES 6**

2 tablespoons Ghee (page 21) or canola oil

1 medium-size red onion, cut in half lengthwise
    and thinly sliced

6 green or white cardamom pods

¼ cup tomato paste

1 tablespoon coriander seeds, ground

1 teaspoon cayenne (ground red pepper)

½ teaspoon ground turmeric

1 teaspoon coarse kosher or sea salt

8 ounces Doodh paneer (page 286), cut into 1-inch cubes

1 cup half-and-half

½ cup finely chopped fresh cilantro leaves
    and tender stems

1. Heat the ghee in a medium-size saucepan over medium heat. Add the onion and cardamom pods, stirring once or twice to coat the onion with the oil. Cover the pan and cook until the onion is honey-brown with a deep purple hue, 15 to 20 minutes. (At first the onion will sweat and then, once the moisture evaporates, it will start to brown.)

2. Stir in the tomato paste, coriander, cayenne, and turmeric. Simmer the thick sauce, uncovered, stirring occasionally, until oil starts to glisten on the surface and around the edges, 3 to 5 minutes.

3. Pour in 1 cup water and scrape the pan to deglaze it, releasing the browned bits of onion and spice. Stir in the salt and *paneer*. Once the curry comes to a boil, reduce the heat to medium-low, cover the pan, and simmer until the cheese has absorbed the sauce's flavors and softened slightly (the pieces will still be very firm-looking), about 15 minutes.

4. Fold in the half-and-half and simmer, uncovered, stirring occasionally and gently, until the sauce thickens, 5 to 10 minutes.

5. Stir in the cilantro, and serve.

Royal Taj Curry
WITH CHILES, POTATOES & CHEESE

mirchi paneer

I tasted a version of this curry while staying at the Taj View Hotel in Agra, when I took a group of people to visit the marbled splendor of the Taj

Mahal, appropriately one of the Seven Wonders of the World. Everything about the palace is sheer perfection, and no book, photo, or movie ever docs true justice to its physical presence and breathtaking beauty, especially when the early morning's rays bathe it in a golden light.

At the hotel I was honored to be served seven curries whipped up by that generous, talented, and warm executive chef Mahipal Singh Rathore (I confess I had mentioned to him that I was writing a curry cookbook). They were all delicious, but this particular one, redolent with chiles and tomato paste, took my breath away as I mopped up every bit of the sauce with piping hot, ghee-laden naan from the hotel's clay oven. **SERVES 4**

2 tablespoons Ghee (page 21) or canola oil

2 tablespoons tomato paste

2 tablespoons finely chopped fresh cilantro leaves
      and tender stems

10 to 12 medium-size to large fresh curry leaves,
      coarsely chopped

4 fresh green Thai, cayenne, or serrano chiles,
      stems removed, thinly sliced crosswise
      (do not remove the seeds)

4 ounces Doodh paneer or Malai paneer
      (pages 286, 287), cut into 1-inch cubes

1 pound russet or Yukon Gold potatoes, peeled,
      cut into ½-inch cubes, and submerged
      in a bowl of cold water to prevent browning

1½ teaspoons coarse kosher or sea salt

½ cup half-and-half

1. Heat the ghee in a small saucepan over medium-high heat. Stir in the tomato paste, cilantro, curry leaves, chiles, and *paneer*. Cook, uncovered, stirring occasionally, until the tomato paste starts to turn darker, a glistening oily sheen forms on the surface, and the chiles smell pungent, 3 to 5 minutes.

2. Drain the potatoes.

3. Pour 2 cups water into the pan and scrape the bottom to deglaze it, releasing the reddish-brown bits of tomato paste. Add the potatoes and stir in the salt. Heat the curry to a boil. Then reduce the heat to medium-low, cover the pan, and simmer, stirring occasionally, until the potatoes are tender and the sauce has thickened slightly, 15 to 20 minutes.

4. Stir in the half-and-half and simmer, uncovered, stirring occasionally, until it is warmed, 3 to 5 minutes. Then serve.

Cheese Dumplings
IN A SPINACH SAUCE

Chenna Saag

A recent visit to Udaipur, in the northwestern state of Rajasthan, took me to the restaurant at the Lake Palace Hotel. The hotel, originally the summer palace for the king, is situated on an island in Lake Pichola. Of course I ordered the curry that tweaked my interest, the combination that seemed odd and defied all things classically Indian: cheese rounds simmered in a smooth spinach sauce. You see, cheese balls are usually featured in India's classic *Rasmalai*, a sweet ending with a creamy, saffron-kissed sauce. Simmering them in a savory spinach sauce was different but turned out to be equally comforting. So I returned to my not-quite-so-grand home in the United States and created a rendition of this curry—and fell in love with it all over again. My sauce had more body, with the spinach left whole rather than pureed. The cheese balls remind me of matzoh balls—light, creamy, and nosh-able. **SERVES 6**

For the *chenna* (cheese dumplings):

2 quarts whole milk

2 to 3 tablespoons distilled white vinegar

2 tablespoons rice flour

For the sauce:

2 tablespoons canola oil

1 teaspoon cumin seeds

1 cup finely chopped red onion

1 tablespoon finely chopped fresh ginger

4 medium-size cloves garlic, finely chopped

1 can (14.5 ounces) diced tomatoes

1½ teaspoons coarse kosher or sea salt

1 teaspoon ground Deggi chiles (see box, page 290); or ½ teaspoon cayenne (ground red pepper) mixed with ½ teaspoon sweet paprika

1 teaspoon Toasted Cumin-Coriander Blend (page 33)

½ teaspoon ground turmeric

1 pound fresh baby spinach leaves, well rinsed

1. To make the *chenna*, pour the milk into a large saucepan and bring it to a boil over medium-high heat, stirring frequently to prevent the milk from scorching. Once it comes to a boil, stir in 2 tablespoons of the vinegar; if there is not enough curdling, add another tablespoon. (Clumps of white curds should completely separate from the light grayish-green whey.) Remove the pan from the heat and set it aside.

2. Line a colander with a double layer of cheesecloth or a clean dishcloth, making sure there are 2 to 3 inches hanging over the rim of the colander. Place the colander in the sink, then pour the cheese and whey into the colander, and set it aside to drain off all the watery whey, about 1 hour.

3. Transfer the crumbly cheese to a medium-size bowl, and sprinkle the rice flour over it. Wet your hands, and use them to mix the cheese and flour together. The flour is the binding tool and your wet hands will provide enough additional moisture to seal the two to create a bumpy, dough-like mass. Wet your hands as many times as necessary to reach this point (usually two to three times should do it). Then break off walnut-size pieces of cheese and compress them tightly in your fist to form a ball. Set the cheese balls on a plate.

4. To make the sauce, heat the oil in a large saucepan over medium-high heat. Add the cumin seeds and cook until they sizzle, turn reddish brown, and smell nutty, 5 to 10 seconds. Add the onion, ginger, and garlic. Stir-fry until the onion is light brown around the edges, about 5 minutes.

5. Stir in the tomatoes with their juices, and the salt, ground chiles, cumin-coriander blend, and turmeric. Cook, uncovered, stirring occasionally, until some of the oil starts to separate from the chunky sauce, 3 to 5 minutes.

6. Pile the spinach into the pan, cover it, and cook, stirring once or twice, until the leaves start to wilt, about 5 minutes.

7. Stir in 2 cups water. Place the cheese balls in the sauce, and spoon the spinach and sauce over to cover them. Lower the heat to medium and simmer, uncovered, basting the cheese balls without stirring them, until the sauce has thickened slightly, 15 to 20 minutes. Then serve.

legume
curries

to declare that legumes (basically, legumes are seeds that grow within pods) are an Indian vegetarian's lifeline is an understatement. A rich source of essential nutrients (low in fat, no cholesterol, high in fiber, protein, folate, potassium, iron, magnesium, and phytochemicals—a group of compounds that may help prevent cardiovascular disease and cancer), lentils, beans, and peas have been a

part of the Indian diet since 4500 B.C. With over sixty varieties to choose from, legumes are a staple not only for vegetarians but also for those who consume meat—especially when eating meat daily might not be economically feasible. Dried legumes (also called pulses) are inexpensive and have a long shelf life, making them very convenient, especially in a society where refrigeration is still scarce in the smaller towns and villages. Every meal in India includes a legume curry, and like veg-

etables, their importance is evident in the sheer number of recipes in this chapter.

buying & storing legumes

many of the common varieties of legumes (like chickpeas, kidney beans, brown lentils, and yellow split peas) are a cinch to locate in the rice and beans aisle of your neighborhood supermarket. For some of the not-so-common ones (like black lentils, pigeon peas, and cowpeas), seek out an Indian grocery store in your city (or in a larger city nearby), a mail-order or website source (page 773), or a natural foods store. I have been pleasantly surprised to find the unusual ones in a "regular" supermarket in my city; this is the case especially in areas that have a large Indian enclave.

When shopping for legumes, make sure you purchase the specific type called for in the recipe; many legumes have distinct tastes and textures and they are not always interchangeable (a substitution won't ruin a recipe, but it will definitely alter the cooking time and the flavor). The spellings on the packaging might differ slightly—the English words are phonetic interpretations of the Indian terms. When in doubt, pay attention to the color of the legume. For example, black lentils come in three forms: whole, split with skin on, and split and skinned. The whole is labeled *sabud urad* while the split ones, both skinned and skin-on, are called *urad dal*. The skinned ones are cream colored and are markedly different in taste, texture, and cooking time from the ones with the skin on. You'll find that wherever it's needed, I have included information about the color in the recipes' ingredients lists. Also refer to the facing page for a description of the legumes used in this book.

a few words about dal
❖ ❖ ❖

he word **dal** *is a term used in multiple contexts within the Indian kitchen.* Dal *describes split lentils or beans (as in* urad dal *and* masoor dal, *whose whole counterparts are referred to as* sabud urad *and* sabud masoor). *It can also refer to a curry consisting of beans, peas, or lentils (or a combination). And it can be a catchall term for all legumes.*

Most of the legumes found here in the United States are of excellent quality. Nevertheless, packages of certain dried lentils, beans, and peas may contain stones or husks. It's a good idea to sort through the legumes and discard any debris before you cook them. (You wouldn't want to bite into a stone or pebble while relishing your curry.) To sort them, I dump the legumes onto a glass or white plate, where I can see them clearly (as opposed to their being lost in a plate's pattern or color scheme). I quickly discard any loose husks and run my fingers through to feel for any stones or pebbles. That's all it takes!

To store legumes, either leave them in their original packaging or transfer them to an airtight jar, and keep them away from heat and humidity. You do not need to refrigerate them. Use up the old batch before you get to the newly purchased one—the older a legume, the longer it will take to cook.

cooking dried legumes

he form of a legume determines its optimum cooking method. A whole bean, like kidney beans, chickpeas, or black lentils, requires soaking before you cook it. Split legumes, like yellow split peas, split green lentils, or salmon-colored split brown lentils, do not require soaking and thus may be your best bet when you are looking for a speedy, vegetarian-friendly meal on a harried evening. It's always a good idea to wash legumes before you use them, to rid them of dust, loose husks, or other alien matter (I have included washing instructions in each of the recipes that instruct you to do so).

Soaking and cooking legumes: For those legumes that require prior soaking, you have two options: quick-soak or overnight soak.

digesting legumes

❖ ❖ ❖

When my son Robert was almost four years old, he blurted out to his preschool teacher a poem that "Papa taught me," feeling mighty proud of his memory: "Beans, beans, the magical fruit, the more you eat the more you toot." I wasn't sure whether to be proud or to slink away in embarrassment, but I figured that at least he had learned something culinary. There is after all some scientific basis to that rhyme.

Some legumes, especially beans, contain simple sugars called oligosaccharides that are hard for the lower intestines to process and digest, giving the victim a feeling of being bloated and flatulent. Spices and herbs, in the study and practice of the ancient medicine called ayurveda, are known to have healing powers of all sorts. When certain spices and flavorings—especially turmeric, asafetida, Bishop's weed, black salt, and ginger—are added to legume-based curries, they help the body process the legumes better; call it the Indian's Beano. It is for this reason (taste too is a huge plus) that many of our legume dishes contain one or more of these flavorings.

If you are not used to consuming a large amount of legumes in your diet, start out by including them in small amounts until your body gets used to processing them. Eventually the stigma of being a "magical fruit" may disappear, and then you will be able to eat more without any musical notes during the aftermath.

For a quick-soak, place the legumes in a large saucepan, stockpot, or Dutch oven, and cover them with plenty of water (there is no need to rinse them). Bring the water to a rolling boil over high heat. Then remove the pan from the heat and let it sit, covered, until the legumes soften slightly and swell up, 2 to 3 hours. Discard the soaking liquid and give the grains a good rinse. This process will also alleviate some of the discomfort caused by hard-to-digest beans (I'll address this a bit later). Return the legumes to the pan, add at least three to four times the amount of water (at least 6 to 8 cups water for 2 cups soaked legumes), and bring it to a boil over high heat. Discard any foam that forms on the surface. Then reduce the heat to medium-low and simmer the grains, covered, checking occasionally to make sure there is plenty of water, until they are cooked, anywhere from 1 to 2 hours, depending on the legume.

For an overnight soak, place the legumes in a saucepan and cover them generously with hot water. Cover the pan and let it sit on the counter all night, covered, until the legumes appear slightly swollen, at least 8 hours. Discard the soaking liquid, rinse, add fresh water, and cook as described above.

See page 335 for my two cents on using canned beans.

types of legumes

Cowpeas

black-eyed peas—*lobhia*
red cowpeas—*sabud chowli*

Of African origin, this class of peas spread around the world and embedded itself firmly in the Indian kitchen. Black-eyed peas—kidney-shaped and cream-colored with a small spot, or eye, on the inside curve—gained wide acceptance all over India because of their buttery, creamy taste and nutty texture. Try Fresh Greens with Black-Eyed Peas (page 320) or Coconut-Smothered

Black-Eyed Peas (page 318) and you will see why. They are easy to cook in their dry state, but in a pinch, you can find canned cooked black-eyed peas at the supermarket; drain and rinse them before use. Frozen black-eyed peas are also widely available, making for a nice compromise between cooking from scratch and using canned peas.

Red cowpeas are actually reddish brown; they have an oval shape and that same "eye" in the underbelly. Not as buttery as black-eyed peas, these are nutty-tasting and firm-looking when cooked. They are great sprouted and stewed in coconut milk (Sprouted Cowpeas Stewed in Coconut Milk, page 327) or simply cooked and

flavored with spices that make them easy to digest, as in Cowpeas with Bishop's Weed and Toasted Chickpea Flour (page 326). My favorite, hands-down, is my sister-in-law's Cowpeas Coconut with Winter Melon (page 325).

Chickpeas

yellow chickpeas—*kabuli chana*
black chickpeas—*kala chana*
green chickpeas—*hara chana*

Yellow chickpeas, also commonly identified as "garbanzo beans" or "Bengal gram," were consumed in India as early as the Harappan civilization, around 4500 B.C. One of the most popular

using a pressure cooker

So far I have talked about cooking dried legumes the old-fashioned way—in a pot on the stove for a few hours. Let's not forget the pressure cooker, used with fervor across many continents to cook everything from legumes to meats to vegetables. Not as popular in the United States as it should be, this technique is the most expedient way to cook dried legumes, especially the harder-to-cook chickpeas, kidney beans, horse gram, and whole pigeon peas (and you don't even have to presoak some of the legumes). It is also the most nutritious method, because the pressure cooker uses less liquid and requires a shorter cooking time, resulting in the retention of more minerals and vitamins. Visions of bursting pressure cookers, unsafe gaskets, and airborne lids are a thing of the past; the modern-day cookers are designed to be safe (many of them come with at least four safety systems). There are numerous brands on the shelves, ranging from inexpensive models to Cadillac versions, all of which deliver safety and convenience.

The cooker produces pressure by heating water over high heat to generate steam. The steam is kept inside, with only the excess allowed to vent through a tube, which in turn is controlled by a bell-shaped weight. Once the steam has built up within, the pressure control automatically maintains a constant internal pressure (at medium to low heat on the burner), thus expediting the cooking time while maintaining the nutritional value. When you have cooked the legumes for the required time (you'll find this information in the recipes that use a pressure cooker), turn off the burner and let the cooker cool down naturally (usually 10 to 15 minutes), which releases the internal pressure and allows you to release the lid safely.

Every pressure cooker comes with an informative manual, and if you follow the instructions, you will be rewarded with perfectly cooked legumes in 20 percent of the time it takes to cook them the traditional way. When I started, I was apprehensive and wary—as you may be. But once I gave in and trusted it, I couldn't imagine how I had lived without my pressure cooker.

of all the legumes, chickpeas are versatile and are also consumed fresh (the fresh green ones are eaten off the pod as a crunchy snack). The cooked bean's nutty texture and ability to absorb spices and herbs makes it an ideal ingredient in curries like Tart Chickpeas with a Spicy Tomato Sauce (page 333) and Chickpeas with a Coconut Sauce (page 328). Every supermarket carries canned cooked chickpeas, which are priceless in terms of convenience and expediency; drain and rinse them before use.

Dried black chickpeas are much smaller than their yellow sibling and are actually dark reddish brown. Requiring a much longer cooking time, these are best handled in a pressure cooker (see box, page 314). Their nuttiness shines through in the Keralite specialty Black Chickpea Stew Mounded over Steamed Rice Cakes (page 340), and they offer a great contrast in texture in Sweet-Hot Black Chickpeas with Golden Raisins (page 344).

Green chickpeas, comparable in texture to the black ones and cooked very similarly, are addictive in Green Chickpeas with Spinach (page 345).

Ground into a flour—labeled "chickpea flour," *"besan,"* or "gram flour"—chickpeas are turned into a batter for coating vegetables that are then fried golden brown, used as thickeners for curries, or transformed into savory snacks and sweet desserts. Chickpea flour is found in curries like Chickpea Flour Dumplings with Spinach (page 349) and Scrambled Chickpea Flour with Ginger (page 351).

Pigeon Peas
whole—*sabud toovar*
skinned split—*toovar dal*

Even though pigeon peas originated in Africa, today the legume is synonymous with India,

which produces 90 percent of the world's crop. In Indian stores pigeon peas are available under two different names: *toovar* and *arhar.* They are two different varieties of the same species, and either will do for any of the recipes that call for pigeon peas. The oval-shaped whole peas are widely consumed in the northwestern state of Gujarat, fresh when they are in season, when they are immensely popular, and dried when they are not (Whole Pigeon Peas with Tomato and Mustard, page 425). Here in the United States pigeon peas are widely available in the dried form, and lately I have noticed that frozen pigeon peas are appearing in many Indian grocery stores.

When these peas are split, they are sold as *toovar* (or *arhar) dal,* and they are packaged in two different forms: oily and dry. The oily ones are coated with a vegetable oil to prevent any insect infestation and tend to have a longer shelf life; just wash them thoroughly before you use them. Pigeon peas are by far the most popular of all legumes in India; in many regions they are eaten almost daily and also at all festive occasions, like birth celebrations and weddings. Southern Indians use *toovar dal* to make a signature stew called *sambhar* (Coconut-Smothered Pigeon Peas with Pumpkin, page 429), and I love their unusual use in Chile-Hot Dumplings with Buttermilk (page 453). Gujaratis combine them with peanuts (another legume) in Nutty-Sweet Pigeon Peas and Peanuts with Jaggery (page 436), while Maharashtrians offer a simple *Varan*—Pureed Pigeon Peas with Ground Spices and Clarified Butter (page 442).

Yellow Split Peas *(chana dal)* A friend of mine insists on calling these peas "china doll," but there is nothing dainty about them. In fact, even though the peas are split, *chana dal* remains firm-looking, with an almost cornlike taste and

texture, no matter how long you cook it (generally no more than 30 minutes). Also known as *Bengal gram dal,* these look very much like skinned split pigeon peas, but yellow split peas are much nuttier in taste. Try them in Slow-Cooked Sweetened Yellow Split Peas with Fresh Coconut Chips (page 413), Eggplant-Smothered Yellow Split Peas (page 417), or the addictive Stewed Potatoes with Yellow Split Peas (page 418), and you too will incorporate them with more frequency in your kitchen.

Whole Yellow Peas *(safed vatana)*

Not as popular as some of the other peas, these whitish-yellow peas are more common in Gujarati-speaking homes of northwestern India. The dried peas take a long time to cook and do require some soaking. A pressure cooker expedites the process, and once the peas are cooked, you will notice that many of the translucent skins have separated and are floating, flotsamlike, on the surface. The skins are perfectly edible (not to mention a good source of fiber), but if they bother you, by all means discard them. Purchase *safed vatana* at an Indian grocery store and try Whole Yellow Peas with Bishop's Weed (page 410) for an almost chewy, meatlike experience.

Red Kidney Beans *(rajmah)*

Despite its botanical name, *Phaseolus vulgaris,* there is nothing obscene or vulgar about this robust-flavored, kidney-shaped bean, which is very popular in the northern regions of India, especially Punjab. There is mention of these beans as a staple among the Aryans in one of the well-known literary works called *Yajurveda,* dating back to around 800 B.C. Very meatlike in texture and aroma, this bean is a great alternative for someone who is looking to cut back on cholesterol-rich meats; try the nutritionally complete Minty Kidney Beans and Potatoes (page 360). My favorite is the combination in Creamy Black Lentils with Chickpeas and Kidney Beans (page 367). The dried beans do take some time to soak and cook (a pressure cooker is ideal here), but if time is of the essence, the readily available canned cooked beans are a great substitute.

Moth Beans *(moth)*

The English name is derived from the Indian word, *moth,* for this bean. Prolific in the dry climate of Rajasthan, moth beans are diminutive and elongated, resembling a tiny red cowpea. Because they are so small, they need to be checked carefully for stones and pebbles, which are apt to be the same size; so make sure you sort through them before you cook them. Cooking can take less than an hour and requires no prior soaking. Tart Moth Beans with Lime Juice (page 408) showcases the flavors of Gujarat.

Horse Gram *(kulith)*

In use in India even before 1500 B.C., this elliptical-shaped legume (see box, page 356) takes a long time to cook. Very chewy and meatlike, in the United States it is used as cattle feed. Lucky cattle because they sure eat good. As humans, we can savor the sprouted version in Sprouted Horse Gram with a Spicy Coconut-Chile Sauce (page 356), as the curry's robust flavors match the legume's heartiness.

Black Lentils

whole—*sabud urad*
split—*urad dal*

Also known as "black gram," these are very similar in shape and size to the green lentils called mung beans (the Latin word for "lentil" is *lens,* the shape of all the various lentils). This pulse is a very important one, especially among Hindus because of its inclusion in many religious rites. At the Indian grocery store, don't be surprised (or confused) to see these lentils in four different versions: black lentils left whole (*sabud urad*), whole with skin off (also *sabud urad,* off-white and oval-shaped in this form), skin-on and split (*urad dal,* cream-colored on one side, black on the other), and skinned and split (also *urad dal,* cream-colored on both sides). All four forms have a satiny, creamy texture when cooked.

Whole black lentils are used extensively in the north, where the signature Makhani Dal (page 364) is redolent with ginger, garlic, and butter—what's not to love? This curry is a staple in every north Indian restaurant because the slow-cooking lentils, by their nature, are very smooth and creamy. The skinned whole lentils are not that common, but try some Skinned Whole Black Lentils with Browned Onions (page 365) and that might very well change.

Skinned split lentils are very common in the southern and western regions of India. The southerners use them in very interesting ways—

everything from spice blends to steamed cakes, dumplings, fritters, and crepes. I love the western Indian Maharashtrian community's Creamy-Tart Split Black Lentils with Coconut (page 371); they stew the legume and season it simply with tart spices and fresh coconut. When the dried lentils are turned into flour, they are the prime ingredient in many of India's wafer-thin *papads* (lentil wafers).

The skin-on split lentils are more common in northwestern Indian communities, and when combined with yellow split peas, they provide not only abundant protein but also robust body to a curry (Black Lentils and Yellow Split Peas with Cardamom, page 372).

Green Lentils

whole—*sabud moong*
split—*moong dal*

These pulses, also called "green gram," are spelled *mung* in some books and on some packages. This plant is native to India and is fast-growing, yielding several crops per year. Small in size, oval in shape, and olive/forest green in color, these are quick-cooking even in the whole form. As is true of many pulses, they are available in several forms: whole, skin-on and split, and skinned and split. The most popular use for these legumes is in the sprout form (see box, page 328). In fact, the bean sprouts that are found in every supermarket, used extensively in Chinese cooking, are from these lentils.

Whole green lentils don't require soaking before cooking, and in less than 45 minutes they turn creamy and tender, very much like whole black lentils. I love the green theme of Spinach-Smothered Whole Green Lentils (page 380), but don't stop at that; make Turmeric-Flavored Whole Green Lentils with Chiles (page 379) and savor it over rice.

serving legumes

Legumes are the source of protein for India's millions of vegetarians, and therefore all of the curries in this chapter could be the main course. For nonvegetarians they are excellent alongside meat, poultry, and seafood dishes. I've given the recipe servings in cups rather than number of servings to allow for this variation. To serve legumes as a main dish, figure on 1 cup per person with rice or bread. To serve them as a side dish, figure on 1/2 cup per person.

Most of the curries in this chapter can be prepared ahead of time and then reheated—so they make meal preparation easy as well as nutritious!

Split green lentils, both skin-on (yellow on one side, green on the other) and skinned (yellow all over), cook in less than 20 minutes and will turn mushy. And no, that doesn't mean you have overcooked them; that's their nature. Split Green Lentils with Red Chiles and Toasted Spices (page 388) uses the skin-on form, while Cumin-Scented Split Green Lentils with Ginger (page 382) uses the skinned version—similar spices, slightly different versions of the same lentil, markedly different flavors. An unusual technique is used in Rajasthani kitchens, where skinned split lentils are pureed and delicately spiced, piped into "drops" (they actually look like yellow Hershey's Kisses), and sun-dried. This yields a very meatlike texture (almost like cooked hamburger meat), as you will experience when you make Green Lentil "Drops" with Peas (page 396).

Brown Lentils

whole—*sabud masoor*

split—*masoor dal*

These lentils are a familiar ingredient, especially the skinned split version that is salmon in color and is also known as "red lentils." Once red lentils are cooked (which happens in less than 20 minutes), they turn mushy, sauce-like, and yellow in color. This is an ideal legume for an evening meal when you are looking for something quick, meatless, cheap, and tasty. Just whip up some Slow-Roasted Bell Pepper with Red Lentils (page 401) or Tart Red Lentils with Tomatoes, Lime Juice, and Scallions (page 399).

The whole ones (*sabud masoor,* also called *matki*) take longer to cook than their split form. Soaking will of course expedite this, and so will a pressure cooker. Very nutty-tasting, chewy, and musky, these are great in Brown Lentils with Cumin and Turmeric (page 374).

Coconut-Smothered Black-Eyed Peas

Bina's Lobhia

I was intrigued when Bina Toniyat shared this recipe with me in her beautiful bungalow in Bangalore, India. She not only impressed me with her passion for her career in homeopathy (it came in handy when a stray dog bit me outside her gates) but also with her enthusiasm for cooking. This curry is testimony to that talent. Onions, one batch stewed with black-eyed peas, the other pureed and used as a key flavor with fresh coconut, sweeten this curry, made extra-creamy by the slow breakdown of the black-eyed peas. No need to worry about the number of chiles—the coconut and peas tend to absorb some of the peppers' capsaicin. **MAKES 4 CUPS**

1 cup dried black-eyed peas (see box, page 321)

2 small red onions; 1 cut in half lengthwise and thinly sliced, 1 coarsely chopped

4 fresh green Thai, cayenne, or serrano chiles, stems removed; 2 cut in half lengthwise, 2 coarsely chopped (do not remove the seeds)

½ cup shredded fresh coconut; or ¼ cup shredded dried unsweetened coconut, reconstituted (see Note)

1½ teaspoons coarse kosher or sea salt

1 teaspoon cumin seeds

¼ teaspoon ground turmeric

2 tablespoons coconut oil or canola oil

1 teaspoon black or yellow mustard seeds

12 medium-size to large fresh curry leaves

1. Place the black-eyed peas in a pressure cooker. Fill the cooker halfway with water and rinse the peas by rubbing them between your fingertips. The water may appear slightly dirty. Drain this water. Repeat three or four times, until the water remains relatively clear; drain. Now add 3 cups water and bring to a boil, uncovered, over high heat. Skim off and discard any foam that rises to the surface. Stir in the sliced onion and the 2 halved chiles. Seal the cooker shut and allow the pressure to build up. When the cooker reaches full pressure, reduce the heat to medium low and cook for about 20 minutes. Then remove the cooker from the heat and allow the pressure to subside naturally (about 15 minutes) before opening the lid.

2. Meanwhile, pour ½ cup water into a blender jar, and add the chopped onion and the chopped chiles. Add the coconut, salt, cumin seeds, and turmeric. Puree, scraping the inside of the jar as needed, to make a slightly gritty, green-speckled paste. Set it aside until the black-eyed peas are done.

3. Stir the coconut paste into the cooked black-eyed peas and simmer over medium-low heat, uncovered, stirring occasionally, until the flavors mingle, 5 to 10 minutes.

4. Heat the oil in a small skillet over medium-high heat. Add the mustard seeds, cover the skillet, and cook until the seeds have stopped popping (not unlike popcorn), about 30 seconds. Remove the skillet from the heat and add the curry leaves—carefully, as they will spatter upon contact. Pour this aromatic oil mixture into the curry, and stir. Then, serve.

Note: To reconstitute coconut, cover with ¼ cup boiling water, set aside for about 15 minutes, and then drain.

Black-Eyed Peas
WITH MUSHROOMS

dhingri Lobhia

ften, newly converted vegetarians yearn to slip back into carnivore land, especially when the aromas of sizzling, grilling, or broiling meats tempt them to fall off the herbivorous wagon. Here's a solution: Stir-fry meaty-textured, hearty brown mushrooms and fold them into black-eyed peas for a comparable fix without the guilt. **MAKES 4 CUPS**

1 cup dried black-eyed peas (see box, page 321)
2 tablespoons mustard oil or canola oil
8 ounces brown cremini mushrooms, sliced
1½ teaspoons coarse kosher or sea salt
1 teaspoon ground ginger
1 teaspoon ground Kashmiri chiles; or
    ¼ teaspoon cayenne (ground red pepper)
    mixed with ¾ teaspoon sweet paprika
½ cup finely chopped fresh cilantro leaves
    and tender stems

1. Place the black-eyed peas in a pressure cooker. Fill the cooker halfway with water and rinse the peas by rubbing them between your fingertips. The water may appear slightly dirty. Drain this water. Repeat three or four times, until the water remains relatively clear; drain. Now add 3 cups water and bring to a boil, uncovered, over high heat. Skim off and discard any foam that forms on the surface. Seal the cooker shut and allow the pressure to build up. When the cooker reaches full pressure, reduce the heat to medium-low and cook for about 20 minutes. Remove the cooker from the heat and allow the pressure to subside naturally (about 15 minutes) before opening the lid.

2. Meanwhile, heat the oil in a medium-size skillet over medium heat. Add the mushrooms and stir-fry until they shrivel up and start to brown, 5 to 10 minutes. Stir in the salt, ginger, ground chiles, and cilantro. Cook the spices gently without burning them (the mushrooms will cushion them against the direct heat from the skillet), about 1 minute. Set the mixture aside until the black-eyed peas are done.

3. Add the mushroom mixture to the cooked black-eyed peas. Transfer a spoonful of peas and water to the skillet and scrape the bottom to deglaze it, releasing the browned bits of mushrooms and spices. Add this to the curry. Bring the mixture to a simmer over medium heat and cook, uncovered, stirring occasionally, until the black-eyed peas absorb the flavors and the sauce thickens, about 15 minutes. Then serve.

Fresh Greens
WITH BLACK-EYED PEAS

Hyderabadi Waale Lobhia

this is one of those curries that is not only good but also good for you. Mustard greens house an incredibly large amount of iron and provide a hint of bitterness to the mixture. Serve this with a basket of naan (page 729), either homemade or store-bought, for a simple but nutritionally solid meal. **MAKES A GENEROUS 4 CUPS**

1 cup dried black-eyed peas (see box, page 321)

2 tablespoons Ghee (page 21) or canola oil

2 teaspoons cumin seeds

¼ teaspoon ground turmeric

¼ teaspoon ground asafetida

1 large tomato, cored and finely chopped

1½ teaspoons coarse kosher or sea salt

2 fresh green Thai, cayenne, or serrano chiles, stems removed, cut into ¼-inch-wide slices (do not remove the seeds)

4 ounces fresh mustard greens, well rinsed and finely chopped (see Tip, page 606)

4 ounces fresh spinach leaves, well rinsed and coarsely chopped

2 teaspoons Roasted Curry Leaf Spice Blend (page 35)

1. Place the black-eyed peas in a pressure cooker. Fill the cooker halfway with water and rinse the peas by rubbing them between your fingertips. The water may appear slightly dirty. Drain this water. Repeat three or four times, until the water remains relatively clear; drain. Now add 3 cups water and bring to a boil, uncovered, over high heat. Skim off and discard any foam that forms on the surface. Seal the cooker shut and allow the pressure to build up. When the cooker reaches full pressure, reduce the heat to medium-low and cook for about 20 minutes. Remove the cooker from the heat and allow the pressure to subside naturally (about 15 minutes) before opening the lid.

2. Meanwhile, heat the ghee in a medium-size skillet over medium-high heat. Add the cumin seeds and cook until they turn reddish brown and smell fragrant, 5 to 10 seconds. Sprinkle in the turmeric and asafetida, immediately followed by the tomato, salt, and chiles. Simmer over medium heat, stirring occasionally, until the tomato softens, about 5 minutes. Set the mixture aside until the black-eyed peas are done.

3. Stir the mustard and spinach greens into the

cooked black-eyed peas. Sprinkle in the spice blend, and add the tomato mixture. Stir once or twice and simmer over medium heat, uncovered, stirring occasionally, until the greens are wilted and the black-eyed peas have absorbed the incredibly simple but amazing flavors, about 10 minutes. Then serve.

Fenugreek-Perfumed Black-Eyed Peas
WITH A TOMATO SAUCE

Methi Lobhia

If possible, make a trip to your local Indian grocery store to procure fresh or frozen fenugreek leaves for this curry. The dried leaves will do in a pinch, but the perfumed bitterness from the fresh ones lingers much longer with every bite. One night when I had both vegetarians and non-vegetarians for dinner, I served this with Poppy and Mustard Seed–Rubbed Fish Fillets (page 255) and kept everyone happy. **MAKES 4 CUPS**

1 cup dried black-eyed peas (see box)

1 small red onion, coarsely chopped

6 medium-size cloves garlic

4 fresh green Thai, cayenne, or serrano chiles, stems removed

2 tablespoons Ghee (page 21) or canola oil

1 can (14.5 ounces) diced tomatoes

1 cup chopped fresh or frozen fenugreek leaves (thawed if frozen); or ½ cup dried fenugreek leaves, soaked in a bowl of water and skimmed off before use (see box, page 473)

2 teaspoons white granulated sugar

1½ teaspoons coarse kosher or sea salt

½ teaspoon ground turmeric

1. Place the black-eyed peas in a pressure cooker. Fill the cooker halfway with water, and rinse the peas by rubbing them between your fingertips. The water may appear slightly dirty. Drain this water. Repeat three or four times, until the water remains relatively clear; drain. Now add 3 cups water and bring it to a boil, uncovered, over high heat. Skim off and discard any foam that forms on the surface. Seal the cooker shut and allow the pressure to build up. When the cooker reaches full pressure, reduce the heat to medium-low and cook for about 20 minutes. Remove the cooker from the heat and allow the pressure to subside naturally (about 15 minutes) before opening the lid.

using frozen or canned black-eyed peas
❖ ❖ ❖

If you do not wish to cook them from scratch, frozen black-eyed peas are a perfectly acceptable alternative (one 16-ounce package frozen peas equals 1 cup dried). Follow the package directions to cook them. Make sure you retain 1 cup of the cooking liquid with the cooked peas so the curry won't be dry.

If you use canned black-eyed peas (two 15-ounce cans equals 1 cup dried), make sure you drain and rinse them before use. Add 1 cup water to the peas and start at Step 2.

2. Meanwhile, combine the onion, garlic, and chiles in a food processor and pulse until minced (the blend will be teary-eyed pungent).

3. Heat the ghee in a medium-size skillet over medium heat. Add the minced blend to the skillet and stir-fry until it is caramel-brown, 10 to 12 minutes.

4. Add the tomatoes, with their juice, and the fenugreek leaves, sugar, salt, and turmeric. Simmer, uncovered, stirring occasionally, until the tomato has softened and the fenugreek is cooked, about 5 minutes. Set this Christmassy-looking, red-green sauce aside until the black-eyed peas are ready.

5. Add the sauce to the cooked black-eyed peas. Simmer over medium heat, uncovered, stirring occasionally, until the peas have absorbed the flavors, about 5 minutes. Then serve.

Black-Eyed Peas

WITH MUSTARD, CUMIN, AND CURRY LEAVES

ʄuth ɳu dal

Indian black eyed-peas, called *muth,* are much smaller than their American siblings. Like all black-eyed peas, they retain their shape even when they are fully cooked. This dal is a great example of "simple is good." The spices and herbs—typical in Gujarati-speaking homes—highlight the peas' earthy flavors. I especially love it with comforting rice and yogurt if I want something easy for dinner. **MAKES 3 CUPS**

I cup dried black-eyed peas (see box, page 321)
2 tablespoons Ghee (page 21) or canola oil
I teaspoon black or yellow mustard seeds
2 teaspoons coarse kosher or sea salt
I teaspoon cumin seeds, ground
I teaspoon coriander seeds, ground
I teaspoon white granulated sugar
¼ teaspoon ground turmeric
¼ teaspoon ground asafetida
I large tomato, cored and finely chopped
12 medium-size to large fresh curry leaves
2 tablespoons finely chopped fresh cilantro leaves and tender stems for garnishing

1. Place the black-eyed peas in a pressure cooker. Fill the cooker halfway with water and rinse the peas by rubbing them between your fingertips. The water may appear slightly dirty. Drain this water. Repeat three or four times, until the water remains relatively clear; drain. Now add 3 cups water and bring it to a boil, uncovered, over high heat. Skim off and discard any foam that forms on the surface. Seal the cooker shut and allow the pressure to build up. When the cooker reaches full pressure, reduce the heat to medium-low and cook for about 20 minutes. Remove the cooker

cooking black-eyed peas in a saucepan
❖ ❖ ❖

black-eyed peas are quick-cooking and hence do not require soaking before they are cooked. A pressure cooker expedites the cooking, but a saucepan also does the trick: Place the black-eyed peas in a saucepan, add water to cover, and bring to a boil. Then cover the pan, reduce the heat to medium-low, and simmer until the peas are tender, 35 to 45 minutes.

from the heat and allow the pressure to subside naturally (about 15 minutes) before opening the lid.

2. Meanwhile, heat a small skillet over medium-high heat and pour in the ghee. Add the mustard seeds, cover the skillet, and cook until the seeds have stopped popping (not unlike popcorn), about 30 seconds. Then stir in the salt, cumin, coriander, sugar, turmeric, and asafetida. Immediately add the tomato and the curry leaves. Cook, uncovered, stirring occasionally, until the tomato has softened but is still chunky-looking, 2 to 3 minutes. Set this fragrant, tart, pungent, sweet sauce aside until the black-eyed peas are done.

3. Add the sauce to the cooked black-eyed peas, and stir once or twice. Spoon some of the peas and water into the skillet, and scrape up every last bit of sauce; pour this back into the cooker. Cook over medium heat, uncovered, stirring occasionally, until the peas have absorbed the flavors, 8 to 10 minutes.

4. Sprinkle with the cilantro, and serve.

Cinnamon-Flavored Black-Eyed Peas
WITH CARDAMOM

Sabud Garam Masale Waale Lobhia

black-eyed peas are a cinch to cook, and this creamy-tasting curry makes a quick weekday meal when ladled over slightly starchy white rice—the rice enhances the sauce's buttery texture. **MAKES 3 CUPS**

1 cup dried black-eyed peas (see box, page 321)
2 tablespoons Fried Onion Paste (page 16)
2 tablespoons tomato paste
1 tablespoon Garlic Paste (page 15)
2 teaspoons coarse kosher or sea salt
½ teaspoon cayenne (ground red pepper)
¼ teaspoon ground turmeric
2 tablespoons Ghee (page 21) or canola oil
2 cinnamon sticks (each 3 inches long)
2 fresh or dried bay leaves
2 black cardamom pods (see Tip)
2 tablespoons finely chopped fresh cilantro leaves
*   and tender stems for garnishing*

1. Place the black-eyed peas in a pressure cooker. Fill the cooker halfway with water and rinse the peas by rubbing them between your fingertips. The water may appear slightly dirty. Drain this water. Repeat three or four times, until the water remains relatively clear; drain. Now add 3 cups water and bring to a boil, uncovered, over high heat. Skim off and discard any foam that forms on the surface. Seal the cooker shut and allow the pressure to build up. When the cooker reaches full pressure, reduce the heat to medium-low and cook for about 20 minutes. Remove the cooker from the heat and allow the pressure to subside naturally (about 15 minutes) before opening the lid.

2. Meanwhile, combine ½ cup water with the onion and tomato and garlic pastes in a small bowl. Add the salt, cayenne, and turmeric, and whisk to make a slightly thick slurry.

3. Heat the ghee in a small skillet over medium-high heat. Sprinkle in the cinnamon sticks, bay leaves, and cardamom pods, which will instantly sizzle and swell to perfume the ghee. Stir in the reddish-brown slurry and

reduce the heat to medium-low. Simmer the sauce, partially covered to contain the spattering, stirring occasionally, until the ghee starts to separate around the edges and a glossy sheen forms on the surface, 8 to 10 minutes. Set it aside until the black-eyed peas are done.

4. Add the sauce to the cooked black-eyed peas, and stir once or twice. Simmer the curry over medium-low heat, uncovered, stirring occasionally, until the peas absorb the seasonings, about 10 minutes.

5. Remove the cinnamon sticks, bay leaves, and cardamom pods. Sprinkle the cilantro over the curry, and serve.

Tip: The more readily available green or white cardamom pods are an adequate alternative to the smoky black ones.

Sweet-Tart Cowpeas
WITH PEANUTS

Chori Ane Sengdana Nu Dal

Peanuts in this curry will not break down and fall apart, no matter how much you boil them. Their presence imparts a nice crunch to each mouthful. Sweet jaggery, tart kokum, nutty peanuts, pungent chiles, and

Jaggery? Kokum? See the Glossary of Ingredients, page 758.

aromatic curry leaves all come together in a well-balanced curry, with no one flavor dominating the mix. **MAKES 4 CUPS**

1 cup red cowpeas (sabud chowli), picked over
    for stones
6 pieces dried black kokum (each roughly
    2 inches long and 1 inch wide; see Tips)
2 tablespoons unsalted dry-roasted peanuts
1 tablespoon crumbled (or chopped) jaggery or
    firmly packed dark brown sugar
1½ teaspoons coarse kosher or sea salt
¼ teaspoon ground turmeric
¼ teaspoon ground asafetida
2 tablespoons Ghee (page 21) or canola oil
1 teaspoon cumin seeds
1 tablespoon finely chopped fresh ginger
12 medium-size to large fresh curry leaves
4 fresh green Thai, cayenne, or serrano chiles,
    stems removed, cut in half lengthwise
    (do not remove the seeds)

1. Place the cowpeas in a strainer and rinse them under running water to wash off any dust. Drain, and transfer them to a medium-size saucepan. Cover the cowpeas with hot water and set them aside at room temperature to soak until they soften and swell up a bit, 1 to 2 hours.

2. Drain the cowpeas, return them to the saucepan, and add 4 cups water. Bring to a boil over medium-high heat. Skim off and discard any foam that forms on the surface. Stir in the kokum slices. Lower the heat to medium, partially cover the pan, and simmer vigorously, stirring occasionally, until the cowpeas are tender but still firm-looking, 15 to 20 minutes.

3. Add the peanuts, jaggery, salt, turmeric, and asafetida. Cover the pan and simmer, stirring occasionally, until the peas are soft, 15 to 20 minutes. (They will continue to maintain their firm appearance even when soft.)

4. While the cowpeas are cooking, heat the ghee in a small skillet over medium-high heat. Add the cumin seeds and cook until they sizzle, turn reddish brown, and smell nutty, 5 to 10 seconds. Then add the ginger and stir-fry until it is browned, about 1 minute. Carefully throw in the curry leaves and chiles (they will spatter upon contact and instantly infuse the oil with a citrusy pungency).

5. Add this spiced oil mixture to the softened cowpeas and continue to cook the curry, uncovered, stirring occasionally, until the flavors mingle and the sauce thickens slightly, 20 to 25 minutes. (The intense heat of the peas will make the kokum break down into little bits. If larger pieces remain, you can either discard them, leave them in as is, or smash them into a pulpy mass with the back of your cooking spoon and return them to the dal.) Then serve.

Tips:

❖ Slightly unripe firm black plums, cut into ¼-inch-wide strips, make an easy alternative to kokum.

❖ Another alternative to kokum is tamarind. It makes for a darker-colored sauce; stir ½ teaspoon tamarind paste or concentrate into the simmering mixture in Step 5.

❖ I believe ghee provides an intrinsic richness to any curry, especially when an extra tablespoon is swirled in just before you serve it. If the fat calories are not okay for you, however, use vegetable oil for frying the spices and herbs and incorporate that lonesome tablespoon of ghee toward the end.

Coconut Cowpeas
WITH WINTER MELON

☸lan

When she was describing it to me, my sister-in-law Geeta said emphatically that *olan*, a special-occasion curry among the Hindu Brahmins of Kerala, is very simple to make and "should not be cluttered" with aggressive spices—the purity of the coconut milk should shine through. (See page 760 if you want to use fresh coconut milk.) Ladle this curry onto cooked red rice (page 708) for a nutty combination. You will be amazed at the potency of the small amount of chiles, especially with your first mouthful.

SERVES 4

¼ cup red cowpeas (sabud chowli), picked
    over for stones (see Tips)
1½ pounds white winter melon (see Tips), peeled,
    seeded, and cut into 1-inch cubes
¼ teaspoon ground turmeric
½ cup thick coconut milk (see Tips)
10 to 12 medium-size to large fresh curry leaves
1 or 2 fresh green Thai, cayenne, or serrano chiles,
    to taste, stems removed, cut in half lengthwise
    (do not remove the seeds)
1 teaspoon coarse kosher or sea salt

1. Place the cowpeas in a strainer and rinse them under running water to wash off any dust. Drain, transfer them to a small saucepan, and add hot water to cover. Set the pan aside at room temperature and let the cowpeas soak until they soften slightly and swell up, 1 to 2 hours.

2. Drain the cowpeas and return them to the same saucepan. Add 1 cup water and bring it to a boil over medium-high heat. Skim off and discard any foam that forms on the surface. Lower the heat to medium and simmer vigorously, uncovered, stirring occasionally, until the cowpeas are tender but still firm-looking, 12 to 15 minutes. Drain them in a colander.

3. While the cowpeas are cooking, combine 3 cups water, the winter melon, and the turmeric in a medium-size saucepan and bring to a boil over medium heat. Simmer vigorously, uncovered, stirring very occasionally (since the melon pieces are light, they tend to float and stay at the top, and when you move them around you get even-cooked results), until the melon is juicy-tender but still firm, about 10 minutes; drain.

4. Combine the cowpeas and melon in a medium-size saucepan, and add the coconut milk, curry leaves, chiles, and salt. Bring to a boil over medium-high heat. Then reduce the heat to medium-low, cover the pan, and cook until the flavors have mingled, about 5 minutes. Then serve.

Tips:

❖ Red cowpeas are easy to find in Indian grocery stores, but red adzuki beans or even black-eyed peas make perfect alternatives. The cooking time for all of them is relatively the same, give or take a few minutes.

❖ The flesh of the white winter melon reminds me of the light green or white, thick part of watermelon rind. Use that in a heartbeat if winter melon is not available in your favorite Indian grocery store.

❖ In a good-quality canned coconut milk, the thicker part floats to the top while the wheylike thinner liquid stays at the bottom. To get the thicker part of the milk, do not shake the can before you open it. Spoon out the thick milk from the top and leave the thin liquid behind.

Cowpeas
WITH BISHOP'S WEED AND TOASTED CHICKPEA FLOUR

Chowli Nu Dal

Tucked away in a very American-style shopping mall in Mumbai is my favorite restaurant, Rajdhani, which serves vegetarian fare from the northwestern states of Gujarat and Rajasthan. When I had stopped by for brunch on a recent visit, everything was outstanding, but these cowpeas bowled me over with their earthy-rich, thyme-like, sweet, hot, and succulent flavors.

MAKES 2 CUPS

> **B**ishop's weed? See the Glossary of Ingredients, page 758.

¾ cup red cowpeas (sabud chowli), picked over
    for stones
2 tablespoons canola oil
1 teaspoon cumin seeds
½ teaspoon bishop's weed
¼ cup finely chopped fresh cilantro leaves and
    tender stems
1½ teaspoons coarse kosher or sea salt
1 teaspoon coriander seeds, ground
1 teaspoon ground Deggi chiles (see box, page 290);
    or ½ teaspoon cayenne (ground red pepper)
    mixed with ½ teaspoon sweet paprika
¼ cup Toasted Chickpea Flour (page 41)
12 to 15 medium-size to large fresh curry leaves
2 teaspoons white granulated sugar
1 tablespoon Ghee (page 21)

1. Place the cowpeas in a strainer and rinse them under running water to wash off any dust. Drain, transfer them to a small saucepan, and add hot water to cover. Set the pan aside at room temperature and let the cowpeas soak until they soften slightly and swell up, 1 to 2 hours.

2. Drain the cowpeas and return them to the same saucepan. Add 3 cups water and bring to a boil over medium-high heat. Skim off and discard any foam that forms on the surface. Lower the heat to medium, cover the pan, and simmer vigorously, stirring occasionally, until the cowpeas are tender but still firm-looking, 20 to 25 minutes.

3. While the cowpeas are cooking, heat the oil in a small skillet over medium-high heat. Add the cumin seeds and bishop's weed. Cook until the seeds sizzle, turn reddish brown, and smell aromatic, 5 to 10 seconds. Remove the skillet from the heat and stir in the cilantro, salt, coriander, and ground chiles. (The heat from the oil will be just right to cook the spices without burning them.)

4. Pour this spiced oil into the cooked cowpeas, and add the chickpea flour and the curry leaves. Continue to simmer the curry over medium heat, uncovered, stirring occasionally, until the sauce thickens slightly, about 15 minutes.

5. Stir in the sugar and ghee, and serve. The burst of sweetness and the succulence from the ghee will tone down the intensity of the chiles to make for a smooth balance.

Tip: Cooked black-eyed peas are a fine alternative to the cowpeas. Combine the black-eyed peas with 2 cups water in a saucepan, and heat until the peas are warmed through. Start the recipe at Step 3.

Sprouted Cowpeas
STEWED IN COCONUT MILK

Chawli Kokum Chi Dal

Because sprouted peas and beans are tender and chock-full of nutrients, people often eat them raw in salads. Sprouted beans and peas contain even more vitamins and minerals than their dried versions and are a popular choice in regions where a lack of fuel can hinder cooking. **MAKES 3 CUPS**

2 tablespoons canola oil
1 cup finely chopped red onion
4 large cloves garlic, finely chopped
4 fresh green Thai, cayenne, or serrano chiles, stems removed, finely chopped (do not remove the seeds)
3 cups partially sprouted red cowpeas (see box, page 328)
½ teaspoon ground turmeric
1 can (13.5 ounces) unsweetened coconut milk
1½ teaspoons coarse kosher or sea salt
6 pieces dried black kokum (each roughly 2 inches long and 1 inch wide; see Tips)
¼ cup boiling water
½ teaspoon Toasted Cumin-Coriander Blend (page 33)
2 tablespoons finely chopped fresh cilantro leaves and tender stems for garnishing

1. Heat the oil in a medium-size saucepan over medium-high heat. Add the onion, garlic, and chiles, and stir-fry until the mixture is light brown and smells pungent, 5 to 7 minutes.

sprouting

❖ ❖ ❖

It's very easy to sprout peas, beans, and even lentils. Chickpeas, mung beans, and cowpeas are easy to sprout. Even fenugreek seeds yield great, if slightly bitter-tasting, sprouts.

Place the legumes in a strainer and rinse them thoroughly under running water. Then transfer them to a large bowl (the bowl should be large enough to accommodate the legumes' growth in volume during soaking) and fill the bowl more than halfway with warm water. Cover the bowl with plastic wrap and set it aside at room temperature; let the legumes soak until they are tender, 4 to 6 hours or even overnight.

Drain the legumes and transfer them to a glass jar that is large enough to accommodate a six-fold increase in volume. Place a piece of cheesecloth over the mouth of the jar and secure it with the jar's ring (for a Mason-type jar) or with a sturdy rubber band. Place the jar in a dark, humid spot (I keep mine in the cupboard under the kitchen sink). Two or three times a day (if you remember), rinse the legumes by filling the jar with water (pour it through the cheesecloth) and then draining it; return the legumes to their solitary confinement. Within 24 hours, you will notice tiny sprouts emerging from the grains. Two or 3 days of this rinse-drain-store cycle will yield sprouts that are about 2 inches long.

Thoroughly rinse the sprouted legumes, transfer them to a self-seal plastic bag, and store them in the refrigerator for up to 5 days.

2. Add the cowpeas and turmeric, and stir to coat the sprouted peas and to gently cook the yellow spice, about 1 minute. Pour in the coconut milk, and sprinkle in the salt. Once the curry comes to a boil, reduce the heat to medium-low, cover the pan, and simmer, stirring occasionally, until the cowpeas are firm-tender and the sauce is thick, 18 to 20 minutes.

3. While the cowpeas are cooking, place the kokum pieces in a heatproof bowl and pour the boiling water over them. Set the bowl aside letting the kokum steep until the water turns dark brown with a purple hue, about 15 minutes. Discard the kokum pieces.

4. Fold the kokum water and the spice blend into the curry, sprinkle with the cilantro, and serve.

Tips:

❖ If kokum is not available, use ¼ teaspoon tamarind paste or concentrate dissolved in ¼ cup warm tap water.

❖ I started with 1 cup red cowpeas, which yielded about 5 cups sprouted peas.

Chickpeas
WITH A COCONUT SAUCE

Shundal

Comforting *Shundals* make an appearance during the ten days leading up to Hindu India's celebration of lights, called Diwali, celebrated sometime in October and November. Made as an offering to the goddess of learning, these legume-based dishes are wrapped in packets of banana leaves, and accompany the women and children to their homes after they have visited the temples or friends' homes for worshipping. Often not as saucelike as this one, but definitely wet, these coconut-smothered curries incorporate whole legumes; favorites are the curries made with black-eyed peas, black and yellow chickpeas, and whole green lentils. My rendition packs a punch with potent red chiles. Use less if your tolerance for heat is not great, more if you enjoy its endorphin-inducing high. **MAKES 4 CUPS**

- *2 tablespoons unrefined sesame oil or canola oil*
- *2 tablespoons yellow split peas (chana dal), picked over for stones*
- *1 tablespoon coriander seeds*
- *4 dried red Thai or cayenne chiles, stems removed*
- *1 teaspoon tamarind paste or concentrate*
- *1 teaspoon black or yellow mustard seeds*
- *3 cups cooked chickpeas*
- *2 teaspoons coarse kosher or sea salt*
- *¼ teaspoon ground turmeric*
- *¼ teaspoon ground asafetida*
- *12 medium-size to large fresh curry leaves*
- *1 cup shredded fresh coconut; or ½ cup shredded dried unsweetened coconut, reconstituted (see Note)*
- *2 tablespoons finely chopped fresh cilantro leaves and tender stems*

1. Heat the oil in a medium-size saucepan over medium-high heat. Add the split peas, coriander seeds, and chiles, and roast, stirring constantly, until the split peas and coriander seeds are reddish brown and the chiles have blackened slightly, 1 to 2 minutes. Remove the pan from the heat. Using a slotted spoon, skim off the spices and transfer them to a plate to cool; let

them sit for about 5 minutes. Once they are cool to the touch, put them in a spice grinder and grind until the texture resembles that of finely ground black pepper.

2. Pour 2 cups water into a bowl, and add the tamarind paste. Whisk to dissolve the tamarind.

3. Reheat the oil in the saucepan over medium-high heat. Add the mustard seeds, cover the pan, and cook until the seeds have stopped popping (not unlike popcorn), about 30 seconds. Stir in the chickpeas, salt, turmeric, asafetida, and curry leaves. Stir to coat the chickpeas evenly with the spices. Pour in the tamarind water and bring to a boil. Then lower the heat to medium and cook, uncovered, stirring occasionally, until the chickpeas absorb the flavors, 8 to 10 minutes.

4. Stir in the ground spices, coconut, and cilantro, and serve.

Note: To reconstitute coconut, cover with ½ cup boiling water, set aside for about 15 minutes, and then drain.

Gingered Chickpeas

Adrak Lasson Waale Chana Masala

I love how the stir-fried ginger and garlic mingle with their pureed selves in this robustly flavored curry. I admit that folks need another *chana masala* recipe like they need a hole in the head (or another north Indian restaurant, for that matter), but I do think that you will agree that this version is a true winner. You can proudly take it to any Punjabi potluck and accept full credit for all your not-so-hard work—because this simple curry will come across as having been "slaved over."

MAKES 4 CUPS

I large tomato, cored and coarsely chopped
I small red onion, coarsely chopped
8 lengthwise slices fresh ginger (each 2 inches long,
    I inch wide, and ⅛ inch thick); 4 coarsely chopped,
    4 cut into matchstick-thin strips (julienne)
8 medium-size cloves garlic; 4 coarsely chopped,
    4 finely chopped
I or 2 fresh green Thai, cayenne, or serrano chiles,
    to taste, stems removed
I tablespoon coriander seeds
2 teaspoons cumin seeds
I cinnamon stick (3 inches long), broken into pieces
2 tablespoons canola oil
2 teaspoons ground Kashmiri chiles; or ½ teaspoon
    cayenne (ground red pepper) mixed with
    1½ teaspoons sweet paprika
½ teaspoon ground turmeric
½ cup finely chopped fresh cilantro leaves and
    tender stems
3 cups cooked chickpeas
I teaspoon Punjabi garam masala (page 25)
Juice of I medium-size lime

1. Pour ½ cup water into a blender jar, followed by the tomato, onion, coarsely chopped ginger, coarsely chopped garlic, chilcs, coriander seeds, cumin seeds, and cinnamon pieces. Puree, scraping the inside of the jar as needed, to make a smooth, purple-red, spice-speckled sauce.

2. Heat the oil in a medium-size saucepan over medium heat. Sprinkle in the julienned ginger and the finely chopped garlic. Stir-fry until they sizzle and turn light brown, 1 to 2 minutes.

3. Pour in the sauce, which will start to boil within seconds. Then stir in the ground chiles, turmeric, and ¼ cup of the cilantro. Cover the pan partially, and simmer, stirring occasionally, until an oily sheen starts to form around the edges and on the surface, 5 to 10 minutes.

4. Add the chickpeas and 1 cup water, and stir once or twice. Bring the curry to a boil. Then reduce the heat to medium-low and simmer, completely covered, stirring occasionally, until the sauce has thickened slightly and the chickpeas have become more tender and have absorbed the rich flavors, 25 to 30 minutes.

5. Stir in the garam masala, lime juice, and remaining ¼ cup cilantro, and serve.

Chickpeas
WITH MANGO POWDER

Amchur Chana

When a curry relies on the pervasive flavor of a spice, it had better be strong enough to carry the sauce. The ground powder *(chur)* of unripe mango *(aam)* in this dish bears that burden with great fortitude, not to mention earthy tartness. Mango powder is a souring, cooling spice, used heavily in northern India—as are chickpeas, so it is natural that the two come together very often there. I find it interesting that even though crushed tomatoes (another acid) form the base of the sauce, they take a back seat to this beige-colored spice. **MAKES 4 CUPS**

2 tablespoons canola oil

2 teaspoons cumin seeds, I teaspoon whole,
   I teaspoon ground

2 black, green, or white cardamom pods

I or 2 cinnamon sticks (each 3 inches long), to taste

I cup canned crushed tomatoes (see Tip)

2 tablespoons mango powder (see box, page 604) or
   fresh lime juice

I tablespoon coriander seeds, ground

I teaspoon coarse kosher or sea salt

½ teaspoon cayenne (ground red pepper)

¼ teaspoon ground turmeric

3 cups cooked chickpeas

4 tablespoons finely chopped fresh cilantro
   leaves and tender stems

¼ cup finely chopped red onion

1. Heat the oil in a medium-size saucepan over medium-high heat. Sprinkle in the cumin seeds, cardamom pods, and cinnamon sticks, and cook until they sizzle and smell aromatic, 10 to 15 seconds.

2. Add the tomatoes, mango powder, coriander, ground cumin, salt, cayenne, and turmeric. Lower the heat to medium and simmer the sauce, partially covered, stirring occasionally, until some of the oil starts to separate around the edges, 5 to 10 minutes.

3. Stir in the chickpeas, 1 cup water, and 2 tablespoons of the cilantro. Cover the pan and simmer the curry, stirring occasionally, until the flavors blend, the chickpeas absorb the flavors, and the sauce thickens, 20 to 25 minutes.

4. Sprinkle with the onion and the remaining 2 tablespoons cilantro, and serve.

Tip: Some varieties of canned crushed tomatoes are unsalted. If that is what you use for this recipe, add an extra ½ teaspoon salt.

Tea and Ginger Simmered Chickpeas

Chai Patte Waali Chana

This may seem like a fusion dish if you are not familiar with some of India's regional curries. However, ask a northeast Indian about chickpeas in brewed tea, and he or she will nod in that oh-so-Indian way and rattle off many other tasty and unusual concoctions that use the region's world famous tea leaves. Darjeeling's black tea is the cabernet of teas, with unparalleled body, aroma, and color in each hot sip. When added to sauces, it imparts, in addition to color and aroma, a slight perfumed bitterness. A good way to use up leftover brewed tea, wouldn't you agree? **SERVES 6**

2 tablespoons black tea leaves, preferably
   Darjeeling

2 tablespoons mustard oil or canola oil

I tablespoon cumin seeds

2 tablespoons finely chopped fresh ginger

I tablespoon finely chopped garlic

2 to 4 fresh green Thai, cayenne, or serrano chiles,
   to taste, stems removed, thinly sliced crosswise
   (do not remove the seeds)

3 cups cooked chickpeas

¼ cup finely chopped fresh cilantro leaves
   and tender stems

1½ teaspoons coarse kosher or sea salt

½ teaspoon ground turmeric

Juice of I medium-size lime

1. Bring 2 cups water to a rolling boil in a small saucepan over medium-high heat. Sprinkle in the tea leaves, remove the pan from the heat, and allow the tea to steep for about 5 minutes; it will turn the water a deep reddish brown. Strain the infusion, discarding the swollen leaves.

2. Heat the oil in a medium-size saucepan over medium-high heat. Add the cumin seeds and cook until they sizzle, turn reddish brown, and smell fragrant, 5 to 10 seconds. Then add the ginger, garlic, and chiles, and stir-fry until the ginger and garlic are light brown and the chiles smell pungent, 1 to 2 minutes.

3. Stir in the chickpeas, cilantro, salt, and turmeric. Cook, making sure every chickpea gets well coated with the seasonings, until the turmeric is cooked, about 1 minute. Pour in the brewed tea, stir once or twice, and bring to a boil. Then lower the heat to medium and cook, uncovered, until the sauce has thickened slightly, 8 to 10 minutes.

4. Stir in the lime juice, and serve.

quick-soaking chickpeas

❖ ❖ ❖

If you don't have time to soak dried chickpeas for 8 hours, use the quick-soak method: After you have rinsed the beans, bring the beans and water to cover to a rolling boil in a medium-size saucepan over medium-high heat. Remove the pan from the heat and allow the beans to stand in that water, covered, for 1 hour.

Slow-Cooked Chickpeas
WITH BROWNED ONIONS IN AN ONION SAUCE

Vengayam Thana

I was apprehensive, at best, when a slow cooker made its way into my kitchen. Having always used a pressure cooker to tenderize beans, especially long-cooking chickpeas, I tested this curry with great trepidation. The initial prep work to get all the ingredients ready for the slow cooker proved effortless, and the rest was very easy as I let the cooker do its thing. After a good night's sleep, I woke up, not to the usual aroma of freshly brewed coffee, but to the magic of spices in the air. Raising the lid revealed plump chickpeas smothered in an invitingly robust-looking sauce. A quick stir or two and soon I was spooning in mouthfuls of pungent, tart, and surprisingly sweet curry well before I sipped that first mandatory cup of coffee. I was thankful for a new and exciting way to awaken all my senses. And yes, I became a slow-cooker convert for curries that require long simmering times, especially if they contain hard-to-cook legumes or tough cuts of meat. **MAKES 4 CUPS**

1 cup dried chickpeas

2 tablespoons canola oil

1 teaspoon cumin seeds

6 green or white cardamom pods

4 dried red Thai or cayenne chiles, stems removed

2 cinnamon sticks (each 3 inches long)

*2 medium-size red onions: 1 cut in half lengthwise
and thinly sliced, 1 coarsely chopped*

2 teaspoons Sambhar masala (page 33)

1 teaspoon black salt

1 teaspoon coarse kosher or sea salt

1 can (14.5 ounces) diced tomatoes

*1 teaspoon tamarind paste or concentrate
(see Tip)*

*2 fresh green Thai, cayenne, or serrano chiles,
stems removed*

*½ cup finely chopped fresh cilantro leaves and
tender stems*

*½ cup shredded fresh coconut; or ¼ cup shredded
dried unsweetened coconut (no need to
reconstitute it for this recipe)*

12 to 15 medium-size to large fresh curry leaves

1. Place the chickpeas in a medium-size bowl. Fill the bowl halfway with water and rinse the chickpeas by rubbing them between your fingertips. The water will become slightly cloudy. Drain this water. Repeat three or four times, until the water remains relatively clear; drain. Now fill the bowl halfway with hot water and let it sit at room temperature, covered with plastic wrap, until the chickpeas have softened, at least 8 hours or as long as overnight.

2. When the chickpeas are almost tender, heat the oil in a medium-size skillet over medium-high heat. Sprinkle in the cumin seeds, cardamom pods, dried chiles, and cinnamon sticks. Cook until the spices sizzle, smell aromatic, and start to crackle, about 1 minute. Then add the sliced onion and stir-fry until it is light brown around the edges, about 5 minutes. Stir in the *Sambhar masala*, black salt, and coarse salt. Transfer this mixture to a slow cooker.

3. Pour the tomatoes, with their juices, into a blender jar, followed by the coarsely chopped onion, tamarind paste, and fresh chiles. Puree, scraping the inside of the jar as needed, to make a smooth, light red sauce speckled with green and purple flakes. Pour this into the slow cooker. Pour ½ cup water into the blender jar and swish it around to wash it out; add this to the slow cooker. Pour another 1½ cups water into the cooker, and add the cilantro, coconut, and curry leaves.

4. Drain the chickpeas and stir them in. Place the lid on the cooker, set it to "low," and cook for 10 to 12 hours.

5. Remove the cardamom pods, dried chiles, and cinnamon sticks if you like. Stir the curry, and serve.

Tip: Tamarind provides earthy tartness to this curry. If you don't have any, stir the juice of 1 medium-size lime into the curry just before serving for a burst of clean, crisp, puckery flavor.

Chickpeas
WITH A SPICY TOMATO SAUCE

Thana Masala

This curry is as pervasive in northern Indian home kitchens as is macaroni-and-cheese in kitchens all across the United States. Its color reflects the dark spices that paint its flavors. It is best served with bread as an accompaniment, and it appeases even the vegan at the table. Those who don't think it's hot enough can cut up some fresh green Thai, cayenne, or serrano chiles and scatter them atop the onion.

SERVES 8

2 tablespoons Ghee (page 21) or canola oil

2 teaspoon cumin seeds, 1 teaspoon left whole,
   1 teaspoon ground

2 tablespoons Ginger Paste (page 15)

1 tablespoon Garlic Paste (page 15)

2 tablespoons tomato paste

1 tablespoon coriander seeds, ground

1 tablespoons mango powder or
   fresh lime juice

1 teaspoon cayenne (ground red pepper)

½ teaspoon ground turmeric

4 cups cooked chickpeas

4 tablespoons finely chopped fresh cilantro
   leaves and tender stems

1½ teaspoons coarse kosher or sea salt

½ cup finely chopped red onion

1. Heat the ghee in a large saucepan over medium-high heat. Sprinkle in the whole cumin seeds and cook until they sizzle, turn reddish brown, and smell nutty, 5 to 10 seconds. Immediately lower the heat to medium and carefully stir in the ginger and garlic pastes. Stir-fry until the pastes turn light brown, about 2 minutes.

2. Stir in 1 cup water and the tomato paste, coriander, mango powder, cayenne, turmeric, and ground cumin. Simmer, partially covered, stirring occasionally, until the water evaporates from the reddish-brown sauce, 5 to 10 minutes.

3. Pour in 2 cups water, the chickpeas, 2 tablespoons of the cilantro, and the salt. Raise the heat to medium-high and cook, uncovered, stirring occasionally, until the sauce thickens, 15 to 18 minutes.

4. Sprinkle the remaining 2 tablespoons cilantro and the onion over the curry, and serve.

Chickpeas
WITH SPINACH AND MUSTARD SEEDS

Chana Saag

A fine balance, this curry juggles northern techniques and ingredients (onion and ginger pastes) with the southern way of roasting spices and legumes. Savor it ladled over white rice for a well-balanced meal of whole grains, starch, and greens. It is no wonder that so many men, women, and children with Indian roots are content being vegetarians. **MAKES 4 CUPS**

2 tablespoons Ghee (page 21) or canola oil

1 teaspoon black or yellow mustard seeds

1 tablespoon Ginger Paste (page 15)

2 tablespoons Fried Onion Paste (page 16)

2 tablespoons tomato paste

2 teaspoons Sambhar masala (page 33)

2 teaspoons coarse kosher or sea salt

2 cups cooked chickpeas

1 pound fresh spinach leaves, well rinsed and
   finely chopped

1. Heat the ghee in a medium-size saucepan over medium-high heat. Add the mustard seeds, cover the pan, and cook until the seeds have stopped popping (not unlike popcorn), about 30 seconds. Lower the heat to medium and carefully add the Ginger Paste (watch for spattering). Stir-fry until it is light brown, about 30 seconds.

2. Stir in the Fried Onion Paste, tomato paste, *Sambhar masala*, salt, and chickpeas. Stir to coat the chickpeas well with the hot-tart sauce. Add 2 cups water and heat to a boil.

3. Add the spinach, several handfuls at a time, stirring each batch in until wilted. When all the spinach has been added, reduce the heat to medium-low and continue to simmer the curry, covered, stirring occasionally, until the sauce has thickened, 8 to 10 minutes. Then serve.

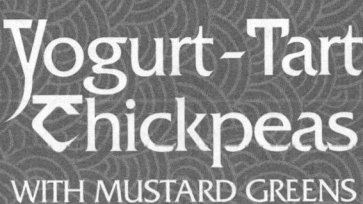

Yogurt-Tart Chickpeas
WITH MUSTARD GREENS

Sorshe Thana

Bengalis are masters at incorporating an underlying pleasant bitterness into their curries. Often mustard paste, pureed from mustard seeds, provides that slap-in-your-face kick, but in this recipe, mustard greens sneak in just a hint, to offer a vibrant base for the chickpeas. **MAKES 7 CUPS**

- 1 small red onion, cut in half lengthwise and coarsely chopped
- 6 to 8 fresh green Thai, cayenne, or serrano chiles, to taste, stems removed
- 6 medium-size cloves garlic
- 3 lengthwise slices fresh ginger (each 2 inches long, 1 inch wide, and ⅛ inch thick)
- 2 tablespoons Ghee (page 21) or canola oil
- 2 fresh or dried bay leaves
- 1 can (14.5 ounces) diced tomatoes
- 2 teaspoons Bangala garam masala (page 26)
- 2 teaspoons coarse kosher or sea salt
- 1 pound fresh mustard greens, well rinsed and finely chopped (see Tips)

using canned legumes
❖ ❖ ❖

Just because I consider myself a gourmet (and a gourmand at times), it doesn't mean I turn my nose up at canned chickpeas and kidney beans (or any other legume). In fact, at any given time, feel free to stop by my house unannounced and open up my pantry cupboards—you'll discover canned beans! I find them perfectly acceptable for inclusion in any of my curries. What I don't like about them is the brine that they sit in. So I drain them and rinse them before I add them to my recipes—and marvel at the convenience of canned goods. Makes it downright expedient to whip up a legume curry at a moment's notice!

- 4 cups cooked chickpeas (see Tips)
- 1 cup plain yogurt
- ¼ cup heavy (whipping) cream
- 1 tablespoon Toasted Cumin-Coriander Blend (page 33)

1. Combine the onion, chiles, garlic, and ginger in a food processor and mince, using the pulsing action, to make a pungent blend.

2. Heat the ghee in a large saucepan over medium-high heat. Add the onion blend and the bay leaves, and cook until the onion starts to brown around the edges, 3 to 5 minutes.

3. Pour in the diced tomatoes, with their juices, the garam masala, and the salt, and stir once or twice. Then add a couple of handfuls of the mustard greens, stirring to coat them with the sauce and letting them wilt in the heat. Repeat until all the greens have been added. Stir in the chickpeas and simmer over medium-low heat, uncovered, until the sauce has thickened slightly, 12 to 15 minutes.

4. While the chickpea mixture is simmering, whisk the yogurt and cream together in a small bowl.

5. When the curry has thickened, fold in the tart-smooth creamy yogurt. Stir in the cumin-coriander blend.

6. Discard the bay leaves, and serve.

Tips:

❖ If you are not wild about mustard greens, substitute spinach greens for half the amount.

❖ Canned chickpeas cut the time spent in the kitchen. Two 15-ounce cans will yield about 4 cups cooked beans. Make sure you drain them and rinse off the brine before using them.

Sweet and Sour Chickpeas
AND KIDNEY BEANS

khatte meethe chanay

ark brown, hot-sweet, and highly tart, this sauce blankets two kinds of beans, chickpeas and kidney beans, both quite widely used in northern Indian cuisine. I often serve this as an appetizer curry with a basket of naan, either store-bought or homemade (page 729), cut into small wedges. Dunk the naan in the addictive sauce, or spoon the legumes over the naan pieces. You will notice that you can't just eat one, which is fine because this is a healthy alternative to deep-fried potato chips. (Don't get me wrong—I love those potato chips.) **MAKES 6 CUPS**

1 medium-size red onion, coarsely chopped

8 medium-size cloves garlic

4 to 6 dried red Thai or cayenne chiles, to taste, stems removed

3 lengthwise slices fresh ginger (each 2 inches long, 1 inch wide, and ⅛ inch thick)

2 tablespoons Ghee (page 21) or canola oil

1 teaspoon cumin seeds

2 tablespoons coriander seeds, ground

2 teaspoons coarse kosher or sea salt

2 teaspoons white granulated sugar

1 teaspoon fennel seeds, ground

½ teaspoon ground turmeric

½ teaspoon cardamom seeds from green or white pods, ground

3 cups cooked chickpeas

2 cups cooked kidney beans

2 teaspoons tamarind paste or concentrate

¼ cup finely chopped fresh cilantro leaves and tender stems

1. Combine the onion, garlic, chiles, and ginger in a food processor, and pulse until minced.

2. Heat the ghee in a large saucepan over medium-high heat. Add the cumin seeds and cook until they sizzle, turn reddish brown, and smell nutty, 5 to 10 seconds. Immediately add the minced blend, and stir-fry until the mixture is pungent (adequate ventilation is a good idea at this point, to prevent upper respiratory discomfort) and light brown around the edges, 5 to 8 minutes.

3. Stir in the coriander, salt, sugar, fennel, turmeric,

and cardamom, and stir until the spices are cooked but not burned, 1 to 2 minutes. Add the chickpeas and kidney beans, and pour in 4 cups water. Stir in the tamarind paste; it will turn the liquid a murky brown. Bring the curry to a boil. Then lower the heat to medium and simmer, uncovered, stirring occasionally, until a lot of the liquid has been absorbed and the sauce has thickened, 25 to 30 minutes.

4. Stir in the cilantro, and serve.

Chickpeas and Potatoes
FLAVORED WITH SINGED SPICES

Pindi Waale Aloo Chana

Short for Rawalpindi, Pindi was the capital city of Pakistan until the 1960s, when Islamabad was constructed—a modern replacement for this overcrowded and unplanned metropolis. Some of the street foods associated with Pindi are extremely popular, not only in Pakistan, but also in India—especially in the northwest. This style of cooking chickpeas highlights the tart flavors of dried mango powder, pomegranate seeds, and sulfur-based black salt. Note the interesting way the spices are cooked: by gently singeing them with hot oil (that's the verb singe, as in searing; you are not required to break into a Bollywood tune).

SERVES 6

Pomegranate seeds? Black salt? See the Glossary of Ingredients, page 758.

1 medium-size russet or Yukon Gold potato, peeled, cut into ½-inch cubes, and submerged in a bowl of cold water to prevent browning
3 cups cooked chickpeas
2 tablespoons mango powder or fresh lime juice
1 tablespoon dried pomegranate seeds, ground
2 teaspoons Toasted Cumin-Coriander Blend (page 33)
1 teaspoon ground Deggi chiles (see box, page 290); or ½ teaspoon cayenne (ground red pepper) mixed with ½ teaspoon sweet paprika
1 teaspoon Punjabi garam masala (page 25)
1 teaspoon coarse kosher or sea salt
1 teaspoon fine black salt
6 tablespoons canola oil
1 cup finely chopped red onion
1 large tomato, cored and finely chopped
2 to 4 fresh green Thai, cayenne, or serrano chiles, to taste, stems removed, cut in half lengthwise (do not remove the seeds) for garnishing
¼ cup finely chopped fresh cilantro leaves and tender stems for garnishing

1. Drain the potato cubes.

2. Pour 3 cups water into a medium-size saucepan, and add the potato, chickpeas, mango powder, pomegranate, cumin-coriander blend, ground chiles, garam masala, coarse salt, and black salt. Bring to a boil over medium-high heat and continue to simmer vigorously, uncovered, stirring occasionally, until the potato is fork-tender and the sauce has thickened, 15 to 20 minutes.

3. While the potato-chickpea mixture is cooking, heat 2 tablespoons of the oil in a medium-size skillet over medium-high heat. Add the onion and stir-fry until it is light brown around the edges, 3 to 5 minutes. Stir in the tomato and continue to simmer, uncovered, stirring occasionally, until it softens but is still firm-looking, 2 to 4 minutes.

4. When the potato-chickpea mixture has thickened, stir in the onion-tomato mixture.

5. Heat the remaining 4 tablespoons oil in a small skillet over medium-high heat until it almost starts to smoke (see Tip). Carefully pour this hot oil into the potato-chickpea mixture, singeing the spices, and stir well.

6. Sprinkle the chiles and cilantro over the curry, and serve.

Tip: This is where you can make re-use use of your canola oil, after having used it multiple times for deep-frying. The flavors that linger in the oil will augment the curry's zest, as long as the oil is not rancid. I usually store my used oil in the refrigerator.

Be careful when you heat used oil. Its smoke point is not as high as fresh oil because of the moisture that has leached into it from the fried foods. As soon as it starts to shimmer, hold the palm of your hand 2 inches above the oil. If your hand feels the heat in less than 5 seconds, it's ready for the singe.

Gujarati-Style Black and Yellow Chickpeas
WITH A SPICY-SWEET SAUCE

Kala Aur Kabuli Chana

I sampled a rendition of this dal at the home of my childhood friend Pinank on a recent visit to Mumbai. His mother, an exceptional cook and compassionate being, filled my stainless steel bowl with this spicy-rich curry and made sure there was an unending supply of her famous handkerchief-thin *rotlis,* smothered with ghee, to go with it. No matter how tight my traveling schedule may be, when I am in India, I always make time for a meal at her table. With fare like this, how could I not?

MAKES 4 CUPS

¼ *cup dried black chickpeas*

¼ *cup dried chickpeas*

¼ *cup dried red kidney beans*

¼ *cup whole black lentils (sabud urad)*

2 tablespoons Ghee (page 21) or canola oil

1 teaspoon black or yellow mustard seeds

2 teaspoon cumin seeds; 1 teaspoon left whole,
  1 teaspoon ground

2 teaspoons white granulated sugar

1½ teaspoons coarse kosher or sea salt

1 teaspoon coriander seeds, ground

½ teaspoon ground turmeric

½ teaspoon ground asafetida

2 dried red Thai or cayenne chiles

1 large tomato, cored and finely chopped

2 to 4 fresh green Thai, cayenne, or serrano chiles,
  to taste, stems removed, cut in half lengthwise
  (do not remove the seeds)

2 tablespoons finely chopped fresh cilantro
  leaves and tender stems for garnishing

1. Place all the chickpeas, beans, and lentils in a medium-size bowl. Fill the bowl halfway with water and rinse the legumes by rubbing them between your fingertips. The water will become slightly cloudy. Drain this water. Repeat three or four times, until the water remains relatively clear; drain. Now fill the bowl halfway with hot water and let it sit at room temperature, covered with plastic wrap, until the legumes soften, at least 8 hours or as long as overnight.

2. Drain the chickpea/bean/lentil mixture, and transfer it to a pressure cooker. Add 3 cups water and bring to a boil, uncovered, over high heat. Skim off and discard any foam that forms on the surface. Seal the cooker shut and allow the pressure to build up. When the cooker reaches full pressure, reduce the heat to medium-low and cook for about 1 hour. Remove the cooker from the heat and allow the pressure to subside naturally (about 15 minutes) before opening the lid.

3. While the legumes are cooking, heat the ghee in a small skillet over medium-high heat. Add the mustard seeds, cover the skillet, and cook until the seeds have stopped popping (not unlike popcorn), about 30 seconds. Remove the skillet from the heat and sprinkle in the whole cumin seeds, sugar, salt, ground cumin, coriander, turmeric, asafetida, and dried chiles. The spices will instantly sizzle and smell aromatic, but the heat of the ghee will be just right to cook them without burning.

4. Immediately add the tomato and the fresh chiles, and return the skillet to medium heat. Cook until the tomato has softened slightly and appears saucelike, about 2 minutes. Set this aside until the legumes are cooked.

5. Add the tomato mixture to the cooked legumes, and stir once or twice. Simmer over medium heat, uncovered, stirring occasionally, until the sauce has thickened and flavored the legumes, 12 to 15 minutes.

6. Sprinkle with the cilantro, and serve.

Black Chickpeas
WITH A COCONUT-CHILE SAUCE

Kala Chana Masala

A robust legume like this one needs assertive spices, and I usually find myself looking to the south (India, that is) for its dried red chiles, coconut, and coriander seeds. Serve this with the other southern (U.S.A., that is) delicacy: warm, jalapeño-kissed corn bread. You'll rethink your traditional chili-corn bread strategy for dinner.

MAKES 4 CUPS

1 cup dried black chickpeas
6 green or white cardamom pods
2 fresh or dried bay leaves
2 cinnamon sticks (each 3 inches long)
4 tablespoons canola oil
½ cup shredded dried unsweetened coconut
1 tablespoon coriander seeds
4 to 6 dried red Thai or cayenne chiles, to taste, stems removed
1 teaspoon black or yellow mustard seeds
15 to 20 medium-size to large fresh curry leaves
1½ teaspoons coarse kosher or sea salt

1. Place the chickpeas in a medium-size bowl. Fill the bowl halfway with water and rinse the chickpeas by rubbing them between your fingertips. The water will become slightly cloudy. Drain this water. Repeat three or four times, until the water remains relatively clear; drain. Now fill the bowl halfway with hot water and let it sit at room temperature, covered with plastic wrap, until the chickpeas have softened, at least 8 hours or as long as overnight.

2. Drain the chickpeas and transfer them to a pressure cooker. Add 3 cups water and bring to a boil, uncovered, over high heat. Skim off and discard any foam that forms on the surface. Add the cardamom pods, bay leaves, and cinnamon sticks. Seal the cooker shut and allow the pressure to build up. When the cooker reaches full pressure, reduce the heat to medium-low and cook for about 1 hour. Remove the cooker from the heat and allow the pressure to subside naturally (about 15 minutes) before opening the lid.

3. Meanwhile, heat a small skillet over medium-high heat and pour in 2 tablespoons of the oil. Add the coconut, coriander seeds, and chiles. Stir-fry until the coconut and coriander seeds are reddish brown and the chiles have blackened, 1 to 2 minutes. Scrape this into a blender jar, and add ½ cup water. Puree, scraping the inside of the jar as needed, to make a thin, gritty paste. Set it aside.

4. Heat the remaining 2 tablespoons oil in the same small skillet over medium-high heat. Add the mustard seeds, cover the skillet, and cook until the seeds have stopped popping (not unlike popcorn), about 30 seconds. Remove the skillet from the burner and add the curry leaves. They will spatter and crackle, so watch out. Set it aside.

5. Add the coconut paste and the spice/oil mixture to the cooked chickpeas. Pour ½ cup water into the blender jar and swirl it around to wash it out; pour the washings into the cooker. Stir in the salt. Simmer the curry over medium heat, uncovered, stirring occasionally, until the chickpeas have absorbed the flavors, 15 to 20 minutes. Then serve.

Tips:

❖ This sauce will not thicken very much because the chickpeas will not break down, even with extensive simmering. If you prefer a thicker sauce, dissolve 1 tablespoon rice flour or 1 teaspoon cornstarch in 2 tablespoons cold water. Add this to the curry in Step 5, after the chickpeas have simmered in the sauce for about 15 minutes. Continue to simmer, uncovered, stirring occasionally, until the sauce thickens, 2 to 4 minutes.

❖ Remove the cardamom pods, cinnamon sticks, and bay leaves before you serve the curry, if you so wish. If not, instruct your family and friends at the table to watch out for the whole spices, should they land on their plate.

Black Chickpea Stew
OVER STEAMED RICE CAKES

Kadala Masala Puttu

this is breakfast food in Kerala, and I cannot think of a better way to perk up your sleeping palate than with these savory rice cakes soused with hot, sweet, coconut-sauced, nutty-tasting, black chickpeas. Serve it as the main course if you have a bunch of vegans over for dinner.
SERVES 6

For the stew:

1 cup dried black chickpeas
2 tablespoons canola oil
1 medium-size red onion, finely chopped

2 fresh green Thai, cayenne, or serrano chiles,
    stems removed, cut in half lengthwise
    (do not remove the seeds)
1 cup shredded fresh coconut; or ½ cup shredded dried
    unsweetened coconut, reconstituted (see Note)
1 tablespoon coriander seeds
2 to 4 dried red Thai or cayenne chiles, to taste,
    stems removed
1 large tomato, cored and finely chopped
1½ teaspoons coarse kosher or sea salt
12 to 15 medium-size to large fresh curry leaves

For the steamed rice cakes:

1 cup long- or medium-grain white rice
¼ cup Cream of Wheat (not instant)
1 teaspoon coarse kosher or sea salt
Vegetable cooking spray
About ¼ cup shredded fresh coconut; or
    2 tablespoons shredded dried unsweetened
    coconut, reconstituted (see Note)

1. To make the stew, place the chickpeas in a medium-size bowl. Fill the bowl halfway with water and rinse the chickpeas by rubbing them between your fingertips. The water will become slightly cloudy. Drain this water. Repeat three or four times, until the water remains relatively clear; drain. Now fill the bowl halfway with hot water and let it sit at room temperature, covered with plastic wrap, until the chickpeas have softened, at least 8 hours or as long as overnight.

2. Drain the chickpeas and transfer them to a pressure cooker. Add 3 cups water and bring to a boil, uncovered, over high heat. Skim off and discard any foam that forms on the surface. Seal the cooker shut and allow the pressure to build up. When the cooker reaches full pressure, reduce the heat to medium-low and cook for about 45 minutes. Then remove the cooker from the heat and allow the pressure to subside naturally (about 15 minutes) before opening the lid.

3. While the chickpeas are cooking, heat the oil in a medium-size saucepan over medium heat. Add the onion and fresh chiles, and stir-fry slowly until the onion is browned, 15 to 20 minutes.

4. While the onion is cooking (keep an eye on it), pour ½ cup water into a blender jar, followed by the coconut, coriander seeds, and dried chiles. Puree, scraping the inside of the jar as needed, to make a slightly gritty, thick paste, with the ground coriander and chiles speckled evenly throughout.

5. Add this paste to the browned onion. Pour 1½ cups water into the blender jar and swish it around to wash it out; add the washings to the pan. Then add the tomato, salt, and curry leaves. Set the pan aside until the chickpeas are ready.

cooking black chickpeas

❖ ❖ ❖

black chickpeas, a close relative of the more common yellow chickpeas (or garbanzo beans) are actually earthy-brown with a reddish tint. The tough skin and small hard grains are hard to cook. This is where a pressure cooker comes in handy, because it ensures tender beans with a meaty texture. If you don't have one, cover the beans with hot water and let them soak overnight. Then drain them, transfer them to a medium-size saucepan, add 3 cups fresh water, cover the pan, and simmer over medium-low heat until the chickpeas are tender, about 2 hours. While they are cooking, check on the water level. If need be, add 2 to 3 cups hot tap water (hot so that you do not lower the temperature of the beans and slow down the cooking time) to maintain the original level.

6. Drain the cooked chickpeas and stir them into the mixture in the saucepan. Bring to a boil. Then reduce the heat to medium-low, cover the pan, and simmer, stirring occasionally, to allow the flavors to mingle, about 15 minutes. Keep warm.

7. Now, make the rice cakes: Heat a medium-size skillet over medium heat. Add the rice and toast the grains, stirring frequently, until they are shriveled and light brown, 5 to 10 minutes. Transfer them to a plate or bowl and set them aside to cool, about 5 minutes. Transfer the cooled rice to a blender, and grind to the consistency of uncooked Cream of Wheat. Pour this into a medium-size bowl, and stir in the Cream of Wheat and the salt.

8. Pour a few tablespoons of warm water over the rice blend, stirring it in (you can use your clean hand) after each addition. The "dough" will always look dry and will start to feel like wet, gritty sand. All in all, you will need to add about ½ cup warm water. If you grab a small handful of the "dough" and compress it in one hand, it should hold its compact shape but be loose enough to fall apart when you apply a little pressure to it.

9. Fill a saucepan halfway with water and insert a steamer basket; or place a bamboo steamer in a wok filled halfway with water. Lightly spray the inside of the steamer with cooking spray. Plop a scant ¼ cup of the "dough" in one hand and compress it tightly into a roundball. Using two fingers, make an indentation in the ball. Press about 1 teaspoon of the coconut into the depression. Place this *puttu* in the steamer basket, and prepare and add 3 more *puttus* to it. Steam, covered, until the rice cakes are firm-looking and have a dull sheen on the surface. Transfer them to a plate and cover to keep them warm. Repeat with the remaining rice cakes (you should have 12 in all), making sure there is enough water in the pan after each batch is steamed.

10. To serve the curry, place 2 steamed *puttus* in each individual serving bowl, and ladle some of the black chickpea stew over them. Encourage folks to break apart the *puttus* and spoon up a combination of *puttu* and curry.

Note: To reconstitute coconut, cover with ½ cup boiling water, set aside for about 15 minutes, and then drain. For 2 tablespoons dried coconut, use 2 tablespoons boiling water.

Tips:

❖ You could use the water the chickpeas cooked in, instead of draining them, in place of the 1½ cups fresh water in Step 5. The cooking water is dark, however, and I prefer this curry to have a lighter appearance.

❖ If you want to sweeten the *puttus*, combine the coconut with 2 tablespoons crumbled (or chopped) jaggery or firmly packed dark brown sugar (for a smoother blend, briefly zap the jaggery in a microwave to melt it). Or for another filling option, mash half an overripe banana and combine it with the coconut.

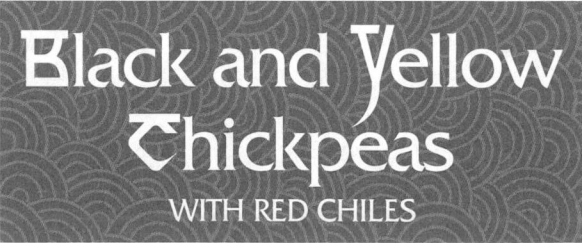

Black and Yellow Chickpeas
WITH RED CHILES

Mirchi Waale Kala Aur Kabuli Chana

A protein powerhouse, this curry is like a hearty vegetarian chili—ladled over steaming white rice, it's perfect for that icy winter night. For a creamier alternative, I have served this atop a mound of buttered mashed potatoes in small bowls, as the soup course of an elegant multi-course curry dinner. **MAKES 4 CUPS**

¼ cup dried black chickpeas
¼ cup dried chickpeas
¼ cup dried kidney beans
¼ cup whole black lentils (sabud urad)
1 medium-size red onion, coarsely chopped
10 whole cloves
6 to 8 dried red Thai or cayenne chiles, to taste,
  stems removed
4 green or white cardamom pods
2 cinnamon sticks (each 3 inches long),
  broken into smaller pieces
2 tablespoons Ginger Paste (page 15)
1 tablespoon Garlic Paste (page 15)
½ teaspoon ground turmeric
2 tablespoons Ghee (page 21) or canola oil
2 tablespoons tomato paste
2 teaspoons coarse kosher or sea salt
¼ cup heavy (whipping) cream or half-and-half
2 tablespoons finely chopped fresh cilantro leaves and
  tender stems for garnishing

1. Place the chickpeas, kidney beans, and lentils in a medium-size bowl. Fill the bowl halfway with water and rinse the legumes by rubbing them between your fingertips. The water will become slightly cloudy. Drain this water. Repeat three or four times, until the water remains relatively clear; drain. Now fill the bowl halfway with hot water and let it sit at room temperature, covered with plastic wrap, until the legumes have softened, at least 8 hours or as long as overnight.

2. Drain the legumes and transfer them to a pressure cooker. Add 3 cups water and bring to a boil, uncovered, over high heat. Skim off and discard any foam that forms on the surface. Seal the cooker shut and allow the pressure to build up. When the cooker reaches full pressure, reduce the heat to medium-low and cook for

about 1 hour. Remove the cooker from the heat and allow the pressure to subside naturally (about 15 minutes) before opening the lid.

3. Meanwhile, pour ¼ cup water into a blender jar. Add the onion, cloves, chiles, cardamom pods, and cinnamon pieces. Puree, scraping the inside of the jar as needed, to make a smooth, reddish-brown paste. Scrape this spiced onion paste into a small bowl, and fold in the Ginger Paste, Garlic Paste, and turmeric.

4. Heat the ghee in a medium-size skillet over medium heat. Add the spiced paste and simmer, partially covered, stirring occasionally, until some of the liquid evaporates and the ghee starts to separate from the sauce (which is starting to look dark brown), 12 to 15 minutes.

5. Stir the tomato paste and salt into the sauce, and set it aside until the legumes are ready.

6. Add the sauce to the cooked legumes. Pour ¾ cup water into the skillet and deglaze it, releasing the browned bits; add this to the curry. Simmer over medium-low heat, covered, stirring occasionally, until the legumes have absorbed the flavors, 20 to 25 minutes.

7. Mix in the cream, sprinkle with the cilantro, and serve.

Tips:

❖ You can prepare the sauce as much as 2 hours ahead if you wish.

❖ For extra crunch, sprinkle finely chopped red onion and thinly sliced fresh green Thai, cayenne, or serrano chiles over the curry just before serving.

❖ I often double the quantity of chickpeas, kidney

beans, and lentils (and double the cooking water), and freeze half for up to 2 months (liquid and all). For a tasty snack, thaw the legumes, season them with a spice blend like *Rajasthani garam masala* (page 26) and a hint of Toasted Chickpea Flour (page 41), and enjoy. Or, of course, use the frozen batch for making this curry another day.

Sweet-Hot Black Chickpeas
WITH GOLDEN RAISINS

kishmish kala Thana

Certain key ingredients shape this curry's final destiny: plump golden raisins provide ample sweetness, and the chiles bring the sweetness down a few notches. You will notice that there is hardly a multitude of spices here, shattering the myth that a curry has to house a plethora of them in order to be palatable. I love this for lunch, with slices of warmed baguette.

MAKES 4 CUPS

1 cup golden raisins
1 cup boiling water
1 small red onion, coarsely chopped
4 large cloves garlic
4 fresh green Thai, cayenne, or serrano chiles, stems removed
2 lengthwise slices fresh ginger (each 2 inches long, 1 inch wide, and ⅛ inch thick)
2 tablespoons canola oil
1 cup tomato sauce, canned or homemade (see page 18)

1½ teaspoons coarse kosher or sea salt
3 cups cooked black chickpeas (see Tips)
4 tablespoons finely chopped fresh cilantro leaves and tender stems
½ cup heavy (whipping) cream
2 teaspoons Toasted Cumin-Coriander Blend (page 33)

1. Place the raisins in a medium-size heatproof bowl, and pour the boiling water over them. Set the bowl aside until the raisins have turned plump and succulent-looking, about 30 minutes.

2. Drain the raisins, reserving the soaking water.

3. Combine the raisins, onion, garlic, chiles, and ginger in a food processor, and pulse until minced.

4. Heat the oil in a medium-size saucepan over medium-high heat. Add the minced blend and stir-fry until the very pungent mixture is honey-brown, 5 to 6 minutes. Pour in the reserved soaking liquid and scrape the bottom of the skillet to deglaze it, releasing the browned bits. Cook, uncovered, stirring occasionally, until the liquid has been absorbed, 2 to 4 minutes.

5. Add the tomato sauce and salt, and mix well. Reduce the heat to medium-low, partially cover the pan, and simmer, stirring occasionally, until the oil starts to separate from the sauce around the edges, 12 to 15 minutes.

6. Stir in the chickpeas, 2 cups water, and 2 tablespoons of the cilantro. Raise the heat to medium and bring to a boil. Simmer vigorously, uncovered, stirring occasionally, until the sauce has thickened slightly, 8 to 10 minutes.

7. Mix in the cream and the spice blend. Simmer, uncovered, until the curry is warmed through, about 2 minutes.

8. Sprinkle with the remaining 2 tablespoons cilantro, and serve.

Tips:

❖ Canned yellow chickpeas (drained and rinsed) are a perfectly acceptable alternative. For more on black chickpeas, see page 341.

❖ To make an interesting soup for a wintry day, add 1 cut-up medium-size bell pepper (½-inch pieces, any color) when you stir-fry the raisin-onion mixture in Step 4. Just before serving, stir in ½ teaspoon *Punjabi garam masala* (page 25).

Green Chickpeas
WITH SPINACH

Palak Hara Chana

If you ever have a chance to sample fresh green chickpeas, I know you will fall in love with their nutty-sweet taste and juicy crunch, as I did during a recent trip to Uttar Pradesh and Rajasthan in northern India. It is common there to see men and women holding bunches of the greens that house the chickpeas, snacking on the fresh legumes as they go about their business. Simply steamed and tossed with a few spices, green chickpeas are delicious. Unfortunately the chances of finding them here, in the United States, are next to none (but to my happy surprise, I have stumbled upon frozen green chickpeas at Trader Joe's). Dried green chickpeas, however, are available in Indian and Pakistani grocery stores. Like their yellow and black siblings, dried green chick-

peas require prior soaking and long hours of cooking to be tender—unless you have a pressure cooker. **MAKES 4 CUPS**

1 cup dried green chickpeas (see Tips)
¼ teaspoon baking soda
2 tablespoons canola oil
1 teaspoon black or yellow mustard seeds
1 teaspoon cumin seeds
½ teaspoon bishop's weed (see Tips)
1 cup finely chopped red onion
1 teaspoon ground Deggi chiles (see box, page 290);
*   or ½ teaspoon cayenne (ground red pepper)*
*   mixed with ½ teaspoon sweet paprika*
½ teaspoon ground turmeric
2 tablespoons crumbled (or chopped) jaggery
*   or firmly packed dark brown sugar*
1½ teaspoons coarse kosher or sea salt
8 ounces fresh spinach leaves, well rinsed and finely
*   chopped; or 1 package (8 to 10 ounces) frozen*
*   chopped spinach, thawed (no need to drain)*
2 teaspoons Toasted Cumin-Coriander Blend
*   (page 33)*
1 teaspoon tamarind paste or concentrate,
*   or the juice of 1 medium-size lime*

1. Place the chickpeas in a medium-size bowl. Fill the bowl halfway with water and rinse the chickpeas by rubbing them between your fingertips. The water will become slightly cloudy. Drain this water. Repeat three or four times, until the water remains relatively clear; drain. Now fill the bowl halfway with hot water and let it sit on the counter, covered with plastic wrap, until the chickpeas have softened, at least 8 hours or as long as overnight.

2. Drain the chickpeas and transfer them to a pressure cooker. Add 4 cups water and the baking soda, and bring to a boil, uncovered, over high heat. Skim off and discard any foam that forms on the surface. Seal the cooker shut and allow the pressure to build up. When the cooker reaches full pressure, reduce the heat to medium-low and cook for about 30 minutes. Remove the cooker from the heat and allow the pressure to subside naturally (about 15 minutes) before opening the lid.

3. While the chickpeas are cooking, heat the oil in a small saucepan over medium-high heat. Add the mustard seeds, cover the pan, and cook until the seeds have stopped popping (not unlike popcorn), about 30 seconds. Sprinkle in the cumin seeds and bishop's weed, and cook until they sizzle, turn reddish brown, and are aromatic, 5 to 10 seconds.

4. Add the onion and stir-fry until it is light brown around the edges, about 5 minutes. Then stir in the ground chiles and turmeric, and cook without burning the ground spices, 5 to 10 seconds. Pour in 2 cups water, and stir in the jaggery and salt. Bring to a boil. Lower the heat to medium and simmer, uncovered, stirring occasionally, until half the liquid has evaporated, 15 to 20 minutes.

5. Stir in the spinach and the spice blend. Cook until the spinach is warmed through and has turned olive-green, about 5 minutes. Set this aside until the chickpeas are ready.

6. Add the spinach mixture to the cooked chickpeas and simmer over medium heat, uncovered, stirring occasionally, until the chickpeas absorb the flavors, 20 to 25 minutes. (The sauce will be fairly thin. If you prefer a thicker sauce, mash some of the chickpeas and continue to simmer the curry, uncovered, stirring occasionally, until the sauce thickens, 5 to 10 minutes.)

7. Add the tamarind paste, stirring to dissolve it, and serve.

Tips:

❖ Frozen green chickpeas are available in many Indian stores in the United States. They don't require a pressure cooker; just follow the package instructions.

❖ If you wish, you can use the more common yellow chickpeas here. Canned ones (drained and rinsed to get rid of the brine) make this curry super-easy: just stir them into the spinach mixture at the end of Step 5.

❖ Bishop's weed imparts a thymelike flavor to the sauce. If you can't locate any, use the same amount of dried thyme leaves as an alternative.

Chickpea Flour Dumplings
IN A SPICY YOGURT SAUCE

Gatte ki Subzi

My friend Radhika Sharma, who was born in Mumbai and has strong familial roots in Rajasthan, India's desert country, talked with me about the way the absence of vegetation has shaped that region's culinary habits. Reliance on dried legumes, flours, milk, and dairy products is the norm, with vegetables being a scarcity, confined to a short growing season. Rajasthan's cuisine, like its people's love for the arts, colorful jewelry, and clothing, reflects a culture that has triumphed over adversity and over the challenges of a difficult topography. No wonder that Radhika, now far removed from that heritage and presently a successful writer in California, takes great pride in preserving the flavors of her childhood. She recommends serving this curry with a basket of rotis (page 727) and a bowlful of soothing plain yogurt for a quick weekday dinner. **SERVES 6**

For the dumplings:

2 cups chickpea flour, sifted, plus extra for the work surface

2 teaspoons coriander seeds, ground

1 teaspoon cumin seeds, ground

1 teaspoon cayenne (ground red pepper)

1 teaspoon coarse kosher or sea salt

½ teaspoon Rajasthani garam masala (page 26)

Canola oil for kneading

For the curry:

2 tablespoons plain yogurt

2 teaspoons coriander seeds, ground

3 teaspoons cumin seeds, 1 teaspoon ground, 2 teaspoons left whole

1½ teaspoons cayenne (ground red pepper)

½ teaspoon ground turmeric

½ teaspoon Rajasthani garam masala (page 26)

½ teaspoon coarse kosher or sea salt

1 tablespoon Ghee (page 21) or melted butter

½ teaspoon ground asafetida

3 lengthwise slices fresh ginger (each 2 inches long, 1 inch wide, and ⅛ inch thick), finely chopped

1. To make the dumplings, combine the 2 cups chickpea flour, coriander, cumin, cayenne, salt, and garam masala in a medium-size bowl. Drizzle ¼ cup warm water over the mixture, and use your hand to bring it together to form a ball. If it's too dry, add a tablespoon or more of warm water. At this point the dough may be sticky and slightly unmanageable. Remove as much of the stuck-on dough from your fingers as you can, and wash and dry your hands. Add about 1 tablespoon oil to the dough and knead it, right in the bowl, until smooth.

2. Lightly flour a hard surface, and place the dough on it. By gently pressing and rolling it under your hands, shape the dough into a log that is roughly 12 inches long and 1½ inches thick. Cut the log crosswise into 4 pieces.

3. Fill a medium-size saucepan halfway with water, and bring it to a rolling boil over medium-high heat. Gently place the pieces of dough in the water, and lower the heat to medium. Simmer, uncovered, turning them occasionally, until they turn light yellow and have bumps all over, about 45 minutes.

4. Using a slotted spoon, transfer the pieces of boiled dough to a plate. Discard the cooking water and fill the saucepan with fresh cold water. Plunge the pieces into the cold water for a few seconds; then return them to the same plate. Using a butter knife or a paring knife, gently scrape off and discard the outer bumpy, slick layer to reveal a smooth, darker-looking, firm, spice-speckled piece of dough.

5. Slice the pieces in half lengthwise, and then cut each length crosswise into ½-inch-thick dumplings. You will end up with about 48 of these dumplings. Place half of them in a freezer-safe self-seal bag and freeze them for up to 2 months (see Tip). Reserve the other half for this curry.

6. To make the curry, combine the yogurt with 1½ cups water in a medium-size bowl, and whisk together to form a wheylike liquid, akin to watered-down buttermilk. Whisk in the coriander, ground cumin, cayenne, turmeric, garam masala, and salt. Drop the dumplings into this spicy liquid.

7. Heat the ghee in a small saucepan over medium-high heat. Add the whole cumin seeds and cook until they sizzle, turn reddish brown, and are aromatic, 5 to 10 seconds. Sprinkle in the asafetida and ginger, and stir-fry to lightly brown the ginger, about 1 minute.

8. Pour the yogurt mixture, including the dumplings, into the saucepan and heat to a boil. Then lower the heat to medium and boil gently, uncovered, stirring occasionally, until the sauce thickens and the ghee forms a red layer on top, 15 to 20 minutes. Then serve.

Tip: By preparing an extra batch of these dense dumplings and freezing them, you have the makings of a quick meal. No need to thaw them, since they will simmer in the sauce you prepare long enough to warm up.

Fenugreek-Flavored Dumplings
WITH CABBAGE

Muthiya bund Gobhi nu Shaak

this is one of those robust-tasting curries that you can serve without hesitation to the vegan at your table, as well as the meat-eating guests. The meaty oomph of the steamed chickpea flour dumplings provides not only essential proteins and fiber, but also textural contrast to the noodle-like cooked cabbage. Serve this with a stack of rotis (page 727). **SERVES 8**

For the dumplings:
- 1 cup chickpea flour, sifted, plus extra for the work surface if needed
- 2 tablespoons roti flour (see Tip, page 728) or whole-wheat flour
- 1 cup chopped fresh or frozen fenugreek leaves (thawed and squeezed dry if frozen); or ½ cup dried fenugreek leaves, soaked in a bowl of water and skimmed off before use (see box, page 473)
- 1 teaspoon coarse kosher or sea salt
- ¼ teaspoon ground turmeric
- 1 tablespoon finely chopped fresh ginger
- 4 to 6 fresh green Thai, cayenne, or serrano chiles, to taste, stems removed, finely chopped (do not remove the seeds)
- 1 tablespoon canola oil, plus extra for greasing your hands

For the curry:
- 1 pound cabbage, thinly shredded (see Tips, page 468 and below)
- ½ teaspoon ground turmeric
- 2 tablespoons canola oil
- 1 teaspoon black or yellow mustard seeds
- 1 teaspoon finely chopped fresh ginger
- 2 to 4 fresh green Thai, cayenne, or serrano chiles, to taste, stems removed, cut crosswise into ¼-inch-thick slices (do not remove the seeds)
- 2 teaspoons coriander seeds, ground
- 1 teaspoon cumin seeds, ground
- ¼ teaspoon ground asafetida
- 1 teaspoon coarse kosher or sea salt
- 1 teaspoon white granulated sugar
- 2 tablespoons finely chopped fresh cilantro leaves and tender stems for garnishing

1. To make the dumplings, combine the two flours, fenugreek leaves, salt, turmeric, ginger, and chiles in a medium-size bowl. Drizzle the oil over the mixture and work it into the flour with your hand. Pour 1 tablespoon warm water over the flour mixture, and try to bring it together to form a ball. If it's too dry, add another tablespoon or two of warm water. At this point, the dough can be sticky and slightly unmanageable. Remove as much of the stuck-on dough from your fingers as you can, and wash and dry your hands. Lightly grease your hand with oil, and knead the bumpy dough until it is glossy-smooth.

2. Shape the dough into a log, about 8 inches long, by rolling and pressing it lightly but firmly on a flat surface. (Flour the surface lightly if the dough is sticky.) Cut the log into ½-inch pieces. Shape each piece into a ball and then press it to form a patty about 1½ inches in diameter and ½ inch thick.

3. Fill a saucepan halfway with water and insert a steamer basket, or place a bamboo steamer in a wok filled halfway with water. Lay the patties in a single layer, or overlapping just a bit, in the steamer basket. Bring the water to a boil, cover the pan, and steam over medium heat until a knife stabbed in a few patties comes out clean, 8 to 10 minutes. Transfer the green-speckled, opaque-looking patties to a plate. Reserve the water in the steamer.

4. Now, make the curry: Pile the cabbage into the reserved hot water in the saucepan or wok. Add 1 cup water and bring to a boil over medium-high heat. Cook until the cabbage wilts, about 5 minutes. Then stir in the turmeric and continue to cook until the yellowed cabbage is fork-tender, about 10 minutes. Reserving 1 cup of the cooking water, drain the cabbage in a colander.

5. Heat the oil in a wok or a large skillet over medium-high heat. Add the mustard seeds, cover the pan, and cook until the seeds have stopped popping (not unlike popcorn), about 30 seconds. Immediately add the ginger, chiles, coriander, cumin, asafetida, salt, and sugar. Stir-fry to lightly brown the ginger and cook the spices, 10 to 15 seconds.

6. Pour in the nutrient-rich reserved cooking water, the drained cabbage, and the steamed patties. Simmer, uncovered, stirring occasionally, until the sauce thickens slightly, 3 to 5 minutes.

7. Sprinkle with the cilantro, and serve.

Tip: If cooked cabbage is not your cup of tea, use ½ pound dried spaghetti and cook al dente in the same fashion as the cabbage in Step 4.

Chickpea Flour Dumplings
WITH SPINACH

Gatte Saag ki Subzi

I sampled a variation of this curry at the dramatic Rambagh Palace hotel, formerly the residence of Rajasthan's renowned Maharani Gayatri Devi, who occasionally graces the facilities with her stunning presence. The chickpea flour dumplings *(gatte)*, a specialty of Rajasthan, provide filling proteins while the spinach-based sauce offers an iron-rich backdrop. This is an easy lunch offering, served with either homemade or store-bought rotis (page 727). **SERVES 6**

For the dumplings:

I cup chickpea flour, sifted, plus extra for dusting
I teaspoon ground Deggi chiles (see box, page 290);
or ½ teaspoon cayenne (ground red pepper)
mixed with ½ teaspoon sweet paprika
I teaspoon coarse kosher or sea salt
½ teaspoon fennel seeds, ground
½ teaspoon ground ginger
¼ teaspoon bishop's weed; or ⅛ teaspoon
dried thyme mixed with ⅛ teaspoon
freshly ground black pepper
About 3 tablespoons plain yogurt
Canola oil for kneading

For the curry:

2 tablespoons canola oil
I cup finely chopped red onion
2 teaspoons coriander seeds, ground
I teaspoon cumin seeds, ground
I teaspoon ground Deggi chiles (see box,
page 290); or ½ teaspoon cayenne
(ground red pepper) mixed with
½ teaspoon sweet paprika
I teaspoon coarse kosher or sea salt
½ teaspoon ground turmeric
¼ teaspoon ground asafetida
I large tomato, cored and finely chopped
8 ounces fresh spinach leaves,
well rinsed and finely chopped

Bishop's weed? See the Glossary of Ingredients, page 758.

1. To make the dumplings, combine the 1 cup chickpea flour, ground chiles, salt, fennel, ginger, and bishop's weed in a medium-size bowl. Spoon the yogurt, 1 tablespoon at a time, over the flour mixture, using your hand to bring it together to form a ball. If it's too dry, add a tablespoon or more of yogurt. At this point, the dough may be sticky and slightly unmanageable. Remove as much of the stuck-on dough from your fingers as you can, and wash and dry your hands. Add about 1 tablespoon oil to the dough and knead it, in the bowl, until smooth. If the dough still feels sticky, dust it with additional chickpea flour as needed.

2. Lightly flour a hard work surface. Divide the dough into 6 portions. By gently pressing and rolling it under your hands, shape each portion into a log that is roughly 6 inches long and ½ inch thick.

3. Fill a small saucepan halfway with water, and bring it to a rolling boil over medium-high heat. Gently add the dough logs, and lower the heat to medium. Simmer, uncovered, turning the logs occasionally, until they turn opaque, are orange-yellow, and appear to have lost their sheen, 12 to 15 minutes. Drain the logs in a colander and run cold water over them. Slice the logs crosswise into ½-inch-thick dumplings, and set them aside. You will have about 72 dumplings.

4. To make the curry, heat the oil in a medium-size saucepan over medium-high heat. Add the onion and stir-fry until it is light brown around the edges, 2 to 3 minutes.

5. Stir in the coriander, cumin, ground chiles, salt, turmeric, and asafetida. The heat from the onion will be just right to cook the spices without burning them. Add the tomato and cook until it is softened but still firm-looking, about 2 minutes.

6. Pour 1 cup water into the pan, and then pile in the spinach. Stir until the spinach is wilted. Then cover the pan, lower the heat to medium, and simmer the curry, stirring occasionally, until the spinach softens and turns olive-green, about 10 minutes.

7. Add the dumplings and continue to simmer, covered, stirring occasionally, until they are warm through, about 5 minutes. Then serve.

Tip: You can make the dumplings ahead of time and refrigerate them, covered with plastic wrap, for up to 4 days. They can be frozen for up to 1 month in a self-seal freezer-safe bag.

Scrambled Chickpea Flour
WITH GINGER

Rajasthani Petla

My friend Radhika Sharma shared this family favorite with me, and I was particularly enamored of the resulting curry's fluffy-soft scrambled-eggs consistency. For those who don't consume eggs, this is an excellent breakfast alternative. The flavors will perk up your sleepy morning taste buds. Radhika recommends serving it with rotis (page 727), but I have been known to cheat (yes, *moi aussi*) and use whole-wheat tortillas instead, especially on a busy morning. For lunch or a simple dinner, add Red Lentils with a Caramel-Sweet Onion Sauce (page 403) for a protein-rich meatless meal. **SERVES 4**

1 cup chickpea flour, sifted

2 teaspoon coriander seeds, ground

1½ teaspoons coarse kosher or sea salt

½ teaspoon Rajasthani garam masala (page 26)

½ teaspoon cayenne (ground red pepper)

½ teaspoon ground turmeric

2 tablespoons canola oil

1 teaspoon black or yellow mustard seeds

¼ teaspoon ground asafetida

1 tablespoon Ginger Chile Paste (page 17)

2 tablespoons finely chopped fresh cilantro leaves and tender stems

1. Combine the chickpea flour, coriander, salt, garam masala, cayenne, and turmeric in a medium-size bowl. Pour in ¾ cup water and whisk quickly to make a thick, lump-free paste. Then add another ¾ cup water and whisk it in to thin the paste into a runny batter.

2. Heat the oil in a medium-size nonstick skillet over medium-high heat. Add the mustard seeds, cover the skillet, and cook until the seeds have stopped popping (not unlike popcorn), about 30 seconds. Sprinkle in the asafetida, which will instantly sizzle and cook. Carefully add the Ginger Chile Paste (there will be a fair amount of spattering) and stir it around to lightly brown it, about 2 minutes.

3. Lower the heat to medium and pour the batter into the hot pan. Stir constantly while the batter starts to clump up and separate from the skillet's sides and bottom, and then to come together to form a soft ball, 5 to 8 minutes. While the batter is cooking, you will need to scrape the spoon or spatula intermittently against the skillet's edges to release the stuck-on dough. Push the dough flat against the bottom with your spoon to ensure even cooking.

4. Remove the skillet from the heat and let the ball of dough cool slightly, 3 to 5 minutes. When you touch it, it will feel silky-smooth and dry. The longer it cools, the drier it will feel.

5. Transfer the ball to a cutting board and sprinkle the cilantro over it. Slice into the dough from all sides, chopping it up to incorporate the cilantro into it and to break it into soft, scrambled egglike pieces. Then serve.

Tips: If you want to incorporate tomatoes, onion, or other chopped vegetables, return the "scrambled" cooked *petla* to the skillet and add the vegetables. Cook them together until the vegetables are warmed through.

Chickpea-Stuffed Taro Leaf
STEWED IN SPICED BUTTERMILK

patra kadhi

I always serve this curry with white basmati rice and pass around some homemade ghee (page 21) so each person can drizzle a spoonful or so of the nutty-flavored fat over it for that silky-rich texture. Flame-toasted papads (page 740) are another favorite accompaniment to this meal. **SERVES 8**

4 cups buttermilk

2 tablespoons chickpea flour

I teaspoon white granulated sugar

I teaspoon coarse kosher or sea salt

½ teaspoon ground turmeric

4 fresh green Thai, cayenne, or serrano chiles, stems removed: 2 sliced crosswise into ½-inch-thick slices, 2 cut in half lengthwise (do not remove seeds in either case)

2 tablespoons canola oil

I teaspoon black or yellow mustard seeds

6 to 8 medium-size to large fresh curry leaves

I bag (about 14 ounces) frozen patra rounds, thawed (see box, page 608, and Tip)

1. Combine the buttermilk and chickpea flour in a medium-size bowl and whisk well to make a lump-free, slightly frothy liquid. Stir in the sugar, salt, turmeric, and the sliced chiles. Set this aside.

2. Heat the oil in a large skillet over medium-high heat. Add the mustard seeds, cover the skillet, and cook until the seeds have stopped popping (not unlike popcorn), about 30 seconds. Throw in the remaining 2 chiles (the ones cut in half) and the curry leaves, and stand back a little because they will spatter on contact.

3. Add the *patra* rounds in a single layer, and cook until the underside is browned, 3 to 5 minutes. Flip the slices over and brown on the other side, 3 to 5 minutes.

4. Pour the buttermilk mixture over the *patra*. The curry will instantly bubble, thanks to the very hot pan. Do not stir it, because the *patra* slices will fall apart. Lower the heat to medium and simmer, uncovered, without stirring, until the sauce thickens, 10 to 15 minutes.

5. Lift the *patra* slices from the sauce, and transfer them to a shallow serving bowl. Pour the sauce over them, and serve. (Some of the slices might fall apart, but trust me, they are just as delicious that way.)

Tip: For your convenience, I have used store-bought *patra* to expedite this curry. If you wish, you can make your own using collard greens instead of taro root leaves (pages 107–108, through Step 5) for an equally satisfying experience.

Yogurt Curry
WITH CUMIN AND CURRY LEAVES

Gujarati kadhi

Gujaratis, masters at whipping up vegetarian meals, do wonders with dairy products—in fact, a large percentage of Gujaratis are dairy farmers. Many of their sauce-based dishes are thin, and this one is no exception. Perhaps the word "curry" was an adaptation of *kadhi*, but in any case, either sip it from small bowls or pour it over steamed rice for the epitome of a comforting meal. **MAKES 4 CUPS**

2 cups plain yogurt

2 tablespoons chickpea flour

I tablespoon white granulated sugar

I teaspoon coarse kosher or sea salt

½ teaspoon ground turmeric

½ teaspoon bishop's weed

½ teaspoon fenugreek seeds

2 tablespoons Ghee (page 21) or melted butter

2 teaspoons cumin seeds

5 dried red Thai or cayenne chiles, stems removed

10 to 12 medium-size to large fresh curry leaves

2 tablespoons finely chopped fresh cilantro leaves and tender stems for garnishing

1. Combine the yogurt with 2 cups water in a medium-size saucepan, and whisk together to make a thin, buttermilk-like liquid. Sprinkle in the chickpea flour, 1 tablespoon at a time, quickly whisking it in to make sure there are no lumps. Then stir in the sugar, salt, turmeric, bishop's weed, and fenugreek seeds. Bring the mixture to a simmer, whisking periodically, and cook until the thin, deep yellow curry thickens ever so slightly and the raw flour taste disappears, about 15 minutes.

2. While the *kadhi* is simmering, heat the ghee in a small skillet over medium-high heat. Add the cumin seeds and chiles, and cook until the seeds turn reddish brown and the chiles blacken slightly, 10 to 15 seconds. Remove the skillet from the heat and add the curry leaves (carefully—they will spatter).

3. Once the *kadhi* is ready, add the ghee mixture and continue to simmer until the flavors permeate the curry, 5 minutes.

4. Sprinkle with the cilantro, and serve.

Toasted Chickpea Flour Curry
WITH SORGHUM FLATBREAD

Zunka bhaakar

Just about every street in Mumbai has a booth selling *Zunka bhaakar*, a Maharashtrian peasant food—very filling, nutritious, and quick to prepare. The velvety texture of this curry can be an acquired taste, especially for those who find the consistency of baby food a challenge. I do think that the sliced onion and chiles in the curry balance out the smoothness, providing a contrast in textures. If you don't wish to make the *bhaakar*, use a store-purchased whole-wheat tortilla as an option. **SERVES 6**

For the *zunka* (curry):

- 1 cup Toasted Chickpea Flour (page 41)
- 1½ teaspoons coarse kosher or sea salt
- ½ teaspoon ground turmeric
- 2 tablespoons canola oil
- 1 teaspoon black or yellow mustard seeds
- 1 teaspoon cumin seeds
- 1 small red onion, cut in half lengthwise and thinly sliced
- 4 to 6 fresh green Thai, cayenne, or serrano chiles, to taste, stems removed, thinly sliced crosswise (do not remove the seeds)
- ¼ cup finely chopped fresh cilantro leaves and tender stems

For the *bhaakar* (flatbread):

- 2 cups sorghum flour or millet flour (see box), plus extra for the work surface if needed
- 1 teaspoon coarse kosher or sea salt
- 2 tablespoons Ghee (page 21) or butter, plus extra for brushing

1. To make the *zunka*, combine the toasted flour, salt, and turmeric in a medium-size bowl.

2. Heat the oil in a large skillet over medium-high heat. Add the mustard seeds, cover the skillet, and cook until the seeds have stopped popping (not unlike popcorn), about 30 seconds. Sprinkle the cumin seeds into the hot oil; they will instantly sizzle, turn reddish brown, and smell nutty. Add the onion and chiles, and stir-fry until the onion is light brown around the edges, 5 to 8 minutes.

3. Pour in 3 cups water. As soon as it starts to simmer, sprinkle in the flour mixture, stirring constantly to prevent any lumps from forming. The mixture will instantly start to thicken, making a pastelike curry that is reddish brown with flecks of purple and green. Stir in the cilantro, and set it aside.

4. To make the *bhaakar*, combine the sorghum flour and salt in a food processor. Add the ghee and cut it into the salted flour by using the pulsing action, turning the ghee into pea-size balls. (It's these clumps of clarified butter that will provide the fat that makes the flatbread nice and flaky.)

5. Gradually drizzle in about ⅔ cup water, a few tablespoons at a time, continuing to pulse the crumbly mixture until it just starts to come together to form a soft ball. Transfer the dough to a cutting board or other dry surface, and knead it gently to form a smooth ball. (Because of the lower amount of protein, it will never have the same consistency as dough made with wheat flour.) If it is a little sticky, lightly flour the work surface. Cut the dough into 8 portions.

6. Preheat a small nonstick skillet over medium heat. Place a portion of dough on a piece of wax paper, and

sorghum and millet

❖ ❖ ❖

Sorghum, a cereal grass with cornlike leaves and clusters of grains at the end of its stalk, is the third-largest grain crop produced in the United States. But in spite of the fact that it has more protein than maize, it is not grown here for human consumption (with the exception of the production of sorghum molasses). Third World nations like India and Africa, on the other hand, feed their poor with sorghum flour.

Millet flour, known as bajra in India, is another example of a grassy cereal that is used the same way as sorghum (jowar). This grain has been sown in China for 5,000 years, making it one of the oldest grains that have benefited humans and animals alike. Both jowar and bajra flour are available in Indian grocery stores and also in natural food stores in the United States.

press it down with your fingers to form a patty. Continue to stretch it out to make an even round that is 4 to 6 inches in diameter and ⅛ inch thick. (It may not be perfectly round, especially the first few times you do this.) Gently peel it off the wax paper and drop the round into the skillet. Cook until the underside has a slight sheen with light brown patches, 2 to 4 minutes. Flip it over and cook the other side for the same results, 2 to 3 minutes. Brush the top of the round with ghee and flip it over to sear it, about 30 seconds. Brush the second side with ghee and sear that side too, about 30 seconds. Wrap the bread in aluminum foil so the steam will keep it moist. Repeat with the other dough rounds.

7. Serve the *zunka* with the *bhakaar.*

Horse gram
WITH POUNDED GARLIC AND FENNEL

kulith ŋu dal

his curry is a mouthful of textures and flavors, its main "chewiness" coming from the legume itself. Because of its assertive nature, I have incorporated a lot of garlic and chiles to offset that. I love this curry ladled over white rice with a squeeze of fresh lime juice. **MAKES 4 CUPS**

- 1 cup horse gram (kulith), picked over for stones
- 8 medium-size cloves garlic
- 6 fresh green Thai, cayenne, or serrano chiles, stems removed
- 2 teaspoons fennel seeds
- 2 tablespoons Ghee (page 21) or canola oil
- 1 teaspoon black or yellow mustard seeds

Rock salt? See the Glossary of Ingredients, page 758.

- 1 small red onion, cut in half lengthwise and thinly sliced
- 12 to 15 medium-size to large fresh curry leaves
- 1½ teaspoons rock salt, pounded

1. Place the horse gram in a pressure cooker. Fill the cooker halfway with water and rinse the legumes by rubbing them between your fingertips. The water may appear slightly dirty. Drain this water. Repeat three or four times, until the water remains relatively clear; drain. Now add 3 cups water and bring to a boil, uncovered, over high heat. Skim off and discard any foam that forms on the surface. Seal the cooker shut and allow the pressure to build up. When the cooker reaches full pressure, reduce the heat to medium-low and cook for about 45 minutes. Remove the cooker from the heat and allow the pressure to subside naturally (about 15 minutes) before opening the lid.

2. Meanwhile, combine the garlic, chiles, and fennel seeds in a mortar. Pound with the pestle, scraping the sides to contain the ingredients in the center, to make a pulpy, gritty mass.

3. Heat the ghee in a small skillet over medium-high heat. Add the mustard seeds, cover the skillet, and cook until the seeds have stopped popping (not unlike popcorn), about 30 seconds. Immediately add the onion and the pounded paste. Stir-fry until the onion is light brown around the edges and the paste is pungent, about 5 minutes. Set the skillet aside.

4. Once the legumes are ready, add the contents of the skillet and stir once or twice. Ladle some of the legume mixture into the skillet and scrape the bottom to deglaze it. Add this to the pressure cooker, and stir in the curry leaves and salt. Simmer over medium heat, uncovered, stirring occasionally, until the flavors meld, about 5 minutes. Then serve.

Sprouted Horse Gram

WITH A SPICY COCONUT-CHILE SAUCE

khili hui kulith

for some reason, some legumes harbor more debris than others, and horse gram is one of those. Sort through the beans very carefully before you get them to sprout. (Sprouted beans cook much faster than if they were used whole.) You can use other, more readily available, partially sprouted beans as an alternative. Their cooking time will be about the same, but their flavor and texture will differ. Sprouted beans generally don't break down, and hence the sauce for this dish (which is robust, chock-full of heat, and nutty-tasting) is on the thin side—

horse gram

Kulath, kulthi, *and* kulith *are some of the terms Indians use for this thin, hearty, muddy-brown, slightly elliptical legume. In the United States and other English-speaking countries, it is known as horse gram, and is often associated with cattle feed (hence its name). This slightly mealy-textured, earthy-flavored legume can stand up to strong flavors and is available wherever Indian groceries are sold. Brown lentils, commonly referred to as French lentils, and also red cowpeas make excellent alternatives, should you wish to make this curry without a trip to the store.*

the coconut in the paste provides a little body.

MAKES 5 CUPS

- 1 cup shredded fresh coconut; or ½ cup shredded dried unsweetened coconut, reconstituted (see Note)
- ¼ cup firmly packed fresh cilantro leaves and tender stems
- ¼ cup firmly packed medium-size to large fresh curry leaves
- 2 teaspoons coriander seeds
- 1 teaspoon cumin seeds
- 4 dried red Thai or cayenne chiles, stems removed
- 2 tablespoons Ghee (page 21) or canola oil
- 1 teaspoon black or yellow mustard seeds
- 1 medium-size red onion, finely chopped
- 2 fresh green Thai, cayenne, or serrano chiles, stems removed
- 3 cups partially sprouted horse gram (see box, page 328)
- 1 small cauliflower, cut into 1-inch florets
- 1½ teaspoons coarse kosher or sea salt

1. Pour ¼ cup water into a blender jar, followed by the coconut, cilantro, curry leaves, coriander seeds, cumin seeds, and dried chiles. Puree, scraping the inside of the jar as needed, to make a pretty, light green paste, red-speckled and gritty to the touch.

2. Heat the ghee in a pressure cooker over medium-high heat. Add the mustard seeds, cover the cooker (do not seal it), and cook until the seeds have stopped popping (not unlike popcorn), about 30 seconds. Immediately add the onion and fresh chiles, and stir-fry until the onion is light brown around the edges, about 5 minutes.

3. Add the coconut paste to the onion mixture and cook, uncovered, stirring occasionally, until the water evaporates from the paste and some of the ghee starts to separate on the surface, 5 to 8 minutes.

4. Stir in 2 cups water, and add the horse gram, cauliflower, and salt. Bring to a boil. Then seal the cooker shut and allow the pressure to build up. When the cooker reaches full pressure, reduce the heat to medium-low and cook for about 15 minutes. Remove the cooker from the heat and allow the pressure to subside naturally (about 15 minutes) before opening the lid.

5. Stir once or twice, and serve.

Note: To reconstitute coconut, cover with ½ cup boiling water, set aside for about 15 minutes, and then drain.

Kidney Beans
WITH A
CARDAMOM-YOGURT SAUCE

dahi elaichi Rajmah

this is a version of a dish I first sampled in the kitchen of a dear woman, Mrs. Kalia, during my first few lonely days in the United States, far away from my mother's home cooking. The simple flavors in this curry, an unconditional offering of comfort in her north Indian kitchen, provided much-needed satisfaction for my palate. Mrs. Kalia served it with a brimming basket of fresh, puffy *pooris* (page 725) and spicy lime pickles. If you would like to make your own pickles, use the Lime Wedges Pickled in Cayenne Pepper and Mustard Oil (page 745).

MAKES 2½ CUPS

2 tablespoons Ghee (page 21) or canola oil
1 small red onion, finely chopped
6 green or white cardamom pods
1 cup plain yogurt
½ teaspoon ground turmeric
2 cups cooked red kidney beans
2 teaspoons coarse kosher or sea salt
2 teaspoons Karuvapillai podi (page 35), or Punjabi garam masala (page 25)
½ teaspoon cayenne (ground red pepper)
2 tablespoons finely chopped fresh cilantro leaves and tender stems for garnishing

1. Heat the ghee in a medium-size saucepan over medium-high heat. Add the onion and cardamom pods, and stir-fry until the onion turns light brown around the edges, 3 to 5 minutes.

2. Stir in the yogurt and continue to cook, uncovered, stirring occasionally, until the watery liquid evaporates from the yogurt and leaves behind reddish-brown curd-like pellets, 12 to 15 minutes.

3. Sprinkle in the turmeric and incorporate it into the tart sauce. Add 2 cups water and the kidney beans, salt, *Karuvapillai podi,* and cayenne. Bring the curry to a boil. Then lower the heat to medium and gently boil the sauce, uncovered, stirring occasionally, until it has thickened, 10 to 15 minutes.

4. Sprinkle the cilantro over the curry, and serve. (Remove the cardamom pods first, if you wish.)

Tip: It would be hard not to notice the unusual technique that creates a sharply tart flavor in this curry without using the ingredients that normally provide tartness—such as tomatoes, lime juice, or tamarind. Cooking the yogurt down accentuates its sharp flavor by letting its wheylike liquid component evaporate, leaving behind lip-puckering curds. Even though you add water later on, the tartness remains, providing a crucial element to this easy curry.

Slow-Stewed Tomato Sauce
WITH KIDNEY BEANS

tamatar malai rajmah

here is a simple technique, developed over centuries in northern India and which I finally mastered during my restaurant days, for creating a surprisingly complex-tasting sauce. The process of reducing the water in the sauce as a way to cook the spices slowly, known as *bhunao*, is repeated in succession to fashion this rich curry. **MAKES 4 CUPS**

2 tablespoons Ghee (page 21) or canola oil

2 black cardamom pods

2 cinnamon sticks (each 3 inches long)

2 fresh or dried bay leaves

5 lengthwise slices fresh ginger (each 2 inches long, 1 inch wide, and ⅛ inch thick), finely chopped

4 large cloves garlic, finely chopped

3 tablespoons tomato paste

1 tablespoon sweet paprika

2 teaspoons coarse kosher or sea salt

2 teaspoons coriander seeds, ground

1 teaspoon cumin seeds, ground

½ teaspoon cayenne (ground red pepper)

¼ teaspoon ground turmeric

¼ cup Fried Onion Paste (page 16)

3 cups cooked red kidney beans

½ cup heavy (whipping) cream

½ teaspoon Punjabi garam masala (page 25)

2 tablespoons finely chopped fresh cilantro leaves and tender stems for garnishing

1. Heat the ghee in a medium-size saucepan over medium-high heat. Add the cardamom pods, cinnamon sticks, and bay leaves, and cook until they sizzle and are aromatic, 5 to 10 seconds. Immediately add the ginger and garlic, and stir-fry to a golden-brown color, about 1 minute.

2. Pour in ½ cup water and the tomato paste, paprika, salt, coriander, cumin, cayenne, and turmeric. Reduce the heat to medium-low, cover the pan, and simmer, stirring occasionally, until the water evaporates and a thin film of oil starts to form on the surface of the sauce, about 5 minutes.

3. Stir in another ½ cup water and continue to simmer the sauce, covered, stirring occasionally, until the water evaporates and the oil film reappears on the surface, about 5 minutes. Repeat the addition and evaporation of water twice more to create a rich-tasting, lush-red sauce. Stir in the onion paste and simmer, covered, to create another layer of complex sweetness, 5 minutes.

4. Add the kidney beans and 1 cup water. Stir the curry and bring it to a boil over medium heat. Continue to simmer it, uncovered, stirring occasionally, until the sauce starts to thicken, 13 to 15 minutes.

5. Pour in the cream and sprinkle in the garam masala. Cook until the cream has warmed through, 1 to 2 minutes.

6. Sprinkle with the cilantro, and serve. (Remove the cardamom pods, cinnamon sticks, and bay leaves first, if you wish.)

Tart-Hot Kidney Beans
WITH TOMATO IN A YOGURT SAUCE

dahiwaale Rajmah

Sindhi-style curry, this packs vibrant flavors into the kidney beans. I, for one, adore the bean's meaty texture and find it a perfect medium for the cool, hot, tart sauce. Once you finish eating *Methi chappatis* (page 733) with this curry, eat the rest over cooked white rice and call it a night. **MAKES 4 CUPS**

1 cup plain yogurt

2 tablespoons chickpea flour

1 teaspoon Garlic Paste (page 15)

1½ teaspoons coarse kosher or sea salt

½ teaspoon ground turmeric

3 or 4 fresh green Thai, cayenne, or serrano chiles, to taste, stems removed, finely chopped (do not remove the seeds)

2 tablespoons canola oil

1 tablespoon finely chopped fresh ginger

1 large tomato, cored and finely chopped

1 teaspoon Punjabi garam masala (page 25)

3 cups cooked red kidney beans

2 tablespoons finely chopped fresh cilantro leaves and tender stems for garnishing

1. Combine the yogurt with 1 cup water in a medium-size bowl, and whisk together. Sprinkle the chickpea flour over the yogurt mixture and whisk it in, making sure there are no lumps (the flour is essential because it will prevent the yogurt from curdling when simmered). Stir in the Garlic Paste, salt, turmeric, and chiles.

2. Heat the oil in a medium-size saucepan over medium-high heat. Sprinkle in the ginger and stir-fry until it is light brown, 1 to 2 minutes.

3. Add the tomato and the garam masala. Cook, uncovered, stirring occasionally, until the tomato softens but is still firm-looking, 3 to 5 minutes.

4. Stir in the kidney beans and the yogurt sauce. Bring the curry to a boil. Then lower the heat to medium and simmer, uncovered, stirring occasionally, until the sauce thickens, 10 to 15 minutes.

5. Sprinkle with the cilantro, and serve.

Hearty Kidney Beans
WITH A TART ONION-CHILE SAUCE

Punjabi Rajmah

from India's heartland, the wheat-growing region, this peasant dish is spicy, dark brown, and tart. Serve it with Punjab's other gift to the Western world: crispy-thin, fluffy, smoky, buttery naan (page 729). **MAKES 4 CUPS**

1 small red onion, coarsely chopped

4 fresh green Thai, cayenne, or serrano chiles,
    stems removed

4 large cloves garlic

2 lengthwise slices fresh ginger (each 2 inches long,
    1 inch wide, and ⅛ inch thick)

1 tablespoon mango powder or fresh lime juice

2 tablespoons Ghee (page 21) or canola oil

½ cup plain yogurt

3 cups cooked red kidney beans

¼ cup finely chopped fresh cilantro leaves and
    tender stems

½ teaspoon Punjabi garam masala (page 25)

1. Combine the onion, chiles, garlic, and ginger in a food processor. Pulse until minced. Add the mango powder and pulse to incorporate it into the blend. (If you were to add the powder at the beginning, it would create a clog, preventing an even mince.)

2. Heat the ghee in a medium-size saucepan over medium-high heat. Add the minced blend and stir-fry until it is pungent (adequate ventilation is a good idea at this point) and is light brown around the edges, 5 to 8 minutes.

3. Stir in the yogurt and continue to cook, uncovered, stirring occasionally, until the watery liquid evaporates from the yogurt and leaves behind reddish-brown curd-like pellets, 12 to 15 minutes.

4. Pour in 1 cup water and add the beans. Bring the curry to a boil. Then lower the heat to medium and continue to simmer, uncovered, stirring occasionally, until the sauce thickens, 10 to 15 minutes.

5. Stir in the cilantro and garam masala, and serve.

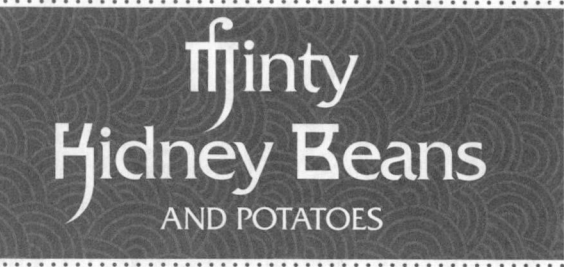

Minty Kidney Beans AND POTATOES

Aloo Pudhina Rajmah

Robust and assertive, this curry packs quite a punch and easily can be the only game in town, especially at your weekday dinner table. For a complete meal, serve it in large individual bowls with either bread or rice on the side. (My preference is a loaf of freshly baked crusty French bread from the bakery. Slice it into ½-inch-thick slices, warm them briefly in the oven, and dunk them into the curry to mop up the sauce between spoonfuls of minty-flavored kidney beans and potatoes.)

MAKES 4 CUPS

1 large tomato, cored and coarsely chopped

1 small red onion, coarsely chopped

¼ cup tightly packed fresh mint leaves

2 lengthwise slices fresh ginger (each 2 inches long,
    1 inch wide, and ⅛ inch thick)

¼ teaspoon black peppercorns

¼ teaspoon ground turmeric

3 to 5 fresh green Thai, cayenne, or serrano chiles,
    to taste, stems removed

1 cinnamon stick (3 inches long), broken into
    smaller pieces

2 tablespoons Ghee (page 21) or canola oil

1 teaspoon cumin seeds

2 medium-size russet or Yukon Gold potatoes,
    peeled, cut into ½-inch cubes, and submerged
    in a bowl of cold water to prevent browning

3 cups cooked red kidney beans

½ cup plain yogurt

2 tablespoons heavy (whipping) cream

1 teaspoon Punjabi garam masala (page 25)

1½ teaspoons rock salt, pounded

2 tablespoons finely chopped fresh cilantro
   leaves and tender stems

1. Put the tomato in a blender jar, and add the onion, mint, ginger, peppercorns, turmeric, chiles, and cinnamon pieces. Puree, scraping the inside of the jar as needed, to make a smooth pink sauce, dusted with specks of purple, green, and brown.

2. Heat the ghee in a medium-size saucepan over medium-high heat. Sprinkle in the cumin seeds and cook until they sizzle, turn reddish brown, and smell nutty, 5 to 10 seconds. Add the pureed sauce; within seconds it will start to bubble and spatter. Lower the heat to medium, partially cover the pan, and simmer, stirring occasionally, until almost all the liquid has evaporated and the oil is starting to separate around the edges and form a very thin, glossy layer on top, 10 to 15 minutes.

3. Drain the potatoes and stir them in. Add the kidney beans and 1 cup water, and bring the curry to a boil. Cover the pan and simmer, stirring occasionally, until the potatoes are fork-tender and the sauce has thickened slightly, 15 to 20 minutes.

4. While the curry is simmering, whisk the yogurt and cream together in a small bowl (the fat in the cream will stabilize the yogurt when it heats, keeping it from curdling).

5. Once the potatoes are tender, fold in the yogurt mixture, garam masala, rock salt, and cilantro. Simmer, uncovered, stirring occasionally, until the yogurt is warmed through, 2 to 4 minutes. Then serve.

Green Peas and Kidney Beans
WITH YOGURT AND CREAM

Rajmah Mutter

the textural difference between the nutty bite of the kidney beans and the soft squish of the green peas appeals to me, particularly against a backdrop of creamy-tart yogurt. If you don't have fresh curry leaves in your refrigerator's vegetable crisper, use ¼ cup firmly packed fresh cilantro leaves and tender stems for a similarly textured but different tasting sauce (although the flavors are very different).

MAKES 4 CUPS

2 teaspoons coriander seeds

1 teaspoon cumin seeds

½ teaspoon black peppercorns

½ teaspoon fenugreek seeds

20 to 25 medium-size to large fresh curry leaves

2 lengthwise slices fresh ginger (each 2 inches
   long, 1 inch wide, and ⅛ inch thick), coarsely
   chopped

2 fresh green Thai, cayenne, or serrano chiles,
   stems removed

2 tablespoons Ghee (page 21) or canola oil

2 cups cooked red kidney beans

2 cups frozen green peas (no need to thaw)

1 teaspoon coarse kosher or sea salt

½ cup plain yogurt

½ cup heavy (whipping) cream or
   half-and-half

2 teaspoons cornstarch (see Tip)

1. Combine the coriander seeds, cumin seeds, peppercorns, fenugreek seeds, curry leaves, ginger, and chiles in a mortar. Pound with the pestle, scraping the sides of the mortar to contain the mixture in the center, to form a wet blend with the texture of cut, wet leaves. The spices will break down, but not completely, which is where the gritty texture comes from.

2. Heat the ghee in a medium-size saucepan over medium heat. Scrape the pounded mixture into the pan and stir-fry to cook the spices without burning them, barely 30 seconds. Stir in the kidney beans and green peas, coating them with the flavorings. Pour in 1 cup water and sprinkle in the salt. Heat to a boil. Then lower the heat to medium and boil, uncovered, stirring occasionally, until the broth is flavored with the seasonings, about 5 minutes.

3. Combine the yogurt and cream in a small bowl, and quickly whisk them together (the fat in the cream stabilizes the yogurt, keeping it from curdling). Pour this into the saucepan and stir once or twice. Continue to boil the curry, uncovered, stirring occasionally, until the kidney beans and peas are tender, 8 to 10 minutes.

4. Dissolve the cornstarch in 2 tablespoons cold water. Pour this into the curry; the sauce will instantly start to thicken. Then serve.

Tip: Cornstarch is not the only thickener you can use for this curry; rice flour or toasted chickpea flour (page 41) will also do the trick. Another option is simply to coarsely mash some of the peas and kidney beans for a thicker-bodied sauce.

Turnips
WITH KIDNEY BEANS

Rajmah Shalgum

Reminiscent of a hearty chili, maybe because of the meaty-plump kidney beans and the wake-me-up sauce, this curry is chock-full of cumin, fennel, sweet turnips, and spicy ground chiles. If it's not hot enough for you, spoon an extra teaspoon of cayenne into the sauce. Go ahead and sprinkle that shredded cheddar cheese on top and savor it with a big slice of jalapeño cornbread—I won't mind. **SERVES 6**

2 tablespoons canola oil

2 cups finely chopped red onion

2 tablespoons Ginger Paste (page 15)

1 tablespoon Garlic Paste (page 15)

4 black cardamom pods

¼ cup tomato paste

2 teaspoons fennel seeds, ground

2 teaspoons cumin seeds, ground

1 teaspoon coriander seeds, ground

1 teaspoon ground Kashmiri chiles; or ¼ teaspoon
    cayenne (ground red pepper) mixed with
    ¾ teaspoon sweet paprika

½ teaspoon ground turmeric

3 cups cooked red kidney beans

4 small or 2 medium-size turnips, peeled and cut into
    1-inch cubes

1½ teaspoons coarse kosher or sea salt

6 tablespoons finely chopped fresh cilantro leaves
    and tender stems

1. Heat the oil in a medium-size saucepan over medium heat. Add the onion, the ginger and garlic pastes, and the cardamom pods. Stir-fry until the onion softens and is light brown around the edges, and a thin brown layer of the pastes starts to form on the bottom of the pan, about 15 minutes.

2. Stir in the tomato paste, fennel, cumin, coriander, ground chiles, and turmeric. Pour in 1 cup water, and scrape the bottom of the pan to deglaze it, releasing the collected bits of onion and spice. Cover the pan and simmer, stirring occasionally, until most of the water in the sauce has evaporated, 8 to 10 minutes. Pour in 1 more cup water and simmer, covered, until some of the water has evaporated and an oily sheen starts to form on the surface, 5 to 8 minutes.

3. Pour in 2 more cups water, and add the kidney beans, turnips, salt, and 4 tablespoons of the cilantro. Heat to a boil. Then reduce the heat slightly and simmer vigorously, uncovered, stirring occasionally, until the turnips are fork-tender and the sauce is thick, 15 to 20 minutes.

4. Remove the cardamom pods if you wish. Sprinkle with the remaining 2 tablespoons cilantro, and serve.

Kidney Beans and Chickpeas
WITH A TART ONION SAUCE

Chana Rajmah

A vegetarian's dream for a wintry night, this is best ladled over long-grain white rice or even over a thick piece of corn bread (not Asian Indian, but passable as American Indian). It'll even please the vegan at the table if you use oil instead of the ghee.

MAKES 4 CUPS

> ½ cup dried chickpeas
> ½ cup dried dark red kidney beans
> 2 tablespoons Ghee (page 21) or canola oil
> 1 teaspoon Panch phoron (page 36)
> ¼ cup Fried Onion Paste (page 16)
> 2 tablespoons Ginger Paste (page 15)
> 1 tablespoon Garlic Paste (page 15)
> 1 tablespoon coriander seeds, ground
> 1½ teaspoons coarse kosher or sea salt
> 1 teaspoon ground Deggi chiles
>   (see page 290); or ½ teaspoon cayenne
>   (ground red pepper) mixed with
>   ½ teaspoon sweet paprika
> ½ teaspoon ground turmeric
> 2 tablespoons tomato paste
> 1 teaspoon white granulated sugar
> 2 tablespoons finely chopped fresh cilantro
>   leaves and tender stems for garnishing

1. Place the chickpeas and the kidney beans in a pressure cooker. Fill the cooker halfway with water, and rinse the legumes by rubbing them between your fingertips. The water may appear slightly dirty. Drain this water. Repeat three or four times, until the water remains relatively clear; drain. Now add 4 cups water and bring to a boil, uncovered, over high heat. Skim off and discard any foam that forms on the surface. Seal the cooker shut and allow the pressure to build up. When the cooker reaches full pressure, reduce the heat to medium-low and cook for 1 to 1¼ hours. Remove the cooker from the heat and allow the pressure to subside naturally (about 15 minutes) before opening the lid.

2. Meanwhile, heat the ghee in a small skillet over medium-high heat. Sprinkle in the *Panch phoron* and cook until the seeds crackle, pop, and smell aromatic, 10 to 15 seconds. Stir in the onion, ginger, and garlic pastes, and lower the heat to medium. Cook, uncovered, stirring occasionally, until some of the ghee separates from the pastes, especially around the edges, 4 to 6 minutes.

3. Stir in the coriander, salt, ground chiles, and turmeric, and allow the ground spices to cook without burning, about 30 seconds. Then stir in the tomato paste and sugar, and cook so the spices can flavor the tart base, about 1 minute.

4. Pour in ½ cup water, and scrape the skillet to release any browned bits of spice and paste. Set the skillet aside until the chickpeas and kidney beans are ready.

5. Pour the sauce into the cooked chickpeas and beans, and stir once or twice. Simmer over medium heat, uncovered, stirring occasionally, until the flavors meld, 10 to 12 minutes.

6. Sprinkle with the cilantro, and serve.

Tips:

❖ If you don't have time to cook the dried legumes, use canned chickpeas and kidney beans—one 15-ounce can of each, rinsed and drained. Eliminate the 4 cups water used to cook the dried beans. Instead, combine the drained legumes with 1 cup water in a medium-size saucepan, and simmer over medium heat to heat the beans. Then start the recipe at Step 2.

❖ The sugar in this curry balances out the acidic tomato paste and the pungent Deggi chiles. For a more full-bodied alternative, substitute 1 tablespoon jaggery or dark brown sugar.

Whole Black Lentils
WITH GINGER, GARLIC, AND BUTTER

Makhani dal

I am fortunate enough to have sampled a few hundred versions of this Punjabi classic, made doubly popular by the plethora of north Indian restaurants that dot the American and European landscapes. It's a "must" at every special-occasion gathering. The curry's flavoring runs the gamut from simple to complex, depending on the cook's mood. Mine gravitates to the keep-it-simple school of thought. Ladle the gingered, creamy-textured curry over white rice or serve a basket of store-bought Indian flatbreads alongside. **MAKES 4 CUPS**

1 cup whole black lentils (sabud urad),
  picked over for stones
¼ cup Ginger Paste (page 15)
2 tablespoons Garlic Paste (page 15)
½ cup plain yogurt
½ cup Whole Milk Solids (page 24); or ½ cup
  heavy (whipping) cream
1½ teaspoons coarse kosher or sea salt
1 teaspoon Punjabi garam masala (page 25)
½ teaspoon cayenne (ground red pepper)
2 to 3 tablespoons unsalted butter or Ghee (page 21)
2 tablespoons finely chopped fresh cilantro leaves
  and tender stems for garnishing

1. Place the lentils in a pressure cooker. Fill the cooker halfway with water and rinse the lentils by rubbing them between your fingertips. The water may appear slightly dirty. Drain this water. Repeat three or four times, until

the water remains relatively clear; drain. Now add 3 cups water and bring to a boil, uncovered, over high heat. Skim off and discard any foam that forms on the surface. Stir in the ginger and garlic pastes. Seal the cooker shut and allow the pressure to build up. When the cooker reaches full pressure, reduce the heat to medium-low and cook for about 45 minutes. Remove the cooker from the heat and allow the pressure to subside naturally (about 15 minutes) before opening the lid.

2. Meanwhile, combine the yogurt, milk solids, salt, garam masala, and cayenne in a blender jar. Puree, scraping the inside of the jar as needed, to make a smooth, batterlike paste, speckled with brown and red spices.

3. Once the lentils are ready, stir in the butter and the creamy paste. Sprinkle with the cilantro, and serve.

Skinned Whole Black Lentils
WITH BROWNED ONIONS

dhuli hui Sabud Urad

When I first sampled skinned whole black lentils, I was amazed to see how quickly they broke down to form a rich, creamy-tasting dal. My friend, colleague, and fellow cookbook author Mary Evans joined me for lunch when we tasted this curry, along with some store-bought onion-filled naans brushed with ghee. We both felt lucky to work for ourselves and, more important, to be able to savor a glass of wine under the hot afternoon sun, both rarities in Minneapolis (the sun and the afternoon glass of wine, that is). **MAKES 3 CUPS**

1 cup skinned whole black lentils (sabud urad),
  picked over for stones
2 tablespoons Ghee (page 21) or canola oil
1 teaspoon cumin seeds
1 small red onion, cut in half lengthwise and thinly sliced
4 medium-size cloves garlic, finely chopped
4 to 6 fresh green Thai, cayenne, or serrano chiles,
  to taste, stems removed, finely chopped
  (do not remove the seeds)
1½ teaspoons coarse kosher or sea salt
½ teaspoon ground turmeric
¼ cup finely chopped fresh cilantro leaves
  and tender stems

1. Place the lentils in a pressure cooker. Fill the cooker halfway with water and rinse the lentils by rubbing them between your fingertips. The water may appear slightly dirty. Drain this water. Repeat three or four times, until the water remains relatively clear; drain. Now add 3 cups water and bring to a boil, uncovered, over high heat. Skim off and discard any foam that forms on the surface. Seal the cooker shut and allow the pressure to build up. When the cooker reaches full pressure, reduce the heat to medium-low and cook for 10 to 15 minutes. Remove the cooker from the heat and allow the pressure to subside before opening the lid.

2. Meanwhile, heat the ghee in a medium-size skillet over medium-high heat. Add the cumin seeds and cook until they sizzle, turn reddish brown, and are aromatic, 5 to 10 seconds. Add the onion, garlic, and chiles, and stir-fry until the onion is light honey-brown around the edges, 3 to 5 minutes.

3. Sprinkle in the salt and turmeric, and stir to cook the spices, about 10 seconds. Then add 1 cup water and deglaze the skillet. Set the skillet aside until the lentils are cooked. Once the lentils are ready, stir in the cilantro and the contents of the skillet. Stir once or twice, and serve.

Slow-Cooked Creamy Black Lentils
WITH WHOLE SPICES

ɱaa di dal

Mother is *maa,* and to call this Punjabi curry "Mother's Lentils" signifies the importance of the dish. There are as many legume and spice combinations as there are cooks in northwestern India, when it comes to *Maa di dal.* This version makes liberal use of cream and clarified butter, along with simple spices and herbs, and allows the natural creaminess of the cooked black lentils to shine. I often serve it as a first course with baskets of either store-bought or homemade naan (page 729), cut into wedges.

MAKES 6 CUPS

1 cup whole black lentils (sabud urad),
   picked over for stones

½ cup yellow split peas (chana dal), picked
   over for stones

8 medium-size cloves garlic

2 lengthwise slices fresh ginger (each 2 inches long,
   1 inch wide, and ⅛ inch thick)

2 to 4 fresh green Thai, cayenne, or serrano chiles,
   to taste, stems removed

4 green, white, or black cardamom pods

2 fresh or dried bay leaves

2 cinnamon sticks (each 3 inches long)

4 tablespoons Ghee (page 21) or unsalted butter

1 teaspoon cumin seeds

1 cup finely chopped red onion

1 cup crushed tomatoes or tomato sauce,
   canned or homemade (page 18)

2 teaspoons coarse kosher or sea salt

½ teaspoon cayenne (ground red pepper)

1 cup cooked red kidney beans, coarsely mashed
   (see Tips)

½ cup heavy (whipping) cream

2 tablespoons finely chopped fresh cilantro
   leaves and tender stems

1. Place the lentils and split peas in a large saucepan. Fill the pan halfway with water and rinse the legumes by rubbing them between your fingertips. The water will become cloudy. Drain this water. Repeat three or four times, until the water remains relatively clear; drain. Now add 6 cups water and bring to a boil, uncovered, over medium heat. Skim off and discard any foam that forms on the surface.

2. While the water is coming to a boil, combine the garlic, ginger, and chiles in a food processor. Pulse until the ingredients are minced.

3. As soon as the water is boiling and you have discarded the foam, add the minced blend and the cardamom pods, bay leaves, and cinnamon sticks. Lower the heat to medium, cover the pan, and simmer, stirring occasionally, until the lentils swell up and soften and the split peas are fall-apart tender, about 1 hour.

4. While the legumes are cooking, heat 2 tablespoons of the ghee in a medium-size skillet over medium-high heat. Sprinkle in the cumin seeds and cook until they sizzle, turn reddish brown, and smell nutty, 5 to 10 seconds. Add the onion and stir-fry until it is light brown around the edges, 3 to 5 minutes.

5. Reduce the heat to medium-low and stir in the tomatoes, salt, and cayenne. Simmer the sauce, partially covered, stirring occasionally, until some of the ghee starts to separate on the surface, 6 to 10 minutes. Set the skillet aside until the legumes are ready.

6. Once the legumes are tender, stir in the sauce, the kidney beans, and the cream. Pour 1 cup water into the skillet and scrape the bottom to deglaze it, releasing any sauce and spices. Add this to the legumes and stir once or twice.

7. Cover the pan and simmer over medium heat, stirring occasionally, until the flavors mingle, 5 to 10 minutes.

8. Stir in the remaining 2 tablespoons ghee and the cilantro, and serve.

Tips:

❖ I often use canned red kidney beans for convenience, after draining them and rinsing off the gelatinous, salty brine.

❖ Coarsely mashing the kidney beans (use a potato masher or the back of a cooking spoon) provides a nutty texture to the curry and thickens it a bit without any need to use flour.

Creamy Black Lentils
WITH CHICKPEAS AND KIDNEY BEANS

teen taal dal

the melody of this *teen* (three) *taal* (tune) *dal* (legume) is pure harmony—its texture creamy-smooth, its flavor sublime. Whole black lentils are naturally velvety when cooked, a smoothness further enhanced by adding yogurt and heavy cream (what's not to love?), staples in Punjabi kitchens. The first time I made this dal, I consumed massive amounts of it, initially dunking flaky *Paranthas* (page 731) into it, and then mounding the rest over steamed white basmati rice (page 707). **MAKES 4 CUPS**

½ cup whole black lentils (sabud urad),
   picked over for stones
¼ cup dried chickpeas
¼ cup dried red kidney beans
2 fresh or dried bay leaves
2 black, green, or white cardamom pods
1 cinnamon stick (3 inches long)
1 small red onion, coarsely chopped
3 large cloves garlic
2 lengthwise slices fresh ginger (each 2 inches long,
   1 inch wide, and ⅛ inch thick)
1 to 3 fresh green Thai, cayenne, or serrano chiles,
   to taste, stems removed
2 tablespoons Ghee (page 21) or melted butter
¼ teaspoon ground turmeric
2 tablespoons tomato paste
1½ teaspoons coarse kosher or sea salt
½ cup plain yogurt
¼ cup heavy (whipping) cream
1 teaspoon Toasted Cumin-Coriander Blend
   (page 33)
2 tablespoons finely chopped fresh cilantro
   leaves and tender stems for garnishing

1. Place the lentils, chickpeas, and kidney beans in a pressure cooker. Fill the cooker halfway with water, and rinse the legumes by rubbing them between your fingertips. The water may appear slightly dirty. Drain this water. Repeat three or four times, until the water remains relatively clear; drain. Now add 3 cups water and bring to a boil, uncovered, over high heat. Skim off and discard any foam that forms on the surface. Add the bay leaves, cardamom pods, and cinnamon stick. Seal the cooker shut and allow the pressure to build up. When the cooker reaches full pressure, reduce the heat to medium-low and cook for about 45 minutes. Remove the cooker from the heat and allow the pressure to subside naturally (about 15 minutes) before opening the lid.

2. Meanwhile, combine the onion, garlic, ginger, and chiles in a food processor. Pulse until the mixture is minced.

3. Heat the ghee in a medium-size skillet over medium-high heat. Add the minced onion blend and stir-fry until it is dark brown, 10 to 12 minutes. (Initially the mixture will sweat, but once the liquid evaporates, the onion will brown and the chiles will smell pungent.)

4. Sprinkle the turmeric over the browned onion blend, add ½ cup water, and scrape the bottom of the skillet to deglaze it, releasing any browned bits of onion and spice. Set the skillet aside.

5. When the lentils are cooked, add the contents of the skillet, the tomato paste, and the salt, and stir once or twice. Simmer over medium heat, uncovered, stirring occasionally, until the creamy-looking dal has absorbed the flavors, about 5 minutes.

6. Stir in the yogurt, cream, and cumin-coriander blend, and continue to simmer, uncovered, stirring occasionally, until the yogurt and cream are warmed through, 2 to 3 minutes.

7. Remove the bay leaves, cardamom pods, and cinnamon stick. Sprinkle the cilantro over the dal, and serve.

Split Black Lentils
WITH CLARIFIED BUTTER

Thilke Waale Urad ki dal

Very buttery, creamy, nutty, and delicate this dal curry's flavors are a perfect match for store-bought or homemade rotis (page 727) and a side dish of thinly sliced fresh green Thai, cayenne, or serrano chiles. **MAKES 4 CUPS**

> 1 cup skin-on split black lentils (urad dal), picked over for stones
> 2 tablespoons canola oil
> 1 teaspoon cumin seeds
> 1 medium-size red onion, finely chopped
> 1½ teaspoons coarse kosher or sea salt
> ½ teaspoon ground turmeric
> 2 to 3 tablespoons Ghee (page 21), to taste

1. Place the lentils in a medium-size saucepan. Fill the pan halfway with water and rinse the lentils by rubbing them between your fingertips. The water will become cloudy and some of the black skins will separate. Drain this water, discarding the skins. Repeat three or four times, until the water remains relatively clear; drain. Now add 3 cups water and bring to a boil, uncovered, over medium heat. Skim off and discard any foam that forms on the surface. Lower the heat to medium and simmer, uncovered, stirring occasionally, until the lentils are soft, 25 to 30 minutes.

2. While the lentils are cooking, heat the oil in a medium-size skillet over medium-high heat. Add the cumin seeds and cook until they sizzle and turn red-

dish brown, 5 to 10 seconds. Add the onion and stir-fry until it is light honey-brown, about 5 minutes. Set the skillet aside.

3. Once the lentils are soft, coarsely mash some of them with a potato masher or the back of a spoon (this will help thicken the curry). Stir in the salt and turmeric, followed by the onion mixture. Cover the pan and simmer over medium heat, stirring occasionally, until the lentils have absorbed the flavors, about 5 minutes.

4. Just before serving, stir in the ghee for that burst of intense, rich flavor.

Skinned Split Black Lentils

WITH CHILES AND BLACK PEPPER

kali Aur hari Mirch Urad dal

You will be amazed at this curry's creamy-smooth texture and mellow heat, even though it is liberally peppered with green chiles and peppercorns. I attribute the mellowness to the lentils, which protect our palates from the fiery burn. If you wish for something tangy, squirt a tablespoon or two of freshly squeezed lime or lemon juice over the finished curry. **MAKES 4 CUPS**

1 cup skinned split black lentils (cream-colored in this form, urad dal), picked over for stones
½ teaspoon ground turmeric
1 teaspoon black peppercorns
6 to 8 fresh green Thai, cayenne, or serrano chiles, to taste, stems removed

2 tablespoons Ghee (page 21) or canola oil
1 teaspoon black or yellow mustard seeds
4 large cloves garlic, finely chopped
¼ cup finely chopped fresh cilantro leaves and tender stems
1½ teaspoons coarse kosher or sea salt
1 teaspoon white granulated sugar

1. Place the lentils in a medium-size saucepan. Fill the pan halfway with water and rinse the lentils by rubbing them between your fingertips. The water will become cloudy. Drain this water. Repeat three or four times, until the water remains relatively clear; drain. Now add 3 cups water and bring to a boil, uncovered, over medium heat. Skim off and discard any foam that forms on the surface. Stir in the turmeric, reduce the heat to medium-low, and cover the pan. Simmer, stirring occasionally, until the lentils are tender but still firm-looking, 15 to 20 minutes.

2. While the lentils are cooking, put the peppercorns in a mortar and add the chiles. Pound the mixture with the pestle to form a coarse, pulpy blend.

3. Heat the ghee in a small skillet over medium-high heat. Add the mustard seeds, cover the skillet, and cook until the seeds have stopped popping (not unlike popcorn), about 30 seconds. Add the garlic and stir-fry until it is light brown around the edges, about 30 seconds. Stir in the pounded pepper-chile blend and stir-fry (with adequate ventilation) for about 30 seconds. Then pour 1 cup water into the skillet, and scrape the pan to deglaze it, releasing any browned bits of spice. Set the skillet aside.

4. When the lentils are ready, pour the contents of the skillet into the saucepan, and add the cilantro, salt, and sugar. Simmer, uncovered, stirring occasionally, until the flavors have mingled and the sauce has thickened, 8 to 10 minutes. Then serve.

Garlic-Infused Split Black Lentils
WITH LIME

Lasoon Urad Chi dal

to me this dal, scooped over a mound of steamed rice and enjoyed with a basket of *Papads* (page 740), makes a perfect simple meal, especially after a day of eating junk food. I love the creamy texture of these black lentils, but if you don't happen to have any in your pantry, use the equally quick-cooking skinned split green lentils *(moong dal)* for a satisfying alternative. **MAKES 4 CUPS**

1 cup skinned split black lentils (cream-colored
   in this form, urad dal), picked over for stones
¼ teaspoon ground turmeric
2 tablespoons Ghee (page 21) or canola oil
1 teaspoon cumin seeds
1 small red onion, cut in half lengthwise and thinly sliced
4 medium-size cloves garlic, finely chopped
4 fresh green Thai, cayenne, or serrano chiles, stems
   removed, cut crosswise into ¼-inch-thick slices
   (do not remove the seeds)
2 teaspoons coarse kosher or sea salt
Juice of 1 medium-size lime
2 tablespoons finely chopped fresh cilantro
   leaves and tender stems for garnishing

1. Place the lentils in a medium-size saucepan. Fill the pan halfway with water and rinse the lentils by rubbing them between your fingertips. The water will become cloudy. Drain this water. Repeat three or four times, until the water remains relatively clear; drain.

Now add 3 cups water and bring to a boil, uncovered, over medium heat. Skim off and discard any foam that forms on the surface. Stir in the turmeric, reduce the heat to medium-low, and cover the pan. Simmer, stirring occasionally, until the lentils are tender but still firm-looking, 15 to 20 minutes.

2. While the lentils are cooking, heat a medium-size skillet over medium-high heat and pour in the ghee. Add the cumin seeds and cook until they sizzle and turn reddish brown, 5 to 10 seconds. Add the onion, garlic, and chiles, and stir-fry until the onion is lightly browned and the chiles are pungent, 3 to 5 minutes. Stir in 1 cup water and the salt. Cook until the onion has softened, about 2 minutes. Set the skillet aside.

3. Once the turmeric-stained lentils are cooked, add the onion mixture and simmer over medium heat, uncovered, stirring occasionally, until the lentils have absorbed the flavors and the dal has thickened slightly, 8 to 10 minutes.

4. Stir in the lime juice, sprinkle with the cilantro, and serve.

Skinned Split Black Lentils
WITH SPINACH

Palak Urad dal

often evening comes along sooner than we expect it, and just like everyone else, we cookbook authors face the question: What's for dinner? When that happens, I have a look at my store of legumes and pick the grain that calls out to me. My criteria are usually that the dish be quick-cooking, not labor-intensive, nutritious, and a one-pot deal. This curry meets all the requirements, and is downright tasty to boot—especially when you serve it with slightly starchy long-grain white rice and a stack of Flame-Toasted Lentil Wafers (page 740). **MAKES 5 CUPS**

> 1 cup skinned split black lentils
>   (cream-colored in this form, urad dal),
>   picked over for stones
> 1 pound fresh spinach leaves, well rinsed and
>   coarsely chopped
> ¼ teaspoon ground turmeric
> ½ teaspoon fenugreek seeds
> 5 large cloves garlic
> 4 fresh green Thai, cayenne, or serrano chiles,
>   stems removed
> 2 lengthwise slices fresh ginger (each 2 inches
>   long, 1 inch wide, and ⅛ inch thick)
> 2 tablespoons Ghee (page 21) or canola oil
> 1 teaspoon cumin seeds
> ¼ cup finely chopped fresh cilantro leaves
>   and tender stems
> 1½ teaspoons coarse kosher or sea salt

1. Place the lentils in a medium-size saucepan. Fill the pan halfway with water and rinse the lentils by rubbing them between your fingertips. The water will become cloudy. Drain this water. Repeat three or four times, until the water remains relatively clear; drain. Now add 4 cups water and bring to a boil, uncovered, over medium heat. Skim off and discard any foam that forms on the surface. Add the spinach, a couple of handfuls at a time, stirring it in until wilted. Then stir in the turmeric, reduce the heat to medium-low, and cover the pan. Simmer, stirring occasionally, until the lentils are tender but still slightly firm-looking, 20 to 25 minutes.

2. While the lentils are cooking, sprinkle the fenugreek seeds into a mortar, followed by the garlic, chiles, and ginger. Pound with the pestle, scraping the sides to contain the mixture in the center, to form a pulpy, slightly gritty paste.

3. Heat a small skillet over medium-high heat and pour in the ghee. Add the cumin seeds and cook until they sizzle, turn reddish brown, and smell nutty, 5 to 10 seconds. Immediately stir in the paste and cook, stirring occasionally, until the garlic and ginger are browned, about 2 minutes. Set the skillet aside.

4. When the lentils are ready, stir in the contents of the skillet, the cilantro, and the salt. Simmer, uncovered, stirring occasionally, until the flavors meld, about 5 minutes. Then serve.

Tip: Use dried red chiles instead of the fresh ones and notice how markedly different the resulting curry tastes: more vibrant, slightly hotter, but still yummy.

Creamy-Tart Split Black Lentils
WITH COCONUT

Urad Kokum Chi Dal

You will find this dal curry is true to its title: The natural creaminess from the *urad dal* offers a mellow backdrop to the fiery chiles, while the tart flavor emerges from the kokum. One night I was bone-tired, so I warmed a stack of frozen homemade rotis (page 727) to serve with this, making a light but truly satisfying dinner. For my son, of course, a bowl of store-bought mango pulp was compulsory. **MAKES 4 CUPS**

1 cup skinned split black lentils (cream-colored in this form, urad dal), picked over for stones

¼ teaspoon ground turmeric

4 pieces dried black kokum (each roughly 2 inches long and 1 inch wide

2 tablespoons Ghee (page 21) or canola oil

2 teaspoons cumin seeds

8 to 10 fresh green Thai, cayenne, or serrano chiles, to taste, stems removed, thinly sliced crosswise (do not remove the seeds)

4 large cloves garlic, finely chopped

1 large tomato, cored and finely chopped

¼ cup shredded fresh coconut; or 2 tablespoons shredded dried unsweetened coconut, reconstituted (see Note)

1½ teaspoons coarse kosher or sea salt

10 to 12 medium-size to large fresh curry leaves

1. Place the lentils in a medium-size saucepan. Fill the pan halfway with water, and rinse the lentils by rubbing them between your fingertips. The water will become cloudy. Drain this water. Repeat three or four times, until the water remains relatively clear; drain. Now add 3 cups water and bring to a boil, uncovered, over medium heat. Skim off and discard any foam that forms on the surface. Stir in the turmeric and kokum, reduce the heat to medium-low, and cover the pan. Simmer, stirring occasionally, until the lentils are tender but still firm-looking, 15 to 20 minutes.

2. While the lentils are cooking, heat a medium-size skillet over medium-high heat and pour in the ghee. Add the cumin seeds and cook until they sizzle and turn reddish brown, 5 to 10 seconds. Add the chiles and garlic, and stir-fry until the garlic is lightly browned, 1 to 2 minutes.

Kokum? See the Glossary of Ingredients, page 758.

3. Immediately add the tomato, coconut, salt, and curry leaves. Lower the heat to medium and simmer, uncovered, stirring occasionally, until the tomato has softened but is still slightly chunky, 2 to 3 minutes. Set the skillet aside.

4. When the lentils are tender, add the sauce and stir once or twice. Pour 1 cup water into the skillet and scrape the bottom to release any stuck-on spices and sauce; pour this into the lentils. Cover the pan and simmer, stirring occasionally, until the flavors have mingled and the sauce has thickened, 8 to 10 minutes.

5. Remove the kokum slices, and serve.

Note: To reconstitute coconut, cover with 2 tablespoons boiling water, set aside for about 15 minutes, and then drain.

Black Lentils and Yellow Split Peas
WITH CARDAMOM

Thilke Waale Urad Aur Thane ki dal

A classic of the hunting community in India's northwestern region, this dal often simmers for hours over an open fire. Once the hunters return from their exhausting day, the dal awaits them, its creamy, mellow flavors a perfect complement to the spice-cured meat from the previous day's kill. My taste buds are just as happy when I ladle this atop white rice with a mound of fiery lime pickles (page 745). **MAKES 4 CUPS**

¾ cup skin-on split black lentils (urad dal), picked over
    for stones

¼ cup yellow split peas (chana dal), picked over for stones

¼ teaspoon ground turmeric

1 large red onion, coarsely chopped

6 medium-size cloves garlic

3 lengthwise slices fresh ginger (each 1½ inches long,
    1 inch wide, and ⅛ inch thick)

3 fresh green Thai, cayenne, or serrano chiles, stems
    removed

2 tablespoons Ghee (page 21) or butter, plus additional
    for drizzling (optional)

2 teaspoons cumin seeds

½ teaspoon ground asafetida

4 black cardamom pods

1½ teaspoons coarse kosher or sea salt

2 tablespoons finely chopped fresh cilantro
    leaves and tender stems for garnishing

1. Place the lentils and split peas in a medium-size saucepan. Fill the pan halfway with water, and rinse the legumes by rubbing them between your fingertips. The water will become cloudy and some of the black lentil skins will separate. Drain this water, discarding the skins. Repeat three or four times, until the water remains relatively clear; drain. Now add 3 cups water and bring to a boil, uncovered, over medium heat. Skim off and discard any foam that forms on the surface. Stir in the turmeric. Reduce the heat to medium-low and simmer, uncovered, stirring occasionally, until the legumes are tender but still firm-looking and most of the water has evaporated from the surface, 30 to 35 minutes.

2. While the legumes are cooking, combine the onion, garlic, ginger, and chiles in a food processor. Pulse until the ingredients are minced.

3. Heat the ghee in a small skillet over medium-high heat. Add the cumin seeds and cook until they sizzle, turn reddish brown, and smell fragrant, 5 to 10 seconds.

Add the onion-chile blend, asafetida, and cardamom pods. Stir-fry until the onion is lightly browned, 8 to 10 minutes.

4. Sprinkle the salt into the onion mixture and stir once or twice. Pour in 1 cup water. Set the skillet aside until the lentils and split peas are ready.

5. When the legumes are tender, pour the onion mixture into the pan and stir once or twice. Cover the pan and boil, stirring occasionally, until the lentils absorb the flavors and soften further, 15 to 20 minutes.

6. Remove the cardamom pods if you wish. Sprinkle the cilantro over the curry, drizzle with the extra ghee if desired, and serve.

Tip: Make an extra effort to sort through the black lentils, as they tend to harbor more than the usual amount of small stones and pebbles. I spread them out on a white plate and rub my fingers over them to feel for gritty stones.

Black and Green Lentils
WITH BAY LEAVES AND CURRY LEAVES

Moong Urad Nu Dal

this spicy, creamy dal is perfect with a stack of fluffy rotis (page 727) and some Avocado Chutney (page 748). I salivate just thinking about it. MAKES 3 CUPS

½ cup skinned split black lentils (cream-colored
*   in this form, urad dal), picked over for stones*
½ cup skinned split green lentils (yellow in this
*   form, moong dal), picked over for stones*
6 lengthwise slices fresh ginger (each 1½ inches long,
*   1 inch wide, and ⅛ inch thick)*
4 to 6 fresh green Thai, cayenne, or serrano chiles,
*   to taste, stems removed*
2 tablespoons Ghee (page 21) or canola oil
1 teaspoon cumin seeds
½ teaspoon ground asafetida
12 medium-size to large fresh curry leaves
6 green or white cardamom pods
4 fresh or dried bay leaves
4 dried red Thai or cayenne chiles, stems removed
1½ teaspoons coarse kosher or sea salt
½ teaspoon ground turmeric
2 tablespoons finely chopped fresh cilantro
*   leaves and tender stems for garnishing*

1. Place both types of lentils in a medium-size saucepan. Fill the pan halfway with water and rinse the lentils by rubbing them between your fingertips. The water will become cloudy. Drain this water. Repeat three or four times, until the water remains relatively clear; drain. Now add 3 cups water and bring to a boil, uncovered, over medium heat. Skim off and discard any foam that forms on the surface. Continue to boil the lentils vigorously, uncovered, stirring occasionally, until they are tender but still firm-looking and most of the water has evaporated from the surface, 12 to 15 minutes.

2. While the lentils are cooking, combine the ginger and the fresh chiles in a food processor and pulse until minced, making a highly aromatic blend.

3. Heat the ghee in a small skillet over medium-high heat. Add the cumin seeds and cook until they sizzle, turn reddish brown, and are fragrant, 5 to 10 seconds. Add the minced blend and the asafetida, curry leaves,

cardamom pods, bay leaves, and dried chiles. Stir-fry until the ginger has browned and the red chiles have blackened, 1 to 2 minutes.

4. Sprinkle in the salt and turmeric, and stir once or twice. Pour in 1 cup water and remove from the heat.

5. When the lentils are tender, add the contents of the skillet and stir once or twice. Simmer over medium heat, uncovered, stirring occasionally, until the flavors permeate the lentils, 3 to 5 minutes.

6. Sprinkle with the cilantro, and serve.

Tip: This curry does contain a number of whole spices and leaves that we Indians don't usually eat—especially the cardamom pods, curry leaves, bay leaves, and dried chiles (although personally, I like to nibble on the smoky-hot chiles between mouthfuls of bread and dal). You can pick them out of the dal before you serve it, or you can leave them in and caution the eaters to watch for them.

Brown Lentils
WITH CUMIN AND TURMERIC

Molu's Sabud Masoor

R.J. Singh (Molu to his loved ones), a boyishly young man in his thirties with a beautiful wife, Tara, and two adorable boys, Ishan and Rohan, set the lentils to cook in a pressure cooker while he laid out the meager spices that he would later add to flavor the curry. "We spiced our foods with few ingredients while growing up in Dehra Dun [in northern India]," he mused as he remembered his ancestors' humble roots in the tiny village of Buland Shehar, in the western part of Uttar Pradesh. Molu talked about his father, who went to college at Agra University and wore shoes for the first time when he attended a master's program there. Molu's deep friendship has touched me over the years. This humble dal balances hot, nutty, and tart flavors. Mound it over boiled red rice (page 708), a favorite in Dehra Dun.

MAKES 3 CUPS

1 cup whole brown lentils (sabud masoor),
  picked over for stones
1½ teaspoons coarse kosher or sea salt
1 teaspoon cayenne (ground red pepper)
1 teaspoon ground turmeric
2 tablespoons Ghee (page 21) or melted butter
2 tablespoons cumin seeds
¼ cup finely chopped fresh cilantro leaves and
  tender stems
Juice of 1 medium-size lime

1. Place the lentils in a pressure cooker. Fill the cooker halfway with tap water and rinse the lentils by rubbing them between your fingertips. The water may appear slightly dirty. Drain this water. Repeat three or four times, until the water remains relatively clear; drain. Now add 4 cups water and bring to a boil, uncovered, over high heat. Skim off and discard any foam that forms on the surface. Seal the cooker shut and allow the pressure to build up. When the cooker reaches full pressure, reduce the heat to medium-low and cook for 25 to 30 minutes. Remove the cooker from the heat and allow the pressure to subside naturally (about 15 minutes) before opening the lid.

2. Stir in the salt, cayenne, and turmeric, and simmer over medium heat, uncovered, stirring occasionally, to allow the spices to flavor the lentils, about 5 minutes.

3. Heat the ghee in a small skillet over medium-high heat. Add the cumin seeds and cook until they sizzle, are aromatic, and turn reddish brown, 10 to 15 seconds. Scrape the contents of the skillet into the dal, add the cilantro, and stir once or twice.

4. Stir in the lime juice, and serve.

Brown Lentils
WITH CHUNKY ONION AND CHILES

Pyaaz Waale Sabud Masoor

the lentils in this brown curry will retain their shape, no matter how long they cook. So if texture is important to you, this is your dal. But let me throw in an additional incentive: the sweet, onion-kissed flavor tweaked with tiny morsels of pungent chiles. Drizzle a tablespoon of ghee over the curry just before serving it for an added richness. **MAKES 4 CUPS**

1 cup whole brown lentils (sabud masoor),
  picked over for stones
1 medium-size red onion, cut in half lengthwise,
  and then cut into 1-inch cubes
2 tablespoons Ghee (page 21) or canola oil
1 teaspoon black or yellow mustard seeds
2 tablespoons tomato paste
2 tablespoons finely chopped fresh cilantro
  leaves and tender stems
1½ teaspoons coarse kosher or sea salt
¼ teaspoon ground turmeric
3 to 5 fresh green Thai, cayenne, or serrano chiles,
  to taste, stems removed, cut crosswise into
  ¼-inch-thick slices (do not remove the seeds)

1. Place the lentils in a medium-size bowl. Fill the bowl halfway with water and rinse the lentils by rubbing them between your fingertips. The water will become slightly cloudy. Drain this water. Repeat three or four times, until the water remains relatively clear; drain. Now fill the bowl halfway with hot water and let it sit on the counter, covered with plastic wrap, until the lentils soften, at least 8 hours or as long as overnight.

2. Drain the lentils and transfer them to a medium-size saucepan. Add the onion and 4 cups water, and bring to a boil over medium-high heat. Skim off and discard any foam that rises to the surface. Lower the heat to medium, cover partially, and simmer, stirring occasionally, until the lentils are tender, about 30 minutes.

3. While the lentils are cooking, heat the ghee in a small skillet over medium-high heat. Add the mustard seeds, cover the skillet, and cook until the seeds have stopped popping (not unlike popcorn), about 30 seconds. Stir in all the remaining ingredients and lower the heat to medium (to prevent excess spattering when the tomato paste hits the hot ghee). Simmer, uncovered stirring occasionally, until some of the ghee starts to separate around the edges, about 2 minutes.

4. Scrape the lush red sauce into the cooked lentils. Transfer a spoonful of the dal to the skillet and stir it around to get every bit of flavor; pour this back into the saucepan. Simmer, uncovered, stirring occasionally, until the lentils have absorbed the seasonings, about 5 minutes. Then serve.

Brown and Green Lentils
WITH A CASHEW-ALMOND SAUCE

Dal Korma

nut-based curries, called *kormas,* are often reserved to bathe expensive cuts of meat and highbrow vegetables. I find this discriminatory practice quite disturbing, especially when there are perfectly rich-tasting legumes that await their just due. So here I pamper them with the same treatment, using two whole legumes for a satisfying result. Any variety of legume will work, but if you choose ones that are split, cut the pressure-cooker time by half. **MAKES 6 CUPS**

½ cup whole brown lentils (sabud masoor),
    picked over for stones
½ cup whole green lentils (sabud moong),
    picked over for stones
I tablespoon Ginger Paste (page 15)
I tablespoon Garlic Paste (page 15)
½ teaspoon ground turmeric
6 green or white cardamom pods
2 cinnamon sticks (each 3 inches long)
¼ cup heavy (whipping) cream or half-and-half
¼ cup slivered blanched almonds
¼ cup raw cashew nuts
2 fresh green Thai, cayenne, or serrano chiles,
    stems removed
2 tablespoons Ghee (page 21) or canola oil
I medium-size red onion, finely chopped
I½ teaspoons coarse kosher or sea salt
½ cup finely chopped fresh cilantro leaves
    and tender stems

1. Place the brown and green lentils in a pressure cooker. Fill the cooker halfway with water, and rinse the lentils by rubbing them between your fingertips. The water may appear slightly dirty. Drain this water. Repeat three or four times, until the water remains relatively clear; drain. Now add 4 cups water and bring to a boil, uncovered, over high heat. Skim off and discard any foam that forms on the surface. Stir in the ginger and garlic pastes, turmeric, cardamom pods, and cinnamon sticks. Seal the cooker shut and allow the pressure to build up. When the cooker reaches full pressure, reduce the heat to medium-low and cook for 25 to 30 minutes. Remove the cooker from the heat and allow the pressure to subside naturally (about 15 minutes) before opening the lid.

2. While the lentils are cooking, pour the cream into a blender jar, followed by the almonds, cashews, and chiles. Puree, scraping the inside of the jar as needed, to form a thick, gritty, green-speckled paste.

3. Heat the ghee in a medium-size skillet over medium heat. Add the onion and stir-fry until it is caramel-brown with a deep purple hue, 10 to 15 minutes. Pour in ½ cup water and scrape the pan to deglaze it, releasing the browned bits of onion (the deglazing technique provides yet another level of complexity to the curry).

4. When the lentils are ready, stir in the contents of the skillet, the pureed nut paste, and the salt. Pour ½ cup water into the blender jar and give the blades a whir to wash it out; add the washings to the dal and stir once or twice. Simmer, uncovered, over medium heat, stirring occasionally, until the flavors marry, 5 to 10 minutes.

5. Stir in the cilantro, and serve. (Fish the cardamom pods and cinnamon sticks out of the curry before you serve it, if you wish.)

BALTI-STYLE
Whole Green Lentils
WITH BAY LEAVES

Sabud Moong ki dal

Remove the sharp-edged bay leaves from the dal before you serve this curry, especially if there are young children at the table. Indian bay leaves are actually much larger than the variety sold here; in fact, they are the leaves of a type of cinnamon tree.

MAKES 4 CUPS

1 cup whole green lentils (sabud moong), picked over for stones
2 tablespoons Ginger Paste (page 15)
2 tablespoons Garlic Paste (page 15)
1 teaspoon cayenne (ground red pepper)
½ teaspoon ground turmeric
2 or 3 fresh or dried bay leaves
2 tablespoons Ghee (page 21) or canola oil
1 tablespoon cumin seeds
1 cup tomato sauce, store-bought or homemade (page 18)
2 teaspoons Balti masala (page 31)
1½ teaspoons coarse kosher or sea salt
¼ cup finely chopped fresh cilantro leaves and tender stems
Additional 1 to 2 tablespoons Ghee (page 21; optional)

1. Place the lentils in a medium-size saucepan. Fill the pan halfway with water, and rinse the lentils by

rubbing them between your fingertips. The water may become cloudy. Drain this water. Repeat three or four times, until the water remains relatively clear; drain. Now add 4 cups water and bring to a boil, uncovered, over medium heat. Skim off and discard any foam that forms on the surface. Reduce the heat to medium-low, cover the pan, and simmer, stirring occasionally, until the lentils are mostly tender but still firm-looking, 30 minutes.

2. Stir in the Ginger Paste, Garlic Paste, cayenne, turmeric, and bay leaves. Raise the heat to medium and continue to simmer the lentils, uncovered, stirring occasionally, until the sauce thickens slightly, about 15 minutes.

3. While the lentils are simmering, heat the ghee in a small skillet over medium-high heat. Add the cumin seeds and cook until they sizzle, turn reddish brown, and smell nutty, 5 to 10 seconds. Stir in the tomato sauce, *Balti masala,* and salt. Reduce the heat to medium-low, partially cover the skillet, and simmer, stirring occasionally, until an oily sheen forms on the surface, about 5 minutes.

4. When the lentils are cooked, add the contents of the skillet and stir once or twice. Reduce the heat to medium-low and continue to simmer, uncovered, stirring occasionally, until the sauce thickens and the flavors meld, about 10 minutes.

5. Stir in the cilantro and the additional ghee (if using), and serve.

Toasted Spices and Onion
WITH GREEN LENTILS

dhania jeera Aur Sabud Moong

I love the nuttiness of cooked whole green lentils and find the spicing in this curry just right to highlight that adoration. With easy-to-find ingredients, quick cooking times, and minimal prep, this curry is a cinch to make for a quick weekday meal. **MAKES 4 CUPS**

1 cup whole green lentils (sabud moong), picked
    over for stones
2 tablespoons Ghee (page 21) or canola oil
½ cup finely chopped red onion
1 medium-size tomato, cored and finely chopped
¼ cup finely chopped fresh cilantro leaves
    and tender stems
1½ teaspoons coarse kosher or sea salt
1 teaspoon Toasted Cumin-Coriander Blend
    (page 33)
1 teaspoon ground Deggi chiles (see box, page 290);
    or ½ teaspoon cayenne (ground red pepper)
    mixed with ½ teaspoon sweet paprika
¼ teaspoon ground turmeric

1. Place the lentils in a medium-size saucepan. Fill the pan halfway with water and rinse the lentils by rubbing them between your fingertips. The water may become cloudy. Drain this water. Repeat three or four times, until the water remains relatively clear; drain. Now add 4 cups water and bring to a boil, uncovered, over medium heat. Skim off and discard any foam that forms on the surface. Reduce the heat to medium-low, cover the pan,

and simmer, stirring occasionally, until the lentils are mostly tender but still firm-looking, 30 minutes.

2. While the lentils are simmering, heat the ghee in a medium-size skillet over medium-high heat. Add the onion and stir-fry until it is light brown around the edges, 3 to 5 minutes.

3. Stir the tomato, cilantro, salt, spice blend, chiles, and turmeric into the onion. Cook until the tomato is softened but still slightly firm, 3 to 5 minutes. Remove the skillet from the heat and set it aside until the lentils are ready.

4. When the lentils are tender, add the tomato sauce. If some of the sauce still adheres to the skillet, pour a scoop of the lentil mixture into the skillet and scrape the bottom to deglaze it, releasing the collected bits of onion, tomato, and spice; add this to the pan. Continue to simmer the dal, uncovered, stirring occasionally, until the sauce thickens, about 15 minutes. Then serve.

Tips:

❖ If the curry is not acidic enough for you, squeeze in the juice of a medium-size lime just before you serve it, for that clean, crisp gusto.

❖ I often cook a batch of whole green lentils, without adding any seasoning, for later use. I refrigerate it for up to 4 days, or freeze it for up to a month, and then I know I have a batch on hand for those days when I don't want to cook dried lentils from scratch. If you happen to have cooked lentils on hand now, by all means use them: Add 1 to 2 cups water to the lentils when you reheat them; this allows the spiced tomato sauce to infuse its seasonings into the curry without drying out the dish. (You will need to add water even if you stored cooked lentils in their cooking liquid, because they have a tendency to absorb any liquid as they stand.)

Turmeric-Flavored Whole Green Lentils
WITH CHILES

haldi Waale Sabud Moong

the first time I made this, it was a "desperation curry" on a harried evening. I had the cooked lentils from another recipe and needed to use them before they spoiled. Spicing them with slightly hot, highly colorful Deggi chiles and Toasted Cumin-Coriander Blend was a quick solution, and soon a brimming bowlful graced the table. I added a basket of Flame-Toasted Lentil Wafers (page 740) and a bowl of Rice with Yogurt and Mustard Seeds (page 710)—and voilà, dinner ready in under an hour. **MAKES 4 CUPS**

1 cup whole green lentils (sabud moong), picked over for stones
2 tablespoons Ghee (page 21) or canola oil
1 teaspoon cumin seeds
½ cup finely chopped red onion
1 large tomato, cored and finely chopped
¼ cup finely chopped fresh cilantro leaves and tender stems
1½ teaspoons coarse kosher or sea salt
1 teaspoon ground Deggi chiles (see box, page 290); or ½ teaspoon cayenne (ground red pepper) mixed with ½ teaspoon sweet paprika
1 teaspoon Toasted Cumin-Coriander Blend (page 33)
1 teaspoon ground turmeric

1. Place the lentils in a pressure cooker. Fill the cooker halfway with water, and rinse the lentils by rubbing them between your fingertips. The water may appear slightly dirty. Drain this water. Repeat three or four times, until the water remains relatively clear; drain. Now add 3 cups water and bring to a boil, uncovered, over high heat. Skim off and discard any foam that forms on the surface. Seal the cooker shut and allow the pressure to build up. When the cooker reaches full pressure, reduce the heat to medium-low and cook for about 20 minutes. Remove the cooker from the heat and allow the pressure to subside naturally (about 15 minutes) before opening the lid.

2. Meanwhile, heat a medium-size skillet over medium-high heat and pour in the ghee. Add the cumin seeds and cook until they sizzle, turn reddish brown, and are aromatic, 5 to 10 seconds. Add the onion and stir-fry until it is light brown around the edges, 3 to 5 minutes.

3. Add the tomato, cilantro, salt, ground chiles, cumin-coriander blend, and turmeric. Cook, uncovered, stirring occasionally, until the tomato breaks down to a saucy consistency and some of the ghee starts to separate on the surface, 5 to 8 minutes. Set the skillet aside until the lentils are cooked.

4. When the lentils are ready, add the sauce. Pour ½ cup water into the skillet and deglaze it, releasing any browned bits; pour this into the lentils. Stir once or twice, and simmer over medium heat, stirring occasionally to prevent the lentils from sticking, until the flavors permeate the legumes, 8 to 10 minutes. Then serve.

Spinach-Smothered Whole Green Lentils

Salak Moong

What I love about this curry is the spinach overload. It gives the lentils a saucelike consistency, and since it is a vegetable combined with protein, I can ladle it over cooked white rice and call it lunch—or dinner. A few pieces of Flame-Toasted Lentil Wafers (page 740) provide crunchy texture, and a side of either homemade (page 745) or store-bought lime pickles would be an added bonus.

MAKES 8 CUPS

1 cup whole green lentils (sabud moong), picked over for stones
2 pounds fresh spinach leaves, well rinsed and coarsely chopped
2 teaspoons cumin seeds
3 to 5 fresh green Thai, cayenne, or serrano chiles, to taste, stems removed
2 tablespoons Ghee (page 21) or canola oil
1 small red onion, finely chopped
1 tablespoon finely chopped fresh ginger
1 large tomato, cored and cut into 1-inch cubes
2 teaspoons coarse kosher or sea salt

1. Place the lentils in a large saucepan. Fill the pan halfway with water and rinse the lentils by rubbing them

between your fingertips. The water may become cloudy. Drain this water. Repeat three or four times, until the water remains relatively clear; drain. Now add 6 cups water and bring to a boil, uncovered, over medium heat. Skim off and discard any foam that forms on the surface.

2. Grab several handfuls of the spinach and add them to the pan, stirring until they wilt. Repeat until all the spinach has been added. Now reduce the heat to medium-low, cover the pan, and simmer, stirring occasionally, until the lentils are mostly tender but still firm-looking, 30 minutes.

3. Uncover the pan, raise the heat to medium, and continue to simmer the lentils, stirring occasionally, until the sauce thickens slightly and the spinach starts to look velvety-soft, about 15 minutes.

4. While the curry is simmering, sprinkle the cumin seeds into a mortar and add the chiles. Pound with the pestle to form a pulpy-gritty blend. The chiles will appear squished, with their veins and seeds released, while the cumin seeds will look bruised but not completely ground.

5. Heat the ghee in a small skillet over medium-high heat. Add the onion and ginger, and stir-fry until the onion is light brown around the edges, 5 to 8 minutes.

6. Stir in the pounded blend, tomato, and salt. Simmer the sauce over medium heat, uncovered, stirring occasionally, until the tomato breaks down and softens and the ghee starts to separate around the edges, 3 to 5 minutes.

7. Add the sauce to the cooked lentils and stir once or twice. Continue to simmer the curry over medium heat, uncovered, stirring occasionally, until the flavors mingle, 8 to 10 minutes. Then serve.

Whole Green Lentils
WITH COCONUT AND TOMATOES

thenga paruppu

generic term in Tamil, *paruppu* usually signifies cooked lentils. This creamy-tasting dal reminds me of my childhood days, when my grandmother would feed me sweet split yellow pigeon peas with yogurt-smothered rice. I have used whole green lentils in this recipe to capture her flavors—in every mouthful. Serve it with the same yogurt rice, *Tayyar shaadum* (page 710), for a winning and comforting combination. **MAKES 6 CUPS**

1 cup whole green lentils (sabud moong), picked over for stones
2 tablespoons Ghee (page 21) or canola oil
1 teaspoon black or yellow mustard seeds
1 medium-size red onion, cut in half lengthwise and thinly sliced
½ teaspoon black or yellow mustard seeds, ground
½ teaspoon fenugreek seeds, ground
1 can (14.5 ounces) diced tomatoes
2 tablespoons finely chopped fresh cilantro leaves and tender stems
2 teaspoons coarse kosher or sea salt
½ teaspoon ground turmeric
15 medium-size to large fresh curry leaves
2 fresh green Thai, cayenne, or serrano chiles, stems removed, cut crosswise into ¼-inch-thick slices (do not remove the seeds)
1 cup shredded fresh coconut; or ½ cup shredded dried unsweetened coconut, reconstituted (see Note)

1. Place the lentils in a pressure cooker. Fill the cooker halfway with water, and rinse the lentils by rubbing them between your fingertips. The water may appear slightly dirty. Drain this water. Repeat three or four times, until the water remains relatively clear; drain. Now add 3 cups water and bring to a boil, uncovered, over high heat. Skim off and discard any foam that forms on the surface. Seal the cooker shut and allow the pressure to build up. When the cooker reaches full pressure, reduce the heat to medium-low and cook for about 20 minutes. Remove the cooker from the heat and allow the pressure to subside naturally (about 15 minutes) before opening the lid.

2. While the lentils are cooking, heat a medium-size skillet over medium-high heat and pour in the ghee. Add the mustard seeds, cover the skillet, and cook until the seeds have stopped popping (not unlike popcorn), about 30 seconds. Add the onion and stir-fry until it is light brown around the edges, 2 to 4 minutes.

3. Sprinkle in the ground mustard and fenugreek, and stir to cook the spices, about 10 seconds. Then add all the remaining ingredients, reduce the heat to medium, cover the skillet, and cook, stirring occasionally, until the tomatoes soften and look saucelike, about 5 minutes.

4. Stir the chunky sauce into the cooked lentils. Add ½ cup water to the skillet and stir to wash it out; add the washings to the lentils. Stir once or twice, and simmer over medium heat, uncovered, stirring occasionally, until the lentils have absorbed the flavors, 8 to 10 minutes. Then serve.

Note: To reconstitute coconut, cover with ½ cup boiling water, set aside for about 15 minutes, and then drain.

Cumin-Scented Split Green Lentils

jeera moong nu dal

This is delicious with thinly rolled rotis (page 727), but you can also serve it as a soup with a loaf of crusty, butter-laden French bread alongside. **MAKES 3 CUPS**

I cup skinned split green lentils (yellow in this form, moong dal), picked over for stones

1½ teaspoons coarse kosher or sea salt

½ teaspoon ground turmeric

4 lengthwise slices fresh ginger (each 1½ inches long, I inch wide, and ⅛ inch thick), coarsely chopped

2 fresh green Thai, cayenne, or serrano chiles, stems removed, coarsely chopped (do not remove the seeds)

2 tablespoons Ghee (page 21) or melted butter

I teaspoon cumin seeds

2 dried red Thai or cayenne chiles, stems removed

½ teaspoon ground asafetida

2 tablespoons finely chopped fresh cilantro leaves and tender stems for garnishing

1. Place the lentils in a medium-size saucepan. Fill the pan halfway with water and rinse the lentils by rubbing them between your fingertips. The water will become cloudy. Drain this water. Repeat three or four times, until the water remains relatively clear; drain. Now add 3 cups water and bring to a boil, uncovered, over medium heat. Skim off and discard any foam that forms on the surface. Sprinkle in the salt, turmeric, ginger, and fresh chiles. Reduce the heat to medium-low, cover the pan, and simmer, stirring occasionally, until the lentils are tender, 18 to 20 minutes.

2. Transfer half the lentils, including the ginger, chiles, and half the cooking water, to a blender and puree until smooth. Pour this creamy yellow blend into a bowl. Repeat with the remaining lentils and water. Then return all the puree to the saucepan. (If you have an immersion blender, you can puree all the ingredients right in the saucepan.)

3. Heat the ghee in a small skillet over medium-high heat. Add the cumin seeds and dried chiles, and cook until the chiles blacken and the seeds sizzle, turn reddish brown, smell aromatic, 10 to 15 seconds. Remove the pan from the heat and sprinkle in the asafetida. Pour this mixture into the pureed lentils. Cover the saucepan and simmer the dal over medium-low heat, stirring occasionally, until the flavors permeate the curry, about 5 minutes.

4. Sprinkle with the cilantro, and serve.

Jaggery? See the Glossary of Ingredients, page 758.

Sweet-Tart Split Green Lentils
WITH MUSTARD

Moong Nu Dal

My sister Lalitha's classmate, Smita, a Gujarati, is an amazing cook. She can create vegetarian magic with minimal

ingredients to balance sweet, hot, and nutty flavors in one lentil-based mouthful. I sampled this dal at Smita's kitchen table in Ohio, and its spicy-pungent memory lingered for weeks. Serve it with a basket of *pooris* (page 725) and the mango puree (*Aamras;* page 751). **MAKES 4 CUPS**

1 cup skinned split green lentils (yellow in this form, moong dal), picked over for stones
2 tablespoons Ghee (page 21) or canola oil
1 teaspoon black or yellow mustard seeds
2 teaspoons cumin seeds
2 teaspoons coarse kosher or sea salt
½ teaspoon cayenne (ground red pepper)
¼ teaspoon ground turmeric
¼ teaspoon ground asafetida
1 large tomato, cored and finely chopped
1 tablespoon crumbled (or chopped) jaggery or firmly packed dark brown sugar
¼ cup finely chopped fresh cilantro leaves and tender stems

1. Place the lentils in a medium-size saucepan. Fill the pan halfway with water and rinse the lentils by rubbing them between your fingertips. The water will become cloudy. Drain this water. Repeat three or four times, until the water remains relatively clear; drain. Now add 3 cups water and bring to a boil, uncovered, over medium heat. Skim off and discard any foam. Continue simmering vigorously, uncovered, stirring occasionally, until the lentils are barely tender, 10 to 12 minutes.

2. While the lentils are cooking, heat a small skillet over medium-high heat and pour in the ghee. Add the mustard seeds, cover the skillet, and cook until the seeds have stopped popping (not unlike popcorn), about 30 seconds. Sprinkle in the cumin seeds and cook until they turn reddish brown, about 5 seconds. Immediately add the salt, cayenne, turmeric, and asafetida. Cook for no more than 5 seconds, and then add the tomato, jaggery, and cilantro. Simmer, uncovered, over medium heat until the tomato pieces appear saucelike, 2 to 3 minutes.

3. Once the lentils are barely tender, add this slightly chunky tomato sauce to the pan, stir once or twice, and reduce the heat to medium-low. Cover the pan and simmer, stirring occasionally, until the dal has absorbed the flavors, 5 to 7 minutes. Then serve.

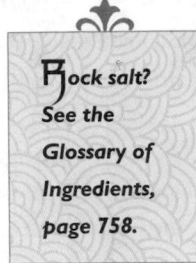

Rock salt? See the Glossary of Ingredients, page 758.

Garlicky Green Lentils

Lasoon Moong ki dal

Garlicky! So do pop in a mint or chew on some cardamom seeds before you come up close and personal to any friends. They will appreciate your thoughtfulness—and you will have enjoyed this curry, especially if you had some Avocado Relish with Tamarind and Chiles alongside (page 748). **MAKES 4 CUPS**

1 cup skinned split green lentils (yellow in this form, moong dal), picked over for stones

¼ teaspoon ground turmeric

2 tablespoons Ghee (page 21) or canola oil

1 teaspoon cumin seeds

¼ teaspoon ground asafetida

6 large cloves garlic, finely chopped

3 fresh green Thai, cayenne, or serrano chiles, stems removed, thinly sliced crosswise (do not remove the seeds)

1½ teaspoons rock salt, pounded

1. Place the lentils in a medium-size saucepan. Fill the pan halfway with water and rinse the lentils by rubbing them between your fingertips. The water will become cloudy. Drain this water. Repeat three or four times, until the water remains relatively clear; drain. Now add 3 cups water and bring to a boil, uncovered, over medium heat. Skim off and discard any foam that forms on the surface. Stir in the turmeric. Reduce the heat to medium-low, cover the pan, and simmer, stirring occasionally, until the lentils are tender, 18 to 20 minutes.

2. While the lentils are cooking, heat the ghee in a small skillet over medium-high heat. Add the cumin seeds and cook until they sizzle, turn reddish brown, and smell nutty, 5 to 10 seconds. Then sprinkle in the asafetida, garlic, and chiles. Stir-fry until the garlic turns light brown, 1 to 2 minutes. Set the skillet aside until the lentils are done.

3. Scrape the contents of the skillet into the cooked lentils, cover the pan, and simmer, stirring occasionally, until the flavors meld, about 5 minutes. Stir in the rock salt, and serve.

the right lentil

❖ ❖ ❖

At the Indian store, whole green lentils are referred to as either sabud moong (or just moong). The ones next to them, labeled split moong dal, are split but the skin is still intact (they have a yellow flat side and rounded dark green side). The third variety, also known as moong dal, is split with no skin, and is creamy-yellow. They are all from the same legume but are different in flavor, texture, and the way they cook.

Split Green Lentils
WITH BITTER MELON

teto dal

In a brightly lit cubicle at a software-consulting firm in Bangalore, India's Silicon Valley, Sangha Mitra Ray chatted with me about Bengali foods from her childhood. The burgundy saree draped around her petite body highlighted her Western-style short haircut. Sangha described how her family's eating habits have changed (olive oil replacing higher-fat mustard oil, for example). She still cooks west Bengal classics for her husband and their daughter as she manages career and home. The sugar in this *teto* (bitter) dal balances the flavor of the bitter melon, aided by nutty roasted mustard seeds. **MAKES 4 CUPS**

4 small to medium-size bitter melons
   (about 1 pound total)
2 teaspoons coarse kosher or sea salt
1 cup skinned split green lentils
   (yellow in this form, moong dal),
   picked over for stones
2 tablespoons canola oil
1 teaspoon black or yellow mustard seeds
2 teaspoons white granulated sugar
1 teaspoon ground turmeric
2 tablespoons finely chopped fresh cilantro
   leaves and tender stems for garnishing

1. Trim off and discard both ends of each melon. Use a swivel peeler or a paring knife to scrape off the bumpy scales and then peel off the skin, to reveal the light green flesh. Slice each melon in half lengthwise, and scoop out and discard the spongy, fleshy seeds. Shred the melons in a food processor or on a box grater.

2. Place the shredded bitter melons in a colander, and set it in an unused sink or in a bowl. Toss the salt with the melon, and leave it until some of the bitterness has leached out, 2 to 3 hours. (You can leave the melon in the colander overnight. When I do that, I usually place the colander in the refrigerator, just to play it safe.)

3. Rinse the melon shreds thoroughly, and squeeze out as much of the liquid as you possibly can. Pat the shreds dry between paper towels.

4. Place the lentils in a medium-size bowl. Fill the bowl halfway with water and rinse the lentils by rubbing them between your fingertips. The water will become cloudy. Drain this water. Repeat three or four times, until the water remains relatively clear; drain.

5. Heat the oil in a medium-size saucepan over medium-high heat. Add the mustard seeds, cover the pan, and cook until the seeds have stopped popping (not unlike popcorn), about 30 seconds. Throw in the bitter melon and stir-fry until it turns light brown, 3 to 5 minutes.

6. Add the drained lentils and 4 cups water. Once it comes to a boil, stir in the sugar and turmeric. Then lower the heat to medium and simmer, uncovered, until some of the liquid has evaporated and the lentils are tender but still firm-looking, 25 to 30 minutes.

7. Sprinkle with the cilantro, and serve.

Tips:

❖ If bitter melon is not your cup of tea, use shredded yellow squash or even zucchini as an alternative—but then there won't be any *teto* in this dal, will there?

❖ Another option for cutting down the bitterness is to squeeze a burst of fresh lime juice over the dal just before you serve it.

Chile-Spiked Split Green Lentils
WITH CAULIFLOWER

Phool Gobhi Kootu

Lentil stews that contain seasonal vegetables are called *kootus*. They are a staple in millions of south Indian homes, often served as the substantial protein-based dish, especially among vegetarians. I like to serve Rice with Yogurt and Mustard Seeds (page 710) with this curry—the fiery chiles curtail their heat in the presence of the yogurt.

MAKES A GENEROUS 6 CUPS

1 cup skinned split green lentils (yellow in this form, moong dal), picked over for stones

1 pound cauliflower, cut into 1-inch florets

2 tablespoons unrefined sesame oil or canola oil

2 tablespoons skinned split black lentils (cream-colored in this form, urad dal), picked over for stones

½ teaspoon fenugreek seeds

4 to 6 dried red Thai or cayenne chiles, to taste, stems removed

1 cup shredded fresh coconut; or ½ cup shredded dried unsweetened coconut, reconstituted (see Note)

1 teaspoon black or yellow mustard seeds

15 medium-size to large fresh curry leaves

1½ teaspoons coarse kosher or sea salt

1. Place the lentils in a medium-size saucepan. Fill the pan halfway with water and rinse the lentils by rubbing them between your fingertips. The water will become cloudy. Drain this water. Repeat three or four times, until the water remains relatively clear; drain. Now add 3 cups water and bring to a boil, uncovered, over medium heat. Skim off and discard any foam that forms on the surface. Stir in the cauliflower and continue simmering vigorously, uncovered, stirring occasionally, until the lentils and cauliflower are barely tender, 10 to 12 minutes.

2. While the lentils and cauliflower are cooking, heat the oil in a small skillet over medium-high heat. Add the split black lentils, fenugreek seeds, and chiles, and stir-fry until the lentils and fenugreek are reddish brown and the chiles have blackened, 1 to 2 minutes. Remove the skillet from the heat, and use a slotted spoon to transfer the mixture to a blender jar. Add ½ cup water and the coconut to the blender. Puree, scraping the inside of the jar as needed, to make a slightly gritty, aromatic, orange-brown speckled paste.

3. Reheat the oil in the skillet over medium-high heat. Add the mustard seeds, cover the skillet, and cook until the seeds have stopped popping (not unlike popcorn), about 30 seconds. Remove the skillet from the heat and add the curry leaves. They will spatter and crackle, so be careful.

4. When the cauliflower and lentils are barely tender, add the coconut paste and the contents of the skillet. Pour 1 cup water into the blender jar, and swirl it around to wash out the jar. Pour this liquid into the pan, and stir in the salt. Simmer the *kootu* over medium heat, uncovered, stirring occasionally, until the curry has absorbed the flavors, 3 to 5 minutes. Then serve.

Note: To reconstitute coconut, cover with ½ cup boiling water, set aside for about 15 minutes, and then drain.

Spicy Split Green Lentils
WITH CHILES AND ONION

Pyaaz Mirchi Moong ki dal

uick-cooking lentils like these come to my rescue whenever I am exhausted after a full day and neither pizza nor any other take-out turns my crank. A plate of quickly steamed long-grain white rice is perfect, along with a small stack of the Flame-Toasted Lentil Wafers more commonly known as *papads* or *pappadums* (page 740). **MAKES 4 CUPS**

1 cup skinned split green lentils (yellow in this form, moong dal), picked over for stones

2 tablespoons Ghee (page 21) or canola oil

1 teaspoon black or yellow mustard seeds

1 teaspoon cumin seeds

¼ teaspoon ground turmeric

¼ teaspoon ground asafetida

1 medium-size red onion, cut in half lengthwise and thinly sliced

12 medium-size to large fresh curry leaves

4 lengthwise slices fresh ginger (each 1½ inches long, 1 inch wide, and ⅛ inch thick), cut into thin matchsticks (julienne)

4 fresh green Thai, cayenne, or serrano chiles, stems removed, sliced in half lengthwise (do not remove the seeds)

2 teaspoons coarse kosher or sea salt

2 tablespoons finely chopped fresh cilantro leaves and tender stems for garnishing

1. Place the lentils in a medium-size saucepan. Fill the pan halfway with water and rinse the lentils by rubbing them between your fingertips. The water will become cloudy. Drain this water. Repeat three or four times, until the water remains relatively clear; drain. Now add 3 cups water and bring to a boil, uncovered, over medium heat. Skim off and discard any foam that forms on the surface. Continue to simmer vigorously, uncovered, stirring occasionally, until the lentils are barely tender, 10 to 12 minutes.

2. While the lentils are cooking, heat a medium-size skillet over medium-high heat and pour in the ghee. Add the mustard seeds, cover the skillet, and cook until the seeds have stopped popping (not unlike popcorn), about 30 seconds. Stir in the cumin seeds, turmeric, and asafetida. Immediately add the onion, curry leaves, ginger, chiles, and salt. Stir-fry until the onion is honey-brown and the chiles smell pungent, 3 to 5 minutes. Then pour in ½ cup water and scrape the bottom of the skillet to deglaze it, releasing any browned bits of onion and spices.

3. Add the sauce to the barely tender lentils and stir once or twice. Continue to simmer, uncovered, stirring occasionally, to allow the seasonings to flavor the lentils, 2 to 4 minutes. Sprinkle with the cilantro, and serve.

Toasted Split Green Lentils
WITH SPINACH

bhaja moong palak

engalis refer to "toasted" or "roasted" as *bhaja.* The process of toasting split green lentils in a dry pan not only creates a nutty flavor but also keeps the firm shape of the legume intact, no matter how long it cooks—certainly not the case with its untoasted counterpart, which breaks down to a mushy consistency very quickly. The spinach makes this dish colorful, but if you would like a slightly more bitter flavor—and a higher dose of iron—use mustard greens or kale instead. **MAKES 4 CUPS**

1 cup skinned split green lentils (yellow in this form, moong dal), picked over for stones

¼ teaspoon ground turmeric

8 ounces fresh baby spinach leaves, well rinsed

1 tablespoon canola oil

1 teaspoon fennel seeds

½ teaspoon whole cloves

2 to 4 dried red Thai or cayenne chiles, to taste, stems removed

1½ teaspoons coarse kosher or sea salt

1 teaspoon white granulated sugar

1 tablespoon Ghee (page 21)

1. Heat a medium-size saucepan over medium-high heat. Add the lentils and toast them, stirring constantly, until they are reddish brown and nutty-smelling, 5 to 8 minutes.

2. Gently pour in 3 cups water, stirring vigorously to break up any clumps that form. The water will immediately come to a boil because of the heat of the pan. Stir in the turmeric. Reduce the heat to medium-low, cover the pan, and simmer, stirring occasionally, until the lentils are firm-tender, 15 to 20 minutes.

3. Pile the spinach into the pan, cover it, and let the steam wilt the greens, 5 to 8 minutes. (If not all the leaves fit in one batch, wilt them in two separate batches.)

4. While the greens are wilting, heat the oil in a small skillet over medium-high heat. Sprinkle in the fennel seeds, cloves, and chiles, and cook until they sizzle and are aromatic, 10 to 15 seconds. Remove the skillet from the heat.

5. When the spinach has wilted, pour the contents of the skillet into the pan. Add the salt and sugar. Continue to simmer the curry, uncovered, stirring occasionally, until the flavors mingle, 5 to 8 minutes.

6. Stir in the ghee, and serve.

Split Green Lentils
WITH RED CHILES & TOASTED SPICES

Chilke Aur dhuli hui moong ki dal

obust and creamy, this curry incorporates two forms of the same green lentils. Because they both are split, they cook in no time at all and break down to a mushlike consistency that offers both a smooth backdrop and a thickening quality. **MAKES 4 CUPS**

½ cup skin-on split green lentils (moong dal),
  picked over for stones
½ cup skinned split green lentils (yellow in this form,
  moong dal), picked over for stones
2 tablespoons Ghee (page 21) or melted butter
2 teaspoons cumin seeds
4 dried red Thai or cayenne chiles, stems removed
10 to 12 medium-size to large fresh curry leaves
2 teaspoons Toasted Cumin-Coriander Blend
  (page 33)
1½ teaspoons coarse kosher or sea salt
¼ teaspoon ground turmeric
2 tablespoons finely chopped fresh cilantro
  leaves and tender stems for garnishing

1. Place both types of lentils in a medium-size sauce-pan. Fill the pan halfway with water and rinse the lentils by rubbing them between your fingertips. The water will become cloudy and some of the loose skins will float to the top. Drain this water, discarding the loose skins. Repeat three or four times, until the water remains relatively clear; drain. Now add 3 cups water and bring to a boil, uncovered, over medium heat. Skim off and discard any foam that forms on the surface. Continue simmering vigorously, uncovered, stirring occasionally, until the lentils are very tender and almost mushy-looking, 20 to 25 minutes.

2. While the lentils are cooking, heat a medium-size skillet over medium-high heat and pour in the ghee. Add the cumin seeds and chiles, and cook until the chiles blacken slightly and the cumin seeds sizzle, turn reddish brown, and are aromatic, 10 to 15 seconds. Immediately remove the skillet from the heat and carefully throw in the curry leaves, which will instantly spatter.

3. Pour the spiced ghee mixture into the cooked lentils, and stir in the cumin-coriander blend, salt, and turmeric. Sprinkle with the cilantro, and serve.

Green and Black Lentils
WITH GARLIC

Urad Moong Dal

It may seem cumbersome to pound herbs and spices in an old-fashioned mortar. It is not. If anything, it is a stress reliever, as you pulverize your tensions away to yield a tasty base for this curry, which is full of comforting heat, aroma, and taste. **MAKES 3 CUPS**

½ cup skinned split black lentils (cream-colored in this
  form, urad dal), picked over for stones
½ cup skinned split green lentils (yellow in this
  form, moong dal), picked over for stones
2 tablespoons finely chopped fresh cilantro
  leaves and tender stems
2 teaspoons cumin seeds
½ teaspoon black peppercorns
12 to 15 medium-size to large fresh curry leaves
6 medium-size cloves garlic
2 fresh green Thai, cayenne, or serrano chiles,
  stems removed
2 tablespoons Ghee (page 21) or canola oil
1½ teaspoons coarse kosher or sea salt
½ teaspoon ground turmeric

1. Place both types of lentils in a medium-size sauce-pan. Fill the pan halfway with water and rinse the lentils by rubbing them between your fingertips. The water will become cloudy. Drain this water. Repeat three or four times, until the water remains relatively clear; drain. Now add 3 cups water and bring to a boil, uncovered, over medium heat. Skim off and discard any foam

that forms on the surface. Continue to boil the lentils vigorously, uncovered, stirring occasionally, until they are tender but still firm-looking and most of the water has evaporated from the surface, 12 to 15 minutes.

2. While the lentils are cooking, pile the cilantro, cumin seeds, peppercorns, curry leaves, garlic, and chiles into a mortar. Pound with the pestle, scraping the sides to contain the ingredients in the center, to form a pulpy paste that is gritty, chunky, and full of aroma.

3. Heat the ghee in a small skillet over medium-high heat. Add the pounded paste and stir-fry until the garlic in the paste has browned lightly and the chiles and peppercorns are nose-tingling pungent. Stir in the salt and turmeric. Pour in ½ cup water and stir to deglaze the skillet, releasing any browned bits of garlic and spice.

4. When the lentils are cooked, add the contents of the skillet and simmer, uncovered, stirring occasionally, until the creamy-textured lentils have absorbed the spicy fire, about 5 minutes. Then serve.

Spicy-Tart Split Green and Red Lentils
WITH COCONUT

Kokum Moong Aur Masoor Dal

As a child in India, it took me a while to fall in love with the essence of slightly astringent, primarily tart kokum. Peculiar to the Maharashtrian community in Goa and Mumbai, the dried dark purple-black skin of this tropical fruit, a close relation to mangosteen (which has nothing to do with mango), provides sour flavor to many of their curries, both vegetarian and non-vegetarian. Here a quantity of the extracted juices, added toward the end, gives the curry a sharp gusto to balance out the pungent chiles and mellow coconut. **MAKES 4 CUPS**

¼ cup dried black kokum pieces
(see Tip, page 427)
½ cup skinned split green lentils
(yellow in this form, moong dal),
picked over for stones
½ cup skinned split brown lentils
(salmon-colored in this form, masoor dal),
picked over for stones
½ cup shredded fresh coconut; or ¼ cup shredded
dried unsweetened coconut, reconstituted
(see Note)
1 tablespoon coriander seeds
1 teaspoon cumin seeds
½ teaspoon ground turmeric
2 dried red Thai or cayenne chiles,
stems removed
2 tablespoons Ghee (page 21) or canola oil
1 small red onion, cut in half lengthwise and
thinly sliced
3 large cloves garlic, thinly sliced

1. Pour ½ cup water into a microwave-safe bowl and bring it to a boil in a microwave oven (or heat it in a small saucepan on the stove). Add the kokum pieces and set the bowl aside until the water is infused with the kokum's tart and slightly astringent juices, 15 to 20 minutes.

2. While the kokum is soaking, place both types of lentils in a medium-size saucepan. Fill the pan

halfway with water and rinse the lentils by rubbing them between your fingertips. The water will become cloudy. Drain this water. Repeat three or four times, until the water remains relatively clear; drain. Now add 3½ cups water and bring to a boil, uncovered, over medium heat. Skim off and discard any foam that forms on the surface. Reduce the heat to medium-low, partially cover the pan, and simmer, stirring occasionally, until the lentils are tender and soft, 12 to 15 minutes.

3. While the lentils are cooking, pour ¼ cup water into a blender jar, followed by the coconut, coriander seeds, cumin seeds, turmeric, and chiles. Puree, scraping the inside of the jar as needed, to form a slightly gritty, spice-speckled sauce.

4. Heat the ghee in a medium-size skillet over medium-high heat. Add the onion and garlic, and stir-fry until the onion is light brown around the edges, 3 to 5 minutes.

5. Pour the coconut puree into the onion mixture and cook, uncovered, stirring occasionally, until the liquid water evaporates, about 5 minutes.

6. Squeeze the kokum skins to make sure you get every juicy bit, and then discard them. Pour the kokum water into the skillet and scrape the bottom to deglaze it, releasing the browned bits of onion and coconut.

7. Add the sauce to the cooked lentils and simmer, uncovered, over medium heat, stirring occasionally, until the flavors mingle, about 5 minutes. Then serve.

Note: To reconstitute coconut, cover with ¼ cup boiling water, set aside for about 15 minutes, and then drain.

PEPPERY
Split Green Lentils and Yellow Peas

Porithu Kootu

Unique to the Tamilian Brahmins from southeastern India, this curry is flavored with a spice blend commonly used in the thin, brothlike, tamarind-based *rasams*. However, with the absence of tart tamarind and the inclusion of onion-smothered multiple legumes and starchy potato, this curry could not be any more different in taste and body than the *rasams* in this book. **MAKES 4 CUPS**

½ cup skinned split green lentils (yellow in this form, moong dal), picked over for stones

2 tablespoons yellow split peas (chana dal), picked over for stones

2 tablespoons oily or unoily skinned split yellow pigeon peas (toovar dal), picked over for stones

1 medium-size russet or Yukon Gold potato, peeled, cut into ¼-inch cubes, and submerged in a bowl of cold water to prevent browning

1 medium-size red onion, cut into ¼-inch cubes

2 teaspoons Rasam powder (page 34)

½ teaspoon ground turmeric

2 tablespoons Ghee (page 21) or canola oil

1 teaspoon black or yellow mustard seeds

¼ teaspoon ground asafetida

2 tablespoons finely chopped fresh cilantro leaves and tender stems

8 to 10 medium-size to large fresh curry leaves

1½ teaspoons coarse kosher or sea salt

1. Put the lentils, split peas, and pigeon peas in a medium-size saucepan. Fill the pan halfway with water and rinse the legumes by rubbing them between your fingertips. The water will become cloudy. Drain this water. Repeat three or four times, until the water remains relatively clear; drain. Now add 4 cups water.

2. Drain the potato, and add it to the legumes along with the onion, *Rasam powder*, and turmeric. Bring to a boil, uncovered, over medium-high heat. Then reduce the heat to medium-low, cover the pan, and simmer, stirring occasionally, until the legumes and vegetables are tender and the sauce is still relatively thin, 20 to 25 minutes.

3. While the legume mixture is simmering, heat the ghee in a small skillet over medium-high heat. Add the mustard seeds, cover the skillet, and cook until the seeds have stopped popping (not unlike popcorn), about 30 seconds. Remove the skillet from the heat and sprinkle in the asafetida, which will sizzle and cook upon contact. Stand back as you throw in the cilantro and curry leaves—they will spatter on contact. Set the skillet aside.

4. When the legumes and vegetables are tender, add the contents of the skillet. Stir in the salt. Raise the heat to medium and boil, uncovered, stirring occasionally, until the flavors mingle and the sauce thickens slightly, about 15 minutes. Then serve.

Tip: For an unusual but equally starchy alternative, use a medium-size plantain instead of the potato.

SWEET Split Green Lentils and Yellow Peas

Mug Chana Nu Dal

the 16th to 18th centuries witnessed much economic success in Surat, a port city within the state of Gujarat, in northwestern India. Inundated by invaders, both foreign and national, this town bore more than its fair share of woes prior to that period. The British East India Company had set roots there before they moved their presence to the other well-known port, Bombay (now Mumbai), in the latter half of the 1600s. True, the quality of its diamonds made Surat appealing, but its varied culinary styles were an equal attraction, at least to the foodies. The phrase *Surat no jhaman ane kasi no maran* ("to indulge in the foods of Surat and to be cremated along the banks of the Ganges") reflects the dreams of this city's Hindus. As is true with many Gujarati dishes, this curry balances cayenne pepper's kick with jaggery's cloying sweetness. **MAKES 5 CUPS**

½ cup skinned split green lentils
    (yellow in this form, moong dal),
    picked over for stones
¼ cup yellow split peas (chana dal),
    picked over for stones
2 tablespoons Ghee (page 21) or canola oil
1 teaspoon black or yellow mustard seeds
2 teaspoons cumin seeds
1½ teaspoons coarse kosher or sea salt
1 teaspoon cayenne (ground red pepper)

½ teaspoon ground asafetida

½ teaspoon ground turmeric

1 can (14.5 ounces) diced tomatoes

¼ cup crumbled (or chopped) jaggery
     or firmly packed dark brown sugar

¼ cup finely chopped fresh cilantro leaves
     and tender stems

10 to 15 medium-size to large fresh
     curry leaves

1. Place the lentils and split peas in a medium-size saucepan. Fill the pan halfway with water and rinse the legumes by rubbing them between your fingertips. The water will become cloudy. Drain this water. Repeat three or four times, until the water remains relatively clear; drain. Now add 3 cups water and bring to a boil, uncovered, over medium-high heat. Skim off and discard any foam that forms on the surface. Reduce the heat to medium-low, cover the pan, and simmer, stirring occasionally, until the lentils are fall-apart soft and the split peas are tender but still firm-looking, 35 to 40 minutes.

2. While the legumes are cooking, heat the ghee in a small skillet. Add the mustard seeds, cover the skillet, and cook until the seeds have stopped popping (not unlike popcorn), about 30 seconds. Remove the skillet from the heat and sprinkle in the cumin seeds, salt, cayenne, asafetida, and turmeric. The spices will instantly sizzle and smell aromatic, and the heat from the oil will be just right to cook but not burn them. Immediately add the tomatoes, with their juices, and the jaggery, cilantro, and curry leaves. Return the skillet to medium-high heat and simmer, uncovered, stirring occasionally, until the ghee starts to separate on the surface, about 5 minutes. Set the sauce aside until the legumes are cooked.

3. When the legumes are cooked, coarsely mash the lentils and some of the split peas with the back of a cooking spoon to create a creamy yellow base for the curry. Stir in the sauce, cover the pan, and reduce the heat to medium. Simmer, stirring occasionally, until the seasonings permeate the curry, about 5 minutes. Then serve.

Tip:

❖ For a recent lunch on a particularly dreary, cold, and dismal day, I heated a bowl of this curry and tossed a mini baguette in the oven to warm it—the only satisfying experience of the day!

❖ If the health police are busy elsewhere, drizzle a bit of ghee over the cooked dal—and over the warmed baguette. You'll feel a whole lot better.

Fried Lentil and Cabbage Dumplings
WITH A TOMATO-CREAM SAUCE

Moong Aur Bund Gobhi Koftay Ki Curry

These dumplings are delicious, and on occasion I have served them, *sans* sauce, as an appetizer. A store-bought salsa or any dipping sauce works well too. But do make the curry and eat the dumplings and sauce together: crisp dumplings coated with juicy tomatoes, sweetened a tad and given a bit of wispy chile-heat.

SERVES 8

For the dumplings:

½ medium-size cabbage (about 1 pound), finely shredded (see Tip)

2 teaspoons coarse kosher or sea salt

½ cup skinned split green lentils (yellow in this form, moong dal), picked over for stones

4 to 6 fresh green Thai, cayenne, or serrano chiles, to taste, stems removed

4 lengthwise slices fresh ginger (each 1½ inches long, 1 inch wide, and ⅛ inch thick)

1 cup finely chopped red onion

½ cup finely chopped fresh cilantro leaves and tender stems

½ cup rice flour

½ cup chickpea flour

Canola oil for deep-frying

For the sauce:

2 tablespoons canola oil

1 teaspoon cumin seeds

½ cup finely chopped red onion

2 large tomatoes, cored and finely chopped

1 teaspoon white granulated sugar

1 teaspoon coarse kosher or sea salt

1 teaspoon ground Deggi chiles (see box, page 290); or ½ teaspoon cayenne (ground red pepper) mixed with ½ teaspoon sweet paprika

1 teaspoon Punjabi garam masala (page 25)

½ cup half-and-half

2 tablespoons finely chopped fresh cilantro leaves and tender stems for garnishing

1. To make the dumplings, combine the cabbage and salt in a medium-size bowl. Cover the bowl with plastic wrap, and let it stand at room temperature to allow the salt to extract the water from the cabbage, 1 to 2 hours.

2. Meanwhile, place the lentils in a medium-size bowl. Fill the bowl halfway with water and rinse the lentils by rubbing them between your fingertips. The water will become cloudy. Drain this water. Repeat three or four times, until the water remains relatively clear; drain. Now fill the bowl halfway with warm water and let it sit at room temperature, covered with plastic wrap, until the lentils soften, 1 to 2 hours.

3. Drain the lentils and transfer them to a food processor. Add the chiles and ginger, and process to form a wet, coarse-breadcrumb-like paste. Transfer this to the same medium-size bowl (why dirty another one?).

4. Drain the cabbage, and then grab handfuls of the cabbage and squeeze them tightly to eliminate as much liquid as possible. Add the squeezed cabbage to the lentils. Mix in the onion, cilantro, and both flours to make a slightly damp, sandlike mixture. Place 2 heaping tablespoons of this mixture in the palm of your hand and squeeze it to condense it and shape it into a tight ball (if it's not tightly compacted, it will fall apart in the hot oil). Repeat with the remaining mixture to make roughly 30 walnut-size balls, speckled with green herbs and purple onion bits.

5. Pour oil to a depth of 2 to 3 inches into a wok, Dutch oven, or medium-size saucepan. Heat the oil over a medium heat until a candy or deep-fry thermometer inserted into the oil (without touching the pan's bottom) registers 350°F.

6. Line a plate or a cookie sheet with three or four sheets of paper towels.

7. Once the oil is ready, gently slide in 8 dumplings. Fry, turning them occasionally, until they are honey-brown and crisp, about 5 minutes. Remove them with a slotted spoon and allow them to drain on the paper towels. Repeat until all the dumplings are fried. You may need to adjust the heat to maintain the oil's temperature at 350°F.

8. To make the sauce, heat the oil in a large saucepan over medium-high heat. Add the cumin seeds and cook until they sizzle and turn reddish brown, 5 to 10 seconds. Immediately add the onion and stir-fry until it is light brown around the edges, 3 to 5 minutes.

9. Stir in the tomatoes, sugar, salt, ground chiles, garam masala, and half-and-half. Gently add the dumplings to the sauce, making sure they do not break apart. Heat the curry over medium heat until the sauce starts to bubble. Then lower the heat, cover the pan, and simmer until the sauce has thickened considerably, about 5 minutes. Refrain from stirring the sauce for fear of breaking up the juicy dumplings.

10. Sprinkle with the cilantro, and serve.

Tips:

❖ To finely shred cabbage in a food processor, cut it into long pieces that are the right width to fit through the feed tube. (I don't bother removing the tough rib since it's perfectly edible, especially when shredded.) If you have two different shredding blades, use the one with the smaller holes for a finer shred. Push the pieces through to shred them.

The medium-size or large holes on a box grater will also do the trick. If you use a chef's knife, finely chop the cabbage, making sure no large pieces sneak their way in.

❖ These dumplings can be made ahead and frozen. Prepare them through Step 7, and then store the fried dumplings in a freezer-safe self-seal bag in the freezer.

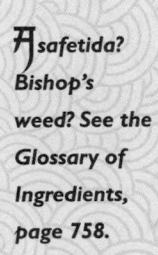

Asafetida? Bishop's weed? See the Glossary of Ingredients, page 758.

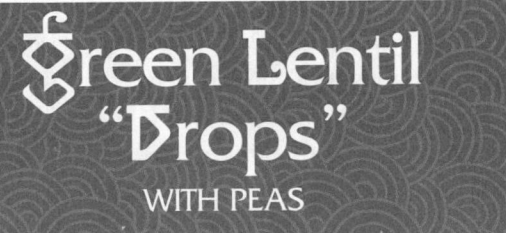

Green Lentil "Drops"
WITH PEAS

Mutter Mangori

What the @#*$% is *mangori?* someone might ask when encountering it at your dinner table. Just explain that these drops, shaped like Hershey's Kisses, are made from a paste of skinned split green lentils that is flavored with turmeric and asafetida and then sun-dried until stone-dry. The meatlike texture will appeal to carnivores and herbivores alike, making for a guilt-free meal. **MAKES 4 CUPS**

I cup mangori (see Tips)
I tablespoon canola oil
I teaspoon black or yellow mustard seeds
2 tablespoons finely chopped fresh ginger
2 teaspoons coriander seeds, ground
I teaspoon cumin seeds, ground
I teaspoon coarse kosher or sea salt
¼ teaspoon ground asafetida
2 to 4 fresh green Thai, cayenne, or serrano chiles,
   to taste, stems removed, thinly sliced
(do not remove the seeds)
   I cup frozen green peas (no need to thaw)
   I large tomato, cored and finely chopped
   2 tablespoons finely chopped fresh cilantro
      leaves and tender stems
   I tablespoon Ghee (page 21; see Tips)

1. Dump the rock-hard *mangori* into a food processor and chop until they are the size of peas.

2. Heat the oil in a medium-size saucepan over medium-high heat. Add the mustard seeds, cover the pan, and cook until the seeds have stopped popping (not unlike popcorn), about 30 seconds. Immediately add the ginger, coriander, cumin, salt, asafetida, and chiles. Stir-fry until the spices are cooked and the ginger is lightly browned, 10 to 15 seconds.

3. Add the *mangori* and stir-fry until they are coated with the seasonings, about 1 minute. Then pour in 4 cups water, stir once or twice, and heat to a boil. Reduce the heat to medium-low, cover the pan, and simmer, stirring occasionally, until the *mangori* are tender but still meaty, not unlike ground beef.

4. Stir in the green peas, tomato, and cilantro. Simmer, uncovered, stirring occasionally, until the green peas are warm and tender 3 to 5 minutes.

5. Stir in the ghee, and serve.

Tips:

❖ *Mangori*, also known as *moong dal vadis,* are available among the dried lentils, beans, and peas in your favorite Indian grocery store. This shelf-stable, rock-hard product will keep for years in your pantry. Rajasthan, north of Mumbai, has a short growing season before it succumbs to desert weather, so the farmers there sun-dry much of their harvested vegetables and legumes, to be reconstituted during the arid months. Skinned split green lentils have a pastelike texture when cooked, but *mangori*, because of its hardened quality, retains its ground-meat-like texture when cracked and cooked.

❖ Even though it is a minimal amount, the ghee that is swirled in just before serving provides a rich flavor.

NUTTY-HOT
Green Lentil "Drops"
WITH TOMATOES

tamatar Mangori

I fell in love with Rajasthan—its topography, its people, and above all, its culinary repertoire. The ability to create magic, like this Rajasthani delicacy, out of barely anything always wins me over. Arid conditions and a short growing season force the Rajasthanis to dry fresh ingredients for later use, as is the case with these lentil drops, which are easy to find in any Indian grocery store.

MAKES 3 CUPS

> 1 cup mangori (see Tip, page 397)
> 2 tablespoons canola oil
> 1 teaspoon cumin seeds
> ½ teaspoon bishop's weed
> ½ teaspoon ground Deggi chiles (see box, page 290);
>   or ¼ teaspoon cayenne (ground red pepper)
>   mixed with ¼ teaspoon sweet paprika
> ¼ teaspoon ground asafetida
> 1 large tomato, cored and finely chopped
> 1½ teaspoons coarse kosher or sea salt
> 2 tablespoons finely chopped fresh cilantro
>   leaves and tender stems
> 1 tablespoon finely chopped fresh ginger
> 1 or 2 fresh green Thai, cayenne, or serrano chiles,
>   to taste, stems removed, finely chopped
>   (do not remove the seeds)
> 1 tablespoon Ghee (page 21)

1. Put the rock-hard *mangori* in a food processor, and

process until they are reduced to the consistency of coarse breadcrumbs.

2. Heat the oil in a small saucepan over medium-high heat. Sprinkle in the cumin seeds and bishop's weed, and cook until they sizzle and smell aromatic (thyme-like because of the bishops' weed), 5 to 10 seconds. Immediately add the processed *mangori*, ground chiles, and asafetida. Stir-fry to cook the spices without burning them, 1 to 2 minutes. Then stir in the tomato, 2 cups water, and the salt. Heat the curry to a boil. Reduce the heat to medium-low, cover the pan, and simmer, stirring occasionally, until the *mangori* are tender but still meaty, not unlike ground beef, 25 to 30 minutes.

3. Stir in the cilantro, ginger, and chiles. Continue to simmer the curry, covered, stirring occasionally, until the flavors meld, about 5 minutes.

4. Stir in the ghee, and serve.

Red Lentils
WITH CHILES

ʄirchi Ⱳaale ʄasoor ʈi ɗal

Beautiful salmon-colored lentils (also known as Egyptian lentils) unfortunately lose their color and turn yellow when they are cooked. They have a mild, delicate flavor, are very quick-cooking, and are an ideal choice should you wish to throw something healthy together at the last minute. I love this for a simple lunch over cooked white rice, with a side of Indian pickles (either homemade or store-bought) and some flame-toasted or deep-fried lentil wafers (page 740). **MAKES 3 CUPS**

1 cup skinned split brown lentils (salmon-colored in this form, masoor dal), picked over for stones
1 tablespoon Ginger Paste (page 15)
1 tablespoon Garlic Paste (page 15)
¼ teaspoon ground turmeric
2 tablespoons canola oil
1 teaspoon cumin seeds
1 small red onion, cut in half lengthwise and thinly sliced
6 fresh green Thai, cayenne, or serrano chiles, stems removed, cut in half lengthwise (do not remove the seeds)
3 dried red Thai or cayenne chiles, stems removed
1 teaspoon coarse kosher or sea salt
2 tablespoons finely chopped fresh cilantro leaves and tender stems
Juice of 1 large lime
1 tablespoon Ghee (page 21; optional)

1. Place the lentils in a medium-size saucepan. Fill the pan halfway with water and rinse the lentils by rubbing them between your fingertips. The water will become cloudy. Drain this water. Repeat three or four times, until the water remains relatively clear; drain. Now add 4 cups water and bring to a boil, uncovered, over medium heat. Skim off and discard any foam that forms on the surface. Stir in the Ginger Paste, Garlic Paste, and turmeric. Reduce the heat to medium-low, cover the pan, and simmer, stirring occasionally, until the lentils are tender, 18 to 20 minutes.

2. While the lentils are cooking, heat the oil in a small skillet over medium-high heat. Add the cumin seeds and cook until they sizzle, turn reddish brown, and smell nutty, 5 to 10 seconds. Add the onion and both fresh and dried chiles. Stir-fry until the onion is light brown around the edges and the chiles smell pungent, 3 to 5 minutes.

3. When the lentils are done, stir in the salt and the contents of the skillet. Continue to simmer, uncovered, stirring occasionally, until the flavors meld, about 10 minutes.

4. Stir in the cilantro, lime juice, and ghee (if using), and serve.

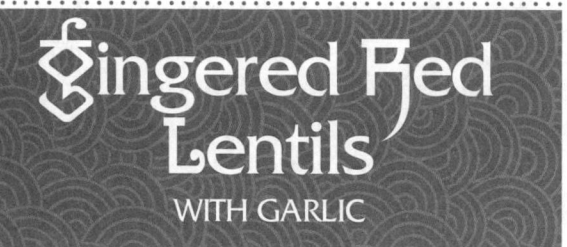

Gingered Red Lentils
WITH GARLIC

Aadrak Lasoon Masoor ki dal

I love the gingery-garlic flavors in this dal—they provide depth to an otherwise ho-hum legume. For a more substantial and colorful presentation, spoon ¼ cup wilted greens (spinach, mustard, kale, or collard) over each serving of dal, and pass around a basket of onion-laced *Pyaaz kulcha* (page 736) as an accompaniment. **MAKES 4 CUPS**

1 cup skinned split brown lentils (salmon-colored in this form, masoor dal), picked over for stones

1 small red onion, coarsely chopped

4 large cloves garlic, coarsely chopped

4 lengthwise slices fresh ginger (each 2 inches long, 1 inch wide, and ⅛ inch thick), coarsely chopped

2 fresh green Thai, cayenne, or serrano chiles, stems removed

2 tablespoons Ghee (page 21) or canola oil

1 teaspoon cumin seeds

2 dried red Thai or cayenne chiles, stems removed

1 medium-size tomato, cored and finely chopped

1 teaspoon coarse kosher or sea salt

¼ teaspoon ground turmeric

¼ cup finely chopped fresh cilantro leaves and tender stems

1. Place the lentils in a medium-size saucepan. Fill the pan halfway with water, and rinse the lentils by rubbing them between your fingertips. The water will become cloudy. Drain this water. Repeat three or four times, until the water remains relatively clear; drain. Now add 3 cups water and bring to a boil, uncovered, over medium heat. Skim off and discard any foam that forms on the surface. Reduce the heat to medium-low, cover the pan, and simmer, stirring occasionally, until the lentils are tender, 18 to 20 minutes.

2. While the lentils are cooking, combine the onion, garlic, ginger, and fresh chiles in a food processor. Mince the ingredients, using the pulsing action. (Letting the blades run constantly will yield a watery blend.)

3. Heat the ghee in a small skillet over medium-high heat. Add the cumin seeds and dried chiles, and cook until the chiles blacken and the seeds turn reddish brown, and smell nutty, 5 to 10 seconds. Immediately add the onion blend, reduce the heat to medium, and stir-fry until the mixture is light brown around the edges, 3 to 5 minutes.

4. Stir in the tomato, salt, and turmeric. Simmer, uncovered, stirring occasionally, until the tomato softens and the ghee starts to separate around the edges of the sauce, 3 to 6 minutes. Stir in the cilantro.

5. Stir the sauce into the cooked lentils. Ladle some of the lentil mixture into the skillet and stir it around to wash it out; add this to the lentils.

6. Cover the pan and simmer over medium heat, stirring occasionally, until the flavors mingle, about 5 minutes. Then serve.

Tart Red Lentils
WITH
TOMATOES, LIME JUICE & SCALLIONS

Ahomya Bilahi dal

Ahoms (the Mongols), warriors of Shan origin from Burma (now Myanmar), arrived in the northeast corner of India in the early 13th century and maintained a strong foothold there for 600 years, adopting Hinduism, the predominant religion of the area. Multiple attempts by the Moghuls to take over the northeast from the Ahoms failed each time. However, the ongoing attacks made the ruling party weak and the Ahoms succumbed to another group from Burma, who ruled Assam for four years before the British usurped the land. The land of Ahom became the English Assam, but its people still adhere to the Ahomya culture and traditions. This dal, made tart with tomatoes, incorporates scallions, which are used more in that region than in others.

I love the complexity of this sauce, created from two types of onion used in three different ways, demonstrating yet again that treating the same ingredient in various ways can yield various flavors. **MAKES 4 CUPS**

1 cup skinned split brown lentils (salmon-colored in this form, masoor dal), picked over for stones (see Tip)
2 small red onions, 1 coarsely chopped,
    1 cut in half lengthwise and thinly sliced
2 lengthwise slices fresh ginger (each 2 inches long, 1 inch wide, and ⅛ inch thick)
2 large cloves garlic
2 tablespoons canola oil

2 teaspoons Panch phoron (page 36)
2 to 4 fresh green Thai, cayenne, or serrano chiles, to taste, stems removed, cut in half lengthwise (do not remove the seeds)
3 scallions (green tops and white bulbs), trimmed, cut crosswise into ¼-inch pieces
1½ teaspoons coarse kosher or sea salt
½ teaspoon ground turmeric
1 medium-size tomato, cored and cut into ½-inch pieces
¼ cup finely chopped fresh cilantro leaves and tender stems
Juice of 1 medium-size lime

1. Place the lentils in a medium-size saucepan. Fill the pan halfway with water and rinse the lentils by rubbing them between your fingertips. The water will become cloudy. Drain this water. Repeat three or four times, until the water remains relatively clear; drain. Now add 3 cups water and bring to a boil, uncovered, over medium heat. Skim off and discard any foam that forms on the surface. Reduce the heat to medium-low, cover the pan, and simmer, stirring occasionally, until the lentils are tender, 10 to 15 minutes.

2. While the lentils are cooking, combine the coarsely chopped onion, ginger, and garlic in a food processor. Pulse until the ingredients are minced.

3. Heat the oil in a medium-size skillet over medium-high heat. Sprinkle in the *Panch phoron* and chiles, and cook until the seeds crackle, sizzle, turn reddish brown, and smell nutty-pungent, 10 to 15 seconds. Add the minced onion blend, the sliced onion, and the scallions. Cook, uncovered, stirring occasionally, until the red onion is honey-brown with a deep purple hue, 8 to 10 minutes.

4. Add the salt, turmeric, tomato, and 2 cups water. Cook, uncovered, stirring occasionally, until the tomato has a saucelike consistency but is still slightly firm, 10 to 15 minutes. (Meanwhile, when the lentils are tender, reduce the heat to the lowest possible setting and keep them warm, covered.)

5. Stir the sauce into the cooked lentils and simmer over medium heat, uncovered, stirring occasionally, until the flavors mingle and the sauce thickens slightly, 8 to 10 minutes.

6. Stir in the cilantro and lime juice, and serve.

Tip: Equally quick-cooking skinned split green lentils *(moong dal)* work as an alternative to the red lentils.

Addictive Red Lentils
WITH GONGURA LEAVES

Gongura Sambhar

This legume curry is a specialty of the Andhra community in Andhra Pradesh, in the south-east of India. On a recent visit to nearby Bangalore to see my brother, I had the opportunity to pay a visit to his neighbor, Ambuja Balaji Rao, who lived for many years in Hyderabad, the capital of Andhra Pradesh, a city that is known for its layered biryanis and strong Muslim influences (in both food and culture). Ambuja maintains her Hindu heritage and weaves her penchant for hot chiles, garlic, and tart gongura leaves into many of her curries, chutneys, and pickles. These leaves are available wherever there are large Indian communities with big grocery stores. My version

is a combination of two different recipes Ambuja provided. **MAKES 4 CUPS**

> 1 cup skinned split brown lentils (salmon-colored in this form, masoor dal), picked over for stones
> ½ teaspoon ground turmeric
> 8 ounces fresh gongura leaves, well rinsed and cut into thin strips (see Tip)
> 2 tablespoons Ghee (page 21) or canola oil
> 1 teaspoon black or yellow mustard seeds
> ½ teaspoon fenugreek seeds
> 6 dried red Thai or cayenne chiles, stems removed
> 6 medium-size cloves garlic, finely chopped
> 1 teaspoon coarse kosher or sea salt
> 2 tablespoons unsalted dry-roasted peanuts, coarsely chopped for garnishing

1. Place the lentils in a medium-size saucepan. Fill the pan halfway with water, and rinse the lentils by rubbing them between your fingertips. The water will become cloudy. Drain this water. Repeat three or four times, until the water remains relatively clear; drain. Now add 4 cups water and bring to a boil, uncovered, over medium heat. Skim off and discard any foam that forms on the surface. Stir in the turmeric, reduce the heat to medium-low, and cover the pan. Simmer, stirring occasionally, until the lentils are tender, 18 to 20 minutes.

2. Add the gongura leaves, a couple of handfuls at a time, stirring them in until wilted. Repeat until all the leaves have been added. Then continue to simmer, uncovered, until the leaves soften, about 5 minutes.

3. Heat the ghee in a small skillet over medium-high heat. Add the mustard seeds, cover the skillet, and cook until the seeds have stopped popping (not unlike popcorn), about 30 seconds. Sprinkle in the fenugreek seeds, chiles, and garlic. Stir-fry until the chiles blacken and the garlic turns light brown, 1 to 2 minutes. Scrape the contents of the skillet into the lentils, and add the salt. Simmer, uncovered, stirring occasionally, until the flavors blend, about 5 minutes.

4. Sprinkle the peanuts over the curry, and serve.

Tip: Gongura leaves are dark green, with a reddish-brown tint on the edges. They look very much like their notorious sibling, marijuana, but have none of marijuana's addictive qualities. The leaves are often cut into thin strips and simmered with legumes, meats, and fish. A member of the hibiscus family, gongura is widely cultivated not only in India, but also in Africa (where it is known as *kenaf*), Thailand, and Eastern Europe. The leaves are very tart and provide an acidic balance to many of Andhra Pradesh's curries. Pickling these leaves in a truckload (and I mean a truckload) of red chiles gives gongura pickles their fiery reputation. If you can't locate fresh gongura, use sorrel or fresh spinach leaves and add ¼ teaspoon tamarind paste or concentrate (or 1 tablespoon fresh lime juice), to each 8 ounces of greens.

SLOW-ROASTED Bell Pepper WITH RED LENTILS

Bhuna Hua Simla Mirch Aur Masoor ki Dal

Many of us, myself included, automatically reach for that onion sitting on the counter as a starting point to build a base for sauces, stews, soups, and even stir-fries. We often overlook the bell pepper (known as *simla mirch* because most of them come from Simla, a picturesque resort just north of Delhi, in the foothills of the Himalayas), which bestows an uncanny, slightly smoky sweetness to a dish. I love the consistency of this curry, and often serve it as a soup course with crusty European bread. Don't hesitate to dunk the bread in it (I am sure Ms. Manners would do the same). **MAKES 5 CUPS**

1 cup skinned split brown lentils (salmon-colored in this form, masoor dal), picked over for stones
2 tablespoons canola oil
1 large green bell pepper, stemmed, seeded, and finely chopped
2 to 4 fresh green Thai, cayenne, or serrano chiles, to taste, stems removed, thinly sliced crosswise (do not remove the seeds)
1 medium-size tomato, cored and cut into ½-inch pieces
1½ teaspoons coarse kosher or sea salt
½ teaspoon ground turmeric
¼ cup finely chopped fresh cilantro leaves and tender stems

1. Place the lentils in a medium-size saucepan. Fill the pan halfway with water and rinse the lentils by rubbing them between your fingertips. The water will become cloudy. Drain this water. Repeat three or four times, until the water remains relatively clear; drain. Now add 3 cups water and bring to a boil, uncovered, over medium heat. Skim off and discard any foam that forms on the surface. Reduce the heat to medium-low, cover the pan, and simmer, stirring occasionally, until the lentils are tender, 10 to 15 minutes.

2. While the lentils are cooking, heat the oil in a medium-size skillet over medium heat. Add the bell pepper and chiles, and cook, uncovered, stirring occasionally until the bell pepper initially releases its water and then starts to brown, and the hot chiles smell

pungent (adequate ventilation will help clear the air), 10 to 12 minutes.

3. Stir in the tomato, salt, and turmeric, and scrape the bottom of the skillet to deglaze it, releasing the browned bits. Pour in 2 cups water and cook, uncovered, stirring occasionally, until the tomato has softened and turned slightly pulpy, 5 to 8 minutes.

4. Once the lentils are tender, pour the bell pepper sauce into the pan. Raise the heat to medium and continue to simmer the dal, uncovered, stirring occasionally, until the flavors mingle and the sauce thickens slightly, 5 to 8 minutes.

5. Stir in the cilantro, and serve.

Minty Red Lentils
WITH
CILANTRO AND RAW ONION

Masaledar Masoor dal

this full-flavored dal is an odd one, in terms of seasoning styles. Normally we slow-cook onions to extract their sweet flavor, and herbs play a minor role in augmenting that. Here, the onion slices are not cooked but the herbs are, which makes every bite of this dal an assertive one. In order to minimize the onion's pungency, I usually serve this with Black Puttu Rice (page 708). The rice has a nutty, brown rice–like quality and tends to soften the dal's tastes and textures. Regular brown rice will also work.

MAKES 4 CUPS

1 cup skinned split brown lentils (salmon-colored in this form, masoor dal), picked over for stones
1 cup firmly packed fresh cilantro leaves and tender stems
½ cup firmly packed fresh mint leaves
4 medium-size cloves garlic
2 to 4 fresh green Thai, cayenne, or serrano chiles, to taste, stems removed
2 tablespoons Ghee (page 21) or canola oil
1 teaspoon cumin seeds
1½ teaspoons coarse kosher or sea salt
½ teaspoon Punjabi garam masala (page 25)
1 small red onion, cut in half lengthwise and thinly sliced for garnishing

1. Place the lentils in a medium-size saucepan. Fill the pan halfway with water and rinse the lentils by rubbing them between your fingertips. The water will become cloudy. Drain this water. Repeat three or four times, until the water remains relatively clear; drain. Now add 3 cups water and bring to a boil, uncovered, over medium heat. Skim off and discard any foam that forms on the surface. Reduce the heat to medium-low, cover the pan, and simmer, stirring occasionally, until the lentils are tender, 10 to 15 minutes.

2. While the lentils are cooking, pile the cilantro, mint, garlic, and chiles into a food processor. Pulse until the mixture is minced, creating a very aromatic, moist blend.

3. Heat the ghee in a small skillet over medium-high heat. Add the cumin seeds and cook until they sizzle, are aromatic, and turn reddish brown, 5 to 10 seconds. Immediately stir in the minced blend and stir-fry until the herbs are cooked and the garlic is browned, 3 to 5 minutes. (The heat will also mellow the cilantro's flavor.)

4. Once the lentils are ready, stir in the contents of

the skillet, the salt, and the garam masala. Simmer over medium heat, uncovered, stirring occasionally, until the flavors meld, 3 to 5 minutes.

5. Scatter the onion slices over the dal, and serve.

Red Lentils
WITH
A CARAMEL–SWEET ONION SAUCE

Masoor Pyaaz dal

What I love about this curry (in addition to its superb flavor, of course) is that while the lentils are simmering, I can quickly prepare the spice mixture and get a pot of rice started on the stove: a vegetarian meal that's ready in under 45 minutes, including prep time. So pour yourself a glass of wine, tune the family out while you cook, and calm yourself down. Having store-bought breads, yogurt, and even pickles on hand will make it even easier for you to put that spread on the table on a weekday evening. **MAKES 4 CUPS**

1 cup skinned split brown lentils (salmon-colored
*   in this form, masoor dal), picked over for stones*
1 teaspoon cumin seeds
1 teaspoon rock salt
½ teaspoon cardamom seeds from green or white pods
½ teaspoon whole cloves
½ teaspoon black peppercorns
3 or 4 fresh green Thai, cayenne, or serrano chiles,
*   to taste, stems removed*
¼ cup Ghee (page 21) or canola oil

1 large red onion, cut in half lengthwise
*   and thinly sliced*
1 large tomato, cored and finely chopped
½ teaspoon ground turmeric

1. Place the lentils in a medium-size saucepan. Fill the pan halfway with water and rinse the lentils by rubbing them between your fingertips. The water will become cloudy. Drain this water. Repeat three or four times, until the water remains relatively clear; drain. Now add 3 cups water and bring to a boil, uncovered, over medium heat. Skim off and discard any foam that forms on the surface. Reduce the heat to medium-low, cover the pan, and simmer, stirring occasionally, until the lentils are tender, 18 to 20 minutes.

2. While the lentils are cooking, combine the cumin seeds, rock salt, cardamom seeds, cloves, peppercorns, and chiles in a mortar. Pulverize the blend with the pestle, scraping the sides to contain the mixture in the center, to form a gritty, pulpy mass.

3. Heat the ghee in a large skillet over medium heat. Add the onion and the pulverized spice mixture. Stir once or twice. Then cover the skillet and cook, stirring occasionally, until the onion turns caramel-brown with a deep purple hue and the spices smell sweet, 20 to 25 minutes. (Meanwhile, when the lentils are tender, simply keep them warm, covered, over very low heat.)

4. Stir the tomato and the turmeric into the onion mixture and cook, uncovered, until the tomato softens a little, 2 to 4 minutes. (The tomato juices will deglaze the skillet, releasing the browned bits of onion and spices.)

5. Add the onion-tomato mixture to the dal, and stir once or twice. Simmer, uncovered, stirring occasionally, until the flavors mingle, 3 to 5 minutes. Then serve.

Mixed Lentils
WITH GINGER AND GARLIC

Moong, Masoor, Aur Urad Dal Fry

This technique of topping creamy, soft cooked lentils with crispy fried onion is typical of *dal fry*, made popular by Iranian restaurant owners in Mumbai; they serve it with hunks of warm yeast breads, similar to dinner rolls, called double roti or *paav*. I recommend that you do the same for a quick, satisfying, sit-by-the-fireplace-on-a-freezing-night dinner with a glass of wine. **MAKES 3 CUPS**

⅓ cup skinned split green lentils (yellow in this form, moong dal), picked over for stones

⅓ cup skinned split brown lentils (salmon-colored in this form, masoor dal), picked over for stones

⅓ cup skinned split black lentils (cream-colored in this form, urad dal), picked over for stones

6 lengthwise slices fresh ginger (each 2½ inches long, 1 inch wide, and ⅛ inch thick), coarsely chopped

3 fresh green Thai, cayenne, or serrano chiles, stems removed, coarsely chopped (do not remove the seeds)

2 teaspoons cumin seeds

4 tablespoons Ghee (page 21) or canola oil

1 small red onion, cut in half lengthwise and thinly sliced

½ teaspoon ground turmeric

1 medium-size tomato, cored and cut into 1-inch cubes

¼ cup finely chopped fresh cilantro leaves and tender stems

1 teaspoon coarse kosher or sea salt

1. Place all the lentils in a medium-size saucepan. Fill the pan halfway with water and rinse the lentils by rubbing them between your fingertips. The water will become cloudy. Drain this water. Repeat three or four times, until the water remains relatively clear; drain. Now add 3 cups water and bring to a boil, uncovered, over medium heat. Skim off and discard any foam that forms on the surface. Reduce the heat to medium-low, partially cover the pan, and simmer, stirring occasionally, until the lentils are tender and soft, 12 to 15 minutes.

2. While the lentils are cooking, combine the ginger, chiles, and cumin seeds in a mortar. Pound the ingredients with the pestle until they have the consistency of a gritty but pulplike paste. (The cumin seeds will bruise and break a little, but most will retain their shape.)

3. Heat a medium-size skillet over medium-high heat. Pour in 2 tablespoons of the ghee and swirl it around to coat the bottom. Add the onion and stir-fry until it is dark brown, 15 to 18 minutes. Transfer the onion slices to a plate.

4. Pour the remaining 2 tablespoons ghee into the same hot skillet. Immediately add the crushed paste and stir-fry until the ginger is lightly browned and the chiles are pungent, 1 to 2 minutes. Sprinkle in the turmeric, and stir once or twice to flavor the paste and cook the yellow spice. Add the tomato, cilantro, and salt, reduce the heat to medium, and simmer, uncovered, until the tomato pieces break down (mash them roughly with the back of the spoon if necessary), 3 to 5 minutes.

5. When the lentils are cooked, add the sauce and stir once or twice. Add ½ cup water to the skillet and deglaze it; add this to the lentils. Reduce the heat to medium-low, cover the pan, and simmer, stirring occasionally, until the lentils have absorbed the flavors, 5 to 7 minutes.

6. Top the dal with the sweet, dark brown onion slices, and serve.

Red and Yellow Lentils

WITH GARLIC AND CURRY LEAVES

Moong Masoor Dal

flavors in this dal reflect Hyderabadi cooking, a cuisine that combines northern Indian ingredients like garlic, ginger, and tomatoes with southern staples like curry leaves. Followers of the predominant Islamic faith in Hyderabad live in close and harmonious quarters with a population of Hindus—much like the marriage of flavors in many of their signature dishes.

MAKES 4 CUPS

½ cup skinned split green lentils
  (yellow in this form, moong dal),
  picked over for stones
½ cup skinned split brown lentils
  (salmon-colored in this form, masoor dal),
  picked over for stones
2 teaspoons cumin seeds
2 lengthwise slices fresh ginger
  (each 2 inches long, 1 inch wide, and
  ⅛ inch thick), coarsely chopped
2 large cloves garlic, coarsely chopped
2 to 4 fresh green Thai, cayenne, or
  serrano chiles, to taste, stems removed
2 tablespoons Ghee (page 21) or canola oil
1 small red onion, finely chopped
1 large tomato, cored and finely chopped
2 tablespoons finely chopped fresh cilantro
  leaves and tender stems
2 teaspoons coarse kosher or sea salt
½ teaspoon ground turmeric
30 medium-size to large fresh curry leaves

1. Place both types of lentils in a medium-size saucepan. Fill the pan halfway with water and rinse the lentils by rubbing them between your fingertips. The water will become cloudy. Drain this water. Repeat three or four times, until the water remains relatively clear; drain. Now add 3 cups water and bring to a boil, uncovered, over medium heat. Skim off and discard any foam that forms on the surface. Reduce the heat to medium-low, partially cover the pan, and simmer, stirring occasionally, until the lentils are tender and soft, 12 to 15 minutes.

2. While the lentils are cooking, combine the cumin seeds, ginger, garlic, and chiles in a mortar, and pound the ingredients with the pestle until they are crushed to a gritty but pulplike paste. (The cumin seeds will bruise and break a little, but most retain their shape.)

3. Heat a medium-size skillet over medium-high heat. Pour in the ghee and immediately add the onion and the crushed paste. Stir-fry until the onion is lightly browned and the chiles are pungent, 3 to 5 minutes. Add the tomato, cilantro, salt, turmeric, and curry leaves. Reduce the heat to medium and simmer, uncovered, until the tomato pieces break down and appear saucelike, 2 to 3 minutes.

4. When the lentils are cooked, add the sauce and stir once or twice. Pour ½ cup water into the skillet and deglaze it; add this to the lentils. Reduce the heat to medium-low, cover the pan, and simmer, stirring occasionally, until the lentils have absorbed the flavors, 5 to 7 minutes. Then serve.

Five-Lentil Stew
WITH CUMIN AND CAYENNE

Panchmela dal

Rajni Kedia is a neighbor and friend of my sister-in-law Geeta in suburban Mumbai. On a recent visit, her passion for the foods of her childhood in Rajasthan, which she still creates daily for her family, came through crystal-clear. It was a sunny Sunday afternoon, the auspicious day called *Makar Sankranti,* and hundreds of kites soared in the warm breeze in celebration of the first day of spring. Rajni's lentil-rich stew simmered on the stove while she sizzled the spices that went into her *baghaar* (a process that perks up clarified butter and swirls it into a curry as the final layer of flavors). "A little ghee before you serve," she said as my eyes widened at her perception of "little." No wonder it tasted so rich, especially when eaten with ghee-soused hard-baked *Baati* (page 739), the perfect match for Rajasthan's classic dal. **MAKES 3 CUPS**

¼ *cup skin-on split black lentils (urad dal), picked over for stones*

¼ *cup skinned split green lentils (yellow in this form, moong dal), picked over for stones*

¼ *cup skin-on split green lentils (moong dal), picked over for stones*

¼ *cup yellow split peas (chana dal), picked over for stones*

¼ *cup oily or unoily skinned split yellow pigeon peas (toovar dal), picked over for stones*

1½ *teaspoons coarse kosher or sea salt*

½ *teaspoon ground turmeric*

4 *fresh green Thai, cayenne, or serrano chiles, stems removed, coarsely chopped (do not remove the seeds)*

2 *lengthwise slices fresh ginger (each 2 inches long, 1 inch wide, and ⅛ inch thick)*

2 *tablespoons Ghee (page 21) or melted butter*

2 *teaspoons cumin seeds*

2 *fresh or dried bay leaves*

½ *teaspoon ground asafetida*

½ *teaspoon cayenne (ground red pepper)*

2 *tablespoons finely chopped fresh cilantro leaves and tender stems for garnishing*

1. Place all the lentils, the split peas, and the pigeon peas in a medium-size saucepan. Fill the pan halfway with water and rinse the legumes by rubbing them between your fingertips. The water will become cloudy and some of the skin from the lentils will separate. Drain this water, discarding the loose skins. Repeat three or four times, until the water remains relatively clear; drain. Now add 3 cups water and bring to a boil, uncovered, over medium heat. Skim off and discard any foam that forms on the surface. Stir in the salt, turmeric, chiles, and ginger. Reduce the heat to medium-low, cover the pan, and simmer, stirring occasionally, until the legumes are tender, about 30 minutes.

2. Remove and discard the pieces of ginger. Then transfer half the legumes, with half their cooking water, to a blender and puree until smooth. Pour this creamy blend into a bowl. Repeat with the remaining legumes and water. Then return all the puree to the saucepan. (If you have an immersion blender, you can puree all the legumes and water right in the saucepan.)

3. Heat the ghee in a small skillet over medium-high heat. Add the cumin seeds and cook until they sizzle and turn reddish brown, 5 to 10 seconds. Remove the pan from the heat and add the bay leaves, asafetida, and cayenne. They will sizzle and smell aromatic upon contact, and the heat will be just right to cook the ground spices without burning. Pour the contents of the skillet over the dal, and stir once or twice.

4. Remove the bay leaves, sprinkle with the cilantro, and serve.

Dried Lentil Wafers
WITH A YOGURT SAUCE

Papad Aur Dahi Ki Kadhi

Unusually textured and thickly sauced, this curry is pure comfort food. I always devour stacks of homemade whole-wheat breads (page 727) and a small mound of pickles, either store-bought or homemade (page 745), along with it. It is no wonder people in Rajasthan snooze for a while in the afternoon, after a lunch like this. **SERVES 4**

I cup plain yogurt

I tablespoon chickpea flour

I teaspoon coarse kosher or sea salt

¼ teaspoon ground turmeric

4 lengthwise slices fresh ginger (each 2 inches long, I inch wide, and ⅛ inch thick), finely chopped

2 fresh green Thai, cayenne, or serrano chiles, stems removed, finely chopped (do not remove the seeds)

2 tablespoons Ghee (page 21) or canola oil

I teaspoon black or yellow mustard seeds

2 teaspoons cumin seeds: I teaspoon left whole, I teaspoon ground

2 teaspoons coriander seeds, ground

¼ teaspoon ground asafetida

3 uncooked lentil wafers (papads or pappadums), at least 6 inches in diameter, broken into bite-size pieces (see box, page 593)

¼ cup finely chopped fresh cilantro leaves and tender stems for garnishing

1. Combine the yogurt, chickpea flour, salt, turmeric, ginger, chiles, and 1 cup water in a medium-size bowl. Stir well.

2. Heat the ghee in a medium-size saucepan over medium-high heat. Add the mustard seeds, cover the pan, and cook until the seeds have stopped popping (not unlike popcorn), about 30 seconds. Remove the pan from the heat and stir in the whole and ground cumin seeds, coriander, and asafetida. (The hot oil will be just right to sizzle and cook the spices without burning them.)

3. Carefully pour the yogurt mixture into the spiced ghee, and stir to combine. Return the pan to the heat and stir in the broken *papads*. Cook, stirring occasionally, until the sauce thickens, about 5 minutes.

4. Sprinkle with the cilantro, and serve.

Creamy Moth Beans
WITH COCONUT MILK

Kokum Moth Chi Dal

Because mung beans are similar in texture and shape to moth beans, you can use them as an alternative; they have the same

cooking times. However, that's where their similarities end: moth beans have an earthier, meatier flavor than mellow-tasting mung. I often serve this as an appetizer with wedges of Flaky Breads Stuffed with Spicy Green Peas (page 737)—it always gets rave reviews. **MAKES 4 CUPS**

1 cup whole moth beans

¼ teaspoon ground turmeric

4 pieces dried black kokum (each roughly 2 inches long
*   and 1 inch wide, see Tip, page 427)*

2 tablespoons Ghee (page 21) or canola oil

2 teaspoons cumin seeds

8 to 10 fresh green Thai, cayenne, or
*   serrano chiles, to taste, stems removed,*
*   thinly sliced crosswise*
*   (do not remove the seeds)*

4 large cloves garlic, finely chopped

1 large tomato, cored and finely chopped

1 cup unsweetened coconut milk

1½ teaspoons coarse kosher or sea salt

10 to 12 medium-size to large fresh curry leaves

1. Place the beans in a pressure cooker. Fill the cooker halfway with water and rinse the beans by rubbing them between your fingertips. The water may appear slightly dirty. Drain this water. Repeat three or four times, until the water remains relatively clear; drain. Now add 3 cups water and bring to a boil, uncovered, over high heat. Skim off and discard any foam that forms on the surface. Stir in the turmeric and kokum. Seal the cooker shut and allow the pressure to build up. When the cooker reaches full pressure, reduce the heat to medium-low and cook for about 10 minutes. Remove the cooker from the heat and allow the pressure to subside naturally (about 15 minutes) before opening the lid.

2. Meanwhile, heat the ghee in a medium-size skillet over medium-high heat. Add the cumin seeds and

cook until they sizzle and turn reddish brown, 5 to 10 seconds. Add the chiles and garlic, and stir-fry until the garlic is lightly browned, 1 to 2 minutes.

3. Immediately add the tomato, coconut milk, salt, and curry leaves. Lower the heat to medium and simmer, uncovered, stirring occasionally, until the tomato appears saucelike but is still slightly chunky, 2 to 3 minutes. Set the mixture aside until the beans are ready.

4. Add the sauce to the cooked beans, and stir once or twice. Simmer, uncovered, stirring occasionally, until the sauce thickens, 5 to 10 minutes.

5. If the kokum pieces have not disintegrated, remove them before you serve the curry.

Tart Moth Beans
WITH LIME JUICE

Moth Nu dal

I was amazed to discover that these light brown oval beans, firm and stonelike, similar in shape to green mung beans, were used as cattle feed in Texas many years ago. I am sure the animals loved them in their raw form, but I would rather boil the beans until they are tender but still firm-looking—they have a creamy texture when cooked just right. These beans, pronounced "moat" in Gujarati, are widely available in Indian and some Pakistani grocery stores. In Maharashtra, these beans are partially sprouted, adding another dimension to this tasty legume. **MAKES 4 CUPS**

with morsels of yeasty, fermented-tasting, chewy sourdough bread—dunk them in the spicy curry.

MAKES 4 CUPS

*3 cups partially sprouted whole moth beans
    (see box, page 328)*

½ teaspoon ground turmeric

*3 pieces dried black kokum (each roughly
    2 inches long and 1 inch wide; see Tips)*

2 tablespoons Ghee (page 21) or canola oil

*1 medium-size red onion, cut in half lengthwise
    and thinly sliced*

4 medium-size cloves garlic, finely chopped

1 teaspoon cumin seeds

*3 to 5 fresh green Thai, cayenne, or serrano chiles,
    to taste, stems removed*

1½ teaspoons coarse kosher or sea salt

*1 teaspoon Maharashtrian garam masala
    (page 28)*

1. Combine 3 cups water and the beans in a pressure cooker, and bring to a boil over medium-high heat. Skim off and discard any foam that forms on the surface. Stir in the turmeric and kokum. Seal the cooker shut and allow the pressure to build up. When the cooker reaches full pressure, reduce the heat to medium-low and cook for about 10 minutes. Remove the cooker from the heat and allow the pressure to subside naturally (about 15 minutes) before opening the lid.

2. While the beans are cooking, heat the ghee in a medium-size skillet over medium heat. Add the onion and garlic, and stir-fry until they are dark brown, soft, and deep purple, 15 to 20 minutes.

3. While the onion is browning, sprinkle the cumin seeds into a mortar and add the chiles. Pound with the pestle to form a pulpy, gritty paste.

4. When the onion and garlic are cooked, scrape the

cumin-chile paste into the skillet and stir-fry to cook the spice blend, about 1 minute. Set the mixture aside until the beans are cooked.

5. When the beans are ready, add the onion mixture to the cooker. Pour 1 cup water into the skillet, and scrape the bottom to deglaze it, releasing any browned bits of onion and spice; add the washings to the beans. Stir in the salt and garam masala, and bring the curry to a simmer over medium heat. Continue to simmer, uncovered, stirring occasionally, until the flavors meld, about 10 minutes. Then serve.

Tips:

❖ The intense heat generated in the pressure cooker might break down the pieces of kokum. If they remain intact, feel free to discard them before you serve the curry.

❖ If you don't have any kokum on hand, stir in ½ teaspoon tamarind paste or concentrate just before you serve the curry. The intense burst of tartness leaves a pleasant aftermath after every bite.

Whole Yellow Peas
WITH BISHOP'S WEED

Ragado

Whole legumes—like chickpeas, or yellow or green peas, cooked with simple spices—are referred to as *ragados* in Gujarati. I once sampled a frozen convenience product labeled *"Ragado"* and said to myself, "I can do better than this." Here is the result, made extra-textural by the raw red onion and sweet golden raisins. Eat it with fluffy thin rotis (page 727) for a simple meal.

MAKES 4 CUPS

1 cup dried whole yellow peas (safed vatana)

2 tablespoons canola oil

1 teaspoon cumin seeds

½ teaspoon bishop's weed

6 tablespoons finely chopped fresh cilantro
   leaves and tender stems

1½ teaspoons coarse kosher or sea salt

1 teaspoon coriander seeds, ground

1 teaspoon ground Deggi chiles
   (see box, page 290); or ½ teaspoon
   cayenne (ground red pepper) mixed
   with ½ teaspoon sweet paprika

2 teaspoons white granulated sugar

1 tablespoon Ghee (page 21)

½ cup finely chopped red onion for garnishing

⅓ cup golden raisins for garnishing

1. Place the peas in a medium-size bowl. Fill the bowl halfway with water and rinse the peas by rubbing them between your fingertips. The water will become slightly cloudy. Drain this water. Repeat three or four times, until the water remains relatively clear; drain. Now fill the bowl halfway with hot water, cover the bowl, and set it aside at room temperature until the peas soften, about 8 hours. (Alternatively, bring the peas and water to a boil in a pressure cooker, without the lid in place. Then remove the cooker from the heat, seal the lid in place, and set the cooker aside for the peas to swell and become tender in that steam room–like environment, 3 to 8 hours.)

Bishop's weed? See the Glossary of Ingredients, page 758.

2. Drain the peas and place them in a pressure cooker. Add 4 cups water and bring to a boil, uncovered, over high heat. Skim off and discard any foam that forms on the surface. Seal the cooker shut and allow the pressure to build up. When the cooker reaches full pressure, reduce the heat to medium-low and cook for about 30 minutes. Then remove the cooker from the heat and allow the pressure to subside naturally (about 15 minutes) before opening the lid. You will see that many of the peas have shed their skin, which has floated to the top. Do not discard the skins.

3. While the peas are cooking, heat the oil in a small skillet over medium-high heat. Add the cumin seeds and bishop's weed, and cook until they sizzle, turn reddish brown, and smell aromatic, 5 to 10 seconds. Remove the skillet from the heat and stir in 4 tablespoons of the cilantro and the salt, coriander, and ground chiles. (The heat from the oil will be just right to cook the spices without burning them.) Set the skillet aside.

4. Once the peas finish doing their thing in the cooker, pour the spiced oil into the cooker. Ladle a scoop of peas and broth into the skillet, and stir to make sure you get every bit of the spices. Add this to the cooker. Continue to simmer the curry, uncovered, over medium heat, stirring occasionally, until the sauce thickens slightly, 10 to 15 minutes.

5. Stir in the sugar and ghee. (The burst of sweetness and the succulence from the ghee tone down the intensity of the chiles to make for a smooth balance.)

6. Top the curry with the onion, raisins, and the remaining 2 tablespoons cilantro, and serve.

Whole Yellow Peas
WITH ONIONS AND GRIDDLE-BROWNED BREAD

Usal Paav

there is a reason why this peasant food, simple in its combination and presentation, appeals to the citizens of Maharashtra, home to the port city of Mumbai. I have seen many a Maharashtrian stop by a vendor's cart next to the bus stop or at the railway station to grab a bowlful of *usal* and *paav* for breakfast on the way to work.

MAKES 3 CUPS

1 cup dried whole yellow peas (safed vatana)
1½ teaspoons coarse kosher or sea salt
2 teaspoons Usha Raikar's garam masala
    (page 27)
½ teaspoon ground turmeric
Butter for griddle cooking
4 sliced white hamburger-style buns
½ cup finely chopped red onion for garnishing
¼ cup finely chopped fresh cilantro leaves
    and tender stems for garnishing

1. Place the peas in a medium-size bowl. Fill the bowl halfway with water and rinse the peas by rubbing them between your fingertips. The water will become slightly cloudy. Drain this water. Repeat three or four times, until the water remains relatively clear; drain. Now fill the bowl halfway with hot tap water, cover it, and let it sit at room temperature until the peas have softened, at least 8 hours.

2. Drain the peas and transfer them to a pressure cooker. Add 4 cups water and bring to a boil, uncovered, over high heat. Skim off and discard any foam that forms on the surface. Seal the cooker shut and allow the pressure to build up. When the cooker reaches full pressure, reduce the heat to medium-low and cook for about 30 minutes. Remove the cooker from the heat and allow the pressure to subside naturally (about 15 minutes) before opening the lid. You will see that many of the peas have shed their skin, which will have floated to the top. Do not discard the skins.

3. Stir in the salt, garam masala, and turmeric. Coarsely mash some of the peas (I use a potato masher to break them up). Bring the curry to a boil over medium-high heat. Continue to boil, uncovered, stirring occasionally, until the sauce thickens slightly and the flavors permeate the peas, about 15 minutes.

4. Butter the cut sides of the buns. Heat a large nonstick skillet or griddle over medium heat. Add the slices, butter side down, and brown them, about 2 minutes.

5. Top the peas with the onion and cilantro, and serve with the crispy-soft bread alongside.

Tip: One time I decided to use frozen green peas as an alternative to the dried yellow peas. I reduced the water to 2 cups and obviously saw no need to either soak them overnight or use a pressure cooker. I brought them to a boil in a medium-size saucepan over medium-high heat and continued to boil them, uncovered, for about 10 minutes. After I seasoned them and coarsely mashed them, I stewed the curry for only 5 minutes because fresh green peas have a thicker "body" when mashed and hence the sauce is quite thick to begin with.

Slow-Cooked Sweetened Yellow Split Peas
WITH FRESH COCONUT CHIPS

Cholar Dal

One Sunday afternoon, my dear friend Mithu re-created this curry for me in her kitchen in suburban Minneapolis. It is the same recipe her late mother, Rekha Mukherjee, used. Mithu explained that Rekha made this dish only on weekends and for special gatherings because "it is so rich and sweet, just like my mother." I took copious notes while I perched on a bar stool at the kitchen counter, listening to Mithu reminisce about her childhood's favorite tastes. She described her mother's cooking techniques and translated from Rekha's notes, written in Bengali. It is no wonder that "Mithu" means "honey-sweet"—a name her parents chose for their beautiful and high-spirited daughter.

MAKES 4 CUPS

1 cup yellow split peas (chana dal), picked over for stones
½ teaspoon ground turmeric
3 cups boiling water
1 tablespoon white granulated sugar
1½ teaspoons coarse kosher or sea salt
½ teaspoon cayenne (ground red pepper)
¼ cup Ghee (page 21) or unsalted butter
2 teaspoons cumin seeds
½ cup finely chopped fresh coconut (see Tip)

1. Place the split peas in a medium-size saucepan. Fill the pan halfway with water and rinse the peas by rubbing them between your fingertips. The water will become cloudy. Drain this water. Repeat three or four times, until the water remains relatively clear; drain. Now add 3 cups water and bring it to a boil, uncovered, over medium-high heat. Skim off and discard any foam that forms on the surface. Stir in the turmeric. Reduce the heat to medium-low, cover the pan, and simmer, stirring occasionally, until the split peas are partially tender, 25 to 30 minutes.

2. Remove the lid and raise the heat to medium. Cook until the remaining water in the pan has been absorbed by the split peas. Then add 1 cup of the boiling water and cook, stirring occasionally, until the split peas absorb it all, 5 to 10 minutes. Repeat twice more (1 cup at a time), using up all the boiling water to create creamy-tasting but firm-looking split peas.

3. Stir in the sugar, salt, and cayenne.

4. Heat the ghee in a small skillet over medium-high heat. Add the cumin seeds and cook until they sizzle, turn reddish brown, and smell nutty, 5 to 10 seconds. Immediately pour this, ghee and all, into the split peas.

5. Stir in the coconut, and serve.

Tip: The day Mithu made this dish, she did not have any fresh coconut on hand, so she used shredded dried coconut instead. It was tasty. But in keeping with her mother's original version, I swirled in fresh coconut when I made this at home, and the results were outstanding. Yes, Mithu will be the first to admit that her mother knew best. (See page 760 for tips on handling fresh coconut.)

Minced Yellow Split Peas
WITH MUSTARD AND CHILES

Vaatli dal

A Maharashtrian staple, this peasant food is anything but pedestrian. It is bursting with pungent chiles, sweet coconut, and nutty-tasting peas, and has a great texture thanks to the mincing. I grab every chance I get to eat this with roti (page 727) or even *Bhaakar* (page 354).

MAKES 4 CUPS

I cup yellow split peas (chana dal), picked over for stones

6 to 8 fresh green Thai, cayenne, or serrano chiles, to taste, stems removed

2 lengthwise slices fresh ginger (each 2 inches long, I inch wide, and ⅛ inch thick)

1½ teaspoons coarse kosher or sea salt

½ teaspoon ground turmeric

2 tablespoons canola oil

I teaspoon black or yellow mustard seeds

I teaspoon cumin seeds

¼ teaspoon ground asafetida

I cup shredded fresh coconut; or ½ cup shredded dried unsweetened coconut, reconstituted (see Note)

¼ cup finely chopped fresh cilantro leaves and tender stems

12 to 15 medium-size to large fresh curry leaves

1. Place the split peas in a medium-size bowl. Fill the bowl halfway with water and rinse the peas by rubbing them between your fingertips. The water will become cloudy. Drain this water. Repeat three or four times, until the water remains relatively clear; drain. Now fill the bowl halfway with warm water and add the chiles. Cover the bowl with plastic wrap, and set it aside at room temperature until the peas and chiles have softened, 1 to 4 hours.

2. Drain the split peas and chiles, and transfer them to a food processor. Add the ginger, and process to form a green-speckled, slightly gritty paste. Scrape this into the same medium-size bowl (why dirty another one?), and stir in the salt and turmeric.

3. Heat the oil in a medium-size saucepan over medium-high heat. Add the mustard seeds, cover the pan, and cook until the seeds have stopped popping (not unlike popcorn), about 30 seconds. Sprinkle in the cumin seeds and asafetida, both of which will instantly sizzle and smell aromatic. Immediately add the split pea mixture, and stir to incorporate the roasted spices, 1 to 2 minutes.

4. Pour in 3 cups water, and stir well to make a thick slurry. Once it starts to boil (it will look like a bubbly mud bath), reduce the heat to medium-low, cover the pan, and simmer, stirring occasionally, until some of the water has been absorbed, 15 to 20 minutes.

5. Stir in the coconut, cilantro, and curry leaves, and serve.

Note: To reconstitute coconut, cover with ½ cup boiling water, set aside for about 15 minutes, and then drain.

Yellow Split Peas
WITH UNRIPE PAPAYA

Cholar Papeeta dal

A hearty, stewlike curry, with a pleasantly spicy bite and mellow tartness, this is a great meal for cold winter nights; just add some slices of crusty store-bought bread. On the other hand, if a multiple-course dinner gathering is on your agenda, serve smaller portions as the soup course. **MAKES 5 CUPS**

1 pound green unripe papaya (see Tips)
1 cup yellow split peas (chana dal), picked over
    for stones
4 fresh green Thai, cayenne, or serrano chiles,
    stems removed, cut in half lengthwise
    (do not remove the seeds)
2 tablespoons Ghee (page 21) or canola oil
2 teaspoons Panch phoron (page 36)
1 small red onion, finely chopped
4 dried red Thai or cayenne chiles, stems removed
    (see Tips)
1 teaspoon Bangala garam masala (page 26)
½ teaspoon ground turmeric
2 teaspoons coarse kosher or sea salt
2 tablespoons finely chopped fresh cilantro leaves
    and tender stems
Juice of 1 medium-size lime

1. Slice off and discard the stem and heel ends of the papaya (¼-inch-thick slices). Peel the papaya with a swivel peeler. Cut the firm, light green fruit in half lengthwise. Discard the white pearl seeds and the thin fibrous material underneath by scraping them off with a spoon. Cut the flesh into ½-inch cubes.

2. Place the split peas in a medium-size saucepan. Fill the pan halfway with water and rinse the grains by rubbing them between your fingertips. The water will become cloudy. Drain this water. Repeat three or four times, until the water remains relatively clear; drain. Now add 3 cups water and bring to a boil, uncovered, over medium-high heat. Skim off and discard any foam that forms on the surface. Stir in the papaya and the fresh chiles. Reduce the heat to medium-low, cover the pan, and simmer, stirring occasionally, until the split peas are partially tender, 25 to 30 minutes.

3. While the split peas are simmering, heat a small skillet over medium-high heat. Add the ghee, which will instantly heat and appear to shimmer. Add the *Panch phoron* and cook until it sizzles and is aromatic, 10 to 15 seconds. Immediately add the onion and dried chiles, and stir-fry until the onion is light brown around the edges and the chiles have blackened slightly, 3 to 5 minutes. Sprinkle in the garam masala and turmeric, and stir to cook the spices, 5 to 10 seconds. Then add ½ cup water and scrape the bottom of the skillet to deglaze it, releasing any browned bits of onion and spice. Remove the skillet from the heat.

4. Uncover the dal and raise the heat to medium-high. Boil, stirring occasionally, until the sauce thickens and the papaya and split peas are tender but still firm-looking, 10 to 12 minutes.

5. Add the onion sauce and the salt. Cook over medium heat, uncovered, stirring occasionally, until the flavors have permeated the dal, about 5 minutes.

6. Stir in the cilantro and lime juice, and serve.

Tips:

❖ Try cubes of rutabaga, potato, or even sweet potato as an alternative to the unripe papaya.

❖ If you desire a greater degree of heat from this curry, increase the number of dried chiles.

Sweet-Hot Yellow Split Peas
WITH GOLDEN RAISINS

Kishmish Waale Chane ki dal

this dal is redolent of ingredients introduced during the Moghal regime. Black cumin, known as *shahi* (royalty) cumin, and golden raisins (brought in by traders from Afghanistan) provide a slightly bitter and sweet balance to the split peas, moving the flavor of this curry up many notches. **MAKES 4 CUPS**

1 cup yellow split peas (chana dal), picked over for stones
½ teaspoon ground turmeric
3 tablespoons Ghee (page 21) or canola oil
1 large red onion, cut in half lengthwise and thinly sliced
½ cup golden raisins
3 fresh or dried bay leaves
1 teaspoon cumin seeds
1 teaspoon black cumin seeds
2 tablespoons Ginger Paste (page 15)
2 tablespoons Garlic Paste (page 15)
1 large tomato, cored and finely chopped
4 to 6 fresh green Thai, cayenne, or serrano chiles, to taste, stems removed, cut crosswise into ½-inch-thick slices (do not remove the seeds)

1½ teaspoons coarse kosher or sea salt
½ teaspoon Punjabi garam masala (page 25)
¼ cup finely chopped fresh cilantro leaves and tender stems for garnishing

1. Place the split peas in a medium-size saucepan. Fill the pan halfway with water and rinse the peas by rubbing them with your fingertips. The water will become slightly cloudy. Drain this water. Repeat two or three times, until the water remains relatively clear; drain. Now add 3 cups water and the turmeric, and bring to a boil over medium-high heat. Skim off and discard any foam that forms on the surface. Lower the heat to medium and continue to simmer the split peas, uncovered, stirring occasionally, until they have absorbed most of the water but are still firm, 25 to 30 minutes.

2. Pour 2 cups water into the split peas and continue to simmer, stirring occasionally, until they are tender and some of them are starting to break down, about 15 minutes.

3. While the peas are simmering, heat 2 tablespoons of the ghee in a large skillet over medium-high heat. Add the onion, raisins, and bay leaves, and stir-fry until the onion is light brown and the raisins are reddish brown and plump, 8 to 10 minutes. Transfer the mixture to a plate. Discard the bay leaves.

4. Heat the remaining 1 tablespoon ghee in the same skillet over medium heat. Sprinkle in both kinds of cumin seeds and cook until they sizzle and are aromatic, 5 to 10 seconds. Carefully spoon in the ginger and garlic pastes (they will spatter), and stir-fry until the blend is a light brown color, 1 to 2 minutes.

5. Add the tomato, chiles, salt, garam masala, and 1 cup water. Stir to deglaze the skillet, releasing all the collected bits of onion and spices.

6. When the split peas are tender, add the sauce and continue to simmer, uncovered, stirring occasionally, until the sauce has thickened and the split peas have absorbed the flavors, about 15 minutes.

7. Top the curry with the onion-raisin mixture and the cilantro, and serve.

EGGPLANT SMOTHERED Yellow Split Peas

baingan chane ki dal

Porridgelike and thick, this curry adroitly balances nutty and pungent flavors. Use more chiles (or fewer) to tilt the scale to suit your taste buds. For added richness, drizzle a tablespoon or more of ghee over the cooked dal. In addition to being downright tasty, the ghee will protect your tongue if you have added one too many red-hot chiles. **MAKES 4 CUPS**

1 cup plus 1 tablespoon yellow split peas (chana dal), picked over for stones

2 tablespoons Ghee (page 21) or canola oil

1 tablespoon coriander seeds

4 dried red Thai or cayenne chiles, stems removed

1 teaspoon black or yellow mustard seeds

½ teaspoon ground asafetida

12 to 15 medium-size to large fresh curry leaves

1 medium-size eggplant (about 1 pound), stem removed, cut into ½-inch cubes

2 teaspoons coarse kosher or sea salt

1. Place the 1 cup split peas in a medium-size saucepan. Fill the pan halfway with water and rinse the peas by rubbing them between your fingertips. The water will become cloudy. Drain this water. Repeat three or four times, until the water remains relatively clear; drain. Now add 3 cups water and bring to a boil, uncovered, over medium-high heat. Skim off and discard any foam that forms on the surface. Reduce the heat to medium-low, cover the pan, and simmer, stirring occasionally, until the split peas are partially tender, 25 to 30 minutes.

2. While the split peas are cooking, heat the ghee in a small skillet over medium-high heat. Sprinkle in the remaining 1 tablespoon split peas, the coriander seeds, and the chiles. Cook, stirring constantly, until the split peas and coriander seeds turn reddish brown and the chiles blacken slightly, about 1 minute. Using a slotted spoon, transfer the mixture to a plate to cool, leaving the oil behind. Set the skillet aside.

3. Once the spice mixture is cool to the touch, transfer it to a spice grinder and grind until the texture resembles that of finely ground black pepper.

4. Reheat the ghee in the skillet over medium-high heat. Add the mustard seeds, cover the skillet, and cook until the seeds have stopped popping (not unlike popcorn), about 30 seconds. Remove the skillet from the heat and sprinkle in the asafetida and curry leaves (be careful, as the leaves will spatter upon contact).

5. Once the split peas are partially tender, stir in the eggplant, the salt, the ground spice blend, and the contents of the skillet. Cover the pan and cook over medium heat, stirring occasionally, until the eggplant is fork-tender, about 10 minutes. Then serve.

Stewed Potatoes
WITH YELLOW SPLIT PEAS

Urulikazhangu kootu

During my childhood days, this was a favorite curry of mine, and when my mother made puffy *pooris* to go with it, it was all I would eat—finishing my dinner with a glass of spiced buttermilk, a must after any meal in southern India because of its stomach-soothing qualities. **SERVES 6**

½ cup yellow split peas (chana dal), picked over
    for stones
2 medium-size russet or Yukon Gold potatoes,
    peeled, cut into ¼-inch cubes, and submerged
    in a bowl of cold water to prevent browning
1 small red onion, cut into ¼-inch cubes
2 teaspoons Sambhar masala (page 33)
1½ teaspoons coarse kosher or sea salt
½ teaspoon ground turmeric
12 to 15 medium-size to large fresh curry leaves
2 tablespoons Ghee (page 21) or canola oil
1 teaspoon black or yellow mustard seeds
1 tablespoon skinned split black lentils
    (cream-colored in this form, urad dal),
    picked over for stones
6 dried red Thai or cayenne chiles, stems removed
¼ teaspoon ground asafetida

1. Place the split peas in a medium-size saucepan. Fill the pan halfway with water and rinse the peas by rubbing them between your fingertips. The water will become cloudy. Drain this water. Repeat three or four times, until the water remains relatively clear; drain. Now add 3 cups water.

2. Drain the potatoes and add them to the split peas. Stir in the onion, *Sambhar masala,* salt, turmeric, and curry leaves, and bring to a boil, uncovered, over medium-high heat. Then lower the heat to medium and simmer, uncovered, stirring occasionally, until the split peas and vegetables are tender and the sauce is much thicker than when you started, 30 to 35 minutes.

3. While the split peas are cooking, heat the ghee in a small skillet over medium-high heat. Add the mustard seeds, cover the skillet, and cook until the seeds have stopped popping (not unlike popcorn), about 30 seconds. Add the lentils and chiles and stir-fry until the lentils turn golden-brown and the chiles blacken, 15 to 20 seconds. Remove the skillet from the heat and sprinkle in the asafetida, which will sizzle and cook upon contact.

4. Once the split peas and vegetables are ready, pour in the spiced oil mixture and stir once or twice. Continue to simmer the curry, uncovered, stirring occasionally, until the flavors blend, about 5 minutes. Then serve.

Yellow Split Peas
AND SPINACH
IN A YOGURT-PEANUT SAUCE

Patli dal

A remarkable physician—vibrant, down-to-earth, and with a passion for good food—Ashlesha Tamboli-Madhok and I (fellow Mumbai-ites) bonded over dishes from her childhood (Marathi foods). Her husband, also a physician, and their lovely daughter share her passion for all things Indian. I was intrigued by this curry, which Ashlesha brought to a potluck dinner. It's a flavorful combination of yellow split peas, yogurt, and spinach.

MAKES 5 CUPS

I cup yellow split peas (chana dal), picked over
   for stones
I bag (10 ounces) fresh spinach leaves,
   well rinsed
2 tablespoons unsalted dry-roasted peanuts
2 fresh green Thai, cayenne, or serrano chiles,
   stems removed
I cup plain yogurt
2 tablespoons chickpea flour
1½ teaspoons coarse kosher or sea salt
¼ teaspoon ground turmeric
12 to 15 medium-size to large fresh curry leaves
2 lengthwise slices fresh ginger
   (each 2½ inches long, I inch wide,
   and ⅛ inch thick), cut into matchstick-thin
   strips (julienne)
2 tablespoons Ghee (page 21) or canola oil
I teaspoon black or yellow mustard seeds
¼ teaspoon ground asafetida

1. Place the split peas in a medium-size saucepan. Fill the pan halfway with water and rinse the peas by rubbing them between your fingertips. The water will become cloudy. Drain this water. Repeat three or four times, until the water remains relatively clear; drain. Now add 3 cups water and bring to a boil, uncovered, over medium-high heat. Skim off and discard any foam that forms on the surface. Add the spinach, a few handfuls at a time, stirring it in until wilted. Once all the spinach has been stirred in, reduce the heat to medium-low, cover the pan, and simmer, stirring occasionally, until the split peas are tender and the spinach is olive green, 30 to 35 minutes.

2. While the split peas are cooking, combine the peanuts and chiles in a mortar. Pound the mixture with the pestle, scraping the sides to contain the ingredients in the center, to form a pulpy mass, still chunky with broken-down pieces of peanuts and chiles.

3. Combine the yogurt and ½ cup water in a medium-size bowl, and whisk together. Sprinkle the chickpea flour over the mixture and whisk it in, making sure there are no lumps. Stir in the salt, turmeric, half of the curry leaves, and the ginger. Then add the pounded peanut mixture.

4. When they are tender, mash the split peas and spinach with the back of a spoon, or with a potato masher, until the leaves break down and some of the peas squish. Stir in the yogurt sauce and bring to a boil over medium-high heat. Then lower the heat to medium and simmer, uncovered, stirring occasionally, until the sauce has thickened and lost its raw floury taste, yielding a nutty-tasting, curdle-free curry, about 15 minutes.

5. Heat the ghee in a small skillet over medium-high heat. Add the mustard seeds, cover the skillet, and cook until the seeds have stopped popping (not unlike popcorn), about 30 seconds. Remove the skillet from the heat and sprinkle in the asafetida and the remaining curry leaves (which will instantly sizzle and spatter in the hot oil). Add this mixture to the curry, stir once or twice, and serve.

Tip: The velvety texture of the sauce is a result of coarsely mashing the spinach and some of the split peas, which also thickens the curry a bit. Of course the flour in the yogurt mixture thickens it further, in addition to stabilizing the yogurt and preventing it from curdling. The burst of ginger with each mouthful is an added bonus (clears your sinuses, too).

Yellow Split Peas
WITH TOMATO AND CHILES

tamatar Chana dal

Simply a breeze to make, this curry requires no advance planning. All the ingredients are readily available. It makes a great meal when mounded over rice or when served as the "dunkee" for wedges of naan (page 729).

MAKES 4 CUPS

- *1 cup yellow split peas (chana dal), picked over*
  for stones
- *1 tablespoon coriander seeds*
- *1 teaspoon cumin seeds*
- *4 fresh green Thai, cayenne, or serrano chiles,*
  stems removed, coarsely chopped
  (do not remove the seeds)
- *4 medium-size cloves garlic*
- *2 tablespoons Ghee (page 21) or melted butter*
- *1 large tomato, cored and finely chopped*
- *1½ teaspoons coarse kosher or sea salt*
- *¼ teaspoon ground turmeric*
- *¼ cup finely chopped fresh cilantro leaves and*
  tender stems

1. Place the split peas in a medium-size saucepan. Fill the pan halfway with tap water and rinse the peas by rubbing them between your fingertips. The water will become cloudy. Drain this water. Repeat three or four times, until the water remains relatively clear; drain. Now add 3 cups water and bring to a boil, uncovered, over medium-high heat. Skim off and discard any foam that forms on the surface. Reduce the heat to medium-low, cover the pan, and simmer, stirring occasionally, until the peas are partially tender, 25 to 30 minutes.

2. While the split peas are simmering, combine the coriander seeds, cumin seeds, chiles, and garlic in a mortar. Pound with the pestle to form a pungent, pulpy mass (some coriander seeds will remain whole).

3. Heat the ghee in a small skillet over medium-high heat. Add the pounded chile blend and stir-fry (with adequate ventilation) until the garlic is honey-brown, 1 to 2 minutes.

4. Add the tomato, salt, and turmeric. Cook over medium heat, uncovered, stirring occasionally, until the tomato softens and the ghee starts to separate around the edges, 5 to 8 minutes. Stir in the cilantro, and set aside.

5. When the split peas are partially tender, add the sauce and ½ cup water, and stir. Ladle a spoonful of the mixture into the skillet and stir to wash it out. Add this to the saucepan. Continue to simmer the dal over medium heat, uncovered, stirring occasionally, until the flavors permeate the split peas, about 5 minutes. Then serve.

Steamed Nuggets
WITH A PEANUT-TOMATO SAUCE

kothimbir Chi Vadi

Some of the more traditional *vadis* I sampled in Marathi-speaking homes in the state of Maharashtra, in western India, were pan-fried medallions of pureed chile-spiked yellow split peas, served as an appetizer with a relish or sauce of some kind. Here I have changed the concept a bit, turning it into a main-course curry and avoiding the pan-frying to make this a healthier alternative while retaining all the flavor.

SERVES 6

For the nuggets:

1 cup yellow split peas (chana dal), picked over
   for stones
½ cup firmly packed fresh cilantro leaves and
   tender stems
1 teaspoon coarse kosher or sea salt
½ teaspoon ground asafetida
4 to 6 fresh green Thai, cayenne, or serrano chiles,
   to taste, stems removed
Vegetable cooking spray

For the curry:

2 tablespoons canola oil
1 cup finely chopped red onion
12 to 15 medium-size to large fresh curry leaves
3 or 4 fresh green Thai, cayenne, or serrano chiles,
   to taste, stems removed, thinly sliced crosswise
   (do not remove the seeds)
1 can (14.5 ounces) diced tomatoes
½ cup firmly packed fresh cilantro leaves and tender
   stems; ¼ cup finely chopped, ¼ cup left as is
1 teaspoon white granulated sugar
1 teaspoon coarse kosher or sea salt
¼ cup unsalted dry-roasted peanuts

1. First, make the split pea nuggets: Place the split peas in a medium-size bowl. Fill the bowl halfway with water and rinse the legumes by rubbing them between your fingertips. The water will become cloudy. Drain this water. Repeat three or four times, until the water remains relatively clear; drain. Now fill the bowl halfway with warm water, cover it with plastic wrap, and set it aside at room temperature until the split peas have softened, 1 to 4 hours.

2. Drain the split peas in a strainer, and transfer them to a food processor. Add the cilantro, salt, asafetida, and chiles. Process to form a green-marbled, slightly gritty paste. Scrape this into the same medium-size bowl (why dirty another one?).

3. Grease the palms of your hands with a little cooking spray or oil. Divide the wet, sandlike, slightly gritty paste in half. Shape each half into a tight log, about 7 inches long.

4. Insert a steamer basket into a saucepan filled halfway with water, or place a bamboo steamer in a wok filled halfway with water. Spray the steamer basket lightly with cooking spray. Lay the logs side by side in the steamer basket. Once the water comes to a boil, cover the pan and steam the logs until they look dry and are firm to the touch, about 30 minutes. Remove the steamer basket from the pan and allow the logs to cool.

5. Once they are cool to the touch, lift the logs onto a cutting board. Slice them in half lengthwise, and then slice each length in half lengthwise again. Cut each strip crosswise into 1-inch nuggets.

6. To make the curry, heat the oil in a medium-size saucepan over medium heat. Add the onion, curry leaves, and chiles, and stir-fry until the onion is honey-brown with a deep purple hue, 10 to 15 minutes.

7. Pour in 2 cups water, and add the tomatoes with their juices, the chopped cilantro, the sugar and salt. Stir in the split pea nuggets. Heat the curry to a boil and continue to boil, uncovered, stirring infrequently and gently, until the sauce starts to thicken, 8 to 10 minutes.

8. While the sauce is boiling, combine the peanuts and the remaining ¼ cup cilantro in a mortar. Pound the mixture to a wet breadcrumb-like texture, scraping the sides of the mortar to contain the mixture in the center.

9. When the sauce has thickened, stir in the peanut-cilantro blend and serve.

Tip: You can prepare the nuggets ahead of time, through Step 5. Cover and refrigerate them for up to 3 days, or freeze the nuggets in freezer-safe self-seal bags for up to 1 month.

Yellow Split and Pigeon Peas
WITH ONION AND GARLIC

Chana toor dal Fry

Even though these are quick-cooking legumes and you really don't need a pressure cooker, I like to use it in order to cook them to a creamy-smooth consistency, with some of the split peas still firm-looking. There's a pleasant textural difference between the sweet, lightly browned onion slices and the pieces of burning chile. I serve this curry with wedges of lime for a fresh tang, especially if the tomatoes are not at their juiciest best. **MAKES 4 CUPS**

½ cup yellow split peas (chana dal),
    picked over for stones
½ cup oily or unoily skinned split yellow pigeon peas
    (toovar dal), picked over for stones

¼ cup Ghee (page 21) or melted unsalted butter
1 teaspoon black or yellow mustard seeds
1 medium-size red onion, cut in half lengthwise
    and thinly sliced
8 medium-size cloves garlic, finely chopped
2 fresh green Thai, cayenne, or serrano chiles,
    stems removed, cut crosswise into ¼-inch-thick
    slices (do not remove the seeds)
2 teaspoons coarse kosher or sea salt
1 teaspoon cumin seeds, ground
½ teaspoon fenugreek seeds, ground
½ teaspoon ground turmeric
1 large tomato, cored and cut into ½-inch cubes
2 tablespoons finely chopped fresh cilantro
    leaves and tender stems

1. Place the split peas and pigeon peas in a pressure cooker. Fill the cooker halfway with water, and rinse the legumes by rubbing them between your fingertips. The water may appear slightly dirty or cloudy. Drain this water. Repeat three or four times, until the water remains relatively clear; drain. Now add 3 cups water and bring to a boil, uncovered, over high heat. Skim off and discard any foam that forms on the surface. Seal the cooker shut and allow the pressure to build up. When the cooker reaches full pressure, reduce the heat to medium-low and cook for about 15 minutes. Remove the cooker from the heat and allow the pressure to subside naturally (about 15 minutes) before opening the lid.

2. While the peas are cooking, heat the ghee in a medium-size skillet over medium-high heat. Add the mustard seeds, cover the skillet, and cook until the seeds have stopped popping (not unlike popcorn), about 30 seconds. Add the onion, garlic, and chiles, and stir-fry until the mixture is a light brown color and smells pungent-sweet, 2 to 3 minutes. Stir in the salt, cumin, fenugreek, and turmeric, and allow the spices to cook, about 30 seconds.

3. Add the tomato, cilantro, and ½ cup water. Simmer the sauce, uncovered, stirring occasionally, until the tomato has softened, about 5 minutes.

4. Add the sauce to the cooked legumes, and stir once or twice. Simmer the curry, uncovered, over medium-low heat until the legumes are infused with the flavors, about 10 minutes. Then serve.

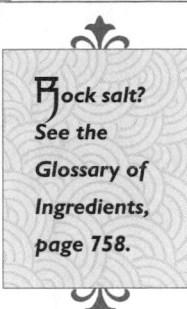

Rock salt? See the Glossary of Ingredients, page 758.

Whole Pigeon Peas
WITH SPINACH

Sabud toor Aur Palak ki dal

I love the fact that there is more spinach than legumes in this curry. Pressure-cooking greens might seem like overkill (and it is, for texture and nutrients), but the silky smooth sauce makes it all right. This recipe makes a huge batch, and if you are like me, you will ladle it over rice, wrap it into flatbreads, and eat it by the spoonful every chance you get until it is all gone. Yes, you can make half the recipe, but then you won't have all those wonderful leftovers! **MAKES 7 CUPS**

I cup whole pigeon peas (sabud toovar),
*   picked over for stones*
I½ pounds fresh spinach leaves, well rinsed
I tablespoon Ginger Paste (page 15)
I tablespoon Garlic Paste (page 15)
½ teaspoon ground turmeric

½ cup firmly packed fresh cilantro leaves
*   and tender stems*
I tablespoon plus I teaspoon cumin seeds
2 teaspoons rock salt
4 medium-size cloves garlic, coarsely chopped
4 dried red Thai or cayenne chiles, stems removed
2 tablespoons canola oil
I teaspoon coriander seeds
2 tablespoons Ghee (page 21) or butter
4 lengthwise slices fresh ginger (each I½ inches long,
*   I inch wide, and ⅛ inch thick), cut into matchstick-*
*   thin strips (julienne)*

1. Place the pigeon peas in a medium-size bowl. Fill the bowl halfway with water and rinse the peas by rubbing them between your fingertips. The water will become slightly cloudy. Drain this water. Repeat three or four times, until the water remains relatively clear; drain. Now fill the bowl halfway with hot tap water and let it sit at room temperature, covered with plastic wrap, until the peas have softened, at least 8 hours or as long as overnight.

2. Drain the pigeon peas and transfer them to a pressure cooker. Add 4 cups water and bring it to a boil, uncovered, over high heat. Skim off and discard any foam that forms on the surface. Add the spinach, several handfuls at a time, stirring it in until it is wilted. When all the spinach has been added, stir in the ginger and garlic pastes and the turmeric. Seal the cooker shut and allow the pressure to build up. When the cooker reaches full pressure, reduce the heat to medium-low and cook for about 1 hour. Remove the cooker from the heat and allow the pressure to subside naturally (about 15 minutes) before opening the lid.

3. Meanwhile, combine the cilantro, the 1 tablespoon cumin seeds, the rock salt, garlic, and chiles in a mortar. Pound with the pestle, scraping down the sides to contain the mixture in the center, until the blend resembles coarse-cut wet grass, feels gritty, and has large specks of red from the chiles. (Yes, you can do this in a food processor, using the pulsing action, but I prefer the texture you get from pounding.)

4. Heat the oil in a small skillet over medium-high heat. Sprinkle in the remaining 1 teaspoon cumin seeds and the coriander seeds. Cook until they sizzle, turn reddish brown, and smell citrus-nutty, 10 to 15 seconds. Add the pounded herb-spice mixture and stir-fry until the garlic in the blend forms a thin brown layer on the bottom of the skillet and the medley smells pungent-hot, about 1 minute. Set the mixture aside until the pigeon peas are done.

5. Once the pigeon peas and spinach are ready, add the contents of the skillet, and stir in the ghee and the ginger. Pour some of this mixture into the skillet and scrape the bottom to deglaze it, releasing every bit of stuck-on herbs and spices; add the washings to the curry.

6. Simmer the olive-green curry, studded with nutty-brown pigeon peas, over medium-high heat, uncovered, stirring occasionally, until the flavors meld, about 10 minutes. Then serve.

Tip: This curry is an excellent example of applying different cooking techniques to the same ingredients to yield diverse tastes and textures. Cumin plays a dual role: first when pounded with the herbs for a slightly nutty taste, the second time sizzled in oil for a sweet and aromatic effect. Ginger, in paste form, is simmered with the peas and spinach, the intense cooking mellowing out its potency; as matchstick-thin strips, it is added towards the end for a palate-kicking effect. Garlic plays a similar initial role as a paste; then garlic cloves are pounded, releasing the oils, and stir-fried to a sweet-spicy aftermath that lingers with each mouthful.

Five-Spiced Whole Pigeon Peas

Sabud toor Aur Panch Phoron

Whole pigeon peas are similar to black-eyed peas in shape, but they have a yellowish-green skin. Unlike their split version, which is more common along India's western and southern coasts, the whole peas are not quick-cooking. And no matter how long they do cook, the whole peas will remain firm, albeit tender. **MAKES 3 CUPS**

1 cup whole pigeon peas (sabud toovar),
*   picked over for stones*
2 tablespoons Ghee (page 21) or canola oil
1 tablespoon Panch phoron (page 36)
1 small red onion, cut in half lengthwise and
*   thinly sliced*
2 teaspoons coriander seeds, ground
1 teaspoon cumin seeds, ground
½ teaspoon ground turmeric
6 dried red Thai or cayenne chiles, stems removed
1½ teaspoons coarse kosher or sea salt
2 tablespoons finely chopped fresh cilantro leaves
*   and tender stems for garnishing*

1. Place the pigeon peas in a medium-size bowl. Fill the bowl halfway with water and rinse the peas by rubbing them between your fingertips. The water will become slightly cloudy. Drain this water. Repeat three or four times, until the water remains relatively clear; drain. Now fill the bowl halfway with hot tap water and let it sit at room temperature, covered with plastic wrap, until the peas soften, at least 8 hours or as long as overnight.

2. Drain the pigeon peas and transfer them to a pressure cooker. Add 4 cups water and bring it to a boil, uncovered, over high heat. Skim off and discard any foam that forms on the surface. Seal the cooker shut and allow the pressure to build up. When the cooker reaches full pressure, reduce the heat to medium-low and cook for about 1 hour. Remove the cooker from the heat and allow the pressure to subside naturally (about 15 minutes) before opening the lid.

3. Meanwhile, heat the ghee in a medium-size skillet over medium-high heat. Sprinkle in the *Panch phoron* and cook until the spices sizzle and turn aromatic, 30 seconds to 1 minute. Add the onion and stir-fry until it turns caramel-brown, 8 to 10 minutes. Then stir in the coriander, cumin, turmeric, and chiles. Cook until they are fragrant, about 1 minute. Set the mixture aside until the pigeon peas are done.

4. Add the onion-spice mixture and the salt to the cooked pigeon peas, and boil vigorously over medium-high heat, uncovered, stirring occasionally, until the curry has absorbed the flavors and the sauce has thickened slightly. (The sauce will never really thicken much. If you prefer a thicker sauce, mash a few of the pigeon peas.)

5. Sprinkle with the cilantro, and serve.

Nutty-Tart Whole Pigeon Peas

Sabud toovar Ane tamatar

The nuttiness of whole pigeon peas appeals to my desire for texture in a curry, and here provides a firm backdrop for tart kokum and tomato. This curry is very mellow, in the absence of chiles or ground pepper of any kind. If you do wish for a little heat, as I often do, serve a few slivers of fresh Thai, cayenne, or serrano chiles alongside the dal, with rice or bread.

MAKES 4 CUPS

1 cup whole pigeon peas (sabud toovar), picked over for stones
6 pieces dried black kokum (each roughly 2 inches long and 1 inch wide; see page 427)
1 tablespoon Ginger Paste (page 15)
1 tablespoon Garlic Paste (page 15)
2 tablespoons Ghee (page 21) or canola oil
1 teaspoon black or yellow mustard seeds
1 teaspoon cumin seeds
¼ teaspoon ground asafetida
¼ teaspoon ground turmeric
1 large tomato, cored and finely chopped
2 tablespoons finely chopped fresh cilantro leaves and tender stems
1½ teaspoons coarse kosher or sea salt
12 to 15 medium-size to large fresh curry leaves

1. Place the pigeon peas in a medium-size bowl. Fill the bowl halfway with water and rinse the peas by rubbing them between your fingertips. The water will become slightly cloudy. Drain this water. Repeat three or four times, until the water remains relatively clear; drain. Now fill the bowl halfway with hot water and let it sit at room temperature, covered with plastic wrap, until the peas soften, at least 8 hours or as long as overnight.

2. Drain the pigeon peas and transfer them to a pressure cooker. Add 4 cups water and bring it to a boil, uncovered, over high heat. Skim off and discard any foam that forms on the surface. Add the kokum, Ginger Paste, and Garlic Paste. Seal the cooker shut and allow the pressure to build up. When the cooker reaches full pressure, reduce the heat to medium-low and cook for about 1 hour. Remove the cooker from the heat and allow the pressure to subside naturally (about 15 minutes) before opening the lid.

3. Meanwhile, heat the ghee in a small skillet over medium-high heat. Add the mustard seeds, cover the skillet, and cook until the seeds have stopped popping (not unlike popcorn), about 30 seconds. Then stir in the cumin seeds, asafetida, and turmeric, which will instantly sizzle and smell aromatic. Remove the skillet from the heat.

4. When the pigeon peas are done, add the ingredients from the skillet. Stir in the tomato, cilantro, salt, and curry leaves. Boil vigorously over medium-high heat, uncovered, stirring occasionally, until the curry has absorbed the flavors and the sauce has thickened slightly, about 10 minutes. (The sauce will never really thicken much. If you prefer a thicker sauce, mash a few of the pigeon peas.) Then serve.

Kokum? See the Glossary of Ingredients, page 758.

Pigeon Peas
WITH CHILES AND JAGGERY

toovar nu dal

Every Gujarati-speaking household with roots in India's northwest has a version of *Toovar nu dal.* The spices vary ever so slightly among households, but the creamy, sweet-hot combination always includes pungent chiles and sweet jaggery. (Sometimes white granulated sugar is used instead, but I prefer the complex, molasses-like jaggery, which you can find in any store that stocks Indian groceries—or failing that, dark brown sugar.) **MAKES 4 CUPS**

1 cup oily or unoily skinned split yellow
    pigeon peas (toovar dal),
    picked over for stones

2 pieces dried black kokum
    (each roughly 2 inches long
    and 1 inch wide; see Tip)

1 tablespoon Ghee (page 21) or canola oil

1 teaspoon black or yellow mustard seeds

1 teaspoon cumin seeds

½ teaspoon fenugreek seeds

¼ teaspoon ground asafetida

1 tablespoon finely chopped fresh ginger

12 to 15 medium-size to large fresh curry leaves

4 fresh green Thai, cayenne, or serrano chiles,
    stems removed, slit in half lengthwise
    (do not remove the seeds)

1 medium-size tomato, cored and finely chopped

2 tablespoons finely chopped fresh cilantro
    leaves and tender stems

I tablespoon crumbled (or chopped) jaggery
   or firmly packed dark brown sugar
1 ½ teaspoons coarse kosher or sea salt
¼ teaspoon ground turmeric

1. Place the pigeon peas in a medium-size saucepan. Fill the pan halfway with water and rinse the peas by rubbing them between your fingertips. The water will become cloudy. Drain this water. Repeat three or four times, until the water remains relatively clear; drain. Now add 3 cups water and the kokum, and bring to a boil, uncovered, over medium-high heat. Skim off and discard any foam that forms on the surface. Reduce the heat to medium-low, cover the pan, and simmer, stirring occasionally, until the peas are tender, 20 to 25 minutes.

2. While the pigeon peas are cooking, heat a small skillet over medium-high heat and pour in the ghee. Add the mustard seeds, cover the skillet, and cook until the seeds have stopped popping (not unlike popcorn), about 30 seconds. Then stir in the cumin seeds, fenugreek seeds, asafetida, and ginger, and cook, stirring constantly, until the ginger turns golden brown and is fragrant, about 30 seconds. Pour in ½ cup water and remove the skillet from the heat.

3. Remove the kokum slices from the cooked pigeon peas, and discard them. (The Gujaratis prefer not to darken the dal and hence remove the kokum. You may choose to keep it in if a darker-colored dal is not a concern.) Transfer half the pigeon peas, with half their cooking water, to a blender and puree until smooth. Pour this creamy blend into a bowl. Repeat with the remaining peas and water. Return all the puree to the saucepan. (If you have an immersion blender, you can puree all the peas and water right in the saucepan.) Pour the contents of the skillet into the puree, making sure to scrape up every bit of spice from the skillet. Then

stir in the curry leaves, chiles, tomato, cilantro, jaggery, salt, and turmeric.

4. Cover the pan and simmer the dal over medium-low heat, stirring occasionally, until it has absorbed the flavors, 5 to 7 minutes. Then serve.

Tip: I find that the fruit of a very firm unripe dark plum is an acceptable alternative if black kokum is not on hand. Mangosteen, a close relative of kokum, is available in Chinese grocery stores at certain times of the year; it works well to provide a tart alternative. Dried tamarind pulp, just one or two similar-size pieces, works too. I don't care for the clean, crisp tartness of lime or lemon juice—they don't have that earthy aftermath found in kokum and tamarind.

Cumin-Scented Pigeon Peas
WITH MANGO

Ambyachi dal

If you are ever in Mumbai at the peak of mango season—especially when the sweet Alphonso variety abounds in the markets—try this dal. In the U.S., I find that the variety known as champagne mango—light yellow skin; firm, juicy, sweet pulp; not too fibrous—is a suitable stand-in. This sweet curry actually has a chile-aftermath, thanks to the garam masala. **MAKES 4 CUPS**

*I cup oily or unoily skinned split yellow pigeon peas
(toovar dal), picked over for stones*

*I medium-size firm, ripe mango, peeled, seeded,
and coarsely chopped (see box, page 641)*

*2 tablespoons Maharashtrian garam masala
(page 28)*

I½ teaspoons coarse kosher or sea salt

½ teaspoon ground turmeric

10 to 12 medium-size to large fresh curry leaves

2 tablespoons Ghee (page 21) or canola oil

2 teaspoons cumin seeds

*¼ cup finely chopped fresh cilantro leaves
and tender stems*

1. Place the pigeon peas in a medium-size saucepan. Fill the pan halfway with water and rinse the peas by rubbing them between your fingertips. The water will become cloudy. Drain this water. Repeat three or four times, until the water remains relatively clear; drain. Now add 3 cups water and bring to a boil, uncovered, over medium-high heat. Skim off and discard any foam that forms on the surface. Reduce the heat to medium-low, cover the pan, and simmer, stirring occasionally, until the peas are partially tender, about 10 minutes.

2. Add the mango, garam masala, salt, turmeric, curry leaves, and 1 cup water to the partially cooked dal. Stir once or twice and continue to cook, covered, stirring occasionally, until the pigeon peas and mango are very tender, 15 to 20 minutes.

3. While the mixture is simmering, heat the ghee in a medium-size skillet over medium-high heat. Add the cumin seeds and cook until they sizzle, turn reddish brown, and smell nutty, 5 to 10 seconds. Immediately remove the skillet from the heat and carefully throw in the cilantro (it will crackle as it transitions from its harsh flavor, which a few find obtrusive, to a gentle, mellow, we-can-all-get-along self).

4. When the pigeon peas and mango are tender, coarsely mash them with the back of a cooking spoon. Scrape the seasoned ghee into the mashed dal, and stir once or twice. Continue to simmer the curry, uncovered, stirring occasionally, until the flavors harmonize, about 5 minutes. Then serve.

Tart Pigeon Peas
WITH TOMATO & MANGO POWDER

Amchur tamatar dal

notice how this curry gets its acidic gusto from two key ingredients: the tomato, which contributes a mild tartness while providing a base for the sauce, and the mango powder, which turns the red sauce muddy-brown and accentuates the sourness with its complex, puckered-lips, earthy flavor. **MAKES 4 CUPS**

*I cup oily or unoily skinned split yellow pigeon peas
(toovar dal), picked over for stones*

2 tablespoons Ghee (page 21) or canola oil

I teaspoon cumin seeds

¼ teaspoon ground asafetida

*I small red onion, cut in half lengthwise
and thinly sliced*

*2 fresh green Thai, cayenne, or serrano chiles,
stems removed, cut in half lengthwise
(do not remove the seeds)*

I large tomato, cored and finely chopped

I tablespoon mango powder or fresh lime juice

I½ teaspoons coarse kosher or sea salt

¼ teaspoon ground turmeric

*2 tablespoons finely chopped fresh cilantro
leaves and tender stems for garnishing*

Mango powder? See the Glossary of Ingredients, page 758.

1. Place the pigeon peas in a medium-size saucepan. Fill the pan halfway with water and rinse the peas by rubbing them between your fingertips. The water will become cloudy. Drain this water. Repeat three or four times, until the water remains relatively clear; drain. Now add 3 cups water and bring to a boil, uncovered, over medium-high heat. Skim off and discard any foam that forms on the surface. Reduce the heat to medium-low, cover the pan, and simmer, stirring occasionally, until the peas are tender, about 20 minutes.

2. While the pigeon peas are cooking, heat a small skillet over medium-high heat, and pour in the ghee. Add the cumin seeds and cook until they sizzle and turn reddish brown, about 5 seconds. Then sprinkle in the asafetida, and add the onion and chiles. Stir-fry until the onion slices are light brown around the edges, 2 to 4 minutes.

3. Add the tomato, mango powder, salt, and turmeric. (If you are using lime juice instead of mango powder, don't add it here.) Cook, stirring occasionally, until the tomato has softened and appears saucelike but is still chunky, 2 to 3 minutes. Set this sauce aside.

4. Transfer half of the cooked pigeon peas, with half of their cooking water, to a blender and puree until smooth. Pour this creamy blend into a bowl. Repeat with the remaining peas and water. Then return all the pureed peas to the saucepan. (If you have an immersion blender, you can puree all the pigeon peas and water right in the saucepan.)

5. Add the onion-tomato sauce to the pureed pigeon peas and bring to a boil over medium heat. Reduce the heat to medium-low, cover the pan, and simmer, stirring occasionally, until the dal absorbs the flavors from the sauce, 5 to 8 minutes. Stir in the lime juice, if using.

6. Sprinkle with the cilantro, and serve.

COCONUT-SMOTHERED
Pigeon Peas
WITH PUMPKIN

Arrachay Uttu Sambhar

When my mother made steamed rice cakes (page 115), she usually prepared this legume curry to go along with them, altering the vegetables to fit the season (as you should). Any vegetables will fit the bill, especially if they are the root variety. We all loved the vegetable called "drumsticks," but it was my brother Bhaskar who always ended up with the biggest pile of fibrous sticks on his plate. We teased him about being as slender as a drumstick.

MAKES 8 CUPS

½ cup oily or unoily skinned split yellow pigeon peas (toovar dal), picked over for stones

1 walnut-size ball dried tamarind pulp, or 1 teaspoon tamarind paste or concentrate

2 teaspoons Sambhar masala (page 33)

½ teaspoon ground asafetida

1 cup cut-up cauliflower (2-inch florets)

4 ounces fresh pumpkin, cut into 1-inch cubes

10 to 12 pieces frozen "drumsticks" (each 3 to 4 inches long; no need to thaw; see box, page 489)

15 to 20 medium-size to large fresh curry leaves

2 tablespoons unrefined sesame oil or canola oil

¼ cup raw cashew nuts

1 tablespoon coriander seeds

4 dried red Thai or cayenne chiles, stems removed

1 cup shredded fresh coconut; or ½ cup shredded dried unsweetened coconut, reconstituted (see Note)

1 teaspoon black or yellow mustard seeds

1½ teaspoons coarse kosher or sea salt

1. Place the pigeon peas in a small saucepan. Fill the pan halfway with water and rinse the peas by rubbing them between your fingertips. The water will become cloudy. Drain this water. Repeat three or four times, until the water remains relatively clear; drain. Now add 2 cups water and bring it to a boil, uncovered, over medium-high heat. Skim off and discard any foam that forms on the surface. Reduce the heat to medium-low, cover the pan, and simmer, stirring occasionally, until the peas are tender, about 20 minutes.

2. While the pigeon peas are cooking, pour 4 cups water into a medium-size saucepan. *If you are using the ball of tamarind,* add it to the water and allow it to soften, 15 to 20 minutes. Then, using your fingers, break it apart and coax the pulp to leach and dissolve into the water as you massage the pieces. Once the water is light chocolate-brown and tastes tart, strain it through a fine-mesh strainer to separate out the pulp and any fibers; discard the pulp and fibers. Reserve the tamarind-infused water. *If you are using tamarind paste,* simply whisk it into the water to dissolve it.

3. Sprinkle the *Sambhar masala* and asafetida over the tamarind water. Add the cauliflower, pumpkin, "drumsticks," and curry leaves. Heat to a boil. Then reduce the heat to medium and simmer the thin brothlike curry, uncovered, stirring occasionally, until the vegetables are fork-tender, 15 to 20 minutes.

4. When the pigeon peas are tender, set the saucepan aside.

5. Heat 1 tablespoon of the oil in a small skillet over medium-high heat. Add the cashews, coriander seeds, and chiles, and stir-fry until the nuts and seeds turn reddish brown and the chiles blacken, 1 to 2 minutes. Scrape the skillet's contents into a blender jar, and add ½ cup water and the coconut. Puree, scraping the inside of the jar as needed, to form a slightly gritty paste. Add

this paste to the pumpkin mixture. Pour ½ cup water into the blender jar, swish it around to wash the jar out, and add this to the pumpkin mixture.

6. Heat the remaining 1 tablespoon oil in the same skillet over medium-high heat. Add the mustard seeds, cover the skillet, and cook until the seeds have stopped popping (not unlike popcorn), about 30 seconds. Add this spiced oil to the pumpkin mixture.

7. Transfer the cooked pigeon peas, with their cooking water, to a blender and puree, scraping the inside of the jar as needed, until smooth. (If you have an immersion blender, you can puree the peas and water right in the saucepan.) Pour this thin, creamy-yellow broth into the pumpkin mixture, and add the salt. Bring to a boil and then reduce the heat. Simmer, uncovered, stirring occasionally, until the flavors blend, about 5 minutes. Then serve.

Note: To reconstitute coconut, cover with ½ cup boiling water, set aside for about 15 minutes, and then drain.

Shallots
WITH PIGEON PEAS & COCONUT MILK

Chinnay Vengayam thengapaal Sambhar

this curry demonstrates a technique that is common in the cuisine of Kerala: separating the thin coconut milk from the thick, and using the two at different points in cooking the dish. The thin milk stews early on in the curry to absorb the simple spices and herbs, while the thick milk finishes the dish with a creamy aftermath. Ladle this over a small bowl of cooked white rice for a soup course, or double the portion and savor it as the one-dish main event for a quiet night alone. **MAKES 5 CUPS**

½ cup oily or unoily skinned split yellow pigeon peas (toovar dal), picked over for stones

1 can (13.5 ounces) unsweetened coconut milk (do not shake the can before opening it)

2 tablespoons unrefined sesame oil, coconut oil, or canola oil

1 teaspoon black or yellow mustard seeds

10 to 12 medium-size to large shallots, thinly sliced

12 to 15 medium-size to large fresh curry leaves

2 fresh green Thai, cayenne, or serrano chiles, stems removed, cut in half lengthwise (do not remove the seeds)

2 dried red Thai or cayenne chiles, stems removed

1½ teaspoons coarse kosher or sea salt

½ teaspoon ground turmeric

½ teaspoon black peppercorns, coarsely cracked

1 large tomato, cored and finely chopped

3 lengthwise slices fresh ginger (each 2½ inches long, 1 inch wide, and ⅛ inch thick), cut into matchstick-thin strips (julienne)

2 tablespoons finely chopped fresh cilantro leaves and tender stems

1. Place the pigeon peas in a small saucepan. Fill the pan halfway with water and rinse the peas by rubbing them between your fingertips. The water will become cloudy. Drain this water. Repeat three or four times, until the water remains relatively clear; drain. Now add 2 cups water and bring it to a boil, uncovered, over medium-high heat. Skim off and discard any foam that forms on the surface. Reduce the heat to medium-low, cover the pan, and simmer, stirring occasionally, until the peas are tender, about 20 minutes.

2. While the pigeon peas are cooking, open the can of coconut milk without shaking it. Carefully scoop out the top thick part of the milk and set it aside for later use. Pour the remaining watery-thin coconut milk into a measuring cup and add enough water to make 2 cups. Set this aside too.

3. Heat the oil in a medium-size saucepan over medium-high heat. Add the mustard seeds, cover the pan, and cook until the seeds have stopped popping (not unlike popcorn), about 30 seconds. Then add the shallots, curry leaves, and fresh and dried chiles. Stir-fry until the shallots turn light brown around the edges, 3 to 5 minutes.

4. Stir in the salt, turmeric, cracked peppercorns, and the thin coconut milk. Heat to a boil and cook, uncovered, stirring occasionally, until the flavors blend, 5 to 10 minutes.

5. Transfer the cooked pigeon peas, with their cooking water, to a blender and puree, scraping the inside of the jar as needed, until smooth. (If you have an immersion blender, you can puree the peas and water right in the saucepan.)

6. Pour the pureed pigeon peas into the shallot mixture, and add the tomato and ginger. Continue to simmer, uncovered, stirring occasionally, until the liquid in the curry is reduced by about 1 cup, 15 to 20 minutes.

7. Stir in the thick coconut milk and the cilantro. As soon as the curry has returned to a boil, remove the pan from the heat and serve.

Tip: To separate thick and thin coconut milk, place the can in the refrigerator and let it chill for about 1 hour. The thicker part will congeal at the top, leaving underneath a wheylike liquid that resembles a frozen lake in the dead of winter.

Slow-Cooked Onion

WITH PIGEON PEAS

dal fry

Some versions of *dal fry* literally swim in clarified butter. Fried onions make up part of the flavor base, along with the cooked dal that "fries" in additional ghee, all of which comes together to make an unhealthy, but mighty tasty, curry. This low-fat version is my sister Mathangi's favorite, and she makes it at least once a week because her family asks for it at every meal.

MAKES 4 CUPS

1 cup oily or unoily skinned split yellow pigeon peas
    (toovar dal), picked over for stones

2 tablespoons Ghee (page 21) or canola oil

1 teaspoon black or yellow mustard seeds

1 small red onion, cut in half lengthwise
    and thinly sliced

4 fresh green Thai, cayenne, or serrano chiles,
    stems removed, cut crosswise into ½-inch-thick
    slices (do not remove the seeds)

1½ teaspoons coarse kosher or sea salt

1 teaspoon cumin seeds, ground

½ teaspoon fenugreek seeds, ground

½ teaspoon black or yellow mustard seeds, ground

¼ teaspoon ground turmeric

1 medium-size tomato, cored and finely chopped

¼ cup finely chopped fresh cilantro leaves and
    tender stems

12 to 15 medium-size to large fresh curry leaves

1. Place the pigeon peas in a medium-size saucepan. Fill the pan halfway with water and rinse the peas by rubbing them between your fingertips. The water will become cloudy. Drain this water. Repeat three or four times, until the water remains relatively clear; drain. Now add 3 cups water and bring to a boil, uncovered, over medium-high heat. Skim off and discard any foam that forms on the surface. Reduce the heat to medium-low, cover the pan, and simmer, stirring occasionally, until the peas are tender, about 20 minutes.

2. While the pigeon peas are cooking, heat a medium-size skillet over medium-high heat and pour in the ghee. Add the mustard seeds, cover the skillet, and cook until the seeds have stopped popping (not unlike popcorn), about 30 seconds. Then add the onion and chiles and lower the heat to medium. Stir-fry until the onion is soft and honey-brown with a deep purple hue, 8 to 10 minutes.

3. Stir in the salt and the ground cumin, fenugreek, mustard, and turmeric. The heat from the onion will be just right to cook the ground spices without burning them, 5 to 10 seconds. Then add the tomato, cilantro, and curry leaves. Cook, uncovered, stirring occasionally, until the tomato has softened but is still firm-looking, 2 to 4 minutes.

4. Transfer the cooked pigeon peas, with their cooking water, to a blender and puree, scraping the inside of the jar as needed, until smooth. Pour this creamy-yellow dal back into the saucepan, and fold in the chunky tomato sauce. If some of the sauce is stuck to the bottom of the skillet, spoon some of the dal into the skillet and scrape the bottom to release the collected bits of spice and tomato; add this to the dal.

5. Lower the heat to medium, cover the pan, and simmer, stirring occasionally, to allow the flavors to get familiar with each other, about 5 minutes. Then serve.

Spicy Pigeon Peas

WITH TOMATOES AND BROWNED ONIONS

hyderabadi toor dal

Color of the setting sun, this orange-yellow curry is smooth, creamy, and stick-to-your-ribs tasty. I like to eat curries like this with thin flatbreads like rotis (page 727) or with warmed store-bought whole-wheat tortillas. For an unusual first course, serve a bowlful of this dal surrounded by slices of toasted French bread, commonly referred to as crostini. Instruct your guests to dunk the toasts in the dal and savor every crunchy, creamy bite. **MAKES 4 CUPS**

1 cup oily or unoily skinned split yellow pigeon peas (toovar dal), picked over for stones

2 tablespoons Ghee (page 21) or canola oil

1 teaspoon black or yellow mustard seeds

1 cup finely chopped red onion

2 tablespoons Ginger Paste (page 15)

1 tablespoon Garlic Paste (page 15)

12 to 15 medium-size to large fresh curry leaves

1 large tomato, cored and finely chopped

1½ teaspoons coarse kosher or sea salt

1 teaspoon ground Kashmiri chiles; or ¼ teaspoon cayenne (ground red pepper) mixed with ¾ teaspoon sweet paprika

½ teaspoon ground turmeric

1. Place the pigeon peas in a pressure cooker. Fill the cooker halfway with water and rinse the peas by rubbing them between your fingertips. The water may appear slightly dirty. Drain this water. Repeat three or four times, until the water remains relatively clear; drain. Now add 3 cups water and bring to a boil, uncovered, over high heat. Skim off and discard any foam that forms on the surface. Seal the cooker shut and allow the pressure to build up. When the cooker reaches full pressure, reduce the heat to medium-low and cook for about 10 minutes. Remove the cooker from the heat and allow the pressure to subside naturally (about 15 minutes) before opening the lid.

2. Meanwhile, heat the ghee in a medium-size skillet over medium-high heat. Add the mustard seeds, cover the skillet, and cook until the seeds have stopped popping (not unlike popcorn), about 30 seconds. Immediately add the onion, ginger and garlic pastes, and curry leaves. Stir-fry until the onion is light brown around the edges, 3 to 5 minutes.

3. Stir in the tomato, salt, ground chiles, and turmeric. Cook, uncovered, stirring occasionally, until the tomato is softened but still firm-looking, 2 to 3 minutes. Set the mixture aside until the pigeon peas are done.

4. Add the tomato mixture to the cooked pigeon peas. Pour ½ cup water into the skillet and scrape the bottom to deglaze it, releasing any remaining bits of sauce. Add this to the peas.

5. Continue to simmer the curry over medium heat, uncovered, stirring occasionally, until the flavors mingle, 3 to 5 minutes. Then serve.

Tip: Split pigeon peas are relatively quick-cooking legumes and usually do not require a pressure cooker. The reason I used a pressure cooker here was to create a creamy, smooth texture without having to puree the peas. The intense heat in the cooker breaks them down to a saucy consistency within minutes, without the need of a blender—one less piece of equipment to clean.

Buttery Pigeon Peas
WITH TURMERIC

ŋayee boram ɲaruppu

It's amusing to see the importance given to this one-spice curry. It is the first solid food fed to babies, especially in south Indian homes. It is also the first course at weddings and special religious functions, where it is ladled over steamed rice mounded on lush banana leaves. "Simply flavorful," my dear friend and fellow cookbook author Mary Evans stated at lunch one day. It reminded her of the split pea soup with ham hock from her childhood, even though this curry has no meat in it. Why? Because ghee, clarified over low heat, has a smoky, nutty taste and when added as a finishing flavor, it is easy to understand the resemblance to musky ham hocks. **MAKES 3 CUPS**

*1 cup oily or unoily skinned split yellow pigeon peas
(toovar dal), picked over for stones
1½ teaspoons coarse kosher or sea salt
½ teaspoon ground turmeric
2 tablespoons Ghee (page 21)*

1. Place the pigeon peas in a medium-size saucepan. Fill the pan halfway with water and rinse the peas by rubbing them between your fingertips. The water will become cloudy. Drain this water. Repeat three or four times, until the water remains relatively clear; drain. Now add 3 cups water and bring to a boil, uncovered, over medium-high heat. Skim off and discard any foam that forms on the surface. Reduce the heat to medium-low, cover the pan, and simmer, stirring occasionally, until the peas are tender, 20 to 25 minutes.

2. Transfer half the cooked pigeon peas, with half their cooking water, to a blender and puree until smooth. Pour this creamy blend into a bowl. Repeat with the remaining peas and water. Return all the puree to the saucepan. (If you have an immersion blender, you can puree all the peas and water right in the saucepan.)

3. Stir in the salt and turmeric. If you wish to thicken the dal a bit more, return it to medium heat and simmer, uncovered, for 3 to 5 minutes.

4. Drizzle in the ghee, and serve.

Tips:

❖ I normally give an alternative for ghee in a recipe, especially if you use it for stir-frying spices or other ingredients. But in this dish there is no alternative. In fact, if you want to splurge, go ahead and drizzle an extra tablespoon or two of ghee over the dal.

❖ The perfect accompaniment for this dal is boiled white rice. For a simple lunch, serve it with Green Beans with Tomato (page 511).

Unripe Mango
WITH PIGEON PEAS

khatte Aam boor ki dal

My dear friend R. J., more affectionately called Molu, remembers this dal from his boyhood days at a boarding school in Dehradun, a city nestled in the Himalayas. Proud agricultural center for world-renowned basmati rice, green and black tea, and sweetly succulent lychee fruit, it is no wonder that this mountain resort became a mecca for the British rulers during the oppressive summer months. I especially enjoy the flavors in this dish, made sweet-tart by stewing unripe mango with pigeon peas, and with a fiery aftermath from the abundance of chiles. You can reduce the number of chiles by two or three—but remember that when this is served over steamed basmati rice (a natural companion), the starch in the rice will mask some of the chiles' potency. **MAKES 4 CUPS**

1 cup oily or unoily skinned split yellow pigeon peas (toovar dal), picked over for stones

1 medium-size rock-firm unripe mango, peeled, seeded, and coarsely chopped (see box, page 641)

2 tablespoons Ghee (page 21) or canola oil

2 teaspoon cumin seeds, 1 teaspoon left whole, 1 teaspoon ground

6 green or white cardamom pods

1 small red onion, cut in half lengthwise and thinly sliced

8 to 10 fresh green Thai, cayenne, or serrano chiles, to taste, stems removed, cut in half lengthwise, each half cut into long, thin strips (do not remove the seeds)

3 lengthwise slices fresh ginger (each 2½ inches long, 1 inch wide, and ⅛ inch thick), cut into matchstick-thin strips (julienne)

¼ cup finely chopped fresh cilantro leaves and tender stems

2 teaspoons coarse kosher or sea salt

1 teaspoon coriander seeds, ground

½ teaspoon ground turmeric

1. Place the pigeon peas in a medium-size saucepan. Fill the pan halfway with water and rinse the peas by rubbing them between your fingertips. The water will become cloudy. Drain this water. Repeat three or four times, until the water remains relatively clear; drain. Now add 3 cups water and bring to a boil, uncovered, over medium-high heat. Skim off and discard any foam that forms on the surface. Reduce the heat to medium-low, cover the pan, and simmer, stirring occasionally, until the peas are partially tender, about 10 minutes.

2. Add the mango and 1 cup water to the partially cooked dal. Stir once or twice, cover the pan, and continue to cook, stirring occasionally, until the pigeon peas and mango are very tender, 15 to 20 minutes.

3. While the peas and mango are simmering, heat the ghee in a medium-size skillet over medium-high heat. Add the whole cumin seeds and the cardamom pods, and cook until the seeds turn reddish brown and the pods smell fragrant, 5 to 10 seconds. Then add the onion, chiles, and ginger, and stir-fry until the onion is lightly browned and the chiles are pungent, 3 to 5 minutes.

4. Add the cilantro, salt, the ground cumin, coriander and turmeric. Stir-fry until the ground spices are cooked, about 1 minute. Set aside.

5. Transfer half the cooked pigeon peas, mango, and cooking water to a blender, and puree until smooth. Pour this creamy blend into a bowl. Repeat with the remaining peas, mango, and water. Return all the puree to the saucepan. (If you have an immersion blender, you can puree all the peas, mango, and water right in the saucepan.)

6. Scrape the contents of the skillet into the dal, and bring it to a boil over medium heat. Then reduce the heat to medium-low, cover the pan, and simmer, stirring occasionally, until the dal absorbs the flavors, 5 to 8 minutes. Then serve.

Pigeon Peas and Peanuts
WITH JAGGERY

toovar mandvishing nu dal

I love the textural difference between the soft, almost creamy-tender pigeon peas and the crunchy peanuts in this curry.

MAKES 6 CUPS

1 cup oily or unoily skinned split yellow pigeon peas (toovar dal), picked over for stones

½ cup raw peanuts (without the skin)

2 cups chopped fresh or frozen fenugreek leaves (no need to thaw if frozen); or ½ cup dried fenugreek leaves, soaked in a bowl of water and skimmed off before use (see box, page 473)

½ cup shredded fresh coconut; or ¼ cup shredded dried unsweetened coconut, reconstituted (see Note)

1 tablespoon crumbled (or chopped) jaggery or firmly packed dark brown sugar

1½ teaspoons coarse kosher or sea salt

1 teaspoon tamarind paste or concentrate

¼ teaspoon ground turmeric

4 to 6 fresh green Thai, cayenne, or serrano chiles, to taste, stems removed, slit in half lengthwise (do not remove the seeds)

2 tablespoons Ghee (page 21) or canola oil

1 teaspoon black or yellow mustard seeds

¼ teaspoon ground asafetida

1. Place the pigeon peas and the peanuts in a medium-size saucepan. Fill the pan halfway with water and rinse the peas by rubbing them between your fingertips. The water will become cloudy. Drain this water. Repeat three or four times, until the water remains relatively clear; drain. Now add 4 cups water and bring it to a boil, uncovered, over medium-high heat. Skim off and discard any foam that forms on the surface. Stir in the fenugreek leaves. Reduce the heat to medium-low, cover the pan, and simmer, stirring occasionally, until the pigeon peas are tender, 20 to 25 minutes.

2. Stir in the coconut, jaggery, salt, tamarind paste, turmeric, and chiles. Continue to simmer the dal, still over medium-low heat, uncovered, stirring occasionally, until the flavors meld, about 5 minutes.

3. Heat the ghee in a small skillet over medium-high heat. Add the mustard seeds, cover the skillet, and cook until the seeds have stopped popping (not unlike popcorn), about 30 seconds. Sprinkle in the asafetida. Pour this into the dal, and serve.

Note: To reconstitute coconut, cover with ¼ cup boiling water, set aside for about 15 minutes, and then drain.

Jaggery? See the Glossary of Ingredients, page 758.

Peppery Pigeon Peas
WITH GARLIC AND CUMIN

menalina saru

Jyotsana Rayadurgh—petite, sharp, highly intelligent, and very friendly—handed me a piece of paper in the parking lot of our children's school one nippy day. "My mother used to make this all the time when we had a cold back in Karnataka," she said as she chased after her beautiful daughters, Shruti and Aditi, into the warm school building. (Karnataka, south of Maharashtra and north of Kerala, is home to Bangalore, India's Silicon Valley.) When I felt the onset of a stuffy nose a few days later, I tried her recipe: The peppery aromas freed up my olfactory canals and the flavors provided soothing comfort. I guess mothers know it all, no matter where they live. And no, you don't have to wait until you are sick to savor this. It's great anytime.

MAKES 4 CUPS

1 cup oily or unoily skinned split yellow pigeon peas (toovar dal), picked over for stones

2 large tomatoes, cored and cut into 1-inch cubes

1 tablespoon cumin seeds

2 teaspoons black peppercorns

1½ teaspoons rock salt

4 medium-size garlic cloves

2 tablespoons Ghee (page 21) or butter

3 to 5 dried red Thai or cayenne chiles, to taste, stems removed

2 tablespoons finely chopped fresh cilantro leaves and tender stems for garnishing

1. Place the pigeon peas in a medium-size saucepan. Fill the pan halfway with water and rinse the peas by rubbing them between your fingertips. The water will become cloudy. Drain this water. Repeat three or four times, until the water remains relatively clear; drain. Now add 3 cups water and bring to a boil, uncovered, over medium-high heat. Skim off and discard any foam that forms on the surface. Stir in the tomatoes. Reduce the heat to medium-low, cover the pan, and simmer, stirring occasionally, until the peas are tender, about 20 minutes.

Rock salt? See the Glossary of Ingredients, page 758.

2. While the pigeon peas are cooking, combine the cumin seeds, peppercorns, rock salt, and garlic in a food processor. Process to form a damp, coarse, potent-smelling blend.

3. Heat the ghee in a small skillet over medium-high heat. Add the chiles and cook until they are slightly blackened, 30 seconds to 1 minute. Then add the peppery blend from the processor, and stir-fry until the mixture sizzles and smells nutty-pungent, and the garlic turns light brown (its color will be hard to detect because of all the black pepper, but you will distinctly smell the aromas), 1 to 2 minutes.

4. Once the pigeon peas are tender, add the chile mixture. Scoop a spoonful of the liquid into the skillet to wash it out, and add the washings to the pan. Raise the heat to medium-high and simmer the curry, uncovered, stirring occasionally, until the flavors mingle, about 5 minutes.

5. Sprinkle with the cilantro, and serve.

Cabbage and Plantains
WITH PIGEON PEAS AND BUTTERMILK

Muttaikose Vazhaipazham kootu

Criteria for a Tamilian *kootu* are not too many: one, two, or as many vegetables as you want to get rid of from the refrigerator; pigeon peas, split green lentils, or yellow split peas as the protein; a coconut- or spice-based sauce; and a *tadka* (whole or ground spices sizzled in hot oil), usually of black mustard seeds and fresh curry leaves. I have included four *kootus* in this section, two with split green lentils (pages 386 and 391) and the other with yellow split peas (page 418). Here, to complete the legume quartet, I've included a *kootu* with pigeon peas. I have swirled in an additional ingredient for tartness—buttermilk. Hope you enjoy it as much as I do. **MAKES 6 CUPS**

> 1 cup oily or unoily skinned split yellow pigeon peas (toovar dal), picked over for stones
> 1 small to medium-size very firm plantain
> 1 cup shredded cabbage
> ½ cup buttermilk
> 2 tablespoons heavy (whipping) cream
> 1 cup shredded fresh coconut; or ½ cup shredded dried unsweetened coconut, reconstituted (see Note)
> 1½ teaspoons coarse kosher or sea salt
> 1 teaspoon black peppercorns
> 4 to 6 dried red Thai or cayenne chiles, to taste, stems removed
> 2 tablespoons coconut oil or canola oil
> 1 teaspoon black or yellow mustard seeds
> 10 to 12 medium-size to large fresh curry leaves

1. Place the pigeon peas in a small saucepan. Fill the pan halfway with water and rinse the peas by rubbing them between your fingertips. The water will become cloudy. Drain this water. Repeat three or four times, until the water remains relatively clear; drain. Now add 4 cups water and bring it to a boil, uncovered, over medium-high heat. Skim off and discard any foam that forms on the surface. Reduce the heat to medium-low, cover the pan, and simmer, stirring occasionally, until the peas are tender, about 20 minutes.

2. As soon as the pigeon peas start to simmer, slice off the stem and heel ends of the plantain (about ¼-inch-thick slices). Cut the plantain in half crosswise. Then, using a paring knife, make a lengthwise slit, ⅛ to ¼ inch deep, in each half. Wedge your fingers just under the slit and peel the skin off in one easy motion. (You can remove the skin with a paring knife, but it is slightly more time-consuming.) Cut the plantain flesh into ½-inch cubes, and add them to the simmering pigeon peas. Add the cabbage too. (If you add the vegetables within 5 minutes of the peas' starting to simmer, the vegetables and peas will finish cooking at the same time.)

3. While they are cooking, pour the buttermilk into a blender jar, followed by the cream (buttermilk's stabilizer), coconut, salt, peppercorns, and chiles. Puree, scraping the inside of the jar as needed, to make a gritty, red-speckled sauce. Some of the peppercorns will be cracked, releasing a slap-in-your-face peppery aroma.

4. When the vegetables and pigeon peas are tender, add the buttermilk mixture and stir once or twice. Continue to simmer, uncovered, stirring occasionally, until the flavors mix, about 5 minutes.

5. Heat the oil in a small skillet over medium-high heat. Add the mustard seeds, cover the skillet, and cook until the seeds have stopped popping (not unlike popcorn), about 30 seconds. Remove the pan from the heat and throw in the curry leaves (carefully, as they will spatter on contact). Pour this spiked oil mixture into the *kootu*, stir once or twice, and serve.

Note: To reconstitute coconut, cover with ½ cup boiling water, set aside for about 15 minutes, and then drain.

Ökra and Shallots
WITH PIGEON PEAS AND TAMARIND

Vendakkai Kozhumbu

Some call it *sambhar*, while others call it *kozhumbu*—these Tamil words are used interchangeably for a stewlike curry made 365 days a year in south Indian home kitchens. So you can understand why I reach for this comforting curry whenever I want to hark back to my childhood days. Serve it over boiled white rice. A tablespoon of ghee drizzled on top is optional (especially if you are watching your calories), but boy, it sure brings it home to mama! **MAKES 4 CUPS**

½ cup oily or unoily skinned split yellow pigeon peas (toovar dal), picked over for stones

1 pound fresh okra, rinsed and thoroughly dried

2 tablespoons unrefined sesame oil or canola oil

1 teaspoon black or yellow mustard seeds

1 cup thinly sliced shallots

1 teaspoon tamarind paste or concentrate

1 tablespoon Sambhar masala (page 33)

1½ teaspoons coarse kosher or sea salt

½ teaspoon ground turmeric

½ teaspoon ground asafetida

12 to 15 medium-size to large fresh curry leaves

2 tablespoons finely chopped fresh cilantro leaves and tender stems

Asafetida? See the **Glossary of Ingredients,** page 758.

1. Place the pigeon peas in a small saucepan. Fill the pan halfway with water and rinse the peas by rubbing them between your fingertips. The water will become cloudy. Drain this water. Repeat three or four times, until the water remains relatively clear; drain. Now add 2 cups water and bring it to a boil, uncovered, over medium-high heat. Skim off and discard any foam that forms on the surface. Reduce the heat to medium-low, cover the pan, and simmer, stirring occasionally, until the peas are tender, about 20 minutes.

2. While the pigeon peas are cooking, slice the caps off the okra without cutting into the pods, and then cut the pods into 1-inch-long pieces.

3. Heat the oil in a large saucepan over medium-high heat. Add the mustard seeds, cover the pan, and cook until the seeds have stopped popping (not unlike popcorn), about 30 seconds. Add the okra and stir-fry until it blisters in spots and the ridged skin is lightly browned, 8 to 10 minutes. Halfway through the stir-frying, toss in the shallots. By the time the okra is ready, the shallots will have turned limp and light brown (as opposed to dark brown and burned if they were added at the same time as the okra).

4. Meanwhile, pour 3 cups water into a bowl and add the tamarind paste. Stir to dissolve it. Add the *Sambhar masala*, salt, turmeric, asafetida, and curry leaves.

5. Pour the spicy-tart tamarind concoction into the okra-shallot mixture, and scrape the bottom of the pan to deglaze it, releasing the browned bits of okra and shallots. Bring the thin curry to a boil and continue to simmer, uncovered, stirring occasionally, until the okra is fork-tender, 5 to 8 minutes.

6. Transfer the cooked pigeon peas, with their cooking water, to a blender and puree, scraping the inside of the jar as needed, until smooth. (If you have an immersion blender, you can puree the peas and water right in the saucepan.) Pour this thin, creamy-yellow broth into the okra curry, and stir in the cilantro. Cook until the flavors mingle, 1 to 2 minutes, and serve.

Tip: What constantly amazes me is how varied *sambhars* can be from day to day. Many *sambhars* contain pigeon peas, but by varying the vegetable, the taste changes significantly. There are also some legume-less *sambhars* that employ buttermilk or tamarind water as the base for the sauce.

Pureed Pigeon Peas
WITH CHILES AND MUSTARD SEEDS

kadaghu toram paruppu

In India mothers introduce their babies to the world of solid foods by spooning pureed pigeon peas, flavored with a mound of clarified butter, a hint of turmeric, and a smidgen of salt, into their mouths. Here I have taken that same offering and blown an intense burst of chiles into the creamy blend. I definitely savor this the only way I can: with a giant pyramid of cooked white rice. Don't be alarmed by the number of chiles. When you slit a chile open but do not chop it, you barely release the capsaicin that runs through the pepper's veins.

MAKES 3 CUPS

1 cup oily or unoily skinned split yellow pigeon peas
    (toovar dal), picked over for stones
2 tablespoons Ghee (page 21) or canola oil
1 teaspoon black or yellow mustard seeds
½ teaspoon ground turmeric
15 to 20 medium-size to large fresh curry leaves

8 to 10 fresh green Thai, cayenne, or serrano chiles,
    to taste, stems removed, slit in half lengthwise
    (do not remove the seeds)
2 teaspoons coarse kosher or sea salt
Juice of 1 medium-size lime

1. Place the pigeon peas in a medium-size saucepan. Fill the pan halfway with water and rinse the peas by rubbing them between your fingertips. The water will become cloudy. Drain this water. Repeat three or four times, until the water remains relatively clear; drain. Now add 3 cups water and bring to a boil, uncovered, over medium-high heat. Skim off and discard any foam that forms on the surface. Reduce the heat to medium-low, cover the pan, and simmer, stirring occasionally, until the peas are tender, 20 to 25 minutes.

2. While the pigeon peas are cooking, heat a small skillet over medium-high heat and pour in the ghee. Add the mustard seeds, cover the skillet, and cook until the seeds have stopped popping (not unlike popcorn), about 30 seconds. Remove the skillet from the heat and sprinkle in the turmeric. Carefully add the curry leaves and chiles (they will spatter). Set the mixture aside until the pigeon peas are ready.

3. Stir the salt into the cooked pigeon peas. Transfer half of the pigeon peas, with half of their cooking water, to a blender and puree until smooth. Pour this creamy blend into a bowl. Repeat with the remaining peas and water; then return all the puree to the saucepan. (If you have an immersion blender, you can puree all the peas and water right in the saucepan.) Stir the spiked ghee mixture into the puree.

4. Place the saucepan over medium-low heat and simmer, uncovered, stirring occasionally, to allow the flavorings to permeate the dal, 5 to 7 minutes.

5. Stir in the lime juice, and serve.

Tamarind Broth
WITH PUREED PIGEON PEAS AND BLACK PEPPER

molagha tanni

hearty mulligatawny soup—the English version—contains meat, stock, and vegetables. Its origin, however, the humble Tamil *molagha* (pepper) *tanni* (water), consists of just that—pepper and water—along with a few other spices, in a no-frills, complex-tasting broth. This is comfort food, poured over a bowlful of slightly starchy cooked white rice and served with a basket of flame-toasted lentil wafers (page 740).

MAKES 5 CUPS

¼ cup oily or unoily skinned split yellow
    pigeon peas (toovar dal), picked over
    for stones

4 tablespoons finely chopped fresh cilantro
    leaves and tender stems

2 teaspoons Rasam powder (page 34)

1½ teaspoons coarse kosher or sea salt

1 teaspoon tamarind paste or concentrate

½ teaspoon ground asafetida

½ teaspoon ground turmeric

15 to 20 medium-size to large fresh curry leaves

2 tablespoons Ghee (page 21) or canola oil

1 teaspoon black or yellow mustard seeds

1. Place the pigeon peas in a small saucepan. Fill the pan halfway with water and rinse the peas by rubbing them between your fingertips. The water will become cloudy. Drain this water. Repeat three or four times, until the water remains relatively clear; drain. Now add 1 cup water and bring it to a boil, uncovered, over medium-high heat. Skim off and discard any foam that forms on the surface. Reduce the heat to medium-low, cover the pan, and simmer, stirring occasionally, until the peas are tender, about 20 minutes.

2. While the pigeon peas are cooking, pour 4 cups water into a medium-size saucepan. Stir in 2 tablespoons of the cilantro and the *Rasam powder*, salt, tamarind, asafetida, turmeric, and curry leaves. Bring the broth to a boil over medium-high heat. Then lower the heat to medium and simmer vigorously, uncovered, stirring occasionally, to allow the spices to cook, about 15 minutes.

3. Transfer the cooked pigeon peas, with their cooking water, to a blender and puree, scraping the inside of the jar as needed, until smooth. (If you have an immersion blender, you can puree the peas and water right in the saucepan.)

4. Heat a small skillet over medium-high heat and pour in the ghee. Add the mustard seeds, cover the skillet, and cook until the seeds have stopped popping (not unlike popcorn), about 30 seconds. Scrape the nutty-smelling oil-seed mixture into the simmering broth, and add the creamy-yellow pigeon pea puree.

5. Sprinkle with the remaining 2 tablespoons cilantro, and serve.

Tip: You can always add tomatoes, bell peppers, and even pearl onions to contribute extra flavor and color. Add about 1 cup of cut-up vegetables to the broth in Step 2, and simmer until tender.

Pureed Pigeon Peas

WITH GROUND SPICES AND CLARIFIED BUTTER

Varan

In the Maharashtrian community, this no-frills curry is served with slightly starchy boiled white rice practically every day. When I was a young boy in Mumbai, I sampled it on many an occasion at my friend Sunil's apartment, across the hallway from ours. Back then, when it always swam in ghee, I adored its richness. Now, years later, my version is not so saturated with clarified butter and instead I find solace in the simple creaminess of the pureed pigeon peas. **MAKES 3 CUPS**

> 1 cup oily or unoily skinned split yellow
>   pigeon peas (toovar dal), picked
>   over for stones
> 2 tablespoons crumbled (or chopped) jaggery or
>   firmly packed dark brown sugar
> 1 teaspoon cayenne (ground red pepper)
> 1 teaspoon ground turmeric
> ½ teaspoon ground asafetida
> 2 tablespoons Ghee (page 21)
> 1½ teaspoons coarse kosher or sea salt

1. Place the pigeon peas in a medium-size saucepan. Fill the pan halfway with water and rinse the peas by rubbing them between your fingertips. The water will become cloudy. Drain this water. Repeat three or four times, until the water remains rela-

tively clear; drain. Now add 3 cups water and bring it to a boil, uncovered, over medium-high heat. Skim off and discard any foam that forms on the surface.

2. Stir in the jaggery, cayenne, turmeric, and asafetida. Reduce the heat to medium-low, cover the pan, and simmer, stirring occasionally, until the peas are tender, 20 to 25 minutes.

3. Transfer half the pigeon peas, with half their cooking water, to a blender and puree until smooth. Pour this creamy blend into a bowl. Repeat with the remaining peas and water. Then return all the puree to the saucepan. (If you have an immersion blender, you can puree all the peas and water right in the saucepan.)

4. Stir in the ghee and salt, and serve.

Plantains and Cabbage

WITH PIGEON PEAS

Vazhaipazham toram Paruppu

Read this recipe carefully, as some of the ingredients sneak their way in in bits and pieces. It's worth the attention when the noodle-like cabbage strips tangle with the cubes of waxy plantain in the smooth sauce of pigeon peas, sweet coconut, and pungent chiles. You will be eloquent in your praise and use highfalutin words like "yum." **SERVES 4**

¼ cup plus 1 tablespoon oily or unoily skinned split
    yellow pigeon peas (toovar dal), picked over
    for stones
2 cups shredded cabbage (see Tip, page 468)
1 large plantain, peeled and cut into ½-inch cubes
2 tablespoons canola oil
2 teaspoons coriander seeds
2 dried red Thai or cayenne chiles,
    stems removed
½ cup shredded fresh coconut; or ¼ cup shredded
    dried unsweetened coconut, reconstituted
    (see Note)
1 teaspoon black or yellow mustard seeds
10 to 12 medium-size to large fresh curry leaves
1 teaspoon coarse kosher or sea salt
2 tablespoons finely chopped fresh cilantro
    leaves and tender stems

1. Place the ¼ cup pigeon peas in a medium-size saucepan. Fill the pan halfway with water and rinse the peas by rubbing them between your fingertips. The water will become cloudy. Drain this water. Repeat three or four times, until the water remains relatively clear; drain. Now add 1½ cups water, the cabbage, and the plantain. Bring to a boil, uncovered, over medium-high heat. Skim off and discard any foam that forms on the surface. Reduce the heat to medium-low, cover the pan, and simmer, stirring occasionally, until the peas are soft and the vegetables are fork-tender, 20 to 25 minutes.

2. While the pigeon peas and vegetables are cooking, heat a small skillet over medium-high heat and pour in the oil. Sprinkle in the remaining 1 tablespoon pigeon peas, the coriander seeds, and the chiles. Stir-fry until the chiles blacken slightly and smell pungent, and the coriander seeds and pigeon peas turn reddish brown, about 1 minute. Using a slotted spoon, transfer the roasted ingredients to a blender jar. Add the coconut and ¼ cup water.

Puree, scraping the inside of the jar as needed, to form a smooth, albeit slightly gritty, paste.

3. Reheat the spice-kissed oil in the skillet over medium-high heat. Add the mustard seeds, cover the skillet, and cook until the seeds have stopped popping (not unlike popcorn), about 30 seconds. Carefully pour the hot oil, including the popped seeds, into the cooked pigeon peas and vegetables. Add the curry leaves, salt, cilantro, and the coconut paste. Pour ¼ cup water into the blender jar and swirl it around to wash it out; add this to the dal and stir once or twice.

4. Cover the pan and simmer the curry over medium-low heat, stirring occasionally, until the flavors mingle, about 5 minutes. Then serve.

Note: To reconstitute coconut, cover with ¼ cup boiling water, set aside for about 15 minutes, and then drain.

Peas and Lentils
WITH PUMPKIN

kaddu dhansaak

A vegetarian-friendly version of a Parsi classic, this combines a plethora of legumes (dhan) and vegetables (saak) to make a more-than-adequate one-dish offering—adequate even for Sunday dinner, as a replacement for the standard pot roast and vegetables. **MAKES 6 CUPS**

½ cup oily or unoily skinned split yellow
   pigeon peas (toovar dal), picked over
   for stones
¼ cup skinned split green lentils (yellow in
   this form, moong dal), picked over for
   stones
¼ cup yellow split peas (chana dal),
   picked over for stones
2 cups cubed fresh red pumpkin (1-inch cubes;
   see Tip, page 141)
2 medium-size red onions; 1 cut into
   ½-inch cubes, 1 cut in half lengthwise
   and thinly sliced
1 medium-size carrot, ends trimmed,
   cut crosswise into ½-inch-thick slices
1 medium-size russet or Yukon Gold potato,
   peeled, cut into ½-inch cubes, and
   submerged in a bowl of cold water
   to prevent browning
1 teaspoon ground turmeric
1 teaspoon ground Kashmiri chiles; or
   ¼ teaspoon cayenne (ground red pepper)
   mixed with ¾ teaspoon sweet paprika
4 tablespoons Ghee (page 21) or canola oil
4 medium-size cloves garlic, thinly sliced
1 can (14.5 ounces) diced tomatoes
2 teaspoons coarse kosher or sea salt
1 teaspoon Sambhar masala (page 33)
1 teaspoon English-style Madras Curry Powder
   (page 24)
½ teaspoon Maharashtrian garam masala
   (page 28)
8 ounces fresh spinach leaves, well rinsed
   and coarsely chopped
¼ cup finely chopped fresh cilantro leaves
   and tender stems

1. Place the pigeon peas, lentils, and split peas in a pressure cooker. Fill the cooker halfway with water, and rinse the legumes by rubbing them between your fingertips. The water may appear slightly dirty. Drain this water. Repeat three or four times, until the water remains relatively clear; drain. Now add 3 cups water and bring to a boil, uncovered, over high heat. Skim off and discard any foam that forms on the surface. Stir in the pumpkin, cubed onion, carrot, potato, turmeric, and ground chiles. Seal the cooker shut and allow the pressure to build up. When the cooker reaches full pressure, reduce the heat to medium-low and cook for about 15 minutes. Remove the cooker from the heat and allow the pressure to subside naturally (about 15 minutes) before opening the lid.

2. Meanwhile, heat 2 tablespoons of the ghee in a medium-size skillet over medium heat. Add the sliced onion and the garlic, and stir-fry until the onion is soft and brown with a deep purple hue, 8 to 10 minutes.

3. Stir in the tomatoes, with their juices, the salt, and the three spice blends. Cook, uncovered, stirring occasionally, until the tomatoes soften and a thin layer of oil starts to separate around the edges and on the surface, 5 to 8 minutes.

4. When the legume-vegetable mixture is ready, add the sauce, the spinach, and the cilantro. Simmer over medium heat, uncovered, stirring occasionally, until the flavors marry, 5 to 10 minutes.

5. Stir in the remaining 2 tablespons ghee, and serve.

Tip: When you see a recipe that calls for multiple spice blends, don't be alarmed. They all take under 5 minutes to put together, and you can prepare them up to a month ahead. You may already have some of the blends on hand, if you've made a curry that used them.

Mango, Bell Pepper, and Onion
IN A PIGEON PEA SAUCE

Maangai Kootan

Certain curries are lodged in my memory bank. Twenty-five years ago, while on a sojourn visiting southern Indian temples, we stopped in Trivandrum, a city in Kerala, where we dined at the home of a family friend. The curry was a rich stew of unripe mangoes peppered with green chiles, ladled over steaming-hot rice noodles. Flash forward to my American home kitchen a quarter of a century later, where the memory of those flavors rushed back. This time the curry is served over red rice (page 708) for equal intensity.

MAKES 5 CUPS

½ cup oily or unoily skinned split yellow pigeon peas (toovar dal), picked over for stones

2 tablespoons coconut oil or canola oil

1 teaspoon black or yellow mustard seeds

½ cup chopped peeled rock-firm unripe mango (½-inch cubes; see box, page 641)

1 large green bell pepper, stemmed, seeded, and cut into ½-inch pieces

1 small red onion, cut in half lengthwise, then cut into ½-inch cubes

12 to 15 medium-size to large fresh curry leaves

6 green or white cardamom pods

6 whole cloves

4 fresh green Thai, cayenne, or serrano chiles, stems removed, cut crosswise into ½-inch-thick slices (do not remove the seeds)

1 teaspoon ground turmeric

1 can (13.5 ounces) unsweetened coconut milk

1½ teaspoons coarse kosher or sea salt

1. Place the pigeon peas in a small saucepan. Fill the pan halfway with water and rinse the peas by rubbing them between your fingertips. The water will become cloudy. Drain this water. Repeat three or four times, until the water remains relatively clear; drain. Now add 2 cups water and bring it to a boil, uncovered, over medium-high heat. Skim off and discard any foam that forms on the surface. Reduce the heat to medium-low, cover the pan, and simmer, stirring occasionally, until the peas are tender, about 20 minutes.

2. While the pigeon peas are cooking, heat the oil in a medium-size saucepan over medium-high heat. Add the mustard seeds, cover the pan, and cook until the seeds have stopped popping (not unlike popcorn), about 30 seconds. Then add the mango, bell pepper, onion, curry leaves, cardamom pods, cloves, and chiles. Cook, uncovered, stirring occasionally, until the mango and vegetables turn light brown around the edges, 5 to 7 minutes.

3. Sprinkle in the turmeric, stirring to cook it without burning as it coats the vegetables with its sun-yellow brilliance, 5 to 10 seconds. Then carefully pour in the coconut milk, which will heat up immediately, thanks to the hot pan. Sprinkle in the salt and stir once or twice. (The curry will be creamy-yellow, rich with chunky vegetables and whole spices. Go ahead and taste the sauce, but do be prepared to say *wow* when it coats your tongue.) Reduce the heat to medium-low, cover the pan, and simmer, stirring occasionally, until the bell pepper and onion are fork-tender, 10 to 15 minutes.

4. While the vegetables are stewing, transfer the cooked pigeon peas, with their cooking water, to a blender and puree, scraping the inside of the jar as needed, until smooth. (If you have an immersion blender, you can puree the peas and water right in the saucepan.)

5. Once the vegetables are tender, stir in the thin, creamy-yellow puree, and serve.

Tip: If you wish, remove the cardamom pods and cloves before serving the curry.

Sweet Pineapple
STEWED IN PIGEON PEA BROTH

Anasi Pazham Rasam

With his nose up in the air, the skeptic at my table pooh-poohed the notion of adding pineapple to the classic tamarind-based curry his mother made daily. I quietly poured a serving of my sweet-tart-hot adaptation over a mound of slightly sticky long-grain rice. A few sips of the broth gave way to approval, as he refilled his bowl three times. I wanted to tell him that his mother did not always know best, but I took the high road and kept my mouth shut.

MAKES 4 CUPS

¼ cup oily or unoily skinned split yellow pigeon peas (toovar dal), picked over for stones

2 cups cubed fresh pineapple (½-inch cubes)

1 medium-size tomato, cored and cut into ½-inch cubes

2 teaspoons Sambhar masala (page 33)

1½ teaspoons coarse kosher or sea salt

½ teaspoon ground asafetida

10 to 12 medium-size to large fresh curry leaves

4 tablespoons finely chopped fresh cilantro leaves and tender stems

2 tablespoons Ghee (page 21) or canola oil

1 teaspoon black or yellow mustard seeds

1 teaspoon cumin seeds

4 dried red Thai or cayenne chiles, stems removed

1. Place the pigeon peas in a small saucepan. Fill the pan halfway with water and rinse the peas by rubbing them between your fingertips. The water will become cloudy. Drain this water. Repeat three or four times, until the water remains relatively clear; drain. Now add 1 cup water and bring it to a boil, uncovered, over medium-high heat. Skim off and discard any foam that forms on the surface. Reduce the heat to medium-low, cover the pan, and simmer, stirring occasionally, until the peas are tender, about 20 minutes.

2. While the pigeon peas are cooking, combine the pineapple, tomato, *Sambhar masala,* salt, asafetida, curry leaves, and 2 tablespoons of the cilantro in a medium-size saucepan. Add 2 cups water and bring it to a boil over medium-high heat. Lower the heat to medium and simmer, uncovered, stirring occasionally, until the pineapple and tomato have softened but are still firm-looking, 10 to 15 minutes.

3. Transfer the cooked pigeon peas, with their cooking water, to a blender and puree, scraping the inside of the jar as needed, until smooth. (If you have an immersion blender, you can puree the peas and water right in the saucepan.)

4. Heat a small skillet over medium-high heat, and pour in the ghee. Add the mustard seeds, cover the skillet, and cook until the seeds have stopped popping (not unlike popcorn), about 30 seconds. Remove the skillet from the heat and sprinkle in the cumin seeds and chiles; the seeds will sizzle, turn reddish brown, and smell fragrant, and the chiles will blacken slightly.

5. Stir this spiced ghee mixture into the sweet-tart pineapple-tomato broth, and add the pureed pigeon peas. Sprinkle with the remaining 2 tablespoons cilantro, and serve.

DR. BELANI'S
Pigeon Pea Broth
WITH SEASONAL VEGETABLES

Sindhi Kadhi

It's rare to see Indian men—especially from my generation and older, and especially back in India—take on an active role in the kitchen, particularly if they are married or live with their mother (yes, I know I will get called on this by many who may disagree). However, there are exceptions. My guests at a recent potluck included Dr. Kiran Belani (a beautiful infectious-disease specialist of slender build and lush white hair) and her husband, the equally charming, soft-spoken Dr. Kumar Belani (an anesthesiologist). Both originally from Sindhi-speaking families in Bangalore, they take turns preparing the meals in their Minneapolis home, each cooking the dishes he or she excels at. This special-occasion curry is Kumar's, and he explained in detail the steps he takes, and the hours of slow simmering required, to create the rich-tasting pigeon pea broth. Two bowlfuls of it that night convinced me that he was a passionate cook who also, I could well imagine, took the same amount of care in treating

his patients. (We use a slow cooker for this recipe. If you don't have one, just check the Tips below.)

MAKES 3 CUPS

1 cup oily or unoily skinned split yellow pigeon peas (toovar dal), picked over for stones
3 tablespoons Ghee (page 21) or canola oil
1 teaspoon black or yellow mustard seeds
2 teaspoons cumin seeds
1 teaspoon fenugreek seeds
10 to 12 medium-size to large fresh curry leaves
3½ cups boiling water
1 medium-size tomato
1 tablespoon shredded fresh ginger
1 teaspoon coarse kosher or sea salt
½ teaspoon cayenne (ground red pepper)
¼ teaspoon ground turmeric
4 pieces (each roughly 2 inches long and 1 inch wide) dried black kokum (see Tips, page 449)
1 cup fresh or frozen cut green beans (no need to thaw)
8 to 10 pieces frozen "drumsticks" (each 3 to 4 inches long; no need to thaw; see box, page 489); or 8 to 10 asparagus spears, cut into 3- to 4-inch lengths
2 medium-size carrots, peeled, ends trimmed, thinly sliced crosswise
2 tablespoons chickpea flour
2 fresh green Thai, cayenne, or serrano chiles, stems removed, cut in half lengthwise (do not remove the seeds)
2 tablespoons finely chopped fresh cilantro leaves and tender stems for garnishing

1. Place the pigeon peas in a small bowl. Fill the bowl halfway with water and rinse the peas by rubbing them between your fingertips. The water will become cloudy. Drain this water. Repeat three or four times, until the water remains relatively clear. Drain the pigeon peas and transfer them to a slow cooker.

2. Heat 2 tablespoons of the ghee in a small skillet

over medium-high heat. Add the mustard seeds, cover the skillet, and cook until the seeds have stopped popping (not unlike popcorn), about 30 seconds. Remove the skillet from the heat and sprinkle in 1 teaspoon of the cumin seeds, the fenugreek seeds, and the curry leaves (careful—they will spatter oil on contact). The seeds will instantly sizzle and turn reddish brown, thanks to the hot oil. Scrape the skillet's contents into the slow cooker, and pour in 3 cups of the boiling water. Stir once or twice.

3. Cover the slow cooker, set it to "low," and simmer the pigeon pea mixture until the legumes are very tender and the broth has acquired intense aromas and flavors, about 3 hours.

4. While the pigeon peas are cooking, fill a small saucepan three-fourths full with water and bring it to a rolling boil. Plunk the tomato into the water and leave it until its skin starts to loosen, 30 seconds. Remove it with a slotted spoon and set it aside to cool a bit. Once the tomato is cool enough to touch, core it and slip off its loosened skin. Place the skinned tomato in a fine-mesh strainer set over a small bowl. Using your fingers, break up and mash the tomato, pressing as much of its juice as you can through the strainer, leaving behind the seeds and some of its pulp. Discard the pulp and seeds, and reserve the clear tomato juice.

5. Put the shredded ginger in a small heatproof bowl, and pour the remaining ½ cup boiling water over it. Let the shreds steep until they release their pungent juices into the water, about 15 minutes. Then set the same strainer over the bowl containing the tomato juice, and strain the ginger water through it, adding it to the tomato juice. Squish the ginger shreds between your fingers to extract all the flavor. Discard the shreds.

6. When the pigeon peas are very tender, place a fine-mesh strainer over a medium-size bowl and pour the contents of the slow cooker into it. Mash the peas to make sure you extract all the juices (see the box below for suggestions on using the smashed peas). The strained broth will be amber-colored and chock-full of flavor. Stir in the salt, cayenne, turmeric, and kokum pieces, and then taste the broth. You will see why a meat stock is unnecessary in this dish. Add the green beans, "drumsticks," and carrots to the broth, and stir in the tomato juice–ginger water blend. Return this vegetable-laden broth to the slow cooker.

7. Heat the remaining 1 tablespoon ghee in the same small skillet over medium heat. Sprinkle in the remaining 1 teaspoon cumin seeds and cook until they sizzle and turn reddish brown. Immediately sprinkle the chickpea flour evenly and slowly into the hot ghee (as if you were dusting a baked good with powdered sugar), quickly stirring it in as you sprinkle. The goal is to make sure there aren't any lumps. Add the fresh

smashed pea patties
❖ ❖ ❖

the smashed pigeon peas, left behind after you extract the broth, brim with nutrients and flavor. Instead of discarding them (I hate to throw food away), I fold in some finely chopped red onion, salt, turmeric, and 2 to 4 tablespoons rice flour. Refrigerate the mixture, covered, for about 2 hours or even overnight. Once chilled, it has a soft dough-like consistency that makes it easy to form walnut-size rounds. Flatten them into patties and pan-fry in vegetable oil until they are crispy brown on both sides. Eat as is for a teatime snack, or serve as an appetizer course with any of the sauces in this book—especially the sauces in the Appetizer Curries chapter (try the sauce for Herb-Stuffed Shrimp, page 96, or the one for Steamed Chickpea-Flour Cake with Mint Sauce, page 111).

chiles and continue to stir until the flour turns light brown and smells nutty, 1 to 2 minutes. Ladle some of the broth from the slow cooker into the skillet, whisking it in to make sure there are no lumps. Once the mixture has a thick, smooth pancake batter–like consistency, transfer it to the slow cooker.

8. Cover the slow cooker, set it on low heat again, and simmer gently until the vegetables are tender, about 2 hours.

9. Sprinkle with the cilantro, and serve.

Tips:

❖ Kokum imparts a pleasant tartness, reminiscent of tamarind, but without the dark brown color that tamarind would leach into the sauce. If kokum is unavailable at your Indian grocery store, cut up a small unripe dark plum and simmer it along with the vegetables.

❖ If you don't have a slow cooker stashed away in your cupboard, don't let that stop you: Use a large covered saucepan set on the lowest setting on your burner.

Lime-Tart Pigeon Pea Broth
WITH COCONUT

Elambuchambu Rasam

Usually tamarind-based broths, *rasams* are an everyday feature of Tamil home kitchens. Sometimes tart fruits like lime juice, pineapple, and unripe mango fill in for the tamarind to provide a change of pace. I love the clean sharpness of lime juice, a polar opposite of the earthy, complex, murky tamarind. I always add it after the broth is fully cooked and seasoned, because if lime juice is exposed to heat for too long, it can turn bitter. Ladle this *rasam* over cooked white rice and serve it as a soup course, or do as I do and devour two large bowls of rice and *rasam* and call it a soul-satisfying "light" lunch. (This would explain why I feel sleepy in the afternoon when I indulge in this passion.)

MAKES 5 CUPS

> ¼ cup oily or unoily skinned split yellow pigeon peas (toovar dal), picked over for stones
> 4 tablespoons finely chopped fresh cilantro leaves and tender stems
> 2 teaspoons Sambhar masala (page 33)
> 1½ teaspoons coarse kosher or sea salt
> ½ teaspoon ground asafetida
> 12 to 15 medium-size to large fresh curry leaves
> 1 cup shredded fresh coconut; or ½ cup shredded dried unsweetened coconut, reconstituted (see Note)
> 2 tablespoons Ghee (page 21) or canola oil
> 1 teaspoon black or yellow mustard seeds
> 1 teaspoon cumin seeds
> Juice of 2 large limes

1. Place the pigeon peas in a small saucepan. Fill the pan halfway with water and rinse the peas by rubbing them between your fingertips. The water will become cloudy. Drain this water. Repeat three or four times, until the water remains relatively clear; drain. Now add 1 cup water and bring it to a boil, uncovered, over medium-high heat. Skim off and discard any foam that forms on the surface. Reduce the heat to medium-low, cover the pan, and simmer, stirring occasionally, until the peas are tender, about 20 minutes.

2. While the pigeon peas are cooking, combine 3 cups

water, 2 tablespoons of the cilantro, and the *Sambhar masala*, salt, asafetida, and curry leaves in a medium-size saucepan. Bring to a boil over medium heat and continue to boil, uncovered, stirring occasionally, until the flavors come together, about 15 minutes.

3. Transfer the cooked pigeon peas, with their cooking water, to a blender. Add the coconut and puree, scraping the inside of the jar as needed, until creamy smooth (albeit a tad gritty, thanks to the coconut).

4. Heat a small skillet over medium-high heat, and pour in the ghee. Add the mustard seeds, cover the skillet, and cook until the seeds have stopped popping (not unlike popcorn), about 30 seconds. Remove the skillet from the heat and sprinkle in the cumin seeds. Let them cook in the residual heat until they sizzle and turn reddish brown and fragrant, about 5 seconds. Scrape this oil-seed mixture into the simmering broth, and stir in the coconut-flavored pigeon pea puree.

5. Stir in the lime juice, sprinkle with the remaining 2 tablespoons cilantro, and serve.

Note: To reconstitute coconut, cover with ½ cup boiling water, set aside for about 15 minutes, and then drain.

Pigeon Pea Broth
WITH UNRIPE MANGO

Maangai Rasam

There are two ways you can enjoy this thin, broth-like curry, chock-full of tart-soft mango: You can pour it over cooked white rice, or you can do as I do during the winter months in the tundra of Minneapolis, which is to serve it with thick slices of oven-warm, crusty sourdough bread slathered with premium butter. **MAKES 4 CUPS**

¼ *cup oily or unoily skinned split yellow pigeon peas (toovar dal), picked over for stones (see Tip)*

1 large rock-firm unripe mango, peeled, seeded, and finely chopped (see box, page 641)

3 teaspoons Rasam powder (page 34) or Sambhar masala (page 33)

1½ teaspoons coarse kosher or sea salt

20 medium-size to large fresh curry leaves

4 tablespoons finely chopped fresh cilantro leaves and tender stems

2 tablespoons Ghee (page 21) or canola oil

1 teaspoon black or yellow mustard seeds

1 teaspoon cumin seeds

1. Place the pigeon peas in a small saucepan. Fill the pan halfway with water and rinse the peas by rubbing them between your fingertips. The water will become cloudy. Drain this water. Repeat three or four times, until the water remains relatively clear; drain. Now add 1 cup water and bring it to a boil, uncovered, over medium-high heat. Skim off and discard any foam that forms on the surface. Reduce the heat to medium-low, cover the pan, and simmer, stirring occasionally, until the peas are tender, about 20 minutes.

2. While the pigeon peas are cooking, combine the mango, *Rasam powder*, salt, curry leaves, and 2 tablespoons of the cilantro in a medium-size saucepan. Add 3 cups water and bring it to a boil over medium-high heat. Lower the heat to medium and simmer, uncovered, stirring occasionally, until the mango is tender, 10 to 15 minutes.

3. Transfer the cooked pigeon peas, with their cooking water, to a blender and puree, scraping the inside of the jar as needed, until smooth. (If you have an immersion blender, you can puree the peas and water right in the saucepan.)

4. Heat a small skillet over medium-high heat, and pour in the ghee. Add the mustard seeds, cover the skillet, and cook until the seeds have stopped popping (not unlike popcorn), about 30 seconds. Remove the skillet from the heat and sprinkle in the cumin seeds. Let them cook until they sizzle and turn reddish brown and fragrant, about 5 seconds. Scrape the nutty-smelling oil-seed mixture into the simmering mango-kissed broth, and add the thin, creamy-yellow pureed pigeon peas.

5. Sprinkle with the remaining 2 tablespoons cilantro, and serve.

Tip: If pigeon peas aren't on hand in your pantry, yellow split peas make an excellent alternative.

Garlic-Flavored Pigeon Pea Broth

WITH "DRUMSTICKS" AND KOKUM

Falidu

Classic to the Bohri Muslim community of northwestern India, this curry infuses a nutty-sweet pigeon pea sauce with slightly tart kokum and woodsy "drumstick." Ranee Munaim's mother, Sakina, shared this recipe with me, and as I cooked it, I couldn't help but notice the similarity to the tamarind-based *rasams* of my southern upbringing. However, one spoonful of this curry and the resemblance ended. The flavors could not be any farther apart. **MAKES 4 CUPS**

Hokum? See the Glossary of Ingredients, page 758.

¼ cup oily or unoily skinned split yellow pigeon peas (toovar dal), picked over for stones
2 tablespoons Ghee (page 21) or canola oil
1 teaspoon cumin seeds
1 teaspoon fenugreek seeds
6 medium-size cloves garlic, finely chopped
1 tablespoon chickpea flour
2 teaspoons Toasted Cumin-Coriander Blend (page 33)
1 teaspoon ground Kashmiri chiles; or ¼ teaspoon cayenne (ground red pepper) mixed with ¾ teaspoon sweet paprika
1 teaspoon coarse kosher or sea salt
12 to 16 pieces frozen "drumsticks" (each 3 to 4 inches long; no need to thaw; see box, page 489)
4 pieces dried black kokum (each roughly 2 inches long and 1 inch wide, see Tips page 449)
2 tablespoons finely chopped fresh cilantro leaves and tender stems for garnishing

1. Place the pigeon peas in a small saucepan. Fill the pan halfway with water and rinse the peas by rubbing them between your fingertips. The water will become cloudy. Drain this water. Repeat three or four times, until the water remains relatively clear; drain. Now add 1 cup water and bring it to a boil, uncovered, over medium-high heat. Skim off and discard any foam that forms on the surface. Reduce the heat to medium-low, cover the pan, and simmer, stirring occasionally, until the peas are tender, about 20 minutes.

2. Transfer the pigeon peas and their cooking water to a blender and puree, scraping the inside of the jar as needed, until smooth. (If you have an immersion blender, you can puree the peas and water right in the saucepan.)

3. Heat the ghee in a medium-size saucepan over medium heat. Sprinkle in the cumin and fenugreek seeds, and cook until they sizzle, turn reddish brown, and smell nutty, 15 to 30 seconds. Add the garlic and stir-fry until it is light brown, 1 to 3 minutes. Sprinkle in the chickpea flour and cook, stirring frequently, until it is lightly browned, 1 to 2 minutes.

4. Pour in the pureed pigeon peas, 3 cups water, and the cumin-coriander blend, ground chiles, salt, and "drumsticks." Bring to a boil. Then reduce the heat to medium-low, cover the pan, and simmer, stirring occasionally, until the "drumsticks" split open when pried with a fork, 15 to 20 minutes.

5. Add the kokum, raise the heat to medium-high, and continue to simmer the curry, uncovered, stirring occasionally, until the sauce is tart, about 5 minutes.

6. Remove the kokum pieces, sprinkle the cilantro over the curry, and serve.

Tip: Substitute a few alternatives for the main characters in this curry (yellow split peas for split pigeon peas, rice flour for chickpea flour, asparagus for "drumsticks," and tamarind or lime juice for kokum), and you have an entirely new curry at no extra charge. Enjoy!

Spicy "Gnocchi"

dal dhoklis

Velvet-soft dumplings called *dhoklis* are easy to make, and when simmered in a pot of pureed pigeon peas, the resulting curry makes for a nutritionally complete meal in one

spicy-hot, creamy-smooth, slightly sweet sauce.

MAKES 4 CUPS

½ cup oily or unoily skinned split yellow pigeon peas (toovar dal), picked over for stones

For the *dhoklis:*

½ cup roti flour (see Tip, page 728)
1 teaspoon coarse kosher or sea salt
1 teaspoon white granulated sugar
½ teaspoon cayenne (ground red pepper)
½ teaspoon ground turmeric
½ teaspoon bishop's weed
2 tablespoons finely chopped fresh cilantro leaves and tender stems
2 tablespoons canola oil

For finishing the dal:

1 teaspoon Toasted Cumin-Coriander Blend (page 33)
1½ teaspoons white granulated sugar
1½ teaspoons coarse kosher or sea salt
½ teaspoon ground turmeric
2 fresh green Thai, cayenne, or serrano chiles, stems removed, cut crosswise into ½-inch pieces (do not remove the seeds)
2 tablespoons Ghee (page 21) or canola oil
1 teaspoon black or yellow mustard seeds
1 teaspoon cumin seeds
½ teaspoon fenugreek seeds
¼ teaspoon ground asafetida
6 to 8 medium-size to large fresh curry leaves
1 medium-size tomato, cored and finely chopped
2 tablespoons finely chopped fresh cilantro leaves and tender stems

1. Place the pigeon peas in a pressure cooker. Fill the cooker halfway with water and rinse the peas by rubbing them between your fingertips. The water may appear slightly dirty or cloudy. Drain this water. Repeat three or four times, until the water remains relatively clear;

drain. Now add 4 cups water and bring to a boil, uncovered, over high heat. Skim off and discard any foam that forms on the surface. Seal the cooker shut and allow the pressure to build up. When the cooker reaches full pressure, reduce the heat to medium-low and cook for about 15 minutes. Then remove the cooker from the heat and allow the pressure to subside naturally (about 15 minutes) before opening the lid.

2. While the pigeon peas are cooking, make the dough for the *dhoklis*: Combine the roti flour, salt, sugar, cayenne, turmeric, bishop's weed, and cilantro in a medium-size bowl and stir well. Drizzle the oil over the flour mixture, and rub the flour through your hands to evenly distribute the oil.

3. Pour a few tablespoons of hot tap water over the flour, stirring it in as you drizzle. Once the flour comes together to form a soft ball, stop adding water (you will use about 4 tablespoons). Using your hand (as long as it's clean, I think it's the best tool), gather the ball, picking up any dry flour in the bottom of the bowl, and knead it to form a smooth, slightly stiff ball of dough. If it's a little too wet, dust it with a little more flour, kneading it in after every dusting until you get the right dry consistency. (If you have been using your hand to make the dough from the start, it will be caked with clumps of dough. Scrape that off your hand back into the bowl. Wash and dry your hands thoroughly, and then return to the dough to knead it. You will get a much better feel for the dough's consistency when you use a dry hand.)

4. Using your hands, roll the dough to form a 12-inch-long log. Cut the log crosswise into ¼-inch-thick pieces, and shape each piece into a marble-size ball. Place a ball in the palm of one hand, and use your thumb to press it down to make a depression, creating a concave shape. Repeat with the remaining balls. Set the *dhoklis* aside.

5. Once the pressure has subsided, check to see if the pigeon peas have completely disintegrated into a soft, creamy texture. If not, transfer half of the peas and half the cooking water to a blender, and puree until smooth. Pour this creamy blend into a bowl. Repeat with the remaining peas and water. Return all the pureed peas to the saucepan. (If you have an immersion blender, you can puree all the peas right in the saucepan.)

6. Now make the dal: Stir the cumin-coriander blend, sugar, salt, turmeric, and chiles into the pigeon peas, and bring to a boil over medium heat. Add the *dhoklis*, stirring gently to make sure they don't stick to one another. Continue to boil the dal, uncovered, stirring occasionally, until the *dhoklis* are cooked, 15 to 20 minutes. (When cooked, they will have expanded, there will be a glossy sheen on their slightly slippery surface, and they will easily crack open to reveal a slightly dry interior.)

7. Heat the ghee in a small skillet over medium-high heat. Add the mustard seeds, cover the skillet, and cook until the seeds have stopped popping (not unlike popcorn), about 30 seconds. Sprinkle in the cumin seeds, fenugreek seeds, asafetida, and curry leaves. Add this to the dal, then stir in the tomato and cilantro, and serve.

Chile-Hot Dumplings
WITH BUTTERMILK

Paruppu Unday More Kozhumbu

Hearty dumplings like these are special-occasion fare in Tamil-speaking kitchens. They are not laborious to make but do take some constant stirring, which can be a bit of a workout because the mixture is dense. The dumplings are often simmered in a tamarind-based curry, but I like the clean-tasting tartness that buttermilk offers in this version. Puffy fried *pooris* (page 725) are an ideal accompaniment to this surprisingly heavy curry.

The number of chiles in the recipe looks alarming, but don't panic. The pigeon peas, buttermilk, half-and-half, and coconut are all instrumental in lowering the heat. **SERVES 8**

For the dumplings:

I cup oily or unoily skinned split yellow pigeon peas (toovar dal), picked over for stones

12 dried red Thai or cayenne chiles, stems removed

¼ cup finely chopped fresh curry leaves

¼ cup rice flour

I teaspoon coarse kosher or sea salt

½ teaspoon ground asafetida

¼ cup canola oil

For the curry:

2 cups buttermilk

¼ cup half-and-half

I cup shredded fresh coconut; or ½ cup shredded dried unsweetened coconut, reconstituted (see Note)

4 to 6 dried red Thai or cayenne chiles, to taste, stems removed

I tablespoon cumin seeds

I teaspoon coriander seeds

½ teaspoon coarse kosher or sea salt

12 medium-size to large fresh curry leaves

I tablespoon canola oil

I teaspoon black or yellow mustard seeds

1. To make the dumplings: Place the pigeon peas in a medium-size bowl. Fill the bowl halfway with water and rinse the peas by rubbing them between your fingertips. The water will become cloudy. Drain this water.

Repeat three or four times, until the water remains relatively clear; drain. Now fill the bowl halfway with warm water and add the chiles. Let it sit at room temperature, covered with plastic wrap, until the pigeon peas have softened, at least 30 minutes or as long as 4 hours.

2. Drain the pigeon peas and chiles, and transfer them to a food processor. Process to form a red-speckled, slightly gritty paste. Scrape this into a medium-size bowl. Fold in the curry leaves, rice flour, salt, and asafetida.

3. Heat a wok or a well-seasoned cast-iron skillet over medium-high heat. Drizzle the oil down its sides. When the oil has formed a shimmering pool at the bottom, add the thick pigeon pea paste. Cook, stirring and spreading it out evenly with the back of a spoon, until it changes from a wet, sticky-feeling, batterlike dough to a dull, dry-feeling, soft, doughlike mass, 3 to 5 minutes. (At first, the paste will stick to the spoon. Keep scraping it off with a spatula. Then, as it cooks, the paste will stop sticking. Don't overcook it, or the dough will dry out, turning into small pebble-like chunks that will be difficult to shape.) Transfer the dough to a plate to cool.

4. Once it is cool to the touch, divide the dough into 16 equal portions. Compress each portion tightly in the palm of your hand, forming a tight walnut-size dumpling. Place the dumplings on a baking sheet, cover them with plastic wrap, and set them aside while you prepare the curry. (You can prepare the dumplings up to 2 days ahead; cover and refrigerate.)

5. Now, make the curry: Whisk the buttermilk and half-and-half together in a medium-size bowl.

6. Pour ¼ cup water into a blender jar, followed by the coconut, chiles, cumin, and coriander. Puree, scraping the inside of the jar as needed, to make a gritty, red-speckled citrus-smelling sauce. Pour this into the buttermilk mixture, and stir in the salt and curry leaves.

7. Heat the oil in a medium-size saucepan over medium-high heat. Add the mustard seeds, cover the pan, and cook until the seeds have stopped popping (not unlike popcorn), about 30 seconds. Immediately (and carefully) pour the buttermilk mixture into the pan, and stir once or twice. Add the dumplings in a single layer. Lower the heat to medium and bring the curry to a gentle boil. As soon as it starts to boil, remove the pan from the heat. You will notice that the curry has instantly started to thicken, thanks to the rice flour in the dumplings and the coconut in the sauce. Gently lift the buttermilk-drenched dumplings and transfer them to a serving bowl or platter. Pour the sauce over them. (One or two dumplings may fall apart, but that's okay. That's the reason why you remove the pan from the heat as soon as the sauce comes to a boil: The more it boils, the more the dumplings will start to disintegrate.) Serve immediately.

Note: To reconstitute coconut, cover with ½ cup boiling water, set aside for about 15 minutes, and then drain.

Sprouted Beans and Peas

WITH CHILES AND LIME JUICE

Mirchi Waale Khili Hui dal

I adore the clean-tasting tartness that lime juice, added at the last minute, provides in this curry. The acidity also helps lower the heat from the chiles, with the able assistance of the toasted chickpea flour. If you wish, a teaspoon or two of white granulated sugar, stirred in with the salt, yields a pleasantly sweet undertone to the curry. Balance rears its pretty head once again. **MAKES 4 CUPS**

2 tablespoons canola oil
1 cup finely chopped red onion
6 fresh green Thai, cayenne, or serrano chiles,
*   stems removed, thinly sliced crosswise*
*   (do not remove the seeds)*
4 cups partially sprouted beans and/or peas
*   (see box, page 328, and Tip)*
½ teaspoon ground turmeric
1½ teaspoons coarse kosher or sea salt
2 tablespoons Toasted Chickpea Flour (page 41)
2 teaspoons Toasted Cumin-Coriander Blend (page 33)
2 tablespoons finely chopped fresh cilantro leaves
*   and tender stems*
Juice of 1 large lime

1. Heat the oil in a medium-size saucepan over medium-high heat. Add the onion and chiles, and stir-fry until the onion is light brown around the edges and the chiles are throat-clearing pungent, 3 to 5 minutes.

2. Stir in the sprouted beans and the turmeric. Continue to stir-fry to coat the beans with the spice, 3 to 4 minutes.

3. Pour in 2 cups water, stir in the salt, and heat to a boil. Then lower the heat to medium, cover the pan, and simmer, stirring occasionally, until the beans are cooked but still have that nutty crunch, 15 to 20 minutes.

4. Sprinkle in the toasted flour and the spice blend. Simmer, uncovered, stirring occasionally, until the sauce thickens a bit and has a nice body to it, 5 to 8 minutes.

5. Stir in the cilantro and lime juice, and serve.

Tip: If you're not into sprouting your own beans and peas, don't let that stop you from making this curry.

There's a perfectly acceptable alternative: natural food stores and large supermarkets stock various sprouted legumes in their produce section. Purchase them without guilt. The more common larger bean sprouts (used in Southeast Asian cooking) are also okay, but note that they require only half the simmering time—you want to maintain that delectable crunch.

Cashew Nuts
STEWED WITH CARDAMOM & CLOVES

Kaaju Curry

Cashew nuts cook up into classic Sri Lankan curry I had the fortune to sample (okay, devour) at Piyumi and Priyantha Samaratunga's house. Piyumi is a successful immigration attorney, Priyantha is an engineer, and both are passionate about food and cooking. Their ancestral roots are deeply entrenched in picturesque Sri Lanka (formerly Ceylon), known for its vibrant curries studded with seafood, fresh coconut, peppercorns, cloves, and cinnamon.

With opposite work schedules to accommodate caring for their three adorable children, Piyumi and Priyantha rarely have time to cook as a team—but when they do, it is magical. With her intuitive cooking style and his scientific approach, their enthusiasm was evident the night they served me their childhood favorites. The table was beautifully set and the banquet of curries perfumed the air. This cashew nut curry caught my eye. She served it with the pearl-like short-grain rice from Sri Lanka called *Muttu sambha* (page 721), which was steeped in lemongrass, turmeric, and coconut milk. **SERVES 8**

2 cups raw cashew nuts
1 can (13.5 ounces) unsweetened coconut milk
1 teaspoon coarse kosher or sea salt
½ teaspoon ground turmeric
½ teaspoon cayenne (ground red pepper)
12 to 15 medium-size to large fresh curry leaves
6 green or white cardamom pods
6 whole cloves
1 or 2 cinnamon sticks (each 3 inches long)

1. Place the cashews in a medium-size saucepan and add water to cover. Bring the water to a rolling boil over high heat, and then remove the pan from the heat. Cover the pan and set it aside until the cashews have softened slightly, about 2 hours.

2. Drain the cashews in a colander and return them to the same saucepan. Add all the remaining ingredients and bring to a boil over medium-high heat. Reduce the heat to medium-low, cover the pan, and simmer, stirring occasionally, until the creamy yellow, highly aromatic sauce has thickened and the cashews are tender but still firm, 30 to 35 minutes. Remove the cardamom pods, cloves, and cinnamon sticks if you wish, and serve.

Boiled Peanuts
WITH RADISH GREENS AND JAGGERY

Mungphalli Aur Mooli ki Bhajee

Nutty-textured, this curry is sweet, hot, bitter, and sour—all flavor profiles that are the hallmarks of complex Indian cuisine, without any laborious effort to create them. Spoon it into small bowls and serve it with either homemade rotis (page 727) or store-bought whole-wheat tortillas that you've warmed. **SERVES 6**

1 cup raw peanuts (without the skins)

2 cups firmly packed radish greens, finely chopped (see Tips)

1 teaspoon coarse kosher or sea salt

½ teaspoon ground turmeric

2 tablespoons Ghee (page 21) or canola oil

1 tablespoon cumin seeds, coarsely chopped (see Tips)

6 medium-size cloves garlic, finely chopped

4 dried red Thai or cayenne chiles, stems removed

2 tablespoons Toasted Chickpea Flour (page 41)

2 tablespoons crumbled (or chopped) jaggery or firmly packed dark brown sugar

½ teaspoon cayenne (ground red pepper)

Juice of 1 large lime

1. Place the peanuts in a medium-size saucepan, add 2 cups water, and bring to a boil over medium-high heat. Lower the heat to medium and simmer vigorously, uncovered, until most of the water has evaporated and the nuts are partially tender, 20 to 25 minutes.

2. Pour in another 2 cups water, and then add the radish greens, salt, and turmeric. Cover the pan and allow the steam to wilt the greens, 2 to 3 minutes. Continue to cook the greens, covered, stirring occasionally, until they are tender and the peanuts are tender but firm-looking, 10 to 12 minutes.

3. While the peanuts and greens are simmering, heat the ghee in a small skillet over medium-high heat. Add the cumin, garlic, and chiles. Stir-fry until the cumin seeds are aromatic, the garlic has turned light brown, and the chiles have blackened, about 1 minute.

4. Add the contents of the skillet to the cooked peanut mixture, and stir in the toasted flour, jaggery, and cayenne. Spoon some of the liquid into the skillet and

scrape up any browned bits of garlic; pour this back into the pan and stir once or twice. Cover the pan and simmer the spicy-sweet-bitter curry, stirring occasionally, until the sauce thickens slightly, 5 to 8 minutes.

5. Stir in the lime juice, and serve.

Tips:

❖ Radish greens are easy to cook and have a slight bitterness, reminiscent of fresh arugula leaves. Slice them off the radishes and dunk them in a bowl filled with cold water. Swish them around to wash them, letting any grit or mud sink to the bottom. Scoop out the greens and discard the water. Repeat once more to ensure grit-free greens. Dry them a bit between paper towels, and then chop them.

❖ To coarsely chop cumin seeds, mound them on a cutting board. Chop them with a sharp chef's knife, trying to contain the seeds on the cutting surface. The texture should resemble that of gritty sand. This chopping injects a slightly more intense flavor into the dish, but not quite as strong as freshly ground cumin seeds.

Peanuts and Yellow Split Peas
WITH SPINACH

Mungphalli Palak Dal

Peanuts, called "groundnuts" in India (because when the plant flowers, the peanuts bury themselves just below the ground), are grown in the western states of

Gujarat and Maharashtra, home of the bustling metropolis Mumbai. At the onset of the monsoons, a flood of peanuts in their muddy shells overflows from many a street vendor's gunnysack in Mumbai's marketplaces. I loved to eat bowlfuls of the sea-salted boiled peanuts that my mother cooked in a pressure cooker. This highly nutritious peanut stew, which combines the nuts with sweet yellow split peas and fresh spinach, makes for a filling meal when served with either steamed rice or fluffy whole-wheat breads (page 727). **SERVES 6**

½ cup raw peanuts (without the skins)

½ cup yellow split peas (chana dal), picked over for stones

1 medium-size tomato, cored and coarsely diced

3 or 4 fresh green Thai, cayenne, or serrano chiles, to taste, stems removed

2 teaspoons coarse kosher or sea salt

1 teaspoon white granulated sugar

2 tablespoons Ghee (page 21), or canola oil

1 teaspoon black or yellow mustard seeds

2 tablespoons chickpea flour

¼ teaspoon ground asafetida

¼ teaspoon ground turmeric

1 pound fresh spinach leaves, well rinsed and cut into thin ribbons

1. Place the peanuts and split peas in a large saucepan. Fill the pan halfway with water and rinse the legumes by rubbing them with your fingertips. The water will become slightly cloudy. Drain this water. Repeat two or three times, until the water remains relatively clear; drain. Now add 4 cups water and bring to a boil, uncovered, over medium-high heat. Skim off and discard any foam that forms on the surface. Reduce the heat to medium-low, cover the pan, and simmer, stirring occasionally, until the peanuts and split peas are tender, about 30 minutes.

2. While the legumes are cooking, place the tomato and chiles in a mortar. Pound gently with the pestle until the tomatoes are coarsely crushed and the chiles are flattened, their seeds released to mix with those of the tomato. Fold in the salt and sugar.

3. Heat a small skillet over medium-high heat and pour in the ghee. Add the mustard seeds, cover the skillet, and cook until the seeds have stopped popping (not unlike popcorn), about 30 seconds. Immediately sprinkle the chickpea flour, asafetida, and turmeric into the hot oil and cook, stirring constantly, until the mixture has a nutty aroma, about 1 minute.

4. Add the tomato-chile mixture and stir until the sauce thickens slightly, 2 to 3 minutes. Set the sauce aside.

5. When the legumes are cooked, add the spinach, a few handfuls at a time, stirring until wilted.

6. Stir the sauce into the legume-spinach mixture. Transfer a few spoonfuls of the liquid to the skillet and deglaze it; add this to the pan. Raise the heat to medium-high and boil the stew vigorously, uncovered, stirring occasionally, until the flavors have blended, about 5 minutes. Then serve.

Tips: The technique of pounding the tomatoes with the chiles provides for a subtle heat from the bruised peppers. The seeds are barely released, and the veins that house the heat-generating capsaicin remain relatively intact. The tomato's skin, along with some meaty pulp, separates from its seeds when you pound it. Your instinct might be to discard the skin, but in India we leave it in. The curry has quite a few interesting textures from the nutty-firm peanuts, yellow split peas, and ribbon shreds of spinach, so the few tomato skins won't interfere in any way (at least, to me they don't; but if they are bothersome to you, by all means discard them).

vegetable curries

i may be biased when I say that Indians are masters at creating magic when furnished with just about any vegetable grown on this planet. Not only are vegetables important in the millions of vegetarian homes across India, they are also a key player in kitchens that simmer meat, fish, and poultry dishes. It is not uncommon to find two or three vegetable dishes

at the family table at any meal, and that significance is evident in this book. This chapter carries a huge weight (literally and figuratively), reflecting the way we eat in India. Often the vegetable is the protagonist with protein-based dishes playing supporting roles, which is quite the opposite of what we find in the European and North American kitchens. In the average kitchen in the United States, vegetables—other than potatoes, onions, tomatoes, green beans, broccoli, and corn—don't

seem to make their presence known. And the vegetables I grew up on—okra, taro root, bottle gourd squash, eggplant, plantain—appear even less often. Vegetables may be sides in American and European kitchens, but in an Indian's home they are an absolute must at every meal, including breakfast, and very often they are featured prominently as the main course. When you consider the role of vegetables in India's rich history, it is easy to understand their significance today.

main-course vegetable curries

❖ ❖ ❖

ranted, most of these curries are great alongside many of the main-course dishes in this book, but there are some that can hold their own, especially when escorted by one of the curry accompaniments. Here is a mere fistful for you to savor:

Chopped Cabbage with a Yellow Split Pea Sauce (page 475)

Tamilian Okra with a Buttermilk-Coconut Sauce (page 523)

One-Pot Potatoes in a Red Lentil Sauce with Lime Juice (page 552)

Stewed Potatoes, Carrots, and Peas in Spiced Coconut Milk (page 565)

Fiery-Tart Potatoes (page 577)

Squash with Taro Leaf "Roulade" (page 608)

Root Vegetables and Pea Pods in a Green Pea–Coconut Sauce (page 629)

Mixed Vegetables with a Potent Coconut-Chile Sauce (page 630)

Seasonal Vegetables with Yellow Split Peas (page 632)

Nine-Jeweled Medley with a Cashew-Raisin Sauce (page 634)

We know that amaranth was a staple in the Harappan civilization of the Indus Valley around 2000 B.C., and it still sneaks into my kitchen via Amaranth Leaves with Peanuts (page 461). Mustard plants blossomed in the northwestern state of Rajasthan around 2800 B.C., and curries like Pureed Mustard Greens with Clarified Butter (page 522), popular back in 500 B.C., are still the rage in Punjabi homes and at roadside eateries called *dhabas*. Today we can experience the same excitement the Aryans felt, when they inhabited India between 1500 and 350 B.C., while gorging on lotus root, bottle gourd, and bitter melon through sauced sensations like Lotus Root with a Roasted Cumin-Yogurt Sauce (page 513), Fried Bottle Gourd Squash Dumplings in a Cashew-Raisin Sauce (page 595), and Bitter Melon with Onion and Tomato (page 465). I would be remiss if I didn't mention the starchy influence of potatoes, introduced to Indians by the Portuguese settlers and traders in the late 16th and early 17th century A.D. No meal is complete without potatoes, in my not-so-humble opinion, and my addiction for these tubers is revealed in Chunky Potatoes with Golden Raisins (page 557), Slow-Cooked Baby Potatoes in a Yogurt-Fennel Sauce (page 559), and Mashed Potatoes with Roasted Red Chiles (page 560). Okra holds similar stature, and I know you will agree with me when you sample Cashew and Coriander Stuffed Okra (page 525) and Pan-Fried Okra with an Onion-Tamarind Sauce (page 531).

Amaranth Leaves
WITH PEANUTS

Thowli Nu Shaak

Red amaranth leaves not only look pretty, they taste delicious, especially when stewed with roasted mustard seeds and peanuts. Filled with nutrients, these stewed leaves are a great side dish with Sweet-Hot Yellow Split Peas with Golden Raisins (page 416) and white rice. I also love the smoky-crunch of Flame-Toasted Lentil Wafers (page 740) as an accompaniment to this simple vegetarian fare for a weekday dinner.

SERVES 4

1 pound fresh red amaranth leaves, well rinsed,
    tough stems discarded (see Tip, page 462)
2 tablespoons peanut or canola oil
1 teaspoon black or yellow mustard seeds
1 teaspoon cumin seeds
½ teaspoon ground turmeric
½ teaspoon cayenne (ground red pepper)
¼ teaspoon ground asafetida
½ cup unsalted dry-roasted peanuts
1 teaspoon coarse kosher or sea salt
1 teaspoon white granulated sugar

1. Stack a dozen or so of the amaranth leaves on top of one another, and cut them into thin strips. Repeat with the remaining bunch.

2. Heat the oil in a large skillet over medium-high heat. Add the mustard seeds, cover the skillet, and cook until the seeds have stopped popping (not unlike popcorn), about 30 seconds. Remove the skillet from the heat and sprinkle in the cumin seeds, turmeric, cay-

serving vegetable curries
❖ ❖ ❖

These vegetable curries are more flexible than other types: all of them can be prepared ahead of time and then reheated when you are ready to serve them. That makes it easy to serve more than one if you choose to—and cuts down on that last-minute rush.

We Indians usually just push aside whole cardamom pods, cloves, dried chiles, and the like when we are eating. But if you prefer, or if your guests aren't used to confronting them, by all means feel free to remove them before serving the curry.

enne, and asafetida, which will instantly sizzle and smell nutty (without burning).

3. Grab a handful of the amaranth strips and stir them into the spiced oil. Allow them to wilt before you add another handful. Once all the leaves have been added and wilted, stir in 1 cup water and the peanuts, salt, and sugar.

4. Bring the curry to a boil. Then lower the heat to medium, cover the skillet, and simmer, stirring occasionally, until the leaves are tender and the sauce has thickened slightly, about 15 minutes. (The sauce will be on the thinner end of the spectrum; so, if you wish to shift it toward the thicker, remove the cover and simmer over medium heat, stirring occasionally, to boil off some more of the brothlike liquid, about 5 minutes.) Then serve.

Tip: If you can't find amaranth at your market—or more likely, at an Asian grocery store—spinach, collard, mustard (slightly more bitter), and kale are all great stand-ins.

Red Amaranth and Spinach
WITH A COCONUT-CHILE SAUCE

Shapu Keerai

*d*eeply pink, this curry sure is pretty to look at—but don't stop there. Dig a spoon into its velvety smoothness and sample it. The initial tartness of the lime will awaken your palate, followed by the silky smooth leaves that will coat your tongue with their buttery texture and slight bitterness. The moment you swallow a mouthful, you will feel the gentle burn of the fiery chiles in the sauce, masked by the sweetness of fresh coconut. You may break into a sweat, but my bets are on you giving in to the addiction. Serve it over nests of rice noodles (page 723) for an even more satisfying experience. **SERVES 6**

2 pounds fresh red amaranth, well rinsed, tough stems discarded (see Tip)

1 pound fresh spinach leaves, well rinsed

4 tablespoons coconut oil or canola oil

½ cup shredded dried unsweetened coconut

1 tablespoon coriander seeds

8 to 10 dried red Thai or cayenne chiles, to taste, stems removed

1 teaspoon black or yellow mustard seeds

1 tablespoon skinned split black lentils (cream-colored in this form, urad dal), picked over for stones

2 teaspoons coarse kosher or sea salt

Juice of 1 medium-size lime

1. Fill a large saucepan three-fourths full with water, and bring it to a rolling boil over medium-high heat. Grab handfuls of the amaranth and spinach leaves, and stir them into the water to wilt them. Repeat until all of the leaves have been added and wilted. Reserving 1 cup of cooking water, drain the leaves in a colander. Run cold water through the leaves to cool them.

2. Pile a few of the heavy, wet leaves on a cutting board and finely chop them. Transfer them to a medium-size bowl. Repeat with the remaining leaves. Don't worry if the leaves continue to be water-drenched.

3. Wash and dry the same saucepan, and heat 2 tablespoons of the oil in it over medium-high heat. Add the coconut, coriander seeds, and 4 to 6 of the chiles. Cook, stirring constantly, until they all turn reddish brown and smell nutty, 2 to 3 minutes. Transfer the ingredients to a blender, and pour in ½ cup of the reserved cooking water. Puree, scraping the inside of the blender jar as needed, to make a slightly gritty reddish-brown paste.

4. Heat the remaining 2 tablespoons oil in the same saucepan. Add the mustard seeds, cover the pan, and cook until the seeds have stopped popping (not unlike popcorn), about 30 seconds. Add the lentils and the remaining dried chiles, stir-fry until the lentils turn golden-brown and the chiles blacken slightly, 15 to 20 seconds. Immediately add the chopped leaves, liquid and all, the coconut paste, and the salt. Pour the remaining ½ cup cooking water into the blender jar and swish it around to wash it out; add this to the curry. Stir once or twice and heat to a boil. Then reduce the heat to medium-low, cover the pan, and cook, stirring occasionally, until the flavors mingle, about 15 minutes.

5. Stir in the lime juice, and serve.

Tip: Bunches of red amaranth are found year-round in the produce section of Chinese markets. Also called "red spinach" or "Chinese spinach," red amaranth has a much more assertive flavor than the mild-tasting green-leafed amaranth. To prep the leaves for cooking, trim off their tough stems. Place the leaves in a large bowl and pour cold water over them. Gently shake the leaves under the water to get rid of the minute particles of grime, which will sink to the bottom. Dump the water, refill the bowl with cold water, and repeat once or twice to thoroughly clean the leaves.

Bamboo Shoots
WITH A SMOKY-TART GARLIC SAUCE

bambalay Curry

bamboo shoots are an unusual ingredient to most Indians except those from the Coorgh and Assamese communities. Bamboo trees grow wild along the southwestern coast of India, and the shoots are available fresh. Fresh bamboo shoots have a very different taste and texture than the canned variety (they are more fibrous, but once cooked are sweet with a juicy crunch). Unfortunately, the only bamboo shoots available here are the canned ones, which are cooked and then immersed in brine. Still, once the canned bamboo shoots are drained and stewed with smoky-tart kudampuli, you won't notice the difference. I usually enjoy this for lunch with puffy-fried *pooris* (page 725). **SERVES 4**

kudampuli? See the Glossary of Ingredients, page 758.

1 whole kudampuli (see Tip, page 248) or
    ½ teaspoon tamarind paste or concentrate
    plus 1 drop liquid smoke
1 cup boiling water

2 tablespoons canola oil
1 teaspoon black or yellow mustard seeds
½ teaspoon fenugreek seeds
8 to 10 dried red Thai or cayenne chiles, to taste,
    stems removed
10 to 12 medium-size to large fresh curry leaves
4 large cloves garlic, thinly sliced
1 can (15 ounces) bamboo shoots, drained
1 teaspoon coarse kosher or sea salt
2 tablespoons rice flour
2 tablespoons finely chopped fresh cilantro
    leaves and tender stems

1. Place the kudampuli in a small heatproof bowl and pour the boiling water over it. Set the bowl aside until a haunting smokiness emanates from the water, about 15 minutes. Then squeeze the dried fruit (it will still be firm to the touch) to extract some more of its juices. (I usually wrap the fruit and refrigerate it for another extraction or two.)

2. Heat the oil in a small saucepan over medium-high heat. Add the mustard seeds, cover the pan, and cook until the seeds have stopped popping (not unlike popcorn), about 30 seconds. Sprinkle in the fenugreek seeds, chiles (yes, they will make you cough as they turn black), curry leaves, and garlic. Cook until the garlic browns, 1 to 2 minutes. Then add the bamboo shoots, salt, and the smoky-tart kudampuli water. Heat the curry to a boil. Then lower the heat to medium and simmer, uncovered, until the shoots absorb the flavors, about 5 minutes.

3. Sprinkle the rice flour over the mixture and stir it in quickly to prevent any lumps from forming. Within seconds, the sauce will start to thicken.

4. Sprinkle with the cilantro, and serve.

Stewed Beets

WITH
BEET GREENS & GINGER

Thukander Aur Saag

beets have an inherent sweetness that plays a crucial role in balancing out the heat from the chiles and the sharp bite of the ginger in this curry. Savor it as a side dish with Seared Shrimp with a Pearl Onion Sauce (page 271) and Fragrant Basmati Rice with Curry Leaves (page 715)—not only a cohesive meal, but also a stunning-looking one. **SERVES 4**

2 large beets with their green tops
   (about 1 pound total)

2 tablespoons canola oil

1 teaspoon black or yellow mustard seeds

6 to 8 medium-size to large fresh curry leaves

2 fresh green Thai, cayenne, or serrano chiles,
   stems removed, cut in half lengthwise
   (do not remove the seeds)

1 teaspoon coarse kosher or sea salt

3 lengthwise slices fresh ginger (each 2 inches long,
   1 inch wide, and 1/8 inch thick), cut into
   matchstick-thin strips (julienne)

1. Separate the greens from the beet bulbs (you can cut them off or twist, yank, and tear them away—whatever your state of mind). Rinse the greens under cold water and shake off the excess water. Arrange the greens in a stack on a cutting board and slice the bunch into thin shreds—including the deep red, juicy stalks. Transfer them to a small bowl. Trim off and discard both ends of each beet bulb. Peel them with a vegetable peeler, and rinse them under running water. Cut the bulbs into 1-inch cubes.

2. Heat the oil in a medium-size saucepan over medium-high heat. Add the mustard seeds, cover the pan, and cook until the seeds have stopped popping (not unlike popcorn), about 30 seconds. Add the beets, curry leaves, and chiles. Stir-fry to coat the deep red beets with the mustard seeds, 1 to 2 minutes. Then reduce the heat to medium-low, cover the pan, and cook, stirring occasionally, until the beets are braised, 10 to 15 minutes. (The beets will sweat, releasing some liquid, in which they will cook.)

3. Add the beet greens, salt, ginger, and 1 cup water. Once the blood-red curry comes to a boil, cover the pan and simmer, stirring occasionally, until the beets have absorbed most of the liquid and are tender when tested (or more appropriately, tasted), 25 to 30 minutes. Then serve.

Tips:

❖ Beets, short for beetroots, have been around since before 300 B.C. Although their botanical name is *Beta vulgaris,* let me tell you, there is nothing crude or obscene about this plant. The leaves and ribs are similar to the Swiss chard so prolific in supermarkets these days. The bulb, which grows under the ground, has a deep reddish-purple skin, numerous whisker-like fibers, and a long tapered root at the opposite end of the stem. Golden and albino (white) beets are also available, and if you wish for a melting pot–like extravaganza, use a combination.

❖ The secret to avoiding red beet stains on your cutting board is to wash it with soap, bleach, and warm water as soon as you have finished cutting up the beets. There is a reason why some natural red dyes are extracted from beets.

Bitter Melon
WITH ONION & TOMATO

Rassedaar Karelay Ki Subzi

My Sindhi-speaking sister-in-law, Anuradha, offered this curry one day when I was visiting my brother and his family in Mumbai. I lamented that I had yet to find a bitter melon recipe I liked, and she pulled this concoction, mottled with spices, onion, and tomato, from her refrigerator. "Salt it for a very long time and pan-fry it," she advised, "and you won't find it to be unpleasantly bitter." Well, Anuradha was right about that, and I found it to be certainly palatable

and manageable. You decide and let me know if you feel the same way. **SERVES 8**

4 small to medium-size bitter melons
   (about 1 pound total)
2 teaspoons coarse kosher or sea salt
4 tablespoons canola oil
1 cup finely chopped red onion
1 large tomato, cored and finely chopped
1 teaspoon Punjabi garam masala (page 25)
1 teaspoon cayenne (ground red pepper)
1 teaspoon white granulated sugar
½ teaspoon ground turmeric
¼ cup finely chopped fresh cilantro leaves
   and tender stems for garnishing

1. Trim off and discard both ends of each melon. Using a swivel peeler or a paring knife, scrape off the

bitter melon

It looks like a small cucumber with bumpy, scaly skin and a rat-like tail at one end; its color ranges from light green to dark green; and its skin spans the thin-to-thick spectrum. There is no way of minimizing the news: Any way you slice, dice, stew, pan-fry, bake, or stuff it, bitter melon is one bitter-tasting vegetable. Billions adore this melon (or gourd)—not only in India, but also in China, Vietnam, Sri Lanka, and Africa. The fact that bitter melon is available year-round even in "regular" grocery stores underscores the rule of supply and demand: millions demand it and the grocery stores supply it. Period.

So, why is this vegetable (technically a fruit but used as a vegetable) so popular? Because bitterness is a taste profile that is prevalent in many of India's regional curries, and bitter melon is an ideal candidate for adding

that taste. Americans of European descent are not big on bitter foods, but much of the rest of the globe craves bitter flavors. Indians know bitter melon as karela (not Kerala, which is a state in the southwest of India) or parakai, and just like squash, it is a truly versatile vegetable.

To prepare bitter melon for cooking (no person in their right mind eats it raw), trim the ends off and peel the bumpy, scaly skin with a swivel peeler or a paring knife. Slice the melon in half lengthwise and scoop out some of the seeds from its fleshy center. I usually salt the melon to leach away its bitterness, then rinse it well and dry it with paper towels before cooking it. Because it retains that salty flavor even when rinsed, there is no need to add any more salt when you incorporate it in a recipe.

bumpy scales and then peel the melon to reveal its light green flesh. Slice the melons in half lengthwise, and scoop out and discard the spongy, fleshy seeds from the center. Cut each half into ¼-inch cubes.

2. Dump the melon cubes into a colander and place it either in a sink or in a bowl. Add the salt and toss it with the melon. Let the melon sit to allow some of the bitterness to leach out (akin to salting eggplant), 2 to 3 hours. (You can leave the melon in the colander overnight; when I do that, I usually place the colander in the refrigerator, just to play it safe.)

3. Rinse the bitter melon thoroughly and then squeeze out as much of the water as you possibly can. Pat the pieces dry between paper towels.

4. Heat 2 tablespoons of the oil in a medium-size skillet over medium-high heat. Add the melon and stir-fry until the pieces are light honey-brown and slightly crispy, 8 to 12 minutes. Transfer them to a plate.

5. Heat the remaining 2 tablespoons oil in the same skillet over medium-low heat. Add the onion and cook until it starts to turn caramel-brown with a deep purple hue, 15 to 20 minutes (the onion will stew first, and then the liquid will evaporate).

6. Add the tomato, garam masala, cayenne, sugar, and turmeric to the onion. Raise the heat to medium and cook, uncovered, stirring occasionally, until the tomato softens, about 5 minutes.

7. Stir in ½ cup water and the fried bitter melon pieces. Heat the curry to a boil. Then reduce the heat and simmer, uncovered, stirring occasionally, until the sauce has thickened slightly and the melon has absorbed the flavors, somewhat masking its bitterness, 5 to 10 minutes.

8. Sprinkle with the cilantro, and serve.

Broccoli
WITH GINGER AND COCONUT

ŋariyal ħare ᵽhool ᵹobhi

Mellow-tasting, this curry makes ho-hum broccoli perk up with the presence of the chiles in the *Sambhar masala* (page 33). Serve it with the easy-to-make, onion-flavored *Pyaaz murghi* (page 153) for a south-north Indian combo. **SERVES 6**

> 2 tablespoons canola oil
> 1 teaspoon cumin seeds
> 2 tablespoons finely chopped fresh ginger
> 1 pound broccoli, cut into 1-inch florets
> 1½ teaspoons coarse kosher or sea salt
> 1 teaspoon Sambhar masala (page 33)
> 1 cup shredded fresh coconut; or ½ cup shredded
>   dried unsweetened coconut, reconstituted
>   (see Note)

1. Heat the oil in a medium-size skillet over medium-high heat. Add the cumin seeds and cook until they sizzle and turn reddish brown, 5 to 10 seconds. Add the ginger and stir-fry until it is golden brown, about 1 minute.

2. Add the broccoli, salt, and *Sambhar masala,* and stir-fry to make sure the spice blend coats the florets, about 1 minute. Pour in 1 cup water and stir once or twice. Once the water boils, lower the heat to medium, cover the skillet, and cook, stirring occasionally, until the broccoli is fork-tender, 8 to 10 minutes.

3. Stir in the coconut, which will thicken the curry almost instantly. Continue to simmer the curry, uncov-

ered, until the coconut is warmed through, about 2 minutes. Then serve.

Note: To reconstitute coconut, cover with ½ cup boiling water, set aside for about 15 minutes, and then drain.

Broccoli and Carrots
WITH ROASTED SPICES AND TOMATO

Pardesi Hare Phool Gobhi Aur Gajar ki Subzi

There is no translation for "broccoli" because it isn't an Indian vegetable. So I came up with *pardesi* (foreign) *hare* (green) *phool* (flower) *gobhi* (cauliflower)! Now, because of trade with countries like the United States, and with Indians traveling more, broccoli has simmered its way into many an Indian curry and stir-fry. This combination provides a simple but incredibly delicious curry. Enjoy it as a side dish with *Lasoon urad chi dal* (page 370), those creamy-tasting, garlic-infused, lime-flavored black lentils, and a mound of red rice (page 708). **SERVES 6**

2 tablespoons canola oil

1 teaspoon black or yellow mustard seeds

1 tablespoon skinned split black lentils (cream-colored in this form, urad dal), picked over for stones

1 pound broccoli, cut into 1-inch florets

1 large carrot, peeled and cut into strips 2 inches long, ½ inch wide, and ¼ inch thick

2 teaspoons Sambhar masala (page 33)

1 teaspoon coarse kosher or sea salt

1 can (14.5 ounces) diced tomatoes

15 medium-size to large fresh curry leaves

1. Heat the oil in a large skillet over medium-high heat. Add the mustard seeds, cover the skillet, and cook until the seeds have stopped popping (not unlike popcorn), about 30 seconds. Add the lentils and stir-fry until they turn golden brown, 15 to 20 seconds. Immediately add the broccoli, carrot, *Sambhar masala,* and salt, and cook to flavor the medley, about 1 minute.

2. Stir in the tomatoes, with their liquid, ½ cup water, and the curry leaves. Bring to a boil. Then reduce the heat to medium-low, cover the skillet, and cook, stirring occasionally, until the broccoli and carrot are fork-tender, 12 to 15 minutes. Then serve.

Shredded Cabbage and Carrots
WITH CHILES

Sambhara

If you are not sweating while eating this curry, there are not enough chiles in it (you certainly have my blessings if you wish to add more). This is one of those well-balanced curries with an initially hot impact that quickly slides down a notch (not everything needs to be "taken up a notch") with the tart lime juice, sweet granulated sugar, and waterlogged cooked cabbage. Some of the *sambharas* I have eaten in Gujarati-speaking homes and kitchens are drier stir-fries, but I like the inclusion of lime juice for its tart quality.

SERVES 6

2 tablespoons peanut or canola oil

I teaspoon black or yellow mustard seeds

I teaspoon fenugreek seeds

¼ teaspoon ground asafetida

I small cabbage, thinly shredded (see Tips)

2 medium-size carrots, peeled, ends trimmed, shredded (see Tips)

6 to 8 fresh green Thai, cayenne, or serrano chiles, to taste, stems removed, thinly sliced lengthwise (do not remove the seeds)

½ teaspoon ground turmeric

2 teaspoons white granulated sugar

½ teaspoon coarse kosher or sea salt

¼ cup finely chopped fresh cilantro leaves and tender stems

Juice of I large lime

1. Heat a wok or a well-seasoned cast-iron skillet over high heat. Drizzle the oil down the sides of the wok. When oil has formed a shimmering pool at the bottom, add the mustard seeds, cover the wok, and cook until the seeds have stopped popping (not unlike popcorn), about 30 seconds. Sprinkle in the fenugreek seeds and asafetida, which will instantly sizzle on contact, the seeds turning reddish brown. Immediately add the cabbage, carrots, chiles, turmeric, sugar, and salt. Stir-fry to coat the vegetables with the spices, 1 to 2 minutes. Continue to cook, uncovered, stirring occasionally, until the cabbage cooks down and releases its water, 5 to 10 minutes.

2. Add ½ cup water and stir once or twice. Reduce the heat to medium-high, cover the wok, and cook, stirring occasionally, until the cabbage has that cooked, noodle-like appearance but is still slightly crunchy, 5 to 10 minutes.

3. Stir in the cilantro and lime juice, and serve. (If you are using an old-fashioned iron wok, transfer the curry to a serving bowl right away, or the acid in the lime will react with the wok to give the curry an unwanted metallic taste.)

Tips:

❖ Bags of shredded cabbage and carrots are readily available in the produce section of any supermarket. You will need 1½ pounds of shredded vegetables (cabbage and carrots combined) to substitute for the cabbage and carrots in this recipe.

❖ When I am doing my own shredding, I prefer to shred the cabbage with a sharp chef's knife, and to shred the carrots against a box grater, in a food processor, or with a mandoline. Cutting the cabbage by hand yields neat, crisp shreds. To do it by hand, slice the head of cabbage in half and remove the core by making a triangular cut at the base. Slice each half in half again. And then cut the cabbage (either lengthwise or crosswise) in pencil-shaving-thin strips.

❖ A food processor can also shred cabbage, but I am not too wild about the results.

Cabbage and Cauliflower
IN A SPICY TOMATO-MINT SAUCE

Pudhinay Waale
Gobhi Aur bund Gobhi ki Subzi

t his thin, mint-flavored curry is mild in heat, despite all those chiles. If it's not hot enough for you, chomp on a few of the whole ones in between mouthfuls to enliven your taste buds. I love the noodle-like texture of cooked cabbage. Serve this with slices of buttered toast for a simple lunch. **SERVES 8**

2 tablespoons canola oil

I small red onion, cut in half lengthwise
   and thinly sliced

6 dried red Thai or cayenne chiles, stems removed

I can (14.5 ounces) diced tomatoes

1½ teaspoons coarse kosher or sea salt

½ teaspoon ground turmeric

I pound cauliflower, cut into 1-inch florets

4 cups shredded cabbage (see Tip, page 468)

¼ cup finely chopped fresh mint leaves

¼ cup finely chopped fresh cilantro leaves and
   tender stems

12 to 15 medium-size to large fresh curry leaves

1. Heat the oil in a large saucepan over medium-high heat. Add the onion and chiles, and stir-fry until the onion is honey-brown and the chiles have blackened slightly, 5 to 8 minutes.

2. Stir in the tomatoes, with their liquid, and the salt and turmeric. Simmer the sauce, uncovered, stirring occasionally, until the flavors meld, 2 to 4 minutes.

3. Stir in the cauliflower, cabbage, and 1 cup water, and bring to a boil. Then lower the heat to medium, cover the pan, and simmer, stirring occasionally, until the cauliflower is fork-tender and the cabbage strips are tender but still slightly firm and noodle-like, 15 to 18 minutes.

4. Stir in the mint, cilantro, and curry leaves, and serve.

Coconut Cabbage
WITH CHILES AND GREEN PEAS

thenga muttaikose

A side dish like this one was always popular in my mother's kitchen because cabbage was one of very few vegetables that were liked by everyone in the family. Cooked cabbage may elicit strong opinions pro or con in this country, but my six-year-old son loves it—so I know he is carrying on the family preferences. **SERVES 6**

I cup shredded fresh coconut; or ½ cup shredded dried
   unsweetened coconut, reconstituted (see Note)

4 fresh green Thai, cayenne, or serrano chiles, stems
   removed

2 tablespoons canola oil

I teaspoon black or yellow mustard seeds

I tablespoon skinned split black lentils
   (cream-colored in this form, urad dal),
   picked over for stones

4 cups shredded cabbage (see Tip, page 468)

2 cups frozen green peas (no need to thaw)

2 teaspoons coarse kosher or sea salt

12 medium-size to large fresh curry leaves

1. Pour 1 cup water into a blender jar, and add the coconut and chiles. Puree, scraping the inside of the jar as needed, to make a creamy-white, thin sauce with flecks of green.

2. Heat the oil in a large saucepan over medium-high heat. Add the mustard seeds, cover the pan, and cook until the seeds have stopped popping (not unlike popcorn), about 30 seconds. Add the lentils and stir-fry until they turn golden brown, 15 to 20 seconds.

3. Immediately add the cabbage, peas, salt, curry leaves, and the sauce. Stir once or twice, and bring the curry to a boil. Then reduce the heat to medium-low, cover the pan, and simmer, stirring occasionally, until the cabbage is just tender, 8 to 10 minutes. Then serve.

Note: To reconstitute coconut, cover with ½ cup boiling water, set aside for about 15 minutes, and then drain.

Cabbage, Potatoes, and Peas

badha kofi torkari

The sauce for this curry is pretty thin because there is no ingredient in the mix to thicken it. The potatoes are cut into large pieces and browned, so they don't break down to thicken the sauce. The clarified butter, folded in after the vegetables cook, combines with the remaining liquid to provide some body. I usually serve a curry like this as a side dish with a legume, meat, or fish curry. The yogurt-based *Doi maach* (page 252) is especially good with it. **SERVES 6**

1 pound russet or Yukon Gold potatoes, peeled, cut into
2-inch cubes, and submerged in a bowl of cold water
to prevent browning
2 tablespoons canola oil
1 teaspoon cumin seeds

1½ teaspoons coarse kosher or sea salt
1 teaspoon grated fresh ginger
½ teaspoon cayenne (ground red pepper)
½ teaspoon ground turmeric
2 fresh green Thai, cayenne, or serrano chiles,
stems removed, thinly sliced crosswise
(do not remove the seeds)
2 fresh or dried bay leaves
4 cups shredded cabbage (see Tip, page 468)
1 cup frozen green peas (no need to thaw)
¼ cup finely chopped fresh cilantro leaves
and tender stems
2 tablespoons Ghee (page 21) or butter
(preferably unsalted)
½ teaspoon Bangala garam masala (page 26)

1. Drain the potatoes and pat them dry with paper towels.

2. Preheat a wok or a well-seasoned cast-iron skillet over medium-high heat. Drizzle the oil down the sides of the wok, and let it heat until it forms a shimmering pool at the bottom. Then sprinkle in the cumin seeds and cook until they sizzle, turn reddish brown, and smell nutty, 5 to 10 seconds. Immediately add the potatoes, salt, ginger, cayenne, turmeric, chiles, and bay leaves. Reduce the heat to medium-low, cover the wok, and cook, stirring occasionally, until the spices roast and the potatoes brown, 8 to 12 minutes.

3. Pour in 2 cups water. Stir, and scrape the bottom of the wok to deglaze it, releasing any browned bits of potato and spice. Stir in the cabbage and bring the curry to a boil over medium heat. Continue to simmer vigorously, uncovered, stirring occasionally, until the vegetables are fork-tender, 15 to 20 minutes.

4. Stir in the peas, cilantro, ghee, and garam masala. Simmer, uncovered, stirring occasionally, until the peas are warmed through, about 5 minutes. Then serve.

Stewed Cabbage, Potato, and Peas

WITH A ROASTED CHILE–LENTIL BLEND

Muttaikose, Urulikazhangu, Patani Bhajee

An easy-to-make curry, this rounds out that epitome of comfort food, Rice with Yogurt and Mustard Seeds (page 710), especially after you've binged on fried foods at the local summer state fair. Add a serving of lime pickles (page 745) and call it a satisfying night. **SERVES 6**

- 1 pound russet or Yukon Gold potatoes, peeled, cut into 1-inch cubes, and submerged in a bowl of cold water to prevent browning
- 2 tablespoons canola oil
- 1 teaspoon black or yellow mustard seeds
- 1 tablespoon skinned split black lentils (cream-colored in this form, urad dal), picked over for stones
- 1 teaspoon fenugreek seeds, ground
- 1 teaspoon black or yellow mustard seeds, ground
- ½ teaspoon ground turmeric
- 1 pound cabbage, thinly shredded (see Tip, page 468)
- 2 cups frozen green peas (no need to thaw)
- 1½ teaspoons coarse kosher or sea salt
- 1 teaspoon Sambhar masala (page 33)
- ¼ cup finely chopped fresh cilantro leaves and tender stems

1. Drain the potatoes and pat them dry with paper towels.

2. Heat the oil in a wok or a large saucepan over medium-high heat. Add the mustard seeds, cover the pan, and cook until the seeds have stopped popping (not unlike popcorn), about 30 seconds. Add the lentils and stir-fry until they turn golden brown, 15 to 20 seconds. Add the potatoes and stir-fry until they turn a honey-brown color, about 5 minutes.

3. Sprinkle the fenugreek, mustard, and turmeric over the potatoes, and stir once or twice; cook for about 30 seconds. Then add 2 cups water and the cabbage, peas, salt, and *Sambhar masala*. Cook over medium heat, uncovered, stirring occasionally, until the vegetables have absorbed most of the thin curry and are fork-tender, 20 to 25 minutes.

4. Stir in the cilantro, and serve.

Cabbage and Peas

WITH ROASTED MUSTARD SEEDS & LENTILS

Muttaikose Pattani

Botanically called *brassica oleracea* this family of cruciferous vegetables includes kale, cauliflower, Brussels sprouts, broccoli, kohlrabi, and cabbage. Tight-headed green cabbage is the most prolific member of this family that is used in Indian cooking, and it is one of the few vegetables Indians eat raw (see Cabbage and Cucumber "Slaw" with Roasted Peanuts, page

741). Nutritionally sound, with a large amount of vitamins (which are unfortunately minimized with cooking), this large-leafed ball of goodness is 90 percent water—which is why this curry does not need any added water. **SERVES 8**

2 tablespoons canola oil

1 teaspoon black or yellow mustard seeds

1 tablespoon skinned split black lentils
    (cream-colored in this form, urad dal),
    picked over for stones

1 small head cabbage (1 to 1½ pounds),
    cut into ½-inch cubes

¼ cup finely chopped fresh cilantro leaves
    and tender stems

2 teaspoons Sambhar masala (page 33)

2 teaspoons coarse kosher or sea salt

10 to 12 medium-size to large fresh curry leaves

2 cups fresh or frozen green peas
    (no need to thaw if frozen)

1. Heat the oil in a large saucepan over medium-high heat. Add the mustard seeds, cover the pan, and cook until the seeds have stopped popping (not unlike popcorn), about 30 seconds. Immediately add the lentils and stir-fry until they turn golden brown, 15 to 20 seconds. Then add the cabbage, cilantro, spice blend, salt, and curry leaves. Cook, uncovered, stirring occasionally, until the spices and herbs coat the cabbage, 2 to 4 minutes.

2. Cover the pan and reduce the heat to medium-low. Cook, stirring occasionally, until the cabbage is tender, 10 to 15 minutes. (The rising steam within and the release of the cabbage's inherent liquid will braise the vegetable.)

3. Stir in the peas and continue cooking, covered, stirring occasionally, until they are warm and tender, 5 to 10 minutes. Then serve.

Cabbage and Potatoes
WITH FENNEL AND CHILES

bund Gobhi Aur Aloo ki Subzi

this mellow-tasting curry highlights the citrusy taste of ground coriander against the mild-flavored cabbage. If you like, thicken the thin, brothlike sauce by mashing a few of the fork-tender potatoes with the back of a spoon. **SERVES 6**

8 ounces russet or Yukon Gold potatoes, peeled,
    cut into ½-inch cubes, and submerged in a
    bowl of cold water to prevent browning

2 tablespoons canola oil

1 teaspoon fennel seeds

1 teaspoon cumin seeds

½ teaspoon fenugreek seeds

4 dried red Thai or cayenne chiles, stems removed

1 tablespoon coriander seeds, ground

4 cups shredded cabbage (see Tip, page 468)

½ cup finely chopped fresh cilantro leaves and
    tender stems

1½ teaspoons coarse kosher or sea salt

1 large tomato, cored and cut into 1-inch pieces

1. Drain the potatoes and pat them dry with paper towels.

2. Heat the oil in a large saucepan over medium-high heat. Sprinkle in the fennel seeds, cumin seeds, fenugreek seeds, and chiles. Cook until they sizzle, the chiles blacken, and the seeds turn reddish brown and smell nutty-pungent, 15 to 20 seconds. Then add the

potatoes and the coriander. Stir-fry until the potatoes are lightly browned, 3 to 5 minutes.

3. Stir in the cabbage, ¼ cup of the cilantro, the salt, the tomato, and ½ cup water. Bring the curry to a boil. Then reduce the heat to medium-low, cover the pan, and simmer, stirring occasionally, until the potatoes are fork-tender, 15 to 20 minutes.

4. Sprinkle with the remaining ¼ cup cilantro, and serve.

Tip: Note the addition of cilantro at two different stages during the cooking: The first batch, thrown in early on and simmered in the sauce, adds flavor while diminishing the controversial herb's gusto. The final addition, sprinkled just before serving, enlivens the curry.

fenugreek leaves

❖ ❖ ❖

fenugreek leaves, widely used in the northern regions of India, contribute a perfumed bitterness to curries. Both fresh and frozen fenugreek leaves are widely available in Indian grocery stores. Fresh leaves are not as common, but the frozen ones (available in 10-ounce packages) are omnipresent. Even more widespread are the dried leaves known as kasoori methi.

To use the dried leaves, I soak them in a bowl of water for about 15 minutes. Then I use my fingers to scoop them up from the water's surface (they are very light and float to the top), leaving behind any dust or dirt, which will have sunk to the bottom of the bowl. When substituting dried for fresh or frozen leaves, use half the amount called for (1/2 cup dried for 1 cup fresh or frozen).

Al Dente Cabbage
WITH POTATOES AND PEAS

Bund Gobhi, Aloo, Aur Mutter ki Subzi

I love cooked cabbage, and in this curry, I especially enjoy its al dente, noodle-like texture against the surprising citrus-crunch of stir-fried coriander seeds. The balance of bitter fenugreek seeds and aromatic fenugreek leaves proves that siblings can co-exist harmoniously, even with disparate personalities. **SERVES 6**

1 pound russet or Yukon Gold potatoes, peeled, cut into 1-inch cubes, and submerged in a bowl of cold water to prevent browning
2 tablespoons canola oil
1 teaspoon coriander seeds
½ teaspoon fenugreek seeds
2 dried red Thai or cayenne chiles, stems removed
2 teaspoons coarse kosher or sea salt
4 cups shredded cabbage (see Tip, page 468)
1 cup frozen green peas (no need to thaw)
2 tablespoons dried fenugreek leaves, soaked in a bowl of water and skimmed off before use (see box)

1. Drain the potatoes.

2. Preheat a wok or a large saucepan over medium-high heat. Pour the oil into the hot pan and then immediately add the coriander seeds, fenugreek seeds, and chiles. Allow them to sizzle until the seeds turn golden brown and the chiles blacken slightly, 30 seconds to 1 minute.

3. Add the potatoes, 1 cup water, and the salt; stir once or twice to evenly distribute the spices. Heat to a boil. Stir in the cabbage and allow the water to come to a boil again. Then lower the heat to medium, cover the wok, and cook, stirring occasionally, until the potatoes are partially cooked, 5 to 8 minutes.

4. Stir in the peas, and add the fenugreek leaves. Continue to simmer the curry, covered, stirring occasionally, until the potatoes are fork-tender, 8 to 10 minutes. Then serve.

Simmered Cabbage and Spinach
WITH PEANUTS

Bund Gobhi Palak Chi Bhajee

Cabbage, when simmered in a sauce, never breaks down enough to thicken it. Therefore cabbage-based curries generally have thin sauces, unless thickening ingredients are added. Don't expect this curry to have much body, but do be prepared to be blown away by its full-bodied, potent flavors. **SERVES 6**

¼ cup raw peanuts (see Tips)
2 tablespoons canola oil
2 tablespoons finely chopped fresh ginger
6 fresh green Thai, cayenne, or serrano chiles,
    stems removed, thinly sliced crosswise
    (do not remove the seeds)
2 teaspoons mustard seeds, ground

2 teaspoons coriander seeds, ground
2 teaspoons cumin seeds, ground
2 teaspoons coarse kosher or sea salt
½ teaspoon ground turmeric
1 pound cabbage, chopped into ¼-inch pieces
1 pound fresh spinach leaves, well rinsed and
    coarsely chopped
Juice of 1 medium-size lime

1. Pulse the peanuts in a food processor until they have the consistency of fine breadcrumbs.

2. Heat the oil in a large saucepan over medium heat. Add the peanuts, ginger, and chiles, and stir-fry until the mixture has a light honey-brown color, 3 to 4 minutes. Sprinkle in the mustard, coriander, cumin, salt, and turmeric, and stir once or twice to cook the spices, about 15 seconds.

3. Pile in the cabbage and stir to coat it with the aromatic spices. Add 1 cup water and heat to a boil. Reduce the heat to medium-low, cover the pan, and braise the cabbage, stirring occasionally, until it is fork-tender, about 15 minutes.

4. Add the spinach, cover the pan, and cook until it has wilted, about 10 minutes.

5. Stir in the lime juice, and serve.

Tips:

❖ If you have no raw peanuts on hand but do have the preroasted kind, use them by all means; just wait to add them along with the cabbage, so as not to burn them.

❖ When you need to grind a few spices for a curry like this, there is no need to grind them individually. Put all the whole spices in a spice grinder and pulverize the mixture to a consistency like that of finely ground black pepper. (However, I do often recommend that my students grind spices one at a time so they can familiarize themselves with each one's distinct aroma. It's always a "wow" moment to smell them one at a time and then collectively, as a blend, because the aromas in a spice mix can be so different than its components.)

Chopped Cabbage
WITH A YELLOW SPLIT PEA SAUCE

Muttaikose Usli

◆ ne of many dishes spooned atop banana leaves, *uslis* are often served at weddings in southern India. Cut-up yard-long green beans are a favorite, but I love the texture of cooked cabbage in this version. The steamed split pea paste not only appeals to the protein-conscious eater but also thickens the sauce. **SERVES 6**

I cup yellow split peas (chana dal), picked over
    for stones
6 dried red Thai or cayenne chiles, stems removed
    (see Tips)
2 teaspoons coarse kosher or sea salt
½ teaspoon ground asafetida
Vegetable cooking spray
2 tablespoons canola oil
I teaspoon black or yellow mustard seeds
I tablespoon skinned split black lentils
    (cream-colored in this form, urad dal),
    picked over for stones
4 cups finely chopped cabbage
½ teaspoon cayenne (ground red pepper)

¼ teaspoon ground turmeric
12 to 15 medium-size to large fresh curry leaves
2 tablespoons finely chopped fresh cilantro
    leaves and tender stems

1. Place the split peas in a medium-size bowl. Fill the bowl halfway with water and rinse the peas by rubbing them between your fingertips. The water will become cloudy. Drain this water. Repeat three or four times until the water remains relatively clear; drain. Now fill the bowl halfway with warm water and add the chiles. Set the bowl aside at room temperature, covered, until the split peas and chiles have softened, 2 to 4 hours.

2. Drain the split peas and chiles, and place them in a food processor. Process to form a red-speckled, slightly gritty paste. Transfer this to the same medium-size bowl (why dirty another one?), and fold in 1 teaspoon of the salt and the asafetida.

3. Lightly spray a steamer basket with cooking spray and insert it into a pan filled halfway with water. (Or, if you are using a bamboo steamer, line the bottom with wax paper and lightly spray the paper with cooking spray; place the steamer in a wok filled halfway with water.) Spread the paste in a ¼- to ½-inch-thick layer in the steamer basket, and bring the water to a boil. Steam, covered, until a knife inserted in the center of the paste comes out clean, 20 to 25 minutes.

4. When the paste is cooked, remove the basket from the steamer and set it aside to cool.

5. While the paste is cooling, heat the oil in a medium-size saucepan over medium-high heat. Add the mustard seeds, cover the pan, and cook until the seeds have stopped popping (not unlike popcorn), about 30 seconds. Add the lentils and stir-fry until they turn golden brown, 15 to 20 seconds. Add the cabbage and stir-fry to coat the leaves with the nutty-tasting oil, about

2 minutes. Sprinkle in the remaining 1 teaspoon salt and the cayenne, turmeric, and curry leaves. Stir once or twice, and add 1 cup water. Remove from the heat.

6. Once the paste is cool to the touch, break the dry, spicy cake into pea-size crumbs. Stir the crumbs into the cabbage mixture, cover, and cook over medium-low heat, stirring occasionally, until the flavors meld and most of the liquid has been absorbed into the now slightly swollen crumbs, 12 to 15 minutes.

7. Stir in the cilantro, and serve.

Tips:

❖ Don't be alarmed by the number of dried chiles in the paste—they will taste not-so-pungent, thanks to the flavor-absorbing split peas. Decrease the number by 1 or 2 chiles, if you must, but no more.

❖ The asafetida in legume-heavy curries like this one helps your body digest them—one of the key reasons why folks in the south use this controversial-smelling (but fine-tasting) spice.

Carrot Slices
IN A DILL SAUCE

₲ajar Suva

ill is not a very popular herb in many regions of India, but it is a favorite in the Sindhi community in the northwest. Stirred in at the very end, the dill retains its sharp, almost grassy essence. Sindhi cooks often combine spinach and dill, but in this recipe, I chose the other natural companion: sweet carrots. The carrots in India are a slightly different variety than those found in the U.S. and are deep red in color. Nutritionally they are quite superior because they contain lycopene—also found in tomatoes—which guards against heart disease and some forms of cancer. **SERVES 6**

2 tablespoons canola oil

1 teaspoon cumin seeds

1 cup finely chopped red onion

1 tablespoon coriander seeds, ground

½ teaspoon cayenne (ground red pepper)

¼ teaspoon ground turmeric

1 pound carrots, peeled, ends trimmed,
    thinly sliced on the diagonal

1 cup frozen green peas (no need to thaw)

¼ cup chopped fresh dill

3 tablespoons Toasted Chickpea Flour (page 41)

1½ teaspoons rock salt, pounded

1. Heat the oil in a medium-size skillet over medium-high heat. Add the cumin seeds and cook until they sizzle, turn reddish brown, and smell nutty, 5 to 10 seconds. Immediately add the onion and reduce the heat to medium-low. Cook slowly, uncovered, stirring occasionally, until the onion turns soft and brown with a deep purple hue, 10 to 12 minutes.

2. Stir in the coriander, cayenne, and turmeric. The heat will be just right to cook but not burn the ground spices, about 30 seconds.

3. Add the carrots, peas, and 2 cups water. Raise the heat to medium-high and simmer the vegetables, uncovered, stirring occasionally, until they are fork-tender and the sauce is somewhat thick, 6 to 8 minutes.

4. Stir in the dill, chickpea flour, and rock salt. The flour will instantly thicken the sauce. Then serve.

Tip: When you fold in pounded rock salt (or sea salt crystals) at the end, it gives a much sharper saltiness to the dish—which I love, especially because toasted chickpea flour can mask much of the mineral's gusto. For more information on rock salt, see the Glossary of Ingredients, page 758.

Carrots and Peas
WITH A ROASTED CHILE-SPICE BLEND

Manjal Mullangi Pattani Kari

This thin-sauced curry is a great side dish with Creamy Black Lentils with Chickpeas and Kidney Beans (page 367). The sweet carrots balance the hot flavors in the *Sambhar masala*, especially when you use either baby or thin, tender carrots—not those gargantuan, flavorless wonders. **SERVES 6**

- 2 tablespoons unrefined sesame oil or canola oil
- 1 teaspoon black or yellow mustard seeds
- 1 cup finely chopped red onion
- 1½ teaspoons coarse kosher or sea salt
- 1 teaspoon cumin seeds, ground
- 1 teaspoon coriander seeds, ground
- ½ teaspoon Sambhar masala (page 33)
- ¼ teaspoon ground turmeric
- 8 ounces carrots, peeled, ends trimmed, thinly sliced crosswise
- 2 cups frozen green peas (no need to thaw; see Tip)
- 2 tablespoons finely chopped fresh cilantro leaves and tender stems

1. Heat the oil in a small saucepan over medium-high heat. Add the mustard seeds, cover the pan, and cook until the seeds have stopped popping (not unlike popcorn), about 30 seconds. Immediately add the onion and stir-fry until it is honey-brown, 2 to 3 minutes. Then sprinkle in the salt, cumin, coriander, *Sambhar masala*, and turmeric. Cook, stirring constantly, for about 1 minute.

2. Add the carrots and peas, and stir to coat them with the onion-spice blend. Pour in 1 cup water and heat to a boil. Then reduce the heat to medium-low, cover the pan, and simmer, stirring occasionally, until the carrots are fork-tender, 12 to 15 minutes.

3. Sprinkle with the cilantro, and serve.

Tip: In India, frozen peas are a convenience that not many can afford. Fresh peas, though seasonal, are plump, sweet, and nutty-tasting. Here in the United States, when you have access to the fresh peas, use them instead of the frozen ones. You don't need to precook them before using them in this recipe.

Carrots
WITH WILTED SPINACH
IN A PEANUT-COCONUT SAUCE

Gajar, Palak, Ane Sengdane Chi Bhajee

Splurge and buy sweet, tender, slender carrots even if they might be a bit more costly than the mealy, gargantuan ones.

Serve this with Tamarind Shrimp with Coconut Milk (page 275) for an easy meal. **SERVES 4**

¼ cup raw peanuts (without the skins)

2 tablespoons white sesame seeds

2 tablespoons shredded dried unsweetened coconut

3 dried red Thai or cayenne chiles, stems removed

2 large cloves garlic

2 tablespoons canola oil

¼ teaspoon ground turmeric

I pound carrots, peeled, ends trimmed, thinly sliced crosswise

I teaspoon coarse kosher or sea salt

I teaspoon white granulated sugar

4 ounces fresh spinach leaves, well rinsed and coarsely chopped

1. Combine the peanuts, sesame seeds, coconut, chiles, and garlic in a food processor, and pulse to form a gritty, sticky, mellow-smelling blend with the consistency of coarse, but moist breadcrumbs.

2. Heat the oil in a medium-size skillet over medium heat. Add the peanut mixture and stir-fry until it is light honey-brown and fragrant, 1 to 2 minutes. Sprinkle the turmeric over it and stir it in.

3. Add the carrots, salt, sugar, and 1 cup water. Heat to a boil. Then reduce the heat to medium-low, cover the skillet, and simmer, stirring occasionally, until the carrots are very tender, 12 to 14 minutes.

4. Add the spinach and stir it in. As soon as the spinach has wilted (3 to 5 minutes), remove the skillet from the heat, and serve.

White poppy seeds? See the Glossary of Ingredients, page 758.

Stewed Cauliflower
IN A COCONUT-CASHEW SAUCE

dum gobhi

surprisingly sweet curry (even without the presence of sugar), this offers a great backdrop to otherwise ho-hum cauliflower. Cinnamon infuses it with an aromatic sweetness in tandem with fresh coconut. Serve it as an accompaniment to Fragrant Ginger Shrimp with Shallots and Curry Leaves (page 260) and a bowl of white rice. **SERVES 6**

I cup shredded fresh coconut; or ½ cup shredded dried unsweetened coconut, reconstituted (see Note)

¼ cup raw cashew nuts

I tablespoon white poppy seeds

I tablespoon coriander seeds

I teaspoon cumin seeds

I½ teaspoons coarse kosher or sea salt

¼ teaspoon ground turmeric

3 dried red Thai or cayenne chiles, stems removed

I cinnamon stick (3 inches long), broken into smaller pieces

2 tablespoons canola oil

I medium-size red onion, finely chopped

4 lengthwise slices fresh ginger (each I½ inches long, I inch wide, and ⅛ inch thick), finely chopped

I pound cauliflower, cut into 2-inch florets

1. Combine the coconut, cashews, poppy seeds, coriander seeds, cumin seeds, salt, turmeric, chiles, and cinnamon pieces in a blender jar. Puree, scraping the inside of the jar as needed, to form a slightly gritty, yellowish-red paste.

2. Heat the oil in a large skillet over medium heat. Toss in the onion and ginger, and stir-fry until the mixture is light brown, 5 to 7 minutes.

3. Add the coconut paste to the skillet and stir-fry for 1 to 2 minutes. Once it starts to stick, pour in ½ cup water and scrape the bottom of the skillet to release the browned bits of paste. Reduce the heat to medium-low and continue to simmer the mixture, uncovered, stirring occasionally, until it acquires a roasted aroma and a yellowish-brown color as some of the oil starts to separate from the sauce, about 15 minutes.

4. Pour in 1 cup water and add the cauliflower. Stir the curry once or twice, cover the skillet, and cook, stirring occasionally, until the florets are fork-tender, 25 to 30 minutes. Then serve.

Note: To reconstitute coconut, cover with ½ cup boiling water, set aside for about 15 minutes, and then drain.

Tips:

❖ Broccoli has now made it into India's marketplaces, flowering its way into the kitchens of those who have traveled in the West and experienced its flavor and versatility. Use it instead of, or in addition to, the cauliflower in this curry to provide a burst of green.

❖ For a nuttier flavor, use roasted cashew nuts, reducing the salt to 1 teaspoon if the nuts are salted.

Cayenne-Spiked Cauliflower
WITH AN ONION-TOMATO SAUCE

Masaaledar Phool Gobhi

Sometimes simpler is better. The few spices in this curry maintain the mellow cauliflower flavor and highlight the caramel-sweet onion. Don't be alarmed by the abundance of cayenne—the slow-cooked onion will absorb some of its heat with the tart assistance of the diced tomatoes. This a perfect side dish to serve with Pigeon Peas with Chiles and Jaggery (page 426) and white basmati rice. **SERVES 6**

2 tablespoons canola oil

1 small red onion, cut in half lengthwise
   and thinly sliced

6 medium-size cloves garlic, cut into
   thin lengthwise slivers

2 lengthwise slices fresh ginger
   (each 2 inches long, 1 inch wide, and ⅛ inch thick),
   cut into matchstick-thin strips (julienne)

2 teaspoons cumin seeds, ground

2 teaspoons coriander seeds, ground

1½ teaspoons coarse kosher or sea salt

1 teaspoon cayenne (ground red pepper)

½ teaspoon ground turmeric

1 can (14.5 ounces) diced tomatoes

1 pound cauliflower, cut into 1-inch florets

2 tablespoons Toasted Chickpea Flour (page 41)

¼ cup finely chopped fresh cilantro leaves
   and tender stems

1. Heat the oil in a large skillet over medium heat.

Add the onion, garlic, and ginger, and stir-fry until the onion is caramel-brown and soft, 10 to 12 minutes.

2. Sprinkle in the cumin, coriander, salt, cayenne, and turmeric. Stir once or twice and cook for about 30 seconds. Then stir in the tomatoes, with their juices, the cauliflower, and 1 cup water. Deglaze the skillet, releasing the browned bits of vegetables and spices. Heat to a boil. Then reduce the heat to medium-low, cover the skillet, and cook, stirring occasionally, until the florets are fork-tender, 12 to 15 minutes.

3. Sprinkle in the chickpea flour and quickly stir it into the sauce to thicken it slightly. Allow the sauce to simmer, uncovered, until it has thickened a bit more, 1 to 2 minutes.

4. Stir in the cilantro, and serve.

Cauliflower
IN AN ONION-CHILE SAUCE

Phool Gobhi Pyaaz

Chunky onions simmering in an onion sauce: sounds almost cannibalistic. But you won't feel an iota of guilt when you inhale this curry. The sweet undertones provide a comforting and flavorful base for mild-tasting cauliflower. **SERVES 6**

1 large red onion; half coarsely chopped,
*   half cut into 1-inch cubes*
2 teaspoons coriander seeds
1 teaspoon cumin seeds
2 tablespoons canola oil

4 fresh green Thai, cayenne, or serrano chiles,
*   stems removed, thinly sliced crosswise*
*   (do not remove the seeds)*
1½ teaspoons coarse kosher or sea salt
1 pound cauliflower, cut into 1-inch florets
1 large tomato, cored and cut into 1-inch cubes
2 tablespoons finely chopped fresh cilantro
*   and tender stems*

1. Pour ¼ cup water into a blender jar, and add the coarsely chopped onion, coriander seeds, and cumin seeds. Puree, scraping the inside of the jar as needed, to form a smooth purple sauce.

2. Heat the oil in a large skillet over medium-high heat. Add the cubed onion and the chiles, and stir-fry until the onion cubes turn light honey-brown around the edges and the chiles blacken (sending you into a coughing-sneezing fit), 5 to 10 minutes. Immediately add the pureed onion mixture. Pour ¼ cup water into the blender jar and swish it around to wash it out. Stir this into the skillet. Cook the sauce over medium heat, uncovered, stirring occasionally, until the water evaporates and the sauce starts to stick to the bottom of the skillet, 6 to 8 minutes.

3. Pour in ½ cup water and scrape the bottom of the skillet to deglaze it, releasing the browned bits of onion and spices. Stir in the salt, and add the cauliflower. Gently toss the florets with the sauce. Reduce the heat to medium-low, cover the skillet, and simmer, stirring occasionally, until the florets are fork-tender, 30 to 35 minutes.

4. Fold in the tomato and cilantro, and continue to cook, covered, until the tomato is warmed through, 1 to 2 minutes. Then serve.

Tip: Cubed potatoes, slightly browned in oil, make an excellent alternative for cauliflower.

Cauliflower and Potatoes
IN A BLACKENED RED CHILE SAUCE

Alur Phulkopir Jhol

fiery-hot, the chiles in this curry are more robust because they are roasted in a bit of oil until blackened. However, don't be alarmed by their number, because the creamy-tasting milk solids tone them down, making the whole experience downright enjoyable—without any of that hurt-so-good pain.

SERVES 6

1 white potato, such as russet or Yukon Gold,
    peeled, cut into 1-inch cubes, and submerged
    in a bowl of cold water to prevent browning
2 tablespoons mustard oil or canola oil,
    plus extra for brushing the skillet
1 pound cauliflower, cut into 1-inch florets
6 dried red Thai or cayenne chiles, stems removed
1 teaspoon cumin seeds
½ cup Whole Milk Solids (page 24; see Tip)
1½ teaspoons coarse kosher or sea salt
2 tablespoons finely chopped fresh cilantro
    leaves and tender stems for garnishing

1. Drain the potatoes and pat them dry with paper towels.

2. Heat the 2 tablespoons oil in a large skillet over medium heat. Add the cauliflower and potatoes, cover the skillet, and cook, stirring occasionally, until they are partially cooked and lightly browned, 12 to 15 minutes.

3. While the vegetables are cooking, brush a small skillet with a little oil and heat it over medium-high heat. Add the chiles and cumin seeds and roast them, stirring constantly, until the chiles blacken and the seeds turn reddish brown, 2 to 3 minutes.

4. Transfer the chiles and cumin seeds to a blender jar, and add ½ cup water and the milk solids. Puree, scraping the inside of the jar as needed, to make a smooth, creamy, chile-speckled sauce.

5. Once the vegetables are lightly browned, pour the sauce over them and sprinkle with the salt. Stir, reduce the heat to medium-low, cover the skillet, and cook, stirring occasionally, until the cauliflower and potatoes are fork-tender, 8 to 10 minutes.

6. Sprinkle with the cilantro, and serve.

Tip: Not having Whole Milk Solids on hand should not preclude you from making this curry. An equal amount of heavy (whipping) cream is an acceptable alternative to cut down the chiles' heat—but I do enjoy the depth that reduced milk solids provide.

Easy Cauliflower and Peas
WITH A CURRY LEAF SAUCE

Cauliflower Pattani

great as an icebreaker, this curry appeals to those who are just starting to explore the Indian way of eating. Most of the spice and herb ingredients are aromatics, and so do not generate pungent heat. The chiles in the spice blend are quite mellow, and whatever wisp it exudes is further tempered by the presence of rice flour, which acts in a double role (like a Bollywood actor). Serve it with some Sweetened Mango Puree with Milk (page 751) and a stack of puffy fried *pooris* (page 725), either for lunch or for a no-frills dinner. **SERVES 6**

2 tablespoons canola oil

I teaspoon black or yellow mustard seeds

I tablespoon skinned split black lentils
   (cream-colored in this form, urad dal),
   picked over for stones

I medium-size head cauliflower, cut into 2-inch-florets

I cup fresh or frozen green peas
   (no need to thaw if frozen)

1½ teaspoons coarse kosher or sea salt

I tablespoon rice flour

2 tablespoons finely chopped fresh cilantro leaves
   and tender stems

2 teaspoons Roasted Curry Leaf Spice Blend (page 35)

1. Heat the oil in a large skillet over medium-high heat. Add the mustard seeds, cover the skillet, and cook until the seeds have stopped popping (not unlike popcorn), about 30 seconds. Add the lentils and stir-fry until they turn golden brown, 15 to 20 seconds.

2. Immediately add the cauliflower, peas, and salt. Stir-fry the medley to allow the salt to coat the vegetables. Then add 1 cup water and bring it to a boil. Cover the pan and simmer over medium heat, stirring occasionally, until the cauliflower is almost fall-apart tender, 12 to 15 minutes.

3. Sprinkle in the rice flour and quickly stir it in to prevent any clumps from forming. The sauce will start to thicken within seconds. Stir in the cilantro and the spice blend, and serve.

Bolly Cauli

Aloo Gobhi

You will see a few versions of this dish in this book, testimony to its popularity in north Indian restaurants all across Europe and North America. And let's not forget its prominence in the movie *Bend It Like Beckham,* where the hockey-stick-wielding tomboy heroine is forced to learn how to make this Punjabi delicacy to prove her capability as a dutiful housewife for her Indian husband. Just-baked naan (page 729)—that buttery, can't-stop-eating-it clay-oven bread—is a must with this curry. **SERVES 8**

1 pound russet or Yukon Gold potatoes, peeled,
   cut into 1-inch cubes, and submerged in a
   bowl of cold water to prevent browning

2 tablespoons canola oil

4 large cloves garlic, finely chopped

3 lengthwise slices fresh ginger (each 2 inches long,
   1 inch wide, and ⅛ inch thick), finely chopped

2 teaspoons Bin bhuna hua garam masala (page 30)

1½ teaspoons coarse kosher or sea salt

¼ teaspoon ground turmeric

1 pound cauliflower, cut into 2-inch florets (see Tip)

1 can (14.5 ounces) diced tomatoes

¼ cup finely chopped fresh cilantro leaves
   and tender stems

1. Drain the potatoes and pat them dry with paper towels.

2. Heat the oil in a large skillet over medium-high heat. Add the garlic and ginger, and stir-fry until they turn light brown, about 1 minute. Lower the

heat to medium and add the potatoes, garam masala, salt, and turmeric. Continue to stir-fry until the spices cook and smell fragrant, about 2 minutes.

3. Toss in the cauliflower and the tomatoes with their juices, and stir once or twice. Cover the skillet and simmer over medium-low heat, stirring occasionally, until the vegetables are fork-tender, 30 to 35 minutes. (The tomatoes keep the vegetables from cooking too quickly, thanks to their acidity.)

4. Stir in the cilantro, and serve.

Tip: You can substitute a 1-pound bag of frozen cauliflower florets; there's no need to thaw them before you add them to the recipe.

Restaurant-Style Cauliflower
AND POTATOES

Rassedaar Aloo Aur Gobhi ki Subzi

north Indian restaurant chefs love to serve their curries as smooth sauces that defy recognition. Creating subtle flavors in pureed tomato-, spinach-, and cream-based sauces is a hallmark of this type of restaurant cooking. These techniques are reminiscent of the royal Moghal-style cuisine made popular by the emperors who influenced northern India's food and cultural scene before the British regime. **SERVES 8**

I pound russet or Yukon Gold potatoes, peeled, cut into 1-inch cubes, and submerged in a bowl of cold water to prevent browning
2 tablespoons canola oil
2 tablespoons Ginger Paste (page 15)
I tablespoon Garlic Paste (page 15)
2 teaspoons coriander seeds, ground
2 teaspoons coarse kosher or sea salt
I teaspoon cumin seeds, ground
I teaspoon cayenne (ground red pepper)
¼ teaspoon ground turmeric
¼ cup Fried Onion Paste (page 16)
2 tablespoons tomato paste
I pound cauliflower, cut into 2-inch florets
I teaspoon Punjabi garam masala (page 25)
2 tablespoons finely chopped fresh cilantro leaves and tender stems

1. Drain the potatoes and pat dry with paper towels.

2. Heat the oil in a large saucepan over medium heat. Add the potatoes and the ginger and garlic pastes. Cook, stirring, until the potatoes have barely browned and a thin honey-brown layer of paste coats the bottom of the pan, 8 to 10 minutes.

3. Sprinkle the coriander, salt, cumin, cayenne, and turmeric over the potatoes, and stir-fry to cook the spices, about 30 seconds. Then add 1½ cups water, the Fried Onion Paste, and the tomato paste. Scrape the bottom of the pan to release the browned bits of potatoes and spices. (The potatoes themselves will not brown as much.)

4. Add the cauliflower, stir once or twice, and bring to a boil. Then reduce the heat to medium-low, cover the pan, and simmer, stirring occasionally, until the potatoes and cauliflower are fork-tender, 25 to 30 minutes.

5. Stir in the garam masala and cilantro, and serve.

Pan-Stewed Cauliflower and Spinach
WITH A SPICY TOMATO SAUCE

Cauliflower keerai kari

Whenever there are curry leaves in a dish, my students, who may never have come across their presence before, ask whether it's okay to eat them. When they are left whole, as in this recipe, we eat around them. They are perfectly edible, but they are used in recipes like this to gently flavor the sauce, so you don't really want to overwhelm the flavor by eating a whole leaf. The more chopped up they are, the more intense the flavor, and eating them in this form is just fine. However, don't let my advice stop you from munching on a whole one to see what it's all about. **SERVES 6**

2 tablespoons unrefined sesame oil or canola oil

1 teaspoon black or yellow mustard seeds

1 tablespoon skinned split black lentils (cream-colored in this form, urad dal), picked over for stones

8 ounces cauliflower, cut into 2-inch florets

1 pound fresh spinach leaves, well rinsed

1 large tomato, cored and cut into 1-inch cubes

1 tablespoon finely chopped fresh cilantro leaves and tender stems

1 teaspoon Sambhar masala (page 33)

1 teaspoon coarse kosher or sea salt

10 to 12 medium-size to large fresh curry leaves

1. Heat the oil in a large saucepan over medium-high heat. Add the mustard seeds, cover the pan, and cook until the seeds have stopped popping (not unlike popcorn), about 30 seconds. Add the lentils and stir-fry them until they turn golden brown, 15 to 20 seconds.

2. Immediately add the cauliflower and stir-fry until the florets are lightly browned around the edges, about 2 minutes. Pour 1 cup water into the pan; it will instantly come to a boil because of the hot pan. Lower the heat to medium, cover the pan, and stew the cauliflower, stirring occasionally, until it is partially cooked, 3 to 5 minutes.

3. Pile the spinach into the pan, cover, and cook until the leaves wilt, about 5 minutes. Then stir in all the remaining ingredients. Continue to cook the curry, uncovered, stirring occasionally, until the tomato is warmed through and the cauliflower is fork-tender, 3 to 5 minutes. Then serve.

Cauliflower and Spinach
IN A BLACK PEPPER–COCONUT MILK SAUCE

Cauliflower keerai thenga paal

Combine two of Kerala's prized ingredients, coconut milk and black peppercorns, to provide a smooth and slightly peppery base to otherwise ho-hum cauliflower and spinach. The addition of slightly tart tomato makes it a festive-looking dish. I serve it the way Keralites do, over a bowl of perfectly cooked rice noodles, either store-bought or, preferably, homemade (see *Idiappam,* page 723). **SERVES 8**

2 tablespoons canola oil

1 teaspoon black or yellow mustard seeds

1 teaspoon cumin seeds

8 ounces cauliflower, cut into 1-inch florets

4 large cloves garlic, finely chopped

1 can (13.5 ounces) unsweetened coconut milk

2 teaspoons coarse kosher or sea salt

1 teaspoon black peppercorns, coarsely cracked

12 medium-size to large fresh curry leaves

1 pound fresh spinach leaves, well rinsed

1 large tomato, cored and cut into ½-inch cubes

1. Heat the oil in a large saucepan over medium-high heat. Add the mustard seeds, cover the pan, and cook until the seeds have stopped popping (not unlike popcorn), about 30 seconds. Sprinkle in the cumin seeds, which will instantly turn reddish brown and smell fragrant.

2. Add the cauliflower and stir-fry until the florets are lightly browned around the edges, about 2 minutes. Add the garlic and stir-fry until it is browned, 1 minute.

3. Pour in the coconut milk, and scrape the pan to deglaze it, releasing the browned bits of spice. The coconut curry will instantly come to a boil because of the hot pan. Sprinkle in the salt, peppercorns, and curry leaves. Reduce the heat to medium-low, cover the pan, and simmer, stirring occasionally, until the cauliflower is fork-tender, 5 to 8 minutes.

4. Pile the spinach into the pan, cover, and cook until the leaves have wilted, about 5 minutes. Then stir in the tomato and raise the heat to medium-high. Allow the curry to boil vigorously, uncovered, stirring occasionally, until the tomato is warmed through and some of the cauliflower has broken down (which will help to thicken the sauce), 3 to 5 minutes. Then serve.

Fenugreek-Perfumed Cauliflower
WITH IVY GOURDS

Methiwaale Gobhi Tindora

I adore the fresh flavor of this sauce and the perfumed bitterness that emanates from the fenugreek greens. Here cauliflower is happy to play second fiddle to the juicy tenderness of ivy gourd squash, which look like small, thin baby cucumbers. This is a great side dish with a shrimp curry. **SERVES 8**

2 tablespoons canola oil

2 teaspoons cumin seeds

1 pound ivy gourd squash (see box, page 611)
  or English cucumbers, ends trimmed off, cut
  lengthwise into 2-inch-long-and-¼-inch-thick strips

1 pound cauliflower, cut into 1-inch florets

1 small red onion, cut in half lengthwise
  and thinly sliced

4 to 6 fresh green Thai, cayenne, or serrano chiles,
  to taste, stems removed, cut lengthwise into
  thin strips (do not remove the seeds)

2 teaspoons coarse kosher or sea salt

1 teaspoon ground turmeric

½ cup chopped fresh or frozen fenugreek leaves
  (thawed if frozen); or ¼ cup dried fenugreek leaves,
  soaked in a bowl of water and skimmed off before
  use (see box, page 473)

1. Heat the oil in a large saucepan over medium-high

heat. Sprinkle in the cumin seeds and cook until they sizzle, turn reddish brown, and smell fragrant, about 10 seconds. Immediately add the ivy gourd, cauliflower, onion, chiles, salt, and turmeric. Stir-fry to cook the turmeric, about 5 minutes.

2. Pour in 1 cup water and stir once or twice. Reduce the heat to medium-low, cover the pan, and cook, stirring occasionally, until the vegetables are fork-tender, 20 to 25 minutes.

3. Stir in the fenugreek and continue to simmer, covered, stirring occasionally, until some of the cauliflower breaks down into smaller pieces and slightly thickens the sauce, about 5 minutes. Then serve.

Sweet Corn
WITH CUMIN, CURRY LEAVES & CHILES

Makkai Nu Shaak

Corn grown in India is not the sweet variety that we so prize here in the United States. Often, when cooking Indian corn, the cook adds sugar—an ingredient I find unnecessary when sweet corn overflows the bins at grocery stores and farmers' markets here during the summer months. Serve this with Pigeon Peas with Chiles and Jaggery (page 426) and some fluffy rotis (page 727) for a simple, healthy vegetarian dinner. **SERVES 6**

I tablespoon Ghee (page 21) or butter
I teaspoon cumin seeds
¼ teaspoon ground turmeric

*Asafetida?
See the
Glossary of
Ingredients,
page 758.*

¼ teaspoon ground asafetida
Kernels from 3 ears fresh corn
   (about 3 cups; see Tip, page 489)
2 tablespoons finely chopped fresh cilantro leaves
   and tender stems
I teaspoon coarse kosher or sea salt
12 medium-size to large fresh curry leaves
2 to 4 fresh green Thai, cayenne, or serrano chiles,
   to taste, stems removed, sliced crosswise into
   ½-inch pieces (do not remove the seeds)

1. Heat the ghee in a medium-size saucepan over medium-high heat. Add the cumin seeds and cook until they sizzle, turn reddish brown, and are aromatic, 5 to 10 seconds. Sprinkle in the turmeric and asafetida.

2. Immediately add the corn, 1 cup water, and all the remaining ingredients. Stir once or twice and bring the curry to a boil. Then reduce the heat to medium-low, cover the pan, and simmer, stirring occasionally, until the corn is juicy and tender and some of the liquid has been absorbed, 8 to 10 minutes. Then serve.

Cob Corn
IN A COCONUT-CHILE SAUCE

Nariyal Bhutta

When I first tested this recipe, I wasn't bowled over by its looks. Halved corncobs bathing in a slightly curdled-looking coconut sauce didn't call out to me. But I did give in and taste it—and I am so glad I did. As I bit into the succulent kernels, sweetness permeated my mouth, followed by a slow, gentle burn.

The sweet backdrop against up-front pungent chiles proved addictive as I grabbed my second helping. My six-year-old son, Robert, surprised me by having seconds too, asking for a small bowl of plain, soothing yogurt to soothe his burning lips between mouthfuls of spicy-sweet corn.

For an unusual first course, serve this curry as a prelude to Lime-Tart Pigeon Pea Broth with Coconut (page 449). **SERVES 4**

1 cup shredded fresh coconut; or ½ cup shredded dried
   unsweetened coconut, reconstituted (see Note)
2 dried red Thai or cayenne chiles,
   stems removed
2 fresh green Thai, cayenne, or serrano chiles,
   stems removed
2 tablespoons canola oil
1 teaspoon black or yellow mustard seeds
1½ teaspoons coarse kosher or sea salt
12 to 15 medium-size to large fresh curry leaves
4 ears fresh corn, shucked and cut in half (see Tip)

1. Pour ½ cup water into a blender jar, and then add the coconut, dried chiles, and fresh chiles. Puree, scraping the inside of the jar as needed, to make a smooth, green-and-red-speckled batter-like sauce.

2. Heat the oil in a medium-size saucepan over medium-high heat. Add the mustard seeds, cover the pan, and cook until the seeds have stopped popping (not unlike popcorn), about 30 seconds. Pour in the spicy coconut sauce, making sure to scrape every last drop into the pan. Stir in the salt, curry leaves, and ½ cup water. Add the corncobs, arranging them in a single layer, and blanket them with the sauce.

3. Reduce the heat to medium-low, cover the pan, and simmer, occasionally bathing the cobs with the sauce, until the kernels are juicy-tender when pierced, 20 to 25 minutes.

4. Transfer the corncobs to a serving platter. Stir the curdled-looking sauce to create a more homogenized-looking curry, pour it over the cobs, and serve.

Note: To reconstitute coconut, cover with ½ cup boiling water, set aside for about 15 minutes, and then drain.

Tip: If fresh corn is not in season, use 3 cups frozen kernels and cook for only 5 to 8 minutes in Step 3. I have also seen frozen corncobs at my neighborhood grocery store; they certainly will do as an alternative too.

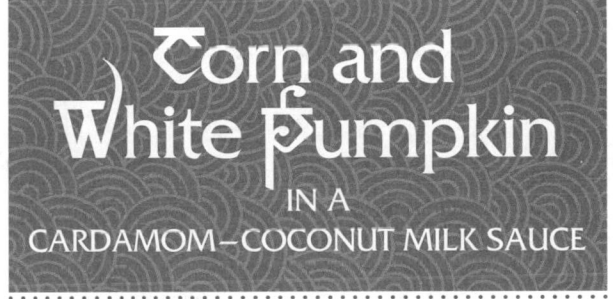

Corn and White Pumpkin
IN A CARDAMOM–COCONUT MILK SAUCE

Makkai Parangikai Kari

Kerala, in addition to being one of the top tourist destinations in the world for its lush green landscape, sensuous beaches, and unhurried way of life, is home to many of India's spices. Cardamom trees brimming with plump pods, vanilla bean orchids, bunches of green peppercorn vines that get processed to make Tellicherry black peppercorns (the world's best), black mustard seeds, and ginger all grow here and supply India's unending thirst for spices. No wonder many of this state's curries incorporate these indigenous spices along with its coastal bounty of coconuts. **SERVES 8**

1 tablespoon finely chopped fresh ginger

¼ teaspoon black peppercorns

¼ teaspoon cardamom seeds from green
   or white pods

2 fresh green Thai, cayenne, or serrano chiles,
   stems removed

1 tablespoon canola oil

1 teaspoon black or yellow mustard seeds

1 cup unsweetened coconut milk (see Tips)

1½ teaspoons coarse kosher or sea salt

2 cups fresh or frozen corn kernels
   (no need to thaw if frozen)

1 pound white pumpkin, peeled, seeded, and cut into
   1-inch cubes (see box, page 586), or the white inner
   rind of watermelon, cut into 1-inch cubes

2 tablespoons finely chopped fresh cilantro leaves
   and tender stems

12 medium-size to large fresh curry leaves

1. Combine the ginger, peppercorns, cardamom seeds, and chiles in a mortar, and pound together to make a coarse but pulpy paste.

2. Heat the oil in a medium-size saucepan over medium-high heat. Add the mustard seeds, cover the pan, and cook until the seeds have stopped popping (not unlike popcorn), about 30 seconds.

3. Immediately pour the coconut milk into the pan, and stir in the salt. Add the pounded ginger paste, changing the curry's color from white to off-white with flecks of black, green, and tan. Remove the pan from the heat and let the delicate flavors mingle for about 30 seconds.

4. Stir in the corn, pumpkin, cilantro, curry leaves, and 1 cup water. Heat to a boil. Then reduce the heat to medium-low, cover the pan, and simmer, stirring occasionally, until the squash is fork-tender but still firm and juicy, about 15 minutes. Then serve.

Tips:

❖ Even though I have used corn and white pumpkin in this recipe, any seasonal vegetable works just as well. Potatoes and pearl onions are an unusual and excellent alternative.

❖ If full-fat coconut milk is an issue for you, by all means use the low-fat variety. It won't compromise the rich flavors present in this milky-white liquid.

Corn
AND TOMATO MEDLEY

Angrezi bhutta

We do thank the British for introducing Madras curry powder to the world. Efforts to capture the flavors of "a spicy curry" resulted in this well-known blend, packaged and sold in many versions around the world. My simplified version re-creates the essence of this effort and is sprinkled into this corn-tomato combination. Even though I recommend kernels stripped off fresh ears of corn, feel free to throw in kernels from leftover roasted cobs. **SERVES 6**

2 tablespoons canola oil

1 small red onion, finely chopped

2 teaspoons English-Style Madras Curry Powder (page 24)

1 large tomato, cored and finely chopped

Kernels from 3 ears fresh corn (about 3 cups; see Tip)

1 teaspoon coarse kosher or sea salt

2 tablespoons finely chopped fresh cilantro leaves
   and tender stems

1. Heat the oil in a medium-size saucepan over

medium-high heat. Add the onion and stir-fry until it is light brown around the edges, 3 to 5 minutes.

2. Sprinkle the curry powder over the onion and stir it in. Cook until it has rid itself of its raw flavors and emerged complexly subtle-tasting, about 30 seconds.

3. Add the tomato and simmer, uncovered, stirring occasionally, until it has softened but is still firm-looking, 2 to 3 minutes.

4. Stir in the corn kernels, salt, and 1 cup water. Bring to a boil. Then reduce the heat to medium-low, cover the pan, and simmer, stirring occasionally, until the sauce thickens, about 10 minutes.

5. Stir in the cilantro, and serve.

Tip: Devour sweet corn within hours of its harvest. Frozen corn is acceptable as a second choice, but please, no metallic-tasting canned corn.

drumsticks

❖ ❖ ❖

y friend Don grew up with "drumsticks" meaning parts of chicken legs, so when a drumstick curry landed at the table, he said, "What, no chicken?" To us Indians this drumstick is a woody vegetable that looks like overgrown okra—about 12 inches long, ½ inch thick, with tapered ends. To eat it (it's usually cut crosswise into smaller pieces), split it open with your finger, scrape the inside pulp against your teeth, and discard the woody exterior. It is juicy and has a slight musky flavor and aroma, reminiscent of fresh asparagus spears. In fact, you can use cut-up asparagus as a perfectly acceptable alternative, should you wish to make the curry on this page without a trip to the Indian grocery store.

"Drumsticks"
IN A SPICY YOGURT SAUCE WITH ROASTED CHICKPEA FLOUR

Sing Pitta

I sampled a version of this Rajasthani delicacy in a Gujarati restaurant in Mumbai on a recent trip to visit family and friends. Theirs was thicker-sauced, with the drumsticks as the center of attention. My adaptation has a more pronounced textural difference, with the slightly crunchy pulp of the drumsticks against the backdrop of an ample, smooth sauce—a combination you can either savor over rice or serve as an accompaniment to fluffy rotis (page 727). **SERVES 4**

1 package (12 to 14 ounces) frozen drumsticks (see box; no need to thaw); or 1 pound fresh asparagus, tough ends discarded, spears cut in half
2 cups plain yogurt
3 tablespoons Toasted Chickpea Flour (page 41)
2 tablespoons Ginger Chile Paste (page 17)
2 teaspoons white granulated sugar
1 teaspoon coarse kosher or sea salt
1 teaspoon Toasted Cumin-Coriander Blend (page 33)
¼ teaspoon ground turmeric
¼ cup finely chopped fresh cilantro leaves and tender stems
6 to 8 medium-size to large fresh curry leaves
2 tablespoons Ghee (page 21) or canola oil
1 teaspoon black or yellow mustard seeds

1. Fill a medium-size saucepan halfway with water, and bring it to a rolling boil over medium-high heat. Dump the frozen drumsticks into the water and bring it to a boil again. Drain the vegetable into a colander. Dry the saucepan with a paper towel.

2. Whisk the yogurt and 1 cup water together in a medium-size bowl. Sprinkle in the chickpea flour, a tablespoon at a time, whisking it in after each addition. Then whisk in the Ginger Chile Paste, sugar, salt, spice blend, and turmeric. Fold in the cilantro and curry leaves. (Don't try to use a wire whisk when you have herbs in the sauce. If you do, be prepared to unclog the greens from the wires when they get tangled.)

3. Heat the ghee in the same saucepan over medium-high heat. Add the mustard seeds, cover the pan, and cook until the seeds have stopped popping (not unlike popcorn), about 30 seconds. Pour in the yogurt sauce and add the drumsticks. Lower the heat to medium and simmer, uncovered, stirring occasionally, until the deep yellow sauce thickens slightly, 10 to 15 minutes. Serve hot.

Eggplant
WITH A TAMARIND-CHILE SAUCE

katarikai goshtu

tamilian *goshtus* are coarsely mashed stews of vegetables like shallots, eggplant, or both—tamarind-tart and chile-hot in flavor. This *goshtu,* even though it is not mashed, has that appearance due to the eggplant's consistency, which naturally breaks down into a pulpy mass. You can mash the eggplant with the back of a spoon for a pulpier look, but I prefer the chunky-smooth texture. **SERVES 6**

2 tablespoons canola oil, plus extra for brushing

2 tablespoons skinned split black lentils (cream-colored in this form, urad dal), picked over for stones

1 tablespoon coriander seeds

4 to 6 dried red Thai or cayenne chiles, to taste, stems removed

1 teaspoon black or yellow mustard seeds

1 large eggplant (about 1½ pounds), stems removed, cut into 1-inch cubes

1½ teaspoons coarse kosher or sea salt

12 to 15 medium-size to large fresh curry leaves

1 teaspoon tamarind paste or concentrate

1. Heat the 2 tablespoons oil in a large skillet over medium-high heat. Sprinkle in the lentils, coriander seeds, and chiles. Roast, stirring constantly, until the lentils and coriander are reddish brown and the chiles have blackened slightly, 2 to 3 minutes. Using a slotted spoon, transfer the spices to a plate, leaving as much of the oil as you can in the skillet. Once the spices are cool to the touch, place them in a spice grinder and grind until they have the texture of finely ground black pepper.

2. Reheat the skillet over medium-high heat. Add the mustard seeds, cover, and cook until the seeds have stopped popping (not unlike popcorn), about 30 seconds. Immediately add the eggplant, salt, and curry leaves, and stir-fry until the fleshy part of the eggplant is light brown, 2 to 4 minutes.

3. Dissolve the tamarind paste in 1 cup water to make a muddy-brown liquid. Pour this over the eggplant, and stir in the ground spices. Reduce the heat to medium-low, cover the skillet, and simmer, stirring occasionally, until the eggplant is very soft, 10 to 12 minutes. Then serve.

Tip: I prefer not to use an iron wok for a curry like this because the harshly acidic tamarind has a tendency to react with the pan (especially when the pan is not properly seasoned), to yield a metallic-tasting sauce. Therefore, if you don't have a stainless steel skillet, use an enamel-coated cast-iron pan.

Mashed Grilled Eggplant
WITH TAMARIND AND CHILES

Puli Katarikai

Vibrant, tart, nutty, spicy-hot and smoky this curry has an almost pickle-like quality to it and packs oomph in every small mouthful. I think the starchy, soothing Rice with Yogurt and Mustard Seeds (page 710) is a perfect combination with this curry—a dollop of the eggplant embedded in the rice and slid into the mouth, just as my grandmother did when she hand-fed us as toddlers. **SERVES 4**

1 large eggplant (about 1½ pounds)
¼ cup finely chopped fresh cilantro leaves
    and tender stems
1 teaspoon tamarind paste or concentrate
1 teaspoon coarse kosher or sea salt
¼ teaspoon ground turmeric
2 fresh green Thai, cayenne, or serrano chiles,
    stems removed, finely chopped
    (do not remove the seeds)
2 tablespoons unrefined sesame oil or canola oil
1 teaspoon black or yellow mustard seeds
1 tablespoon skinned split black lentils
    (cream-colored in this form, urad dal),
    picked over for stones

2 dried red Thai or cayenne chiles, stems removed
¼ teaspoon ground asafetida
12 medium-size to large fresh curry leaves

1. Preheat a gas (or charcoal) grill, or the broiler, to high.

2. Prick the eggplant in multiple spots with a fork or knife (this prevents it from bursting when you grill or broil it). Don't bother to remove the stem since it will be discarded once you skin the eggplant. *If you are grilling it,* place the eggplant on the grill grate, cover the grill, and cook, turning the eggplant periodically to ensure even grilling, until its skin is evenly charred, about 25 minutes. *If you are using the broiler,* set the broiler rack so the eggplant will be about 6 inches from the heat, place the eggplant directly on the rack, or on a rack in a broiler pan, and broil, turning it periodically, until its skin is evenly charred, about 25 minutes.

3. Remove the grilled eggplant and transfer it to a bowl. Cover the bowl with plastic wrap and let the eggplant sweat in its own heat until the skin appears shriveled, about 15 minutes. Once the eggplant is cool to the touch, peel and discard the skin along with the stem. You will notice that there are eggplant juices in the bowl—make sure you do not discard them. Mash the eggplant well with a potato masher. (I often use my clean hands if a masher is not handy.)

4. Mix in the cilantro, tamarind paste, salt, turmeric, and fresh chiles.

5. Heat the oil in a medium-size skillet over medium-high heat. Add the mustard seeds, cover the skillet, and cook until the seeds have stopped popping (not unlike popcorn), about 30 seconds. Add the lentils and stir-fry until they turn golden brown, 15 to 20 seconds. Stir in the dried chiles, asafetida, and curry leaves (which will instantly spatter). Immediately add the mashed

eggplant mixture and lower the heat to medium. Cook, uncovered, stirring occasionally, until some of the oil starts to separate from the mixture, especially along its edges, about 15 minutes. Then serve.

Smoky Eggplant
WITH GARLIC AND RED CHILES

baingan ŋu bharto

ere is an example that shatters the myth of turmeric as the omnipresent curry spice. Armed with only five ingredients, this recipe shows the layers of complexities you can create with a few readily available ingredients. I break the mold and serve this as a fascinating appetizer, slathered onto pieces of crostini (toasted slices of French or Italian bread), along with a glass of wine as a precursor to a full-blown, robust curry dinner. **SERVES 6**

2 medium-size eggplants (2 to 2½ pounds total)

2 teaspoons rock salt

4 large cloves garlic

3 fresh red Thai or cayenne chiles, stems removed (see Tip)

2 tablespoons Ghee (page 21) or melted butter

1. Preheat a gas (or charcoal) grill, or the broiler, to high.

2. Prick the eggplants in multiple spots with a fork or knife (this prevents them from bursting when you grill or broil them). Don't bother to remove the stems, since they will be discarded once you skin the eggplants. *If you*

are grilling, place the eggplants on the grill grate, cover the grill, and cook, turning them periodically to ensure even grilling, until the skin is evenly charred, about 25 minutes. *If you use the broiler,* position the broiler rack so the eggplants will be about 6 inches from the heat. Place the eggplant directly on the rack, or on a rack in a broiler pan, and broil, turning them periodically, until the skin is evenly charred, about 25 minutes.

3. While the eggplants are grilling, sprinkle the rock salt into a mortar and add the garlic and chiles. With the pestle, pound the contents into a pulpy mass, frequently scraping the paste from the bottom and folding it within itself to ensure an even mix.

4. Place the grilled eggplants in a bowl, cover with plastic wrap, and let them sweat in their own heat until the skin appears shriveled, about 15 minutes. Once the eggplants are cool to the touch, peel them and discard the stems along with the skin. You will notice that there are eggplant juices in the bowl—make sure you do not discard them. Mash the eggplants well with a potato masher. (I often use a clean hand to do this if a masher is not handy.)

5. Fold the garlic-chile paste into the smoky-smelling eggplant.

6. Heat the ghee in a wok or a large skillet over medium heat. Add the eggplant pâté and stir-fry for 10 to 12 minutes. This creates a second layer of roasted flavor and also roasts the garlic without burning it. Then serve.

Tip: Stop by any Asian grocery store to find mounds of fresh Thai chiles in the refrigerated produce section. Hand-pick the fiery reds for this recipe. If you don't have access to such a store, go to the spice aisle of your supermarket, where you will find a jar or bag of dried red chiles labeled Chiles Japones (means Japanese but these are Thai chiles) or Chile de Arbol (cayenne). Soak the required number of chiles in a bowl of hot water until reconstituted, about 30 minutes.

Stewed Eggplant
WITH A COCONUT-CHILE SPICE BLEND

kolhapuri Vanghi

Addictive and robust, this eggplant curry brings home the tastes and aromas of the Kolhapuri kitchen through dried coconut (also known as *copra* in this form), red chiles, and sesame seeds—all roasted in the spice blend. The spice blend is a cinch to make, and so is the curry. **SERVES 4**

2 tablespoons canola oil

4 medium-size cloves garlic, finely chopped

1 small eggplant (about 8 ounces), stem removed, cut into ½-inch cubes

2 medium-size tomatoes, cored and cut into ½-inch cubes

2 teaspoons Kolhapuri masala (page 32)

1 teaspoon white granulated sugar

1 teaspoon coarse kosher or sea salt

½ teaspoon ground turmeric

¼ cup finely chopped fresh cilantro leaves and tender stems

1. Heat the oil in a medium-size saucepan over medium-high heat. Add the garlic and stir-fry to take away its raw edge, about 30 seconds. Add the eggplant and cook, stirring occasionally, until it releases its liquid and starts to appear shriveled (at which point it starts to brown), 5 to 10 minutes.

2. Add the tomatoes, masala, sugar, salt, and turmeric. Cook, scraping the bottom of the pan to deglaze it, releasing any browned bits of eggplant and garlic. Once the curry comes to a boil, lower the heat to medium and simmer, uncovered, stirring occasionally, until the eggplant is very soft and the tomatoes have broken down to a saucelike but firm-looking consistency, 8 to 10 minutes.

3. Stir in the cilantro, and serve.

Tip: If eggplant doesn't turn your crank, use turnips, potatoes, or parsnips (all pound for pound) instead. Because these vegetables don't contain as much moisture as eggplant, you will need to add ½ cup water when you add the tomato.

Fried Baby Eggplant
WITH A PEANUT-COCONUT SAUCE

baghare baingan

No special Hyderabadi meal is complete without this rich peanut-coconut curry smothering pan-fried baby eggplant. A specialty of the Hindu community in that charming bi-religious city, this curry can be "slightly laborious to make, but well worth it," said Preeti Mathur, a reporter whose roots are deeply embedded in the city. She often makes it for her father, now a widower, who lives with her in the U.S., in one of the suburbs of the Twin Cities. Her father's approval of her culinary prowess means the world to Preeti because she finds it comforting to know she can provide the tastes he was so used to when her mother was alive. **SERVES 6**

½ cup raw peanuts (without the skins)

2 tablespoons white sesame seeds

1 tablespoon white poppy seeds

1 tablespoon coriander seeds

½ cup shredded dried unsweetened coconut

6 tablespoons canola oil

1 small red onion, cut in half lengthwise
    and thinly sliced

2 teaspoons ground Deggi chiles (see box, page 290);
    or 1 teaspoon cayenne (ground red pepper) mixed
    with 1 teaspoon sweet paprika

1½ teaspoons coarse kosher or sea salt

½ teaspoon ground turmeric

12 small purple Indian eggplants, or 1 large
    Italian eggplant (about 1½ pounds)

2 tablespoons Ghee (page 21)

1 teaspoon cumin seeds

12 to 15 medium-size to large fresh curry leaves

4 dried red Thai or cayenne chiles, stems removed

3 tablespoons Ginger Paste (page 15)

2 tablespoons Garlic Paste (page 15)

1. Preheat a large skillet over medium-high heat. Sprinkle in the peanuts and cook, stirring constantly, until they turn light brown and acquire a light oily sheen, 3 to 4 minutes. Transfer the toasty brown nuts to a medium-size bowl.

2. Sprinkle the sesame, poppy, and coriander seeds into the same hot skillet and cook, stirring constantly, until they turn reddish brown and are aromatic, 1 to 2 minutes. Add the seeds to the peanuts.

3. Add the coconut to the skillet and stir constantly until it (very quickly) turns toasty brown, about 30 seconds. Add the coconut to the peanut-spice blend.

4. Drizzle 2 tablespoons of the oil into the same skillet. Add the onion and stir-fry until it is light honey-brown, 5 to 10 minutes. Place the onion, oil and all, on top of the coconut-peanut-spice blend in the bowl.

5. Pour 1 cup water into a blender jar, and add the ingredients in the bowl. Add the ground chiles, salt, and turmeric. Puree, scraping the inside of the jar as needed, to make a thick, nutty-gritty paste.

6. *If you are using small eggplants,* remove the stems. Slit each eggplant three-quarters of the way through by making two crosswise slits, forming an X. (Make sure you do not accidentally cut through the entire length. This keeps them held together and makes the pan-frying a bit easier.) *If you are using one large eggplant,* remove the stem. Slice the eggplant crosswise into 2-inch-thick rounds. Slit each piece three-quarters of the way through by making two crosswise slits, forming an X. Make sure you do not accidentally cut through the skin.

7. Heat the remaining 4 tablespoons oil in the skillet you've been using over medium heat. Add the eggplant, cover the skillet to contain the spattering, and sear, shaking the skillet occasionally to move the eggplants around, until they blister, some of the skin blackens, and they are fork-tender, about 15 minutes. Transfer the eggplants to a plate.

8. Heat the ghee in the same skillet over medium heat. Sprinkle in the cumin seeds, curry leaves, and dried chiles, and immediately cover the skillet to contain the spattering. Cook until the cumin is reddish brown and the chiles have blackened slightly, 5 to 10 seconds. Immediately add the gin-

ger and garlic pastes, and cover the skillet again. Once the spattering dissipates, remove the lid and stir-fry until the pastes are light brown and have absorbed the colors and aromas from the skillet, 2 to 3 minutes.

9. Add the peanut-coconut paste from the blender jar. Pour ½ cup water into the blender and swish it around to wash it out; add this to the skillet. Add the eggplant, stirring it gently to coat it with the sauce. Reduce the heat to medium-low, cover the skillet, and simmer, stirring occasionally, until the eggplant has absorbed the rich, nutty flavors, about 5 minutes. Then serve.

Eggplant
WITH APPLES, FENNEL & BLACK CUMIN

kashmiri baingan

Wild apples studded the northwestern Himalayas in Kashmir in the 19th century. A variety known as the Wilson, large and juicy, made its appearance around 1850, and today the Red and Golden Delicious varieties are more popular in the marketplace. Apples, having made their way into many of Kashmir's dishes, provide a great source of tartness. In this curry fennel seeds sneak in some mellow sweetness, while black cumin, also known as *shahjeera* (royal cumin), provides a hint of bitterness, all coming together in harmony with the delectable combination of eggplant and apples. **SERVES 8**

2 tablespoons mustard oil or canola oil
2 teaspoons fennel seeds
I teaspoon black cumin seeds (see Tips)

4 dried red Thai or cayenne chiles, stems removed
2 small eggplants (about 8 ounces each), stems removed, cut into 1-inch cubes (see Tips)
2 large tart-sweet apples, such as Braeburn or Granny Smith, cored and cut into 1-inch cubes
2 teaspoons coarse kosher or sea salt
I teaspoon coriander seeds, ground
I teaspoon cumin seeds, ground
½ teaspoon ground turmeric
¼ cup finely chopped fresh cilantro leaves and tender stems

1. Heat the oil in a large skillet or in a wok over medium-high heat. Add the fennel seeds, black cumin seeds, and chiles. Cook until they sizzle, crackle, and smell fragrant, 10 to 15 seconds.

2. Immediately add the eggplants and apples. Sprinkle with the salt and the ground coriander, cumin, and turmeric. Stir-fry to coat the vegetable-fruit medley with the spices, and to cook the ground spices without burning them, 2 to 4 minutes.

3. Pour in 1 cup water, and stir to release any browned bits from the bottom of the skillet. Heat to a boil. Then reduce the heat to medium, cover the skillet, and cook, stirring occasionally, until the eggplant is fall-apart tender and the apple is slightly firm and very succulent (and, unusually, more tart), about 15 minutes.

4. Sprinkle with the cilantro, and serve.

Tips:

❖ If you don't have any black cumin, use the common white variety (which is actually grayish) for an equally satisfying result.

❖ The most common variety of eggplant in the grocery stores here in the United States is the Italian-American: dark purple, tough-skinned, and bell-shaped. I don't bother either peeling them or salting them (to leach away excess bitterness). In fact, their bitterness offers a great balance to this curry—bitterness being a flavor of choice for many Indians, especially in the Kashmir region. To cut the eggplant, first remove its stem. Then slice it in half lengthwise, and cut each half, lengthwise again, into 1-inch-thick slices. Stack 2 or 3 slices and cut them, white flesh side up, into 1-inch cubes. (It's easier for the knife to slice from the flesh side through the slightly tough skin as opposed to the other way around.) Feel free to use any variety of eggplant.

Cashew-Stuffed Baby Eggplant
WITH TOMATOES AND SPICES

bharela baingan

baby eggplants are not bitter at all, as the gargantuan ones (the Italian variety), widely available in American super-markets, can be. These bell-shaped, light purple varieties, roughly 2 to 3 inches long, are easy to find in Asian grocery stores. They can also be found at neighborhood farmers' markets at the tail end of summer, especially in areas where there are concentrations of Asian immigrants. If they are unavailable, however, you can use the standard large variety. **SERVES 4**

½ cup raw cashew nuts, ground
3 tablespoons finely chopped fresh cilantro leaves and tender stems
1 tablespoon mango powder or fresh lime juice

Raw cashew nuts? Mango powder? See the Glossary of Ingredients, page 758.

2 teaspoons cumin seeds, ground
1½ teaspoons coarse kosher or sea salt
½ teaspoon cayenne (ground red pepper)
½ teaspoon Punjabi garam masala (page 25)
8 to 10 small purple Indian (or 1 medium-size Italian) eggplants (about 1 pound total)
¼ cup canola oil
1 cup canned crushed tomatoes
1 teaspoon white granulated sugar

1. Combine the ground cashews, 2 tablespoons of the cilantro, the mango powder, cumin, salt, cayenne, and garam masala in a small bowl. Stir together thoroughly.

2. *If you are using small eggplants,* wash them well but do not remove the stems. Slit each eggplant three-quarters of the way through by making two crosswise slits, forming an X. (Make sure you do not accidentally cut through the entire length. This keeps them held together and makes the pan-frying a bit easier.) *If you are using one large eggplant,* rinse it well and remove the stem. Slice the eggplant crosswise into 2-inch-thick rounds. Slit each piece three-quarters of the way through by making two crosswise slits, forming an X. Make sure you do not accidentally cut through the skin. You can use kitchen twine to tie them closed after you stuff them.

3. Stuff each eggplant with the spice-nut mixture (as much as you can push into the slits). Don't worry if some of the filling falls out; most of it will remain inside.

4. Heat the oil in a large skillet over medium-high heat. Add the stuffed eggplants, arranging them in a single layer, and sear them on the underside, 1 to 2 minutes. Sprinkle any remaining filling over the eggplants, reduce the heat to low, and cover the skillet. Roast the

eggplants, turning them occasionally (gently) with a pair of tongs, until they are fork-tender, about 30 minutes. As much as you are tempted, do not raise the heat to expedite the roasting; you will burn the spices and make the eggplant unpalatable.

5. Carefully lift the eggplants out of the skillet and transfer them to a serving platter.

6. Pour the crushed tomatoes and the sugar into the pan, and scrape the bottom of the skillet to incorporate all those wonderful pan drippings left behind after roasting the eggplant. Turn up the heat to medium-high and bring the sauce to a boil. Cook, stirring occasionally, until the sauce thickens, about 3 minutes.

7. Stir in the remaining 1 tablespoon cilantro, pour the sauce over the eggplant, and serve.

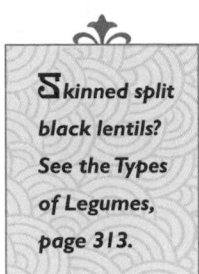

Skinned split black lentils? See the Types of Legumes, page 313.

Eggplant
WITH ROASTED CHILES AND TOMATO

katarikai bhajee

Potently spiced, this curry is delicious when mixed with white basmati rice. If you're not watching your calories, drizzle a tablespoon or more of ghee (page 21) over it all to balance out the pungent chiles. I like to take this along for a summer picnic—it transports well and is just as delicious at room temperature. A bowl of plain yogurt alongside is soothing and also provides that complementary protein, making it a nutritionally well-balanced meal. **SERVES 6**

2 tablespoons canola oil

3 tablespoons skinned split black lentils
    (cream-colored in this form, urad dal),
        picked over for stones

1 tablespoon coriander seeds

5 dried red Thai or cayenne chiles, stems removed

1 teaspoon black or yellow mustard seeds

1 medium eggplant, (about 1 pound) stem
        removed, cut into ¼-inch cubes

12 to 15 medium-size to large fresh curry leaves

1½ teaspoons coarse kosher or sea salt

½ teaspoon ground turmeric

1 medium-size tomato, cored and finely chopped

¼ cup finely chopped fresh cilantro leaves
    and tender stems

1. Heat the oil in a medium-size skillet over medium-high heat. Sprinkle in 2 tablespoons of the lentils, the coriander seeds, and the chiles. Roast, stirring constantly, until the lentils and coriander are reddish brown and the chiles have blackened slightly, 2 to 3 minutes. Using a slotted spoon, transfer the spices to a plate, leaving as much of the oil as you can in the skillet. Once the spices are cool to the touch, place them in a spice grinder and grind until they have the texture of finely ground black pepper.

2. Reheat the skillet over medium-high heat. Add the mustard seeds, cover the skillet, and cook until the seeds have stopped popping (not unlike popcorn), about 30 seconds. Add the remaining 1 tablespoon lentils and stir-fry until they turn golden brown, 15 to 20 seconds. Immediately add the eggplant and curry leaves. Stir-fry to coat them with the spiced, nutty oil and to partially cook them, about 5 minutes.

3. Stir in the salt and turmeric. Add 1 cup water, which will instantly come to a boil, thanks to the hot pan. Continue to simmer the curry vigorously, uncovered, stirring occasionally, until the eggplant is soft and tender and most of the sauce has been absorbed, 8 to 10 minutes.

4. Mix in the tomato, ground spice blend, and cilantro, and serve.

Stuffed Baby Eggplant
WITH COCONUT AND ROASTED LEGUMES

thenga katarikai

Cooks in every region of India stuff baby eggplants—the fillings range from minced meat to mashed vegetables. The Tamils in southern India fill their baby purples with fresh coconut and roasted legumes, both hallmark ingredients of this area's cuisine. I served this as a side with Roasted Leg of Lamb with Raisin-Mint Sauce (page 184) for a recent Christmas dinner. The bold flavors worked well with the equally robust lamb, and even a die-hard eggplant-hater was converted. **SERVES 6**

5 tablespoons canola oil

2 tablespoons skinned split black lentils (cream-colored in this form, urad dal), picked over for stones

2 tablespoons yellow split peas (chana dal), picked over for stones

2 tablespoons raw cashew nuts

1 tablespoon coriander seeds

4 dried red Thai or cayenne chiles, stems removed

1 cup shredded fresh coconut; or 1/2 cup shredded dried unsweetened coconut, reconstituted (see Note)

1 1/2 teaspoons coarse kosher or sea salt

12 small eggplants (1 1/2 pounds total; see Tip)

1 teaspoon black or yellow mustard seeds

10 to 12 medium-size to large fresh curry leaves

1. Heat 1 tablespoon of the oil in a large skillet over medium-high heat. Add the lentils, split peas, cashews, coriander seeds, and chiles. Stir-fry until the legumes and nuts are reddish brown and the chiles have blackened, 1 to 2 minutes. Using a slotted spoon, transfer the ingredients to a plate, leaving behind any residual oil. Once they are cool to the touch, place the ingredients in a spice grinder and grind until the texture resembles that of finely ground black pepper.

2. Place the coconut, salt, and the ground blend in a small bowl, and combine thoroughly.

3. Rinse the eggplants well but do not remove the stems. Slit each eggplant three-quarters of the way through by making two crosswise slits, forming an X. (Make sure you do not accidentally cut through the entire length. This keeps them held together and makes the pan-frying a bit easier.)

4. Stuff each eggplant with this spice-nut blend (as much as you possibly can push into the slits). Don't worry if some of the filling falls out; most of it will remain inside.

5. Heat the remaining 4 tablespoons oil in the same skillet over medium-high heat. Add the mustard seeds, cover, and cook until the seeds have stopped popping (not unlike popcorn), about 30 seconds. Immediately add the eggplants, arranging them in a single layer, and lower the heat to medium. Cook, uncovered, turning them gently every 2 to 4 minutes, until the eggplants have seared and appear slightly blotchy, about 10 minutes.

6. Pour in 1 cup water, which will instantly come to a boil in the hot skillet. Reduce the heat to medium-low, cover the skillet, and braise the eggplant, turning them occasionally, until they are very soft when pierced with a fork or spoon, about 1 hour. The eggplant will have absorbed most of the liquid. Lift them gently onto a platter and keep warm.

7. Pour 1 cup water into the skillet, sprinkle in the curry leaves, and raise the heat to medium-high. Boil the sauce, uncovered, stirring occasionally, until it is thick, about 5 minutes.

8. Pour the sauce over the eggplant, and serve.

Note: To reconstitute coconut, cover with ½ cup boiling water, set aside for about 15 minutes, and then drain.

Tip: If small eggplants are not available in your grocery store, purchase the large variety. Remove the stem, and cut the eggplant into 2-inch-thick rounds. Slit each piece three-quarters of the way through by making two crosswise slits, forming an X. Make sure you do not accidentally cut through the skin. Stuff the eggplant rounds, and use kitchen twine to hold them shut if necessary.

sweat-frying

❖ ❖ ❖

the term I use to describe my method for slow-cooking red onions is "sweat-frying." The onions—chopped or sliced—are cooked in a covered pan over medium or medium-low heat. At first the onions sweat, releasing their liquid. Then, as the liquid evaporates, they start to brown, releasing their sugars. After 15 to 20 minutes, the onions are soft and caramel-brown with a deep purple hue. Yum!

Eggplant and Okra
WITH FENUGREEK AND MUSTARD

baingan bhindi ki subzi

the textural difference between these two vegetables—one soft, the other earthy—may prove to be the major topic of conversation at the dinner table when you serve this curry. The first time I served it, half of the group loved the texture, some were indifferent, and others didn't care for it at all. As the cook, you have two choices: either you can substitute two different, firm-fleshed vegetables (like green beans, potatoes, carrots, bell peppers, sweet potatoes, or green papaya), or you can invite more adventuresome guests to join you at the table! **SERVES 4**

2 tablespoons canola oil
1 small red onion, cut in half lengthwise
    and thinly sliced
4 fresh green Thai, cayenne, or serrano chiles,
    stems removed, thinly sliced crosswise
    (do not remove the seeds)
8 ounces fresh okra, rinsed and thoroughly dried
1 small eggplant (about 8 ounces), stem removed,
    cut into 1-inch cubes
1½ teaspoon coarse kosher or sea salt
1 teaspoon fenugreek seeds, ground
1 teaspoon black or yellow mustard seeds, ground
½ teaspoon ground turmeric
2 tablespoons finely chopped fresh cilantro
    leaves and tender stems for garnishing

1. Heat the oil in a medium-size saucepan over medium heat. Add the onion and chiles, and stir once or twice. Cover the pan and cook until the onion is soft

and honey-brown with a deep purple hue, 10 to 15 minutes. (The onion will sweat first, and then start to brown once the liquid evaporates. This lets it release its sugars, providing a sweet balance to the hot chiles.)

2. While the onion and chiles are cooking, trim the caps off the okra without cutting into the pods, and then cut the pods crosswise into 1-inch lengths.

3. Add the okra to the onion mixture and stir-fry until it is partially cooked and has acquired some brown spots, about 15 minutes.

4. Stir in the eggplant, salt, fenugreek, mustard, and turmeric. Cook for 2 minutes (the vegetables will protect the ground spices from burning and let them cook gently).

5. Pour in 1 cup water and scrape the pan to deglaze it, releasing any browned bits of onion and spice. Continue to cook, uncovered, stirring occasionally, until the sauce thickens, about 15 minutes. Then cover the pan, lower the heat a notch, and simmer until the vegetables are cooked through, about 5 minutes.

6. Sprinkle with the cilantro, and serve.

Pan-Blistered Eggplant
WITH ONION

kaanda Vangi

perfect curry for a gloomy, cloudy day—the colors certainly match! The good news is that underneath the darkness there is a smoky flavor that is incredibly complex, even with so few ingredients. The cilantro provides a splash of green as well as flavor. Cilantro-haters, however, can leave it out. Tomatoes would both add some color and contribute a mellow acidic element to the sauce: use 1 medium-size tomato, cored and cut into 2-inch pieces, stirring it in after the eggplant has cooked.

SERVES 8

> 2 tablespoons canola oil
>
> I teaspoon black or yellow mustard seeds
>
> 12 small purple Indian (or I large Italian) eggplants (about 1½ pounds total), stems removed, cut into pieces 2 inches long, I inch wide, and ½ inch thick
>
> I large red onion, cut into pieces 2 inches long and I inch wide
>
> I tablespoon Maharashtrian garam masala (page 28)
>
> 2 teaspoons coarse kosher or sea salt
>
> 2 tablespoons finely chopped fresh cilantro leaves and tender stems for garnishing

1. Heat the oil in a wok, Dutch oven, or large saucepan over medium-high heat. Add the mustard seeds, cover the pan, and cook until the seeds have stopped popping (not unlike popcorn), about 30 seconds. Immediately add the eggplant and onion pieces, and stir-fry until the eggplant starts to blister and the onion turns light honey-brown, 8 to 10 minutes.

2. Sprinkle in the garam masala and salt, and continue to stir-fry to incorporate the spices into the dark blend of eggplant and onion, about 30 seconds. Then add 1 cup water, stir once or twice, and bring to a boil. Lower the heat to medium, cover the pan, and stew, stirring occasionally, until the eggplant is tender, 8 to 10 minutes.

3. Sprinkle with the cilantro, and serve.

Grilled Eggplant Pâté
WITH MANGO POWDER

baingan bharta

Northerners hanker for smoky-flavored eggplant like this one for many a special-occasion meal. Back in India (and even in commercial north Indian restaurants around the globe), the eggplant is often dropped directly onto the hot coals of a tandoor (a clay oven) to char its skin. The grilled eggplant is then peeled, mashed with herbs and spices, and stir-fried with ghee to create sublime flavors. **SERVES 6**

1 large eggplant (about 1½ pounds)
1 small red onion, coarsely chopped
6 large cloves garlic
2 to 4 fresh green Thai, cayenne, or serrano chiles, to taste, stems removed
1 cup crushed tomatoes (see Tips)
4 tablespoons finely chopped fresh cilantro leaves and tender stems
2 tablespoons mango powder or fresh lime juice
1 teaspoon coarse kosher or sea salt
¼ teaspoon ground turmeric
2 tablespoons Ghee (page 21) or canola oil
1 tablespoon Toasted Cumin-Coriander Blend (page 33)
½ cup finely chopped red onion, for garnishing (optional)

1. Preheat a gas (or charcoal) grill, or the broiler, to high.

2. Prick the eggplant in multiple spots with a fork or knife (this prevents it from bursting when you grill or broil it). Don't bother to remove its stem, since it will be discarded once you skin the eggplant. *If you are grilling,* place the eggplant on the grill grate, cover the grill, and cook, turning it periodically to ensure even grilling, until its skin is evenly charred, about 25 minutes. *If you use the broiler,* position the broiler rack so the eggplant will be about 6 inches from the heat. Place the eggplant on the rack and broil it, turning it periodically, until its skin is evenly charred, about 25 minutes.

3. While the eggplant is grilling, combine the onion, garlic, and chiles in a food processor. Pulse until minced.

4. Place the grilled eggplant in a bowl, cover it with plastic wrap, and let it sweat in its own heat until the skin appears shriveled, about 15 minutes. Once it's cool to the touch, peel the eggplant and discard the stem along with the skin. You will notice that there are eggplant juices in the bowl—make sure you do not discard them. Mash the eggplant well with a potato masher. (I often use a clean hand to do this if a masher is not handy.)

5. Stir the minced onion mixture into the mashed eggplant. Add the tomatoes, 2 tablespoons of the cilantro, and the mango powder, salt, and turmeric. Mix thoroughly.

6. Preheat a wok or a large skillet over medium-high heat. Pour in the ghee (which should immediately heat up because of the preheated pan) and add the eggplant pâté. Roast, stirring occasionally, until the eggplant loses some of its excess liquid and starts to get dry, 15 to 18 minutes. Then reduce the heat to medium-low and continue to cook, uncovered, stirring occasionally, until some of the oil starts to separate from the pâté, 8 to 10 minutes.

Mango powder? See the Glossary of Ingredients, page 758.

7. Stir in the cumin-coriander blend. Sprinkle with the remaining 2 tablespoons cilantro, and with the chopped onion if desired, and serve.

Tips:

✤ Canned crushed tomatoes are readily available, and I splurge on the organic variety for their fresh taste.

✤ An alternative (albeit a messy one) to grilling or broiling the eggplant is to hold it with a pair of tongs over a gas burner, directly over the flame, turning it often to ensure even charring. The problem is that the juices that leach from the grilling eggplant can muddle the burner's flame.

Grilled Eggplant
WITH PEAS AND BUTTER

baingan mutter makhani

Maybe this is a restaurant's way to use up leftover Grilled Eggplant Pâté with Mango Powder (page 501) from the previous day's buffet—just swirl in some green peas for the all-you-can-eat offering! My version actually makes the effort to create an entirely new sauce with nutty almonds and sweet golden raisins, among other ingredients. Serve this mashed goodness with wedges of buttery naan (page 729).

SERVES 8

2 medium-size eggplants (2 to 2½ pounds total)
2 cups fresh or frozen green peas (no need to thaw)
½ cup finely chopped fresh cilantro leaves and tender stems
1½ teaspoons coarse kosher or sea salt
½ teaspoon ground turmeric
6 tablespoons Ghee (page 21) or butter
1 medium-size red onion, cut in half lengthwise and thinly sliced
¼ cup slivered blanched almonds
2 tablespoons golden raisins
4 large cloves garlic, coarsely chopped
4 fresh green Thai, cayenne, or serrano chiles, stems removed, cut in half crosswise (do not remove the seeds)
2 lengthwise slices fresh ginger (each 2 inches long, 1 inch wide, and ⅛ inch thick), coarsely chopped
2 tablespoons tomato paste
½ cup heavy (whipping) cream or half-and-half

1. Preheat a gas (or charcoal) grill, or the broiler, to high.

2. Prick the eggplants in multiple spots with a fork or knife (this prevents them from bursting when you grill or broil them). Don't bother to remove the stems, since they will be discarded once you skin the eggplants. *If you are grilling*, place the eggplants on the grill grate, cover the grill, and cook, turning them periodically to ensure even grilling, until the skin is evenly charred, about 25 minutes. *If you use the broiler*, position the broiler rack so the eggplants will be about 6 inches from the heat. Place the eggplants directly on the rack, or on a rack in a broiler pan, and broil, turning them periodically, until the skin is evenly charred, about 25 minutes.

3. Place the grilled eggplants in a bowl, cover with plastic wrap, and let them sweat in their own heat until the skin appears shriveled, about 15 minutes. Once the eggplants are cool to the touch, peel them and discard the stems along with the skin. You will notice that there are eggplant juices in the bowl—make sure you do not discard them. Mash the eggplants well with a potato masher. (I often use a clean hand to do this if a masher is not handy.) Stir in the peas, cilantro, salt, and turmeric.

4. Heat 2 tablespoons of the ghee in a large skillet, or in a wok, over medium heat. Add the onion, almonds, raisins, garlic, chiles, and ginger. Stir, cover the skillet, and cook, stirring occasionally, until the onion is caramel-brown with a deep purple hue, 15 to 20 minutes. (The steam will rise, gather under the lid, and drip back into the skillet, providing enough moisture to prevent the onion slices from blackening but not enough to stew the onion, making for a perfect balance to create that honey-rich flavor.)

5. Add ½ cup water, scraping the skillet to deglaze it, releasing the browned bits of onion and other ingredients. Transfer this, liquid and all, to a blender jar. Add the tomato paste and puree, scraping the inside of the jar as needed, to make a gritty, nutty, sweet-hot puree, reddish brown in color.

6. Wash and dry the skillet. Heat 2 tablespoons of the ghee over medium heat. Add the pea-studded eggplant pâté and cook, uncovered, stirring occasionally, until all the moisture has been absorbed and there is a slight oily sheen on the surface, 10 to 15 minutes.

7. Add the onion paste to the eggplant. Pour the cream into the blender jar and swish it around to release any paste stuck to the inside. Add the cream to the skillet. Simmer the eggplant, uncovered, stirring occasionally, until the sauce has flavored the pâté, 5 to 8 minutes.

8. Stir in the remaining 2 tablespoons ghee, and serve.

Tips:

❖ You may wonder why I have you thinly slice the red onion (and not the garlic or ginger) when you are going to be pureeing it. When you thinly slice it, you create an even surface area for the slices to brown and thus yield a sweeter sauce. The ginger and garlic

pieces are small enough that they won't make a huge impact even if they brown unevenly.

❖ You can always reduce the amount of ghee in the recipe if fat is an issue. But honestly, if you plan to make this on rare occasions, why not splurge and relish a smaller, albeit satisfying, portion?

Stuffed Baby Eggplants
WITH CRUSHED PEANUTS AND CHILES

Bharlele Vanghi

the time it takes to make the spice blend: 5 minutes. The time it takes to prep the eggplant: 5 minutes. The time it takes to roast the eggplant: 30 minutes. The time it takes to make the sauce: 5 minutes. The time it takes for your guests to smile: 1 bite. What makes it so easy? The same ingredients are used in the filling and in the sauce. **SERVES 6**

½ cup unsalted dry-roasted peanuts
2 tablespoons Kolhapuri masala (page 32)
1½ teaspoons coarse kosher or sea salt
12 small purple Indian (or 1 large Italian) eggplants
*   (about 1½ pounds total)*
¼ cup canola oil
1 teaspoon black or yellow mustard seeds
2 tablespoons finely chopped fresh cilantro
*   leaves and tender stems*

1. Place the peanuts in a food processor and pulse until they have the consistency of coarse breadcrumbs.

Transfer the ground peanuts to a small bowl, and stir in the spice blend and salt.

2. *If you are using small eggplants,* wash them well but do not remove the stems. Slit each eggplant three-quarters of the way through by making two crosswise slits, forming an X. (Make sure you do not accidentally cut through the entire length. This keeps them held together and makes the pan-frying a bit easier.) *If you are using one large eggplant,* rinse it well and remove the stem. Slice the eggplant crosswise into 2-inch-thick rounds. Slit each piece three-quarters of the way through by making two crosswise slits, forming an X. Make sure you do not accidentally cut through the skin. You can use kitchen twine to tie them closed after you stuff them.

3. Stuff each eggplant with the spice-nut blend (as much as you can push into the slits). Don't worry if some of the filling falls out; most of it will remain inside. You will have almost half the peanut-spice filling left over. Set it aside for the sauce.

4. Heat the oil in a large skillet over medium-high heat. Add the mustard seeds, cover the skillet, and cook until the seeds have stopped popping (not unlike popcorn), about 30 seconds. Arrange the stuffed eggplant in a single layer in the skillet, reduce the heat to low, and cover the skillet. Roast the eggplants, turning them occasionally (gently) with a pair of tongs, until they are fork-tender, about 30 minutes. As much as you are tempted, do not raise the heat to expedite the roasting; you will burn the spices and make the eggplant unpalatable.

5. Carefully lift the eggplants out of the skillet and transfer them to a serving platter.

6. Sprinkle the remaining filling into the skillet, and add 1 cup water. Scrape the bottom of the skillet to deglaze it, releasing any stuck-on bits of nuts and spice. Raise the heat to medium-high and cook, uncovered,

stirring occasionally, until the sauce is thick, 5 to 8 minutes. Stir in the cilantro, spoon the sauce over the eggplants, and serve.

Mashed Grilled Eggplant
WITH POTATOES, CHILES & TAMARIND

Aloo baingan ka bharta

My dear friend Molu's family regularly enjoyed this version of the more traditional eggplant pâté (page 501). The mashed potatoes bulk up the curry and also absorb some of the excess liquid from the eggplant, to make a thickly sauced pâté that is perfect when scooped up with pieces of ghee-laced naan (page 729). **SERVES 4**

I large eggplant (about 1½ pounds)

I pound russet or Yukon Gold potatoes, peeled, cut into 1-inch pieces, and submerged in a bowl of cold water to prevent browning

6 to 8 dried red Thai or cayenne chiles, to taste, stems removed

4 lengthwise slices fresh ginger (each 2 inches long, 1 inch wide, and ⅛ inch thick)

I teaspoon tamarind paste or concentrate

I teaspoon coarse kosher or sea salt

½ teaspoon ground turmeric

2 tablespoons Ghee (page 21) or canola oil

I teaspoon cumin seeds

¼ cup finely chopped fresh cilantro leaves and tender stems for garnishing

1. Preheat a gas (or charcoal) grill, or the broiler, to high.

2. Prick the eggplant in multiple spots with a fork or knife (this prevents it from bursting when you grill or broil it). Don't bother to remove its stem, since it will be discarded once you skin the eggplant. *If you are grilling,* place the eggplant on the grill grate, cover the grill, and cook, turning it periodically to ensure even grilling, until its skin is evenly charred, about 25 minutes. *If you use the broiler,* position the broiler rack so the eggplant will be about 6 inches from the heat. Place the eggplant on the rack and broil it, turning it periodically, until its skin is evenly charred, about 25 minutes.

3. While the eggplant is charring, prepare the potatoes: Fill a medium-size saucepan with water and bring it to a boil over medium-high heat. Drain the potatoes and add them to the boiling water. Bring it to a boil again. Then lower the heat to medium and cook, partially covered, until the potatoes are very tender, 8 to 10 minutes. Drain the potatoes and mash them in a medium-size bowl.

4. Remove the grilled eggplant and transfer it to a large bowl. Cover the bowl with plastic wrap and let the eggplant sweat in its own heat until the skin appears shriveled, about 15 minutes.

5. While the eggplant is sweating, combine the chiles and ginger in a food processor, and mince them.

6. Once the eggplant is cool to the touch, peel and discard the skin along with the stem. You will notice that there are eggplant juices in the bowl—do not discard them. Mash the eggplant well with a potato masher. (I often use a clean hand to do this if a masher is not handy.) Mix in the mashed potatoes. Then add the chile-ginger blend, tamarind paste, salt, and turmeric, and stir well.

7. Preheat a wok or a large skillet over medium-high heat. Pour in the ghee (which should immediately heat up in the hot pan), and add the cumin seeds. Stir-fry until they sizzle, turn reddish brown, and are aromatic, 5 to 10 seconds. Then add the eggplant-potato pâté and roast, uncovered, stirring occasionally, until the eggplant loses some of its excess liquid and starts to dry out a bit, 15 to 18 minutes.

8. Sprinkle with the cilantro, and serve.

Tips:

❖ Molu recommends serving this with some finely chopped red onions, slivers of fresh green chiles, and wedges of lime. A burst of fresh lime juice accentuates the tamarind's super-tart flavor.

❖ For an unusual but surprising burst of flavor, fold in a teaspoon of rock salt, barely pulverized, at the end of Step 7. If you do this, eliminate the coarse salt in Step 6.

Saucy Eggplant and Green Tomato

Ringana tamatar nu Shaak

Green tomatoes provide an acidic balance to the eggplant here, creating a nice solution for the "what can I do with these unripe tomatoes" question. If the sauce is a little too tart for your taste buds, sprinkle in a teaspoon of white granulated sugar before serving it. This makes a great side dish when served with

Sweet Split Green Lentils and Yellow Peas (page 392) and rotis, either store-bought or homemade (page 727). **SERVES 6**

2 tablespoons peanut or canola oil

I teaspoon black or yellow mustard seeds

I teaspoon cumin seeds

12 small purple Indian (or I large Italian) eggplants (about I½ pounds total), stems removed, cut into pieces 2 inches long, I inch wide, and ½ inch thick

8 ounces unripe green tomatoes, cored and cut into pieces 2 inches long and I inch wide

¼ cup finely chopped fresh cilantro leaves and tender stems

4 fresh green Thai, cayenne, or serrano chiles, stems removed, cut in half lengthwise (do not remove the seeds)

2 teaspoons coriander seeds, ground

I teaspoon cumin seeds, ground

¼ teaspoon ground turmeric

1. Heat the oil in a large saucepan over medium-high heat. Add the mustard seeds, cover the pan, and cook until the seeds have stopped popping (not unlike popcorn), about 30 seconds. Sprinkle in the cumin seeds, which will instantly sizzle. Immediately add the eggplant, tomatoes, cilantro, and chiles. Stir-fry until the vegetables are seared, 3 to 5 minutes.

2. Stir in the coriander, ground cumin, and turmeric, and cook the spices without burning (thanks to the cushioned protection from the vegetables), about 1 minute.

3. Pour in ½ cup water. Reduce the heat to medium-low, cover the pan, and simmer, stirring occasionally, until the vegetables are very tender, 5 to 10 minutes.

4. Coarsely mash the vegetables with the back of a spoon. Continue cooking, now uncovered, stirring occasionally, until the sauce thickens, 3 to 5 minutes. Then serve.

Eggplant
WITH TOMATO AND GARLIC

katarikai thakkali kari

An easy-to-prep-and-cook curry, this is delicious with a bowl of white or red rice tossed with plain yogurt. **SERVES 8**

2 tablespoons unrefined sesame oil or canola oil

I teaspoon black or yellow mustard seeds

I tablespoon skinned split black lentils (cream-colored in this form, urad dal), picked over for stones

I small red onion, cut in half lengthwise and thinly sliced

4 medium-size cloves garlic, finely chopped

12 small purple Indian (or I large Italian) eggplants (about I½ pounds total), stems removed, cut into pieces 2 inches long, I inch wide, and ½ inch thick

2 large tomatoes, cored and cut into 2-inch cubes

2 tablespoons finely chopped fresh cilantro leaves and tender stems

2 teaspoons coarse kosher or sea salt

I teaspoon Sambhar masala (page 33)

15 medium-size to large fresh curry leaves

1. Heat the oil in a large saucepan over medium-high heat. Add the mustard seeds, cover the pan, and cook until the seeds have stopped popping (not unlike popcorn), about 30 seconds. Add the lentils and stir-fry until they turn golden brown, 15 to 20 seconds. Immediately add the onion and garlic, and stir-fry until the onion slices are light brown around the edges, 3 to 5 minutes.

2. Add the eggplant, tomatocs, and 1½ cups water. Stir in the cilantro, salt, *Sambhar masala,* and curry leaves. Lower the heat to medium and heat to a boil. Cook, uncovered, stirring occasionally, until some of the eggplant breaks down and thickens the sauce, 18 to 20 minutes. Then serve.

Tip: This curry reminds me of ratatouille, that robust-flavored eggplant stew from southern France. Try tossing it with fresh cooked pasta for a package deal that will please even the finicky eaters at your table.

Flat Beans and Dried Berries
WITH MANGO POWDER

ker Sangar

Rajasthan's signature dish, this curry makes perfect sense, especially when you realize how arid that state's climate is for most of the year. To optimize the short growing season for fruits, vegetables, and herbs, Rajasthanis use the very same sun to dry them out for later use—and then reconstitute them in dairy products, which can be more plentiful there than water. So when flat, thin beans and desert berries blossom, they are plucked and sun-parched, to be soaked later in buttermilk and cooked with spices. My adaptation uses water all the way, but feel free to soak them in

buttermilk (don't heat it, though) in Step 1. (Discard the buttermilk before you proceed with the recipe.) See the Tips at the end of the recipe to see my substitute ingredients suggestions. Now I realize that if you make this curry with all the alternatives, it is no longer *ker sangar.* My goal is to introduce you to the classic, but in the absence of the key ingredients, I didn't want you to stop enjoying the flavors in this tart curry. So enjoy already! **SERVES 4**

½ cup dried flat beans (see Tips)
¼ cup dried fruit berries (see Tips)
2 dried red Kashmiri or guajillo chiles (see Tips), stems removed
I large clove garlic
2 tablespoons Ghee (page 21) or canola oil
I teaspoon cumin seeds
¼ teaspoon ground asafetida
2 teaspoons coriander seeds, ground
I teaspoon mango powder (see Tips)
I teaspoon coarse kosher or sea salt
½ teaspoon ground turmeric
½ teaspoon cayenne (ground red pepper)

1. Place the beans, berries, and chiles in a medium-size bowl. Add hot water to cover, and let them soak until reconstituted, 1 to 2 hours. Drain.

2. Combine the reconstituted mixture with 2 cups water in a small saucepan, and bring to a boil over medium heat. Then reduce the heat, cover the pan, and simmer, stirring occasionally, until the beans and berries are tender, 10 to 15 minutes. Drain the medley in a colander, reserving 1 cup of the cooking water.

3. Remove the chiles from the drained mixture and transfer them to a mortar. Add the garlic and pound, scraping the sides to contain the mixture in the center, to form a deep red pulpy paste.

4. Dry out the saucepan and heat the ghee in it over medium-high heat. Add the cumin seeds and cook until they sizzle, turn reddish brown, and smell nutty, 5 to 10 seconds. Immediately sprinkle in the asafetida, and then add the drained beans and berries, the chile-garlic paste, and the coriander, mango powder, salt, turmeric, and cayenne. Cook, stirring occasionally, for 2 to 4 minutes.

5. Pour in the reserved cooking water and scrape the bottom of the pan to deglaze it, releasing any bits of spice and vegetable. Boil the curry, uncovered, stirring occasionally, until the sauce thickens slightly, about 5 minutes. Then serve.

Tips:

❖ The thin, light green dried beans known as *sangar* are barely 2 to 3 inches long and ¼ to ½ inch thick. *Ker*, the dried form of desert berries, look like small radishes; they are tart, with a seedy pulp inside (like a cross between the graininess of unripe figs and gelatinous cucumber seeds). Whenever I can, I bring some *ker* and *sangar* back from my travels to India; they are very shelf-stable. But here's the bad news: Outside of Rajasthan, it is very hard to find these dried beans and berries. So, what's a mother to do? Well, mama, use 1 cup frozen French-style cut green beans for the *sangar* and 3 or 4 slightly unripe fresh figs (or reconstituted dried ones) for the *ker*. Start the recipe at Step 2.

❖ Dried Kashmiri chiles, used whole, impart a shocking red color with gentle heat. A similar chile, called guajillo, is stout and dark blood-red when dry. When reconstituted in boiling water, guajillos have the same color and heat intensity as the Kashmiri chiles, making them an ideal alternative.

❖ I normally recommend an equal amount of lime juice as an alternative for mango powder; if you want to use it, add it toward the end, just before you serve the curry.

Aromatic Green Beans
WITH POUNDED MUSTARD AND CARDAMOM

farasvi Chi bhajee

While I was making the paste for this curry, I kept singing Jerry Lee Lewis's song, switching "poundin'" for "shakin'." The rhythmic beat of the pestle thumping against the herbs and spices, releasing intense aromas, made the experience not only pleasurable but also highly cathartic. Serve this with Herb-Stuffed Shrimp (page 96) and some black rice (page 708) for a stunning-looking (not to mention -tasting) plate. **SERVES 4**

I teaspoon rock salt (see Tip)

½ teaspoon black or yellow mustard seeds

½ teaspoon cardamom seeds from green or white pods

3 dried red Thai or cayenne chiles, stems removed

¼ cup firmly packed fresh cilantro leaves and tender stems

½ cup shredded fresh coconut; or ¼ cup shredded dried unsweetened coconut, reconstituted (see Note)

2 tablespoons fresh lime juice

I teaspoon white granulated sugar

¼ teaspoon ground turmeric

12 to 15 medium-size to large fresh curry leaves

2 tablespoons peanut or canola oil

I teaspoon cumin seeds

I pound green beans, trimmed and cut into 2-inch lengths

1. Combine the rock salt, mustard seeds, cardamom seeds, and chiles in a mortar. Pound the dry blend with the pestle to break down the spices. Then add the cilantro and pound the aromatic herb, using a spatula to scrape the sides and contain the blend in the center for a more concentrated clobbering. Alternatively, use a food processor. Once it breaks down to a pulpy mass, add the coconut and do the same. Finally, fold in the lime juice, sugar, turmeric, and curry leaves.

2. Heat the oil in a medium-size skillet over medium-high heat. Add the cumin seeds and cook until they sizzle, turn reddish brown, and smell nutty, 5 to 10 seconds. Add the green beans and stir-fry until they start to blister and acquire brown spots, 5 to 7 minutes.

3. Pour in the ½ cup water and deglaze the skillet, releasing any brown bits. Reduce the heat to medium-low, cover the skillet, and simmer the thin brown broth, stirring occasionally, until the beans are fork-tender, 12 to 15 minutes.

4. Stir in the pounded mixture and raise the heat to medium-high. Simmer, uncovered, stirring occasionally, until the coconut is warmed and the sauce is thick, 2 to 3 minutes. Then serve.

Note: To reconstitute coconut, cover with ¼ cup boiling water, set aside for about 15 minutes, and then drain.

Tip: Rock salt has a delicate mineral-like flavor and a pleasant saltiness, and I adore its grainy texture. By all means use coarse kosher salt as an alternative if you have no rock salt at hand. (Any upscale grocery store should stock rock salt right next to the regular salt, if they value their salt and your business.)

Spicy Green Beans
WITH SAUCY RED ONIONS

Vengayam Avarai

Watch out when you dive into this curry, because hidden among those greens beans are hot chiles, sliced the same way as the beans. The rice flour, in addition to thickening the sauce, mellows out the chiles' pungency with its starchy presence.

SERVES 6

2 tablespoons canola oil

I teaspoon black or yellow mustard seeds

I tablespoon skinned split black lentils (cream-colored in this form, urad dal), picked over for stones

I small red onion, cut in half lengthwise and thinly sliced

2 fresh green Thai, cayenne, or serrano chiles, stems removed, sliced diagonally into ½-inch pieces (do not remove the seeds)

½ teaspoon black or yellow mustard seeds, ground

½ teaspoon fenugreek seeds, ground

¼ teaspoon ground turmeric

I pound green beans, trimmed and sliced diagonally into ½-inch lengths

1½ teaspoons coarse kosher or sea salt

10 to 12 medium-size to large fresh curry leaves (see Tips)

I tablespoon rice flour

1. Heat the oil in a large skillet over medium-high

heat. Add the mustard seeds, cover the skillet, and cook until the seeds have stopped popping (not unlike popcorn), about 30 seconds. Add the lentils and stir-fry until they turn golden brown, 15 to 20 seconds. Immediately add the onion, chiles, ground mustard, fenugreek seeds, and turmeric. Stir-fry until the spices are fragrant, about 1 minute.

2. Toss in the green beans, salt, and curry leaves, and continue to stir-fry until the curry leaves have released their delicate aroma, about 30 seconds. Pour in 1 cup water and stir once or twice to deglaze the skillet, releasing any browned bits of spices and onion. Reduce the heat to medium-low, cover the skillet, and stew the beans, stirring occasionally, until they are fork-tender, 10 to 12 minutes.

3. Remove the lid and sprinkle the rice flour over the watery curry. Stir three or four times, and remove the skillet from the heat. The sauce will instantly thicken, bringing together the delectably sweet onions, pungent chiles, and tender-but-firm green beans. Serve.

Tips:

❖ During the warm summer months, in my otherwise frozen state of Minnesota, I throw this curry together for a quick weekday side dish, using a combination of bright green and yellow wax beans, purchased at the farmers' market.

❖ We Indians normally don't eat the curry leaves that are left whole in a dish, but by all means try a few—it won't kill you. The leaves are left intact in the curry because they continue to provide flavor and aroma.

Green Beans, Potatoes, and Eggplant
WITH A CILANTRO-ONION SAUCE

Sem, Aloo, Aur Baingan ki Subzi

Here's an excellent example of a curry with no spices in it—just herbs. Feel free to either add or drop any vegetable from this combination if one does or doesn't appeal to you. Just adjust the cooking time to suit the vegetables you use. **SERVES 6**

1 large tomato, cored and coarsely chopped
1 medium-size red onion, coarsely chopped
½ cup firmly packed fresh cilantro leaves and tender stems
4 fresh green Thai, cayenne, or serrano chiles, stems removed
1 large white potato, such as russet or Yukon Gold, peeled, cut into 2-inch cubes, and submerged in a bowl of cold water to prevent browning
2 tablespoons canola oil
12 small purple Indian (or 1 large Italian) eggplants (about 1½ pounds total), stems removed, cut into pieces 2 inches long, 1 inch wide, and ½ inch thick
4 ounces fresh green beans, trimmed, cut into 1-inch lengths
2 teaspoons coarse kosher or sea salt

1. Plop the tomato into a blender jar, and then add the onion, cilantro, and chiles. If the tomato is juicy, it will provide ample liquid for the blender blades to function.

If it isn't, you might need to add ¼ cup water. Puree to form a light purple-red sauce with flecks of green.

2. Drain the potato and pat it dry with paper towels.

3. Heat the oil in a large saucepan over medium heat. Carefully add the potato and stir it around. Cover the pan to contain the spattering, and cook, stirring occasionally, until the potato cubes are evenly browned with a slightly crispy skin, 5 to 10 minutes.

4. Pour in the sauce, and scrape the bottom of the pan to deglaze it, releasing any browned bits of potato. Stir in the eggplant, green beans, and salt. Heat to a boil. Then reduce the heat to medium-low, cover the pan, and simmer, stirring occasionally, until the vegetables are fork-tender, 20 to 25 minutes. Then serve.

Green Beans
WITH TOMATO

Lilva ŋu Shaak

Make sure the green beans you purchase are of top-notch quality. When bent, they should snap with a slight crisp sound. If they are limp, don't waste your money on them—they may have a fibrous texture when cooked, which will make the experience unremarkable. If you can't find really good fresh beans, you are better off using a bag of frozen green beans. During the growing season, I have made this curry with yellow wax beans. **SERVES 6**

2 tablespoons canola oil
1 teaspoon black or yellow mustard seeds
1 teaspoon cumin seeds
2 teaspoons coriander seeds, ground
1½ teaspoons coarse kosher or sea salt
1 teaspoon cumin seeds, ground
1 teaspoon cayenne (ground red pepper)
1 teaspoon white granulated sugar
½ teaspoon ground turmeric
½ teaspoon ground asafetida
1 pound green beans, trimmed and cut into
* ½-inch lengths*
1 medium-size tomato, cored and cut into
* ½-inch cubes*
2 tablespoons finely chopped fresh cilantro
* leaves and tender stems for garnishing*

1. Heat the oil in a medium-size saucepan over medium-high heat. Add the mustard seeds, cover the pan, and cook until the seeds have stopped popping (not unlike popcorn), about 30 seconds. Sprinkle in the cumin seeds, which will instantly turn reddish brown and smell fragrant.

2. Remove the pan from the heat and add the coriander, salt, ground cumin, cayenne, sugar, turmeric, and asafetida. The heat from the oil will be just right to cook the ground spices without burning them. Add the beans to the mixture and return the pan to the heat. Stir to coat the beans with the spices.

3. Pour in 1 cup water, and stir in the tomato. Heat the curry to a boil. Then reduce the heat to medium-low, cover the pan, and stew the beans, stirring occasionally, until they are fork-tender, 10 to 12 minutes.

4. Sprinkle with the cilantro, and serve.

Tip: For a much sweeter depth, try 1 tablespoon crumbled or chopped jaggery or firmly packed dark brown sugar instead of the white sugar. It also helps to thicken the sauce a bit more.

Young Jackfruit
WITH ONION AND TOMATO

kathal chi bhajee

This Maharashtrian delicacy is a sure winner—especially if you wish to fool your guests into thinking they are eating meat. Young (green) jackfruit is firm and slightly fibrous, its chewy, meaty quality further enhanced when you deep-fry the pieces in oil. In this country, you are more likely to find the canned version, sold in Southeast Asian and Indian grocery stores. It is perfectly acceptable, especially if you treat it this way. Serve it with either *pooris* (page 725) or rotis (page 727), homemade or store-bought, for a quick lunch. **SERVES 6**

Canola oil for deep-frying
1 can (20 ounces) young, unripe jackfruit, drained, patted dry between paper towels, and cut into 1-inch pieces (see box below)
2 tablespoons Ghee (page 21) or canola oil
1 teaspoon cumin seeds
1 small red onion, finely chopped
1 or 2 fresh green Thai, cayenne, or serrano chiles, to taste, stems removed, finely chopped (do not remove the seeds)
1 medium-size tomato, cored and finely chopped
4 tablespoons finely chopped fresh cilantro leaves and tender stems

jackfruit

Babar, the founding father of India's Moghal empire and a forefather of Shah Jahan, of Taj Mahal fame, described the inside of the jackfruit as resembling a sheep's stomach with its compartments. This description may not appeal to a herbivore, but it certainly provides a vivid picture of the inside of this enormous fruit (one can weigh up to 100 pounds). A close sibling to breadfruit, jackfruit has a rough skin with several hexagonal-shaped "scales" that grow out into horns when ripe, and that exude a strong aroma that is considered foul by some, while others employ more favorable terms like ripe pineapple and bananas. Whichever side of the perfume debate you are on, you will agree about the sweetness of the numerous fleshy, yellow, smooth-skinned fruit bulbs when they are ripe. The fruit encases an oval nut and continues to ripen even when cut, developing a yeasty flavor within a short time. It is best to eat ripe jackfruit as soon as the vendor excavates the fleshy bulbs, should you be in a part of the world where it is sold fresh. (Extracting the fruit is a messy, sticky project, best left to folks who know how to do it, employing gigantic cleavers and vegetable oil.)

It is the unripe jackfruit that is consumed as a starchy vegetable, providing a meatlike texture in some of India's curries. If the canned vegetable is not within reach where you live, my dear friend and colleague David Joachim, in his mind-boggling Food Substitutions Bible, recommends plantains, potatoes, winter melon, fuzzy gourd, or even summer squash as an acceptable alternative. Whichever vegetable you end up using, follow the techniques described in this recipe for a comparable texture and flavor.

2 teaspoons Kolhapuri masala (page 32)

1 teaspoon coarse kosher or sea salt

4 scallions (green tops and white bulbs),
   finely chopped

1. Pour oil to a depth of 2 to 3 inches into a wok, Dutch oven, or medium-size saucepan. Heat the oil over medium heat until a candy or deep-fry thermometer inserted into it (without touching the pan's bottom) registers 350°F. (An alternative way to see if the oil is at the right temperature for deep-frying is to gently flick a drop of water over it. If the pearl-like drop skitters across the surface, the oil is ready.)

2. Line a plate or a cookie sheet with three or four sheets of paper towels.

3. Once the oil is ready, gently add the jackfruit (I use a slotted spoon to lower the pieces into the oil). Stand back a little, as the fruit will initially make the oil spatter and bubble. Then it will subside. Fry gently, turning occasionally, until the pieces are light honey-brown and crisp, about 5 minutes. Remove them with a slotted spoon and allow them to drain on the paper towels.

4. Heat the ghee in a medium-size saucepan over medium-high heat. Sprinkle in the cumin seeds and cook until they sizzle, turn reddish brown, and are aromatic, 5 to 10 seconds. Immediately add the onion and chiles. Stir-fry until the onion is light brown, 5 to 8 minutes.

5. Add the tomato, 2 tablespoons of the cilantro, the masala, and the salt. Lower the heat to medium and cook, uncovered, stirring occasionally, until the tomato has softened but is still firm-looking, about 5 minutes.

6. Pour in 1 cup water and add the fried jackfruit. Heat the curry to a boil. Then reduce the heat to medium-low, cover the pan, and simmer, stirring occasionally, until the jackfruit is fork-tender, 15 to 20 minutes.

7. Stir in the scallions and the remaining 2 tablespoons cilantro, and serve.

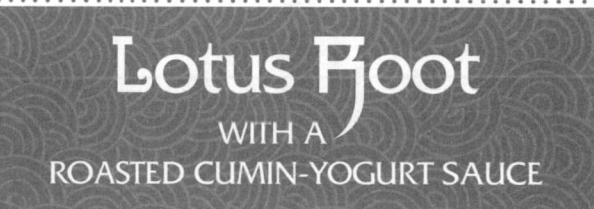

Lotus Root
WITH A
ROASTED CUMIN-YOGURT SAUCE

Zeera Kamal Kakadi

Lotus root (technically a rhizome, from which the roots emerge) looks like tapered, stout sausage links. A swivel peeler can easily remove the light creamy-brown skin. When it is sliced, you can see the petal-like patterns of holes that run the length of the rhizome. Lotus root is a perfect match for the stunning burgundy-tinted flower that floats sensuously atop its wide leaves in the water. The flavor and texture of the root slices resembles the sweetness of fresh water chestnuts and the crispy, juicy crunch of jicama. These rhizomes—links, peel, and all—are a common sight at markets that stock Chinese, Vietnamese, and Thai groceries. And on many occasions, I have been pleasantly surprised to spot peeled, shrink-wrapped fresh lotus root at my suburban neighborhood's supermarket, right next to the other Asian vegetables. Flash-frozen peeled slices (½ inch thick) are readily available in every Indian and Pakistani grocery store. **SERVES 6**

4 medium-size cloves garlic

3 lengthwise slices fresh ginger (each 2 inches long,
 1 inch wide, and ⅛ inch thick)

3 fresh green Thai, cayenne, or serrano chiles,
 stems removed

2 tablespoons mustard oil or canola oil

1½ teaspoons coarse kosher or sea salt

1 pound fresh lotus root, peeled and cut into
 ½-inch-thick rounds; or 1 pound frozen
 sliced lotus root (no need to thaw)

½ cup plain yogurt

2 tablespoons heavy (whipping) cream

1 teaspoon cumin seeds, toasted and ground
 (see Tip, page 294)

2 tablespoons finely chopped fresh cilantro
 leaves and tender stems for garnishing

1. Combine the garlic, ginger, and chiles in a food processor and pulse to mince the mixture.

2. Heat the oil in a large skillet over medium-high heat. Add the minced garlic mixture and stir-fry until the ginger and garlic are light reddish brown, 1 to 2 minutes.

3. Pour in 1 cup water and scrape the bottom of the skillet to deglaze it, releasing any browned bits. Stir in the salt, followed by the lotus root. Heat the curry to a boil. Then reduce the heat to medium-low, cover the skillet, and simmer, stirring occasionally, until the lotus slices are fork-tender, 15 to 20 minutes.

4. While the lotus root is simmering, whisk the yogurt, cream, and ground toasted cumin together in a small bowl.

5. When the lotus root is tender, pour the yogurt mixture into the curry. Allow the sauce to rewarm, uncovered, stirring occasionally, 2 to 5 minutes.

6. Sprinkle with the cilantro, and serve.

Tip: Because water chestnuts are similar in texture, you can use them as an alternative to the fresh lotus root. If you resort to the canned variety, make sure to drain and rinse them before you add them to the curry.

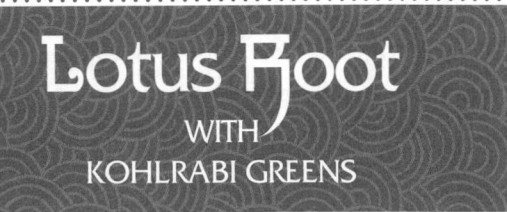

Lotus Root
WITH
KOHLRABI GREENS

ŋadru ħaak

both these vegetables are native to Kashmir and come alive in the presence of sweet fennel, pungent ginger, hot chiles, and smoky cardamom. This dish is a great sidekick to the robust lamb curry called *Roghan josh* (page 214); serve some basmati rice too. **SERVES 6**

2 tablespoons canola oil

2 dried red Thai or cayenne chiles, stems removed

2 black cardamom pods

6 cups thinly shredded fresh kohlrabi leaves
 (see box, facing page)

8 ounces fresh lotus root, peeled and cut crosswise
 into ½-inch-thick slices; or 8 ounces frozen
 sliced lotus root (no need to thaw; see Tip,
 page 516)

1 teaspoon fennel seeds, ground

1 teaspoon ground ginger

1 teaspoon coarse kosher or sea salt

¼ cup heavy (whipping) cream

1. Heat the oil in a medium-size saucepan over medium-high heat. Add the chiles and cardamom pods,

and cook until they sizzle and smell smoky-pungent, 10 to 15 seconds. Then add the kohlrabi leaves, a handful at a time, stirring them in until wilted.

2. Stir in the lotus root, fennel, ginger, and salt. Stir to coat the vegetables with the spices, 1 to 2 minutes.

3. Pour in 1 cup water and heat to a boil. Then reduce the heat to medium-low, cover the pan, and simmer, stirring occasionally, until the lotus root is fork-tender, 15 to 20 minutes.

4. Stir in the cream and simmer, uncovered, stirring occasionally, until the sauce has thickened slightly, 3 to 5 minutes.

5. Remove the chiles and cardamom pods if you wish, and serve.

Lotus Root and Yams
WITH A SHALLOT-GINGER SAUCE

kamal kakadi Aur Suran ki Subzi

the literal translation of *kamal kakadi* is "lotus cucumber," and once you work with this water-chestnut-like vegetable, you will see why it is called that. Its juicy crunch is a wonderful backdrop to the shallot-ginger-chile sauce, and the yams provide an underlying sweetness to the curry. **SERVES 6**

kohlrabi

kohlrabi is delicious in place of, or in addition to, crunchy lotus root. I think kohlrabi is a vegetable that has been overlooked, and unjustly so. It is a member of the cabbage family and looks very much like its sibling, the turnip (in fact, kohlrabi also grows in shades of green and purple). Elizabeth Schneider, in her book *Vegetables from Amaranth to Zucchini*, describes its flavor as a cross between that of "broccoli stalks, water chestnuts, and cucumbers," and I couldn't agree more. Kashmiris adore the complete package—bulb and leaves—steeped in milk, yogurt, cream, and aromatic spices like cardamom, ginger, and fennel.

When you purchase a bunch of kohlrabi (usually three or four bulbs banded together) with their leaves (similar to collard greens, but not as wide), there usually is not much left to the greens. To get the 6 cups needed for Lotus Root with Kohlrabi Greens (page 514), you will probably need about 3 bunches. During the summer months, when you visit your neighborhood farmers' market (especially if there is a strong immigrant community from southeast and southwest Asia), you will find bundles of kohlrabi greens cascading from vendors' carts.

To prepare the leaves for cooking, rinse them under cold water. Then fold the leaves in half, along the tough rib that runs north-south. Cut out and discard the rib. Stack a few of the leaves together, and slice them into thin shreds.

8 ounces fresh lotus root, peeled and cut crosswise into
  ½-inch-thick slices; or 8 ounces frozen sliced lotus
  root (no need to thaw; see Tips)

4 cups frozen cubed yams (no need to thaw), or 4 cups
  cubed fresh yams (½-inch cubes; see box, below)

½ teaspoon ground turmeric

6 medium-size to large shallots, coarsely chopped

4 lengthwise slices fresh ginger (each 2 inches long,
  1 inch wide, and ⅛ inch thick)

2 to 4 fresh green Thai, cayenne, or serrano chiles,
  to taste, stems removed

2 tablespoons canola oil

¼ cup raw pine nuts

1½ teaspoons coarse kosher or sea salt

2 tablespoons Toasted Chickpea Flour (page 41)

Juice of 1 medium-size lime

1. Combine the lotus, yams, and turmeric in a
medium-size saucepan, and add water to cover. Bring to
a boil over medium heat. Then reduce the heat, cover
the pan, and simmer, stirring occasionally, until the vegetables are fork-tender, about 15 minutes.

2. While the vegetables are cooking, combine the
shallots, ginger, and chiles in a food processor, and
pulse until minced.

3. Drain the vegetables in a colander, reserving 2 cups
of the cooking water.

4. Give the saucepan a quick wipe with a paper towel
to dry it out, and then heat the oil in the pan over
medium-high heat. Add the minced blend and the
pine nuts. Stir-fry until the "flavor packet" is light brown
around the edges, the nuts are reddish brown, and the
chiles are making you cough (come on, live a little—
but do have proper ventilation to ease the discomfort),
3 to 5 minutes.

5. Pour in the reserved cooking water and add the
drained vegetables. Stir in the salt. Heat the curry to a
boil. Then reduce the heat to medium-low, cover the
pan, and simmer, stirring occasionally, until the flavors
meld, about 15 minutes.

6. Sprinkle the chickpea flour over the mixture and
stir it in quickly to prevent any lumps from forming.
Once the sauce thickens, which will be mere seconds,
stir in the lime juice and serve.

Tips:

❖ Sliced lotus root and cubed yams are both easy to
locate in handy freezer packs at your Indian grocery
store and are perfectly acceptable and downright
convenient.

❖ Fresh lotus root and yams will be piled in boxes
right next to the onions and potatoes. Trim off their
ends and peel them to get at their fleshy interior.
Thoroughly wash them before you cook them.

yams

❖ ❖ ❖

Yams are part of the genus Dioscorea, so named
because of a toxin, dioscorine, that is found in
the uncooked tubers. These tubers have been
used medicinally for centuries—to make poultices
and more recently as a source of steroids. Their skin
is generally tough, gnarly, and hairy, ranging in color
from brown and black to blackish-purple. When
peeled, they reveal shades of yellow (this variety goes
by the name suran in Hindi), white, and deep purple
(called kand in Gujarat and a key root vegetable in
their signature curry, Undhiyu, found on page 629).
Many folks consider yams bland, but in the right hands,
they are yummy. If you savor a spiced dish like this
curry—assertive with chiles, ginger, and shallots—you
just might fall in love with yams (or with the Indian).

Brown Cremini Mushrooms
WITH CHIVES

dhingri josh

May I make a confession? The texture of mushrooms bothers me; it reminds me of overcooked meat. However, I do enjoy the mushroom's wild, earthy flavors, especially when braised in a spicy tomato-based sauce like this one. Latte-colored cremini mushrooms are very similar—in shape only, mercifully—to mundane button mushrooms. They have a deeper flavor and are easy to find year-round in most supermarkets. **SERVES 6**

2 tablespoons mustard oil or canola oil

I teaspoon cumin seeds

I teaspoon black cumin seeds

4 black cardamom pods

3 fresh or dried bay leaves

2 cinnamon sticks (each 3 inches long)

2 dried red Thai or cayenne chiles,
    stems removed

I cup finely chopped red onion

I tablespoon Ginger Paste (page 15)

I tablespoon Garlic Paste (page 15)

I can (14.5 ounces) diced tomatoes

I teaspoon ground Kashmiri chiles; or ¼ teaspoon
    cayenne (ground red pepper) mixed with
    ¾ teaspoon sweet paprika

I teaspoon coarse kosher or sea salt

8 ounces brown cremini mushrooms, quartered

½ teaspoon Punjabi garam masala (page 25)

I cup finely chopped fresh chives

1. Heat the oil in a large skillet over medium-high heat. Sprinkle in both kinds of cumin seeds and the cardamom pods, bay leaves, cinnamon sticks, and chiles. Cook until the spices sizzle and are aromatic, 10 to 15 seconds. Add the onion and stir-fry until it is honey-brown, about 5 minutes.

2. Stir in the ginger and garlic pastes, which will spatter when they hit the hot oil, and stir-fry to barely remove their harsh edge, about 30 seconds.

3. Add the tomatoes, with their juices, the ground chiles, and the salt. Lower the heat to medium and simmer the sauce, partially covered, stirring occasionally, until most of the tomato liquid has evaporated and some of the oil is starting to separate, 8 to 10 minutes.

4. Pour ½ cup water into the curry and continue to simmer, partially covered, until the water is absorbed and a little oil is starting to separate from the deep-red sauce, 5 to 10 minutes.

5. Pour in ½ cup water, and add the mushrooms. Cook, covered, stirring occasionally, until the mushrooms are tender but still succulent when bit into, about 10 minutes.

6. Remove the cardamom pods, bay leaves, and cinnamon sticks. Stir in the garam masala and chives, and serve.

Tip: Before you serve this curry, I recommend removing the cardamom pods, bay leaves, and cinnamon sticks—especially the cardamom pods. They closely resemble the mushrooms, and if you bite into one, it makes for an unpleasant experience. The pod's smokiness can overpower your taste buds and dull the flavors of the other ingredients.

Morel Mushrooms
WITH
GREEN PEAS

Gucchi Mutter

You may have to take out a bank loan for this dish, but it is well worth it. Found in the wild in Kashmir and revered for their meaty texture and woodsy flavor, morels have a characteristic cone-shaped cap with honeycomb-like chambers. These crevices harbor dirt and insects. To rid the mushrooms of any unwanted "extras," slice them open lengthwise, then dunk them repeatedly in a bowl of cool water, letting the grime sink to the bottom. Dry them with paper towels.

Morels are not eaten raw. They require a longer cooking time than other varieties of mushroom, making them an ideal candidate for the robust flavors in this slow-stewed curry.

SERVES 4

4 tablespoons Ghee (page 21) or canola oil

½ small red onion, coarsely chopped

¼ cup slivered blanched almonds

3 medium-size cloves garlic, coarsely chopped

2 lengthwise slices fresh ginger (each 2 inches long,
    1 inch wide, and ⅛ inch thick), coarsely chopped

2 tablespoons tomato paste

8 ounces fresh morel mushrooms, cleaned and
    sliced in half (see Tips)

1 teaspoon coarse kosher or sea salt

1 teaspoon ground Kashmiri chiles; or ¼ teaspoon
    cayenne (ground red pepper) mixed with
    ¾ teaspoon sweet paprika

½ teaspoon Kashmiri garam masala (page 29)

¼ teaspoon ground turmeric

1 cup frozen green peas (no need to thaw)

2 tablespoons finely chopped fresh cilantro
    leaves and tender stems for garnishing

1. Heat 2 tablespoons of the ghee in a medium-size saucepan over medium-high heat. Add the onion, almonds, garlic, and ginger, and stir-fry until the nuts are browned and the onion is light brown around the edges, 4 to 6 minutes.

2. Pour ½ cup water into a blender jar, followed by the onion mixture and the tomato paste. Puree, scraping the inside of the jar as needed, to form a slightly gritty terra-cotta-colored sauce.

3. Heat the remaining 2 tablespoons ghee in the same saucepan over medium-high heat. Add the morels and stir-fry until their woodsy, musky aroma fills the air and they are a bit shriveled, 4 to 6 minutes.

storing mushrooms

Store mushrooms in paper bags in the refrigerator—not in plastic bags, which expedite that "slime factor" which is oh-so-neither-desirable-nor-edible. They will keep in the refrigerator for up to a week. I personally do not recommend freezing mushrooms.

Which leads me to the next question: Do I wash the mushrooms? Some food pundits shun washing them for fear of water seeping into the flesh. They recommend, instead, that you scrub them with a brush to get rid of excess dirt, and peel the stem ends if they are tough and mud-caked. For a curry like Dhingri josh, where the mushrooms are sauce-soused, I wash them.

4. Add the sauce to the mushrooms, and stir in the salt, ground chiles, garam masala, turmeric, and peas. Cover the pan, reduce the heat to medium-low, and simmer, stirring occasionally, until the mushrooms are fork-tender, 10 to 15 minutes.

5. Sprinkle with the cilantro, and serve.

Tips:

❖ Dried morels are slightly cheaper than fresh ones. Put 4 ounces of dried morels in a heatproof bowl, cover them with boiling water, and set them aside for about 1 hour, until they swell up and feel spongy-soft when touched. Then wash them well.

❖ If morels are not in your budget, try slices of portobello mushrooms, which are equally meaty if not as uniquely flavorful.

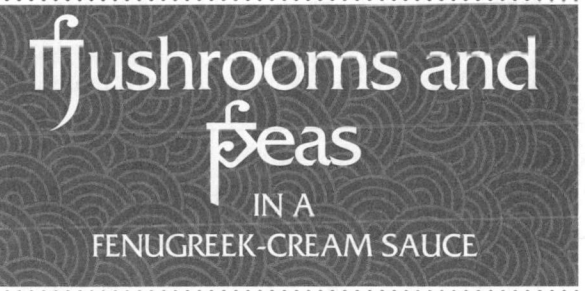

Mushrooms and Peas
IN A
FENUGREEK-CREAM SAUCE

Malai Waale Dhingri Mutter

It's amazing how you can take humdrum peas and common button mushrooms, stir in the right herb, and *voilà* (as my eight-year-old son exclaims), you have a rich-tasting, complex-looking vegetable side dish. This goes well with Cashew Chicken with a Cilantro Sauce (page 155) and some white rice. **SERVES 6**

¼ cup raw cashew nuts

6 medium-size cloves garlic

4 to 6 fresh green Thai, cayenne, or serrano chiles, to taste, stems removed

2 tablespoons canola oil

I cup finely chopped red onion

8 ounces button or brown cremini mushrooms (see Tip)

I cup chopped fresh or frozen fenugreek leaves (thawed if frozen); or ½ cup dried fenugreek leaves, soaked in a bowl of water and skimmed off before use (see box, page 473)

I cup frozen green peas (no need to thaw)

½ cup half-and-half

I teaspoon coarse kosher or sea salt

1. Combine the cashews, garlic, and chiles in a food processor, and process until minced; the blend will be coarse, gritty, and gummy-textured.

2. Heat the oil in a large skillet over medium-high heat. Add the onion and the garlic-cashew blend, and stir-fry until a thin, light brown film of garlic and cashews forms on the bottom of the skillet, 2 to 3 minutes.

3. Stir in the mushrooms and continue to stir-fry for 1 to 2 minutes. Then pour in ½ cup water and scrape the bottom of the skillet to deglaze it, releasing the brown layer and incorporating its rich flavors into the sauce.

4. Stir in the fenugreek leaves, peas, half-and-half, and salt, and heat the curry to a boil. Lower the heat to medium and simmer, uncovered, stirring occasionally, until the sauce thickens slightly (to the consistency of whole milk), 8 to 10 minutes. Then serve.

Tip: For a sinful indulgence, and if your wallet can bear the price, use morel mushrooms instead. Any combination of wild mushrooms will also do the trick.

East Indian Spiced Mustard
AND
FENUGREEK GREENS

Sarson Aur Methi Ki Bhajee

You would think that if you combined bitter mustard greens with equally bitter (but perfumed) fenugreek leaves, your curry might be unpalatable—but wouldn't you know it, your instincts fail you once again. You'll realize this the moment you taste that first mouthful, redolent with the sweet spices in the *bottle masala*. The second time I made this curry, I had run out of *bottle masala*, but I did have the sweeter, three-spice *Bangala garam masala* (page 26) in my pantry. It was a perfectly acceptable substitute, even though it lacked the subtleties of the twenty-spice blend. **SERVES 4**

- 2 tablespoons canola oil
- 1 tablespoon finely chopped fresh ginger
- 8 ounces fresh mustard greens, well rinsed and finely chopped (see Tip, page 606)
- ½ cup chopped fresh or frozen fenugreek leaves (thawed if frozen); or 2 tablespoons dried fenugreek leaves, soaked in a bowl of water and skimmed off before use (see box, page 473)
- ¼ cup finely chopped fresh cilantro leaves and tender stems
- 2 fresh green Thai, cayenne, or serrano chiles, stems removed, cut in half lengthwise (do not remove the seeds)
- 1 medium-size tomato, cored and finely chopped
- 2 teaspoons East Indian bottle masala (page 37)
- 1 teaspoon coarse kosher or sea salt

1. Heat the oil in a medium-size saucepan over medium-high heat. Sprinkle in the ginger, and stir-fry until it sizzles and starts to turn light brown, 30 seconds to 1 minute.

2. Add the mustard greens, a couple of handfuls at a time, stirring until they wilt, 2 to 4 minutes per batch. When all the leaves have wilted, stir in all the remaining ingredients. Add ½ cup water and bring to a boil. Lower the heat to medium, cover the pan, and simmer, stirring occasionally, until the leaves are olive-green and soft, about 15 minutes. Then serve.

Mustard Greens
WITH SWEET CORN

Sarson Aur Makai Ki Subzi

I am fortunate to live in the state of Minnesota, which proclaims itself the "corn capital" of the world. Late summer heralds the arrival of sweet, plump white and yellow corn, bursting with flavor. This curry provides a subtle hint of bitterness from the mustard greens, balanced with the naturally sugary sweet corn—a winning combination in my book. Serve it with a basketful of rotis (page 727) and some spicy lime pickles, either store-bought or homemade (page 745), for a satisfying lunch. **SERVES 6**

- 2 tablespoons canola oil
- 1 teaspoon cumin seeds
- 1 small red onion, cut in half lengthwise and thinly sliced
- 1 pound fresh mustard greens, well rinsed and finely chopped (see Tip, page 606)
- 1 can (14.5 ounces) diced tomatoes

I ½ teaspoons coarse kosher or sea salt
I teaspoon Punjabi garam masala (page 25)
Kernels from 3 ears fresh corn (about 3 cups;
   see Tip, page 489)

1. Heat the oil in a large skillet over medium-high heat. Add the cumin seeds and cook until they sizzle, turn reddish brown, and smell aromatic, 5 to 10 seconds. Immediately add the onion and stir-fry until it is light brown, 2 to 3 minutes.

2. Add the mustard greens and continue to stir-fry until the greens wilt, 1 to 2 minutes. Then stir in the tomatoes, with their liquid, the salt, and the garam masala. Reduce the heat to medium and cook, uncovered, until the tomatoes are warmed through, 2 to 3 minutes.

3. Stir in the corn, cover the skillet, and cook, stirring occasionally, until it is warmed through and barely cooked, 3 to 5 minutes. Then serve.

Mustard Greens and Spinach

Sarson Aur Palak ka Saag

Vegetable greens are called *saag*, and here two of northern India's favorites, especially among Punjabi-speaking homes, offer bitter and buttery-mellow flavors in one smoothly pureed mouthful. Serve it with flaky, ghee-laden griddle-cooked cornbread called *Makkai ki roti* (page 728), a bowl of cool yogurt, and a giant serving of fiery, chile-smothered pickles (*Hari aur lal mirchi ki achar,* page 744). **SERVES 8**

8 large cloves garlic
4 fresh green Thai, cayenne, or serrano chiles,
   stems removed
2 lengthwise slices fresh ginger (each 2 inches long,
   I inch wide, and ⅛ inch thick)
2 tablespoons Ghee (page 21) or canola oil
I teaspoon cumin seeds
I pound fresh mustard greens, well rinsed
   and coarsely chopped (see Tip, page 606)
I pound fresh spinach leaves, well rinsed
   and coarsely chopped
I can (14.5 ounces) diced tomatoes
2 teaspoons coarse kosher or sea salt
I teaspoon Punjabi garam masala (page 25)

1. Combine the garlic, chiles, and ginger in a food processor, and pulse until minced.

2. Heat the ghee in a large saucepan over medium-high heat. Add the cumin seeds and cook until they sizzle, turn reddish brown, and smell nutty, about 15 seconds. Add the garlic-chile blend and stir-fry until the garlic is light brown and the chiles smell pungent, about 1 minute.

3. Add several handfuls of the greens to the pan (about half should fit). Cover the pan and cook until the greens wilt, about 3 minutes. Repeat with the remaining greens. Then stir in the tomatoes, with their liquid, the salt, and the garam masala. Cook, uncovered, until the tomatoes are warmed through, about 5 minutes. Remove the olive-green curry from the heat and let it cool slightly, 5 to 7 minutes.

4. Spoon half the chunky curry into a blender and puree, scraping the inside of the jar as needed, until smooth. Transfer the puree to a serving bowl. Repeat with the remaining batch, and serve.

Pureed Mustard Greens
WITH CLARIFIED BUTTER

Sarson da Saag

A classic *dhaba* (truck-stop roadside eatery) food, these pureed greens offer nutritious respite to Punjabi lorry (truck) drivers when they step down from their ornately painted vehicles and wipe their brows under the hot afternoon sun. A simple meal of *Sarson da saag, Makkai ki roti* (page 728), homemade pickles, and conversation provides fuel for the long, lonely journey ahead. **SERVES 6**

2 tablespoons mustard oil or canola oil

1 teaspoon cumin seeds

4 large cloves garlic, coarsely chopped

2 dried red Thai or cayenne chiles, stems removed

2 fresh green Thai, cayenne, or serrano chiles, stems removed

1 pound fresh mustard greens, well rinsed and coarsely chopped (see Tip, page 606)

1 teaspoon coarse kosher or sea salt

2 tablespoons Ghee (page 21) or butter, plus additional melted ghee or butter for serving (optional)

2 tablespoons yellow or white cornmeal

Juice of 1 medium-size lime

1. Heat the oil in a large saucepan or skillet over medium-high heat. Add the cumin seeds and cook until they sizzle, turn reddish brown, and are aromatic, 5 to 10 seconds. Immediately throw in the garlic and the two varieties of chiles. Stir-fry to take the raw edge off the garlic and to gently blister the chiles (especially the green ones), 1 to 2 minutes.

2. A handful at a time, drop the mustard greens into the spiced oil and stir-fry until they wilt. Repeat until all the greens have been added and wilted. Continue to cook the greens, uncovered, stirring occasionally, until their liquid evaporates and leaves a slight sheen on the leaves, 8 to 12 minutes. Stir in the salt.

3. Pour in 2 cups water, scraping the pan to deglaze it, releasing any browned bits of spice and greens. Bring to a boil. Then lower the heat to medium, cover the pan, and simmer, stirring occasionally, until the greens are tender and olive green, about 15 minutes. Remove the pan from the heat.

4. Transfer the greens, liquid and all, to a blender jar. Puree, scraping the inside of the jar as needed, to make a smooth puree. Return the puree to the pan, and fold in the 2 tablespoons ghee and the cornmeal. Place the pan over low heat, cover, and cook, stirring the greens occasionally, until the cornmeal has absorbed the liquid and the mixture has thickened, about 15 minutes.

5. Fold in the lime juice and transfer the puree to a serving bowl. If you like, pass extra ghee to drizzle atop the tart, slightly bitter, curiously nutty-tasting *saag* for added succulence.

Tip: Would it surprise you to know that there are more than fifteen varieties of mustard greens in the world, with quite a few of them available in today's marketplace? The most common American mustard, with curly leaves, is not as bitter as its Asian counterpart, a variety known as wrapped-heart mustard or *dai gai choy*. This Asian kind closely resembles the varieties of mustard that are eaten in large quantities all around the northern regions of India. See the Tip on page 606 for advice on cleaning mustard greens for cooking.

Sliced Okra
BATHED IN BUTTERMILK

bhindi kadhi

One school of thought has it that the word "curry" is an anglicized pronunciation of the yogurt- or buttermilk-based dish called *kadhi*. *Kadhis* have been in existence all around the Indian subcontinent for eons, and they have a reputation as a cure for digestive ailments: a scoop of delicately spiced *kadhi* over a mound of hot white rice will do the trick. This version, from the northwestern state of Gujarat, uses thick slices of okra fried in ghee and simmered until tender in spiced, herbed buttermilk, thickened with chickpea flour. One eloquent word describes this combination: yum! **SERVES 6**

1 pound fresh okra, rinsed and thoroughly dried

4 cups buttermilk

2 tablespoons chickpea flour

2 teaspoons white granulated sugar

2 teaspoons coarse kosher or sea salt

1 teaspoon cayenne (ground red pepper)

¼ teaspoon ground turmeric

2 tablespoons finely chopped fresh cilantro
    leaves and tender stems

12 medium-size to large fresh curry leaves

2 tablespoons Ghee (page 21) or melted butter

1 teaspoon cumin seeds

1 teaspoon fenugreek seeds

1. Trim the caps off the okra without cutting into the pods, and then cut the pods into 1-inch lengths.

2. Whisk the buttermilk, chickpea flour, sugar, salt, cayenne, and turmeric together in a medium-size bowl, making sure the flour is completely incorporated, with no lumps. Then stir in the cilantro and curry leaves.

3. Heat the ghee in a large saucepan over medium-high heat. Sprinkle the cumin and fenugreek seeds into the pan and cook until they sizzle, turn reddish brown, and are fragrant, about 10 seconds.

4. Immediately add the okra and stir-fry until the slices blister in spots and acquire a light brown coloration on their ridged skin, 8 to 10 minutes.

5. Pour in the spiced buttermilk mixture and stir once or twice to deglaze the pan, releasing any browned bits of spices and okra. Lower the heat to medium and simmer, uncovered, stirring occasionally, until the okra is fork-tender and the curry has thickened slightly, 10 to 12 minutes. The transformation from a pale, cream-colored curry to a robust, sun-yellow one is beautiful to watch. Enough, eat already.

Tamilian Okra
WITH A BUTTERMILK-COCONUT SAUCE

Vendakkai Morekozhumbu

This is one of those Tamilian curries that evoke warm, fuzzy, mother-knows-how-to-comfort-you-during-down-and-out-days memories. Rice flour, the thickener of choice in rice-growing south India, not only helps give body to the curry but also stabilizes the buttermilk and prevents it from curdling. **SERVES 6**

1 pound fresh okra, rinsed and thoroughly dried

2 tablespoons canola oil

2 teaspoons coriander seeds

½ teaspoon fenugreek seeds

1 teaspoon black or yellow mustard seeds

2 cups buttermilk

2 tablespoons rice flour

1½ teaspoons coarse kosher or sea salt

¼ teaspoon ground turmeric

*½ cup shredded fresh coconut; or ¼ cup shredded
dried unsweetened coconut, reconstituted
(see Note)*

*2 fresh green Thai, cayenne, or serrano chiles,
stems removed*

12 medium-size to large fresh curry leaves

1. Trim the caps off the okra without cutting into the pods, and cut the pods into 1-inch lengths.

2. Heat a large skillet over medium-high heat. Add the oil and swirl it around to coat the bottom evenly. Sprinkle the coriander and fenugreek seeds into the hot oil, and roast, stirring constantly, until they turn reddish brown, about 1 minute. Using a slotted spoon, transfer the seeds to a blender jar and set it aside.

3. Add the mustard seeds to the same hot, smoky oil, cover the skillet, and cook until the seeds have stopped popping (not unlike popcorn), about 30 seconds. Immediately add the okra, lower the heat to medium, and stir-fry until the pieces blister in spots and acquire a light brown coloration on their ridged skin, 12 to 15 minutes.

4. While the okra is browning, whisk the buttermilk, rice flour, salt, and turmeric together in a medium-size bowl.

5. Add the coconut, ½ cup water, and the chiles to the seeds in the blender jar. Puree, scraping the inside of

the jar as needed, to make a slightly gritty, freckly paste. Add the paste to the buttermilk mixture. Pour ¼ cup water into the blender jar and swish it around to wash it out. Pour this into the coconut-buttermilk mixture and whisk to blend.

6. When the okra has browned, pour in the coconut-buttermilk mixture, and add the curry leaves. Stir once or twice and cook, uncovered, stirring occasionally, until the curry thickens slightly, 3 to 5 minutes. Then serve.

Note: To reconstitute coconut, cover with ¼ cup boiling water, set aside for about 15 minutes, and then drain.

Okra
WITH A
CASHEW-VINEGAR SAUCE

Goan Bhindi

Some Indians feel that assigning ethnicity to a particular dish is too restrictive, but I feel that this curry captures the essence of Goan Portuguese cooking, balancing tart-sweet malt vinegar and plump cashew nuts. In India this would be prepared with Goa's other claim to fame, fermented palm toddy vinegar, but it's hard to come by even in other areas of India. I have substituted malt vinegar and find it a perfectly acceptable alternative. **SERVES 8**

*1 pound fresh okra, rinsed and thoroughly
dried*

4 tablespoons canola oil

¼ cup raw cashew nuts

I small red onion, coarsely chopped

4 medium-size cloves garlic

2 lengthwise slices fresh ginger (each 2 inches long,
   I inch wide, and ⅛ inch thick)

2 dried red Thai or cayenne chiles, stems removed

¼ teaspoon ground turmeric

¼ cup malt vinegar

I teaspoon coarse kosher or sea salt

I large tomato, cored and finely chopped

2 tablespoons finely chopped fresh cilantro
   leaves and tender stems

1. Trim the caps off the okra without cutting into the pods, and slice the pods into ½-inch-thick rounds.

2. Heat 2 tablespoons of the oil in a large skillet over medium heat. Add the okra and stir-fry until the pods blister in spots and acquire a light brown coloration on their ridged skin, 12 to 15 minutes.

3. While the okra is browning, combine the cashews, onion, garlic, ginger, and chiles in a food processor, and pulse until minced.

4. Transfer the browned okra to a plate.

5. Heat the remaining 2 tablespoons oil in the same skillet over medium heat. Add the spicy-hot onion blend and stir-fry (with adequate ventilation) until it is light brown, 5 to 8 minutes. Stir in the turmeric.

6. Pour in ½ cup water, the vinegar, and the salt, and stir once or twice. Add the okra, cover the skillet, reduce the heat to medium-low, and braise until it is fork-tender, 8 to 10 minutes.

7. Stir in the tomato and cilantro, and simmer, uncovered, stirring occasionally, until the tomato is warmed but still firm-looking, 2 to 3 minutes. Then serve.

Raw cashew nuts? See box, page 228.

Cashew and Coriander Stuffed Okra

Bharlele Masala Bhindi

Recently I served this curry with Green Peas and Kidney Beans with Yogurt and Cream (page 361), some plain yogurt (yes, I made my own), and white rice. Nat King Cole crooned in the background while we ate . . . "Unforgettable." **SERVES 6**

I pound fresh okra, rinsed and thoroughly dried

½ cup raw (unroasted) cashew nuts, ground
   (see Tips)

2 teaspoons ground Deggi chiles (see box,
   page 290); or I teaspoon cayenne
   (ground red pepper) mixed with I teaspoon
   sweet paprika

2 teaspoons coriander seeds, ground

1½ teaspoons coarse kosher or sea salt

I teaspoon cumin seeds, ground

¼ cup canola oil

I teaspoon black or yellow mustard seeds

I small red onion, cut in half lengthwise
   and thinly sliced

12 to 15 medium-size to large fresh curry leaves

I large tomato, cored and cut into I-inch cubes (see Tips)

1. Trim the caps off the okra without cutting into the pods. Then form a small cavity in each okra by cutting a slit down three quarters of the length, making the slit about ¼ inch deep. Be careful not to cut all the way through the pod. This cavity will hold the stuffing.

2. Combine the cashews, ground chiles, coriander, salt, and cumin in a small bowl, and mix well.

3. Using your fingers, stuff each okra pod with approximately ½ teaspoon of this spice blend. (You can safely stuff the okra a day ahead. Cover with plastic wrap and refrigerate.) There shouldn't be any blend left over, but if there is, either sprinkle it over the stuffed okra or save it, stored in a jar or a self-seal plastic bag, on a cool pantry shelf for future use; it will keep for up to 2 months.

4. Heat the oil in a large skillet over medium-high heat. Add the mustard seeds, cover the skillet, and cook until the seeds have stopped popping (not unlike popcorn), about 30 seconds. Stir in the onion, and add the okra along with the curry leaves. Lower the heat to medium and roast the mixture, uncovered, occasionally stirring gently, until the onion softens and the now olive-green okra is partially tender, 15 to 20 minutes.

5. Stir in the tomato, cover the skillet, and simmer, stirring occasionally, until the okra is tender, 10 to 15 minutes. Then serve.

Tips:

❖ To grind the cashews powder-fine, use a spice grinder or a blender. If some kernels refuse to pulverize, empty some of the ground nuts into a bowl, freeing up space for the blades to do their thing.

❖ When you rely on the juiciness of a tomato to provide essential moisture to a curry, it had better be perfectly ripe, bursting with sweet succulence—none of those waxy, pale pink specimens that remain firm even after squatting on the kitchen counter for days. If you can't find that just-right fresh tomato, use 1 can (14.5 ounces) diced tomatoes, juice and all, instead.

Pan-Fried Okra
WITH
SHREDDED COCONUT AND CHILES

Thenga Vendakkai

Savor this delicious curry alongside Nimmy Paul's Fish Fillets Poached in a Tomato-Vinegar Sauce (page 254). If okra does not suit your fancy, use green beans, diced potatoes, any summer squash, or even fresh spinach leaves. Each of these vegetables turns fork-tender at a different time, with spinach being the quickest to get there. **SERVES 6**

I pound fresh okra, rinsed and thoroughly dried

I cup shredded fresh coconut; or ½ cup shredded dried unsweetened coconut, reconstituted (see Note)

I tablespoon coarsely chopped fresh cilantro leaves and tender stems

3 or 4 fresh green Thai, cayenne, or serrano chiles, to taste, stems removed

2 tablespoons unrefined sesame oil or canola oil

I teaspoon black or yellow mustard seeds

I tablespoon skinned split black lentils (cream-colored in this form, urad dal), picked over for stones

12 to 15 medium-size to large fresh curry leaves

I teaspoon coarse kosher or sea salt

1. Trim the caps off the okra without cutting into the pods, and cut the pods into ½-inch-thick rounds.

2. Combine the coconut, cilantro, and chiles in a food processor, and pulse to cut the coconut into smaller bits and to mince the cilantro and chiles. (This textural grittiness offers a great backdrop to the softened okra, which is why I don't suggest pureeing it in a blender.)

3. Heat the oil in a large skillet over medium-high heat. Add the mustard seeds, cover the skillet, and cook until the seeds have stopped popping (not unlike popcorn), about 30 seconds. Add the lentils and stir-fry until they turn golden brown, 15 to 20 seconds. Immediately add the okra and the curry leaves. Lower the heat to medium, and stir-fry until the okra pieces blister in spots and acquire a light brown coloration on their ridged skin, 15 to 20 minutes.

4. Stir the coconut mixture into the okra and sprinkle with the salt. Simmer, uncovered, stirring occasionally, to warm the sauce, 2 to 3 minutes. Then serve.

Note: To reconstitute coconut, cover with ½ cup boiling water, set aside for about 15 minutes, and then drain.

Okra Curry
WITH TOASTED CHICKPEA FLOUR

Sindhi Curry

While growing up in a traditional vegetarian Brahmin home in Mumbai (known as Bombay in those days), I was keenly aware of the aromas that wafted in from our neighbor's kitchen, Mrs. Chandwani's foreign garlic and toasted flours mingling with our familiar fresh curry leaves and roasted mustard seeds. I truly never appreciated the marriage of culinary traditions back then. But now, years later, when I return to my birth land, I stop by her house to visit (talking in a loud voice because of her fierce opposition to hearing aids) and to enjoy the fla-

vors and aromas of her kitchen, today the domain of her beautiful daughter-in-law, Varsha. **SERVES 4**

½ cup oily or unoily skinned split yellow pigeon peas (toovar dal), picked over for stones
1 cup fresh okra, rinsed and thoroughly dried
1 medium-size russet or Yukon Gold potato, peeled, cut into 2-inch cubes, and submerged in a bowl of cold water to prevent browning
2 tablespoons canola oil
1 teaspoon cumin seeds
½ cup sliced fresh or frozen lotus root (½-inch pieces; no need to thaw if frozen; see Tip, page 516)
10 to 12 medium-size to large fresh curry leaves
5 to 8 pieces frozen "drumsticks" (each 3 to 4 inches long; no need to thaw; see Tip)
4 to 6 fresh green Thai, cayenne, or serrano chiles, to taste, stems removed, cut lengthwise into thin matchstick-like strips (do not remove the seeds)
1 small Japanese eggplant (about 6 inches long and 1 inch in diameter), stem removed, cut lengthwise in half, and then cut into 2-inch lengths
8 ounces fresh spinach leaves, well rinsed and finely chopped; or 1 package (8 to 10 ounces) frozen chopped spinach, thawed (no need to drain)
1 large tomato, cored and cut into 2-inch pieces
2 teaspoons coarse kosher or sea salt
½ teaspoon ground turmeric
½ teaspoon tamarind paste or concentrate
2 tablespoons Toasted Chickpea Flour (page 41)
¼ cup finely chopped fresh cilantro leaves and tender stems

1. Place the pigeon peas in a small saucepan. Fill the pan halfway with tap water and rinse the peas by rubbing them between your fingertips. The water will become cloudy. Drain. Repeat three or four times, until the water remains relatively clear; drain. Now add 1 cup water and bring it to a boil, uncovered, over medium-high heat. Skim off and discard any foam that rises to the surface. Reduce the heat to medium-low, cover the pan, and simmer, stirring occasionally, until the pigeon peas are tender, about 20 minutes.

2. While the pigeon peas are cooking, prepare and cook the vegetables: Trim the caps off the okra without cutting into the pods. Drain the potato and pat it dry with paper towels.

3. Heat the oil in a large saucepan over medium-high heat. Add the cumin seeds and cook until they start to sizzle, turn reddish brown, and smell nutty, 10 to 15 seconds. Immediately throw in the okra, lotus root, curry leaves, drumsticks, chiles, potato, and eggplant. Stir-fry until some of the vegetables have browned lightly, 8 to 10 minutes. Then lower the heat to medium and continue to cook, uncovered, stirring occasionally, until the vegetables are partially tender and there is a thin brown layer on the bottom of the pan, 10 to 15 minutes.

4. Stir in the spinach, tomato, salt, and turmeric. The spinach and the tomato will release enough liquid to deglaze the pan, releasing the browned bits of vegetable. Stir to incorporate those robust flavors into the mixture. Pour in 1½ cups water, and stir once or twice. Bring the curry to a boil. Then reduce the heat to medium-low, cover the pan, and simmer, stirring occasionally, until the vegetables are fork-tender, 12 to 15 minutes.

5. While the vegetables are simmering, return to the now-cooked pigeon peas. Transfer the peas and their cooking water to a blender, and puree, scraping the inside of the jar as needed, until smooth. (If you have an immersion blender, you can puree the peas and water right in the saucepan.)

6. Pour the thin, creamy-yellow pigeon pea puree into the cooked vegetables. Stir in the tamarind paste and cook until it dissolves and adds its tart flavor, about 2 minutes.

7. Stir in the toasted chickpea flour and cilantro, and serve.

Tip: Within India's borders, "drumsticks" (also called *murangakai, saragova, sahjan,* and *setka ni sing*) have nothing to do with poultry parts. This is a vegetable, so named because it resembles the sticks used to beat on drums. Its fibrous, olive-green exterior, akin to tough overgrown okra (ridges and all), houses a jelly-like pulp that blankets slightly crunchy seeds. The tree's tart-tasting leaves also are edible, especially when stewed with shredded fresh coconut and dried red chiles. To eat drumsticks, pry each piece open and scrape the pulp against your teeth to savor its sweetness, leaving a neat pile of fibrous skin in a corner of your dinner plate.

If fresh or frozen drumsticks are unavailable, use asparagus for its slight resemblance in flavor.

Onion-Stuffed Okra
WITH MANGO POWDER

Bharee Amchur Bhindi

Sounds laborious, but it's not really. The payoff is well worth any extra effort. Just make sure you thoroughly wash your hands with soap and warm water when done, because the chiles in the blend can cause great discomfort if you touch your face—and especially the area around your eyes—without washing off the capsaicin.

Serve this as a side dish alongside the spicy-sweet, coconut-flavored *Jhinga mutter* (page 273) and some roti (page 727). **SERVES 6**

1 pound fresh okra, rinsed and thoroughly
 dried (see box, page 530)

1 small red onion, coarsely chopped

5 lengthwise slices fresh ginger (each 2 inches
 long, 1 inch wide, and 1/8 inch thick)

4 large cloves garlic

4 to 6 fresh green Thai, cayenne, or serrano
 chiles, to taste, stems removed

2 tablespoons mango powder or fresh lime juice

2 teaspoons cumin seeds, ground

2 teaspoons coriander seeds, ground

1 1/2 teaspoons coarse kosher or sea salt

1/2 teaspoon cardamom seeds from green
 or white pods, ground

1/2 teaspoon whole cloves, ground

1/4 cup canola oil

1 large tomato, cored and finely chopped

2 tablespoons finely chopped fresh cilantro
 leaves and tender stems for garnishing

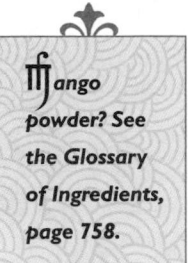

Mango powder? See the Glossary of Ingredients, page 758.

1. Trim the caps off the okra without cutting into the pods. Then form a small cavity in each okra by cutting a slit down three quarters of the length, making the slit about 1/4 inch deep. Be careful not to cut all the way through the pod. This cavity will hold the stuffing.

2. Combine the onion, ginger, garlic, and chiles in a food processor and pulse to mince the mixture, creating a pungent, slightly wet blend. Transfer this to a small bowl, and stir in the mango powder, cumin, coriander, salt, cardamom, and cloves.

3. Using your fingers, stuff each okra pod with approximately 1/2 teaspoon of this onion-spice blend. (You can safely stuff the okra a day ahead. Cover with plastic wrap and refrigerate.)

4. Heat the oil in a large skillet over medium heat. Arrange the stuffed okra in a single layer and reduce the heat to medium-low. Roast, uncovered, turning the okra occasionally, until they are halfway cooked, 15 to 20 minutes.

5. Pour in 1/2 cup water and scrape the bottom of the skillet to deglaze it, releasing any browned bits of spice. Add the tomato, cover the skillet, and cook, stirring occasionally, until the okra is fork-tender, 15 to 18 minutes.

6. Sprinkle with the cilantro, and serve.

Sweet-Hot Okra
IN A MUSTARD-POPPY SAUCE

Sorshe Bata diyea Bhindi

Slightly curdled-looking, this sauce may be unappealing in appearance, but remember the oft-heard adage "Don't judge a book by its cover"—especially a "book" that offers sweet-hot flavors without the okra getting slimy. Wrap pieces of thin whole-wheat rotis (page 727) around the tasty slices. **SERVES 6**

2 tablespoons black or yellow mustard seeds

1 tablespoon white poppy seeds

1 pound fresh okra, rinsed and thoroughly dried

2 dried red Thai or cayenne chiles, stems removed

2 tablespoons mustard oil or canola oil

1/4 teaspoon ground turmeric

1 1/2 teaspoons coarse kosher or sea salt

1 teaspoon white granulated sugar

1. Sprinkle the mustard and poppy seeds into a small bowl and cover them with hot tap water. Set the bowl aside until the seeds soften, about 30 minutes.

2. While the seeds are soaking, trim the caps off the okra, being careful not to cut into the pods. If the pods are long, cut them into 2-inch-long pieces.

3. Drain the soaked seeds and transfer them to a mortar. Add the chiles and pound the mixture to form a gritty, cream-colored paste with reddish-brown speckles.

4. Heat the oil in a large skillet over medium-high heat. Add the okra and stir-fry until the slices are slightly browned and blistered in patches, 8 to 10 minutes.

5. Add the pounded mustard paste and stir-fry to cook the spices, about 1 minute. Stir in the turmeric and continue to stir-fry for 5 seconds.

6. Add 1 cup water, the salt, and the sugar. Once the curry comes to a boil, reduce the heat to medium-low, cover the skillet, and simmer, stirring occasionally, until the okra is fork-tender, 5 to 8 minutes.

7. Remove the lid and raise the heat to medium-high. Cook until the sauce has thickened slightly, about 5 minutes. Then serve.

selecting okra

❖ ❖ ❖

fresh okra is generally available year-around in supermarkets in this country. Your favorite Indian store will definitely stock okra at all times. Choose medium-size okra pods—no more than 2 inches long—and test them for freshness: when you bend the tip (opposite the cap end), it should snap off with a slight crunch, similar to the sound of a matchstick being snapped in half. Large okra pods are usually woody and fibrous, and can make for an unpleasant experience when eaten.

Tart Okra
WITH MUSTARD SEEDS & TAMARIND

Vendakkai Bhajee

During my childhood years, okra was a staple in my mother's kitchen, served at least once a week. This curry was by far my favorite: The spices in the *Sambhar masala*, which are assertive yet mellow, and the tart tamarind create a harmonious balance that only abets my obsession with okra. **SERVES 6**

I pound fresh okra, rinsed and thoroughly dried
2 tablespoons canola oil
I teaspoon black or yellow mustard seeds
I tablespoon skinned split black lentils
   (cream-colored in this form, urad dal),
   picked over for stones
15 to 20 medium-size to large fresh curry leaves
I teaspoon tamarind paste or concentrate
I½ teaspoons coarse kosher or sea salt
I teaspoon Sambhar masala (page 33)
¼ teaspoon ground turmeric

1. Trim the caps off the okra without cutting into the pods, and cut the pods into ½-inch-thick rounds.

2. Heat the oil in a large skillet over medium-high heat. Add the mustard seeds, cover the skillet, and cook until the seeds have stopped popping (not unlike popcorn), about 30 seconds. Add the lentils and stir-fry until they turn golden brown, 15 to 20 seconds. Immediately add the okra and the curry leaves. Lower the heat to medium and stir-fry until the okra slices blister in spots and acquire a light brown coloration on their ridged skin, 15 to 20 minutes.

3. Whisk the tamarind paste into ½ cup water, and pour this tart tamarind water over the okra. Add the salt, *Sambhar masala,* and turmeric. Reduce the heat to medium-low, cover the skillet, and cook, stirring occasionally, until the okra is fork-tender, about 15 minutes. Then serve.

Pan-Fried Okra
WITH AN ONION-TAMARIND SAUCE

bhindi pyaaz

Maybe when Roy Blount Jr., in his "Song to Okra," crooned, "You can have strip pokra, give me a nice girl and a dish of okra. . ." he meant this tart, onion-based okra curry. This vegetable, a member of the hibiscus family, is known as "lady's finger" in India. If I were a lady (no smart-aleck comments please), I don't think I would want my slender fingers compared to a fibrous, ridged-skin vegetable. This prehistoric plant, found growing wild in Sudan and Ethiopia, made its way into India's kitchens via traders and invaders and holds a special place in the subcontinent's culinary repertoire. **SERVES 4**

¼ *cup canola oil*
1 pound fresh okra, rinsed, thoroughly dried,
 caps pared off without cutting into the pods
1 teaspoon cumin seeds
1 medium-size red onion, cut in half lengthwise
 and thinly sliced

1 tablespoon coriander seeds, ground
1½ teaspoons coarse kosher or sea salt
½ teaspoon cayenne (ground red pepper)
¼ teaspoon ground turmeric
½ teaspoon tamarind paste or concentrate
2 tablespoons finely chopped fresh cilantro
 leaves and tender stems for garnishing

1. Heat the oil in a large skillet over medium-high heat. Add half the okra pods and pan-fry, stirring them around frequently, until they blister and acquire reddish-brown patches on their woody skin, about 5 minutes. (The spattering from the oil will make for a messy stovetop, but soap and water will take care of that.) Transfer the okra to a plate. Add the remaining okra pods to the skillet and stir-fry until they blister and acquire reddish-brown patches on their woody skin, about 5 minutes. Add them to the first batch.

2. Sprinkle the cumin seeds into the hot oil; they will instantly sizzle and turn reddish brown. Add the onion and stir-fry until it is light brown around the edges, 3 to 5 minutes.

3. Dust the browned onion with the coriander, salt, cayenne, and turmeric. Allow the spices to cook without burning, stirring occasionally, 1 to 2 minutes.

4. Quickly whisk the tamarind paste into ½ cup water in a small bowl, dissolving the paste. Return the okra to the skillet and pour the tart tamarind water over it. Stir once or twice.

5. Lower the heat to medium and simmer, uncovered, stirring occasionally, until most of the liquid has been absorbed into the okra and the pods appear drenched, about 5 minutes. The okra should be fork-tender by now.

6. Sprinkle with the cilantro, and serve.

Seared Okra
WITH POTATOES AND TOMATO

Aloo Bhindi ki Subzi

Either you love okra or you hate it—for exactly the same reason. Its slimy quality elicits strong opinions on either side of this slippery dispute. I, for one, like okra in any size, shape, or form. I do think Indians have cornered the market on cooking okra without letting its slime factor ooze into the mix. This tomato-based curry combines pan-fried potatoes and okra in a dish that wins over everyone on the debate teams. (The secrets to eliminating okra's objectionable nature are to wash and to dry the pods completely before cutting them, and to fry them before you simmer them in a sauce.)

SERVES 8

1 pound fresh okra, rinsed and thoroughly dried

4 tablespoons canola oil

1 pound russet or Yukon Gold potatoes, peeled, quartered, thinly sliced crosswise, and submerged in a bowl of cold water to prevent browning

2 teaspoons coarse kosher or sea salt

½ teaspoon cayenne (ground red pepper)

¼ teaspoon ground asafetida

¼ teaspoon ground turmeric

1 large tomato, cored and cut into 1-inch pieces

1. Trim the caps off the okra without cutting into the pods.

2. Heat 2 tablespoons of the oil in a large nonstick skillet over medium-high heat. Add the okra pods and fry, turning them occasionally with a pair of tongs, until they are soft and evenly browned all over, about 10 minutes. Transfer them to a plate.

3. Drain the potatoes and pat them dry with paper towels.

4. Heat the remaining 2 tablespoons oil in the same skillet. Add the potatoes and fry, tossing them occasionally, until they are crisp and brown, 5 to 10 minutes. Return the okra to the skillet, and add the salt, cayenne, asafetida, and turmeric. Continue to stir-fry the combination until the spices start to roast, about 1 minute.

5. Add the tomato and ½ cup water. Stir once or twice, and bring to a boil. Then reduce the heat to medium-low, cover the skillet, and simmer, stirring occasionally, until the potatoes are fork-tender, 8 to 10 minutes. Serve immediately.

Braised Okra
AND TOMATOES

Masala Bhindi Tamatar

One day I selected all my students who weren't familiar with okra and had them execute this recipe. Hesitant bites gave in to "I can't eat fast enough"—proving yet again that the right recipe can change the ways of the most doubtful doubting Thomas.

SERVES 4

1 pound fresh okra, rinsed and thoroughly dried

2 tablespoons canola oil

1 teaspoon cumin seeds

2 dried red Thai or cayenne chiles, stems removed

1 tablespoon coriander seeds, ground

1½ teaspoons coarse kosher or sea salt

½ teaspoon cayenne (ground red pepper)

¼ teaspoon ground turmeric

1 large tomato, cored and cut into 1-inch pieces

2 tablespoons finely chopped fresh cilantro leaves and tender stems for garnishing

1. Trim the caps off the okra, being careful not to cut into the pods. Cut the pods into 1-inch lengths.

2. Heat the oil in a large skillet over medium heat. Add the cumin seeds and cook until they sizzle and turn reddish brown, 5 to 10 seconds. Then stir in the chiles and cook until they blacken slightly and smell pungent, about 5 seconds.

3. Immediately add the okra and stir-fry until the pieces blister in spots and acquire a light brown coloration on their ridged skin, 10 to 12 minutes.

4. Stir in the coriander, salt, cayenne, and turmeric, and continue to stir-fry to cook the spices, about 1 minute.

5. Add the tomato and ½ cup water, stirring once or twice. Once the sauce starts to boil, reduce the heat to medium-low, cover the skillet, and cook, stirring occasionally, until the okra is fork-tender, 12 to 15 minutes.

6. Sprinkle with the cilantro, and serve.

Sliced Onions
IN A FENUGREEK-TAMARIND BROTH

Vengayam Mendium Kozhumbu

Comfort food to millions of Tamilians around the globe, this southern Indian classic reminds me curiously of the European favorite, beef broth–laden (oh Hindu horrors!) French onion soup. The broth is assertive, the onion is slow-cooked to yield sugary sweetness, and the spices provide complex heat—all coming together to yield that meatlike taste (*umami*) so endearing to the southies (and maybe to the French too). I usually ladle this over a bowl of white rice, and for added richness, I swirl in a teaspoon of ghee. **SERVES 6**

2 tablespoons canola oil

1 teaspoon black or yellow mustard seeds

1 teaspoon fenugreek seeds

¼ teaspoon ground asafetida

1 large red onion, cut in half lengthwise and thinly sliced

1 tablespoon Sambhar masala (page 33)

12 to 15 medium-size to large fresh curry leaves

1½ teaspoons tamarind paste or concentrate

1½ teaspoons coarse kosher or sea salt

1. Heat the oil in a medium-size saucepan over medium-high heat. Add the mustard seeds, cover the pan, and cook until the seeds have stopped popping (not unlike popcorn), about 30 seconds. Sprinkle in the fenugreek seeds and asafetida, which will instantly sizzle and turn reddish brown. Add the onion and stir-fry to allow the spices to coat the slices, about 1 minute. Then reduce the heat to

medium-low, cover the pan, and cook, stirring occasionally, until the onion's liquid dissipates and the slices start to turn caramel-brown, 25 to 30 minutes.

2. Stir in the *Sambhar masala* and curry leaves, and roast the spices without worrying about burning them, thanks to the cushion provided by the onion, for about 1 minute.

3. Quickly whisk the tamarind paste into 4 cups water. Pour this over the onion mixture, sprinkle in the salt, and stir to deglaze the pan. Raise the heat to medium-high and boil the broth vigorously, stirring occasionally, until the liquid is reduced by about 1 cup, about 15 minutes. (The broth will remain thin, but the flavors will be assertive.) Then serve.

Pearl Onions
WITH SPINACH AND TOMATOES

Thinnay Vengayam Kari

Pearl onions are readily found in every grocery store. For a colorful curry, use a combination of yellow, red, and white pearl onions. Biting into these succulent onions enriched with spices and spinach makes the peeling worthwhile. **SERVES 6**

2 tablespoons canola oil
1 pound pearl onions, peeled
1 can (14.5 ounces) diced tomatoes
1 teaspoon coarse kosher or sea salt
¼ teaspoon ground turmeric
8 ounces fresh spinach leaves, well rinsed
*   and coarsely chopped*

1 teaspoon Sambhar masala (page 33)
½ teaspoon Punjabi garam masala (page 25)

1. Heat the oil in a medium-size saucepan over medium-high heat. Add the pearl onions and stir-fry until they are light brown, 3 to 5 minutes.

2. Add the tomatoes, salt, and turmeric. Reduce the heat to medium and simmer, uncovered, stirring occasionally, until the tomatoes are stewed and the spices are cooked, 5 to 7 minutes.

3. Add the spinach, cover the pan, and cook until the spinach has wilted, 2 to 3 minutes. Stir and continue to braise, covered, stirring occasionally, until the onions are fork-tender, about 5 minutes.

4. Sprinkle in the two spice blends, stir the curry once or twice, and serve.

Tip: In a pinch, use frozen pearl onions. Thaw them and pat them dry with paper towels. Then stir-fry as described in Step 1.

Green Peas
WITH A
SPINACH-FENUGREEK SAUCE

Mutter, Methi,
Aur Palak ki Subzi

When you look at the ingredients in this curry, all you see is green. Your neighbors will be green too—with envy—should you bring this along as your contribution to a neighborhood potluck. In addition, this will keep more greens of the paper variety in your wallet, proving that an inexpensive curry does not have to be frugal on flavor. **SERVES 6**

2 tablespoons canola oil

I teaspoon cumin seeds

I small red onion, finely chopped

6 medium-size cloves garlic, finely chopped

4 lengthwise slices fresh ginger (each 1½ inches long, 1 inch wide, and ⅛ inch thick), finely chopped

I pound fresh spinach leaves, well rinsed and finely chopped (see Tips)

I cup finely chopped fresh or frozen fenugreek leaves (thawed if frozen)

4 to 6 fresh green Thai, cayenne, or serrano chiles, to taste, stems removed, finely chopped (do not remove the seeds)

2 cups frozen green peas (no need to thaw)

I cup finely chopped fresh cilantro leaves and tender stems

2 teaspoons coarse kosher or sea salt

½ cup heavy (whipping) cream (see Tips)

1. Heat the oil in a large saucepan over medium-high heat. Add the cumin seeds and cook until they sizzle, turn reddish brown, and smell fragrant, 5 to 10 seconds. Immediately toss in the onion, garlic, and ginger, and stir-fry until they are light brown, 2 to 3 minutes.

2. Pile in the spinach, fenugreek, and chiles, and cover the pan. Cook, stirring once or twice to thoroughly mix the greens, until the steam has wilted the spinach, about 5 minutes.

3. Pour in 2 cups water and bring it to a boil. Lower the heat to medium and gently boil the thin, grassy-smelling curry, uncovered, stirring occasionally, until the greens are cooked and the sauce has thickened slightly, 12 to 15 minutes.

4. Stir in the peas, cilantro, and salt, and cover the pan. Simmer, stirring occasionally, until the peas are warmed through, 5 to 8 minutes.

5. Mix in the cream and simmer, uncovered, until it is warmed through, about 5 minutes. Then serve.

Tips:

❖ Frozen chopped spinach is a totally acceptable alternative. Thaw it before using it, but don't worry about squeezing any water out of it. The extra water will not affect the curry's texture.

❖ If heavy cream is a sensitive issue for your health, leave it out. To create a creamy texture, puree some of the greens before you add the peas: guilt-free pleasure.

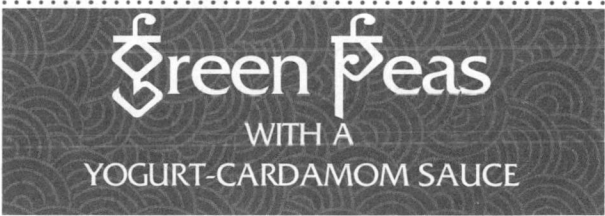

green peas
WITH A
YOGURT-CARDAMOM SAUCE

khoya elaichi mutter

Sometimes a simple technique can make a world of a difference; the reduced milk solids (if you can boil milk, you can reduce milk solids) provide an unparallel depth in this curry that not even heavy cream can. The menthol-like cardamom perfumes its way into each creamy, spicy mouthful. **SERVES 6**

½ cup plain yogurt

¼ cup Whole Milk Solids (page 24)

½ teaspoon cardamom seeds from green
or white pods

2 tablespoon Ghee (page 21) or canola oil

1 teaspoon cumin seeds

2 teaspoons ground Deggi chiles (see box, page 290);
or 1 teaspoon cayenne (ground red pepper)
mixed with 1 teaspoon sweet paprika

1 teaspoon coarse kosher or sea salt

1 pound frozen green peas (no need to thaw)

½ teaspoon Punjabi garam masala (page 25)

2 tablespoons finely chopped fresh cilantro
leaves and tender stems for garnishing

1. Combine the yogurt, milk solids, and cardamom in a blender jar. Puree, scraping the inside of the jar as needed, to form a smooth blend speckled with cracked cardamom.

2. Heat the ghee in a medium-size saucepan over medium-high heat. Add the cumin seeds and cook until they sizzle and are aromatic, 5 to 10 seconds. Pour in the yogurt puree, and sprinkle in the ground chiles and salt. Simmer over medium heat, uncovered, stirring occasionally, until some of the ghee starts to separate from the orange sauce, 3 to 5 minutes.

3. Pour in 1 cup water, and add the peas. Raise the heat to medium-high and bring to a boil. Continue to boil vigorously, uncovered, stirring occasionally, until the sauce thickens, 12 to 15 minutes.

4. Stir in the garam masala, sprinkle with the cilantro, and serve.

Tip: Do not be alarmed by the amount of ground chiles. The sweet peas and the yogurt mixture tone the curry down just right, so it leaves a pleasant burn that lingers on your palate.

Anaheim Peppers
STUFFED WITH PEANUTS AND SESAME SEEDS

Mungphalli Til Chi Mirchi

Spending a few extra minutes in the kitchen will prove truly worthwhile when you taste this curry, which incorporates spices, ingredients, and techniques common to many Marathi-speaking homes. The slightly pungent Anaheims, along with the potent fresh green chiles, prove a great balance to the nutty peanuts and naturally sweet coconut. Serve this as a side dish with beef vindaloo (page 174) and basmati rice. **SERVES 4**

8 large Anaheim peppers (each 6 to 8 inches long;
do not remove the stems)

3 tablespoons canola oil

½ cup raw peanuts (without skin)

2 tablespoons white sesame seeds

1 large red onion, coarsely chopped

2 to 4 fresh green Thai, cayenne, or serrano chiles,
to taste, stems removed

1½ teaspoons coarse kosher or sea salt

4 tablespoons finely chopped fresh cilantro
leaves and tender stems

1 cup shredded fresh coconut; or ½ cup shredded dried
unsweetened coconut, reconstituted (see Note)

½ teaspoon Maharashtrian garam masala (page 28)

¼ teaspoon ground turmeric

1. Working with a sharp paring knife, slit each pepper, starting from the stem end, down three-fourths of its

length, taking extra care not to cut through the other side of the pepper. Slide your fingers into the cavity and remove most of the seeds, vein, and ribs. (Make sure to wash your hands thoroughly with soap and warm water afterwards, since the capsaicin is quite potent even in this mild variety of pepper. Use gloves if you have sensitive skin.)

2. Heat 1 tablespoon of the oil in a small skillet over medium heat. Scatter the peanuts into the hot oil and roast, stirring, until they are nutty-brown, 2 to 3 minutes. Scoop them out with a slotted spoon and place them on a plate to cool, leaving as much of the browned oil in the skillet as possible.

3. While the peanuts are cooling, return the skillet to medium heat. Sprinkle the sesame seeds into the oil and stir-fry until they start to crackle and turn honey brown, 1 to 2 minutes. Transfer them to a small bowl.

4. Once the peanuts are cool, transfer them to a food processor and pulse to process them to the consistency of coarse breadcrumbs. Add the peanuts to the bowl containing the sesame seeds.

5. Without washing out the food processor, place the onion and chiles in it and pulse to mince them (continuous processing would create excess moisture). Add this eyes-tearing blend to the sesame-peanut mixture, and stir in 1 teaspoon of the salt and 2 tablespoons of the cilantro. Stir well. This is the filling for the peppers.

6. Stuff each pepper with the filling, dividing it equally among them.

7. Pour 1 cup water into a blender jar, and add the coconut, garam masala, turmeric, and remaining ½ teaspoon salt. Puree, scraping the inside of the jar as needed, to form an almost smooth, albeit slightly gritty, sauce.

8. Heat the remaining 2 tablespoons oil in a large skillet over medium-high heat. Add the peppers, arranging them in a single layer. Cook, turning them every 2 minutes, until they are evenly seared and blistered, 6 to 10 minutes. (Don't worry if a little stuffing oozes out and browns. It'll simply add flavor to the sauce.)

9. Pour the coconut sauce over the peppers, making sure it coats the bottom of the skillet so it can deglaze it, releasing the browned bits of peppers and stuffing. Reduce the heat to medium-low, cover the skillet, and simmer, basting the peppers every 1 to 2 minutes with the sauce, until they are fork-tender, 20 to 25 minutes.

10. Carefully transfer the tender peppers to a serving platter, and cover them with aluminum foil to keep them warm.

11. Pour 1 cup water into the skillet and bring it to a boil over medium-high heat. Cook, uncovered, stirring occasionally, until the sauce thickens, 5 to 8 minutes. Stir in the remaining 2 tablespoons cilantro.

12. Pour the sauce over the peppers, and serve.

Note: To reconstitute coconut, cover with ½ cup boiling water, set aside for about 15 minutes, and then drain.

Tips:

❖ Roasting the peanuts intensifies their flavor, but don't be deterred if you don't have any raw peanuts on hand. Simply use unsalted roasted peanuts and skip Step 2, eliminating the oil from the recipe.

❖ Feel free to use any garam masala from your pantry, should you not have the Maharashtrian one called for in this recipe.

Spicy Banana Peppers
WITH A COCONUT–SESAME SEED SAUCE

Mirch ka Salan

thick-sauced curries called salans are from the south-central city of Hyderabad, a culinary hotspot that hugs two regional cooking styles—the north and the south. One school of thought feels that *salans* captured the British attention and fascination for spicy food, and hence catapulted the concept of curries to the Western world. A pretty hefty responsibility, but this sauce can shoulder the burden with its robust body, bold flavors, and tart aftermath. It's easy to see why it may have bowled over an entire nation. **SERVES 8**

1 tablespoon white sesame seeds

1 teaspoon cumin seeds

1 cup shredded fresh coconut; or ½ cup shredded dried unsweetened coconut, reconstituted (see Note)

¼ cup unsalted dry-roasted peanuts

1 teaspoon tamarind paste or concentrate

2 tablespoons canola oil

1 pound banana peppers, cut in half lengthwise, stems and seeds removed (see Tips)

1½ teaspoons coarse kosher or sea salt

2 tablespoons finely chopped fresh cilantro leaves and tender stems

1. Preheat a large skillet over medium-high heat. Sprinkle in the sesame and cumin seeds, and cook, shaking the pan frequently, until the seeds crackle, smell nutty, and are reddish brown, 1 to 2 minutes. Quickly transfer them to a blender jar, and pour in ½ cup water followed by the coconut, peanuts, and tamarind paste. Puree, scraping the inside of the jar as needed, to form a thick, gritty sauce.

2. Heat the oil in the same skillet over medium-high heat. Add the banana peppers and stir-fry (with adequate ventilation) until some of them acquire blisters on their skin, about 5 minutes.

3. Add the sauce to the skillet. Pour 1 cup water into the blender jar, and swish it around to wash it out. Add this to the skillet, sprinkle in the salt, and stir once or twice. Reduce the heat to medium-low, cover the skillet, and simmer, stirring occasionally, until the peppers are fork-tender, 8 to 10 minutes.

4. Remove the lid and raise the heat to medium-high. Allow the sauce to boil vigorously, stirring it occasionally, until it thickens, 5 to 8 minutes.

5. Stir in the cilantro, and serve.

Note: To reconstitute coconut, cover with ½ cup boiling water, set aside for about 15 minutes, and then drain.

Tips:

❖ Banana peppers have some heat, which will rub off onto your hands. Make sure to wash your hands (cutting board and knife too) with soap and warm water before rubbing your eyes, touching your mouth, or any other sensitive skin.

❖ Bell peppers, more readily available than banana peppers, are an acceptable substitute, but I recommend adding 1 or 2 fresh green Thai, cayenne, or serrano chiles, stems removed, to the coconut sauce while you puree it to provide an oomph similar to banana peppers.

Nutty-Tart Bell Peppers

WITH PEANUTS

ʃirchi ŋu Shaak

In Surat, the birthplace of this curry, they say that two things are most important in a Hindu's life: to eat the foods of Surat and to die in Kashi (now Varanasi), the holy city for Hindus. (There is no cause and effect there, I assure you.) This Surati curry came to me from Bharati Sindhvad, whose ancestral roots are deeply entrenched in this city in northwestern India. Serve this with Yogurt Curry with Cumin and Curry Leaves (page 353) and white rice for an I-have-eaten-the-best-and-now-am-ready-to-die-in-Kashi experience. **SERVES 4**

2 tablespoons canola oil

2 large bell peppers (1 pound total), any color or combination of colors, stemmed, seeded, and cut into 1-inch pieces

6 whole cloves

1 or 2 fresh or dried bay leaves

2 tablespoons chickpea flour

1 teaspoon Toasted Cumin-Coriander Blend (page 33)

1 teaspoon coarse kosher or sea salt

1 teaspoon white granulated sugar

½ teaspoon cayenne (ground red pepper)

2 tablespoons unsalted dry-roasted peanuts, ground to the texture of fine breadcrumbs (see Tip)

2 tablespoons finely chopped fresh cilantro leaves and tender stems

Juice of 1 medium-size lime

1. Heat the oil in a large skillet over medium-high heat. Throw in the bell peppers, cloves, and bay leaves. Roast, uncovered, stirring occasionally, until the peppers soften and acquire brown spots, 15 to 18 minutes.

2. Sprinkle in the chickpea flour and cook, stirring, until it browns lightly, 3 to 5 minutes.

3. Pour in 1 cup water and scrape the bottom of the skillet to deglaze it, releasing any browned bits of pepper and flour. Stir in the cumin-coriander blend, salt, sugar, and cayenne. Reduce the heat to medium-low and simmer, uncovered, stirring occasionally, until the flavors mingle, 5 to 8 minutes.

4. Stir in the peanuts and cilantro. Just before you serve the curry, remove the cloves and bay leaves, and stir in the lime juice.

Tip: To grind that small quantity of peanuts, use a spice grinder or even a mortar and pestle.

Pan-Blistered Bell Peppers

WITH LUFFA SQUASH SAUCE

ʁudai ʃolagha Peerkangai ʁari

My mother used to make a chutney with ridged luffa squash, serving it alongside plain steamed white rice drizzled with clarified butter. Here that same chutney is the base for these pan-blistered bell peppers, adding an element of sweetness to the curry. My favorite accompaniment for this dish is the highly comforting *Tayyar shaadum* (page 710), a mound of rice drenched with yogurt, chiles, and mustard seeds. **SERVES 4**

1 pound ridged luffa squash, peeled and diced (see box, page 613); or 1 pound yellow squash, ends trimmed, and diced

2 tablespoons canola oil

1 tablespoon skinned split black lentils (cream-colored in this form, urad dal), picked over for stones

1 teaspoon coriander seeds

1 teaspoon fenugreek seeds

1 or 2 dried red Thai or cayenne chiles, to taste, stems removed

¼ cup tightly packed fresh cilantro leaves and tender stems

1 teaspoon coarse kosher or sea salt

½ teaspoon tamarind paste or concentrate

1 teaspoon black or yellow mustard seeds

2 large bell peppers (1 pound total), any color or combination of colors, stemmed, seeded, and cut into 1-inch pieces

1. Place the squash in a small saucepan, add 1 cup water, and bring to a boil over medium-high heat. Lower the heat, cover the pan, and simmer until the squash is fork-tender, 3 to 5 minutes.

2. While the squash is cooking, preheat a large skillet over medium-high heat. Pour the oil into the skillet and swirl it around to coat the bottom evenly. Sprinkle the lentils, coriander seeds, fenugreek seeds, and chiles into the skillet and roast, stirring constantly, until the lentils turn toasty brown, the coriander and fenugreek seeds are reddish brown, and the chiles have blackened slightly, about 1 minute. Remove the skillet from the heat and, using a slotted spoon, scoop out the lentils and spices and dump them into the steaming squash.

3. Once it is tender, transfer the squash and the now-spiced cooking water to a blender jar. Add the cilantro, salt, and tamarind paste, and puree, scraping the inside of the jar as needed, to form a smooth, red-speckled olive-green sauce.

4. Reheat the oil in the skillet over medium-high heat. Add the mustard seeds, cover, and cook until the seeds have stopped popping (not unlike popcorn), about 30 seconds. Immediately add the bell peppers and stir-fry until they blister and acquire brown spots, about 5 minutes.

5. Pour the squash sauce over the peppers and stir once or twice. Reduce the heat to medium-low and cook, uncovered, stirring occasionally, until the sauce has thickened and the peppers are fork-tender, 5 to 8 minutes. Then serve.

Roasted Bell Peppers
WITH CHILES

Simla Mirch Fry

This sweet curry—sweet thanks to the slow-roasted peppers—is a great side dish to offset a spicier curry such as Wok-Cooked Beef Cubes with a Chile-Yogurt Sauce (page 90). **SERVES 4**

2 tablespoons canola oil

1 teaspoon black or yellow mustard seeds

2 large red or green bell peppers (1 pound total), stemmed, seeded, and cut into 1-inch pieces

4 fresh green Thai, cayenne, or serrano chiles,
    stems removed, cut in half lengthwise
    (do not remove the seeds)
¼ cup finely chopped fresh cilantro leaves and
    tender stems
1 teaspoon Toasted Cumin-Coriander Blend (page 33)
1 teaspoon coarse kosher or sea salt

1. Heat the oil in a medium-size saucepan over medium-high heat. Add the mustard seeds, cover the pan, and cook until the seeds have stopped popping (not unlike popcorn), about 30 seconds. Reduce the heat to medium-low and add the bell peppers and chiles. Roast, uncovered, stirring occasionally, until the peppers sweat, their juices evaporate, their skin acquires blotchy brown spots, and they soften, 15 to 18 minutes.

2. Add the cilantro, cumin-coriander blend, and salt, and stir once or twice.

3. Pour in ½ cup water and bring the thin curry to a boil. Then serve.

Resort Bells
WITH ONIONS, POTATOES, AND MUSTARD SEEDS

simla mirch ki bhajee

Simla, a resort community in the hills of northern India, was once the getaway spot for British dignitaries escaping the oppressive heat in the plains below. The weather there is pleasantly cool year-round, making it an ideal vacation choice. Simla is also the source of India's bell peppers. **SERVES 6**

1 medium-size white potato, such as russet
    or Yukon Gold, peeled, cut into ½-inch cubes,
    and submerged in a bowl of cold water to
    prevent browning
2 tablespoons canola oil
1 teaspoon black or yellow mustard seeds
1 tablespoon skinned split black lentils
    (cream-colored in this form, urad dal),
    picked over for stones
1 large green or red bell pepper, stemmed,
    seeded, and cut into ½-inch pieces
1 medium-size red onion, cut into ½-inch cubes
2 teaspoons Sambhar masala (page 33)
1 teaspoon coarse kosher or sea salt
¼ teaspoon ground turmeric
1 medium-size tomato, cored and cut into ½-inch cubes
2 tablespoons finely chopped fresh cilantro leaves
    and tender stems
12 to 15 medium-size to large fresh curry leaves

1. Drain the potato and pat it dry with paper towels.

2. Heat the oil in a medium-size saucepan over medium-high heat. Add the mustard seeds, cover the pan, and cook until the seeds have stopped popping (not unlike popcorn), about 30 seconds. Add the lentils and stir-fry until they turn golden-brown, 15 to 20 seconds. Immediately add the bell pepper, potato, onion, *Sambhar masala*, salt, and turmeric. Stir to coat the vegetables with the spices, and cook for 1 to 2 minutes.

3. Pour in 1 cup water, and add the tomato, cilantro, and curry leaves. Reduce the heat to medium-low, cover the pan, and simmer, stirring occasionally, until the vegetables are fork-tender, 15 to 20 minutes. Then serve. (If the sauce is not thick enough, mash some of the potato cubes with the back of a spoon. The starch will give the sauce more body.)

Stuffed Bell Peppers
IN A TOMATO-CREAM SAUCE

bharee Simla Mirchi

India's bell peppers are generally smaller than their gargantuan American counterparts. It's amazing to see such complex flavors emerge from each savory bite of these stuffed peppers, in a recipe that uses fewer than ten ingredients. For a gorgeous presentation, use a variety of different colored peppers. **SERVES 8**

2 pounds russet or Yukon Gold potatoes, peeled,
   cut into large chunks, and submerged in a
   bowl of cold water to prevent browning
½ cup firmly packed fresh cilantro leaves and
   tender stems
8 fresh green Thai, cayenne, or serrano chiles,
   stems removed
8 medium-size cloves garlic
I cup frozen green peas (no need to thaw)
2 teaspoons coarse kosher or sea salt
4 large bell peppers, any color or combination
   of colors, cut in half lengthwise, stems
   and seeds removed
2 cans (15 ounces each) tomato sauce
½ cup dried fenugreek leaves, soaked in a bowl of
   water and skimmed off before use (see box, page 473)

1. Bring a pot (or at least a large saucepan) of water to a boil over medium-high heat. Drain the potatoes, and add them to the boiling water. Bring back to a boil. Then lower the heat to medium, cover the pot, and cook until the potatoes are very tender, 12 to 15 minutes.

2. While the potatoes are cooking, combine the cilantro, chiles, and garlic in a food processor, and pulse until minced.

3. Using a slotted spoon, transfer the potatoes to a medium-size bowl. (Do not discard the cooking water.) Mash the potatoes with a potato masher. Add the minced cilantro-chile mixture to the mashed potatoes, along with the peas and salt. Thoroughly mix the combination (I use my clean hands).

4. Place 4 of the pepper halves in the pot containing the potato cooking water, and bring it to a boil over medium-high heat. Cook, uncovered, until the pepper halves are limp, about 2 minutes. Remove them with tongs and place them on a cookie sheet. Repeat with the remaining 4 pepper halves.

5. Once the pepper halves are cool to the touch, pack them with the spicy, garlicky mashed potatoes.

6. Preheat the oven to 350°F.

7. Combine the tomato sauce and fenugreek leaves in a medium-size bowl. Pour some of the spiked tomato sauce into a baking dish, coating the bottom. Place the stuffed peppers on the bed of sauce, and then cover the peppers with the remaining sauce, making sure you use every last drop. Cover the dish with aluminum foil and bake until the sauce has thickened, about 30 minutes.

8. Serve immediately, or set aside to cool. (See Tip.)

Tip: These peppers don't freeze well—when they are thawed out, they have an unpleasant spongy texture. However, they will keep, covered with plastic wrap, for up to 4 days in the refrigerator.

Spicy-Tart Bell Peppers
AND PEAS

Simla Mirch Kadhi

I believe that you should enjoy yogurt-based *kad his* first with thin rotis (page 727), and then when you feel you are about to reach that bursting point, dump the rest over cooked white rice and savor the combination, until you really cannot eat even one more mouthful. (It's okay. We all need to make a pig of ourselves once in a while.) This curry not only tastes hot (with a slightly sweet aftermath) but also looks delicious, with its salmon-orange sauce, small chunks of bell peppers (multicolored if you want that confetti look), and plump green peas. **SERVES 4**

1 cup plain yogurt
1 tablespoon chickpea flour
1½ teaspoons rock salt
1 teaspoon white granulated sugar
4 fresh green Thai, cayenne, or serrano chiles,
    stems removed, coarsely chopped
    (do not remove the seeds)
2 lengthwise slices fresh ginger
    (each 2 inches long, 1 inch wide,
    and ⅛ inch thick), coarsely chopped
1 cup frozen green peas (no need to thaw)
2 tablespoons finely chopped fresh cilantro
    leaves and tender stems
1 teaspoon ground Deggi chiles (see box, page 290);
    or ½ teaspoon cayenne (ground red pepper)
    mixed with ½ teaspoon sweet paprika

1 teaspoon Toasted Cumin-Coriander Blend
    (page 33)
½ teaspoon ground turmeric
2 tablespoons canola oil
1 teaspoon black or yellow mustard seeds
1 teaspoon cumin seeds
2 medium-size bell peppers (any color), stemmed,
    seeded, and finely chopped
10 to 12 medium-size to large fresh curry leaves
1 tablespoon Ghee (page 21; optional)

1. Combine the yogurt with 1 cup water in a medium-size bowl, and whisk together. Sprinkle the chickpea flour over the mixture, and whisk it in quickly to prevent any lumps from forming.

2. Spoon the rock salt and sugar into a mortar. Add the chiles and ginger, and pound to form a pulpy, gritty, slightly watery paste. Add this to the yogurt mixture. Then stir in the peas, cilantro, ground chiles, cumin-coriander blend, and turmeric.

3. Heat the oil in a medium-size saucepan over medium high heat. Add the mustard seeds, cover the pan, and cook until the seeds have stopped popping (not unlike popcorn), about 30 seconds. Sprinkle in the cumin seeds; they will sizzle and turn reddish brown instantly. Immediately add the bell peppers and curry leaves, and stir-fry until the peppers are blistered and the leaves are crinkly-dry, 8 to 10 minutes.

4. Carefully add the yogurt mixture to the pan, and stir once or twice. Lower the heat to medium and simmer, uncovered, stirring occasionally, until the sauce thickens and the raw taste of the flour disappears, 15 to 20 minutes.

5. Stir in the ghee, if using, and serve.

Chile-Spiked Bell Peppers
AND SPINACH

Mirch Palak ki Subzi

Hot-sweet and addictive this curry is a great dish to serve alongside Rice with Yogurt and Mustard Seeds (page 710)—the mellow yogurt tones down the sauce's spiciness. The chickpea flour helps to thicken the sauce and makes it smooth and satiny. Use red bell peppers for a red-green curry that would be a perfect accompaniment during the Christmas holidays. **SERVES 6**

2 tablespoons canola oil

1 teaspoon cumin seeds

2 large green or red bell peppers (1 pound total), stemmed, seeded, and cut into 1-inch pieces

2 large cloves garlic, finely chopped

1 or 2 fresh green Thai, cayenne, or serrano chiles, to taste, stems removed, finely chopped (do not remove the seeds)

2 tablespoons chickpea flour

¼ teaspoon ground turmeric

1½ teaspoons coarse kosher or sea salt

8 ounces fresh spinach leaves, well rinsed

1. Heat the oil in a large skillet or wok over medium-high heat. Sprinkle in the cumin seeds and cook until they sizzle and turn reddish brown, 5 to 10 seconds. Add the bell peppers, garlic, and chiles, and stir-fry until the peppers blister, the garlic browns (it won't burn because the peppers will cushion it), and the chiles are throat-clearing pungent (so be sure to use adequate ventilation), about 5 minutes.

2. Sprinkle in the chickpea flour and turmeric, and stir to cook and lightly brown the flour, about 1 minute.

3. Pour in 1 cup water. Stir, scraping the bottom of the skillet to deglaze it, releasing any collected bits of browned vegetable. Pour in another 1 cup water to make a thin, yellowish-brown sauce. Stir in the salt and heat to a boil. Reduce the heat to medium-low, cover the skillet, and cook, stirring occasionally, until the peppers are fork-tender, 8 to 10 minutes.

4. Add the spinach, a couple of handfuls at a time, stirring until it is wilted (about 3 minutes per batch). Then raise the heat to medium-high and simmer, uncovered, stirring occasionally, until the sauce has thickened, 8 to 10 minutes. Then serve.

Plantains
WITH
SESAME SEEDS AND PEPPERCORNS

Yellu Molaghu Vazhaipazham

Memorable and special to me, we make this once a year in honor of a loved one's death anniversary. Known as *teva-sam* (memorial) food, the blend of sesame seeds and black peppercorns replaces the more traditional spice blends. Simple combinations create complex layers of flavors to remind us of our own multifaceted relationships with our loved one's departed being. **SERVES 6**

2 large, very firm green plantains
(about 1 pound; see Tip)

¼ teaspoon ground turmeric

2 tablespoons canola oil

2 tablespoons black peppercorns

1 tablespoon white sesame seeds

1 teaspoon black or yellow mustard seeds

1 tablespoon skinned split black lentils (cream-colored
in this form, urad dal), picked over for stones

1½ teaspoons coarse kosher or sea salt

12 medium-size to large fresh curry leaves

1. Slice off the stem and the heel of each plantain, making a ¼-inch-thick slice. Cut each plantain in half crosswise. With a paring knife, make a lengthwise slit, ⅛ to ¼ inch deep, in each half. Wedge your fingers just under the slit and peel off the skin in one easy motion. (You can peel the entire skin with a paring knife, but it is slightly more time-consuming.) Cut the light beige flesh into ½-inch cubes.

2. Bring a medium-size (or larger) saucepan of water to a boil over medium-high heat. Add the plantain cubes and the turmeric, and bring to a boil again. Continue to boil, uncovered, stirring occasionally, until the plantain pieces are fork-tender but still firm-looking, 8 to 10 minutes.

3. While the plantains are cooking, heat the oil in a medium-size skillet over medium-high heat. Sprinkle in the peppercorns and sesame seeds, and roast, stirring constantly, until the sesame seeds turn reddish brown and smell nutty, 1 to 2 minutes. Use a slotted spoon to transfer the spices to a mortar. Crush and grind the blend with the pestle to form a complex-smelling, nutty-pungent mix with the texture of slightly coarse ground black pepper. (Reserve the oil in the skillet.)

4. Reserving 1 cup of the turmeric water, drain the plantains.

5. Reheat the oil in the skillet over medium-high heat. Add the mustard seeds, cover the skillet, and cook until the seeds have stopped popping (not unlike popcorn), about 30 seconds. Add the lentils and stir-fry until they turn golden brown, 15 to 20 seconds. Add the plantains, reserved cooking water, pounded spice blend, salt, and curry leaves. Heat the curry to a boil and cook, uncovered, stirring occasionally, until the sauce thickens, 2 to 3 minutes. Then serve.

Tip: Plantains are found in many supermarkets, right next to the bananas. This fruit, primarily used as a vegetable in south Indian and Jain households, is very starchy and waxy. Because it has an extremely dry mouth-feel, it is a perfect choice to drown in a heavily spiced curry. Choose plantains that are very firm, leaving even slightly soft ones behind, as the softness signals the start of a ripening process that sweetens this tropical delicacy—which is fine for dessert dishes, but not for use as a vegetable.

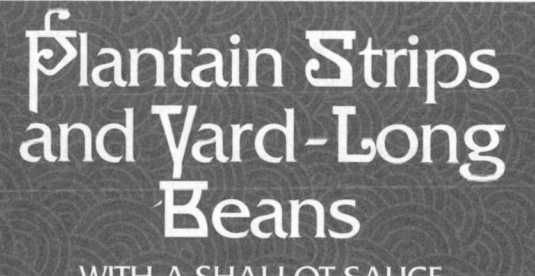

Plantain Strips and Yard-Long Beans
WITH A SHALLOT SAUCE

Vazhaipazham Avarai Kari

Waxy plantains and juicy green beans shine in a potent shallot-chile sauce that's made more interesting with fresh coconut "chips." I recommend serving this over the steamed rice nests called *Idiappam* (page 723) for a downright tasty meal. **SERVES 8**

I large, very firm green plantain (about 8 ounces)

I teaspoon coarse kosher or sea salt

¼ teaspoon ground turmeric

4 cups cut-up yard-long beans (2-inch pieces)

2 medium-size shallots, coarsely chopped

4 medium-size cloves garlic

4 dried red Thai or cayenne chiles, stems removed

1½ teaspoons rock salt

2 tablespoons coconut oil or canola oil

I teaspoon black or yellow mustard seeds

I small red onion, cut in half lengthwise
and thinly sliced

¼ cup finely chopped fresh coconut (see Tip, page 760)

12 to 15 medium-size to large fresh curry leaves

2 lengthwise slices fresh ginger (each 2½ inches
long, 1 inch wide, and ⅛ inch thick), cut into
matchstick-thin strips (julienne)

2 fresh green Thai, cayenne, or serrano chiles,
stems removed, cut in half lengthwise
(do not remove the seeds)

1. Cut a ¼-inch slice off both ends of the plantain. Cut the plantain in half crosswise. Using a paring knife, make a lengthwise slit, ⅛ to ¼ inch deep, in each half. Wedge your fingers just under the slit and peel off the skin in one easy motion. (You can peel the entire skin with a paring knife, but it will be slightly more time-consuming.) Cut the light beige flesh into thin strips about 2 inches long, ¼ inch thick, and ¼ inch wide (see Tip).

2. Fill a medium-size or larger saucepan with water and bring it to a boil over medium-high heat. Sprinkle in the coarse salt and turmeric. Add the beans and bring the water to a boil again. Continue simmering vigorously, uncovered, until the beans are slightly underdone and still firm, 8 to 10 minutes.

3. Add the plantains and stir gently. Continue to boil until both vegetables are fork-tender, 5 to 8 minutes.

yard-long beans
❖ ❖ ❖

dark green yard-long beans (yes, they can grow up to 3 feet in length, but they are usually harvested when they reach half that size) are easy to find in any Asian grocery store and even in some upscale supermarkets. When snapped, this prehistoric member of the legume family (native to China) is not as crispy-crunchy as the garden-variety green beans or wax beans. In fact, they are quite limp. Trim off their woody ends and cut them into smaller pieces before you stir-fry, boil, stew, braise, or steam them. If they're unavailable, use green beans or yellow wax beans for an equally satisfying flavor.

4. While the vegetables are cooking, combine the shallots, garlic, dried chiles, and rock salt in a mortar. Pound, scraping the sides to contain the blend in the center, to create a wet, pulpy mass.

5. Heat the oil in a medium-size skillet over medium-high heat. Add the mustard seeds, cover the skillet, and cook until the seeds have stopped popping (not unlike popcorn), about 30 seconds. Carefully stir in the pounded shallot blend (the liquid in it will splatter when it comes in contact with the hot oil). Stir-fry until the shallots and garlic are browned and the chiles smell pungent-hot, 1 to 2 minutes.

6. Add the onion, coconut, curry leaves, ginger, and fresh chiles, and stir-fry to take the raw edge off the onion, 2 to 3 minutes.

7. When the plantain and beans are done, reserve 1½ cups of the cooking water and then drain them in a colander.

8. Pour the reserved cooking water into the skillet and scrape the bottom to release the browned bits of spice, shallots, and garlic. Add the plantain and beans, and heat the curry to a boil. Continue to simmer, uncovered, stirring occasionally, until the vegetables are warmed through, about 5 minutes. Then serve.

Tip: To cut plantains into thin strips, cut them crosswise in half after peeling them. Slice each half lengthwise into ¼-inch-thick slices. Stack 2 slices and cut them lengthwise into ¼-inch-wide strips. Cut the strips to the desired length. (If you keep them the same thickness as the beans in this recipe, they will be equally tender when cooked. Plantains cook much faster than the tough beans, and so I like to give the beans a head start when boiling the two together.)

Rock salt? See the Glossary of Ingredients, page 758.

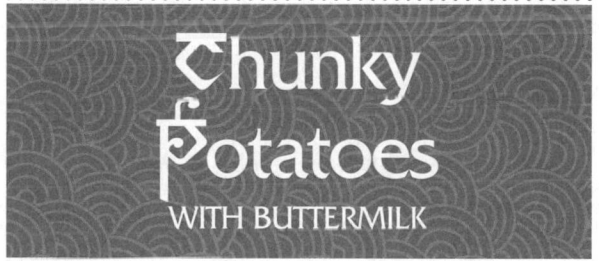

Thunky Potatoes WITH BUTTERMILK

Aloo Thaas

It dawned on me the other day that if I had to follow a carbohydrate-free diet, I would most definitely contemplate end-of-life decisions. I know that sounds extreme, but that's how passionate I am for potatoes. I am forever willing to be the spud's poster child, as long as I receive a steady supply to fry, mash, sauté, stuff, stew, simmer, bake, and braise (of course, money would be nice too). This curry balances the chiles' fiery potency with soothing-cool buttermilk laced with cream, a perfect blanket for my tuberous compulsion. **SERVES 4**

4 dried red Thai or cayenne chiles, stems removed
1 cup boiling water
½ cup firmly packed fresh cilantro leaves and tender stems
1 teaspoon rock salt
8 medium-size cloves garlic, coarsely chopped
1 pound russet or Yukon Gold potatoes, peeled, cut into 2-inch cubes, and submerged in a bowl of cold water to prevent browning
2 tablespoons canola oil
¼ teaspoon ground turmeric
½ cup nonfat buttermilk
2 tablespoons heavy (whipping) cream

1. Place the chiles in a heatproof bowl and pour the boiling water over them. Set the bowl aside until they are reconstituted, about 15 minutes. Then remove the softened chiles, reserving the spicy water. Coarsely chop the chiles, making sure you do not remove the seeds.

2. Pile the cilantro, rock salt, garlic, and chiles in a mortar. Pound the ingredients to a pulpy, red-speckled, pungent mass with the pestle, using a spatula to contain the mixture in the center for a concentrated pounding.

3. Drain the potatoes.

4. Heat the oil in a medium-size skillet over medium-high heat. Add the pounded paste and stir-fry until the flecks of garlic are honey-brown and the chiles are throat-constricting pungent, 1 to 2 minutes. (Make sure to use adequate ventilation.)

5. Add the potatoes and turmeric, and stir-fry to coat the tubers with the yellow spice, about 1 minute.

6. Pour in the reserved chile water and heat to a boil. Then reduce the heat to medium-low, cover the skillet, and cook, stirring occasionally, until the potatoes are fork-tender, 15 to 20 minutes.

7. While the potatoes are cooking, whisk the buttermilk and cream together in a small bowl.

8. When the potatoes are tender, add the buttermilk blend and stir once or twice. Continue to simmer the curry, uncovered, to warm the buttermilk, 2 to 3 minutes. Then serve.

Tip: The cream provides fat, which in turn prevents the buttermilk from curdling when it is heated. The combination mellows the pungent chiles, balancing out the curry. A great example of a chain reaction that helps one and all.

Mrs. Joshi's Potatoes
WITH A FRESH COCONUT–LIME SAUCE

batata bhajee

For a number of years during my childhood, Mrs. Joshi worked as a registered nurse with my physician sister Lali and pricked me with many an injection. She always knew how to make me happy after a needle poke: a bar of Cadbury's chocolate or a small bag of wafer-thin cayenne-coated potato chips. On a recent visit to Mumbai, I stopped by Mrs. Joshi's house for breakfast—which turned out to be small chunks of potatoes bathed in a coconut-lime sauce, with perfectly round, puffy *pooris* alongside. Mrs. Joshi had remembered my potato habit and rewarded me with that combination.

SERVES 8

1½ pounds russet or Yukon Gold potatoes, peeled, cut into ½-inch cubes, and submerged in a bowl of cold water to prevent browning

2 tablespoons peanut or canola oil

2 teaspoons cumin seeds

½ teaspoon ground asafetida

½ teaspoon ground turmeric

12 to 15 medium-size to large fresh curry leaves

4 to 6 fresh green Thai, cayenne, or serrano chiles, to taste, stems removed, cut crosswise into ¼-inch-thick slices (do not remove the seeds)

1½ teaspoons coarse kosher or sea salt

1 teaspoon white granulated sugar

½ cup shredded fresh coconut; or ¼ cup shredded dried unsweetened coconut, reconstituted (see Note)

2 tablespoons finely chopped fresh cilantro leaves and tender stems

Juice of 1 large lime

1. Drain the potatoes and pat them dry.

2. Heat the oil in a medium-size saucepan over medium-high heat. Add the cumin seeds and cook until they sizzle, turn reddish brown, and are aromatic, 5 to 10 seconds. Sprinkle in the asafetida and turmeric. Immediately add the potatoes, curry leaves, and chiles. Stir-fry until the potatoes are coated with the spices, 1 to 2 minutes.

3. Pour in 2 cups water, and stir in the salt and sugar.

Bring to a boil. Then lower the heat to medium, cover the pan, and cook, stirring occasionally, until the potatoes are fork-tender, 18 to 20 minutes.

4. Stir in the coconut and cilantro, and simmer, uncovered, stirring occasionally, until the sauce thickens, 3 to 5 minutes.

5. Just before you serve the curry, stir in the lime juice.

Note: To reconstitute coconut, cover with ¼ cup boiling water, set aside for about 15 minutes, and then drain.

Tip: For an interesting alternative, substitute sweet potatoes. The sugars in that root vegetable offer a sweet backdrop to the fiery chiles and make it unnecessary to use the granulated sugar called for in the recipe.

Potatoes
WITH FRESH COCONUT AND CHILES

Chenga Urulikazhangu

The coconut in this dish provides a sweet balance to the pungent chiles, especially because it is added toward the end. For an even sweeter alternative, use sweet potatoes instead of the white potatoes. Either way, serve the curry with either rotis (page 727) or *pooris* (page 725). **SERVES 8**

2 pounds russet or Yukon Gold potatoes, peeled, cut into 1-inch cubes, and submerged in a bowl of cold water to prevent browning

2 tablespoons canola oil
1 teaspoon black or yellow mustard seeds
1 tablespoon skinned split black lentils (cream-colored in this form, urad dal), picked over for stones
4 dried red Thai or cayenne chiles, stems removed
¼ teaspoon ground asafetida
¼ teaspoon ground turmeric
¼ cup finely chopped fresh cilantro leaves and tender stems
2 teaspoons coarse kosher or sea salt
12 medium-size to large fresh curry leaves
4 fresh green Thai, cayenne, or serrano chiles, stems removed, cut in half lengthwise (do not remove the seeds)
½ cup shredded fresh coconut; or ¼ cup shredded dried unsweetened coconut, reconstituted (see Note)

1. Drain the potatoes and pat them dry.

2. Heat the oil in a large saucepan over medium-high heat. Add the mustard seeds, cover the pan, and cook until the seeds have stopped popping (not unlike popcorn), about 30 seconds. Add the lentils and stir fry until they turn golden brown, 15 to 20 seconds. Immediately add the dried chiles, asafetida, and turmeric. Stir-fry until the chiles smell pungent and are slightly blackened, about 10 seconds.

3. Add the potatoes, 2 cups water, and the cilantro, salt, curry leaves, and fresh chiles. Stir once or twice and bring to a boil. Then reduce the heat to medium-low, cover the pan, and cook, stirring occasionally, until the potatoes are fork-tender, 8 to 10 minutes.

4. Raise the heat to medium-high, uncover the pan, and cook, stirring occasionally, until the sauce thickens slightly, 3 to 5 minutes. Some of the potato pieces will disintegrate, which is okay because this will provide more body to the sauce.

5. Stir in the coconut, and serve.

Note: To reconstitute coconut, cover with ¼ cup boiling water, set aside for about 15 minutes, and then drain.

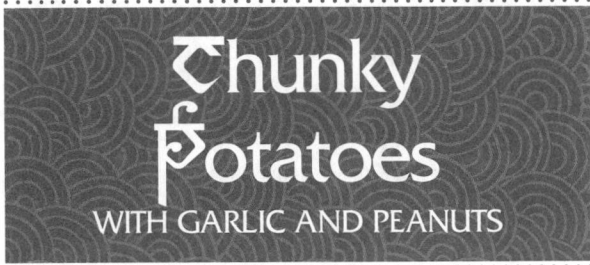

Thunky Potatoes
WITH GARLIC AND PEANUTS

lasoon Sengdane Batate Chi Bhajee

Once in a great while a curry comes along that blows everyone's palate, including my own. This Maharashtrian-influenced potato dish will appeal to all, and I have no qualms betting my first-born on it. Even though it is a great side dish, I often stuff it into slices of pita bread for a substantial lunch, along with a bowl of creamy kidney beans (pages 357–359). **SERVES 8**

- 2 tablespoons white sesame seeds
- 2 tablespoons raw peanuts (without ths skin)
- 4 medium-size cloves garlic
- 3 dried red Thai or cayenne chiles, stems removed
- 2 tablespoons peanut or canola oil
- 1 pound russet or Yukon Gold potatoes, peeled, cut into 1-inch cubes, and submerged in a bowl of cold water to prevent browning
- ½ teaspoon ground turmeric
- 1 can (14.5 ounces) diced tomatoes
- 2 teaspoons coarse kosher or sea salt
- 2 tablespoons finely chopped fresh cilantro leaves and tender stems
- 12 medium-size to large fresh curry leaves

1. Combine the sesame seeds, peanuts, garlic, and chiles in a food processor, and pulse to form a gritty, sticky, mellow-smelling blend.

2. Heat the oil in a medium-size saucepan over medium-low heat. Scrape the sesame-peanut blend into the warmed oil and roast the mixture, stirring, until it starts to release its own oils and loosen, turning crumbly and nutty brown, 5 to 8 minutes.

3. Meanwhile, drain the potatoes.

4. Stir the turmeric into the sesame-peanut blend and cook for 5 seconds. Then add the potatoes, tomatoes (with their juices), 1 cup water, and the salt. Stir once or twice, raise the heat to medium-high, and bring to a boil. Then reduce the heat to medium-low, cover the pan, and cook, stirring occasionally, until the potatoes are fork-tender and the sauce has thickened, 25 to 30 minutes.

5. Stir in the cilantro and curry leaves, and serve.

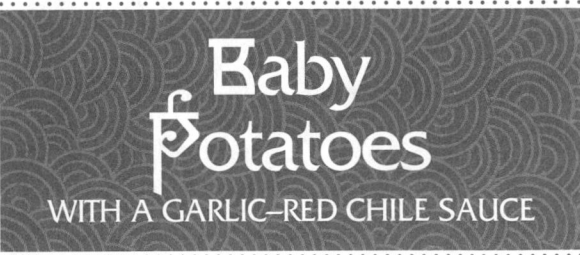

Baby Potatoes
WITH A GARLIC–RED CHILE SAUCE

ŋepalese dum loo

Bhavesh Kumar Thapa spent his childhood days in the Darjeeling district, near Siligury, the commercial capital of the area that comprises northern West Bengal, Sikkim, Bhutan, Nepal, and Bangladesh. The pristine weather in these rolling hills, covered with tea plantations, was a beacon of respite for the British when they ruled India, and the cluster of resort cities proved perfect getaways from the oppressive summer heat that scorched the rest of India. Now Bhavesh, with his wife, Shalini, and their two daughters, lives in south-central Bangalore. Even though they happily indulge in the crepes, pancakes, and steamed cakes of the south, they still have a strong preference for the foods of their Nepalese heritage, including these chile-hot, garlicky baby potatoes. **SERVES 6**

1 ¼ *pounds baby new potatoes, scrubbed clean*
  (do not peel)
10 *medium-size cloves garlic*
2 or 3 *dried red Thai or cayenne chiles, to*
  taste, stems removed (see Tips)
2 *tablespoons mustard oil or canola oil*
½ *teaspoon cumin seeds*
½ *teaspoon fennel seeds*
½ *teaspoon nigella seeds*
½ *teaspoon bishop's weed; or ¼ teaspoon*
  dried thyme mixed with ¼ teaspoon fresh
  ground black pepper
2 *fresh or dried bay leaves*
1½ *teaspoons coarse kosher or sea salt*
1 *teaspoon ground Kashmiri chiles; or ¼ teaspoon*
  cayenne (ground red pepper) mixed with
  ¾ teaspoon sweet paprika
½ *teaspoon ground turmeric*
10 to 12 *medium-size to large fresh curry leaves*

1. Fill a medium-size (or larger) saucepan with water and bring it to a boil over medium-high heat. Add the potatoes to the boiling water and bring it to a boil again. Lower the heat to medium and cook, partially covered, until the potatoes are tender but firm-looking, 5 to 8 minutes.

2. While the potatoes are cooking, combine the garlic and chiles in a food processor, and pulse until minced.

3. Reserving 1 cup of the cooking water, drain the potatoes.

4. Heat the oil in a medium-size saucepan over medium-high heat. Sprinkle in the cumin, fennel, and nigella seeds. Add the bishop's weed and bay leaves. Cook until the herbs and spices sizzle and are aromatic, 15 to 30 seconds. Add the garlic-chile blend and stir-fry until the garlic is light brown and the chiles smell pungent, 1 to 2 minutes. Then immediately remove the pan from the heat and sprinkle in the salt, ground chiles, turmeric, and curry leaves. Stir once or twice. The heat from the oil will be just right to cook the ground spices without burning them.

5. Add the reserved cooking water and the potatoes to the pan and return the pan to the heat. Once the water comes to a boil, reduce the heat to medium-low, cover the pan, and simmer, stirring occasionally, until the potatoes are fall-apart tender and the sauce has thickened, 10 to 12 minutes. Then serve.

Tips:

❖ If baby potatoes are not available at the market, use any variety of white potato, such as russet or Yukon Gold. Peel them and cut them into 1-inch cubes for a perfectly acceptable alternative.

❖ These chiles are potent, so do use adequate ventilation when you are frying them. Reduce the number of chiles if you can't handle the heat, but if you happen to be on the other end of the spectrum, throw in an additional 1 or 2 chiles, especially if you enjoy that endorphin euphoria often associated with these macho chiles. You may thump your chest with your two fists after all!

Bishop's weed? Nigella? See the Glossary of Ingredients, page 758.

Tender Potatoes
WITH GROUND FENUGREEK

Aloo Subzi

here's a curry with an unusual base for its sauce: oil. A larger-than-usual amount of oil and briefly stir-fried onion yield a thick curry that enhances the potato's succulence. I love this dish even when it's served at room temperature. It's especially delicious when taken along for a picnic, with a stack of *pooris* (page 725) and a dish of fresh chile slivers with thinly sliced raw onions sprinkled with coarse sea salt. **SERVES 6**

¼ cup canola oil (see Tip)

1 teaspoon black or yellow mustard seeds

1 medium-size red onion, finely chopped

2 teaspoons coarse kosher or sea salt

1 teaspoon cumin seeds, ground

1 teaspoon fenugreek seeds, ground

¼ teaspoon ground turmeric

3 to 5 fresh green Thai, cayenne, or serrano chiles, to taste, stems removed, sliced crosswise into ¼-inch-thick pieces (do not remove the seeds)

1 pound russet or Yukon Gold potatoes, peeled, cut into ½-inch cubes, and submerged in a bowl of cold water to prevent browning

¼ cup finely chopped fresh cilantro leaves and tender stems

15 to 20 medium-size to large fresh curry leaves

1. Heat the oil in a medium-size saucepan over medium-high heat. Add the mustard seeds, cover the skillet, and cook until the seeds have stopped popping (not unlike popcorn), about 30 seconds. Immediately add the onion, salt, cumin, fenugreek, turmeric, and chiles. Stir-fry until the onion is translucent, the spices have cooked and turned aromatic, and the chiles smell pungent, about 2 minutes.

2. Drain the potatoes and add them, along with ½ cup water, the cilantro, and the curry leaves. Stir once or twice and bring to a boil. Reduce the heat to medium-low, cover the pan, and cook, stirring occasionally to prevent sticking, until the potatoes are tender, 8 to 10 minutes. Then serve.

Tip: I am one who never likes to throw anything away, even used canola oil. I recycle cooking oil three or four times, straining it after each use and refrigerating it to prevent rancidity. Then when a recipe calls for oil for stir-frying and seasoning spices, I use "gently used" oil to add even more flavor. Call me frugal, call me cheap, but please don't call me unimaginative.

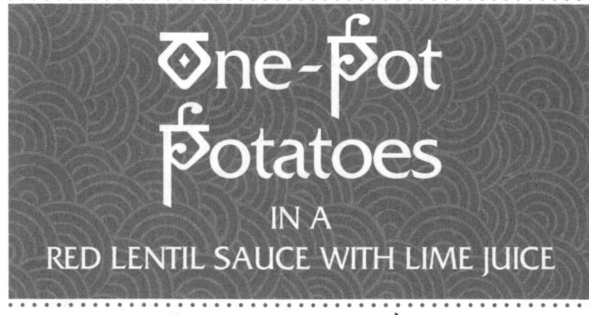

One-Pot Potatoes
IN A
RED LENTIL SAUCE WITH LIME JUICE

Aloo Masoor Dal

quick-cooking, this curry combines starch and protein to make an easy, light, nutritionally complete vegetarian meal. Serve it with one of the salads in the Curry Cohorts chapter and some store-bought flatbreads for a weekday dinner. **SERVES 6**

I cup red lentils (masoor dal), picked over for stones

2 tablespoons canola oil

2 teaspoons cumin seeds

I small red onion, finely chopped

I tablespoon finely chopped fresh ginger

2 or 3 fresh green Thai, cayenne, or serrano chiles,
    to taste, stems removed, finely chopped
    (do not remove the seeds)

I pound russet or Yukon Gold potatoes, peeled,
    cut into ½-inch cubes, and submerged in a
    bowl of cold water to prevent browning

2 teaspoons coarse kosher or sea salt

2 teaspoons cumin seeds, ground

I teaspoon coriander seeds, ground

I teaspoon ground turmeric

I tablespoon finely chopped fresh cilantro leaves
    and tender stems

Juice of I medium-size lime

1. Place the lentils in a medium-size saucepan. Fill the pan halfway with tap water and rinse the lentils by rubbing them between your fingertips. The water will become cloudy. Drain this water. Repeat three or four times, until the water remains relatively clear; drain. Now add 2 cups water and bring to a boil, uncovered, over medium heat. Skim off and discard any foam that rises to the surface. Reduce the heat to medium-low, cover the pot, and simmer, stirring occasionally, until the lentils are tender, 10 to 12 minutes. Remove the pan from the heat.

2. While the lentils are cooking, heat the oil in a large skillet over medium heat. Add the cumin seeds and cook until they sizzle, turn reddish brown, and are fragrant, 10 to 15 seconds. Add the onion, ginger, and chiles, and stir-fry until the onion is caramel-brown, 8 to 10 minutes.

3. Drain the potatoes and add them to the skillet. Stir in the salt, ground cumin, coriander, turmeric, and cilantro. Stir-fry to cook the spices as they turn fragrant, 1 to 2 minutes. Then add ½ cup water, scraping the bottom of the skillet to deglaze it, releasing any collected bits of onion and spice. Reduce the heat to medium-low, cover, and cook, stirring occasionally, until the potatoes are fork-tender, 8 to 10 minutes.

4. Transfer half of the lentils, with half of the cooking water, to a blender and puree until smooth. Pour this creamy blend over the potatoes. Repeat with the remaining lentils and water. (If you have an immersion blender, you can puree the lentils and water right in the saucepan.)

5. Stir this protein-rich sauce into the mixture, allowing the potatoes to absorb some of its flavors and vice-versa.

6. Just before you serve the curry, stir in the lime juice.

Tips:

❖ Salmon-colored *masoor dal*, also known as red Egyptian lentils, turn yellow when cooked. Because they are quick-cooking, prior soaking is unnecessary.

❖ For an interesting alternative, use turnips instead of, or in addition to, the potatoes in this curry.

❖ For an even more nutritious curry, stir in a cup of fresh spinach greens when the potato (or turnip) is tender, at the end of Step 4, and cook the greens until just wilted.

Green-Chile Potatoes

haree bharee Aloo

The Hindi words *haree bharee* describe anything that is lush-green and bountiful. These potatoes fill the bill with fresh mint, cilantro (made mellow by cooking), and pungent green chiles. For an unusual combination, I have served this robust curry with bowls of steamed couscous and a side of *Kachumber* (page 741).

SERVES 4 TO 6

- 1 pound russet or Yukon Gold potatoes, peeled, cut into ½-inch cubes, and submerged in a bowl of cold water to prevent browning
- 1 cup tightly packed fresh mint leaves
- 1 cup tightly packed fresh cilantro leaves and tender stems
- 3 to 5 fresh green Thai, cayenne, or serrano chiles, to taste, stems removed
- 1 tablespoon canola oil
- 1 teaspoon cumin seeds
- 1 cup finely chopped red onion
- 1 tablespoon Ginger Paste (page 15)
- 2 teaspoons Garlic Paste (page 15)
- 2 teaspoons coarse kosher or sea salt

1. Drain the potatoes.

2. Combine the mint, cilantro, and chiles in a food processor and pulse until minced, scraping the inside of the bowl as necessary to ensure an even blend.

3. Heat the oil in a medium-size saucepan over medium-high heat. Sprinkle in the cumin seeds, which will instantly turn reddish brown and fragrant. Add the onion, Ginger Paste, and Garlic Paste, and cook, stirring occasionally, until the onion is translucent, about 1 minute.

4. Add the potatoes, 1 cup water, the salt, and the minced herbs. Stir once or twice and bring to a boil. Lower the heat to medium, cover the pan, and cook, stirring occasionally to prevent the potatoes from sticking, until they are fork-tender and the sauce has thickened slightly, 15 to 18 minutes. Then serve.

Tips:

❖ I do not recommend freezing chunky, potato-based curries because when you thaw them, the potatoes' texture becomes quite spongy. This curry will keep in the refrigerator for up to 4 days, so polishing it off in that time frame should not be a problem.

❖ In the summer, fresh herbs are inexpensive, especially at farmers' markets. Off-season, I tend to go to Asian grocery stores, where the fresh herbs are one-third the price you would expect to pay in larger supermarkets.

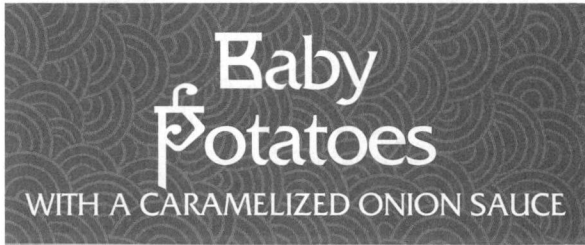

Baby Potatoes
WITH A CARAMELIZED ONION SAUCE

Punjabi dum Aloo

The technique of trapping steam in a pan by sealing it closed with a piece of wheat flour dough stretched across the top is called *dum*; the contraption sits atop hot coals. This not only provides essential moisture but also contributes a smoky flavor to the dish. In India, some upscale north Indian restaurants offer menu items, such as this one, cooked in this fashion, and the server brings the dish to the table with the dough cover intact. When he pierces it, enticing aromas are released. I have not applied the *dum* technique to this recipe, but I have found this version to be equally satisfying. **SERVES 6**

1¼ pounds baby new potatoes, scrubbed clean
    (do not peel) and patted dry
2 tablespoons Ghee (page 21) or canola oil
1 tablespoon cumin seeds
1 large red onion, finely chopped
6 fresh green Thai, cayenne, or serrano chiles,
    stems removed, cut crosswise into ¼-inch-thick
    slices (do not remove the seeds)
1 can (14.5 ounces) diced tomatoes
2 teaspoons coarse kosher or sea salt
1 teaspoon ground turmeric
1 tablespoon mango powder or fresh lime juice
1 tablespoon Toasted Cumin-Coriander Blend (page 33)
2 tablespoons finely chopped fresh cilantro
    leaves and tender stems for garnishing

1. Prick each potato in multiple places with a fork or the tip of a knife (this allows it to vent steam so it doesn't burst into pieces when being stir-fried).

2. Heat 1 tablespoon of the ghee in a medium-size nonstick skillet over medium-low heat. Add the potatoes and stir-fry until they are partially cooked and the skin appears shriveled, about 15 minutes. Transfer the potatoes to a plate.

3. Heat the remaining 1 tablespoon ghee in the same skillet over medium heat. Add the cumin seeds and cook until they sizzle and turn reddish brown, 5 to 10 seconds. Add the onion and chiles, and stir-fry until the onion is caramel-brown, 10 to 12 minutes.

4. Pour in the tomatoes, with their juices, and stir in the salt and turmeric. Simmer, covered, over medium-low heat, stirring occasionally, until the tomato softens to make a chunky sauce, 5 to 8 minutes.

5. Stir in the potatoes, cover the skillet, and cook, stirring occasionally, until they are fork-tender, 25 to 30 minutes.

6. Fold in the mango powder and the cumin-coriander blend. Sprinkle with the cilantro, and serve.

Tip: Baby new potatoes, with either red jackets or white, are usually about 1 inch or less in diameter. They are sweet and easy to cook. I wait for their appearance in my farmers' market in mid-spring or early summer with unabashed greed. During the months when these babies are absent, choose the smallest potatoes you can find for this recipe. The cooking times will vary according to their size.

Spring Baby Potatoes
WITH FRIED ONION SAUCE AND MINT

Sudhine Waale Naye Aloo

Spring's first crop unearths sweet baby potatoes. Combine them with another under-the-ground crop, red onions, and above-ground mint leaves, and you have the makings of a sensuous curry. **SERVES 6**

2 tablespoons canola oil

I teaspoon cumin seeds

I pound baby new potatoes (about ½ to
    I inch in diameter), scrubbed and rinsed

¼ cup Fried Onion Paste (page 16)

I tablespoon tomato paste

1½ teaspoons coarse kosher or sea salt

½ cup firmly packed fresh mint leaves, finely chopped

I teaspoon Kashmiri garam masala (page 29)

1. Heat the oil in a large skillet over medium-high heat. Add the cumin seeds and cook until they sizzle, turn reddish brown, and are aromatic, 5 to 10 seconds. Then add the potatoes and stir-fry until they turn reddish brown and are partially tender, about 10 minutes.

2. While the potatoes are cooking, whisk the onion paste, tomato paste, salt, and 1 cup water together in a medium-size bowl.

3. Pour the reddish-brown tomato-onion liquid over the potatoes and stir once or twice. Reduce the heat to medium-low, cover the skillet, and cook, occasionally basting the potatoes with the sauce, until they are fork-tender, 15 to 20 minutes.

4. Stir in the mint and the garam masala, and serve.

Tips:

❖ If baby potatoes are not available (or you want to prepare this in the middle of winter), use any kind of potatoes and cut them into smaller pieces. Watch the cooking time, however, since cut-up potatoes may become fork-tender a bit faster than whole baby ones.

❖ You can use store-bought garam masala if you have not had the time to make the *Kashmiri garam masala*. But it takes only 1 or 2 minutes to put it together, so do yourself a favor and make the spice blend. You will be grateful you did.

Potato Cubes
IN A SWEET ONION SAUCE

Aloo Kaanda Bhajee

Onions are the star in this simple, robust curry. As much as you might want to crank up the heat and hurry the browning process, don't give in to temptation. This technique of slowly stewing the onions yields amazing sweetness while the chiles keep the sugars at bay to make their pungent presence known. Enjoy this with a stack of puffy fried *pooris* (page 725). **SERVES 8**

¼ cup canola oil

I teaspoon black or yellow mustard seeds

I teaspoon cumin seeds

I large red onion, cut in half lengthwise
    and then into ½-inch cubes

¼ cup firmly packed medium-size to large
    fresh curry leaves

4 fresh green Thai, cayenne, or serrano chiles,
    stems removed, cut crosswise into ½-inch-thick
    slices (do not remove the seeds)

1½ pounds russet or Yukon Gold potatoes, peeled,
    cut into ½-inch cubes, and submerged in a
    bowl of cold water to prevent browning

2 teaspoons coarse kosher or sea salt

I teaspoon ground turmeric

2 tablespoons finely chopped fresh cilantro
    leaves and tender stems for garnishing

1. Heat the oil in a medium-size saucepan over medium-high heat. Add the mustard seeds, cover the pan, and cook until the seeds have stopped popping (not unlike popcorn), about 30 seconds. Sprinkle in the cumin seeds, which will instantly turn reddish brown and fragrant.

2. Toss in the onion, curry leaves, and chiles. Reduce the heat to medium-low and stir-fry for 1 to 2 minutes. Then cover the pan and cook, stirring occasionally, letting the onion stew in its own juices and release its sugars, until the cubes split when cut with a fork, 18 to 20 minutes.

3. Drain the potatoes. Add the potatoes, salt, and turmeric to the pan, and stir to coat the vegetables with the turmeric, a few seconds. Then add 1 cup water, stir once or twice, and cover the pan. Stew, stirring occasionally, until the potatoes are fork-tender and the curry has thickened, 15 to 20 minutes.

4. Sprinkle with the cilantro, and serve.

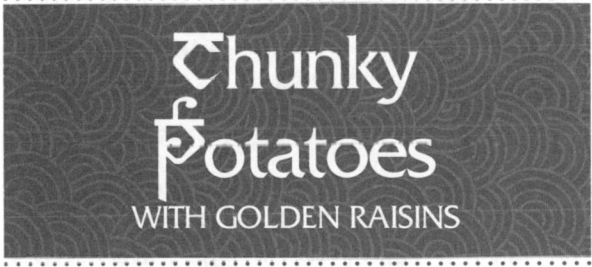

Chunky Potatoes
WITH GOLDEN RAISINS

Aloo Kishmish Ki Subzi

I love the burst of sweetness that plump golden raisins offer this mélange of spicy ingredients. Serve it with puffy *pooris* (page 725) for a private pamper-yourself lunch. Go ahead and treat yourself to a glass of Viognier, Sancerre, or pinot blanc with the simple meal. You deserve it, don't you?

SERVES 6

1 can (14.5 ounces) diced tomatoes
1 small red onion, coarsely chopped

¼ cup firmly packed fresh cilantro leaves and tender stems
4 large cloves garlic
3 dried red Thai or cayenne chiles, stems removed
2 lengthwise slices fresh ginger (each 2 inches long, 1 inch wide, and ⅛ inch thick)
2 tablespoons canola oil
1 teaspoon cumin seeds
1 pound russet or Yukon Gold potatoes, peeled, cut into ½-inch cubes, and submerged in a bowl of cold water to prevent browning
½ cup frozen green peas (no need to thaw)
½ cup golden raisins (see Tip)

1. Combine the tomatoes, with their juices, and the onion, cilantro, garlic, chiles, and ginger in a blender jar. Puree, scraping the inside of the jar as needed, to make a reddish-green sauce.

2. Heat the oil in a large skillet over medium-high heat. Add the cumin seeds and cook until they sizzle, turn reddish brown, and smell nutty, 5 to 10 seconds. Immediately add the pureed tomato-onion sauce. Lower the heat to medium and cook, partially covered to contain some of the spattering, stirring occasionally, until the liquid evaporates and some oil starts to separate from the sauce, 15 to 20 minutes.

3. Stir in 1 cup water. Drain the potatoes and add them. Cook, covered, stirring occasionally, until the potatoes are fork-tender, 20 to 25 minutes.

4. Stir in the peas and cook, uncovered, until they are warmed through, 2 to 3 minutes.

5. Top the curry with the raisins, and serve.

Tip: Are there some golden raisins on your pantry shelf that have hardened over time? Soak them in a bowl of hot water for about an hour to soften them up before you add them to the curry. There's nothing worse than chewing on a combination of rubbery raisins and tender potatoes. Well, actually, what's worse is not having any potatoes in your pantry—now, that *is* cause for alarm.

Shredded Potatoes
WITH PEANUTS AND CHILES

batata kheema

Ground meat is called *kheema,* but there is none in this recipe. The shredded potatoes—crispy brown on the outside and tender, soft, and chewy on the inside—provide the succulence associated with ground meat. This is the perfect alternative to those ordinary breakfast hash browns. **SERVES 6**

¼ *cup raw peanuts (without the skins)*
4 tablespoons canola oil
I pound russet or Yukon Gold potatoes, peeled, shredded, and submerged in a bowl of cold water to prevent browning (see Tip)
I small red onion, cut in half lengthwise and thinly sliced
I medium-size tomato, cored and finely chopped
¼ *cup finely chopped fresh cilantro leaves and tender stems*
I½ teaspoons coarse kosher or sea salt
¼ *teaspoon ground turmeric*
6 fresh green Thai, cayenne, or serrano chiles, stems removed, thinly sliced crosswise (do not remove the seeds)

1. Place the peanuts in a food processor and pulse until they have the texture of coarse breadcrumbs.

2. Heat 2 tablespoons of the oil in a large nonstick skillet over medium heat. Add the ground peanuts and stir-fry until they are golden brown and smell nutty, 2 to 3 minutes. Transfer the roasted nuts to a small plate. Wipe out the skillet with a dry paper towel to remove any nutty crumbs.

3. Drain the potatoes and pat them dry.

4. Heat the remaining 2 tablespoons oil in the same skillet over medium heat. Add the onion and potatoes, and stir-fry until they are a honey-brown color (similar to hash browns), about 15 minutes.

5. Stir in the tomato, cilantro, salt, turmeric, and chiles. Add 1 cup water and the roasted ground peanuts. Bring to a boil and cook until the sauce thickens—which will happen quickly, thanks to the peanuts and the starchy potatoes. Then serve.

Tips:

❖ You can shred the potatoes either in a food processor or against the large holes of a box grater. Just remember to drop the shreds immediately into cold water to prevent any discoloration. If you like, you can also purchase those convenient bags of pre-shredded potatoes (the plain variety), found in the refrigerated section at your neighborhood supermarket.

❖ If you have a peanut allergy, please accept my condolences. I hate to see you left out, so use raw cashew nuts as an alternative. "No nuts," you say? Then leave them out, I'll love you anyway!

Potatoes
WITH A
SPICY TOMATO-CILANTRO SAUCE

dhaniawale Aloo

Fuffy fried *kachoris* (page 737) are an ideal match for these addictive, thick-sauced potatoes. Break the crisp-tender breads apart and use them as a scoop to spoon the curry into your eager mouth. What's a good time for this combination? Breakfast, of course. That is when I indulged in it recently—after a visit to the Taj Mahal in Agra, where a roadside vendor has made a reputation, and millions, selling this combination of *aloo* and *kachoris*. **SERVES 8**

2 pounds russet or Yukon Gold potatoes, peeled,
 cut into ½-inch cubes, and submerged in a
 bowl of cold water to prevent browning
2 tablespoons canola oil
I teaspoon cumin seeds
2 teaspoons coarse kosher or sea salt
I teaspoon cumin seeds, ground
I teaspoon cayenne (ground red pepper)
½ teaspoon ground turmeric
I cup tomato sauce, canned or homemade (see page 18)
I cup firmly packed cilantro leaves and tender stems

1. Drain the potatoes and pat them dry.

2. Heat the oil in a large skillet over medium-high heat. Add the cumin seeds and cook until they sizzle, turn reddish brown, and are aromatic, 5 to 10 seconds. Carefully add the potatoes (there will be some spattering), and stir-fry until they are light brown around the edges, about 5 minutes.

3. Stir in the salt, ground cumin, cayenne, and turmeric. Reduce the heat to medium-low, cover the skillet, and cook, stirring and scraping the bottom of the pan occasionally, until the potatoes are partially cooked, about 20 minutes. (The steam that builds up in the pan provides enough moisture not only to cook the potatoes, but also to deglaze the pan and prevent the spices from burning.)

4. While the potatoes are cooking, pour the tomato sauce into a blender jar. Add the cilantro and puree, scraping the inside of the jar as needed, to form a smooth, olive-green sauce.

5. When the potatoes are partially cooked, add the tomato-cilantro sauce. Pour ¼ cup water into the blender jar and swish it around to wash it out. Add this to the skillet, and stir once or twice. Continue to simmer, covered, stirring occasionally, until the potatoes are tender, 10 to 12 minutes. Then serve.

Slow-Cooked
Baby Potatoes
IN A YOGURT-FENNEL SAUCE

kashmiri dum Aloo

Life in Kashmir is slow-moving, as its inhabitants take that extra moment to stop and bask in the state's pristine natural beauty, its lush green fields of basmati rice, and the snow-capped Himalayan mountains. So it is no wonder that they let the new spring potatoes cook slowly in mild ground Kashmiri chiles, yogurt, and onions. Traditionally the pan is sealed tight with a piece of dough stretched across the top as a lid and then set atop ash-covered coals to cook (the technique referred to as *dum*). **SERVES 6**

¼ cup Ghee (page 21) or canola oil

2 pounds baby (new) potatoes, scrubbed and pierced in multiple spots with a fork or knife

1 tablespoon cumin seeds

½ teaspoon whole cloves

4 black cardamom pods

2 fresh or dried bay leaves

1 small red onion, cut in half lengthwise and thinly sliced

½ cup plain yogurt

2 teaspoons fennel seeds, ground

2 teaspoons ground Kashmiri chiles; or ½ teaspoon cayenne (ground red pepper) mixed with 1½ teaspoons sweet paprika

1 teaspoon Kashmiri garam masala (page 29)

1½ teaspoons coarse kosher or sea salt

½ teaspoon cayenne (ground red pepper)

1. Heat the ghee in a large skillet over medium-high heat. Add the potatoes and fry, stirring them occasionally, until the skin appears shriveled and partially browned and the potatoes are just a bit tender, 12 to 15 minutes. Transfer the potatoes to a plate, leaving behind as much of the ghee as possible.

2. Sprinkle the cumin seeds, cloves, cardamom pods, and bay leaves into the skillet. Cook until the spices perfume the ghee, 15 to 30 seconds. Then add the onion and stir-fry until it is light honey-brown, 5 to 8 minutes.

3. Add the yogurt, fennel, ground chiles, garam masala, salt, and cayenne. Simmer, uncovered, stirring occasionally, until most of the liquid from the yogurt has evaporated and a deep red film of ghee is starting to separate from the sauce, 5 to 10 minutes.

4. Pour in 1 cup water and return the potatoes to the skillet. Stir once or twice, cover the skillet, and cook over medium-low heat, basting the potatoes every 5 minutes or so with the sauce, until they are tender, 1 to 1½ hours.

5. Remove the cardamom pods, bay leaves, and whole cloves before serving.

Tips:

❖ Piercing the tubers prevents them from bursting open in the hot oil and also provides tiny pores for the lush flavors to seep into—making for machismo-curried potatoes.

❖ If you wish for a touch of green, sprinkle 2 tablespoons finely chopped fresh cilantro leaves and tender stems over the curry just before you serve it.

Mashed Potatoes
WITH ROASTED RED CHILES

Podi Maas

When I was growing up in a vegetarian family, this curry was our hands-on favorite. It was a perfect accompaniment to *pooris* (page 725) on long train journeys or on daylong picnics to one of the beaches that dot Mumbai's coast. Fiery hot, potent, and highly addictive, this thick-sauced potato curry is flavored with a *podi* (pounded blend) that makes you see red in more ways than one. **SERVES 4**

1 pound russet or Yukon Gold potatoes, peeled, diced, and submerged in a bowl of cold water to prevent browning

2 tablespoons canola oil

8 to 10 dried red Thai or cayenne chiles, to taste,
stems removed

2 tablespoons skinned split black lentils (cream-colored
in this form, urad dal), picked over for stones

1 teaspoon black or yellow mustard seeds

2 tablespoons finely chopped fresh cilantro
leaves and tender stems

1 teaspoon coarse kosher or sea salt

8 to 10 medium-size to large fresh curry leaves

1. Fill a medium-size (or larger) saucepan with water and bring it to a boil over medium-high heat. Drain the potatoes and add them to the boiling water. Bring it to a boil again. Lower the heat to medium and cook, partially covered, until the potatoes are very tender, 5 to 8 minutes. Drain the potatoes, reserving ½ cup of the cooking water. Transfer them to a medium-size bowl and coarsely mash them. Cover the mashed potatoes to keep them warm.

2. Heat the oil in a small saucepan over medium-high heat. Add the chiles and 1 tablespoon of the lentils, and stir-fry until the chiles are slightly blackened and the lentils are honey-brown, 1 to 2 minutes. Using a slotted spoon, transfer the chiles and lentils to a mortar. Pound the blend, potent and red-hot, with the pestle, scraping it into the center with a spatula to contain it for a concentrated pounding until it has the consistency of coarsely ground black pepper.

3. Reheat the oil over medium-high heat. Add the mustard seeds, cover the pan, and cook until the seeds have stopped popping (not unlike popcorn), about 30 seconds. Add the remaining 1 tablespoon lentils and stir-fry until they turn golden brown, 15 to 20 seconds. Scrape this nutty-smelling oil into the potatoes, and add the pounded spice blend, cilantro, salt, curry leaves, and the reserved cooking water. Stir well to combine, making a thick-sauced curry mottled with chiles. Then serve.

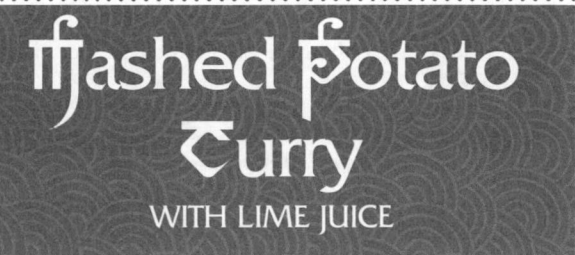

Mashed Potato Curry
WITH LIME JUICE

Limboo Podi Maas

A quick-cooking potato curry and a small stack of *pooris* (page 725) from the night before helped to ease my mother's workload and satiate our appetites, as she was rushing to prepare both breakfast and a light carry-along lunch for us children. **SERVES 4**

1 pound russet or Yukon Gold potatoes, peeled,
diced, and submerged in a bowl of cold water
to prevent browning

2 tablespoons canola oil

1 teaspoon black or yellow mustard seeds

1 tablespoon skinned split black lentils
(cream-colored in this form, urad dal),
picked over for stones

¼ teaspoon ground turmeric

¼ cup finely chopped fresh cilantro leaves and
tender stems

1½ teaspoons coarse kosher or sea salt

10 medium-size to large fresh curry leaves

2 fresh green Thai, cayenne, or serrano chiles,
stems removed, cut crosswise into ¼-inch-thick
slices (do not remove the seeds)

Juice of 1 medium-size lime

1. Fill a medium-size (or larger) saucepan with water and bring it to a boil over medium-high heat. Drain the potatoes and add them to the boiling water. Bring it to a boil again. Lower the heat to medium and cook, partially covered, until the potatoes are very tender, 5 to 8

minutes. Reserving 1 cup of the cooking water, drain the potatoes into a colander. Coarsely mash them in the same colander.

2. Heat the oil in a medium-size saucepan over medium-high heat. Add the mustard seeds, cover the pan, and cook until the seeds have stopped popping (not unlike popcorn), about 30 seconds. Add the lentils and stir-fry until they turn golden brown, 15 to 20 seconds. Sprinkle the turmeric into the hot oil. Immediately add the mashed potatoes, reserved cooking water, and all the remaining ingredients except the lime juice. Lower the heat to medium, cover the pan, and cook, stirring occasionally, until the thick curry is warmed through, 8 to 10 minutes.

3. Stir in the lime juice, and serve.

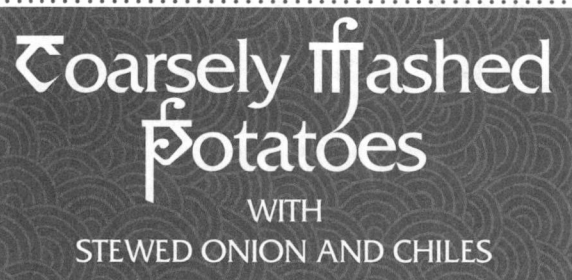

Coarsely Mashed Potatoes
WITH
STEWED ONION AND CHILES

Masala Bhajee

traditionally, this curry is a stuffing for southern India's signature bread called *dosa*. The unleavened bread, made with fermented rice-lentil batter, is lacy-thin and crepe-like. Torn into bite-size pieces and wrapped around these saucy potatoes, it is consumed with unabashed glee at all times of the day. **SERVES 6**

2 tablespoons yellow split peas (chana dal), picked over for stones

1 pound russet or Yukon Gold potatoes, peeled, diced, and submerged in a bowl of cold water to prevent browning

2 tablespoons canola oil

1 teaspoon black or yellow mustard seeds

1 medium-size red onion, cut in half lengthwise and thinly sliced

½ teaspoon ground turmeric

¼ teaspoon ground asafetida

¼ cup finely chopped fresh cilantro leaves and tender stems

2 teaspoons coarse kosher or sea salt

12 medium-size to large fresh curry leaves

6 fresh green Thai, cayenne, or serrano chiles, stems removed, cut in half lengthwise (do not remove the seeds)

4 lengthwise slices fresh ginger (each 1½ inches long, 1 inch wide, and ⅛ inch thick), cut into thin matchsticks (julienne)

1. Place the split peas in a small bowl and add hot tap water to cover. Let them soak for 15 minutes. Then drain and pat them dry with paper towels.

2. Fill a medium-size (or larger) saucepan with water and bring it to a boil over medium-high heat. Drain the potatoes and add them to the boiling water. Bring it to a boil again. Lower the heat to medium and cook, partially covered, until the potatoes are very tender, 5 to 8 minutes. Reserving 1 cup of the cooking water, drain the potatoes into a colander. Coarsely mash them in the same colander.

3. Heat the oil in a medium-size skillet over medium-high heat. Add the mustard seeds, cover the skillet, and cook until the seeds have stopped popping (not unlike popcorn), about 30 seconds. Add the split peas and stir-fry until they turn reddish brown, 1 to 2 minutes.

4. Add the onion and stir-fry just long enough to take away its raw flavor and still maintain its slight crunch, 1 to 2 minutes. Sprinkle in the turmeric and asafetida, stir, and cook for 15 to 20 seconds. Then add the reserved cooking water. Reduce the heat to medium-low, cover the skillet, and cook, stirring occasionally, until the onion has softened, 10 to 15 minutes.

5. Stir in the potatoes and all the remaining ingredients. Cover the skillet and cook, stirring occasionally, until the potatoes have warmed and absorbed the sweet onion flavor, 3 to 5 minutes. Then serve.

Tip: It is common to set aside the chiles, ginger, and curry leaves when you eat this curry. However, if you enjoy a burst of heat from the chiles and the pungency from the ginger, by all means consume them. We usually don't eat the curry leaves.

Garlic-Chile Potato Dumplings
IN A RAISIN-TOMATO SAUCE

tari daar Aloo kofta

I struggled with where to place this curry—in the appetizer chapter or in the vegetable chapter. I would hate to see these dumplings get lost as a side dish in a curry dinner because the combination of chiles and garlic (the two prominent flavors in *koftas*) is phenomenal against the nutty, sweet, tart backdrop of the sauce. Start a formal dinner with this *kofta* curry, and set the expectations high for the following courses. **SERVES 6**

For the *koftas* (dumplings):
- *1 pound russet or Yukon Gold potatoes, peeled, diced, and submerged in a bowl of cold water to prevent browning*
- *½ cup firmly packed fresh cilantro leaves and tender stems*
- *4 or 5 fresh green Thai, cayenne, or serrano chiles, to taste, stems removed*
- *6 medium-size cloves garlic*
- *1½ teaspoons coarse kosher or sea salt*
- *½ teaspoon Punjabi garam masala (page 25)*
- *1 cup chickpea flour, sifted*
- *¼ teaspoon ground turmeric*
- *Canola oil for deep-frying*

For the sauce:
- *2 tablespoons Ghee (page 21) or canola oil*
- *1 medium-size red onion, coarsely chopped*
- *2 lengthwise slices fresh ginger (each 2 inches long, 1 inch wide, and ⅛ inch thick), coarsely chopped*
- *½ cup raw cashew nuts*
- *¼ cup golden raisins*
- *1 can (15 ounces) tomato sauce*
- *½ teaspoon coarse kosher or sea salt*
- *2 tablespoons finely chopped fresh cilantro leaves and tender stems for garnishing*

1. To make the dumplings, bring a medium-size (or larger) saucepan of water to a boil over medium-high heat. Drain the potatoes and add them to the boiling water. Bring to a boil again. Then lower the heat to medium and cook, partially covered, until the potatoes are very tender, 5 to 8 minutes. Reserving 1 cup of the cooking water, drain the potatoes. Transfer them to a medium-size bowl, and mash them.

2. Combine the cilantro, chiles, and garlic in a food processor, and pulse until minced. Transfer this herb mix to the potatoes, and sprinkle in 1 teaspoon of the salt and the garam masala. Using clean hands or a spoon, thoroughly mix the spiced potatoes to form a soft, slightly bumpy, doughlike mass.

3. Scoop up 2 tablespoons of the potato dough and compress it in your hand to shape it into a tight, egg-shaped dumpling. Lay it on a plate or tray. Repeat with the remaining dough. You should end up with about 12 light-green *koftas*.

4. Combine the chickpea flour, turmeric, and the remaining ½ teaspoon salt in a medium-size bowl. Whisk in ½ cup warm tap water to make a smooth, yellow batter, a bit thicker than pancake batter.

5. Pour oil to a depth of 2 to 3 inches into a wok, Dutch oven, or medium-size saucepan. Heat the oil over medium heat until a candy or deep-fry thermometer inserted into the oil (without touching the pan's bottom) registers 350°F. (An alternative way to see if the oil is at the right temperature for deep-frying is to gently flick a drop of water over it. If the pearl-like drop skitters across the surface, the oil is ready.)

6. Line a plate or a cookie sheet with three or four sheets of paper towels. Once the oil is ready, gently coat each *kofta* completely with the batter. Slide 4 *koftas* into the hot oil and fry, turning them occasionally, until they are yellowish brown and crispy, 5 to 8 minutes. Remove them with a slotted spoon and set them on the paper towels to drain. Repeat with the remaining dumplings. You may need to adjust the heat to maintain the oil's temperature at 350°F.

7. To make the sauce, heat the ghee in a large saucepan over medium-high heat. Add the onion, ginger, cashews, and raisins, and stir-fry until the onion turns light brown around the edges, the nuts are brown in patches, and the raisins have plumped up, about 5 minutes.

8. Pour in the tomato sauce, and scrape the bottom

of the pan to deglaze it, releasing the browned bits of onion and sugar. Reduce the heat to medium-low, cover the pan, and simmer, stirring occasionally, until the onion has softened, about 5 minutes.

9. Transfer the sauce to a blender jar and puree, scraping the inside of the jar as needed, to make a smooth, albeit slightly gritty, sauce. Return the sauce to the saucepan. Pour the reserved 1 cup potato cooking water into the blender jar, and swish it around to wash it out. Pour this into the saucepan, add the salt, and stir. Reheat the sauce gently over medium-low heat.

10. Lower the fried dumplings into the sauce, and cover them completely with the sweet-tart, red blanket. Cover the pan and simmer, without stirring (or the *koftas* will fall apart), for 5 to 7 minutes.

11. Sprinkle with the cilantro, and serve.

Potatoes and Carrots
WITH A CORIANDER-FENUGREEK SAUCE

Urulikazhangu Manjal Mullangi Kari

familiar potatoes and carrots dot this curry, but use any other combination of root vegetables that might appeal to you. Sweet potatoes, yams, taro, parsnips, and turnips are all fair game, but remember to adjust the cooking times to fit the vegetable. **SERVES 6**

vegetable curries

I pound russet or Yukon Gold potatoes, peeled,
   cut into 2-inch cubes, and submerged in a
   bowl of cold water to prevent browning
1 tablespoon plus 1 teaspoon unrefined sesame
   oil or canola oil
1 teaspoon black or yellow mustard seeds
1 tablespoon skinned and split black lentils
   (cream-colored in this form, urad dal),
   picked over for stones
3 medium-size carrots, peeled and cut into
   short French-fry strips (about 2 inches long,
   ¼ inch wide, and ¼ inch thick)
2 teaspoons coarse kosher or sea salt
¼ teaspoon ground turmeric
12 to 15 medium-size to large fresh curry leaves
1 tablespoon coriander seeds
1 teaspoon fenugreek seeds
2 or 3 dried red Thai or cayenne chiles, to taste,
   stems removed
1 cup shredded fresh coconut; or ½ cup shredded
   dried unsweetened coconut, reconstituted
   (see Note)

1. Drain the potatoes.

2. Heat the 1 tablespoon oil in a large saucepan over medium-high heat. Add the mustard seeds, cover the pan, and cook until the seeds have stopped popping (not unlike popcorn), about 30 seconds. Add the lentils and stir-fry until they turn golden brown, 15 to 20 seconds. Immediately dump in the potatoes, carrots, 1 cup water, and the salt, turmeric, and curry leaves. Stir, and bring the water to a boil. Then reduce the heat to medium-low, cover the pan, and simmer, stirring occasionally, until the vegetables are fork-tender, 15 to 18 minutes.

3. While the vegetables are cooking, drizzle the remaining 1 teaspoon oil into a small skillet and heat it over medium-high heat. Sprinkle in the coriander

seeds, fenugreek seeds, and chiles. Roast the spices by stirring them constantly until they are reddish brown and smell nutty with a citrus undertone, 1 to 2 minutes. Transfer the spice mixture, oil and all, to a blender jar. Add ½ cup water and the coconut. Puree, scraping the inside of the jar as needed, to make a gritty, reddish-brown-speckled coconut paste.

4. Once the vegetables are tender, add the coconut paste. Pour ½ cup water into the blender jar and swish it around to wash it out. Add the washings to the vegetables and stir once or twice. Raise the heat to medium-high and simmer vigorously, uncovered, stirring occasionally, until the sauce thickens slightly, 8 to 10 minutes. Then serve.

Note: To reconstitute coconut, cover with ½ cup boiling water, set aside for about 15 minutes, and then drain.

Stewed Potatoes, Carrots, and Peas
IN SPICED COCONUT MILK

kai ishto

A perfect match for this curry is Kerala's signature nests of coconut-dusted rice noodles called *Idiappam* (page 723). I pipe the "from-scratch" rice noodles (so easy to make that I am almost embarrassed to share that recipe with you) into a steamer while the curry stews.

The vegetables are redolent with cardamom, peppercorns, cloves, and cinnamon—all spices from Kerala's sprawling plantations. **SERVES 6**

> 3 medium-size russet or Yukon Gold potatoes,
>   peeled, cut into ½-inch cubes, and submerged
>   in a bowl of cold water to prevent browning
> 3 medium-size carrots, peeled, ends trimmed,
>   cut lengthwise into quarters, and cut crosswise
>   into ½-inch pieces
> 1 teaspoon black peppercorns
> ¼ teaspoon whole cloves
> ¼ teaspoon cardamom seeds from green or white pods
> 1 cinnamon stick (3 inches long), broken into smaller
>   pieces
> 2 tablespoons coconut oil or canola oil
> 1 small red onion, cut in half lengthwise
>   and thinly sliced
> 12 to 15 medium-size to large fresh curry leaves
> 4 medium-size cloves garlic, cut into thin slivers
> 3 lengthwise slices fresh ginger (each 1 inch long,
>   1 inch wide, and ⅛ inch thick), cut into matchstick-
>   thin strips (julienne)
> 2 fresh green Thai, cayenne, or serrano chiles,
>   stems removed, cut lengthwise into thin strips
>   (do not remove the seeds)
> 1 cup unsweetened coconut milk
> 1 cup frozen green peas (no need to thaw)
> 1½ teaspoons coarse kosher or sea salt

1. Drain the potatoes and put them in a medium-size saucepan. Add the carrots and water to cover, and bring to a boil over medium-high heat. Continue to boil, uncovered, stirring occasionally, until the vegetables are tender but still firm-looking, 8 to 10 minutes.

2. While the vegetables are cooking, combine the peppercorns, cloves, cardamom seeds, and cinnamon pieces in a mortar. Pound with the pestle until the blend has the texture of coarse sawdust.

3. Heat the oil in a medium-size skillet over medium heat. Add the onion, curry leaves, garlic, ginger, chiles, and the pounded spices. Stir-fry to barely take the raw edge off the onion and to gently cook the spices, 2 to 4 minutes.

4. Drain the carrots and potatoes in a colander, and then return them to the same saucepan. Add the onion mixture.

5. Pour the coconut milk into the skillet and deglaze it, releasing any browned bits of the onion mixture. Then pour the coconut milk into the pan containing the vegetables, and stir in the peas and salt.

6. Cover the pan and simmer the curry over medium heat, stirring occasionally, until the flavors marry and the sauce has thickened slightly, 5 to 8 minutes. Then serve.

Spicy Potatoes
WITH CHILES AND TOMATOES

Molagha Urulikazhangu

ven though this spicy potato curry uses twelve chiles, half dried and half fresh, to create heat, it also has an addictive complexity. The chiles are left whole, making the resulting curry actually quite mellow-spiced. Savor this with a stack of onion-filled *Pyaaz kulcha* (page 736) and a small bowl of pureed mangoes sweetened with a hint of sugar (page 751). **SERVES 4**

1 pound russet or Yukon Gold potatoes, peeled,
    cut into 1-inch cubes, and submerged in a
    bowl of cold water to prevent browning

2 tablespoons canola oil

1 teaspoon black or yellow mustard seeds

1 tablespoon skinned split black lentils (cream-colored
    in this form, urad dal), picked over for stones

½ teaspoon ground turmeric

¼ teaspoon ground asafetida

6 dried red Thai or cayenne chiles, stems removed

1 large tomato, cored and cut into 1-inch cubes

¼ cup finely chopped fresh cilantro leaves and
    tender stems

2 teaspoons coarse kosher or sea salt

6 fresh green Thai, cayenne, or serrano chiles,
    stems removed, cut in half lengthwise
    (do not remove the seeds)

1. Fill a medium-size (or larger) saucepan with water and bring it to a boil over medium-high heat. Drain the potatoes and add them to the boiling water. Bring it to a boil again. Lower the heat to medium and cook, partially covered, until the potatoes are very tender, 5 to 8 minutes. Reserving 1 cup of the cooking water, drain the potatoes.

2. Heat the oil in a large skillet over medium-high heat. Add the mustard seeds, cover the skillet, and cook until the seeds have stopped popping (not unlike popcorn), about 30 seconds. Add the lentils and stir-fry until they turn golden brown, 15 to 20 seconds. Sprinkle the turmeric, asafetida, and dried chiles into the hot oil and allow them to sizzle for 5 to 10 seconds.

3. Immediately pour in the reserved cooking water, the potatoes, and the tomato, cilantro, salt, and fresh chiles. Bring the curry to a boil. Then reduce the heat to medium and cook, uncovered, stirring occasionally, until the sauce has thickened, 3 to 5 minutes. Remove the dried chiles if desired, and serve.

Cumin-Spiced Potatoes AND TOMATOES

bateta nu Shaak

Yes, this simple potato curry and a basketful of *pooris* (page 725) or green-pea-laced *Mutter kachoris* (page 737) is the antithesis to the Atkins diet, but in my opinion, bread and potatoes is a match made in heaven. During mango season (just before the monsoons in June), Gujaratis often serve pureed mangoes alongside this curry. Sweet, hot, and savory flavors are the trademark of the cuisine from India's northwestern region. **SERVES 6**

1 pound russet or Yukon Gold potatoes, peeled,
    cut into ½-inch cubes, and submerged in a
    bowl of cold water to prevent browning

1 tablespoon canola oil

1 teaspoon black or yellow mustard seeds

2 teaspoons cumin seeds, 1 whole, 1 ground

1½ teaspoons coarse kosher or sea salt

1 teaspoon white granulated sugar

1 teaspoon coriander seeds, ground

½ teaspoon cayenne (ground red pepper)

¼ teaspoon ground turmeric

¼ teaspoon ground asafetida

1 can (14.5 ounces) diced tomatoes

2 tablespoons finely chopped fresh cilantro
    leaves and tender stems

12 to 15 medium-size to large fresh curry leaves

1. Drain the potatoes.

2. Heat the oil in a small saucepan over medium-high heat. Add the mustard seeds, cover the pan, and cook until the seeds have stopped popping (not unlike popcorn), about 30 seconds. Sprinkle in the whole cumin seeds, which will instantly turn reddish brown and fragrant. Toss in the potatoes, salt, sugar, ground cumin, coriander, cayenne, turmeric, and asafetida. Stir-fry to cook the ground spices until they turn fragrant, about 1 minute.

3. Add the tomatoes with their liquid, 1 cup water, and the cilantro and curry leaves. Stir once and bring to a boil. Then reduce the heat to medium-low, cover the pan, and simmer, stirring occasionally, until the potatoes are fork-tender, about 15 minutes.

4. Remove the lid, raise the heat to medium-high, and continue to cook, stirring occasionally, until the sauce thickens slightly, 7 to 10 minutes. Then serve.

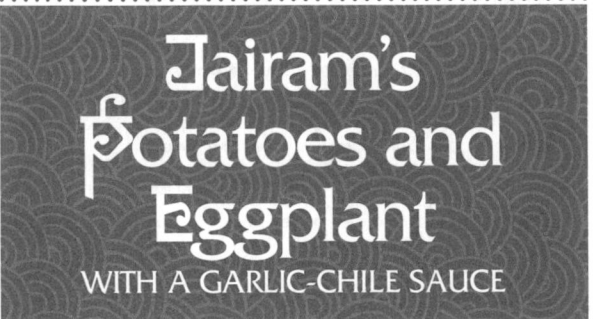

Jairam's Potatoes and Eggplant
WITH A GARLIC-CHILE SAUCE

bihari Aloo baingan

tall, animated, wiry man with a pencil-thin, Errol Flynn–like moustache, Jairam Das clearly takes great pride in his nighttime security job at my brother's Information Technology office in Bangalore. As we chatted, he described how he and his brother had left a small village in Bihar—leaving behind his wife, kids, parents, and a small but bountiful farm—to come to Bangalore to make ends meet and to provide monetary support for those left behind. Jairam loves to cook, and he does so daily, his diet rich with vegetables, legumes, and the occasional meat. His manner of speech is slow and precise, just like his cooking techniques, and his flavors are bold and strong. Jairam insists that you eat this curry with griddle-hot rotis (page 727), slices of raw red onion, and slivers of fresh green chiles.

SERVES 6

1 pound russet or Yukon Gold potatoes, peeled, cut into ½-inch cubes, and submerged in a bowl of cold water to prevent browning

½ cup firmly packed fresh cilantro leaves and tender stems

4 large cloves garlic

3 dried red Thai or cayenne chiles, stems removed (see Tips)

2 lengthwise slices fresh ginger (each 2½ inches long, 1 inch wide, and ⅛ inch thick)

2 tablespoons canola oil

1 teaspoon cumin seeds

1 medium-size red onion, cut in half lengthwise and thinly sliced

5 small purple Indian (or 1 small Italian) eggplants (about 8 ounces total), stems removed, cut into ½-inch cubes (see Tips)

1½ teaspoons coarse kosher or sea salt

1. Drain the potatoes.

2. Combine the cilantro, garlic, chiles, and ginger in a food processor, and pulse until the ingredients are minced.

3. Heat the oil in a large skillet over medium-high

heat. Add the cumin seeds and cook until they sizzle and turn reddish brown, about 5 seconds. Immediately add the onion and stir-fry until the slices are light brown around the edges, 3 to 5 minutes.

4. Add the cilantro-garlic blend and continue to stir-fry until the garlic is lightly browned and the chiles are pungent, about 30 seconds.

5. Toss in the potatoes and eggplant, and stir until they are coated with the seasonings, 1 to 2 minutes. Then add 1 cup water and scrape the pan to deglaze it, releasing the browned bits of onion and garlic. Stir in another 1 cup water, and add the salt. Bring to a boil (which will happen quickly in the hot skillet). Then reduce the heat to medium-low, cover the skillet, and simmer, stirring occasionally, until the vegetables are fall-apart tender and the sauce is glossy and slightly thickened, 20 to 25 minutes. Then serve.

Tips:

❖ Jairam used dried round red chiles, the size of a marble, which he referred to as *gol* (round) *mirchi* (chiles). This is a bit confusing because in many other regions in India, people call black peppercorns *gol mirchi*. The red chiles that Jairam used (which I managed to procure and bring back with me to the United States) are a variety known as Tinnevelly chiles. If you can find them here, by all means use them instead of the Thai or cayenne.

❖ You can certainly submerge the eggplant in the water along with the potatoes if you are concerned about it discoloring. However, when you simmer it in the curry, it will turn blackish purple anyway, so I wouldn't bother if I were you!

❖ If eggplant is not your thing, use yellow squash; the cooking time will be the same.

Braised Potatoes and Eggplant
WITH TOASTED CUMIN

Aloo Baingan

Slowly braising the vegetables in this curry yields a sweetness that is further enhanced by a rather large amount of ground toasted cumin seeds. If you want to balance this sweetness with increased pungency, use more than the four chiles called for. This side dish is great with spicy Yogurt-Marinated Lamb (page 214) and Perfumed Basmati Rice with Black Cardamom Pods (*Kala elaichi pulao,* page 709).
SERVES 8

2 tablespoons canola oil
1 teaspoon cumin seeds
¼ teaspoon ground turmeric
1½ pounds russet or Yukon Gold potatoes, peeled, cut into ½-inch cubes, and submerged in a bowl of cold water to prevent browning
10 small purple Indian (or 1 large Italian) eggplants (about 1¼ pounds total), stems removed, cut into pieces 2 inches long and 1 inch wide
2 to 4 fresh green Thai, cayenne, or serrano chiles, to taste, stems removed, cut crosswise into ¼-inch-thick slices (do not remove the seeds)
1 tablespoon cumin seeds, toasted and ground (see Tip, page 294)
2 teaspoons coarse kosher or sea salt
1 can (14.5 ounces) diced tomatoes
2 tablespoons finely chopped fresh cilantro leaves and tender stems for garnishing

1. Heat the oil in a large saucepan over medium-high heat. Add the cumin seeds and cook until they sizzle, turn reddish brown, and are aromatic, 5 to 10 seconds. Immediately sprinkle the turmeric into the hot oil, followed by the potatoes, eggplant, and chiles.

2. Lower the heat to medium and stir-fry the vegetables to coat them with the spices, 3 to 5 minutes. Pour in ½ cup water and scrape the bottom of the pan to deglaze it, releasing any browned bits of spice and vegetable. Reduce the heat to medium-low, cover the pan, and braise the vegetables, stirring occasionally, until they are fork-tender, about 30 minutes.

3. Add the ground toasted cumin, salt, and tomatoes with their juices. Continue cooking, covered, stirring occasionally, until the sauce is warmed through, 5 to 8 minutes.

4. Sprinkle with the cilantro, and serve.

Half-Moon Potatoes
WITH FENUGREEK GREENS

Aloo Methi Subzi

In this curry, fenugreek leaves take the limelight, breathing their perfumed bitterness into every half-moon slice of the humble potato. Whenever possible, I serve this curry with an unobtrusive-tasting flatbread like roti (page 727) or *poori* (page 725), or even with mellow-tasting Rice with Yogurt and Mustard Seeds (page 710).

SERVES 6

1 pound russet or Yukon Gold potatoes
2 tablespoons canola oil
1 tablespoon cumin seeds
1 teaspoon ground Deggi chiles (see box, page 290);
*   or ½ teaspoon cayenne (ground red pepper)*
*   mixed with ½ teaspoon sweet paprika*
½ teaspoon ground turmeric
¼ teaspoon ground asafetida
1 cup chopped fresh or frozen fenugreek leaves,
*   (thawed if frozen); or ½ cup dried fenugreek leaves,*
*   soaked in a bowl of water and skimmed off before*
*   use (see box, page 473)*
1½ teaspoons coarse kosher or sea salt

1. Peel the potatoes and cut them in half lengthwise. Then slice them crosswise to form ¼-inch-thick half-moons. If you won't be cooking them immediately, submerge the slices in a bowl of cold water and set it aside. When you are ready to use them, drain the potatoes and pat them dry.

2. Heat the oil in a medium-size saucepan over medium-high heat. Add the cumin seeds and cook until they sizzle, turn reddish brown, and smell nutty, 5 to 10 seconds.

3. Remove the pan from heat and sprinkle in the ground chiles, turmeric, and asafetida. (The heat from the oil will be just right to cook the ground spices without burning them.) Quickly add the potatoes and fenugreek (this will stop the spices from starting to burn).

4. Pour in 1 cup water and add the salt. Bring the curry to a boil. Then reduce the heat to medium-low, cover the pan, and simmer, stirring occasionally, until the potatoes are fall-apart tender, 15 to 18 minutes. Then serve.

Stewed Potatoes

WITH TOMATOES AND GARLIC

tamatar bateta

Chock-full of herbs and spices, these thick-sauced potatoes nestle together in a tart tomato blanket. I find this curry particularly appealing when it is served with homemade rotis (page 727); if you don't want to make your own, store-bought whole-wheat tortillas are an acceptable alternative. During the season, add some chunky mangoes to the combination, as many Gujaratis do. Or add some canned mango pulp, imported from India; the pulp made from Alphonso mangoes has a haunting sweetness and no fibers. (That's why my son loves this dinner arrangement.) **SERVES 6**

1 pound russet or Yukon Gold potatoes, peeled,
   cut into ½-inch cubes, and submerged in a
   bowl of cold water to prevent browning
2 tablespoons canola oil
1 teaspoon black or yellow mustard seeds
8 medium-size cloves garlic, thinly sliced
1 teaspoon cumin seeds, ground
1 teaspoon coriander seeds, ground
¼ teaspoon ground asafetida
¼ teaspoon ground turmeric
4 to 6 fresh green Thai, cayenne, or serrano
   chiles, to taste, stems removed, crushed
   (do not remove the seeds)
1 pound tomatoes, cored and cut into
   1-inch cubes

¼ cup finely chopped fresh cilantro leaves
   and tender stems
2 teaspoons white granulated sugar
2 teaspoons coarse kosher or sea salt
12 to 15 medium-size to large fresh curry leaves

1. Drain the potatoes and pat them dry.

2. Heat the oil in a large skillet over medium-high heat. Add the mustard seeds, cover the skillet, and cook until the seeds have stopped popping (not unlike popcorn), about 30 seconds. Add the potatoes, lower the heat to medium, and partially cover the skillet to contain some of the spattering. Cook, stirring occasionally, until the potatoes turn light sunny-brown and are partially cooked, 5 to 8 minutes.

3. Stir in the garlic, cumin, coriander, asafetida, turmeric, and chiles. The heat from the potatoes will be just right to cook the spices without burning them, about 30 seconds.

4. Add all the remaining ingredients and stir once or twice. Reduce the heat to medium-low, cover the skillet, and cook, stirring occasionally, until the potatoes are fork-tender, 15 to 20 minutes. Then serve.

Tip: If your tomatoes are naturally juicy, the curry does not need any added moisture in the form of water. But if you are forced to use those waxy-looking, anemic, winter-season tomatoes that never change firmness or color even after weeks at room temperature, throw in ½ cup water to give the potatoes enough moisture to braise. Another alternative is to use canned chopped tomatoes, with their liquid.

Potatoes and Mustard Greens
WITH GINGER AND GARLIC

Aloo Aur Sarson ka Saag

I love the starchy pieces of potato nestled among the bitter-tasting greens, and find this curry to be a great accompaniment to Wok-Seared Chicken Breasts with a Fennel-Tomato Sauce (page 149). Unless a vegetable curry has legumes in it, I consider it a side dish and match it with a protein-based main course. **SERVES 6**

I pound russet or Yukon Gold potatoes, peeled,
cut into I-inch cubes, and submerged in a
bowl of cold water to prevent browning
2 tablespoons canola oil
4 lengthwise slices fresh ginger (each 2 inches long,
I inch wide, and 1/8 inch thick), finely chopped
4 large cloves garlic, finely chopped
I pound fresh mustard greens, finely chopped
(see Tip, page 606)
2 tablespoons tomato paste
2 teaspoons coarse kosher or sea salt
I teaspoon cayenne (ground red pepper)
I teaspoon Punjabi garam masala (page 25)

1. Drain the potatoes and pat them dry with paper towels.

2. Heat the oil in a large skillet over medium heat. Add the potatoes, ginger, and garlic, and stir-fry until the potatoes are light brown around the edges, 8 to 10 minutes.

3. Add a few handfuls of the mustard greens, cover the skillet, and let the greens wilt in the built-up steam, 3 to 5 minutes. Add the remaining greens, and repeat.

4. Stir in the tomato paste, salt, and cayenne. Pour in 1 cup water to make a thin curry. Cook, covered, over medium-low heat, stirring occasionally, until the potatoes are fork-tender and the sauce has thickened slightly, 18 to 20 minutes.

5. Mix in the garam masala, and serve.

Potato-Onion Curry

Urulikazhangu Vengayam Bhajee

During my childhood in Mumbai, if my mother asked me what curry she should make for the evening meal on a day when she had made those addictive, puffy fried breads called *pooris,* I always answered *"Urulikazhangu vengayam bhajee."* Soon she stopped asking me and automatically made this potato-onion dish each time she made *pooris.* You do the same in your kitchen (tear off a piece of *poori,* scoop up some potato curry with it, and wrap the torn bread around it)—you will see why the combination works so well. (See page 725 for *pooris.*) **SERVES 6**

1 1/2 pounds russet or Yukon Gold potatoes, peeled,
cut into 1/2-inch cubes, and submerged in a
bowl of cold water to prevent browning
I tablespoon canola oil

½ teaspoon fennel seeds

6 whole cloves

2 dried red Thai or cayenne chiles, stems removed

1 cinnamon stick (½-inch long), broken into
    smaller pieces

1 tablespoon coarsely chopped fresh ginger

2 fresh green Thai, cayenne, or serrano chiles,
    stems removed

1 teaspoon black or yellow mustard seeds

1 tablespoon yellow split peas (chana dal),
    picked over for stones

1 medium-size red onion, cut into ½-inch cubes

1½ teaspoons coarse kosher or sea salt

¼ teaspoon ground turmeric

¼ cup finely chopped fresh cilantro leaves and
    tender stems

1. Bring a medium-size (or larger) saucepan of water to a boil over medium-high heat. Drain the potatoes and add them to the boiling water. Bring to a boil again. Then lower the heat to medium and cook, partially covered, until the potatoes are barely cooked, 2 to 4 minutes. (Cut into such small cubes, the potatoes will cook quickly, so be careful not to overcook them.) Reserving 1 cup of the cooking water, drain the potatoes.

2. Preheat a wok over medium-high heat. Add ½ teaspoon of the oil and sprinkle in the fennel seeds, cloves, dried chiles, and cinnamon pieces. Stir-fry until the chiles blacken slightly and the spices are fragrant, about 1 minute. Transfer the roasted mixture to a mortar, and add the ginger and fresh chiles. Using the pestle, pound the mixture and grind it into a fairly smooth paste. (The spices will break down easily because they turn brittle when roasted. I don't recommend using a blender to make this paste because of the small quantity of ingredients.)

3. Reheat the same wok over a medium-high heat. Pour in the remaining 2½ teaspoons oil, and add the mustard seeds. Cover the wok and cook until the seeds have stopped popping (not unlike popcorn), about 30 seconds. Then add the split peas and stir-fry until they turn golden brown, about 30 seconds.

4. Add the onion and the spice-ginger paste and stir-fry until the onion turns golden brown and the mixture smells nutty-pungent, 2 to 3 minutes. Stir in the salt and turmeric. Pour in the reserved potato cooking water, and add the potatoes. Heat to a boil. Then reduce the heat to medium, cover the wok, and cook, stirring occasionally, until the potatoes are fork-tender, about 5 minutes.

5. Coarsely mash the potatoes with the back of a cooking spoon, and fold in the cilantro. Then serve.

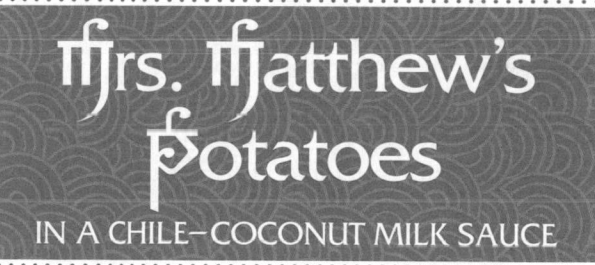

Mrs. Matthew's Potatoes
IN A CHILE–COCONUT MILK SAUCE
ulli tai

Shirley Matthew, a Syrian Christian with roots in Kerala, settled in Bangalore, where she works as (you guessed it) an IT consultant. She works the night shift, solving the problems of callers from the other side of the world in the United States. Juggling a fast-paced job (her husband works in the same company during the day), young children, and their home seems to be the way of life for Shirley and the burgeoning number of young women who labor literally around the clock. Her late-night dinner/breakfast/snack is this potato curry, which she likes to spoon over rice noodles, re-warmed in a microwave. Simple, hearty, and tasty. **SERVES 6**

> *2 tablespoons coconut oil or canola oil*
> *1 medium-size red onion, cut in half lengthwise*
>   *and thinly sliced*
> *1 tablespoon Ginger Chile Paste (page 17)*
> *1 cup unsweetened coconut milk*
> *1½ teaspoons coarse kosher or sea salt*
> *10 to 12 medium-size to large fresh curry leaves*
> *1 pound russet or Yukon Gold potatoes, peeled,*
>   *cut in half lengthwise, and thinly sliced,*
>   *submerged in a bowl of cold water to*
>   *prevent browning*
> *½ cup finely chopped fresh cilantro leaves*
>   *and tender stems*

1. Heat the oil in a large skillet over medium heat. Add the onion and stir-fry until it is dark brown, 10 to 12 minutes.

2. Stir in the Ginger Chile Paste and continue to stir-fry (with adequate ventilation) until the chiles in the paste start to smell pungent, about 1 minute.

3. Pour in the coconut milk, salt, and curry leaves, and stir to deglaze the skillet, releasing any browned bits of onion, ginger, and chiles. The green-and-red-speckled coconut milk will start to boil quickly.

4. Drain the potatoes and add them, stirring once or twice. Cover the skillet, reduce the heat to medium-low, and cook, stirring occasionally, until the potatoes are fork-tender, 10 to 12 minutes.

5. Stir in the cilantro, and serve.

Pan-Roasted Potatoes and Onion
WITH TURMERIC

bhuna Kua Aloo Pyaaz

I have a very discerning palate and am apt to be overly critical of my culinary creations. Nevertheless, every once in a while, I have to admit I surprise myself. This simple curry bowled me over, all because of the simple technique of slow-roasting the potatoes and onion while sweating them at the same time. The crusty layer that forms on the bottom of the pan (which is why a nonstick pan will not work) yields robust, nutty-sweet flavors that are incorporated into the curry when the pan is deglazed. *Mutter kachoris* (page 737)—savory ginger-chile–spiked green peas nestled in flaky fried bread—makes a winning combination. **SERVES 6**

> *1 pound russet or Yukon Gold potatoes, peeled,*
>   *cut into ½-inch cubes, and submerged in a*
>   *bowl of cold water to prevent browning*
> *¼ cup canola oil*
> *1 large red onion, cut into ½-inch cubes*
> *¼ cup finely chopped fresh cilantro leaves*
>   *and tender stems*
> *1½ teaspoons coarse kosher or sea salt*
> *1 teaspoon ground turmeric*
> *1 teaspoon ground Deggi chiles (see box, page 290);*
>   *or ½ teaspoon cayenne (ground red pepper)*
>   *mixed with ½ teaspoon sweet paprika*

1. Drain the potatoes and pat them dry.

2. Heat the oil in a large skillet, or in a wok, over medium heat. Add the potatoes and onion, and stir once or twice. Cover the skillet, and let the vegetables slowly roast and "sweat," stirring them occasionally, until a thin brown layer of crust has formed on the bottom of the skillet and the potatoes are tender (some of the cubes should almost fall apart when pierced), 15 to 20 minutes. If the skillet seems too hot and the crust appears to be burning, lower the heat a notch.

3. Stir in the cilantro, salt, turmeric, and ground chiles. Pour in 1 cup water, and scrape the skillet to release the dark brown layer of onion and potatoes. (Once the water warms, the layer will loosen much faster.) Bring the orange-yellow curry to a boil and cook, uncovered, until it thickens, about 2 minutes. Then serve.

Imperial Potatoes

Moghalai Aloo
Aur Simla Mirch

Moghal emperors, who ruled parts of India just before the British regime, introduced the plump, sweet, sun-yellow raisins known as sultanas, appropriately named after the Sultans. Stir-frying the raisins releases their inherent sugars, making them even sweeter, which provides a sugary balance to the spicy hint of ground red pepper in this curry.

Serve this as a side dish with Yogurt-Marinated Lamb (page 214) and Kabuli *Chana biryani* (page 697). A stack of flame-roasted lentil wafers (*Papads*, page 740) will round out this special menu. **SERVES 6**

2 tablespoons canola oil

I teaspoon cumin seeds

2 black cardamom pods

2 cinnamon sticks (each 3 inches long)

2 fresh or dried bay leaves

I small red onion, cut into I-inch pieces

¼ cup raw cashew nuts

¼ cup golden raisins

I pound russet or Yukon Gold potatoes, peeled, cut into I-inch cubes, and submerged in a bowl of cold water to prevent browning

2 medium-size green or red bell peppers (8 ounces total), stemmed, seeded, and cut into I-inch pieces

2 teaspoons coarse kosher or sea salt

¼ teaspoon ground turmeric

2 tablespoons finely chopped fresh cilantro leaves and tender stems

½ teaspoon Balti masala (page 31)

½ teaspoon cayenne (ground red pepper)

1. Heat the oil in a medium-size saucepan over medium-high heat. Add the cumin seeds, cardamom pods, cinnamon sticks, and bay leaves, and cook until they are fragrant, 10 to 15 seconds.

2. Immediately add the onion, cashews, and raisins, and stir-fry until the onion turns light brown, the nuts are reddish brown, and the raisins swell, 2 to 3 minutes.

3. Drain the potatoes and add them, along with the bell peppers. Pour in 1 cup water, and sprinkle in the salt and turmeric. Bring the curry to a boil. Then reduce the heat to medium-low, cover the pan, and cook, stirring occasionally, until the potatoes are fork-tender, 12 to 15 minutes.

4. Stir in the cilantro, garam masala, and cayenne, and serve.

Tips:

❖ If you wish, remove the cardamom pods, cinnamon sticks, and bay leaves before you serve the curry.

❖ For those who are allergic to any kind of nuts, leave out the cashews. Even though yellow split peas are never used as a flavoring spice or as a nut in northern Indian cooking, you could use them here as an acceptable crunchy alternative.

Savory Cinnamon Potato and Bell Pepper Strips

Urulikazhungu Molagha Bhajee

When someone at the table complains that this curry is spicy-hot, you will know that that person is predisposed to think that all Indian food is hot—because there is nothing in the curry that generates spicy heat. Just shake your head and help yourself to seconds, or better yet, feed it to a young toddler, who will probably savor every morsel. **SERVES 6**

1 pound russet or Yukon Gold potatoes, peeled, cut into French-fry strips (2 inches long and ½ inch thick), and submerged in a bowl of cold water to prevent browning

2 tablespoons plus ½ teaspoon canola oil

1 large green or red bell pepper, stemmed, seeded, and cut into ½-inch-wide strips

12 to 15 medium-size to large fresh curry leaves

1½ teaspoons coarse kosher or sea salt

1 tablespoon skinned split black lentils (cream-colored in this form, urad dal), picked over for stones

1 tablespoon yellow split peas (chana dal), picked over for stones

1 tablespoon coriander seeds

1 cinnamon stick (3 inches long), broken into smaller pieces

Juice of 1 medium-size lime

2 tablespoons finely chopped fresh curry leaves

1. Drain the potatoes and pat them dry with paper towels.

2. Heat the 2 tablespoons oil in a large skillet over medium-high heat. Add the potatoes, bell pepper strips, and whole curry leaves, and stir-fry until the potatoes are lightly browned around the edges, 3 to 5 minutes.

3. Pour in 1 cup water and sprinkle in the salt. Stir once or twice and bring to a boil. Then reduce the heat to medium-low, cover the skillet, and simmer, stirring occasionally, until the potatoes are fork-tender, 10 to 12 minutes.

4. While the vegetables are cooking, drizzle the remaining ½ teaspoon oil into a small skillet and heat it over medium-high heat. Add the lentils, split peas, coriander seeds, and cinnamon pieces and cook, stirring constantly, until they turn reddish brown and smell nutty, 2 to 3 minutes. Transfer the mixture to a plate and let it cool. Once it is cool to the touch, transfer the mixture to a spice grinder and grind until it has the texture of coarsely ground black pepper.

5. When the vegetables are tender, stir in the spice blend and the lime juice.

6. Stir in the chopped curry leaves, and serve.

Nutty Spuds and Bells

besan Aloo Mirchi ki Subzi

Simple ingredients and interesting techniques pack in many flavors in this thick-sauced curry. The roasted chickpea flour not only thickens the sauce but also provides a nutty flavor that tones down the heat from the cayenne pepper. **SERVES 6**

I pound russet or Yukon Gold potatoes, peeled,
   quartered lengthwise, then thinly sliced
   crosswise, and submerged in a bowl of
   cold water to prevent browning
2 tablespoons canola oil
I teaspoon cumin seeds
I large red or green bell pepper, stemmed, seeded,
   and cut into I-inch pieces
2 tablespoons Toasted Chickpea Flour
   (page 41)
1½ teaspoons coarse kosher or sea salt
I teaspoon cayenne (ground red pepper)
2 tablespoons finely chopped fresh cilantro
   leaves and tender stems

1. Drain the potatoes and pat them dry with paper towels.

2. Heat the oil in a large skillet over medium-high heat. Add the cumin seeds and cook until they sizzle, turn reddish brown, and smell nutty, 5 to 10 seconds. Immediately add the potatoes and place a lid on the skillet to contain the spattering. Let the potatoes sweat-fry, covered, stirring occasionally, until the slices are golden brown, slightly crispy, and partially tender, 5 to 8 minutes.

3. Remove the lid and add the bell pepper. Stir-fry until the pepper pieces blister and acquire brown spots, about 5 minutes.

4. Sprinkle the chickpea flour, salt, and cayenne over the vegetables, and stir to incorporate. Add 1 cup water and heat to a boil. Cook, uncovered, stirring occasionally, until the curry thickens nicely, about 2 minutes.

5. Stir in the cilantro, and serve.

Fiery-Tart Potatoes

Aloo toor ki Subzi

You'll find the surprise crunch of roasted coriander seeds appealing, with its short burst of intense, orange-peel-like citrus flavor with sweet undertones. (It seems natural to attribute winelike descriptions to spices, since they possess such layered complexities.) Each bite of the curry sneaks in one of these seeds mingled with starchy potatoes and burning-hot chiles. **SERVES 8**

1 cup oily or unoily skinned split yellow pigeon peas
   (toovar dal), picked over for stones

2 tablespoons mustard oil or canola oil

1 tablespoon coriander seeds

1 medium-size red onion, cut into ¼-inch cubes

4 to 6 fresh green Thai, cayenne, or serrano chiles,
   to taste, stems removed, cut crosswise into ¼-inch-
   thick slices (do not remove the seeds)

1½ pounds russet or Yukon Gold potatoes, peeled,
   cut into 1-inch cubes, and submerged in a bowl of
   cold water to prevent browning

2 tablespoons finely chopped fresh cilantro leaves and
   tender stems

2 teaspoons ground Deggi chiles (see box, page 290);
   or 1 teaspoon cayenne (ground red pepper) mixed
   with 1 teaspoon sweet paprika

2 teaspoons coarse kosher or sea salt

1 teaspoon ground turmeric

1 teaspoon tamarind paste or concentrate

1. Place the pigeon peas in a small saucepan. Fill the pan halfway with tap water and rinse the peas by rubbing them between your fingertips. The water will become cloudy. Drain this water. Repeat three or four times, until the water remains relatively clear; drain. Now add 2 cups water and bring it to a boil, uncovered, over medium-high heat. Skim off and discard any foam that rises to the surface. Reduce the heat to medium-low, cover the pan, and simmer, stirring occasionally, until the pigeon peas are tender, about 20 minutes.

2. While the pigeon peas are cooking, heat the oil in a large saucepan over medium-high heat. Add the coriander seeds and cook until they sizzle, turn reddish brown, and smell slightly citrusy with nutty undertones, 10 to 15 seconds. Quickly add the onion and fresh chiles, and stir-fry until the onion turns light brown around the edges and the chiles are pungent, 5 to 8 minutes.

3. Meanwhile, drain the potatoes.

4. Stir the potatoes, cilantro, ground chiles, salt, and turmeric into the onion mixture. Lower the heat to medium, cover the pan, and cook gently, stirring occasionally, until the potatoes are lightly browned, 15 to 20 minutes.

5. When the pigeon peas are tender, transfer them, with their cooking water, to a blender jar. Add the tamarind paste. Puree, scraping the inside of the jar as needed, until smooth. (If you have an immersion blender, you can puree the peas, water, and tamarind right in the saucepan.)

6. Pour the puree into the potato mixture. Stir, cover the pan, and stew, stirring occasionally, until the potatoes are fork-tender, 8 to 10 minutes. Then serve.

Thunky Potatoes
WITH SPINACH

Aloo Palak

When time is of the essence, this thick-sauced curry is a cinch to make. It is a great side dish with Lamb with Yellow Split Peas (page 197). If you like, serve some cooked rice and avocado chutney (page 748) alongside. **SERVES 6**

2 tablespoons canola oil

1 teaspoon black or yellow mustard seeds

1 tablespoon cumin seeds

½ teaspoon ground turmeric

1 pound russet or Yukon Gold potatoes, peeled,
   cut into 1-inch cubes, and submerged in a
   bowl of cold water to prevent browning

2 teaspoons coarse kosher or sea salt

8 ounces fresh spinach leaves, well rinsed
   and coarsely chopped

1 cup shredded fresh coconut; or ½ cup shredded
   dried unsweetened coconut, reconstituted
   (see Note)

8 to 10 fresh green Thai, cayenne, or serrano
   chiles, to taste, stems removed, cut crosswise
   into ¼-inch-thick slices (do not remove
   the seeds)

10 medium-size to large fresh curry leaves

1. Heat the oil in a large saucepan over medium-high heat. Add the mustard seeds, cover the pan, and cook until the seeds have stopped popping (not unlike popcorn), about 30 seconds. Sprinkle in the cumin seeds and cook until they sizzle and turn reddish brown, about 5 seconds. Add the turmeric, which will immediately turn the oil yellow. Then pour in 1 cup water, which will instantly boil because of the hot pan.

2. Drain the potatoes, and add them to the pan along with the salt. Reduce the heat to medium-low, cover the pan, and simmer, stirring occasionally, until the potatoes are fork-tender, 8 to 10 minutes.

3. Pile the spinach into the pan, cover it, and let the spinach wilt, about 2 minutes. Then add the coconut, chiles, and curry leaves. Stir, and continue to simmer, covered, until the sauce is warmed through, 3 to 5 minutes. Then serve.

Note: To reconstitute coconut, cover with ½ cup boiling water, set aside for about 15 minutes, and then drain.

Spicy Potatoes and Spinach
WITH BLACKENED CHILES AND COCONUT MILK

Ulli Ishto

When I put together a recipe, I try to incorporate not only compatible flavors but also attuned colors. Food should appeal to all your senses to make it memorable. In addition, if it is ready in under 30 minutes, it will add to your satisfaction. This curry delivers all that—and with potatoes to boot, which have to be one of the world's favorite tubers (in my "potatoholic" opinion). Serve this over rice noodles (*Idiappam*, page 723) for a delicious carbohydrate overload. **SERVES 4**

1 pound russet or Yukon Gold potatoes, peeled,
   cut into ½-inch cubes, and submerged in a
   bowl of cold water to prevent browning

2 tablespoons canola oil

1 tablespoon Panch phoron
   (page 36)

3 dried red Thai or cayenne chiles,
   stems removed

1½ teaspoons coarse kosher or sea salt

½ teaspoon ground turmeric

1 cup unsweetened coconut milk

8 ounces fresh spinach leaves, well rinsed
   and coarsely chopped

1. Drain the potatoes.

2. Heat the oil in a large skillet over medium-high heat. Sprinkle in the *Panch phoron* and cook until it sizzles and is aromatic, 10 to 15 seconds. Add the chiles and stir-fry until they blacken and are highly pungent, 10 to 15 seconds. Immediately add the potatoes and cover the pan briefly. (The water clinging to the potatoes will make the hot oil spatter upon contact, so the lid helps contain the spattering.) Remove the lid once the din subsides, and stir the potatoes once or twice. Then cover the skillet again, reduce the heat to medium, and cook, stirring occasionally, until the potatoes are partially cooked, about 5 minutes.

3. Stir in the salt and turmeric. Pour in the coconut milk, and stir to deglaze the skillet, releasing any collected browned bits of spice and vegetable. Heat to a boil. Then reduce the heat to medium-low, cover the skillet, and cook, stirring occasionally, until the potatoes are fork-tender, 12 to 15 minutes.

4. Pile in the spinach and cover the skillet. Cook until the steam has wilted the leaves, about 2 minutes.

5. Stir the curry once or twice to incorporate the wilted greens, and serve.

Tips:

❖ Dried red chiles are hot, but to a southerner, not hot enough. So to make this dish more pungent, they blacken the chiles in hot oil to sharpen their potency.

❖ The coconut milk acts as a mellow, sweet, creamy base for the potatoes. Cans of light (as in reduced-fat) coconut milk are now widely available in supermarkets, and are a perfectly acceptable alternative to the full-fat variety.

New Potatoes and Spinach
IN A GARLIC–RED CHILE SAUCE

Lasoon batata palak

It's amazing how you can take one ingredient, a chile, and extract so many levels of heat from it. Use it whole and unbroken: experience a wispy level of heat. Roast it to blacken the skin: watch its pungency creep up the heat scale. Coarsely chop it and then blacken it: break into a subtle sweat. The sweat-breaking version heats the curry here, but the starchy potatoes tone it down to make for a pleasant balance. **SERVES 8**

Jaggery? See the Glossary of Ingredients, page 758.

2 tablespoons canola oil

1 teaspoon cumin seeds

6 medium-size cloves garlic, finely chopped

6 dried red Thai or cayenne chiles, stems removed, coarsely chopped (do not remove the seeds)

¼ teaspoon ground turmeric

1 pound baby new potatoes, scrubbed and sliced in half

1 large tomato, cored and cut into 1-inch pieces

¼ cup finely chopped fresh cilantro leaves and tender stems

1 tablespoon crumbled (or chopped) jaggery or firmly packed dark brown sugar

1½ teaspoons coarse kosher or sea salt

8 ounces fresh spinach leaves, well rinsed and coarsely chopped

1. Heat the oil in a medium-size saucepan over medium-high heat. Add the cumin seeds and cook until they turn reddish brown and smell nutty, 5 to 10

seconds. Immediately throw in the garlic and chiles. Stir-fry until the garlic turns honey-brown and the chiles blacken, about 1 minute.

2. Sprinkle in the turmeric, and carefully pour in 1 cup water. Stir to deglaze the pan, releasing any browned bits of garlic. Add the potatoes, tomato, cilantro, jaggery, and salt. Stir once or twice, and heat to a boil. Then reduce the heat to medium-low, cover the pan, and simmer, stirring occasionally, until the potatoes are fall-apart tender, 20 to 25 minutes.

3. Add the spinach, a couple of handfuls at a time, stirring until wilted (about 1 minute per batch). Then serve.

Tip: If baby potatoes are not in season, use white or yellow-skin potatoes and cut them into 1½- to 2-inch chunks. The cooking time should be the same as the baby ones if the sizes are comparable.

Cumin-Scented Potatoes
WITH TOMATOES

Shurma Aloo

f Iranian origin, *ghurmas* are thick-sauced, long-simmered stews, spiked with dry herbs and thickened with vegetables. My close friend R. J. Singh, more affectionately called Molu, remembers this particular curry from his days at boarding school, where there was a cook of Iranian ancestry.

Serve this curry with a stack of *Malabar paranthas* (page 731) and a bowl of Peanuts and Yellow Split Peas with Spinach (page 457). **SERVES 6**

> 1½ pounds russet or Yukon Gold potatoes, peeled, cut into ½-inch cubes, and submerged in a bowl of cold water to prevent browning
> 2 tablespoons canola oil
> 1 tablespoon cumin seeds
> 1 small red onion, cut in half lengthwise and then into ½-inch cubes
> 1 teaspoon ground turmeric
> 2 teaspoons coarse kosher or sea salt
> 1 teaspoon cayenne (ground red pepper)
> 1 medium-size tomato, cored and cut into 1-inch cubes
> 2 tablespoons finely chopped fresh cilantro leaves and tender stems

1. Drain the potatoes and pat them dry.

2. Heat the oil in a medium-size saucepan over medium-high heat. Add the cumin seeds and cook until they sizzle, turn reddish brown, and are fragrant, 5 to 10 seconds. Add the potatoes, onion, and turmeric, and stir-fry until the potatoes and onion are lightly browned around the edges, 4 to 6 minutes.

3. Sprinkle in the salt and cayenne, and stir once or twice. Pour in 1 cup water and bring to a boil. Reduce the heat to medium-low, cover the pan, and cook, stirring occasionally, until the potatoes are almost fall-apart tender, 18 to 20 minutes.

4. Stir in the tomato and cilantro, and cover the pan. Simmer, stirring occasionally, until the tomato is warmed through, about 2 minutes. Then serve.

Tip: For a thicker sauce, coarsely mash some of the potato cubes.

Chile-Spiked Potatoes
WITH TURNIP GREENS

Aloo Shalgam ka Saag

turnip greens are usually found in the supermarket in late fall or early winter. These giant green leaves are slightly bitter but are a rich source of essential nutrients. The greens are never eaten raw. Braised, they turn buttery-smooth with a slight hint of pleasant bitterness. The turnips themselves are delicious sliced, diced, and cubed in savory stews like Tender Braised Lamb with Turnips (page 198). The more available mustard or collard greens are excellent alternatives for turnip greens. **SERVES 6**

> *1 pound russet or Yukon Gold potatoes, peeled,*
> *cut into ½-inch cubes, and submerged in a*
> *bowl of cold water to prevent browning*
> *2 tablespoons canola oil*
> *4 to 6 dried red Thai or cayenne chiles, to taste,*
> *stems removed*
> *1 pound fresh turnip greens, rinsed and cut into*
> *thin strips (chiffonade; see Tips)*
> *1 bunch (6 to 8) scallions (green tops and*
> *white bulbs), finely chopped*
> *1 teaspoon coarse kosher or sea salt*
> *½ teaspoon Bangala garam masala*
> *(page 26)*
> *½ teaspoon cayenne (ground red pepper)*

1. Drain the potatoes and pat them dry with paper towels.

2. Heat the oil in a wok or a large saucepan over medium-high heat. Add the potatoes and chiles, and stir-fry until they are lightly browned, about 5 minutes.

3. Pile the turnip greens, with some of the rinse water still clinging to them, atop the potatoes. Stir once or twice, cover, and cook, stirring occasionally, until most of the liquid released from the greens has been absorbed and the potatoes are fork-tender, 10 to 12 minutes.

4. Add the scallions, salt, garam masala, and cayenne, and stir once or twice.

5. Pour in ½ cup water and simmer the curry, uncovered, stirring occasionally, until the sauce is warmed through, about 2 minutes. Then serve.

Tips:

❖ To prepare turnip greens for cooking, cut out and discard the tough rib that runs through three-quarters the length of each leaf. Stack 2 or 3 similar-length leaves and roll them tightly into a tube shape. Cut the tube into thin slices, unfold them to yield ribbons (called a chiffonade), and place them in a large bowl. Once they are all sliced, cover them with cold water. Briefly dunk the leaves under the water. Grab fistfuls of the leaves and gently lift them, letting any sand or grit sink to the bottom. Repeat once or twice to ensure that the leaves are completely clean and grit-free.

❖ If you are looking for a low-carbohydrate option, try cubes of the lightly browned creamy cheese called *Malai paneer* (page 287) as an alternative to the potatoes.

Double the Potatoes

WITH CUMIN AND CHILES

Zeera Waale Aloo Aur Rataloo ki Subzi

I f you savor flavor differences, then you will love the effect of the hot ground chiles against the smooth, bland backdrop of white and sugary sweet potatoes. Opposites attract and can have a harmonious balance—you'll see. **SERVES 4**

> 2 medium-size russet or Yukon Gold potatoes,
>   peeled, cut into 1-inch cubes, and submerged
>   in a bowl of cold water to prevent browning
> 1 large sweet potato, peeled, cut into 1-inch
>   cubes, and submerged in a bowl of cold
>   water to prevent browning
> 2 tablespoons canola oil
> 1 tablespoon cumin seeds
> 1½ teaspoons coarse kosher or sea salt
> 1 teaspoon ground Deggi chiles (see box, page 290);
>   or ½ teaspoon cayenne (ground red pepper)
>   mixed with ½ teaspoon sweet paprika
> ¼ cup finely chopped fresh cilantro leaves
>   and tender stems

1. Drain the white potatoes and the sweet potato, and pat them dry with paper towels.

2. Heat the oil in a large skillet over medium-high heat. Add the cumin seeds and cook until they sizzle, turn reddish brown, and smell nutty, 5 to 10 seconds. Immediately add the white and sweet potatoes and cook, stirring occasionally, until they turn light brown around the edges, about 5 minutes.

3. Sprinkle the salt and the ground chiles over the potatoes, and stir them in. Cook the spices without burning them, about 30 seconds. Then add 1 cup water and stir to deglaze the skillet, releasing the collected bits of spice and vegetable. Reduce the heat to medium-low, cover the skillet, and simmer, stirring occasionally, until the vegetables are fork-tender, 8 to 10 minutes.

4. Uncover the skillet, raise the heat to medium, and cook, stirring occasionally, until the sauce thickens, about 5 minutes (some of the potato cubes will break down, helping to thicken the sauce).

5. Stir the cilantro into the lush orange-red curry, and serve.

Whites & Sweets

WITH PEAS

Shakarai Urulikazhangu Kari

F ault me for being one of those people who would much rather help myself to a savory second helping than to a sweet one. So it took me a few years to learn to love sweet potatoes—until my mother fried them and tossed them with cayenne pepper and pounded rock salt. Then I became an addict. No wonder this curry calls to me: it's sweet, hot, and nutty. Ladle it into bowls and serve it alongside multi-lentil pancakes (page 724). **SERVES 6**

2 medium-size russet or Yukon Gold potatoes, peeled,
cut into 1-inch cubes, and submerged in a bowl of
cold water to prevent browning
1 large sweet potato, peeled, cut into 1-inch cubes,
and submerged in a bowl of cold water to prevent
browning
2 tablespoons sesame oil or canola oil
1 teaspoon black or yellow mustard seeds
1 tablespoon skinned split black lentils (cream-colored
in this form, urad dal), picked over for stones
2 tablespoons finely chopped fresh cilantro
leaves and tender stems
12 to 15 medium-size to large fresh curry leaves
2 fresh green Thai, cayenne, or serrano chiles,
stems removed, cut in half lengthwise
(do not remove the seeds)
1 cup frozen green peas, thawed
1½ teaspoons coarse kosher or sea salt

1. Drain the white and sweet potatoes. Combine them in a large saucepan, add 3 cups water, and bring to a boil over medium-high heat. Lower the heat to medium and simmer vigorously, uncovered, stirring once in a great while, until the potatoes are tender but still firm-looking, 8 to 10 minutes. Reserving 1 cup of the cooking water, drain the potatoes in a colander.

2. Dry the saucepan with paper towels, and add the oil. Heat it over medium-high heat. Add the mustard seeds, cover the pan, and cook until the seeds have stopped popping (not unlike popcorn), about 30 seconds. Add the lentils and stir-fry until they turn golden brown, 15 to 20 seconds.

3. Throw in the cilantro, curry leaves, and chiles, and allow them to spatter in the smoking-hot oil. Immediately add the potatoes, reserved cooking water, peas, and salt. Bring to a boil. Then reduce the heat to medium and simmer, uncovered, stirring occasionally, until the sauce has thickened slightly, 4 to 6 minutes. Then serve.

A Potato Mix
WITH A
CRACKED PEPPERCORN SAUCE

Molaghu Urulikazhangu Bhajee

because I use such highly starchy ingredients as white potato and sweet potato in this curry, I can afford the heat from ground Kashmiri chiles and black peppercorns. (On a recent trip to Kerala, I brought back vibrantly potent Malabar peppercorns. I admit I find it hard to share them with friends, for fear of depleting my stock.) I enjoy the burst of pungent heat, like a slap in the face, when I occasionally bite into the coarsely pounded peppercorns. Wrap morsels of tortilla-thin rotis (page 727) around this curry for a simply great lunch. **SERVES 6**

3 medium-size russet or Yukon Gold potatoes,
peeled, cut into ½-inch cubes, and submerged
in a bowl of cold water to prevent browning
1 medium-size sweet potato, peeled, cut into
½-inch cubes, and submerged in a bowl
of cold water to prevent browning
1½ teaspoons rock salt
1 teaspoon black peppercorns
¼ teaspoon whole cloves
¼ teaspoon cardamom seeds from green
or white pods
1 cinnamon stick (3 inches long), broken
into pieces
1 teaspoon ground Kashmiri chiles;
or ¼ teaspoon cayenne (ground red pepper)
mixed with ¾ teaspoon sweet paprika
2 tablespoons canola oil

1 teaspoon black or yellow mustard seeds

12 grape tomatoes, sliced in half; or 1 medium-size
   tomato, cored and cut into 1-inch pieces

12 to 15 medium-size to large fresh curry leaves

2 tablespoons finely chopped fresh cilantro leaves
   and tender stems

1. Place both varieties of potato in a medium-size saucepan, add 3 cups water, and bring to a boil over medium-high heat. Lower the heat to medium and simmer vigorously, uncovered, stirring once in a great while, until the potatoes are tender but still firm-looking, 8 to 10 minutes.

2. While the potatoes are cooking, combine the rock salt, peppercorns, cloves, cardamom seeds, and cinnamon pieces in a mortar. Pound with the pestle until the texture resembles coarse sawdust. Stir in the ground chiles.

3. Reserving ½ cup of the cooking water, drain the potatoes.

4. Dry out the saucepan, add the oil, and heat it over medium-high heat. Add the mustard seeds, cover the pan, and cook until the seeds have stopped popping (not unlike popcorn), about 30 seconds. Then throw in the tomatoes, curry leaves, and the spice mixture, and stir once or twice. Cook, uncovered, stirring occasionally, until the tomatoes have softened but are still firm-looking, 2 to 4 minutes.

5. Pour in the reserved cooking water and scrape the bottom of the pan to deglaze it, releasing any browned bits. Add the potatoes and stir once or twice. Simmer until the potatoes are warmed through, 2 to 4 minutes.

6. Stir in the cilantro, and serve.

Rock salt? See the Glossary of Ingredients, page 758.

White Pumpkin

WITH COCONUT, CHILES, AND CURRY LEAVES

Parangikai Curry

Lush yellow and green-flecked, this curry blankets succulent bits of white pumpkin that squirt little bursts of juice with each bite. The fresh coconut is an added bonus and provides a soothing bed for the potent chiles.

SERVES 6

1 cup shredded fresh coconut; or ½ cup shredded
   dried unsweetened coconut, reconstituted
   (see Note)

2 fresh green Thai, cayenne, or serrano chiles,
   stems removed

2 tablespoons unrefined sesame oil
   or canola oil

1 teaspoon black or yellow mustard seeds

1½ pounds white pumpkin, peeled, seeded,
   and cut into 1-inch cubes
   (see box, page 586)

¼ teaspoon ground turmeric

2 tablespoons finely chopped fresh cilantro
   leaves and tender stems

1 teaspoon coarse kosher or sea salt

10 medium-size to large fresh curry leaves

1. Pour 1 cup water into a blender jar, and add the coconut and chiles. Puree, scraping the inside of the jar as needed, to make a slightly gritty green-speckled paste.

2. Heat the oil in a medium-size skillet over medium-high heat. Add the mustard seeds, cover the skillet, and cook until the seeds have stopped popping (not unlike popcorn), about 30 seconds. Immediately add the pumpkin and turmeric, and stir-fry to coat the pieces evenly with the yellow spice and the mustard-seed–spiked oil, about 1 minute.

3. Add the coconut-chile paste, making sure you get every spicy bit from the blender jar. Stir in the cilantro, salt, and curry leaves. Heat to a boil. Then reduce the heat to medium-low, cover the skillet, and stew the pumpkin, stirring occasionally, until it is fork-tender, 12 to 15 minutes. Then serve.

Note: To reconstitute coconut, cover with ½ cup boiling water, set aside for about 15 minutes, and then drain.

white pumpkin

❖ ❖ ❖

White pumpkin, called *parangikai* in Tamil, "ash gourd" or "winter melon" in English, is available in Indian grocery stores; look for wedges wrapped in plastic wrap in the refrigerated section. The whole vegetable is large, rather like a gargantuan watermelon, with a light green exterior and the firm off-white or pale green flesh with numerous flat seeds entrapped in the weblike spongy pulp. Remove the tough skin with a chef's knife—a swivel peeler may not be strong enough to cut through the winter skin. A good substitute for white pumpkin is the light green inner rind of watermelon.

Radishes and Greens
WITH
GINGER AND GARLIC

Mooli ka Saag

Radishes used in India are the variety known as daikon—white, long, slender, with a slightly pungent bite, reminiscent of horseradish. The radish greens too have an edge of bitterness to them, and when they all come together with a bit of sugar and some aromatic spices, you can understand why this nutritionally sound curry is considered a treat by the Punjabi community. (In this country it's easier to find red radishes with their greens still on—the daikon are usually trimmed—so that's what I have suggested here.) This is a great side dish with any of the lamb curries in the book; its assertive flavors stand up to lamb's gamey flavor. **SERVES 4**

2 bunches red radishes with their green tops (about 1 pound total)
2 tablespoons canola oil
1 teaspoon cumin seeds
4 medium-size cloves garlic, finely chopped
2 lengthwise slices fresh ginger (each 2 inches long, 1 inch wide, and ⅛ inch thick), finely chopped
1 teaspoon coarse kosher or sea salt
1 teaspoon Punjabi garam masala (page 25)
½ teaspoon white granulated sugar

1. Separate the green tops from the radishes. Trim off and discard the root end of the radishes, and wash them thoroughly under cold water. Cut them in half, either lengthwise or crosswise (to create about 1-inch pieces).

2. To clean the green tops, tear the leaves off their tough stems. Fill a bowl with cold water, and submerge the leaves in it. Give the leaves a good shake in the water. They are usually very gritty, and the grit and mud will sink to the bottom of the bowl. Scoop the leaves out and transfer them to a colander. Dump out the dirty water, rinsing the bowl to wash out the grit. Fill it with cold tap water again, and repeat the dunking of the leaves. Repeat once or twice more to eliminate every grain of dirt—a cumbersome process for which you will thank yourself when you eat the greens without the crunch of gritty grime. Once they are completely washed, finely chop the greens and set them aside in a small bowl.

3. Heat the oil in a medium-size skillet or saucepan over medium-high heat. Add the cumin seeds and cook until they sizzle, turn reddish brown, and smell nutty, 5 to 10 seconds. Add the garlic and ginger, and stir-fry until the mixture is light brown, 1 to 2 minutes.

4. Dump in the radish halves. Lower the heat to medium and stir-fry for 1 to 2 minutes. Then simmer, uncovered, stirring occasionally, until the radishes release a bit of their liquid, 3 to 5 minutes.

5. Pile in the greens and add 1 cup water, the salt, and the garam masala and sugar. Heat the curry to a boil. Then cover the pan and simmer, stirring occasionally, until the radishes are fork-tender, 15 to 20 minutes. Then serve.

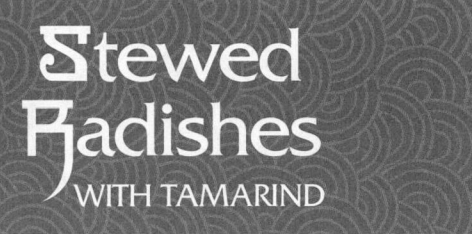

Stewed Radishes
WITH TAMARIND

imli Waale Mooli

Pretty in pink, and no, it's not the movie. It's this sensuous-looking curry, chock-full of slightly bitter flavor made sweet by a hint of sugar and finished off with tart tamarind—just a touch. I have seen bunches of Easter egg-colored radishes at the supermarket; use them to make a rainbow-splashed curry (the flavors will be the same). Don't discard the green radish tops: cooked with garlic, onions, and a splash of lime juice, they make a great stew. **SERVES 6**

> 2 tablespoons canola oil
>
> 6 whole cloves
>
> 2 to 4 dried red Thai or cayenne chiles, to taste, stems removed
>
> 2 cinnamon sticks (each 3 inches long)
>
> 10 to 12 medium-size red radishes, ends trimmed, cut in half lengthwise
>
> 1 teaspoon white granulated sugar
>
> 1 teaspoon coarse kosher or sea salt
>
> ½ teaspoon tamarind paste or concentrate

1. Heat the oil in a medium-size saucepan over medium-high heat. Sprinkle in the cloves, chiles, and cinnamon sticks, and cook until they sizzle and smell sweet-hot, 10 to 20 seconds. Immediately add the radishes.

2. Lower the heat to medium and stir-fry the radishes for 1 to 2 minutes. Then cover the pan and simmer, stirring occasionally, until the radishes are fork-tender, 15 to 20 minutes (they will release their liquid and then stew in its juices).

3. Stir in the sugar, salt, and tamarind paste. Simmer, uncovered, stirring occasionally, to allow the added flavors to mingle, 3 to 5 minutes.

4. Remove the cloves, chiles, and cinnamon sticks if you wish, and serve.

Stewed Shallots
WITH TAMARIND AND CHILES

Chinnay Vengayam Goshtu

this shallot *goshtu* (*gotsu* in other parts of southern India) was a presence at our Sunday brunch table during my childhood days in Mumbai. Its regular accompaniment, my favorite *Uppama* (page 722)—spiced Cream of Wheat with green peas—provided a mellow base for the surprisingly sweet-tart-hot shallot stew. Slow-cooking the shallots is the secret to infusing the curry with their natural sweetness. The acidic tamarind reduces the effect of the capsaicin from all those potent dried chiles. **SERVES 4**

*1 teaspoon plus 2 tablespoons unrefined
    sesame oil or canola oil*
2 teaspoons coriander seeds
1 teaspoon fenugreek seeds
*6 dried red Thai or cayenne chiles,
    stems removed*
1 teaspoon black or yellow mustard seeds
⅛ teaspoon ground asafetida

2 cups thinly sliced shallots
8 to 10 medium-size to large fresh curry leaves
1 teaspoon tamarind paste or concentrate
1 teaspoon coarse kosher or sea salt

1. Heat the 1 teaspoon oil in a small saucepan over medium-high heat. Sprinkle in the coriander seeds, fenugreek seeds, and chiles, and roast, stirring constantly, until the chiles blacken and the seeds turn reddish brown, 1 to 2 minutes. Transfer the mixture to a mortar and pound it with a pestle to form a slightly coarse blend. (Alternatively, transfer the mixture to a plate to cool. Once it is cool to the touch, put the mixture in a spice grinder and pulverize until the texture resembles that of coarsely ground black pepper.)

2. Heat the remaining 2 tablespoons oil in the same saucepan over medium-high heat. Add the mustard seeds, cover the pan, and cook until the seeds have stopped popping (not unlike popcorn), about 30 seconds. Sprinkle in the asafetida, which will instantly sizzle. Reduce the heat to medium-low and immediately add the shallots and the curry leaves. Stir-fry until the shallots soften and turn light brown around the edges, about 20 minutes.

3. While the shallots are cooking, whisk the tamarind paste into 1 cup water.

4. As soon as the shallots are ready, pour the tamarind liquid into the pan. Add the pounded spices and the salt.

5. Raise the heat to medium-high and cook, uncovered, stirring occasionally, until some of the liquid has been absorbed and the curry is slightly thickened, 3 to 5 minutes. Then serve.

Tip: Red onions make a great alternative to the shallots. If you use red onions, add 1 garlic clove, finely chopped, when you add the onions for that shallotlike flavor.

Stewed Spinach
WITH COCONUT, CHILES, AND CURRY LEAVES

keerai masiyal

When my mother prepared this curry, she bought numerous bunches of spinach from the vegetable vendor, who sold them from his pushcart. She would plunk them on large pieces of old newspaper, and proceed to pull the tender leaves from their thick stems while the dirt collected on the paper. Then she repeatedly dunked the leaves in a large bowl of water, letting any remaining dirt sink to the bottom. Soon the greens, stewed with chile-spiced coconut, were spooned into bowls set on dinner plates, where they waited for handkerchief-thin rotis (page 727) to engulf them and point them toward our eager mouths. **SERVES 6**

I pound fresh spinach leaves, well rinsed

I cup shredded fresh coconut; or ½ cup shredded dried unsweetned coconut, reconstituted (see Note)

¼ cup medium-size to large fresh curry leaves

4 dried red Thai or cayenne chiles, stems removed

2 tablespoons Ghee (page 21) or canola oil

I teaspoon black or yellow mustard seeds

I tablespoon skinned split black lentils (cream-colored in this form, urad dal), picked over for stones

I teaspoon coarse kosher or sea salt

1. Bring a large pot of water to a vigorous boil over medium-high heat. Grab handfuls of the spinach leaves and dump them into the boiling water, stirring until they wilt, 3 to 5 minutes. Repeat until all the spinach has wilted in the water. Then, reserving ½ cup of the cooking water, drain the (wimpy-looking) leaves in a colander. Run cold water through them to shock them, so they retain their bright green color. Transfer the spinach to a cutting board and chop it fine. Don't worry about squeezing all the excess water from the spinach.

2. Pour the reserved cooking water into a blender jar and add the coconut, curry leaves, and 2 of the chiles. Puree, scraping the inside of the jar as needed, to make a paste the color of Christmas—very light green with flecks of red.

3. Heat the ghee in a small skillet over medium-high heat. Add the mustard seeds, cover the skillet, and cook until the seeds have stopped popping (not unlike popcorn), about 30 seconds. Add the lentils and the remaining 2 chiles, and stir-fry until the lentils turn golden brown and the chiles blacken, 15 to 20 seconds.

4. Immediately add the spinach, including any water from the greens. Add the salt and the coconut paste. As soon as the mixture starts to boil, lower the heat to medium, cover the skillet, and simmer vigorously, stirring occasionally, to allow the spinach to stew in the coconut paste, absorbing its sweet-hot flavors, about 10 minutes. Then serve.

Note: To reconstitute coconut, cover with ½ cup boiling water, set aside for about 15 minutes, and then drain.

Perfumed Spinach
WITH FRESH DILL

Palak Suva

Sindhis from the northwestern region of India, hugging the Pakistan border, devour combinations of field greens and fresh dill. Spinach and mustard, radish, and kohlrabi greens are all fair game, with fresh dill being the steadfast flavoring. Dill seeds spice up many of their curries, but the fresh herb plays a role as crucial as the other greens, to provide not only flavor but also nutrition, especially when used in large quantities. India's ancient ayurvedic medicine holds that fresh dill aids in digestion, sleep, eliminating halitosis, calming cranky babies, and growing healthy nails. No wonder the Sindhis imbibe this herb and its seeds by the kilo! **SERVES 6**

2 tablespoons canola oil
2 teaspoons cumin seeds
2½ pounds fresh spinach leaves, well rinsed
1½ teaspoons coarse kosher or sea salt
1 teaspoon ground Deggi chiles (see box, page 290); or ½ teaspoon cayenne (ground red pepper) mixed with ½ teaspoon sweet paprika
½ teaspoon Kashmiri garam masala (page 29)
1 cup chopped fresh dill

1. Heat the oil in a large saucepan over medium-high heat. Add the cumin seeds and cook until they sizzle, turn reddish brown, and smell nutty, 5 to 10 seconds. Immediately grab handfuls of the spinach and stir it in as the heat wilts the leaves. Repeat until all the spinach has wilted.

2. Stir in the salt, ground chiles, and garam masala. Reduce the heat to medium and continue to stew the spinach in its own juices, uncovered, stirring occasionally, until the leaves break down and become pulpy, 10 to 15 minutes.

3. Stir in the dill, and serve.

Creamy Spinach and Fenugreek Leaves
WITH PINE NUTS

Chilgozae Waale Palak Aur Methi Saag

Pine-nut-studded greens sounds too good to be true, but it is both delicious and real. Fenugreek leaves play a significant role here in providing great flavor, with a slight bitterness, and a perfumed aroma. In this particular recipe, dried fenugreek leaves are not comparable to fresh or frozen ones—that's why I did not recommend that as an alternative. If you wish, you can use mustard, collard, or kale greens as a passable alternative to the fenugreek. **SERVES 6**

1 pound fresh fenugreek leaves, rinsed, blanched in hot water until wilted, and chopped; or 1 pound frozen chopped fenugreek leaves, thawed (no need to drain)
1 pound fresh spinach leaves, rinsed, blanched in hot water until wilted, and chopped; or 1 pound frozen chopped spinach leaves, thawed (no need to drain)

2 tablespoons mustard oil or canola oil

1 small red onion, cut in half lengthwise and thinly sliced

4 medium-size cloves garlic, cut into thin slivers

¼ cup raw pine nuts

2 teaspoons ground Kashmiri chiles; or ½ teaspoon
   cayenne (ground red pepper) mixed with
   1½ teaspoons sweet paprika

1 teaspoon coarse kosher or sea salt

½ teaspoon Kashmiri garam masala (page 29)

½ cup heavy (whipping) cream

1. Grab handfuls of the chopped fenugreek and spinach greens and squeeze them tightly between the palms of your hands over a 2-cup measuring cup. You should have at least 1½ cups liquid; if not, add enough water to bring it up to the correct measure.

2. Heat the oil in a medium-size saucepan over medium-low heat. Add the onion, garlic, and pine nuts, and stir once or twice. Cover the pan and cook until the onion is browned to a caramel color with a deep purple hue, 18 to 20 minutes. (The onion will sweat first, and then brown after the moisture evaporates.)

3. Add the greens, ground chiles, salt, and garam masala. Stir-fry to gently cook the spices without burning them, about 5 minutes.

4. Pour in the reserved liquid and bring the curry to a boil. Then reduce the heat, cover the pan, and simmer, stirring occasionally, until the greens are soft, about 15 minutes.

5. Stir in the cream and cook, uncovered, stirring occasionally, until it is warmed through, 3 to 5 minutes. Then serve.

Tip: The Indian chilgoza pine is one of 115 varieties of pine around the world. The nuts from this evergreen tree's cones are rich in carbohydrates and proteins. The tree is prolific in the mountainous northwestern Himalayan regions of Himachal Pradesh, Pakistan, and Afghanistan. The pine nuts available in this country will do just fine for this recipe, so you don't have to trek to the Himalayas for your stash of Indian chilgoza. But on the other hand, if I insisted that you have to go to India for them, that wouldn't be such a bad thing to do, would it?

MRS. VAKHARIA'S
Peanutty Spinach

Palak Sengdana Nu Shaak

An old friend of the family, Mrs. Vakharia was an opinionated cook. If she didn't like something, she did not hesitate to let you know. Because she was exceptional in the kitchen and cooked the vegetarian fare of her original Gujarati home kitchen with such expertise, she expected the same from others. I always enjoyed my occasional weekend visits to her home in Flint, Michigan, a culinary oasis during my days as an impoverished college student at Michigan State University. This wet *shaak* was one of her recipes, and I clearly remember her sitting next to me at the kitchen table, making sure my *thali* was kept full with a bowlful of the curry, handkerchief-thin *rotlis* (unleavened whole-wheat breads), and sweet Gujarati *kadhi* (yogurt curry). The texture of the satin-soft spinach against the crunch of freshly roasted peanuts is a great reminder of Mrs. Vakharia's munificent heart and grainy comments. **SERVES 6**

1 pound fresh spinach leaves, well rinsed

2 tablespoons peanut or canola oil

2 teaspoons cumin seeds, 1 teaspoon whole
* and 1 teaspoon ground*

½ cup unsalted dry-roasted peanuts

2 teaspoons coriander seeds, ground

1 teaspoon white granulated sugar

1 teaspoon coarse kosher or sea salt

½ teaspoon cayenne (ground red pepper)

¼ teaspoon ground asafetida

¼ teaspoon ground turmeric

1 tablespoon finely chopped fresh ginger

1. Bring a large pot of water to a vigorous boil over medium-high heat. Grab handfuls of the spinach leaves and dump them into the boiling water, stirring until they wilt, 3 to 5 minutes. Repeat, using up all the spinach. When it is all wilted, reserve 1 cup of the cooking water and drain the leaves into a colander. Run cold water through them to shock them, so they retain their bright green color. Transfer the spinach to a cutting board and chop it fine. Don't worry about squeezing excess water from the spinach.

2. Heat the oil in a small saucepan over medium-high heat. Add the cumin seeds and cook until they sizzle, turn reddish brown, and smell nutty, 5 to 10 seconds. Then add the peanuts, coriander, ground cumin, sugar, salt, cayenne, asafetida, and turmeric. Allow the spices to cook without burning (the peanuts will cushion them to some extent), about 5 seconds.

3. Immediately pour in the reserved spinach cooking water, the chopped spinach, and the ginger. Cook, uncovered, stirring occasionally, until some of the liquid has boiled off, 15 to 20 minutes. The curry will still be fairly thin. Then serve.

Tips: I love the way freshly roasted peanuts perfume my kitchen. Blanched (skin removed) small raw peanuts, the type known as Spanish peanuts, are easy to find in any supermarket or Asian grocery store. Pour a teaspoon of peanut oil or canola oil into a small skillet and heat it over medium heat. Add ½ cup blanched raw peanuts and roast them, stirring constantly, until they are honey-brown and nutty-smelling, 4 to 6 minutes. Immediately transfer them to a paper-towel-lined plate to drain and cool.

For a more even, store-bought-looking brown color, you can deep-fry raw peanuts in oil. I find the process a little messy, and if I have no plans for deep-frying anything else, I use the pan-frying method.

And yes, you can always buy the unsalted dry-roasted peanuts from the store (as I have specified in this recipe). If you are using the salted variety, reduce the salt in the list to ½ teaspoon.

Chopped Spinach
WITH DRIED LENTIL WAFERS

Palak Papad ki Subzi

A recent trip to Jaipur, in the state of Rajasthan, unveiled many surprises, including this curry, which I sampled at the palatial Rambagh Hotel. Creating magic out of nothing proved to be the norm in this desert region of India, and this dish was no disappointment. The curry's texture intrigued me, and I hope it will do the same for you. Satin-soft pieces of simmered lentil wafers provide not only flavor and texture but also body to the sauce. My version

lentil wafers

Southern Indians call them pappadums. The rest of the nation refers to them as papads. Whatever they're called, these wafer-thin crackers made with various lentil flours are a must in every household in India. A great snack and a good substitute for bread, they are often flavored with cumin, garlic, black pepper, cayenne, or green chiles. Regional preferences usually dictate which lentil flour is used to prepare the papads. The south uses skinned split black lentils, while the Gujaratis of the northwest make papads with skinned split green lentils. Papads are also made with tapioca pearls, rice flour, and even potato starch. The

Sindhis from northwestern India take pride in making these delicate wafers at home, a process that is often laborious and time-consuming. A Sindhi will welcome you with a glass of water and airily crisp papads. Papads are available in the ethnic food section of supermarkets, natural food stores, and specialty stores. Indian grocery stores often carry hundreds of varieties and half the fun is trying them all. They can be fried, baked, broiled, flame-roasted (which is often the case in India), or cooked in a microwave. Or they can be added, uncooked, to a curry, as in the spinach recipe on these pages.

incorporates fresh spinach, and when it is served with white rice and a bowl of plain yogurt, it makes for an easy, simple weekday dinner—satisfying even if you are not a vegetarian. **SERVES 4**

2 tablespoons canola oil

1 teaspoon black or yellow mustard seeds

1 teaspoon cumin seeds, ground

1 teaspoon coriander seeds, ground

½ teaspoon ground Deggi chiles
   (see box, page 290) or hot paprika

8 to 10 medium-size to large fresh curry leaves

2 fresh green Thai, cayenne, or serrano chiles,
   stems removed, cut in half lengthwise
   (do not remove the seeds)

½ teaspoon coarse kosher or sea salt

8 ounces fresh spinach leaves, well rinsed
   and coarsely chopped

3 uncooked lentil wafers (pappadums), at least
   6 inches in diameter, broken into bite-size pieces
   (see box, above)

1. Heat the oil in a medium-size saucepan over medium-high heat. Add the mustard seeds, cover the pan, and cook until the seeds have stopped popping (not unlike popcorn), about 30 seconds. Remove the pan from the heat and stir in the cumin, coriander, ground chiles, curry leaves, and fresh chiles. They will instantly sizzle and spatter in the hot oil.

2. Pour in 1½ cups water, and add the salt. Return the pan to the burner, and once the spiced water starts to boil, grab a few handfuls of the spinach and submerge them in the watery curry, stirring until they are wilted. Repeat with the remaining spinach.

3. Stir in the pappadum pieces. Lower the heat to medium and simmer, uncovered, stirring occasionally, until the pappadum pieces are soft and jelly-like and the sauce has thickened, about 5 minutes. Then serve.

Palghat Spinach

keerai molaghutal

A specialty of the Palghat Iyers (a community of Brahmin Iyers from Palghat) on the coast of the lush green state of Kerala, this curry, with a pigeon pea–coconut sauce, I warn you, is quite addictive. They often serve it as a side dish on special occasions, to highlight what they love: coconut and chiles. This version is an adaptation of Vidya Subramani's family favorite. (Vidya, a consumer researcher for a national chain of electronics stores, is an accomplished south Indian classical Bharata Natyam dancer.)

A word of caution: Be very careful to follow the recipe exactly. Some of the ingredients are used in multiple steps, at different times and in various ways, to achieve diverse flavors. **SERVES 6**

1 pound fresh spinach leaves, well rinsed (see Tip)
¼ cup plus 1 tablespoon oily or unoily skinned split
   yellow pigeon peas (toovar dal), picked over for stones
2 tablespoons skinned split black lentils (cream-colored
   in this form, urad dal), picked over for stones
1 teaspoon coriander seeds
1 teaspoon fenugreek seeds
5 dried red Thai or cayenne chiles, stems removed
2 tablespoons canola oil
½ cup shredded fresh coconut; or ¼ cup shredded
   dried unsweetened coconut, reconstituted
   (see Note)
1 teaspoon black or yellow mustard seeds
1½ teaspoons coarse kosher or sea salt

1. Bring a large pot of water to a vigorous boil over medium-high heat. Grab handfuls of the spinach leaves and dump them into the boiling water, stirring until they wilt, 3 to 5 minutes. Repeat until all the spinach has wilted in the water. Then drain the leaves in a colander. Run cold water through them to shock them, so they retain their bright green color. Transfer the spinach to a cutting board and chop it fine. Don't worry about squeezing all the excess water from the spinach.

2. Place the ¼ cup pigeon peas in a small saucepan. Fill the pan halfway with tap water, and rinse the peas by rubbing them between your fingertips. The water will become cloudy. Drain this water. Repeat three or four times, until the water remains relatively clear; then drain. Now add 1 cup water and bring it to a boil, uncovered, over medium-high heat. Skim off and discard any foam that rises to the surface. Reduce the heat to medium-low, cover the pan, and simmer, stirring occasionally, until the pigeon peas are tender, about 20 minutes.

3. While the peas are cooking, combine the remaining 1 tablespoon pigeon peas, 1 tablespoon of the black lentils, the coriander and fenugreek seeds, 3 of the chiles, and about ½ teaspoon of the oil in a small bowl. (The oil coats the legume-spice blend evenly to facilitate an even roasting.)

4. Heat a medium-size saucepan over medium-high heat. Add the legume-spice blend and stir-fry until the pigeon peas and lentils turn light brown, the spices are fragrant, and the chiles blacken slightly, 2 to 3 minutes. Transfer the mixture to a blender jar, and add the coconut. Set this aside until the simmering pigeon peas are tender.

5. Add the cooked pigeon peas and their cooking water to the mixture in the blender. Puree, scraping the inside of the jar as needed, to form a thick, albeit slightly gritty, nutty-smelling paste.

6. Heat the remaining 5½ teaspoons oil in the same

medium-size saucepan over medium-high heat. Add the mustard seeds, cover the pan, and cook until the seeds have stopped popping (not unlike popcorn), about 30 seconds. Add the remaining 1 tablespoon black lentils and the remaining 2 chiles, and stir-fry until the lentils turn golden brown and the chiles blacken, 15 to 20 seconds.

7. Immediately dump in the spinach, the salt, and the coconut paste. Pour 1 cup water into the blender jar, swish it around to wash it out, and stir this into the spinach. Reduce the heat to medium-low and simmer the curry, uncovered, stirring occasionally, to allow the spinach to cook and absorb the nutty-hot flavors, 8 to 10 minutes. Then serve.

Note: To reconstitute coconut, cover with ¼ cup boiling water, set aside for about 15 minutes, and then drain.

Tip: Frozen chopped spinach (thawed but not drained) is a totally acceptable alternative, but, oh please, no canned spinach.

Fried Bottle Gourd Squash Dumplings
IN A CASHEW-RAISIN SAUCE

ɖudhi ƙofta ʈurry

I know squash can be boring at times, especially when used in mundane stir-fries. But leave it up to us Indians to turn this vegetable into a special-occasion curry that takes prominence in many of our wedding meals! Savor these moist, rich-tasting dumplings with equally elegant saffron-perfumed rice, *Zarda chaawal* (page 716). Of all my recipes, this is the one my mother always asked me to make whenever I went to see her in Mumbai. **SERVES 8**

For the dumplings:

2 pounds bottle gourd squash (see box, page 596, and Tips)

2 teaspoons coarse kosher or sea salt

1 small red onion, coarsely chopped

2 tablespoons raw cashew nuts

4 large cloves garlic

4 lengthwise slices fresh ginger (each 2 inches long, 1 inch wide, and ⅛ inch thick)

4 fresh green Thai, cayenne, or serrano chiles, stems removed

¼ cup chickpea flour

2 tablespoons rice flour

2 tablespoons finely chopped fresh cilantro leaves and tender stems

Vegetable oil for deep-frying

For the sauce:

2 tablespoons Ghee (page 21) or canola oil

1 teaspoon cumin seeds

1 small red onion, coarsely chopped

4 fresh green Thai, cayenne, or serrano chiles, stems removed, coarsely chopped (do not remove the seeds)

2 tablespoons raw cashew nuts

2 tablespoons golden raisins

1 can (14.5 ounces) diced tomatoes

1 teaspoon coarse kosher or sea salt

¼ teaspoon ground turmeric

½ cup half-and-half

1 teaspoon Punjabi garam masala (page 25)

2 tablespoons finely chopped fresh cilantro leaves and tender stems for garnishing

1. To make the dumplings: Cut off and discard the stem and heel ends of the squash. Peel the squash with a vegetable peeler and cut it in half lengthwise. Scoop out the seeds and the surrounding spongy mass with a spoon or a melon baller, creating firm-fleshed, pale green squash "boats." Shred the squash boats in a food processor or using a box grater. Collect the shreds in a medium-size bowl and mix in the salt. Allow the squash mixture to stand for about 30 minutes to release its liquid.

2. Meanwhile, place the onion, cashews, garlic, ginger, and chiles in a food processor. Pulse until the mixture forms a slightly chunky blend.

3. Grab a handful of the shredded squash and squeeze it tightly between the palms of your hands to drain the liquid completely. Transfer this handful to a separate medium-size bowl, and repeat with the remaining squash. (Discard the drained liquid.) Add the minced onion mixture, and sprinkle in the two flours and the cilantro. Combine quickly to form a slightly wet, potato-latke-like batter. Working quickly, place a heaping tablespoon of this batter in the palm of your hand and squeeze it to condense it into a ball. Repeat, using up the remaining batter. You should have about 25 rounds. (The longer you let the batter stand without shaping it into rounds, the more liquid the squash will continue to leach, making it quite impossible to handle. If you add more flour, it will make it manageable, but it will also make the dumplings too dense.)

4. To cook the dumplings: Pour oil to a depth of 2 to 3 inches into a wok, Dutch oven, or medium-size saucepan. Heat the oil over medium heat until a candy or deep-fry thermometer inserted into it (without touching the pan's bottom) registers 300°F.

5. Line a plate or a cookie sheet with three or four sheets of paper towels. Once the oil is ready, gently slide 8 dumpling rounds into the pan. Fry, turning them occa-

bottle gourd squash
❖ ❖ ❖

*S*haped like a bottle or a bowling pin, this squash is often eaten before it reaches maturity. A light green summer squash, it has a thin skin, juicy texture, and sweet flavor when cooked. The young vegetable's mellow flesh is used as a base for many of India's herbs and spices. Once the gourd matures, its light woodlike skin is shaped to form bowls and the exterior casings for musical instruments. Bottle gourd squash is widely available at supermarkets and Asian grocery stores. Use yellow summer squash (unpeeled and unseeded) as an alternative.

sionally, until they are honey-brown and crisp, about 5 minutes. Remove the dumplings with a slotted spoon and allow them to drain on the paper towels. Repeat until all the rounds are fried. You may need to adjust the heat to maintain the oil's temperature at 300°F.

6. To make the sauce: Heat the ghee in a large saucepan over medium-high heat. Add the cumin seeds and cook until they sizzle and turn reddish brown, 5 to 10 seconds. Immediately add the onion, chiles, cashews, and raisins. Stir-fry until the onion is dark brown, the chiles are pungent, the cashews have turned honey-brown, and the raisins have swelled and darkened, about 5 minutes.

7. Add the tomatoes, salt, and turmeric to the sauce, stirring once or twice. Then transfer the mixture to a blender jar and puree, scraping the inside of the jar as needed, to make a smooth and spicy-sweet red sauce. Pour this back into the saucepan. Pour ½ cup water into the blender jar and swish it around to wash it out. Add this to the pan. Stir in the half-and-half and the garam masala.

8. Gently add the dumplings to the sauce, making sure they do not break apart. Heat the curry over medium heat until the sauce starts to bubble. Then lower the heat, cover the pan, and simmer until the dumplings are warmed through and have absorbed some of the sauce, about 5 minutes (do not stir the sauce, for fear of breaking up the dumplings).

9. Sprinkle with the cilantro, and serve.

Tips:

✤ Zucchini makes an excellent alternative to the bottle gourd squash in this dish. Moreover, the beauty of zucchini is that you do not have to peel or seed it before you shred it. Just make sure you slice off the stem and the tail ends of this pervasive American summer squash.

✤ It looks like a lot of steps, but this curry really is a cinch to make. If time is of the essence, you can fry the dumplings and make the sauce a day ahead. (If you do this, cover and refrigerate them separately; you don't want the dumplings sitting in the sauce for a long time because they will absorb too much of it.)

Squash
WITH A CHICKPEA FLOUR–LIME SAUCE

dudhi besan chi bhajee

browning flour in oil, then slowly adding the liquid to it, is an easy way to thicken a sauce. Since bottle gourd squash has no starch in it, nutty-tasting chickpea flour comes to the rescue here, not only giving body to the curry but also taming the chiles a bit. The acidity from the lime juice also cuts the capsaicin heat further, resulting in a clear burst of citrus after each mouthful. **SERVES 6**

> 1½ pounds bottle gourd squash (see box, facing page, and Tip)
> 1½ teaspoons coarse kosher or sea salt
> ¼ teaspoon ground turmeric
> 2 tablespoons canola oil
> 1 teaspoon cumin seeds
> 4 medium-size cloves garlic, finely chopped
> 2 or 3 fresh green Thai, cayenne, or serrano chiles, to taste, stems removed, cut in half lengthwise (do not remove the seeds)
> 1 tablespoon chickpea flour
> 8 to 10 medium-size to large fresh curry leaves
> 2 teaspoons white granulated sugar
> 2 tablespoons finely chopped fresh cilantro leaves and tender stems
> Juice of 1 medium-size lime

1. Cut off and discard the stem and heel ends of the squash. Peel the squash with a vegetable peeler and cut it in half lengthwise. Scoop out the seeds and the surrounding spongy mass with a spoon or a melon baller, creating firm-fleshed, pale green squash "boats." Cut the squash boats into ½-inch pieces.

2. Place the squash in a medium-size saucepan and add water to cover. Stir in 1 teaspoon of the salt and the turmeric. Bring the water to a boil. Reduce the heat to medium-low, cover the pan, and simmer, stirring once in a while, until the squash is firm but juicy-tender, about 15 minutes. Reserving 1 cup of the yellow-hued cooking water, drain the squash.

3. Wipe the saucepan dry with a paper towel, place it over medium-high heat, and add the oil. Sprinkle in the cumin seeds and cook until they sizzle, turn reddish brown, and smell nutty, 5 to 10 seconds. Add the garlic and chiles, and stir-fry until the garlic is light brown and the chiles smell pungent, about 1 minute.

4. Sprinkle in the chickpea flour, and stir until it smells nutty and is reddish brown, about 30 seconds. Pour in the reserved cooking water, quickly whisking it in to prevent any lumps from forming. Then stir in the curry leaves, drained squash, sugar, remaining ½ teaspoon salt, and the cilantro. Lower the heat to medium and allow the curry to simmer, uncovered, stirring occasionally, until the flavors mingle, 2 to 4 minutes.

5. Stir in the lime juice just before serving.

Tip: Garden-variety yellow squash is an easy substitute for bottle gourd. There is no need to peel it or to remove its seeds before use. Zucchini also is okay, but I find the yellow squash a little closer in texture, color, and flavor to the bottle gourd.

Coconut-Chile Squash

Shorrakai Avial

My mother often made this curry and served it with puffy fried *pooris* (page 725) for a late lunch on Sunday afternoons—nothing else as an accompaniment. If you do that, just be prepared to assign one or two people to make the *pooris* as hungry folks come back again and again, wolfing down the combination. **SERVES 6**

1½ *pounds bottle gourd squash*
  (see box, page 596)
2 *tablespoons coconut oil or canola oil*
1 *teaspoon black or yellow mustard seeds*
1 *tablespoon skinned split black lentils*
  (cream-colored in this form, urad dal),
  picked over for stones
2 *fresh green Thai, cayenne, or serrano chiles,*
  stems removed, cut crosswise into ¼-inch pieces
  (do not remove the seeds)
1½ *teaspoons coarse kosher or sea salt*
¼ *teaspoon ground turmeric*
12 *to 15 medium-size to large fresh curry leaves*
1 *cup shredded fresh coconut; or ½ cup shredded*
  dried unsweetened coconut, reconstituted
  (see Note)
2 *tablespoons finely chopped fresh cilantro leaves*
  and tender stems

1. Cut off and discard the stem and heel ends of the squash. Peel the squash with a vegetable peeler and cut it in half lengthwise. Scoop out the seeds and the surrounding spongy mass with a spoon or a melon baller, creating firm-fleshed, pale green squash "boats." Cut the squash boats into 2-inch cubes.

2. Heat the oil in a large skillet over medium-high heat. Add the mustard seeds, cover the skillet, and cook until the seeds have stopped popping (not unlike popcorn), about 30 seconds. Add the lentils and stir-fry until they turn golden brown, 15 to 20 seconds. Immediately add the squash (this will stop the lentils from browning further) and the chiles. Sprinkle in the salt and turmeric. Stir-fry the mixture to allow the spices to cook, about 30 seconds.

3. Pour in ½ cup water and add the curry leaves. Reduce the heat to medium-low, cover the skillet, and simmer, stirring occasionally, until the squash is fork-tender but still juicy-firm, 12 to 15 minutes.

4. Stir in the coconut and cook, covered, stirring occasionally, until it warms through and the sauce appears thick, about 5 minutes.

5. Sprinkle with the cilantro, and serve.

Note: To reconstitute coconut, cover with ½ cup boiling water, set aside for about 15 minutes, and then drain.

Bottle gourd Squash
WITH
COCONUT AND CURRY LEAVES

thenga Shorrakai

My mother's coconut sauce is a perfect match for this squash (coconut plays a dual role, masking the pungent chiles and thickening the sauce)—but her mother-in-law, if she were alive today, still wouldn't approve.

SERVES 6

1½ pounds bottle gourd squash (see box, page 596)

2 tablespoons canola oil

½ cup shredded fresh coconut; or ¼ cup shredded
dried unsweetened coconut, reconstituted
(see Note)

1 tablespoon coriander seeds

2 dried red Thai or cayenne chiles, stems removed

¼ cup finely chopped fresh cilantro leaves
and tender stems

1 teaspoon coarse kosher or sea salt

10 to 12 medium-size to large fresh curry leaves

1. Cut off and discard the stem and heel ends of the squash. Peel the squash with a vegetable peeler and cut it in half lengthwise. Scoop out the seeds and the surrounding spongy mass with a spoon or a melon baller, creating firm-fleshed, pale green squash "boats." Cut the squash boats into 1-inch pieces and place them in a medium-size saucepan. Pour in 1 cup water and bring it to a boil over medium-high heat. Reduce the heat to medium-low, cover the pan, and steam the squash until it is juicy-tender, 8 to 10 minutes.

2. While the squash is cooking, heat the oil in a small skillet over medium heat. Add the coconut, coriander seeds, and chiles, and stir-fry until the coconut is light brown and a thin brown crust is starting to form on the bottom of the skillet, 3 to 5 minutes. Pour in ½ cup water and scrape the skillet to release the crusty brown bits of coconut and coriander. Transfer this coconut-spice mixture to a blender and puree, scraping the inside of the jar as necessary, to make a smooth, but slightly gritty, paste.

3. Add the coconut paste to the cooked squash. Scoop about ½ cup liquid out of the saucepan and pour it into the blender jar; swish it around to wash out the blender, and then return it to the saucepan.

4. Stir in the cilantro, salt, and curry leaves. Raise the heat to medium-high and cook, uncovered, stirring occasionally, until most of the liquid has been absorbed and the spicy, nutty sauce has thickened to a gravy-like consistency, 5 to 8 minutes. Then serve.

Note: To reconstitute coconut, cover with ¼ cup boiling water, set aside for about 15 minutes, and then drain.

Bengali Squash
IN COCONUT MILK

Lauki Narkol

on't be fooled by this simple Bengali curry that contains very few spices: Its flavor is not so simple! Given the right spice, the appropriate cooking technique, and a suitable sauce, an easy, homespun dish can be nothing short of spectacular. You don't have to take my word for it: It speaks for itself when you taste that first spoonful (or finger-full if you use your hand to eat, just like a good little Indian).

SERVES 6

1½ *pounds bottle gourd squash (see box,*
   page 596)
2 *tablespoons mustard oil or canola oil*
2 *teaspoons Panch phoron (page 36)*
2 *to 4 dried red Thai, cayenne, or serrano chiles,*
   to taste, stems removed
1 *teaspoon coarse kosher or sea salt*
½ *teaspoon ground turmeric*
1 *can (13.5 ounces) unsweetened coconut milk*
2 *tablespoons finely chopped fresh cilantro*
   leaves and tender stems

1. Cut off and discard the stem and heel ends of the squash. Peel the squash with a vegetable peeler and cut it in half lengthwise. Scoop out the seeds and the surrounding spongy mass with a spoon or a melon baller, creating firm-fleshed, pale green squash "boats." Cut the squash boats into 1-inch pieces and place them in a medium-size bowl (I usually use a bowl that I can serve the cooked squash in, eliminating the need to dirty yet another bowl).

2. Heat the oil in a medium-size skillet over medium-high heat. Sprinkle in the *Panch phoron* and chiles, and stir-fry until the chiles blacken and the seeds crackle, pop, and are aromatic, about 1 minute.

3. Add the squash, salt, and turmeric. Cook, stirring, until the squash is coated with the spices, 1 to 2 minutes. Pour in the coconut milk and stir once or twice. As soon as the creamy-yellow liquid starts to boil, reduce the heat to medium-low, cover the skillet, and simmer, stirring occasionally, until the squash is juicy-tender, 20 to 25 minutes.

4. Remove the chiles if you wish. Stir in the cilantro, and serve.

Robust Squash
WITH A
GINGER-CHILE PASTE

Masaledar Lauki

sually when I have purchased a large amount of an ingredient for testing recipes, I create multiple dishes with that ingredient so that nothing goes to waste (that is one of my pet peeves—wasting food). So, one Saturday afternoon when I happened to be knee-deep in bottle gourd squash (a good predicament, mind you), I concocted a number of curries, including this one. I especially like the final sweet balance that the coconut gives the sauce, in spite of the generous dose of potent Ginger Chile Paste.

SERVES 4

1½ pounds bottle gourd squash (see box, page 596)

2 tablespoons Ginger Chile Paste
   (page 17)

½ teaspoon ground turmeric

2 tablespoons canola oil

1 teaspoon black or yellow mustard seeds

1 teaspoon coarse kosher or sea salt

6 to 8 medium-size to large fresh curry leaves

1 cup shredded fresh coconut; or ½ cup shredded
   dried unsweetened coconut, reconstituted
   (see Note)

2 tablespoons finely chopped fresh cilantro
   leaves and tender stems

1 teaspoon Rajasthani garam masala (page 26)

1. Cut off and discard the stem and heel ends of the squash. Peel the squash with a vegetable peeler and cut it in half lengthwise. Scoop out the seeds and the surrounding spongy mass with a spoon or a melon baller, creating firm-fleshed, pale green squash "boats." Cut the squash boats into 1-inch pieces, and place them in a medium-size bowl.

2. Add the Ginger Chile Paste and the turmeric to the squash, and toss to coat the squash pieces with the seasonings.

3. Heat the oil in a medium-size saucepan over medium-high heat. Add the mustard seeds, cover the pan, and cook until the seeds have stopped popping (not unlike popcorn), about 30 seconds. Add the squash and stir-fry until the spice paste is lightly browned, about 2 minutes.

4. Pour in 1½ cups water and scrape the bottom of the pan to deglaze it, releasing the browned bits. Stir in the salt and the curry leaves. Once the curry comes to a boil, reduce the heat to medium-low, cover the pan, and simmer, stirring occasionally, until the squash is fork-tender with a juicy squish, about 15 minutes.

5. Stir in the coconut, cilantro, and garam masala, and serve.

Note: To reconstitute coconut, cover with ½ cup boiling water, set aside for about 15 minutes, and then drain.

Peanut-Coconut Squash

dudhi moongphalli chi bhajee

this spicy-hot curry gets its oomph from the dried red chiles. If it's too hot for you, simply reduce the number of chiles by one or two. However, I find that the coconut and peanuts come together to alleviate some of the chiles' heat. A sprinkling of white granulated sugar, stirred into the coconut mixture after you stir-fry it, will also help alleviate the heat but adds a layer of sweetness that may not appeal to everyone. **SERVES 8**

2 pounds bottle gourd squash (see box, page 596)

½ cup unsalted dry-roasted peanuts

½ cup shredded fresh coconut, or ¼ cup shredded
   dried unsweetened coconut (see Tip)

1 tablespoon white sesame seeds

4 dried red Thai or cayenne chiles, stems removed

1 tablespoon canola oil

1 teaspoon black or yellow mustard seeds

1 teaspoon cumin seeds

1½ teaspoons coarse kosher or sea salt

¼ teaspoon ground turmeric

2 tablespoons finely chopped fresh cilantro
   leaves and tender stems

1. Cut off and discard the stem and heel ends of the squash. Peel the squash with a vegetable peeler and cut it in half lengthwise. Scoop out the seeds and the surrounding spongy mass with a spoon or a melon baller, creating firm-fleshed, pale green squash "boats." Cut the squash boats into 1-inch pieces.

2. Pour 1 cup water into a medium-size saucepan, and add the squash. Bring the water to a boil over medium-high heat. Then reduce the heat to medium-low, cover the pan, and simmer, stirring occasionally, until the squash pieces are fork-tender, 15 to 20 minutes.

3. While the squash is cooking, pour the peanuts into a food processor and pulse until they have the consistency of coarse breadcrumbs. (A constant grind, rather than on-and-off pulsing, will yield peanut butter, not a desirous product for this curry.)

4. Preheat a small skillet over medium heat. Add the coconut, sesame seeds, and chiles, and stir-fry until the coconut and sesame turn nutty-brown and the chiles smell pungent and glisten with the oil emanating from the other ingredients. Transfer this mixture to a plate to cool. Once it is cool to the touch, place half of the mixture in a spice grinder and grind until the texture resembles that of finely ground black pepper. Transfer the ground mixture to a bowl, and repeat with the other half.

5. Heat the oil in a medium-size saucepan over medium-high heat. Add the mustard seeds, cover the pan, and cook until the seeds have stopped popping (not unlike popcorn), about 30 seconds. Stir in the cumin seeds. As soon as the cumin sizzles, turns reddish brown, and smells nutty, add the ground peanuts. Stir-fry until the nuts have warmed and smell fresh, about 2 minutes. Then stir in the salt and turmeric.

6. Scrape the coconut blend and the peanuts into the cooked squash, and stir together. Simmer the curry over medium heat, uncovered, stirring occasionally, until the sauce thickens, about 5 minutes.

7. Stir in the cilantro, and serve.

Tip: You'll notice that I have not recommended reconstituting shredded dried coconut in this recipe; the moisture might make it take longer for the coconut to brown. If you are using fresh shreds, they will be fine because they don't contain excess liquid.

Cubed Squash
WITH UNRIPE MANGO

Lauki Aur Kucchey Aam ki Subzi

Mango contributes an appealing tartness to this sauce and to the succulent squash, whose texture I oh-so-love. Note the double flavors that cumin provides: the first in its seed form when it's sizzled in hot oil, the other in its ground form when it's briefly cooked in the same hot oil. **SERVES 6**

1½ pounds bottle gourd squash (see box, page 596)
2 tablespoons canola oil
2 teaspoons cumin seeds, 1 teaspoon whole,
*   1 teaspoon ground*
3 lengthwise slices fresh ginger (each 2½ inches
*   long, 1 inch wide, and ⅛ inch thick),*
*   cut into matchstick-thin strips (julienne)*
2 fresh green Thai, cayenne, or serrano chiles,
*   stems removed, thinly sliced crosswise*
*   (do not remove the seeds)*

2 teaspoons coriander seeds, ground

½ teaspoon ground asafetida

½ teaspoon ground turmeric

1 large green (unripe) mango, peeled, seeded,
and cut into ½-inch cubes (see box,
page 641)

½ cup chopped fresh or frozen fenugreek leaves
(thawed if frozen); or 2 tablespoons dried
fenugreek leaves, soaked in a bowl of water
and skimmed off before use (see box,
page 473)

1 teaspoon coarse kosher or sea salt

1. Cut off and discard the stem and heel ends of the squash. Peel the squash with a vegetable peeler, and then cut it in half lengthwise. Scoop out the seeds and the surrounding spongy mass with a spoon or a melon baller, creating firm-fleshed, pale green squash "boats." Cut the squash boats into 1-inch cubes.

2. Heat the oil in a large skillet over medium-high heat. Add the cumin seeds and cook until they sizzle and turn reddish brown, 5 to 10 seconds. Add the ginger and chiles, and stir-fry until the ginger is light brown and the chiles smell pungent, about 1 minute.

3. Remove the skillet from the heat and stir in the ground coriander, ground cumin, asafetida, and turmeric. (The heat from the oil will be just right to cook but not burn the ground spices.) Immediately pour in 1 cup water (this will stop the cooking).

4. Return the skillet to the heat, and add the squash, mango, fenugreek leaves, and salt. Stir once or twice, and heat to a boil. Then reduce the heat to medium-low, cover the skillet, and simmer, stirring occasionally, until the pale green vegetables are fork-tender, 25 to 30 minutes. Then serve.

Squash
WITH MANGO POWDER

Amchur Lauki

A friend of mine looked at the name of this recipe and blurted, "What's armchair loo-kee?" Once I picked myself off the floor and stopped laughing, I explained that this succulent summer squash perks up in the presence of pungent chiles and tart mango powder, and yes, he could certainly eat this seated in his armchair, with rotis (page 727) and a side of pickles, while watching TV. An unusual and tasty alternative to a TV dinner, *n'est-ce pas?* **SERVES 6**

1½ pounds bottle gourd squash (see box,
page 596)

1 tablespoon canola oil

1 teaspoon cumin seeds

¼ teaspoon ground turmeric

2 fresh green Thai, cayenne, or serrano chiles,
stems removed, cut crosswise into ¼-inch-thick
slices (do not remove the seeds)

1 medium-size tomato, cored and cut into
1-inch cubes

1 tablespoon mango powder (see box, page 604)
or fresh lime juice

1½ teaspoons coarse kosher or sea salt

1. Cut off and discard the stem and heel ends of the squash. Peel the squash with a vegetable peeler, and then cut it in half lengthwise. Scoop out the seeds and the surrounding spongy mass with a spoon or a melon baller, creating firm-fleshed, pale green squash "boats." Cut the squash boats into 2-inch pieces and place them in a medium-size bowl.

2. Heat the oil in a large skillet over medium-high heat. Add the cumin seeds and cook until they start to sizzle, turn reddish brown, and smell nutty, 5 to 10 seconds. Immediately add the squash, turmeric, and chiles. Cook, uncovered, stirring occasionally, until the squash is coated with the sun-yellow turmeric and is lightly browned, 5 to 8 minutes.

3. Stir in the tomato, *amchur,* and salt. Pour in 1 cup water and scrape the bottom of the skillet to deglaze it, releasing any browned bits of vegetable and spice. Once the water comes to a boil, lower the heat to medium, cover the skillet, and simmer, stirring occasionally, until the squash is juicy-tender, 10 to 15 minutes. Then serve.

Pan-Fried Bottle Gourd Slices
WITH YOGURT & AROMATIC SPICES

Shia Yakhani

this Kashmiri delicacy is easy to make. The star of the show, the ingredient that makes it a *yakhani,* is the yogurt. The generous sauce packs tart flavors without looking curdled, thanks to the heavy cream. The juicy succulence of the tender squash is great over basmati rice. **SERVES 8**

2½ pounds bottle gourd squash (see box, page 596)
6 tablespoons canola oil
¾ teaspoon ground asafetida
6 whole cloves
1 teaspoon coarse kosher or sea salt
1 cup plain yogurt

mango powder (amchur)

Amchur (also spelled amchoor) is the souring spice of choice in the northern, northwestern, and northeastern regions of India. Very tart and rich in vitamins, this earthy-tasting light brown powder is made by grinding slices of sun-dried green (unripe) mangoes. Some Indian and Pakistani grocery stores stock packages of the dried slices; grind them in a spice grinder or in a blender for a clean burst of earthy tartness.

¼ cup heavy (whipping) cream
1 teaspoon ground ginger
½ teaspoon coarsely ground black pepper
1 teaspoon cumin seeds, toasted (see Tips page 294) and ground
¼ teaspoon ground cinnamon
2 tablespoons finely chopped fresh cilantro leaves and tender stems for garnishing

1. Cut off and discard the stem and heel ends of the squash. Peel the squash with a vegetable peeler and cut it in half lengthwise. Scoop out the seeds and the surrounding spongy mass with a spoon or a melon baller, creating firm-fleshed, pale green squash "boats." Cut the squash boats crosswise into ¼-inch-thick slices. (When you get to the hollowed-out part, the slices will be thick at the ends but very thin in the middle.)

2. Heat 2 tablespoons of the oil in a large skillet over medium heat. Add about a third of the squash slices, arranging them in a single layer, and sprinkle ¼ teaspoon of the asafetida and 2 of the cloves over them. Cook until the slices are lightly browned and blistered on the underside, 3 to 5 minutes. Flip them over and let the other side blister and brown, 3 to 5 minutes. Transfer the slices to a medium-size bowl and pour 2 cups of water over them. Repeat with two more batches, using the remaining oil, squash slices, asafetida, and cloves (don't add any more water). Add the browned slices to the first batch. Stir in the salt.

3. Return the squash and the salted soaking water to the same skillet, and bring to a boil over medium-high heat. Quickly whisk together the yogurt, cream, ginger, and black pepper. Pour this over the curry and stir once or twice. Continue boiling it vigorously, uncovered, stirring occasionally, until the sauce thickens slightly, 15 to 20 minutes.

4. Remove the cloves if you wish, and stir in the cumin and cinnamon. Sprinkle with the cilantro, and serve.

> **A**safetida? See the Glossary of Ingredients, page 758.

Bottle Gourd Squash
WITH MUSTARD GREENS AND SPINACH

Lauki, Sarson, Aur Palak ki Subzi

My body often craves leafy greens, especially spinach, when I have not had any in more than a week. This combination fills that void, especially when you throw in iron-rich mustard greens. The juicy squash offers a wonderful textural contrast to the grassy greens in a sauce that balances tart tomatoes and smooth half-and-half. The spices are readily available ones, but the combination is unusual. This is a great side dish with a lamb curry or a lentil-based curry and a mound of basmati rice. **SERVES 6**

1½ pounds bottle gourd squash (see box, page 596)
2 tablespoons canola oil
1 teaspoon black or yellow mustard seeds
1½ teaspoons coarse kosher or sea salt
1 teaspoon cumin seeds, ground
1 teaspoon coriander seeds, ground
1 teaspoon fenugreek seeds, ground
1 teaspoon cayenne (ground red pepper)
¼ teaspoon ground asafetida
¼ teaspoon ground turmeric
1 can (14.5 ounces) diced tomatoes
1 pound fresh spinach leaves, well rinsed and cut into thin slivers (chiffonade; see Tip)
1 pound fresh mustard greens, well rinsed and cut into thin slivers (chiffonade; see Tip)
½ cup half-and-half

1. Cut off and discard the stem and heel ends of the squash. Peel the squash with a vegetable peeler, and then cut it in half lengthwise. Scoop out the seeds and the surrounding spongy mass with a spoon or a melon baller, creating firm-fleshed, pale green squash "boats." Cut the squash boats into 1-inch cubes.

2. Heat the oil in a large saucepan over medium-high heat. Add the mustard seeds, cover the pan, and cook until the seeds have stopped popping (not unlike popcorn), about 30 seconds. Immediately add the squash, salt, cumin, coriander, fenugreek, cayenne, asafetida, and turmeric. Stir-fry to cook the spices, about 1 minute.

3. Pour in the tomatoes, with their liquid, and add half of the spinach and mustard greens. Cover the pan and let the greens wilt in the built-up steam,

about 3 minutes. Add the remaining greens, cover again, and cook until the new batch has wilted, 3 minutes.

4. Pour in the half-and-half, and stir once to incorporate it into the curry. Reduce the heat to medium-low, cover the pan, and cook, stirring occasionally, until the squash is fork-tender and juicy, 12 to 15 minutes. Then serve.

Tip: Fresh mustard greens are available in most supermarkets. To prepare them for cooking, cut out and discard the tough rib that runs through three-quarters the length of each leaf. Stack 2 or 3 similar-length leaves and roll them tightly into a tube shape. Cut the tube into thin crosswise slices and unfold them to yield ribbons (called a chiffonade). Place them in a large bowl. Once all the greens are sliced, cover them with cold water. Dunk the leaves briefly under the water. Grab handfuls of the leaves to lift them out of the water. The sand or grit will sink to the bottom. Repeat once or twice to ensure that the leaves are completely clean and grit-free.

Potato Stuffed Squash

bharwan Lauki

festive-looking, unusual, and a definite party-pleaser, these potato-stuffed squash halves are a cinch to make, and you can assemble them up to two days before you plan to serve them. And did I say it was delicious? **SERVES 6**

1 medium-size to large (1½ to 2 pounds) bottle gourd squash (see box, page 596)
2½ teaspoons coarse kosher or sea salt
2 medium-size russet or Yukon Gold potatoes, peeled, diced, and submerged in a bowl of cold water to prevent browning
2 teaspoons coriander seeds, ground
1 teaspoon cumin seeds, ground
½ teaspoon ground Deggi chiles (see box, page 290); or ¼ teaspoon cayenne (ground red pepper) mixed with ¼ teaspoon sweet paprika
¼ teaspoon ground turmeric
2 tablespoons canola oil
1 small red onion, finely chopped
1 tablespoon finely chopped fresh ginger
1 can (14.5 ounces) diced tomatoes
2 teaspoons Maharashtrian garam masala (page 28)
2 tablespoons finely chopped fresh cilantro leaves and tender stems for garnishing

1. Preheat the oven to 350°F.

2. Cut off and discard the stem and heel ends of the squash. Peel the squash with a vegetable peeler and cut it in half lengthwise. Scoop out the seeds and the surrounding spongy mass with a spoon or a melon baller, creating firm-fleshed, pale green squash "boats."

3. Place the squash halves in a flameproof casserole or Dutch oven. Fill the casserole with enough water to completely submerge the squash. Sprinkle in 2 teaspoons of the salt, and bring the water to a boil over medium-high heat. Then lower the heat to medium, cover the casserole, and simmer until the squash is slightly opaque and limp, about 5 minutes. Using tongs, lift the squash halves out of the water and place them in an oval ovenproof dish, hollowed side up.

4. Drain the potatoes and add them to the casserole. Bring the water to a boil again over medium-high heat. Then lower the heat to medium, partially cover the casserole, and cook until the potatoes are very tender, 5 to 8 minutes.

5. Drain the potatoes, reserving ½ cup of the cooking water. Place them in a bowl and coarsely mash them. Stir in the coriander, cumin, ground chiles, remaining ½ teaspoon salt, and turmeric.

6. Heat the oil in a medium-size skillet over medium-high heat. Add the onion and ginger, and stir-fry until they are light brown around the edges, 3 to 5 minutes.

7. Stir in the spiced potatoes and cook, uncovered, stirring occasionally, until there is a very thin layer of browned potatoes lining the bottom of the skillet, 5 to 8 minutes.

8. Pour in the reserved ½ cup cooking water and allow it to run under the potatoes. Scrape the bottom of the skillet to release the browned layer, stirring to incorporate it into the onion-potato stuffing.

9. Divide the filling equally between the squash boats, spreading it so it fills the cavities and covers the entire surface.

10. Combine the tomatoes and garam masala in a medium-size bowl. Pour this over the stuffed squash halves, lifting them a little to allow the juices to run under and form a thin layer (this will prevent the squash from drying out when baked).

11. Cover the baking dish and bake until the potatoes are warm, the squash is tender, and the tomatoes have softened, about 1 hour.

12. Sprinkle the cilantro over the stuffed squash. Then cut each half into 3 pieces and serve, making sure each piece is brimming with potatoes and tomatoey sauce.

Tip: When I served this with Chicken Thighs with a Peanut Sauce (page 159), it was a big hit with my family.

Savory Squash
WITH SPINACH AND COCONUT MILK

Shorrakai Keerai Ishto

A word derived from the English "stew," *ishto* is a favorite type of curry in Kerala. This coconut milk–based savory dish can include meat, seafood, vegetables, and even grains. This vegetarian version, combining bottle gourd squash and spinach, is incredible when poured over freshly steamed rice noodles (page 723). A starchy long-grain white rice is equally tasty with this spicy-sweet *ishto,* and so is the more unusual nutty-black variety called black *puttu* rice (page 708). **SERVES 6**

1½ pounds bottle gourd squash (see box, page 596)

2 tablespoons coconut oil or canola oil

1 teaspoon black or yellow mustard seeds

2 to 4 fresh green Thai, cayenne, or serrano chiles, to taste, stems removed, cut crosswise into ¼-inch-thick slices (do not remove the seeds)

1 cup unsweetened coconut milk

1½ teaspoons coarse kosher or sea salt

1½ pounds fresh spinach leaves, well rinsed and coarsely chopped

2 tablespoons finely chopped fresh cilantro leaves and tender stems

10 medium-size to large fresh curry leaves

1. Cut off and discard the stem and heel ends of the squash. Peel the squash with a vegetable peeler, and then cut it in half lengthwise. Scoop out the seeds and the surrounding spongy mass with a spoon or a melon baller, creating firm-fleshed, pale green squash "boats." Cut the squash boats into ¼-inch cubes.

2. Heat the oil in a large saucepan over medium-high heat. Add the mustard seeds, cover the pan, and cook until the seeds have stopped popping (not unlike popcorn), about 30 seconds. Immediately add the squash and chiles, and stir-fry for 1 to 2 minutes.

3. Pour in the coconut milk and salt. Grab a third of the spinach and add it to the mixture. Cover the pan and cook until the greens are wilted, 2 to 4 minutes. Repeat with the remaining spinach. Once all the spinach is wilted, reduce the heat to medium-low and cook, covered, stirring occasion-ally, until the squash is tender but still firm, 15 to 20 minutes.

4. Uncover the pan and raise the heat to medium-high. Cook, stirring occasionally, until the coconut milk thickens, about 5 minutes.

5. Stir in the cilantro and curry leaves, and serve.

patra

❖ ❖ ❖

patra is a delicacy among the Gujarati-speaking communities of northwestern India. It consists of large elephant-ear taro leaves that are layered with a spiced chickpea-flour paste, rolled into a tight log, and steamed. The cement-like quality of the flour holds everything in place. Once they are steamed, we cut the logs into 1/2-inch-thick rounds and pan-fry them with roasted mustard seeds. The steamed pinwheels are widely available—either in cans or frozen—in Indian grocery stores. I prefer the frozen ones, but the canned ones will do in a pinch. If fresh taro leaves are in season, I often make patra from scratch. It is not as labor-intensive as you might think.

Squash
WITH TARO LEAF "ROULADE"

Lauki Patra Nu Shaak

I adore the textural difference between the juicy squish of perfectly cooked squash and the leafy bite of steamed taro leaves. The *patra* also helps to thicken the sauce, thanks to its layers of spiced chickpea flour paste. I wait until after the squash is tender to add it because if it is simmered too long, it will fall apart in the curry—which is not all bad. For a firmer texture from the *patra*, pan-fry the rounds on both sides (per the package instructions). As always, yellow squash works well as an alternative to bottle gourd. The other "vegetable" that works well here is the light green or white, fleshy rind of watermelon (the meat between the exterior dark green skin and the interior juicy red fruit). It has the same color and texture as bottle gourd squash.

SERVES 8

1½ *pounds bottle gourd squash (see box, page 596)*
2 *tablespoons peanut or canola oil*
1 *teaspoon black or yellow mustard seeds*

2 teaspoons cumin seeds, I teaspoon whole,
   I teaspoon ground

2 teaspoons coriander seeds, ground

I teaspoon white granulated sugar

I teaspoon coarse kosher or sea salt

½ teaspoon Rajasthani garam masala
   (page 26)

½ teaspoon cayenne (ground red pepper)

½ teaspoon ground turmeric

I bag (about 14 ounces) frozen patra rounds,
   thawed (see box, facing page)

1. Cut off and discard the stem and heel ends of the squash. Peel the squash with a vegetable peeler, and cut it in half lengthwise. Scoop out the seeds and the surrounding spongy mass with a spoon or a melon baller, creating firm-fleshed, pale green squash "boats." Cut the squash boats into 1-inch pieces and place them in a medium-size bowl.

2. Heat the oil in a large saucepan over medium-high heat. Add the mustard seeds, cover the pan, and cook until the seeds have stopped popping (not unlike popcorn), about 30 seconds. Remove the pan from the heat and sprinkle in the cumin seeds, coriander, ground cumin, sugar, salt, garam masala, cayenne, and turmeric. The spices will instantly sizzle and smell aromatic. Immediately toss in the squash and stir to coat the pieces with the spices. Return the pan to medium heat, and stir-fry for 1 to 2 minutes.

3. Pour in 3 cups water and bring the curry to a boil. Then reduce the heat, cover the pan, and simmer, stirring occasionally, until the squash is fork-tender, 20 to 25 minutes.

4. Fold in the *patra* and simmer, covered, until the rounds are warmed through and the sauce has thickened, 5 to 7 minutes. Then serve.

Bottle Gourd Squash
WITH
TOMATO AND FENUGREEK LEAVES

Lauki Methi

fenugreek's perfumed bitterness is a perfect match to the juicy pieces of tender squash in this easy-to-make curry. Because of its subtle tastes, I often find myself using fewer herbs and spices when I cook this squash. **SERVES 6**

1½ pounds bottle gourd squash
   (see box, page 596)

½ teaspoon ground turmeric

2 tablespoons canola oil

I large tomato, cored and cut into 1-inch cubes

2 cups chopped fresh or frozen fenugreek leaves
   (thawed if frozen; see box, page 473)

2 teaspoons coarse kosher or sea salt

I teaspoon cayenne (ground red pepper)

1. Cut off and discard the stem and heel ends of the squash. Peel the squash with a vegetable peeler and cut it in half lengthwise. Scoop out the seeds and the surrounding spongy mass with a spoon or a melon baller, creating firm-fleshed, pale green squash "boats." Cut the squash boats into 1-inch pieces and place them in a medium-size bowl. Add the turmeric and toss to coat the squash with the spice.

2. Heat the oil in a large skillet over medium-high heat until it starts to shimmer, about 30 seconds. Add the squash and stir-fry until the pieces turn light brown, 1 to 2 minutes.

3. Add the tomato, fenugreek leaves, salt, and cayenne, and stir once or twice. Reduce the heat to medium-low, cover the skillet, and cook, stirring occasionally, until the squash is fork-tender, 20 to 25 minutes. Then serve.

Tip: For a refreshing alternative, I have made this dish with finely chopped fresh cilantro instead of the fenugreek leaves (but then of course the dish is not *Lauki methi*).

Coconut Gourd

WITH CURRY LEAVES

kovakkai kari

When I was working on this book, I had an uneasy feeling that my steadfast friends would wander off as soon as I finished testing the recipes. After all, there was no way I could continue to churn out curry after curry, day in and day out, to keep them happy. I feared that once I stopped, they would disappear, never to come back . . . at least until the next book project came along. All right, I confess—it was a figment of my Bollywood imagination, as I imagined myself the fallen hero, abandoned by one and all, a violin stringing a tragic tune in the background.

Actually I know that my friends will continue to stand by me, especially as long as I am able to make curries like this one, the hands-down favorite out of five tested one evening. They loved the tender squash's juicy crunch, accented with fresh coconut and nutty-hot spices. **SERVES 4**

2 tablespoons canola oil

1 teaspoon black or yellow mustard seeds

1 tablespoon skinned split black lentils (cream-colored in this form, urad dal), picked over for stones

1 pound ivy gourd (see box, facing page), sliced crosswise into ¼-inch-thick slices, or 1 pound English cucumbers, ends trimmed off, cut lengthwise into quarters, each quarter cut into ¼-inch-thick slices

1 cup shredded fresh coconut; or ½ cup shredded dried unsweetened coconut, reconstituted (see Note)

2 teaspoons Sambhar masala (page 33)

1½ teaspoons coarse kosher or sea salt

12 to 15 medium-size to large fresh curry leaves

2 tablespoons finely chopped fresh cilantro leaves and tender stems for garnishing

1. Heat the oil in a small saucepan over medium-high heat. Add the mustard seeds, cover the pan, and cook until the seeds have stopped popping (not unlike popcorn), about 30 seconds. Then add the lentils and stir-fry until they turn golden brown, 15 to 20 seconds.

2. Stir in the ivy gourd, coconut, ½ cup water, and the *Sambhar masala,* salt, and curry leaves. Bring the curry to a boil. Reduce the heat to medium-low, cover the pan, and simmer, stirring occasionally, until the gourd pieces are fork-tender, 20 to 25 minutes.

3. Sprinkle with the cilantro, and serve.

Note: To reconstitute coconut, cover with ½ cup boiling water, set aside for about 15 minutes, and then drain.

Garlicky Gourd

Lasoon tindora

I love the juicy crunch of ivy gourd when it is cooked al dente. The tart yogurt in this curry provides a smooth backdrop to the cayenne pepper, and the fat in the cream prevents the yogurt from curdling when it is heated. **SERVES 4**

1 tablespoon canola oil

8 ounces ivy gourd (see box, below), cut crosswise into ¼-inch-thick slices; or 8 ounces English cucumbers, ends trimmed off, cut lengthwise into quarters, each quarter cut into ¼-inch-thick slices

6 medium-size cloves garlic, cut in half lengthwise and thinly sliced

2 tablespoons plain yogurt

2 tablespoons heavy (whipping) cream

2 tablespoons finely chopped fresh cilantro leaves and tender stems

2 teaspoons Toasted Cumin-Coriander Blend (page 33)

½ teaspoon coarse kosher or sea salt

½ teaspoon cayenne (ground red pepper)

1. Heat the oil in a medium-size skillet over medium-high heat. Add the gourd and garlic, and stir-fry until the garlic starts to turn light brown, about 2 minutes.

2. Pour in ½ cup water (which will instantly start to boil). Reduce the heat to medium-low, cover the skillet, and simmer until the gourd slices are tender and the water has been absorbed, 8 to 10 minutes.

3. While the gourd is cooking, mix the yogurt, cream, cilantro, spice blend, salt, and cayenne together in a small bowl.

4. Once the ivy gourd is tender, stir in the spiced yogurt. Cook, uncovered, until the sauce is warmed through, about 2 minutes. Then serve.

Ivy Gourd
WITH POMEGRANATE AND MANGO POWDER

tindora masaledaar

For a simple vegetarian dinner, I often serve this tart-sweet curry alongside Black Chickpeas with a Coconut-Chile Sauce (page 339) and some Perfumed Basmati Rice with Black Cardamom Pods (page 709). Long English cucumbers, cut into thick strips, will work as an alternative to the squash. **SERVES 6**

ivy gourd
❖ ❖ ❖

Cute mini-cucumber-looking gourds, 2 to 3 inches in length and ½ to 1 inch in girth, these are also called tindla (in Gujarat) and kovakkai (in Chennai). Some refer to them as "gentlemen's toes," but I have yet to meet a gentleman who has appendages quite like these. The gourds contain gelatinous seeds, and their color, when they are slit open, can range from pale green to orange-red, depending on ripeness. Ivy gourd has an underlying bitterness, and we normally don't consume them raw. They are easy to spot in the refrigerated section of Indian grocery stores throughout the year, and I have noticed that they also come frozen.

1 teaspoon coriander seeds

½ teaspoon cumin seeds

½ teaspoon dried pomegranate seeds

¼ teaspoon cardamom seeds from green
or white pods

1 pound ivy gourd (see box, page 611),
cut in half lengthwise; or 1 pound English
cucumbers, ends trimmed off, peeled, and cut into
strips 2 inches long and ½ inch thick

1 tablespoon mango powder or lime juice

1 tablespoon Ginger Paste (page 15)

2 teaspoons Garlic Paste (page 15)

1 teaspoon coarse kosher or sea salt

½ teaspoon cayenne (ground red pepper)

¼ teaspoon ground turmeric

2 tablespoons Ghee (page 21) or
canola oil

2 tablespoons Fried Onion Paste
(page 16)

1 medium-size tomato, cored and cut into
1-inch pieces

¼ cup finely chopped fresh cilantro leaves and
tender stems

1. Place the coriander, cumin, pomegranate seeds, and cardamom seeds in a spice grinder, and grind until the texture resembles that of finely ground black pepper.

2. Place the ivy gourd halves in a medium-size bowl, and sprinkle the ground spices over them.

3. Add the mango powder, ginger and garlic pastes, salt, cayenne, and turmeric. Combine to coat the squash with the robust spice blend.

4. Heat the ghee in a large skillet over medium-high heat. Add the squash and stir-fry until it is lightly browned and the ginger and garlic pastes coat the bottom of the skillet, 3 to 5 minutes.

5. Quickly combine the Fried Onion Paste with ¾ cup water to make a murky-looking liquid. Pour this over the vegetable, and scrape the skillet to deglaze it, releasing the thin pasty layer and the browned spices to create an intensely flavored sauce. Bring the curry to a boil. Then reduce the heat to medium-low, cover the skillet, and simmer, stirring occasionally, until the squash is juicy-tender, 20 to 25 minutes.

6. Stir in the tomato and continue simmering, uncovered, stirring occasionally, until it is warmed through, 3 to 5 minutes.

7. Stir in the cilantro, and serve.

Mango powder? See the box on page 604.

Ridged Luffa Squash
WITH GREEN PEAS

toori mutter

Jainism and Buddhism both arose in the 6th century in India, and the Jains, especially the ones who are quite orthodox, adhere to particularly strict guidelines about what they can and cannot eat. Anything that grows under the ground is taboo, as the teachings of Mahavira forbid disturbing living things under the earth. (Also taboo are meat, fish, poultry, and eggs.) This rules out garlic, onions, potatoes, and root vegetables, and hence their cooking relies on spices like asafetida (for that onion-garlic flavor) and vegetables like plantains (a starchy stand-by for the tuber the rest of us cannot do without). The blend of flavors here is so complex and appealing that I for one don't even miss the ingredients that we normally think we must have to make things taste better. I have used ridged squash and peas, but any other combination will be okay too. **SERVES 6**

2 tablespoons peanut or canola oil

2 teaspoons cumin seeds; 1 teaspoon whole,
   1 teaspoon ground

1½ pounds ridged luffa squash (see box); or English
   cucumber, ends trimmed off, peeled, quartered
   lengthwise, each quarter cut into 2-inch pieces

2 teaspoons coriander seeds, ground

1 teaspoon white granulated sugar

1 teaspoon coarse kosher or sea salt

½ teaspoon cayenne (ground red pepper)

¼ teaspoon ground turmeric

¼ teaspoon ground asafetida

12 to 15 medium-size to large fresh curry leaves

2 fresh green Thai, cayenne, or serrano chiles,
   stems removed, cut in half lengthwise
   (do not remove the seeds)

1 cup frozen green peas (no need to thaw)

2 tablespoons finely chopped fresh cilantro
   leaves and tender stems

1 teaspoon Toasted Cumin-Coriander Blend
   (page 33)

1. Heat the oil in a medium-size saucepan over medium-high heat. Add the cumin seeds and cook until they sizzle, turn reddish brown, and smell nutty, 5 to 10 seconds. Immediately add the squash, coriander, ground cumin, sugar, salt, cayenne, turmeric, asafetida, curry leaves, and chiles. Stir-fry to coat the squash with the spices and cook them without burning, 1 to 2 minutes.

2. Pour in 1 cup water and add the peas. Lower the heat to medium and simmer, uncovered, stirring occasionally, until the squash is fork-tender, 10 to 15 minutes.

3. Stir in the cilantro and the cumin-coriander blend, and serve.

Tip: This curry "walks the talk" of extracting multiple flavors from a single ingredient. Here you see cumin used three ways: whole seeds sizzled in oil, ground raw seeds cooked with the squash, and toasted ground seeds in the cumin-coriander blend. Coriander also plays a double role, and in conjunction with the cumin, it makes for a layered curry that is complex in flavor without being cumbersome to prepare.

luffa

❖ ❖ ❖

this vegetable does look like a luffa (or loofah) sponge—fibrous, with many ridges and sharp edges. The ridges run the length (8 to 10 inches) of the dark green squash. After you cut off about 1/2 inch on each end, use a paring knife to peel off the tough skin. The off-white, slightly spongy flesh (imagine a cucumber-zucchini hybrid) is very bitter when eaten raw (which I don't recommend), but once cooked, it is sweet and mellow. The seeds inside are fairly tender, so you can leave them. The flesh cooks quickly, so make sure you do not overcook it. Any Asian grocery store will carry this squash, which is also known as Chinese okra—but if it's unavailable, use 2 large English cucumbers (peeled and seeded) instead.

Ridged Luffa Squash
WITH
ONION AND CILANTRO

toori nu shaak

Gujaratis are masters at preparing vegetables, even simple-tasting squashes like this one, with great creativity. I especially love the textural contrast between the matchstick-thin ginger and the softness of cooked luffa squash. This makes a great side dish to any of the legume curries in this book, along with a bowl of white rice. **SERVES 6**

1½ *pounds ridged luffa squash (see box, page 613);*
   or English cucumber, ends trimmed off, peeled,
   quartered lengthwise, each quarter cut into
   2-inch pieces
1 *teaspoon cumin seeds, ground*
1 *teaspoon coriander seeds, ground*
1 *teaspoon coarse kosher or sea salt*
½ *teaspoon cayenne (ground red pepper)*
¼ *teaspoon ground turmeric*
¼ *teaspoon ground asafetida*
2 *tablespoons canola oil*
1 *teaspoon black or yellow mustard seeds*
1 *small red onion, cut in half lengthwise*
   and thinly sliced
4 *lengthwise slices fresh ginger*
   (each 1½ inches long, 1 inch wide,
   and ⅛ inch thick, cut into thin matchstick
   strips (julienne)
2 *tablespoons finely chopped fresh cilantro*
   leaves and tender stems

1. Place the squash pieces in a medium-size bowl, and add the cumin, coriander, salt, cayenne, turmeric, and asafetida. Toss to coat the squash with the spices.

2. Heat a large skillet over medium-high heat, and add the oil. Add the mustard seeds, cover the skillet, and cook until the seeds have stopped popping (not unlike popcorn), about 30 seconds. Immediately add the onion and ginger, and stir-fry until they turn light brown around the edges, 3 to 5 minutes. Don't worry if there are browned bits of onion stuck to the bottom of the skillet.

3. Add the squash mixture to the skillet, and continue to stir-fry until the spices turn aromatic and are cooked, about 2 minutes.

4. Pour ½ cup water into the skillet and scrape the bottom to deglaze it, releasing the browned bits of onion and spice. Stir the curry once or twice, and heat it to a boil. Then reduce the heat to medium-low, cover the skillet, and simmer, stirring once or twice, until the squash is fork-tender, 8 to 10 minutes.

5. Stir in the cilantro, and serve.

Tips:

❖ It is important to cook the spices, but ground spices are never tossed directly into hot oil because they will burn upon contact. If you coat a vegetable or meat with the spices and then cook them, you can rest assured that they will cook quickly and not burn. Burning makes spices unpalatable.

❖ If you wish for a more festive-looking curry, after the squash cooks, stir in 1 medium tomato, cored and cut into 1-inch cubes.

Sweet Potato and Plantain

IN A SAUCE OF FRESH AND ROASTED COCONUT

brussery

My sister-in-law Geeta is a great cook. She is a "foodie" in the true sense. She knows where to go for the best of the best. Her Keralite specialties—vegetarian offerings from her upbringing—pepper her kitchen, much to her husband's and son's satisfaction. This curry, reserved for special gatherings, is a harvest-season favorite and consumes a bit more of her time in the kitchen. "Because the coconut [a must in many of her dishes] is used in multiple ways to create the sauce's complexity, pay extra attention to the what, when, and how," she cautions. Well worth it, you will agree, once you sample the results. **SERVES 5**

- 1 very firm large plantain (about 8 ounces)
- 1 teaspoon coarse kosher or sea salt
- ½ teaspoon ground turmeric
- 1 large sweet potato, peeled, cut into 1-inch cubes, and submerged in a bowl of cold water to prevent browning
- 1 cup shredded fresh coconut; or ¼ cup shredded dried unsweetened coconut, reconstituted (see Note) and ¼ cup shredded dried unsweetened coconut left as is
- 3 fresh green Thai, cayenne, or serrano chiles, stems removed
- 1 dried red Thai or cayenne chile, stem removed
- 2 tablespoons coconut oil or canola oil
- 1 teaspoon black or yellow mustard seeds
- 1 tablespoon skinned split black lentils (cream-colored in this form, urad dal), picked over for stones
- 12 to 15 medium-size to large fresh curry leaves
- ½ teaspoon rock salt, pounded

1. Cut a ¼-inch-thick slice off both ends of the plantain. Cut the plantain in half crosswise. With a sharp paring knife, make a lengthwise slit, ⅛ to ¼ inch deep, down the length of each half. Wedge your fingers just under the slit, and peel off the skin in one easy motion. (You can peel the entire skin with a paring knife, but it is slightly more time-consuming.) Cut the light beige flesh into 1-inch cubes.

2. Bring a pot (at least a medium-size saucepan) of water to a boil over medium-high heat. Sprinkle in the coarse salt and the turmeric. Drain the sweet potato cubes and add them, along with the plantain. Bring to a boil again. Cover the pot and continue to boil over medium heat, stirring occasionally, until the vegetables are tender but still firm, 8 to 10 minutes.

3. While the vegetables are cooking, scoop out ½ cup of the cooking water and pour it into a blender jar. Add half of the coconut (½ cup fresh or the ¼ cup reconstituted) along with the fresh and dried chiles. Puree, scraping the inside of the jar as needed, to make a sauce; it will be slightly gritty to the touch.

4. Heat the oil in a small skillet over medium-high heat. Add the mustard seeds, cover the skillet, and cook until the seeds have stopped popping (not unlike popcorn), about 30 seconds. Add the lentils and stir-fry until they turn golden brown, 15 to 20 seconds. Remove the lentils and mustard seeds with a slotted spoon and add them to the pureed coconut mixture.

5. Add the remaining coconut (½ cup fresh or the ¼ cup dried) and the curry leaves to the oil remaining in the skillet. Roast, stirring frequently, until the coconut is toasty-brown and the curry leaves are dry and crinkly, 3 to 5 minutes. Add this to the pureed coconut mixture.

6. When the potato and plantain are cooked, reserve ½ cup cooking water and drain the rest. Return the vegetables to the same saucepan, and add the reserved cooking water, the coconut puree, and the pounded rock salt. Stir once or twice to incorporate them in one spicy harmony, and serve.

Note: To reconstitute coconut, cover with ¼ cup boiling water, set aside for about 15 minutes, and then drain.

Tip: The life of shredded fresh coconut (or thawed frozen coconut) is not that long. It will last maybe 2 days in the refrigerator, but beyond that, be prepared to discard it if it has turned rancid or to use it quickly before it does. Dried shredded coconut, on the other hand, will keep in the refrigerator for months. Incidentally, a large coconut will yield 2 to 3 cups of shredded meat.

Taro Leaves
WITH PEANUTS

Arbi Patte Chi Bhajee

My first sight of these gigantic leaves evoked images of Dumbo's ears. Heavily used in the cuisines of the Caribbean Islands, West Indies, Hawaii, and the western regions of India, taro leaves are bright green on the front side and olive green on the back. They are available seasonally in Caribbean, West Indian, and Indian markets—you'll find them in the refrigerated produce section. Taro leaves are never eaten raw because they contain a high percentage of calcium oxalate crystals. They are often stewed for long periods of time or steamed (as is the case in some Punjabi, Marathi, Gujarati, and Tamilian curries) until the leaves turn very limp. But once they are thoroughly cooked, their almost buttery flavor can prove highly addictive. I especially enjoy the wonderful textural differences in this curry, where the leaves are cooked with peanuts. I have had equal success using collard greens whenever taro leaves are hard to come by. **SERVES 4**

¼ cup yellow split peas (chana dal); picked over
*   for stones*
3 to 5 medium-size to large taro leaves
½ teaspoon tamarind paste or concentrate
2 tablespoons canola oil
¼ cup raw peanuts (without the skins)
¼ cup shredded dried unsweetened coconut
2 tablespoons chickpea flour
¼ teaspoon ground asafetida
1 teaspoon coarse kosher or sea salt
1 teaspoon white granulated sugar
1 teaspoon coriander seeds, ground
½ teaspoon cumin seeds, ground
2 dried red Thai or cayenne chiles, stems removed

1. Place the split peas in a small bowl and add hot water to cover. Let them soak for 15 minutes. Then drain them and pat them dry between paper towels.

2. Rinse the taro leaves under cold water. Slice each along each side of each leaf's central vein, ending up with two long halves; discard the veins. Stack similar-length halves and roll them into a tube shape. Slice the tube crosswise into thin strips, which will unfold into ribbons (chiffonade). You should have 3 cups of loosely packed ribbons. Set them aside.

3. Combine the tamarind paste with 2 cups water, and whisk them together thoroughly. Set this aside too.

4. Heat the oil in a medium-size saucepan over medium-high heat. Add the peanuts and split peas, and stir-fry until they turn honey-brown and smell nutty, 3 to 4 minutes. Stir in the coconut, chickpea flour, and asafetida, and continue to stir-fry until the coconut and flour turn reddish brown and aromatic, 2 to 4 minutes.

5. Add the salt, sugar, coriander, cumin, and chiles, and stir-fry until the spices are cooked and the chiles have blackened slightly, 20 to 30 seconds.

6. Pour in the tamarind water, and stir in the taro-leaf ribbons. Heat to a boil. Then lower the heat to medium and boil, uncovered, stirring occasionally, until the leaves are limp and tender and the sauce has thickened slightly, 8 to 10 minutes.

7. Remove the chiles if you wish, and serve.

Tip: I like to serve this along with the *Arbi curry* (below), both as side dishes, to show my guests the markedly different flavors and textures from the same plant—the leaves so buttery and full of tender crunch, the root very starchy, soft, and succulent.

Taro Root
WITH CURRY LEAVES AND CHILES

Arbi Curry

this curry starts off watery-looking, but within minutes, thanks to the starchy taro, the sauce turns smooth and velvety. And what a picture: a tinge of purple peeking out from under a bright yellow sauce splashed with green herbs.

SERVES 6

- *1 pound taro root (see box, page 619)*
- *2 tablespoons canola oil*
- *1 teaspoon black or yellow mustard seeds*
- *1 tablespoon skinned split black lentils (cream-colored in this form, urad dal), picked over for stones*
- *¼ teaspoon ground turmeric*
- *¼ cup finely chopped fresh cilantro leaves and young stems*
- *1 teaspoon coarse kosher or sea salt*
- *10 to 12 medium-size to large fresh curry leaves*
- *2 to 4 fresh green Thai, cayenne, or serrano chiles, to taste, stems removed, thinly sliced crosswise (do not remove the seeds)*

1. Peel the gnarly-looking taro roots with a swivel peeler or a paring knife, and rinse them thoroughly under running water. They will be extremely starchy and slippery (no matter how much you rinse, the slipperiness will never go away). Slice each root in half lengthwise, and then cut each half in half crosswise, making 1-inch (or so) pieces.

2. Place the taro pieces in a small saucepan, add water to cover, and bring to a boil over medium-high heat. Reduce the heat to medium-low, cover the pan, and cook until the pieces are fork-tender, 8 to 10 minutes. Drain.

3. Heat the oil in a medium-size skillet over medium-high heat. Add the mustard seeds, cover the skillet, and cook until the seeds have stopped popping (not unlike popcorn), about 30 seconds. Add the lentils and stir-fry until they turn golden-brown, 15 to 20 seconds. Sprinkle in the turmeric and allow it to cook and color the oil, about 5 seconds. Then immediately add the cooked taro, 1 cup water, and the cilantro, salt, curry leaves, and chiles. Stir once or twice and bring to a boil. Lower the heat to medium and cook, uncovered, stirring occasionally, until the sauce thickens, about 5 minutes. (Because taro contains a very high amount of starch, the sauce will thicken quickly.) Then serve.

Batter-Fried Taro Root

WITH A PEANUT-GARLIC SAUCE

Arbi Pakode Chi Bhajee

frankly, I could eat the batter-fried taro root as is, without sousing it with the equally addictive peanut-garlic sauce. Go ahead and snatch a fried piece or two, and do take note of how much firmer (albeit slightly dry) this tastes when compared to the steamed pieces in the other curry recipes. **SERVES 6**

1 pound taro root (see box, facing page)
¼ cup chickpea flour
2 teaspoons coarse kosher or sea salt
1 teaspoon cayenne (ground red pepper)
Canola oil for deep-frying, plus 2 tablespoons
*   for the sauce*
¼ cup fresh cilantro leaves and tender stems
2 tablespoons salted dry-roasted peanuts
4 large cloves garlic
4 fresh green Thai, cayenne, or serrano chiles,
*   stems removed*

1. Peel the gnarly-looking taro roots with a swivel peeler or a paring knife. Thoroughly rinse them under running water. They will be extremely starchy and slippery (no matter how much you rinse, the slipperiness will never go away). Cut each root into 2-inch cubes. Place them in a medium-size saucepan, add water to cover, and bring to a boil over medium-high heat. Reduce the heat to medium-low, cover the pan, and cook until the pieces are fork-tender, 8 to 10 minutes. Drain.

2. Transfer the warm taro pieces to a medium-size bowl, and sprinkle with the chickpea flour, 1 teaspoon of the salt, and the cayenne. Toss well to coat the pieces. (The dampness of the taro will provide enough moisture to make the flour stick.)

3. Pour oil to a depth of 2 to 3 inches into a wok, Dutch oven, or medium-size saucepan. Heat the oil over medium heat until a candy or deep-fry thermometer inserted into it (without touching the pan's bottom) registers 350°F. (An alternative way to see if the oil is at the right temperature is to gently flick a drop of water over it. If the pearl-like drop skitters across the surface, the oil is ready.)

4. Line a plate or a cookie sheet with three or four sheets of paper towels.

5. Once the oil is ready, gently slide the taro pieces into the pan. Fry, turning them occasionally, until they are reddish brown and crispy, about 5 minutes. Remove them with a slotted spoon and allow them to drain on the paper towels.

6. Combine the cilantro, peanuts, garlic, and chiles in a mortar, and pound with the pestle to form a coarse paste.

7. Heat the remaining 2 tablespoons oil in a medium-size skillet over medium-high heat. Add the peanut-garlic paste and stir-fry until it is light brown and some of the garlic is starting to stick to the bot-

tom of the skillet, about 1 minute. Pour in 1 cup water and scrape the bottom of the skillet to deglaze it, releasing the browned bits of paste. Add the taro pieces and stir once or twice to coat them with the thin sauce. Heat to a boil. Then lower the heat to medium and cook, uncovered, stirring occasionally, until the sauce thickens and clings to the taro pieces, 6 to 8 minutes. Then serve.

Garlicky Taro Root
WITH TAMARIND

Lasoon Arbi Chi Bhajee

ut the purple-hued tender roots into 1-inch cubes for this incredibly easy and robust curry. It is dynamite with slices of warm buttered toast.

For an alternative cooking method, see the Tip on page 621. **SERVES 6**

1 pound taro root (see box, below)

1½ teaspoons coarse kosher or sea salt

1 teaspoon cumin seeds

4 large cloves garlic

2 to 4 fresh green Thai, cayenne, or serrano chiles, to taste, stems removed

¼ teaspoon ground turmeric

1 teaspoon tamarind paste or concentrate

1 tablespoon canola oil

1 teaspoon black or yellow mustard seeds

2 tablespoons finely chopped fresh cilantro leaves and tender stems

1. Peel the gnarly-looking roots with a swivel peeler or a paring knife. Thoroughly rinse them under running water. They will be extremely starchy and slippery (no matter how much you rinse, the slipperiness will never go away). Cut each root into 1-inch cubes. Place them in a medium-size saucepan, add water to cover, and bring to a boil over medium-high heat. Reduce the heat to medium-low, cover the pan, and cook until the pieces are fork-tender, 8 to 10 minutes. Drain.

2. While the taro root is cooking, combine the salt, cumin seeds, garlic, and chiles in a mortar and pound

taro root
❖ ❖ ❖

You've seen it in the supermarket, next to the root vegetables, fleetingly wondered what it was, and walked right by, put off by its rough, gnarly, hairy, odd-shaped appearance. Now that I have trashed its looks, I will talk about the inner beauty that lies underneath taro root's rough exterior (it's technically not a root but rather a bulbous rhizome). Taro's white, slippery flesh reminds me of potatoes and fresh water chestnuts, but of course it tastes like neither. It has a wonderful aroma when boiled or steamed, and turns light beige with a purple hue (if it were a paint, it would have a "foufou" name). It pan-fries, braises, deep-fries (my favorite), steams, boils, and mashes, to show its versatility as a favorite Old World tuber. The skin contains toxins (calcium oxalate crystals), as do its leaves, which make handling taro an itchy situation for people with sensitive skin; use disposable gloves if you are not sure—I am okay with my bare hands. So, for the same reason, please don't eat taro uncooked.

with the pestle to form a pulpy blend. (You will be amazed at the complex aromas that emanate from the mortar, even with these pedestrian ingredients.) Fold in the turmeric.

3. Combine the tamarind paste and 1 cup water, and whisk them together to dissolve the tamarind.

4. Heat the oil in a small saucepan over medium-high heat. Add the mustard seeds, cover the pan, and cook until the seeds have stopped popping (not unlike popcorn), about 30 seconds. Immediately add the pounded garlic paste and stir-fry until the garlic turns caramel-brown and bits of the paste are sticking to the bottom of the pan, about 1 minute.

5. Pour in the tamarind water and scrape the bottom of the pan to deglaze it, releasing the stuck-on bits of garlic, chile, and cumin. Stir in the taro root and bring the dark brown, watery curry to a boil. Lower the heat to medium and cook, uncovered, stirring occasionally, until the sauce turns velvet-smooth and viscous, 3 to 5 minutes.

6. Fold in the cilantro, and serve.

Lime-Tart Taro Root

Limboo Arbi

When I tried this recipe the first time, I realized why I can look beyond taro root's slippery texture so easily. It's because the flavor reminds me of the source of my primary food addiction: the potato. I feel guilty about wanting to eat potatoes every day, and taro is a pleasant alternative. **SERVES 4**

> 1 pound taro root (see box, page 619)
> 2 tablespoons finely chopped fresh cilantro leaves and tender stems
> 2 teaspoons Sambhar masala (page 33)
> 2 teaspoons coarse kosher or sea salt
> ½ teaspoon ground turmeric
> ¼ teaspoon ground asafetida
> 12 medium-size to large fresh curry leaves
> 2 tablespoons canola oil
> 1 teaspoon black or yellow mustard seeds
> 1 tablespoon skinned split black lentils (cream-colored in this form, urad dal), picked over for stones
> Juice of 1 medium-size lime

1. Peel the gnarly-looking roots with a swivel peeler or a paring knife. Thoroughly rinse them under running water. They will be extremely starchy and slippery (no matter how much you rinse, the slipperiness will never go away). Slice each root in half lengthwise and then cut each half crosswise into 2-inch pieces. Place them in a medium-size saucepan, add water to cover, and bring to a boil over medium-high heat. Reduce the heat to medium-low, cover the pan, and cook until the taro is fork-tender, 8 to 10 minutes. Drain, and let it cool for 5 to 10 minutes. (Or see Tip, below.)

2. Combine the taro, cilantro, *Sambhar masala*, salt, turmeric, asafetida, and curry leaves in a bowl, and toss to coat the taro with the seasonings.

3. Heat the oil in a medium-size skillet over medium-high heat. Add the mustard seeds, cover the skillet, and cook until the seeds have stopped popping (not unlike popcorn), about 30 seconds. Add the lentils and stir-fry until they turn golden brown, 15 to 20 seconds. Immediately add the taro mixture and stir-fry to cook some of the raw spices, 1 to 2 minutes. Pour in 1 cup

water, which will immediately come to a boil on contact with the hot skillet. Lower the heat to medium and cook, uncovered, stirring occasionally, until the sauce thickens, 3 to 5 minutes. (Because taro has a very high amount of starch, it will quickly thicken the sauce.)

4. Stir in the lime juice, and serve.

Tip: There is another, hassle-free, way to cook taro root. Scrub it with a vegetable brush, ridding it of some of its hairlike fibers. Cover it with ample water in a saucepan and bring to a boil. Cook, covered, over medium-low heat until a fork pierces the vegetable with ease, about 15 minutes. Drain it and allow it to cool. Peel the skin either with your fingers or with a paring knife to reveal a purple-hued white flesh that is not sticky or slimy to the touch. Cut it as the recipe recommends.

Beefy Stuffed Tomatoes

WITH
FENUGREEK-PERFUMED POTATOES

bharwan tamatar

Even though the title indicates "beefy," there is nothing here to turn the vegetarian—or the vegan—away from the table. The terminology has more to do with the oomph the curry delivers. This is a curry that uses simple ingredients, simply put together, to yield, well, simply spectacular flavors. It's great as a side dish with Bone-In Chicken with Squash and Pickling Spices (page 141). **SERVES 6**

1 pound russet or Yukon Gold potatoes, peeled, cut into 1-inch pieces, and submerged in a bowl of cold water to prevent browning

1 cup frozen green peas (no need to thaw)

½ cup chopped fresh or frozen fenugreek leaves (thawed if frozen); or 2 tablespoons dried fenugreek, soaked in a bowl of water and skimmed off before use (see box, page 473)

2 teaspoons Rajasthani garam masala (page 26)

2 teaspoons coarse kosher or sea salt

6 medium-size to large ripe but firm tomatoes, such as the beefsteak variety (6 to 8 ounces each)

1 tablespoon white granulated sugar

2 teaspoons ground Kashmiri chiles; or ½ teaspoon cayenne (ground red pepper) mixed with 1½ teaspoons sweet paprika

2 tablespoons canola oil

1 medium-size red onion, finely chopped

6 green or white cardamom pods

1. Fill a medium-size saucepan with water and bring it to a boil over medium-high heat. Drain the potatoes and add them to the boiling water. Bring it to a boil again. Then lower the heat to medium and cook, partially covered, until the potatoes are very tender, 8 to 10 minutes. Drain the potatoes and mash them in a medium-size bowl.

2. Add the peas, fenugreek leaves, garam masala, and 1 teaspoon of the salt to the potatoes, and stir together thoroughly.

3. To prepare the tomatoes for stuffing, cut a ½-inch-thick slice off the stem end of each tomato; discard. Working with one tomato at a time, use a serrated paring knife to cut around the inner wall, leaving a ¼-inch-thick shell; make sure you don't cut through the skin. Use a spoon to scoop out the pulp and seeds;

place them in a medium-size bowl. When you have hollowed out all the tomatoes, mash the pulp and seeds in the bowl with a potato masher. (I actually use my hand, because that's what cooks in India use. Squishy, seedsy, wet, it appeals to my inner child.) Stir in the sugar, ground chiles, and the remaining 1 teaspoon salt.

4. Preheat the oven to 350°F.

5. Fill the tomato cavities with the potato mixture.

6. Heat the oil in a medium-size skillet over medium-high heat. Add the onion and cardamom pods, and stir-fry until the onion is light brown around the edges, 5 to 8 minutes. Stir in the tomato pulp. *If your skillet is ovenproof,* place the stuffed tomatoes in the skillet and spoon some of the sauce over them. Cover the skillet and bake in the oven until the tomatoes soften, about 30 minutes. *If your skillet is not ovenproof,* transfer the sauce to an ovenproof baking dish and then arrange the stuffed tomatoes on the sauce. Spoon some of the sauce over the tomatoes, cover the dish, and bake until the tomatoes soften, about 30 minutes.

7. Remove the cardamom pods if you wish, and serve.

green Tomatoes
AND POTATOES WITH GARLIC

hare tamatar Aur Aloo ki Subzi

reen tomatoes should never be eaten raw because they contain an alkaloid called tomatine, which is a toxin, similar to the one found in potatoes that turn green.

When purchasing unripe green tomatoes, pick ones that are very firm to the touch and blemish-free, with a smooth, light green skin. (Some heirloom varieties remain green even when ripe. You want unripe tomatoes.)

Because of tomatoes' acidic nature (ripe or unripe), I recommend that when you cook curries containing them, you use only nonreactive cookware like stainless steel. Avoid aluminum, iron, and brass cookware, which can create a metallic reaction that will leave an unpleasant taste in your mouth. **SERVES 4**

2 tablespoons canola oil

4 large cloves garlic, finely chopped

8 ounces russet or Yukon Gold potatoes, peeled, cut into ½-inch cubes, and submerged in a bowl of cold water to prevent browning

8 ounces unripe green tomatoes, cored and cut into pieces 2 inches long and 1 inch wide

2 teaspoons Bin bhuna hua garam masala (page 30)

1½ teaspoons coarse kosher or sea salt

¼ teaspoon ground turmeric

2 tablespoons finely chopped fresh cilantro leaves and tender stems

1. Heat the oil in a medium-size skillet over medium-high heat. Add the garlic and stir-fry until it is reddish brown, the color of toasted nuts, 1 to 2 minutes.

2. Drain the potatoes and add them to the skillet with the tomatoes, garam masala, salt, and turmeric. Lower the heat to medium and cook, stirring, to gently cook the spices and slowly brown the potatoes, 8 to 10 minutes.

3. Pour in 1 cup water and scrape the bottom of the

skillet to deglaze it, releasing the browned bits. Once the liquid comes to a boil, reduce the heat to medium-low, cover the skillet, and simmer, stirring occasionally, until the potatoes and tomatoes are tender, 12 to 15 minutes.

4. If the sauce is not as thick as you would like it, mash a few of the potato and tomato pieces with the back of a cooking spoon.

5. Stir in the cilantro, and serve.

Tip: Don't mistake tomatillos (often called Mexican tomatoes) for regular green tomatoes. Tomatillos, which look like small green tomatoes except that they are enclosed in papery husks, are eaten both cooked and raw. For this recipe you want regular tomatoes—unripe.

Sesame-Flavored Green Tomatoes

hare tamatar til chi bhajee

Yes, fried green tomatoes are delicious (and I am the first in line at the local state fair to devour them), but this peanut-flavored sauce wrapped around slightly tart tomatoes is just as addictive. It shows us that we can do something different with green tomatoes. I had it with leftover Coconut-Smothered Pigeon Peas with Pumpkin (page 429) and some white rice for lunch.

SERVES 6

2 tablespoons peanut or canola oil

¼ cup raw peanuts (without the skin), coarsely chopped

1 tablespoon white sesame seeds

1 teaspoon cumin seeds

1 pound unripe green tomatoes, cored and cut into pieces 2 inches long and 1 inch wide

1½ teaspoons coarse kosher or sea salt

½ teaspoon cayenne (ground red pepper)

¼ teaspoon ground turmeric

¼ cup finely chopped fresh cilantro leaves and tender stems

1 teaspoon white granulated sugar

1. Heat the oil in a small saucepan over medium-high heat. Sprinkle in the peanuts, sesame seeds, and cumin seeds. Roast, stirring the mixture constantly, until the nuts and seeds are light honey-brown and smell nutty, 1 to 2 minutes.

2. Add the tomatoes, salt, cayenne, and turmeric. Stir to coat the tomatoes with the spices and cook them gently without burning, 1 to 2 minutes.

3. Pour in 1 cup water and bring it to a boil. Lower the heat to medium and continue to simmer vigorously, uncovered, stirring occasionally, until the tomato is partially cooked and some of the water has evaporated, thickening the sauce slightly, 6 to 8 minutes.

4. Stir in the cilantro and sugar. Reduce the heat to medium-low, cover the pan, and simmer, stirring occasionally, until the tomato pieces are tender but not mushy, 8 to 10 minutes. Then serve.

Tomatoes
WITH A MUSTARD SAUCE

Sorshe tamatar

the key flavor in this curry comes from pungent mustard paste, a delicacy enjoyed in the eastern states of India and an acquired taste among folks from other parts of the country. Bitter flavors maybe a hallmark of Bengali cooking (and are featured at the start of a meal), but foods that counterbalance the bitterness usually follow, making sure you do not leave the table with an unpleasant experience. This curry incorporates a burning glow from the chiles while cloyingly sweet jaggery keeps it under control, all coming together with acidic tomatoes in a delectable medley that goes well with Bottle Gourd Squash with Shrimp and Chiles (page 266). **SERVES 6**

> Jaggery? See the **Glossary of Ingredients,** page 758.

- *2 tablespoons black or yellow mustard seeds, ground*
- *¼ cup boiling water*
- *2 tablespoons mustard oil or canola oil*
- *3 or 4 dried red Thai or cayenne chiles, to taste, stems removed*
- *I pound (about 2 large) tomatoes, cored and cut into 2-inch pieces*
- *I tablespoon crumbled (or chopped) jaggery or firmly packed dark brown sugar*
- *I teaspoon coarse kosher or sea salt*
- *½ teaspoon ground turmeric*
- *¼ cup finely chopped fresh cilantro leaves and tender stems*

1. Combine the ground mustard and the boiling water in a small heatproof bowl, and stir well to make a thick yellow paste. (Even if you are using black mustard seeds, the paste will be yellow because the seeds are yellow inside.)

2. Heat the oil in a medium-size saucepan over medium heat. Sprinkle in the chiles and roast until they blacken and smell cough-inducing pungent, 15 to 30 seconds. Add the tomatoes, mustard paste, jaggery, salt, and turmeric. Once the curry comes to a boil, reduce the heat slightly and continue simmering vigorously, uncovered, stirring occasionally, until the tomatoes have softened but still maintain some firmness and the sauce has thickened slightly, 10 to 12 minutes.

3. Remove the chiles if you wish, stir in the cilantro, and serve.

Nutty-Hot Tomatoes
WITH GARLIC

tamatar Chi bhajee

for a truly comforting meal, serve this nutty tomato curry with fluffy thin rotis (page 727) and a side of store-purchased pickles. Add some Rice with Yogurt and Mustard Seeds (page 710), and the comfort will be complete. **SERVES 6**

- *2 tablespoons peanut or canola oil*
- *¼ cup raw peanuts (without the skin; also see Tips)*
- *4 medium-size cloves garlic, coarsely chopped*
- *2 dried red Thai or cayenne chiles, stems removed*

1½ teaspoons rock salt

1 teaspoon cumin seeds

1 pound (about 2 large) tomatoes, cored
*   and cut into 2-inch pieces (see Tips)*

¼ cup finely chopped fresh cilantro leaves
*   and tender stems*

1 teaspoon white granulated sugar

12 to 15 medium-size to large fresh curry
*   leaves*

Rock salt? See the Glossary of Ingredients, page 758.

1. Heat the oil in a small saucepan over medium-high heat. Add the peanuts and stir-fry until they are honey-brown and nutty-smelling, 2 to 3 minutes. Scoop them out of the skillet with a slotted spoon, leaving behind as much of the oil as possible. Transfer the peanuts to a mortar and add the garlic, chiles, and rock salt.

2. Pound the mixture with the pestle, scraping the sides of the mortar as needed to contain the mass in the center, until it forms a pulpy, gritty blend with the texture of slightly dry chunky peanut butter.

3. Reheat the oil remaining in the saucepan over medium heat. Add the peanut blend and stir-fry to allow the garlic to lose its sharp, pungent aroma, about 1 minute.

4. Stir in the tomatoes, cilantro, sugar, and curry leaves. Pour in ½ cup water and stir once or twice. Heat the curry to a boil. Reduce the heat slightly and continue to simmer it vigorously, uncovered, stirring occasionally, until the tomatoes have softened but still maintain some firmness and the sauce has thickened, 10 to 12 minutes. Then serve.

Tips:

❖ If you use preroasted peanuts, eliminate the first step. If they are salted, reduce the amount of added salt by ½ teaspoon.

❖ I cannot overstress the importance of using juicy, fresh, succulent-looking tomatoes for this recipe; they provide an intrinsic sweetness to the curry. Refrain from purchasing those waxy-looking tomatoes that never change color, no matter how long they sit in the bowl on the kitchen counter. If those are your only option, you are far better off using a pound of canned tomatoes. Substitute the juice in the can for the ½ cup water.

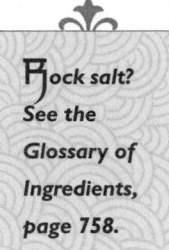

Turnips
WITH GARLIC AND BLACK CUMIN

Lasoon Waale Shalgam

A thin-sauced dish like this is great alongside a robust curry like Black-Eyed Peas with Mustard, Cumin, and Curry Leaves (page 322). Choose small turnips—they will be less bitter after the long simmering time than large turnips would be. **SERVES 8**

1 teaspoon black cumin seeds

6 medium-size cloves garlic, finely chopped

3 dried red Thai or cayenne chiles, stems removed

2 tablespoons canola oil

1½ pounds turnips, peeled and cut into 2-inch cubes

1½ teaspoons coarse kosher or sea salt

¼ teaspoon ground turmeric

¼ cup firmly packed fresh mint leaves, finely chopped

¼ cup finely chopped fresh cilantro leaves
*   and tender stems*

1. Combine the cumin seeds, garlic, and chiles in a mortar. Pound the mixture with the pestle, scraping

the sides of the mortar as needed to contain the ingredients in the center, to form a pulpy, gritty paste.

2. Heat the oil in a large skillet over medium-high heat. Scrape the garlic-chile paste carefully into the oil and stir-fry until the garlic browns and the chiles smell pungent, 1 to 2 minutes.

3. Stir in the turnips, reduce the heat to medium, and cover the skillet. Cook, stirring occasionally, until the turnips brown, 5 to 8 minutes. The chiles will smell even more pungent, so do make sure you have adequate ventilation.

4. Pour in 1 cup water, and sprinkle in the salt and turmeric. Scrape the bottom of the skillet to deglaze it, releasing any browned bits. Once the liquid comes to a boil, reduce the heat to medium-low, cover the skillet, and simmer, stirring occasionally, until the turnips are tender-crisp, 20 to 25 minutes.

5. Fold in the mint and cilantro. Simmer, uncovered, anointing the turnips with the sauce, until some of the liquid has been absorbed, 5 to 8 minutes. Then serve.

> **B**lack cumin seeds? See the **Glossary of Ingredients, page 758.**

ffixed Vegetables
WITH A PEPPERY LENTIL SAUCE

khatkhatem

A mixture of vegetables translates to *khatkhatem* and is Hindu Goa's signature dish, kin to the southern Indian *Aviyal* (page 630), but is unknown to most non-Goans.

(Nivedita Dempo, who married my dear friend Polu and is the daughter of a well-known industrialist from Goa, screamed with glee, *"Arre,* how do you know about *khatkhatem?"* when I mentioned that I had just made this curry after a recent trip to her homeland.) Its unique flavor derives from the spice called *tirphal,* a close sibling to the Sichuan peppercorn. The assortment of vegetables I have used in this recipe is typical, but by no means should you feel bound by it. The spice-coconut combination makes it memorable, and not necessarily the choice of vegetables (although I confess these are good together). **SERVES 8**

¼ cup oily or unoily skinned split yellow pigeon peas (toovar dal), picked over for stones

½ cup cubed unripe green papaya (1-inch cubes; see Tip)

1 medium-size white potato, such as russet or Yukon Gold, peeled, cut into 1-inch cubes, and submerged in a bowl of cold water to prevent browning

1 small Japanese eggplant (about 6 inches long and 1 inch in diameter), stem removed, cut in half lengthwise, and then cut crosswise into 1-inch pieces

1 medium-size carrot, peeled and sliced crosswise into 1-inch pieces

1 cup cut-up fresh green beans (1-inch pieces)

½ cup canned raw jackfruit, drained and rinsed, cut into 1-inch pieces (see box, page 512)

½ cup cubed fresh red pumpkin (1-inch pieces; see Tip, page 141)

5 to 8 pieces frozen "drumsticks," each 3 to 4 inches long (see box, page 489; no need to thaw)

1 teaspoon ground turmeric

½ cup shredded fresh coconut; or ¼ cup shredded dried unsweetened coconut, reconstituted (see Note)

6 to 8 dried red Thai or cayenne chiles, to taste, stems removed

1½ teaspoons coarse kosher or sea salt

1 teaspoon tamarind paste or concentrate

8 to 10 teflam seeds (see box, this page)

1. Place the pigeon peas in a small saucepan. Fill the pan halfway with water and rinse the peas by rubbing them between your fingertips. The water will become cloudy. Drain this water. Repeat three or four times, until the water remains relatively clear; drain. Now add 1 cup water and bring it to a boil, uncovered, over medium-high heat. Skim off and discard any foam that rises to the surface. Then reduce the heat to medium-low, cover the pan, and simmer, stirring occasionally, until the pigeon peas are tender, about 20 minutes.

2. While the pigeon peas are cooking, combine the papaya and all the vegetables in a large saucepan. Add water to cover, and stir in the turmeric. Bring to a boil over medium-high heat. Continue to boil, uncovered, stirring gently occasionally, until the fruits and vegetables are fork-tender, 12 to 15 minutes. Drain the ingredients in a colander, reserving 1 cup of the cooking water. Then return them to the saucepan, cover, and place over very low heat to keep warm.

3. When the pigeon peas are tender, dump them, liquid and all, into a blender jar. Add the coconut, chiles, salt, and tamarind paste. Puree, scraping the inside of the jar as needed, to make a spicy-hot sauce that is slightly gritty to the touch, thanks to the coconut.

4. Pour this sauce over the vegetables in the saucepan. Pour the reserved cooking water into the blender jar, and swish it around to wash it out. Add this to the vegetables.

5. Heat a small skillet over medium-high heat. Add the teflam seeds and cook, stirring them constantly by shaking the skillet, until they are slightly ashen and very

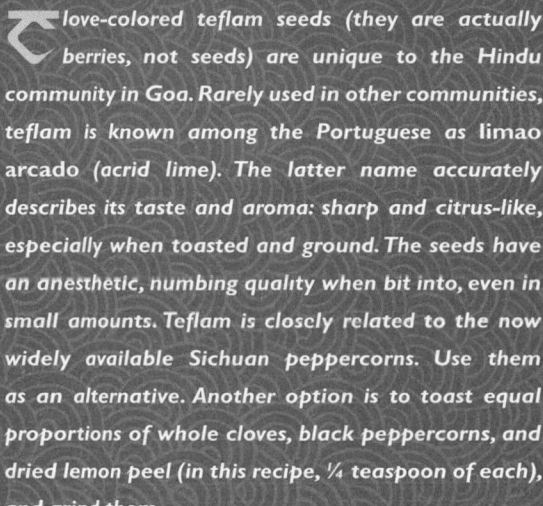

teflam

❖ ❖ ❖

Clove-colored teflam seeds (they are actually berries, not seeds) are unique to the Hindu community in Goa. Rarely used in other communities, teflam is known among the Portuguese as limao arcado (acrid lime). The latter name accurately describes its taste and aroma: sharp and citrus-like, especially when toasted and ground. The seeds have an anesthetic, numbing quality when bit into, even in small amounts. Teflam is closely related to the now widely available Sichuan peppercorns. Use them as an alternative. Another option is to toast equal proportions of whole cloves, black peppercorns, and dried lemon peel (in this recipe, ¼ teaspoon of each), and grind them.

fragrant, about 1 minute. Transfer them to a mortar or a spice grinder, and grind—which will release an incredible pepper-like aroma with a strong citrus perfume. The tougher hulls will not break down completely, so discard them.

6. Stir the ground teflam into the curry, and serve.

Note: To reconstitute coconut, cover with ¼ cup boiling water, set aside for about 15 minutes, and then drain.

Tip: To prepare the papaya, slice off and discard the stem and heel ends (about ¼-inch, crosswise, from each end). Peel the papaya with a vegetable peeler. Slit the firm, light green fruit lengthwise. Discard the white pearl seeds and the thin fibrous material underneath, scraping it off with a spoon. Cut the flesh into 1-inch cubes.

Three C's
IN A ROASTED LENTIL-CHILE SAUCE

Gajar, Bund Aur Phool Gobhi Ki Subzi

One day I brought several dishes to a friend's book club dinner. The group enjoyed them all, but this curry spoke to many with its bold flavors, unique combinations, and quick-cooking abilities. I personally love the inclusion of two acidic ingredients (tomato and tamarind)—one injects a clean, fruity taste, the other an earthy, molasses-like complexity. **SERVES 6**

2 cups chopped cabbage (roughly ½-inch pieces)

1 medium-size carrot, peeled, ends trimmed, cut lengthwise in half, and cut crosswise into ½-inch pieces

1 small cauliflower, cut into 1-inch florets

½ teaspoon ground turmeric

12 to 15 medium-size to large fresh curry leaves

2 tablespoons canola oil

1 tablespoon yellow split peas (chana dal), picked over for stones

1 tablespoon skinned split black lentils (cream-colored in this form, urad dal), picked over for stones

1 teaspoon coriander seeds

3 to 5 dried red Thai or cayenne chiles, to taste, stems removed

½ teaspoon tamarind paste or concentrate

1 medium-size tomato, cored and coarsely chopped

1½ teaspoons coarse kosher or sea salt

1 teaspoon black or yellow mustard seeds

1 tablespoon rice flour

2 tablespoons finely chopped fresh cilantro leaves and tender stems for garnishing

1. Combine the cabbage, carrot, and cauliflower in a medium-size saucepan. Add water to cover, and bring it to a boil over medium-high heat. Stir in the turmeric and curry leaves. Lower the heat to medium, cover the pan, and simmer, stirring occasionally, until the vegetables are fork-tender, 12 to 15 minutes.

2. While the vegetables are cooking, heat the oil in a small skillet over medium-high heat. Sprinkle in the split peas, lentils, coriander seeds, and chiles. Roast until the legumes and seeds turn reddish brown and the chiles blacken, 2 to 3 minutes. Using a slotted spoon, transfer the legume-spice blend to a blender jar, leaving as much oil in the skillet as possible.

3. Steal about 2 tablespoons of the cooking water from the simmering vegetables and pour it into a small bowl. Add the tamarind paste and stir to dissolve it. Pour this tart liquid over the spices in the blender jar, and add the tomato. Puree, scraping the inside of the jar as needed, to make a gritty, reddish-brown paste.

4. Drain the vegetables in a colander, reserving 1½ cups of the cooking water. Then return the vegetables to the saucepan. Add the lentil paste. Pour the reserved cooking water into the blender and give the blades a quick whir to wash out the jar. Add the washings to the pan, sprinkle in the salt, and stir once or twice.

5. Reheat the oil remaining in the skillet over medium-high heat. Add the mustard seeds, cover the skillet, and cook until the seeds have stopped popping (not unlike popcorn), about 30 seconds. Stir this seedy oil into the vegetables.

6. Heat the curry over medium heat, uncovered, stirring occasionally, to allow the flavors to marry, 3 to 5 minutes. Sprinkle the rice flour over the mixture and quickly stir it in. Cook until the curry has thickened, 1 to 2 minutes. Sprinkle with the cilantro, and serve.

Root Vegetables and Pea Pods

IN A GREEN PEA–COCONUT SAUCE

Surti Undhiyu

When fresh pigeon peas and their pods are in season, *undhiyu* stews its way into many a Gujarati kitchen, with purple and yellow yams, sweet potatoes, baby potatoes, eggplants, and plantains bubbling along with the peas in a spicy-sweet coconut sauce fortified with coarse mashed pigeon peas. I have been fortunate to sample many versions of this seasonal curry, with most of them swimming in ghee (clarified butter—oy, what's not to love?). My version is low in fat, but if you want that silky richness that ghee offers, drizzle a tablespoon or two over the stew just before you serve it. Fluffy thin rotis (page 727) or *pooris* (page 725) are a must, as is a big bowl of sweet pureed mangoes (page 751). **SERVES 8**

1 cup frozen green peas (no need to thaw)
½ cup shredded fresh coconut; or ¼ cup shredded
  dried unsweetened coconut, reconstituted
  (see Note)
½ cup firmly packed fresh cilantro leaves and
  tender stems
2 teaspoons white granulated sugar
1½ teaspoons coarse kosher or sea salt
2 to 4 fresh green Thai, cayenne, or serrano chiles,
  to taste, stems removed
Juice of 1 small lime
2 tablespoons canola oil
1 teaspoon black or yellow mustard seeds
½ teaspoon ground asafetida
1 bag (12 ounces) frozen Surti undhiyu mix
  (no need to thaw; see Tip)
1 large tomato, cored and cut into 1-inch pieces

1. Dump the peas into a food processor, and add the coconut, cilantro, sugar, salt, chiles, and lime juice. Process to form a wet minced blend, bumpy to the touch.

2. Heat the oil in a medium-size saucepan over medium-high heat. Add the mustard seeds, cover the pan, and cook until the seeds have stopped popping (not unlike popcorn), about 30 seconds. Sprinkle in the asafetida, which will instantly sizzle and smell slightly garlicky. Immediately add the pea mixture and simmer, uncovered, stirring occasionally, until a thin film of sauce sticks to the bottom of the pan, 3 to 5 minutes.

3. Pour in 1½ cups water, and scrape the bottom of the pan to deglaze it, releasing the film of cooked-on sauce. Empty the bag of *undhiyu* mix into the curry, and stir once or twice. Bring it to a boil. Then reduce the heat to medium-low, cover the pan, and simmer, stirring occasionally, until the vegetables are fork-tender and the sauce is clinging-thick, 30 to 35 minutes.

4. Stir in the tomato and continue to simmer, uncovered, stirring occasionally, until it is warmed through, 2 to 4 minutes. Serve.

Note: To reconstitute coconut, cover with ¼ cup boiling water, set aside for about 15 minutes, and then drain.

Tip: Bags of frozen *Surti undhiyu* mix are found in the freezer at every Indian grocery store. The mix usually contains shelled pigeon peas and flat pods (called *lilva papdi*), chunks of purple and orange-yellow yams, baby potatoes, cubes of small eggplant, plantains, and ovals of fried flour dumplings. In its absence, you can make up your own blend using seasonal root vegetables, snow-pea pods, and frozen green peas (totaling 12 ounces) for equally spectacular results.

Mixed Vegetables
WITH A
POTENT COCONUT-CHILE SAUCE

Aviyal

there's a reason why this precision-cut vegetable curry is relished at South Indian weddings. The time spent in cutting nine different vegetables, some of them of the root variety, warrants a sauce that will cling, letting the potent chiles, nutty cumin seeds, and sweet-fresh coconut adhere. My accompaniment of choice, hands down, is Rice with Yogurt and Mustard Seeds (page 710), a creamy rice treat that serves as a capsaicin-lowering backdrop for the potent chiles in the sauce. **SERVES 8**

1 cup cut-up fresh green beans (2-inch lengths)

1 cup cauliflower florets (2-inch pieces)

1 cup French-fry-cut fresh red pumpkin
(pieces about 4 inches long, ¼ inch wide,
and ¼ inch thick; see Tips, page 141)

½ cup frozen green peas (no need to thaw)

½ cup cubed frozen yams (no need to thaw)
or fresh yams (½-inch pieces; see Tip)

8 to 10 pieces (3 to 4 inches long) frozen
"drumsticks" (no need to thaw; see box,
page 489)

1 medium-size russet or Yukon Gold potato, peeled
and cut into French-fry pieces (about 4 inches
long, ¼ inch wide, and ¼ inch thick)

1 medium-size sweet potato, peeled and
cut into French-fry pieces (about 4 inches
long, ¼ inch wide, and ¼ inch thick)

1 medium-size carrot, peeled, ends trimmed,
cut into French-fry pieces (about 4 inches
long, ¼ inch wide, and ¼ inch thick)

2 teaspoons coarse kosher or sea salt

1 teaspoon ground turmeric

1 tablespoon canola oil

1 tablespoon yellow split peas (chana dal),
picked over for stones

15 to 20 medium-size to large fresh curry leaves

1 cup shredded fresh coconut; or ½ cup shredded
dried unsweetened coconut, reconstituted
(see Note)

1 teaspoon cumin seeds

6 to 8 fresh green Thai, cayenne, or serrano chiles,
to taste, stems removed

1 teaspoon rock salt, pounded

2 tablespoons coconut oil or Ghee
(page 21; optional)

1. Dump all the vegetables (the green beens through the carrot) into a large saucepan and add water to cover. Sprinkle in the coarse salt and the turmeric, and bring to a boil over medium-high heat. Continue to boil, uncovered, stirring gently occasionally, until the vegetables are fork-tender, 12 to 15 minutes.

2. While the vegetables are simmering, heat the canola oil in a small skillet over medium-high heat. Add the yellow split peas and roast them, stirring constantly, until they are nutty-brown and aromatic, 1 to 2 minutes.

Scoop out the split peas with a slotted spoon and transfer them to a blender jar. Set the blender aside for the moment.

3. Quickly throw the curry leaves into the same hot oil; they will spatter and perfume the oil within seconds. Scrape the oil and the leaves into the simmering vegetables.

4. When the vegetables are fork-tender, reserve 1 cup of the cooking liquid and drain the vegetables.

5. Pour half of the reserved cooking liquid into the blender jar, over the split peas, and add the coconut, cumin seeds, and chiles. Puree, scraping the inside of the jar as needed, to make a slightly gritty sauce, mottled with chiles.

6. Return the drained vegetables to the same saucepan. Pour in the spicy coconut puree. Add the remaining reserved cooking liquid to the blender jar, and swish it around to wash it out; add this to the pan. Stir in the rock salt and coconut oil.

7. Bring the thick-sauced vegetables to a simmer over medium-high heat and cook, uncovered, stirring occasionally, until they are warmed through, about 5 minutes. Then serve.

Note: To reconstitute coconut, cover with ½ cup boiling water, set aside for about 15 minutes, and then drain.

Tip: Packages of cubed yams (yellow and purple varieties) can be found in the freezer of your city's Indian grocery store. Those same stores, along with African, Latin American, and Chinese grocery stores, also stock the fresh tubers. Peel off the tough exterior with a paring knife to reveal the fleshy root vegetable underneath.

Vinegar-Kissed Vegetables
WITH FRESH WHEAT NOODLES

thupa

I wanted to call this "Bhavesh Kumar Thapa's Thupa," but that would have been too cute (see page 550 for more about Bhavesh). Make a double or triple batch of fresh noodles and freeze the extras. For a curry that does not contain many spices, this is remarkably complex-tasting, the sharp vinegar pleasingly tart. **SERVES 4**

For the noodles:
- ½ cup unbleached all-purpose flour
- ½ teaspoon coarse kosher or sea salt
- ½ teaspoon Bangala garam masala (page 26)
- About 3 tablespoons boiling water

For the vegetable curry:
- 1 cup cut-up cauliflower florets (1-inch pieces)
- 1 cup thinly shredded cabbage
- ½ cup frozen green peas (no need to thaw)
- ½ cup fresh or frozen cut green beans (about 1-inch pieces; no need to thaw if frozen)
- 1 small carrot, peeled, ends trimmed, thinly sliced on an angle
- 1½ teaspoons coarse kosher or sea salt
- 2 tablespoons Ghee (page 21) or canola oil
- 2 tablespoons distilled white vinegar
- 2 tablespoons finely chopped fresh cilantro leaves and tender stems
- 1 teaspoon Garlic Paste (page 15)
- ½ teaspoon cayenne (ground red pepper)

1. To make the noodles: Combine the flour, salt, and garam masala in a small bowl. Add the boiling water, 1 tablespoon at a time, and stir the flour mixture until it just comes together into a soft ball. Use your hand to knead the dough to a smooth, satin-soft texture. If you feel you have over-watered it, dust it with a little flour and knead it again, repeating until you get the right texture. Wrap the dough in plastic wrap to keep it from drying out while you continue to work.

2. Fill a medium-size saucepan three-quarters full with water, and bring it to a rolling boil over medium-high heat.

3. Push the dough into the cylindrical cavity of a noodle press (see Tip) or a cookie press (use the plate with the larger round holes). Holding the press over the boiling water, press the dough down to extrude spaghetti-like noodles, letting them fall directly into the water. Allow them to cook briefly, until they have a wet sheen on the surface and are tender but still firm (al dente) when either bit into or cut with a fork. Drain the noodles in a colander and run cold water through them to prevent further cooking.

4. Set the noodles aside while you make the curry: Combine the cauliflower, cabbage, peas, beans, and carrot in a medium-size saucepan. Add water to cover, and stir in 1 teaspoon of the salt. Bring to a boil over medium-high heat and continue to boil, uncovered, until the vegetables are tender-crunchy, about 5 minutes. Drain them in a colander and run cold water through them to stop them from continuing to cook.

5. Heat the ghee in a large skillet over medium-high heat. Add the drained vegetables, vinegar, cilantro, Garlic Päste, cayenne, and the remaining ½ teaspoon salt. Stir-fry until the vegetables are warmed through, 2 to 3 minutes.

6. Add the noodles and toss the mixture to warm up the noodles, 2 to 3 minutes. Then serve.

Tips:

❖ The Indian noodle press (known as a *chakli press* or *sevai nari*) can be found in the equipment aisle in Indian grocery stores. Available either in brass, wood, or stainless steel, it is usually cylindrical in shape, about 4 inches long and 3 inches wide. The bottom of the press has four removable plates with variously shaped perforations. Use the mold that has the largest holes to extrude these spaghetti-thick noodles. Cookie presses, also known as spritzers, work equally well and are sold in kitchenware stores.

❖ Store-bought fresh or dried spaghetti is a perfect alternative.

Seasonal Vegetables
WITH YELLOW SPLIT PEAS

Subzi Dalcha

I love the completeness of this vegetarian version of a Hyderabadi classic from south-central India. Protein-rich yellow split peas combined with fresh seasonal vegetables yields a hearty, stew-like curry—perfect for a cold winter night by the fireplace, with a loaf of crusty French bread and a bottle of Côtes-du-Rhône. **SERVES 8**

½ cup yellow split peas (chana dal), picked over
for stones

I large russet or Yukon Gold potato, peeled,
cut into ½-inch cubes, and submerged in a
bowl of cold water to prevent browning

2 cups shredded cabbage

I cup cut green beans, frozen or fresh
(1-inch lengths)

I medium-size carrot, peeled, ends trimmed,
cut into ½-inch-thick rounds

1½ teaspoons coarse kosher or sea salt

½ teaspoon ground turmeric

2 tablespoons Ghee (page 21) or butter

I teaspoon cumin seeds

¼ teaspoon ground asafetida

6 to 8 fresh green Thai, cayenne, or
serrano chiles, stems removed, thinly
sliced crosswise (do not remove the
seeds)

6 medium-size cloves garlic, thinly sliced

2 tablespoons Toasted Chickpea Flour
(page 41; Tips)

¼ cup finely chopped fresh cilantro leaves
and tender stems

4 lengthwise slices fresh ginger (each 2½ inches long,
I inch wide, and ⅛ inch thick), cut into
matchstick-thin strips (julienne)

1. Place the split peas in a large saucepan. Fill the pan halfway with water, and rinse the peas by rubbing them between your fingertips. The water will become cloudy. Drain. Repeat three or four times, until the water remains relatively clear; drain. Now add 4 cups water and bring to a boil, uncovered, over medium-high heat. Skim off and discard any foam that rises to the surface.

2. Drain the potato and add it to the split peas. Pile in the cabbage, beans, and carrot. Cover the pan and cook until the cabbage wilts, 5 to 8 minutes. Then stir in the salt and turmeric. Lower the heat to medium, cover the pan, and simmer until the vegetables are fork-tender and the split peas are soft but firm-looking, 12 to 15 minutes.

3. While the vegetables are simmering, heat the ghee in a small skillet. Add the cumin seeds and cook until they sizzle, turn reddish brown, and smell fragrant, 15 to 20 seconds. Stir in the asafetida, chiles, and garlic. Stir-fry until the garlic is light brown and the chiles smell pungent, 1 to 2 minutes.

4. Once the vegetables and split peas are cooked, stir in the garlic-spiked ghee. Scoop a ladleful of cooking water from the saucepan, add it to the skillet, and swish it around. Pour the washings back into the pan, making sure you get every bit of spice. Stir in the chickpea flour, cilantro, and ginger. Raise the heat to medium-high and simmer the curry, uncovered, stirring occasionally, until the sauce thickens and the flavors mingle, about 5 minutes. Then serve.

Tips:

❖ Any combination of seasonal vegetables works here. Try sweet potatoes, winter squash, and spinach for a sweeter offering during the autumn months.

❖ Don't be alarmed by the number of chiles. All those vegetables, the split peas, and the toasted chickpea flour bring the heat level down to make each bite addictive without excess heat.

❖ If you don't have chickpea flour on hand, use 1 tablespoon cornstarch dissolved in 2 tablespoons cold water. Stir this slurry into the curry in Step 4 instead of the chickpea flour.

Nine-Jeweled Medley

WITH A CASHEW-RAISIN SAUCE

navratan korma

A special-occasion curry, this exemplifies the flavors that emanated from the royal palaces' kitchens in Moghal India. Today this nine-jeweled *(navratan)* offering is found on every north Indian restaurant menu around the world, often in a tomatoey and nutless rendition. My nut-based version stays true to the rich sauce that graced the royal table, as it will yours. **SERVES 6**

½ cup cut-up cauliflower florets (½-inch pieces)

¼ cup frozen green peas (no need to thaw)

¼ cup cut-up fresh green beans (½-inch pieces)

¼ cup cut-up yard-long beans (½-inch pieces);
    or ¼ cup cut-up frozen French-cut green beans
    (no need to thaw; ½-inch pieces)

¼ cup cut-up bottle gourd squash (½-inch cubes;
    see box, page 596)

1 small carrot, peeled, ends trimmed, cut into
    ½-inch cubes

1 small white potato, such as russet or Yukon Gold,
    peeled, cut into ½-inch cubes, and submerged
    in a bowl of cold water to prevent browning

1 small green or red bell pepper, stemmed, seeded,
    and cut into ½-inch pieces

2 tablespoons Ghee (page 21) or canola oil

1 small red onion, coarsely chopped

¼ cup raw cashew nuts

¼ cup golden raisins

1 teaspoon Ginger Paste (page 15)

1 teaspoon Garlic Paste (page 15)

¼ teaspoon whole cloves

¼ teaspoon cardamom seeds from green or white pods

1 or 2 fresh or dried bay leaves

1 tablespoon tomato paste

1½ teaspoons coarse kosher or sea salt

½ teaspoon cayenne (ground red pepper)

¼ teaspoon ground turmeric

½ teaspoon Punjabi garam masala (page 25)

4 ounces Doodh paneer (page 286), cut into ½-inch
    cubes and pan-fried (see box, page 286)

2 tablespoons finely chopped fresh cilantro leaves
    and tender stems for garnishing

1. Combine the cauliflower, peas, both kinds of beans, squash, carrot, potato (after you drain it), and bell pepper in a medium-size saucepan. Add water to cover and bring to a boil over medium-high heat. Lower the heat to medium and continue to simmer vigorously, uncovered, stirring occasionally, until the vegetables are tender-firm, 5 to 8 minutes.

2. Reserving 2 cups of the cooking water, drain the vegetables in a colander. Then return the drained vegetables to the saucepan. Leave the saucepan off the heat while you prepare the sauce.

3. Heat the ghee in a medium-size skillet over medium heat. Add the onion, cashews, raisins, ginger and garlic pastes, cloves, cardamom seeds, and bay leaves. Reduce the heat to medium-low and cover the skillet. Cook, stirring occasionally, until the onion and nuts are browned and the raisins have swelled, 10 to 12 minutes. Pour in ½ cup of the reserved cooking water, and scrape the bottom of the skillet to deglaze it, releasing any browned bits.

4. Transfer the onion blend, liquid and all, to a blender jar. Add the tomato paste, salt, cayenne, turmeric, and garam masala. Puree, scraping the inside of the jar as needed, to make a thick, reddish-brown sauce.

Add this sauce to the vegetables in the saucepan. Pour the remaining 1½ cups reserved cooking water into the blender jar, and whir the blades to wash out the inside of the jar. Add the washings to the saucepan.

5. Fold in the fried *paneer*. Cover the pan and simmer the curry over medium heat, stirring occasionally, until the vegetables and *paneer* are warmed through, 5 to 8 minutes.

6. Sprinkle with the cilantro, and serve.

Vegetable Medley
WITH A MINT-CASHEW SAUCE

Pudhina Kaaju Subzi

We Indians like our vegetables cooked a little beyond the al dente stage. This curry from my childhood days, as it is traditionally cooked, fits that almost-mushy requirement. But having spent more than half my life in the United States, I have gotten used to crisper vegetables. So when I make this in my Western kitchen, I tend not to overcook them, and as a result they provide a balanced textural contrast to the creamy mint-cilantro sauce.

SERVES 8

1 large white potato, such as russet or Yukon Gold, peeled, cut into 2-inch cubes, and submerged in a bowl of cold water to prevent browning

1 medium-size carrot, peeled, sliced in half lengthwise, and cut into 2-inch lengths

2 large green tomatoes, cored and cut into 2-inch pieces

8 ounces cauliflower, cut into 2-inch florets

8 ounces fresh spinach leaves, well rinsed

¼ cup raw cashew nuts

¼ cup firmly packed fresh mint leaves

¼ cup firmly packed fresh cilantro leaves and tender stems

1 or 2 fresh green Thai, cayenne, or serrano chiles, to taste, stems removed

2 tablespoons canola oil

1 teaspoon cumin seeds

1 small red onion, cut in half lengthwise and thinly sliced

1½ teaspoons coarse kosher or sea salt

1. Drain the potato and combine it with the carrot and tomatoes in a medium-size saucepan. Add 1½ cups water and bring to a boil over medium-high heat. Reduce the heat to medium-low, cover the pan, and simmer, stirring occasionally, until the vegetables are tender but still very firm-looking, 10 to 12 minutes.

2. Stir in the cauliflower and continue to simmer, covered, until the vegetables are fall-apart tender, 5 to 10 minutes.

3. Add the spinach, a couple of handfuls at a time, and stir it in until wilted (about 3 minutes per batch). (Don't worry about breaking up the cooked vegetables, as that will provide some body to the sauce.) Place the pan, covered, over very low heat to keep warm.

4. Pour ¼ cup water into a blender jar and add the cashews, mint, cilantro, and chiles. Puree, scraping the inside of the jar as needed, to make a slightly gritty, creamy, pesto-looking sauce.

5. Heat the oil in a medium-size skillet over medium-high heat. Add the cumin seeds and cook until they sizzle, turn reddish brown, and smell nutty, 5 to 10 seconds. Then add the onion and stir-fry until it is honey-brown, 5 to 8 minutes.

6. Add the herb-cashew puree to the onion. Pour ¼ cup water into the blender jar and swish it around to wash it out; add this to the onion mixture. Lower the heat to medium and cook the sauce, uncovered, stirring occasionally, until some of the oil starts to separate and a thin brown layer forms on the bottom of the skillet, 10 to 15 minutes.

7. Add the sauce to the vegetables in the saucepan. Spoon some of the liquid from the saucepan into the skillet, and scrape the bottom of the skillet to deglaze it, releasing the browned layer. Add this to the vegetables.

8. Stir in the salt and simmer the curry, uncovered, to allow the flavors to mingle and the vegetables to reheat, 3 to 5 minutes. Then serve.

Tip: You can substitute the vegetables I call for with a combination that suits your fancy. Adjust your cooking time to accommodate them.

Sweet Bananas
WITH CHILES AND CUMIN

kela ŋu Shaak

Swetal Sindhvad's father was a hardworking man from a not-so-prosperous background in Ahmedabad, in northwestern India. He was blessed with a supportive wife and beautiful children, and he worked in numerous jobs in unhygienic conditions so that his family would have a successful life—a life that he made possible when he immigrated to the United States. Swetal talks warmly about her father—and about this banana curry, which her father made whenever he had to fend for himself. **SERVES 4**

2 tablespoons Ghee (page 21) or butter
    (preferably unsalted)
1 teaspoon cumin seeds
2 fresh green Thai, cayenne, or serrano chiles,
    stems removed
2 firm but ripe bananas, peeled, sliced lengthwise
    in half, and cut into ½-inch pieces
½ teaspoon coarse kosher or sea salt
¼ teaspoon ground turmeric
¼ teaspoon cayenne (ground red pepper)
2 tablespoons finely chopped fresh cilantro
    leaves and tender stems for garnishing

1. Heat the ghee in a medium-size skillet over medium-high heat. Add the cumin seeds and chiles, and cook until the seeds sizzle and turn reddish brown and the chiles blister, 10 to 20 seconds. Immediately add the bananas, salt, turmeric, and cayenne.

2. Lower the heat to medium, cover the skillet, and simmer, stirring occasionally, until the bananas soften but are still firm-looking and the mixture has a bit of a sauce, 10 to 15 minutes.

3. Sprinkle with the cilantro, and serve.

Tip: Sweetness, either added or inherent, is a hallmark of Gujarati curries. White granulated sugar and unrefined cane sugar (jaggery) are the usual choices, but when sweet bananas are the main attraction, you need neither. Ripe bananas also contain plenty of moisture and make it unnecessary to add any liquid. I wouldn't use overripe bananas because they will turn the curry mushy and unattractive.

Guava and Pomegranate
WITH MUSTARD SEEDS

Peru Anardana Nu Shaak

Nothing evokes the tropics more than musky-smelling, tennis-ball-size guavas with their seedy pulp and red pomegranates with their juicy ruby-red seeds. Bring them together in a chile-hot curry and you have an unusual package that is sure to pique the interest of even the hard-core gourmet at your dinner table. The pomegranate will start to lose its lush red color if it sits in the sauce for too long, so don't stir it in until just before you serve the curry. **SERVES 8**

2 tablespoons canola oil

1 teaspoon black or yellow mustard seeds

1 teaspoon cumin seeds

1 teaspoon ground Deggi chiles (see box, page 290); or ½ teaspoon cayenne (ground red pepper) mixed with ½ teaspoon sweet paprika

1 teaspoon coarse kosher or sea salt

½ teaspoon ground turmeric

¼ teaspoon ground asafetida

2 medium-size to large fresh ripe but firm guavas, cut into ½-inch cubes (see Tip, page 638)

2 cups fresh pomegranate seeds (see box, page 106)

2 tablespoons finely chopped fresh cilantro leaves and tender stems

1. Heat the oil in a medium-size saucepan over medium-high heat. Add the mustard seeds, cover the pan, and cook until the seeds have stopped popping (not unlike popcorn), about 30 seconds. Remove the pan from heat and sprinkle in the cumin seeds, ground chiles, salt, turmeric, and asafetida. The spices will instantly sizzle and smell aromatic. Pour in 1 cup water.

2. Return the pan to the heat and add the guava. Bring to a boil. Then reduce the heat to medium-low, cover the pan, and simmer, stirring occasionally, until the fruit is fork-tender, like firm-cooked apples, 15 to 20 minutes. Some of the guava's pulp will break down and thicken the sauce slightly.

3. Stir in the pomegranate seeds and cilantro, and serve.

guavas

Guavas, evidence of which has been discovered in the excavations of the ancient civilizations of Peru, made their journey to India in the 17th century, thanks to the Portuguese traders and settlers. Numerous varieties exist, ranging from pear-shaped to round ones, their flesh colors spanning from creamy white to yellow to pink (the pink kind contains lycopene, the same antioxidant found in tomatoes, which lowers the risk of heart disease and certain forms of cancer). When guavas are in season in India, vendors push carts loaded with the strong-smelling fruit (strong-smelling because of the essential oil eugenol, also found in cloves), and on request cut them and smother them with cayenne and black salt, a spice blend that elevates their sweetness. That same principle is applied in Guava and Pomegranate with Mustard Seeds, a dish found in Gujarati-speaking homes, where sweet and hot flavors are hallmarks of the cuisine.

Tip: I have stumbled across fresh guavas in Indian and Southeast Asian grocery stores, pretty much all year round. If you wish, use firm pears or slightly tart apples as an alternative to the guavas.

green Mangoes
WITH A YOGURT-TOASTED COCONUT SAUCE

kalan

My sister-in-law, Geeta, has a passion for food. If you need to know where to go for the best samosas or the sweetest mangoes, she can rattle off the appropriate vendors. Her cooking reflects her enthusiastic culinary meanderings, and this curry with unripe mangoes also mirrors her familial heritage as a Palghat Iyer from Kerala. *Kalan* is also made with winter melon, but I find this version far more interesting. **SERVES 6**

Jaggery? See the Glossary of Ingredients, page 758.

2 large green (unripe) mangoes, peeled, seeded, and cut into ½-inch cubes (see box, page 641)

1 teaspoon coarse kosher or sea salt

¼ teaspoon ground turmeric

2 tablespoons canola oil

1 cup shredded fresh coconut; or ½ cup shredded dried unsweetened coconut, reconstituted (see Note)

1 tablespoon yellow split peas (chana dal), picked over for stones

1 teaspoon black peppercorns

1 or 2 fresh green Thai, cayenne, or serrano chiles, to taste, stems removed

1 or 2 dried red Thai or cayenne chiles, to taste, stems removed

1 tablespoon crumbled (or chopped) jaggery or firmly packed dark brown sugar

½ cup Thick Yogurt (page 22)

½ teaspoon black or yellow mustard seeds

¼ teaspoon fenugreek seeds

1. Combine the mangoes, salt, turmeric, and 3 cups water in a medium-size saucepan and bring to a boil over medium heat. Continue to boil, uncovered, stirring occasionally, until the mangoes are tender but still firm-looking, 8 to 10 minutes.

2. While the mangoes are cooking, heat 1 tablespoon of the oil in a medium-size skillet over medium-high heat. Add the coconut, split peas, peppercorns, and the fresh and dried chiles, and stir-fry until the coconut is toasty brown and the chiles have blistered slightly, about 5 minutes.

3. Drain the mangoes, reserving 1 cup of the yellow broth.

4. Pour ½ cup of the reserved mango broth into the coconut mixture and scrape the bottom of the skillet to deglaze it, releasing any browned bits of coconut. Transfer this mixture to a blender jar and puree, scraping the inside of the jar as needed, to make a gritty, light brown, spice-speckled paste.

5. Return the drained mangoes to the same saucepan they cooked in, and add the coconut paste. Pour the remaining ½ cup reserved broth into the blender jar and swish it around to wash it out. Add the washings to the pan. Add the jaggery and stir once or twice. Cook the curry over medium heat, uncovered, stirring occasionally, until the jaggery dissolves, 3 to 5 minutes. Remove the pan from the heat and stir in the Thick Yogurt. (If the yogurt curdles in the heat, don't worry—the gritty coconut paste in the curry will camouflage it.)

6. Heat the remaining 1 tablespoon oil in a small skillet over medium-high heat. Add the mustard seeds, cover the skillet, and cook until the seeds have stopped popping (not unlike popcorn), about 30 seconds. Add the fenugreek seeds, which will instantly sizzle and smell nutty-bitter. Pour this oil-seed combination into the curry, stir it once or twice, and serve.

Note: To reconstitute coconut, cover with ½ cup boiling water, set aside for about 15 minutes, and then drain.

Fragrant Mangoes
WITH A COCONUT–CURRY LEAF SAUCE

Maangai Morekootan

I love the tart-hot-sweet flavors of this curry ladled over Kerala's other delicacy: nests of steamed rice noodles called *Idiappam* (page 723). It's actually a great breakfast combination—try it for an unusual Sunday morning wake-up call instead of maple syrup–smothered pancakes. **SERVES 6**

¼ cup oily or unoily skinned split yellow pigeon peas (toovar dal), picked over for stones

1 large green (unripe) mango, peeled, seeded, and cut into ½-inch cubes (see box, page 641)

1 cup shredded fresh coconut; or ½ cup shredded dried unsweetened coconut, reconstituted (see Note)

1 teaspoon cumin seeds

25 medium-size to large fresh curry leaves

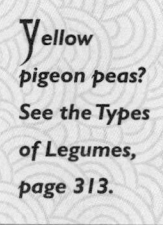

Yellow pigeon peas? See the Types of Legumes, page 313.

3 dried red Thai or cayenne chiles, stems removed

1 tablespoon coconut oil or canola oil

1 teaspoon black or yellow mustard seeds

1 tablespoon skinned split black lentils (cream-colored in this form, urad dal), picked over for stones

1. Place the pigeon peas in a small saucepan. Fill the pan halfway with water and rinse the peas by rubbing them between your fingertips. The water will become cloudy. Drain this water. Repeat three or four times, until the water remains relatively clear; drain. Now add 1 cup water and bring it to a boil, uncovered, over medium-high heat. Skim off and discard any foam that rises to the surface. Reduce the heat to medium-low, cover the pan, and simmer, stirring occasionally, until the pigeon peas are tender, about 20 minutes.

2. While the pigeon peas are cooking, combine 1 cup water and the mango in a medium-size saucepan, and bring to a boil over medium-high heat. Lower the heat to medium and cook, uncovered, until most of the water has evaporated and the mango is very tender, 12 to 15 minutes.

3. Once the pigeon peas are tender, pour them, with their cooking water, into a blender jar. Add the coconut, cumin seeds, 15 curry leaves, and the chiles. Puree, scraping the inside of the jar as needed, to form a slightly gritty, creamy yellow paste speckled with red and green. Add this to the cooked mango.

4. Heat the oil in a small skillet over medium-high heat. Add the mustard seeds, cover the skillet, and cook until the seeds have stopped popping (not unlike popcorn), about 30 seconds. Add the black lentils and stir-fry until

they turn golden brown, 15 to 20 seconds. Remove the skillet from the heat and carefully stir in the remaining 10 curry leaves, which will splatter. Pour this mixture into the mango curry and stir once or twice.

5. Heat the curry over medium heat, uncovered, stirring occasionally, until the flavors mingle, about 5 minutes. Then serve.

Note: To reconstitute coconut, cover with ½ cup boiling water, set aside for about 15 minutes, and then drain.

Tart-Hot Mangoes
WITH A COCONUT–RED CHILE SAUCE

Maangai Masiyal

When you live in a country that has over 125 varieties of mangoes, of course you will use them every which way possible, including in curries. The small green Asian mango (roughly half the size of the mango you typically see at the grocery store here in the United States) offers a pleasant tartness to this dish and eliminates the need to incorporate tamarind, which imparts sourness to southern Indian curries. Asian supermarkets here also stock a much larger variety of mango known as the Haitian mango; its shape resembles the beak of a macaw. Use this or go to your mainstream supermarket and choose the firmest, greenest mango there. The key is "unripe"—that's more important than the variety. **SERVES 6**

I pound green unripe mangoes, peeled, seeded, and cut into ½-inch cubes (see box, facing page)

¼ teaspoon ground turmeric

¼ teaspoon ground asafetida

2 tablespoons canola oil

I teaspoon coriander seeds

2 or 3 dried red Thai or cayenne chiles, to taste, stems removed

I cup shredded fresh coconut; or ½ cup shredded dried unsweetened coconut, reconstituted (see Note)

I teaspoon black or yellow mustard seeds

I tablespoon skinned split black lentils (cream-colored in this form, urad dal), picked over for stones

10 medium-size to large fresh curry leaves

I teaspoon coarse kosher or sea salt

1. Pour 1 cup water into a small saucepan, and add the mango, turmeric, and asafetida. Bring to a boil over medium-high heat. Then reduce the heat to medium-low, cover the pan, and cook, stirring occasionally, until the mango is very tender, 5 to 7 minutes.

2. While the mango is cooking, preheat a small skillet over medium-high heat. Pour the oil into the skillet and swirl it around to coat the bottom evenly. Sprinkle the coriander seeds and the chiles into the hot oil, and roast, stirring constantly, until the coriander turns reddish brown and the chiles blacken slightly, about 1 minute. Remove the skillet from the heat. Using a slotted spoon, transfer the nutty, pungent-smelling spices to a blender jar. Set the skillet aside. Add the coconut and ½ cup water, and puree, scraping the inside of the jar as needed, to make a slightly gritty, reddish-brown speckled paste.

3. Add the coconut paste to the mango mixture. Pour ¼ cup water into the blender jar, swish it around to wash the jar, and add this to the mango mixture, stirring once or twice.

4. Reheat the spiced oil in the skillet over medium-high heat. Add the mustard seeds, cover, and cook until the seeds have stopped popping (not unlike popcorn), about 30 seconds. Add the lentils and stir-fry until they turn golden brown, 15 to 20 seconds. Remove the skillet from the heat and add the curry leaves. Scrape this perfumed, slightly citrus-smelling oil and lentil mixture into the mango curry. Add the salt and simmer, uncovered, stirring occasionally, until the flavors mingle, about 5 minutes. Then serve.

Note: To reconstitute coconut, cover with ½ cup boiling water, set aside for about 15 minutes, and then drain.

Tip: This is a great curry to serve with the savory lentil pancakes known as *Vengayam adai* (page 724). But when I don't have any pancakes, I serve it with slices of hot buttered toast with equal satisfaction.

how to handle a mango

❖ ❖ ❖

What do I do with it, how do I eat it, and—a much more desperate question—how do I cut it up? Here is how to handle an unripe mango.

The peeling part is easy: just use a swivel vegetable peeler to remove the skin.

Now you need to separate the light green, firm flesh from the large flat seed. Holding the peeled fruit firmly with one hand, set it so its tip is resting on the cutting board. Slice down the length of the broad side of the mango, running the knife as close as possible to the seed, to yield an oval, concave slice. Swivel the mango on its tip and repeat on the other side. Now slice off the narrower sides. (Frugal moi then continues to shave off as many slices as I possibly can, to leave behind a bald seed, not unlike my own pate.)

green Papaya
WITH GARLIC & CHICKPEA FLOUR

besan Waale kaccha Papeeta

I love the juicy texture of unripe papaya when it's cooked just right—it's similar to the bite of a perfectly ripe grape. The mellow-flavored fruit, used as a vegetable in this curry, is the ideal companion to perky spices. I like to serve this alongside Cardomom-Scented Chicken (page 157) and Sweet-Hot Basmati Rice with Jaggery and Chiles (page 715). **SERVES 6**

- 1 pound green unripe papaya
- 2 tablespoons canola oil
- 1 teaspoon cumin seeds
- 2 large cloves garlic, finely chopped
- 1 or 2 fresh green Thai, cayenne, or serrano chiles, to taste, stems removed, finely chopped (do not remove the seeds)
- 2 teaspoons Bin bhuna hua garam masala (page 130)
- 1 teaspoon coarse kosher or sea salt
- 2 tablespoons Toasted Chickpea Flour (page 41)
- ¼ cup finely chopped fresh cilantro leaves and tender stems

1. Slice off and discard the stem and heel ends of the papaya (about ¼ inch, crosswise, from each end). Peel the papaya with a vegetable peeler. Slice the firm, light green flesh in half lengthwise. Discard the white seeds and the thin fibrous material underneath by scraping it off with a spoon. Cut the flesh into 1-inch cubes, and set them aside.

2. Heat the oil in a medium-size saucepan over medium-high heat. Add the cumin seeds and cook until they sizzle, turn reddish brown, and are fragrant, 5 to 10 seconds. Add the garlic and chiles, and stir-fry until the garlic is light brown and the chiles smell pungent, about 1 minute.

3. Sprinkle in the garam masala and salt, and stir to cook the spices, 30 seconds to 1 minute. Pour in 1 cup water, and add the papaya. Stir once or twice. Heat the curry to a boil. Then reduce the heat to medium-low, cover the pan, and cook, stirring occasionally, until the fruit is fork-tender, 12 to 15 minutes.

4. Sprinkle 1 tablespoon of the chickpea flour over the curry and stir it in quickly to prevent any lumps from forming. Repeat with the remaining 1 tablespoon flour. The sauce will thicken instantly.

5. Stir in the cilantro, and serve.

Tips:

❖ If unripe papaya is unavailable, the more readily available bottle gourd squash (see page 596) provides the same succulent texture.

❖ The garam masala used in this recipe is the spicy kind. If you prefer less heat, eliminate the fresh chiles.

Peanutty Green Papaya

kacchu Papeeta Nu Shaak

Papaya makes a stunning transformation as it ripens from a light green–fleshed fruit (used primarily as a vegetable) to the salmon-colored sweet sensation we consume as a fruit. Even the pearl-like seeds change from snow-white to deep caviar-black, giving the fruit that exotic look we all admire. Unripe papaya is widely available in Asian and Indian supermarkets almost year-round, so you can make this peanut-rich curry weekly if you like. This Gujarati specialty proves once again that they are truly masters at creating delectable vegetarian fare. Savor it as a side dish with fluffy-thin rotis (page 727). **SERVES 6**

1 pound green unripe papaya (see Tips)
½ teaspoon cayenne (ground red pepper)
¼ teaspoon ground turmeric
¼ teaspoon ground asafetida
¼ cup raw peanuts (without the skin; see Tips)
2 tablespoons peanut or canola oil
1 teaspoon black or yellow mustard seeds
1½ teaspoons coarse kosher or sea salt
1 teaspoon white granulated sugar
1 large tomato, cored and finely chopped
2 tablespoons finely chopped fresh cilantro
  leaves and tender stems

1. Slice off and discard the stem and heel ends of the papaya (about ¼ inch, crosswise, from each end). Peel the papaya with a vegetable peeler. Slice the firm, light green flesh in half lengthwise. Discard the white seeds and the thin fibrous material underneath by scraping it off with a spoon. Cut the flesh into ½-inch cubes.

2. Place the papaya in a medium-size bowl, and sprinkle it with the cayenne, turmeric, and asafetida. Toss to coat the cubes with the spices.

3. Place the peanuts in a mortar and pound them with the pestle, or pulse them in a food processor, to the consistency of coarse breadcrumbs.

4. Heat the oil in a medium-size saucepan over medium-high heat. Add the mustard seeds, cover the pan, and cook until the seeds have stopped popping (not unlike popcorn), about 30 seconds. Reduce the heat to medium-low, add the peanuts, and stir-fry until they turn golden brown and smell nutty, 20 to 30 seconds.

5. Immediately add the spiced papaya cubes and stir-fry to cook the ground spices, about 1 minute. Pour in 1 cup water, and stir in the salt and sugar. Bring to a boil. Then reduce the heat, cover the pan, and simmer, stirring occasionally, until the papaya is fork-tender but still firm-looking and the sauce has thickened, 25 to 30 minutes.

6. Stir in the tomato and cilantro, and cook until the tomato has warmed, 1 to 2 minutes. Then serve.

Tips:

❖ If unripe papaya is not easy to find where you live, use zucchini as a passable alternative. Zucchini cooks more quickly, so check it after 15 minutes of simmering in Step 5. Once the zucchini is tender, remove the lid, raise the heat to medium-high, and continue to cook, stirring occasionally, until the sauce thickens, about 5 minutes.

❖ When you roast raw peanuts, as we do in Step 4, it provides a fresh, nutty flavor. You can use preroasted peanuts, but do stir-fry them too, for 5 to 10 seconds, for a burst of that same nutty taste.

❖ If peanuts are an issue, use raw cashews instead. If you don't eat nuts, leave them out (what a pity!).

Bengali-Style Green Papaya
WITH TOMATO AND CHILES

kancha pepe jhol

Common in Bengali-speaking kitchens, this thin, stewlike curry (*jhol*), combines unripe papaya with bitter, hot, sweet spices to create a surprisingly sweet and highly complex-tasting sauce. Watch out for those chiles, should one land on your plate. I love to bite into them with mouthfuls of cooked rice in between to absorb some of the heat. **SERVES 6**

1½ pounds green unripe papaya
2 tablespoons Ginger Paste (page 15)
½ teaspoon ground turmeric
½ teaspoon white granulated sugar
2 fresh green Thai, cayenne, or serrano chiles, stems removed, cut crosswise into ½-inch thick slices (do not remove the seeds)
2 tablespoons mustard oil or canola oil
1 tablespoon Panch phoron (page 36)
2 or 3 dried red Thai or cayenne chiles, to taste, stems removed
1½ teaspoons coarse kosher or sea salt
1 large tomato, cored and cut into 1-inch cubes
2 tablespoons finely chopped fresh cilantro leaves and tender stems

1. Slice off and discard the stem and heel ends of the papaya (about ¼ inch, crosswise, from each end). Peel the papaya with a vegetable peeler. Slice the firm, light green flesh in half lengthwise. Discard the white seeds and the thin fibrous material underneath by scraping it off with a spoon. Cut the flesh into 1-inch cubes.

2. Place the papaya in a medium-size bowl, and add the Ginger Paste, turmeric, sugar, and fresh chiles. Toss to mix.

3. Heat the oil in a medium-size saucepan over medium-high heat. Sprinkle in the *Panch phoron* and cook until the spices sizzle, crackle, and are aromatic, 10 to 15 seconds. Stir in the dried chiles and cook until they blacken slightly and smell pungent, about 5 seconds.

4. Add the papaya, and stir-fry until some of the ginger turns light brown and sticks to the bottom of the pan, 2 to 3 minutes.

5. Stir in 1 cup water and the salt. Scrape the bottom of the pan to deglaze it, releasing the collected bits of ginger paste and spices. The water will quickly come to a boil because of the pan's intense heat. Reduce the heat to medium-low, cover the pan, and simmer, stirring occasionally, until the papaya is fork-tender but still firm-looking, 15 to 20 minutes.

6. Stir in the tomato and cilantro, and continue to cook, now uncovered, stirring occasionally, until the tomato is warmed through, 3 to 5 minutes. Then serve.

Tip: For an unusual alternative to the papaya, use the white rind of watrmelon instead. It has the same juicy tenderness when cooked for a similar length of time.

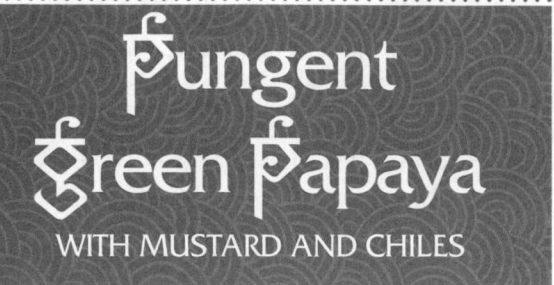

Pungent Green Papaya
WITH MUSTARD AND CHILES

Omita Khaar

he bitter flavor in this curry (*khaar* means "bitter") comes from baking powder, which helps to break down the vegetable and blanket it with a thick, slightly chalky sauce. Mustard oil and mustard seeds both augment that bitterness, chiles balance it with gentle heat, and they all come together with the juicy bite of tender, cooked green papaya. Monica Kataky (see page 237) told me she could eat this every day, and she did, growing up in Assam. A compound extracted from banana peel and burnt leaves (which contain potash and soda salts) is used in Assam to make *khaar,* but here in her home outside Minneapolis/ St. Paul, Monica resorts to baking powder to give that same flavor and texture to the curry. **SERVES 6**

1½ pounds green unripe papaya
2 tablespoons mustard oil or canola oil
½ teaspoon black or yellow mustard seeds
2 fresh green Thai, cayenne, or serrano chiles,
    stems removed, cut in half lengthwise
    (do not remove the seeds)
2 teaspoons baking powder
1½ teaspoons coarse kosher or sea salt

1. Slice off and discard the stem and heel ends of the papaya (about ¼ inch, crosswise, from each end). Peel the papaya with a vegetable peeler. Slice the firm, light green flesh in half lengthwise. Discard the white seeds and the thin fibrous material underneath by scraping it off with a spoon. Cut the flesh into 1-inch cubes.

2. Heat the oil in a medium-size saucepan over medium-high heat. Add the mustard seeds, cover the pan, and cook until the seeds have stopped popping (not unlike popcorn), about 30 seconds. Add the papaya and the chiles. Stir-fry until the papaya is very light brown around the edges, 2 to 4 minutes.

3. Sprinkle in the baking powder and salt. Continue to stir-fry, coating the papaya with the baking powder, until the vegetable is broken down, 2 to 4 minutes.

4. Pour in 2 cups water and stir once or twice. Cover the pan and simmer, stirring occasionally, until the papaya is fork-tender but still firm-looking, 15 to 20 minutes. Then serve.

Sweet Pineapple
WITH COCONUT MILK AND COFFEE

Anasi Curry

When Piyumi Samaratunga served this curry as part of her Sri Lankan dinner (see page 282), what caught my attention was the inclusion of ground coffee. We never used it in any of our curries, and I discovered that the slightly bitter flavor and deep color it brewed was a great balance to the pineapple's sweet-tart tastes. Piyumi served it with the lemongrass-flavored pearl rice called *Muttu sambha* (page 721), and I suggest that you do the same.

SERVES 8

2 tablespoons canola oil

1 teaspoon black or yellow mustard seeds

1 cup finely chopped red onion

2 teaspoons Untoasted Sri Lankan Curry Powder (page 40)

2 teaspoons finely ground coffee

12 to 14 medium-size to large fresh curry leaves

3 cups cubed fresh pineapple (1-inch cubes)

1 cup unsweetened coconut milk

1 teaspoon coarse kosher or sea salt

½ teaspoon cayenne (ground red pepper)

1. Heat the oil in a medium-sized saucepan over medium-high heat. Add the mustard seeds, cover the pan, and cook until the seeds have stopped popping (not unlike popcorn), about 30 seconds. Add the onion and stir-fry until it is light brown around the edges, 3 to 5 minutes.

2. Stir in the curry powder, coffee, and curry leaves, and cook until the ground spices are aromatic, about 30 seconds. Then add the pineapple, coconut milk, salt, and cayenne. Stir once or twice.

3. Once the curry comes to a boil, reduce the heat to medium-low, cover the pan, and simmer, stirring occasionally, until the flavors meld and the pineapple is cooked but still be firm-looking, about 30 minutes. Then serve.

Tips:

❖ Fresh pineapple is ideal for this curry—I don't particularly care for the metallic tang of canned pineapple. It is easy to cut your own chunks from the tropical fruit, but if that seems daunting, pick up precut cubes in the fruit and produce section of your supermarket.

❖ Fresh mango, papaya, and even nectarines are great alternatives, should you wish to try something different.

Sweet Watermelon
WITH GARLIC AND RED CHILES

barbooz ki subzi

In this delicacy from the desert region of Rajasthan, in northwestern India, common watermelon is transformed into an unusual curry—sweet, pungent, and juicy. I like to serve this watery curry with puffy fried *pooris* (page 725) and pungent chile pickles (either store-bought or homemade, page 744. **SERVES 6**

1 piece (about 3 pounds) seedless watermelon

2 tablespoons canola oil

½ teaspoon cumin seeds

½ teaspoon bishop's weed; or ¼ teaspoon
    dried thyme mixed with ¼ teaspoon
    ground black papper

½ teaspoon nigella seeds

4 dried red Thai or cayenne chiles, stems
    removed

4 large cloves garlic, finely chopped

¼ teaspoon ground turmeric

1 teaspoon coarse kosher or sea salt

2 tablespoons finely chopped fresh cilantro
    leaves and tender stems for garnishing

1. Cut off and discard the outer dark green skin of the watermelon, leaving as much of the light green rind intact as possible, along with the red, juicy flesh. Separate the red fruit from the rind by slicing it where the color changes. Cut the rind into 1-inch cubes and

the fruit into 1-inch cubes as well, keeping them in separate bowls.

2. Heat the oil in a medium-size saucepan over medium-high heat. Sprinkle the cumin seeds, bishop's weed, nigella seeds, and chiles into the shimmering oil and cook until they sizzle and smell nutty and the chiles blacken slightly, 10 to 15 seconds. Immediately add the garlic and stir-fry until it is golden brown, about 30 seconds. Sprinkle in the turmeric.

3. Immediately add the watermelon rind and the salt. Stir once or twice to incorporate the whole spices into the squashlike pieces. Continue to stir-fry until the rind is light brown around the edges, about 5 minutes.

4. Pour 1 cup water into the pan, cover the pan, and reduce the heat to medium-low. Simmer the curry, stirring occasionally, until the rind is fork-tender, 5 to 10 minutes.

bishop's weed? Nigella seeds? See the Glossary of Ingredients, page 758.

5. Add the red watermelon cubes and stir once or twice. Raise the heat to medium-high and simmer vigorously, uncovered, to allow the spices to flavor the watery curry, about 5 minutes. (The watermelon will lose a lot of its water, providing a thin broth for the curry, and still maintain its firm, juicy texture and taste. If you prefer a thicker sauce, coarsely mash some of the red fruit, providing instant body to the curry.)

6. Sprinkle with the cilantro, and serve.

Tip: Use the entire amount of chiles called for in this curry. The heat they generate is very mild because they are left whole—keeping the heat-producing capsaicin trapped in its long, curvaceous prison. If you want, remove them before serving the curry.

contemporary curries

aving lived in two countries (India and the United States) for over twenty years each, I consider myself a perfect hybrid of two cultures. So it is no surprise that I often combine the spices and herbs of my birth land with recipes and cooking techniques that are markedly Western. Pork Ribs with a Sweet-Sour Glaze (page 663) grills on the "barbie" for a lazy Sunday summer picnic, and

Leg of Lamb with an Onion-Coconut Sauce (page 660) perfumes my springtime kitchen. Looking for something different for a hearty winter stew, I serve a bowl of Three-Bean Chili with a Cashew-Pistachio Sauce (page 671) and some crusty French bread by the fireside. You have picky children? Expand their palates with a saucy rendition of Spaghetti with a Spicy Tomato Sauce (page 672) or Macaroni and Paneer (page 678). For a romantic Indo-French celebration with a loved one, savor Tandoori Mignon

with a Mushroom Cream Sauce (page 666) and a side of Scalloped Potatoes with Coconut Milk and Chiles (page 686).

With the influence of Chinese immigrants in India, it is easy to savor that culinary presence—even in remote village roadside restaurants that boast Gobhi Manchurian (page 683) or Hakka Noodles (page 675). You will not go wrong with any of these contemporary curries for any occasion. Hybrid is in, especially in this global community of ours.

Yellow Split Pea Soup

WITH BROWNED RED ONIONS, YOGURT, AND CHILES

A hearty first-course soup, this is delicious either hot or cold and makes an ideal introduction to an Indian-inspired meal. I often enjoy it all on its own, with a thick slice of rustic Italian bread or a slice of jalapeño corn bread, for a quick weekday meal.

SERVES 6 (4 AS A MAIN COURSE)

1 cup yellow split peas (chana dal), picked over
   for stones
4 medium-size cloves garlic, coarsely chopped
2 tablespoons canola oil
1 teaspoon cumin seeds
1 medium-size red onion, cut in half lengthwise
   and thinly sliced
2 lengthwise slices fresh ginger (each 2 inches long,
   1 inch wide, and ⅛ inch thick), coarsely chopped
2 fresh green Thai, cayenne, or serrano chiles,
   stems removed, coarsely chopped
   (do not remove the seeds)
1 teaspoon coarse kosher or sea salt
½ teaspoon ground turmeric
1 medium-size tomato, cored and coarsely
   chopped
½ cup plain yogurt
¼ cup heavy (whipping) cream
2 tablespoons finely chopped fresh cilantro leaves
   and tender stems for garnishing

1. Place the split peas in a medium-size saucepan. Fill the pan halfway with water and rinse the split peas by rubbing them between your fingertips. The water will become cloudy. Drain this water. Repeat three or four times, until the water remains relatively clear; drain. Now add 4 cups water and bring to a boil, uncovered, over medium-high heat. Skim off and discard any foam that forms on the surface. Stir in the garlic, reduce the heat to medium-low, and cover the pan. Simmer, stirring occasionally, until the split peas are partially tender, 25 to 30 minutes.

2. Meanwhile, heat the oil in a medium-size skillet over medium-high heat. Add the cumin seeds and cook until they sizzle, turn reddish brown, and smell nutty, 5 to 10 seconds. Then add the onion, ginger, and chiles, and stir-fry until the onion turns light brown around the edges, 5 to 8 minutes.

3. Stir in the salt, turmeric, tomato, and ½ cup water. Cook, uncovered, stirring occasionally, until the tomato appears saucelike but is still firm-looking, 3 to 5 minutes.

4. Add the contents of the skillet to the partially tender split peas.

5. Continue to simmer the split peas, partially covered, stirring occasionally, until the flavors marry, about 5 minutes. Remove the pan from heat and let the soup cool for 15 to 20 minutes.

6. Transfer half the split peas, with half the cooking water, to a blender and puree until smooth. Pour this creamy blend into a bowl. Repeat with the remaining peas and cooking water. Return all the puree to the saucepan. (If you have an immersion blender, you can puree all the peas and water right in the saucepan.)

7. Fold in the yogurt and cream. Gently warm the

dal

❖ ❖ ❖

dal is a cornerstone of many an Indian meal, in both vegetarian and nonvegetarian kitchens. Dal means many things to an Indian—it refers to legume varieties whose grains are split; it also signifies seasoned stewlike dishes. Dal, which is very accessible and inexpensive, is a humble man's source of essential nutrients, especially when combined with wheat flatbread or steamed rice. It is never served as a soup course in Indian meals (since multiple-course menus are not common—all the dishes are served at once).

I enjoy introducing classic Indian flavors in packages that are recognizable to the average American. Dal has often evoked the concept of "soup" to many of my students and dinner guests, and instead of continually trying to educate them to savor it as we Indians do (with flatbreads or over steamed rice), I decided to step out of my box and present it as a soup here, complete with traditional Indian seasonings of onions, chiles, and cumin seeds.

soup over medium-low heat, covered, stirring occasionally, 3 to 5 minutes.

8. Ladle the chowder-thick soup into individual bowls, sprinkle with the cilantro, and serve.

Tips:

❖ The Indian yellow split peas are slightly different in flavor (a bit sweeter) than their American counterpart, but the yellow split peas in your neighborhood supermarket will do just fine. Because they are split, they do not require pre-soaking and are quick to cook, making this an ideal legume for harried weekday meals.

❖ If yogurt is not your cup of tea, or you are lactose-intolerant or following a vegan diet, eliminate it and the cream from the recipe. Soy alternatives won't work here—they just don't have the same depth as their dairy counterparts.

mulligatawny

◆

I can only imagine what those blokes from the newly formed British East India Company must have thought when they first sampled south India's tamarind-tart, black-pepper-smothered *molagha tanni* ("pepper water," see page 441). Perhaps it was a shock to their senses, much like India itself—too many disparate flavors commingling in one thin-bodied broth. Over the course of time, the south Indian cooks learned to appease their sahibs by toning down the slap-in-your-face heat with cream (from coconut), even resorting to the inclusion of a commercial "curry powder" (invented by a canny south Indian businessman who had the vision to fulfill the Englishman's desire to capture the allure of India in one spicy concoction). Variations abounded over the years as meats, stock, celery, fruits, and nuts dotted this soup to conform to each cook's personal taste buds. My version keeps some of the original ingredients of Tamilian *molagha tannis* (like the pigeon peas and freshly pounded black peppercorns) and embraces one of India's oldest fusion curries with creamy passion. **SERVES 10**

½ cup oily or unoily skinned split yellow pigeon peas (toovar dal), picked over for stones

2 tablespoons canola oil

I teaspoon black or yellow mustard seeds

I medium-size red onion, finely chopped

I medium-size green bell pepper, stemmed, seeded, and cut into ½-inch pieces

I large carrot, peeled, ends trimmed, finely chopped

4 large cloves garlic, finely chopped

1½ pounds boneless, skinless chicken breasts, cut into ½-inch cubes

¼ cup finely chopped fresh cilantro leaves and tender stems

I tablespoon English-style Madras curry powder (page 24)

1½ teaspoons coarse kosher or sea salt

I cup unsweetened coconut milk

I cup frozen green peas (no need to thaw)

I large tomato, cored and cut into ½-inch cubes

½ teaspoon black peppercorns, coarsely cracked

1. Place the pigeon peas in a small saucepan. Fill the pan halfway with water and rinse the peas by rubbing them between your fingertips. The water will become cloudy. Drain this water. Repeat three or four times, until the water remains relatively clear; drain. Now add 2 cups water and bring to a boil, uncovered, over medium-high heat. Skim off and discard any foam that forms on the surface. Reduce the heat to medium-low, cover the pan, and simmer, stirring occasionally, until the peas are tender, about 20 minutes.

2. While the pigeon peas are cooking, heat the oil in a large saucepan over medium-high heat. Add the mustard seeds, cover the pan, and cook until the seeds have stopped popping (not unlike popcorn), about 30 seconds. Add the onion, bell pepper, carrot, and garlic. Cook, uncovered, stirring occasionally, until the vegetables start to turn light brown, 10 to 15 minutes. (At first they will release their liquid. Then, as it evaporates, they will start to brown.)

3. Add the chicken and stir-fry until the meat is seared, 2 to 4 minutes.

4. Sprinkle in the cilantro and curry powder, and stir occasionally to let the ground spices cook without burning, about 1 minute. Pour in 3 cups water and scrape the bottom of the pan to deglaze it, releasing any browned bits of vegetable, chicken, and spices. Stir in the salt. Once the broth comes to a boil, continue to boil it, uncovered, stirring occasionally, until the flavors meld, 10 to 15 minutes.

5. Meanwhile, transfer the cooked pigeon peas, with their cooking water, to a blender. Puree, scraping the inside of the jar as needed, until smooth. (If you have an immersion blender, you can puree the peas and water right in the saucepan.)

6. Add the thin, creamy-yellow pigeon pea puree to the chicken mixture, and stir in the coconut milk, peas, and tomato. Continue to simmer the soup, uncovered, stirring occasionally, to let the flavors blend, 5 to 10 minutes.

7. Stir in the pepper, and serve.

Tips:

❖ If pigeon peas are not on hand, use yellow split peas or red lentils as alternatives. Yellow split peas are thicker when pureed than pigeon peas, and so provide more body to the broth.

❖ If you wish, pass a bowl of chopped apples and/or golden raisins for folks to include as a sweet garnish.

Spinach Soup
WITH RED LENTILS

Pulsing the soup (as opposed to pureeing it) yields a nutty crunch that offsets the presence of the tender chiles. Barely cooking the spinach maintains its lush green color, which makes for an appealing-looking curry. It is delicious with slices of warm, crusty, sourdough bread and makes for a nutritionally sound meal. It's an especially good choice for cooler weather, when soup is what everyone wants for dinner.

SERVES 6 (8 IF SERVED AS A SOUP COURSE)

1 cup skinned split brown lentils (salmon-colored in this form, masoor dal), picked over for stones

2 teaspoons cumin seeds

2 teaspoons coriander seeds

4 to 6 fresh green Thai, cayenne, or serrano chiles, to taste, stems removed

2 tablespoons canola oil

1 small red onion, cut in half lengthwise and thinly sliced

6 medium-size cloves garlic, finely chopped

1½ pounds fresh spinach leaves, well rinsed

2 teaspoons coarse kosher or sea salt

1 teaspoon Balti masala (page 31)

1. Place the lentils in a small saucepan. Fill the pan halfway with water and rinse the lentils by rubbing them between your fingertips. The water will become cloudy. Drain this water. Repeat three or four times, until the water remains relatively clear; drain. Now add 3 cups water and bring to a boil, uncovered, over medium heat. Skim off and discard any foam that forms on the surface. Reduce the heat to medium-low, cover the pan, and simmer, stirring occasionally, until the lentils are tender, 18 to 20 minutes.

2. While the lentils are cooking, place the cumin, coriander, and chiles in a mortar and pound to form a pulpy, slightly gritty mass.

3. Heat the oil in a large saucepan over medium-high heat. Add the onion and garlic, and stir-fry until the onion is light brown around the edges, 5 to 10 minutes. Add the pounded spice-chile blend and stir-fry to cook the spices, 1 to 2 minutes.

4. Add the spinach, a few handfuls at a time, stirring until wilted, 1 to 2 minutes per batch. Repeat until all the spinach has been added.

5. Add the cooked lentils, with their cooking water, to the spinach mixture. Stir in 1 cup water.

6. Spoon half the mixture into a food processor or blender, and pulse to create a minced puree. Do not overprocess—you want some texture. Pour this into a medium-size saucepan. Repeat with the remaining mixture, and add it to the saucepan. Stir in the salt and masala.

7. Simmer the soup over medium heat, stirring occasionally, for about 5 minutes, and serve.

Tip: For a slightly bitter flavor, substitute mustard, kale, collard, or radish greens for half the spinach in the recipe.

Matzo Ball Soup

For my dear friend Jeff Mandel, a successful and compassionate internist (did I mention that he is handsome and single, ladies?), nothing evokes a stronger childhood memory of family, comfort, ritual, and tradition (including the search for the *afikomen*—the hidden matzo) than a bowl of matzo ball soup at the yearly Passover meal. The first time I sampled his classic version was at his house, at my first Passover, when his boisterous sister's outburst, "My, Jeff, your balls are light and fluffy," helped me realize the significance of the matzo ball's texture as a benchmark of a good cook (not to mention my almost-choking reaction to the double entendre).

On a recent trip to Cochin, in southwestern India, Jeff accompanied me on a visit to a section of the town called "Jew Town." This area, known for its spice markets (where black peppercorns and ginger are traded wholesale), antiques stores, and an active Jewish synagogue that was built in the 1700s but has a cemetery dating from the 1300s, is popular among tourists from all over the world. The few remaining Jewish families take care of the synagogue and are a dwindling remnant of the once populous community of Cochini Jews, who arrived on the Malabar shores around 370 C.E.

This version of the traditional Passover soup is Jeff's creation, incorporating spices and ingredients common to the coast of Malabar—his tribute to the Jews of Kerala. **SERVES 6**

For the matzo balls:

¼ teaspoon cumin seeds
¼ teaspoon black or yellow mustard seeds
¼ teaspoon fennel seeds
1 dried red Thai or cayenne chile, stem removed
½ cup matzo meal
2 extra-large or jumbo eggs, slightly beaten
2 tablespoons canola oil
½ teaspoon coarse kosher or sea salt

For the soup:

2 tablespoons canola oil
1 medium-size red onion, finely chopped
½ teaspoon ground turmeric
2 to 4 fresh green Thai, cayenne, or serrano chiles, to taste, stems removed, cut in half lengthwise (do not remove the seeds)
8 cups low-sodium chicken (or vegetable) stock
1 large parsnip, peeled, ends trimmed, quartered
2 large carrots, peeled, ends trimmed, cut crosswise into 1-inch-thick pieces
4 medium-size to large ribs celery, ends trimmed, cut into ½-inch-thick pieces
1 teaspoon coarse kosher or sea salt
2 tablespoons finely chopped fresh cilantro leaves and tender stems for garnishing

1. To make the matzo balls, heat a small skillet over medium-high heat. Add the cumin seeds, mustard seeds, fennel seeds, and chile, and cook, stirring them every few seconds or shaking the skillet very often, until the mustard seeds crackle and maybe pop, the cumin and fennel seeds turn reddish brown, and the chile blackens, 1 to 2 minutes.

2. Immediately transfer the nutty-smelling spices to a plate to cool. (The longer they sit in the hot skillet, the more likely it is that they will burn, making them bitter and unpalatable.) Once they are cool to the touch, place them in a spice grinder and grind until the

texture resembles that of finely ground black pepper. (If you don't allow the spices to cool, the ground blend will acquire unwanted moisture from the heat, making the final blend slightly "cakey.") Alternatively, use a mortar and pestle; it might work even better because of the small quantity of ingredients.

3. Transfer the nutty-smelling spice blend to a medium-size bowl and add the matzo meal to it. Stir in the eggs, oil, and salt. Place the bowl in the refrigerator to allow the matzo meal to absorb the liquid and the mixture to chill, about 15 minutes.

4. Bring about 2 quarts salted water to a rolling boil in a large saucepan over medium-high heat. While the water is heating, place a heaping tablespoon of the chilled matzo blend in the palm of your hand. Shape it lightly (without compressing it tightly) into a ball, and set it on a plate. Repeat with the remaining matzo blend. You should have 12 matzo balls.

5. Once the water is boiling, gently slide the matzo balls into the pan. Reduce the heat to medium-low, cover the pan, and simmer, stirring very gently maybe once or twice, until the balls swell up and are firm-looking (akin to a piece of water-logged sponge), 20 to 25 minutes. Remove the pan from the heat and keep it covered while you prepare the broth. (The matzo balls can keep in the water, refrigerated, for about 2 days. You can also freeze them for up to a month, drained and stored in an airtight, freezer-safe container.)

6. To make the soup, heat the oil in a large saucepan over medium heat. Add the onion and stir-fry until it is soft but not brown around the edges, 2 to 4 minutes. Stir in the turmeric and chiles.

7. Pour in the stock, and add the parsnip, carrots, celery, and salt. Bring to a boil. Drain the matzo balls, add them to the stock, and reduce the heat to

medium-low. Cover the pan and simmer, stirring very gently maybe once or twice, until the carrots are fork-tender, 10 to 12 minutes. Remove and discard the parsnips and chiles.

8. Place two matzo balls in each soup bowl, and ladle some of the broth and vegetables over them. Sprinkle with the cilantro, and serve.

Tip: The matzo balls must be light and fluffy. "Firm pressure when rolling the balls in your palms, and lifting the lid too often while they simmer, guarantee tough balls," Jeff cautions, "so be very gentle." May your balls be light and fluffy!

Potato–Coconut Milk Soup
WITH LEMONGRASS AND CHILES

A hearty soup, this gathers together ingredients that are common in Sri Lanka, the tear-shaped island south of India. The flavors in this curry are simply amazing, using aromatics like curry and screwpine leaves, salty dried Maldive fish, tart tamarind, hot chiles, and lemony lemongrass. It all adds up to a somewhat salty, perfumed, irresistible bowlful. I often serve it as a main-course soup, with slices of warmed baguette alongside, during the winter months. A glass of Vouvray, Sancerre, or sauvignon blanc would be perfect with these flavors. **SERVES 8**

4 medium-size to large shallots, coarsely chopped

½ teaspoon kewra water, or 1 piece (2 inches) of fresh
    screwpine leaf (optional; see Tips)

10 to 12 medium-size to large fresh curry leaves

4 to 6 fresh green Thai, cayenne, or serrano chiles,
    to taste, stems removed

2 tablespoons finely chopped lemongrass (see Tip,
    page 722)

1 pound russet or Yukon Gold potatoes, peeled,
    cut into ¼-inch cubes, and submerged in a bowl
    of cold water to prevent browning

2 tablespoons canola oil

1 teaspoon black or yellow mustard seeds

1½ teaspoons coarse kosher or sea salt

1 can (13.5 ounces) unsweetened coconut milk

1 tablespoon dried salted Maldive fish, pounded (see Tips)

½ teaspoon tamarind paste or concentrate

1 large tomato, cored and finely chopped

½ cup finely chopped fresh cilantro leaves and
    tender stems

1. Place the shallots in a food processor, and add the *kewra* water, curry leaves, chiles, and lemongrass. Pulse until minced. (If you want to smell the blend, do so with caution because the fumes from the chiles can be quite powerful.)

2. Drain the potatoes and pat them dry with paper towels.

3. Heat the oil in a medium-size saucepan over medium-high heat. Add the mustard seeds, cover the pan, and cook until the seeds have stopped popping (not unlike popcorn), about 30 seconds. Add the potatoes and the minced shallot mixture, and cook, uncovered, stirring frequently, until the shallots and herbs are cooked without burning, 2 to 4 minutes.

4. Pour in 3 cups water, stir in the salt, and heat to a boil. Then reduce the heat to medium-low, cover the

pan, and cook, stirring occasionally, until the potatoes are tender but still firm-looking, 15 to 20 minutes.

5. Stir in the coconut milk, Maldive fish, tamarind paste, tomato, and cilantro. Raise the heat to medium and boil, uncovered, stirring occasionally, to allow the coconut milk to mellow out some of the harsh heat from the chiles, about 5 minutes. Then serve.

Tips:

❖ Aromatic *kewra* water (see page 206), the extract of a variety of screwpine, is used in parts of northern India and Pakistan. It is a shelf-stable product, found among the extracts and flavorings in Indian and Pakistani stores. If you wish, leave it out.

❖ Screwpine leaves, also known as pandanus leaves, are an essential flavoring in many of Sri Lanka's dishes, along with curry leaves and lemongrass. If the leaves are available in your area's Asian market (screwpine is also common in the cuisines of Vietnam and China), use a piece about 2 inches long. If not, leave it out.

❖ Maldive fish has many aliases, including *bomeloe, bummalow, pla pak khom,* and the best known, *Bombay duck.* A large-headed fish with sharp teeth and a long, thin body, its vicious-looking visage gives clue to its predatory nature. Very rarely eaten fresh (because it has a very short shelf life once it is netted), its thin fillets (and even the entire fish) are salted and hung on bamboo along Mumbai's beachfronts, creating nose-holding smells as they flap in the tropical winds. If your Asian store does not stock the fish (whole or chunks), use any salted dried fish as an alternative. To pound the dried fish pieces, plunk them into a mortar and pound them with the pestle until the sharp aromas pervade your breathing space.

Stuffed Chicken Breasts
WITH AVOCADO AND CHEESE IN AN EGGPLANT SAUCE

definitely not a classic curry, this contemporary presentation does pack in some of the classic flavors and ingredients from northern India—in conjunction with avocado, which is actually found in southern India (although not the Hass variety). The eggplant gives the sauce a slightly meaty texture, to make the whole package an excellent main-course offering for an elegant "fusion" dinner.

SERVES 4

For the chicken:

4 boneless, skinless chicken breasts (1½ pounds total)

4 ounces Doodh paneer (page 286), shredded (see Tips)

1 medium-size ripe but slightly firm Hass avocado, seeded, peeled, and cut into ⅛-inch cubes

2 tablespoons finely chopped fresh cilantro leaves and tender stems

1 teaspoon coarse kosher or sea salt

2 fresh green Thai, cayenne, or serrano chiles, stems removed, finely chopped (do not remove the seeds)

2 tablespoons canola oil

For the sauce:

1 medium-size eggplant (about 1¼ pounds), stem removed, finely chopped (see Tips)

1 small red onion, finely chopped

2 teaspoons English-style Madras curry powder (page 24)

1½ teaspoons coarse kosher or sea salt

1 teaspoon Punjabi garam masala (page 25)

2 cups low-sodium chicken stock or water

1 medium-size tomato, cored and finely chopped

2 tablespoons finely chopped fresh cilantro leaves and tender stems for garnishing

1. To make the chicken, place a chicken breast between two sheets of plastic wrap and pound it to thin it out evenly, until it is roughly ¼ inch thick. Repeat with the remaining 3 breasts.

2. Combine the *paneer*, avocado, cilantro, salt, and chiles in a medium-size bowl. Mix thoroughly.

3. Lay 1 pounded chicken breast on a cutting board. Spread one fourth of the filling across the lower third of the breast. Roll it up, tucking the ends under, to form a tight log, burrito-style. Repeat with the remaining chicken and filling.

4. Heat the oil in a large skillet over medium heat. Arrange the stuffed breasts, seam side down, in the skillet and sear them until they are light brown, 2 to 4 minutes. Using a pair of tongs, gently turn them over, taking care not to let the filling spill out (once you sear the seam side, it should firm up and somewhat seal the edge). Cook until they are browned all over, 2 to 4 minutes. Lift the breasts out of the skillet and set them aside on a plate.

5. To make the sauce, add the eggplant and onion to the same skillet. Cook, stirring occasionally, until the eggplant starts to release its liquid, and then starts to brown lightly along with the onion, 12 to 15 minutes.

6. Stir in the curry powder, salt, and garam masala. Let the spices cook gently without burning (the vegetables will provide cushioning), about 1 minute.

7. Pour some of the stock into the skillet and scrape the bottom to deglaze it, releasing the browned bits of chicken and vegetable. Then pour in the remaining stock, and add the tomato.

8. Raise the heat to medium-high and cook, uncovered, stirring occasionally, until some of the stock has been absorbed, 5 to 8 minutes.

9. Return the chicken breasts to the skillet and spoon the sauce over them (the blanket of stewlike sauce will prevent them from drying out). Reduce the heat to medium-low, cover the skillet, and simmer, without stirring, until the breasts are no longer pink inside (carefully slice into one to check for doneness), 15 to 20 minutes.

10. Using a spatula, transfer the chicken breasts to a platter. Spoon every last bit of the sauce over them, sprinkle with the cilantro, and serve.

Tips:

❖ Not having *paneer* in your refrigerator should not preclude you from making this unbelievably simple but elegant-looking curry. Crumbled feta, shredded farmer's cheese, or even mozzarella makes for a perfectly acceptable alternative. These cheeses are usually fairly salty, so I recommend reducing the salt in the filling to ½ teaspoon.

❖ To finely chop an eggplant, slice it lengthwise into ¼-inch-thick slices. Stack 2 or 3 slices together and cut them into thin lengthwise strips. Then slice the strips crosswise into very small pieces (about ⅛ inch). I do not recommend pulsing eggplant in a food processor because too much liquid will be released if you over-pulse it.

Chicken
WITH LEMONGRASS AND KAFFIR LIME LEAVES

Based on flavors associated with Thai food, and in the absence of coconut milk, the chiles do deliver a bite in this curry. I sampled a version of this at an upscale Thai restaurant in Goa. My version contains half-and-half (or you can use heavy cream) to help thicken the sauce and to calm the heat from the chiles. **SERVES 6**

2 tablespoons Ginger Paste (page 15)
1 tablespoon Garlic Paste (page 15)
1 teaspoon coarse kosher or sea salt
1 chicken (3½ pounds), skin removed, cut into 8 pieces (see box, page 121)
⅛ cup finely chopped lemongrass (see Tip, page 722)
2 large kaffir lime leaves (see box)
2 to 4 fresh green Thai, cayenne, or serrano chiles, to taste, stems removed
2 tablespoons canola oil
1 large tomato, cored and finely chopped
1 small red onion, cut in half lengthwise and thinly sliced
½ cup half-and-half

1. Combine the Ginger Paste, Garlic Paste, and salt in a medium-size bowl. Add the chicken pieces and stir to coat them with the spices. Refrigerate, covered, for at least 30 minutes, or even overnight, to allow the flavors to permeate the meat.

2. Combine the lemongrass, lime leaves, and chiles in

a food processor, and pulse until minced. When you uncover the processor bowl, the intense lemony, spicy-hot aromas will guarantee a "wow."

3. Heat the oil in a large skillet over medium-high heat. Arrange the chicken pieces, including the paste, in a single layer, meat side down, in the skillet. Cook until the chicken is seared and light brown on the underside, 3 to 6 minutes. Turn the pieces over and brown the meat on the other side, 3 to 6 minutes. Some dark brown bits of meat will stick to the skillet.

4. Turn the chicken over again, so the pieces are meat side down in the skillet. Spread the minced mixture over the chicken pieces, and scatter the tomato and onion over them. Cover the skillet, reduce the heat to medium-low, and cook for about 20 minutes. (The juices from the tomato and the onion will deglaze the skillet and incorporate the drippings from the chicken.)

kaffir lime

❖ ❖ ❖

Kaffir lime leaves, a must in many of Thailand's curries, have a distinct lime aroma and flavor. Called Citrus hystrix, the fruits have a dark green, bumpy rind; its lemony aromatic oils are used in many cosmetic products. Only the leaves and rind are used for cooking purposes—not the fruit itself—and they have no substitute, although the rind of limes makes for a not-so-perfect alternative. The FDA has banned the import of kaffir lime leaves, but locally grown ones are available (especially from Florida), albeit at a premium price. I have had no problem finding them in my neighborhood's Asian grocery stores. I usually buy a bunch of the leaves and keep them in self-seal bags in the freezer, where they retain their strong aroma and flavor for up to 3 months.

5. Turn the chicken over and continue to simmer, covered, until the thickest parts of the chicken, when pierced, are no longer pink and the juices run clear, 5 to 8 minutes. Transfer the chicken to a serving platter.

6. Pour the half-and-half into the skillet and simmer over medium-high heat, uncovered, stirring occasionally, until the sauce thickens, 5 to 8 minutes (it will have a slightly curdled appearance, thanks to the slightly acidic lemongrass and lime leaves).

7. Pour the sauce over the chicken, and serve.

Wok-Seared Chicken
WITH MUSTARD GREENS AND SPICY SOY SAUCE

It never fails to amaze me to see the influence of the Chinese community, and more specifically their foods, in *all* of India. Of course, the Indianization of classic Chinese flavors is bound to happen, especially when you combine the quick-cooking, stir-frying techniques from the Far East with the subcontinent's propensity to "spice things up." This thick-sauced Indo-Chinese dish pays homage to a street vendor near my childhood home in Mumbai. For decades he has never failed to set up his one-man stall—and his reward is the throngs who gather to sample his chile-hot fare well past midnight. **SERVES 4**

I tablespoon tomato paste

I tablespoon soy sauce

½ teaspoon coarse kosher or sea salt

¼ teaspoon Chinese five-spice powder (see Tips)

I pound boneless, skinless chicken breasts,
*   cut into ½-inch cubes*

I tablespoon cornstarch

8 tablespoons peanut or canola oil

8 ounces fresh mustard greens, well rinsed, finely
*   chopped (see Tip, page 606), and patted dry*

2 large cloves garlic, finely chopped

3 to 5 fresh green Thai, cayenne, or serrano chiles,
*   to taste, stems removed, cut in half lengthwise*
*   (do not remove the seeds)*

2 tablespoons finely chopped fresh cilantro leaves
*   and tender stems*

3 scallions (green tops and white bulbs), cut into
*   2-inch lengths*

1. Stir the tomato paste, soy sauce, salt, and five-spice powder together in a small bowl.

2. Toss the chicken and the cornstarch together in a medium-size bowl.

3. Heat a wok, or a well-seasoned cast-iron skillet, over high heat. Drizzle 2 tablespoons of the oil down the sides of the wok. When it forms a shimmering pool in the bottom, add the chicken and fry, stirring constantly (the definition of stir-frying), until the chicken turns reddish brown and is no longer pink inside, 5 to 8 minutes. Transfer the chicken to a plate.

4. Trickle 2 more tablespoons of the oil down the sides of the wok, and add half the mustard greens. Stir-fry until they are wilted, 2 to 4 minutes. Add this to the chicken. Repeat with another 2 tablespoons oil and the remaining greens.

5. Now drizzle the remaining 2 tablespoons oil into the wok and quickly stir-fry the garlic and chiles. (The pungent chiles will permeate your breathing space, so adequate ventilation is an absolute must.) The garlic will brown within seconds. Add the tomato paste mixture and stir to warm it, about 30 seconds.

6. Return the chicken and greens to the wok, and stir well to combine the ingredients and to season the meat and vegetable with the not-so delicate sauce. Once the chicken feels hot to the touch, 2 to 4 minutes, stir in the cilantro and scallions, and serve.

Tips:

❖ To double or triple this recipe and still get that wok-seared, smoky flavor, cook the dish in two or three separate batches. If you crowd the pan, the ingredients will stew, as opposed to being stir-fried and seared, and the consequence will be blah-tasting fare. Don't say I didn't warn you.

❖ "Five-spice" indicates the number of ingredients in this blend but fails to convey its complexity. This highly aromatic and strong-tasting blend has been in existence for centuries and balances flavors of sour, bitter, sweet, pungent, and salty, in keeping with age-old Chinese tradition. The classic version consists of equal quantities of ground fennel, cloves, cinnamon, Sichuan peppercorns, and star anise, but other blends have included cardamom, cassia (instead of cinnamon), ginger, nutmeg, and even licorice root. Some of China's signature dishes, such as Peking duck, barbecued spare ribs, and roast pork, are flavored with the classic blend. It is available in supermarkets and in Asian grocery stores. To make your own, combine in a spice grinder 1½ teaspoons fennel seeds, 1½ teaspoons whole cloves, 1½ teaspoons Sichuan peppercorns (or 2 teaspoons ground), 6 star anise (or 2 teaspoons ground), and three 3-inch-long cinnamon sticks, broken into smaller pieces. Grind until the texture resembles that of finely ground black pepper.

Tortillas
WITH A SPICED TURKEY FILLING

exican-influenced corn tortillas, stacked and filled with delicately spiced ground turkey and black beans, sprinkled with cheese, and soused with a macho guajillo chile sauce: This bellows out its layered flavors and textures in each mouthful. A glass of Spanish Rioja wine is perfect with this meal, as is a side of Sautéed Spinach with Yogurt (page 743). **SERVES 6**

For the sauce:

12 dried guajillo chiles, stems removed

3 cups boiling water

2 teaspoons Dabeli masala (page 39)

1 teaspoon coarse kosher or sea salt

For the turkey filling:

2 tablespoons canola oil

1 small red onion, finely chopped

1 pound ground turkey

1 can (15 ounces) black beans, drained and rinsed

2 teaspoons Dabeli masala (page 39)

1 teaspoon coarse kosher or sea salt

1 or 2 fresh green Thai, cayenne, or serrano chiles, to taste, stems removed, finely chopped (do not remove the seeds)

For assembling:

Vegetable cooking spray

18 corn tortillas (6-inch size)

About 2 cups shredded cheese (such as cheddar, mozzarella, or a blend)

About ½ cup finely chopped fresh cilantro leaves and tender stems

1. To make the sauce, put the guajillo chiles in a heatproof bowl and pour the boiling water over them. The chiles are light and buoyant, so to keep them submerged, weight them down with a pan. (If you don't, they won't soften evenly.) Set the bowl aside until the chiles have softened, 15 to 20 minutes.

2. Pick the chiles out of the red-stained water (do not discard the water) and put them in a blender jar. Pour ½ cup of the soaking liquid into the jar and puree, scraping the inside of the jar as needed, to make a thick, blood-red sauce.

3. Place a strainer over a small saucepan. Pour the sauce into the strainer, and using a spatula, stir it frequently to extract as much liquid as possible. Pour 1 cup of the reserved soaking liquid into the blender jar and swish it around to wash it out. Add this to the strainer. Once the level in the strainer goes down, pour in the remaining 1½ cups reserved soaking liquid and stir with the spatula again. Discard the residual pulp in the strainer.

4. Bring the strained sauce to a boil over medium-high heat. Stir in the *Dabeli masala* and the salt. Remove the pan from the heat.

5. Now make the filling: Heat the oil in a large skillet over medium-high heat. Add the onion and turkey, and cook, uncovered, stirring to break up the turkey, until they start to brown, 15 to 20 minutes. (They will release some liquid at first, and then as the liquid starts to evaporate, start to brown.)

6. Stir in the beans, masala, salt, and chiles. Cook, stirring, until the beans are warmed through, about 5 minutes. Remove the skillet from the heat.

7. Preheat the oven to 350°F. Spray the bottom of a large baking pan with cooking spray. (You can bake the

tortillas in several batches in the same pan, or you can prepare one or two more baking pans and bake them all at once. The baking pans need to accommodate a total of six stacks of tortillas.)

8. Place 1 tortilla in the prepared baking pan, and spread some of the filling over it. Follow that with a sprinkling of cheese and cilantro. Place another tortilla on top, and layer it similarly with filling, cheese, and cilantro. Place the third tortilla on top, and pour a ladleful of the sauce over the stack, letting it run over the edges and pool at the bottom. Repeat with the remaining tortillas, filling, cheese, cilantro, and sauce—but reserve some cheese and cilantro for sprinkling on top later.

9. Cover the baking pan(s) with aluminum foil, and bake until the stacks are warmed through and the sauce is bubbling and thickened, 10 to 15 minutes.

10. Sprinkle some cheese on top of each hot stack so it melts evenly. Lift each stack onto an individual serving plate, and spoon some of the sauce over it. Sprinkle with a smidgen of cilantro for color, and serve.

Tip: These tortilla stacks will keep in the refrigerator, covered, for up to 4 days, or in the freezer for up to a month. Rewarm them in a microwave oven for 3 to 4 minutes and frozen, add another 2 to 4 minutes.

Leg of Lamb
WITH AN ONION-COCONUT SAUCE

I love combining regional tastes. The flavors in this nut-studded roast are characteristic of northern India's Moghul cuisine, while its sauce is typical of the East Indian community in Mumbai, where seafood, not meat, is the dietary staple. Even though I have used lamb, a beef roast would be perfectly acceptable and would have the same cooking time. **SERVES 6**

For the lamb:

1 bone-in leg of lamb (2½ to 3 pounds),
    preferably the loin portion
¼ cup plain yogurt
¼ cup slivered blanched almonds
¼ cup raw cashew nuts
¼ cup raw shelled pistachio nuts
2 tablespoons Ginger Paste (page 15)
1 tablespoon Garlic Paste (page 15)
2 teaspoons ground Kashmiri chiles; or ½ teaspoon
    cayenne (ground red pepper) mixed with
    1½ teaspoons sweet paprika
1½ teaspoons coarse kosher or sea salt
Vegetable cooking spray

For the sauce:

2 tablespoons canola oil
1 cup finely chopped red onion
2 large cloves garlic, finely chopped
2 tablespoons tomato paste
2 teaspoons East Indian bottle masala (page 37)
1 teaspoon coarse kosher or sea salt
1 can (13.5 ounces) unsweetened coconut milk
2 tablespoons finely chopped fresh cilantro leaves
    and tender stems

1. To prepare the lamb, make four to six ¼-inch-deep gashes, well spaced, in the meat. Set the roast in a shallow baking pan.

2. Pour the yogurt into a blender jar, followed by the almonds, cashews, and pistachios. Puree, scraping the inside of the jar as needed, to make a slightly gritty, light green sauce. Make sure all the nuts are pulver-

ized. Pour the sauce into a small bowl, and stir in the ginger and garlic pastes, ground chiles, and salt.

3. Pour this marinade over the lamb, and using your hands, massage it into the meat; make sure you get it into the gashes. Cover the roast with plastic wrap and refrigerate it overnight, to allow the yogurt to tenderize the lamb and the spices to permeate the meat.

4. When you are ready to cook the lamb, preheat the oven to 425°F. While the oven is preheating, bring the lamb to room temperature by setting the baking pan on the kitchen counter (I usually place it close to the warming oven to quicken the process).

5. Set a rack in a roasting pan, and spray the rack with cooking spray. Place the lamb on the rack, including any marinade that clings to its surface. (Reserve the remaining marinade for basting.) Place the pan in the oven and roast until the lamb is seared and lightly browned on the outside, 10 to 15 minutes.

6. Lower the oven temperature to 325°F, and continue to roast the lamb for another 15 minutes or so. Then spread the reserved marinade over it. Continue to roast the lamb until the meat registers around 135°F (for medium-rare) when you insert a meat thermometer into its thickest part, about 1 hour. While it is roasting, occasionally check the pan to see if the meat drippings are starting to burn off. If they are, pour a little water into the pan to allow for some moisture, which will maintain the meat's succulence without diluting its flavors.

7. While the lamb is roasting, prepare the sauce: Heat the oil in a medium-size saucepan over medium-high heat. Add the onion and garlic, and stir-fry until the onion is caramel-brown with a deep purple hue, 10 to 15 minutes.

8. Stir in the tomato paste, bottle masala, and salt, and

simmer, uncovered, stirring occasionally, until a thin film starts to form on the bottom and the paste acquires an oily sheen on its surface, 1 to 2 minutes.

9. Pour in ¼ cup water and scrape the bottom of the pan to deglaze it, releasing the browned bits of sauce, onion, and spices. Stir in the coconut milk. Once the sauce comes to a boil, lower the heat to medium and continue to boil rather vigorously, uncovered, stirring occasionally, until it has reduced by almost half and thickened, 20 to 25 minutes. Keep the sauce warm, covered, over very low heat.

10. When the lamb is done, remove the baking pan from the oven and let it rest on the counter for about 10 minutes. The meat's internal temperature will rise about 5 degrees.

11. Transfer the lamb to a cutting board. Cut the meat into ½-inch-thick slices and arrange them on a serving platter.

12. Stir the cilantro into the sauce. Serve the lamb and sauce separately, allowing the diners to spoon on as much sauce as they wish.

Loin Lamb Chops
WITH AN APRICOT SAUCE

Resembling small T-bone steaks, these thick chops, do take a while to cook, unlike the cuts from the rib rack. So when you grill them, use medium heat to allow the inside to reach the right temperature (for medium-rare, a meat thermometer inserted into the densest part, without touching any bone, should register between 130° and 135°F). Lamb's gamey flavor is played down a bit here, in part due to the sweetness of the apricots. **SERVES 4**

2 tablespoons Ginger Paste (page 15)

2 tablespoons Garlic Paste (page 15)

1 teaspoon coarse kosher or sea salt

8 bone-in loin lamb chops (cut 2 inches thick), excess fat trimmed

6 dried apricots, cut into ¼-inch-thick slices

1 cup boiling water

2 tablespoons canola oil

1 small red onion, cut in half lengthwise and thinly sliced

6 medium-size cloves garlic, thinly sliced

1 teaspoon black peppercorns

½ teaspoon rock salt

¼ teaspoon whole cloves

¼ teaspoon cardamom seeds from green or white pods

1 cinnamon stick (3 inches long), broken into pieces

1 teaspoon ground Kashmiri chiles; or ¼ teaspoon cayenne (ground red pepper) mixed with ¾ teaspoon sweet paprika

Vegetable cooking spray

2 tablespoons finely chopped fresh cilantro leaves and tender stems for garnishing

1. Combine the Ginger Paste, Garlic Paste, and salt in a small bowl; stir well. Divide the paste equally among the 8 lamb chops, smearing the broad sides with the strong-smelling blend. Refrigerate, covered, for at least 30 minutes, or as long as overnight, to allow the flavors to permeate the meat.

2. When you are ready to cook the chops, put the apricot slices in a small heatproof bowl and pour the boiling water over them. Set the bowl aside until the apricots are reconstituted, 15 to 30 minutes. Drain the apricots, reserving the soaking liquid.

Rock salt? See the Glossary of Ingredients, page 758.

3. Heat the oil in a medium-size saucepan over medium heat. Add the onion and garlic and stir once or twice. Cover the pan and cook, stirring occasionally at first and more frequently once they start to brown, until the onions are caramel-brown with a deep purple hue, 15 to 20 minutes.

4. While the onions and garlic are cooking, combine the peppercorns, rock salt, cloves, cardamom seeds, and cinnamon pieces in a mortar. Pound with the pestle until the mixture has the texture of coarse sawdust. Stir in the ground chiles.

5. Transfer the browned onion and garlic to a blender jar, and add the softened apricot slices. Pour half of the apricot soaking water into the jar. Puree, scraping the inside of the jar as needed, to make a smooth, light brown sauce with purple specks. Return the sauce to the same saucepan. Pour the remaining soaking liquid into the blender jar and swish it around to get every bit of the sauce. Add the washings to the pan, and stir in the pounded spices. Keep the sauce over low heat, covered, while you grill the lamb chops.

6. Preheat a gas or charcoal grill, or the broiler, to medium heat.

7. *If you are grilling,* spray the grill grate lightly with cooking spray. Place the chops, paste and all, on the grate and grill on both sides until the meat is seared and is still medium-rare in the center, 6 to 8 minutes on each side. *If you are broiling,* set the oven rack so the top of the chops will be 4 to 6 inches from the heat. Lightly spray the rack of a broiler pan with cooking spray, and arrange the chops, marinade and all, on the rack. Broil until the meat is seared and is still medium-rare in the center, 6 to 8 minutes on each side.

8. Transfer the chops to a serving platter and ladle the sauce over them. Sprinkle with the cilantro, and serve.

Pork Ribs
WITH A SWEET-SOUR GLAZE

here's one for you lovers of grilled ribs. The technique is familiar, while the seasonings are an array of spices, herbs, and ingredients common to the southwestern regions of India. A great summer picnic offering, these succulent, fall-apart ribs are delicious even at room temperature. If you don't feel like firing up the outdoor grill, see the Tip for an alternative baking method. Use any kind of ribs, either beef or pork, for equally spectacular results. **SERVES 8**

For the ribs:

2 tablespoons Ginger Paste (page 15)
1 tablespoon Garlic Paste (page 15)
1½ teaspoons coarse kosher or sea salt
½ teaspoon ground turmeric
4 pounds pork baby back ribs

For the glaze:

¼ cup tomato paste
¼ cup crumbled (or chopped) jaggery or
    firmly packed dark brown sugar, dissolved
    in ¼ cup boiling water
1 tablespoon cider vinegar or malt vinegar
1 tablespoon canola oil
2 teaspoons ground Kashmiri chiles; or ½ teaspoon
    cayenne (ground red pepper) mixed with
    1½ teaspoons sweet paprika
2 teaspoons Balti masala (page 31)
1 teaspoon coarse kosher or sea salt

For the sauce:

4 medium-size cloves garlic
2 or 3 fresh green Thai, cayenne,
    or serrano chiles, to taste,
    stems removed
2 tablespoons canola oil
1 cup finely chopped red onion
2 tablespoons tomato paste
2 tablespoons cider vinegar or malt vinegar
2 teaspoons white granulated sugar
½ teaspoon coarse kosher or sea salt
½ teaspoon ground turmeric
2 tablespoons finely chopped fresh cilantro leaves
    and tender stems

Vegetable cooking spray for grilling

1. To prepare the ribs, mix the ginger and garlic pastes, salt, and turmeric together in a small bowl. Smear this yellow paste over the meaty side of the ribs. Cover the ribs and refrigerate overnight to allow the flavors to permeate the meat. (I usually put the ribs on a sheet pan or cookie sheet, as they are easily contained in one tray and don't take up that much room in the refrigerator.)

2. When you are ready to cook the ribs, combine all the glaze ingredients in a small bowl, and stir thoroughly.

3. Next, make the sauce: Combine the garlic and chiles in a mortar. Pound the two together with the pestle, scraping the sides to contain the ingredients in the center, to form a wet, pulpy mass.

4. Heat the oil in a small saucepan over medium-high heat. Add the onion and stir-fry until it is dark brown around the edges, 5 to 8 minutes.

5. Add the pounded chile-garlic blend and stir it around to lightly brown the garlic, about 1 minute.

6. Stir in the tomato paste, vinegar, sugar, salt, and turmeric. Cook the sharp-smelling sauce, uncovered, stirring occasionally, until the vinegar evaporates and there is an oily sheen on the surface and around the edges, 3 to 5 minutes.

7. Pour in 1 cup water, and scrape the bottom of the pan to deglaze it. Once the sauce comes to a boil, lower the heat to medium and simmer, uncovered, stirring occasionally, until it thickens, 5 to 8 minutes. Remove the pan from the heat.

8. To grill the ribs, heat a gas or charcoal grill to high. Lightly spray the grill grate with cooking spray. *If you are using a gas grill,* lower the heat to medium. *If charcoal is the name of your game,* spread the hot charcoal pieces to the sides for indirect heat.

9. Place the slabs of ribs on the grill grate, meat side down, and cover the grill. Cook for 35 to 45 minutes. Check the ribs periodically to make sure the meat drippings don't flame up and burn them (if they do, I usually move them to the top grill grate for a few seconds until the flames die down).

10. Turn the ribs over, so they are meat side up, and cover the grill. Cook for 20 to 25 minutes.

11. Once the meat is tender and almost falling off the bone, liberally brush the ribs with the spicy-sweet-tart glaze, using it all up. Continue to grill, covered, meat side up, until the glaze has a slightly opaque look to it and the meat is very tender, 10 to 15 minutes.

12. Remove the ribs from the grill, set them on a cutting board, cover them with aluminum foil, and let them rest for 5 to 10 minutes.

13. While the ribs are resting, rewarm the sauce and stir in the cilantro.

14. Slice the ribs between the bones (it's okay to lick your fingers when no one is watching), and transfer them to a serving platter. Either brush the sauce over the ribs or pass it around separately for people to dip their ribs into (this is a good time for those bibs to surface).

Tips:

❖ If you like, you can prepare the glaze a day ahead. Refrigerate it, covered with plastic wrap.

❖ If you don't have a grill (or it's freezing outside), use your oven to roast the ribs: Position a rack in the center of the oven and preheat the oven to 325°F. Lightly spray a broiler pan, or a rack set in a roasting pan, with cooking spray. Arrange the ribs, meat side down, on the rack and roast them for about 45 minutes. Flip the ribs over, and roast for 30 to 45 minutes. Once the meat is tender and almost falling off the bone, liberally brush the ribs with the spicy-sweet-tart glaze, using it all up. Continue to roast, meat side up, until the glaze has a slightly opaque look to it and the meat is very tender, 10 to 15 minutes. Remove the ribs from the grill, set them on a cutting board, cover them with aluminum foil, and let them rest for 5 to 10 minutes.

Grilled Pork Tenderloin
DRENCHED WITH AN ONION SAUCE

t he simple marinade that coats this pork tenderloin is as yellow as prepared mustard and when grilled, creates a crusty coating around a tender interior. The pork is served atop a mound of fluffy garlic mashed potatoes. The spinach surrounding it all provides both color and a tender texture. The simple onion sauce that drenches everything brings it all together with every moist, succulent, yummy bite. **SERVES 6**

For the pork:

1 tablespoon Ginger Paste (page 15)
1 tablespoon Garlic Paste (page 15)
2 teaspoons English-Style Madras Curry Powder
     (page 24)
1 teaspoon coarse kosher or sea salt
1½ pounds pork tenderloin
Vegetable cooking spray

For the potato-spinach bed:

1 pound russet or Yukon Gold potatoes, peeled,
     each cut into four quarters, and submerged
     in a bowl of cold water to prevent browning
4 medium-size cloves garlic
1 teaspoon coarse kosher or sea salt
2 tablespoons Ghee (page 21) or butter
8 ounces fresh spinach leaves, well rinsed

For the sauce:

2 tablespoons canola oil
1 cup finely chopped red onion
2 teaspoons English-Style Madras Curry Powder
     (page 24)
½ teaspoon salt
1 teaspoon cornstarch

1. To prepare the pork, stir the Ginger Paste, Garlic Paste, curry powder, and salt together in a small bowl. Smear the dark yellow marinade all over the meat. Place the meat in a baking dish and cover it with plastic wrap. Refrigerate it for at least 1 hour, or as long as overnight, to allow the flavors to permeate the pork.

2. When you are ready to grill the meat, preheat a gas or charcoal grill to high heat.

3. Lightly spray the grill grate with cooking spray, and place the meat on the grate. *If your grill is a gas one,* lower the heat to medium. *If charcoal is the name of your game,* spread the hot charcoal pieces to even out the heat. Cover the grill and cook, turning the meat occasionally, until all the sides have the grill marks and a meat thermometer stuck in the thickest part of the meat registers 155° to 160°F, 25 to 30 minutes.

4. While the pork is grilling, prepare the potatoes: Bring a medium-size or larger saucepan of water to a boil over medium-high heat. Drain the potatoes and add them, along with the garlic, to the boiling water. Bring to a boil again. Then lower the heat to medium, partially cover the pan, and cook until the potatoes are very tender, 5 to 8 minutes. Scoop the potatoes and garlic out with a slotted spoon, and plunk them into a medium-size bowl. (Do not discard the cooking water.) Sprinkle ½ teaspoon of the salt over the potatoes, and drizzle with the ghee. Mash the potatoes and garlic. Then quickly cover the bowl to contain the heat.

5. When the meat is done, transfer it from the grill to a warmed platter and cover it with aluminum foil.

6. Bring the potato cooking water back to a boil. Drop several handfuls of the spinach into the boiling water and stir them in until wilted, 1 to 2 minutes. Repeat until all the spinach has been wilted. Reserving 1 cup of the cooking water, drain the spinach in a colander. Sprinkle the remaining ½ teaspoon salt over the spinach, and toss to mix. Transfer the spinach to a bowl and cover it with plastic wrap to keep it warm.

7. Now make the sauce: Heat the oil in a medium-size saucepan. Add the onion and stir-fry until it is light brown around the edges, 3 to 5 minutes.

8. Sprinkle the curry powder over the onion and cook, stirring to cook the spices and coat the onion with them, about 15 seconds. Immediately pour in the reserved 1 cup cooking water, and stir once or twice to deglaze the pan, releasing the collected browned bits of onion.

9. Quickly stir the cornstarch and 2 tablespoons cold water together in a small bowl, and pour this into the boiling sauce, which will instantly start to thicken.

10. Transfer the pork to a cutting board and cut it into ¼-inch-thick slices.

11. Spoon the mashed potatoes onto the center of a serving platter, and surround them with the spinach. Arrange the sliced pork across the potato bed. Pour the onion sauce over the meat and the spinach, and serve.

Tip: You'll notice that I do not suggest broiling as an alternative to grilling the meat in this recipe. If you don't have a grill, use the oven: pork tenderloin works better when roasted, initially at a high temperature, then at a lower one, until the internal temperature reaches 155°F. To roast the pork, place an oven rack on the highest level and preheat the oven to 450°F. Lightly spray the rack of a roasting pan with vegetable cooking spray. Place the marinated pork on the rack and roast it for about 15 minutes. Then reduce the oven temperature to 300°F and continue to roast until a thermometer stuck in the thickest part of the meat registers 155° to 160°F, 35 to 45 minutes. Remove the pork from the oven and proceed with the recipe.

Tandoori Mignon
WITH
A MUSHROOM CREAM SAUCE

When you work with the best cut of meat from the prized (and did I say pricey?) tenderloin of beef, you want to make sure you not only cook it right (if you can, serve it medium-rare but definitely no more than medium) but also use spices that complement the meat's assertive presence. I cannot think of a better marinade than slightly tart yogurt fortified with pungent ginger, garlic, and mellow Kashmiri chiles. When you sample a grilled piece of this filet as is, with no sauce, you will find it quite spicy-hot; but drape a morsel with the creamy mushroom sauce, and you will notice a velvety balance that makes this combination a winning and noticeable main course at your special-occasion dinner table.

SERVES 4

For the meat:
¼ cup plain yogurt
1 tablespoon Ginger Paste (page 15)
1 tablespoon Garlic Paste (page 15)
1 teaspoon Balti masala (page 31)
1 teaspoon ground Kashmiri chiles;
   or ¼ teaspoon cayenne (ground red pepper)
   mixed with ¾ teaspoon sweet paprika
1 teaspoon coarse kosher or sea salt
4 filets mignons (each 6 to 8 ounces,
   cut 3 to 3½ inches thick)

For the mushroom sauce:

8 ounces brown cremini mushrooms,
coarsely chopped

I small red onion, coarsely chopped

4 medium-size cloves garlic,
coarsely chopped

2 tablespoons canola oil

4 dried red Thai or cayenne chiles,
stems removed

I teaspoon Toasted Cumin-Coriander Blend
(page 33)

I teaspoon coarse kosher or sea salt

½ cup heavy (whipping) cream or half-and-half

Vegetable cooking spray

2 tablespoons finely chopped fresh cilantro leaves
and tender stems for garnishing

1. To put together the marinade, combine the yogurt, ginger and garlic pastes, masala, ground chiles, and salt in a small bowl. Whisk together well.

2. Smear the creamy, reddish-orange marinade over both sides of each filet. Cover and refrigerate for at least 1 hour, or as long as overnight, to allow the flavors to permeate the beef.

3. When you are ready to cook the filets, make the sauce: Pile the mushrooms, onion, and garlic into a food processor, and pulse until minced. The blend will be quite damp, thanks to the liquid in the mushrooms.

4. Heat the oil in a medium-size skillet over medium-high heat. Add the chiles and stir them around until they blacken, 30 seconds to 1 minute. Then add the mushroom blend. Simmer, stirring occasionally, until the vegetables turn light brown, 12 to 15 minutes. (The water within the mushrooms will boil off first.)

5. Pour in ½ cup water, and scrape the skillet to deglaze it, releasing any browned bits of mushrooms, onion, and garlic. The water will instantly start to boil. Stir in the cumin-coriander blend and the salt, followed by the cream. Remove the skillet from the heat.

6. Preheat a gas (or charcoal) grill to high heat.

7. Lightly spray the grill grate with cooking spray, and place the filets, including whatever marinade is clinging to them, on the grate (reserve any remaining marinade). *If yours is a gas grill,* lower the heat to medium. *If charcoal is the name of your game,* spread out the hot charcoal pieces to even out the heat. Cover the grill and cook, basting the filets occasionally with the remaining marinade, for 8 to 12 minutes on each side (120°F for rare, 125° to 130°F for medium-rare, 135° to 140°F for medium).

8. While the filets are grilling, gently rewarm the mushroom sauce.

9. Ladle some of the creamy mushroom sauce on each plate. Place a grilled filet atop the saucy bed, sprinkle with the cilantro, and serve.

Tips:

❖ Rib lamb chops or pork tenderloin medallions will also work with this marinade. Lamb chops take much less time to cook (about 2 minutes on each side for medium-rare) and so does pork. But then you won't be calling this curry a "mignon," *non?*

❖ I use brown cremini mushrooms, but you could use a medley of wild mushrooms, especially if these earthy delights are in season, for a meatier option.

Catfish
WITH A
CHUNKY AVOCADO-TOMATO SAUCE

atfish fillets are usually about half an inch thick and are easy to find fresh (or even frozen) in your supermarket. Catfish has an unobtrusive flavor that lends itself well to assertive seasonings, as is the case in this curry, which combines ingredients and spices typical of the cooking in Kerala. **SERVES 4**

1 teaspoon ground turmeric

1 pound skinless catfish fillets, cut into 2-inch pieces

2 tablespoons canola oil

1 teaspoon black or yellow mustard seeds

1 large ripe Hass avocado, seeded, peeled, and cut into ½-inch cubes

½ cup canned diced tomatoes

12 medium-size to large fresh curry leaves

4 fresh green Thai, cayenne, or serrano chiles, stems removed, cut in half lengthwise (do not remove the seeds)

3 lengthwise slices fresh ginger (each 1½ inches long, 1 inch wide, and ⅛ inch thick), cut into matchstick-thin strips (julienne)

1½ teaspoons coarse kosher or sea salt

1. Sprinkle the turmeric over the catfish pieces and rub it in, coating both sides. Cover and refrigerate for at least 30 minutes or even overnight.

2. Heat the oil in a large skillet over medium-high heat. Add the mustard seeds, cover the skillet, and cook until the seeds have stopped popping (not unlike popcorn), about 30 seconds. Immediately add the turmeric-coated fish in a single layer, and cook until each side is lightly browned, about 15 seconds per side. Transfer the catfish pieces to a plate.

3. Add the avocado, tomatoes with their juices, curry leaves, chiles, ginger, salt, and ½ cup water to the skillet. Heat the chunky sauce to a boil, uncovered. Return the fish pieces to the skillet and spoon the sauce over them. Cover the skillet and poach the fish until it barely starts to flake, about 5 minutes.

4. Using a slotted spatula, gently transfer the fish to a serving platter. Continue to simmer the sauce, uncovered, stirring occasionally, until it starts to thicken, 1 to 2 minutes.

5. Spoon the sauce over the catfish, and serve.

Salmon
WITH HOLY BASIL IN A
TAMARIND-HONEY SAUCE

hat happens when a prostitute falls in love with an iconic persona like Krishna, the reincarnation of Vishnu the Preserver? He is married and she really wants to be close to him, at least be able to see him, so he allows her entry into his courtyard, where she devotedly remains. (Yes, Bollywood even made a movie from that story: *Main Tulsi Tere Aangan Ki* [I Am the Basil Plant of Your Courtyard].) Thus the holy basil plant, *tulsi* ("the incomparable one"), became the representation of that dedication and to this day holds a pivotal spot in the entryway of any

Hindu temple, before the devotee even crosses the threshold to the inner sanctum. As you prepare to taste this curry, experience that same up-front devotion as holy basil mingles with rich-tasting salmon, made tart-sweet by tamarind and honey. **SERVES 4**

½ teaspoon ground turmeric

1 pound boneless, skinless salmon fillet

1 tablespoon honey

1 teaspoon coarse kosher or sea salt

½ teaspoon tamarind paste or concentrate

2 tablespoons mustard oil or canola oil

½ cup finely chopped scallions
    (green tops and white bulbs)

3 lengthwise slices fresh ginger (each 2½ inches
    long, 1 inch wide, and ⅛ inch thick), cut into
    matchstick-thin strips (julienne)

2 fresh green Thai, cayenne, or serrano chiles, stems
    removed, cut in half lengthwise
    (do not remove the seeds)

½ cup finely chopped fresh holy basil or sweet
    basil leaves (see Tip)

1. Sprinkle the turmeric over both sides of the salmon and massage it into the flesh. Cover and refrigerate for at least 30 minutes, or even overnight, to allow the yellow spice to flavor the fish.

2. Combine the honey, salt, tamarind paste, and ¼ cup water in a small nonreactive bowl, and whisk to blend.

3. Heat the oil in a medium-size skillet over medium heat. Add the fish and sear it on both sides until light brown, about 2 minutes per side. Pour the tamarind-honey sauce over the fish, and sprinkle the scallions, ginger, and chiles on top. Cover the skillet and braise the fish, without stirring, until the salmon barely starts to flake, 3 to 5 minutes. While it is cooking, periodically tilt the pan and scoop a little of the sauce over the fish.

4. Lift the fish onto a serving platter, and stir the basil into the sauce. Spoon this herb-rich sauce over the fish, and serve.

Tip: Holy basil *(Osimum sanctum)* is widely available in Asian grocery stores. These leaves are narrower than the common sweet basil, and have a dull reddish-purple tint to their edges and tips. They have a peppery taste with a sharp pungency that dissipates when simmered in sauces. If unavailable, sweet basil makes a perfectly acceptable alternative.

holy basil

❖ ❖ ❖

oly basil is used extensively in Ayurveda, India's ancient medicinal practice, to cure everything from stomach upsets (soothing when its leaves brew with tea leaves), to fever, to even malaria (in South Africa, this variety of basil is called the "mosquito plant").

Wild Salmon Fillets

POACHED WITH CHILES, SCALLIONS, AND TOMATO

he difference between farm-raised salmon and wild salmon does not stop at the price. Aficionados of wild salmon adore its deep red-orange color and meatlike marbling, a result of the fish swimming upstream for miles to spawn, when it depends on its fat reserves to make the long journey. A prized delicacy from the Northern Hemisphere, particularly the Pacific Northwest, this seasonal fish excels when it is poached in creamy coconut milk flavored with pungent chiles, tart vinegar, aromatic curry leaves, festive tomato, and perky-crisp scallions.

SERVES 4

½ teaspoon ground turmeric

1½ pounds boneless, skin-on wild salmon fillet
   (such as Alaskan or Copper River)

1 cup unsweetened coconut milk

1 tablespoon Balchao masala (page 17)

1 teaspoon coarse kosher or sea salt

12 to 15 medium-size to large fresh curry leaves

2 tablespoons canola oil

12 grape tomatoes, sliced in half; or 1 medium-size
   tomato, cored and cut into 1-inch pieces

2 scallions (green tops and white bulbs),
   thinly sliced crosswise

1. Sprinkle the turmeric over the skinless side of the salmon fillet, and pat it into the firm, meaty, deep red-orange flesh. Cover and refrigerate to allow the turmeric to flavor the fillet, at least 30 minutes or as long as overnight (since there is no acid, the fish won't break down).

2. When you are ready to cook the fish, combine the coconut milk, masala, salt, and curry leaves in a small bowl.

3. Heat the oil in a large skillet over medium heat. Add the salmon, flesh side down, and cook until it browns and seals in the juices, 2 to 4 minutes. Turn the fish over and briefly sear the skin side, 1 to 2 minutes.

4. Give the spicy coconut milk mixture a stir,

and then pour it over the fish. Lift the fillet to allow the liquid to coat the bottom of the skillet. Once the curry comes to a boil, spread the tomatoes and scallions over the fillet. Continue to poach the salmon, uncovered, occasionally tilting the pan and scooping some of the sun-yellow sauce over the fish to baste it, until the fillet barely starts to flake, 5 to 8 minutes.

5. Lift the fish onto a serving platter, spoon the sauce over it, and serve.

Shrimp
WITH BASIL-PEANUT PESTO

Changing one or two ingredients in a classic dish can be enough to catapult it into another continent's flavor boundary. I am talking about Italy's basil pesto, which includes sweet basil, pine nuts, and olive oil. Switch the pine nuts to peanuts (India's favorite nut from its northwestern region), incorporate chiles into the puree, and you have a chutney-like sauce. It not only makes succulent shrimp a joy to eat but also offers a beautiful light green backdrop. Serve this with either store-bought rice noodles or the homemade ones called *Idiappam* (page 723). **SERVES 4**

1 pound large shrimp (16 to 20 per pound),
   peeled and deveined, but tails left on

½ teaspoon ground turmeric

4 medium-size cloves garlic, finely chopped

1 cup unsalted dry-roasted peanuts

½ cup firmly packed fresh holy basil or sweet
   basil leaves

2 teaspoons white granulated sugar

1 teaspoon coarse kosher or sea salt

2 or 3 fresh green Thai, cayenne, or serrano chiles,
   to taste, stems removed

Juice of 1 medium-size lime

2 tablespoons canola oil

1. Toss the shrimp, turmeric, and garlic together in a medium-size bowl. Cover and refrigerate for at least 30 minutes, or as long as overnight, to allow the flavors to permeate the delicate shellfish.

2. Put the peanuts in a food processor, and pile in the basil, sugar, salt, and chiles. Turn the processor on and mince the ingredients, drizzling ½ cup water through the chute to form a thick, gritty paste. Then, with the machine still running, drizzle in the lime juice.

3. Heat the oil in a medium-size skillet over medium-high heat. Add the shrimp and sear them evenly, about 30 seconds per side. Add the pesto and stir to coat the shrimp with it. Lower the heat to medium, cover the skillet, and simmer, stirring occasionally, until the shrimp are salmon-orange, curled, and tender, 3 to 5 minutes. Then, serve.

Three-Bean Chili
WITH A CASHEW-PISTACHIO SAUCE

When I look at what Americans have consumed over the years in the name of chili, I can't help but think that this combination of beans, sauce, and spices is the perfect curry.

My meatless version will appeal to vegetarians and nonvegetarians alike. It contains plenty of protein, thanks to the nuts, and is chock-full of spices and vegetables. Serve it the way you would bowls of chili—with cheese, chopped scallions, and sour cream. Or why not try, instead, thick yogurt (page 22), shredded *paneer* (page 286), and chopped unripe mango for an unusual alternative that can be the main attraction at the dinner table. **SERVES 8**

¼ cup canola oil

1 large red onion, finely chopped

2 medium-size ribs celery, finely chopped

1 medium-size carrot, peeled, ends trimmed,
   finely chopped

6 medium-size cloves garlic, finely chopped

4 fresh green Thai, cayenne, or serrano chiles,
   stems removed, finely chopped

1 can (14.5 ounces) diced tomatoes

2 teaspoons ground Kashmiri chiles; or
   ½ teaspoon cayenne (ground red pepper)
   mixed with 1½ teaspoons sweet paprika

2 teaspoons Toasted Cumin-Coriander Blend
   (page 33)

1½ teaspoons coarse kosher or sea salt

½ teaspoon ground turmeric

½ cup raw pine nuts

½ cup raw cashew nuts

½ cup raw shelled pistachio nuts

1 can (15.5 ounces) pinto beans, drained
   and rinsed

1 can (15.5 ounces) red kidney beans, drained
   and rinsed

1 can (15.5 ounces) black beans, drained
   and rinsed

¼ cup finely chopped fresh cilantro leaves
   and tender stems for garnishing

1. Heat the oil in a large saucepan over medium-high heat. Add the onion, celery, carrot, garlic, and fresh chiles, and cook, uncovered, stirring occasionally, until the vegetables soften, the onion browns, and browned bits stick to the bottom of the pan, about 20 minutes.

2. Stir in the tomatoes, with their juices, and the ground chiles, cumin-coriander blend, salt, and turmeric. Lower the heat to medium and cook, uncovered, stirring occasionally, until the tomato is softened, about 5 minutes.

3. While the mixture is cooking, pour ¼ cup water into a blender jar, and then add the three kinds of nuts. Puree, scraping the inside of the jar as needed, to make a thick, slightly gritty paste.

4. Add the nut paste to the vegetable mixture. Pour 2¾ cups water into the blender jar and whir the blades to wash it out, making sure you get every bit of the nut paste. Add the washings to the pan. (If you added all the water to the blender with the nuts, the excess liquid would prevent the nuts from grinding evenly. They would be coarsely crushed, giving a very different texture and flavor to the curry.) Add the pinto, kidney, and black beans, and stir once or twice.

5. Once the chili comes to a boil, lower the heat to medium-low, cover the pan, and simmer, stirring occasionally, for about 15 minutes. At about this time, the sauce might start to stick on the bottom, so turn the heat to low and continue to simmer, covered, stirring occasionally, until the sauce is thick, another 15 minutes.

6. Sprinkle with the cilantro, and serve.

Spaghetti
WITH A
SPICY TOMATO SAUCE

I sampled good Indo-Italian food in the temple city of Orcha, in the state of Madhya Pradesh, during a recent road trip to visit the sensual stone carvings of Khajuraho. The Rajput Bundela dynasty built the city of Orcha, with its sprawling temples and forts, in the 16th century, and its remnants now serve as a must-see tourist attraction. In this princely setting I enjoyed a spicy rendition of *spaghetti arrabbiata* at a eatery at the foot of the Raj Mahal fort. Here is my version. **SERVES 8**

2 tablespoons canola oil

I teaspoon cumin seeds

2 or 3 dried red Thai or cayenne chiles,
    to taste, stems removed

I medium-size red onion, finely chopped

¼ cup tomato paste

I tablespoon Ginger Paste (page 15)

I tablespoon Garlic Paste (page 15)

2 teaspoons ground Deggi chiles
    (see box, page 290); or I teaspoon cayenne
    (ground red pepper) mixed with I teaspoon
    sweet paprika

2 teaspoons white granulated sugar

1½ teaspoons coarse kosher or sea salt

½ teaspoon Kashmiri garam masala (page 29)

4 cups finely chopped tomatoes

½ cup finely chopped fresh cilantro leaves
    and tender stems

I pound spaghetti

Freshly grated Parmigiano-Reggiano cheese
    (see Tips, page 675)

1. Heat the oil in a large saucepan over medium-high heat. Add the cumin seeds and chiles, and cook until the chiles blacken and the seeds turn reddish brown and smell nutty, 10 to 15 seconds. Immediately throw in the onion, and stir-fry until it is light brown around the edges, 5 to 8 minutes.

2. Add the tomato paste, ginger and garlic pastes, ground chiles, sugar, salt, and garam masala. Simmer the thick paste over medium heat, uncovered, stirring occasionally, until a thin film of paste starts to coat the bottom of the pan and there is an oily sheen on the surface, 2 to 4 minutes.

3. Pour in 2 cups water, and scrape the bottom of the pan to deglaze it, releasing the coating of paste. Heat the curry to a boil and continue to simmer, uncovered, stirring occasionally, until it starts to thicken slightly, 5 to 10 minutes.

4. Stir in the tomatoes and cilantro. Cook, uncovered, stirring occasionally, until the tomatoes are warmed through, 3 to 5 minutes. Keep the sauce warm, covered, over very low heat.

5. Fill a large saucepan or stockpot with water and bring it to a rolling boil over medium-high heat. Add the spaghetti and cook until it is tender but firm to the bite (al dente), following the package instructions.

6. Drain the spaghetti and immediately toss it with the sauce. (The bit of water that clings to the pasta is perfect, as it will provide enough moisture to allow the sauce to adhere to the pasta.)

7. Sprinkle with the cheese, and serve.

penne
WITH A CASHEW-DILL SAUCE

nutty sauce blankets these penne (quill-shaped pasta) and contains a hint of smokiness with more than a wisp of heat from the blackened chiles. Dairy-rich half-and-half balances it all and helps to thicken the sauce, with the able assistance of the starchy pasta. The sun-dried tomatoes provide tartness while the dill perfumes it with a hint of bitterness and vibrant green. All hallmarks of an addictive weekday dish. And did I say how easy it is to make? **SERVES 4**

2 cups penne pasta
½ cup sun-dried tomatoes
2 tablespoons olive oil
¼ cup raw cashew nuts
3 to 5 dried red Thai or cayenne chiles, to taste, stems removed
1 cup half-and-half
1 teaspoon coarse kosher or sea salt
6 medium-size cloves garlic, finely chopped
4 cups firmly packed fresh spinach leaves, well rinsed
¼ cup chopped fresh dill

1. Fill a medium-size saucepan with water and bring it to a boil. Add the penne pasta and cook until it is tender but still firm (al dente), following the package instructions. Reserving 1 cup of the pasta water, drain the penne in a colander. Run cold water through the penne to quickly cool them down and stop the cooking.

2. Place the sun-dried tomatoes in a small bowl, pour the reserved hot pasta water over them, and set the

bowl aside until the tomatoes are reconstituted, about 15 minutes. Once the tomatoes have softened, drain them and slice the pieces into matchstick-thin strips.

3. Heat the oil in a large skillet over medium-high heat. Add the cashews and chiles, and stir-fry until the nuts are reddish brown and the chiles have blackened, 1 to 2 minutes. Using a slotted spoon, transfer the nuts and chiles to a blender jar. Pour in ½ cup of the half-and-half, add the salt, and puree, scraping the inside of the jar as needed, to make a smooth, reddish-brown paste.

4. Reheat the oil in the skillet over medium-high heat. Add the garlic and stir-fry until it is light brown, about 1 minute. Add a couple of handfuls of the spinach, and stir-fry until it is wilted. Repeat until all the spinach has been added and wilted. Add the cashew-chile paste to the skillet. Pour the remaining ½ cup half-and-half into the blender jar and swish it around to wash it out. Add this to the skillet. Stir in the cooled penne, the dill, and the sun-dried tomato strips.

5. Simmer the curry, uncovered, stirring occasionally, until the pasta and the sauce are warmed through, 3 to 5 minutes. Then serve.

Ziti
WITH ARUGULA AND JAGGERY

Pasta—egg or semolina—a staple in almost every kitchen in America, is markedly absent in classic Indian cooking. However, when tossed with saucy cumin and fennel-kissed tomatoes, pasta makes a great starchy substitute for the more popular Indian basmati or long-grain rice. We Indians love to create subtle balances in our curries, with bitter, hot, tart, sweet, astringent, and nutty flavors, taste profiles that we extract from spices like red chiles, fennel, jaggery, and cumin. Arugula, classic to Italian cuisine, provides that essential source of bitterness and appeals to the Indian palate. When these players take center stage in the American home kitchen, their resulting performance is truly award-worthy. My guests and students inhale it each time I prepare this dish, marveling at how easy it is to make. **SERVES 6**

- *1 pound ziti pasta (see Tips)*
- *1 pound fresh arugula, washed, stems discarded, large leaves torn (see Tips)*
- *2 tablespoons olive oil*
- *2 teaspoons cumin seeds*
- *1 teaspoon fennel seeds*
- *2 to 4 dried red Thai or cayenne chiles, to taste, stems removed*
- *3 large tomatoes, cored and finely chopped (see Tips)*
- *¼ cup crumbled (or chopped) jaggery or firmly packed dark brown sugar*
- *1½ teaspoons coarse kosher or sea salt*
- *Freshly grated Parmigiano-Reggiano cheese (see Tips)*

1. Bring a large pot of water to a rolling boil over medium-high heat. Add the ziti and cook until it is fork-tender but not mushy, following the package instructions. (Some cookbooks recommend adding salt to the water, and/or adding a few tablespoons of oil to prevent the pasta from sticking together. I don't do either—there's enough flavor in the sauce, and the few tablespoons of oil are unnecessary because if you cook the pasta in plenty of water, it won't stick.)

2. Stir in the arugula, and as soon as it wilts, drain the pasta and greens in a colander. Run cold water over them to prevent the pasta from continuing to cook.

(The cold water will also "shock" the leaves and keep them bright green.)

3. Heat the oil in a large saucepan over medium-high heat. Sprinkle in the cumin seeds, fennel seeds, and chiles, and cook until the chiles blacken slightly and the seeds sizzle, turn reddish brown, and smell nutty sweet, 20 to 30 seconds. Stir in the tomatoes and jaggery, and simmer, uncovered, stirring occasionally, until the tomatoes are warmed through, about 5 minutes. Then stir in the salt.

4. Toss the pasta and arugula into the sauce and simmer until the pasta rewarms, 3 to 5 minutes.

5. Sprinkle with the cheese, and serve.

Tips:

❖ Macaroni, mostaccioli, and even orecchiette are equally exciting alternatives to ziti.

❖ Arugula, also known as "rocket" or "roquette," are usually available in bunches in large supermarkets and natural food stores. These bitter greens, similar in taste to mustard greens, usually have a lot of grit in the leaves, so they need to be thoroughly rinsed before use. I usually dunk the leaves in a large bowl of cold water to get rid of the grit; then I scoop the leaves out and dry them in a salad spinner if I plan to use them in salads. They have a relatively short shelf life (usually 2 to 3 days) if you don't wash and dry the leaves, but when they are rinsed, spun-dried, and stored in an airtight self-seal bag, they maintain their crisp texture for almost a week. A rich source of iron and vitamins A and C, arugula is also available prewashed, much like those bags of triple-washed spinach leaves. Use spinach, mustard, kale, or even collard greens (or a combination) if arugula is unavailable.

❖ I prefer canned tomatoes to those waxy-looking, unappealing "fresh" ones during the long winter months. Fresh organic or vine-ripened hydroponic tomatoes are great too. During the summer, when heirloom tomatoes appear in the markets, I use several varieties for an even more flavorful presentation.

❖ For heaven's sake, spend the extra dollars and buy the real deal when it comes to Parmesan cheese. Parmigiano-Reggiano, the naturally aged, crumbly cheese, is quite expensive, but when wrapped in parchment paper and stored in an airtight self-seal bag in the refrigerator, it will keep for up to a month. Buy the smallest chunk possible, so you are assured of a fresh supply of this fruity, piquant cheese. And no matter what, don't ever buy that stuff in the green can.

Hakka Noodles

Hakka, who live at the junction of Guangdong, Fujian, and Jiangxi provinces in China, trace their roots back to the early 3rd century B.C., the era of the Qin dynasty. Fleeing natural disasters, they migrated from the northern provinces to the south—and the southerners coined the name *Hakka*, which means "guest families." An ethnically diverse group, many Hakka migrated to various corners of the world, including Calcutta, after the onset of Kuomintang rule and the Second World War.

Calcutta has one of the largest Chinese communities in India and has eagerly adopted the flavors and cuisines of the early settlers, artisans, and industrious business folks, some of whom (the Hakka) immigrated over 200 years ago. The sharp smell of the fermented soy-based ingredients that salted many of the immigrants' dishes piqued the Indians' curiosity. The aromas of stir-fried meats in hot woks further tempted the Calcuttans, and ropes of fresh noodles, ready to boil and toss into bowls, became a common sight. The immigrants, on the other hand, incorporated many of India's spices and chiles into their cooking styles, creating an Indo-Chinese revolution within the depths of their woks. Fusion noodle dishes became insanely popular, and Hakka noodles came into being. Today they are found at street-corner stalls, on restaurant menus, and in home kitchens all over India. **SERVES 4**

8 ounces fresh or dried fettuccini-type egg noodles
(available in Asian markets)
¼ cup tomato ketchup
¼ cup soy sauce
1 tablespoon malt or cider vinegar
2 teaspoons ground Kashmiri chiles; or ½ teaspoon
cayenne (ground red pepper) mixed with
1½ teaspoons sweet paprika
½ teaspoon coarse kosher or sea salt
2 tablespoons canola oil
4 ounces Doodh paneer (page 286), cut into thin strips
1 cup cut-up cauliflower florets (2-inch florets)
1 large carrot, peeled, ends trimmed, thinly sliced crosswise
4 medium-size cloves garlic, finely chopped
½ cup finely chopped fresh cilantro leaves
and tender stems (see Tip)
1 large tomato, cored and cut into ½-inch cubes
4 scallions (green tops and white bulbs), cut into
1-inch lengths
2 lengthwise slices fresh ginger (each 2½ inches
long, 1 inch wide, and ⅛ inch thick), cut into
matchstick-thin strips (julienne)
1 cup bean sprouts

1. Fill a large saucepan three-fourths full with water, and bring it to a rolling boil over medium-high heat. Add the noodles and cook until they are tender but still firm to the teeth (al dente), following the package instructions.

2. While the noodles are cooking, whisk the ketchup, soy sauce, vinegar, ground chiles, and salt together in a small bowl.

3. Drain the noodles into a colander and run cold water through them to cool them off and stop the cooking.

4. Preheat a wok or a well-seasoned cast-iron skillet over medium-high heat. Drizzle the oil down the sides of the wok, and when it forms a shimmering pool at the bottom, add the *paneer*, cauliflower, carrot, garlic, and ¼ cup of the cilantro. Stir-fry until the cheese and vegetables are browned and crunchy-tender, 5 to 8 minutes.

5. Fill a large bowl with warm water and dunk the cooled noodles into it to loosen them (and to provide the moisture that helps to rewarm them quickly). Drain them again and immediately add them to the wok (a little dripping water is just fine). Cook, stirring, until the noodles are warmed though, 2 to 4 minutes.

6. Add the sauce and stir to coat the noodles and vegetables with its hot, salty, slightly sweet flavors. Stir in the tomato, scallions, and ginger. Cook, uncovered, stirring frequently, to warm the tomato, 2 to 4 minutes.

7. Top with the bean sprouts and the remaining ¼ cup cilantro, and serve.

Tip: That's a lot of cilantro, but when you add it at

two separate stages, the effect isn't so extreme: half of it cooks with the vegetables and turns mellow, while the other batch is scattered over the noodles just before you serve them, to impart a sharper taste.

Cheese-Filled Tortellini
WITH A SPICY MUSHROOM-CREAM SAUCE

My mushroom sauce is a creation from years gone by, when I had sampled a vegetarian version of Russian-influenced stroganoff over thick slices of pan-fried tofu. My Indianized adaptation includes dried red chiles, Sindhi-swayed dill, and a touch of *Kashmiri garam masala,* spices that stand up to the assertive flavor of mushrooms. Don't worry about the chiles—the sour cream (not to mention the cheese in the tortellini) will squelch their heat. **SERVES 6**

2 tablespoons canola oil

1¼ pounds brown cremini mushrooms, finely chopped

6 medium-size cloves garlic, finely chopped

4 dried red Thai or cayenne chiles, gently pounded to release some of the seeds

1½ pounds light sour cream

1½ teaspoons coarse kosher or sea salt

½ teaspoon Kashmiri garam masala (page 29)

½ cup finely chopped fresh dill

1½ pounds dried or fresh cheese-filled tortellini

1. Heat the oil in a large saucepan over medium-high heat. Add the mushrooms, garlic, and chiles, and cook, uncovered, stirring occasionally, until the mushrooms release their liquid and then start to shrink and brown, forming a thin brown layer on the bottom of the pan, 12 to 15 minutes.

2. Stir in the sour cream and scrape the pan to deglaze it, turning the sauce muddy-brown. Stir in the salt and garam masala. Cover the pan and simmer over medium-low heat, stirring occasionally, until the flavors mingle, about 15 minutes.

3. Stir in the dill and remove the pan from the heat. Keep it covered while you cook the pasta.

4. To cook the tortellini, fill a large saucepan halfway with water and bring it to a boil over medium-high heat. Cook the tortellini until tender but still firm, following the package instructions.

5. Drain the tortellini and transfer it to a large serving bowl. Add the mushroom sauce, toss, and serve.

Saffron-Marinated Cheese
WITH BASIL, PEANUTS, AND POMEGRANATE

Very few things in life, especially in the food category, at first glance, make you blurt out "sexy." This dish fairly begs for you to spend some quiet time with it, and when you are finished, you may very well wish for a cigarette, even if you don't smoke. The whole presentation is an orgasmic joy: soft creamy fingers of grilled cheese sheathed in velvety yellow sauce bursting with slender orange saffron threads and aromatic green herbs that permeate the curry with their strong flavors, topped with succulent, ruby-red pomegranate. Now don't you wish your curry were hot like this? Don't you? **SERVES 4**

½ cup half-and-half
½ teaspoon saffron threads
1 teaspoon salt
2 fresh green Thai, cayenne, or serrano chiles, stems removed, cut in half lengthwise (do not remove the seeds)
8 ounces Doodh paneer (page 286), cut into finger-like pieces about 3 inches long, 1 inch wide, and 1 inch thick
Vegetable cooking spray
½ cup finely chopped scallions (green tops and white bulbs)
¼ cup finely chopped fresh holy basil or sweet basil leaves
¼ cup finely chopped fresh cilantro leaves and tender stems
½ cup fresh pomegranate seeds (see box, page 106)
¼ cup unsalted dry-roasted peanuts, coarsely crushed

1. Pour the half-and-half into a small saucepan and bring it to a boil over medium heat. Remove the pan from the heat. Sprinkle in the saffron and stir it in to allow the heat to extract its deep orange-yellow color and sweet-smelling aroma. Stir in the salt and chiles.

2. Add the *paneer* fingers and make sure they are completely submerged in the cream. Cover the pan and refrigerate it for at least 30 minutes or as long as 1 hour, to allow the cheese to soak in the mixture. It will turn spongy-soft when poked with a finger.

3. Preheat a gas (or charcoal) grill, or the broiler, to high. *If you are grilling,* lightly spray the grill grate with cooking spray. Lift the *paneer* fingers from the marinade (keep the marinade in the saucepan) and arrange them on the grill. Cover the grill and cook, turning them every 2 to 3 minutes, until the grill marks are reddish brown, 8 to 12 minutes. *If you are broiling,* set the oven rack so the top of the *paneer* will be 2 to 3 inches from the heat. Lightly spray the rack of a broiler pan with cooking spray. Arrange the *paneer* fingers on the broiler pan and broil, turning them every 2 to 3 minutes, until light reddish brown, 8 to 12 minutes.

4. Transfer the *paneer* to a serving platter and cover it with plastic wrap.

5. Return the pan of saffron cream to medium heat, and bring it to a boil. Continue to boil it, uncovered, stirring occasionally, until it thickens, 3 to 5 minutes. Then stir in the scallions, basil, and cilantro.

6. Pour the sauce over the grilled *paneer*. Sprinkle with the pomegranate seeds and peanuts, and serve.

Macaroni and Paneer

Macaroni and cheese, much loved by both children and adults in the United States, is revered for its comforting qualities, its cheesy silkiness a perfect match for satiny-textured macaroni. So when my sister Mathangi, in Mumbai, quipped, "Your nephew loves macaroni and cheese the way I make it, and he asks for it all the time," I was instantly intrigued. Of course her version was Indianized, the homemade creamy *paneer* a sit-in for cheddar and mozzarella, fortified with aromatic garam masala and leafy spinach. A few bites convinced me of the global appeal of this comfort food.

SERVES 8

  2 cups elbow macaroni

  2 tablespoons canola oil

  1 teaspoon black or yellow mustard seeds

  1 tablespoon finely chopped fresh ginger

  8 ounces fresh spinach leaves, well rinsed and
      finely chopped

  1 large tomato, cored and finely chopped

  1½ teaspoons coarse kosher or sea salt

  1 teaspoon ground Kashmiri chiles; or
      ¼ teaspoon cayenne (ground red pepper)
      mixed with ¾ teaspoon sweet paprika

  1 teaspoon Punjabi garam masala (page 25)

  ¼ teaspoon ground turmeric

  8 ounces Malai paneer (page 287), crumbled or
      shredded (see Tip)

  1 cup finely chopped scallions
      (green tops and white bulbs)

  ¼ cup freshly grated Parmigiano-Reggiano cheese

1. Fill a medium-size saucepan three-quarters full with water, and bring it to a rolling boil over medium-high heat. Add the macaroni and cook until it is just tender, following the package instructions.

2. Reserving 2 cups of the pasta water, drain the macaroni into a colander. Run cold water through it to stop the cooking.

3. Heat the oil in a large saucepan over medium-high heat. Add the mustard seeds, cover the pan, and cook until the seeds have stopped popping (not unlike pop-

corn), about 30 seconds. Immediately add the ginger and stir-fry until it is light brown around the edges, 30 seconds to 1 minute.

4. Grab about two handfuls of the spinach, add it to the pan, and stir-fry until it wilts, about 1 minute. Continue to add the remaining greens in small batches, stir-frying each addition until just wilted.

5. Stir in the tomato, salt, chiles, garam masala, and turmeric. Cook, stirring occasionally, until the tomato softens, 3 to 5 minutes.

6. Pour in the reserved 2 cups pasta water and heat to a boil. Add the macaroni and the *paneer*. Simmer the curry, uncovered, stirring occasionally, until the pasta and cheese are warmed through, 3 to 5 minutes.

7. Stir in the scallions and cheese, and serve.

Tip: Crumbled soft tofu or crumbled feta cheese makes a great alternative to the *paneer*. If you do use feta, reduce the salt in the recipe to 1 teaspoon since the cheese is quite salty.

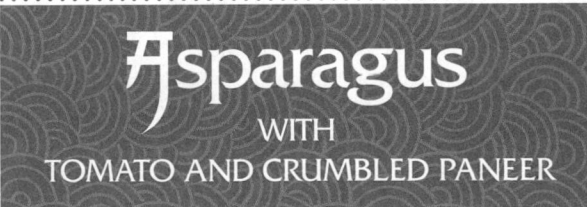

Asparagus
WITH
TOMATO AND CRUMBLED PANEER

An easy-to-do side dish, this is great when fresh asparagus is in season during the spring and early summer months. Crumbled tofu is an acceptable alternative if you don't feel like making your own *paneer*—or even making a trip to the Indian grocery store. **SERVES 8**

2 tablespoons canola oil

I cup finely chopped red onion

2 teaspoons English-Style Madras Curry Powder
    (page 24)

I½ pounds asparagus, tough ends discarded,
    cut into 2-inch lengths

I cup crumbled Doodh paneer
    (page 286)

I teaspoon coarse kosher or sea salt

I large tomato, cored and finely chopped

2 tablespoons finely chopped fresh cilantro leaves
    and tender stems for garnishing

1. Heat the oil in a large skillet over medium-high heat. Add the onion and stir-fry until it is light brown around the edges, 3 to 5 minutes.

2. Sprinkle in the curry powder and stir it around to cook the spices without burning, about 15 seconds. Add the asparagus and stir to coat it with the onion and spices. Then add ½ cup water and bring the curry to a boil. Lower the heat to medium, cover the skillet, and simmer, stirring occasionally, until the asparagus is fork-tender, 15 to 20 minutes.

3. Stir in the *paneer*, salt, and tomato. Cook, uncovered, stirring occasionally, until the cheese is warmed through and the tomato has softened, 3 to 5 minutes.

4. Sprinkle with the cilantro, and serve.

Tip: Any seasonal green vegetables will be equally tasty instead of the asparagus. Adjust your cooking times accordingly.

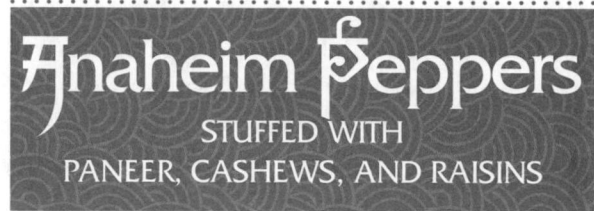

Anaheim Peppers
STUFFED WITH
PANEER, CASHEWS, AND RAISINS

great side dish, this can be a part of an elegant dinner featuring any of the shrimp curries in this book. I have also served it with Breaded Ginger Beef with a Cucumber–Pigeon Pea Sauce (page 87) and a small mound of buttered egg noodles. **SERVES 4**

8 large fresh Anaheim peppers (each about
    6 inches long; do not remove the stems)

¼ cup raw cashew nuts

¼ cup golden raisins

I cup crumbled Doodh paneer or Malai paneer
    (pages 286, 287)

½ teaspoon Kashmiri garam masala (page 29)

I teaspoon coarse kosher or sea salt

2 tablespoons mustard oil or canola oil

I cup finely chopped red onion

I teaspoon fennel seeds, ground

I teaspoon ground Kashmiri chiles; or ¼ teaspoon
    cayenne (ground red pepper) mixed with ¾
    teaspoon sweet paprika

½ teaspoon ground ginger

I cup half-and-half

1. Slit each pepper open lengthwise to expose the cavity. Make sure you do not cut all the way through the pepper. Gently pull out and discard most of the seeds and veins.

2. Combine the cashews and raisins in a food processor, and pulse until the mixture has the consistency of coarse breadcrumbs.

3. Combine the *paneer*, cashew-raisin blend, garam masala, and ½ teaspoon of the salt in a medium-size bowl, and stir well. Divide the filling into 8 portions and stuff the cavity of each pepper with a portion.

4. Heat the oil in a large skillet over medium heat. Add the peppers, cover the skillet (to contain the spattering), and sear them, turning them occasionally to ensure an even roast, until their skin is blistered and slightly shriveled, 10 to 12 minutes. Remove the skillet from the heat and set it aside, covered, to allow the peppers to steam and soften, about 5 minutes. Using tongs, carefully lift the peppers out of the skillet, making sure the filling stays inside. A tiny bit will spill out, and that's okay.

5. Add the onion to the same skillet and stir-fry it, scraping the bottom to release any browned bits of the stuffing, until it is reddish brown, 5 to 7 minutes. Then add the fennel, ground chiles, ground ginger, and the remaining ½ teaspoon salt. Cook, stirring, so the spices cook without burning, about 10 seconds.

6. Pour in the half-and-half, which will instantly acquire a deep red color from the chiles and turn the sauce a lush orange. Return the peppers to the skillet and spoon some of the sauce over them. Raise the heat to medium-high and cook, uncovered, until the sauce thickens, 3 to 5 minutes.

7. Transfer the peppers to a serving platter, spoon the thick orange sauce over them, and serve.

Tips:

❖ Be careful when you reach in to extract the veins and seeds from the chiles. They contain a lower level of capsaicin (the chemical that generates heat) than other varieties, but it's still enough to require that you wash your hands with soap and warm water afterwards, before you touch any part of your body—especially your face.

❖ You can substitute crumbled feta for the *paneer*. If you do, eliminate the salt from the filling because feta is salty as is.

Broccoli and Bell Peppers
WITH ENGLISH-STYLE CURRY POWDER

this colorful curry will look very festive at your holiday table, with its green and red combination. The smoky sweetness of seared peppers and the chile-heat in the anglicized curry powder come together to flavor a well-balanced sauce. Serve it alongside the equally celebratory roasted leg of lamb called *Raan* (page 184). **SERVES 6**

2 tablespoons canola oil

3 medium-size green bell peppers, stemmed, seeded, and cut into 1-inch pieces

6 medium-size cloves garlic, thinly sliced

2 teaspoons English-Style Madras Curry Powder (page 24)

1 can (14.5 ounces) diced tomatoes

1½ teaspoons coarse kosher or sea salt

8 ounces broccoli, cut into 1-inch florets

1. Heat the oil in a large skillet over medium-high heat. Add the bell peppers and garlic, and stir-fry until the peppers sear and blister and the garlic is sunny-brown, 5 to 8 minutes.

2. Sprinkle in the curry powder and stir it around to

lightly cook the spices without burning them, about 30 seconds. Then add the tomatoes, with their juices, and the salt. Cook, uncovered, stirring occasionally, until the tomato has softened, 3 to 5 minutes.

3. Stir in the broccoli and 1 cup water. Bring the curry to a boil. Then reduce the heat to medium-low, cover the skillet, and simmer, stirring occasionally, until the broccoli is fork-tender and succulent-tasting, 8 to 12 minutes. Then serve.

Tip: For a slight variation, you can use the broccoli stem along with the florets. Peel off the tough, fibrous, light green exterior with a swivel peeler. Then cut the stem into thin slices (either crosswise or into long, matchstick-thin pieces) for a pleasant crunch. If you do this, stir-fry the stem pieces with the peppers, not with the florets, because they take a little longer to cook.

Chile-Spiked Eggplant
WITH LEMONGRASS AND SCALLIONS

because this curry tastes great even when eaten cold or at room temperature, during the summer months, I serve the thick-sauced eggplant at room temperature over slices of toasted French baguette as an appetizer, with mint juleps or salt-crusted margaritas. Makes for an interesting alternative to the French ratatouille, *n'est-ce pas?* **SERVES 6**

¼ cup firmly packed fresh cilantro leaves
   and tender stems
2 tablespoons finely chopped lemongrass
   (see Tip, page 722)
1 teaspoon coarse kosher or sea salt
4 medium-size cloves garlic
2 to 4 fresh green Thai, cayenne, or serrano chiles,
   to taste, stems removed
2 large kaffir lime leaves
   (see box, page 657)
2 tablespoons canola oil
1 large eggplant (about 1½ pounds),
   stem removed, cut into French-fry-style
   fingers
1 large tomato, cored and cut into
   1-inch cubes
½ cup finely chopped scallions
   (green tops and white bulbs)
½ cup finely chopped fresh sweet basil leaves

1. Put the cilantro in a food processor bowl, followed by the lemongrass, salt, garlic, chiles, and kaffir lime leaves. Pulse until minced. The mixture's citrus-hot aromas will enliven your senses the moment you open the processor's lid.

2. Heat a wok or a well-seasoned cast-iron skillet over high heat. Drizzle the oil down the sides of the wok. As soon as it forms a shimmering pool at the bottom, add the eggplant and spread the minced blend over it. Stir-fry to partially cook the eggplant and the herbs, 1 to 2 minutes. (Adequate ventilation is a good idea, as the chiles may cause a coughing fit.)

3. Add the tomato and continue to cook, uncovered, stirring frequently, until the tomato softens and the eggplant is fall-apart tender, 10 to 15 minutes.

4. Stir in the scallions and basil, and serve.

Gobhi Manchurian

I am not quite sure where this name came from, but if you mention Indo-Chinese food in India, Gobhi Manchurian will be the first one mentioned—always. Crispy-battered cauliflower nestled in a dark brown sauce with fiery heat describes this favorite, and contrary to a widely held misconception, it is a cinch to make. A wok, high heat, and simple ingredients are all you need to re-create this restaurant classic at home. Yes, this is India's chop suey. Chinese restaurateurs all over the world are masters at giving their customers what they want (heavy sauces, sweet flavors, starchy foods, and local spicing techniques)—not necessarily what they themselves eat in their own home kitchens or back in China. **SERVES 4**

For the fried cauliflower:

3 tablespoons unbleached all-purpose flour

3 tablespoons cornstarch

½ teaspoon coarse kosher or sea salt

1 egg white, slightly beaten

Canola oil for deep-frying

1 small cauliflower, cut into 1-inch florets

For the sauce:

2 tablespoons tomato ketchup

2 tablespoons soy sauce

1 tablespoon rice vinegar

6 fresh green Thai, cayenne, or serrano chiles, stems removed, cut crosswise into ¼-inch-thick slices (do not remove the seeds)

1 teaspoon cornstarch

2 tablespoons peanut or canola oil

1 tablespoon finely chopped fresh ginger

2 large cloves garlic, finely chopped

1 small red bell pepper, stemmed, seeded, and cut into ½-inch pieces

1 cup chicken or vegetable stock

¼ cup finely chopped fresh cilantro leaves and tender stems

2 scallions (green tops and white bulbs), cut into 2-inch lengths

1. To make the cauliflower, combine the flour, cornstarch, and salt in a medium-size bowl. Beat in the egg and 3 tablespoons water to make a smooth, pancake-type batter.

2. Pour oil to a depth of 2 to 3 inches into a wok, Dutch oven, or medium-size saucepan. Heat the oil over medium heat until a candy or deep-fry thermometer inserted into the oil (without touching the pan's bottom) registers 350°F. (An alternative way to see if the oil is at the right temperature for deep-frying is to gently flick a drop of water over it. If the drop skitters across the surface, the oil is ready.)

3. Line a plate or a cookie sheet with three or four sheets of paper towels.

4. When the oil is ready, coat half the cauliflower with the batter. Gently lower the florets into the hot oil and fry, turning them occasionally, until they are caramel-brown and crispy, about 5 minutes. Remove them with a slotted spoon and allow them to drain on the paper towels. Repeat with the remaining florets and batter. You may need to adjust the heat to maintain the oil's temperature at 350°F.

5. To make the sauce, whisk the ketchup, soy sauce, vinegar, and chiles together in a small bowl.

6. In another small bowl, stir the cornstarch into 2 tablespoons cold water until it dissolves.

7. Heat a wok or a well-seasoned cast-iron skillet over high heat. Drizzle the oil down the sides of the wok. When the oil has formed a shimmering pool in the bottom, add the ginger, garlic, and bell pepper. Stir-fry until the bell pepper is partially seared and blistered and the ginger and garlic are browned, 1 to 2 minutes.

8. Add the ketchup-soy mixture to the wok and stir-fry to cook it, about 30 seconds. Pour in the stock and heat to a boil. Then add the cauliflower florets and cook, stirring occasionally, to rewarm them, 1 to 2 minutes.

9. Add the cilantro, scallions, and the cornstarch mixture (stir it first, because the cornstarch tends to settle). Toss and cook until the sauce thickens, about 1 minute. Then serve.

Tip: If you like an even crisper crust, you can refry the cauliflower pieces one more time, just before you add them to the sauce. It makes for a great textural contrast. If you do that, they may not need as much rewarming time in Step 8.

Potato-Stuffed Peppers
IN A GUAJILLO CHILE SAUCE

My idea for this Mexican-influenced Indian curry came from a lunch at a Mexican restaurant in Mumbai. The restaurant's chile-based sauces, beans, and rice dishes are a natural extension of similar ingredients in many of India's dishes. My favorite there has always been their chiles rellenos—Anaheim chiles stuffed with manchego cheese, batter-fried, and bathed in a red chile sauce. My version plays on that theme: peppers filled with garlic-flavored mashed potatoes, coated in a chickpea-flour batter and fried, then smothered with a sauce made with guajillo chiles, Toasted Cumin-Coriander Blend, and cilantro. **SERVES 6**

For the sauce:
- 12 dried guajillo chiles, stems removed (see Tip)
- 3 cups boiling water
- ¼ cup finely chopped fresh cilantro leaves and tender stems
- 2 teaspoons Toasted Cumin-Coriander Blend (page 33)
- 1 teaspoon coarse kosher or sea salt

For the peppers:
- 1 pound russet or Yukon Gold potatoes, peeled, boiled until tender, and mashed
- 1 teaspoon coarse kosher or sea salt
- ¼ cup firmly packed fresh cilantro leaves and tender stems
- 4 large cloves garlic
- 4 fresh green Thai, cayenne, or serrano chiles, stems removed
- 6 large fresh Anaheim peppers (each 6 to 8 inches long; do not remove the stems)

For the batter:
- 1 cup chickpea flour, sifted
- ½ cup rice flour
- 1 teaspoon coarse kosher or sea salt
- ½ teaspoon ground turmeric
- About ¾ cup warm water

- Canola oil for deep-frying
- 2 tablespoons finely chopped fresh cilantro leaves and tender stems for garnishing

1. To make the sauce, put the guajillo chiles in a heatproof bowl and pour the boiling water over them. The chiles are light and buoyant, so to keep them submerged, weight them down with a pan. (If you don't, they won't soften evenly.) Set the bowl aside until the chiles have softened, 15 to 20 minutes.

2. Pick the chiles out of the red-stained soaking liquid (do not discard the liquid) and put them in a blender jar. Pour ½ cup of the reserved liquid into the jar and puree, scraping the inside of the jar as needed, to make a thick, deep-red sauce.

3. Place a strainer over a small saucepan. Pour the sauce into the strainer and stir it with a spatula to extract as much of the liquid as possible. Pour 1 cup of the remaining reserved soaking liquid into the blender jar and swish it around to wash it out. Add this to the strainer. Then pour in the last 1½ cups soaking liquid. Discard the residual pulp in the strainer.

4. Bring the strained sauce to a boil over medium-high heat. Stir in the cilantro, spice blend, and salt. Continue to boil the sauce, uncovered, stirring occasionally, until it thickens to the consistency of maple syrup, 20 to 25 minutes. Remove the pan from the heat. As the sauce sits, it will thicken some more.

5. To prepare the peppers, stir the mashed potatoes and salt together in a medium-size bowl.

6. Combine the cilantro, garlic, and chiles in a food processor, and pulse until minced. Add this to the potatoes and thoroughly mix it in.

7. Using a paring knife, slit each pepper along three fourths of its length, starting from the stem end. Be careful not to cut all the way through the pepper. Slide your fingers into the cavity and extract most of the seeds, veins, and ribs; discard them. (Now make sure to wash your hands thoroughly with soap and warm water since the capsaicin is quite potent, even in this mild variety of chile. Use gloves to work with the chiles if you have sensitive skin.)

8. Stuff the peppers with the garlicky mashed potatoes, and set them aside while you make the batter.

9. To make the batter, mix the two flours, salt, and turmeric together in a medium-size bowl. Pour in about ⅓ cup of the warm water and whisk to start forming a thick batter. Continue adding warm water, a few tablespoons at a time, whisking them in after each addition, until you have a smooth batter that is thick enough to coat the peppers when you dip them in it. You will use about ¾ cup warm water altogether.

10. Pour oil to a depth of 2 to 3 inches into a wok, Dutch oven, or medium-size saucepan. Heat the oil over medium heat until a candy or deep-fry thermometer inserted into the oil (without touching the pan's bottom) registers 350°F. (An alternative way to see if the oil is at the right temperature for deep-frying is to gently flick a drop of water over it. If the pearl-like drop skitters across the surface, the oil is ready.)

11. Line a plate or a cookie sheet with three or four sheets of paper towels.

12. Once the oil is ready, dip 2 stuffed peppers into the batter, coating them well. Carefully slide each pepper into the hot oil as you finish coating it. Fry, turning them occasionally, until they are golden brown and crispy, 5 to 8 minutes. Using a slotted spoon, transfer the peppers to the paper towels and allow them to drain. Repeat with the remaining peppers. You may need to adjust the heat to maintain the oil's temperature at 350°F.

13. To assemble the curry, arrange the golden-brown

peppers on a serving platter. Just before you serve them, pour the sauce over them. (If you sauce them too far ahead of serving time, the crusty batter will turn soggy.)

14. Sprinkle with the cilantro, and serve.

Tip: Dried guajillo chiles are sold in almost every grocery store in the United States. These smooth-skinned, deep red chiles have a tough, leather-like skin when dry and hence require soaking to soften it. Puree the peppers and strain the puree for a smooth, velvety-textured sauce with a blood-red color. It has a slightly pungent flavor, complex-tasting, with immense depth. If you like it hotter, throw 2 to 4 dried red Thai or cayenne chiles into the mix.

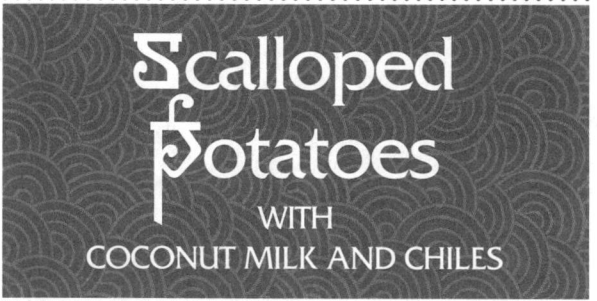

Scalloped Potatoes
WITH
COCONUT MILK AND CHILES

An Indian-inspired version of the French classic, layered with eye-opening flavors (yes, it hurts so good), this is a great side dish with any of the meat offerings in this book. I love to serve it for Sunday brunch, as a piquant alternative to hash browns. **SERVES 6**

1 can (13.5 ounces) unsweetened coconut milk
2 tablespoons Balchao masala
   (page 17)
1½ teaspoons coarse kosher or sea salt
Vegetable cooking spray
1 pound russet or Yukon Gold potatoes, peeled,
   cut crosswise or lengthwise (depending on
   their size) into ¼-inch-thick slices, and
   submerged in a bowl of cold water to
   prevent browning
4 scallions (green tops and white bulbs),
   thinly sliced crosswise
8 to 10 medium-size to large fresh curry leaves

1. Preheat the oven to 350°F.

2. Whisk the coconut milk, masala, and salt together in a small bowl.

3. Lightly spray a casserole dish with cooking spray. Drain the potatoes. Cover the bottom of the casserole with a layer of potatoes, and sprinkle a third of the scallions over them. Stir the sauce (the masala tends to sink to the bottom, so a good stir helps to mix everything evenly) and drizzle a third of it over the layer. Repeat the layers of potatoes, scallions, and masala two more times, using up all the ingredients.

4. Spread the curry leaves over the top layer. Cover the dish and bake until the potatoes are fork-tender, about 45 minutes.

5. Remove the cover and continue to bake until the potatoes are browned, 10 to 15 minutes. Then serve.

biryani
curries

biryanis (from the Persian term *biriyan*—to fry before cooking), of which there are more than thirty-five different styles across India, were introduced and made popular by several invaders—the Moghuls being of prime influence, having gathered the taste for them from the Persians. The Nawabs of Lucknow and the Nizams of Hyderabad popularized these layered meat-rice-nuts

dishes all across India. The fancier the occasion, the more elaborate the biryani—some even included pounded silver leaves. I consider these biryanis to be meals in themselves; the only accompaniments they need are a simple yogurt-based *raita* (even a bowl of plain yogurt will suffice), pickles (either homemade or store-bought), and flame-toasted lentil wafers (*papads*).

The constitution of a biryani is rather simple. First, meat, if it is included,

is marinated and braised, spiced and simmered in various sauces. Second, to prepare the rice layer, ghee is perfumed with whole spices, and sometimes with nuts and raisins, and then basmati rice is steeped in the butter (with water) to partially cook it. Finally, alternating layers of the meat curry and rice *pulao* are spread in a casserole and baked until the flavors mingle and the rice grains are tender. Saffron Rice Layered with Lamb-Tomato Curry (page 688) is a good example of this technique. The exception to pre-cooking the meat separately and then combining it with rice is the Hyderabadi classic Yogurt-Marinated Lamb with Rice, Saffron, and Mint (page 690), where uncooked (but marinated) lamb is combined with partially cooked rice and baked to completion. Although many of the biryanis are meat-based, vegetarians have adapted these dishes to include legumes and vegetables—for example, Rajasthani Dumpling-Studded Basmati Rice (page 695), Rice and Lentil Casserole with Onions (page 702), and Garlicky Festive Rice (page 698).

Now that you are familiar with the components of a biryani, its ease of preparation, and its "do-ahead" qualities, you'll see that these one-pot meals are your ticket to effortless and tasty entertaining.

Saffron Rice
LAYERED WITH LAMB-TOMATO CURRY

ǧosht dum biryani

I associate biryanis with Sunday dinners, family gatherings, and special-occasion meals. In restaurants in India, *dum biryanis* are always served in individual clay or copper-bottomed pots with a crisp layer of pastry sealing the top. The waiter breaks it open at the table to reveal mouthwatering, perfume-spiced layers of meat, vegetables, and rice, and ladles out a portion for you to wolf down with a yogurt-based *raita* on the side. This perfect one-pot meal can be the only dish at the table. Those of you who don't eat lamb can try any of the other vegetarian, chicken, or seafood biryanis in this chapter. **SERVES 6**

For the lamb curry:

1 pound boneless leg of lamb, fat trimmed off, cut into 1-inch cubes
2 tablespoons Ginger Paste (page 15)
1 tablespoon Garlic Paste (page 15)
2 tablespoons canola oil
1 can (15 ounces) tomato sauce, canned or homemade (page 18)
1 cup Fried Onion Paste (page 16)
2 teaspoons ground Kashmiri chiles; or ½ teaspoon cayenne (ground red pepper) mixed with 1½ teaspoons sweet paprika
1½ teaspoons coarse kosher or sea salt
½ teaspoon ground turmeric
1 teaspoon Punjabi garam masala (page 25)

For the rice:

1 cup Indian or Pakistani white basmati rice
2 tablespoons Ghee (page 21) or butter
1 teaspoon cumin seeds
2 black cardamom pods
2 fresh or dried bay leaves
2 cinnamon sticks (each 3 inches long)
1 small red onion, cut in half lengthwise and thinly sliced
½ teaspoon saffron threads
1 teaspoon coarse kosher or sea salt

Vegetable cooking spray

For the pastry lid:

Unbleached all-purpose flour for dusting
1 sheet frozen puff pastry, completely thawed

1. First, make the lamb curry: Combine the lamb, Ginger Paste, and Garlic Paste in a bowl, and toss to coat the lamb with the pastes. Refrigerate, covered, for at least 30 minutes or as long as overnight, to allow the flavors to permeate the meat.

2. Heat the oil in a large skillet over medium-high

heat. Add the lamb, with the pastes, and cook, stirring occasionally, until the meat sears, then releases its liquid, and then starts to brown, 8 to 10 minutes.

3. While the lamb is browning, whisk the tomato sauce, onion paste, ground chiles, salt, turmeric, garam masala, and 1 cup water together in a medium-size bowl.

4. Once the lamb has browned, pour the sauce into the skillet and scrape the bottom to deglaze it, releasing the browned bits. Reduce the heat to medium-low, cover the skillet, and simmer, stirring occasionally, until the lamb is fork-tender, 25 to 30 minutes. Set the curry aside.

5. While the lamb is cooking, prepare the rice: Place the rice in a medium-size bowl. Fill the bowl halfway with water, to cover the rice. Gently rub the slender grains through your fingers, without breaking them, to wash off any dust or light foreign objects (like loose husks), which will float to the surface. The water will become cloudy. Drain this water. Repeat three or four times, until the water remains clear; drain. Now fill the bowl halfway with cold water and let it sit at room temperature until the grains soften, about 1 hour; drain.

6. Heat the ghee in a medium-size saucepan over medium-high heat. Sprinkle in the cumin seeds, cardamom pods, bay leaves, and cinnamon sticks. Cook until they sizzle, turn reddish brown, and smell nutty, 15 to 20 seconds. Then immediately add the onion and stir-fry until it is light brown around the edges, 3 to 5 minutes.

7. Stir in the saffron and let the heat from the ingredients unleash its perfume, 30 seconds to 1 minute. Add the drained rice and toss gently to coat the grains with the orange-tinted onion. Pour in 1 cup cold water, add the salt, and stir the rice once to incorporate the ingredients. Bring to a boil, still over medium-high heat. Cook until the water has evaporated from the sur-

face and craters are starting to appear in the rice, 5 to 8 minutes. Remove the pan from the heat.

8. Position a rack in the center of the oven and preheat the oven to 350°F. Lightly spray the interior of a medium-size casserole dish with cooking spray.

9. Spoon half the lamb curry into the prepared casserole dish, and spread it out evenly to form the bottom layer. Spread half of the rice mixture over the curry. Repeat the lamb and rice layers.

10. Lightly dust a clean, dry cutting board or countertop with flour. Roll out the sheet of puff pastry to form a rectangle measuring approximately 12 inches by 10 inches. Dust with additional flour as necessary. Drape the sheet of puff pastry over the casserole, and trim the edges to leave an overhang of about 1 inch. Press the puff pastry securely around the outside edge, making sure the dish is sealed. Place the casserole in the oven and bake until the puff pastry is honey-brown and crisp, 35 to 45 minutes.

11. Remove the casserole from the oven and break open the pastry to reveal the steaming hot, perfectly cooked rice with succulent, tender lamb underneath. When you serve the biryani, scoop out portions that contain all four layers, along with some of the puff pastry.

Tips:

❖ For biryanis, I soak the basmati rice longer than I do for other rice dishes. The amount of cooking water is much less than the usual, and since I need the rice to be half-cooked by the time the water evaporates, the extra soaking gives me that assurance.

❖ You can assemble this biryani as much as 2 days ahead. Roll out the puff pastry sheet just before you bake it, or it won't be flaky-crisp.

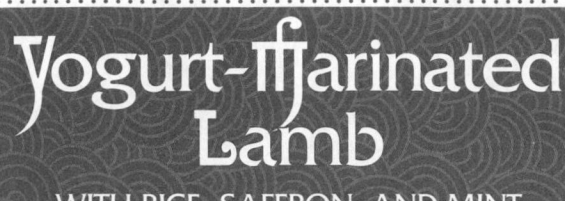

Yogurt-Marinated Lamb

WITH RICE, SAFFRON, AND MINT

kacchi biryani

A Hyderabadi specialty, this comes to me by way of my old college soulmate Abdul Contractor, who is still a close friend. His mother was a master at preparing biryanis. In this recipe, uncooked lamb *(kacchi)* is layered with partially cooked rice, and then the biryani is baked in the oven to create pure magic. Some of Abdul's mother's versions included cashew nuts, golden raisins, and fried onion slices. This simplified version pays respect to her flavors. **SERVES 6**

For the lamb:

1 pound boneless leg of lamb, fat trimmed off,
*   cut into 1-inch cubes*
1 cup plain yogurt
½ cup firmly packed fresh mint leaves, finely chopped
¼ cup firmly packed fresh cilantro leaves and
*   tender stems, finely chopped*
2 tablespoons Ginger Paste (page 15)
1 tablespoon Garlic Paste (page 15)
2 teaspoons ground Kashmiri chiles; or ½ teaspoon
*   cayenne (ground red pepper) mixed with*
*   1½ teaspoons sweet paprika*
1½ teaspoons coarse kosher or sea salt
1 teaspoon Punjabi garam masala (page 25)
½ teaspoon ground turmeric

For the rice:

1 cup Indian or Pakistani white basmati rice
2 tablespoons Ghee (page 21) or unsalted butter

1 teaspoon cumin seeds
2 black cardamom pods
2 fresh or dried bay leaves
2 cinnamon sticks (each 3 inches long)
1 small red onion, cut in half lengthwise and
*   thinly sliced*
½ teaspoon saffron threads
1 teaspoon coarse kosher or sea salt

Vegetable cooking spray
2 tablespoons Ghee (page 21) or unsalted butter,
*   melted*
2 tablespoons finely chopped fresh mint leaves
*   for garnishing*

1. First, marinate the lamb: Combine the lamb, yogurt, mint, cilantro, Ginger Paste, Garlic Paste, chiles, salt, garam masala, and turmeric in a bowl, and toss to coat the lamb. Refrigerate, covered, for at least 3 hours or as long as overnight, to allow the flavors to permeate the meat and also to tenderize it.

2. An hour before you are ready to start assembling the biryani, prepare the rice: Place the rice in a medium-size bowl. Fill the bowl halfway with water, to cover the rice. Gently rub the slender grains through your fingers, without breaking them, to wash off any dust or light foreign objects (like loose husks), which will float to the surface. The water will become cloudy. Drain this water. Repeat three or four times, until the water remains clear; drain. Now fill the bowl halfway with cold water and let it sit at room temperature until the grains soften, about 1 hour; drain.

3. Heat the ghee in a medium-size saucepan over medium-high heat. Sprinkle in the cumin seeds, cardamom pods, bay leaves, and cinnamon sticks. Cook until they sizzle, turn reddish brown, and smell nutty, 15 to 20 seconds. Then immediately add the onion and stir-fry until it is light brown around the edges, 3 to 5 minutes.

4. Stir in the saffron and let the heat from the ingredients unleash its perfume. Add the drained rice and toss gently to coat the grains with the orange-tinted onion. Pour in 1 cup cold water, add the salt, and stir the rice once to incorporate the ingredients. Bring to a boil, still over medium-high heat. Cook until the water has evaporated from the surface and craters are starting to appear in the rice, 3 to 5 minutes. Remove the pan from the heat.

5. Position a rack in the center of the oven and preheat the oven to 350°F. Lightly spray the interior of a medium-size casserole dish with cooking spray.

6. Spread the lamb (including any pooled marinade) across the bottom of the casserole dish and drizzle the melted ghee over it. Add the rice mixture, spreading it evenly over the lamb. Cover the casserole, place it in the oven, and bake until the rice kernels are perfectly cooked and the lamb underneath is fork-tender, about 1 hour.

7. Serve topped with the mint. While serving the biryani to your guests, caution them to eat around the whole spices.

Grilled Chicken
LAYERED WITH SAFFRON RICE

tandoori murghi biryani

Here's the best of northern India's creations, Tandoori chicken curry and saffron-scented basmati rice, piled into a casserole to make a luscious meal. I often serve it with a yogurt-based *raita* and with flame-toasted *Papads* (page 740) for a delicious Sunday supper. The recipe asks you to prepare the rice in two stages, but don't judge a book (except mine) by its cover. It's actually a very easy dish to prepare and can be assembled as much as a day in advance. Bake it just before you plan to serve it; the aromas emanating from the oven will make you appreciate it even more. **SERVES 6**

⅓ cup plain yogurt
1 tablespoon Ginger Paste (page 15)
1 tablespoon Garlic Paste (page 15)
2 teaspoons Balti masala (page 31)
2 teaspoons ground Kashmiri chiles; or ½ teaspoon
  cayenne (ground red pepper) mixed with
  1½ teaspoons sweet paprika
Coarse kosher or sea salt
1 chicken (3½ pounds) skin removed,
  cut into 8 pieces (see box, page 121)
1 cup Indian or Pakistani white basmati rice
Vegetable cooking spray
2 tablespoons Ghee (page 21) or butter
½ cup tomato sauce, canned or homemade
  (see page 18)
½ cup chopped fresh or frozen fenugreek leaves
  (thawed if frozen); or 2 tablespoons dried
  fenugreek leaves, soaked in a bowl of water
  and skimmed off before use (see box, page 473)
½ teaspoon cayenne (ground red pepper)
¼ teaspoon saffron threads
2 tablespoons heavy (whipping) cream or
  half-and-half, warmed

1. Combine the yogurt, Ginger Paste, Garlic Paste, *Balti masala*, Kashmiri chiles, and 1 teaspoon salt in a small bowl, and whisk to blend. Smear this orange-red marinade over the chicken pieces. Cover and refrigerate for at least 1 hour, or as long as overnight, to allow the flavors to permeate the meat.

2. Start the rice: Place the rice in a medium-size bowl. Fill the bowl halfway with water, to cover the rice. Gently rub the slender grains through your fingers, without breaking them, to wash off any dust or light foreign objects (like loose husks), which will float to the surface. The water will become cloudy. Drain this water. Repeat three or four times, until the water remains relatively clear; drain. Now fill the bowl halfway with cold water and let it sit at room temperature until the grains soften, about 30 minutes; drain.

3. While the rice is soaking, prepare the chicken: Heat a gas or charcoal grill to high, or preheat the oven to 350°F.

4. *If you are grilling,* spray the grill grate with cooking spray. Place the chicken, meat side down, on the grate. (Reserve any marinade for basting the chicken.) Cover, and grill the chicken, basting it occasionally with the remaining marinade and turning the pieces over halfway through, until the meat in the thickest parts is still slightly pink inside and half-cooked, 10 to 15 minutes. Transfer the chicken to a plate while you quickly make the sauce.

If you are oven-roasting the chicken, place a rack in a roasting pan and spray it with cooking spray. Place the chicken, meat side down, on the rack. (Reserve any marinade for basting the chicken.) Roast, basting it occasionally with the remaining marinade and turning the pieces over halfway through, until the meat in the thickest parts is still slightly pink inside and half-cooked, about 15 minutes. Transfer the chicken to a plate while you quickly make the sauce.

5. To make the sauce, heat the ghee in a small saucepan over medium heat. Add the tomato sauce, fenugreek leaves, cayenne, and ¼ teaspoon salt. Cover and simmer, stirring occasionally, to allow the flavors to meld, 5 to 10 minutes. Add the partially cooked chicken pieces and stir them in to make sure they are well coated.

6. Meanwhile, back to the rice: Stir the saffron into the warmed cream and let it steep for about 5 minutes; the sun-orange threads will tint the cream with their sensuous color.

7. Fill a medium-size saucepan three-fourths full of water, and bring it to a rolling boil over medium-high heat. Sprinkle in 1 teaspoon salt, add the drained rice, and stir once or twice to separate the grains. Once the water comes to a boil again, reduce the heat and simmer, uncovered, stirring very infrequently, until the rice is partially cooked, 3 to 5 minutes. Quickly drain the rice in a colander and then dump it back into the same saucepan. Pour the saffron-kissed cream into it and stir well to coat the grains.

8. Position a rack in the center of the oven and preheat the oven to 300°F. Lightly spray the interior of a medium-size casserole dish with cooking spray. (If you have a clear glass dish, use it; the layers will be beautifully visible when you serve the biryani.)

9. Spread half of the saffron rice evenly in the prepared casserole, forming the bottom layer. Spread the chicken curry over the rice, and then spread the remaining saffron rice over the curry. (The saffron threads tell your guests that not only have you made something special for them, you have also splurged on expensive ingredients.) Cover the casserole with its lid or with aluminum foil, sealing it tightly.

10. Place the dish in the oven and bake until the meat in the thickest parts of the chicken is no longer pink inside and its juices run clear, 45 minutes to 1 hour.

11. Remove the dish from the oven and uncover it to reveal the steaming hot, perfectly cooked rice with spicy-hot chicken underneath. When you serve the biryani, scoop out portions that contain all three layers.

Baked Spicy Rice

WITH COCONUT AND SHRIMP

jhinga biryani

A richly layered rice dish, this features flavors typical of Hyderabadi cooking—an interesting mix of southern ingredients (coastal shrimp and fresh coconut) and the northern Moghalai technique of flavoring clarified butter (here with nuts, raisins, bay leaves, black cardamom, and cinnamon) to make one huge, lasting impression on the folks who are lucky enough to eat it. If shellfish poses a problem, cubes of salmon, cod, or sole are fair game. **SERVES 8**

For the shrimp curry:

1 pound large shrimp (21 to 25 per pound), peeled and deveined, but tails left on

1 teaspoon coarse kosher or sea salt

½ teaspoon cayenne (ground red pepper)

¼ teaspoon ground turmeric

2 tablespoons Ghee (page 21) or canola oil

1 teaspoon cumin seeds

1 teaspoon fennel seeds

1 pound fresh mustard greens, well rinsed, patted dry, and finely chopped (see Tip, page 606)

1 cup shredded fresh coconut; or ½ cup shredded dried unsweetened coconut, reconstituted (see Note)

For the rice:

1 cup Indian or Pakistani white basmati rice

4 tablespoons Ghee (page 21) or butter (preferably unsalted)

½ cup raw cashew nuts

½ cup golden raisins

2 or 3 fresh or dried bay leaves

2 green, white, or black cardamom pods

2 cinnamon sticks (each 3 inches long)

1 medium-size red onion, cut in half lengthwise and thinly sliced

½ teaspoon saffron threads

1 teaspoon coarse kosher or sea salt

Vegetable cooking spray

1. To make the shrimp curry, combine the shrimp, salt, cayenne, and turmeric in a medium-size bowl, and toss. Refrigerate, covered, for about 30 minutes or as long as overnight.

2. Heat the ghee in a large skillet over medium-high heat. Sprinkle in the cumin and fennel seeds, and cook until they sizzle, turn reddish brown, and smell nutty-sweet, 5 to 10 seconds. Immediately add several handfuls of the mustard greens and stir until they are wilted, 5 to 10 minutes. Repeat until all the greens have been added.

3. Stir in the spice-rubbed shrimp and the coconut, and remove the skillet from the heat.

4. Prepare the rice: Place the rice in a medium-size bowl. Fill the bowl halfway with water, to cover the rice. Gently rub the slender grains through your fingers, without breaking them, to wash off any dust or light foreign objects (like loose husks), which will float to the surface. The water will become cloudy. Drain this water. Repeat three or four times, until the water remains relatively clear; drain. Now fill the bowl halfway with cold water and let it sit at room temperature until the grains soften, about 1 hour; drain.

5. Heat 2 tablespoons of the ghee in a medium-size saucepan over medium-high heat. Add the cashews and

biryani curries

raisins, and stir-fry until the nuts are reddish brown and the raisins are swollen, 2 to 3 minutes. Using a slotted spoon, transfer them to a plate.

6. Pour the remaining 2 tablespoons ghee into the same pan and add the bay leaves, cardamom pods, and cinnamon sticks. Cook until they crackle, sizzle, and perfume the clarified butter (not to mention the air), 15 to 20 seconds. Immediately add the onion and stir-fry until it is light brown around the edges, 3 to 5 minutes.

7. Add the drained rice and the saffron, and carefully stir-fry the rice to coat the grains with the world's most expensive spice. Pour in 1½ cups water, add the salt, and stir once to incorporate the ingredients. Bring to a boil, still over medium-high heat. Cook until the water has evaporated from the surface and craters are starting to appear in the rice, 5 to 8 minutes. Remove the pan from the heat.

8. Position a rack in the center of the oven and preheat the oven to 350°F. Lightly spray the interior of a medium-size casserole dish with cooking spray.

9. Spoon half the shrimp mixture into the prepared casserole, and spread it out evenly to form the bottom layer. Spread half the rice mixture over the shrimp. Repeat the shrimp and rice layers.

10. Cover the casserole, place it in the oven, and bake until the rice is perfectly cooked and the shrimp are salmon-pink and curled, 45 minutes to 1 hour.

11. Remove the dish from the oven and sprinkle the roasted cashews and raisins over the top. When you serve the biryani, scoop out portions that contain all four layers. (Remove the bay leaves, cardamom pods, and cinnamon sticks as you serve it, or just remind folks to eat around them.)

Note: To reconstitute coconut, cover with ½ cup boiling water, set aside for about 15 minutes, and then drain.

Nimmy Paul's Tomato Rice

tamatar biryani

When Nimmy Paul made this rice biryani (it's not a layered casserole, but the saucelike tomato curry makes it a biryani), she used an *urli,* a traditional round-bottomed, heavy pan with a generous lip. I salivated not only at the beautifully colored biryani but also at her antique *urli,* its patina harboring aromatic spices that had perfumed hundreds of curries over the years. To re-create those earthy tastes, I used my clay *urli,* which I had brought back from India as carry-on luggage. The tastes were incredible. I served it with Nimmy's fish curry, *Meen pullikaach* (page 254). **SERVES 6**

1 cup Indian or Pakistani white basmati rice
2 tablespoons Ghee (page 21) or butter
¼ teaspoon whole cloves
6 green or white cardamom pods
2 cinnamon sticks (each 3 inches long)
2 blades mace
1 small red onion, cut in half lengthwise and thinly sliced
1 teaspoon shredded fresh ginger
4 medium-size cloves garlic, thinly sliced

· 694 ·

2 or 3 fresh green Thai, cayenne, or serrano chiles,
to taste, stems removed, cut lengthwise into
thin strips (do not remove the seeds)
1 can (14.5 ounces) diced tomatoes
1 teaspoon coarse kosher or sea salt
¼ teaspoon ground turmeric
¼ cup finely chopped fresh cilantro leaves
and tender stems

1. Place the rice in a medium-size bowl. Fill the bowl halfway with water, to cover the rice. Gently rub the slender grains through your fingers, without breaking them, to wash off any dust or light foreign objects (like loose husks), which will float to the surface. The water will become cloudy. Drain this water. Repeat three or four times, until the water remains relatively clear; drain. Now fill the bowl halfway with cold water and let it sit at room temperature until the kernels soften, 20 to 30 minutes; drain.

2. Heat the ghee in a medium-size saucepan over medium-high heat. Sprinkle in the cloves, cardamom pods, cinnamon sticks, and mace. Cook until they sizzle, crackle, and smell aromatic, 15 to 30 seconds. Then add the onion and stir-fry until it is light brown around the edges, 5 to 7 minutes.

3. Mix in the ginger, garlic, and chiles. Cook, stirring, for about 1 minute. (You don't want the garlic to brown because its nutlike crunch is important to the rice's texture.) Stir in the tomatoes, with their juices, and the salt and turmeric. Simmer, uncovered, stirring occasionally, until the tomatoes soften, 5 to 7 minutes.

4. Add the drained rice and toss gently to coat the grains with the tomato sauce. Pour in 1½ cups cold water, and stir once to incorporate the ingredients. Bring to a boil, still over medium-high heat. Cook until the water has evaporated from the surface and craters are starting to appear in the rice, 5 to 8 minutes. Then (and not until then) stir once to bring the partially cooked layer from the bottom of the pan to the surface. Cover with a tight-fitting lid and reduce the heat to the lowest possible setting. Cook for 8 to 10 minutes (10 minutes for a gas burner). Then turn off the heat and let the pan stand on that burner, undisturbed, for 10 minutes.

5. Remove the lid, fluff the rice with a fork, sprinkle with cilantro, and serve. (Remove the cloves, cardamom pods, and cinnamon sticks before you serve it, or just remind folks to eat around them.)

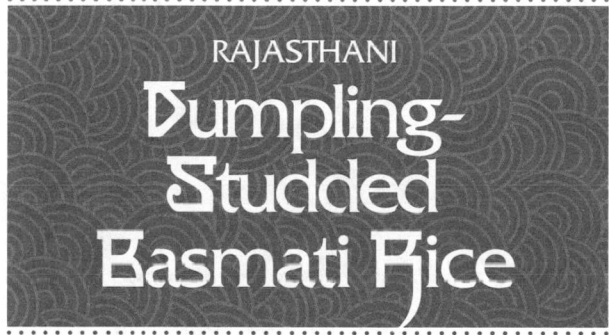

RAJASTHANI
Dumpling-Studded Basmati Rice

gatte ki behri

Chickpea dumplings *(gatte)* are easy to put together, and the recipe makes a double batch; freeze half and use them later in Chickpea Flour Dumplings with Spinach (page 349)—or make a double batch of the *pulao* (pilaf) if you're expecting a crowd. This is a hearty dish that has the starch and protein rolled into one. All you need for a simple meal is some Perfumed Spinach with Tamarind and Chiles (page 590) and Chopped Radish with Chile-Spiked Yogurt (page 742). The combination looks very pretty on the plate. **SERVES 6**

For the dumplings:

2 cups chickpea flour, sifted

2 teaspoons coriander seeds, ground

1 teaspoon cumin seeds, ground

1 teaspoon cayenne (ground red pepper)

1 teaspoon fine kosher or sea salt

½ teaspoon Rajasthani garam masala (page 26)

About ¼ cup warm water

About 1 tablespoon canola oil

For the *pulao*:

1 cup Indian or Pakistani white basmati rice

2 tablespoons Ghee (page 21) or canola oil

*3 teaspoons cumin seeds; 2 teaspoons whole,
    1 teaspoon ground*

½ teaspoon ground asafetida

1 teaspoon cayenne (ground red pepper)

1 teaspoon coarse kosher or sea salt

½ teaspoon ground turmeric

*½ teaspoon Rajasthani garam masala
    (page 26)*

½ cup boiling water

*¼ cup finely chopped fresh cilantro leaves
    and tender stems for garnishing*

1. To make the dumplings, combine the chickpea flour, coriander, cumin, cayenne, salt, and garam masala in a medium-size bowl. Drizzle ¼ cup warm water over the flour mixture, and use your hand to bring it together to form a ball. If it's too dry, add an extra tablespoon or more of water. At this point, the dough can be sticky and slightly unmanageable. Remove the stuck-on dough from your fingers, and wash and dry your hands. Then add about 1 tablespoon oil to the dough, and knead it until smooth. (Do this right in the bowl.)

2. Shape the dough into a log, roughly 12 inches long and 1½ inches in diameter, by gently pressing and rolling it under your hands on a hard surface (lightly flour

Asafetida? See the Glossary of Ingredients, page 758.

the surface if the dough is a little sticky). Cut the log crosswise into 4 pieces.

3. Fill a medium-size saucepan halfway with water, and bring it to a rolling boil over medium-high heat. Gently add the dough pieces, and lower the heat to medium. Simmer, uncovered, turning them occasionally, until they turn light yellow and have bumps all over, about 45 minutes.

4. Using a slotted spoon, gently transfer the dough pieces to a plate. Dump out the cooking water, and fill the saucepan with fresh cold water. Submerge the pieces in the cold water for a few seconds. Then return them to the plate. Using a butter knife or a paring knife, gently scrape off the outer slick, bumpy layer, revealing a smooth, darker-looking, firm, spice-speckled dumpling underneath. (Discard the pared-off dough.)

5. Slice the dumplings in half lengthwise. Cut each half crosswise into ½-inch-thick nuggets. You will end up with about 48 of these nuggets. Set aside half of the nuggets for this curry. Place the other half in a freezer-safe self-seal bag and freeze them for up to 2 months.

6. To make the *pulao,* place the rice in a medium-size bowl. Fill the bowl halfway with water, to cover the rice. Gently rub the slender grains through your fingers, without breaking them, to wash off any dust or light foreign objects (like loose husks), which will float to the surface. The water will become cloudy. Drain this water. Repeat three or four times, until the water remains relatively clear; drain. Now fill the bowl halfway with cold water and let it sit at room temperature until the kernels soften, 20 to 30 minutes; drain.

7. Heat the ghee in a medium-size saucepan over medium-high heat. Sprinkle in the cumin seeds and cook until they sizzle, turn reddish brown, and smell nutty, 5 to 10 seconds. Then stir in the drained rice and the asafetida, cumin, cayenne, salt, turmeric, and garam masala. Stir in 2 cups cold water, and bring to a boil. Cook, without stirring, until the water has evaporated from the surface and craters are starting to appear in the spice-speckled rice, 5 to 8 minutes.

8. Pour the boiling water into the rice mixture, add the dumplings, and stir once to bring the partially cooked layer on the bottom of the pan to the surface. Cover with a tight-fitting lid and reduce the heat to the lowest possible setting. Cook for 8 to 10 minutes (10 minutes for a gas burner). Then turn off the heat and let the pan stand on the burner, undisturbed, for 10 minutes.

9. Remove the lid and fluff the rice with a fork. Sprinkle with the cilantro, and serve.

Minty Rice
LAYERED WITH CHICKPEAS AND GREENS

Kabuli Thana Biryani

The first time I tested this recipe, I happened to have some cooked black chickpeas in the freezer, so I used them. They looked very pretty against the backdrop of green, orange, and red colors, nestled in the dish. If you have some cooked black chickpeas on hand, by all means use them—but regular canned chickpeas are perfectly acceptable. **SERVES 8**

For the chickpea-spinach curry:

2 large tomatoes, cored and coarsely chopped
2 small red onions; 1 coarsely chopped, 1 cut in half lengthwise and thinly sliced
8 to 10 fresh green Thai, cayenne, or serrano chiles, to taste, stems removed
4 tablespoons Ghee (page 21) or canola oil
½ cup raw cashew nuts
½ cup golden raisins
2 teaspoons cumin seeds
4 black, green, or white cardamom pods
4 fresh or dried bay leaves
2 cinnamon sticks (each 3 inches long)
2 teaspoons coarse kosher or sea salt
2 teaspoons Sambhar masala (page 33)
½ teaspoon Punjabi garam masala (page 25)
½ teaspoon ground turmeric
8 ounces fresh spinach leaves, well rinsed and coarsely chopped
8 ounces cauliflower, cut into ½-inch florets
2 cups cooked chickpeas (drained and rinsed if canned)

For the rice:

1 cup Indian or Pakistani white basmati rice
2 tablespoons Ghee (page 21) or butter
½ teaspoon saffron threads
1 teaspoon coarse kosher or sea salt

Vegetable cooking spray
1 cup firmly packed fresh cilantro leaves and tender stems, finely chopped
1 cup firmly packed fresh mint leaves, finely chopped

1. To make the curry, spoon the tomatoes into a blender jar, followed by the coarsely chopped onion and the chiles. Puree, scraping the inside of the jar as needed, to make a smooth, reddish-pink sauce.

2. Heat 2 tablespoons of the ghee in a large skillet over medium-high heat. Add the cashews and raisins,

and stir-fry until the nuts are reddish brown and the raisins have swollen, 2 to 3 minutes. Using a slotted spoon, transfer them to a plate.

3. Add the remaining 2 tablespoons ghee to the same skillet; it will heat up instantly because of the hot pan. Sprinkle in the cumin seeds, cardamom pods, bay leaves, and cinnamon sticks, and cook until they sizzle and smell aromatic, about 1 minute. Add the sliced onion and stir-fry until it is light brown around the edges, 3 to 5 minutes.

4. Carefully pour in the pureed tomato blend, and lower the heat to medium. Simmer the sauce, partially covered, stirring occasionally, until the ghee starts to separate around the edges of the skillet, 15 to 20 minutes.

5. Stir in the salt, the two spice blends, and the turmeric. Pour in 2 cups water and bring to a boil. Add the spinach, a couple of handfuls at a time, stirring it in until wilted, 2 to 3 minutes. Repeat until all the spinach has been added. Add the cauliflower and chickpeas, and remove the skillet from the heat. Cover it and set it aside.

6. Prepare the rice: Place the rice in a medium-size bowl. Fill the bowl halfway with water, to cover the rice. Gently rub the slender grains through your fingers, without breaking them, to wash off any dust or light foreign objects (like loose husks), which will float to the surface. The water will become cloudy. Drain this water. Repeat three or four times, until the water remains relatively clear; drain. Now fill the bowl halfway with cold water and let it sit at room temperature until the kernels soften, about 1 hour; drain.

7. Heat the ghee in a medium-size saucepan over medium-high heat. Add the drained rice and the saffron, and carefully stir-fry to coat the rice with the saffron. Pour in 1 cup cold water, add the salt, and stir once

to incorporate the ingredients. Bring to a boil, still over medium-high heat. Cook until the water has evaporated from the surface and craters are starting to appear in the rice, 5 to 8 minutes. Remove the pan from the heat.

8. Position a rack in the center of the oven and preheat the oven to 350°F. Lightly spray the interior of a medium-size casserole dish with cooking spray.

9. Spoon half the chickpea curry into the prepared casserole, and spread it out evenly to form the bottom layer. Spread half of the rice mixture on top of the curry. Repeat the layers of curry and rice. Scatter the cilantro and mint over the top. Cover the casserole, place it in the oven, and bake until the rice is perfectly cooked, about 1 hour.

10. Remove the dish from the oven and sprinkle the roasted cashews and raisins over the top. When you serve the biryani, scoop out portions that contain all four layers. (Remove the bay leaves, cardamom pods, and cinnamon sticks as you serve it, or just remind folks to eat around them.)

Garlicky Festive Rice

Subzi Biryani

festive and colorful, this biryani is perfect for weddings—and for the people you want to impress and please the most (which, in my mind, should be you). It's not hard to put together, and in fact you can assemble it the day before you plan to serve it. For a very special meal, bake it an hour or two before you plan to serve it (to make life easy), and offer it with one of the legume curries (for vegetarians) or meat curries (for the carnivores), with a yogurt-based cucumber *raita* (page 743) and some Flame-Toasted Lentil Wafers (page 740) alongside. **SERVES 6**

For the vegetable curry:

- 2 tablespoons Ghee (page 21) or canola oil
- I teaspoon cumin seeds
- I teaspoon black cumin seeds
- 6 green or white cardamom pods
- 6 whole cloves
- 2 or 3 fresh or dried bay leaves
- 2 cinnamon sticks (each 3 inches long)
- I medium-size red onion, cut in half lengthwise and thinly sliced
- 6 medium-size cloves garlic, cut into thin slivers
- I cup cauliflower florets (½-inch florets)
- I cup fresh or frozen cut green beans (about 1-inch pieces; no need to thaw if frozen)
- 2 small carrots, peeled, ends trimmed, cut in half lengthwise, and cut into ½-inch cubes
- 2 teaspoons Punjabi garam masala (page 25)
- 1½ teaspoons coarse kosher or sea salt
- ½ cup fresh or frozen green peas (no need to thaw if frozen)

For the rice:

- I cup Indian or Pakistani white basmati rice
- ¼ teaspoon saffron threads
- 2 tablespoons heavy (whipping) cream or half-and-half, warmed
- I teaspoon coarse kosher or sea salt
- I teaspoon ground Kashmiri chiles; or ¼ teaspoon cayenne (ground red pepper) mixed with ¾ teaspoon sweet paprika

Vegetable cooking spray

1. To make the vegetable curry, heat the ghee in a medium-size saucepan over medium-high heat. Sprinkle in the two kinds of cumin seeds and the cardamom pods, cloves, bay leaves, and cinnamon sticks. Cook until they sizzle, crackle, and perfume the ghee, 30 to 45 seconds. Then add the onion and garlic, and stir-fry until they are light brown around the edges, 5 to 8 minutes.

2. Add the cauliflower, green beans, and carrots. Cook, stirring frequently to coat the vegetables with the spiced onion and garlic, for 1 to 2 minutes.

3. Sprinkle in the garam masala and salt. Add 1 cup water, and stir to deglaze the pan, releasing the browned bits of vegetables. As soon as it comes to a boil, reduce the heat to medium-low, cover the pan, and simmer, stirring occasionally, until the vegetables are almost fork-tender but still have a little crunch left, 10 to 12 minutes.

4. Stir in the peas, cover the pan, and remove the pan from the heat.

5. Prepare the rice: Place the rice in a medium-size bowl. Fill the bowl halfway with water, to cover the rice. Gently rub the slender grains through your fingers, without breaking them, to wash off any dust or light foreign objects (like loose husks), which will float to the surface. The water will become cloudy. Drain this water. Repeat three or four times, until the water remains relatively clear; drain. Now fill the bowl halfway with cold water and let it sit at room temperature until the grains soften, about 30 minutes; drain.

6. Stir the saffron into the warm cream and let it steep for about 5 minutes; the sun-orange threads will tint the cream with their sensuous color.

7. Fill a medium-size saucepan three-fourths full of water, and bring it to a rolling boil over medium-high heat. Sprinkle in the salt, add the drained rice, and stir

once or twice to separate the grains. Once the water comes to a boil again, reduce the heat and simmer, uncovered, stirring very infrequently, until the rice is partially cooked, 3 to 5 minutes.

8. Quickly drain the rice into a colander and divide it evenly between two small bowls. Pour the saffron-kissed cream into one bowl and stir well to coat the grains. Sprinkle the ground chiles into the other bowl, and stir to color the rice a deep vermilion-red.

9. Position a rack in the center of the oven and preheat the oven to 300°F. Lightly spray the interior of a medium-size casserole dish with cooking spray.

10. Spread the red-colored rice evenly in the prepared casserole, forming the bottom layer. Spread the vegetable curry over the rice, and then spread the saffron rice over the curry. (The saffron threads tell your guests that not only have you made something special for them, you have also splurged on expensive ingredients). Cover the casserole with its lid or with aluminum foil, sealing it tightly.

11. Place the dish in the oven and bake until the rice is perfectly cooked and the vegetables are tender, 45 minutes to 1 hour.

12. Remove the dish from the oven and uncover it to reveal the steaming hot, perfectly cooked rice with spicy-hot vegetables underneath. When you serve the biryani, scoop out portions that contain all three layers. (Discard the cloves, cardamom pods, bay leaves, and cinnamon sticks if you wish, or just remind your guests to push them aside.)

Tip: If you have a clear glass casserole dish, by all means use it for the layered biryanis. The layers will be beautifully visible when you bring the biryani to the table.

Five-Jeweled Vegetable Rice
TOPPED WITH PUFF PASTRY

Panjaratan dum biryani

Decked with five *(panj)* vegetables that provide jewel-precious *(ratan)* flavor, this biryani, has a definite nutty-hot undertone to its curry layer, thanks to the presence of southern India's signature blend, *Sambhar masala.* Tomato sauce contains a high amount of lycopene, an antioxidant thought to lower the risk of cancer, so here is an excuse for you to pile on multiple helpings of this biryani (not that you'll need an excuse). **SERVES 6**

For the vegetable curry:

I medium-size russet or Yukon Gold potato, peeled, cut into ½-inch cubes, and submerged in a bowl of cold water to prevent browning

2 tablespoons canola oil

I medium-size red onion, cut in half lengthwise and thinly sliced

I cup cauliflower florets (1-inch florets)

½ cup fresh or frozen green peas (no need to thaw if frozen)

2 small carrots, peeled, cut in half lengthwise, and cut into ½-inch cubes

I small green bell pepper, stemmed, seeded, and cut into ½-inch pieces

2 teaspoons Sambhar masala (page 33)

1½ teaspoons coarse kosher or sea salt

I cup tomato sauce, canned or homemade (see page 18)

I cup Fried Onion Paste (page 16)

For the rice:

1 cup Indian or Pakistani white basmati rice

2 tablespoons Ghee (page 21) or butter

1 teaspoon cumin seeds

2 black cardamom pods

2 fresh or dried bay leaves

2 cinnamon sticks (each 3 inches long)

*1 small red onion, cut in half lengthwise
  and thinly sliced*

½ teaspoon saffron threads

1 teaspoon coarse kosher or sea salt

Vegetable cooking spray

For the pastry lid:

Unbleached all-purpose flour for dusting

1 sheet frozen puff pastry, completely thawed

1. To make the vegetable curry, first drain the potato cubes and pat them dry with paper towels. Set them aside for the moment.

2. Heat the oil in a medium-size saucepan over medium-high heat. Add the onion and stir-fry until the slices are light brown around the edges, 3 to 5 minutes.

3. Drain the potato and add it with the cauliflower, peas, carrots, bell pepper, *Sambhar masala,* and salt. Stir-fry to cook the spices gently without burning them (the vegetables will provide cushioning), 1 to 2 minutes.

4. Stir in the tomato sauce, onion paste, and 1 cup water, and heat to a boil. Then reduce the heat to medium-low, cover the pan, and simmer until the vegetables are fork-tender, 25 to 30 minutes. Set the curry aside.

5. While the curry is simmering, start the rice: Place the rice in a medium-size bowl. Fill the bowl halfway with water, to cover the rice. Gently rub the slender grains through your fingers, without breaking them, to wash off any dust or light foreign objects (like loose husks), which will float to the surface. The water will become cloudy. Drain this water. Repeat three or four times, until the water remains relatively clear; drain. Now fill the bowl halfway with cold water and let it sit at room temperature until the grains soften, about 1 hour; drain.

6. Heat the ghee in a medium-size saucepan over medium-high heat. Sprinkle in the cumin seeds, cardamom pods, bay leaves, and cinnamon sticks. Cook until they sizzle, turn reddish brown, and smell nutty, 15 to 20 seconds. Immediately add the onion and stir-fry until the slices are light brown around the edges, 3 to 5 minutes.

7. Stir in the saffron and let the heat from the ingredients gently unleash its full-perfumed potential, 30 seconds to 1 minute. Add the drained rice and toss to coat the grains with the onion mixture. Pour in 1 cup cold water, add the salt, and stir once to incorporate the ingredients. Bring to a boil, still over medium-high heat. Cook until the water has evaporated from the surface and craters are starting to appear in the rice, 5 to 8 minutes. Remove the pan from the heat.

8. Position a rack in the center of the oven and preheat the oven to 350°F. Lightly spray the interior of a medium-size casserole dish with cooking spray.

9. Spoon half the vegetable curry into the prepared casserole, and spread it out evenly to form the bottom layer. Spread half the rice mixture over the curry. Repeat the layers of curry and rice.

10. Lightly dust a clean, dry cutting board or countertop with flour. Roll the puff pastry out to form a rectangle measuring approximately 12 inches by 10 inches. Dust it with additional flour as necessary. Drape the sheet of puff pastry over the casserole dish and trim the edges, leaving an overhang of about 1 inch. Press the overhang firmly around the outside edge, making sure the dish is well sealed.

11. Place the dish in the oven and bake until the puff pastry is honey-brown and crisp, 35 to 45 minutes.

12. Remove the dish from the oven, and break open the pastry to reveal the steaming hot, perfectly cooked rice with spicy-hot vegetables underneath.

13. When you serve the biryani, scoop out portions that contain all four layers, along with some of the flaky-crisp pastry. (Remove the bay leaves, cardamom pods, and cinnamon sticks as you serve it, or just remind folks to eat around them.)

Rice and Lentil Casserole
WITH ONIONS

bisi bele bhaat

A classic rice casserole from southeastern India, this is pure comfort food. Serve it with Buttery Pigeon Peas with Turmeric (page 434), yogurt, spicy *Nimboo ka achar* (page 745), and a good supply of freshly fried pappadums—those airily crisp lentil wafers (page 740). **SERVES 6**

1 cup Indian or Pakistani white basmati rice
¼ cup oily or unoily skinned split yellow pigeon peas (toovar dal), picked over for stones
3 tablespoons Ghee (page 21) or canola oil
1 teaspoon black or yellow mustard seeds
1 tablespoon yellow split peas (chana dal), picked over for stones
1 tablespoon skinned split black lentils (cream-colored in this form, urad dal), picked over for stones
1 cup finely chopped red onion
2 tablespoons white granulated sugar
2 teaspoons coarse kosher or sea salt
2 teaspoons Sambhar masala (page 33)
1 teaspoon Punjabi or Maharashtrian garam masala (pages 25, 28)
1 teaspoon tamarind paste or concentrate
½ teaspoon ground turmeric
4 to 6 fresh green Thai, cayenne, or serrano chiles, to taste, stems removed, finely chopped (do not remove the seeds)
¼ cup finely chopped fresh cilantro leaves and tender stems
2 to 3 tablespoons Ghee (page 21) or butter (optional)
3 slices firm white bread, cut into ½-inch cubes and toasted (see box, facing page); or 2 cups store-bought unflavored salad croutons

1. Place the rice in a medium-size bowl. Fill the bowl halfway with water, to cover the rice. Gently rub the slender grains through your fingers, without breaking them, to wash off any dust or light foreign objects (like loose husks), which will float to the surface. The water will become cloudy. Drain this water. Repeat three or four times, until the water remains relatively clear; drain. Now fill the bowl halfway with cold water and let it sit at room temperature until the grains soften, 20 to 30 minutes; drain.

2. Place the pigeon peas in a medium-size saucepan. Fill the pan halfway with water, and rinse the peas by rubbing them between your fingertips. The water will become cloudy. Drain this water. Repeat three or four times, until the water remains relatively clear; drain. Now add 4 cups water and bring to a boil, uncovered, over medium-high heat. Skim off and discard any foam that forms on the surface. Reduce the heat to medium-low, cover the pan, and simmer, stirring occasionally, until the peas are partially tender, about 10 minutes.

3. Raise the heat to medium-high, stir in the drained rice, and bring to a boil. Then reduce the heat to low, cover the pan, and simmer without stirring until the rice and lentils have absorbed all the water and are swollen and tender, 15 to 20 minutes.

4. Meanwhile, heat the ghee in a medium-size skillet over medium-high heat. Add the mustard seeds, cover the skillet, and cook until the seeds have stopped popping (not unlike popcorn), about 30 seconds. Add the split peas and the lentils, and stir-fry until they turn golden-brown, 15 to 20 seconds. Add the onion and stir-fry until it is light brown around the edges, 3 to 5 minutes. Stir in the sugar, salt, the two spice blends, and the tamarind paste, turmeric, and chiles.

5. Add the onion mixture to the cooked rice mixture, and stir it in thoroughly. Stir in the cilantro and the extra ghee, if using. Sprinkle the toasted bread cubes over the top, and serve.

Cracked-Wheat Porridge
WITH BEEF, LEGUMES, AND RICE

khichda

A dish found in all the Muslim communities in India is *khichdas*. This particular version is favored by the Bohri Muslims, who converted from their Gujarati Brahmin backgrounds to Islam during the 11th and 12th centuries. This recipe comes to me via Ranee Munaim and Zohair Motiwalla (*Motiwalla* means "pearl merchant"—in Bohri households, ancestral last names often reflect their trade). Ranee is an occupational therapist, Zohair an information systems specialist, and their passion for food is evident in their remodeled kitchen in their charming home in Minneapolis. They meticulously wrote down some recipes from their childhood for me—including this porridge, which is a complete meal in itself. You can cook this in a slow cooker or in a pressure cooker (see the Tip). **SERVES 8**

toasting bread cubes
❖ ❖ ❖

To toast bread cubes, toss them in a bowl with oil, melted butter, or ghee, coating them well. Preheat a wok or a large skillet over medium-high heat. Add the drenched cubes and stir-fry until they are reddish brown, 4 to 6 minutes. Then spread them out on paper towels to drain and cool. Once cooled, they will be nicely crunchy. Store them in a self-seal plastic bag for up to 2 weeks.

1 cup cracked wheat

½ cup long-grain white rice

¼ cup yellow split peas (chana dal), picked over
   for stones

¼ cup oily or unoily skinned split yellow
   pigeon peas (toovar dal), picked over for stones

1¼ pounds cut-up beef (1-inch cubes) for stew
   (I use boneless chuck short ribs)

½ cup Ginger Chile Paste (page 17)

2 tablespoons Toasted Cumin-Coriander Blend
   (page 33)

2 teaspoons black cumin seeds

2 teaspoons coarse kosher or sea salt

¼ cup Ghee (page 21) or butter
   (preferably unsalted)

1 tablespoon cumin seeds

6 large cloves garlic, finely chopped

¼ cup finely chopped fresh cilantro leaves
   and tender stems for garnishing

1. Place the cracked wheat in a medium-size bowl. Fill the bowl halfway with water and rinse the grains by rubbing them between your fingertips. The water will become slightly cloudy. Drain this water. Repeat three or four times, until the water remains relatively clear; drain. Now pour 6 cups water over the wheat, cover the bowl, and let it sit at room temperature for 6 to 8 hours, or as long as overnight, until the wheat has softened and swelled.

2. Pour the wheat, with its soaking water, into a slow cooker. Stir in the rice, split peas, pigeon peas, beef, Ginger Chile Paste, cumin-coriander blend, black cumin seeds, and 1 teaspoon of the salt. Place the lid on the cooker, set it to low, and cook for 6 hours.

3. When the meat, rice, and legumes are very tender, heat the ghee in a small skillet over medium-high heat. Add the cumin seeds and cook until they sizzle, turn reddish brown, and smell nutty, 5 to 10 seconds. Immediately add the garlic and stir-fry until it is light brown, about 1 minute. Scrape the contents of the skillet into the *khichda* (porridge). Add the remaining 1 teaspoon salt, and stir once or twice.

4. Sprinkle with the cilantro, and serve from the slow cooker.

Tip: The desired texture of a porridge like this one—oatmeal-mushy—is an obvious reason why pressure-cooking is the medium of choice in India, especially when you consider that the meat that is normally used is tough goat meat. My version uses beef stew meat, a cut that can be tough, but the cooking technique yields fall-apart results, thanks to the slow cooker. If you prefer a quick-cooking option, use a pressure cooker: At Step 2, place the ingredients in a pressure cooker and bring to a boil, uncovered, over high heat. Skim off and discard any foam that forms on the surface. Seal the cooker shut and allow the pressure to build up. Once the weight begins to jiggle or whistle, reduce the heat to medium-low and cook for 1 hour. Remove the pressure cooker from the heat and allow the pressure to subside naturally (about 15 minutes) before you open the lid. Proceed with Step 3.

curry cohorts

You've heard of the old lyric that love and marriage go together like a horse and carriage. Have you also heard of the older adage that talks about curries and rice (breads, *raitas,* and chutneys too) being twins? Didn't think so. But let me be the one to break it to you: curries and rice are inseparable and if divided will most certainly be sad and forlorn. Curries in India are not stand-alone creatures but are always part

of a family of dishes that consists of rice, bread, chutneys, and yogurt-based *raitas* (and let's not forget dessert and beverages) at any given meal.

Steamed white rice (basmati or any other kind) is the perfect sidekick for any of this book's sauce-y dishes, but do sample red rice or Sri Lankan pearl rice for a more unique experience. Once in a while you want a little something to balance out a curry with an added oomph. Look no further than Lime-Flavored Rice with Roasted Yellow Split Peas (page 717) for that tart edge, or perfumed Saffron-Laced Basmati Rice (page 716) if you want to splurge. I love the texture of Coconut-Dusted Rice Noodles (page 723) for any one of my rich, coconut milk–based curries from the south—they are not only easy to make but are also easy on the pocketbook (if you ever were a poor college student, as I once was, you know what I mean).

India's flatbreads (no yeast in them) are our edible utensil of choice for

cooking rice

there are many ways to cook basmati (and all other kinds of rice). The two ideal ways are the absorption/steeping method and the open-pot pasta method. Some people use rice cookers and even pressure cookers to cook this delicate grain, and I find that they generate too intense a heat, resulting in a mushy, overcooked texture. To salt or not to salt the rice is the Shakespearean query. In my curry recipes I use just enough salt to bring out the flavors, so I do recommend salting.

absorption/steeping method:

1 cup Indian or Pakistani white basmati rice
1½ teaspoons coarse kosher or sea salt

1. Place the rice in a medium-size saucepan. Fill the pan halfway with water, to cover the rice. Gently rub the slender grains through your fingers, without breaking them, to wash off any dust or light foreign objects, like loose husks, which will float to the surface. The water will become cloudy. Drain this water. Repeat three or four times, until the water remains relatively clear; drain. Now add 1½ cups cold water and let it sit at room temperature until the grains soften, 20 to 30 minutes.

2. Stir in the salt, and bring to a boil over medium-high heat. Cook until the water has evaporated from the surface and craters are starting to appear in the rice, 5 to 8 minutes. Now (and not until now), stir once to bring the partially cooked layer from the bottom of the pan to the surface. Cover the pan with a tight-fitting lid, reduce the heat to the lowest possible setting, and cook for 8 to 10 minutes (8 for an electric burner, 10 for a gas burner). Then turn off the heat and let the pan stand on that burner, undisturbed, for 10 minutes.

3. Remove the lid, fluff the rice with a fork, and serve.

Makes 3 cups

open-pot pasta method:

1 cup Indian or Pakistani white basmati rice
1½ teaspoons coarse kosher or sea salt

1. Fill a large saucepan halfway with water, and bring it to a rolling boil over medium-high heat.

2. While the water is heating, place the rice in a medium-size saucepan. Fill the pan halfway with water, to cover the rice. Gently rub the slender grains through your fingers, without breaking them, to wash off any dust or light foreign objects, like loose husks, which will float to the surface. The water will become cloudy. Drain this water. Repeat three or four times, until the water remains relatively clear; drain.

3. Add the rice to the boiling water, and stir once or twice. Bring the water to a boil again and continue to boil the rice vigorously, uncovered, stirring very rarely and only to test the kernels, until they are tender, 5 to 8 minutes. Immediately drain the rice into a colander and run cold water through it to stop the rice from continuing to cook. (The problem with his method is that the grain will go from just-right to overcooked in mere seconds if you are not attentive.)

4. Transfer the rice to a microwave-safe dish and stir in the salt. Just before you serve it, rewarm it at full power, covered, for 2 to 4 minutes.

Makes 3 cups

scooping up those vibrant curries (read: no spoon or fork). Fluffy Griddle-Cooked Whole-Wheat Flatbread, called roti (page 727), is ubiquitous in Indian homes, but it's not the only choice. The Punjabi delicacy Griddle-Cooked Corn Bread with Onion and Chiles (page 728) is *it* to serve alongside Pureed Mustard Greens with Clarified Butter (page 522). And who in their right mind could pass up hot, buttered, chewy naan (page 729) or airily crisp *Papads* (page 740)?

It is true that I could write a book on just pickles, condiments, and relishes—better known to us Indians as *achars, raitas,* and chutneys. Their role is to perk up a curry with either a hurt-so-good slap like Green and Red Chiles with Cracked Mustard (page 744) or with a sweet-tart-hot punch like Pineapple Stewed with Raisins and Chiles (page 744). Soothing Sautéed Spinach and Yogurt (page 743) or Soused Cucumbers in Yogurt and Fresh Mint (page 743), on the other hand, will provide cooling relief to a chile-hot curry.

Water is the beverage of choice with any meal in India, but a cool glass of Fresh-Squeezed Lime Juice with Soda and Pepper (page 755) is perfect for that summer thirst. Don't forget to end your curry meal with a cup of steaming hot Cardamom-Scented Green Tea with Saffron (page 755) and a slice of Mango Cardamom Cheesecake with a Pistachio Crust (page 751). One eloquent word can summarize your entire experience: Yum!

a mini primer
on indian rices

Rice plays a very important role in India, and this book would not be complete without a brief description of some of the more common varieties that are consumed with curries. But let me begin by saying that there are 100,000 varieties of rice, and about a tenth of them are cultivated for human consumption—making this one of the most popular grains in the world. Terraced hills, typical of rice cultivation, dated to around 10,000 B.C., have been found in Kashmir, and the grain itself has been traced around 6000 B.C. in Thailand and China. India's soil and rainy weather are perfect for rice and it is now cultivated all over, with the south producing massive amounts for everyday use. Goa grows its classic red rice, and farther south you will find a black cultivar called black *puttu* rice. The pearl rice of Sri Lanka, called *muttu sambha,* is similar to Japanese short-grain rice and is very starchy.

Basmati Rice

Discovered and cultivated in the foothills of the Himalayas, this much-sought-after aromatic variety (*basmati* means "the perfumed one") is the world's most expensive rice. Naturally aged for many years, like a fine wine, before it graces your kitchen, basmati is less starchy and more slender than other long-grain varieties. Not only is it a complex carbohydrate, but it is also rich in amino acids and other essential nutrients, including iron, niacin, phosphorus, potassium, riboflavin, and thiamine. Basmati from India or Pakistan is not fortified with minerals, unlike the varieties grown in the United States. The kind most widely used has the outer husk and bran removed. Brown basmati is also available, but it is rarely used in India because of its short shelf life (the bran and husk harbor oil that can turn rancid rather quickly). Incidentally, if the label does not say "Indian [or Pakistani] basmati," it isn't true basmati. California basmati and Texmati are facsimiles (poor ones in my opinion); and I find these grains to be stout, short, and starchy.

Basmati is delicious when boiled, lightly buttered (optional), and salted. It's much desired in *pulao* and biryani recipes because of its low starch content.

Oftentimes white basmati rice is stored in gunnysacks and sold in sacks, which means it needs to be washed. It is important to wash the rice gently, so the grains—extremely thin, long, and tapering at each end—remain intact. This makes the rice less starchy and does not wash away any valuable nutrients. It is not necessary to soak basmati rice before you cook it, but I do; it guarantees a quicker-cooking, dry, single-grained, fluffy product.

Govindo bhog Rice

This rice is Calcutta's favorite grain, and it seems to be prevalent in that community alone. It looks like miniature basmati rice and has a creamy, nutty texture. The cooking method is the same as for basmati, but I recommend soaking the *govindo-bhog* rice for an additional 15 minutes and adding another ¼ cup water if you use the absorption method. Some large Indian grocery stores stock it, as do specialty mail-order sources. I got my stash in New York City, at a store called Kalustyan's (see page 773).

Brown Rice

In a nutshell, the main difference between white rice and brown is that the grains of brown rice still have their bran layer intact. Only the outer hulls are milled, leaving behind a more nutritious grain that is rich in complete proteins, vitamins, and minerals. This nutty-tasting, slightly chewy variety is cultivated and sold in the United States as long, medium, and short grain, the first two being the more popular ones.

More recently, packages of brown rice, including brown basmati rice, have found equal shelf space in major supermarkets and grocery stores, and there are even wider choices in natural food stores, especially in the bulk bins.

Purchase small quantities of brown rice (if you don't use it often) and refrigerate any unused portion. These grains have a higher oil content and hence a greater possibility of turning rancid. Brown rice is not fortified with minerals, so wash the grains once or twice, especially when using rice sold in bulk, to get rid of the dust. (Packaged rice is relatively clean, so you can use it without washing.) Soaking the rice is also not necessary, but if time is not of the essence, do so for 1 to 2 hours: add the required amount of water to the rice and let it soak before you cook it in the same water (for 1 cup brown rice, use 2 cups cold water). Soaking tenderizes the grain and makes for more even cooking. If you don't soak the rice, add 1 extra cup water (3 cups total) to 1 cup rice when you cook it.

To cook 1 cup brown rice, stir 1 teaspoon coarse kosher or sea salt into the rice and water. Bring to a boil over medium-high heat, and stir once or twice to prevent the kernels from sticking together. Then reduce the heat to low, cover the pan, and simmer, without stirring, until the rice has absorbed all the water and become nutty-tender, about 30 minutes. Turn off the heat and let the pan stand on the same burner, undisturbed, for 15 minutes. Remove the lid, fluff the rice with a fork, and serve.

Red Rice

Bhutanese and Goan red rices are common in India: the former is grown in Bhutan, a country just northwest of Assam, in the far northeast, and the latter is native to Goa, in the far southwest of India. These are medium-grain rices and are cooked like brown rice, with the same rice-to-water ratio (either the absorption or the open-pot method will work). Many specialty stores stock these varieties.

Black Rice

I have seen black rice labeled as "black *puttu* rice" in Kerala. Some larger Indian and Pakistani stores stock this variety, which actually turns the water dark purple when cooked. I love the nutty flavor of this rice and find that I obtain the best texture when I cook it like brown rice (the absorption method), using the same ratio of rice to water. This is not to be confused with Native American wild rice (which is not really rice but a grass), which is not indigenous to India.

Parboiled Rice

Southern Indians use a lot of parboiled rice (they just call it boiled rice) for everyday cooking. To process the rice, it is first boiled and then cooled with its hull intact. The rice is then milled for an extended shelf life. The parboiling process makes rice nutritionally sound (more like brown rice) and when steamed by the home cook, it delivers fluffy, nonsticky, single-grain rice. In addition to steaming (1 cup rice to 1½ cups water) or cooking it in a large volume of water, you can also use a rice cooker for parboiled rice (in which case, use equal amounts of water and rice). Incidentally, converted rice is parboiled rice that has been cooked a little more before being packaged for that quick convenience. In the south there is a common variety of parboiled rice called *rosematta*. In the uncooked state, this rice is yellowish brown with a red tint, but when cooked, the grains are mostly white with flecks of red. This rice does tend to have a stronger flavor, making it a suitable bed for some of the more assertive meat curries.

Perfumed Basmati Rice
WITH
BLACK CARDAMOM PODS

Kala Elaichi Pulao

Indians call spice-flavored rice dishes *pulaos*, while many in the Western world refer to them as *pilafs*. This side dish combines three of Kashmir's prized ingredients—basmati rice, black cardamom pods, and saffron—to create smoky magic. I usually serve this with *Roghan josh* (page 214), that lamb classic from the same region, full of potent flavors and deep red color. Kashmiris will use their fingers (of the right hand—the left usually reserved for "other" uses) to spoon morsels of rice and curry into their mouths, never afraid to lick their fingers to get every bit. **SERVES 6**

1 cup Indian or Pakistani white basmati rice
2 tablespoons Ghee (page 21) or butter
5 black cardamom pods
2 fresh or dried bay leaves
1 small red onion, cut in half lengthwise
   and thinly sliced
½ teaspoon saffron threads
1 teaspoon coarse kosher or sea salt

1. Place the rice in a medium-size bowl. Fill the bowl halfway with water, to cover the rice. Gently rub the slender grains through your fingers, without breaking them, to wash off any dust or light foreign objects (like loose husks), which will float to the surface. The water will become cloudy. Drain this water. Repeat three or four times, until the water remains relatively clear;

drain. Now fill the bowl halfway with cold water and let it sit at room temperature until the grains soften, 20 to 30 minutes; drain.

2. Heat the ghee in a medium-size saucepan over medium-high heat. Sprinkle in the cardamom pods and bay leaves. Cook until they sizzle, swell up (the pods especially), and smell aromatic, 15 to 30 seconds. Immediately add the onion, and stir-fry until the slices are light brown around the edges, 3 to 5 minutes.

3. Stir in the saffron. The heat from the ingredients in the pan will allow the saffron to gently unleash its full-perfumed potential. Add the drained rice, and coat the grains with the orange-tinted onion by tossing them together gently. Pour in 1½ cups cold water, and add the salt. Stir the rice once to incorporate the ingredients. Allow the water to boil, still over medium-high heat, until it has evaporated from the surface and craters are starting to appear in the rice, 5 to 8 minutes. Now (and not until now) stir once to bring the partially cooked layer from the bottom of the pan to the surface. Cover the pan with a tight-fitting lid and reduce the heat to the lowest possible setting. Cook for 8 to 10 minutes (8 for an electric burner, 10 for a gas burner). Then turn off the heat and let the pan stand on that burner, undisturbed, for an additional 10 minutes.

4. Uncover the pan, fluff the rice with a fork, and serve.

Tip: Either remove the cardamom pods and bay leaves before you serve the rice, or make sure the folks at the table are alerted to set them aside. Otherwise, your people will be calling my people to complain that I did not have the decency to post that warning. The pods especially are very strong-tasting if bit into, and might leave an unpleasant bitterness that prevents future mouthfuls from being at all pleasant.

Rice
WITH
YOGURT AND MUSTARD SEEDS

tayyar Shaadum

Whenever I serve spicy curries, this is my choice as the accompaniment because it will absorb some of the heat. When I get homesick, I reach for a plateful of this rice with a mound of spicy pickles. And if I've been indulging in junk food at the local state fair (oh, those tubs of French-fried potatoes), I look forward to ending the day with this stomach-settling, soul-satisfying offering. This is my comfort food, my nirvana, my escape after a long day. **SERVES 6**

1 cup Indian or Pakistani white basmati rice
2 cups plain yogurt, whisked
1½ teaspoons coarse kosher or sea salt
2 tablespoons canola oil
1 teaspoon black or yellow mustard seeds
1 tablespoon skinned split black lentils
   (cream-colored in this form, urad dal),
   picked over for stones
2 tablespoons finely chopped fresh cilantro
   leaves and tender stems
12 to 15 medium-size to large fresh curry leaves
3 to 5 fresh green Thai, cayenne, or serrano
   chiles, to taste, stems removed, cut crosswise
   into ¼-inch-thick slices (do not remove
   the seeds)

1. Place the rice in a small saucepan. Fill the pan halfway with water, to cover the rice. Gently rub the slender

grains through your fingers, without breaking them, to wash off any dust or light foreign objects (like loose husks), which will float to the surface. The water will become cloudy. Drain this water. Repeat three or four times, until the water remains relatively clear; drain. Now add 1½ cups cold water and let it sit at room temperature until the grains soften, 20 to 30 minutes; drain.

2. Place the saucepan over medium-high heat and bring to a boil. Cook until the water has evaporated from the surface and craters are starting to appear in the rice, 5 to 8 minutes. Now (and not until now) stir once to bring the partially cooked layer from the bottom of the pan to the surface. Cover the pan with a tight-fitting lid and reduce the heat to the lowest possible setting. Cook for 8 to 10 minutes (8 for an electric burner, 10 for a gas burner). Then turn off the heat and let the pan stand on that burner, undisturbed, for 10 minutes.

3. While the rice stands undisturbed, combine the yogurt and salt in a medium-size bowl.

4. Heat the oil in a small skillet over medium-high heat. Add the mustard seeds, cover the skillet, and cook until the seeds have stopped popping (not unlike popcorn), about 30 seconds. Add the lentils and stir-fry until they turn golden-brown, 15 to 20 seconds. Remove the skillet from the heat and carefully throw in the cilantro, curry leaves, and chiles (they will spatter upon contact with the hot oil). Scrape this concoction into the salted yogurt.

5. Add the yogurt mixture to the cooked rice and mix well but gently, being careful not to break the rice grains. Then serve.

Dirty Rice
WITH CARAMELIZED ONIONS

"Mitty" Chawal

Earthly dirt in Hindi is *mitty*, but don't worry—this rice doesn't taste of dirt. It is, however, dirt-colored—and packed with intense flavors and aromas, thanks to the highly fragrant cloves, cinnamon, and cardamom. Slow-roasting the onion, fuelled by the sugar, creates the rice's muddy-brown color and gives the grain an earthy sweetness that provides an embracing backdrop to many of the curries in this book.
SERVES 6

1 cup Indian or Pakistani white basmati rice
½ teaspoon black peppercorns
8 to 10 green or white cardamom pods, to taste
6 whole cloves
2 cinnamon sticks (each 3 inches long), broken into smaller pieces
2 tablespoons Ghee (page 21) or canola oil
1 large red onion, finely chopped
1 teaspoon white granulated sugar
1½ teaspoons coarse kosher or sea salt

1. Place the rice in a medium-size bowl. Fill the bowl halfway with water, to cover the rice. Gently rub the slender grains through your fingers, without breaking them, to wash off any dust or light foreign objects (like loose husks), which will float to the surface. The water will become cloudy. Drain this water. Repeat three or four times, until the water remains relatively clear; drain. Now fill the bowl halfway with cold water and let it sit at room temperature until the grains soften, 20 to 30 minutes.

2. While the rice is soaking, combine the peppercorns, cardamom pods, cloves, and cinnamon pieces in a mortar. Pound the spices with the pestle, breaking them down into smaller chips and releasing their aromatic oils.

3. Heat the ghee in a medium-size saucepan over medium heat. Add the onion, sugar, and pounded spices, and stir-fry until the onion turns dark purple-brown and soft, 10 to 15 minutes.

4. Drain the rice and add it to the onion mixture, tossing them together gently. Pour in 1½ cups cold water, and add the salt. Stir the rice once to incorporate the ingredients. Raise the heat to medium-high and cook until the water has evaporated from the surface and craters are starting to appear in the rice, 5 to 8 minutes. Now (and only now) stir once to bring the partially cooked layer from the bottom of the pan to the surface. Cover the pan with a tight-fitting lid and reduce the heat to the lowest possible setting. Cook for 8 to 10 minutes (8 for an electric burner, 10 for a gas burner). Then turn off the heat and let the pan stand on that burner, undisturbed, for 10 minutes.

5. Remove the lid, fluff the rice with a fork, and serve.

Nutty Rice
WITH CASHEWS, ALMONDS, AND FRESH MINT

Kaaju Badam Chawal

Swirling fresh mint in after the rice has cooked provides not only color but also a great flavor when you bite into those ten-der leaves. I am a nutty kind of guy (I left myself open with that one), and I especially love the toasty crunch of the cashews and almonds against the rice's tender-soft backdrop. Try this rice with Yogurt Curry with Cumin and Curry Leaves (page 353) for a hurry-up-and-eat lunch. **SERVES 6**

1 cup Indian or Pakistani white basmati rice
2 tablespoons Ghee (page 21) or butter
1 small red onion, cut in half lengthwise and
*   thinly sliced*
¼ cup slivered blanched almonds
¼ cup raw cashew nuts
4 fresh or dried bay leaves
1 teaspoon coarse kosher or sea salt
½ cup firmly packed fresh mint leaves, finely chopped
1 teaspoon coarsely cracked black peppercorns

1. Place the rice in a medium-size bowl. Fill the bowl halfway with water, to cover the rice. Gently rub the slender grains through your fingers, without breaking them, to wash off any dust or light foreign objects (like loose husks), which will float to the surface. The water will become cloudy. Drain this water. Repeat three or four times, until the water remains relatively clear; drain. Now fill the bowl halfway with cold water and let it sit at room temperature until the grains soften, 20 to 30 minutes; drain.

2. Heat the ghee in a medium-size saucepan over medium-high heat. Add the onion, almonds, cashews, and bay leaves. Stir-fry until the nuts turn reddish brown and the onion is light brown around the edges, 3 to 5 minutes.

3. Add the drained rice and coat the grains with the onion-nut blend by tossing them together gently. Pour in 1½ cups cold water, and add the salt. Stir the rice once to incorporate the ingredients. Boil, still over medium-high heat, until the water has evaporated from the surface and craters are starting to appear in the rice, 5 to 8 minutes. Now (and only now) stir once to bring the partially cooked layer from the bottom of the pan to the surface. Cover the pan with a tight-fitting lid and reduce the heat to the lowest possible setting. Cook for 8 to 10 minutes (8 for an electric burner, 10 for a gas burner). Then turn off the heat and let the pan stand on that burner, undisturbed, for 10 minutes.

4. Remove the lid and fluff the rice with a fork. Remove the bay leaves. Stir in the mint and pepper, and serve.

Buttery Basmati Rice
WITH SPINACH AND ONION

Palak Pulao

Once a month we all try to gather around the stove—close friends who have a passion for food, fellowship, and frolic. There are two rules: We only cook the Indian way, and this is an all-men gathering (no spouses or partners invited). This is how we bond, talk, and just be. We chip in to prep, cook, clean, eat, and of course drink. When it is time to make the rice, we all turn to our resident physician, Jeff Mandel, an extraordinary internist and a warm, caring man, who happens to make perfect rice. "What, sun-dried tomatoes in the rice again?" we joke, knowing that it is a favorite ingredient in his pantry. This time I asked Jeff to do something with spinach, onions, and one spice—

I wanted to keep it simple in order to highlight the flavors of the curries we had prepared. This was his offering, and the result was just right: fluffy long-grain rice, drenched with spinach and onions that have been slow-roasted in clarified butter and cumin seeds. **SERVES 6**

1 cup Indian or Pakistani white basmati rice
2 tablespoons Ghee (page 21) or butter
1 teaspoon cumin seeds
1 medium-size red onion, cut in half lengthwise
*   and thinly sliced*
3 cups firmly packed fresh spinach leaves,
*   well rinsed, patted dry, and coarsely chopped*
1½ teaspoons coarse kosher or sea salt

1. Place the rice in a medium-size bowl. Fill the bowl halfway with water, to cover the rice. Gently rub the slender grains through your fingers, without breaking them, to wash off any dust or light foreign objects (like loose husks), which will float to the surface. The water will become cloudy. Drain this water. Repeat three or four times, until the water remains relatively clear; drain. Now fill the bowl halfway with cold water and let it sit at room temperature until the grains soften, 20 to 30 minutes; drain.

2. Heat the ghee in a medium-size saucepan over medium-high heat. Add the cumin seeds and cook until they sizzle, turn reddish brown, and smell aromatic, 5 to 10 seconds. Then stir in the onion and add a handful of spinach. Lower the heat to medium and stir until the greens wilt, about 1 minute. Repeat until all the spinach has been added. Then cook the onion-spinach mixture until all the liquid has evaporated and the onion has turned soft and honey-brown, 15 to 20 minutes.

3. Add the drained rice and toss it gently with the onion-spinach mixture. Pour in 1½ cups cold water, and add the salt. Stir the rice once to incorporate the ingredients. Raise the heat to medium-high and cook until the water has evaporated from the surface and craters are starting to appear in the rice, 5 to 8 minutes. Now (and only now) stir once to bring the partially cooked layer from the bottom of the pan to the surface. Cover the pan with a tight-fitting lid and reduce the heat to the lowest possible setting. Cook for 8 to 10 minutes (8 for an electric burner, 10 for a gas burner). Then turn off the heat and let the pan stand on that burner, undisturbed, for 10 minutes.

4. Remove the lid, fluff the rice with a fork, and serve.

Rice
WITH
POTATOES AND PANEER

Aloo Paneer Pulao

With this protein-rich rice (thanks to the *paneer*, which also provides a meaty texture), I usually serve a vegetable curry, a yogurt-based *raita* like Sautéed Spinach and Yogurt (page 743), and some Flame-Toasted Lentil Wafers (page 740). **SERVES 6**

1 cup Indian or Pakistani white basmati rice
1 medium-size russet or Yukon Gold potato, peeled, cut into ¼-inch cubes, and submerged in a bowl of cold water to prevent browning
2 tablespoons Ghee (page 21) or butter
1 teaspoon cumin seeds
4 ounces Doodh paneer (page 286), cut into ¼-inch cubes
1 small red onion, finely chopped
4 fresh green Thai, cayenne, or serrano chiles, stems removed, thinly sliced (do not remove the seeds)
1½ teaspoons coarse kosher or sea salt

1. Place the rice in a medium-size bowl. Fill the bowl halfway with water, to cover the rice. Gently rub the slender grains through your fingers, without breaking them, to wash off any dust or light foreign objects (like loose husks), which will float to the surface. The water will become cloudy. Drain this water. Repeat three or four times, until the water remains relatively clear; drain. Now fill the bowl halfway with cold water and let it sit at room temperature until the kernels soften, 20 to 30 minutes; drain.

2. Drain the potato cubes and pat them dry with paper towels.

3. Heat the ghee in a medium-size saucepan over medium-high heat. Add the cumin seeds and cook until they sizzle, turn reddish brown, and smell nutty, 5 to 10 seconds. Toss in the *paneer*, potato cubes, onion, and chiles. Stir-fry until the mixture turns light brown and the chiles start to smell pungent-hot (proper ventilation is a good idea), 8 to 10 minutes.

4. Add the drained rice and coat the grains with the vegetable-cheese mixture by tossing them together gently. Pour in 1½ cups cold water, and add the salt. Stir the rice once to incorporate the ingredients. Continue to boil, still over medium-high heat, until the water has evaporated from the surface and craters are starting to appear in the rice, 5 to 8 minutes. Now (and only now) stir once to bring the partially cooked layer from the bottom of the pan to the surface. Cover the pan with a tight-fitting lid and reduce the heat to the lowest possible setting. Cook for 8 to 10 minutes (8 for an electric burner, 10 for a gas burner). Then turn off the heat and let the

pan stand on that burner, undisturbed, for 10 minutes.

5. Remove the lid, fluff the rice with a fork, and serve.

Fragrant Basmati Rice
WITH CURRY LEAVES

Karuvapillai Shaadum

You never want to overwhelm the delicate flavors of basmati rice. The subtle seasonings in this blend preserve that fragile nuttiness to provide an elegant backdrop for many of the curries in this book. Try it with one of my favorites: Garlic Shrimp with a Coconut Sauce (page 264). **SERVES 6**

- *I cup Indian or Pakistani white basmati rice*
- *2 tablespoons canola oil*
- *I teaspoon black or yellow mustard seeds*
- *2 tablespoons Roasted Curry Leaf Spice Blend (page 35)*
- *I teaspoon coarse kosher or sea salt*

1. Place the rice in a medium-size bowl. Fill the bowl halfway with water, to cover the rice. Gently rub the slender grains through your fingers, without breaking them, to wash off any dust or light foreign objects (like loose husks), which will float to the surface. The water will become cloudy. Drain this water. Repeat three or four times, until the water remains relatively clear; drain. Now fill the bowl halfway with cold water and let

it sit at room temperature until the kernels soften, 20 to 30 minutes; drain.

2. Heat the oil in a medium-size saucepan over medium-high heat. Add the mustard seeds, cover the pan, and cook until the seeds have stopped popping (not unlike popcorn), about 30 seconds.

3. Add the drained rice and coat the grains with the nutty-smelling mixture by tossing them together gently. Pour in 1½ cups cold water, and sprinkle with the spice blend and salt. Stir the rice once to incorporate the spices. Continue to boil, still over medium-high heat, until the water has evaporated from the surface and craters are starting to appear in the rice, 5 to 8 minutes. Now (and only now) stir once to bring the partially cooked layer from the bottom of the pan to the surface. Cover the pan with a tight-fitting lid and reduce the heat to the lowest possible setting. Cook for 8 to 10 minutes (8 for an electric burner, 10 for a gas burner). Then turn off the heat and let the pan stand on that burner, undisturbed, for 10 minutes.

4. Remove the lid, fluff the rice with a fork, and serve.

Sweet-Hot Basmati Rice
WITH JAGGERY AND CHILES

Gud Bhaat

Sweet-hot flavors of this rice dish reflect the spicing techniques employed in the kitchens of Gujarati- and Marathi-speaking homes. You may choose to discard the chiles before you serve the rice (I will certainly understand), but I for one love to bite into them between mouthfuls. Serve this rice with Black-Eyed Peas with Mustard, Cumin, and Curry Leaves (page 322). **SERVES 6**

1 cup Indian or Pakistani white basmati rice

2 tablespoons canola oil

1 teaspoon black or yellow mustard seeds

1 small red onion, cut in half lengthwise
    and thinly sliced

6 dried red Thai or cayenne chiles, stems
    removed

2 tablespoons crumbled (or chopped)
    jaggery or firmly packed dark
    brown sugar

1 teaspoon coarse kosher or sea salt

1. Place the rice in a medium-size bowl. Fill the bowl halfway with water, to cover the rice. Gently rub the slender grains through your fingers, without breaking them, to wash off any dust or light foreign objects (like loose husks), which will float to the surface. The water will become cloudy. Drain this water. Repeat three or four times, until the water remains relatively clear; drain. Now fill the bowl halfway with cold water and let it sit at room temperature until the grains soften, 20 to 30 minutes; drain.

2. Heat the oil in a small saucepan over medium-high heat. Add the mustard seeds, cover the pan, and wait until the seeds have stopped popping (not unlike popcorn), about 30 seconds. Immediately add the onion and chiles, and stir-fry until the onion is caramel-brown, 8 to 10 minutes.

3. Add the drained rice and coat the grains with the sweet onion mixture by tossing them together gently. Pour in 1½ cups cold water, and add the jaggery and salt. Stir the rice once to incorporate the ingredients. Continue to boil, still over medium-high heat, until the water has evaporated from the surface and craters are starting to appear in the rice, 5 to 8 minutes. Now (and only now) stir once to bring the partially cooked layer from the bottom of the pan to the surface. Cover the pan with a tight-fitting lid and reduce the heat to the lowest possible setting. Cook for 8 to 10 minutes (8 for an electric burner, 10 for a gas burner). Then turn off the heat and let the pan stand on that burner, undisturbed, for 10 minutes.

> Jaggery? See the Glossary of Ingredients, page 758.

4. Remove the lid, fluff the rice with a fork, remove the chiles, if desired, and serve.

Saffron-Laced Basmati Rice

Zarda Thaawal

Uncluttered, this recipe highlights the rich flavors of basmati rice and saffron, both prized commodities in India. The sugar coaxes the saffron's perfumed flavor to shine, drenching the rice with its sunny disposition. I recommend some of the mellow nut-based curries, such as Razia Syed's Chicken with an Almond Yogurt Sauce (page 130), as perfect matches for this rice. **SERVES 4**

1 cup Indian or Pakistani white basmati rice

2 tablespoons Ghee (page 21) or butter

½ teaspoon saffron threads

2 teaspoons white granulated sugar

1 teaspoon coarse kosher or sea salt

1. Place the rice in a medium-size bowl. Fill the bowl halfway with water, to cover the rice. Gently rub the slender grains through your fingers, without breaking them, to wash off any dust or light foreign objects (like loose husks), which will float to the surface. The water will become cloudy. Drain this water. Repeat three or four times, until the water remains relatively clear; drain. Now fill the bowl halfway with cold water and let it sit at room temperature until the grains soften, 20 to 30 minutes; drain.

2. Heat the ghee in a medium-size saucepan over medium-high heat. Add the drained rice and the saffron and stir gently, being careful not to break the delicate rice grains while you coat them with the spice, for 1 to 2 minutes.

3. Pour in 1½ cups cold water, and scrape the bottom of the pan to loosen any stuck-on rice kernels. Stir in the sugar and salt. Cook, still over medium-high heat, until the water has evaporated from the surface and craters are starting to appear in the rice, 5 to 8 minutes. Now (and only now) stir once to bring the partially cooked layer from the bottom of the pan to the surface. Cover the pan with a tight-fitting lid and reduce the heat to the lowest possible setting. Cook for 8 to 10 minutes (8 for an electric burner, 10 for a gas burner). Then turn off the heat and let the pan stand on that burner, undisturbed, for 10 minutes.

4. Remove the lid, fluff the rice with a fork, and serve.

Lime-Flavored Rice
WITH
ROASTED YELLOW SPLIT PEAS

Elambuchambu Shaadum

At south Indian weddings, this rice is packed in banana leaves for the groom's party to eat on the way to the ceremony, should their journey be long. It can easily be eaten as is (which is normally the case for the groomsmen), but it also is the perfect accompaniment for Mixed Vegetables with a Potent Coconut-Chile Sauce (page 630), another wedding favorite.

SERVES 6

1 cup Indian or Pakistani white basmati rice (see Tips)

2 tablespoons unrefined sesame oil or canola oil

1 teaspoon black or yellow mustard seeds

¼ cup yellow split peas (chana dal), picked over for stones, soaked in hot water for 15 minutes, drained, and patted dry between paper towels

2 dried red Thai or cayenne chiles, stems removed (see Tips)

1½ teaspoons coarse kosher or sea salt

Juice of 1 large lime

½ teaspoon ground turmeric

12 medium-size to large fresh curry leaves

2 fresh green Thai, cayenne, or serrano chiles, stems removed, cut crosswise into ½-inch-thick slices (do not remove the seeds)

1. Place the rice in a medium-size bowl. Fill the bowl halfway with water, to cover the rice. Gently rub the

slender grains through your fingers, without breaking them, to wash off any dust or light foreign objects (like loose husks), which will float to the surface. The water will become cloudy. Drain this water. Repeat three or four times, until the water remains relatively clear; drain. Now fill the bowl halfway with cold water and let it sit at room temperature until the grains soften, 20 to 30 minutes; drain.

2. Heat the oil in a medium-size saucepan over medium-high heat. Add the mustard seeds, cover the pan, and cook until the seeds have stopped popping (not unlike popcorn), about 30 seconds. Then add the split peas and dried chiles. Stir-fry until the split peas are reddish brown and the chiles have blackened, 2 to 4 minutes.

3. Add the drained rice and coat the grains with the spice-legume mixture by tossing them together gently. Pour in 1½ cups cold water, and add the salt. Stir the rice once to incorporate the ingredients. Continue to boil, still over medium-high heat, until the water has evaporated from the surface and craters are starting to appear in the rice, 5 to 8 minutes. Now (and only now) stir once to bring the partially cooked layer from the bottom of the pan to the surface. Cover the pan with a tight-fitting lid and reduce the heat to the lowest possible setting. Cook for 8 to 10 minutes (8 for an electric burner, 10 for a gas burner). Then turn off the heat and let the pan stand on that burner, undisturbed, for 10 minutes.

4. While the rice is standing, combine the lime juice, turmeric, curry leaves, and fresh chiles in a small bowl.

5. Remove the lid and fluff the rice with a fork. Pour the lime juice mixture into the rice, stir it well to color the kernels a beautiful shade of sun-yellow mottled with green herbs, and serve.

Tips:

❖ Even though I have recommended basmati rice, any long-grain white variety will work as an alternative.

❖ You may want to skirt around the dried chiles, but I usually eat them, nestled in the lime-flavored rice grains to mask their heat.

Rice-Lentil Porridge
WITH GHEE AND CUMIN

moong dal kichidi

Long before risottos became the craze here in the United States, creamy *kichidis* were providing comfort to millions of Indians, who often eat them simply with some pickles, yogurt, and lentil wafers. I find that the smooth, starchy porridge is a perfect bed for many of this book's curries—especially its ideal consort, Spicy Ground Beef with Peas and Chiles (page 182). **SERVES 8**

1 cup skinned split green lentils (yellow-colored in this form, moong dal), picked over for stones

1 cup long-grain white rice (see Tips)

2 teaspoons coarse kosher or sea salt

½ teaspoon ground turmeric

4 cups boiling water

3 tablespoons Ghee (page 21) or unsalted butter

1 tablespoon cumin seeds

1. Place the lentils in a medium-size saucepan. Fill the pan halfway with water, and rinse the lentils by rubbing them between your fingertips. The water will become cloudy. Drain this water. Repeat three or four times, until the water remains relatively clear; drain. Now add the rice and 4 cups cold water. Bring the water to a boil over medium-high heat. Skim off and discard any foam that forms on the surface.

2. Stir in the salt and turmeric. Reduce the heat to medium and cook, uncovered, stirring occasionally, until all the water has been absorbed by the rice and lentils, 8 to 10 minutes.

3. Pour 1 cup of the boiling water into the rice-lentil mixture and continue to cook, stirring occasionally, until that water is absorbed too. Repeat with the remaining 3 cups boiling water, 1 cup at a time, until the porridge is creamy-smooth, the rice kernels are swollen and puffy, and all the water has been absorbed. This entire process may take 35 to 40 minutes.

4. Heat the ghee in a small skillet over medium-high heat. Add the cumin seeds and cook until they sizzle, turn reddish brown, and smell nutty, 5 to 10 seconds. Pour the nutty butter over the *kichidi*, stir once or twice, and serve.

Tips:

❖ The technique for making porridge is very similar to the one used for succulent risottos with arborio rice, a short-grain, starchy, creamy rice. The rice I use here is not the pricey basmati, which is less starchy.

❖ Long-grain rice available in the United States is fortified with iron, phosphate, niacin, thiamine, and folic acid, and so I don't recommend that you wash the rice before cooking, since it will leach out these beneficial additives.

Rice-Lentil Porridge
WITH
CURRY LEAVES AND GINGER

Ven Pongal

Southern Indians usually indulge in this moist, creamy rice-lentil accompaniment at the end of the harvest season, to celebrate the bounty of their water-filled, rich soil, ideal for cultivating rice. Although any of the curries in this book is great with *pongal*, my favorites are the root vegetable stew called *Aviyal* (page 630) and Eggplant with a Tamarind-Chile Sauce (page 490). **SERVES 8**

½ cup skinned split green lentils (yellow-colored in this form, moong dal), picked over for stones

1 cup long-grain white rice (see Tip, this page)

1½ teaspoons coarse kosher or sea salt

½ teaspoon ground turmeric

4 tablespoons Ghee (page 21) or butter (preferably unsalted)

2 teaspoons cumin seeds

1 teaspoon black peppercorns

3 lengthwise slices fresh ginger (each 1½ inches long, 1 inch wide, and ⅛ inch thick), cut into matchstick-thin strips (julienne)

¼ cup finely chopped fresh cilantro leaves and tender stems

12 to 15 medium-size to large fresh curry leaves

1. Place the lentils in a medium-size saucepan. Fill the pan halfway with water and rinse the lentils by rubbing them between your fingertips. The water will become cloudy. Drain this water. Repeat three or four times, until the water remains relatively clear; drain. Now add the rice and 3 cups cold water. Bring the water to a boil over medium-high heat. Skim off and discard any foam that forms on the surface.

2. Stir in the salt and turmeric. Continue to cook, uncovered, stirring occasionally, until the water has evaporated from the surface and craters are starting to appear in the rice, 5 to 8 minutes. Now (and only now) stir once to bring the partially cooked layer from the bottom of the pan to the surface. Cover the pan with a tight-fitting lid and reduce the heat to the lowest possible setting. Cook for 8 to 10 minutes. Then turn off the heat and let the pan stand on that burner, undisturbed, for 10 minutes.

3. While the rice-lentil mixture is steeping, heat 2 tablespoons of the ghee in a small skillet over medium-high heat. Sprinkle in the cumin seeds and peppercorns, and cook until they sizzle, the cumin seeds turn reddish brown, and the spices smell nutty-hot, 20 to 30 seconds. Transfer the spices, ghee and all, to a mortar, and let the mixture cool for 2 to 3 minutes. Pound the mixture with the pestle until the spices are coarsely cracked.

4. Heat the remaining 2 tablespoons ghee in the same skillet over medium-high heat. Add the ginger and cook until it sizzles and is aromatic, 10 to 15 seconds. Then carefully add the cilantro and curry leaves—step back a little, as they will spatter upon contact and send hot grease up in the air. Set it aside.

5. Once the porridge is ready, remove the lid and stir in the contents of the skillet and the pounded spices. Stir to mix. (I usually plop a little porridge into the skillet and the mortar, and stir it around to make sure I get every bit of ghee, spice, and herb. Then I return this to the pot, stirring it all in to ensure an even blend.) Then serve.

Tip: Mortars and pestles (see page 13) are great for some tasks, especially when the texture of the blend is important to the recipe's success. But I wouldn't want you to not make this dish just because you don't have a reliable mortar and pestle. Scoop the roasted seeds and peppercorns into a spice grinder (try not to get too much of the ghee in the mix, for fear of your particular grinder not being able to accommodate "wet" grinding). Use a pulsing action to create the coarse texture called for in the recipe. Although the bowl of a standard-size food processor might be too large for the few teaspoons of spices here, a mini chopper or mini processor might work.

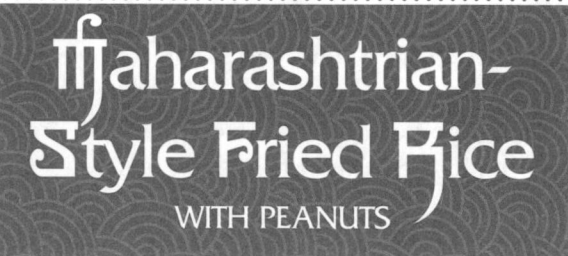

Maharashtrian-Style Fried Rice
WITH PEANUTS

Masala Bhaat

Robust-flavored and -textured accompaniments like this work very well with many of the fish and chicken curries in this book. Leftover cooked white rice is the best choice because the starch, when cold, keeps the grains from sticking together and makes the rice easier to stir-fry. Any other variety of rice (brown, red, or black) will be fine, but do realize that they all provide an added nuttiness (with respect to texture) to the dish, due to their intact bran. **SERVES 6**

I medium-size russet or Yukon Gold potato, peeled, cut into ¼-inch cubes, and submerged in a bowl of cold water to prevent browning

2 tablespoons peanut or canola oil

1 teaspoon black or yellow mustard seeds

1 teaspoon cumin seeds

1 medium-size red onion, finely chopped

⅓ cup raw peanuts (without the skin)

1 tablespoon white sesame seeds

3 cups cooked white rice

1 cup frozen green peas (no need to thaw)

1 teaspoon Sambhar masala (page 33)

12 to 15 medium-size to large fresh curry leaves

1 medium-size tomato, cored and finely chopped

*2 tablespoons finely chopped fresh cilantro leaves
    and tender stems for garnishing*

1. Drain the potato cubes and pat them dry with paper towels.

2. Preheat a wok or a well-seasoned cast-iron skillet over medium-high heat. Drizzle the oil down its sides, and when it forms a shimmering pool at the bottom, add the mustard seeds. Cover the wok and cook until the seeds have stopped popping (not unlike popcorn), about 30 seconds. Sprinkle in the cumin seeds, which will instantly sizzle and turn reddish brown.

3. Add the onion, peanuts, sesame seeds, and potatoes. Stir-fry until the peanuts, onion, and sesame seeds are reddish brown, and the potatoes are crispy brown and tender, 5 to 10 minutes.

4. Break the rice up gently, if it is in clumps, separating as many of the grains as you can without splitting the grain. Add the rice to the wok, along with the peas, masala, and curry leaves. Stir-fry until the rice feels warm to the touch, about 5 minutes.

5. Fold in the tomato and continue to cook, uncovered, stirring frequently, until the tomato is warmed through, 2 to 4 minutes.

6. Sprinkle with the cilantro, and serve.

Tips:

❖ If you have a frozen vegetable mixture that you want to use up, add it to the wok at the end of Step 3, after the potatoes have browned. (If you add it before, the water from the vegetables may prevent the potatoes from browning and delay that process.)

❖ If there are peanut allergies in your home, use vegetable oil. Any other nut, particularly cashews (the unroasted kind), might be a great alternative to the peanuts. Also try slivered blanched almonds.

Sri Lankan Pearl Rice
WITH LEMONGRASS

Muttu Sambha

Pearls in Sinhalese is *muttu*. This short-grain, pearl-like rice is slightly starchy, especially when you compare it to Indian basmati rice. A special-occasion dish, this creamy rice steeps in rich coconut milk, perfumed lemongrass, and aromatic cardamom—providing a comforting base for many of this country's fragrant curries. Serve it with Pan-Seared Shrimp with a Spicy-Hot Chile Vinegar Paste (page 270) for a well-balanced combination of flavors. **SERVES 6**

1 cup white Sri Lankan sambha rice (see Tip)

2 tablespoons canola oil

1 cup finely chopped red onion

2 tablespoons finely chopped lemongrass
   (see Tips)

4 to 6 green or white cardamom pods

4 whole cloves

1 cinnamon stick (3 inches long)

1 teaspoon coarse kosher or sea salt

¼ teaspoon ground turmeric

1 cup unsweetened coconut milk

1. Place the rice in a medium-size bowl. Fill the bowl halfway with water, to cover the rice. Gently rub the stout grains through your fingers, without breaking them, to wash off any dust or light foreign objects (like loose husks), which will float to the surface. The water will become cloudy. Drain this water. Repeat three or four times, until the water remains relatively clear; drain. Now fill the bowl halfway with cold water and let it sit at room temperature until the grains soften, 45 minutes to 1 hour; drain.

2. Heat the oil in a medium-size saucepan over medium-high heat. Add the onion, lemongrass, cardamom pods, cloves, and cinnamon stick. Stir-fry until the onion is light brown around the edges and the spices perfume your breathing space, 3 to 5 minutes.

3. Add the rice, salt, turmeric, coconut milk, and 1 cup cold water. Stir once or twice, and bring to a boil. Cook until the water has evaporated from the surface and craters are starting to appear in the light yellow rice, 6 to 8 minutes. Now (and only now) stir once to bring the partially cooked layer from the bottom of the pan to the surface. Cover the pan with a tight-fitting lid, reduce the heat to the lowest possible setting, and cook for 10 to 15 minutes (10 for an electric burner, 15 for a gas burner). Turn off the heat and let the pan stand on that burner, undisturbed, for 10 minutes.

4. Remove the lid, fluff the rice with a fork, and serve.

Tips:

❖ *Sambha* rice, sometimes spelled *samba*, is widely available in Indian grocery stores that also cater to Sri Lankan communities. The short-grain, starchy rice is almost round, with a translucent edge and a creamy white center. Because of its denser quality, it does take a little bit longer to cook than some of the other long-grain varieties—and for this reason, I soak it longer to tenderize the grain. Slow cookers, pressure cookers, and rice cookers are all fair game for this rice. Any other short-grain variety that is available in your grocery store is an acceptable alternative.

❖ Lemongrass imparts not only tang but also aroma. The grated zest of 1 small lime or lemon will do, but it will lack the complexity of lemongrass.

Spiced Cream of Wheat

Uppama

I think Italy's answer to *Uppama* is polenta, and maybe that is why I find the European version equally comforting. *Uppama* is very common as a breakfast offering in south India, and I think its slightly mealy, porridge-like texture also lays out a great bed for many of this book's curries. I especially love the layer that forms, sticks, and browns crispy-thin on the bottom of the pan after it steeps. As a child, I fought for this layer (and won), called *kaandal* in Tamil, with my siblings. Being the youngest does have its advantages. **SERVES 6**

2 tablespoons unrefined sesame oil or canola oil

I teaspoon black or yellow mustard seeds

¼ cup raw cashew nuts

I tablespoon skinned split black lentils
   (cream-colored in this form, urad dal),
   picked over for stones

6 dried red Thai or cayenne chiles, stems removed

2 cups frozen green peas (no need to thaw)

½ teaspoon ground turmeric

10 to 12 medium-size to large fresh curry leaves

1½ teaspoons coarse kosher or sea salt

4 fresh green Thai, cayenne, or serrano chiles,
   stems removed, cut in half lengthwise
   (do not remove the seeds)

2 tablespoons finely chopped fresh cilantro
   leaves and tender stems

I cup uncooked Cream of Wheat (not instant)

1. Heat the oil in a medium-size skillet over medium-high heat. Add the mustard seeds, cover the skillet, and cook until the seeds have stopped popping (not unlike popcorn), about 30 seconds. Add the cashews, lentils, and dried chiles, and stir-fry until the nuts and lentils turn golden-brown and the chiles blacken, 1 to 2 minutes.

2. Add the peas and turmeric, and stir to coat the peas evenly with the spice. Pour in 2 cups water and bring it to a boil. Lower the heat to medium, cover the skillet, and simmer until the peas are tender, 3 to 5 minutes. Stir in the curry leaves, salt, chiles, and cilantro.

3. Reduce the heat to medium-low and stir in the Cream of Wheat. It will instantly absorb the water and start to swell up. Let it cook, covered, until the grains soften and swell up, about 5 minutes. Fluff the mixture with a fork or spoon, and serve.

Coconut-Dusted Rice Noodles

idiappam

◆

If you want to impress the folks at the dinner table, make these noodles and observe the reactions and comments. I guarantee that they will be impressed when you let them know that you made them from scratch. You don't need to reveal the fact that these snowy-white noodles took mere minutes to make. Just enjoy the accolades as they come your way. **SERVES 6**

2 tablespoons canola oil

1½ teaspoons coarse kosher or sea salt

2 cups rice flour

Shredded fresh coconut or shredded dried
   unsweetened coconut, for sprinkling

1. Combine 2 cups water, the oil, and the salt in a medium-size saucepan, and bring to a vigorous boil over medium-high heat. Remove the pan from the heat and add the flour, stirring quickly and constantly as you add it. The flour will instantly absorb the water and come together to form a satin-soft ball.

2. Transfer the dough to a clean, dry countertop or cutting board. Knead the dough to smooth it. Wrap the dough with plastic wrap to prevent it from drying out while you get the *idli* pan or a steamer basket ready for steaming.

3. Shove the dough into the cylindrical cavity of a noodle press (see Tip) or a cookie spritzer (use the

plate with the smaller round holes). *If you are using an idli pan* (see page 116), sprinkle a scant teaspoon of coconut shreds in the individual concave-shaped indentations. Push the dough down to extrude vermicelli-thin noodles directly into the molds, and slice the strands as they fold into a nest. Stack the *idli* plates (there are usually four plates per pan, each with four indentations) around the *idli* stand, placing the small metal rod between the plates to separate them. Fill a large stockpot with hot water to a depth of about ½ inch, and set the device in it. Cover, and steam over medium-high heat until the nests appear dry and are slightly opaque, 10 to 12 minutes. Transfer the nests to a serving platter and keep them under plastic wrap to maintain their moist al dente texture.

If you are using a steamer insert, scatter about 2 tablespoons coconut over the bottom of the steamer basket. Push the dough down to extrude vermicelli-thin noodles, making small piles in the basket and slicing the strands as they fold into nests. Cover, and steam over medium-high heat until the nests appear dry and are slightly opaque, 10 to 12 minutes. Transfer the nests to a serving platter as above.

4. Repeat with the remaining dough.

5. Use right away, or reheat later: in the microwave, covered, for about 30 seconds, or in the steamer basket for 1 to 2 minutes. You can also freeze the nests in sealed plastic bags or containers for up to 1 month.

Tip: The noodle press is available in brass, wood, or stainless steel at any Indian grocery store. It is cylindrical in shape, about 4 inches long and 3 inches wide. The bottom of the press has 4 removable plate molds with variously shaped holes.

Multi-Lentil Pancakes
WITH ONIONS AND TOMATOES

Vengayam Adai

Accompaniments are not supposed to be the main attraction during a curry performance. They are designed to highlight and enhance the curry, by being either a utensil that wraps around the sauce-y offering or by being a starchy bed to mop up the spicy-hot flavors. However, this particular bread, a favorite in Tamil home kitchens, refuses to play a subservient role; its dominant hot chiles, pungent onion, and tart-sweet tomato shine through the soft interior and crispy exterior. To tame the shrew, serve the bread alongside Coconut-Chile Squash (page 598) and Garlicky Shrimp with Chiles and Sesame Seeds (page 278) for a riveting Saturday night presentation. **MAKES ABOUT 12 PANCAKES**

½ cup long-grain white rice

¼ cup yellow split peas (chana dal), picked over for stones

¼ cup skinned split green lentils (yellow in this form, moong dal), picked over for stones

¼ cup oily or unoily skinned split yellow pigeon peas (toovar dal), picked over for stones

2 teaspoons coriander seeds

4 to 6 dried red Thai or cayenne chiles, to taste, stems removed

2 to 4 fresh green Thai, cayenne, or serrano chiles, to taste, stems removed

1 cup plain yogurt

1 cup finely chopped red onion

1 large tomato, cored and finely chopped

¼ cup finely chopped fresh cilantro leaves and tender stems

25 to 30 medium-size to large fresh curry leaves, coarsely chopped

1½ teaspoons coarse kosher or sea salt

½ teaspoon ground asafetida

Canola oil for pan-frying

1. Place the rice, split peas, lentils, and pigeon peas in a medium-size bowl. Fill the bowl halfway with water, and rinse the legumes by rubbing them between your fingertips. The water will become cloudy. Drain this water. Repeat three or four times, until the water remains relatively clear; drain. Now fill the bowl halfway with warm water and add the coriander seeds and the dried chiles. Cover the bowl with plastic wrap, and let it sit at room temperature until the legumes and spices soften, at least 1 hour or as long as 4 hours.

2. Drain the legume mixture.

3. Pour ½ cup water into a blender jar, followed by the drained legume mixture and the fresh chiles. Puree, scraping the inside of the jar as needed, to make a thick paste. With the blender running, slowly drizzle in another ½ cup water to thin the paste to a pancake-batter consistency. It will be slightly gritty, with red and green speckles. Pour this back into the same medium-size bowl (why dirty another one?).

4. Stir in the yogurt, onion, tomato, cilantro, curry leaves, salt, and asafetida.

5. Tear off a large sheet of aluminum foil and fold it in half lengthwise. Set this aside.

6. Heat 1 teaspoon oil in a medium-size nonstick skillet over medium heat. Pour ½ cup of the chunky batter (I use a ladle that holds that much) into the skillet and quickly spread it out with the back of the ladle to form a slightly wider round, about 6 inches in diameter. Cook until little bubbles start to form on top and the glossy-looking batter loses its sheen, turning a dull yellow, 5 to 7 minutes. Flip the pancake over and cook the other side, 2 to 4 minutes. Repeat with the remaining batter, adding oil to the skillet as needed. As they are cooked, slide the pancakes between the layers of aluminum foil to keep them warm. Then serve.

Tips:

❖ These pancakes are optimum in flavor and texture when hot off the griddle. Unused batter will keep in the refrigerator for a week to 10 days. You can freeze it, but once it is thawed, the onion in the batter will have a slightly rubbery texture.

❖ If the pan gets too hot, the batter will clump up when it is ladled in, making it difficult to spread it out. If this happens, wet a piece of paper towel with cold water and wring it out. Wipe the skillet to lower the temperature.

Puffy Whole-Wheat Breads

poori

When these *pooris* puff up, you know you have done a good job rolling the dough out to an even thickness. They will collapse, like a soufflé, if they sit around after they are fried—but don't get too bent out of shape if that happens, because the flavor will still be the same. I particularly love these treats with some of the potato curries in this book.

MAKES 10 BREADS

> 2 cups roti flour (see Tip, page 728), plus extra
>   for dusting
> 1½ teaspoons coarse kosher or sea salt
> 2 tablespoons canola oil, plus more for deep-frying
> About ¾ cup warm water

1. Thoroughly combine the flour and salt in a medium-size bowl. Then drizzle the 2 tablespoons oil over the salted flour, rubbing the flour through your hands to evenly distribute the oil.

2. Drizzle a few tablespoons of the water over the flour, and stir it in. Repeat until the flour comes together to form a soft ball; you will use about ¾ cup warm water altogether. Using your hand (as long as it's clean, I think it's the best tool), gather the ball, picking up any dry flour in the bottom of the bowl, and knead it to form a smooth, soft ball of dough (do this in the bowl or on a lightly floured surface). If it's a little too wet, dust it with a little more flour, kneading it in after every dusting until you get the right soft, dry consistency. (If you used your hand to make the dough from the start, it will be caked with dough. Scrape it back into the bowl. Wash and dry your hands, and return to the dough to knead it. You will get a much better feel for the dough's consistency with a dry hand.)

3. Cover the dough with plastic wrap or a slightly dampened cloth, and set it aside to rest for about 30 minutes. (After 30 minutes, you can refrigerate the dough, wrapped in plastic wrap, for up to 4 days. Bring it back to room temperature before you proceed.)

4. Using your hands, roll the dough out to form a 10-inch-long log (lightly flour the work surface if that helps). Cut the log crosswise into 10 pieces, and shape each piece into a ball. Press each ball out to form a patty. Cover the patties with plastic wrap.

5. Line a plate or a cookie sheet with three or four sheets of paper towels.

6. Pour oil to a depth of 2 to 3 inches into a wok, Dutch oven, or medium-size saucepan. Heat the oil over medium heat until a candy or deep-fry thermometer inserted into the oil (without touching the pan's bottom) registers 375° to 400°F. (An alternative way to see if the oil is at the right temperature for deep-frying is to gently flick a drop of water over it. If the pearl-like drop skitters across the surface, the oil is ready.)

7. While the oil is heating, lightly flour a small work area near the stove and place a dough patty on it. (Keep the remaining patties covered with plastic wrap while you work on this one.) Roll it out to form a round about 3 to 4 inches in diameter, dusting it with flour as needed. Make sure the round is evenly thin, with no tear on its surface. Repeat with the remaining rounds, stacking them as you make them, and flouring between the layers to prevent them from sticking to one another.

8. Once the oil is ready, slide a dough round into the pan. It will sink to the bottom, and then within seconds it will start to bubble and rise to the top. With the back of a spoon, gently keep submerging the round when it rises to the surface, to enable the dough to puff from the inside. It will be done in less than a minute. Remove the golden-brown *poori* with a slotted spoon, and set it on the paper towels to drain.

9. Repeat with the remaining rounds. Then serve.

Griddle-Cooked Whole-Wheat Flatbread

Roti

Roti to an Indian is what a flour tortilla is to a Mexican. The main difference between the two is the kind of flour used: rotis are made with a light whole-wheat grain, while tortillas rely on all-purpose flour. The all-purpose flour has more protein than the Indian *atta,* and as a result tortillas can be far chewier than rotis. (Nevertheless, if I am rushed for time, I will make a trip to the local Mexican restaurant, which makes its tortillas in-house, and serve them with my curries.) Rotis are also known as *chappatis* in certain parts of India, and their thickness can vary among households. They are an Indian's silverware, used to wrap around succulent curries, stir-fries, pickles, and condiments—an easy, addictive, and functional flatbread. **MAKES 12 BREADS**

2 cups roti flour (see Tips), plus extra for dusting

1½ teaspoons coarse kosher or sea salt

About ¾ cup warm water

Ghee (page 21) or melted butter for brushing

1. Thoroughly combine the flour and salt in a medium-size bowl.

2. Drizzle a few tablespoons of the warm water over the salted flour, stirring it in as you do so. Repeat until the flour comes together to form a soft ball; you will use about ¾ cup warm water altogether.

Using your hand (as long as it's clean, I think it's the best tool), gather the ball, picking up any dry flour in the bottom of the bowl, and knead it to form a smooth, soft ball of dough (do this in the bowl or on a lightly floured surface). If it's a little too wet, dust it with a little extra flour, kneading it in after every dusting until you get the right soft, dry consistency. (If you used your hand to make the dough from the start, it will be caked with clumps of dough. Scrape them back into the bowl. Wash and dry your hands thoroughly, and return to the dough to knead it. You will get a much better feel for the dough's consistency with a dry hand.)

3. Wrap the ball of dough in plastic wrap, or cover it with a slightly dampened cloth, and let it rest at room temperature for about 30 minutes.

4. When you are ready to cook the roti, use your hands to roll the dough into a 12-inch-long log. Cut it crosswise into 12 pieces, and shape each piece into a ball. Press each ball flat to form a patty. Cover the patties with plastic wrap. (At this juncture, if you wish, you can refrigerate the dough for up to 4 days. Bring it back to room temperature before you proceed.)

5. Place the ghee close to the stove, with a pastry brush handy. Tear off a large sheet of aluminum foil, fold it in half lengthwise, and set it aside. Tear off 13 sheets of wax paper, each about 8 inches wide.

6. Lightly flour a small work area near the stove, and place a dough patty on it (leaving the others under cover). Roll it out to form a round roughly 5 to 6 inches in diameter, dusting it with flour as needed. Make sure the round is evenly thin, with no tears on the surface. Lift the round, plop it onto a sheet of wax paper, and cover it with a second sheet. Repeat with the remaining dough patties, stacking them between sheets of wax paper as they are rolled.

7. Heat a medium-size skillet (preferably nonstick or cast iron) over medium heat. *If you have a gas stove,* light another burner and keep the flame on medium heat. *If yours is an electric stove,* place a heat diffuser on a separate burner, with the heat set to medium. (If you don't have a heat diffuser, place a skillet over medium heat.)

8. Transfer a round to the hot skillet. Cook until the surface forms some bumps and bubbles, and the underside looks cooked and has some brown spots, 2 to 3 minutes. Immediately flip the round over directly onto the other burner's open flame (or the heat diffuser or skillet). It will puff up and cook on the underside in barely 15 to 30 seconds. Lift it off with a pair of tongs and place it on the piece of foil. Brush one or both sides with ghee. Fold the sheet of foil over the roti to keep it warm.

9. Continue cooking the rounds, brushing them with ghee and keeping them warm under the foil. Then serve.

Tips:

❖ Roti flour, also labeled *atta* ("flour"), is packaged in small, medium, and large bags, and can be found in Indian, Pakistani, Middle Eastern, and other Asian grocery stores. It is a low-protein flour, and is ideal for making these fluffy-thin flatbreads. (When you knead dough made with high-protein flour, it forms gluten—which gives European yeast breads their structure, an unwanted constitution in rotis.)

❖ Rotis are a cinch to freeze, should you decide to make a large stack for future use. Don't brush them with ghee before you freeze them. Keep them tightly wrapped, either in foil or in plastic wrap, and then secure the package in a freezer-safe self-seal bag. They thaw beautifully in a microwave oven (thanks once again to the low protein content, which means they won't toughen like other breads): wrap a roti in a moist paper towel and microwave it for barely 1 minute. Once it is warmed, brush it with ghee.

Griddle-Cooked Corn Bread
WITH CHILES

Makkai ki Roti

You say "*Makkai ki roti*" to a Punjabi, and he or she will reply, "*Sarson da saag.*" This flaky, grainy, succulent bread is a must for scooping up mounds of ghee-drenched mustard greens (see page 522), providing a perfect balance to the greens' bitterness. This simple food satisfies the hardworking individual, especially at lunchtime: All that's needed is a stack of these breads, a mound of pureed greens, and a few fresh green cayenne chiles to bite into in between mouthfuls of addiction. **MAKES 10 BREADS**

*2 cups finely ground yellow corn flour
   (like the Mexican masa harina; see Tip)
1½ teaspoons coarse kosher or sea salt
8 lengthwise slices fresh ginger (each 2 inches long,
   1 inch wide, and ⅛ inch thick)
8 fresh green Thai, cayenne, or serrano chiles,
   stems removed
About ½ cup warm water
Ghee (see page 21) or melted butter
   for brushing*

1. Combine the corn flour and salt in a medium-size bowl.

2. Combine the ginger and chiles in a food processor, and pulse until minced. Add this to the flour mixture.

3. Drizzle a few tablespoons of the warm water over the mixture, stirring it in as you do so. Repeat until the mixture starts to come together to form a ball; you will use about ½ cup warm water altogether. Feel the ball: It should be slightly moist, and there should be no flour in the bottom of the bowl. With your clean, dry hand, gently knead the ball to form a soft dough—which will feel bumpy, thanks to the ginger and chiles (do this in the bowl or on a lightly floured surface).

4. Divide the dough into 10 portions, and shape each portion into a ball. Keep the balls covered with plastic wrap or with a slightly damp paper towel.

5. Tear off a large sheet of aluminum foil, fold it in half lengthwise, and set it aside. Tear off 1 sheet of wax paper about 12 inches wide, plus 11 sheets, each about 8 inches wide.

6. Place a ball of dough on the 12 inch piece of wax paper (leaving the others under cover). Press it down to form a patty, and then use your fingers to stretch it out as you press it into an evenly thin round, roughly 4 to 6 inches in diameter and ⅛ inch thick (the shape might be not be a perfect round, especially the first few times you try this). Gently peel the round off the paper, plop it onto a smaller sheet of wax paper, and cover it with a second sheet. Repeat with the other dough rounds, stacking them between sheets of wax paper as they are formed.

7. Preheat a small nonstick skillet over medium heat.

8. Transfer a round to the hot skillet. Cook until the underside has a slight sheen with light brown patches, 2 to 4 minutes. Flip it over and cook the other side, 2 to 3 minutes (this side won't get that sheen; instead, it will look like a parched landscape). Brush the sheen side with ghee and flip it over to sear it, about 30 seconds. Brush the parched side with ghee and sear that side too, about 30 seconds. Slip the round between the layers of foil to keep it warm. (The steam created inside the foil will drench the parched side and make it just as appealing as the pretty side.) Continue cooking with the remaining rounds. Then serve.

Tip: Look for bags of *masa harina* (corn flour) in the ethnic-foods aisle of your supermarket. You can also find it in Indian and Pakistani markets, as well as Hispanic stores. Regular cornmeal yields a grainier texture and does not hold together as well to make a spreadable dough.

Salt-Crusted Grilled Flatbread
WITH GHEE

ŋaan

Along with tandoori chicken, this clay oven-baked flatbread catapulted northern Indian foods (especially foods from Punjab and the Moghalai way of cooking) into the Western European and North American restaurant scene. A huge burden to bear, I think, for this thin, crispy-back, slightly chewy flatbread that glistens with ghee. The tandoor is truly the master here, seething with a temperature of 700°F, its clay-lined walls retaining that heat to bake the slapped-on dough within seconds—but that doesn't mean we can't bake naan without one, as you will see. Traditionally the naan is tear shaped, but here it is round.

MAKES 4 BREADS

> 3 cups unbleached all-purpose flour, plus extra
>   for dusting
> 2 teaspoons baking powder
> 1 teaspoon coarse kosher or sea salt
> ½ cup buttermilk, at room temperature
> About 1 cup warm water
> Canola oil
> Ghee (page 21) or melted butter for brushing
> Rock salt, gently pounded, for sprinkling

1. Thoroughly combine the flour, baking powder, and salt in a large bowl.

2. Pour the buttermilk over the flour mixture and quickly stir it in. The flour will still be very dry, with a few wet spots.

3. Pour a few tablespoons of the warm water over the flour, stirring it in as you go. Repeat until the flour comes together to form a soft ball; you will use about 1 cup warm water altogether. You want the dough to be very soft, close to being slightly sticky, so if you add an extra tablespoon or so, it won't hurt it. Using your hand (as long as it's clean, I think it's the best tool), gather the ball, picking up any dry flour in the bottom of the bowl, and knead it to form a smooth, soft ball of dough. If it's a little too sticky to handle, dust your hand with flour, but do not add any more flour to the dough if possible. Knead it for a minute or two. (If you used your hand to make the dough from the start, it will be caked with clumps of dough. Scrape them back into the bowl. Wash and dry your hands thoroughly, and return to the dough to knead it. You will get

a much better feel for the dough's consistency with a dry hand.)

4. Cut the dough into 4 equal portions. Lightly grease a plate with oil. Shape one portion into a round resembling a hamburger bun, and put it on the plate. (To get a smooth round, cup the dough in the palm of your hand and use your fingers to fold and tuck the edges underneath; then rotate it, folding and tucking all around to get an evenly smooth ball.) Repeat with the remaining dough.

5. Brush the tops of the rounds with ghee, cover them with plastic wrap or a slightly dampened cloth, and let them sit at room temperature for about 30 minutes.

6. Place a pizza stone or unglazed pottery tiles (see Tip, facing page) on the grill rack. *If it is a gas grill,* heat it to the highest heat setting. *If it is a charcoal grill,* build an intensely hot fire and allow the charcoal to turn ash-white and red-hot. The temperature should hover between 600° and 700°F.

7. Tear off a large piece of aluminum foil, fold it in half lengthwise, and set it aside. Tear off 5 sheets of wax paper, each about 8 inches wide.

8. Lightly flour a small work area near the grill, and place a dough round on it. Press it down to form a patty. Roll the patty out to form a round roughly 3 to 5 inches in diameter, dusting it with flour as needed. Make sure the round is evenly thin, with no tears on the surface. Sprinkle a little rock salt over the top, and gently press it into the dough. Lift the round, plop it on a sheet of wax paper, and cover it with a second sheet. Repeat with the remaining dough rounds, stacking them between sheets of wax paper as they are rolled.

9. Transfer a round, salt side down, onto the hot pizza stone. Within seconds, the dough will start to bubble in

spots. Cover the grill and cook until the dough turns crispy brown on the underside and the top acquires light brown patches, 2 to 3 minutes. Remove it from the stone, liberally brush the top with ghee, and slide it between the layers of foil to keep it warm.

10. Continue cooking with the remaining rounds, stacking them on top of the previously grilled naans.

11. Cut each naan into four pieces, and savor them with any of the curries.

Tips:

❖ Unless you are among the very few folks here in the United States who have a tandoor in the kitchen or backyard, you will have to fashion a tandoor-like environment to cook naan. Look no further than your handy-dandy outdoor grill (or for a less effective result, your oven) and a pizza stone (or unglazed pottery tiles) to re-create those conditions. I have given you explicit instructions in the recipe on how to do it. It is hard to generate that same intense heat in a kitchen oven because they are not designed to generate more than 550°F, but you can bake the flatbread in it if you don't have a grill (or if it's snowing outside). If yours is a conventional oven, place the pizza stone on the lowest rack and preheat it at the highest bake setting. A convection oven generates the same heat but distributes it more evenly, and you can place the pizza stone on any of the racks. You will need to bake the bread a little longer than you would on an outdoor grill.

❖ The moisture in the dough is a key factor in ensuring slightly moist, tender, but chewy bread. If the dough is too dry, the heaviness will deter the characteristic puffing that actually steams the bread from within. That's why I insist that the dough be really soft, almost to the point of stickiness. When Indian cooks shape this dough, they slap it between their palms, all the while stretching it with their thumbs to yield that characteristic tear-shaped naan—and it's much easier to do that with a soft dough.

❖ I like to include buttermilk in the dough because it contributes an appealing sourdough-like flavor, and because the dairy further contributes to the dough's softness.

Flaky Griddle-Cooked Breads

Malabar Parantha

When I first witnessed a street vendor in Chennai (formerly Madras) making these flaky breads, I was mesmerized by his speedy technique as he shaped the dough by hand and rolled it into a coil. He then rerolled it into a round, slapped it onto a hot griddle and let it brown on both sides, and then slathered it with liberal amounts of ghee. A corner of his flat griddle held two large pots of curries, one vegetarian and the other a chicken curry. Both curries were coconut milk–based, redolent with spices from the Malabar coast: green cardamom, hand-crushed black Tellicherry peppercorns, and thin furls of cinnamon bark. I sampled the vegetable stew with the *paranthas,* not quite sure which was better, the bread or the creamy curry. **MAKES 6 BREADS**

3 cups unbleached all-purpose flour,
   plus extra for dusting
2 teaspoons baking powder
1 teaspoon coarse kosher or sea salt
2 tablespoons Ghee (page 21) or vegetable oil
½ cup buttermilk, at room temperature
About 1 cup warm water
Ghee (page 21) or melted butter
   for brushing

1. Thoroughly combine the flour, baking powder, and salt in a large bowl. Drizzle the ghee over the flour mixture, rubbing the flour through your hands to evenly distribute the ghee.

2. Pour the buttermilk over the flour mixture and quickly stir it in. The flour will still be very dry, with a few wet spots.

3. Pour a few tablespoons of the warm water over the flour, stirring it in as you do so. Repeat until the flour comes together to form a soft ball; you will use about 1 cup warm water altogether. Using your hand (as long as it's clean, I think it's the best tool), gather the ball, picking up any dry flour in the bottom of the bowl, and knead it to form a smooth, soft ball of dough (do this in the bowl or on a little floured surface). If it's a little too wet, dust it with a little flour, kneading it in after every dusting until you get the right soft, dry consistency. (If you used your hand to make the dough from the start, it will be caked with clumps of dough. Scrape them back into the bowl. Wash and dry your hands thoroughly, and return to the dough to knead it. You will get a much better feel for the dough's consistency with a dry hand.)

4. Cover the dough with plastic wrap or a slightly dampened cloth, and let it rest at room temperature for about 30 minutes.

5. Using your hands, roll the dough into an 18-inch-long log (lightly flour the work surface if necessary). Cut it crosswise into 6 pieces, and shape each piece into a ball. Press each ball flat to form a patty. Cover the patties with plastic wrap.

6. Tear off a large sheet of aluminum foil, fold it in half lengthwise, and set it aside. Tear off 7 sheets of wax paper, each about 8 inches wide. Place the ghee near the stove, with a pastry brush handy.

7. While the skillet is heating, lightly flour a small work area near the stove, and place a dough patty on it (leave the others under cover). Roll it out to form a round roughly 5 to 6 inches in diameter, dusting it with flour as needed. Make sure the round is evenly thin, with no tears on the surface. Brush the top liberally with ghee. Lift the edge closest to you and roll the dough into a tight cigar-shaped log. Form the log into a tight coil. Then flatten the log to form a patty, and reroll it to form a round roughly 5 to 6 inches in diameter, dusting it with flour as needed. Lift the round, plop it onto a sheet of wax paper and cover it with a second sheet. Repeat with the remaining dough, stacking the rounds between sheets of wax paper as they are rolled.

8. Heat a medium-size skillet (preferably nonstick or cast iron) over medium heat.

9. Transfer a round to the hot skillet. Cook until the surface has some humps and bubbles, and the underside has some brown spots and looks cooked, 2 to 3 minutes. Immediately flip it over and cook until the other side has brown spots, 2 to 3 minutes.

10. Brush the round with ghee and flip it over to sear it, about 30 seconds. Brush the top with ghee and flip it over to sear it, about 30 seconds. Slip the *parantha* between the layers of foil to keep it warm.

11. Continue cooking the remaining rounds, stacking the finished *paranthas* under the foil. Then serve.

Fenugreek-Scented Griddle-Cooked Flatbread

Methi Chappati

Pillow-soft and pleasantly bitter, these flatbreads are the perfect eating tool for many of this book's curries. Tear off a bite-size morsel of the bread, wrap it around your favorite curry, and devour the combination. Fenugreek leaves perfume the bread in this recipe, but you can use any herb or ground spice (or a combination) for a different flavor. *Chappatis* are easy to make once you get your rhythm, and the cooked breads freeze well.

If you plan to freeze *chappatis,* do not brush them with ghee. Separate them with pieces of wax paper, stick them in a self-seal freezer bag, and freeze them for up to a month. To reheat them, cover them with a slightly damp paper towel and microwave on high power for barely a minute, until they are back to their fluffy-soft self. After they are warmed, brush them with ghee for a fresh-cooked taste. **MAKES 14 BREADS**

2 cups roti flour (see Tip, page 728), plus extra for
   dusting
2 teaspoons coarse kosher or sea salt
¼ teaspoon ground turmeric
1 cup chopped fresh or frozen fenugreek
   leaves (thawed and squeezed dry if frozen);
   or ½ cup dried fenugreek leaves, soaked
   in a bowl of water and skimmed off
   before use (see box, page 473)
About ¾ cup warm water
Ghee (page 21) or melted butter for brushing

1. Thoroughly combine the flour, salt, and turmeric in a medium-size bowl. Stir in the fenugreek leaves.

2. Pour a few tablespoons of the warm water over the flour mixture, stirring it in as you do so. Repeat until the flour comes together to form a soft ball; you will need about ¾ cup warm water altogether. Using your hand (as long as it's clean, I think it's the best tool), gather the ball, picking up any dry flour in the bottom of the bowl, and knead it to form a smooth, soft ball of dough (do this in the bowl or on a lightly floured surface). If it's a little too wet, dust it with a little flour, kneading it in after every dusting until you get the right soft, dry consistency. (If you have used your hand to make the dough from the start, it will be caked with clumps of dough. Scrape them back into the bowl. Wash and dry your hands thoroughly, and return to the dough to knead it. You will get a much better feel for the dough's consistency with a dry hand.)

3. Cover the dough with plastic wrap or a slightly dampened cloth, and let it rest at room temperature for about 30 minutes.

4. When you are ready to cook the *chappati,* use your hands to roll the dough into a 14-inch-long log. Cut it crosswise into 14 pieces, and shape each piece into a ball. Press each ball flat to form a patty. Cover the patties with plastic wrap.

5. Place the ghee near the stove, with a pastry brush handy. Tear off a large sheet of aluminum foil, and set it aside. Tear off 15 sheets of wax paper, each 8 inches wide.

6. Lightly flour a small work area near the stove, and place a dough patty on it (leave the others under cover). Roll it out to form a round roughly 5 to 6 inches in diameter, dusting it with flour as needed. Make sure the round is evenly thin, with no tears on the surface. Lift up the green-speckled round, plop it onto a sheet of wax paper, cover it with a second sheet. Repeat with the remaining dough, stacking the rounds between sheets of wax paper as they are rolled.

7. Heat a medium-size skillet (preferably nonstick or cast iron) over medium heat. *If you have a gas stove,* light another burner and keep the flame on medium heat. *If yours is an electric stove,* place a heat diffuser on a separate burner, with the heat set to medium (or set a skillet on the burner).

8. Transfer a round to the hot skillet. Cook until the surface has some bumps and bubbles, and the underside has brown spots and looks cooked, 2 to 3 minutes. Immediately flip the *chappati* over directly onto the other burner's open flame (or the heat diffuser). It will puff up and cook the underside, in barely 15 to 30 seconds. Lift it off with a pair of tongs and place it on the piece of foil. Brush one or both sides with ghee, and fold the foil over the *chappati* to keep it warm.

9. Continue cooking the remaining rounds, stacking the finished *chappatis* under the foil. Then serve.

Mango powder? See the Glossary of Ingredients, page 758.

Flaky Breads
STUFFED WITH SPINACH AND CHEESE

Palak Paneer Parantha

ull-flavored breads like this one are fun to eat as soon as they come, piping hot and flaky, off the griddle. I serve them, cut into wedges for dipping, with some of the simple dal curries in this book for an elegantly simple prelude to a multiple-course curry dinner. **MAKES 6 BREADS**

For the dough:

> 3 cups roti flour (see Tip, page 728)
> 1 teaspoon coarse kosher or sea salt
> 2 tablespoons canola oil
> About 1 cup warm water

For the filling:

> 8 ounces fresh spinach leaves, well rinsed, patted dry, and finely chopped; or 1 box (10 ounces) frozen chopped spinach, thawed, drained, and squeezed dry (see Tips)
> 4 ounces Doodh paneer (page 286), crumbled
> 1 tablespoon mango powder, or the grated zest of 1 lime or lemon
> 1 teaspoon coarse kosher or sea salt
> 3 or 4 fresh green Thai, cayenne, or serrano chiles, to taste, stems removed, finely chopped (do not remove the seeds)

For filling and cooking the bread:

> Ghee (page 21) or melted butter for brushing
> Roti flour for dusting

1. To make the dough, stir the roti flour and salt together in a medium-size bowl. Drizzle the oil over the flour mixture, rubbing the flour through your hands to evenly distribute the oil.

2. Drizzle a few tablespoons of the warm water over the flour mixture, stirring it in as you do so. Continue drizzling warm water until the flour comes together to form a soft ball; you will need about 1 cup warm water altogether. Using your hand (as long as it's clean, I think it's the best tool), gather the ball, picking up any dry flour in the bottom of the bowl, and knead it to form a smooth, soft ball of dough (do this in the bowl or on a lightly floured surface). If it's a little too wet, dust it with a little flour, kneading it in after every dusting, until you get the right soft, dry consistency. (If you used your hand to make the dough from the start, it will be caked with clumps of dough. Scrape them back into the bowl. Wash and dry your hands thoroughly, and return to the dough to knead it. You will get a much better feel for the dough's consistency with a dry hand.)

3. Wrap the dough with plastic wrap or cover it with a slightly dampened cloth, and let it rest at room temperature for about 30 minutes.

4. While the dough is resting, make the filling: Combine the spinach, *paneer*, mango powder, salt, and chiles in a medium-size bowl. Stir well.

5. When the dough has rested, roll it with your hands to form an 18-inch-long log (lightly flour the work surface if necessary). Cut it crosswise into 6 pieces, and shape each piece into a ball. Press each ball flat to form a patty. Cover the patties with plastic wrap.

6. Place the ghee near the stove, with a pastry brush handy. Tear off a large sheet of aluminum foil and set it aside. Tear off 7 sheets of wax paper, each about 8 inches wide.

7. Lightly flour a small work area near the stove and place a dough patty on it (keep the others under cover). Roll it out to form a round roughly 5 to 6 inches in diameter, dusting it with flour as needed. Make sure the round is evenly thin, with no tears on the surface. Spoon 2 to 3 tablespoons of the spinach filling onto the center. Gather the edges of the dough, bring them together over the center, and pinch them together to seal the dough, forming a pouch shape. Flip the pouch over, pinched side down, and gently press it to flatten it. Reroll the dough, dusting it with flour as needed, to form a round roughly 5 to 6 inches in diameter. Lift the green-speckled round, plop it onto a sheet of wax paper, and cover it with a second sheet. Repeat with the remaining dough, stacking the patties between sheets of wax paper as they are rolled.

8. Heat a medium-size skillet (preferably nonstick or cast iron) over medium heat.

9. Transfer a patty to the hot skillet. Cook until the surface has some bumps and bubbles, and the underside has brown spots and looks cooked, 2 to 3 minutes. Immediately flip it over and cook until the other side has some brown spots, 2 to 3 minutes.

10. Brush the surface with ghee and flip it over to sear it, about 30 seconds. Brush the top with ghee and flip it over to sear it, about 30 seconds. Transfer the *parantha* to the piece of foil, and fold the foil over it to keep it warm.

11. Continue cooking the remaining filled dough, stacking the finished *paranthas* under the foil as they are cooked. Then serve.

Tips:

❖ If you plan to use frozen chopped spinach, make sure you thaw it completely and squeeze out as much water as you can before you use it for the filling. The drier the filling, the less chance that the dough will tear when you roll it out.

❖ *Paranthas* (like the other breads in this book) are a cinch to make even days before you plan to serve them. Just rewarm them, wrapped in a damp paper towel, in a microwave oven for barely a minute. Because the flour is a low-protein one, the microwave will not toughen the bread. As long as you do not overheat the *paranthas* in the microwave, they will be as good as fresh. Alternatively, you can wrap them in aluminum foil and rewarm them in a preheated 300°F oven for about 10 minutes.

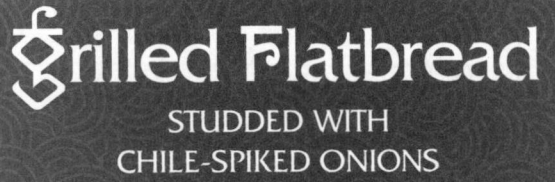

Grilled Flatbread
STUDDED WITH CHILE-SPIKED ONIONS

Pyaaz kulcha

Wedges of these spicy *kulchas* are great as an appetizer, when served with any of the legume curries or with Sautéed Spinach and Yogurt (page 743). Of course they are best when they are hot off the grill, but you can make a batch ahead of time: wrap them in foil and rewarm them in a preheated 300°F oven for about 10 minutes. Like many of the Indian flat-breads, this freezes very well for up to 2 months.

MAKES 4 BREADS

For the dough:
3 cups unbleached all-purpose flour, plus extra for dusting
2 teaspoons baking powder
1 teaspoon coarse kosher or sea salt

Rock salt? Black salt? See the Glossary of Ingredients, page 758.

½ cup buttermilk, at room temperature
About 1 cup warm water
Canola oil
Ghee (see page 21), for brushing

For the filling:
1 cup finely chopped red onion
¼ cup finely chopped fresh cilantro leaves and tender stems
4 to 6 fresh green Thai, cayenne, or serrano chiles, to taste, stems removed
½ teaspoon black salt, coarse kosher, or sea salt

For grilling or baking:
Rock salt, gently pounded, for sprinkling
Ghee (page 21) or melted butter for brushing

1. To make the dough, thoroughly combine the flour, baking powder, and salt in a large bowl.

2. Pour the buttermilk over the flour mixture and quickly stir it in. The flour will still be very dry, with some wet spots.

3. Drizzle a few tablespoons of the warm water over the flour mixture, stirring it in as you do so. Repeat until the flour comes together to form a soft ball; you will use about 1 cup warm water altogether. The dough should be very soft, close to being slightly sticky, so if you add an extra tablespoon or so of water, it won't hurt it. Using your hand (as long as it's clean, I think it's the best tool), gather the ball, picking up any dry flour in the bottom of the bowl, and knead it to form a smooth, soft ball of dough. If it's a little too sticky to handle, dust your hand with flour to handle the dough, but do not add any more flour to the dough if possible. Knead it for a minute or two. (If you used your hand to make the dough from the start, it will be caked with clumps of dough. Scrape them back into the bowl. Wash and dry your hands thoroughly, and return to the dough to knead it. You will get a much better feel for the dough's consistency with a dry hand.)

4. Cut the dough into 8 equal portions. Lightly grease a plate with oil. Shape one portion into a round resembling a hamburger bun and put it on the plate. (To get a smooth round, cup the dough in the palm of your hand and use your fingers to fold and tuck the edges underneath; then rotate, folding and tucking all around to get an evenly smooth ball.) Repeat with the remaining dough.

5. Brush the tops of the rounds with ghee, cover them with plastic wrap or a slightly dampened cloth, and let them sit at room temperature for about 30 minutes.

6. While the dough is resting, make the filling: Combine the onion, cilantro, chiles, and salt in a medium-size bowl, and stir together well.

7. Place a pizza stone or unglazed pottery tiles (see Tip) on the grill rack. *If it is a gas grill,* heat it to the highest heat setting. *If it is a charcoal grill,* build an intensely hot fire and allow the charcoal to turn ash white and red-hot. The temperature should hover between 600° and 700°F.

8. Tear off a large piece of aluminum foil, fold it in half lengthwise, and set it aside. Tear off 5 sheets of wax paper, each about 8 inches wide.

9. Lightly flour a small work area near the grill, and place a dough round on it. Press it down to form a patty. Roll the patty out to form a round roughly 3 to 5 inches in diameter, dusting it with flour as needed. Make sure the round is evenly thin, with no tears on the surface. Spread one fourth of the onion filling over the dough. Take another dough round and roll it out in the same fashion. Drape this round over the filling and press the edges of the dough together, pinching them as hard as

you can to seal them. Sprinkle a little rock salt over the top, and gently press it into the dough. Lift the filled dough round, flip it, plop it on a sheet of wax paper, and cover it with a second sheet. Repeat with the remaining dough rounds and filling, stacking them between sheets of wax paper as they are filled.

10. Transfer a filled round, salt side down, onto the hot pizza stone. Within seconds, the dough will start to bubble in spots. Cover the grill and cook until the dough turns crispy brown on the underside, 3 to 5 minutes. Turn the *kulcha* over and cook until that side turns light brown, 1 to 3 minutes. Remove it from the stone, liberally brush the salted side with ghee, and slide it between the layers of foil to keep it warm.

11. Continue cooking the remaining rounds, stacking them on top of the previously grilled *kulcha.*

12. Cut each one into four quarters, and savor them with any of the curries.

Tip: See the Tips in the Naan recipe (page 729) for advice on kneading the dough, and for an alternative way of baking the bread in the oven.

Flaky Breads
STUFFED WITH SPICY GREEN PEAS

ṁutter ḳachoris

A breakfast presence in parts of north-central and northwestern India, *kachoris* are often eaten with spicy potato curries. *Kachori* street vendors taunt you with their aromas as you walk by, and it is next to impossible to resist the temptation—which is okay; because they are fried at a high temperature, these foods are safe to eat at the roadside stalls. The filling alone has such intense flavors that *kachoris* are equally delicious on their own, without any accompanying curry. **MAKES 6 BREADS**

For the bread dough:

1¼ cups unbleached all-purpose flour

1 teaspoon coarse kosher or sea salt

1 teaspoon nigella seeds

4 tablespoons (½ stick) cold butter (preferably unsalted), cut into thin slices

About ¼ cup ice water

For the filling:

4 to 6 fresh green Thai, cayenne, or serrano chiles,

*   to taste, stems removed*

3 lengthwise slices fresh ginger (each 2½ inches long, 1 inch wide, and ⅛ inch thick)

1 cup frozen green peas, thawed and drained

1 tablespoon canola oil

½ teaspoon Toasted Cumin-Coriander Blend (page 33)

½ teaspoon coarse kosher or sea salt

For assembling and cooking:

Unbleached all-purpose flour for dusting

Canola oil for deep-frying

1. To make the dough, combine the flour, salt, and nigella seeds in the bowl of a food processor. Add the butter slices, and pulse until the butter forms pea-size balls. (It's these clumps of butter that will provide the fat needed for a flaky bread.)

2. Drizzle the ice water, a tablespoon or two at a time, over the mixture, and continue to pulse until it just starts to come together to form a soft ball.

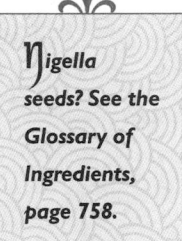

Nigella seeds? See the Glossary of Ingredients, page 758.

3. Transfer the dough to a cutting board or other dry surface, and knead it gently to form a smooth ball (if it seems sticky, lightly flour the work surface). Then, using your hands, roll the dough to form a 6-inch-long log. Cut it into 6 pieces, shaping each piece into a ball. Press each ball flat to form a patty. Wrap them in plastic wrap and refrigerate until ready to use. (They will keep for up to 3 days.)

4. To make the filling, combine the chiles and ginger in a food processor, and pulse until minced. Add the peas, and pulse to cut them into minuscule pieces and to blend the filling together. (If you allow the processor to run continuously, rather than pulsing, you will end up with a watery, gloppy mass—which you really don't want, trust me.)

5. Heat the oil in a small skillet or saucepan over medium heat. Add the pea mixture and cook, stirring frequently, until all moisture has evaporated and the mixture seems dry to the touch, about 5 minutes.

6. Stir in the cumin-coriander blend and the salt. Transfer the filling to a plate and allow it to cool for about 5 minutes.

7. To assemble the *kachoris,* remove a chilled dough patty from the refrigerator and place it on a lightly floured board (keep the others refrigerated). Roll it out to form a round about 5 to 6 inches in diameter, dusting it with flour as needed. Spoon 1 tablespoon of the filling onto the center of the round. Then gather the edges of the dough and bring them together over the center, pinching them together to seal the dough and form a pouch shape. Flip the filled pouch over, pinched side down, and gently press it to flatten it. Reroll the dough, dusting it with flour as needed, to form a round roughly 5 to 6 inches in diameter. Set it aside while you repeat with the remaining dough and filling.

8. Line a plate or a cookie sheet with three or four sheets of paper towels.

9. Pour oil to a depth of 2 to 3 inches into a wok, Dutch oven, or medium-size saucepan. Heat the oil over medium heat until a candy or deep-fry thermometer inserted into the oil (without touching the pan's bottom) registers 375° to 400°F. (An alternative way to see if the oil is at the right temperature for deep-frying is to gently flick a drop of water over it. If the pearl-like drop skitters across the surface, the oil is ready.)

10. Once the oil is ready, slide a filled *kachori* into the pan. It will sink to the bottom, and then within seconds it will start to bubble and rise to the top. With the back of a spoon, gently keep submerging the *kachori* when it rises to the surface, to enable the dough to puff from the inside. In less than a minute, the cooked *kachori* will be honey-brown, with a light green hue in the background from the filling. Remove it with a slotted spoon and set it on the paper towels to drain.

11. Repeat with the remaining *kachoris*. Then serve.

Grilled Steamed Buns

baati

Humble peasant food, *baati* is common in Rajasthani kitchens in northwestern India. These are crusty buns, rather dry and mealy, that are meant to be broken apart and soused (and I mean it) in warm ghee. *Baati* is an accompaniment for many Rajasthani legume-based curries, including Five-Lentil Stew with Cumin and Cayenne (page 406), offering a crunchy but rich-tasting bed for the potent curry.

MAKES 6 BUNS

1 cup roti flour (see Tip, page 728)
2 tablespoons chickpea flour
1 teaspoon coarse kosher or sea salt
1 teaspoon white granulated sugar
½ teaspoon baking soda
½ teaspoon cumin seeds
2 tablespoons canola oil
About ¼ cup warm water
Vegetable cooking spray
Ghee (page 21) for soaking

1. Thoroughly combine the the two flours, salt, sugar, baking soda, and cumin seeds in a medium-size bowl. Drizzle the oil over the mixture, rubbing the flour through your hands to evenly distribute the oil.

2. Drizzle a couple tablespoons of the warm water over the flour mixture, stirring it in as you do so. Continue drizzling warm water until the flour comes together to form a ball; you will need only about ¼ cup warm water. Using your hand (as long as it's clean, I think it's the best tool), gather the ball, picking up any dry flour in the bottom of the bowl, and knead it to form a smooth, albeit stiff, ball of dough. If it's a little too wet, dust it with a little flour, kneading it in after every dusting until you get the right dry consistency. (If you used your hand to make the dough from the start, it will be caked with clumps of dough. Scrape them back into the bowl. Wash and dry your hands thoroughly, and return to the dough to knead it. You will get a much better feel for the dough's consistency when you use a dry hand.)

3. Shape the dough into a 12-inch-long log, and cut the log into 6 pieces. Shape each piece into a tight ball (it will be the size of a lime). Pressing with your fingertip, make a small indentation in the top of each ball. Cover the balls with plastic wrap or a slightly damp-ened cloth, and let them rest at room temperature for about 30 minutes.

4. Fill a pan halfway with water and insert a steamer basket, or place a bamboo steamer in a wok filled half-way with water. Lightly spray the interior of the basket with cooking spray. Place the buns in the steamer bas-ket, cover the pan, and steam until they look opaque and spring back when gently poked, 15 to 20 minutes.

5. Meanwhile, heat a gas or charcoal grill to medium, or the oven to 350°F. *If you are grilling,* spray the grill grate with cooking spray. Arrange the buns on the grate, cover the grill, and cook until they are dark brown and

crusty, 15 to 20 minutes. *If you are baking,* lightly spray a cookie sheet with cooking spray. Arrange the buns on the sheet and bake until they are dark brown and crusty, 30 to 40 minutes.

6. To serve the *baati,* break each one in half (or in pieces) and pour a liberal amount of ghee (I usually like 1 tablespoon per *baati*) onto the pieces.

deep-frying *papads*

❖ ❖ ❖

1. Pour canola oil to a depth of 2 to 3 inches into a wok, Dutch oven, or medium-size saucepan. Heat the oil over medium heat until a candy or deep-fry thermometer inserted into the oil (without touching the pan's bottom) registers 375° to 400°F. (An alternative way to see if the oil is at the right temperature for deep-frying is to gently flick a drop of water over it. If the pearl-like drop skitters across the surface, the oil is ready.)

2. Line a plate or a cookie sheet with three or four sheets of paper towels. If you wish, break the papads in half before you fry them. Lower a piece into the oil and keep it submerged with a pair of tongs until it expands, turns yellowish brown, and loses its dry, opaque look, about 5 seconds. Transfer the papad to the paper towels to drain. Repeat with the remaining papad pieces.

Flame-Toasted Lentil Wafers

papads

When you want something quick and crunchy to accompany a curry instead of one of the breads, these papads fit the bill. I have been known to serve these as an appetizer, too, when I am not in the mood to cook anything else. (For all you need to know about *papads,* see page 593.) **MAKES 6 PAPADS**

6 uncooked lentil wafers (papads/papadums), made from skinned split black lentil (urad dal) flour, at least 6 inches in diameter

1. *If you are using a gas stove,* set the flame of a burner at medium-high. Holding 1 *papad* with a pair of tongs, flip it back and forth over the open flame until bumps start to appear on the surface and the *papad* turns light brown, 1 to 2 minutes. Remember to shift the tongs in order to toast the part initially covered by them. Repeat with the remaining *papads.* Set them aside to cool. *If* *you are using an electric stove,* place a rack as close as possible to the heating element, and preheat the broiler to high. Toast the *papads* until bumps appear on the surface and they turn light brown, 2 to 3 minutes. Set them aside to cool.

2. The *papads* will turn crisp and brittle as they cool. You can store them in airtight self-seal plastic bags at room temperature for up to 2 weeks (but I bet they will be gone long before that).

Tip: If you leave cooked *papads* exposed to humidity, they will turn soft. To re-crisp them, either zap them in a microwave oven for 30 seconds or rewarm them in a preheated 250°F oven until crisp, about 5 minutes.

Chopped Cucumber, Tomato, and Onion
WITH LIME JUICE

kachumber

I used to serve this as an accompaniment when I worked as a kitchen manager at an Indian restaurant in a previous life. The crunchy vegetables, tart marinade, and the zing from the chiles perk up many curries, and I especially like it with some of the seafood recipes in this book; its citrus prominence balances the richness of shrimp or scallops. You can even grill a piece of fish fillet, seasoned with just a little salt and pepper,

and serve some of the *kachumber* on top as a cold, chunky sauce, full of vibrant tastes. **SERVES 8**

1 large English cucumber, ends trimmed off,
*   peeled, cut in half lengthwise, seeds scooped out,*
*   cut into ¼-inch cubes*
1 medium-size tomato, cored and cut into ¼-inch cubes
1 small red onion, finely chopped
¼ cup finely chopped fresh cilantro leaves
*   and tender stems*
1 or 2 fresh green Thai, cayenne, or serrano chiles,
*   to taste, stems removed, finely chopped*
*   (do not remove the seeds)*
Juice of 1 medium-size lime
1 teaspoon Chaat masala (page 39)

1. Combine all the ingredients in a medium-size bowl, and toss together thoroughly.

2. Serve at room temperature or chilled. (It will keep, covered, in the refrigerator for up to 3 days. Longer than that, and the juice will develop a fermented flavor. Don't try to freeze *kachumber:* The vegetables will become mushy and rubbery when thawed.)

Cabbage and Cucumber "Slaw"
WITH ROASTED PEANUTS

bund gobhi kakadi nu salade

There are very few vegetables that Indians savor in their raw form. Two of them, cabbage and cucumbers, are featured in this juicy-crunchy salad. One year I served this as an accompaniment to the Roasted Leg of Lamb with Raisin-Mint Sauce (page 184) for Christmas dinner. If you are looking for a meatless option, any legume-based curry will work really well with this. **SERVES 8**

1 small head cabbage, thinly shredded (see Tip, page 468)

1 large English cucumber, ends trimmed off, peeled, cut in half lengthwise, seeds scooped out, thinly sliced crosswise

½ cup shredded fresh coconut; or ¼ cup shredded dried unsweetened coconut, reconstituted (see Note)

¼ cup finely chopped fresh cilantro leaves and tender stems

1 tablespoon white granulated sugar

1 teaspoon coarse kosher or sea salt

½ cup raw peanuts (without the skins)

2 tablespoons canola oil

1 teaspoon black or yellow mustard seeds

¼ teaspoon ground asafetida

Juice of 1 large lime

1. Combine the cabbage, cucumber, coconut, cilantro, sugar, and salt in a large bowl. Toss well to mix.

2. Heat a small skillet over medium-high heat. Toss in the peanuts and cook, stirring them just occasionally, until they turn golden-brown in patches, 3 to 4 minutes. Transfer the peanuts to a mortar and pound them with the pestle until they have the consistency of coarse breadcrumbs. (If you use a food processor or spice grinder, allow the nuts to cool before you pulse them or the moisture from the heat will turn the nuts cakey.) Add the nuts to the cabbage mixture.

3. Heat the oil in the same skillet over medium-high heat. Add the mustard seeds, cover the skillet, and cook until the seeds have stopped popping (not unlike popcorn), about 30 seconds. Remove the pan from the

Asafetida? See the Glossary of Ingredients, page 758.

heat, and sprinkle the asafetida into the hot oil. The instant onion-garlic aroma is pleasant and surprisingly mellow, quite the contrast from its raw state. Add the contents of the skillet to the cabbage mixture.

4. Add the lime juice and stir the salad well. Enjoy it either cold or at room temperature (my preference).

Note: To reconstitute coconut, cover with ¼ cup boiling water, set aside for 15 minutes, and then drain.

Chopped Radish
WITH CHILE-SPIKED YOGURT

Mooli Raita

Yogurt-based accompaniments, called *raitas*, are pervasive in all of India. The key reason for including a *raita* as part of a meal is to minimize the heat from chiles—fresh, dried, or ground. Yogurt soothes the digestive tract, acting as a sealant against pungent-hot foods. It also cools the body down during intensely hot days. This *raita* is studded with cool, crisp daikon radish, which is quite mild in flavor—daikon is often considered to be a cross between the familiar red radish and pungent horseradish. **MAKES 3 CUPS**

2 cups plain yogurt, whisked

½ teaspoon coarse kosher or sea salt

1 cup finely chopped peeled daikon radish; or 5 medium-size red radishes, finely chopped

1 tablespoon canola oil

1 teaspoon black or yellow mustard seeds

2 tablespoons finely chopped fresh cilantro leaves
   and tender stems

8 to 10 medium-size to large fresh curry leaves

1. Combine the yogurt, salt, and radish in a medium-size bowl. Stir well.

2. Heat the oil in a small skillet over medium-high heat. Add the mustard seeds, cover the skillet, and cook until the seeds have stopped popping (not unlike popcorn), about 30 seconds. Remove the skillet from the heat and carefully throw in the cilantro and the curry leaves (they will spatter when they come in contact with the hot oil).

3. Pour the contents of the skillet into the yogurt mixture, and fold it in. This will keep, covered, in the refrigerator for up to 4 days.

Soused Cucumbers
IN YOGURT AND FRESH MINT

Kakadi Raita

reece's yogurt-based sauce called *tzatziki*. reminds me of this condiment. A cooling balance to fiery curries, it is very common in north Indian home kitchens. If you decide to make your own yogurt (page 23), it will be even tastier. **SERVES 8**

1½ cups plain yogurt, whisked

1 teaspoon coarse kosher or sea salt

1 large English cucumber, ends trimmed off, peeled,
   cut in half lengthwise, seeds scooped out, shredded

½ cup firmly packed fresh mint leaves, finely chopped

1 teaspoon cumin seeds, toasted and ground

2 or 3 fresh green Thai, cayenne, or serrano chiles,
   to taste, stems removed, finely chopped
   (do not remove the seeds)

Thoroughly combine all the ingredients in a medium-size bowl. Serve chilled or at room temperature. This will keep, covered, in the refrigerator for up to 4 days.

Sautéed Spinach and Yogurt

Keerai Pachadi

he secret to achieving the smoky flavor in this *raita* lies in allowing the dried chiles to roast in the oil until they are blackened. The smoky heat leaves a lasting impression even when masked by the heat-lowering, creamy-tart yogurt. **SERVES 8**

1½ cups plain yogurt, whisked

1 teaspoon coarse kosher or sea salt

2 tablespoons canola oil

1 teaspoon black or yellow mustard seeds

4 to 6 dried red Thai or cayenne chiles, to taste,
   stems removed

8 ounces fresh spinach leaves, well rinsed, patted dry,
   and finely chopped

1. Whisk the yogurt and salt together in a medium-size bowl.

2. Heat the oil in a medium-size skillet over medium-high heat. Add the mustard seeds, cover the skillet, and cook until the seeds have stopped popping (not unlike popcorn), about 30 seconds. Stir in the chiles and cook until they blacken, 15 to 20 seconds.

3. Add a couple of handfuls of the spinach to the hot oil, and stir until wilted, 1 to 2 minutes. Repeat until all the spinach has been added. Then continue to cook the spinach in its own water, uncovered, stirring occasionally, until the leaves are softened and olive-green in color, 5 to 8 minutes.

4. Add the spinach mixture to the yogurt, and stir well. Then serve.

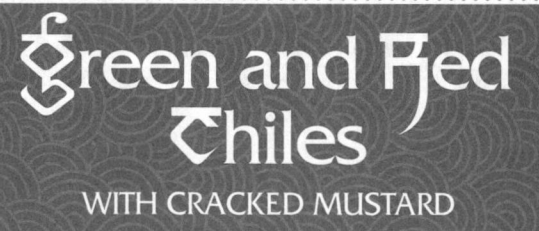

Green and Red Chiles
WITH CRACKED MUSTARD

Hari Aur Lal Mirchi Ki Achar

nly minutes to prepare, these pickles don't have to steep for days before you can use them to perk up curries, breads, and rice. If fresh red chiles aren't easy to come by, make the recipe with all green ones.

MAKES ALMOST 2 CUPS

4 ounces fresh green and red Thai, cayenne, or serrano
chiles, stems removed, cut crosswise into ¼-inch-
thick slices (do not remove the seeds)
¼ cup mustard oil or canola oil

1 tablespoon black or yellow mustard seeds,
coarsely cracked
1 tablespoon coarse kosher or sea salt
1 teaspoon ground turmeric
Juice of 1 medium-size lime

1. Place the chiles in a clean, dry glass jar.

2. Warm the oil in a small skillet over medium heat. Stir in the cracked mustard seeds and allow them to steep (but not sizzle) for 1 to 2 minutes.

3. Pour the seedy oil over the chiles, and sprinkle in the salt and turmeric. Squirt the lime juice into the jar. Screw the top shut and shake the jar vigorously to allow the ingredients to mix thoroughly.

4. Leave the jar on the counter for 4 to 6 hours so the chiles can soak up the flavors.

5. If you don't use them right away, refrigerate the pickles for up to 2 months.

Stewed Pineapple
WITH RAISINS AND CHILES

Anaras Ambol

weet, tart, and hot, this accompaniment from Monica Kataky's kitchen rounded out the fish curry called *Maasor tenga* (page 237) and the white rice she served at dinner. The guests at the table voted it a hands-down winner, the empty bowl a testimony to that conviction. This chutney takes center stage beautifully when served atop a piece of grilled wild salmon.

SERVES 8

2 tablespoons canola oil

1 teaspoon black or yellow mustard seeds

2 cups cubed fresh pineapple (½-inch cubes)

½ cup golden raisins

6 to 8 dried red Thai or cayenne chiles, to taste,
stems removed

½ cup crumbled (or chopped) jaggery
or firmly packed dark brown sugar

¼ teaspoon coarse kosher or sea salt

1. Heat the oil in a small saucepan over medium-high heat. Add the mustard seeds, cover the pan, and cook until the seeds have stopped popping (not unlike popcorn), about 30 seconds. Add the pineapple, raisins, and chiles. Reduce the heat to medium and cook, uncovered, stirring occasionally, until the raisins are plump and the pineapple is lightly browned, 5 to 8 minutes.

2. Add the jaggery and cook, stirring so it melts, 2 to 4 minutes.

3. Pour in 1 cup water, and sprinkle in the salt. Cook, uncovered, stirring occasionally, until the sauce turns syrupy-thick, 10 to 15 minutes.

4. Serve immediately, or cover and refrigerate for up to 1 week. Reheat to warm it before serving.

Tip: For an unusual presentation, ladle a tablespoon of this potent fruit over two scoops of your favorite premium vanilla ice cream.

Lime Wedges
PICKLED IN CAYENNE PEPPER AND MUSTARD OIL

Nimboo ka Achar

Pickling is often defined as sousing any vegetable, fruit, meat, or fish in some kind of acidic liquid flavored with spices for an extended period; the acid tenderizes the food and the salt preserves it. *Larousse Gastronomique* describes pickles as originating in India, where they were a means of preserving food to be consumed months later. Indian pickles pack strong spices in concentrated amounts and are used to enhance, perk up, and complement many stir-fries, stews, and breads. **MAKES 32 WEDGES**

2 large limes, each cut into 16 thin wedges
(see Tips)

1 tablespoon coarse kosher or sea salt

¼ cup cayenne (ground red pepper)

2 teaspoons black or yellow mustard seeds, ground

1 teaspoon fenugreek seeds, ground

1 teaspoon ground turmeric

¼ cup mustard oil or canola oil, slightly warmed
(see Tips)

1. Squeeze some of the juice from each of the lime wedges into a clean, dry glass jar. Add the limes to the jar and top them off with the salt. Screw the lid shut and shake the jar vigorously to allow the salt to get dispersed evenly. The limes should be submerged in their own juice (you can always add some lime juice if the limes were not juicy enough).

2. Place the jar in a warm, sunny spot. During the hot

summer months, I place it on my deck under direct sunlight. Every few hours, if you remember, walk by and shake the jar to "baste" the limes. Bring the jar inside at night and if it starts to rain. Continue this ritual until the limes are tender when cut with a fork, 5 to 8 days.

3. Add the cayenne, mustard, fenugreek, and turmeric to the salted limes and shake the jar again to incorporate the ingredients. Allow the jar to sunbathe for another day or two, shaking it every so often, and bringing it in, as above.

4. Pour the oil into the jar and give it a good shake. Allow it to rest for 4 to 6 hours.

5. The pickles are now ready to eat. You can certainly store them in a cool spot on your countertop. Or if you are uneasy about leaving them at room temperature, by all means refrigerate them. They will keep indefinitely (but it is my sincere hope that you will eat them every excuse you get).

Tips:

❖ The limes in the U.S. are usually tough-skinned and hard when pressed with your fingers. To loosen up its juices, place a lime on a hard surface and roll it back and forth under the palm of your hand, pressing down hard, until the skin appears to give in and the lime feels tender and juicy. Some books recommend zapping them for a few seconds in a microwave oven, but in my opinion the microwave cooks the lime, especially if you are not careful. The heat from your palms is all that's needed to achieve satisfactory results.

❖ I love the mustard oil in these pickles, which in addition to providing succulence gives them that pungent flavor, an ingredient quite essential in almost all store-bought Indian pickles.

Rock salt? See the Glossary of Ingredients, page 758.

Unripe Mango
WITH GINGER, CHILES, AND POUNDED ROCK SALT

Maangai Urughai

Pickles like this one pack strong flavors in minute quantities and yield larger-than-life gusto, making them an ideal match for any curry, rice, and bread. **MAKES 3 CUPS**

1 large, rock-firm unripe mango, peeled, seeded, and cut into ¼-inch cubes (see box, page 641)
¼ cup coarsely chopped fresh curry leaves
2 teaspoons rock salt, pounded
1 teaspoon ground turmeric
6 fresh green Thai, cayenne, or serrano chiles, stems removed, thinly sliced (do not remove the seeds)
4 lengthwise slices fresh ginger (each 2½ inches long, 1 inch wide, and ⅛ inch thick), cut into matchstick-thin strips (julienne)
¼ cup canola oil
1 tablespoon skinned split black lentils (cream-colored in this form, urad dal), picked over for stones
1 teaspoon fenugreek seeds
2 teaspoons black or yellow mustard seeds

1. Combine the mango, curry leaves, rock salt, turmeric, chiles, and ginger in a medium-size bowl.

2. Heat the oil in a small skillet over medium-high heat. Sprinkle in the lentils and fenugreek seeds, and

fresh mangoes

❖ ❖ ❖

Mangoes are the world's most heavily consumed fruit, a fact that's not surprising when you consider that there are over 1,000 varieties. I was fortunate to have been born in India, home to more than 125 varieties of mangoes, cultivated there for over 4,000 years. Dusseri, Payaree, Totapuri, and Langada are some varieties that elicit passionate debates as to which one is the best. Of course no one will be the loser with any of them. The one that stands out in my memory is the Alphonso from western India, salmon-orange and musky-smelling. When perfectly ripe, the flesh melts in your mouth, its sweetness overpowers your palate, and no fibers to get in the way of nirvana.

In my suburban supermarket in these United States, I see a mere handful of common mango varieties like the Hayden, Tommy Atkins, Kent, Champagne, and Keitt, grown and shipped from Florida, California, or Mexico. This tropical king of fruits, seasonal in India but available year-round here, is widely accessible at local supermarkets, natural food stores, and Asian and Latino groceries. Mangoes are usually picked green off the tree because, if they are allowed to tree-ripen, chances are the insects will get to them before we can. Ripen them on the kitchen counter, or enclose them in a brown paper bag to create the gases essential for speedier maturation. Or do as my mother used to do: completely submerge the fruit in uncooked rice grains until ripe.

roast, stirring constantly, until they are reddish brown and nutty-smelling, 1 to 2 minutes. Using a slotted spoon, scoop the lentils and seeds out of the hot oil and transfer them to a mortar. Pound them with the pestle, scraping the sides of the mortar to contain the blend in the center, until the mixture has the consistency of coarse black pepper. Scatter this over the mango mixture.

3. Reheat the oil in the skillet over medium-high heat. Add the mustard seeds, cover the skillet, and cook until the seeds have stopped popping (not unlike popcorn), about 30 seconds. Pour the contents of the skillet over the mango mixture, and stir well.

4. The pickles will keep in the refrigerator, covered, for up to 3 weeks. I usually store them in a dry glass jar or plastic container.

Fried Plantain, Eggplant, and Cashews
WITH A CAYENNE-VINEGAR SAUCE

batu moju

A Sri Lankan pickle, this is not only delicious with the cashew nut curry (page 456), but it also perks up plain white rice and the more exciting, pearl-like rice steeped in coconut milk called *Muttu sambha* (page 721).

SERVES 6

Canola oil for deep-frying
1 very firm medium-size plantain
1 small eggplant, stem removed, cut into 1-inch cubes
½ cup raw cashew nuts
½ cup malt or cider vinegar
2 teaspoons white granulated sugar
2 teaspoons black or yellow mustard seeds, ground
1 teaspoon cayenne (ground red pepper)
1 teaspoon coarse kosher or sea salt
1 teaspoon Ginger Paste (page 15)
1 teaspoon Garlic Paste (page 15)
½ teaspoon coarsely cracked black
*   peppercorns*

1. Line a plate or a cookie sheet with three or four sheets of paper towels.

2. Pour oil to a depth of 2 to 3 inches into a wok, Dutch oven, or medium-size saucepan. Heat the oil over medium heat until a candy or deep-fry thermometer inserted into the oil (without touching the pan's bottom) registers 375° to 400°F. (An alternative way to see if the oil is at the right temperature for deep-frying is to gently flick a drop of water over it. If the pearl-like drop skitters across the surface, the oil is ready.)

3. While the oil is heating, slice off the stem and heel ends of the plantain (¼-inch slices). Cut the plantain in half crosswise. Using a paring knife, make a lengthwise slit, ⅛ to ¼ inch deep, in each half. Wedge your fingers just under the slit and peel off the skin in one easy motion. (You can peel the entire skin with a paring knife, but it is slightly more time-consuming.) Cut the light beige flesh into 1-inch cubes.

4. When the oil is ready, add the plantain cubes and fry, turning them occasionally, until they are sunny-brown and crisp, 5 to 8 minutes. Remove them with a slotted spoon and place them on the paper towels to drain.

5. Add the eggplant cubes to the oil and fry them in a similar fashion, until the cubes are shriveled and slightly crisp, 5 to 8 minutes. Add the eggplant to the plantains.

6. Add the cashews to the hot oil and roast them until they turn reddish brown, 2 to 3 minutes. Add them to the vegetables.

7. Whisk the vinegar, sugar, mustard, cayenne, salt, Ginger Paste, Garlic Paste, and black pepper together in a medium-size bowl. Add the fried vegetables and nuts, and toss well to coat them with the sweet-hot-pungent vinegar. This will keep in the refrigerator for up to 2 weeks. I do not recommend freezing it.

Tip: If deep-frying scares you, try pan-frying the vegetables and nuts separately in a nonstick skillet. They will take a little bit longer to cook through and brown (an additional 5 minutes or so).

Kerala-Style Avocado Relish
WITH
TAMARIND AND CHILES

Avocado Chutney

Condiments like this one play the dual role of curry consort and appetizer. For an appetizer, serve it with either Flame-Toasted Lentil Wafers (page 740) or, my favorite, salty kettle-cooked potato chips (yes, yes, yes).

MAKES A GENEROUS 1 CUP

avocados

Avocados grow in the southwestern state of Kerala—both cultivated and wild. Called makhan phul ("butter fruit") in Hindi, there are three original varieties of avocados in the world: the Mexican, Guatemalan, and West Indian (as in the West Indies islands). The name is an adaptation of ahuacacuauhitl, the Aztec word for "testicle tree" (no comments, please). Spanish traders introduced this fruit to India in the 18th century. The quality of that fruit was not the best, but years of cross-pollination have resulted in popular cultivated varieties (at least 500 kinds in the world) like the Hass and Fuerte.

Choose an avocado that is slightly soft when gently pressed. The more pervasive Hass variety has a slightly thicker, blackish green skin, while the Fuerte is larger, with a light green complexion and thinner skin. If the avocado is firm, leave it at room temperature and it will ripen in a day or two. Once it ripens, store it in the refrigerator; it will keep for up to 2 days.

To cut it open, score the fruit deeply along its length (your paring knife will feel the stone in the center), cutting all the way around. Holding the avocado with both hands, twist each half in the opposite direction to cleanly separate the two; the stone pit will be embedded in one half's cavity. Hold that half in one hand and carefully whack the knife into the pit so that its blade gets wedged in. With the knife still in the pit, twist the avocado half and lift the pit from its bed. Be very careful removing the pit from the knife. Score the fruit by making crisscross cuts into it. Using a spoon, scoop out the cubes.

By the way, it turns out that the notion of leaving the pit embedded in the bowl of avocado cubes (or mashed avocado) to prevent discoloration is hogwash. In the wide expanse of a bowl, avocado flesh is defenseless against the air that discolors it quickly. However, in the Avocado Relish it is not an issue because the highly acidic tamarind imparts its own dark brown color (not to mention tartness) to the chutney.

---

3 medium-size ripe Hass or Fuerte avocados, pitted and
    cut into ¼-inch cubes (see box, above)
¼ cup finely chopped fresh cilantro leaves
    and tender stems
1 teaspoon tamarind paste or concentrate
1 teaspoon coarse kosher or sea salt
2 to 4 fresh green Thai, cayenne, or serrano chiles,
    to taste, stems removed, finely chopped
    (do not remove the seeds)
1 tablespoon coconut oil or canola oil
1 teaspoon black or yellow mustard seeds
12 medium-size to large fresh curry leaves

1. Combine the avocados, cilantro, tamarind paste, salt, and chiles in a medium-size bowl. Toss well to mix.

2. Heat the oil in a small skillet over medium-high heat. Add the mustard seeds, cover the skillet, and cook until the seeds have stopped popping (not unlike popcorn), about 30 seconds. Remove the skillet from the heat and add the curry leaves. (They will crackle and spatter, so watch out.)

3. Scrape the contents of the skillet into the avocado mixture, and fold it in. Then serve.

Luffa Squash Relish
WITH SHALLOTS

Peerkangai Chutney

this curry mate is equally tasty when mixed with cooked white rice and a drizzle of ghee. One night I served this with Batter-Fried Taro Root with a Peanut-Garlic Sauce (page 618) and Goan-Style Spicy Pork Sausage with Vinegar (page 233). Rice was at the table too, of course.

MAKES I CUP

I pound ridged luffa (or loofah) squash,
    ends trimmed, peeled and diced
    (see box, page 6513)
4 dried red Thai or cayenne chiles,
    stems removed
¼ cup firmly packed fresh cilantro leaves
    and tender stems
12 medium-size to large fresh curry leaves
I teaspoon coarse kosher or sea salt
½ teaspoon tamarind paste or concentrate
I tablespoon canola oil
I teaspoon black or yellow mustard seeds
I tablespoon skinned split black lentils
    (cream-colored in this form, urad dal),
    picked over for stones
4 medium-size shallots, thinly sliced

1. Combine the squash, 2 of the chiles, and 1 cup water in a small saucepan, and bring to a boil over medium-high heat. Lower the heat to medium, cover the pan, and simmer, stirring occasionally, until the squash is fork-tender, 5 to 10 minutes.

2. Pour the contents of the pan into a blender jar and pile in the cilantro, 6 of the curry leaves, and the salt and tamarind paste. Puree, scraping the inside of the jar as needed, to make a smooth, olive-green, tart-hot sauce. Pour it into a serving bowl.

3. Heat the oil in a small skillet over medium-high heat. Add the mustard seeds, cover the skillet, and cook until the seeds have stopped popping (not unlike popcorn), about 30 seconds. Add the lentils and the remaining 2 chiles, and stir-fry until the lentils turn golden-brown and the chiles blacken, 15 to 20 seconds.

4. Add the shallots and the remaining 6 curry leaves, and stir-fry until the shallots are light brown around the edges, 4 to 6 minutes.

5. Scrape the contents of the skillet over the chutney, and stir it to mix it in. This will keep in a lidded plastic, glass, or stainless steel container in the refrigerator for up to a week, or in the freezer for up to 2 months. Thaw it in the refrigerator.

Tips:

❖ Yellow summer squash is a great alternative to the luffa squash in this particular chutney. It will take a few minutes longer to cook, so make sure you add an extra ¼ cup water to the pan and allow another 5 minutes or so for it to become fork-tender.

❖ Tamarind paste provides an earthy tartness to this relish. For a fresher acidic burst, substitute a squeeze of fresh lime juice.

❖ The chiles and curry leaves are added at two separate stages to create a complex-tasting chutney.

❖ If you reheat this in a microwave, it will cook the herbs in the chutney to yield a mellow-tasting relish.

Sweetened Mango Puree
WITH MILK

Aamras

Mangoes are low in calories and laced with vitamins, minerals, and antioxidants, making them a guilt-free pleasure for a snack or a center-stage feature at any meal. With qualities like these, no wonder this fruit and its leaves play such a prominent role in many of India's auspicious and religious functions. In India we devour ripe mangoes as is and turn them into ice creams, puddings, and shakes. (The unripe green ones usually end up in curries, seafood-combined stir-fries, pickles, condiments, and chutneys.) This simple puree is popular in Gujarati home kitchens and restaurants, especially in peak mango season, just before the monsoons arrive in early summer. Serve puffy fried *pooris* (page 725) with it. My son adores this combination and I am often surprised at how many *pooris* he can consume this way. (He also makes me save the mango seeds so that he can suck on them until all you see is the bald pith with straggly fibers around it—no comments about any resemblance to my own pate, thank you very much!) **SERVES 4**

3 large ripe mangoes, seeded, peeled, and coarsely diced (see Tip, page 641)
1 cup half-and-half or whole milk
¼ cup white granulated sugar

1. Put the mangoes into a blender jar and add the half-and-half and sugar. Blend, scraping the inside of the jar as needed, to make a smooth, albeit fibrous, puree.

2. Transfer the puree to a serving bowl and serve it at room temperature or chilled. It will keep in the refrigerator, covered, for up to a week. You can also freeze it for up to 2 months.

Tip: Cans of Alphonso mango puree are omnipresent in Indian, Pakistani, Middle Eastern, and some Asian grocery stores. Use them in a heartbeat instead of fresh mangoes (it is far superior in taste and texture to the fresh varieties available here). Three cups of the canned pulp will do in this recipe.

Mango Cardamom Cheesecake
WITH A PISTACHIO CRUST

Aam Elaichi "Cheesecake"

A smooth cheesecake like this one will earn the utmost respect from even your pickiest of friends, and will give them the (false) impression that you slaved for hours over the stunning combination of colors, flavors, and textures.

Mangoes, pistachio nuts, and cardamom are stalwarts in many an Indian dessert. Here they are showcased in the delectable dessert that is so beloved by many of us: cheesecake. This American classic brimming with Indian-inspired ingredients makes for an enlightened ending to a multiple-course curry dinner.

SERVES 12

For the pistachio crust:

Unsalted butter or vegetable cooking spray

2 cups shelled raw unsalted pistachio nuts (see Tips)

¼ cup white granulated sugar

¼ teaspoon coarse kosher or sea salt

4 tablespoons unsalted butter, melted

For the mango–cream cheese filling:

1 pound cream cheese, at room temperature

1 cup white granulated sugar

2 large eggs, at room temperature

2 large egg yolks, at room temperature

1 cup canned mango pulp (see Tips)

1 teaspoon cardamom seeds from green or white pods, ground

For baking and serving:

Boiling water or very hot tap water

1 pint fresh raspberries, or the seeds from 1 large pomegranate

Canned mango pulp for drizzling

1. First, make the pistachio crust: Position one rack in the lowest position and another in the center of the oven, and preheat the oven to 375°F. Lightly butter or spray the bottom and sides of a 9-inch springform pan.

2. Put the pistachios in a food processor and pulse until they are ground to the consistency of fine breadcrumbs. (If the pieces are too large, you will have a problem making them stick together when you pat the crust into the pan.) Transfer the ground nuts to a medium-size bowl, and stir in the sugar and salt.

3. Pour the melted butter into the nut mixture, and use your hand to thoroughly combine the ingredients. The mixture should have the texture of slightly coarse wet sand. With your fingertips, spread and pat the mixture evenly across the bottom and about ½ inch up the sides of the prepared springform pan. Make sure the bottom is completely covered so the filling doesn't leak through while it is baking.

4. Place the pan on the center oven rack and bake until the crust is golden-brown, 10 to 12 minutes. Remove the pan from the oven and set it aside to cool. Reduce the oven temperature to 350°F.

5. Before you start the filling, be sure that the cream cheese is completely softened and that the eggs are at room temperature. (If the cream cheese is not completely softened to begin with, you will end up with a lumpy blend.) If you have a stand mixer, fit it with the paddle attachment; otherwise use a hand-held mixer with the whipping blade attachment.

6. Place the cream cheese in a mixer bowl. With the mixer on medium speed, beat it, adding the sugar, ¼ cup at a time, and beating until the mixture is smooth and creamy. Occasionally stop the mixer and scrape the sides of the bowl with a spatula. At this point, don't worry about overbeating.

7. Turn the mixer off, add 1 egg, and then beat on low speed until the egg has just blended into the cheese. Turn off the mixer, add the second egg, and repeat. Do the same with the 2 egg yolks, adding them one at a time. During this process you do want to be careful, because overbeating the eggs can result in a cheesecake with deep cracks in it.

8. Scrape any batter off the paddle (or whips) and add it to the bowl. Pour the mango pulp into the bowl, and sprinkle the ground cardamom evenly over it. Stir until the pulp blends into the batter. Pour the batter into the baked crust.

9. Fill a shallow pan with boiling water and place it on the lower oven rack. This will provide steam, essential for ensuring a creamy filling and an unburned crust. Place the springform pan on the center oven rack, and bake for 30 minutes.

10. Reduce the oven temperature to 325°F and continue to bake the cheesecake until the center jiggles when slightly nudged, 20 to 30 minutes.

11. Carefully remove the springform pan from the oven and set it on a cooling rack. Let the cheesecake cool completely at room temperature before you refrigerate it. (Otherwise, the jarring temperature difference between the oven and the refrigerator might split the cheesecake.)

12. Refrigerate the cheesecake, uncovered, for at least 12 to (but no longer than) 24 hours before serving it.

13. To serve, run a sharp knife around the sides of the springform pan to loosen the cheesecake. Open and remove the springform sides. To get picture-perfect slices, cut the cheesecake into quarters, using a clean long-bladed knife. Wipe the knife blade clean between cuts. Now slice each quarter into three slices, to get twelve even slices. To ensure clean-looking servings, remember to wipe the knife blade clean each time you slice through the cheesecake.

14. Top each slice with fresh raspberries or pomegranate seeds. Drizzle extra mango pulp around the slices, and serve.

Tips:

❖ If you have problems finding unsalted pistachio nuts, use the salted ones and eliminate the salt called for in the crust.

❖ There is a variety of mango called Alphonso that hails from Maharashtra. The pulp is extremely smooth and fiber-free, and its flavor is incredibly sweet. Of course any other kind will also do. However, a word of advice: For this cheesecake, canned mango pulp will give a better flavor, especially if you don't have access to an excellent fresh variety like the Alphonso. Canned mango pulp is widely available in Indian, Greek, Mexican, and Middle Eastern grocery stores.

If you use a ripe fresh mango, here's how to remove the pulp: First, peel the mango with a paring knife. Then score the pulp in a crisscross fashion, inserting the knife until it hits the hard, fibrous pit. Slice off the pulp, sliding your knife down through the flesh alongside the pit. Plunk the mango cubes into a food processor and process it until smooth—a food processor will work better than a blender for this.

Cardamom and Nutmeg-Flavored Baked Custard
WITH ALMONDS

Lagan Nu Custard

Parsis devour this delicacy (thank you, Perinne Medora), which gets its name from the weddings *(lagan)* it traditionally graces. Very Western in its concept, but with a package of flavors that is passionately Indian, this is a perfect light finale after a curry extravaganza. **SERVES 6**

4 cups whole milk

½ cup white granulated sugar

½ teaspoon cardamom seeds from green or white pods, ground

¼ teaspoon grated nutmeg

¼ cup slivered blanched almonds

1 teaspoon pure vanilla extract

Vegetable cooking spray

3 large eggs, lightly beaten

Premium vanilla ice cream, for serving (optional)

1. Pour the milk into a large saucepan and bring it to a boil over medium-high heat, stirring frequently to prevent it from scorching. Once it comes to a boil, lower the heat to medium. Continue to boil the milk, occasionally scraping down the milk solids that stick to the sides of the pan, until it has reduced by half, 30 to 35 minutes.

2. Remove the pan from the heat, and stir in the sugar, cardamom, nutmeg, almonds, and vanilla. The heat of the milk will be enough to dissolve the sugar. Let the mixture cool to lukewarm as it rests at room temperature, about 30 minutes.

3. While the milk mixture is cooling, position a rack in the center of the oven and preheat the oven to 350°F. Bring either a teakettle or a medium-size saucepan of water to a rolling boil. Lightly spray the bottom and sides of six individual custard cups, or a single small, shallow baking dish, with cooking spray.

4. When the milk has cooled (you don't want scrambled eggs), whisk the eggs into the creamy mixture. Stir to ensure that the nuts and spices get evenly dispersed, and pour it into the prepared custard cups. Place the cups in a deep-sided baking pan (like a cake pan). Pour boiling water into the baking pan, making sure you don't get any in the custard cups, so that the bottom half of the cups are submerged in the water bath.

5. Place the baking pan on the center oven rack and bake, uncovered, until a knife inserted in the custard comes out clean, the center of the custard jiggles when the cup is gently nudged, and the top of the custard is light brown, 20 to 30 minutes.

6. Remove the cups from the water bath and set them aside to cool.

7. Serve at room temperature. When no one's looking, why not go ahead and plop a scoop of premium vanilla ice cream on each custard cup, and dig in (hey, it's a wedding).

Tip: Many Indian and Middle Eastern grocery stores stock a variety of tropical extracts, including mango, guava, and pistachio. Use any of these lieu of the vanilla for an even more exotic dessert. Alternately, sprinkle 3 or 4 saffron threads into each cup before adding the custard; as the custard bakes, the saffron will form orange-red ribbons around it. Scatter a few organic fresh or dried rose petals on the custards after they bake for a sensuous touch.

Cardamom-Scented Green Tea
WITH SAFFRON

kehawa

Kashmiris brew this delicacy for esteemed visitors at weddings, family gatherings, and special meals, especially after a rich curry dinner. Manu Madhok served this the day he and his family invited me for a Kashmiri lunch—a perfect finale to a scrumptious meal.

SERVES 4

¼ *cup loose green tea leaves*
¼ *teaspoon saffron threads*
4 to 6 green or white cardamom pods
1 or 2 cinnamon sticks (each 3 inches long)
4 teaspoons white granulated sugar
¼ *cup slivered blanched almonds,*
    ground

1. Bring 5 cups water to a rolling boil in a medium-size saucepan over medium-high heat. Add the tea leaves, saffron, cardamom pods, and cinnamon sticks. Stir once or twice.

2. Allow the water to come to a boil again, uncovered, and cook, stirring occasionally, until the leaves release their flavor and the spices perfume the tea (not to mention the air), about 5 minutes.

3. Stir in the sugar and remove the pan from the heat.

4. Spoon 1 tablespoon of the ground almonds into each mug. Setting a tea strainer over each mug, strain the tea into the mugs. Serve immediately, and pass around teaspoons to let the folks stir the tea before they sip it.

Tips:

❖ Manu's father described the green tea leaves in his homeland (Assam) as having a hibiscus like aroma. Any specialty tea store in your area should have green tea leaves from India or Assam. If not, use green tea bags as an acceptable alternative.

❖ If sugar is an issue for you, leave it out of the recipe.

Fresh-Squeezed Lime Juice
WITH SODA AND PEPPER

nimboo Paani

I cannot think of a better drink to serve as a precursor to a curry meal than this one. Clear-tasting, tart, sweet with peppery undertones, this drink is delicious poured over ice—or you can add a peg (or two) of high-quality gin or vodka for a refreshing cocktail. Guests are always offered a cool beverage as they enter an Indian's home, and this is a favorite. The salt and pepper in the drink elevates the beverage's sweetness and quenches thirst during the oppressive summer months.

SERVES 4

Juice of 3 medium-size limes
½ cup white granulated sugar
3½ cups cold club soda or cold water
½ teaspoon coarse kosher or sea salt
½ teaspoon black peppercorns,
    coarsely cracked

1. Whisk the lime juice and sugar together in a pitcher, making sure the sugar dissolves completely.

2. Stir in the club soda, salt, and pepper.

3. Plop a few ice cubes in each glass, give the drink a good stir, and pour.

eating, indian style

❖ ❖ ❖

ow that you've mastered the art of curry making, having spiced, stir-fried, and stewed your way through all 660 saucy wonders, next time you make one, why not eat it the Indian way (we call it desi style). We Indians wash our hands, sit at the table, tear off pieces of bread (with one hand only, and yes, it's the right one because the left is considered "unclean," best reserved for other body functions—no need to go further), wrap them around morsels of curry, and in it goes. We repeat this until we're done with "breaking bread." Then we mix the leftover curry with rice and, using the fingers of the right hand, we scoop up little mouthfuls and devour until we can eat no more. If you're left-handed "Oy veh, you are so out of luck!" as my friend the cookbook author Judy Kancigor would say. Or you'll just have to resort to the pardesi (foreign) manner. And yes, the foreign way would be to use fork, knife, and spoon to transport your curry meal. Of course, I say eating with silverware is like making love through an interpreter; something is lost in the translation, n'est-ce pas?

Metric Conversion Charts

Tablespoons and Ounces
(U.S. CUSTOMARY SYSTEM)

Grams
(METRIC SYSTEM)

1 pinch = less than ⅛ teaspoon (dry)	0.5 grams
1 dash = 3 drops to ¼ teaspoon (liquid)	1. 25 grams
1 teaspoon (liquid)	5.0 grams
3 teaspoons = 1 tablespoon = ½ ounce	14.3 grams
2 tablespoons = 1 ounce	28.35 grams
4 tablespoons = 2 ounces = ¼ cup	56.7 grams
8 tablespoons = 4 ounces = ½ cup (1 stick of butter)	113.4 grams
8 tablespoons (flour) = about 2 ounces	72.0 grams
16 tablespoons = 8 ounces = 1 cup = ½ pound	226.8 grams
32 tablespoons = 16 ounces = 2 cups = 1 pound or 0.4536 kilogram	453.6 grams
64 tablespoons = 32 ounces = 1 quart = 2 pounds or 0.907 kilogram	907.0 grams
1 quart = roughly 1 liter	

Temperatures: °Fahrenheit (F) to °Celsius (C)

−10°F = −23.3°C (freezer storage)	300°F =148.8°C
0°F = −17.7°C	325°F =162.8°C
32°F = 0°C (water freezes)	350°F =177°C (baking)
50°F = 10°C	375°F =190.5°C
68°F = 20°C (room temperature)	400°F =204.4°C (hot oven)
100°F = 37.7°C	425°F =218.3°C
150°F = 65.5°C	450°F =232°C (very hot oven)
205°F = 96.1°C (water simmers)	475°F =246.1°C
212°F = 100°C (water boils)	500°F =260°C (broiling)

Conversion Factors

ounces to grams: multiply ounce figure by 28.3 to get number of grams

grams to ounces: multiply gram figure by 0.0353 to get number of ounces

pounds to grams: multiply pound figure by 453.59 to get number of grams

pounds to kilograms: multiply pound figure by 0.45 to get number of kilograms

ounces to milliliters: multiply ounce figure by 30 to get number of milliliters

cups to liters: multiply cup figure by 0.24 to get number of liters

Fahrenheit to Celsius: subtract 32 from the Fahrenheit figure, multiply by 5, then divide by 9 to get Celsius figure

Celsius to Fahrenheit: multiply Celsius figure by 9, divide by 5, then add 32 to get Fahrenheit figure

inches to centimeters: multiply inch figure by 2.54 to get number of centimeters

centimeters to inches: multiply centimeter figure by 0.39 to get number of inches

glossary of ingredients

Note that I've included an ingredient's Hindi translation whenever possible.

Amaranth: Bunches of red amaranth are found year-round in the produce section of Chinese markets. Also called "red spinach" or "Chinese spinach," red amaranth has a much more assertive flavor than the mild-tasting green-leafed amaranth.

Asafetida (*hing*): A member of the carrot family, asafetida is a gumlike resin made from a combination of three giant fennel species. The plant's rhizome is tapped to extract a milky liquid, which is then dried. The mass changes in color from white to yellow to the final translucent brown. Asafetida hardens as it ages, and it is usually sold in powdered form, but because producers often include gum arabic (to absorb moisture), flour (to prevent clumping in humid conditions), and even turmeric (for a little color), purists reach for it in block form. I have used it in its store-bought ground form in all the recipes that call for it.

I always caution my students that this spice does not taste the way it smells (*asafetida* means "nasty-smelling resin," basically). Tasting it raw may preclude you from ever wanting to use it! One student smelled it and shrieked, "*Eeew,* stinking onion and dirty socks." Nevertheless, I had her sprinkle a small amount in hot oil, just as the recipe instructed, and when she sat down to taste the curry, she exclaimed, "Wow, tastes oniony-garlicky." Thus asafetida finds gainful employment in numerous curries within the Jain community, where onion and garlic are prohibited. In the south, many legume-based stews and broths steep with this ground spice (without sizzling it in oil) for a stronger astringent flavor.

Baking powder (*khaar*): This acid-alkali mix is best known for its baking prowess, leavening batters and doughs with its ability to produce carbon dioxide in the presence of moisture. However, in India it is also used as a spice. Baking powder's astringent flavor is prime in Pungent Green Papaya with Mustard and Chiles (page 644).

Bay leaves (*tez patta*): The Indian bay leaf is the sharp-edged leaf of the cassia tree (*Cinnamomum aromaticum* or *zeylanicum*), not the Mediterranean *Laurus nobilis*. Indian and Pakistani stores stock large bags of Indian bay leaves, but feel free to use the Mediterranean variety if you can't locate a source or happen to have some growing in your yard. When sizzled in oil, these leaves infuse it with an aromatic sweetness, and they continue to release their aroma as long as they stew in a curry. I always recommend removing bay leaves from the dish before you serve it, so that someone at the table does not accidentally swallow one.

We toast or roast these leaves in many of our spice blends (such as *Punjabi garam masala,* page 25), and pound them to accentuate their aroma. Bay leaves are an intrinsic part of garam masalas, as their presence generates internal warmth. Fresh bay leaves have an incredibly long shelf life in the refrigerator. If weeks go by and you forget they are in there, don't worry, as they will dry and further extend their use by months.

Bishop's weed (*ajowan/ajwan/ ajwain*): Also known as carom or lovage (not true, because lovage is a separate member of the same family), bishop's weed is indigenous to India and has a peppery-hot taste with undertones of oregano and thyme (because it contains the same essential oil, called thymol). Because of its strong digestive qualities, it is sizzled in oil to assertively flavor many of Gujarat's legume-based curries.

If you can't locate bishop's weed, substitute dried thyme leaves, but use only half the amount (for 1 teaspoon bishop's weed, use ½ teaspoon dried thyme). Add ½ teaspoon ground black pepper for every teaspoon of thyme, and mix the two together.

Bitter melon (*karela*): This vegetable is also known as balsam pear, *foo gua*, and *balsamina*. I consider this light to dark green, bumpy, scaly, cucumber-like squash, with its characteristic rat's-tail stem, to be the King of Bitter. Bitter melon is never eaten raw. Instead, it is salted to leach out its excess bitterness and then fried, stir-fried, or stewed with assertive spices.

Buttermilk. *See* Yogurt.

Cardamom seeds (*elaichi*): The cardamom tree, a close relation to ginger, is indigenous to southern India (especially Kerala, where the variety is known as Mysore) and Sri Lanka (where it is called the Malabar variety or wild cardamom). The world's spice bins overflow with a variety from Allepey (Kerala), the plump green pods considered the true cardamom. (These same green pods are also sun-bleached white and sold in grocery stores as white cardamom; besides aesthetics, I really don't see any reason why, since the flavors remain unaffected.) Another large kind, with black pods and big black seeds, grows in eastern India, in Assam and Bengal; it is called black cardamom or *kala elaichi*. The green ones are menthol-like, aromatic, subtle, and sweet-smelling, while the black ones are smoky, strong, and slightly bitter.

Whole green cardamom pods are sizzled in hot oil or dunked into a sauce to infuse it with their sweet, delicate aromas. When the seeds are pried out of the pods and gently pounded, they release a stronger aroma. Toasting and grinding extracts their optimum strength for spice blends like *Punjabi garam masala* (page 25). If you don't wish to take the trouble to pry the seeds out of the pods, purchase the seeds in jars labeled "decorticated cardamom." Green cardamom and its seeds scent many of India's desserts, and when you pop a few raw seeds into your mouth, they make your breath smell fresh and facilitate digestion (call it an Indian's antacid).

The black pods, on the other hand, infuse smoky aromas into many of the savory dishes favored in the north. The black pods and seeds are never used in desserts, but the seeds do make their presence felt when toasted and ground with other spices to make England's *Balti masala* (page 31). When either the black or green pods appear in your portion of curry, eat around them; their flavor is overpowering and will eclipse every taste and aroma in many subsequent mouthfuls.

Cashews (*caju*): Portuguese settlers introduced the cashew to India, where it thrives in the southwestern state of Goa. The nut is encased within a double shell that contains a toxic substance; the shell is carefully broken open by roasting or boiling. The inside nut is white, sweet, and delicious. Cashews are as versatile as peanuts. The cashew nuts in my recipes are raw (unroasted).

Chiles, red and green (*lal aur hara mirch*): Now look, can you even *think* of Indian curries without the heat from chiles? In this book I have

limited my selection to just a few, chosen primarily for their availability in the Western world.

In the world of Indian curries, two fresh chiles stand out: cayenne and Thai. The cayenne (named after the city of Cayenne in French Guiana, and green when fresh, red when dried) is long and slender—usually 4 to 8 inches long and about ½ inch thick. The Thai chile (sometimes erroneously called bird's-eye) is the green of a bell pepper and about 2 inches long (true bird's-eye chiles are much smaller and two to three times hotter). The serrano chile—also bell-pepper-green, but about 3 inches long and thicker than the other two peppers—is the mildest of the three, and an alternative I recommend because of its wider availability.

Discard the stem and slit the chile open to reveal the veins and the seeds. Removing the veins and seeds will diminish the chile's heat, but we never do so in India because we regard that as criminally wasteful. We do slit the chiles open but leave the vein and seeds intact, to release a gentler heat. Chopping a fresh chile releases the capsaicin, and the finer you chop it, the hotter the taste.

how hot is hot?

❖ ❖ ❖

What makes a chile hot is the chemical capsaicin, which is housed in the membrane-like vein that runs through the chile. The heat is measured in Scoville Units, named after a pharmacist who invented the way of measuring capsaicin content. Pure capsaicin registers at 16,000,000 Scoville Units.

Serrano chile:	5,000 to 15,000 Scoville Units
Cayenne chile:	30,000 to 50,000 Scoville Units
Thai chile:	50,000 to 100,000 Scoville Units

Dried chiles are plentiful in India, and we use cayenne and Kashmiri chiles in large amounts. (When fresh green cayenne chiles vine-ripen to red and then are sun-dried, they become dried red cayenne.) In grocery stores in the U.S., they are also available as *chile de arbol*. These are hot as is, but treat them with heat (by blackening them in a dry skillet or in oil), and the dried capsaicin unleashes a more fiery taste. True Kashmiri chiles, rarely found outside the states of Jammu and Kashmir, are small, finger-long, and about 1 inch thick. These are prized for their color and gentle heat, a trademark of Kashmir's classic curry, *Roghan josh* (page 214). Boxes of ground Kashmiri chiles are widely available in Indian and Pakistani grocery stores across the United States (as well as from many mail-order sources). The combination of cayenne (ground red pepper) and sweet paprika gives you the color of these chiles.

Cilantro (*taaza dhania*): Either you are
a lover of cilantro (also known as fresh coriander or Chinese parsley) or you despise it. More often than not, Indian curries include these leaves, used in various ways to extract flavors ranging from subtle to sharp. Many of the curries use cilantro as a garnish, as one would use parsley, just before they reach the table (and you can always leave it out). Many also incorporate cilantro at various stages in the cooking, and in the presence of heat, the sharp, soapy aroma and taste dissipate (or even disappear), surprising even the naysayers. Cilantro is beneficial for its anticoagulant properties, and the leaves have detoxifying properties. So do give it a chance, will you?

(For the seed of the cilantro plant, *see* Coriander seeds, page 764.)

Cinnamon and cassia (*dalchini*): True
cinnamon, from the bark of *Cinnamomum verum* or *zeylanicum*, indigenous to Sri Lanka and parts of southern India, is highly aromatic, its dried bark unfurling in hot oil to suffuse perfumed sweetness. Most of the cinnamon

we see in the Western world comes from the less expensive *Cinnamomum cassia*, cultivated in China for export. In India, cinnamon sticks most commonly perfume oils in which meats, vegetables, and legumes simmer; they are also used in layered rice bakes. Because of its warming feature (as in internal body warmth) when toasted and ground, cinnamon is a popular spice in many of our garam masalas, including the complex *East Indian bottle masala* (page 37).

Clove (*lavang*):

The mention of pungent cloves in a sauce described by Valmiki in the Hindu epic *Ramayana* (2nd century B.C.) gives a clue to their early presence in India. This evergreen tree bears nail-shaped flower buds; when dried, these buds yield the highly aromatic black cloves. The spice's oils (eugenol) are the source of aroma and heat in Indian curries, especially in the northern regions. The oil also has a certain numbing quality, contributing to that sense of hot pungency on your tongue. As a spice, clove bouquets our curries with its aroma and flavor when sizzled in hot oil. When gently pounded and steeped in coconut milk (see Stewed Potatoes, Carrots, and Peas in Spiced Coconut Milk, page 565), its presence is hushed. It is a warming spice when toasted with other spices and ground to make *Punjabi garam masala* (page 25). Clove's strength is evident in *Bangala garam masala* (page 26), where it is one of only three spices in this blend from the east coast. Both of these blends assert their presence in numerous curries from those regions.

Coconut (*nariyal/thenga*):

The dark brown coconut houses thick white meat that is used for daily cooking along India's coastal areas. The question students ask me the most is how you can tell whether the coconut's meat is sweet without having to crack it open. Here are a few pointers: Choose a fruit that has dry eyes (the three indentations on the end of the coconut, where it attached to the tree). Lift the coconut to feel its weight; it should be heavy. Shake it to

hear its water splashing against the shell; if you hear nothing, chances are the meat is rotten. However, you still have to crack it open to determine whether the meat is okay. Once home, rinse the shell under water. Holding the coconut over a bowl, gently but firmly tap it around its midsection with a hammer or a meat pounder, moving the coconut around as you keep tapping. When the shell cracks open, the off-white water inside will gush out into your bowl. Taste it: If it is sweet, the meat will be too. If the water tastes rancid, the meat could very well be rotten.

Now that you know the meat is sweet, use a sharp paring knife to score it in large pieces, cutting all the way through to the shell. Gently pry out the pieces with a firm butter knife. Peel off the thin, dark brown skin and place the white meat in a food processor. Pulse it into small shreds. (In India we use a coconut grater—a barbaric-looking implement—to get the meat from the shell without any hassles.) A medium-size coconut will yield 2 to 3 cups shredded meat. Freeze any unused coconut meat for up to 2 months.

Indian and Southeast Asian grocery stores stock freshly shredded coconut meat in their freezers. Dried unsweetened shredded coconut (sometimes sold as powder) is also available in major supermarkets and natural food stores; ½ cup dried unsweetened is comparable to 1 cup freshly shredded. I often reconstitute ½ cup dried unsweetened coconut in ½ cup boiling water for about 15 minutes for that freshly shredded taste (drain off the excess water before use). If you are desperate, purchase sweetened shredded coconut and soak it in hot water; drain; and repeat three or four times to get rid of as much sugar as possible.

To make coconut milk, puree 1 cup shreds in a blender with 1 cup water, and then strain through a fine-mesh strainer. This thick, milky liquid has a concentrated flavor. If you dilute the coconut milk one more time, with 1 cup water, and strain that through, you get a weaker-tasting liquid, often referred to as thin coconut milk.

Shopping Cheat Sheet

ENGLISH	HINDI	Would you need to make a trip (online or in person) to an indian store?
SPICES AND FLAVORINGS		
asafetida	hing	yes
bishop's weed	ajowan/ajwan/ajwain	yes
black peppercorns	kala mir	no
black cardamom pods	badi elaichi	yes
black salt	kala namak	yes
cinnamon	dalchini	no
cloves	laung/lavang	no
coconut	nariyal	no
coriander seed	sabud dhania	no
cumin seed	sabud zeera	no
dried chiles	lal mirch	no
dried fenugreek leaves	kasoori methi	yes
dried pomegranate seed	anardana	yes
dried unsweetened coconut shreds	sukha nariyal/copra	no
fennel seed	saunf	no
fenugreek seed	methi	yes
frozen unsweetened shredded coconut	taaza nariyal	yes
garcinia camboge	kudampuli	yes
garcinia indica	kokum	yes
ginger	adrak/sonth	no
green cardamon pods	choti elaichi	no
jaggery	gur	yes
kewra extract	kewra paani	yes
mace	javitri	no
mustard seed	rai	no
nigella seed	kalonji	yes
nutmeg	jaiphal	no
rose extract	gulab paani	yes
saffron threads	zaffran/kesar	no
star anise	badiyan	no
tamarind	imli	yes
teflam seeds	tirphal	yes
turmeric	haldi	no
white poppy seeds	khus khus	maybc
white sesame seeds	safed til	no
FRESH HERBS		
bay leaves	tez patta	yes
coriander (cilantro) leaves	taaza dhania	no
curry leaves	kadipatta	yes
dill	suva	no
fenugreek leaves	taaza methi	yes (available frozen)
fresh green chiles	hara mirchi	no
holy basil	tulsi	maybe
mint leaves	pudhina	no

ENGLISH	HINDI	Would you need to make a trip (online or in person) to an indian store?
FRESH VEGETABLES		
baby eggplant	choti baingan	yes
daikon radish	mooli	no
drumstick	sing/murungakkai	yes
green (unripe) jackfruit	katthal	yes (mostly canned)
green papaya	kaccha papeeta	yes
kohlrabi greens	haak	no
lotus root	kamal kakadi	yes (frozen and canned)
mustard greens	sarson ka saag	no
okra	bhindi	no
plantain	kaccha kela	no
squash (bitter melon)	karela	no
squash (bottle gourd)	dudhi/lauki	no
squash (ivy gourd)	tindora	yes
squash (luffa)	toori	no
squash (white pumpkin)	safed bhopla/parangikai	yes
taro leaves	arbi ke patte	yes
taro root	arbi	no
turnips	shalgam	no
yam	suran	no
LEGUMES		
black chickpeas	kala chana	yes
black-eyed peas	lobhia	no
cow peas	chowli	maybe
dew gram	moth	yes
horse gram	kulith	yes
kidney beans	rajmah	no
skinned and split black lentils (cream-colored)	urad dal	yes
skinned and split brown lentils (salmon-colored)	masoor dal	no
skinned and split green lentils (yellow-colored)	moong dal	maybe
skinned and split yellow pigeon peas (oily or unoily)	toovar/toor/tur/arhar dal	yes
whole black lentils	sabud urad	yes
whole brown lentils	sabud masoor	maybe
whole green lentils	sabud moong	maybe
whole pigeon peas	sabud toor	yes
whole yellow peas	sabud vatana	yes
yellow chickpeas	kabuli chana	no
yellow split peas	chana dal	no
NUTS AND FLOURS		
garbanzo/chickpea/gram flour	besan	maybe
raw (unroasted) cashew nuts	kaaju	no
raw (unroasted) pistachio nuts	pista	no
rice flour	chaawal ka atta	no
roti/chappati flour	chappati ka atta	maybe
OILS		
clarified buter/ghee	ghee	no
coconut oil	copray ka tel	yes
mustard oil	sarson ka tel	yes
unrefined sesame oil	til ka tel/gingelly oil	yes

The taste of fresh coconut milk is amazing, but canned coconut milk is perfectly acceptable. Some brands are better than others, and once you are able to settle on the one that suits your curries, it will definitely make your life easier. Look for a canned product that has the consistency of heavy cream. Shelf-stable coconut powder is also available; you can mix this with water to get not-bad milk.

Coconut is very versatile. Shredded coconut meat, folded into a sauce just before you serve the curry, is sweet. The toasted shreds are nutty and spic-elike, and the milk acts as a creamy sauce for the strong spices in the dish. Pureed coconut also helps to thicken sauces.

Coriander seeds (*sabud dhania*):

The citruslike, brownish-yellow seed of the cilantro plant (see page 760) is nowhere similar in taste or aroma to the leaves. One is not a substitute for the other in a curry, but on numerous occasions they appear together, complementing each other. Unlike the leaves, the seed is noncontroversial. Cumin and coriander go hand-in-hand in many of our curries, the toasted blend (page 33) indicative of that cozy relationship.

Cumin (*zeera/safed zeera*) and black cumin (*shahi zeera*): Native to the

Mediterranean and upper Egypt, cumin is India's favorite spice. Depending on how it gets used, it is capable of having eight distinct flavors, and sizzles, toasts, roasts, soaks, and grinds its way into numerous curries. Cumin is truly a national treasure.

Black cumin is called *shahi* (meaning "kingly") *zeera*, pointing to its affiliation with Moghul India's royal kitchens. Brownish black in color, the seeds are wispy-thin, and have a smoky aroma and a caraway-like undertone. For a more pronounced impact, try curries that include the spice blend *Rajasthani garam masala* (page 26).

Curry leaves (*kadipatta*): Now don't go

shaking your finger at me and say "See, this is where curry powder comes from." The leaves of this small tree, a member of the citrus family, are widely used in sauces along much of India's coastal areas. We use them just as we do bay leaves, simmering a few of the leaves in the sauce to delicately perfume it (see Fragrant Ginger Shrimp with Shallots and Curry Leaves, page 260). We don't eat the leaves, but they are perfectly edible, so go ahead and try some. Blends like Roasted Curry Leaf Spice Blend (page 35) feature them prominently; they still are very subtle even in such large amounts. When sizzled in hot oil, curry leaves have a more intense taste, especially in the Kerala-Style Avocado Relish with Tamarind and Chiles (page 748). Many Indian stores, and also Southeast Asian stores that cater to Malaysian-Americans, stock these fresh in their produce section. If you can only find dried curry leaves, don't bother—they have an insipid aroma. Just do without.

Dill (*suva*): Grasslike dill leaves, widely used in

India's northwestern regions, have a delicate, anise-like flavor that tells you it is part of that family of herbs (Umbelliferae). Very often dill is the main attraction in a curry, and when used in large amounts, it crosses the herbaceous threshold to that of a vegetable.

Fennel seeds (*saunf*): Indigenous to the

Mediterranean countries, fennel (*Foeniculum vulgare*) is a member of the parsley family. Its seeds are used in Indian spice blends, while the feathery leaves and the bulbous stem are abundantly consumed in Mediterranean cultures. When you leave an Indian restaurant, you see a bowl of toasted sugar-coated fennel seeds, waiting for you to pop a spoonful into your mouth. This spice is a great breath freshener—anise-like, refreshing—and a powerful digestive. The seeds are light green and resemble caraway and cumin. In curries they can be toasted, roasted in oil, or simply ground in spice blends to weave their sweet magic.

Some of the curries, especially those that start with mustard oil, rely on fennel seeds to lower the oil's pungently bitter taste. When ground, the seeds assert a stronger, weaving sweet magic in many of the curries they spice.

Fenugreek (*methi*):

Prized in India for both its cloverlike leaf and dark yellowish-brown, triangular, stone-hard seeds—that are very bitter when roasted or toasted—I regard the aroma and taste of fenugreek as "perfumed bitterness." The seed, considered medicinal (some were found in Tutankhamen's tomb), provides commercial curry powders with that distinctive aroma. Whenever I demonstrate recipes that incorporate fenugreek seed, students say, "Oooh, smells like curry."

Many sauces in southern India use toasted and oil-roasted seeds (and their ground versions, as in *Sambhar masala*, page 33), to create bitter balance. The eastern regions put the bitterness to work by stir-frying the seeds (they get more bitter when browned in oil). Cooks along the northern regions cherish the grass-green leaves. Because they have a short shelf life, the young leaves are dried and sold in packages labeled *kasoori methi*. Refer to page 473 for tips on cleaning and preparing fresh leaves for use. Frozen chopped fenugreek leaves are now available in Indian and Pakistani groceries.

Gingelly oil. *See Sesame seeds.*

Ginger (*adrak*):

Although ginger did not come into India until about 1300 B.C., once it did, its pungency (a highly aromatic one too) became a popular taste ingredient, especially in the paste form, for hundreds of our curries and marinades. Steeping slices of ginger in a pot of legumes, stir-frying it with other bulbs to form a sauce's base, smashing it along with herbs and spices for juicy pungency, shredding the ginger and squeezing its juice for a mellow broth, adding julienne of ginger to curries just before serving—these are just a few ways we bring out ginger's various levels of pun-

gency. For information on buying, storing, and using ginger, see the recipe for Ginger Paste (page 15).

Gongura (*methi*):

Similar in looks to their notorious sibling, marijuana, but with none of marijuana's seductive qualities, gongura leaves are dark green, with a reddish-brown tint on the edges. The leaves are often cut into thin strips and simmered with legumes, meats, and fish. The leaves are very tart and provide curries with an acidic balance. If you can't locate fresh gongura, use fresh sorrel or spinach leaves and add ¼ teaspoon tamarind paste or concentrate (or 1 tablespoon fresh lime juice) to each 8 ounces of greens.

Holy basil (*tulsi*):

Used extensively in Ayurveda, India's ancient medicinal practice, holy basil (*Osimum sanctum*) is thought to cure everything from stomach upsets (soothing when its leaves brew with tea leaves), to fever, to even malaria. These small leaves, widely available in Asian grocery stores, are narrower than the common sweet basil, and have a dull reddish-purple tint to their edges and tips. They have a peppery taste with a sharp pungency that dissipates when simmered in sauces. If unavailable, sweet basil makes a perfectly acceptable alternative.

Jaggery (*gur*) and sugar (*chini*):

In Gujarat and Rajasthan, fields of bamboolike sugarcane dot the landscape, its hardened stem masking its yellowish-white, juicy, and extremely fibrous flesh. Its juice is boiled down and dried to yield clumps of dark brown jaggery, which is sold all over the world, especially in Indian grocery stores. Mexican stores stock a similar product they call *piloncillo* (in cone form, which you can use, teaspoon for teaspoon, as a substitute for jaggery). Jaggery is cloyingly sweet, with a molasseslike flavor. I recommend packed dark brown sugar as a very close alternative to jaggery in all my recipes that call for it.

Kokum: Kokum (*Garcinia indica*) is a slender ever-green tree found growing wild in the tropical rain forests along the Konkan coast in southwestern India. Just before the monsoons arrive, the tree bears round fruits that are dark purple when ripe. The fruit has five to eight seeds inside, and the pulp is sweet-tart. The juices extracted from the fruit are sold as a concentrate and are used to make cooling beverages during the oppressive summer months. The dried form, black kokum, is prepared by drying the outer rind, soaking it in the pulpy juice, and then sun-drying it.

Kudampuli: *Garcinia camboge* or *Garcinia gummi-gutta*, also known as Malabar tamarind, is a tree that is found in abundance in Kerala, off the coast of Malabar. I have not often found this fruit—which is dried, then smoked—in the United States, even in Indian stores. Its acidic compound of hydroxy citric acid is considered beneficial in the treatment of obesity. (In the United States, where every weight-loss gimmick gets tested, I hope this compound will get its fair share of attention, making it much easier to procure kudampuli in stores!) Some large Indian supermarkets stock the fruit, as do some Thai and Vietnamese grocery stores. (Sri Lankans call it *goraka*.) If you can't find it, use tamarind paste dissolved in water, and for that distinct smoky flavor, stir in a drop or two of natural smoke flavor.

Lime (*nimbu*): The Indian lime, which originated in Malaysia, is the archetype of the citrus family, its acidity and taste familiar to those who savor Key limes from Florida. It is small, its skin is thin, and its acidity is quite strong. These limes are pickled in assertive spices (page 745) and breathe their tart, fiery-hot breath when served alongside many of our curries. The lime juice provides a clean, crisp tartness and is usually stirred in after the curry has cooked, just before serving. When limes are called for in my recipes, regular ones work perfectly well, but if Key limes are available, give them a try.

Mace. *See* Nutmeg.

Mango, unripe (*khatte aam*) and mango powder (*amchur*): The mango is the most consumed fruit in the world. When you realize there are over 125 varieties in India alone, the multitude of ways they can, and do, sneak into many of our curries should come as no surprise. Growers cultivate certain varieties to use in their unripe form for their sour taste. Green, rock-firm, and tart, they are sliced, then sun-dried.

A more common form is mango powder, the ground dried slices, sold in Indian and Pakistani grocery stores as *amchur* or *amchoor*. Light brown, dusty-looking, and very tart, mango powder showers stews, broths, and sauces, or folds into marinades, particularly in the northern regions of India, to create a sour presence. In the finger-licking blend of spices called *Chaat masala* (page 39), mango powder is one of two key spices.

When the unripe fruit is chopped and used as a vegetable, it plays a dual role to provide not only tartness but also nutrients (it is low in calories and loaded with vitamins, minerals, and antioxidants). Mango pickles and chutneys, from the unripe and ripe fruit, are synonymous with India. While the rest of the world imagines mangoes to be sweet, we Indians usually pickle the unripe fruit with potent ground red pepper (cayenne) and spices to mitigate its tartness.

As with numerous unique ingredients, there is no substitute for the unripe mango's earthy sourness. An alternative, depending on the recipe, is plain lime juice. Some cooks suggest lime zest, but I find that more bitter than sour.

Mint (*pudhina*): This perennial herb is cultivated all over the world, boasting over twenty-four species with hundreds of varieties, peppermint and spearmint being the most popular. The dried leaves make their strong aromatic presence known in spice blends like *Rajasthani garam masala* (page 26). Mint is bold enough to stand up to assertive herbs like fenugreek and mustard, but can also take a subtle backseat, especially when cooled with yogurt. Its digestive properties soothe the cantankerous stomach, especially when chopped mint leaves are steeped in a tea to brew a favorite after-dinner beverage.

Mustard (*rai*):

Fields of mustard sway in northwestern India, in the state of Rajasthan, and in numerous northeastern states, making this a cash crop in those areas. The greens are a delicacy in the northern regions, but the seeds are equally versatile, and there are three kinds of mustard that are primarily harvested for their seeds. *Brassica nigra* produces brownish-black seeds, *Brassica juncea* yields reddish-brown ones, and *Brassica alba* (white mustard) is the source of light yellowish-brown seeds. The first two are widely used in Indian cooking, but the yellow one is an acceptable alternative. When ground, the seeds are potent, but roast the seeds in oil and let them pop (just like popcorn), and they become nutty-sweet. This seed possesses a Jekyll-and-Hyde personality, because it swings between two primary taste elements: When pounded, cracked, or ground, and combined with a liquid, it yields that nose-tingling sharpness. But when you apply heat, as in popping the seeds in oil, it stops that reaction and results in a nutty-sweet taste.

Pure mustard oil, which is viscous, amber-colored, and very bitter, is extracted from the *juncea* variety. It is available in Indian and Pakistani grocery stores. However, if you look closely, you will find the words "for external use only" on the label. The FDA has issued a health warning about the presence of toxic erucic acid. Considering that they deem this unfit for human consumption, it fascinates me that humans have used it in India for 6,000 years. In response to that warning, mustard-flavored blended oil (usually blended with bland soybean oil) is now commonly found in those same stores, and safe to use. Heating mustard oil releases its pungent aroma into the air, and if you happen to stand in the direction of its smoke, be prepared to shed a few tears. This oil is a must in Indian pickles (the oil acts as a preservative), and it is also used to massage the scalp to promote hair growth (it obviously failed in my case). Many of the curries from the eastern, northern, and northwestern regions call for mustard oil.

Nigella (*kalonji*):

Nigella (no, sorry, unrelated to the television personality) is also called black cumin, which is a constant source of confusion to Indians and non-Indians alike. Nigella is a different species altogether, its black seeds used to dot breads in many Middle Eastern countries. In India they go by *kalonji* (mistakenly called "onion seeds," possibly because of a remote resemblance to the flavor of onions). The almost triangular-shaped, charcoal-black seeds sizzle in many curries in India's eastern states; one example is Onion-Studded Lentil and Split Pea Fritters with a Chunky Tomato-Nigella Sauce (page 55).

Nutmeg (*jaiphal*) and mace (*jaipatri*):

It's always nice when a tree yields one useful spice, but when it gives you two, you just might become a tree hugger. The nutmeg tree, indigenous to Indonesia, is cultivated along India's western shores. The pear-shaped nutmeg fruit is revered for its seed. Pry the fruit apart and you can see a beautiful orange-brown web that wraps its tentacles around a hard, dark brown shell. The web is the spice known as mace; it is found in pieces ("blades") in Indian grocery stores and is available from many mail-order sources. Ground mace is more common, but it loses its sweet, musky flavor within a short time (two months after grinding, in my opinion). When the shell dries and is broken open, a hard, light brown nut with little specks of white emerges: This is nutmeg. Just like mace, nutmeg is best when freshly ground (or in this case grated).

Peanuts (*sengdana*):

Of all the nuts, peanuts are the most popular (and affordable) in curries, especially in the western and northwestern regions of India. We always start with raw peanuts, which we then toast or roast. This draws out the oils from within, which provides succulence for the tongue (see *Umami*, page 6). The peanuts may be coarse-cracked, ground, or pureed; each technique elicits a different taste sensation.

When toasted and ground with spices, peanuts have a slightly nutty presence, thus helping to tone down some of the more assertive ingredients in the mix (see *Maharashtrian garam masala*, page 28). They provide nutty texture and protein in Steamed Chickpea Flour Cake with Peanuts and Spinach (page 112), a thickening quality to the sauce in Nutty-Hot Tomatoes with Garlic (page 624), and a leguminous background when stewed with radish greens in Boiled Peanuts with Radish Greens and Jaggery (page 456).

Peppercorns (*kali mirchi*): I am not being
overly dramatic when I say, "This is the spice that created the waves for the spice trade, paving the way for the discovery of seas, civilizations, and the shaping of history as we know it." I admit, it is a hefty burden for this tiny, black, oily, hot, berrylike spice, but when you read about pepper once being traded for gold, you realize its position in the world of flavors. India's indigenous plant, dating back to 4000 B.C., was *Piper longum,* the ancestor of the modern *Piper nigrum* (black pepper). Long peppers are still available in India; but their levels of the volatile oil (piperine) that generates heat are less than those of black peppercorns. The world's top-quality black pepper is grown and processed off the coast of Malabar (now known as Kerala). Once called Malabar peppercorns, they are now more specifically labeled according to the regions that produce them: Allepey and Tellicherry (the latter being superior). As the green peppercorn berries start ripening to a red color on the vine (a creeping plant that is entwined around mango, betel nut, and palm trees), they are plucked and piled in heaps to ferment, then spread out to sun-dry; the heat turns them into the familiar black peppercorns. Their volatile oils are best when just released, and the recipes for many of the southwestern curries instruct you to do just that. Toasted, roasted, ground, coarsely cracked, or pounded, peppercorns exhibit different personalities, but their role of heat inducer is constant.

Pineapple (*anaras*): Pineapple plays a role
similar to unripe mangoes in some curries, but this fruit is used when ripe, so its sour taste comes with its own built-in sweet balance. Perked up with chiles and stewed with sweet golden raisins (page 744), pineapple becomes a great accompaniment to our curries, especially in the northeastern corner of India.

Pomegranate (*anardana*): Fresh pome-
granate and its sun-dried seeds are prevalent in curries in the northern and northwestern regions of India. The juicy fresh seeds (sweet-tart) make a great topping for a street food from Mumbai (Spiced Potatoes and Pomegranate Sandwiches, page 105). Drying the seeds accentuates their tartness, making them a souring choice for curries like Chickpeas and Potatoes Flavored with Singed Spices (page 337).

Poppy seeds (*khus-khus*): If you expect
to intoxicate yourself by imbibing large quantities of the seeds from the opium poppy (*Papaver somniferum*), think again; the narcotic agent loses its hallucinogenic quality when the poppy matures. This legal spice from an illicitly used plant is off-white in India (it's a variety that comes from Persia). The blue-gray seed so common in the U.S. is not found in most Indian curries. The white poppy seed acts as a sauce thickener, and the nutty nature of the seed puts it in the umami (see page 6) category. When toasted or roasted in oil, the seed is extremely strong-tasting, as compared to its innocuous raw form. Its backseat personality comes into play in many of Bengal's curries, where mustard-poppy seed

combinations are popular to highlight mustard's bitterness with poppy's thickening.

Rose. *See* Screw pine.

Saffron (*zaffran/zarda/kesar*): Harvested in Cyprus as early as 1600 B.C. and later brought to Kashmir (the world's best saffron comes from Kashmir, and if someone is kind enough to share some with you, offer your firstborn as a thank-you gift), this is unequivocally the world's most expensive spice. It is the hand-picked, dried stamen of the *Crocus sativa* blossom (70,000 blossoms yield a pound of beautiful reddish-orange saffron threads), and just two to four threads can perfume a curry that feeds four. Never purchase ground saffron, as it is inferior in quality and may be adulterated. Use saffron threads sparingly (heat will bring out its aroma) and guard it with your life.

Salt (*namak*) and black salt (*kala namak*): I add salt during various cooking stages, using one kind of salt while simmering the curry and swirling in a second variety just before serving it (see Sweet Potato and Plantain in a Sauce of Fresh and Roasted Coconut, page 615).

The three main types of "white" salt used in curries are rock salt, sea salt, and table salt. Rock salt is a mined product, processed and purified for human consumption, and sold in, you guessed it, rock form. The extent of purification depends on its end use: The coarser (and cruder) it is, the more industrial its use. You can pulverize rock salt into a gritty powder and sprinkle it into and over many curries. Adding it just before serving highlights its earthy quality.

Sea salt is the most popular salt in Indian curries (with three large oceans surrounding the country's west, south, and eastern coasts, one would hope so), and it is widely available in crystal and powder forms in American supermarkets. This is what I use in all my dishes, with the even more widely available kosher salt as an alternative. Kosher salt (which is slightly coarse), conforming to Jewish dietary laws, is a processed product with no additives, its crystals uneven in shape.

Table salt fills saltshakers all over the United States; it is a heavily processed ingredient, often supplemented with iodine, an essential trace element required by the body. It's very fine in texture and I find it saltier in taste when compared to coarse kosher or sea salt. If you are using table salt for the recipes in this book, I suggest reducing the amount specified by 10 to 15 percent. One of the most interesting works on salt is Mark Kurlansky's *Salt: A World History*; it is definitely worth a read.

Black salt is more purplish-pink with gray undertones than black. It is sold in both rock crystal and powdered form. If you are a purist, procure the rock form and pulverize it in a mortar. If convenience is the name of the game, use the powdered variety (which is what I have used in the recipes here). Packages of powdered black salt may have some lumps, which can be broken apart by pinching them. Black salt is very popular in Indian snacks, curries, and chutneys because of its earthy, addictive, and slightly smoky edge. This is one of the main ingredients in *Chaat masala* (page 39), that finger-licking spice blend sprinkled on many of the chaat recipes in this book. Black salt has digestive qualities, and because of its lower sodium content, it is a better choice for those on a low-sodium diet. It's available in Indian grocery stores.

Screw pine (*kewra*) and Rose (*gulab*): In their extract form these infuse north Indian and Pakistani curries and are prized for their aroma. Kewra water, a highly perfumed clear liquid, is derived from the tropical screw pine tree. Its aroma, which is the main reason why it is used in sweet and savory dishes, has been described as a cross between rose and sandalwood. Although the plant is pervasive in India, its usage is limited to the northern regions including Pakistan; hence its wide availability in Indian and Pakistani grocery stores.

is roasted and ground into a spice blend called *bottle masala*, which perfumes many curries in Mumbai (see page 37).

a saucy aside

❖ ❖ ❖

ere's an interesting tidbit I learned from Professor Elizabeth Collingham: When a British governor, stationed in British India, fell in love with a tamarind-based sauce, he brought a recipe of sorts for chemists Lea and Perrin to re-create. Once during their experimentation, they allowed the sauce to mature. The taste knocked their socks off, enough to motivate them to purchase the original recipe from the governor and start manufacturing the sauce now so familiar to the world as don't-know-quite-how-to-say-it-but-love-it Worcestershire.

Tamarind (*imli*): The tart fruit of this evergreen tree is what we use, extracting its acidity. When fresh, the beanlike pods have an olive-green, tough, hide-like skin. When dried, the skin becomes brittle and greenish brown. Inside is the chocolate-colored pulp that shrouds the hard, dark brown seeds. Indian and Southeast Asian grocery stores carry tamarind in two forms: blocks of dried tamarind pulp (with or without seeds) and jars of tamarind paste or concentrate.

To create tamarind juice from the block form, soak a walnut-size chunk of the dried pulp in ½ cup warm water; this yields the same tartness as 1 teaspoon tamarind paste or concentrate dissolved in ½ cup water. After softening the pulp in water, break it up with your fingers; then mash it to release the tart brown juices while you loosen the intertwined pulp. Continue to soak and mash it until the liquid has a cloudy, muddy-brown appearance. Pour the liquid and pulp through a fine-mesh strainer placed over a small stainless steel, plastic, or glass bowl. (The highly acidic tamarind will react with metals like copper, iron, and tin, resulting in a metallic taste.) Mash and push the pulp through the strainer, and use the juice to sour curries. The pulp and its fibers may be used for a second, albeit weaker, extraction. As an added benefit, because of its high acidity, you can use the tamarind pulp to touch up polished brass and copper tchotchkes with pleasing results.

Rose is revered for its sensual aroma and beauty. When the dried petals bouquet a creamy sauce laced with saffron threads, that opulence is a reflection of the historic Moghul kitchens. The curry not only smells sensuous, but its beauty makes you—at least briefly—hesitate to eat it (see Ground Lamb with Scallions in a Saffron-Rose Sauce, page 95).

Sesame seeds (*til*):

K. T. Achaya, in his *Indian Food: A Historical Companion,* places sesame seeds in India around 20 million years B.C.! White sesame seeds have a nutty flavor, which is accentuated when toasted or roasted in India's myriad curries. The oil from the unrefined seed, called *gingelly oil* in southern India, also imparts a delicate nutty flavor.

Some spice blends call for toasting the dried pulp in a skillet to dry it out completely before grinding. This yields a slight smoky-tart quality to the sauce. I therefore buy both forms of tamarind—block and paste—and store them in airtight jars at room temperature. Kept away from humidity and light, they will keep for six months to a year (even longer at times). Many Thai, Hispanic, and Latino grocery stores sell

Star anise (*badiyan*) :

Even though star anise, which is related to the magnolia, has nothing to do with anise (a relative of fennel), it has an aniselike quality because of its inherent oil, anethole—the same oil found in anise. This star-shaped spice (it has eight "spokes," each with a hard brown seed in its center)

sugar-coated fresh tamarind pods (called candied tamarind) for a tart-sweet snack.

Teflam seeds (*tirphal*): Clove-colored
teflam seeds (they are actually berries, not seeds) look like the animated Pacman from the well-known video game. Unique to the Hindu community of Goa, along the Konkan coast in southwestern India, teflam seeds are rarely used in other communities. The Portuguese call the spice *limao arcado*, "acrid lime," which accurately describes its flavor and aroma: sharp and citruslike, especially when toasted and ground. The seeds have an anesthetic, numbing quality when bit into, even in small amounts. Teflam is closely related to Sichuan peppercorns, which can be used as an alternative. If you don't have either teflam or Sichuan peppercorns, toast equal proportions of whole cloves, black peppercorns, and dried lemon peel, and then grind the mixture.

Turmeric (*haldi*): This deep yellow rhizome,
a very close sibling to ginger, is probably native to India. It is mentioned in ancient Sanskrit literature and has yellowed its way into not only our foods, but also religion, medicine, and as a dye for fabrics, especially the robes worn by Hindu priests and Buddhist monks. Ground into paste form and wrapped in a bandage over a wound, it has anti-inflammatory properties. The chemical curcumin in turmeric (which gives commercial curry powders that yellow color) is the subject of recent medical research in the fight against Alzheimer's disease and certain forms of breast and prostate cancer. Turmeric, sold most often in ground form in the United States, is harsh-tasting when raw, a reason why it is rarely used this way. Nevertheless, sprinkle it in oil (cushioned with other ingredients), and its astringent taste diminishes in the resulting sauce. Coat fish fillets with ground turmeric, and it removes fishy odors. Also known as poor man's saffron (believe me, it is nowhere close to the flavors of saffron) or *safran d'Inde*, turmeric is a strong-tasting and -coloring spice that we use sparingly but frequently in many of our dishes.

The fresh root is also delicious when thinly sliced and pickled in bitter mustard oil, salt, and chopped fresh green chiles. In the western regions of India, turmeric's large leaves are used to wrap steamed fish, infusing the flesh with a hint of astringency.

Vinegars (*sirka*): Vinegars are widely used in
the western areas of India, the most popular being the vinegar curries in the Portuguese-influenced Goan Christian communities. Vegetables, fruits, and pickles, preserved in vinegars, also influence Indian curries, yielding acidic sweetness because of their fruity origins.

Yogurt (*dahi*) and buttermilk (*chaas/ more*): Writings from as early as 2100 B.C. describe
the magic of these tart ingredients. They lend not only sourness to our *karis* and *kadhies* but also digestive comfort. It is customary, even now, to end a meal with either plain yogurt mixed with rice (page 710) or a glass of thin buttermilk.

Yogurt has multiple personalities, and all its incarnations affect curries in different ways. Take the example of Slow-Cooked Baby Potatoes in a Yogurt-Fennel Sauce (page 559), where yogurt is "stir-fried" long enough to evaporate all its moisture, turning the curd pellets very sharp-tasting. When used as a base for marinating meats, yogurt not only imparts a pleasant tartness to the curry but balances out the heat of the chiles. It also tenderizes the meat with its acidity and enzymes. When dolloped atop finished dishes, yogurt blankets the mélange with a creamy, cooling presence.

True buttermilk is the watery whey that is separated from freshly churned butter. In this country it is sold as a cultured dairy product, creamier and sharper-tasting than its Indian counterpart. However, I find our commercial buttermilk perfectly acceptable.

the elements of a curry: flavor = taste + aroma

Seven Asian taste elements (see also pages 5–8)

BITTER	SOUR	SALTY	SWEET	UMAMI	HOT (pungent)	ASTRINGENT
Bitter melon	Tamarind	Rock salt	Jaggery	Monosodium	Black	Asafetida
Fenugreek	Kokum	Sea salt	White	glutamate	peppercorns	Turmeric
leaves	Kudampuli	Table salt	granulated	Meats	Fresh and dried	Baking powder
Fenugreek	Tomatoes	Kosher salt	sugar	Fish and seafood	chiles	Teflam seeds
seed	Yogurt	Black salt	Golden raisins	Poultry	Ginger	
Mustard	Buttermilk		Dried apricots	Milk and milk	Cloves	
greens	Limes		Dried plums	solids		
Mustard seed	Unripe mango		(prunes)	Cream		
Mustard oil	Pineapple		Sweet mango	Yogurt		
	Vinegars		Pineapple	Buttermilk		
	Dried		Fennel seed	Butter and ghee		
	pomegranate		Star anise	(clarified butter)		
	seed		Nutmeg	Almonds		
	Fresh		Mace	Cashew nuts		
	pomegranate			Peanuts		
	seed			Pistachio nuts		
				Walnuts		
				Pine nuts		
				Coconut		
				Poppy seed		
				Sesame seed		
				Mushrooms		
				Legumes		

Five More Essentials

AROMATICS	OILS	BULBS	SAUCY BASES	THICKENERS & STABILIZERS
FRESH HERBS:	**VEGETABLE OILS:**	Garlic	Water	Chickpea flour
Bay leaves	Canola	Onion	Tomato sauce	Rice flour
Coriander (cilantro) leaves	Sunflower	Shallots	Tomato paste	Wheat flour
Dill	Corn	Scallions	Tomato puree	Cornstarch
Curry leaves	Peanut		Yogurt	Nut purees
Mint leaves	Coconut		Buttermilk	Vegetable purees
Fenugreek leaves	Unrefined		Cream or half-and-half	Fruit purees
Holy and sweet basil	sesame		Milk solids	Legume purees
	Mustard		Nut purees	Coconut
DRIED SPICES:			Vegetable purees	
Cardamom pods and seeds			Fruit purees	
Cumin seed			Legume purees	
Nigella seed			Coconut milk	
Coriander seed			Vinegars	
Cinnamon				
Bishop's weed				
Saffron threads				
Kewra extract				
Rose extract				

mail-order sources for spices and legumes

Asia Imports
1840 Central Ave NE
Minneapolis, MN 55418
612-788-4571
www.asiaimportsinc.com

Ethnic Grocers – web site only
www.ethnicgrocer.com
www.indianblend.com

Marhaba International, Inc. (Kalustyan's)
123 Lexington Avenue
New York, NY 10016
212-685-3451
www.kalustyans.com

Penzey's Spices
Multiple locations
800-741-7787
www.penzeys.com

Vanns Spices Ltd.
6105 Oakleaf Avenue
Baltimore, MD 21215
800-583-1693
www.vannsspices.com

To locate any Indian grocery store near you, use
www.thokalath.com/grocery/index.php

bibliography

Achaya, K. T. *Indian Food: A Historical Companion*. India: Delhi Oxford University Press, 1994.

Ammal, S. M. *Cook and See* (Parts 1 and 2). India: Samaithu Par House, 1968.

Baker, L. Interview with Prof. Elizabeth Collingham. "Curries Lost Favour with the British in India." http://info.anu.edu.au/mac/Newsletters_and_Journals/ANU_Reporter/_pdf/vol_33_no_06.pdf.

Baljekar, M. *Curry Lover's Cookbook*. London: Anness Publishing, 2003.

Baljekar, M., et al. *Complete Indian Cooking*. London: Lorenz Books/Anness Publishing, 2004.

Batmanglij, N. *Silk Road Cooking: A Vegetarian Journey*. Washington, D.C.: Mage Publishers, 2004.

Batra, N. *1,000 Indian Recipes*. New York: Wiley Publishing, 2002.

Beard, J. *James Beard's Theory & Practice of Good Cooking*. New York: Alfred A. Knopf, 1977.

Better Homes and Gardens. *Better Homes and Gardens New Cook Book*. Des Moines: Meredith Publishing, 1953.

Bharadwaj, M. *Indian in Minutes*. San Diego: Laurel Glen Publishing, 2000.

Bladholm, L. *The Indian Grocery Store Demystified*. Los Angeles: Renaissance Books, 2000.

Brennan, J. *Curries and Bugles*. New York: HarperCollins, 1990.

Brennan, J. *The Original Thai Cookbook*. New York: Perigee Books, 1981.

Collingham, L. *Curry: A Tale of Cooks and Conquerors*. New York: Oxford University Press, 2006.

Corriher, S. *Cookwise*. New York: William Morrow, 1997.

Dalby, A. *Dangerous Tastes: The Story of Spices*. Berkeley/Los Angeles: University of California Press, 2000.

Davidson, A. *The Oxford Companion to Food*. New York: Oxford University Press, 1999.

Evans, M. *Bistro Chicken*. New York: Broadway Books, 2004.

Fernandes, J. *Goan Cookbook*. Goa: New Age Printers, 1977, 2002.

Fraser, L. *The Book of Curries and Indian Foods*. New York: HP Books, 1989.

Goodman, M. *Jewish Food: The World at Table.* New York: HarperCollins, 2005.

Hamlyn Complete Indian Cooking. London: Octupus Publishing Group, 1999.

Hiremath, L. *The Dance of Spices: Classic Indian Cooking for Today's Home Kitchen.* Hoboken, NJ: John Wiley & Sons, 2005.

Ingram, C. *Cooking Ingredients.* London/New York: Hermes House/Anness Publishing, 2002.

Israel, R. R. *The Jews of India.* New Delhi: Mosaic Books, 2002.

Iyer, R. *Betty Crocker's Indian Home Cooking.* New York: Wiley Publishing, 2001.

———*The Turmeric Trail: Recipes and Memories from an Indian Childhood.* New York: St. Martin's Press, 2002.

Jaffrey, M. *An Invitation to Indian Cooking.* New York: Vintage Books, 1973.

———*A Taste of India.* New York: Atheneum, 1988.

———*Flavors of India.* New York: Carol Southern Books, 1995.

———*From Curries to Kebabs: Recipes from the Indian Spice Trail.* New York: Clarkson Potter, 2003.

———*Madhur Jaffrey's Far Eastern Cookery.* New York: Harper & Row, 1989.

———*Madhur Jaffrey's Indian Cooking.* New York: Barron's, 1983.

———*Madhur Jaffrey's Spice Kitchen.* New York: Carol Southern Books, 1993.

———*Taste of the Far East.* New York: Carol Southern Books, 1993.

Joachim, D. *The Food Substitutions Bible.* Toronto, Robert Rose, 2005.

Johari, H. *The Healing Cuisine.* Rochester, VT: Healing Arts Press, 1994.

Kaimal, M. *Savoring the Spice Coast of India: Fresh Flavors from Kerala.* New York: HarperCollins, 2000.

Katzer, G. *Gernot Katzer's Spice Pages.* uni-graz.at/~katzer/engl/.

Levy, F. Faye. *Levy's International Jewish Cookbook.* New York: Warner Books, 1991.

Lin, F. *Florence Lin's Complete Book of Chinese Noodles, Dumplings and Breads.* New York: William Morrow, 1986.

Loh-Yien Lau, A. *Asian Greens.* New York: St. Martin's Griffin, 2001.

MacMillan-Kaimal, M. *Curried Favors.* New York: Abbeville Press, 1996.

Monroe, J. *Star of India.* West Sussex, England: John Wiley & Sons, 2004.

Montagne, P. *Larousse Gastronomique.* New York: Clarkson Potter, 2001. (American edition of a French book published by Auguste Escoffier and Phileas Gilbert in 1938.)

Mulherin, J. *The Macmillan Treasury of Spices and Natural Flavorings.* New York: Macmillan, 1988.

Padmanabhan, C. *Dakshin: Vegetarian Cuisine from South India.* Boston: Periplus, 1994.

Passmore, J. *The Encyclopedia of Asian Food and Cooking.* New York: Hearst Books, 1991.

Perkins, W. L. *Fannie Farmer Boston Cooking School Cookbook,* 10th ed. Boston: Little, Brown, 1959.

Punjabi, C. *Great Curries of India.* New York: Simon & Schuster, 1995.

Rao, S. R. *Time-Life Foods of the World: The Cooking of India.* New York: Time-Life Books, 1969.

Rombauer, I., et al. *The All New Joy of Cooking.* New York: Scribner, 1997.

Sahni, J. *Classic Indian Cooking.* New York: William Morrow, 1980.

Schneider, E. *Vegetables from Amaranth to Zucchini.* New York: William Morrow, 2001.

"The Spice Trade: A Taste of Adventure." Originally published in *The Economist;* in "The Encyclopedia of Spices" on theepicentre.com.

Tannahill, R. *Food in History.* New York: Stein and Day, 1973.

Trager, J. *The Enriched, Fortified, Concentrated, Country-Fresh, Lip-Smacking, Finger-Licking, International, Unexpurgated Foodbook.* New York: Grossman, 1970.

Usgaokar, K. et al. *Traditional Taste of Goa.* Goa: Fomento Foundation, 2000.

Venkatachary, V. *How to Cook.* Madras: The Little Flower Company, 1987.

index

index

index

index

index

index

index

index

index